BERNARD SHAW
Collected Letters
1926–1950

Shaw in Moscow *(detail)* July 1931
(British Library, Add. Mss. 50586, fol. 5)

BERNARD SHAW

Collected Letters
1926–1950

EDITED BY DAN H. LAURENCE

VIKING

PENGUIN BOOKS
Published by the Penguin Group
Viking Penguin Inc., 40 West 23rd Street,
New York, New York 10010, U.S.A.
Penguin Books Ltd, 27 Wrights Lane,
London W8 5TZ, England
Penguin Books Australia Ltd, Ringwood,
Victoria, Australia
Penguin Books Canada Ltd, 2801 John Street,
Markham, Ontario, Canada L3R 1B4
Penguin Books (N. Z.) Ltd, 182–190 Wairau Road,
Auckland 10, New Zealand

Penguin Books Ltd, Registered Offices:
Harmondsworth, Middlesex, England

First published in 1988 by Viking Penguin Inc.
Published simultaneously in Great Britain

LIBRARY OF CONGRESS CATALOGING IN PUBLICATION DATA
(Revised for vol. 4)
Shaw, Bernard, 1856–1950.
Collected letters.
Includes indexes.
Contents: [1] 1874–1897—[2] 1898–1910—[3] 1911–1925
—[4] 1926–1950.
1. Shaw, Bernard, 1856–1950—Correspondence.
2. Dramatists, Irish—19th century—Correspondence.
3. Dramatists, Irish—20th century—Correspondence.
4. Critics—Great Britain—Correspondence.   5. Reformers
—Great Britain—Correspondence.   I. Laurence, Dan H.
II. Title.
PR5366.A4   1985   822'.912   84-40399
ISBN 0-670-80543-2 (v. 1)
ISBN 0-670-80544-0 (v. 2)
ISBN 0-670-80545-9 (v. 3)
ISBN 0-670-82109-8 (v. 4)

Printed in the United States of America by
Haddon Craftsmen, Scranton, Pennsylvania

To the editor's editor
Barney Blackley

" Too little payment for so great a debt"

Contents

Illustrations

ix

ILLUSTRATIONS IN TEXT

INTRODUCTION

Twenty-seven years ago I received an invitation to edit the correspondence of Bernard Shaw—and declined. It was not that I was not interested; I had, in fact, informed Max Reinhardt, Director of the Bodley Head, when he first interviewed me in London (at the suggestion of my publisher Rupert Hart-Davis) that there was nothing in the world I'd rather do than take on the challenge of the Shaw letters. It was, however, necessary that I meet with the American publishers of the proposed venture before a final decision could be made. And here the difficulty arose.

Dodd, Mead & Co., Shaw's American publishers since 1932, though conceding that I had the credentials for the job, insisted it was necessary to appoint an editor with "name value." They therefore, after plying me sumptuously with food and drink at New York's exclusive Players Club, proposed a bizarre working arrangement. I was to take on the preparatory work—the collecting of the correspondence, the editing of the texts, the research for the annotations, the footnoting—for a fee (which was, as I recall, to be $1500 per volume), after which the manuscript would be handed over to the well-known New York theatre critic John Mason Brown. He would polish any rough edges he found, supply an introduction, and place his name on the title page as nominal editor, followed by a credit "assisted by Dan H. Laurence."

As I had been educated by my parents to be polite to my elders I didn't tell Edward Dodd and Raymond Bond (President of Dodd, Mead) what they could do with their offer. I simply stated, with as much restraint as was possible at the moment, that if they didn't think Shaw's name was sufficient advertisement for a successful sale of his correspondence, they oughtn't to be his publishers—or anybody else's. And I made a dramatic exit.

About a fortnight later, after transatlantic telephonic conversations between the two publishing houses, I received a surprise communication from Dodd, Mead, indicating they were now prepared to reconsider their offer. If I were to agree to "certain conditions," I could have the appointment, as sole editor of the letters. I responded that I would accept the appointment only if it were guaranteed that I would have the final say on all editorial decisions. Eventually we compromised in a few matters, such as house style, which was to be British, except in those instances when it conflicted with Shaw's own stylistic preferences. For the most part, however, we did it my way—blessed by Shaw, who had (as I noted in the introduction to the first volume of the edition) written to Frederick Evans in 1895 about a contemplated edition of his music criticism: "I charge you by all your gods to be guided by *what YOU like*, even if it seems to you that nobody else will like it."

No editor could possibly have hoped for a more rapturous critical reception than both Shaw and I received from reviewer and reader of the first and subsequent volumes of the *Collected Letters*. The publishers' principal problem seemed to be which encomiums to select for quotation! There were, inevitably, a few critics who carped, and it is amusing now to look back over the yellowing cuttings to review their remarks. Leading the pack was a great journalistic snob, who haughtily declined to mention me by name, referring snidely to the "American editor," as he decried a faulty reference to Lady Bell as Lady Hugh Bell, and complained, "Should not a Professor of English Literature have mugged up the quaint niceties of English nomenclature?" I accepted the criticism, and laughed at the hint of xenophobia. A Scottish reviewer of the second volume, also distressed by "American usages," labelled the editing "idiosyncratic" (which I accepted as an unintended compliment and adopted, in the manner of the "decadents"), and faulted my annotations as "occasionally otiose and more often inadequate," on grounds that I did not sufficiently often, to his taste, place a letter in context by citing the other side of the correspondence. Despite the unresolvable problem of Shaw often not having preserved correspondence, I find to my amusement, in going through the second volume, that I quoted (sometimes extensively) pertinent passages from letters by more than forty correspondents.

I don't recall that any reviewers quarrelled with my decision to reproduce Shaw's text as near as possible, in letterpress, to the original manuscript, retaining the unorthodox spellings, the persistent misspelling of people's names, the omission of apostrophes and (to Shaw) other extraneous punctuation, and the insertion of facsimiles of odd-sized or -shaped lettering and of Shaw's quirky little drawings. Less satisfying to them was the decision to dispense with conventional footnotes and to substitute concisely packaged headnotes, which often served as bridges between letters.

"For some reason that has nothing to do with readability," commented one of the detractors in 1985, "[the editor] puts all the notes to each letter in a lump at the start, like a squashed card index." Nothing to do with readability? I might have expatiated on that myopic conclusion if a second reviewer, on the same date, hadn't done it for me by astutely and succinctly noting precisely what I was aiming for: "[The editor] has adopted a neat device to give minimum interruption to Shaw's divine flow. He dispenses entirely with footnotes and instead provides a brief explanation of references and allusions in a continuous paragraph *before* each letter. This works like a dream and preserves much of the alternating surprise, delight, shock, exasperation, and laughter which these letters must have produced when they were first opened."

Unlike those authors and editors who claim that they are never affected by reviews because they never read them, I do read my notices, and try to learn from them. When flaws are indicated ("Books are like men," said Walt Whitman; "the best of them have flaws"), I conscientiously make note of them and record them in a list of errata published at the end of each volume. Though I may disagree with what is said, I respect the integrity of the critic, who has as much right to an opinion as I have. As a consequence I have never (until now) in all my years of publishing responded publicly to a criticism, even on those occasions when a reviewer, through his own ignorance, has taken me to task unwarrantedly.

An example of this is a criticism of a couple of years ago in which a reviewer stated, "Only when [the editor] attempts to list places where letters have been previously published . . . does his bibliographical mania get the better of him. . . . [A] letter to Charles Sarolea is listed as having been published in a magazine called *Everyman* in November 1914. This . . . does not inform us of the more practical point that it is readily available in *What I Really Wrote about the War*, published in the Collected Edition of *The Works of Bernard Shaw*. The irony is that so much time has been spent on getting some of these remoter inessentials correct that the information has in the meantime become out of date. There is little object, for instance, in referring us to the London School of Economics for a quotation from Beatrice Webb's [manuscript] diaries when these diaries are now published and in the bookshop."

The misconceptions embodied in this polemic reflect a pathetic naïveté. It is precisely because I wished to *avoid* "bibliographical mania" that I did not cite any of the later published sources as "readily available" editions. The intent in providing a list of sources was to indicate to an interested scholar whether a letter had had prior publication and, if so, where and when it first appeared. What would be the point of recording a "readily available" reprint of a letter when the reader at that moment is holding in his hands as reliable a reprinted text as he is likely to find? As for the Beatrice Webb diaries, while it is true that they are published, the citation of the manuscript diaries and their source was designed to provide evidence that the editor had fulfilled what scholars consider to be a sacred responsibility, the consultation of a primary text, when it exists, as guarantee against inadvertent retention of another scholar's possible errors.

Having established that I take reviews seriously, I now make the admission that I have avoided as completely as possible the influence, in my work, of the perversity of thought that has been creeping into recent Shavian scholarship through a revisionist school of humourless pseudo-psychiatrists. These, insensitive to Shaw's ironies, extravagances, and comic effusions, have literal-mindedly concocted a "dark side" portrait of him that startlingly rivals the picture of Dorian Gray. We are told that Shaw frantically sought to conceal a deep-rooted fear that his mother had, between trills, cohabited with her Svengalian singing teacher, in the process illegitimately conceiving GBS; that he was anally fixated as a child, and was into the bargain a latent homosexual; that Harley Granville-Barker (and perhaps T.E. Lawrence too) was his illegitimate son; that his flirtation with Molly Tompkins was more than a harmless platonic affair, which resulted in 1927 in her pregnancy and a subsequent abortion; that he was a life-long sadist, never so content as when torturing innocent female victims.

Those who seek to uncover the dark Hyde in the present crop of letters are welcome to their searches. Shaw, having thus far survived a full century of disapprobation, dissection, and predictions of his imminent disappearance from the literary pantheon, by once-eminent critics whose own names turn out to have been writ in water, is likely to outlast the current crop of biographical paparazzi and frenetic Freudians. The rest of us will see in these 740 pieces of correspondence (two-thirds of them hitherto unpublished and many others published in extract only) an aged man touchingly struggling to remain in tune with his times, sharing his precious remaining hours with nearly 350 correspondents—friends, strangers, and foes—giving each the courtesy of serious attention, supplying advice, sharing his bank account, and, with intelligence, honesty, astonishing zest, and vast good humour, succeeding in implanting in the recipient the feeling of being treated as an equal rather than of being patronised.

There are two significant departures in this volume from earlier ones. Because a considerable number of Shaw's correspondents, as well as persons mentioned in the correspondence, or their offspring, are yet living, some sensitive passages have been deleted in fulfilment of Shaw's testamentary request, and in two instances identification has been concealed. Additionally, the editor has had to take cognizance of the loss of dexterity in Shaw's ageing fingers, which resulted in a deterioration in his writing and typing. Frequently in the late correspondence there are skipped letters (as in *kindnss* and *becuse*) or accidentally repeated ones (like *enclossed*), omissions of punctuation, duplicated words, or typed lines running beyond the right margin of the paper, cutting off words in the middle or losing them entirely. Rather than retain the errors created by faulty manipulation of pen or keyboard, as if they were standard misspellings like *wierd* and *ebulition*, I have silently corrected them. Missing words or letters and omitted punctuation have been restored in square brackets, these editorial insertions evidencing graphically the gradual deterioration in the writing.

Throughout the years, in the preparation of this edition and many other works, I have been able to count on at-the-ready guidance, assistance, and moral support from many friends and colleagues, notably my editor Barney Blackley of The Bodley Head; the ever-supportive Bernard F. Burgunder (until his death in 1985); my friend and first publisher Sir Rupert Hart-Davis; and the late John O'Donovan. Frederick McDowell and Charles Sharp were helpful proofreaders. T. F. Evans, as a personal favour, undertook the indexing of the final two volumes of the edition, which have thus been skilfully enhanced. Warren F. Michon, Senior Librarian of the New York Public Library Music Division, has contributed most generously to the *Collected Letters* as well as to *Shaw's Music* and the Shaw bibliography through his painstaking and thorough researches. And I could always count on helpful response from Jacques Barzun, Edward Connery Lathem, Valerie Delacorte (widow of Gabriel Pascal), Maureen Halligan, Felix F. Strauss, Lola L. Szladits, the late Raymond Mander and his partner Joe Mitchenson, James Tyler, Roma Woodnutt, Samuel N. Freedman, Anthony Rota, Cathy Henderson, and Samuel A. Weiss. To all of these my extreme gratitude.

In the deciphering of Shaw's shorthand, problematic in the late years through his accidental omission of words essential to the sense and completeness of a sentence, wrong positioning of dots and reversal of hooks, or reversion to antiquated grammalogues, I have been blessed with several expert Pitman phonographers: John Wardrop, Barbara Smoker, and the late Georgina Musters, Blanche Patch, and Sir James Pitman. In one notable instance, that of a 1946 letter to Winston Churchill, it required the combined expertise of all five to decipher the torn and repaired shorthand draft manuscript.

Acknowledgment of debt has been made in earlier volumes to those who aided in their preparation. To the long roll I now add with deepest thanks the following additional names:

Maurice Adelman Jr; Jean-Claude Amalric; Robert Ashe; Joanne Trautman Banks; Mrs N.F.Barford; Nicolas Barker; James M. Barnes; Elske Bater; the late Hugh Beaumont; James Bennett, Curator of the Elgar Birthplace; E.G.W.Bill, Librarian, Lambeth Palace Library; Trudy Lady Bliss; Michael Bott, Curator of Manuscripts, Reading University Library; Nancy Butler and Helen Lothian, Librarians, The Shaw Festival; Ann Casson Campbell; Margaret Campbell; Mary Clark, Archivist, Dublin Corporation; Sunniva Clarke; L.W.Conolly; Dame Felicitas Corrigan, Stanbrook Abbey; Francis Dobo; Roberta Engleman, Rare Books Department, University of North Carolina at Chapel Hill; H.M.Fletcher; Reavley Gair; Fraser and Vera Gallie; Peggy Gosschalk; Ronald Gow; Norbert Greiner; Nicholas Grene; Alastair Grieve; August Grodzicki.

Rev. Canon A.T.Hanson; Rt. Rev. R.C.P.Hanson; Walter D'Arcy Hart; Mark Haymon, Basic English Foundation; Rev. Brendan Haythornthwaite; Dame Wendy Hiller; H.C.Holloway; Michael Holroyd; the late Denis Johnston; Ernest Jokl; J.Jomaron; Kyre Kalanyos, Rare Books Department, University of North Carolina at Chapel Hill; Jacqueline M.Kavanagh, Written Archives Officer, B.B.C.; Lord Kennet; Raymond Kilgarriff, Archivist, Antiquarian Booksellers' Association; H.P.Kraus; Ravinder Kumar, Director, Nehru Memorial Library; Sylvia Lady Latham; Bernard Lenowitz; Heather McCallum, former Head, Theatre Department, Metropolitan Toronto Library; Niell McLaughlin, Consultant, Arthur Cox & Co., Dublin; Deirdre McMahon; Dorothy Martin, University of British Columbia Library; R. Russell Maylone, Curator of Special Collections, Northwestern University Library; Bernard Meehan, Keeper of Manuscripts, Trinity College, Dublin; Sean Morrow; M.B.Nicholson, Archivist, Dartington Hall Trust; Nigel Nicolson; Deirdre O'Connor; James N.O'Connor, Editor, *Irish Advocate*; Nora O'Sullivan.

Kenneth Parker; Leslie Parris, Deputy Keeper, British Collection,

Tate Gallery; Ellen Pollock; D.S.Porter, Senior Assistant Librarian, Bodleian Library; Colin Prestige, Executor of the Estate of Charlotte F.Shaw; Michael Purcell; Max Reinhardt; Peggy Lady Richardson; the late Harold F.Rubinstein; Ann Saddlemyer; Michael J.Santoro; L.F.Schuster; Peter Schuyten; the late J.W.Robertson Scott; A.P. Sharkey, Town Clerk, Carlow Urban Council; Richard Shrader, Assistant Director, Southern Historical Collection, University of North Carolina at Chapel Hill; Ann Simmons; Peter Smith; Colin Smythe; Lady Strabolgi; David C.Sutton, Senior Research Officer, Location Register of the Twentieth Century English Literary Manuscripts and Letters, Reading University Library; Dorothy L.Swerdlove, Curator, Billy Rose Theatre Collection, New York Public Library; Ethel Thwaites; J.R.Till; William and Ann Bowden Todd; J.C. Trewin; Malcolm Turner, Deputy Music Librarian, British Library; Christopher Wall and Robert Latham, The National Trust; Robin Whitworth; Stephen E.Wilhite.

Also the British Broadcasting Corporation Reference and Registry Services and the staff of the Written Archives Centre; Carlow County Heritage Society; College of Tagore Studies and Research and the Rabindra-Sadana Memorial Museum, Santiniketan, W. Bengal; Dwight D.Eisenhower Library; Greater London Record Office; Irish Academy of Arts and Letters; Irish Architectural Archive; Leeds District Archive; Liddell Hart Centre for Military Archives, King's College, London; Mills Memorial Library, McMaster University, Hamilton, Ontario; Nehru Memorial Museum and Library, New Delhi; New York Historical Society; Orthological Foundation; Ellen Terry Memorial Museum, Smallhythe; Alexander Turnbull Library (National Library of New Zealand), Wellington; Board of Trustees, Victoria and Albert Museum. To the staff of the Music Division of the New York Public Library a special salute, and my gratitude to Richard Nickson, Dennis Peck, Trevor West, J.L.Wisenthal, and five others whose names appear elsewhere in the acknowledgments for their alertness in spotting errors in the third volume that are corrected in the list of errata at the end of this volume.

For permission to publish Bernard Shaw's correspondence I acknowledge the generous co-operation of the librarians and trustees of all of the libraries and institutions recorded in the Code of Sources. For a letter to H.A.Gwynne I am grateful to Vice-Admiral Sir Ian Hogg. Shaw's letter to Herbert Brewer is published by courtesy of the Eugenics Society and of the Wellcome Trustees of the Contemporary Medical Archives Centre, London (MAC:SA/EUG C.43). A letter to

A. Troyte Griffith is published by permission of the City of Birmingham Leisure Services Committee and of the Manchester Central Library. As the Public Records Office, London, requires that correspondence in its collections be identified by document reference number, be it noted that the number for Shaw's letter to Harry Snell is PRO 30/69/1438, fol. 1577, and those for letters to J. Ramsay MacDonald are PRO 30/69/1172/2, fols. 536–7.

For permission to publish from their own correspondence, and for transcriptions of drafts or carbon copies supplied by them, I am indebted to the late Georgina Musters, the late Blanche Patch, the late Allan M. Laing, and the late Denis Johnston. Kind permission to quote from letters of Shaw's correspondents has been received from the following executors or heirs: Quentin Bell (Virginia Woolf); Lady Mairi Bury and the Deputy Keeper of Records, Public Records Office of Northern Ireland (Lady Londonderry); the late Canon Adam Fox (the Very Rev. W. R. Inge); John Freeman (Kingsley Martin); Armina Marshall (Lawrence Langner); Passfield Trust (Beatrice and Sidney Webb); Stanbrook Abbey (Dame Laurentia McLachlan). Extracts from letters by Charlotte F. Shaw appear by generous consent of the Trustees of her Will. A translation of Albert Einstein's seventieth birthday tribute is used by permission of the Estate of Albert Einstein. John Farleigh's drawing and woodcut of Shaw are reproduced through the generosity of Barbara Kane.

There appear to be no surviving executors or living heirs to the Estates of Emily Pethick-Lawrence, Mabel Shaw, or J. E. Whiting, and I have been unsuccessful in efforts to locate anyone who could authorise quotation of letters from the Rev. H. Cotton-Smith, Julius Gold, V. O. Plenazár, William Rowbottom, and J. R. Titterton. I have published these passages on the assumption that such permission would in any event have been forthcoming.

Finally, I should like to express my enormous gratitude for the enthusiastic co-operation of the staff of the library of the University of Guelph, with especial thanks to John B. Black, Librarian, Ellen Pearson, Associate Librarian, and Nancy Sadek, Sarah Funston-Mill, Tim Sauer, Robert A. Logan, and Bernard Katz.

If I have overlooked anyone, please forgive me and be assured that I am grateful.

DAN H. LAURENCE

London
20 May 1987

Code to description of correspondence

A Holograph letter
B Holograph letter-card
C Holograph postcard
D Holograph correspondence card
E Holograph note or "Compliments of Bernard Shaw" enclosure card
F Shorthand draft or copy
G Holograph draft or copy
H Typewritten letter
I Typewritten draft
J Typewritten letter-card
K Typewritten postcard
L Dictated letter, in holograph of Charlotte Shaw, signed by Shaw
M Dictated letter-card, in holograph of Charlotte Shaw, signed by Shaw
N Dictated postcard, in holograph of Charlotte Shaw, signed by Shaw
P Dictated letter, in holograph of secretary, signed by Shaw
Q Dictated letter-card, in holograph of secretary, signed by Shaw
R Dictated postcard, in hand of secretary, signed by Shaw
S Transcription: original unlocated
T Transcription: original located but unavailable for examination
U Photographic reproduction: original unlocated
V Photographic reproduction: original located but unavailable for examination
W Facsimile publication
X Published text
Y Telegram or cablegram
Z Holograph playlet
c Carbon copy
e Extract
hc Holograph corrections
t Typed signature
u Unsigned

NOTE

"Diary" refers to the thirteen shorthand diary volumes kept by Shaw between 1885 and 1897, now in the British Library of Political and Economic Science. (These were published, 1986, by Penn State Press.)

Code to sources of ownership of letters in this volume

The placement of an "e" after a code number in the body of this work indicates that, in prior publication, only an extract or severely truncated text of the letter has appeared.

1 Privately owned
2 British Library (formerly British Museum)
3 General Collections, Harry Ransom Humanities Research Center, University of Texas
4 T.E.Hanley Collection, Harry Ransom Humanities Research Center, University of Texas
5 Henry W. and Albert A.Berg Collection, New York Public Library
6 Houghton Library, Harvard University
7 Beinecke Rare Book and Manuscript Library, Yale University Library: Collection of American Literature
8 De Coursey Fales Library, New York University (Bobst) Library
9 Bernard F.Burgunder Collection, Cornell University Library
10 Library of Congress
11 Princeton University Library
13 British Library of Political and Economic Science, London School of Economics
14 Passfield Trust Papers, British Library of Political and Economic Science, London School of Economics
17 King's College Library, Cambridge University
18 National Library of Scotland
23 Baker Library, Dartmouth College
24 Estelle Doheny Collection, Edward Laurence Doheny Memorial Library, St John's Seminary, Camarillo
25 The Huntington Library
26 University of Illinois Library at Urbana-Champaign
35 Fabian Society Archive, Nuffield College, Oxford
36 British Theatre Association (formerly British Drama League)
37 University Libraries, State University of New York at Buffalo: Poetry/Rare Books Collection
38 Rare Book and Manuscript Library, Columbia University

Code to sources of prior publication

xxii

350 "Drapery as Job for Men," *Sunday Chronicle*, 20 February 1927

351 Benjamin C. Rosset, *Shaw of Dublin* (1964)

352 *New York Times Book Review*, 28 January 1951

353 "Shaw Denounces Ox-Roasts," *New York Times*, 19 July 1931

354 *Lidové Noviny*, Prague, 28 October 1928

355 Evan Charteris, *The Life and Letters of Sir Edmund Gosse* (1931)

356 A. Fenner Brockway, *Inside the Left* (1942)

357 Parke-Bernet Galleries: Sale No. 665 (1945), quotation; Sale No. 1935 (1959), full transcription

358 Eileen Quelch, *Perfect Darling: The Life and Times of George Cornwallis West* (1972)

359 G. W. Bishop, "A Walk and a Talk with Mr. Shaw," *The Observer*, 8 September 1929

360 "A National Theatre," *The Times*, 28 October 1929

361 Huntly Carter, *The New Spirit in the Cinema* (1930)

362 "Mr. Bernard Shaw and the Old Vic," *The Times*, 21 February 1930

363 *Man and Superman*, souvenir programme, Royal Shakespeare Company, Savoy Theatre, August 1977

364 Irene Vanbrugh, *To Tell My Story* (1948)

365 E. Merrill Root, *Frank Harris* (1947)

366 J. N. Moore (ed.), *Music and Friends: Seven Decades of Letters to Adrian Boult* (1979)

367 John Reith, *Into the Wind* (1949)

368 John Farleigh, *Graven Image* (1940)

369 Dame Felicitas Corrigan, *The Nun, the Infidel and the Superman* (1985)

370 Clara Leiser, *Jean de Reszke and the Great Days of Opera* (1933)

371 *Letters to W. B. Yeats*, eds. R. J. Finneran, G. M. Harper, and William Murphy (1978)

372 *The Hindu*, Madras, 19 January 1933; Krishna Kripalani, *Tagore* (1962)

373 Hesketh Pearson, *G. B. S.: A Full Length Portrait* (1942)

374 Bernard Shaw, *Everybody's Political What's What?* (1944)

375 *World's Press News*, 4 May 1933

376 "Mr. Shaw Shuns 'Women's Rights' Meeting," *Daily Telegraph*, 3 November 1933

377 Leslie M. Henderson, *The Goldstein Story* (1973)

378 Dan H. Laurence, *The Fifth Gospel of Bernard Shaw* (1981), reproduced from an unidentified, undated newspaper cutting

379 Gene Fowler, *Good Night, Sweet Prince* (1944)

380   *Chronicle and Echo*, Northampton, 16 January 1934
381   William H. Reed, *Elgar as I Knew Him* (1936)
382   *Publishers' Circular*, 3 November 1934
383   Hesketh Pearson, *Gilbert and Sullivan: A Biography* (1935)
384   J. Barlow Brooks, *Lancashire Bred*, II (1951)
385   George W. Bishop, *My Betters* (1957)
386   A. A. Roback, *Freudiana* (1957)
387   Allan Chappelow, *Shaw the Villager* (1961)
388   Bernard F. Dukore, *Bernard Shaw, Director* (1971)
389   Nicolas Slonimsky, *Music since 1900* (1937)
390   Raymond Mander and Joe Mitchenson, *Theatrical Companion to Shaw* (1954)
391   Dan H. Laurence, *Bernard Shaw: A Bibliography* (1983)
392   J. M. Keynes, *Collected Writings*, XXVIII (1982)
393   Annette T. Rubinstein, *The Great Tradition in English Literature from Shakespeare to Shaw* (1953)
394   Mary Hyde (ed.), *Bernard Shaw and Alfred Douglas: A Correspondence* (1982)
395   G. S. Viereck, *The Kaiser on Trial* (1938)
396   Valerie Pascal, *The Disciple and His Devil* (1970)
397   *Vegetarian News* (London Vegetarian Society), July 1938
398   Ignace Paderewski and Mary Lawton, *The Paderewski Memoirs* (London, 1939)
399   Reproduced in facsimile in Dodd, Mead & Co. advertisement, *New York Times Book Review*, 1 November 1942
400   Bernard Shaw, "Comments" (introduction), *Pygmalion* (New York, 1939)
401   Kenneth Barnes, *Welcome, Good Friends* (1958)
402   S. N. Behrman, *The Suspended Drawing Room* (1965)
403   H. Thal-Jantzen, Catalogue No. 10, November 1958
404   *Leicester Mail*, 8 January 1930
405   "A Generous Opponent," *Mark Twain Quarterly*, Spring 1937
406   "Bernard Shaw and France," *Adam: International Review*, Nos. 255–6 (1956)
407   H. Montgomery Hyde, *The Londonderrys* (1979)
408   Virginia Woolf, *Roger Fry* (1940)
409   Leonard Woolf, *Beginning Again* (1964)
410   *Picture Post*, 22 March 1941
411   J. C. Trewin, *Robert Donat: A Biography* (1968)
412   "The Personal Touch," *Family Circle*, New York, 19 September 1941

413 *The Examiner*, Warrington, 9 August 1941
414 Cole Lesley, *The Life of Noël Coward* (1976)
415 Anthony Weymouth (pseud. of I. Geikie-Cobb), *Journal of the War Years and One Year Later* (1948): letter misdated 19 January 1942
416 O. B. Clarence, *No Complaints* (1943)
417 *Forward*, Glasgow, 18 September 1943
418 *Daily Herald*, 3 November 1950
419 Field Marshal the Viscount Montgomery of Alamein, *Memoirs* (1958)
420 Margot Peters, *Mrs. Pat* (1984)
421 *Forward*, Glasgow, 17 June 1944
422 Arthur Bliss, *As I Remember* (1970)
423 *The Nationalist and Leinster Times*, Carlow, 3 June 1944
424 Marjorie Deans, *Meeting at the Sphinx* (1946), except penultimate paragraph
425 "The Women's Vote," *Manchester Guardian*, 5 July 1945
426 *Sunday Mail*, Glasgow, 9 December 1945
427 *Irish Times* and (in facsimile) *Evening Herald*, Dublin, 19 February 1946
428 *Sunday Pictorial*, 26 May 1946; in facsimile, *Socialist Leader*, 11 November 1950
429 *Irish Press*, Dublin, 26 July 1946
430 Charles Hamilton, *Collecting Autographs and Manuscripts* (1961)
431 *Irish Independent*, Dublin, 8 August 1946
432 Arthur C. Clarke, "Shaw and the Sound Barrier," *Virginia Quarterly Review*, Winter 1960
433 *Irish Press*, Dublin, 1 May 1947
434 "Consummate Love" (letter to editor), *The Listener*, 28 November 1974
435 *Tailor and Cutter*, 5 September 1947
436 *News Chronicle*, 21 November 1950
437 *Daily Express*, 1 May 1958
438 *Empire News*, Manchester, 25 July 1948
439 Ted Berkman, *The Lady and the Law* (1976)
440 *Shaw Society Bulletin*, London, September 1952
441 *Irish Times*, Dublin, 21 September 1948
442 Jawaharlal Nehru, *A Bunch of Old Letters* (1958)
443 *Cycling Magazine*, 10 November 1948
444 Janet Dunbar, *Flora Robson* (1960)
445 *Irish Times*, Dublin, 29 March 1969

446 *The Times*, 12 March 1949
447 Ruari McLean, *Modern Book Design* (1958)
448 *Daily Graphic*, Eire edition, 11 July 1949
449 William White, "Irish Antitheses: Shaw and Joyce," *The Shavian*, February 1961
450 Eileen O'Casey, *Sean* (1971)
451 *The Shavian*, February 1964
452 Wolfgang Goetz, *Werner Krauss* (1954)
453 *Daily Mail*, 19 November 1926
454 Hesketh Pearson, "My Uninvited Collaborator: GBS," *Horizon*, November 1958
455 "Shaw Tours City But Dodges Press," *New York Times*, 12 April 1933

PART I

1926–1930

I

(1926–1930)

Shaw was capped with laurel three times in his life, precisely at twenty year intervals. The first instance was in 1906, following the critical acclamation of his plays in the Court Theatre repertory under the banner of J. E. Vedrenne and Granville Barker. "The Shavian boom," GBS announced to Vedrenne, "has at last reached a pitch of absolute insanity," with hundreds of performances of the plays worldwide, in nearly a dozen languages. His sermons too, he noted, "have an eclectic vogue," a circumstance which temporarily kept the Fabian Society solvent.

When in 1926 he reached the age of seventy ("the only ordinary thing that Mr. Shaw has ever done," commented *The Observer*), his birthday was noted ceremoniously abroad, but with only modest attention at home, though the Prime Minister, Ramsay MacDonald, had quietly suggested a knighthood, which he declined. His political colleagues of the Left gave him the inevitable testimonial dinner (his unscripted speech being barred from broadcast by the B.B.C. when he characteristically declined to give an assurance that it would not be politically controversial). The British press dutifully marked the occasion with leaders and articles that treated him with the dignity and deference due to an Eminent Victorian, pointedly noting that he had outlived Shakespeare, Congreve, and Sheridan, yet oblivious of the fact that, alone among British dramatists of the past three centuries, he had attained international supremacy in the theatre, and was probably the most famous person in the world.

From Germany, however, came a fanfare of acclamation. Productions of his plays outnumbered even those of the revered Bard of Avon; testimonials to his artistry and philosophy poured forth from Albert Einstein, Richard Strauss, the German foreign secretary, the director of the Berlin Opera, Thomas Mann, Spengler, Schönberg, and Arthur Schnitzler; the press published spacious supplements filled with lavish praise from the likes of Bertolt Brecht, Feliks Salten, and Gerhart Hauptmann, and poetic paeans from Emil Ludwig and Franz Werfel. All this was dutifully reported in the British papers, whose readers were for the most part unimpressed. So was GBS, who quietly slipped off to Italy for a holiday on Lake Maggiore.

Thus it came as a shock when the Swedish Academy announced on 12th November that the Nobel Prize for Literature for 1925 had been awarded to Bernard Shaw. It had been widely expected that, if the honour were to come to Britain for the first time in nearly two decades, it would be bestowed upon Thomas Hardy, who alone, in the opinion of *The Bookman*, stood "upon a quite unassailable peak of literary eminence," being "generally regarded at this day as the greatest living creative writer."

The usually unflappable and self-assured Shaw was equally astonished and, at first, speechless when notified that he had been selected as the first British Nobel laureate since Kipling in 1907 (Yeats having pointedly and politically accepted it in 1923 as an award to the literature of the newly created Irish Free State). "I have never given the Nobel Prize very deep consideration," Shaw admitted to journalists when he at last faced them; "I am surprised, I don't know what it means. . . . I always understood that it was awarded for the best book of the year. I produced nothing in 1925." His first impulse was to reject the Prize, having been told that he could not accept the honour while refusing the unneeded and undesired monetary award. It was Charlotte Shaw who, insisting that the Prize was a tribute to Ireland that must not be sacrificed, convinced him that he must devise a way out of the impasse. As a consequence the funds were accepted momentarily, then transferred to a specially created Anglo-Swedish Literary Foundation, under the patronage of Gustav Adolf, Crown Prince of Sweden, for the encouragement of Swedish literature in English translation. Shaw did not go to Stockholm for the presentation; the medal and diploma were accepted for him at the ceremonies on 10th December by the British Ambassador, Sir Arthur Grant Duff, who expressed particular appreciation of the fact that the Prize money would be used to strengthen the cultural relations between Sweden and Great Britain.

In addressing the assembly the Chairman of the Nobel Committee for the Swedish Academy, Dr Per Hallström, made the interesting point in his tribute that Shaw

> showed in the novels of his youth the same conception of the world and the same attitude to social problems that he has ever since maintained. This provides a better defence for him than anything else against the long-current [mostly British] accusation of lack of honesty and of acting as a professional buffoon at the court of democracy. From the very beginning his convictions have been so firm that it seems as if the general process of development, without having any substantial influence on himself, has carried him along

to the tribune from which he now speaks. His ideas were those of a somewhat abstract logical radicalism: hence they were far from new, but they received from him a new definiteness and brilliance. In him they were united with a ready wit, a complete absence of respect for any kind of convention, and the merriest humour—all gathered together in an extravagance which has scarcely ever before appeared in literature.

A consequence of the Nobel Prize laureateship was for Shaw an insufferable celebrity and an unprecedented invasion of privacy. "Those who see me now," he wrote to his childhood friend Ada Tyrrell, "are those who shove and insist and will not take no for an answer." Finding no peace at home or abroad, fighting vainly the tide of publicity and attention that now threatened to engulf him, Shaw stoically succumbed, offering the "smilings and wavings and posings and speech makings" expected of a National Institution whose plays had become "England's Greatest Export-Commodity." Like the celebrated author of Henry James's tale "The Private Life," he talked, he circulated, he flirted, until his reputation became "a kind of gilded obelisk, as if he had been buried beneath it; the body of legend and reminiscence of which he was to be the subject had crystallised in advance."

Moreover, with the advent of the wireless and sound films Shaw could reach vaster audiences than ever before. One of the first to recognise the enormous potential of the talking picture for political advantage, GBS urged Ramsay MacDonald to study a sound newsreel of the Italian dictator Mussolini that he himself had recently seen. Invited by Movietone News in 1928 to make a similar film appearance, Shaw leaped at the opportunity to cavort before the camera. He prepared his own scenario, stage-managed his entrance and movements, positioned the camera at the end of the garden path at Ayot so that he might step out from behind a shrub and amble amiably toward it, then suddenly "discover" his audience with a gasp of mock surprise. Whereat he introduced himself, offered a few light quips, then concluded the appearance with a devastatingly comic impersonation of Il Duce. Within the space of five minutes millions of people throughout the world were given an opportunity to witness, spellbound, Shaw's charm, geniality, skilful use of dramatic and vocal techniques, and sense of humour.

In America sales of his published works soared, and several were circulated in tens of thousands by the Book-of-the-Month Club. In England his thirty-volume Collected Edition, following a single

advertisement, was oversubscribed. Ramsay MacDonald exuberantly declared Shaw's *Intelligent Woman's Guide to Socialism and Capitalism* to be the world's most important book since the Bible, and Winston Churchill, in a similar hyperbolic burst of enthusiasm, categorised GBS as "the greatest living master of letters in the English-speaking world." Every word he uttered, every move he made was deemed worthy of mention in every newspaper in the world—except, of course, *The Times* of London.

Twenty years later, when he reached ninety, Shaw would, even in *The Times*, be elevated to a state of Veneration.

To WILLIAM MAXWELL

[A/3]

Falmouth Hotel. Falmouth
1st January 1926

[The Shaws had returned to Falmouth on 22nd December to enable GBS to work uninterruptedly on his new book, *The Intelligent Woman's Guide to Socialism and Capitalism.* Maxwell had just set the first chapter as an experiment in format.]

Dear Mr Maxwell

You have solved all the difficulties and made a really handsome book of it. The worst of it, as you will see by the enclosed revise, is that I find myself, like Morris, playing tricks with my text solely to avoid ending a paragraph with a short line[.]

I think I shall divide the book into sections within which the chapters can run without a break after each. The number of pages will be at least 350 pages, possibly 400.

I enclose copy for chapters 2 & 3, so that you can carry on to the end of the sheet at once if you care to.

In haste to catch the post
G. Bernard Shaw

To MOLLY TOMPKINS

[H/1; W/319]

Ayot St Lawrence. Welwyn
27th January 1926

[Mozart's "Little Night Music" ("Eine kleine Nachtmusik") is Serenade No. 13 in G. (K.525). Hazel Lady Lavery (1887–1935), a striking beauty from Chicago married to the Irish portrait painter Sir John Lavery, modelled for her husband for the colleen on the first Irish Free State banknotes in 1923. Mary Borden (1886–1968), later Lady Spears, was also a Chicagoan, author of several successful novels. The meeting with one of Tolstoy's three daughters probably occurred at the Stage Society matinée of Chekhov's *Ivanoff* on 9th December 1925. The *Romeo and Juliet* reference is to the Nurse's recollection of the child Juliet, in I.iii.48 and 57: "It stinted, and said 'Aye.' " Forte dei Marmi is a town on the Italian Riviera, south of La Spezia. Molly's son Peter was by this time five or six years of age.]

Dearest Molly

Yes: I am distracted by the slowness with which the book is proceeding through the press. However, it does me good to have to do a real hard literary job, all brains, instead of writing plays. Writing letters is impossible: this is only to explain why I cannot write them.

I snatch this moment late in the evening, when I should not write at all. I am alone here, my wife having gone up to town. It is the anniversary of Mozart's birth in 1756 (I followed in 1856); and his Little Night Music is coming through on the wireless. It is a mild night; and I am sitting at the fire with my typewriter on my knees, like a sailor with his lass.

When Lady Lavery went to New York lately our parting so affected her that—more enterprising than you—she kissed me in broad daylight before all the world in Cromwell Place. But it was spoilt by our meeting again next day at lunch at Mary Borden's. When the party broke up Lady Lavery said "I kissed him yesterday in the middle of the street." "Kiss him again by all means," said Mary. "I can't" said Lady Lavery: "he struggles so."

All three ladies are American. The third is you. But you, being the youngest, do not understand that dotards of seventy must not assume that beautiful females who admire their works would like to be pawed by them. There is a shyness of age as there is a shyness of youth. And that is only the cheapest out of a dozen reasons why a man, especially an old man, does not always devour his natural prey.

And then, your romance has lasted a long time without spoiling. There are moments, of course, when you want to consummate it. But they pass; and the romance remains. You get tired of waiting; but suppose there were no longer anything to wait for!

But these things do not fit into words and arguments. They belong to the Elysian Fields (not those through which you rush the Renault, but those that Gluck set to music in Orfeo) into which we both want to escape to meet each other, and in which we never shall meet except in imagination. But we shall do as well on this solid earth as we need; for next time you will not be so tongue tied, to say the least.

You do not say how Lawrence is. After all, Lawrence has to be considered. Do not have another operation either. When you have a pain, and money, the doctors say they will open you up, and cut the pain out. They open you up accordingly, and cut out anything that they think you will not miss; but the pain comes back all the same until it cures itself.

Tolstoy's daughter told me terrible things about the Bolsheviks the

8

other day; but when I asked her whether she would exchange the Moscow Government for the French or English or American one, she stinted (like Juliet) and said No.

Write when you please and how you please. Your letters are extremely readable (my wife is quite keen on them) and they make me feel romantic at times, which is pleasant at my age. After all, I shall not be completely seventy until July.

Are you really going back to Forte? As a rule, it is a mistake to go back anywhere. When you read my book to Lawrence and Baby it is they and not you who will go asleep. By the way, stop calling him Baby: the other children will laugh at him; and boys are frightfully sensitive. I remember how I hated being called Sonny. You yourself want to be called Marie instead of Molly; but I think Mary should be reserved for the Blessed Virgin, or rather the Blessed Mother.

As you are in Paris, why not take lessons in declamation? We are no good at that in Gower St [Royal Academy of Dramatic Art].

GBS

To ARCHIBALD HENDERSON

[H/7]

10 Adelphi Terrace WC2
30th January 1926

[In *Table-Talk of G.B.S.* (1925), written jointly with Henderson, Shaw inadvertently libelled the Welsh author Caradoc Evans (1879–1945) by stating erroneously that his book *My People* had been "suppressed after publication in England." Shaw, accepting full responsibility despite a contractual protection that made the publishers Chapman & Hall liable, paid a £100 settlement for damages and costs plus £20 for publication of an apology in several newspapers. Henderson had been contemplating a revised and expanded version of his biography of Shaw, eventually to be published in 1932 as *Bernard Shaw: Playboy and Prophet*.]

My dear Henderson

There is nothing in the whole history of literature so disgracefully procrastinative as my treatment of your letter of September the 21st last, in which you sent me a cheque in full for all the costs and damages of the Caradoc Evans affair, and took all the blame on your own shoulders, besides offering to advertise your sole responsibility and exonerate me in the Press here. That is the sort of thing the best kind of American white man does; and I was not in the least surprised at your doing it.

My only excuse is that I put the money on deposit to keep it safe for you, though I took no precaution against my dropping dead and leaving you with no claim on my executors. The amount was $585.13. On deposit for twenty weeks it has grown to $596.38, draft for which I accordingly enclose.

You need not hesitate to let me have my own way in this matter. The responsibility I took in the matter was not yours, but Chapman's; and for seeing them through I had reasons peculiar to myself and in no way binding on you. The original agreement was made on your behalf by your agent and signed by Chapman's. Then I came in and upset the whole affair. I cut your agent clean out of it. I tore up the agreement and drew up an entirely new one myself, which I forced on all the parties. As it happened, I insisted in it that Chapman's should be responsible for any libellous matter contained to their knowledge in the book, which they were bound to examine with that in view before publishing. In short, I walked over everybody; and of course there was an element entirely personal to myself in Chapman's humoring me and leaving the matter in my hands. Finally I took over the copy for the printer and virtually undertook to get it right, altering your stuff as well as my own; and to this Chapman's obtained your full consent. In this way, though technically Chapman's remained responsible for the reading of the copy before publication, I became really responsible, as I took it on myself, and they left it to me, as you did also. I should have spotted the dangerous page; but I did not; and the result was that I let you and Chapman's in. Now my personal relations with W. L. Courtney and Arthur Waugh make it impossible for me to let them go to their Board of Directors and say that they have incurred a debt of $500 by trusting to me. This reason for seeing them through does not touch you at all.

There is another reason. Evans's case against you was such a very poor one that even if there were no Welshmen on the jury he could hardly have hoped for more than a farthing damages. When I read the book I immediately marked certain pages, the reading of which in court would have finished him as far as the sympathies of the jury or the bench were concerned. To pay him $500 damages would have been quite ridiculous: it would have been difficult for him even to insist on a withdrawal of the offending statement except in terms that would have amounted to a repetition of the disparagement. All he had to complain of was that his book had been destroyed by a magistrate's order instead of "suppressed": that is, that you had spared him instead of rubbing the truth in. As between him and you, there wasn't a twenty pound note in it.

But as between him and me it was different. I am a thrice censored author; and the effect on public opinion of my setting up in the censorious line would be too like that of the pot calling the kettle black. I felt that though Evans had no grievance against you, he might with some countenance turn round on me, and ask me was it playing the game to take the side of conventional morality against him, or at least to let the attack on him pass without comment, when I had so often defied it, in however different a way. I thought I owed him a solatium for that if he chose to demand it, and therefore offered a tip that I should never have proposed on your account. That was my own affair.

Finally, there was the pure business aspect of the case. I was so circumstanced that the time and thought it would have taken to fight him instead of building a bridge of silver for him to retreat across would have cost me more than the $500 he demanded. To give him $500 was very good business for me. But there is no reason why you should pay to save my time. I threw down the money and drafted the withdrawal solely with a view to get the affair off my hands at once without spending another hour on it. I did not consider you on this point at all; and I could not have justified the settlement if it had been made at your expense.

If you had been in any way at fault—if your statement had been false or malicious or made without evidence, then I might allow you to appease your conscience by fineing yourself. But as what you said, in so far as it departed from the technical legal fact, was a softening of it, and Evans had no real grievance at all (his book was only on sale for a shilling a copy at a big multiple store which had bought the unsold remainder as junk) it is quite intolerable that you should suffer in the matter.

Now for the reason of my long delay in writing this letter. I am working hard to get this Intelligent Woman's Guide to Socialism and Capitalism through the press. It is a tremendous job of real literary work: not like play writing. I have sent 70,000 words to the printer; and I have to send 70,000 more. I find as a matter of invariable experience that if I answer letters or relax in my desperate resolution to let everything else slide, the book stops dead. As to thinking of the biography until I am through with the book, it is out of the question. But when I get comparatively free, which I hope to within the next few months, I shall tackle the collected edition of my works, and, incidentally, read the biography and send you an annotated copy. . . .

ever
G. Bernard Shaw

To OTTO KYLLMANN

10 Adelphi Terrace WC2
[A(inc.).u/1]   10th February 1926
[Kyllmann had been prodding Shaw to commence work for Constable & Co. on the edition of his collected works that had been hanging fire for several years.]

My dear Kyllmann
    I should say on the face of it that this is worth careful consideration; but then I do not know how Collected Editions are worked: that is, what the alternatives are. It is evident that the number of people who will pay from £20 to £30 down for library furniture (which they never take down from the shelf) is small compared to those who will buy it on the instalment plan for the sake of reading it, especially if they don't know that they can buy it all at the nearest bookshop for a third of the money; but ordinary publishing does not get at them: one needs a special canvassing and advertising organisation like the Enc. Britt. Co. to do the job. There must be others. In America they run Kiplings and Mark Twains in this way; and I have had proposals which I thought worth following up; but Brentanos always choked them off somehow.
    I imagine the thing to do is to launch the Collected Edition (when it is ready—O God!) in the usual way, and then, having the type available, let the E.B. or any similar organization make us an offer for a thousand sets or whatever quantity they think they can dispose of through their advertisements and their tallymen. As they do their own binding and choose their own paper it would really mean simply authorising Clark to print so many sets to their order at their expense, they paying us for the authorisation only.—But, as I said, I am not conversant with the business.

[Balance of letter missing]

12

To CHARLES SAROLEA

[H/76; X/339]

Ayot St Lawrence. Welwyn
20th February 1926

[The University of Edinburgh, through Sarolea, head of its department of romance languages, had offered Shaw an honorary degree of Doctor of Laws. Nearly ten years later he declined a similar offer from Harvard University on the occasion of its tercentenary, writing to the proposer, Dr John B. Sears, on 23rd November 1935, "I cannot pretend that it would be fair for me to accept university degrees when every public reference of mine to our educational system, and especially to the influence of the universities on it, is fiercely hostile. If Harvard would celebrate its 300th anniversary by burning itself to the ground and sowing its site with salt, the ceremony would give me the liveliest satisfaction as an example to all the other famous old corrupters of youth, including Yale, Oxford, Cambridge, the Sorbonne etc. etc. etc." (*Harvard Magazine*, January 1986)]

My dear Sarolea

What have I done to deserve this? Nothing could induce me to take part in such a farce. If the University cannot take its degrees seriously I can. To pick out the one academic department which my work has never touched, and offer me a degree in that, is an insult to me and to Law, an undignified caper which makes light of learning and its institutes. No doubt the same caper has been cut so often that nobody now supposes that an Edinburgh honorary degree means anything; but if this is so, then how dare the University offer it to me? However, it serves me right: I have played the clown in so many harlequinades that it is perhaps unfair for me to suddenly strike a serious attitude; but the University ought to know better.

I am not snubbing the University: I am rebuking it, as it ought to rebuke your frivolous committee for making a tomfoolery of its graduations.

yours, on a very high horse indeed,
G. Bernard Shaw

To G. S. VIERECK

[C/1]

10 Adelphi Terrace W C 2
24th February 1926

[A motto, "Thay haif said. / Quhat say thay? / Lat Thame say!" adorned the mantelpiece in Shaw's Adelphi Terrace flat. It was a charm (later found on rings at Pompeii) often inscribed over doors of houses in sixteenth-century

Scotland. *Physical Culture* was an American journal published by Shaw's friend Bernarr MacFadden.]

That motto is not mine: I spend a large part of my life explaining that it was in the house before I came into it.

There are contributions of mine in back numbers of Physical Culture, which gives far too much prominence to advertisements of overmuscled strong men. Eugen Sandow wanted to overmuscle me; but I told him I never wanted to stand my piano on my chest, nor did I consider it the proper place for three elephants. I remained a weakling; but I am alive and Eugen is dead.

Let not my example be lost on you, nor his fate. The pen is mightier than the dumbbell.

G.B.S.

To ARTHUR BOURCHIER

[A/9]

10 Adelphi Terrace WC2
3rd March 1926

[*Mrs Warren's Profession*, after a twenty-eight year proscription by the Lord Chamberlain's censor, had been licensed for public performance. It opened at the Strand Theatre, London, under the joint management of Arthur Bourchier and Charles Macdona, staged by Esmé Percy, on 3rd March. An invited audience attended a dress rehearsal the previous evening. The cast included Bourchier as Sir George Crofts, Agatha Kentish as Vivie, Carleton Hobbs as Frank, and J. Fisher White as Praed. Shaw's letter in the *Daily News* was a statement in reply to a leader that had charged Shaw with acquiescing "in the decrees of the Censor."]

My dear Bourchier

But for you I don't know what would have happened last night. It was a very near thing, in spite of the curtain calls. The frost was appalling until you came on. Let it be a lesson to both of us never to let any human soul into a theatre again unless he (or she) wants to come badly enough to pay for it. Tonight, with a real audience, it will be much better. The heroine will have got over her panic.

The young uns were magnificently steady. I am writing to F.W. to warm up the opening a little. He was unintentionally tragic as he entered, like the Bearer of Evil Tidings.

The Daily News having given me an opening, I have annexed three quarters of a column of it this morning for publicity.

Many thanks for everything. The part looks six times its natural size in your hands; and I hope it will keep the shop open until Easter, at all events.

ever
G.B.S.

To EDYTH GOODALL

10 Adelphi Terrace WC2
[A/1]   3rd March 1926

[Edyth Goodall (1882–1929) played Kitty Warren in the new production opening that night. Gladys Cooper (1888–1971), a musical comedy actress who later became a celebrated star in drawingroom comedy, had recently appeared in Frederick Lonsdale's *The Last of Mrs. Cheyney*.]

My dear Edyth

What a horrid audience! My heart bled for you. Why didnt you put out your tongue at them? However, tonight it will be quite different. The people will be there because they want to be there and have paid to be there.

You must let yourself rip accordingly. Last night was only cup-and-saucer comedy. Tonight you can give them the rough stuff, as broad, vulgar, and vigorous as you can make it. Never mind if you drop a line or two: nobody will know except the author; and HE don't matter. Play strongly at Crofts in your bits of temper in the first act; for if you make it too light you will not get in on top of Praed and Vivie, who have been leading up to you in a fairly energetic scene. Exaggerate the contrasts: don't smooth them out: too much trade finish takes the life out of my lines.

What you missed was the climaxes on "I despise such women &c.", "What's a woman worth without self respect," which should come out with overwhelming conviction. They are the keynotes of the part: character, self-respect, resistance to temptation &c. Unless these come out triumphantly, and Mrs Warren is morally wiping the floor with Vivie, Mrs Warren appears a mere snivelling apologist for her career instead of a victorious vindicator of it. You can do this if you get hold of the idea, and put all your *joyous* force into it (not, O God! your pathos); and if you don't, I'll kill you.

And for your life dont forget to turn the tears off after "I meant to see you oftener." The only moment when I was really terrified last night was when you turned on your fortissimo with your throat full of tears, and, of course, your voice went. You must not go on trusting to the emotion of the moment, and being taken by surprise by my quick changes every time. There is time to make the effect, but not to wallow in it—do you hear, Edyth, to wallow in it?—the next change is on you before you can say knife; so you must get it all mechanically, knowing everything and feeling nothing. If you try to play those two acts on your feelings you will be in an asylum in a fortnight: it's utterly impossible.

What business has an actress with feelings?

Tonight I will stimulate you from my box with shouts of Attaboy! or whatever it is that modern producers say. I want fifty thousand million times as much energy on and after "Oh, *I'll* sit down." If you play that scene quietly I'll get Gladys Cooper to do it. Dont do what ANYBODY can do: do what only Edyth Goodall can do. What are you afraid of?

Why dont [you] say a prayer before you enter? God will not desert you then.

If you dont make an *enormous* success tonight I will throw thunderbolts and reduce you to a little heap of ashes in the middle of the stage. This time you will have a house worth playing to. The ball is at your toe. Kick it hard, Edyth, *hard*; and live happily ever after.

GBS

[A postcard, written just after the performance on 3rd March, proclaimed: "Hooray, Edyth! GBS."]

To THE EDITOR OF THE *SÄCHSISCHES VOLKSBLATT*

10 Adelphi Terrace WC2

[H/1; W/340]   3rd March 1926

[The *Sächsisches Volksblatt*, Zwickau, on 11th February 1926, published a short story, "Das Kind" by Max Hayek, in which a beautiful but stupid woman and a small, misshapen but highly intelligent man mate eugenically, to create a beautiful and intellectual child. The female offspring, however, proves to have her father's physique and her mother's brain. A reader, accusing Hayek of plagiarism, cited earlier publication in the Milan *Corriere della Sera* of the now-celebrated anecdote in which the dancer Isadora Duncan seeks Shaw's consent to have a child by her. "You," she supposedly said, "have the greatest brain in the world, and I the most graceful body. Let us produce the perfect child." "What," Shaw allegedly replied, "if it turned out to have my body and your brain?" A furious Hayek insisted he had based his story on a real life situation involving a Budapest baron and a society beauty who had wed on eugenic grounds, and that he had never heard the Shavian account. In response to the editor's query, Shaw exonerated Hayek by insisting the story was foisted on him by the Italian journalist, with no basis in fact. Yet he subsequently assured an interviewer, Sewell Stokes, "The story has been told about me in connexion with several famous women, particularly Isadora Duncan. But I really received the strange offer from a foreign actress whose name you wouldn't know, and which I've forgotten. *But I did make that reply*" (*Hear the Lions Roar*, 1931).]

Dear Sir

You ask me to clear up the case of Herr Max's story Das Kind and the paragraph in the *Corriere della Sera* headed Bernard Shaw und die schone Tanzerin. Which is the original and which the plagiarism? Clearly the Bernard Shaw story is the plagiarism, and Das Kind the original. No plagiarist would turn a *verkäuflich* stroke of topical journalism into a literary fable. Any smart journalist might turn a literary fable into a *verkäuflich* topical paragraph. It is as plain as the sun in the heavens that this is what has happened.

But Herr Max must not blame me. No beautiful American dancer has ever proposed marriage to me, on eugenic or any other grounds. The Italian journalist invented the dancer and her proposal; stole the witty reply from Herr Max; and chose me for the hero of his tale because newspapers always buy stories about me. 99% of these stories are flat falsehoods. 1/2% are half true. The remaining 1/2% are true, but spoilt in the telling.

faithfully
G. Bernard Shaw

To RUTLAND BOUGHTON

10 Adelphi Terrace WC2
6th March 1926

[H/2]

[Rutland Boughton joined the Communist Party in February 1926, resigning in June 1929. In 1945 he rejoined the party, but withdrew finally in 1956, disillusioned by the Hungarian revolt. Mr Winkle is a character in Dickens's *Pickwick Papers*. General Miguel Primo de Rivera y Orbaneja (1870–1930) became dictator of Spain in 1923 as the result of a coup d'état. The Independent Labour Party, at its conference in October 1924, decisively rejected the

17

Communists' application for membership. Louis-Adolphe Thiers (1797–1877), French politician, aided in the rehabilitation of France after the Franco-Prussian war, negotiating a peace treaty with Germany (1871). He became first president of the Third Republic. Volney Constantin-François Chasseboeuf (1757–1820), Comte de Volney, was a French scholar and politician, founder of the republican journal *La Sentinelle du peuple* (1788). Grigory Zinoviev (1883–1936), Russian Communist leader, was president of the Third International (1919). An alleged letter from him to British Communists was responsible for the defeat of Ramsay MacDonald's first Labour Government in 1924. Shaw's attack on Zinoviev was contained in a letter to *Izvestia*, published in Moscow in full on 25th December 1924, which first appeared in the *Daily Herald*, London, on 8th December.

Boughton composed and published in 1925 a setting of Walt Whitman's "Pioneers" for chorus and orchestra. His marital relations were complex. In 1903 he married Florence Hobley, from whom he separated in 1910 when he became involved with Christina Walshe, a student at the Birmingham School of Art whom he passed off as his wife. In 1923 she was supplanted by Kathleen Davies, one of Boughton's pupils, with whom he had been enamoured since 1920, and whom he eventually married, in spite of the refusal of Florence, a Catholic, to recognise a secular dissolution.]

My dear Rutland

No: I am not the anonymous donor of the £100. I don't hold with the Communist Party. I happen to be a Communist; and as far as I can make out the Party's speciality is not Communism but Coup d'État-ism, the coup d'état to have no ulterior aim, but to be struck for its own sake as a sort of Marxian ceremony, and also to be announced beforehand in the manner of Mr Winkle, who took off his coat slowly declaring that he was just going to begin. By sensibly omitting this preliminary, Mussolini, General Primo di Rivera, and Lenin got away with their coups d'état, the circumstances being favorable. Our coup d'état-ists, having piously insisted on it in wildly unfavorable circumstances, got twelve months, which served them right for their hopeless failure to measure the situation.

The Labor Party made a serious mistake in expelling them as Communists. It should have simply imposed a test for membership like the signing of the Fabian basis, which would have excluded all the coup d'état-ists without repudiating Robert Owen, William Morris, and myself.

There is something pathetic in hearing these Clydeside men, all quite genuine in their social indignation and revolt against the capitalist world, spouting absurd muddled translations of Marx's 1848 German in the firm persuasion that they are uttering important economic and historical truths of the most advanced school. One man whom I heard doing this presently obliged the company with a song, and turned out to be a vocal genius with a rare basso profundo. I asked him why he persisted in talking obsolete foreign stuff that was neither English nor German nor good broad Scotch, and had absolutely no meaning for his audiences, when he could sing to them so well. All this Marxian resurrection pie is pitiable, almost tragic. They must be laughed out of it. Even Trotsky, a writer of splendid ability, and a most powerful realist critic, makes the most appalling gaffes occasionally because he really believes that what Marx was struggling to formulate in his academic way 75 years ago, and the phase of capitalism (employers' capitalism) that confronted him, are still not only fresh but startling and ultra-advanced, and that Webb is a belated Thiers, Wells a petit bourgeois Volney, and I, who passed through this Marxian phase forty years ago, and had it so acutely that I know the symptoms thoroughly, a benighted farceur to be spared the epithets he applies to Macdonald only because I am so sound on the subject of Trotsky's genius, and stood up for the Soviet right through its worst ill fame, until I let Zinovieff have it with both hands as a pretentious and mischievous noodle (one of Z's feats having been the rustication of Trotsky).

When you intimated that instead of composing you intended to devote yourself to a polemic against me, I was out of all patience; so much so that I had no time to tell you off in black and white. Fortunately you appeased me by sending me that new Whitman setting, which seemed quite healthy as far as I could judge from reading it away from the piano. I was away in Cornwall for weeks. When I play it over and sing it, I will know more about it.

One Kathleen Davis writes to me from Harrow to speak there. How is *your* Kathleen? Chris also wants to see me about something—not you this time, some journalistic stunt. She implies that I owe her reparation for your misdeeds, which I consider rather hard on me.

I note that as you know a hundred times as much about music as I, and I know a hundred times as much about Communism than you, you listen with the greatest docility to my views on orchestration, and are eager to undertake my reproof and instruction on Communism. Human, human, all too human!

ever
GBS

To SIEGFRIED TREBITSCH

[L/5; X/341]

Ayot St Lawrence. Welwyn
19th March 1926

[Shaw, ill with influenza, dictated the letter to Charlotte. Samuel Fischer and Trebitsch were busily arranging a German tribute to Shaw for his seventieth birthday in July, which would take the form of a large album containing contributions from most of Germany's principal intelligentsia. The album is still at Ayot St Lawrence. "Bilin Wasser" was a mineral water obtained from a spa in the Bohemian city of Bilin.]

My dear Trebitsch

You must not let this birthday business worry you. If the German Nation, which celebrated neither my youth nor my prime, wishes to celebrate my dotage by all means let it enjoy itself in that strange fashion as much as it pleases. Perhaps it is desirable that the world should be reminded that I am old & past my work, though I certainly need no such reminder myself. The only condition I make is that they shall not ask me to join in the festivities. I have done the work, but I positively refuse to do the shouting.

There is no reason whatever why you should not be as prominent in the affair as you please. Nothing could be more against my wishes than that all the gentlemen who have been assuring me for the last 30 years that your infamous translations have ruined my reputation in Germany & that they themselves are the true high priests of the Shavian culte, should now gorge themselves at public banquets in my honour from which you are absent, and send me albums of autographs from which your own is missing. Even honest devotees like Julius Bab must not be allowed to take your place in the sun. It must be a case of "Trebitsch, Trebitsch über alles." So do not step an inch out of the limelight under the mistaken impression that I desire your effacement. So you, & the faithful Fischer, may make the most of the occasion.

This is all I have to say for the moment. I have been in bed for 10 days & am ten feet long in consequence. When I have recovered my natural s[t]ature & activity I can attend to business.

Meanwhile give my love to Tina & tell her not to let you overdo the banquets. My health should be always drunk reverently in Billin Wasser after a simple vegetarian meal.

ever
G. Bernard Shaw

To APSLEY CHERRY-GARRARD

Hammels. Boar's Hill. Oxford
[A/3]   1st May 1926

[After his bout of influenza for a fortnight in March, Shaw had become indisposed at Malvern, recording in his engagement diary on 10th April "Very ill." En route to Ayot, he and Charlotte stopped to visit Sir Frederick Keeble and his wife Lillah McCarthy. The *Encyclopaedia Britannica* article, "Socialism: Principles and Outlook," appeared in the 13th edition (1926). An action against Shaw had been commenced in March in the Supreme Court of the City of New York by a young American lawyer Jesse Levinson, for reasons that will be clarified in the headnote to Shaw's letter to Levinson on 22nd August 1927. Shaw was dismissed from the New York suit, after a writ had been served on him at Malvern on 14th April, on the ground that service of the writ in England was not legally effective.

Fred Day (1883–1959), who had been employed by Shaw since 1918, had now become his chauffeur. Shaw had purchased a Bianchi car on 12th February from Arthur Roberts (1875–1950) of C. and A. Roberts (Whitwell) Ltd., his correspondence indicating a concern primarily for accessories: a klaxon horn to work from a button on the steering wheel, a mechanical windscreen wiper, and a spotlight with a mirror on its reverse. He was concerned too about appearances, informing Roberts on 15th February "I want the car to look as nice as possible to please my wife" (C/1).]

My dear Cherry

I am half alive: no more. The live half is all right; but which half is going to prevail is an open question. My inside is deranged; and when they analysed my secretions I was ulcerating somewhat; but except for a sense of indigestion that does not prevent my digesting in some strange fashion there is nothing that hurts. I am thirsty, and take in and put out unnatural volumes of fluid. I am decrepit and crawl about and sleep. On arriving here I started a headache, and am therefore at my lowest.

At Malvern I was making headway, and should have almost recovered if I could have taken it easily; but, besides some rather crowded normal work, I had to write an article on Socialism for the Encyclopedia Brit. before the end of the month; and in the middle of the time I had reserved for it I was served with a writ from the Supreme Court of America (by a film pirate) which put three days extra hard work on me. Then, presuming on my improvements, I did a couple of ascents of the Malvern Hills with great vigor at the cost of complete disablement through deferred fatigue on the following day. However, my temperature does not go above 99; and I drive the car as usual instead of sitting huddled up beside Day; so I suppose I am better than I was. But parts of me are still as dead as a doornail.

The Bianchi people have calmly sent for the car to replace all the timing gears, and differential gears[,] with properly cut helical pinions from Italy. Apparently they tried a dud car on me to see whether I would know the difference; and, when they found that I did, magnanimously offered to give me the real thing "without charge"! Such is business in the motor trade.

We shall be back on Monday; so the rest of my news can be communicated viva voce.

ever
G.B.S.

To KATHLEEN HILTON YOUNG

[H.t/1]

Ayot St Lawrence. Welwyn
20th May 1926

[Since 1922 Kathleen Scott had been married to Edward Hilton Young (1879–1960), a barrister, Liberal (later Conservative) M.P. 1915–35, and Financial Secretary to the Treasury 1921–22, who was created first Baron Kennet of the Dene in 1935. The phrase "the korps should be ready!" appears in "Edwin Forrest as Othello," in *Artemus Ward: His Book* (1862) by Charles Farrar Browne.]

My dear Kathleen

Yes: I know: I have left your letter unanswered for months and months. But has nobody told you that this old thing is busted at last? On the very threshold of seventy I have fallen through with a crash into ninety, and am no more fit to gambol with you and Peter [Scott] and Peterkin and Peter the Great on the shores of Cornwall than to win a Marathon. At the beginning of March I got ill; and though I am working again (too much; but I cant help it: the work wont wait) I have left half of me behind. Unluckily it is the half that enabled you to tolerate me. If you could offer me a nursing home, now, and give poor Charlotte a holiday, I might consider it.

I havnt had the slightest pain; I havnt had a stroke; I have had nothing but temperatures and disablement and something wrong with my inside that doesnt hurt; so you must not weep for me. If I go to see you some afternoon you will notice nothing about me except that I have become an old bore.

The bathing is a temptation: I have an obscure fire within me that craves for cold water.

If only I could finish my confounded book for women on Socialism! When you read it you will be able to lord it over H.Y. with your grasp of finance.

You can start my monument as soon as you please. As Artemus Ward used to say, the corpse will be ready.

However, I am not always as macabre as this. Some days I am quite jolly; and I may beat the darned thing yet, whatever it is.

ever
G.B.S.

To J. E. VEDRENNE

Ayot St Lawrence. Welwyn
[H.t/4]   27th June 1926

[Negotiations for a film version of *The Devil's Disciple* came to nought, as did all other efforts to film Shaw's plays until the emergence of the talking picture a few years later.]

My dear Vedrenne

Probably nobody else on earth could have induced me to reconsider this film business. I think I shall let The Devil's Disciple go if I can guard myself against having it spoiled by turning it into a love story. How to do that requires more consideration than I can give it by return of post. I am out of sorts and can do nothing today. But you may sound your principals as to whether the D's D. would suit them.

Pygmalion is all nonsense: if they had read or seen the play they would know that it must be *heard* to be intelligible.

ever
G.B.S.

To STANLEY W. BULL

[Ayot St Lawrence. Welwyn]
[E/60; X/350]   6th July 1926

[Stanley Bull of Epsom informed Shaw he had been querying "a number of well known personalities" to determine if they considered drapery "essentially a man's job." H.G.Wells had written in agreement "that

23

drapery is a man's job, provided that the drapers insist upon being treated like men and belong to a proper trades organisation to protect their rights and dignity."]

I do not see that drapery is a man's or woman's job any more than saddlery is a horse's job, or a mare's. Drapery requires considerably more athleticism than authorship, which is considered masculine enough. There are departments of drapery in which women prefer to be attended to by women and men by men, which seems to prove that both men and women are indispensable. The male draper, like the male hairdresser, the male greengrocer, and the tailor, are represented as comic in fiction; but as in fact all men are comic, especially deans, bishops, and drum majors (who dress their parts), I don't think this need worry you.

G. Bernard Shaw

To J. C. W. REITH

[Ayot St Lawrence. Welwyn]
[E/99]   11th July 1926

[J.C.W. Reith (1889–1971), knighted in 1927 and created First Baron Reith of Stonehaven in 1940, was managing director of the British Broadcasting Corporation. In 1927 he became first director general of the B.B.C. On 30th June Reith informed Shaw that a small committee was being formed to advise the B.B.C. on pronunciation, and that the poet laureate Robert Bridges and Sir Johnston Forbes-Robertson joined him in inviting Shaw to become a member of the committee. From 1930 to 1937 Shaw was chairman of this Advisory Committee on Spoken English.]

I accept, and suggest (offhand) the following additions to the list of recent problems.

Cowardice, facile, fertile, isolate, Jacobean, exemplary.

G. Bernard Shaw

To HARRY SNELL

10 Adelphi Terrace WC2
[A/68]   15th July 1926

[A Complimentary Dinner in honour of Shaw's seventieth birthday was organised by his Socialist colleagues at the Hotel Metropole on 26th July, with J. Ramsay MacDonald in the chair, Harry Snell (1865–1944), later First

Baron Snell of Plumstead, a Labour M.P. long associated with the Fabian Society, apparently was a member of the arrangements committee. As a consequence of Shaw's refusal to give assurance he would not be controversial, the B.B.C. cancelled the scheduled broadcast of his talk, arguing that it was bound by its licence not to broadcast political speeches sponsored by partisan organisations. To Shaw, in a letter to the *Manchester Guardian* published on 17th August, it was "an embargo on criticism of the Government ... specially applied to the Labour Opposition ... It is a shameless abrogation of the British right of free speech. ... And, incidentally, but for it I should not have mentioned the Government in my speech."]

My dear Snell

Tell the B.B.C. and "the authorities" what they know very well already: that my speech, like all my speeches, will consist from beginning to end of violently controversial arguments on questions of public policy, and that the only undertaking I will give is to use my own best judgment as to what I ought or ought not to say. If any authority pretends to be a better judge, the public will be glad to know his or her name.

Should I abuse the right of free speech, the authorities have their legal remedy. That is the only security to which they are entitled.

faithfully
G. Bernard Shaw

To FRIEDRICH STHAMER

[X/342]

[10 Adelphi Terrace W C2]
28th July 1926

[This is a response to a letter of congratulations on Shaw's seventieth birthday from Dr Gustav Stresemann (1878–1929), German Minister of Foreign Affairs and winner in 1926 of the Nobel Peace Prize, delivered to Shaw by Friedrich Sthamer (1856–1931), German Ambassador in London 1920–30.]

My dear Sthamer

The public honor done me by the message of the German Minister of Foreign Affairs is enhanced by its coming through your hands. It is the sort of thing that would never occur to a British Foreign Secretary, because, as you well know, we are a barbarous nation in matters of culture. We have a genuine dread of intellect in any form, and a conviction that Art, though highly enjoyable clandestinely, is essentially immoral. Therefore the sole notice taken of my seventieth birthday by the British Government was its deliberate official prohibition of the broadcasting of any words spoken by me on that occasion.

The contrast between this attitude and that of the German Government would be a painful one for a nation with cultural traditions; but our governing classes are rather proud of it. To them I owe my reputation as a dangerous and disreputable person: to Germany I owe my recognition in Europe as a thinker and dramatic poet. What is more important, Europe owes to Germany such European sense as exists of the importance of thought and dramatic poetry, and the value of lives devoted to them. Therefore, a tribute from Germany confers on me a distinction that no other nation in the world could give me.

If I were a German I should be justifiably proud of this. As I am, if not an Englishman (as you know, I am an Irishman), at least a lifelong and faithful servant of the English people, I am sorry that it should be so. But it is so; and I am none the less grateful to Germany.

These, however, are merely national considerations. There is a supernational republic of Thought and Art, to the great German members and masters of which my debt is incalculable; and that their countrymen should admit my claim to be a member of it is a triumph which enables me to face without blushing all the eulogies and congratulations showered on me on the first birthday I have ever celebrated, and the last I intend ever to celebrate.

I am fortunate in having the privilege of your personal friendship, which enables me to speak more frankly than I could if our relations were merely official.

faithfully
G. Bernard Shaw

To HENRY ARTHUR JONES

Regina Palace Hotel. Stresa
[A/4; X/124]   27th August 1926

[The Shaws departed for Stresa, Italy, on 4th August, not returning to London until 4th October. Upon learning that his erstwhile friend Henry Arthur Jones was ill, Shaw sent a fence-mending consolatory letter. Jones apparently was moved by the letter, passing it round to family and close friends, but he did not respond. "I think," Doris Arthur Jones wrote in a biography of her father, "he felt that if he answered . . . the old dear friendly relations must inevitably be resumed, and that this would be a betrayal of all his years of work and of the confidence and encouragement given to him by so many of his old friends, and also by enormous numbers of the general public here and in America" (X/124). Jones's article to which Shaw alludes was "My Religion," on 24th September 1925, in a series in the *Daily Express*.]

My dear H. A. J.

I meant to congratulate you on my 70th birthday, but was afraid of sending your temperature up 10 degrees at a critical moment. I am assured now by Max that you are well enough to stand anything; so I insist on affirming that the news of your illness gave me as much concern, and of your safe deliverance as much relief, as if we were still the best of friends. Our quarrel has always been a hopelessly one-sided affair; and I have rejoiced in your vigorous invective far too much to feel any malice at the back of it. Some of it, by the way, was very sound Shavian economics[.]

I was particularly delighted with an article of yours on Religion, in a series in—wasn't it the Daily Express? Anyhow, it was by far the best of the lot, and I have always since cited it to prove that what you suffer from occasionally is an excess of mental vigor, and by no means a deficiency in essential friendliness for me personally.

People who obviously pity my dotage have a well meant but disagreeable habit of reminding me that Sophocles wrote his best plays at 80. I suppose they say the same to you. They know nothing about it; but you seem to me to have more drive and style than ever. I wish I could say the same for myself; but at present I feel that my bolt will be shot when I have got through the final struggle to finish my book on Socialism, with every word of which you will agree. The truth is, I am for the moment so completely done up by work on top of illness (the result of an accident) that the writing of this letter would tire me for the rest of the day if the feeling it expresses were not so nourishing. So you really are doing me good.

Do not bother to reply—though I warn you I shall put the friendliest interpretation on silence. This birthday business, involving as many congratulations (on being 70! Good God!!!) as your recovery is bringing on you, has shewn me how easy it is to kill a strong man by a full broadside from the post office. Just note that I am not to be shaken off, and turn over for another nap with a groan of resignation.

ever

G.B.S.

To KATHLEEN HILTON YOUNG

Regina Palace Hotel. Stresa
[C(4 cards)/1]   2nd October 1926

[Each of the four postcards on which this message was written bore a photo-graphic portrait of Shaw on the reverse. Prince Paul Troubetskoy (1866–1938), Russian sculptor, created his first bust of Shaw during a hurried pair of sittings, totalling three hours, in John Singer Sargent's London studio in 1908. Shaw later presented it to the Theatre Guild. The Shaw statuette (1926) is now at Ayot St Lawrence. A life-size statue of GBS by Troubetskoy (1927) stands today on the lawn at the entrance to the National Gallery of Ireland, Dublin. Troubetskoy's Villa Cabianca was built on the shore of Lago Maggiore. Albert Coates (1882–1953) was a Russian-born orchestral conductor of the Imperial Opera House, St Petersburg, from 1910 until the Revolution, as well as a teacher and composer. Shaw and he became good friends.]

These are the next most interesting postcards I have: handsomer than your ceratosaurus anyhow.

The dreadful truth is that one day on the lake the barcaiuolo [boat-man] pointed to a Villa and said "Troubetskoy." And presently Troubetskoy had us to lunch; and after lunch we went up to the studio to look at my 20-years-ago bust (which he had *not* smashed). I was hardly inside when he grabbed potfuls of plasticine—"Six minutes seulement"—and was half way through a statuette before I could pro-test. I had my arms folded just as in that old greenhouse by the river; and in a moment he had infringed your copyright. Then his wife produced a sacred volume in which T. had made a drawing of Tolstoy and Tolstoy had written his autograph. No other celebrity had ever been allowed to profane its otherwise virgin pages. Naturally I insisted on his drawing ME in that book; and he *did*, and I autographed the drawing and snuffed Tolstoy out.

But the drawing caused him to spend 20 minutes scrutinizing my face; and when we went back to the statuette he was dissatisfied with it, and dashed into a life size head, which was "nearly ready" in 40 minutes, but which after several repetitions of "encore un petit moment" has at last ended in a capo lavoro. Now there is the old bust which Charlotte despised (being jealous for her Rodin) and the new bust and the statuette, which serves you right for putting my nose out of joint with your hasty hammer.

My only hope is that you will think them so despicably lacking in trade finish that you will pass them over with Praxitelian complacency.

The gentleman on the other side [of the postcard] who is playing

Beethoven to my Shakespear is Albert Coates, who is much more completely clothed than usual. He has a villa on the clean side of the lake;
and I swim there with him every morning.

But the winter has set in; and we depart on Monday the 4th, reaching London next afternoon. I should go straight to B.P. [Buckingham
Palace] Road if I did not feel treacherous about Troubetskoy. You still
have your hammer.

G.B.S.

To SAMUEL FISCHER

10 Adelphi Terrace WC2

[H/1; X/343]   3rd November 1926

[German tributes to Shaw on his seventieth birthday consisted, not just of
the handsomely bound album prepared and sent by his German publisher
Fischer, but of lavish tributes in the press, notably from Bertolt Brecht in the
Neue Freie Presse and from Albert Einstein in *Die Literarische Welt*, the
latter proclaiming on 23rd July: "There are few human beings sufficiently
independent to recognize the weakness and foolishness of their contemporaries but to remain untouched thereby themselves. However, once they
have come to perceive the stubbornness of human beings, most of these
few soon lose the courage to work toward an improvement of those conditions. Only very few are fortunate enough to impress the people of their own
generation by their delicate and gracious wit and, by the impersonal power
of artistic expression, make these people see themselves in their true light.
Today, I salute with sincere sympathy the greatest master of that art who
has blessed and educated all of us." (Translation by Dr Otto Nathan;
published by permission of the Estate of Albert Einstein.)]

My dear Herr Fischer

You must have been surprised by my long silence concerning the
magnificent tribute you sent to me on the occasion of my 70th birthday, signed as it was by so many names eminent not only in Germany
but in Europe and indeed throughout the civilized world, and including
as it did the signatures of some valued personal friends. But the effect
was as if you had hung a massive gold chain round the neck of a goose,
and, with the best intentions, sunk the poor bird to the bottom of the
pond.

Had I been in perfect health and in the fullest vigor of my prime, I
should have recovered from the avalanche sooner; but I was 70, and,
as it unluckily happened, only half recovered from a long and serious

29

illness. What was I to do? I could have thanked you with a cordial handshake as I do now most heartily thank you for your friendly labors in organising the tribute. I could have embraced Trebitsch, to whom I owe my reputation in Germany. But how is one to shake hands with a range of mountains, or embrace Valhalla? Picture the old man wagging his overwhelmed head and mumbling Bitte, bitte, sehr verbunden, tausend Dank etc. etc. until he falls asleep exhausted!

I confess I got out of the difficulty by simply running away. A speech at a banquet, a letter to Herr Stresemann which provoked the most gratifying expressions of jealousy in the London press, and I fled to Italy and gave instructions that all journalists and all persons who looked as if they intended to congratulate me were to be informed that I had been drowned that morning whilst bathing in the Lago Maggiore.

On my return I hoped that everybody had forgotten all about my seventieth birthday; but the remonstrances of my wife, who has to see that I behave properly, and a visit from Trebitsch, awakened my lulled conscience, and made me feel that I must write to you and beg you to do what you can to convey to the signatories of the tribute that not a line of it was lost on me. Apart from the warm personal gratification it has given me I shall treasure it as an unchallengeable certificate of my success as a servant of European literature. If when I come to the final judgment I am reported—as I certainly shall be if the Recording Angel happens to be an Englishman—for having presumptuously thought myself a writer of some merit, I shall reply "Germany thought so," and that will settle the case.

faithfully
G. Bernard Shaw

To JOHN MARTIN-HARVEY

10 Adelphi Terrace WC2
11th November 1926

[H/9]

[Martin-Harvey had revived *The Shewing-up of Blanco Posnet* in variety at the Coliseum on 18th October, with himself as Blanco, Wilfred Shine as Elder Daniels, Gordon McLeod as the Sheriff, Mary Gray as the Woman, and N. de Silva (Martin-Harvey's wife) as Feemy. The Rev. Mr Stiggins is a drunken, hypocritical preacher in Dickens's *Pickwick Papers*. The text revision suggested by Shaw was subsequently added to the text published in 1930 in the Collected Edition. Feemy's "audacious" costume was designed by Florence Dyball. Martin-Harvey successfully produced *The Devil's*

Disciple in London, September 1930, and later on tour. Electric recordings had recently supplanted the less effective acoustical ones. The ever-resourceful Shaw appears to have been the first major theatrical personage to contemplate the use of "canned music" in a production.]

My dear Sir John

I squeezed in at the Coliseum one night, and was glad to find a house that left the management nothing to complain of. Blanco is all right for you; and you are all right for Blanco.

Just a hasty note or two on the performance. Tell the Sheriff that he must not dress and make-up as one of the boys: he should be clean, respectably dressed, wellspoken, and obviously a substantial man and the boss. At the Coliseum there was no distinction between him and the foreman of the jury. Both were rowdies, with the result that they killed one another.

Shine is too like a comic British Stiggins, quite out of the atmosphere. He is too good an actor to need that sort of tomfoolery: the effect will be far better if he is a credible mining camp elder-cum-publican.

The woman must not jump at her cue when she denies that Blanco is the man. You see, he *is* the man; and she is about to say so quite naturally when, as she looks at him, she suddenly realises that she is going to hang him. There must be a pause of suspense—will she give him away or not?—before she decides to tell a lie and save him.

But this was partly your fault. I warned you carefully not to use an old copy of the play, or, if you did, to say to Feemy "It's come over me again, same as when the kid touched me, *same as when you swore a lie to save my life.*" Without that line the audience thinks that Feemy did not see Blanco on the horse and was perjuring herself at the beginning, whereas the whole point of the thing is that she was telling the truth, but at the last moment "went soft" and called on God to strike her dead (at the risk of being taken at her word) if she ever saw him or the horse. I believe Lady Harvey herself was wrong about this; for the one point that she missed in a very clever performance was that she waited for a laugh at "It's you and your snivelling face that has put me off it." The saving lie should come out right on top of this with the recklessness of a woman who is going to tell a lie and shame the devil. She rises to telling a lie instead of falling to a confession of the truth. She will understand this all right when she gets the idea.

I was a bit startled by the Russian Ballet dress: it was audacious, but, like Wilfred's shabby clerical get-up, out of the picture. However, audacity always tickles me; and I shall not protest, though I had better warn Feemy that it destroys the disgusted pity that a realistic Feemy inspires, and finally gets that terrible laugh in the wrong place. It makes her a figure of fantasy and fun instead of a squalid tragedienne.

You must emphasize Blanco's delirium tremens a bit in the two places where it explodes. First, when the elder moves to the door and Blanco is afraid to be left alone. You fail to give the requisite touch of the horrors: it looked as if you were keeping the elder merely out of devilment. And again, when the trial is interrupted, and Strapper says "No: it's a woman," Blanco should scream and go all to pieces. His voice should be broken with abject terror when he blubbers "That woman aint real etc," so as to give an unmistakeable and urgent cue for the Sheriff's "Shut your mouth, will you. You have got the horrors." Of course you must *act* this: don't let yourself go and do it on your nerves or it will knock you out for the rest of the performance; but you must produce the illusion of being frantic.

These are the only useful tips I can give you in a hasty letter. I enjoyed the performance, though I am anything but a Shaw fan. If you never have a worse play and I never have a worse star, we shall do very well.

I should recommend you to read *The Devil's Disciple* if it were not for that confounded military band at the end, to say nothing of the crowd of supers. They cost too much. But have you heard the new gramophones and the new records. They may solve the military band problem with a little management.

faithfully
G. Bernard Shaw

To EBBA LOW

Ayot St Lawrence. Welwyn
14th November 1926

[A/5]

[Lady Low, as Shaw's Swedish translator, was among the first to congratulate him on being awarded the Nobel Prize for Literature for 1925. Shaw initially had informed the Swedish Consulate, however, that he would decline the honour since it required that he accept an unneeded and unwanted monetary award of 118,165 Sw. Kr. (approximately £6500).]

My dear Ebba

. . . I will not accept the Nobel Prize; but I will not throw it back at their heads until the distracted Baron Palmstierna has had an opportunity of discussing the terms of my refusal with me.

I gather from your letter that you will not be surprised. If the prizes are to be reserved on Safety First principles for old men whose warfare is accomplished, the sooner they are confiscated and abolished by the Swedish Government, the better.

ever

G.B.S.

To THE PERMANENT SECRETARY OF THE ROYAL SWEDISH ACADEMY

[10 Adelphi Terrace WC2]

[H/88; X/453]   18th November 1926

[After conferring with Baron Erik Kule Palmstierna (1877–1959), Swedish Minister to England, Shaw eventually agreed to accept the monetary award provided the money be channelled to a newly-established Anglo-Swedish Literary Foundation for translation into English of works by neglected Swedish writers. This use of the money was ironic in view of a statement made by Shaw to Frederic Whyte on 21st January 1926: "The Swedes have a very high level of mediocrity: higher than the Swiss. But—bar the accident of Strindberg—no genius" (C/74). The Trust Deed, made on 21st March 1927, called for three trustees, the initial appointees being Baron Palmstierna; the Rt. Hon. Viscount Burnham (Harry Lawson); and Admiral Henry Lindberg, President of the Svensk-Engelska Föreningen, Stockholm. The Foundation also contributed financially to the production of Strindberg's *The Ghost Sonata* at the Globe Theatre in June 1927 and to the Anglo-Swedish Players' production of Oscar Rydquist's *His Majesty Must Wait*, at the Arts Theatre Club, in February 1928. It has quietly functioned to the present time. The Nobel Prize medal and diploma were delivered to Shaw by Palmstierna in February 1927, after he declined to attend the formal ceremonies in Stockholm on 10th December.]

To the Permanent Secretary of the Royal Swedish Academy,

The Award of the Nobel Prize for the year 1925 to an English work is a very welcome reinforcement of the cordial understanding between British and Swedish culture established by the famous bequest of Alfred Nobel. It will not be lost on my native country, Ireland, which already claims one distinguished Nobel prizeman [Yeats]. It is naturally very gratifying to me personally that it has fallen to my lot to furnish the occasion for such an act of international appreciation.

I must, however, discriminate between the award and the prize. For the award I have nothing but my best thanks. But after the most careful

33

consideration I cannot persuade myself to accept the money. My readers and audiences provide me with more than sufficient money for my needs; and as to my renown it is greater than is good for my spiritual health. Under these circumstances the money is a lifebelt thrown to a swimmer who has already reached the shore in safety. I therefore respectfully and gratefully beg the Swedish Royal Academy to confer on me the additional and final honour of classing my works in that respect *hors concours*.

Should this event have been unforseen and unprovided for by the founder of the prizes, it may have the effect of placing at the disposal of the Nobel Directors a sum as to which they are not bound by the difficult and occasionally impossible conditions of prizegiving. May I therefore seize this opportunity to call the attention of the Board to the following consideration.

Some of the most advantageous sites in London are being rapidly filled up with agencies in which not only the British Dominions Oversea, but the European Powers, exhibit their choicest products and advertise the attractions and travelling facilities of their countries. Fruits, cereals, stuffed animals and birds, fabrics of all sorts tempt the importer. The one thing that is rarely exhibited is a book. Sweden invites us to buy her paper; but there is nothing printed on it: the function of Swedish paper, it seems, is to wrap Australian apples in. And yet Sweden's most valuable export is her literature, of which we in Britain are deplorably ignorant.

The Swedish Minister in London, Baron Palmstierna, who is a proved friend of British men of letters and an indefatigable champion of Swedish literature in our country, has informed me of Swedish books of great value which for lack of means cannot be translated and of organs working for the intellectual intercourse between us which are in need of support.

I therefore venture to propose to you that the money which accompanies the award be funded by the Royal Academy or by the Swedish Minister in London and the annual proceeds be used to encourage intercourse and understanding in literature and art between Sweden and the British Isles.

It would be desirable for many reasons that the Swedish Minister should be a member of the Board controlling the fund.

G. Bernard Shaw

To C. B. McCULLOCH

[E/1]

[10 Adelphi Terrace WC2]
18th November 1926

[Christina B. McCulloch had written to point out an apparent anachronism in the surrealistic Epilogue to *Saint Joan*. Shaw's reply was written at the end of her three-page letter.]

Dreams are prophetic in Scripture, to which class of literature, I take it, the Gospel of St Joan must be assigned.

G.B.S.

To CHARLES McEVOY

[A/83]

Grosvenor Hotel. Shaftesbury
23rd December 1926

[The Shaws were en route to Torquay, where they holidayed for a month. Impervious to Shaw's earlier criticism and protestations (see letter of 26th March 1916), Charles McEvoy continued to pressure him for loans. And although he seemed adamant in his refusal, the softhearted GBS continued to dig into his bank account, undertaking in 1928, for example, to pay to the landlord McEvoy's arrears of rent.]

Dear McEvoy

You are certainly a naïve creature. You think you must have mortally offended me because I dont pay your rates. There are forty millions of people in this country whose rates I dont pay. There are thousands of people all over Europe who are clamoring in all their languages at me to give them the Nobel Prize or some of it. You are on velvet compared to most of them. I am like a man with a plank in the sea amid universal shipwreck, kicking other people off it, and becoming as insensible to prayers and pleadings, to age and sex, to despair and death agonies, as a professional executioner. Do you suppose all those unfortunate people have mortally offended me? Not one of them. Why dont you appeal to some *nouveau riche*, whose expenditure has not yet swelled to his income, and to whom no one dreams of applying? He (or she) will pay your rates for the mere novelty and swank of being a benefactor. *I* can no more afford to help all the people who ask me than I can afford to answer their letters. Besides I *hate* giving people money; and they hate me if I give it, though they do not hate me in the least if I tell them to go to the devil. If I refuse to discuss money

35

with you or to be bothered with your worries, the relations between us will be pleasant to both of us. If I become merely the Relieving Officer our relations will be detestable. Every time you borrow five shillings you sell a friend for that sum; and the bargain is a bad one. In your case there is not the excuse of being a worm or a blackguard; but for some reason you can steel yourself to borrow from your friends money you know you cannot repay, and yet cannot steel yourself to insist on proper prices for your work. What screw is it that is loose in you?

I once told a man off (I knew him to be an infernal scoundrel) when he tried to borrow £5 from me by a choice collection of lies. He listened with exemplary patience, and then said "After all that I do not see how you can offer me less than half a sovereign." I recognized the justice of this, and parted with the coin. And now, having told *you* off, I suppose I must pay for my whistle. But I am not sympathetic about your illness, because I believe it has been brought on by borrowing. You are not the sort of man who can inflict psychic injuries on yourself with impunity.

I write this in a moment of leisure at a wayside inn on my way to Devon. How many such moments do you think I have for five years? Charles: you are a Bother; and good men say Damn! when they see your handwriting. Need this be, oh, NEED this be?

GBS

To KENNETH BARNES

[Y/3; X/289]

[The Hydro] Torquay
4th January 1927

[Kenneth Barnes (1878–1957), brother of Irene and Violet Vanbrugh, was appointed administrator of the Academy of Dramatic Art in 1909, and served as principal of what became RADA until his retirement in 1955. He was knighted in 1938. Shaw's telegram was in response to a request to be god-father to Barnes's son Michael, born in mid-December.]

AFTER CONSCIENTIOUS STUDY OF PRAYERBOOK FIND CANNOT COMPLY WITHOUT GROSS PERJURY BESIDE[S] WHY TAR HELPLESS INFANT WITH MY BRUSH NEUTRAL TINTED SPONSOR SAFER

BERNARD SHAW

To SIEGFRIED TREBITSCH

[H/5; X/341]

The Hydro. Torquay
13th January 1927

[The *Neue Freie Presse* on 30th December had reported a forthcoming film version of *Saint Joan*, with Shaw to appear in a prologue. In actuality Shaw was merely experimenting with scraps of dialogue to be spoken by Sybil Thorndike for a Lee De Forrest phono-film in which her husband Lewis Casson and Shaw would also make brief appearances. Archibald Henderson's extended article "My Friend Bernard Shaw" was world-syndicated, appearing serially from 2nd January to 20th February in the *New York American* and almost simultaneously in the *Sunday Chronicle*, Manchester, and the *Neue Freie Presse*. Cyril Maude's new play was Walter Hackett's *The Wicked Earl*.]

My dear Trebitsch

The report about filming St Joan is a lie, as usual; but it is true that I have been investigating the phono-film, and think it may have a great future. You should do all you can to encourage it, because it makes the translator as indispensable as the author. If St Joan was filmed in the ordinary way you would be, as you say, ruined; but if it were phono-filmed there would have to be a special film of your translation for all the German speaking countries.

I do not know what this new "Mein Freund Bernhard Shaw" of Henderson's is: he has told me nothing about it; but he is selling the serial rights; and editors are writing to know whether I approve. I echo your comment.

Cyril Maude is returning to the stage, and is announced to appear in a new play, not Jitta. I have very little hope of his interest in Lenkheim ever coming to anything.

I am in Torquay at present working hard at the book on Socialism. Only by neglecting everything else shall I finish it; but it is almost complete now.

Is Tina quite well?

In great haste
G.B.S.

To AUGUSTIN HAMON

[H/1]   2nd February 1927

[*Getting Married* (*Le Mariage*) was performed in Paris, in English, in June 1930; there is, however, no record of a French production. *La Grande Catherine*, starring Paulette Pax, on a double bill with Roger Ferdinand's *7, Rue de la Parvisse*, was first performed in Monaco, at the Théâtre de Monte-Carlo, on 27th November 1926. It opened at the Théâtre des Arts, Paris, on 8th March 1927. Georges Pitoëff, noted for avant garde theatre at his Théâtre des Arts, had been criticised for cashing in on Shaw's *Saint Joan*. Later in 1927 he took over the larger Théâtre des Mathurins for a season, where in early 1928 he produced *Heartbreak House*. Maxime Jacob (1906–77), composer of comic operas and incidental theatre music, converted to Roman Catholicism in 1929 and took holy orders. Hamon scissored Shaw's signature from the letter for a young friend Georges Sim, better known today by his real name: Georges Simenon.]

My dear Hamon

When two breaks are made in the performance of Getting Married, the first occurs at the end of the scene between the three Bridgenorth brothers; and the play is resumed with the first entrance of Hotchkiss. The second is made at the entry of Mrs George, who appears at the door. The curtain then descends; and when it rises the stage is exactly as before, and she says "Voici mon anneau, monseigneur etc."

But the play must not be described as in three acts. The program must state that the play is [not] divided into acts, but that for the convenience of the audience the curtain will descend twice during the performance for the customary intervals. Of course the Société [des Auteurs] must charge for it as for a full length play.

I cannot translate Bounder: it is pure slang. Fifty years ago, when the word rastaquouère had lost its original special meaning [foreign nobleman of doubtful antecedents], and Rasta was a general term of abuse, it would perhaps have served to translate Bounder; but Rasta seems now obsolete, and I do not know what slang word has supplanted it.

A bounder is a snob of the aggressive, pompous, pretentious, purse-proud, hochnäsig type. Mussolini's enemies would call him a bounder. Mazzini's enemies would never have dreamt of calling him a bounder. But the general expression "week-end bounders" used by Boxer means only the sort of people who have a lot of money to spend, and who pass the week-end in golfing or jazzing hotels, but are not de vieille race, like the Bridg[e]norths. . . .

38

"Two starving men cannot be twice as hungry as one" [one of the "Maxims for Revolutionists" in *Man and Superman*] is perfectly correct. Reflessichez un peu. Two men six feet high each do not constitute a man twelve feet high. Human stature can never exceed the stature of the tallest person living. And human hunger can never exceed the hunger of the hungriest person living. But two men can do much more than twice as much mischief as one by co-operation. A thief with a confederate is much more formidable than a single thief.

I agree that it is much better for Pitoeff to be ereinté for producing plays that pay than to receive a cool "Thank you for doing your duty" for ruining himself. But until some building speculator realizes that there is money in large theatres and low prices of admission and "highbrow" drama, and the old theatres with their war-inflated rents are superseded except for the sort of entertainments the rich people like, there will be nothing but heartbreak and ruin in Paris for artists like the Pitoeffs.

My book on Socialism has been advancing fairly rapidly for the last two months. I hope to have it ready for publication in the spring.

The Nobel Prize was a hideous calamity for me. All Europe wrote to me for loans, mostly of the entire sum, when the news was announced. When the further news came that I had refused it another million or so wrote to say that if I was rich enough to throw away money like that, I could afford to adopt their children, or pay off the mortgages on their houses, or provide them with a dot, or let them have £xxxx to be repaid punctually next May, or to publish a priceless book explaining the mystery of the universe. It says a good deal for female virtue that only two women proposed that I should take them on as mistresses. It was really almost as bad as my 70th birthday. Your regret that you have not f50,000 to give to the Pitoeffs proves that God knew what he was about when he gave you every gift except money. Decidedly you will mourir sur la paille. Never put a farthing into a theatre. Take money out of it if you can get it. Besides, as the sea is nearer to you than Paris you can always throw your money into it if you want to get rid of it. The Pitoeffs must suffer vicissitudes that would drive anyone but an actor mad: c'est leur sort—leur métier. Either Ludmila must learn birth control or Pitoeff selfcontrol. Writing sympathetic letters to actors is waste of time, because though they are in despair when you write, they are in the seventh heaven when your letter arrives.

I must have mislaid the letter in which you ask about Maxime Jacob and the music for Great Catherine; for I cannot find it, nor remember anything about it. But last year an immense improvement in the gramophone and in the methods of recording for it made it possible for the first time to use it effectively on the stage as a substitute for a full military band. Indeed the very latest invention, the Panatrope, costing £20,000, is so powerful that it is unbearable when it is thundering away at full blast. Now in Catherine all that is needed is to have one of the new gramophones to play the ballroom music with the effect of a first rate military band whenever the curtains are opened in the last scene. We cannot afford to share our tantièmes with a composer: they are split in half already. . . .

I think this is all. I have been in the west of England for four weeks, and my correspondence suffered as usual.

[ever
G. Bernard Shaw]

To LILY NIGHTINGALE DUDDINGTON

[A/6]

Ayot St Lawrence. Welwyn
3rd February 1927

[Mrs Duddington (*c.* 1875–1958) was the sister-in-law of John N. Duddington, former rector at Ayot, 1905–11, who had sub-let to the Shaws the New Rectory that they eventually purchased and called Shaw's Corner. The friend for whom she was seeking assistance was Ivan Bunin (1870–1953), Russian poet and novelist, who received the Nobel Prize for Literature in 1933.]

Dear Mrs Duddington

I am sorry for your friend, or would be if the correspondence brought upon me by the Nobel Prize had left a scrap of sensibility in me. The entire European professional class, and a huge section of the middle and pensioned official class, are now reduced to beggary; and as I am unfortunately a prominent mark for begging letters they all shoot at me, first because I accepted (as they thought) the Nobel money, and then because I must be enormously rich to be able to refuse it. You can imagine the result. One feels sympathetic about the first case, impatient about the twentieth, furious about the fiftieth, and indifferent about the hundredth. The letters go into the waste paper basket after a glance at "verzweiflung" "bitte bitte Herr Schaw" "M. 250 (or 250,000)" and so forth. Then the secretary has orders to tear them up at sight.

All well known people soon get like this. The rich unknown, especially the newly rich who have not yet expanded their outlay to their incomes, are the people to try, especially if their consciences are uneasy enough to make them anxious to ransom themselves from the devil.

I am glad to have a hail from you, though I have to shake my head heartlessly in reply.

faithfully
G. Bernard Shaw

To W. S. KENNEDY

[H.c.u/13; X/344]
[10 Adelphi Terrace WC2]
7th February 1927

[The *Daily News* had recently serialized Mussolini's "My Twenty-four Hours: Life and Work," as told to Thomas B. Morgan, Rome correspondent of the British United Press, in ten parts, from 6th to 17th January. A number of letters from readers was published, including one from the solicitor W. S. Kennedy, Shaw's longtime Stage Society colleague, on the 19th, and one by Shaw on the 24th captioned "Bernard Shaw on Mussolini: A Defence":

"The clear self-consciousness and unaffected self-judgment of Signor Mussolini certainly make an amusing contrast with the self-delusion and mock-modesty with which we lecture him for doing in Italy what we have never hesitated to do in England and Ireland on half the provocation he has had.

"One would think that our Cabinets of Oligarchs had never suspended the Habeas Corpus Act, suppressed a newspaper, or persecuted a Cobbett or a Kirkwood. The British Oligarch, it seems, may steal a horse where the Italian Dictator may not look over a hedge.

"Yet the only visible difference is that the British Oligarch kicks constitutional rights out of his way to secure the ascendancy of his class, whereas the Italian Dictator does it to get public business done diligently for the public benefit.

"All the people I discussed him with in Italy last year admitted this, and gave it as their reason for supporting him in spite of his disregard of the items in our Bill of Rights.

"They, as we would say, 'hold no brief for Mussolini'; but they enjoyed the punctuality of the trains, and the compulsion of the Civil Service to earn its pay, instead of regarding a public office as a place where fortunate bureaucrats take their ease and their tips at the expense of the Treasury and inert sexagenarians sit on young men's jobs.

"Why else should the Italians tolerate the Duce? His Blackshirts could no more stand against public disapproval than against the London Metropolitan Police; indeed it is clear that it is Mussolini who protects the Blackshirts and not they who protect him.

"He is not popular as our demagogues are popular; people are too much afraid of him. They think him indispensable, which must mean that they find him useful. They are so tired of indiscipline and muddle and Parliamentary deadlock that they feel the need of a strenuous tyranny, and think Mussolini the right sort of tyrant.

"At least that was how it struck my very superficial tourist's contemplation of the situation. They may tire of him and swing back to Parliamentarianism, or he will in the course of nature die, as Cromwell died, leaving them to relapse, as we relapsed after Cromwell.

"But in the meantime, let us remember that it did not pay to be uncivil to Cromwell while he lasted; and as we did not dare to call Signor Mussolini's bluff at Corfu, and are clearly afraid of him, we had better treat him with distinguished consideration as a matter of policy, no less than of good manners."

Speaking of the sub-head to the published letter, "*I* did not call it A Defence," Shaw informed Graham Wallas on 7th February; "I should have called it a plea for civility if I had called it anything. . . . I'm sorry for Salvemini, Turati & Co [anti-Fascist Italian exiles]; but their polemics are very like those of Kautsky against Lenin, futilely pious" [A/13]. Enclosed was a private rejoinder Shaw had written to Kennedy on the same date, a letter that he released to the press for publication the following October: see 2nd October 1927, to Friedrich Adler.

Giacomo Matteoti (1885–1924), secretary-general of the Socialist Party of Italy, denounced the Fascist Party on 30th May 1924. Twelve days later he was murdered by Fascists, creating an international scandal and threatening Mussolini's recently established regime. Emmanuel-Joseph Sieyès (1748–1836), French revolutionary leader, was a principal organiser of the 1799 coup that raised Napoleon to first consul. The Benckendorffs, a Russian family of German origin, served under several tsars, and took part in the assassination of one of them. The last of the pre-revolutionary line, Aleksandr Konstantinovich (1849–1917), ambassador to Britain 1903–16, was active in the forming of the Triple Entente (1907). Walther Rathenau (1867–1922), German industrialist, writer, and statesman, was foreign minister when assassinated by nationalist reactionaries. Karl Liebknecht (1871–1919) and Rosa Luxemburg (1870–1919) were German socialist radicals, murdered en route to prison after their arrest during the insurrection of the Spartacus League (later the German Communist Party) that they had founded during the war. Thomas Wentworth (1593–1641), first Earl of Strafford, was Lord deputy of Ireland under Charles I. He was beheaded for the alleged intention of using Irish soldiers to war against the British.

The Greek island of Corfu was occupied briefly and bloodily by the Italians in 1923, shortly after Mussolini's rise to power, in supposed retaliation for the murder of an Italian general working with an international boundary commission on Greek territory. The international protests and anti-Fascist public opinion that followed the action antagonised the Duce to the extent of his ordering his naval heads to prepare for possible war with Britain, threatening "that if the London press did not become more favourable to fascist Italy he would find ways of making them regret it, adding that the British, by sympathising with the Greeks, were defying 'every principle of international morality'" (Denis Mack Smith, *Mussolini: A Biography*, 1982).]

My dear Kennedy

I am very sorry my comment on The Daily News articles on Mussolini, which the sub-editor headed A Defence, distressed you as it did. You were not the only one who jumped to the conclusion that I must have been unaware of the Matteotti affair, and of the other revolting incidents of the Fascist terror. This is quite a mistake. I knew about them. Even if the Liberal press in Britain had been reticent on the subject, which it certainly was not, I have been in touch with the Italian refugee whose letter you have sent me, and already knew all that letter told me, besides a great deal more that I can infer from my experience and historical knowledge just as certainly as if I had witnessed it.

But you cannot dispose of Mussolini by simply repeating in a tone of virtuous indignation the admitted and even vaunted fact that he owes his power to a *coup d'état*. Since Augustus founded the Roman Empire, with himself as emperor, by a *coup d'état* which began with the assassination of Cæsar, until Lenin became Dictator of Russia by a violent overthrow of Kerenskyist Liberal democracy involving the very unpleasant operations of the Tcheka, there have been dozens of great usurpations effected by *coups d'état*; and everyone of the coups has been a filthy business in which honest and loyal men have been shouted down in court by perjured witnesses and timeserving magistrates, and have been beaten, tortured, and murdered out of it by gangs of infernal blackguards. All liberties of speech or the press have been suspended until the object of the *coup* had been attained by a thorough reign of terror. The only novelty in the Italian case was the castor oil; and most men would rather be dosed with castor oil than be tarred and feathered.

Now it is clear that our attitude towards a new regime cannot be determined by the means employed to establish it. It is no use fighting Augustus or provoking him to fight you merely because Antony points eloquently to the gashes on Cæsar's body. You cannot ignore Napoleon because he kicked out the excessively constitutional Abbe Sieyès. You cannot demand the reconquest of the Irish Free State because it has passed a Co-ercion Act that would have horrified Lord Salisbury, sweeping away the democratic councils established by the London

43

Parliament and replacing them by autocratic triumvirates such as Dublin Castle at its worst would never have dared to set up. It is silly to refuse to trade with Russia because the Soviet connived at regicide and made an end of the nice dinners given by the dear Benckendorffs. It would be absurd to pretend that the Kaiser is still the rightful ruler of Germany because the substitution of a republic was accompanied by the murder of Rathenau as well as of Liebknecht junior and Rosa Luxembourg.

It is equally irrelevant and silly to refuse to acknowledge the dictatorship of Il Duce because it was not achieved without all the usual villainies. The only question for us is whether he is doing his job well enough to induce the Italian nation to accept him *faute de mieux*. They do accept him, some of them *faute de mieux*, several of them with enthusiasm. His enemies—if you like, his victims—cannot pretend that they had not as good a chance as he. They actually make it a reproach to him that he offered to lead them on any program that would bring order out of chaos. But they were incapable of taking any chance. They could neither lead nor follow. They plead that they had post-war neurasthenia, and that if Mussolini had only waited until they got well, everything would have settled down into its old rut, with themselves enjoying their delightful position of eloquent revolutionary leaders guaranteed against revolution. If that did not seem good enough for Mussolini, and he finally had to come down on the side of a militarist Fascism which was at all events ready to do something, have they, of all people, the right to blame him. It is true that it was only as a sort of unbeheaded and successful Strafford that he could obtain his command of the Fascists; but as an unsuccessful Lenin he could have done nothing except lose his life.

Some of the things Mussolini has done, and some that he is threatening to do go further in the direction of Socialism than the English Labor Party could yet venture if they were in power. They will bring him presently into serious conflict with Capitalism; and it is certainly not my business nor that of any Socialist to weaken him in view of such a conflict. As to cocking snooks at him as the British aristocracy did at George Washington long after they had been forced to accept him as President of the independent United States of America, what good will that do? As long as he can say "J'y suis, et j'y reste," and the Italian people say "So you shall: viva il Duce!" we must accept the situation, and we may as well do it with a good grace. I repeat, we had our chance of challenging him over Corfu; and when we funked that we practically admitted that we must put up with him.

As he has not succeeded in keeping his enemies at home, I think he would do well to be more liberal of passports to his friends, because the Italian refugees who have escaped to Paris and London have it all their own way there when they represent Italy as groaning under an unbearable tyranny. All the tyranny I saw was of the kind which our Capitalist press denounces as characteristic of Socialism; and I do not boil with indignation at it as Liberals do. But that is not my point, which was and is that the campaign of abuse against the Mussolini dictatorship is just as stupid as the campaign against the Soviet dictatorship in Russia. I am sorry my fellow Socialists in Italy were totally unable to take command after the war; and I loathe the savageries which attended the establishment of Fascism. But I shall not waste my energies and compromise my reputation for good sense by refusing to accept an accomplished fact. If I did I should lose the right to criticize Mussolini's rule, which I am quite ready to do whenever I think I can do any good by it.

I hope I have made my position clear to you.

ever faithfully
[G. Bernard Shaw]

To LADY RHONDDA

10 Adelphi Terrace W C 2
[H/8]   9th February 1927

[Margaret Haig Thomas (1883–1958), Viscountess Rhondda of Llanwern, an ardent feminist, was editor of *Time and Tide* and chairman of its publishing company. On 27th January she debated with G. K. Chesterton on "The Menace of the Leisured Woman," with Shaw in the chair. Margaret Bondfield (1873–1953), trade unionist, labour leader, and M.P., became Minister of Labour 1929–31, the first female minister in the British Government. Shaw used her as a model for the Powermistress General in *The Apple Cart*. Annie Besant had returned from India in May 1924, becoming involved in an endless round of dinners, meetings, and speeches, the *Daily News* calling her "probably the best woman speaker in the Empire." In 1926 she returned to England again, at which time she gave a series of four lectures in the Queen's Hall on "The Coming of the World Teacher, as seen by Ancient and Modern Psychology."

Mrs Siddons's biographer relates that the noted actress, "bargaining for some calico" in a shop in Bath, and "hearing the mercer pour forth a hundred commendations of the cloth . . . put the question to him, '*But will it*

45

wash?' in a manner so electrifying as to make the poor shopman start back from his counter" (Thomas Campbell, *The Life of Mrs. Siddons*, 1839). Hannah Pritchard (1711–68), an actress who performed with David Garrick for many years, was considered to be the best Lady Macbeth on the stage before Mrs Siddons. Boswell reported Dr Johnson as saying, on 7th August 1775, "it is wonderful how little mind she had," and telling Sarah Siddons and John Philip Kemble, in October 1783, that Mrs Pritchard "in common life, was a vulgar ideot; she would talk of her *gownd* [gown]: but, when she appeared upon the stage, seemed to be inspired by gentility and understanding."]

My dear Lady Rhondda

Now that you have rashly given me a chance I think I'll give you a talking-to. If you are going into public life as a platform speaker and propagandist you must give up your business habits and take to artistic and intellectual ones. On the platform business habits are No Earthly.

What are business habits? First, complete disregard of technique, which can all be left to the clerk and the calculating machine, the telephone girl, the commercial traveller, and the shop assistant. Second, complete disregard of the nature of the article traded in, the only question to be considered being how much money it will make. The successful woman of business, like her male colleague, may be a clumsy, unpresentable, ill-mannered muddler, who, if she tried to get employment in any of the capacities I have just mentioned, would never even get the chance of being "fired": she would be turned down at sight, or, the moment she opened her mouth, at sound.

On the platform you must have the smart appearance of the clerk, the articulation of the telephone girl, the address of the shop assistant, and the knowledge of your wares and of their talking points of the commercial traveller, all in more than Bond Street perfection.

These accomplishments constitute style; and if you are Margaret Bondfield the public will ask for nothing more. But if you are a peeress a supercharge of style will be expected. If I were you I should, when addressing a popular audience[,] always wear my coronet (or whatever a viscountess wears), and get myself up as if for the Peeress's gallery when the King opens Parliament. Or at least I should put up enough flash to make the audience believe that I had them all on, and that I was every inch a peeress, though condescending amiably to be their affable friend and faithful public servant. And this cannot be done without style: the peeress's distinction cannot be expressed on the platform without the accomplishments of the telephone girl and the shop assistant. I hope you noticed the other night what an excellent shop walker I should make, and how carefully I took the first opportunity of making a little joke just to see by the response whether everyone could hear me. Now the technique of the business is simple enough. Your speaking at present is a public disgrace: lazy, slovenly, not merely unfinished but unbegun, the speaking of a fine lady with an unathletic mouth and no consideration for the poor woman at the back of the hall who has paid her hard earned money to hear every syllable. Also with no notion of what is wrong. But a few weeks exercises (mostly repeating the alphabet) will put you up to what to do; and a few months of actual practice on the platform or in Hyde Park will get up your articulatory muscles until your lips are like Paderewski's fingers. I could put you up to the whole thing in an hour. No brains are needed.

But it is with the commercial traveller's part of the business that the brains come in hard. If a bagwoman came to you and said "Can I interest you, Moddam, in a very special line of drinks?", and you said "Well, what sorts of drinks?", and you then found that all she could tell you was that she was travelling in some sort of fluid without knowing exactly what it was, and talked one moment about tea, and the next about coffee, and the next about cherry brandy, you would say "This woman is an idiot: shew her out."

Now that is just how you talked about the leisured woman. One moment she was the idle woman, the next the domestic woman, the next the stupid woman, the next the maternal voluptuary, the next the malingerer etc., etc., etc.; and it was evident that you have never sat down and drawn up an ideal working day for any woman, and modified it to suit all the different sorts of women who exist.

Chesterton has never done that either: his power of improvisation enables him to come on the platform and find something interesting to say on all occasions, relevant or not; but he got at your disparagement of domestic work for women, and recommendation of general non-domestic business; and he proceeded to disparage extra-domestic business and glorify home activities accordingly, the debate turning on whether a woman should spend her entire life in a nursery or in an office without ever taking a walk, each of you defending an idiotic position against an idiotic alternative. If you had both made up your minds as to exactly how much specialization you wanted, and how it was to be modified to suit cases which vary from born old maids to (saving your ladyship's presence) born whores, you could have driven him from his impossible position instead of letting him drive you into an equally impossible one.

I was furious with you for not developing some positions which you

47

just touched and left: for instance, the appalling effect of the whole-time-job on its victim the child. However, one always does that until one has been over the ground so often as to know every inch of it. I have inflicted all this on you because I think you can succeed in the art of public life. But five-sixths of your ability and earnestness will be thrown away unless you recognize that, like acting, or painting, it is an art and not a business, and that a thorough technique is indispensable to success. The first time I ever tried to read a paper to an audience I was a ghastly failure simply because I did not know that any technique was necessary, and thought that because I could read and speak in private I had nothing to do but continue the two operations in public. I even thought that the audience must be fools because I failed to "put it across." It was an old Alsatian opera-singer [Richard Deck] who enlightened me; and I worked at my alphabet until I could put a candle out with a consonant.

Go and listen to Mrs Besant. I have heard her say on the platform "A rose is not a violet" with such quiet force that the audience took it as a revelation of a new truth, and went home believing that they had never noticed the difference between a rose and a violet before. That was pure technique: without it she might have revealed the secret of the philosopher's stone without anyone noticing that she was saying anything particular. No doubt you have read of how Mrs Siddons terrified the shop assistant with the three words "Will it wash?" and how Mrs Pritchard, who talked in private about her gownd (to the disgust of Dr. Johnson), thrilled the house as Lady Macbeth without having ever read or listened to a line of the play except her own part and its cues. But this old story is full of significance for you. When you are able to say to Chesterton "It wont wash" as unanswerably and terribly as Mrs Siddons asked her innocent little question, then you will be the best platform speaker in England.

too sincerely, I am afraid,
G. Bernard Shaw

To ASHLEY DUKES

10 Adelphi Terrace WC2
[H/4]   [Undated: assigned to 6th April 1927]

[The letter to Janet Achurch was that of 23rd April 1895, in which Shaw outlined for her a lecture on Ibsen. Dukes's article, containing two Shaw letters to Janet, was "A Doll's House and the Open Door," *Theatre Arts*, New York, January 1928.]

Dear Ashley Dukes

I am a bit shy about allowing that letter to Janet to be published. If you write a really nice article round it, you can, I think, make its publication pardonable; but I could not stand an American featuring. You could get a substantial price for the first serial right to such an article; and you could let me see it before it was passed for press.

At that time I played the ghost for more than one actress who had a speech to make; but Janet and I were on special terms (quite innocent ones by the way, but completely intimate). Someone ought to write an article about her. She was a very remarkable actress; and now that she is dead, and her daughter dead, and Charrington dead, nobody's feelings can be hurt by a fairly frank explanation of why she never could secure the position that her genius entitled.

Suppose you try your hand at it.

faithfully
G. Bernard Shaw

To ASHLEY DUKES

Ayot St Lawrence. Welwyn
[A/9]   6th April 1927

Although Titian's masterwork *The Assumption of the Virgin* was painted for the Chiesa Santa Maria dei Frari in Venice, it was exhibited from 1875 to 1919 in the Accademia, where Shaw had viewed it. Candida Bartolucci (1855–1925), C.B.E., daughter of Vincenzo Bartolucci, married William Montagu Hay (1826–1911), tenth Marquis of Tweeddale, in 1878.]

Dear Ashley Dukes

I forgot to say that the notion that Janet was the original of Candida is screamingly off the mark. I wrote the play after an Italian tour; and Titian's Virgin of the Assumption in the Accademia in Venice, and Correggio's in the dome of the cathedral in Parma, boiled down into cockney Candida.

When I was a boy in Dublin we knew an opera-struck Italian named Bartolucci, who sang the part of the Count de Luna in Il Trovatore with amazing ferocity. He had a daughter, Candida Bartolucci. I never saw her; but her name charmed me; and I concluded that because she was an Italian she must be romantically beautiful. She afterwards

49

became the Marchioness of Tweeddale. I wonder whether she ever knew that she was Candida's godmother, or whether she ever heard of her godchild.

> In haste,
> ever
> G.B.S.

To MAURICE LEAHY

10 Adelphi Terrace W C2

[H/1; X/345] 8th April 1927

[Maurice Leahy (b. 1900) was secretary of the University of London Catholic Society; he later emigrated to the United States. Leahy had written to Shaw to report that "a woman had just commissioned a Jesuit Father to say Mass for the immediate conversion of Bernard Shaw, 'so that he might write a really smashing book in defence of Catholicism.'" The "old lady" mentioned by Shaw was Mrs E.A.Collier: see letter of 1st November 1878 to Pakenham Beatty.]

Dear Sir

Lots of people pray for me; and I have never been any the worse for it. One old lady made me wear a medal of the Blessed Virgin for a year as an experiment. The only valid argument against the practice is the Glasite one that God knows his own business without any prompting; but this, at best, overlooks the good it does to people to pray for others.

I cannot very well join any separate Church because a dramatist must be impartial, and make no distinction between Allah, Brahma, or any of the other names; but I need the prayers of all the Churches, and beg you to continue as long as you can keep up sufficient interest in so limited a mortal.

> faithfully
> G.Bernard Shaw

To AUGUSTIN HAMON

Ayot St Lawrence. Welwyn

[H/1] 9th April 1927

[Henri Bernstein and Shaw had clashed in 1925 over the alleged provincialism of Parisian audiences, resulting in the French dramatist-critic charging Shaw with anti-Semitism: see letter of 3rd December 1925 to Hamon. The

Comédie Française did not produce *Man and Superman,* nor any other Shaw play. The term "partition" in music means a full score for instruments or voices.]

My dear Hamon

Heureusement l'affaire Bernstein est raccommodée. On Friday last he came to London, and was entertained by the Anglo-French Luncheon Club. I could not go, as I had to entertain some people at home; but I sent a letter expressing my particular wish to have my name associated with the welcome due to H.B. I also sent a private note to be handed to him, assuring him that my absence had nothing to do with our polémique, and begging him, if I could be in any way useful to him during his stay in London, to count on me sans façons as on a friend. The result was that Henri, with perfect savoir faire, called on me immediately on rising from the lunch, and made himself very agreeable. He is not only an exceptional man, but an exceptional Jew: he reminded us both of Walter Rathenau, who was a very first class Jew indeed. Both of them have (or, in poor Walter's case, had) an admirable social talent for combining an unquestionable authority with the most genial and disarming frankness. He made a great success of our meeting by his tact.

So that is all right. I hate to leave an enemy behind me, though I do not care how many I have in front of me. . . .

H.B. had seen Great Catherine; but he did not think it as good as the original English performance by Gertrude Kingston and McKinnel, which, to my surprise, he had seen and remembered.

As to the Comédie Française I agree with you that as Tanner is the nearest thing in my gallery to the misanthrope, and as his old fashioned tirades are just in the T.F. [Théâtre Français] tradition, Man & Superman would suit better than anything else. You had better terrify them by suggesting that they should, on special nights, give the entire play, including the third act. The Macdona players always do this once a week, beginning the performance at 5; *and it always draws a crammed house.* BUT—what was the objection to letting them have St Joan? Are there not some unreasonable conditions attached to performances at the Francais?

It is true that as we grow older we grow more revolutionary; but in practical politics that effect is counteracted by our realization of the fact that government is such a complicated and skilled business that any departure from its established routine will wreck society unless it is conducted by persons of extraordinary originality and ability, having at their command a highly trained civil service and sufficient military force to defeat the reaction towards normality. Precisely the same realism that confirms my Socialism as I grow older dispels my democratic illusions as to the power of mere idealists to establish it.

However, my disposal of the Nobel money was not a political demonstration. I should not have accepted the money at all but for the fact that my refusal created an impossible situation in which the money was hung up in the air belonging to nobody. The Swedish Minister here is Baron Palmstierna, an old colleague of Branting's, and, being an aristocrat, much more advanced than most Radicals. I accepted the money formally in order to be able to give it to him to obtain decent translations of Strindberg and other modern Swedish authors. I was determined that the money should be virtually returned to Sweden or used for Swedish purposes under Swedish public control, as the spectacle of other nations begging prizes from a Swedish dynamite millionaire for their art and literature and science is a revolting one. So Palmstierna and I devised the trust, making it as undemocratic— that is, as independent—as possible: and he and his successors can now do as they like with the money subject to the general terms of the trust. What would you have done? . . .

Tell Maxime Jacob that he must on no account compose incidental music to my pieces or anyone else's pieces unless and until he receives a commission from the producing manager to do so. I cannot hamper my performing rights with any conditions as to music. In the case of Caesar there is hardly any time for music beyond an overture, one entr'acte, and a certain quantity of what is called *melodrame* to accompany the action without delaying it. I have no objection to this: on the contrary I think it would help the play greatly; but I cannot impose it on any manager, nor, if he wants music, insist on his making use of Jacob's or anyone else's partition. Consequently, if Jacob composes without a commission from Pitoeff he will risk having his partition left on his hands unperformed.

ever
G.B.S.

To G. S. VIERECK

Malvern Hotel. Malvern
[A/3; X/289.e]   15th April 1927
[Viereck not infrequently conjured up interviews with Shaw and other celebrities. The interview in question was "Shaw Looks at Life at 70," published in *Liberty*, New York, on 13th August 1927 with extensive revision by Shaw.]

52

My dear Viereck

You have spoiled my Easter holiday (this is Good Friday) by a frightful job.

I really must protest against these faked interviews which I am forced to rewrite to avoid a fresh addition to the mass of legends and misunderstandings under which my reputation groans.

How could you write such reckless muck about me?

As I have now left it it will do no harm; but you really must not do it again. Above all, you must not put statements in my mouth about other people—Frank Harris or anyone else—who are still living to be hurt by them.

weary and worn out
G.B.S.

To J. E. WHITING

[Ayot St Lawrence. Welwyn]
[E/6; X/346]   18th May 1927

[J.E.Whiting (1853–1932), a Quaker, former partner in a Leeds wholesale drapery firm, was chairman of the Arthington Trust, a body formed to disburse money to various missionary organisations, including the London Missionary Society. Through the latter he became a friend and confidant of the missionary Mabel Shaw, soon to inspire Shaw to write *The Adventures of the Black Girl in Her Search for God*.]

As I am more nearly a Quaker than anything else that has a denomination, and Joan was the spiritual mother of George Fox, I can hardly refuse an infinitesimal percentage of the money I have made out of her.

G.B.S.

To H. G. WELLS

Ayot St Lawrence. Welwyn
[A/26]   30th May 1927

[Wells had just learned that his wife Catherine Amy ("Jane") Wells was suffering from an advanced stage of cancer. Charlotte, deeply distressed, wrote to Wells on 30th May: "It is one of the most tragic things that has come into my life, for, as you say, she is *valiant* & has been the gayest & pluckiest person

I have ever known, I think" (Norman and Jeanne MacKenzie, *The Time Traveller*, 1973). Although Shaw's letter of the same date was viewed by Wells as insensitive, the genuineness of his concern cannot be questioned. As he wrote to Beatrice Webb on 13th July, after a visit to the Wellses, "The doctors and the nurse, having committed themselves to the opinion that Jane is a goner, are naturally creating an atmosphere calculated to produce that effect even on a perfectly healthy woman; and H.G's confounded scientific education makes him susceptible to such suggestions. It makes me feel like Hercules tearing the wife of Admetus out of the grip of death; and I am trying to make her defy science and have a turn at all the empiricisms as aids to curing herself." (H/14). Jane Wells died on 6th October. At the cremation services at Golder's Green four days later, Shaw encouraged Gyp Wells to follow the coffin into the furnace room. "Take the boys and go behind," he said. "It's beautiful." When Gyp hesitated, Shaw added "I saw my mother burnt there. You'll be glad if you go." This, said Gyp, "was a wise counsel and I am very grateful for it. . . . It was indeed very beautiful. I wished she could have known of those quivering bright first flames, so clear they were and so like eager yet kindly living things" (G.P.Wells, ed., *H.G.Wells in Love*, 1984).

Raphael Roche (1857–1945) was a well known homeopath, who claimed, as Shaw reported in *Doctors' Delusions* (1931), "that chronic malignant conditions are amenable to treatment by drugs in infinitesimal doses." At the end of July Wells frantically turned to Roche belatedly, using Arnold Bennett as intermediary. Dr Robert Bell (1845–1926) was superintendent of cancer research at Battersea Hospital.]

My dear H.G.

I could hardly refrain from writing to you when I heard about it: I couldn't stand getting it as gossip; but I concluded that you had better choose your own moment.

Of course I am as helpless as everybody else. I am greatly relieved at the verdict of inoperable. Operation is as useless as it is horrible. Incurable means only that the doctors and surgeons can't cure it, which we knew beforehand. Whether Jane (or God) cannot cure it is not so certain. Cancer means that the life force has taken the wrong turning and finds it easier than the right turning, as it is downhill. It is making a lower class of tissue; and the problem is to get it back to the right road and the higher tissue. Instead of facing this problem the doctors have been wasting time and money in trying to give cancer to mice, and find a microbe. They found one, and succeeded in establishing that it was entirely innocent, and that the mischief lay in the conditions in which it was found, but couldn't define them.

When we are blankly ignorant, there is nothing for it but reckless empiricism. Raphael Roche insists that he has cured cancers by empirical homeopathy, his theory being that the moment you have a theory you are wrong. He once gave me some sugar for an exceedingly nasty lump in my scrotum; and whether by pure coincidence or not, the lump dissolved into lymph in three weeks and troubled me no more. In Jane's case I should be incurably sceptical about Roche; but I should spree £20 on him, and take his pinches of apparently harmless sugar. I should try starvation on water and orange juice, not very hopefully, but on the calculation that at worst it is as good a way to die as the other. I should let Lady Astor Christian Science me into pretending that there was nothing the matter with me. I should not bother much about Dr Bell and the Battersea Hospital methods, because I know that vegetarianism does not protect. The one thing I should not do is follow medical advice, as that is known now to be at best useless and at worst mischievous.

We shall look in on Thursday: Charlotte has written to settle when. I cannot express any feelings: the thing is quite beyond that. There it is, blast it!

G. B. S.

To J. E. WHITING

[A/6]

Ayot St Lawrence. Welwyn
5th July 1927

[Whiting had supplied Shaw with extracts of letters to the London Mission Society from the non-related Mabel Shaw (1889–1973), who served the Society from 1915 to 1940 at the London Mission Station, Mbereshi, Northern Rhodesia (now Zambia). "Her letters," Whiting informed Shaw on 13th July, "are not written for publication, but dashed off late at night . . . obviously without revision. She has sent to my wife the story of her life, or as she calls it the 'History of God's dealings with her.' It is wonderfully written, and must be published some day, but not in her life time, or that of some others" (typed transcript, Harvard). The influence of these letters on Shaw is evidenced in his inscription to Mabel Shaw in a first edition copy of *The Adventures of the Black Girl in Her Search for God* in 1932: "I send you this story, for which you are really responsible, as it was you who set me thinking about the contact of black minds with white religions . . ." (Parke-Bernet Auction Galleries, sale of 10th February 1970). Miss Shaw was later awarded the O.B.E.]

Dear Mr Whiting

I have read the enclosed with great interest. I waive the point that the Shaws have considerable literary talent and are not behindhand as liars, taking it that you can answer for the lady's address being correct, and her activities real. She makes it clear that a negro girl is much less of a savage than an average post war flapper. But I feel pretty angry with her for putting up that cross. When will people learn to introduce Christ as a teacher and not as a figure from the Chamber of Horrors? When the negroes have learnt to worship The Crucified, they have got no further than their worship of their own black king because he buried people alive under the doorposts of his hut.

Charlotte Corday may be a heroine among Assassins, especially as she was a goodlooking young woman, and made a hefty job of it; but I do not like the tribe. She could not resent injustice without murderous rancor, which was exactly Marat's case; but to do Marat justice he never took the law into his own hands, though he had quite as much to exasperate him as she. I really could not associate Charlotte Corday with Joan.

Miss Shaw's letters ought to be printed. Many thanks for sending them to me.

faithfully
G. Bernard Shaw

[Upon receipt of a copy of Shaw's letter, Mabel Shaw wrote to Whiting:

"I am so amused at G.B.S's remarks that Shaws are not behindhand as liars. I should like to tell him why that Cross is in our school. There is no shadow of a thought of the Chamber of Horrors. It is a symbol of the only way of Life that takes us home to God, having nothing, yet possessing all things, dying to live, losing life to save it—except the grain of wheat fall into the ground and die—all that is in the Cross, and to know our Lord as a Teacher one must know Him in His Life and Death—the teaching He taught can only be learnt from Him as a person—you cannot divorce His Life and Death from His teaching, and unless we understand His death, we can never fully understand His teaching.

"No it is not of any horrors the Cross is symbolic—but of all that is fair and lovely—high and courageous—passionate and pure—love to the very uttermost—reaching to the heights of Heaven—and to the depths of Hell...*

"I saw St. Joan when I was at home—and I saw God. The man who wrote that can never have been an agnostic. There are bits in St. Joan I turn to when I need to be near the heart of God" (undated typed transcription, Harvard).]

* The ellipsis is Mabel Shaw's or Whiting's.

To J. E. WHITING

10 Adelphi Terrace WC2

[C/6]   16th July 1927

[Replying to Shaw's comments on Charlotte Corday and Joan of Arc, Whiting argued on 13th July: "Charlotte, like Joan, was a pure minded high souled young woman, who was inspired by the troubles of her country to offer herself a willing sacrifice in an endeavour to save it from destruction. In her case death was certain, though to Joan remained strong hope of survival. As for the killing, the one did it in combination, and called it 'War,' the other individually, and it is called 'Assassination.' . . . She died with a smile on her lips, having as she conceived done her duty, and saved many thousands of innocent lives. As she wrote to her father, in the words of her ancestor Corneille, 'Crime makes the shame, not the scaffold.' All honour both to her and to Joan" (typed transcript, Harvard).

Sir Walter Scott's denunciation of Marat may be found in his nine-volume *Life of Napoleon Buonaparte* (1827), which contains "a Preliminary View of the French Revolution." E.Belfort Bax's *Jean-Paul Marat: The People's Friend*, first published as a biographical sketch in 1879, was revised and enlarged in 1882 and in 1900.]

Joan would have had the sense to see that stabbing him was the way to make sure that "they must all be guillotined," and to add to the number. Scott's denunciation is mere hue & cry against a man whom he regarded as a mad dog. Have you read Belfort Bax's Life of Marat? It gives you the case against Scott.

Joan was a fair fighter, and "saved her country" as they call it. Charlotte was a homicidal egotist who did no good whatever—quite the contrary—by the sanguinary scene she made. You really mustnt worship her.

Tell Miss Shaw to publish her life *now*. All that about waiting until she and all her generation are dead should not count if the book will help people.

G.B.S.

To H. G. WELLS

Regina Palace Hotel. Stresa

[A/26]   4th August 1927

[The Shaws revisited Stresa, leaving London on 24th July and returning on 6th October, during which time the servants supervised the removal of their furnishings from 10 Adelphi Terrace to a service flat at 4 Whitehall Court.

Meanwhile, Wells's most recent novel, dealt with the Rylands clan, "a third perhaps of [whose] millions is in coal," in the Vale of Edensoke, in Yorkshire. Geoffrey is a nephew of Lord Edensoke, head of the Rylands clan. Mr Lewisham is the central figure of Wells's 1899 novel *Love and Mr. Lewisham*. An article by Wells, "The Way the World is Going," appeared in the *Sunday Express* on 24th July; Shaw's reply, "These Scoundrels!" was published on 7th August. The articles were reprinted jointly as *Experiments on Animals* (1927) by the British Union for the Abolition of Vivisection. Galen (130?–200?) was a Greek physician and medical writer. Sir Jagadis Chandra Bose (1858–1937) was an Indian physicist and plant physiologist.]

My dear H.G.

I have just devoured Meanwhile. The fiction of a disgusted spectator of the strike telling his wife what he thinks of its protagonists in intimate letters not intended for publication serves its turn extremely well. As long as Baldwin and Macdonald do not know exactly where they are they will not be able to tell their respective right and left wings to go to hell; and we shall have nothing but guerilla warfare. Baldwin's position is not ascertainable: he is in the air between Capitalism become impossible and Socialism not yet become comprehensible. Macdonald's position *is* ascertainable; but we have to ascertain it for him: the men of action and the parliament men have no time to think. That is why I have left 12 1/2 plays unwritten to produce this book on Socialism with which the printer is now in travail.

You should now pick up some dropped strands from Mr Lewisham, and deal with the appalling corruption of learning, of science, and of thought in every department except that which is fortified by an impregnable *chevaux de frise* of transcendental mathematics, by Edensoke-cum-Geoffreyism in the professions. You must grasp the horror of your own scientific education, by which the material side of physiology and anatomy was imposed on you as biology. Here I am face to face with Troubetskoy, who never reads, and is left desolate by the death of his wife. "What did you make of the Paris surgeons?" I asked. He replied in one word "Assassins." These poor devils did what they had been taught and trained to do; and that is what it came to. And so I shall have to pose to him for a statue (he has done three of me already) because in no other way can I take his mind off the assassination; and I have already had to sacrifice a week of my holiday to answer your paraphrase of Lister's reply to Victoria in the Sunday Express. Why do you do it, H.G.? How can I ask you about Jane after it?

For heaven's sake, if you must believe that doctors are gods, call in

Roman Catholic doctors. They too hold that as animals are for the use of Man, Man has no moral duty to animals. But they also hold that a woman is fundamentally different from a mouse, and that to treat a woman as a mouse or even think of her as a mouse is a mortal sin. The others make no such distinction. To them Jane is mechanically and chemically a morphologic variation on a mouse. Having investigated many thousands of mice they assure you that they know all about her. *I* say that having investigated so many mice they know nothing even about mice, or about anything; and to do them justice they dont pretend to when they talk to me.

I have met an old lady here: an Italian countess, who has turned her place into a menagerie, her speciality being vampire bats. I suspect this humanitarian of being your mother. Her features are not particularly like yours; but her eyes and her expression are so extraordinarily like yours in your sunniest moments that she gives you away. The dismal and uneasy apologist of vivisection is not the real man.

But all that you have said and all that I have said has been said over and over again and left things just where they have been since Galen, the father of lies. What we have to do is the positive work of suggesting experiments in genuine biology. Nothing else will overcome the inertia of the established routine. Bose has done something to bridge the change; but it is not enough to shew what a homeopathic dose of snake poison does to a plant, or even to reduce our common shop vivisection to utterly contemptible clumsiness and savagery by the contrast with his methods. We are not plants; and we must get to direct experiment on the human subject, leaving nothing to analogy and as little as possible to inference, before we can make our biological fictions and speculations (including your books and mine) scientific. Digging into the entrails of dogs and guinea pigs, and seeing what will happen when you extirpate this or ligature that is only ancient Roman augury pithed: I should have no patience with it even if it caused no suffering and did not turn decent medical students into the demoralized blackguards they are.

I don't know whether you have any clinical instinct: anyhow, it is not cultivated; and you cannot take Jane wholly into your own hands. But you can watch and wait with an undarkened mind. The official diagnosis comes to nothing, not only because none of the cases are identical, but because there is a "pseudo" which saves face when the medical verdict has been wrong. If Jane is curing herself—if she has given up making the wrong sort of tissue and is replacing it with the right sort—then you have nothing to do but encourage her, and write nothing that will plunge her into despair. But if not, you must first ascertain whether she is being prevented by some purely physical lesion of the sort that the osteopaths are trained to feel and correct. It is no use putting the question to a registered doctor: he has not the technique: it takes a couple of years to acquire it. If the osteo. finds nothing, or his correction will not stay put, then Bose's snake trick seems to indicate that a homeopathic stimulus might give the life force (*vis medicatrix natura*) a lift. I, in your place, would then try Roche, as a pure empiric; for there is no science of drugs; and he is clever enough to know it. . . .

Here are three stones which you ought not to leave unturned if all is not well. Of course there are all sorts of professed healers about with more or less plausible systems and theories; but there is not time to try them all as last resources; and you could not reasonably reproach yourself for neglecting them. But there is evidence enough to try (1) osteopathy on a definite tissue, (2) homeopathy as a drug stimulus, and (3) the opinion of an up-to-date beginner with a tiptop qualification. To leave these obvious resources untouched simply because the Assassins can do nothing would leave you a prey to remorseful doubts if Jane were to perish at their hands. Besides, there are plenty of qualified men, inside and outside the Battersea Hospital set, who agree with me.

Charlotte says I can do no good by worrying you, as you will only be made more miserable. But I do not regard you as a miserable person; and I have had too many of my friends assassinated to feel easy about Jane whilst the Thugs are in command of her situation. If I worry you you can easily take it out of me without hurting my feelings in the least: I am just as pigheaded as you are.

But it would be very jolly to hear that Jane is all right. Send us a bulletin, however brief. Blank verse, *that*.

G.B.S.

[On 1st September Charlotte wrote to Wells:

"I have been anxiously waiting for a line from you to G.B.S. in answer to his letter—& it hasn't come.

"I didn't want G.B.S. to send that letter, & I did all I could to stop him from writing it. I thought it might vex you, just when I dont want you worried!

"Please H.G. dont be angry with him. You know he is like that—he must sometimes let himself go in this aggravating way—& he means it all so more than well! He is very fond of you & Jane. I do think you are our most special friends, & G.B.S. is really worrying about you both dreadfully just now &

60

would do anything in his power to help you. Then—by some evil fate he is impelled to do what I fear has hurt you.

"Do—*do*—write a line—to *me*, even—& say you ar'nt angry" (A/26). There apparently was no reply.]

To JESSE LEVINSON

[A/1]

Regina Palace Hotel. Stresa
22nd August 1927

[In March 1927 Jesse Levinson had brought an action against Shaw, this time in the Chancery Division of the High Court, seeking a declaration that he was entitled to film *The Chocolate Soldier*, of which he had obtained rights from the operetta's librettist, without Shaw's consent, arguing that the libretto did not reproduce Shaw's text substantially. The court dismissed the action, with Shaw awarded costs. As Levinson, however, failed to make payment beyond the security of £300 he had been obliged to pay into court, the case cost Shaw, who did not seek redress, about one thousand pounds. It was cheaper, he later told F.E. Loewenstein (undated typewritten note, HRC), to buy off plaintiffs than to contest their actions.]

Dear Mr Levinson

Your cable of the 18th has reached me here. You will not find me in London on your arrival. But this does not matter, as your proposal to submit an adaptation of The Chocolate Soldier for my approval is quite out of the question, and would not help you even if I could consent to it. If your adaptation infringes any existing film rights you will have to deal with the holder to whom the author sells them, and not with the author. The question whether the adaptation is an infringement or not is a question of law and fact to be decided by the courts without the slightest reference to my opinion or yours.

I need not remind you of the losses this ill advised affair has already brought on both of us; and the prospect of its revival is extremely disagreeable to me. If you are still going on with it you must not ask me to see you or correspond with you or inspect or express an opinion on any document connected with The Chocolate Soldier. You must proceed on your own responsibility and at your own risk, without communicating with me or with my secretary on that subject until it is finally disposed of. This situation is a legal necessity, and is of course not an expression of personal feeling.

faithfully
G. Bernard Shaw

61

To MICHAEL WILLIAMS

[X/347]

[Regina Palace Hotel. Stresa]
[Undated: *c.* September 1927]

[Michael Williams (1875–1958), religious writer and editor of *The Common-weal*, a New York Catholic weekly review he helped to found in 1924, had been commissioned by a newspaper syndicate to obtain an interview with Pius XI (1857–1939), who had been elected pope in 1922, succeeding Benedict XV. When Williams secured a message from the Holy Father to the world on the Mexican persecution of Catholics under President Plutarco Calles (1877–1945), which the Pope declared was worse even than those suffered under Nero, Domitian, and Caligula, the syndicate rejected the article on the grounds that it was Catholic propaganda. Williams appealed to Shaw to "take the lead in this crusade of mercy on behalf of martyrized Mexico" by using his influence to force publication of the article.]

Dear Sir

I cannot imagine what the American Press is thinking of in refusing to publish what is practically an interview with the Pope. It is news, and official news from a person of overwhelming importance.

[On] The mere fact that the Pope is a Roman Catholic and not a Baptist from Dayton, and that his views are therefore inadmissible in American newspapers, no European comment is possible: Europe cannot make comments if its breath is taken away.

There is an old story of a devout man who, on arriving in Heaven after his death, and asking to be led into the presence of his Maker, whom he had served so long without hope of any greater reward, was told that it was impossible as his Maker had just gone mad. We in Europe are feeling something of what that man felt as it dawns on us that America has gone out of its mind.

I have never been able to understand why the subject of the pitched battle between Church and State in Mexico was dropped so suddenly by the British Press after it had been featured with the prominence its importance deserved for several days.

If the Russian government, which openly repudiates the teachings of the Greek Church as dope, can nevertheless afford to tolerate it, however contemptuously, one would like to know why the Mexican government cannot afford to be equally broadminded, instead of behaving like Queen Elizabeth.

It owes it not only to the Pope but to itself to welcome an inquiry and report; and for the American newspapers to suppress the Pope's demand for such an inquiry as a matter of no interest naturally sets the world asking whether these newspapers are written for children under five or for grown-up citizens of the greatest federation of modern States— the nearest thing on earth to the Holy Roman Empire—in the world.

faithfully
G. Bernard Shaw

To G. S. VIERECK

[Regina Palace Hotel. Stresa]
[S/52]   7th September 1927

[Another of Viereck's alleged interviews with Shaw, which first appeared in the *New York American* on 10th and 17th July 1927, created disquiet in England when an *Evening Standard* correspondent quoted, on 24th August, some controversial remarks from a translation published in the *Neue Freie Presse*, Vienna. Shaw, in a letter from Stresa that was printed in the *Evening Standard* on 14th September, repudiated the interview as a fake. "Extraordinary interviews with me," he wrote, "are like pictures by Rembrandt; they sell so well that a considerable trade in forgeries has sprung up, and is apparently flourishing."

The Battle of Jutland, the only major naval battle between British and German forces in the Great War, took place on 31st May 1916. Vice-Admiral Sir David Beatty (1871–1936) was Senior Officer of the Battle-Cruiser Fleet and head of the squadron that first made contact with a German squadron. Admiral Sir John Jellicoe was Commander-in-Chief of the British Grand Fleet. The "German admiral" was Vice-Admiral Reinhard von Scheer (1863–1928), Commander-in-Chief of the German High Seas Fleet. The Germans, outnumbered, used brilliant tactics to minimise losses. The battle was indecisive.]

My dear Viereck

... The interview in the Neue Freie Presse was quoted by the Evening Standard, and provoked a protest from an Admiral to which I had to reply. In future I shall avoid you like the plague if you persist in publishing what you can remember of our conversations. You represented me as saying that the British Fleet had been completely useless throughout the war: that is, as telling a senseless and obvious lie for the mere sake of lying. I told you that the people at the Admiralty here were divided into a Beatty party and a Jellicoe party: the dispute being as to which of the two made a mess of the Battle of Jutland and let the German admiral get away with the honors of war. You reported me as saying that we disputed as to which of the two *won* the Battle of Jutland. There were other things which obliged me to repudiate the whole interview. In future you must let me speak for myself: I am, like you, a journalist, and need no intermediary. There are nuances both in English politics and in my position which you do not understand; and when you try to explain me you make a horrible mess of it. I got your first interview right by practically rewriting it, which took me longer than a correct statement by myself at first hand would have done; and you will see that I cannot do this for you again. Therefore it must be understood that our intercourse henceforward is not for publication. In short, I forgive you this time; but dont do it again.

your extremely illused
G. Bernard Shaw

To CYRIL CLEMENS

[H/1; X/348]

[Regina Palace Hotel. Stresa]
[Undated: assigned to 15th September 1927]

[Cyril Clemens (b. 1902), a cousin, once-removed, of Samuel L. Clemens, founded the International Mark Twain Society in 1927 and the *Mark Twain Quarterly* in 1936. The Society's "Knight of Mark Twain" honour was bestowed upon Shaw, Churchill, and Mussolini, among countless others. Shaw also received the Mark Twain Gold Medal in 1937.]

Dear Mr Clemens

I met Mark Twain, late in his lifetime, on two occasions. On one of the visits to London made by my biographer Archibald Henderson, I met him at the railway station, and found that Mark had come over in the same boat and was in the same train. There was a hasty introduction amid the scramble for luggage which our queer English way of handling passengers' baggage involves; and after a word or two I tactfully took myself and Henderson off.

Some days later he walked into our flat in Adelphi Terrace. Our parlormaid, though she did not know who he was, was so overcome by his personality that she admitted him unquestioned and unannounced, like the statue of the Commandant [in *Don Giovanni*].

Whether it was on that occasion or a later one that he lunched with us I cannot remember; but at any rate he did lunch with us, and told us stories of the old Mississippi storekeepers. He presented me with one of his books, and autographed the inside of the cloth case on the ground that when he autographed fly leaves they were torn out and sold.

64

He had a complete gift of intimacy which enabled us to treat one another instantly as if we had known one another all our lives, as indeed I had known him through his early books, which I read and revelled in before I was twelve years old. As to what impression he made on me all I can say is that he was himself, and exactly what I expected. We got on together perfectly.

faithfully
G. Bernard Shaw

To DOUGLAS HAMILTON

Regina Palace Hotel. Stresa
[U(A)/52]   29th September 1927

[Douglas Hamilton was a son of Shaw's aunt Constance Ann (Mrs William) Hamilton (d. 1944), née Gurly, half sister of Lucinda Elizabeth Shaw, who had emigrated to America, settling in Pittsburgh, Pa. Hamilton was at this time attending the University of Pittsburgh, where he majored in economics. He later became a real estate agent. The two cousins whose education Shaw paid for were Judy Gillmore (Musters) and Georgina Rogers (Meredith). The two aunts he was supporting were Arabella Gillmore and Charlotte Rogers.]

Dear Douglas Hamilton

You are a young sap—or whatever they call you in Pittsburgh.

I have had to educate two of your cousins; and I still have to support two of your aunts because they were left destitute by your maternal grandfather, whose estate, consisting of a collection of mortgages and pawnbrokers' duplicates, I was unlucky enough to inherit.

You have been fortunate enough to select a financially solid and substantial father. What possible excuse have you for coming to me and asking to be put on the destitute list? Your father, you say, believes in the school of life, not in University education. I agree with him so entirely (not having been through a university course myself, and being to this day—though I have been educating myself for 71 years—incapable of passing the lowest standard examination in an elementary school) that I half suspect him of reading my books secretly. But he knows very well that natural capacity and taste for business are necessary for success in business. The opportunities and experiences that make one youth a millionaire leave another crushed and good-for-nothing.

But between these two extremes come youths who do very well if they have college degrees. They do not build up businesses for themselves; but they find berths, and sometimes very good berths, in modern big business combinations, which are not nowadays so foolish as to staff their offices and departments with casual illiterates, ignorant of mathematics and science and literature, merely because they are the sons of their friends. They will not look at a young man who has not a university record. If he has an exceptionally good one they sometimes take him on at a high salary to do nothing but *think* about their business, which the practical men have no time to do. Even the big Trade Unions are beginning to do this.

Then there are the born artists and the born hoboes. The artists must starve it out as best they can if their fathers cannot or will not finance them. If the hoboes have rich fathers they can always blackmail them by threatening to steal and disgrace the family.

I take it that you belong to the second class. Well, go to your father and tell him so. Tell him that if he wanted you to build up a successful business as he did he should have made you a chip of the old block, but that as he neglected that precaution he must take you as he (or God or your mother) made you, and see you through a university course. If he thinks that what is the matter is that you are lazy and snobbish and self indulgent: well, you *are* lazy and snobbish and self indulgent, and nothing good can come of treating you as energetic, democratic, and hard-living. All parents have to put up with these crosses; for it takes all sorts to make a world; and if all sons were reproductions of their fathers the world would crash for want of the mathematicians and physicists and college cranks who are at the bottom of everything that business men handle, from landaulets to Brooklyn bridges.

Of course it will be up to you to make good; but even if you do not achieve anything extraordinary you will be more credit and less expense to him in the long run than you would be as an ordinary business failure losing money to born men of business.

That is all the comfort I can give you.

faithfully
G. Bernard Shaw

To FRIEDRICH ADLER

Regina Palace Hotel. Stresa

[X/344]   2nd October 1927

[Friedrich Adler (1879–1960), Austrian Socialist politician, was sentenced to death in 1916 for a political assassination of the Austrian prime minister. The sentence subsequently was commuted to a term of imprisonment, and he was liberated at the end of the war, settling in Switzerland. His father Victor was a founder of the Austrian Social Democratic Party (1888). Krastyu G. Rakovsky (1873–1941), Bulgarian-born Bolshevik, was a member of the Central Committee of the Soviet Communist Party from 1919, and Soviet *chargé d'affaires* in London 1923–24. "Rakovsky's safe" is a Shavian jibe at the blowing open of safes in a police raid ordered by the Home Secretary, William Joynson-Hicks, on the premises of Arcos Ltd. and the Soviet Trade Delegation on 12th May 1927, which effectively ended diplomatic relations with Russia. Gaetano Salvemini (1873–1957), Italian historian, was an anti-Fascist who fled the country in 1925, later becoming an American citizen. His letter of attack on Shaw was published in the *Manchester Guardian* on 19th October, with Shaw's reply appearing on the 28th. In 1955 Salvemini published a book, *G. B. Shaw e il Fascismo*.

The Irishwoman who refused to acknowledge political realities probably was Hanna Sheehy-Skeffington (1877–1946), an extreme Republican, who broke with De Valera in 1927 when he decided to take the Oath of Allegiance to the British Crown which made it possible for him to take a seat in Dáil Éireann. Other candidates, less likely, are Maud Gonne McBride and Charlotte Despard, a strange old woman who actively supported the extreme Republican cause. Karl Kautsky (1854–1938) was a German Marxist, private secretary to Engels, who opposed Bolshevism and the Russian revolution. Pius IX was Giovanni Mastai-Ferretti (1792–1878), a reactionary pope who reigned from 1846 to 1878. It was he who proclaimed the dogma of the Immaculate Conception, and it was his Vatican Council of 1869–70 that promulgated the dogma of papal infallibility. Kevin O'Higgins (1892–1927) was at the time of his assassination on 10th July Vice President and Minister of Justice of the Irish Free State and since 1923 a member of Dáil Éireann.

Adler, after reading "with real indignation" a copy of Shaw's 7th February letter to W. S. Kennedy, following the *Daily News* letter of 24th January, wrote that the standpoint taken by Shaw was "very adequate to a Buddha sitting with a fixed stare" but a startling one for a supposedly militant Socialist. "The idea that a people should accept absolutism *faute de mieux* can only be put forward by someone for whom absolutism is merely a mental exercise in history, but not a real experience. In the notice which I wrote about your letter in the *Daily News* I attempted to depict your error as due to the defects of your qualities. But in your second letter [to Kennedy] it is hard to find any good side, because there is really nothing good in it. You come dangerously near to the point of view of the British ruling class. . . .

We are for the *restoration of democracy* in Russia as well as in Italy, and accordingly we have a moral right to fight against Fascism with all our strength" (from a news release of correspondence, authorised by Shaw, issued to the press by the Labour Party publicity department: *Daily News*, 13th October 1927).

The London *Times* correspondent, writing from Milan on 12th October, labelled Shaw's letter, after reading a translation in the *Gazzetta del Popolo* (Turin), "a brilliant defence of Fascism based principally on the arguments used by Mrs Warren in *Mrs Warren's Profession*, when, in order to defend herself, she endeavours to persuade 'Vivie' that all the ladies of society are neither better nor worse than herself" (*The Times*, 13th October).]

Dear Friedrich Adler

On the 24th March last you were kind enough to write me a letter which I was unable to answer at the time. Now that I find myself in Italy again with an hour to spare, I must not leave it longer unanswered.

My article in the *Daily News* was, I am informed, published in the Italian Press after it had been threatened with complete suppression by the Mayor of Milan, and then drastically expurgated. Whether this is true I do not know, as I did not see the Italian newspapers in which it appeared. However, it does not greatly matter. The article was, in the main, a remonstrance with the Daily News for writing contemptuously of Mussolini as if the whole situation in Italy could be disposed of by representing the country as writhing in the grip of a brutal egotist. It was a demand for common sense and common civility in dealing with a foreign statesman who had achieved a dictatorship in a great modern state without a single advantage, social, official, or academic, to assist him, after marching to Rome with a force of Black shirts which a single disciplined regiment backed by a competent government could have routed at any moment. To tell us that this extraordinary success was achieved by murdering one hostile deputy and administering castor oil to his supporters is childish. The obvious retort to it is "If dictatorships can be established in Italy so easily, why did not the communists establish the dictatorship of the proletariat by the same simple means?" They have as much castor oil at their disposal as the Fascisti; and they have not hesitated to shoot and throw bombs.

In your letter you speak of the *restoration* of democracy in Russia and Italy. But do you seriously attach any value to the *status quo ante* in Russia and Italy? I take it that after the war, Italy was left in a condition not unlike that in which Napoleon found France under the Directory when he returned from his Egyptian campaign. The Directory, nominally revolutionary and popular, really doctrinaire, incompetent, and corrupt, could not govern. Napoleon turned the Directory

68

out; put the most capable men he could find at the head of the departments; codified the law and brought it up to date; stabilized the currency; disciplined the public services; forced the press to support him; and incidentally kidnapped the Bourbonnist Duc d'Enghien on foreign territory and shot him. The benefit to the ordinary French citizens was so great that they would have allowed Napoleon to shoot fifty Bourbon dukes, and suppress a hundred anti-Napoleonic newspapers. The Sieyès Liberal doctrinaires and the foreign governments who hated the revolution and dreaded Napoleon's military genius, immediately set up a prolonged howling against the tyrant, the suppressor of popular liberties, the murderer of d'Enghien, insisting that France was groaning under a ruthless despotism when she was in fact enjoying some of the realities of settled liberty after a long stretch of harassing uncertainty.

Are the Italian liberals going to persist in the same mistake? After the war the government of Italy was so feeble that silly Syndicalists were seizing factories, and fanatical devotees of that curious attempt at a new Catholic church called the Third International were preaching a *coup d'état* and a Crusade in all directions, and imagining that this sort of thing was Socialism and Communism. Mussolini, without any of Napoleon's prestige, has done for Italy what Napoleon did for France, except that for the Duc d'Enghien you must read Matteotti.

Are we to give him credit for his work and admit its necessity, and the hopeless failure of our *soi-disant* Socialists, Syndicalists, Communists, Anarchists, etc. etc. etc., to achieve it or even to understand it, or are we to go on shrieking that the murderer of Liberty and Matteotti is trampling Italy under foot?

You say that "we" can never accept the situation, never submit spiritually. But what, exactly, is it that "we" cannot accept and will not submit to? Is it the fact that the despotic lira is worth threepence in English money whilst the democratic franc is worth only twopence? Is it that Italy is governed by a man of the people, whilst France, libertarian, égalitarian and fraternian, is governed by Monsieur Poincaré? Is it that Mussolini, with all his dramatic gestures, has not yet threatened to dam the Nile and cut off the water supply of Egypt, nor broken open Rakovsky's safe like the English Government, which so liberally tolerates our friend Salvemini? Is it because the Corriere della Sera seems to be much more accessible to news that is unpalatable to the bourgeoisie than most of the London papers? Of course, if you compare Italy with a Mazzinian Utopia, it is full of abuses and tyrannies. So is America, so is France, so is England, so is Russia. In liberated Ireland, my native country, liberty has been established by throwing the shibboleths of liberalism to the winds; superseding routine democratic bodies by autocratic Commissions; and passing Coercion Acts such as England never dared to impose. There is a lady in Ireland who declares that she will never accept these facts, never submit to them spiritually. But the facts remain; and the Irish people will not return that lady to the Irish Parliament.

Do you seriously ask me to talk about Mussolini's regime as that impossible countrywoman of mine talks about the Irish Free State? Do you believe, or expect me to believe, that if the black shirts were replaced by red ones, or by cylinder hats and frock coats, Italy would become an earthly paradise? Because I face the facts in the full knowledge that the democratic idealism of the XIXth century is as dead as a door nail, you say that I come dangerously near the point of view of the British ruling class. But are you not delighted to find at last a Socialist who speaks and thinks as responsible rulers do and not as resentful slaves do? Of what use are socialists who can neither rule nor understand what ruling means? Do you expect me to lecture Mussolini as Kautsky lectured Lenin, as Marx lectured Thiers, as Victor Hugo lectured Napoleon III and Pius IX, as all the Socialists who have never had to administer a farthing of public expenditure or employ a single workman (to say nothing of signing a death warrant) lecture the Cabinets of Europe, especially the Socialist ones?

You can hardly believe that the brutalities and retaliations, the assassinations and counter-assassinations, which accompany the eternal struggle of government with anarchy do not disgust me as much as they disgust you. If they were peculiar to Fascism our continual harping on them would have some excuse. As it is, the murder of Matteotti is no more an argument against Fascism than the murder of St Thomas-à-Becket is an argument against Feudalism. In Ireland the new Free State found itself obliged to hang many of its old ultra-patriotic comrades for this sort of thing; and the minister who ordered the executions was assassinated by their sympathisers. Mussolini may have to hang some of the cruder Fascists for *trop de zèle* before order is completely restored in Italy. Meanwhile nothing is to be gained by pretending that any indictment can be brought against him by us or anyone else that he cannot meet by a crushing *tu quoque*. The blots on his rule are neither specifically Fascist nor specifically Italian: they are blots on human nature.

faithfully
G. Bernard Shaw

To FRIEDRICH ADLER

4 Whitehall Court S W 1
[S/13]   11th October 1927

[On 7th October Adler replied to Shaw: "After your letter of the 2nd inst.,
I regard it as hopeless that we should come to any understanding as to an
attitude towards Fascism. Accordingly, there would be no point in my
restating the general views developed in my letter of March 4" (*Daily News,*
13th October 1927). The "distinguished friend" to whom Shaw showed the
letter written to Adler was a neighbour at Stresa, Carlo Emanuele Basile
(1885–1946), Fascist bureaucrat, author of *Discorsi Fascisti* (1930), and
federal secretary of Novara since 1925, who entered parliament in 1929.
Condemned in 1945 to thirty years' imprisonment for war crimes, he did not
live to serve the sentence.

Nicola Sacco (1891–1927) and Bartolomeo Vanzetti (1888–1927), Italian-
born political radicals in the United States, were convicted in 1921 of the
murder of a factory paymaster and guard and the theft of a $16,000 payroll.
Theirs became a *cause célèbre* as radicals and liberals, convinced of their
innocence, rallied worldwide in protest and support of the doomed men.
They were electrocuted, eventually, on 23rd August 1927. Shaw, asked for a
message to be read at a last-ditch rally by the Independent Labour Party,
wrote: "The friends of Sacco and Vanzetti have made out a strong case in
England for their view that these two accused are the victims of a 'frame-up.'
I do not know how this case has been met by the prosecution, and even if I
did, I should still not be in a position to criticise the judgment of the American court. I can only say that if the English courts hesitated for five years to
carry out a capital sentence it would not be carried out at all. It is impossible
for us on this side to feel that execution would have been so long deferred if
the case were clear enough to justify its infliction" (*Manchester Guardian,*
3rd June 1927).

William Halse R. Rivers (1864–1922), English physiologist and writer, was
founder of the Cambridge school of experimental psychology.]

Dear Friedrich Adler

I made three copies of my letter. One of them I sent to the editor of
the Daily Herald, asking him to keep it by him in case the letter should
be published in the continental papers, so that he could give the
original English text, and not have to translate a translation. The
second copy I gave to a distinguished Italian friend of mine, who took
an active part in establishing Fascism after the war, and still governs
his native district, not by popular election, but simply as a High
Commissioner or deputy dictator according to the Fascist procedure.
As he does not read English he had an Italian translation made. I have
no doubt whatever that this translation will find its way into the

71

Italian papers, and that the Daily Herald will then publish its copy of the original; so that the letter will become an open letter. It is impossible for us to converse across Europe in whispers on such a subject as the attitude and policy of Socialism confronted with Bolshevism, Fascism, the Spanish *coup d'état*, and all the other reactions against the futilities of democratic idealism.

We must get the Socialist movement out of its old democratic grooves. After the war, in Italy and [the] central empires, any capable and resolute body of men could have established a Socialist government. The movement had its chance; and it proved just as incapable of seizing it as the Paris Commune of 1871. It waved red flags, made endless speeches, called on the workers to do what it was too ignorant, lazy and cowardly to do itself, and was finally shoved out of the way, shot down, flung into prison, suppressed and squashed with the greatest ease by the men of action of all shades of opinion. And it can do nothing in its disgrace and defeat but wail about Matteotti and Sacco and Vanzetti and any other martyrs it can pick up, and protest that Fascism and Bolshevism and Riversism are undemocratic, and that human society must wait paralysed until everything it does is understood and sanctioned and approved by a majority of the proletariat, of whom ninety per cent are unable to make a living without direction. If we can do nothing better than this we are only leading them to their ruin.

You must have thought of all this. Something must be done to waken the movement to it.

By all means deal with the correspondence as you think best. I have no objection to its publication.

faithfully
G. Bernard Shaw

P.S. Your letter of the 7th has just reached me. I can only add that the fact that government is not a natural monopoly of the bourgeoisie and aristocracy is very conclusively proved by Mussolini himself who is a man of the people, and *knows them*. But if you are waiting for "the assured support of the majority of the people" you will die peacefully in your bed like a good bourgeois whilst "the sons of hell" govern the country. Oh Friedrich, Friedrich!!!

To FRIEDRICH ADLER

4 Whitehall Court SW1

[S/13]   14th October 1927

[Shaw's Fabian Society lecture was titled "Democracy as a Delusion," in the series "Political Democracy: Will It Prevail?" Filippo Turati (1857–1932), founder of the Italian Socialist Party (1892), was an anti-Fascist, exiled in 1926.]

Dear Dr Adler

The correspondence broke out in the London press yesterday. As I have not yet received the weeks cuttings from the Press Cutting Bureau I do not know how far it has gone; but you will see by the enclosed paragraph and portrait from the Daily News that we have received as much publicity as we could expect.

I intend to deal with the question further in a public lecture which I am to deliver for the Fabian Society here on 23rd November; and I hope it will be taken up by the Movement generally. I can now look back, like your father and Liebknecht and Bebel and Vandervelde on a blameless career as a propagandist of Social-Democracy, with the success of the Socialism completely neutralised by the futility of the democracy. I remember the boast of Bebel as to the splendid organisation and extension of the party in Germany, with his reproach to France for lagging so far behind, and the retort of Jaurès "Ah, if we had all that in France *something would happen.*" I recollect how, consequently, we never did anything but preach. I remember Liebknecht's son, in violent and contemptuous opposition to the majority of the German people, being imprisoned by them for four years for taking their part, and finally being shot in open warfare. I remember Adler's son refusing to wait like his father for a mandate of the majority, and on his own responsibility shooting the reactionary Prime Minister [Karl von Stürgkh] out of hand. I remember the war upsetting the empires and placing them at the mercy of any organised and determined party that was capable of seizing the opportunity, and the total and disgraceful inability of the Social-Democrats to rise to the occasion. And I am looking on, as you are, at the accumulating proofs of what I said years ago; that the difficulty in governing by consent of the people was that the people would never consent to be governed because they were too ignorant and personal in their views to grasp what government means, and are very carefully kept in that ignorance by the schools of the capitalist State. It is impossible that they should understand Socialism or escape from the inculcated opinion that

73

Socialism is a criminal conspiracy against the public welfare. Even those who have been reached by our propaganda, and vote for Socialist candidates (most of whom do not understand Socialism, and mean by it nothing but the Labour-Capitalism of the Trade Unions) are merely partisans in the class war which they conceive as a struggle for liberty like the 1848 revolutions.

Now we, as Socialists, have nothing to do with liberty. Our message, like Mussolini's, is one of discipline, of service, of ruthless refusal to acknowledge any natural right of competence. We admit no liberty whatever until the daily debt to society is paid by the day's work. Liberty belongs, not to the day's work which it is a business of a Socialist government to organise, but the day's leisure, as to which there is plenty of room for Liberal activity. Where we differ from the Fascists is that we insist on equality of income and therefore of State Control of production and distribution, which is being entirely lost sight of in the liberal quarrel about Matteotti and Turati. We are, in short, allowing Socialism to be absorbed by Liberalism and letting the whole movement relapse to 1850.

For the rest I can only say that if we cannot meet organisation by organisation, agitation by agitation, and public opinion by public opinion, so much the worse for us. If we can do nothing but run round Europe crying for sympathy and describing how we have been ill used by a bold bad monster named Mussolini, we may get a little contemptuous pity and give Liberal politicians everywhere a chance of making Gladstonian speeches about Italian atrocities; but that will not help us, and it will cost us the little respect that we have not already forfeited by our impotence after the war.

faithfully
G. Bernard Shaw

To J. RAMSAY MacDONALD

[A/68]

4 Whitehall Court SW 1
21st October 1927

[William Joynson Hicks (1865–1932), later first Viscount Brentford, known to all as "Jix," was Home Secretary 1924–29. Leopold S. Amery (1873–1955) was Secretary of State for the Colonies and for Dominion Affairs 1924–29. Frederick E. Smith (1872–1930), first Earl of Birkenhead, controversial right-wing Conservative, former Lord Chancellor, was Secretary of State for India 1924–28.]

My dear Macdonald

We shall not come to tea on Sunday because Charlotte has lumbago, and is not likely to shake it off completely enough to enjoy motoring until next week. Later on we will blow in.

My letters about Mussolini, which have raised a considerable flutter, were really written *at* our own people. At bottom the people know that what they need is not more paper liberty and democracy, but more discipline; and Mussolini's grip of this fact is the whole secret of his command.

In Italy I discussed Fascism with only *one* Fascist, to whom I took my letter *after* writing it. I will tell you what he told me when we meet: it was instructive, which the utterances of Salvemini and Turati certainly are not. Our own Salveminis would not be much use against Hicks & Amery, Churchill & Birkenhead, with their military and financial backing if we had a crisis here.

However————————————————————!

G.B.S.

To FRANCIS FLETCHER VANE

[X/349]

4 Whitehall Court S W 1
5th November 1927

[Sir Francis Fletcher Vane (1861–1934), fifth Baronet, of Hutton, who fought meritoriously in both the Boer War and the Great War, was the founder and leader of the Italian boy scouts, in Venice. In December 1926 the government issued a decree suppressing all scouts in Italy. A protest by the Pope caused modification of the decree to exclude Catholic Scouts, but these were suppressed later. "Haro!" (not Italian, but Middle English, derived from Old and Middle French) is a cry expressing alarm or distress. "Balillas" were members of a Fascist youth organization Opera Nazionale Balilla, for youngsters aged eight to fourteen.]

Dear Sir Francis

I am much obliged to you for your letter of the 18th October. I knew nothing of this very significant Boy Scout business, because our old Liberals, instead of criticising Fascism warily and intelligently, and keeping on speaking terms with Mussolini, will do nothing but scream "Tyranny! Murder! Castor Oil! Matteotti!" etc. etc. On all these talking points Mussolini can say "Mind your own business," or "You can attend to the mote in my eye when you have taken the beam out of your own." An Italian exile may be excused because, as an Italian, he has the right to cry Haro! as loud as he can. But we have no such *locus standi*: it is only when Fascism threatens the peace of Europe that we can *demander la parole* with any propriety. I, therefore, have to tell our Libertarian Impossibilists to stop pestering me with their eternal Matteotti and Sacco and Vanzetti and all the rest of it, and address themselves to serious politics, including, for the good of their own souls, the question why both the workers and the Liberals were so hopelessly incompetent that Italy gave Mussolini *carte blanche* to extirpate them. I have no patience with this futile squealing and atrocity mongering. It produces remarkable examples of literary invective; but meanwhile the Capitalists keep their seats; and we have actually to support them against our own fools to avert a mere wreck of human society.

I confess I am surprised to hear that Mussolini, instead of playing without any reservation his trump card of Nationalising the Boy Scouts as Balillas, spared so many of them at your instance. You see how hard it is in the face of this to accuse him of having abolished an international body of Boy Fascists to replace them with incipient aggressive Nationalists. . . .

faithfully
G. Bernard Shaw

To GEORGES PITOËFF

[T/1]   [4 Whitehall Court SW 1]
                                   16th November 1927

[*Maison crèvecoeurs* (*Heartbreak House*) was produced at the Théâtre des Mathurins on 17th January 1928 as *La maison des coeurs-brisés*. Although Shaw's programme note was drafted in the third person to conceal authorship, his name was appended at the foot. *L'argent n'a pas d'odeur* (*Widowers' Houses*) was eventually produced by Pitoëff at the Mathurins on 16th September 1938, with the then 43-year-old Ludmilla Pitoëff as Blanche, despite Shaw's warning to Pitoëff (in French) on 18th October 1927 that the play "does not concern you. Madame Pitoëff cannot transform herself into that brutal baggage, Blanche Sartorius. [The rôle] is for concierge's daughters." Shaw's French obviously was uncorrected by Charlotte.]

Cher Monsieur Pitoëff

Hamon vous a envoyé le texte de *Maison Crèvecoeur* corrigé. Je lui enverrai quelque chose pour insérer dans le programme.

"Comoedia" annonce (on m'a dit) *Crèvecoeur*, sans la maison, une chose impossible, parce que la maison—espèce de palais enchanté—est le sujet de la pièce. Sans cela, pas d'atmosphère, pas de magique, rien qu'un drame vulgaire manqué qui ne commence jamais, ne finit jamais, ne réussit jamais; bref, qui n'a aucun sens.

On m'assure que nous aurons un four noir. C'est très possible: mes pièces sont dangereuses, et même fatales dans les mains des gens de théâtre comme il faut. Au point de vue du boulevard on les approche comme maux d'être raccourci aussi que possible. On fait des coupures, ce qui est très facile, vu que la plupart de mes lignes sont sans raison d'être. La pièce même est sans raison d'être; d'abord on coupe quelques lignes qui n'ont utilité apparente, mais le procédé poussé au bout finit par couper toute la pièce et substituer un chef d'oeuvre de Scribe ou Augier. Il faut absolument que la réprésentation soit aussi longue que possible—que les spectateurs s'y intéressent au point de se laisser fatiguer atrocement plutôt que de perdre un seul mot. Il faut qu'ils racontent leurs souffrances pendant au moins une semaine après à leurs amis et connaissances; c'est-à-dire qu'ils parlent [de] Pitoëff-Ludmilla-Shaw-Mathurins sans cesse.

Cela veut dire que le jeu shawien est précisément le contraire du jeu du boulevard. Tout effort de concilier le boulevard doit fatalement manquer son but et mettre assez de l'eau dans le breuvage pour le rendre incapable d'enivrer.

Mais gardez-vous bien de fatiguer les gens en les ennuyant au lieu de les intéresser. Il faut surtout éviter les entr'actes longues. Le changement de l'intérieur à l'extérieur de la maison doit être presque instantané. Impossible, vous direz; et vous aurez raison; mais faites-le aussi vite que possible car si cela dure dix minutes vous serez perdu. Trois minutes sera beaucoup mieux que cinq. Les conditions ne sont pas favorables. Un four est prédit parce que:

1) l'auteur est un sale Anglais qui ne sait [pas] construire une pièce de théâtre;

2) vous êtes, comme tous les maris des grandes actrices, un acteur infâme;

3) vous avez un accent de boyar;

4) Madame Pitoëff ne vous permet d'engager que les actrices vieilles et sans talent; et au lieu de l'ensemble demandé par *Maison Crève-Coeur*, vous me donnerez "ma femme et quelques poupées";

5) 6) 7) 8) &c &c. vous pouvez les imaginer. C'est terrible mais enfin je risquerai toute cela; d'ailleurs de telles histoires n'ont pas pour moi le charme de la nouveauté; et il me faut surtout une pierre de touche

77

pour m'assurer que ces dernières pièces ultra-shawiennes sont votre affaire. *Sainte Jeanne*, étant "sui generis," ne prouve rien.

L'Argent n'a pas d'odeur a un succès fou à Berlin, wo es heisst Zinsen? Incroyable, cela: peut-être Hamon avait raison. Excellence extraordinaire de l'ensemble, on dit.

tout à vous
G. Bernard Shaw

To OTTO KYLLMANN

[4 Whitehall Court SW1]
[E/52; X/116] 24th November 1927

[Shaw's note was written at the foot of a letter of 21st November from Thomas Nelson & Sons, requesting permission to include the Loire scene from *Saint Joan* in a textbook intended for the Middle Forms of secondary schools. In an accompanying letter to Kyllmann, director of Constable's, Shaw added: "I return Nelson's enquiry with as mild a comment as I can persuade myself to make. . . . Blast all schools and schoolbooks! They are making literature loathed" (A/64).]

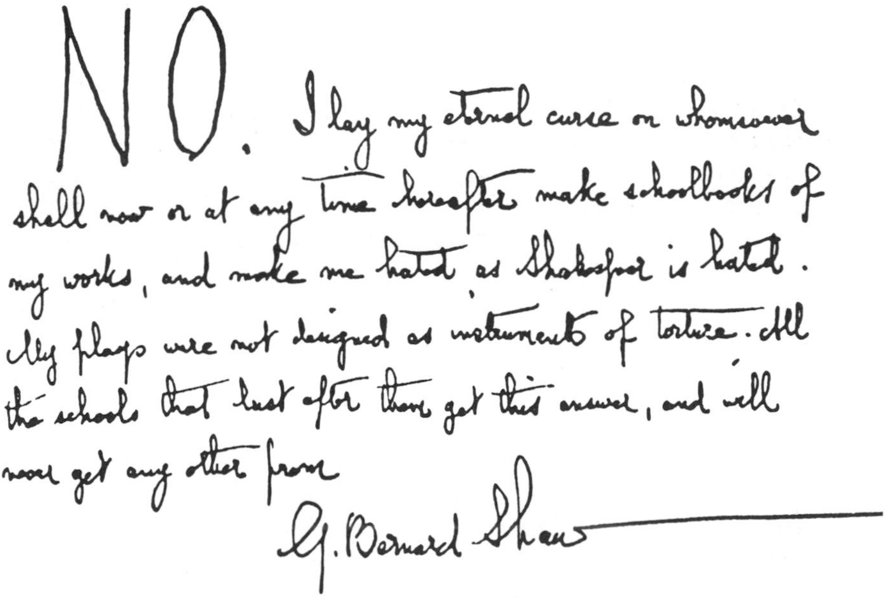
NO. I lay my eternal curse on whomsoever shall now or at any time hereafter make schoolbooks of my works, and make me hated as Shakespear is hated. My plays were not designed as instruments of torture. All the schools that lust after them get this answer, and will never get any other from

G. Bernard Shaw

To J. RAMSAY MacDONALD

[C/68]
4 Whitehall Court SW1
26th November 1927

[Shaw's Movietone "stunt" was a talking film interview at Ayot St Lawrence, eventually made in 1928, in which he gave a comic impersonation of Mussolini.]

If they are still performing the Movietone Voices of Italy at the New Gallery, go and hear it even at the cost of missing a full dress debate. It is of *enormous* political importance. The audience both sees and hears Mussolini ten times more distinctly and impressively than any audience has ever seen and heard *us*; and the political party that wakes up to the possibilities of this method of lecturing will, if it has money enough, sweep the floor with its opponents.

Order the whole Labor Cabinet to go.

As the Movietone people have been very pressing about it to me, I have offered to do a stunt for them as a private experiment.

G.B.S.

To AUGUSTIN HAMON

[H/1]
4 Whitehall Court SW1
[Undated: assigned to 28th November 1927]

My dear Hamon

The enclosed scrap of yellow paper contains what I suggest for the Heartbreak House program.

The other enclosure, in pencil, is a draft of a letter I sent to Pitoeff. As he is a Roumanian he will not be shocked by my bad French. You will notice that I have told him that if he does not make a success of H.H. I shall conclude that he is not the manager for me....

When you tell me that Chateau Chevauche does not make sense you are of course right; but then Horseback Hall does not make sense either. If I were an Academician I should have had to call it Hall Inhabited By Persons Accustomed To Ride On Horseback. You will find on the Seine a ruin called Chateau Gaillard, built by Richard Coeur de Lion. This is a regrettable solecism: it should be Chateau des Gaillards or Chateau Dont Les Habitués Sont Des Viveurs. Similarly, to call a Building For The Accommodation of Superannuated Soldiers Les Invalides is ridiculous. The Arc de Triomphe is not an arc de triomphe: it is an arc de pierre bati pour commemorer les triomphes de Napoléon. These ungrammatical titles are traditions from the troubadours and knights errant. But they serve their turn, and have some poetry about them, or, failing poetry, some fun. On the other hand, Manoir du Cavalier—Manor House of the Rider—is wrong: it should be at least Manoir des Cavaliers. But why be pedantic? Maison Crevecoeur is nonsense just as much as Chateau Chevauche. And both express what is meant, which is more than can be said for Maison ou les coeurs se brisent, or Manoir du Cavalier.

Anyhow, I am at the end of my suggestions: I can think of nothing better than Chevauche.

If when you are in Paris the Cinemas are exhibiting MOVIETONE, do not fail to visit them. The political possibilities are enormous. I have just seen Mussolini far more distinctly than any Italian crowd has ever seen him, and heard him more distinctly too. The scowl which intimidates Europe is a pure accident: he has a forehead of bronze which he cannot change; and his voice quite belies it. As a dictator I greatly prefer him to Poincaré.

In haste, ever
G. Bernard Shaw

To GRAHAM WALLAS

Cliveden. Taplow
(chez Nancy Astor)
24th December 1927

[A/13]

[Wallas had read proofs of the *Intelligent Woman's Guide to Socialism and Capitalism*, which had swollen to nearly 225,000 words by the time of its completion in late March 1927. Edward Hugh Dalton (1887–1962), later Baron Dalton of Forest and Frith, Co. Palatine of Durham, Welsh-born politician, was at this time Labour M.P. for Camberwell (Peckham Division). Gamage's, a department store, was in High Holborn. Hamleys, an internationally famous toy shop, was (and is) in Regent Street. The Burlington Arcade, built in 1819, is a covered shopping promenade of exclusive shops off Piccadilly, the first of its kind in England.]

My dear Wallas

I have made all your corrections except that concerning Lord Hugh Cecil. I have no doubt he said that Labor could not govern; but it was Churchill who made a newspaper stunt of it. It was one of the cries against him at the Westminster election [a by-election, 1924, in which Churchill stood as an independent anti-socialist candidate, losing by 43 votes].

I am now at a standstill for want of a capable indexer. I have indexed 200 pages myself, enough to shew the sort of index I want; but it is an intolerable drudgery; and I want somebody to finish it. . . . Do you know of any intelligent and sufficiently literate female who is at a loss for a job? If you do, drop me a line to the Royal Hotel, Capelcurig, Carnarvon, where we intend to put up for a while to recover from a Xmas of overcrowded splendor here, where I have already nearly talked myself to death.

I shall have to let the book go now as it is. I think another book is badly wanted on Democracy (incidentally) and generally on the forms of government appropriate to a Socialist State. In this Mussolini business people talk of nothing but castor oil, whereas the man, being a Big Simpleton, is trying to organize an Imperial Antonine State by organizing all the conspiracies: the professions, the trades &c &c., without the ghost of a notion that any work has ever been put into the subject by the likes of us. And the eloquent Salvemini denounces the tyrant and explains that he himself is a Socialist because, like Napoleon, he believes in the career open to the talents: *alias* Equality of Opportunity. Well, he has had equality of opportunity with Benito at all events; and he has not found its results enjoyable. You could make up out of your works a special prescription for Italy at present that might make the Daily News & the Manchester Guardian useful on the subject instead of hysterically mischievous.

I hope my book will cure at least some of the wretched wobble that aff[l]icts the Labor Party. As none of them knows what Socialism is, it is necessary to plank something definite down and say "Let that be Socialism," very much as Queen Elizabeth planked down the prayer book. But I suppose they will go on wobbling. I have knocked the Capital Levy out of them; and immediately Snowden revives it in the sacred name of Taxation of Land Values.

Webb, having at a mild estimate about ten times the total having of all the rest in ability and knowledge, gets no grip in parliament because he is neither an actor nor an ambitious scoundrel. He will not take the trouble even to make himself commonly audible to the adoring Fabians in Kingsway Hall, much less bully and impress the St Stephens mob. Besides, he has something better to do and does not intend to go on with front benching. And of course we are all too old, and seem even to Macdonald (to say nothing of Dalton and the younger generation) about 20 years older than we really are.

I finish this on Xmas morning amid an orgy of presents. The place looks like Gamage's or Hamleys or the Burlington Arcade. They have presented me with a mouth organ! I deserve it. God! how I have talked since my arrival on Friday!

You have been a friend in need over those confounded proofs; and I am truly thankful.

ever
GBS

To ARNOLD DOLMETSCH

Cliveden. Taplow
3rd January 1928

[S(C)/24]

[Andrés Segovia (1893–1987), self-taught Spanish musician, won worldwide respect for the guitar as a recital instrument and acclaim for his performance skills.]

In jazz the banjo is used merely as a percussion instrument to mark the rhythm, just as the tabor was. It is really a development of the tambourine.

The lute, as far as my knowledge goes, has no successor: there has been nothing at all like it since it died of its own difficulty. The mandoline might be regarded as a very cheap sort of toy lute. The guitar, in the hands of a player like Segovia, challenges the lute as a fully equipped musical instrument (as distinct from a mere strummer); but its quality is quite different. The lute is *sui generis*.

G.B.S.

To MOLLY TOMPKINS

Cliveden. Taplow
8th January 1928

[A/1; X/319]

["Ballyhooleys" is presumably a comic reference to Shaw's request on 5th November 1927 for a word as to the Tompkins's experience concerning the Balillas in Italy. Charles W. J. Tennant (d. 1942) was district manager of Christian Science committees on publication for Great Britain and Ireland until 1937. In 1931 he accompanied Shaw and the Astors on their visit to the USSR. The American lady at King's College, mentioned later in the letter as Sister Helen (an allusion to D. G. Rossetti's poem of that title), was Granville

Barker's second wife, Helen Huntington. Granville Barker had lectured on Shakespeare to the British Academy on 13th May 1925, following which Shaw seconded Forbes-Robertson's proposal of a vote of thanks. Peter Tompkins was attending a boarding school in Lausanne.]

My dear Mrs Tompkins

I have to thank you for your kind and informative reply to my inquiry concerning the Ballyhooleys.

We have been snowed up in this famous countryhouse since Xmas Eve. We leave tomorrow; but I use the address because I would have you know that the Isolino and its chatelaine are not the only pebbles on the beach.

Further, Lady Astor is a devotee of Christian Science. One day, when we were discussing it, I told her the story of the American lady who sat behind me at Kings College on a celebrated occasion, hating me horribly, and how when I rose to go away I found my spine all rusty and my occiput grating on it, so that I was ill for 30 days, and then recovered suddenly and miraculously. Lady Astor and her guest Mr Tennant, an eminent exponent and practitioner of Christian Science, had no doubt whatever that the American lady's hatred had blasted and bewitched my spine: such happenings were commonplaces to them.

Then I began to think. For there is another American lady who loved me, and then gave me a shock by looking at me with hatred in her eyes and speaking with it in her voice. I nearly ran back to London (we were in Italy); but I unfortunately could not obey this salutary impulse. And, as I now remember, I presently got ill, in spite of swimming and sunbathing. And I cannot get really well, as I was the year before, when the heavens were void of hatred. That wicked woman is giving me absent treatments of hatred. Perhaps she has made a wax figure of me and is sticking pins into it, like Sister Helen. Only by casting her out utterly can I escape the spell; and I find that somehow I cannot do that. The old tenderness gives the witch her grip; and I languish and must presently die of her hatred. Unless she relents and sends a message of love I am a lost man, though a most innocent one. Innocent or not, her adoration was an indispensable Vitamin in my bread of life; and if I perish my blood will be upon her head.

So that is how I am inside, though externally I "peacock" here (Charlotte's expression) amid week end crowds of visitors. Except for this funny Xmas episode I have no news. The book is finished and will appear as soon as its index and chapter headings go to press.

How is Laurence? and how is his malignant merciless wife? Did the great snowstorm reach you on the lake? Did the boy come home for Xmas? and was he much changed by his prison? You must relieve my uneasy soul by a sign of life.

GBS

To FLORENCE EMILY HARDY

4 Whitehall Court SW1

[A/100]   16th January 1928

[Thomas Hardy's remains (except for his heart, buried simultaneously at Stinsford) were laid to rest in a magnificent funeral ceremony in Westminster Abbey that afternoon, escorted by an assortment of eminent pallbearers, including Shaw. "You should have seen me," he wrote to Henry S. Salt on 20th January. "After posing all last summer to Troubetskoy for a full length statue in a sublime attitude I was in full practice; and Galsworthy and I played everybody else off the stage. . . . Kipling fidgeted like the devil, and did his best, by changing step continually, to make me fall over him, which I jolly nearly did until I became wary. [Ramsay] Macdonald's word to us was invaluable—'Look out when you come to the choir entrance or the bier will catch you in the side of the head.' He is quite used to the Abbey by this time" (A/5).]

My dear Mrs Hardy

It was a fine show; and I tried to look as solemn as possible; but I didn't feel solemn a bit. I rejoice in Hardy's memory; and I felt all the time that he was there—up in the lantern somewhere—laughing like anything at Kipling and me and Galsworthy and the rest of us. Probably he shook hands with Handel at the end: his only link with that sort of thing now.

If you only knew how I wanted at the end to swoop on you; tear off all that villainous crape (you should have been like the lilies of the field); and make you come off, *with him*, to see a Charlie Chaplin film! But of course we wouldn't have dared. I had to be content with nudging Cockerell disrespectfully as I passed him.

You must feel lost for the moment with nobody to take care of; but you know, there are lots of things for you to arrange; and before you arrange them just go to bed and stay there until all your arrears of sleep are made up and you feel the return of spring making you jolly and selfish and lazy. That may not seem possible yet; but it is inconceivable that Thomas Hardy's widow should be unhappy or unblest.

Only, don't marry another genius: they are not all so sound at the core; and anyhow he would be an anti-climax. Marry somebody who has nothing else to do than to take care of *you*.

Meanwhile, what an adventure it was, wasn't it?

Hooray! It's not proper; but that's how he makes me feel.

> enthusiastically
> *and*
> affectionately
> G. Bernard Shaw

To FLORENCE EMILY HARDY

4 Whitehall Court SW1
[A/5]   27th January 1928

["Fall not a single tear" is apparently a reference, consciously or otherwise, to "Fall not a tear, I say ..." in Shakespeare's *Antony and Cleopatra*, III.ii.69. Max Gate was Hardy's home in Dorset.]

My dear Mrs Hardy

You see, a man like T.H. does not belong entirely to himself; and he cannot leave his widow more than he owned. When a nation of poor devils who are not T.Hs, rise up in their poverty and claim their part in him with all the Pities at their back, what can he do? What can you do? What can any of us do? Nothing but just give it to them. That is what the Abbey meant. But for that he would not have been there; you would not have been there; I should not have been there. As it was, we *had* to be there. T.H. would not have grudged it to them: it was only the large scale edition of receiving the American pilgrim at Maxgate. Galsworthy never goes to funerals: he feels, as I do, that it is an intrusion; but when the whole country in a manner rises up and intrudes, what can we do but our best to make it a dignified and—in its ceremonial way—a beautiful intrusion?

T.H. puts up with it kindly, you may be sure, just as he put up with the pilgrims. I don't think the "splendor" imposed on him: I still feel that he must have chuckled when Kipling (who is a frightful fidget) changed step and twice very nearly made me fall over him, and that his sole distress was that you should have had such an ordeal or any misgivings as to his understanding the position and the practical compulsion on you to share him with the nation. He would have said "Fall not a single tear: let them have ten funerals if they like."

85

And so, away with melancholy; and thank you for your very kind letter; for I, too, needed just a scrap of consolation.

Don't answer this: in fact, don't answer anybody: no reasonable person will expect it.

ever
G.B.S.

To ADA TYRRELL

Ayot St Lawrence. Welwyn
[H/1; X/351.e]   28th January 1928

[Ada Tyrrell (1854–1955) was a daughter of a Trinity College Senior Fellow, Dr George Ferdinand Shaw (1821–99) and his wife Ellen (Shinkwin), non-related Dublin neighbours of GBS's family. One of their daughters, Constance (known as "Barnacle"), was Lucy Carr Shaw's closest friend. Ada married the classical scholar Robert Yelverton Tyrrell (1844–1914). T.C.D. is Trinity College Dublin. The Dowling sisters and their brother, friends of Shaw in his youth, resided at 30 Upper Leeson Street.]

My dear Ada

I hope I have not delayed answering too long. I have so much writing to do that I never have time to write.

Quite a lot of people have been writing to me lately from America, claiming relationship with your father and assuming that I am his son. In one or two cases where they seemed to want harmless information I have referred them to you, giving your address as 53 Waterloo Road.

Your mother was certainly a remarkable woman, who would have filled a larger place in a larger world than that into which she was dropped. Her scale of values was not that of Harrington Street. Also she was a siren, and, as such, could not be confined within the ordinary circle of home interests. Apparently your father could not reconcile himself to being only one among many men whom she interested and in whom she was interested; and so the household went to pieces, leaving her in a freedom which was rather barren because she had not duties enough to balance her privileges. But why bother about/her? Children never know anything about their parents; and I dont think their occasional attempts to reconstruct them after their death are ever quite successful.

I do not remember any character in my books and plays modelled consciously on your mother. I always had a vision of her as the mother of Cashel Byron in an early novel of mine called Cashel Byron's

Profession (he was a prizefighter); but it was a visual impression mostly. Still, now you mention it, I daresay the visual impression led to a touch of caricature from the living model here and there.

You, I should say, are your father's daughter in so far as you are anybody but yourself. He deserves your sympathy more than she did; for he was literally what Shakespear called "A Fellow [of T.C.D.]* almost damned in a fair wife [*Othello*, I.i.21]."

Yes: I remember the Dowlings. I had a curious sort of romantic friendship with their brother who was drowned. My earliest efforts in fiction were monstrous exploits which I attributed to him: in fact I made him a character in an endless tale of impossible adventures which I used to tell to a boy named Bellhouse, who had an inappeasable appetite for Dowling stories.

But do not remind them of me: they can have no very pleasant recollections of me; and I shudder to think that they might begin to invent an imaginary past. Besides, it is rather awful to think of those two girls pulling the devil by the tail all these years. No doubt they are as happy as most people; but it would have suited me so badly that the thought of it makes me feel suicidal. Except in my secret self I was not happy in Dublin; and when ghosts rise up from that period I want to lay them again with the poker. You, however, are not one of these unwelcome ones.

My life has rushed through very quickly: I have seen very little of anyone who has not worked with me. Except with my wife I have no companionships: only occasional contacts, intense but brief. I spring to intimacy in a moment, and forget in half an hour. An empty life is peopled with the absent and the imagined: a full one has to be cleared out everyday by the housemaid of forgetfulness or the air would become unbreathable. Those who see me now are those who shove and insist and will not take no for an answer, with, of course, the great people who must be seen because they have earned a right of entry everywhere.

I wonder whether you will get this. I see by your letter that your travelling address holds good only until the end of the month; so it looks as if I should be just a day after the fair. Perhaps I had better send a card to Waterloo Road to warn you. I should not like you to suppose that your letter had not elicited an answer.

yours, dear Ada, ever
G.B.S.

* The editorial insertion is Shaw's.

87

To MABEL SHAW

Ayot St Lawrence. Welwyn
[H/83; X/352, 317]   30th January 1928

[J.E.Whiting had supplied Shaw with copies of some of Mabel Shaw's letters, suggesting that he evaluate her writing skills and give her advice. Shaw's letter indicates a lack of awareness that two books by Miss Shaw (*Children of the Chief*, 1921, and *Dawn in Africa*, 1927) had been published in London, and that she had, in addition, a reputation by this time as an educationist, "being the pioneer of a type of education for girls that sought to combine what she considered to be 'traditional' elements in African society with a Christian and English style of education. She was quite widely known in her day in missionary and educational circles for her work at Mbereshi" (Sean Morrow, postgraduate student at the University of Sussex, who did an historical study of the Mbereshi mission, to Dan H. Laurence, 15th May 1980).

Margaret Macmillan (1860–1931), American-born campaigner for the cause of physical education and an early member of the Independent Labour Party, served on the Bradford School Board for several years. In 1904, with backing from the millionaire Joseph Fels, she was enabled to develop a scheme for a health centre that led to the opening of a children's clinic at Deptford in 1910 and a pioneer open-air nursery school in 1917. In the latter year she was awarded a C.B.E.]

Dear Miss Shaw

A friend of yours has shewn me some of your letters, and asked me —as I found them interesting— to let you know whether I thought you qualified to take up literature as a profession.

As far as mere literary faculty is concerned I should say decidedly Yes. You have evidently no difficulty in putting into writing anything you want to say or describe, and in such a way that the reader reads willingly and expectantly. No more than this is required of the greatest authors as professional qualification.

But success in literature depends on what you have to say as well as on how you say it. For instance, of Bunyan's two romances, The Pilgrim's Progress and The Holy War, the second is, if anything, more skilfully written than the first, the hand being more experienced. But the first is universally readable by people whose tastes rise above the football page of the evening paper; and the second ends by making theology ridiculous and unreadable even to a specialist of Bunyan's own persuasion.

Whether you are enough of a freethinker to be successful in literature outside your own sect I cannot say. We are none of us complete freethinkers (least of all sometimes the professed ones): we all have our superstitions and our complexes, the difference between a rather mad writer like Saint Paul and a rather sane one like Voltaire being only one of degree. One can only say that it would have been better for the world if Paul had never been born, and that it would have been a great misfortune—a religious misfortune—to have missed Voltaire, who at least loved justice and did mercy and walked humbly with his God, and believed that no further theology was required of him. Also he certainly loved mercy and, as far as his temperament would let him, tried to do justly. That is why he is still so readable. Besides, as the wickednesses which he exposed and which he called on the world's conscience to renounce were too frightful to be contemplated without some sort of anaesthetic, he used his sense of fun to make people come to scoff, knowing that that was the only chance of getting them to remain to pray.

Now it is clear from what you have written that you are one of the would-be saviors, like Bunyan and Voltaire. Having found happiness with God (so to speak) you wish to bring others to him. Jesus, who was strongly anti-missionary, as his warning about the tares and the wheat shews, would probably tell you to mind your own business and suffer little children to find their own way to God even if it were a black way; but he certainly would not demur to your describing your own pilgrimage and testifying that you had found God in your own white way. That is, if he had any patience with you after discovering that you had set up in the virgin forest the horrible emblem of Roman cruelty and Roman terrorism as an emblem of Christianity. Even Rome itself would have set up the image of a mother and child.

The question is, then, would your descriptions of your own discovery of God please a sufficient number of bookbuyers to make a profit for a publisher and bookseller and a living for you. I think it quite likely they would. I have found your scraps interesting; and I am not in sympathy with you at all. I am not in the least what modern psychologists call a masochist: that is, a person with a queer lust for being tortured; so that when your parents no longer tortured you you tortured yourself. You are not satiated even with the horrible things they did to Christ: you must heap on him a broken body, though the story insists so strongly on the fact that his body was not broken as the bodies of the thieves were. You meet a young man with whom you fall in love, and who falls in love with you. There was nothing to prevent you making him and yourself happy by naturally and unaffectedly marrying him and filling your lap with babies. But no: that would not have been any fun for you: you must break his heart and break your own (if you have one) on the ridiculous pretext that the negro children needed you, though your own country was swarming with little white heathens who needed you as badly as they need Margaret Macmillan in Deptford. And then comes your artistic impulse. You must write about it and make a propaganda of voluptuous agony. Well, there are plenty of people who find agony voluptuous on paper; and they will make a reading public for you. But I, who loathe torture, and object most strongly to being tortured, my lusts being altogether normal, should take you and shake you were it not that you are out of my reach and that you would rather enjoy being shaken if it hurt you enough.

It may be that this psychosis (pardon the jargon) will pass away as your glands mature. At the bottom of this African business there may be a young woman with a healthy taste for travel, novelty, adventure, and salutary hardening hardship. You may not really have wanted that unfortunate young parson whom you smashed up. You are, after all, the granddaughter of your delightful old humbug of a grandmother as well as the daughter of your (as I gather) detestable parents. I call your grandmother a humbug in the friendliest sense because she made a child happy by flattering God, and pretending that he had not a great deal to answer for. She spoilt you; but she saved your soul alive for the time when you will be strong enough to face adult life and grow out of the pastime of playing with the souls of little children as your soul was played with.

And that is all I have to say to you on the little information I have about you. You may think I have said a great deal too much; but I assure you the question of becoming a professional writer is a pretty deep one when the intention behind it extends to becoming a prophet as well. I am in that line myself; and I KNOW.

And anyhow you brought it on yourself. I wonder what you expected me to say.

faithfully

G. Bernard Shaw

[After a year of delay Mabel Shaw finally replied to Shaw's letter on 17th February 1929, informing him that the letter had "at first roused much hot protest," but with the passage of time it "gives me more and more enjoyment as I read it, that deep quiet enjoyment that endures" (BL).]

To MRS PATRICK CAMPBELL

[A/37; X/160]

Ayot St Lawrence. Welwyn
6th February 1928

["Oh Joey dear you are potty," wrote Stella Campbell on 3rd February; "I 'staccato'—the idea!" Not surprisingly, considering the illegibility of her scrawl, Shaw misread the statement.]

Petty! Woman: you are profane: the prophet speaks not without weighing his words.

I said *that* because you are trying to teach (being incapable of learning, which is sometimes not a bad qualification); and the first thing you have to knock into a stage novice is staccato alphabet so staccatissimo that every consonant will put out a candle at the back of the gallery. Not until her tongue and lips are like a pianist's fingers should she begin to dare think of speaking to an audience. I do not know who taught you to articulate; but whoever gave you your staccato gave you the power that, with your unaccountable fascination, enabled you, until you were found out, to persuade people that you were the supreme actress of your generation: no small feat for a woman who could not act at all except in fantasies of her own, like Irving. *His* elocution, by the way, though so pedantic that every slovenly tongued cockney ridiculed it, was half the secret of his illusory distinction.

Such music as your pupils may have must come from within them:

all you can teach them is the value of your 𝄞 *martellato molto.*

That is the foundation of my platform effectiveness. The laugh comes from the back row of the gallery as heartily as from the front of the stalls.

Only, if your pupils want to be trained for the phono–film or Movietone, they must, after learning the staccato, renounce all its sforzandos, and learn a delicacy of touch and subtlety of nuance which would never "get across" viva voce, but which the microphone and the wireless amplifier will carry to the remotest cheap seats of the world.

Oh, if only you could learn—but I waste words. Farewell.

GBS

To HARRIET COHEN

[H/2; X/321.e]

4 Whitehall Court SW1
8th [5th?] February 1928

[Harriet Cohen's concert in the Wigmore Hall on Saturday afternoon, 4th February, with Sir Henry J. Wood and Cohen alternately conducting a chamber orchestra, included performances of de Falla's "Nights in the Gardens of Spain" and Bach's D-major Brandenburg concerto, with Cohen performing on a Bechstein piano. The composer Arnold Bax (1883–1953), later to be Master of the King's Music, and Harriet Cohen were lovers. He gave most of his music manuscripts to her; she subsequently presented them to the British Library. Sigismond Thalberg (1812–71), one of the most celebrated piano virtuosos of his day, was less successful as a composer. For an explanation of the probable misdating of this letter, see the headnote to the letter that follows.]

My dear Harriet

That concert was a brilliant success; but Arnold (the Bax one, not the Bennett), whom I found jilted in the doorway, must have chuckled. To explain why, I must resume my old role of critic and talk to you seriously.

The first thing you have to grasp is that the modern steel concert grand pianoforte, though a triumph of ironmongery, is so plainly inferior in tone to violin and flute (for instance) that it should never be brought into immediate rivalry with them, and should be used at an orchestral concert only as an instrument of percussion like the zylophone (for which many of De Falla's passages were evidently intended) or, in melodic passages, when the melody is carefully enriched with its own characteristic pianoforte harmonies.

Now this means that you should never never never play a Bach or Mozart concerto on a Bechstein. No artifice of touch that you can possibly employ can give you a dog's chance when, in Bach, you have to follow a solo flute and solo violin in a single-line melody with an answer on the piano. You cannot disguise the atrocious inferiority of the tone. You must play on a harpsichord, where the tone is so completely different that it never sounds like a bad imitation of the flute. Bechstein tries to make the piano as like a flute in the middle and upper octaves as possible, and no harm is done at a recital where there is no flute to compare it with; but in a Bach concerto the effect of bad imitation is terrible.

In Mozart [in] the old form of concerto, in which the orchestra begins by playing the themes with all the beauty of Mozart's peculiar scoring, and then the wretched pianiste is asked to repeat them in their simplicity, the case is hopeless. There is nothing for it but either to revive the old wooden piano, which had individual care, and on which Thalberg could get the singing tone with which he enchanted my mother, or else avoid Mozart's concertos as you would avoid the plague.

You will see that in your musical enthusiasm you handicapped your piano frightfully by that gorgeous program, which you conducted, as usual, with great vigor. I believe you are a born conductor, and will abandon virtuosity for that at last, as Albert Coates did at first.

By the way you are developing a wonderful personal beauty, apparently from within, without any make-up. I never thought tuppence about your good looks; but now—really!

You need not bother to answer this; but think over it—not the last bit, but the sound doctrine about that blasted Bechstein.

> ever
> G.B.S.

To ARNOLD DOLMETSCH

4 Whitehall Court SW1
[H/24]   8th [5th?] February 1928

[Shaw had attended Dolmetsch's lecture on lutes and flutes on 3rd February. In November 1927 he was present at a Dolmetsch concert in which Dolmetsch's son Rudolf (1906–42) performed on the harpsichord and viol and, with his brother Carl (b. 1911), on the recorder. Joseph Joachim (1831–1907) and Pablo de Sarasate (1844–1908) were eminent violinists, who had performed frequently in London. Shaw, who first heard and reviewed a Joachim performance in *The Hornet* in 1877, preferred him to Sarasate, whom he first reviewed in *The Star* in 1889.

The dating of this letter is problematic. It is clearly dated 8th February, but the reference to Harriet Cohen's performance of 4th February as occurring "yesterday" confounds this. As noted in the introduction to the third volume of the *Collected Letters*, Shaw frequently sent on to Blanche Patch in London shorthand drafts of letters written at Ayot, to be transliterated. Miss Patch apparently affixed to this letter the date on which she typed it, rather than the date (unprovided by Shaw in the shorthand) on which it was composed.]

My dear Dolmetsch

I could not make the real point of my question about Segovia clear in public. It was this. If it really took forty years to master the lute it would be waste of time to make one, and folly to suggest its revival.

But the famous lute players were no older than Segovia. Their secret, from your point of view, was simply that they did not make lutes. No man who makes lutes can ever by any possibility play them as Segovia plays the guitar. He does it because he has never used his fingers for anything else, and has acquired a touch which enables him to produce a perfectly homogeneous scale from top to the bottom of the instrument automatically, without thinking about it. He listens, not to the instrument, but *for* the music. You, with your entirely different and not less marvellous workman's hand, pluck every string to see whether it sounds right by itself; and the result is that when you play a piece of music every string seems to be a different instrument, each perfect in its way, and each calling attention to itself and seeming to claim that it is not as the other strings are. And the more consummate lute maker you become the more impossible it will be for you to play as Segovia plays. What I really wanted to know was whether you had induced Segovia to try a lute to see what it would sound like if played as he plays the guitar.

People won't buy lutes if you tell them that it will take them forty years to learn it. If you explain that you can no more play it than Stradivarius could have played Brahms' Concerto and that it is in the nature of things impossible that the craftsman's hand should ever do the work of a virtuoso, they would be as ready to experiment with the lute as with the ukalele. After all, the lute cannot be more difficult, or even *as* difficult, as the violin. It is this business point of view that must be my excuse for writing this.

The Morley thing on the recorders was wonderful. But the recorders bring out the fact that not only do scales vary from nation to nation, so that Sarasate played a Latin scale which was quite different from Joachim's Teutonic scale, but no two individuals play the same scale. The recorder, being quite unmechanical, brings this out startlingly. One would expect that all the members of a musical family would play the same scale; but it is not so: Rudolph's scale is *my* scale; but his brother's scale is not the same; and yours differs from both. To get a perfect consort of recorders the players would have to begin by shedding their idiosyncratic scales and adopting one common to them all. How to arrive at that scale, God knows. The old mean tone scale as distinguished from the equally tempered scale is, I suppose, proper to the old pre-Bach music; but I need hardly say I have no artistic faith in scientific scales; and I suspect that good consorts, like happy marriages, can be made only between players to whom the same scale is congenial.

94

Yesterday I heard the Bach concertos and a Mozart one played on a Bechstein grand, and the effect of the melodic passages, played first on flute and violin and answered by the Bechstein, was abominable, whereas in a piece by De Falla, where the piano was used like a xylophone or pair of castanets, as a percussion instrument, it was most exhilarating. Can you not make a wooden piano for Mozart?

Don't trouble to answer. The evening at Queen Square was most enjoyable.

faithfully
G. Bernard Shaw

PS   By the way, when you make a recorder, how *do* you arrive at your scale? I presume you feel for it. But how far does your ear get corrupted by tuning clavichords in a series of flat fifths, resulting in sharp thirds &c &c ?

However, this would involve an answer; so keep it until next we meet.

People still buy and sell and play flageolets. When we were producing Heartbreak House, in which Eric Maturin [as Randall Utterword] was supposed to play the flute, he astonished me by appearing at rehearsal with a *new* flageolet, and playing it precariously but very appropriately.

To ST JOHN ERVINE

Ayot St Lawrence. Welwyn
12th March 1928

[H/3; X/136]

[Ervine's article, "Mr. Moses Shaw," was a review of Parts I and II of the *Back to Methuselah* revival at the Court Theatre, in *The Observer*, 11th March, in which he commented: "The singular fact about this revival is that the second part, which appeared to be pointless and even dull at the first performance [1923], is now full of point and provokes plenty of laughter. Mr. Shaw, like all great dramatists, does not reveal the whole of his mind at the first exhibition of it. I imagine that the stupendous power of this play will only be apparent on the day when a continuous performance of the entire piece is given."]

My dear Ervine

I have just been reading your article on Methuselah in the Observer; and much as I always enjoy your bursts of utter inconsiderateness, or rather inconsideration (for you are not in the idiomatic sense inconsiderate) I cannot have you running about the country lecturing on my religion with such ragged holes in your knowledge of my Anschauung. Think, boy: think.

I estimate the post-Eden families at ten children: that is, five couples. Eve had fifty grandchildren, and lived to see them all grow up. She had two hundred and fifty great-grandchildren, and lived to see them all grow up. She had one thousand two hundred and fifty great-great-grandchildren, and lived to see them all grow up. She had six thousa— but enough. We will take it that at the period of the play, when she was three hundred years old, there were so many thousands that if it had been possible for them all to live within reach of her and keep up the acquaintance, she and Adam would have died of hunger if they had stopped working long enough to kiss the lot once a week.

And you complain because I have not represented her as a grand-mother spoiling her first grandchild!!! Blush for yourself.

You contend further that I am a misogynic St Paul because I have represented a woman in a state of complete pre-sex innocence as making a wry face when it is explained to her that in consequence of the indelicacy with which Nature, in a fit of economy, has combined a merely excretory function with a creatively ejaculatory one in the same bodily part (she knowing only the excretory use of it), she is to allow herself to be syringed in an unprecedented manner by Adam. You say that I should have made her jump for joy. Ask Leonora, you idiot. My play is not a biography of Isadora Duncan. It is true that the indignity has compensations which, *when experienced*, overwhelm all the objections to it; but Eve had not experienced them. I am myself only too susceptible to them; yet I always feel obliged, as a gentleman, to apologize for my disgraceful behaviour; and I would be shot rather than be guilty of it in public. In this I am the normal heterosexual man describing, in Eve, the normal heterosexual woman. Yet you describe me, in an ecstasy of reaction against Victorianism (contemporary with Eve's clothes, which I did not design) as a morbid and impotent Pauline monster. Stuff!

You will have noticed that the arrangement leaves Eve unsatisfied. It leaves the redblooded he-man Cain unsatisfied. You, in a hearty manner, imply that it leaves you satisfied. I don't believe it. Nobody is satisfied; everybody is apologetic; we would all like to detach the ecstasy from the indecency. My suggestion is that the passion of the body will finally become a passion of the mind. Already there is a pleasure in thought—creative thought—that is entirely detached from ridiculous and disgusting acts and postures. Shakespear could not have written of the ecstasies of St Thomas in his sonnet [No. 129] about

96

"the expense of spirit in a waste of shame." The Aberdonian cannot say of the achievements of Einstein that "the position is ridiculous, the pleasure but momentary, and the expense damnable." There is no reduction, no disgust, no love changed to hate. The pleasure falls very short of the pleasure of sex in intensity; but you have only to conceive an intensification of the pleasure of thought as it becomes more and more a vital necessity to evolving society and humanity, accompanied by a reduction of intensity in physically reproductive pleasure, to understand why, 30,000 years hence, the naked and physically comfortless Ancient says to the dancing, lovemaking boy that a moment of life lived as the Ancients live it, in a chronic ecstasy of thought, would strike a boy dead. Also why the dancing boy cannot conceive how the Ancients can endure their (to him) apparently joyless existence.

Grasp this, and you will no longer talk to me as the boy talks to the Ancient.

When I began, Archer complained that my plays were reeking with sex. Now that I am ending you complain that I am an anchorite. Women have never complained of me either way. *They* know that I know what I am talking about.

After this it seems to me an anti-climax to add that Charlotte is now out of bed after half-past-twelve, and downstairs; but it is still very doubtful whether she will be able to come up to town this week. However, if she doesn't I will; so you may expect me to lunch on Thursday anyhow. We will keep you informed of her progress.

ever
GBS

[*On reverse of envelope*] Since closing this the doctor has been; and he says that Charlotte cannot and must not and shall not leave the house until the middle of next week. So Thursday is decidedly off as far as she is concerned. I shall be up on Thursday morning at 11 in case you wish to make any change.

To ST JOHN ERVINE

[C.u/3; X/136]   Ayot St Lawrence. Welwyn
                                                    13th March 1928

After posting my letter I amused myself by adding up the number of Eve's descendants available when she was 300 years old, assuming families of 10 and no deaths.

It comes to four million, eight hundred and eighty two thousand, eight hundred and ten persons, allowing 33⅓ years per generation.

4,882,810

To AUGUSTIN HAMON

4 Whitehall Court SW1

[H/1]   25th May 1928

[Attinger *frères* was a Swiss publishing house interested in issuing Shaw's plays in Hamon's translation at the rate of two a year for ten years, as well as tying up all non-dramatic publications. Nothing came of the negotiations. Eventually a contract was signed with Aubier, Éditions Montaigne, which published the *Intelligent Woman's Guide* in 1929, commencing an edition of the "Œuvres de Bernard Shaw" issued in more than two dozen volumes, until and beyond Shaw's death. The Tournées Ch. Baret toured the French provinces with *Saint Joan* in the spring of 1928, a Mlle Couvières appearing as Joan, to tepid notices. The Pitoëffs retained *Saint Joan* in their repertoire, reprising it in Paris eleven times between 1925 and 1934, and performing it frequently on tour, bringing the production to London in June 1930.]

My dear Hamon

It seems to me that the most immediate thing is to find a publisher for the Guide. It will be published in London and New York on the 1st of June. Fifty thousand copies have been sold in America already before publication. The edition of 10,000 which I ordered to be printed here is already sold; and the printers are working hard to provide more copies. Even in Sweden I am offered £100 for an edition of 3000 copies. What does Attinger say? Will he take it on? I will not make an agreement with him, nor with any publisher, about the plays until the Guide is published; for I think the publisher who takes on the plays ought to have the Guide as a bonne bouche.

The news about the tour of St Joan is worse than I expected. Of course it has to establish its reputation in the provinces, and should do much better on a second than on a first visit; and so on until it becomes a sort of institution. But are you sure that they are not playing tricks with it—playing it in several acts with long intervals for the sake of the refreshment bars, and cutting it all to pieces to shorten it for this purpose? Then as to the actress. You alarmed me by saying that she had a power of expressing sadness. If she does that in Joan, then all is lost. The old conventional Joan with the sad eyes, half burnt before

98

she makes her first entrance, and reeking with pious pathos, will kill any play dead. Joan must be bright, dominantly energetic, full of force and full of fun, with no touch of sentimentality about her, sweeping the play along whenever she is on the stage, or no actress without the special personal charm of Ludmila can succeed in it.

I do not believe that the prejudices you mention can have much to do with the failure of the play. Provincial playgoers will go to a play if they like it, no matter who the author is. St Joan, *properly* done, is the sort of play that gets past all the cliques and all the prejudices. Have you seen a performance? When I was in Italy a provincial company touring with St Joan was announced as coming to Stresa. The moment they heard I was there they cancelled the engagement. This meant, of course, that they had cut the play to pieces and did not want me to find them out. As I have heard nothing of them since I presume their tour was a failure. I cannot help suspecting that the failure at Rennes and Rouen must have the same explanation.

G.B.S.

To MOLLY TOMPKINS

chez Lady Astor at Restharrow
(O gelosia!)
[A/1; X/319]   31st May 1928
Henry was Molly Tompkins's brother-in-law. Storm Jameson (1897–1986) was a popular novelist in her first vogue.]

My dear Mollikins
... Henry is right as to the island [San Giovanni Island on Lake Maggiore]. It is a place to spend six weeks a year in, but not a place to live in. You have no business there—no roots in it. The life you are leading is horribly wicked You cannot keep blasting your soul without blasting your body as well: that is what is the matter with your lungs: the warning colds will develop into tuberculosis, accelerated by drugs and self-hatred; and you will perish miserably. I can do nothing. Other American women save themselves by Christian Science, public work, motherhood (called matriarching by Storm Jameson) and not being prettier than they can help. But you are a predestinate damned soul, a Vamp fiend, neither doing justice, loving mercy, nor walking humbly with your God. You will prowl round that lake, making men's wives miserable; tormenting yourself whenever their glances wander

99

from you for a moment, until the lake water changes to fire and brimstone and rises up and scorches you into nothingness.

Lawrence works and fences; Troubetskoy sculpts; Albert [Coates] and Cecil [Lewis] work like negroes and have no use for women who do not work; Basile overworks and has married a gentlewoman who will hold him when he will post policemen to whistle when you are coming so that he may fly; but *you*—what do you do? what will become of you? how will you face old age? With a "lifted" face, with grease paints and an iceball and rouge, with peroxided hair, an old hag desperately pretending to be a young witch. Oh Molly, Molly, Molly, Molly, I must not think about you; for I cannot save you: I have done my best and only made matters worse.

Can you not learn how to live in the world? You are not a thing evil in itself; and it is impossible to believe that you *must* go to the devil by natural necessity, though my experience tells me that you will. For Mephistopheles whispers to me as he did to Faust "She is not the first." Before you were born I have had to do with sirens as seductive as you. And now! You will go their way unless you can relegate love affairs to very occasional distractions, and then not spend more than an hour a fortnight or so on them. What sort of creature do you suppose I should be now if I had done nothing but exploit my celebrated fascination all my life? Would you have looked twice at so repulsive an object? And yet you thought that when you had secured your Ogygia and lured me to its shores you could play Calypso to my Odysseus and make a hog of me. Arn't you glad you didn't succeed? After all, you have some brains in your upper half. This erotic-romantic attitude to life doesn't make you happy.

If only you had a sense of humor! You could write plays if you had.

I have no use for a woman who can't laugh at herself.

Your spiritual values are all wrong.

It seems such a pitiful waste—a woman of quite considerable capacity and vitality thrown on the scrap heap for want of one trifling ingredient, and because some fool invented looking glasses.

Well, I am not going to start another sheet. Besides, the hostess calls: some social game or other is in hand.

a te, O cara
GBS

To RUTLAND BOUGHTON

[U(H)/2]

4 Whitehall Court S W1
28th June 1928

[Boughton's article in *The Sackbut*, "Is It Life or Death for the Arts?", was published in three parts, in May, June, and August. Shaw added a postscript to the "encyclical" on artists and politics, under the same title, in October. The opera *The Immortal Hour* is Boughton's most celebrated work. The "Guards' Waltz" was a popular Victorian melody by Dan Godfrey. The "Cockaigne Overture" is by Elgar. Shaw was one of several prominent socialists who put up bail money for William Gallacher and other British communists arrested on 21st October 1925 in a raid on their headquarters (see letter of 11th November 1925 to J. Ramsay MacDonald). James Maxton (1885–1946), Independent Labour Party organiser in Scotland, had been the I.L.P.'s chairman since 1926. Arthur James Cook (1885–1931), secretary of the Miners' Federation of Great Britain, was an instigator of the coal miners' strike and the General Strike in 1926.]

My dear Rutland

I have only just had time to read your Sackbut article (in the train); and I rejoice in it, though I am a little scandalised by one or two of the good bits because they suggest that you do not always compose as well as you write, which seems entirely wrong. However, on reflection, I perceive that literature can say things that music cannot; so that Wagner had to get many things off his chest by writing.

When you are writing about politics you must remember that Marxism has now become a mass of phrases dating from 1848 and translated and retranslated until they have come to mean considerably worse than nothing. It is a century out of date, saturated with the idolatry of the proletariat invented by the bourgeois idealists when they could no longer idealise God, king, country, capital or even progress. Today the same sort of idealists, having found out the proletariat as a result of enfranchising it (the realisation of democracy), are idealising Big Business, Big Business Men, and Big Blue Beef, a certain poetry being given to the new idol by H. G. Wells's Clissold stories.

All these idealisations end in disillusion. When Lenin praised the new Russian literature as unquestionably revolutionary and proletarian, and expressed his regret that he found it totally unreadable and must make an exception to the canon of pure Marxism by admitting bourgeois literature—when he told his people that their principles were sound but that there was not a clerk who had been in an office for ten years in Moscow who did not know more about business than they did, he was confessing this disillusion, and insisting that they must face it and clear their minds of the old literary junk inherited from 1848, and from men who, like Marx, combined extraordinary literary and even prophetic power with an inexperience of practical administration which made them useless as guides when their propaganda suddenly (as in Russia) turned into power and public responsibility.

You are still in the before-Lenin phase. You say that I seem to be "entirely out of touch with what is happening today in the minds of the industrial workers." By this I think you mean, not out of touch with the crowds at the cup-ties and the clients of the Swindon bookmakers, but with the composer of The Immortal Hour, and, say, our friend Gallacher from the Clyde. I once heard Gallacher come out on top of a public meeting with a speech which was as much in advance of the common stuff the others talked as Richard Strauss's Dance of the Seven Veils was in advance of the old Guards Waltz. Yet I had later on to go bail for him at Bow Street on a charge of sedition which should have been a charge of political childishness. Under the impression that he was promoting a world revolution, he had taken money from Russia and wasted it on getting himself and his friends into prison in the silliest possible way, because, with all his Marxian culture, he was so completely out of touch with any reality except that of poverty and injustice that at any moment the Home Secretary could pluck him from his home like a daisy and throw him into a prison dustbin. I remember my own early ignorances too well to fail in diagnosing his. And I do not want to see you in the same mess.

Your objection to the Cockaigne overture (perhaps the best of its kind in existence) is simply that there is no Marxism in it. From its impression of the London streets the voices of Maxton and Cook are missing; and the bass is not the ground swell of revolution. It is as if the Bishop of London were to say "Mr Boughton is no doubt a clever musician; but he has no message for England: you listen to his scores in vain for the Church of England." In Moscow they tell their professors of literature that lectures on Shakespear must demonstrate that Shakespear was a sound Marxist.

And you ask me to devote a whole day to discussing that sort of flapdoodle with you. Not five seconds, Rutland. How can you expect me to? You will work your way out of them as Wagner did, and the rest of us have done. Besides, we should talk, not about Marx, but about your lawless private life, and the mess you have made of your private affairs by trying to mix Marx with St. Matthew.

This is all I have time for. Why not organise an orchestra for the

Labor Party, and extinguish Cockaigne by writing a Cardiff overture, with Cook and the General Strike and all the rest of it in full blast?

ever

G.B.S.

To RUTLAND BOUGHTON

[H/2]
Ayot St Lawrence. Welwyn
1st July 1928

[Shaw's memory is faulty: the book he inscribed for Lenin was *Back to Methuselah*, on 16th June 1921, in which he had written: "to Nicolas Lenin the only European ruler who is displaying the ability, character and knowledge proper to his responsible position from Bernard Shaw." The volume, containing Lenin's marginal notes, gained the stature of a religious relic in the USSR, where the inscription is frequently circulated in facsimile reproductions. The article on the slaughter of Tsar Nicholas and his family was "Trotsky, Prince of Pamphleteers," a review-article on Trotsky's *The Defence of Terrorism*, in *The Nation*, 7th January 1922. The date of the Russian Embassy reception has not been determined. Shaw met Leonid Krassin, head of a trade delegation seeking to conclude a commercial treaty with Britain, on 20th June 1920. He also dined with the Rakovskys at Claridge's on 24th May 1928, a fact he does not mention.]

My dear Rutland

What on earth are you talking about? I have backed up the Soviet against White scurrility at every opportunity that presented itself. In 1917 (or was it 18?) I sent a copy of my latest book to Lenin with an inscription that would have flattered an Antonine Emperor. I went to the first grand reception at the Russian embassy and got flashlighted at it with Clare Sheridan, though wild horses would not drag me to such a thing ordinarily. Before that I had entertained Krassin during his first struggles for recognition in London. I actually wrote and published an article pointing out that the slaughtering of the Tsar and his family compared very favorably in point of consideration for the victims with the precedents set in the cases of Charles I and Louis XV [error for XVI]. My going to hear you at Ecclestone Square was only one incident in my efforts to inform myself of what was happening in Russia, so that I might be in a position to refute the White bugaboo on the subject. My bailing of Gallacher, which was quite unnecessary as there was plenty of other bail available, was a gesture in the same direction. Look at page 374 of my book! Can you honestly go a step farther than I have gone there? I am like Falstaff backing up Pistol, I am damned in hell for swearing to gentlemen my friends that greenhorns were tall fellows [*The Merry Wives of Windsor*, II.ii.10–11, with Shavian variation]. Get out.

ever
GBS

To RUTLAND BOUGHTON

4 Whitehall Court SW1

[H/2]   5th July 1928

[William Martin Conway (1856–1937), Baron Conway of Allington, professor of art, explorer, and Unionist M.P., published *The Art Treasures in Soviet Russia* (1925). The N.E.P. was the New Economic Policy.]

My dear Rutland

My attitude "as of a very wise person to a clumsy well meaning idiot" is my attitude to the whole silly world: the grievance is not peculiar to Russia. I have also been reproached for not having given credit to Co-operation in England. Every Quixote in the country defies me for having failed to do justice to his particular Dulcinea. I cannot help that: *my* Dulcinea is equality of income; and my instruction on that point is just as necessary to Stalin & Co as to Baldwin & Co or to Macdonald & Co.

I was asked by William Randolph Hearst to go to Russia on handsome terms and tell the truth about it! I did not go because people were expecting miracles from Soviet Communism (even the Capitalist gibes implied that if Russia were anything short of paradise Communism had failed ignominiously); and I knew, for the reasons in my book [the *Intelligent Woman's Guide*], that things must be in a ghastly mess there for the moment. Wells went, and had to confess to the mess, and be duly denounced as a petit bourgeois because he laughed at Marxolatry. The Webbs are going; and by this time there will be something better than an apparently hopeless mess for them to describe. Meanwhile there have been lots of visitors; and it is noteworthy that those of honest anti-Bolsheviks like Martin Conway have been very much more useful in bringing us to our senses about Russia than the visits of out-and-out Bolshies like Clare Sheridan and Rutland Boughton.

Rutland, by the way, has a future as a front bench man. When I said in my brutal Bolshevik way that Lenin had to climb down and fall back on the private employer (the N.E.P.) Rutland replied in perfect Government Department language, and with the right thump on the despatch box, that my statement was untrue, as "what had happened was simply that they had had so to modify their immediate policy that production could proceed with a minimum of opposition from those capitalist interests which were sabotaging production" (Hear, Hear and loud cheers from the back benches). The encouraged minister proceeds "The effect of that policy has been enormously to increase co-operative production with a steady relative decrease in private capitalism["] (renewed cheers from the Government benches, and derisive counter-cheers from the Trotskyites).

Oh Rutland, Rutland, you have got the official counterpoint beautifully. What about an oratorio for the Three Choirs [Festival]?

Get out.

I suppose you must write a book about Bach if you cannot make enough by composing. But please observe that I am not writing a book about Shakespear. There cannot be anything left to say about Bach that cannot be said in twenty pages. But of course if the book is a book about Boughton with Bach's name on the cover, then there may be something in it.

ever
G.B.S.

To FRANK HARRIS

Hotel Beau Site. Cap d'Antibes

[A/4; X/279]   31st July 1928

[Shaw and Charlotte spent six weeks at Cap d'Antibes, from 20th July to 2nd September, followed by a fortnight in Geneva. It was their most relaxing holiday since Madeira in 1922, both of them enjoying long swims in the warm sea and sunbathing on the rocks. Shaw eventually dined with Harris in Nice on 11th August. Helen O'Hara (Nellie) Harris (1886?–1955) was Harris's second wife.]

My dear F.H.

Many thanks for the proffered lunch on Friday; but I had better come over to Nice some day instead. You will perhaps guess the reason of this evasion; and if you don't, Nellie will.

The villas here regard a set of your confounded life and loves as an indispensable item of furniture. My wife read the first volume when you sent it to me (illustrations and all), and, as mistress of a house where all the books were accessible to a highly respectable female staff, promptly burnt it page by page so that not a comma should escape the flames. Of the subsequent volumes she knows nothing except what she infers from your promise in that first one to outCasanova Casanova in them. She has no doubt that you have been as good (or as bad) as your word.

There is no arguing about these things. You are off her visiting list; and rather than be entertained by you at the Hotel du Cap with all the publicity that my limelight inflicts on her she will go home by the next blue train and take me with her. It cannot be helped. Il faut souffrir pour être Casanova. For a Victorian lady she has given her proofs of Liberalism and even of intransigéance by marrying ME. She leaves me entirely free to maintain our old relations without protest. She hopes that it will be understood that her attitude has nothing to do with Nellie. But Frank Casanova she will not entertain on any terms.

So that's that. Any attempt to disguise the situation would be an indelicacy which you would (very properly) never forgive. My explicitness may provoke you to a dozen buccaneering oaths and epithets; but they will leave no trace.

My notion is that I should lunch with you and Nellie and anyone else you like at your favorite restaurant in Nice. We can then talk at large.

ever
G.B.S.

To HALL CAINE

4 Whitehall Court SW1
[S/2]   21st September 1928

[A new edition of Hall Caine's *Recollections of Rossetti*, first published in 1882 and subsequently revised, had been issued in an expanded version in 1928 for the Rossetti centenary. Theodore Watts(-Dunton) (1832–1914), critic and poet, had added his mother's surname to his name in 1897. An intimate friend of Dante Gabriel Rossetti, he had fostered Swinburne and nursed him in his declining years. J.L.Joynes, poet friend of William Morris, was a member of the Social Democratic Federation. The eccentric young Morris at Oxford having affected a mop of curly black hair and unkempt dress,

Rossetti and Edward Burne-Jones bestowed upon the youth the nickname Topsy, after the endearing character in *Uncle Tom's Cabin*; Shaw in a review of a life of Morris in 1899 deprecated this as patronising. Morris's wife Jane (1838–1914) was the model for many of Rossetti's most celebrated drawings and paintings.

Virginia Surtees's *catalogue raisonné* of Rossetti's works does not record a painting entitled "The Rose of Sharon," and Rossettian experts at the Tate Gallery and the School of Art History at East Anglia have been unable to identify it. The "netted calf" picture is "Found" (begun in 1854, frequently re-worked, but unfinished), in which a young farmer encounters a former love, now a prostitute (modelled by Rossetti's lifelong friend Fanny Cornforth). "If love were what the rose is" is from the first stanza of Swinburne's poem "A Match" (1866). Elizabeth Siddal, a favourite model of the Pre-Raphaelite Brotherhood, married Rossetti in 1860. After her death two years later, of laudanum poisoning, the grief-stricken Rossetti interred with her the sole manuscripts of all of his unpublished poems. In 1869 he arranged quietly for their exhumation from the coffin and subsequent publication. The painter Ford Madox Brown (1821–93), associated with the Pre-Raphaelites, was Rossetti's early teacher and close friend.]

My dear Hall Caine

I returned to England last Tuesday, having been away for two months, and found an unusually interesting stack of books waiting for me. I immediately seized your Rossetti and read it straight through.

Of course it does not finally dispose of Gabriel: the hand of friendship is not rough enough, nor its heart malicious enough for that; but it adds something to the record that nobody else could supply.

I never met Rossetti, but Socialism brought me into a certain intimacy with Morris and, through him, into occasional contacts with Theodore Watts, who lunched me one day at The Pines in the presence of Swinburne. Watts (I never could fit Dunton onto him) had lost his early poetic appearance then to such an extent that when I first met him at Morris's Hammersmith house, J. L. Joynes, asking Morris who he was, described him as looking like "a little infantry major," which was evidently a staggeringly new view of him to Morris.

The truth is, Morris was so enormously bigger than most of the old pre-Raphaelite set, and Socialism seemed then so far above their literary and pictorial enthusiasms, that to us they were only figures of fun except when they called Morris Topsy, which made us feel that the insects were going too far. You too had outgrown them sensationally and become a centre instead of a satellite; and this was why, though your friendship with Rossetti was well known, we never thought of you as one of that lot.

Morris respected Rossetti, who had evidently dominated him, as far as he was dominable, in his early days as an artist-craftsman. He certainly did not love him as he loved Burne-Jones; but he was impressed by Rossetti's diplomacy and power of selling pictures without sending to the Exhibitions. I still remember the tone of awe with which he said "He (R) actually *likes* writing letters." But he said that he had become quite impossible personally. In your book you confine your account of his persecution mania to the reviewers, and leave it to be inferred that his confinement to the house had no specific reason; but Morris conveyed to me that this neurosis had reached such a point that Rossetti believed that everyone who looked at him in the street was insulting him, and was apt to resent it with personal violence. Strindberg had the same craze, and never went out until past midnight. As Morris was impatient of unreason and had a volcanic temper he could, I presume, have kept on good terms with Gabriel only by keeping out of his reach.

Rossetti, by the way, wanted to adopt May Morris.

You did not lose anything conversationally by not talking to Mrs. Morris. She was a wonderful figure at first sight; for she existed until then as an invention of Rossetti's; and when you saw the picture live and walk the effect was supernatural. But you did not hear it talk. She maintained her strong horse sense through all the adoration of that circle, and let the men talk and adore. I remember only two sentences of hers, completing a whole dialogue. It was at a meal at Hammersmith. SHE. "Have some more pudding?" G.B.S. "Thank you: I will. I can't resist it." And then, when I had finished, SHE. "That will do you good: there is suet in it."

All her sensible contempt for the duped vegetarian came out in her tone. I liked her; but she wasted no more words on me, even when I was staying with them at the manor up the river.

I heard enough, however, to appreciate the forbearance, amounting, I must add, to voluntary inadequacy, which prevented you from adding to your mention of that one decent and magically beautiful woman, more than the faintest hint of the raging red haired trollops who seem so enchanting in The Rose of Sharon and in that picture with the netted calf in the cart. I never knew anything accurately about this; but there was a Fanny, or some such name, without a very vivid picture of whom in her tantrum no account of Gabriel would be complete.

Now that I think of it, Morris always spoke of him as Rossetti, never as Gabriel. Morris had no respect for Swinburne, whom he set down, rightly, I think, as a man with a conscience of literature and none of life. He pointed out that Swinburne wrote about the sea like a man who had never seen it, although he was a confirmed bather and swimmer. And he used to quote "If love were what the rose is" as an example of verse without sense.

For my own part the chloral made Rossetti uninteresting to me as a man. The exhumation affair which was the first I heard of him, struck me as a revolting anticlimax; and somehow I divined, underneath the romance of the Siddal woman, Madox Brown's terrible Tolstoyan description of the laudanum addict sitting for hours staring into the fire "with her feet in the fender" (perfect Tolstoy, that). I like sane people, and loathe drunk people, drugged people, crazy people. Your book has therefore done me good in making me take Rossetti more seriously as a man, even though I know that you have left out all the shadows except the ones that give dignity and tragic beauty to the portrait.

I really must stop: this is a ridiculously long letter to inflict on you. I hope it will reach you in an idle moment (if you have any); and in any case it is a letter to be put among those to be answered when you are in the humor once in five years: that is, the sort that doesn't need an answer at all.

ever

G. Bernard Shaw

To IVOR NICHOLSON

[F.u/4]   [4 Whitehall Court SW1]
[Undated: *c.* 21st September 1928]

[Ivor Nicholson (1891–1937), a director of William Randolph Hearst's London-based National Magazine Company, had on 17th September invited Shaw to a "small and entirely private party" being given for the actress Marion Davies (1897–1961). Hearst, he said, would be there if he arrived in England in time. Shaw, in a note on the letter, advised Blanche Patch to reply that he "never heard of Marion Davies, and would not go to a little dinner at the Savoy if she were all the 11000 virgins of St Ursula rolled into one. I am no good for games of that sort" (E/4). On the 20th Nicholson wrote again, remarking he had been distinctly given the impression that Shaw "wished to meet Mr. William Randolph Hearst, who is coming to this party . . . Mr. Hearst has expressed more interest in your work than that of any living writer."]

Dear Mr Nicholson

I have now ascertained that Miss M[arion] D[avies] is a film star. Do you seriously believe that these young and beautiful ladies want to meet old gentlemen of 65 and 72, or to be made an excuse for their meeting oneanother. If so you must be more innocent than the woolliest lamb in Hamley's toyshop.

I just wont go. Mr Hearst and I, old as we are, have still gumption enough left to be able to meet without making Miss Davies yawn and spoiling your festivities.

faithfully
[G. Bernard Shaw]

To STANLEY J. RUBINSTEIN

Ayot St Lawrence. Welwyn

[H/1]   9th October 1928

["Sir William Joynson-Hicks has imposed a secret censorship on the English publication of Miss Radclyffe-Hall's 'The Well of Loneliness,'" reported the *Daily Herald* on 6th October, "and copies of an edition published in Paris have been seized by the Customs officials at Dover." Shaw, asked for an opinion, and obviously disturbed that the English publisher Jonathan Cape, at the behest of the government, had voluntarily suspended publication of the book after review copies were distributed, remarked to the *Daily Herald*: "If this sort of thing is going to happen and no protest be made against it, no books will be published at all in England. To begin with, I don't understand why the publisher withdrew the book. I read it, and read it carefully, and I repeat that it ought not to have been withdrawn. There can be no reason for it. The book speaks of certain things that people ought to know about. Apart from that, the voluntary withdrawal of [the novel] does not imply any legal right to prohibit the importation of an edition of it into this country."

Shortly thereafter the government took formal legal action to suppress the novel, by which time Stanley J. Rubinstein (1890–1975), a solicitor of the firm of Rubinstein, Nash & Co., had been engaged by the author to undertake a defence. Rubinstein's principal strategy was to line up 57 notable witnesses to give evidence on behalf of the book. The presiding magistrate, however, ruled that such evidence was inadmissible, and *The Well of Loneliness* was condemned on 16th November as an obscene libel, all copies of which were to be destroyed. Re-published in Paris, the novel was eventually translated into eleven languages. It was also successfully issued in the United States, where it sold 100,000 copies annually for many years thereafter.

Marguerite Radclyffe Hall (1886–1943), poet and novelist, had published four previous novels, one of which, *Adam's Breed* (1926), had won the prestigious James Tait Black Memorial Prize. Although the subject of *The Well of Loneliness*, lesbianism, was distasteful to many of the reviewers, the book received a generally positive press. The *Times Literary Supplement* reviewer, on 29th July, though judging that the novel failed as a work of art "through divided purpose," yet recognised that it was "sincere, courageous, high-minded and often beautifully expressed," and that "against any feelings of repugnance at her uncompromising sincerity must be set respect for her intentions, frequent admiration for her treatment, and only regret that the statement of an insoluble problem so passionately presented itself as a theme." The *Daily Telegraph* on 7th August called it "a truly remarkable book . . . in the first place as a work of art finely conceived and finely written. Secondly . . . as dealing with an aspect of abnormal life seldom or never presented in English fiction—certainly never with such unreserved frankness." The *Liverpool Post* summed up the dilemma on 15th August: "It is an essentially clean-minded book, yet it may easily antagonize certain normally and perhaps selfishly minded folk who are unwilling, or unable, to recognize the existence and the claims of the abnormal." James Douglas, editor of the *Sunday Express*, presumably had been one of the "normally minded" who labelled the book indecent.

Shaw's letter was in response to a circular letter received from Rubinstein, Nash & Co. soliciting opinions and assistance.]

Dear Mr Rubinstein

When you call witnesses to character be very careful always that their own characters are above suspicion. One of my plays [*Mrs Warren's Profession*] has been denied a license by the Lord Chamberlain on the ground of its indecency; and in America the police have twice arrested theatrical companies for performing it. Another [*The Shewing-up of Blanco Posnet*] has been banned for blasphemy. Another [*Pygmalion*] is notorious because the heroine uses an unmentionable expletive. If Miss Radclyffe Hall can find no better security than mine for her propriety her case is hopeless.

You have to face the fact that the book *is* indecent for all who consider homosexuality an indecent subject. If I were counsel for the Customs I should ask why Miss R.H., if her book is decent, did not sue Mr James Douglas for libel, or lay a criminal information against him. I should ask what better ground the Post Office and the customs have for seizing books and photographs as indecent than that responsible writers in responsible newspapers have denounced them as such in the strongest terms, and that the author has not sought her legal remedy. What reply would you have to that? None, I think, that would convince a British jury.

If you are proceeding merely to recover the seized copies you must plead, not that the book is decent, but that it is indecent only in the sense in which the story of Lot and his wife is indecent, or Pericles of Tyre, or the innumerable essays on psycho-analysis and psychiatry now on the market are indecent. The security of trade would be destroyed if books which are indecent in this sense could be seized whenever they were made the subject of a newspaper stunt. In this case a book has been published by a reputable publisher, printed by a reputable printer, distributed by reputable libraries and booksellers, reviewed without protest by reputable newspapers and critical journals. Neither the Customs nor the postal authorities can reasonably treat such a book as unfit for circulation unless and until it has been prosecuted successfully as such. If the Home Secretary agrees with his one witness (Mr Douglas) let him prosecute and put his witness into the box for cross examination. It is not for a reputable author to take private action against a hysterical journalist and a newspaper with fifty times any author's resources raising a public question: it is for the public authorities to take action if the case is a valid one; and if they do not move the assumption of the Customs should be that the case is not valid.

On these lines you might possibly get a decision that the grounds for the seizure were insufficient; but you will not get a decision that the book is decent. Your application to the courts must be without prejudice on that question; and you will run the risk of provoking a prosecution on it.

This is all I can usefully say in reply to your letter.

faithfully
G. Bernard Shaw

To KAREL ČAPEK

[Ayot St Lawrence. Welwyn]
[W(H)/354]   14th October 1928
[Karel Čapek (1890–1938), Czech playwright and journalist, was on the staff of the *Lidové Novińy*, Prague, in which paper Shaw's remarks were published on 28th October, the tenth anniversary of the founding of the Czech Republic. Informed by his Hungarian agent Emile Szalai that his comments were injudicious and probably would damage his standing in Hungary, Shaw published an amended and more tactful statement in the Budapest *Pester Lloyd* on 14th November.]

My dear Capek

It is very difficult for a foreigner to interfere in any national question without doing the cause with which he sympathizes more harm than good. It is true that Lord Rothermere has no such delicacy; but he is not considering the effect of his championship on Europe: he is simply gratifying his natural sympathy with the traditional policy of Hungary. For my own part I shall restrict myself to saying that if I had to choose between being a Magyar under Tchekoslovakian rule or a T-Slovakian under Magyar rule I should choose to be a Magyar every time. Hungary has a very bad record for its treatment of subject aliens; and Tcheko-slovakia has set up an unprecedentedly enlightened one, though the enlightenment is not to Lord Rothermere's taste. Tchekoslovakia is now the model European State in this respect; and I heartily wish that Italy would take its example to heart in the Tyról.

More than this it would not become me to say. I hope all differences between Hungary and TS will be amicably settled; but I should not advise either State to choose Lord Rothermere as an arbitrator.

faithfully
G. Bernard Shaw

To CHRISTABEL McLAREN

[H/2]

Ayot St Lawrence. Welwyn
22nd October 1928

[The Hon. Christabel McLaren was one of Charlotte's friends. The enclosure was an article "The De-Bunking of John Bunyan" by the Rev. John A. Hutton (1868–1947), published on 18th October in the *British Weekly*, of which he was editor, in recognition of the Bunyan Tercentenary. Alfred Noyes (1880–1958), the poet, had published "Bunyan: A Revaluation" in *The Bookman* for October. *The Holy War* (1682) was one of Bunyan's late works. Shaw's antipathy to the Athanasian Creed was expressed frequently: see particularly the preface to *Misalliance*. He failed, however, to recognise that the author of the creed was not St Athanasius (*c.* 293–373), but an unknown writer of two centuries later, as is evidenced in the Inquisitor's statement in the trial scene of *Saint Joan*: "The blessed St Athanasius has laid it down in his creed that those who cannot understand are damned." Apollyon in *Pilgrim's Progress* (1678) is a satanic spirit who is vanquished by Christian.]

My dear Mrs Christabel

Is the enclosed the sort of thing you feel you want? I doubt it. For my own part I rather rejoice in Alfred Noyes's splurge. It serves John

113

right. What business had he to believe all that muck that he dirtied his mind with? If you want to see where it landed him, read the utterly unreadable last half of The Holy War, with its Election Doubters and "those that rode Reformadoes" and ask yourself could any gift of literary genius excuse it. When he is giving us the Bible we wonder that its literary power could impose on a man who was himself a magazine of literary power; but when it comes to Baptist theology it is really time to wake Bunyan up with a hearty kick and ask him what he supposes God gave him his brains for.

[*Two lines of irregular typing XXXed out*]

DAMN! Not you: the typewriter.

Noyes underrates his man (he always does) and makes a poor job of it accordingly. Bunyan went as deep when he damned poor Ignorance as Athanasius did when he damned all who are too stupid to see anything in the Trinity but an arithmetical impossibility. He knew by experience that Talkative would have nothing to say when he came up against people with something to say. All that about Christian being fiendishly selfish in pursuit of his own salvation will not impose on any woman: all women have been told that it is their duty to stay in the City of Destruction for the sake of their husbands and children. Even Apollyon did not stoop to play that off on Christian: he accused him of rebellion against his prince, not against his wife. On these points you can crack Alfred between your thumbnails if you meet him. But better let be. Somebody had to say that the Pilgrim's Progress is a wicked book to put into children's hands without warning them that the hobgoblins are not real and that John suffered from the horrors because they told him lies about hell when he was a helpless baby.

Why were you not at Antibes? Though indeed if you had been I should have asked you why you were in such a maddening place.

I am writing this after dark in my garden shelter. It is raining cats and dogs; and my hooded candle is inadequate.

With this clue to my mood

I conclude, affectionately
G.B.S.

To STANLEY J. RUBINSTEIN

Ayot St Lawrence. Welwyn
[H/1]   23rd October 1928

[Sir Chartres Biron (1863–1940), a barrister, was Chief Magistrate at Bow Street Police Court from 1920 to 1933.]

Dear Mr Rubinstein

It will be waste of time to play me off on Chartres Biron: he knows me. An exhibition of celebrities for the Press will only irritate him.

The line to be taken seems to me obvious. You quote the "tends to corrupt those whose minds are open to immoral influence and who are likely to see the work": that is, the entire British public, not to say the human race. Counsel must say that there is not a work of literature in existence which he could defend as being outside that all-embracing definition, least of all the Bible, the publication of which in the vernacular produced centuries of warfare. He must admit that The Well of Loneliness may corrupt those whose minds are open to immoral influences as much as Johnson's Dictionary, in which ladies used to look for improper words. He must say that he cannot put witnesses into the box to testify that The Well is absolutely inert morally, because that is a natural impossibility, and could not be claimed for David Copperfield, The Vicar of Wakefield, or The Pilgrim's Progress.

What then is the use of the Act (or whatever it is)? It has exactly the same use as the Motoring Acts, which lay down twenty miles an hour as the utmost speed permissible to a mechanically propelled vehicle. To all practical intents and purposes this is an impossible requirement, like the requirement that a book shall not tend to &c. &c. But it enables the authorities to lay their hands at any moment on any motorist and charge him with breaking the law. He is certain to be in contravention; and if the magistrate is convinced that he has been making a nuisance of himself in some way that cannot be classified as "to the public danger" the magistrate will inflict a suitable penalty. This practice is so convenient that neither the magistrates nor the motorists move for a change in the law as long as it is not abused to make motoring impossible.

In the same way anyone trafficking in obscene photographs and vulgar pornography can always be pounced upon and charged with marketing works that tend to &c &c. It is true that these words apply not only to obscene photographs but to photographs of Raphael's pictorial history of Cupid and Psyche and to the photographs sold by the Government to the public in the National Gallery. An impartial and literal administration of the law would make fine art impossible, and lead to the repeal of the law. But in our common sense way we contrive to make the law at once useful and harmless by leaving art and literature untouched and bringing it into operation against unmistakeable blackguards only.

The Home Office, in relying on the words of the Act to suppress The Well, is either not playing the game, and thereby reducing the Act to absurdity, or else it is alleging that Miss R.H. is a common blackguard whose work is to be classed with obscene photographs and Secrets of The Alcove and the like. As against that allegation counsel puts in the perfectly respectful reviews of the work in the leading literary journals, the unquestioned position of the authoress, and a marked passage in the solitary review which has frightened the Home Secretary into his hasty action, the said passage being of so extravagant a character as to deprive it of all judicial authority and to shew that the writer had from some cause entirely lost his self-control when he penned it.

The final decision and responsibility rests with the magistrate, who has to judge, not whether the book tends to &c. &c., as every work of art necessarily does, but whether it belongs to that class of work for which the Act is by general consent kept in reserve. Nobody is better qualified to make this decision than Sir Chartres Biron, who is a man of letters as well as a lawyer; and the defendant places the book in his hands for his own perusal with every confidence in his judgment.

That's your case as I see it. Probably counsel will refuse to plead it, and insist on blethering for three days on the purity of the book and its authoress, and calling witnesses (of whom I shall not be one) to declare that they have read the book and felt ennobled and emasculated by its perusal. Counsel likes a hopeless case because the judge always encourages and compliments him, knowing that the result is a foregone conclusion, and hating to be bothered by serious arguments. As I cannot plead the case myself I can be of no further use.

faithfully
G.Bernard Shaw

PS I have no objection to the witness box. I rather like it.

To STANLEY J. RUBINSTEIN

[C/1]

Ayot St Lawrence. Welwyn
29th October 1928

No: as at present advised, if Counsel thinks I ought to go into the box I shall simply disagree with him.

GBS

To DENIS WENNLING

[E/4]

[4 Whitehall Court SW1]
16th November 1928

[Denis Wennling wrote on 15th November, from southeast London, to acknowledge receipt of biographical data for "my little work," entitled "Appreciation of G.B.Shaw & His Work," and to request clarification of Shaw's position on religion.]

Yes: Freethinker is the best term.

When the Shelley Society was founded back in the 1880s by Dr Furnivall a great meeting of Shelley enthusiasts (mostly pious old ladies) assembled at University College. My speech began "Like Shelley, I am a Socialist, an Atheist, and a Vegetarian." Two old ladies resigned.

In those days an Atheist was intellectually one who had doubts about the capacity of the ark to hold all the animals, and, politically, one who sympathized with Bradlaugh in his claim to sit in the House of Commons as a professed atheist.

But I do not protest against the tradition. A Creative-Evolutionist *is* an atheist, though he is not a materialist. I do not believe in Blake's Old Nobodaddy. Do you?

G.B.S.

To THE VERY REV. ALBERT VICTOR BAILLIE

[A/9]

4 Whitehall Court SW1
24th November 1928

[On 19th November Desmond MacCarthy distributed a letter drafted by Shaw and himself "which we and many others feel ought to be published in the Press before 'The Well of Loneliness' case again becomes sub judice.

Whatever our individual feelings about this particular book may be, you will agree that a principle is at stake which is of grave importance to literature. We wish to make the protest as weighty as possible and we are therefore anxious to include your name. We very much hope that you will allow us to do so" (draft letter and MacCarthy's accompanying letter are in the Vera Brittain collection, Mills Memorial Library, McMaster University, Hamilton, Ontario).

The letter was published on 22nd November in most of the principal London and provincial daily newspapers, with forty-five signatories, including Virginia Woolf, Granville Barker, Julian Huxley, T. S. Eliot, E. M. Forster, Arnold Bennett, Lytton Strachey, Rose Macaulay, and the Dean of Windsor, the Very Rev. Albert Victor Baillie (1864–1955), who was also domestic chaplain to the King. Shortly after the publication of the letter the Dean was recipient of what apparently was an obscene hate letter, which he worriedly passed along to Shaw.]

My dear Dean

I think the letter is a leg-pull. My wife has no doubt that it is. Whether or no, it is impossible to take any notice of or action upon it.

The letter we sent to the papers was drafted by me very carefully so as to keep us completely off the ground of any sympathy with the propaganda of homosexualism (I write *ism* advisedly) which goes on, and not to commit us even on the point of the book's appeal for the humane consideration of inversion as a natural misfortune. It might have been signed by persons who had not read the book, and did not know nor care what it was about.

We had better leave it at that. It would be impossible to go further without involving ourselves and one another in the discussion we have evaded. We are in the difficulty that the least expression of emotional abhorrence contributes to the morbid atmosphere in which all sexual aberrations flourish and make their practitioners feel heroic, whilst anything less than that—unless at volume length on the Havelock Ellis scale—is interpreted as sympathetic.

I read the book and formed an estimate of it which is practically your own. The attempt in it to make out that bachelor couples and spinster couples preferring the society of their own sex and keeping house together decently are so ostracised and persecuted that they are hounded into the circles in which homosexualism is a cult, seemed to me to be on the face of it blazing nonsense. It proves, I think, that the authoress has what I may call the insanity of her mission. But there was nothing that could justify the classing of the book with obscene photographs and the sort of pornographic trash that dealers in such things stock.

My own experience of life has led me—as a matter of necessary practice—to treat sexual life as outside the scope of the judgments we have to pass on one another for social, political, and business purposes. I have not found that even the most absurd aberrations are necessarily associated with any general depravity of character, or that intemperance in their practice has any other results than the intemperance in normal sexual intercourse which visibly damages many respectably married persons. I should say that a dishonored cheque is a safer index to character for worldly purposes than inversion. But this is only a rule of thumb; for the impossibility of getting at the facts on any statistical scale puts anything like a scientific generalisation out of the question. I have all the normal repugnances to aberrations; but I have found that they are untrustworthy guides in estimating character. Normally sexed people are sometimes as devoid of conscience as it is humanly possible to be: homosexualists are sometimes conspicuously able and highminded. Denunciations of homosexuality as depraving and detestable may have an unsuspected and deeply wounding effect on one's most justly valued friends. The wisest and best inverts never tell; but they can cherish a deep grudge against those who would, if they knew, turn against them, and attribute to them general vices of which they are conspicuously innocent.

I hope you will not let the letter distress you. Such letters are a favorite amusement of mischievous persons; and I, who am a butt for such missiles, can assure you that they are quite negligible. One Dean courageous enough to make a protest against the abuse of the law against unpopular victims does more good than an infinity of obscene letters.

I am just off to the country until the end of next week. I had rather not talk to you about the affair, because I dont want you to think about it further than to dismiss from your mind all thought of allowing those two rapscallions (my wife says a man and a girl) to move you to the smallest gesture of consciousness; but if you are not convinced I am entirely and very willingly at your service. I shall not return to town until Thursday; and my address meanwhile will be Ayot St Lawrence, Welwyn, Herts.

faithfully
G. Bernard Shaw

To LEWIS WYNNE

Ayot St Lawrence. Welwyn
26th November 1928

[U(E)/10]

[Lewis Wynne was the professional name of John Stuart Lewis Wynne Bostock (1896–1969), a free-lance journalist, who had asked Shaw for biographical information for a book supposedly nearing completion. When Shaw responded, not once but two or three times, Bostock warmly expressed gratitude for his being "so kindly and forbearing," then proceeded to forge a considerable number of Shaw letters and manuscripts (craftily creating them from genuine Shavian utterances in interviews, prefaces, and tracts), which circulated in the market between 1929 and 1931. Boldly he addressed some of them to himself, both as Lewis Wynne and as L. Bostock, and identified himself to sceptical dealers, aware that if they made inquiry Shaw, assuming it was the genuine letters that were being offered, would confirm that he had been in correspondence with Bostock. Examples of the forgeries eventually found their way into virtually every major Shaw collection (one American collector, T.E. Hanley, actually purchased, at great cost, *two* "original" manuscripts of the Fabian tract *The League of Nations*, 1928). When the bookseller Gilbert Fabes, who had been one of the credulous purchasers, belatedly questioned the authenticity of the letters and called Shaw's attention to them, Shaw indicated he had long been aware of their existence and of the identity of the forger. He had done nothing, however, to hinder their continued circulation, amusedly looking on at the spectacle of rabid collectors shelling out sizeable sums for spurious relics. The forgeries came to an abrupt end in 1931, not because they were at last recognised as such, but because the forger was apprehended for a crime of a different nature.

On 20th June 1931 Bostock was taken into custody by the Brighton police in connection with the theft and wilful damage of manuscripts and books from the Dickens Fellowship House, in Doughty Street, London, to which he had gained access as "a Dickens scholar" for research purposes. Over a period of months he had appropriated a number of invaluable documents, including the preface to *Dombey and Son*; thirty letters from such illustrious correspondents as Queen Victoria, Disraeli, Gladstone, Thackeray, Carlyle, and Hugo; twenty-five Dickens letters; photogravure plates; and book leaves containing notes. Fifteen items had been sent to America; most of these were recovered. The balance was acquired by a London autograph firm, Myers and Co., from which they subsequently were confiscated. Tried at Bow Street Police Court before the chief magistrate Sir Chartres Biron, Bostock was swiftly found guilty. As it was his second offence (he had served four months in 1920 for forgery and fraud while employed by the London War Pensions Committee), he was sentenced to twelve months' imprisonment with hard labour.

The engraving of Dickens offered to Shaw very likely was one of the book illustrations purloined from the Dickens Fellowship.]

I know the photograph too well to deprive you of it. It was engraved on steel and used for the Charles Dickens edition in red covers with the gilt autograph which prevailed during my boyhood, and which I read as Gnarks &c before I knew what autographs were.

I used to paint heads of Mephistopheles on the whitewashed walls of our Dalkey cottage with penny paints in my childhood, with the curious result that when I grew a moustache it turned up instead of down; and so did my eyebrows. Nature always "creeps up" (Whistler's expression) after Art.

When I was in my twenties an old Alsatian opera singer [Richard Deck] pointed out to me that in Greek statues the hair was always brushed up from the brow so as to form a sort of natural coronet, and asked me why I pasted my hair down, like a Victorian matron. I experimented with my brushes and comb, and found that the Greek plan was feasible and much more picturesque; so I adopted it. There was therefore really a deliberate change; but it had nothing to do with Mephistopheles.

The cape (of some Irish cloth that took my fancy) has never been worn in London—never been there, in fact. But I posed for a photograph in it once at the request of an American camera artist. Hence the legend.

G.B.S.

To MATTHEW EDWARD McNULTY

[H/4]

Ayot St Lawrence. Welwyn
4th December 1928

[George Bernard McNulty, son of Shaw's longtime friend, was at this time working in Hollywood as an assistant to the director John Ford at the William Fox Studios. Nothing is known of his later activities, except that he apparently never married and lived an itinerant existence. Even his death is uncertain, for Bernard Dukore was led, in researches for the Shaw *Collected Screenplays*, to believe that he fell or was pushed from a tall building in Los Angeles in 1980–81, whereas his nephew Bernard Talbot Gargan in Dublin in 1983 claimed that McNulty had jumped or fallen from a Canadian cross-country railroad train, on which he had been employed as a steward, in the 1930s. Nature again creeping up after Art? *Vide* the "suicides" of the Archbishop in *Back to Methuselah*.

Pola Negri (1894–1987), sultry Polish film siren, had unsuccessfully tried her wiles on Shaw in London only a month earlier, seeking screen rights to

Cæsar and Cleopatra. Gabriel Wells (1862–1946) was a Hungarian who emigrated to New York in 1896; after a start as a grain merchant he became a successful bookseller in New York and London. Over the years he built a large personal collection of Shaviana, acquired after his death by T.E. Hanley and now in Texas. The South Dublin Union, long since vanished, was a well-known almshouse, the subject of much music hall humour. Shaw's article "The Censorship," on the proposed Irish Censorship of Publications Act, enacted by the *Dáil* in 1929, was published in the *Irish Statesman* on 17th November.]

My dear Mac

You should not bring up your infants to cherish immoderate ambitions like these. If George Bernard McNulty could lay hold of the film rights of one of my plays, he would, as a businesslike youth, at once and without the smallest difficulty trade it off to Fox or another for fifteen thousand pounds spot cash. If the play were Caesar & Cleopatra the Princess Mdivani (known to the mob as Pola Negri) would fall to it for twenty thousand. And George Bernard would be ruined for life by getting a fortune for nothing without having been brought up to it.

What is he? a producer? And how old? Any experience in film work? Ever been in America? Married or single? Any good, generally speaking, or in artistic work because he is no good at business?

For a long time I refused to allow my plays to be filmed because a screened play is a dead one in the ordinary theatre. But the value of my film rights commercially is so great that unless I realize them before I die my executors will sell them for twopencehalfpenny. Therefore I am now quite prepared to sell for five years the rights of those plays which have had a big revival lately and are consequently likely to go to sleep again for some years in the theatre. Besides, I am artistically interested. Owing to the fact that in filming you can select all the perfect bits from your rehearsals (every rehearsal hits off some passage to perfection) and piece them together into a perfect performance the screen can reach a point of excellence unattainable by the stage. Only, you must know which are the best bits. If, like many American producers, you prefer the worst, and piece *them* together, the result is a sustained atrocity beyond the possibilities of a penny gaff.

Answer my questions about G.B.; and do not on any account send him this letter. He would sell it to Gabriel Wells for several hundred pounds, and buy a studio of his own, which would throw him on your hands with debts which would remove you to the South Dublin Union.

122

How are you? I have come through the shadows and am enjoying a hardy and unscrupulous old age in insufferable celebrity.

ever

G.B.S.

PS Did you see my article on the Censorship Bill in The Irish Statesman?

To LUDMILLA and GEORGES PITOËFF

Ayot St Lawrence. Welwyn

[H/1]   13th January 1929

[Pitoëff had produced *César et Cléopatre* at the Théâtre des Arts (now the Hébertot) on 18th December 1928, with himself as Cæsar and Ludmilla as Cleopatra. The elaborate scenery and costumes were designed by Pitoëff, who also staged the production. In France the "répétition générale" is equivalent to a final dress rehearsal, a preview to which the critics are invited. Thus the reviews in the daily newspapers appear before the next evening's opening performance (the "première représentation"). François-Joseph Talma (1763–1826), classic French actor, was one of the great stars of the Comédie Française. Rodolphe Darzens was managing director of the Théâtre des Arts.]

Mes Chères Pitoeffs

Quel desespoir!

Bah !!!!!!!!!!!!!!!!!!!!!!!!!!!!! ? !!!

Quand vous aurez eu autant des échecs, et, bien pire, des demi-succès que moi, vous vous ficherez de pareilles vétilles.

Le Père Hamon is ready to hang himself. He is not accustomed to the vicissitudes of theatrical adventure, and declares to heaven that all the Press is in a malignant conspiracy to destroy him and you and me —that Georges is greater than Talma and Chaliapine rolled into one— that the décor is worthy of the Celestial City—that I must send him a million francs at once—for what?—to post on every wall in Paris an affiche to assure the public that all the papers, all the critics, all the authors, all the capitalists and Poincarists have pronounced Caesar an atrocious failure, but that this is a LIE, a dastardly, infamous, abominable, corrupt envious L I E.

Why do you not console this worthy man instead of letting him write me frantic letters, ten pages long, accusing me of being corrupted

123

by my fabulous wealth, and of being a party to the conspiracy against you?

It is impossible for me to give you any advice in the matter because I have not seen the production, and do not know what has happened. I can only guess that if there were any likelihood of success M. Darzens, rather than risk having it said that nothing can succeed at his theatre, would save the situation even if he had to depend on your tour to recover his outlay.

Assuming, then, that the failure is for the moment irretrievable, you must bear in mind that the chances were heavily against its succeeding. When all is done that can be done for Caesar & Cleopatra by artistic production, it still remains essentially a star play: that is, a pedestal for an actor who not only *is* a great actor, but who has come to be accepted as one of the great figures—indeed as THE great figure —of the national stage.

When Georges, by casting himself for Caesar, claimed this position, he was putting an enormous strain on public opinion. Ludmilla had attempted this and succeeded. She, a foreigner, had snatched the part of Joan of Arc, France's national heroine, from the French theatre. But for Georges to snatch Caesar from le Talma de nos jours (if such a person exists) was too much. Georges needs ten years more work before he can impose himself so prodigiously on Paris. Well, ten years soon pass; and meanwhile one can play Britannicus or else let the play alone.

I do not like the décor. It is amusing enough in itself; but it does not give the right atmosphere for Caesar. Georges is like all producers: he does not want the audience to attend to the play or to the acting, but to his scenery. And when he tries to produce a play and to act a big part at the same time the work is so hard that at the répétition générale he is half asleep, and the critics soon are wholly asleep. Thus the producer betrays the actor and both of them betray the author, who is fortunately accustomed to be betrayed in this manner and does not waste time complaining about it.

It is evident that the Sphinx was so bad that you did not dare to send me a picture of it. Yet Caesar's whole success depends on the opening soliloquy for which the Sphinx provides the atmosphere and the inspiration. As the critics say, you must have suggested a sort of Slavonic Belle Helène, and this was a fatal mistake, because the fun in Caesar is entirely natural fun: if by the scenery you suggest that the fun is grotesque and voulu you kill it instead of helping it. The scenery may be as brilliant and beautiful as you like; but it must create an

Egypt in which there is nothing comic or modern: it must be through-out the Egypt of the Sphinx to whom Caesar speaks at night, comparing it with himself in his most secret moments. So take all that stuff and sell it, pawn it, burn it, and let it never be seen again on your stage.

I grieve for your disappointment; but one learns everything from disappointments: success is the end of everything and should be put off until one's funeral.

What are you going to try next?

I write this in English because Hamon assures me you read it much better than I write French.

à vous toujours
G. Bernard Shaw

PS How ungrateful you are to the critics! They were very kind, considering what we made them suffer.

To AUGUSTIN HAMON

[H/1]

4 Whitehall Court SW1
17th January 1929

[Shaw's new play was *The Apple Cart*, commenced on 5th November 1928 and completed on 29th December. The prologue to *Cæsar and Cleopatra* performed in Paris had been written for Forbes-Robertson's Farewell Tour revival, 1912–13. It was first published in the Hamons' translation of the play in 1926.]

My dear Hamon

The Pitoeffs have written me a most dismal letter, evidently believing that I am no longer their friend because they have made a mess of Caesar. I have replied in a manner that will make them understand that I am as friendly as ever, and told them to sell or pawn or burn the décor and try again ten years hence, when Georges has either reached the point as an actor at which Paris will accept him as Caesar or else discovered that he has mistaken his vocation and contented himself with producing. I have also reproached the two of them for practising on the innocence of le Père Hamon in these matters and inducing him to try and persuade me that it was all the fault of the Capitalist Press.

Before you hurl another letter at me ask yourself this question. Why was it that Joan, face to face with the same Press, the same critics, the same generalization of capitalist civilization as described so brilliantly in your last letter, nevertheless succeeded triumphantly. The difference between that success and the failure of Caesar was clearly not the Press, not the jealousy of the critics, not the illwill of the newspaper proprietors, not the corruptions of capitalism, but quite simply the fact that Ludmilla, though a foreigner, can act well enough to impose herself in a part which according to every prejudice should have been played by a leading French actress and not by a Russian, whereas Georges, not being a Talma or a Chaliapine, and being obviously not a Frenchman, could not impose himself in a part in which anyone else than a great actor and an established national favorite, must bore the audience to distraction. The fact that he had played Hamlet with success suggested that he had half a chance; and we let him try; but he has failed, and that is all there is to it: no expenditure of money can make a success of that sort of failure. You either hit or miss; and if you miss you simply "cut your loss" and produce another play that is within your capacity.

I am not sorry that you have had a thundering disappointment: it will teach you never again to count your chickens before they are hatched. As to Pitoeff, his loss is all in the day's work for him: Ludmilla's next success will recoup him. You must not encourage him to think that he has been the victim of circumstances. He has overrated his talent and his authority with the Paris public; and he must take the consequences. Nothing on earth could make Caesar fail in the hands of a great actor, nor make it succeed in the hands of a small one.

Do not worry yourself about the prologue. Of course it has been spoken at the last two London revivals, and in the American revival— ever since it has been written, in fact. There is no sign in the press notices (apart from the one or two inevitable silly ones that do not count) that it did any harm.

I have written a new play, which will perhaps please you, as it consists almost entirely of political discussion in the third quarter of the twentieth century. But it will be of no use to Pitoeff. So you see I have not been wasting my time crying over spilt milk.

ever
G. Bernard Shaw

To PHILIP GOSSE

[4 Whitehall Court S W 1]
18th January 1929

[Philip Gosse (1879–1959) was gathering material for a biography of his father Sir Edmund Gosse, who had died the previous year, to be written by Evan Charteris. Sir George Etherege (1634–91) was the first dramatist in England to attempt the kind of social comedy that Congreve and Sheridan later improved on.]

Dear Mr. Gosse

I have no letters. My intercourse with your father was always viva voce. Until very late in our careers we used to meet only at committees; and as he was a most combative man and had a sense of humour which he could never control we sparred and chaffed rather than communed on these occasions. Four or five years ago, when I was in Scotland at Gleneagles, I met him at Cloan, where he was staying with the Haldanes. As I had never had any opportunity of talking to him about his work and shewing him that I knew it and valued it, I took the opportunity to discuss the condition which the history and criticism of the literature of the Restoration had been in when I started (silly tales about Etheredge and the like) and what a difference his studies made. This appreciation was perhaps rather unexpected: at all events he sent me a copy of his *Life of Congreve* with a friendly inscription.

The last time we met was at Hardy's funeral, where he introduced me to Kipling, whom I had never met. We left the Abbey together; and I told him I had just been staying at Cliveden with the Astors, and, finding in my bedroom there a copy of *Father and Son*, had read it straight through. He said, "Had you not read it before?" I said, "Yes, of course: I read it when it first appeared; but this second time was the test; for I could not lay it down until I had been right through it again; and though I had always sworn by it I found it even better—more important—than I thought." "It is," I said, "one of the immortal pages of English literature." He stopped in the roadway and said, "Oh, my dear Shaw, you are the *only* one who ever encourages me."

I was greatly pleased by this. It was one of those occasions on which men of our age wonder which of them will be the next to go; and I am very glad that we parted affectionately and that he finally classed me among his friends. In my opinion he, too, should have been buried in the Abbey; for the little room that is left there should not be reserved for Best Sellers whose work has been fully recognized and rewarded during their lifetime, but allotted for preference to those workers who have loved literature for its own sake and done the things for it that only scholars appreciate, leaving big-drum celebrity to people like myself, for whom literature is only a means of self-expression.

faithfully
G. Bernard Shaw

To THERESA HELBURN

4 Whitehall Court SW1
[H/7]   8th February 1929

[Although Shaw appears to have admired George Arliss as a performer, the actor never performed in a Shaw play. Millamant is a principal character in Congreve's *The Way of the World*. The contemplated "Bühnenfestspiel" became the Malvern Festival, co-founded and jointly managed by Barry Jackson and Roy Limbert (1893–1954), drawing upon the resources of the Birmingham Repertory Company. The midsummer festival ran initially for two weeks, soon being extended to three weeks and then to four, with Shaw in attendance at each through Jackson's final season in 1937. There were two additional seasons before the interruption of war and one unsuccessful postwar season in 1949, under the sole management of Limbert (lessee of the Malvern Theatre); Shaw attended for the last time in 1938. In all, twenty-two Shaw plays were presented, six of them for the first time in England and one a world première.]

My dear Terry

By this time reports of my new play should have appeared in the American press, as it is some weeks since I wrote a letter about it to a lady in Detroit to whom I wanted to do a good turn, authorizing her to communicate the relevant parts of it to the papers and telling her how to set about it.

It is a play in three acts: the first long, the second only a twenty minutes interlude, and the third nearly but not quite as long as the first. The period is towards the end of the present century. With the exception of the interlude, which is a duet for the leading man and his lady (who, by the way, does not otherwise appear), the action consists of a Cabinet meeting at which the King of England is present. The King is the principal man and has the sort of part that George Arliss shines in. Beside him there are two of his private secretaries, both of whom must be pretty good walking gentlemen. Two of the Cabinet ministers are women. The Prime Minister has a strong part; and there are five other ministers with character parts which you will have no difficulty in casting. There is also a young princess with one short scene. In all, nine men and four women, of whom one is a brilliant Millamant, one serious, one musical comedy, and the princess as aforesaid.

These are, of course, business details, not for publication. The book is at the printers. I expect proofs daily, and can let you have one ready for production as soon as your arrangements permit.

The name of the play is The Apple Cart; and it is as unlike St Joan as it possibly can be.

ever

G. Bernard Shaw

PS The play will be produced in England next August at a provincial Bühnenfestspiel, with Methuselah, Heartbreak House, & possibly St Joan [eventually *Cæsar and Cleopatra* was substituted], the particular Bayreuth in question being Malvern in Worcestershire, near the Welsh border. Reinhardt may produce it first in Berlin; but I am rather dissuading him, as the politics in the play are very English.

If L. L. [Lawrence Langner] is about, tell him all this.

To WILLIAM MAXWELL

Ayot St Lawrence. Welwyn

10th February 1929

[C/3]

[William Maxwell was attempting to persuade a reluctant Shaw to abandon the Caslon handset type he had used for his books since 1898 and to substitute a more readable linotype. Despite his initial inflexibility Shaw eventually bowed to Maxwell's expertise, accepting not only this stylistic change, but allowing Maxwell to convince him to scrap the long-used Venetian blind green binding cloth in favour of a non-fading Venetian red sailcloth fabric for the new Standard Edition of his works commencing in 1931.]

The Scotch Roman is nice; and I could design a very pretty edition in thinner volumes and half calf and marbled covers like the Johnson-Malone Shakespears of auld lang syne.

But they are all unbearable after the Caslon; and to break a thirty years tradit on—now an INSTITUTION and a venerable one—for them would be like a gracious old white haired lady suddenly painting her face and sticking on a red wig.

I shall stick to the Caslon and the Venetian blind green until I die. . . .

G.B.S.

To NORMAN CLARK

4 Whitehall Court SW1
[X/293]   21st February 1929

[Unable to attend a luncheon honouring the American heavyweight boxing
champion Gene Tunney (1898–1978) because of his absence at Cap d'Antibes,
Shaw wrote to Tunney on 31st August 1928 offering to arrange a meeting
after his return to London in mid-September if Tunney were still "on this
side of the Atlantic . . . [and] not by that time tired of literary people" (A/9).
Norman Clark (1892—?), the boxing enthusiast (see letter to him of *c.* 15th
December 1919), himself a veteran of fifty amateur contests, had drafted a
report of an interview with Shaw on prizefighting, which he submitted for
correction and inevitable revision. Having learned in the course of the interview that Tunney and his wife Polly had lunched at Whitehall Court on
14th November, Clark had inserted references in his interview to the visit
and to Shaw's opinion of Tunney as a boxer. These were deleted from the
manuscript by Shaw.]

Dear Norman Clark

It is quite out of the question for me to give to the press anything
that passes between me and my private guests, or to criticize them in
public in any way.

Besides, you have not got the hang of Tunney at all. On the evidence
of the films I should say that he is an extraordinarily difficult man to
hit. Carpentier's rights looked as fatal as ever; but as they produced
absolutely no effect they cannot have got home. Tunney never crouches,
always has his head as far back as it will go, and has a peculiar biff that
stalls off every attempt to rush him.

He systematically gets away and makes his opponent miss until
disappointment and exhaustion have brought him down to a condition
of definite inferiority. When Dempsey, after three get-aways, had him
against the ropes and managed to get his arms round him for his
terrible rabbit punch, Tunney simply held him until the referee inter-
posed, in spite of every arm-breaking trick that Dempsey knew. His
confidence in himself and his system amounts to something like contempt for his most famous adversaries; reputations cannot frighten
him; personalities cannot hypnotize him. He does not need to be a
brilliant boxer like Carpentier or a terror like Dempsey: he wins by
mental and moral superiority, combined with plenty of strength, an
inaccessible head, and that very disheartening biff that sickened
Dempsey when he rushed for an apparently certain victory after the
count in the seventh round. With Tunney's character Carpentier
could have beaten Dempsey. Carpentier never looked like a baby in

Dempsey's hands, though he was smashed in the first ten seconds; but Dempsey, in the first fight with Tunney, after the first two rounds, did look like a schoolboy larking with an instructor. I never said to you that Tunney was the only big man who can box. I don't know that he can box better than you can. In an exhibition spar with soft gloves Carpentier could outshine him. He does not knock out his opponents: he wears them out. In short, he is neither the smartest boxer nor the hardest puncher of his time; but he most certainly is the most remarkable character; and it is on character that he has won. You might say that he wins because he has the good sense to win. Fifty years ago he would have had too much good sense to be in the ring; but today no other profession could have done as much for him.

There! You see it's no use trying to report me unless you take it down in shorthand. An attempt to paraphrase me only ends in twaddle.

faithfully
G.B.S.

To NORMAN CLARK

4 Whitehall Court SW1
[C/7]   27th March 1929

[Clark had submitted the revised interview to Shaw, in which he had incorporated the letter of 21st February. The book presumably was Clark's *How to Box* (1922). Edward (Ned) Donnelly's "little treatise" was *Self-Defence; or, The Art of Boxing*, ed. J.M. Waite (1879). For reference to Jem Mace and Tom King, see letter of 29th July 1921 to Lawrence Langner. Tom Sayers (1826–65), known as the Little Wonder (he weighed 155 pounds), became middleweight champion of England in 1857. A class of heavy guns issued from the Royal Arsenal at Woolwich became known as Woolwich Infants. The term came to be applied to anything of impressive size and strength.]

It would have saved you a lot of ink to say that you quite agreed with me. Why must you always have it in your own words? Mine are just as good.

The book is much the best since Donnelly's little treatise—God knows who wrote it!

In the bare knuckle days heavy weights were not fancied. Mace & Sayers were middle weights; and big men (Woolwich Infants) were mere punching bags for them. Nobody then would have given odds on Carpentier because he did not weigh a ton. By the way I never said that he would beat Dempsey: what I did say was that 4 to 1 on

Dempsey was absurd, as no boxer could be four times as good as Carpentier. I was careful to say that I knew nothing of Dempsey, and that as at worst he might knock C. out as Tom King knocked out Mace all the betting that was being worked up on form, weight, measurements, and gorilla scares was mere dope for duffers.

Your physics made me gasp by their staggering non sequiturs; but I havn't time to be precise. Again, thanks for the book.

G.B.S.

To A. FENNER BROCKWAY

[Ayot St Lawrence. Welwyn]

[E/1; X/356] 3rd April 1929

[A. Fenner Brockway (b. 1888), later Lord Brockway, was a journalist and Socialist leader, General Secretary (later Chairman) of the I.L.P., and Labour M.P. for East Leyton 1929–31. When The Masses Stage and Film Guild, founded by the I.L.P., sought in 1929 to show the Russian film *Potemkin*, directed by Sergei Eisenstein, at a private showing for its members, the Home Office refused permission. A number of other revolutionary films were similarly banned from screening in Britain, but Shaw had been able to view these through the efforts of the Hon. Ivor Montagu (1904–84), founder of the London Film Society, who as a member of the Communist Party with ties to the Russian Embassy was able to arrange surreptitious screenings in a Wardour Street film projection room. A few years later Montagu brought Eisenstein to Whitehall Court to meet Shaw.]

Potemkin was exhibited to me privately. It is, artistically, one of the very best films in existence. Its suppression is an undisguised stroke of class censorship, utterly indefensible and inexplicable on any other ground. Simply an incident in the class war, as waged by our governing classes. Remind them of it when they next wax indignant against Soviet censorship. In great haste

G.B.S.

To MRS PATRICK CAMPBELL

4 Whitehall Court SW1

[A/37; X/160] 6th April 1929

[Although Shaw had read *The Apple Cart* to several mutual acquaintances, including Edith Lyttelton ("D.D."), he withheld the play as long as possible from Stella Campbell, anticipating a negative reaction to his fictional usage of her as Orinthia in the play's Interlude. Informed by D.D. that "G.B.Shaw has put you into his play as the Egeria of the King—1960," Mrs Campbell wrote to Shaw on 5th April to "please come and read it to me before you go away. It doesn't look nice of you to refuse, after saying you would, and you have no legal right to put me in a play without my knowledge, or permission—damn you! ... I ran away from you at Sandwich [1913] because I wanted to remain Queen of the Kingdom of my heart—but I suppose you mustn't humble the King in your play like that—" (*Bernard Shaw and Mrs Patrick Campbell: Their Correspondence*, 1952).

"Sissy Cholmondeley died this morning between 9 & 10," Shaw noted in his pocket diary on 5th April, "at her club in London."]

D D remembers the ending [of the Interlude] only too jolly well. It is not for nothing that you call me Joey. It is an ending of the red hot poker order: wildly disgraceful.

Of course the scene isn't true; but you will recognize bits and scraps of it. And there are perhaps gleams of truth in it here and there. Which of us knows the whole truth? Not I.

But I can't read it to you now because I do not possess a copy. I had to send the only one in my hands to Barry Jackson this morning to shew to the Lord Chamberlain on Monday. I am trying to retrieve another somewhere; but I doubt whether I shall succeed before our departure for Italy on the 14th. It has been put off for a week by the death yesterday of my sister-in-law. The funeral will take us to Shropshire on Monday.

However, when I come back I will read the scene to you. The shyness has in it, perhaps, a fear lest you should set me expanding the scene and upsetting the balance of the play; but I will risk it.

Yes: you were right, Sandwich and all. And wrong, I suppose, to get married.

GBS

To ANTHONY ASQUITH

[C/3]

Ayot St Lawrence. Welwyn
10th April 1929

[Anthony Asquith (1902–68), son of the former prime minister, had gone to Hollywood following graduation from Oxford to study filmmaking, returning to England in 1926 to commence a highly successful screen career as a director. He eventually directed film versions of three of Shaw's plays: *Pygmalion*, *The Doctor's Dilemma*, and *The Millionairess*. Barrie's *A Kiss for Cinderella*

(1926) was directed by Herbert Brenon, with Betty Bronson and Tom Moore in the film leads. "L.B." is unidentified; he may have been Lionel Barrymore.]

Well, what is to prevent Paramount making me an offer? The shop is open, the occasion propitious. I approved highly of Cinderella. I have your personal testimonial to L.B's capacity. Pygmalion has had its New York revival by the Theatre Guild and is presumably as dead as mutton there for the next five years. The characteristic American bashfulness of Paramount is misplaced.

I am just off to Italy for—probably—about six weeks; so personal paramount powwows are for the moment impossible; but letters will reach me.

G.B.S.

What about the British firms? Hopeless, I suppose.

To EDWARD GORDON CRAIG

4 Whitehall Court SW1
12th April 1929

[H/3]

[Hearing that the Ellen Terry Estate was contemplating sale of Shaw's letters to Ellen and copyright rights in Ellen's letters, the American lawyer and publisher Elbridge L. Adams (1866–1934), of the Fountain Press, approached Ellen's daughter Edith Craig for publication rights. Aware of Edie's need for money for the establishment of the Ellen Terry Memorial Institute at Smallhythe, her home in Kent, Shaw encouraged her to negotiate. This, however, necessitated that Ellen's son Gordon Craig, for ethical reasons, be approached for approval. On 4th April Craig wrote a friendly-seeming letter to Shaw seeking clarification as to whether or not Shaw wanted the correspondence to be published, adding perversely that he considered the good parts of the letters were too fine to allow the public to share in them. Upon receipt of Shaw's reply, he noted at the foot "The letter of a cockatrice."

Shaw undertook the draft of a preface to the correspondence while holidaying in Italy, completing it on 26th June. Twelve copies were printed in September, the wrapper (labelled "Very Private"), being captioned *Preface to be attached to the Correspondence of Ellen Terry and Bernard Shaw should it ever be published*. It was considerably revised for publication in 1931.

Shaw was under a misconception concerning copyright. As unpublished manuscripts the letters were protected *until* published and for an additional fifty years *from* publication.]

134

Dear Gordon Craig

If there were no money involved I think I should advise that the correspondence should be sent to the British Museum with instructions to withhold it from the general public, though not, subject to the discretion of the Trustees of the Museum, from inspection by the serious biographer or theatrical historian, until we are all dead. But the present mania for literary relics makes it possible to do any or all of three things. 1. Sell the letters without the copyright, as autographs. 2. License the publication of a limited collectors' edition to be sold at some price like five guineas a copy. 3. Publish the correspondence as an ordinary book with an unlimited circulation. No 1 would possibly bring in several thousand pounds. No 2, at least one thousand pounds. No 3. A pretty good harvest in royalties. No 2 would not exclude No 3, provided the collectors' edition were given a fair start of, say, six months. And No 1 is compatible with both or either.

The legal position is that the writers of the letters or their executors own the copyright; but the recipients own the sheets of paper on which the letters are written. Thus I own the sheets of paper on which Ellen wrote to me; and her executors own the copyright in what she wrote. The executors own the sheets of paper on which I wrote; but I own the copyright in what I wrote.

Now for the sentimental position. In the correspondence Ellen and I were the principals; and neither of us could, I think, be really forgiven for making money out of it. But Ellen's executors, even though they are her children, are not in that position. There is no indelicacy in their publishing the correspondence with my consent if they think, on the whole, that it ought to be given to the world for the sake of its interest as theatrical biography or theatrical history. Of course there is always the natural shrinking from the publication of intimate letters that were never meant for publication; but this very fact gives the letters a peculiar value and consequently a peculiar claim to be published sooner or later, *as they certainly will be unless they are destroyed with all existing copies: an act which none of us contemplate.* Therefore in encouraging Edy to frankly make the most of their market value for the benefit of the estate I do not feel that I am advising her to do anything that I would not have done in her position. If the letters are published I will license the publication as far as my copyright is concerned; and I will write a preface for the volume in which I will try to make Ellen's career much more intelligible than even you could make it, because I go back a generation before you to a time when Irving was undreamt of. His beginnings as a big Shakesperean actor were very dreadful to that generation. You have no notion of what his first attempts looked like after the sort of thing that began, one guesses, with Burbage, and ended with Barry Sullivan.

There have been, as yet, no commitments. I start for Italy for six weeks on the 14th, and shall complete the preface there. Meanwhile there are bidders in the field; and one of them has actually deposited £1000 as a pledge that he means business. The rest lies practically with the executors.

There are to be considered not only Edy's circumstances (to say nothing of yours) but the proposed Institute at Tenterden. If the decision be to publish there is still the question as to what should be omitted. Ellen comes out most extraordinarily well from the correspondence; but she describes a contemporary leading lady (still living) as her "idea of hell"; and the fairly numerous references to you and Edy were not meant for the public eye, especially one in which she describes you as demanding whether she expected you to support your wife like any common man, Ellen's comment being that she sometimes could not help wishing that her wonderful boy were a little commoner. However, unless we are all prepared to face things like that, the whole correspondence will have to be suppressed. Still, there it is.

It all comes to this. Unless we destroy the correspondence thoroughly, its publication is only a matter of time. Can Edy? can you?—afford to postpone it until it is no longer under your control in any way? Copyright will expire eventually.

faithfully
G. Bernard Shaw

To NANCY ASTOR

4 Whitehall Court S W 1
[A/101]   13th April 1929

[Marion Phillips (1881–1932), who called herself chief woman officer of the Labour Party, was M.P. for Sunderland 1929–31. Plymouth was Nancy Astor's constituency.]

Dear blessedest Nancy

Charlotte is all right. I went down with her to the funeral at the lovely little old village church of Edstaston on a lovely day with a mountain of lovely flowers. I contributed enough comic relief to wipe the black off without going so far as to turn the afternoon tea into a wake. Still, I think we all enjoyed ourselves. The Intelligent Woman had lived her life well out, and exhausted her health so much through her struggle with asthma that it would really have been terrible if she had recovered and had to die all over again. Those who cared felt that all was well. Those who didnt had a pleasant outing, and were relieved to find that long faces were not expected.

If Charlotte ever has more distress than I can pull her through I will send for you. She is very fond of you. So am I. I dont know why.

What the devil was Marion Phillips doing in Plymouth? Sunderland is her shop; and when she goes out raiding she might at least raid a man's constituency. The worst of Plymouth is that it lives by selling drink to sailors, though it has to keep sober itself to do so effectually and profitably.

I have just registered our luggage. All day yesterday I could think of nothing but

> As there seems to be plenty of room in the box
> I may as well take some additional socks.

Packing is a distracting task; but when it is done it is done. If you have a valet or a maid to do it you are never done with them, and might as well stay at home. That is Charlotte's philosophy of travelling.

Brioni Hotel, Brioni, Istria, Italy is our next address. It was recommended to us as a desert island. We learn now that it is one of the most overcrowded "resorts" on earth. I wonder how long we will be able to stand it.

ever & ever
G.B.S.

To GABRIEL WELLS

Hotel Brioni
Brioni. Istria
20th April 1929

[T(A)/1]

[The Shaws had departed for Italy on 14th April, travelling by the Orient Express to Trieste, where they remained for two days before proceeding to Brioni (until 14th May), to join the Tunneys. This was followed by twelve days in Yugoslavia (Dubrovnik and Split) and a fortnight in Venice, with excursions to Padua, Ferrara, and Ravenna. They arrived back in London on 13th June.

The book to which Shaw refers was a copy of John Locke's *Essay on the Human Understanding* (1841), which had been advertised in the catalogue of the Thomas Hatton sale at the American Art Association, New York, as Shaw's own copy, in which he had "annotated the work in the margins of nearly every page, underscoring the significant passages in pencil." The book was purchased by an American bookseller for $1500. Shaw had inadvertently sold it with a large quantity of rough proofs of his plays, foreign translations, pamphlets and tracts, for £90, when vacating Adelphi Terrace, to Gilbert Fabes (1894–1973), manager of the rare books division of Foyle's. Actually, as Shaw indicated in a note published as "Bernard Shaw's 'Relics,'" in *The Observer* on 24th March 1929, the volume belonged to Charlotte, an inheritance from her father Horace Townsend (his wife affected the name Payne-Townshend), who was the annotator.

Floryan Sobieniowski, an inveterate cadger, had taken to scouting London shops for out-of-the-way Shaw publications, then bringing them to Shaw to annotate and sign. As this was cheaper than indulging Sobieniowski by paying out royalty advances that would never be recovered, Shaw wrote reminiscences and comments on dozens of tracts, pamphlets, and leaflets, most of which were acquired by Wells. Despite Shaw's assertion that he had torn up the shorthand manuscripts of *Saint Joan* and *The Apple Cart*, both survive in library collections, the former in the British Library, the latter in the Humanities Research Center of the University of Texas.]

Dear Mr Gabriel Wells

I assure you I was not in the least annoyed by the Locke's Essay incident. My letter to The Observer was not meant to express any feeling of the kind. But I could not allow the book to pass from auction to auction, drawing large sums from Shavian collectors, without a word of warning.

Mr Fabes explains that he made a present of the book to a good customer who expressed a wish to possess it. I have no doubt that this is true, and that Mr Fabes did not represent the marginalia in the book as being my handiwork. But as the good customer was a dealer, I cannot help wondering what Mr Fabes supposed he wanted the book for. If Mr Fabes has among his valued customers a burglar, and he ever obliges him by presenting him with a jemmy, and that jemmy is subsequently found sticking in one of the safes of the Bank of England, Mr Fabes will certainly be asked whether he thought the burglar wanted the jemmy to stir his tea with.

Miss Patch tells me that you object to my encouraging Floryan S. This from you to me! It is you who encourage him by paying him monstrous sums for first editions and scraps of my handwriting. He sets his relatives to work to hunt out the books, and then brings them to me and tells me, in effect, that if I do not write in them and thus enable him to sell them to you he will have to borrow more money from me. I know that if I give him nothing to sell to you he will borrow your last penny. He is a stupendous, colossal, incorrigible borrower. What can he do, poor fellow, with a wife and child to feed, and nothing to feed them on but his quite genuine but not yet very saleable literary talent? I refuse again and again; but he is so pathetically helpless that in the end he gets something out of me, as I dare say he does out of you too. You may curse the day you ever met him, and curse me for sending him to you; but that will not bury him; and even if it did we should have to lend him the price of his funeral. Probably he will ask us to do that some day; and then he won't die. I have both prayed and paid for his repatriation; but he turns up in Maida Vale again, having gone to Poland only to borrow his fare back to London.

I shall always disparage relics, because I am an Irish Protestant in the marrow of my bones. I tear up manuscripts with savage glee, though I suppose you could sell them all for me at £300 an ounce. I tore up St Joan except for ten pages which had dates on them; and I did the same with The Apple Cart. So if ever you are offered the complete original manuscript for a million or so, beware! they will be forgeries.

I expect to be at this address for some weeks to come.

> faithfully
> G. Bernard Shaw

To BLANCHE PATCH

Hotel Brioni
Brioni. Istria
29th April 1929

[A/4]

I have begun to work at the Ellen Terry preface, but am leaving it to gad about the island on every pretext.

The terrible bora has ceased blowing now for some days and some glorious *looking* weather has ensued; but it is not real summer yet.

I presume Edy has determined to print the letters in spite of Teddy's teeth, and that Ellen's will has excluded him from power to interfere with her. I do not think I can let it go beyond a limited edition. This will secure the thousand pounds at least. But I must look at the thing as a whole when I have finished the preface.

I enclose cheque for Clark.

> GBS

To ALBERT COATES

Brioni. Istria
5th May 1929

[A/9]

[Informed that Coates was contemplating an operatic treatment of *Saint Joan*, Shaw amused himself by drafting a scenario for the work.]

St Joan
A Grand Opera
by
Albert Coates
Lyrics by Madelon Coates

_____   _____

Act I
Overture. ad lib.

1. Duetto buffo – The Steward & Baudricourt. Style – The Three Oranges
    Tenor & Baritone
            The Two Eggs (zylophone obbligato)
2 Cavatina – The Steward. Style "Celeste Aida."
    Tenor
        "A Maiden Fair."
        introducing
3 Soldiers' Chorus (outside) – solos by Baudricourt – Style "Per me ora fatale" Count di Luna (Trovatore)
4 Scena. Joan.
        "Tending my Father's Sheep at Eve." (cor anglaise obbligato)
            introducing
    Celestial voices of SS Michael, Catherine & Agnes with Grand Transparency. (Instrumentation – Harps, with Organ effects on Gramophone).
5   Encore of the Preceding number
6 Another Cavatina. De Poulengy. *Alto!* Style – The Lost Chord.
        "Surely an angel she."
7 Duo. De P & Baudricourt – Canto fermo for baritone with florid alto descant.
        "Think'st thou so, Polly?"
8 Finale
        1st movement – Maestoso – Trio in canon for Steward, de P., & B, taken up by Soldiers' Chorus   Style – The Meistersinger quintet plus the Fidelio quartet.
        "Go, and God's blessing with thee."

140

2nd movement – Presto Vivacissimo – scappamento libero. Style – Offenbachissimo. Accompaniment, saxophones, side drums, sleigh bells, and eight Klaxons.

"Off we go to Chin-Chon-Chinon."

9 Curtain, & frantic calls for the Composer-Conductor, who appears hand in hand with de Poulengy, whose alto voice has had a *succès fou de rire*.

10. Jealousy of prima donna – Lied ohne Musik.

When the score of the above is completed I will supply the rest of the scenario.

Heaven bless you, dear Albert & Madelon. Would we were with you at Intragnola. This is the coldest place we ever struck.

ever
G.B.S.

To NANCY ASTOR

Dubrovnik. Yugoslavia
18th May 1929
Next week—Hotel Danieli. Venice

[A/101]

[Nancy Astor represented the Sutton division of Plymouth in Parliament from 1919 to 1945. Although she was the first woman to take her seat in the House of Commons she was not the first to be elected, this honour belonging to the Sinn Féin leader Constance Countess Markievicz, elected from St Patrick's, Dublin, 1918. Enclosed with Shaw's letter was an undated cutting of a "Special Message" for the Housing number of the *East End Star*, captioned "George Bernard Shaw on the Slums." Ramsay MacDonald contributed articles throughout May to *Forward* (Glasgow). In the General Election of June 1929 Labour was returned with 287 seats to 260 for the Conservatives and 59 for the Liberals, obliging Stanley Baldwin to resign. MacDonald was able handily to form another minority government, which served until July 1931. The "late Speaker" of the dissolved House of Commons was the Rt. Hon. E. A. FitzRoy (1869–1943), re-elected in June, having the confidence of all the parties. The word "jonnick" is British dialect connoting one who is upright, straightforward, fair.]

Dearest Nancy

You will see by the enclosed that I also have had a turn at what I presume to be your main occupation at present. Heaven forgive us both. I gather from an article by Ramsay Macdonald that the election

141

has fallen flat so far; but this can hardly last: the excitement will rise as the candidates strip nakeder and nakeder (nuder, the Americans call it) until they have shed the last ray of scruple and don't care what they say or do to get in. All the better for you; for when the Trade has stooped to its last infamy in reviling you, you need only fold your arms like a Christian martyr and leave chivalrous indignation to do its work. All the same, it is an error to suppose that mud is pleasant when it does not stick, and that lies do not matter as they are not true. On the contrary you get finished without the satisfaction of having deserved it, or the benefit of expiation.

Besides, you are in a difficult situation: a violently Radical Conservative, a recklessly unladylike Lady, a Prohibitionist member of The Trade party, and all sorts of contradictory things, including (on the authority of the late Speaker) the most turbulent member of the Party of Order. The only tune to which you can win in a seafaring constituency is Jack's Delight Is His Lovely Nan. In that sign you will probably conquer in spite of all the sober and virtuous publicans and brothel keepers who minister to the paid-off mariners of our historic port. Knowing that you are on the side of the angels they will give you a vote to set against their profits in the books of the recording angel, believing that you are too jonnick to cut any ice in parliament on your own account. Therefore be extreme on the Drink Question; for if you compromise they will be afraid you might really hurt them, whereas if you go all out for a Dry England they will laugh at pretty Nancy's way and feel sure that you might as well try to dry England with blotting paper as with Prohibition. On the social question, just read chapters of my book at random and give them chunks of it: they will neither know nor care whether it is Socialism or Conservatism if you dont tell them. Give them what you like, and they'll probably like it too; and leave it to the others to "give em muck" (peche Melba). Tell them you are making enemies all the time because you can't suffer fools gladly and are up against 600 of them every working night of your life, and that under God your refuge is Plymouth, and if Plymouth turns you down it will shut the gates of mercy on mankind. In short, dear Nancy, let yourself rip, and wear all your pearls: prudence is not your game; and if you ride hard enough for a fall you won't get it. And if you want a poster—

ever & ever
G.B.S.

To SYDNEY C. COCKERELL

Royal Hotel S. Marco. Ravenna
[X/277]   6th June 1929

[Parkins & Gotto, Ltd., were Britain's court stationers, printers, and engravers, in Oxford Street, London.]

Dear Sydney Cockerell

Having regretted all these years that we missed Ravenna when we were in Italy together [in 1891], here I am at last.

The famous mosaics are very smart indeed, but soul-less after Torcello, which I revisited the other day and found more magical than ever. There is not a scrap of magic about the Ravenna stuff, which is the very best Parkins-and-Gotto by the royal tradesmen of the Imperial court. The figures are obviously fashionable relatives of Pontius Pilate doing their best to look like good Christians. As copied a century or two later in St. Mark's in Venice (my present headquarters—Danieli) they have become real saints. The Torcello Virgin is to the best attempt at her in Ravenna as the deep sea is to a drop of eau de Cologne; but still the architecture is jolly good; there are lots of very well preserved Byzantine things; and the place is a sell only to those who don't know that Christianity is like wine in respect of the fact that though the older it is the better up to a certain point, yet, that point once passed, it deteriorates with age. This fifth century Christianity was an article of fashion, not of faith, for people with money enough to commission mosaics. The real stuff was bought with Peter's pence.

I return to Venice tomorrow, and to London next week, arriving on the 12th. I have explored the Adriatic a little—Ragusa, Spalato, Trau, Sebeneg, Cettinje, Cattaro, etc. etc. and found the Jugoslavians a remarkably affable, easy-going, good-looking people, and the places

143

fascinating. But the feeling between Italy and Jugoslavia could hardly be worse. The Dalmatian coast is very tempting commercially because, like the west coast of Ireland, it is crammed with amazing natural harbors at which the trading mouth waters. Charlotte is with me, of course. We both hope all is well with you. More when we meet.

ever

G.B.S.

To ALBERT COATES

Royal Hotel S. Marco
Ravenna
6th June 1929

[A/9]

[*Maritana*, by the Irish composer Vincent Wallace, was a popular opera known to Shaw from his youth. Beckmesser is the pedantic town clerk (a bass rôle) in Wagner's *Die Meistersinger*. In his early operas Verdi frequently scored several accompaniments to arias, duets and ensembles for the string section of the orchestra playing pizzicato, creating a sound like that of a huge guitar. The melodic line was often doubled by woodwinds playing in unison, in thirds and/or in sixths. (I am indebted to Warren F. Michon of the New York Public Library Music Division for this information.)]

My dear Albert

How is Maritana—St Joan getting on? I feel apologetic about the way I laugh when I think of St Joan as an opera; but at the back of my merriment there is a conviction that we are all tired of symphonic operas that are not really symphonic, only continuous, and that the old string of separate numbers, each a complete piece of music capable of being encored, with a finale, could stage a come-back if anyone would venture on it. As encores are a nuisance the full closes would have to be concealed in the theatre; but they ought to be available for sale of the separate numbers as sheet music with composers' royalties.

Take that in its crudity as a starting point; and admit that a serious opera could not now go back to the Beggar's Opera or even to Don Giovanni. Still, an historical opera (rejected by Wagner as a monstrosity) could and in fact should go back to Meyerbeer; for an attempt to recompose the 3rd act of the Hugenots (uncut) symphonically would only muddle it. The Beethoven–Wagner system is all very well when the subject is the moods of an individual soul (the Beethoven symphony) or the contacts and conflicts of several individual souls (the

Wagnerian music drama); but to apply it to a Rataplan chorus ["Prenant son sabre de bataille," in *The Huguenots*], or to what is now called community singing, in which all the individual souls are reduced to a common impulse, would be ridiculous. Joan's part ought to be a Beethovenian symphony, with characteristic obbligati for the others and a Beckmesseresque Dauphin; but to try to weave them all up into a single emotional tissue like the score of Tristan would end in disaster.

So there really is something in my silly scenario after all.

I must say the Italian conductors do earn their salaries. In Venice (my present headquarters) the conductor of the big municipal band (no strings except to reinforce the bass) beats, in the hottest weather, every crotchet and every triplet. In moments of excitement he madly tries to beat semiquavers. In short, he does more hard physical jerks in ten bars than you ever did in all your lazy life. Even at the opera here in Ravenna, where the conducting was comparatively Coatesian, I never looked at the conductor without being able to tell from his beat whether he was in the middle of a bar or at the beginning of it. They play all their notes, these Italians. The opera was Otello, with a magnificent baritone and a very good tenor, both good actors. The duet at the end of the second act came off to perfection: a thing I never expected to hear. In the first act there was only one constellation, the Great Bear (or Plough) with one pointer missing, and a blazing star, unknown at Greenwich, within two inches of the other. The stars in the G.B. wobbled about until I felt as drunk as Cassio. When the ignorant Moor declared that the Great Bear was the Pleiades, and finally hailed the unknown star as Venus, my cup was full. I went home after the second act as there was no chance of their finishing before three in the morning.

It was very noticeable that when Verdi got away from his old Italian scoring—big guitar for strings and full wind in unisons thirds & sixths with the singers—he did not know how to get his effects, and mostly underscored. With Wagner they would have been sure fire. There is something in being a Kapellmeister after all.

I went to high mass at St Mark's on Sunday and discovered a new (to me) organ stop which must be added to the orchestra at all costs. It is a trumpet. Not the horrible English trumpet stop (which is like a cheap accordion trying to imitate a braying donkey and only succeeding in being a bastard cornet) but something quite new. Imagine a muted trumpet, not wierd nor comic to accompany Mime [in Wagner's *Der Ring des Nibelungen*], but with the tone not only close but beautiful! That is what it is like; and the effect when the organist let it go for a climax was magnificent and delicious. We must find out about it.

In the course of this letter I have returned with Charlotte from Ravenna to Venice. We start for home on Tuesday next, the eleventh, and hope to be in London on the following day. Our loves to Madelon. How is Tamara?

I have just looked out of the window over the lagoon, and as I live by vegetables there's a FOG!

G.B.S.

To FLORYAN SOBIENIOWSKI

[Hotel Danieli. Venice]
[C/4; X/289.e]   [Undated: assigned to 8th June 1929]

[Shaw had, to the consternation both of Siegfried Trebitsch and Barry Jackson, authorised the Teatr Polski to stage the world première of *The Apple Cart* (*Wielki Kram*) in Warsaw on 14th June, in Sobieniowski's translation. The producer (i.e., director) was Karol Borowskiego. The Hungarian playwright Melchior Lengyel, who had encountered Shaw in his travels, apparently had published a report of the meeting, which Shaw implies was semi-fictional.]

Your producer is an artist, and therefore does not understand political emotions. The king's announcement of his intention to enter parliament is an earthquake shock to the old parliamentary hands in the Cabinet, because they at once see what it means. They must all spring to their feet as if a bomb had exploded in the middle of the room. Boanerges, a novice and an egotist, does not understand, and thinks the king in parliament cannot hurt him. The ladies are delighted: they lean back in their chairs and laugh at their dismayed colleagues. If everyone rose the effect would be unmeaning and ridiculous. I have arranged the business of rising and sitting most carefully; and any attempt to change it on *general* principles of etiquette will play the devil with the comedy by giving equal emphasis to every speech. Contrast—continual contrast—is essential to my dialogue: if the performers take their tone and speed from one another, all glibly picking up their cues and rattling on in the same way, the scene will be unintelligible. Unless every actor speaks and behaves as if he had never heard his cue before, and is surprised by it, or wounded, or pleased— all involving some change of tone or pace, however subtle—the whole affair will be about as amusing as a gabbled-through church service.

146

I did not speak to Lengyel for publication. I did not say anything about you. I did not say I had rather go to Vienna or Berlin. I never had the slightest intention of going to either city. I always avoid places where my plays are being performed. Contradict all this nonsense flatly. On the 14th I shall be in London.

G.B.S.

To E. V. LUCAS

4 Whitehall Court S W 1

[X/357]   14th June 1929

[Edward Verrall Lucas (1868–1938), author and chairman of the publishing house Methuen & Co., had sent to Shaw, for autographing, a copy of the first edition of *Widowers' Houses* (1893) donated by Conal O'Riordan for an auction to raise income for the Royal Literary Fund. Shaw provided the volume with a long autograph letter covering both sides of the half-title leaf. When first published, *Widowers' Houses* was apparently issued simultaneously in both olive brown (which Shaw recalled as "citrine") and blue cloth bindings. Despite his insistence that blue copies were unknown to him, only one of the 1893 presentation copies has been discovered in "citrine" binding; all the rest are cased in blue! The inscribed volume fetched £80 at Sotheby's in November.]

My dear Lucas

What puzzles me about this book is its blue cover. Henry & Co. published it in a green colored cloth case of the shade called citrine. Publishing books by me—or plays by anybody—was in those days a sign of inexperienced optimism on the part of a publisher (except at the author's expense) and was generally followed by bankruptcy or retirement from business. When Henry & Co. honorably retired in due course, they very magnanimously presented me with the unsold and unbound remainder of the edition; and I had this remainder bound for myself in mauve cloth to distinguish it from the sold copies.

And now Conal comes along with this BLUE copy which he says he bought from Henry & Co. But one does not buy books from the publisher but from the bookseller, who in 1893 allowed a discount of threepence in the shilling from the price, whereas the publisher only allowed thirteen copies at the price of twelve. Now I cannot believe that Conal bought thirteen: neither of us could afford such extravagances 35 years ago. Nor is it any more credible that Henry & Co. sold enough to involve two successive orders to the binders. Besides, I never saw or heard of any blue copies.

147

Consequently, though I am actually writing these words in a blue copy I deny its existence, and reject Conal's yarn as incompatible with the evidence of the author, who surely ought to know more about it.

As to Conal's estimate of £50 as its value, it is an insult to the book market. It is quite the rarest of my published first editions and has never been reprinted, the later versions of the play being revised into something quite different, and the preface and appendices remaining peculiar to this edition, not to mention that the mysterious blue cover stamps this copy as a sort of literary ghost. Judging by the latest lunacies of the collectors of such curiosities I should suggest a reserve price of fifty millions as nearer the mark. The printing, which I designed myself, is alone well worth the money; and the paper is of the best. William Morris had taught me to be particular about such things.

The purchaser will have the satisfaction of knowing that the Royal Literary Fund will use the money to tide many a member of our ruthlessly sweated and—even at that—heartbreakingly precarious profession over those spells of starvation which are inevitable in a country where benefit of clergy has been abolished as a medieval superstition, and replaced by something not unlike contempt, in spite of the awe inspired by best sellers as such.

G. Bernard Shaw

To MRS PATRICK CAMPBELL

4 Whitehall Court S W 1

[A/37; X/160.e]   20th June 1929

[Bridget Guinness (1871–1931), whose financier husband was chairman of the British and Foreign Travel Trust Ltd., was one of Stella's socialite friends and benefactors. George was Stella Campbell's second husband, George Cornwallis-West, who had abandoned her ten years earlier. Mrs Campbell had scored a "come-back" success in May in G. B. Stern's play *The Matriarch*, at the Royalty Theatre, where it ran for several months.]

... Bridget must not talk too much. There is of course nothing [in the Interlude] that could give any clue to the public—above all to the Press. It can be a secret between us.

As if *I* did not know better than anyone what may or may not be done, and exactly how to do it! The presumption of these infinitesimals!

I have just had a talk with George! He is in love again: not this time with the lady whose fortune vanishes with her marriage, but with a new flame equally opulent, but unconditionally so. He wants to marry her, naturally; for he is living precariously by his pen. As under present circumstances you will have to support him if his pen fails him (such is our quaint law) you might turn over in your mind the advisability of escaping this responsibility by making him happy and at the same time placing him in a strong financial position. I take it that you are prosperous at present; but he isn't; and the *status quo* is so ridiculous that I cannot believe it will last.

However, it's no business of mine. As you know, I never meddle in other people's private affairs, being a model of delicacy and gentlemanly feeling.

Still, there's your future. The Matriarch won't run forever. Forgive me. Not another word—I promise.

I should read that scene to Bridget if I could trust her not to hide you behind the curtains. Though, after all, why shouldn't she?

Goodnight
GBS

To MRS PATRICK CAMPBELL

[A/37; X/160.e]

4 Whitchall Court SW1
27th June 1929

["How can it be a 'secret' between us," Mrs Campbell asked on 25th June, "when Edith Evans told me she was playing *me*? It is unkind of you not to keep your promise to read this play, or to send it to me. A husband cheats—a friend tricks—and the comic thing is human dignity" (*Bernard Shaw and Mrs. Patrick Campbell: Their Correspondence*, 1952).

George Cornwallis-West's desertion of her had been a painful and humiliating experience for Stella Campbell, and it was doubly damnable, by her lights, that Shaw should exploit the circumstance in a play and simultaneously accept George's account of the marriage and take his part in a divorce effort. In passages deleted from correspondence of this period by the editor Alan Dent at the insistence of Mrs Campbell's daughter, she now revealed to Shaw details of her marriage that she previously had withheld. George, she insisted, had not abandoned her because she had made life miserable for him, as he caddishly claimed, but because he was being pressed for repayment of a bank loan borrowed on false security and seeking a wealthier woman than the impecunious Stella to help him out of his troubles. She had paid debts of his to the tune of £4500, by her reckoning, and she was determined to have full repayment before she would allow him his freedom. (For much of the deleted matter in Mrs Campbell's letters, see Margot Peters's article, "Shaw vs. Stella: The battle of 'The Apple Cart,'" *Harvard Magazine, Discovery* supplement, March–April 1984.)

In a passage expunged from her 25th June letter, Mrs Campbell admonished Shaw not to believe everything Cornwallis-West said.]

My dear Stella

I don't. I don't believe anything any man says. But the account of the breaking-off of the old business was circumstantial enough to sound convincing; and the anxiety as to whether the new would wait for him if he could not grasp it without unreasonable delay was, if not genuine, very well acted for an amateur.

In Russia people *must* divorce those they don't live with, and *must* marry those they do live with. I don't expect the Labor Government to Russianize our institutions to that extent; but I do think it possible that some measure of relief for the unhappy ones who are in G's situation and his wife's may be passed when the marriage laws are next touched. Chains breed hatred. Are you quite sure you will never want to marry again? And do you like being in such a situation that no man dare approach you lest some private detective should make a co-respondent of him. Have you thought it all out?

Edith guessed, of course. DD knows; Bridget knows; Nancy [Astor] knows; perhaps half a dozen others know (or think they know; for only you and I will ever know); but the Press must not get hold of it. The lady in Warsaw [Marja Przybylko-Potocka] got stage fright and forgot her lines, making a mess of it, as far as I can ascertain, on the first night. It puzzled the audience considerably.

I ought to know whether you will like it or not; but I don't.

Do you go to America with the Matriarch? Presumably Shubert included you in his bargain.

First rehearsal of the Apple Cart [for Malvern] on Monday. I have to read it to them: a killing job, and I am so old.

GBS

To GEORGE CORNWALLIS-WEST

4 Whitehall Court SW1

[A/2; X/358]   27th June 1929

Dear G. C-W.

I mentioned the matter in the course of a reply to a letter about other things, stressing the precariousness of the literary profession and the legal obligation on the wives of literary men to support them. This ingenious inversion of the risks of the situation elicits the unruffled remark "You must not believe all that George says," and nothing more. However, the facts have their own weight and will no doubt sink in by themselves.

ever

G.B.S.

To MRS PATRICK CAMPBELL

4 Whitehall Court SW1

[A/37; X/160.e]   11th July 1929

[Perceiving belatedly that his failure to read the play to Mrs Campbell had only served to exacerbate the situation and magnify her doubts, Shaw cancelled an urgent appointment at the London School of Economics on the 11th to hurry round to Pont Street. Stella listened stolidly as he read, until the moment when Orinthia offers, as a trump card in her effort to win King Magnus from his dowdy wife, her ability to give him "beautiful, wonderful children." Had he, she asks, "ever seen a lovelier boy than my Basil?" Her impassivity quickly changed to outrage as Magnus responded, "Basil is a very good-looking young man, but he has the morals of a tramp." Though Shaw undoubtedly was right, it is incredible that he could have been so insensible to the passionate, almost incestuous love Stella Campbell bore for her "Beloved One," who, despite his irresponsibility and self-conceit, his gambling and philandering, had been lavishly indulged even when it meant privation for his mother and sister. Shaw had besmirched Beo's memory, for which Stella would never forgive him, no matter how much fence-mending he attempted that same evening.]

Stella

When it comes to the point I can't take Beo out: it's like killing him over again. Do you mind if it runs this way?

> ORINTHIA. I can give you beautiful, wonderful children: have you ever seen a lovelier boy than my Basil?
> MAGNUS. Your children are beautiful; but they are fairy children; and I have several very real ones already. A divorce would not sweep them out of the way of the fairies.

I did not say that he had the morals of a tramp in mere callousness, but because long before my immortal play is dead people will have come to think that tramp morals were the only decent ones in the XIX century.

And to make it *our* immortal play I have changed "Orinthia: It is

151

out of the question: your dream of being queen must remain a dream" to "Orinthia: We are only two children at play; and you must be content to be my queen in fairyland."

Does that cure the soreness at your heart? It makes mine feel much better.

GBS

To MRS PATRICK CAMPBELL

Ayot St Lawrence. Welwyn
[A/37; X/160.e]   12th July 1929

["You hit below the belt when you juggle with gossip picked up about my dead son," Mrs Campbell replied; "it damns you as nothing else can" (Peters, *Harvard Magazine*). Beo's crushing debt, Shaw had learned from her earlier, was £10,000, borrowed from Lord Savile for a theatrical venture and lost to a couple of con men. Mrs Campbell had managed to repay the sum. *Lady Patricia* was a play by Rudolf Besier in which she had appeared at the Haymarket in 1911. At the foot of Stella's letter of the 12th, which he was answering, Shaw at some time pencilled, "Think of what it is for a boy to have such a mother!" (Peters, *Harvard Magazine*).]

Dearest Stella

Fret not thyself because of evildoers. Here are some of the bare facts which are magnifying themselves to torment you. Since the flight of George I have seen him exactly three times at long intervals. First, accidentally at the theatre for five minutes between the acts, when he was evidently relieved to find me as friendly as usual. Second, also accidentally, on the golf links at Sandwich, where I was with Lady Astor. Third, by appointment on your business at his invitation at his house, when he told me what I told you. Add to that a correspondence about a play which I persuaded him was useless to Gladys Cooper or anyone else, and which told me nothing about you which I did not know; and you have the whole history of my relations with him since Tedworth Square. He may be the most abandoned reincarnation of [Thackeray's] Barry Lyndon on earth for all I know; but as you keep all the blarney he ever wrote to you, and you do not seem to mind being his wife, I cannot help suspecting that he is just George and nobody else.

Now as to Beo. I have never gossiped about him, nor ever learnt one single fact concerning him beyond what I saw for myself, and what I was told by his Mother of Sorrows when the young scamp threw on her a crushing debt, which she was in no way bound to accept, under utterly conscienceless circumstances. Well, for her sake I will let him go as a beautiful child; but he doesn't deserve it. Still, as he suffered for other people's sins, the balance of justice is struck.

There are no personalities in the narrower sense in the scene. Orinthia's husbands are not Patrick or George: they are items in the many millions of men and women who, seduced by a splendor that dazzles them, bite off more than they can digest. The story is as old as Jupiter and Semele. Do you not know that though you are marvellous, as all the flappers say, you are gey ill to live with: indeed impossible. You cannot have it both ways. I have made a superb picture of you, God forgive me! and you must play the game.

But you must also be as discreet as human nature allows. You talked in a restaurant; and your celebrated voice carried as far as Warsaw, where I had to choke off a story about the name in the English version being Stella, and Orinthia being you, and Heaven knows what.

Do not think of the scene as having been projected into a vacuum. We must not be handed down to history by ignoble gossip and venomous slander. The world may very well laugh at us; but it had better have splendid fun than dirty fun. Our parts are fine parts; and if you really prefer Lady Patricia to Orinthia you deserve to be whipped at the cart's tail from Sloane Square to Drury Lane.

As to your postscript [Mrs Campbell had written: "As you sat in my room yesterday and read to me—I suddenly knew you—saw you"], could I help it? Perhaps I should not have come; but how else could you have heard the scene? I held off long enough, knowing well enough that an old ruffian of 73 cannot shelter himself in a mist of illusion. But my vanity prevailed; for even the wreck of G.B.S. must be more interesting than an average coaling schooner in full sail. I'll send you a copy of the play presently, if I may. In fact I will whether you like it or not. The test will be how you take it.

GBS

To V. O. PLENAZÁR

[E/78]

[Ayot St Lawrence. Welwyn]
15th July 1929
[Plenazár was a Hungarian admirer, distressed by a report reprinted from a London newspaper that Shaw had stated he married for money. "[W]e need men & women of great vision, [of] spiritual insight," he insisted, "who

will sacrifice & live in poverty if need be, in order that their genius may unfold and lead the present day starved & sinned against youth, to great heights." Shaw's reply was written at the foot of the letter.]

What a tiresome idiot you are! Can you not live your life according to circumstances and the nature of things instead of attempting to realize ideals? Have you never read Ibsen on that subject? Life is an adventure, not the compounding of a prescription. Money and sex have their place in life with all the other things. A man who marries for money is a fool if he has any other means of subsistence. So is a woman. For either, it is simple prostitution; but women very often have to make money, or the capacity for making it, the determining factor in their choice of a husband. If they had property they would either not marry or marry somebody else. This also happens to men, but less often, as men are still the economically self-sufficient sex. "Marrying for money" is a vulgar and silly expression, as marrying for children, for comfort, for company, for rank, for sexual intercourse, and for love, are all contingent to some extent on money except as between tramps who have nothing to gain by marrying at all.

Any artificial principle of living which reduces those who practise it to asking "What is the use of anything?" is evidently destructive of vitality. If people dont realize your ideals the fault is not in them but in your ideals. Spend your life, if you like, in trying to change people's minds; but dont waste your time in complaining that they are not already changed to suit your fancy.

To the British Post Office the name G.B.Shaw means nothing. Bernard is the trade mark; and if you had been intelligent enough to use it (you really *are* an idiot) your letter would have reached me.

G. Bernard Shaw

To O. A. FORSYTH-MAJOR

[H/102]   4 Whitehall Court SW1
                                                                16th July 1929

[Odo Alexander Forsyth-Major (1884–1977), a former army officer, was the author of *Elements of Tactics* (1916) and a vast number of unpublished novels and plays. Shaw, as on numerous other occasions, drafted a reply on the sender's letter for Blanche Patch to recast in the third person and post as her own response. Shaw's interest in Oliver Cromwell as a play subject may be traced as early as the autumn of 1902, when he jotted down in the Henry

Sweet system of shorthand he was then practising: "Cromwell. The two points with which he horrifies the chaplain are first that he declares that it is not God who will call him to account, but he Cromwell who will call God to account; and second that he asks what Jesus Christ would have done, had he, like Cromwell (or Mahomet), become a ruler and a captain" (Burgunder Collection, Cornell University: transliteration by M. K. C. MacMahon).

In 1904, responding to a report in the American press that he was writing a Cromwell play for Arnold Daly, Shaw self-drafted an interview (*Daily Mail*, 30th August) in which he reported that though he had contemplated a short play with Cromwell as subject, to be a curtain-raiser to his Napoleon play *The Man of Destiny*, he had instead composed *How He Lied to Her Husband*. There was, said Shaw, "only one possible Cromwell drama; and that is a single scene, in which Oliver, after his experiment in trying to govern England on reasonable terms instead of duping it by State idols and melodramatic humbug, receives a friendly visit from the ghost of Charles the Martyr, and owns his failure. I shall write that some day . . . when I have a week to spare." When John Drinkwater anticipated him with a Cromwell play (1923) Shaw abandoned the subject. Yet, in 1927, he announced in Italy (*The Observer*, 28th August) he was "at work on a historic drama, entitled 'Oliver Cromwell,' in which I shall not speak badly of England." The play was not written.]

Dear Sir

Mr Bernard Shaw desires me to say that the only dramatic value he feels in Cromwell is the tragi-comedy of his being forced, step by step, from the democratic-theocratic convictions with which he began to the assumption of precisely the attitude of irresponsible (save to God) autocracy for which he executed Charles. Mr Shaw once planned a short play to consist of a visit from Charles's ghost to Cromwell the night before his death to discuss this matter; but he never carried it out.

> yours faithfully
> Blanche Patch
> Secretary

To MRS PATRICK CAMPBELL

[E.u/6; X/160]

[Ayot St Lawrence. Welwyn]
[Undated: *c.* 23rd July 1929]

["Tear it up," Stella Campbell wrote on the 22nd July, "and re-write it with every scrap of the mischievous vulgarian omitted, and all suburban backchat against Charlotte and suggested harlotry against me, and the inference of your own superiority wiped out. .... Please do as I say—you will feel strangely relieved" (*Bernard Shaw and Mrs. Patrick Campbell: Their Correspondence*, 1952). Shaw's reply was written on Mrs Campbell's letter, which he returned to her.]

I don't feel it to be a bit wrong. It plays magnificently. Orinthia never loses her distinction and beauty even when she rolls on the floor. If she did I would amputate her without a moments hesitation, and be ashamed of her. But I'm not. So stand she shall to all eternity. Besides Orinthia is not a portrait: she is a study for which you sat as a model in bits only—though the magnificence of the picture is due to you. And again I am an artist and as such utterly unscrupulous when I find my model—or rather when she finds me.

To MRS PATRICK CAMPBELL

[A/37; X/160.e]

Ayot St Lawrence. Welwyn
28th July 1929

Belovedest

How troublesome you are!

Very well: he shall not say he would rather be in hell: I have changed it to "he said no man could call his soul his own in the same house with you." I admit it is an improvement; for it is a serious statement: the other was obviously only an expletive which any man might use in a fit of temper after a tiff. I did not know that George had used it: the phrase he wrote to me was much more poignant. Stella, Stella, don't you KNOW that you are so exacting, so exciting, so absorbing, so incessant that only a wooden Highlander from a tobacconist's shop could bear the enormous strain of living with you? Can you blame your runaway husbands? Poor Patrick flying to South Africa for sleep (you told me you had kept him ecstatically awake for years) and finding it there from a Boer bullet, or George pretending to fly from the police (so you now tell me): dare you pretend that Orinthia was Candida?— that I have lied?

When I suggest that you are an Orinthia you repudiate the likeness as an outrage. When I introduce any detail that differentiates her from you, you want me to alter it and make the portrait complete and recognizable. However, I shall now be able to say that you revised it yourself, and dictated some of the best bits.

Of course we are a pair of mountebanks; but why, oh why do you get nothing out of me, though I get everything out of you? Mrs Hesione Hushabye in Heartbreak House, the Serpent in Methuselah, whom I always hear speaking with your voice, and Orinthia: all you, to say nothing of Eliza, who was only a joke. You are the Vamp and I the victim; yet it is I who suck your blood and fatten on it whilst you lose everything!

It is ridiculous! There's something wrong somewhere.

GBS

To G. W. BISHOP

[H/9; X/359]

Malvern Hotel. Malvern
4th September 1929

[George W. Bishop (1886–1965) was a special correspondent for *The Observer* and a free-lance journalist. *The Apple Cart* had its first English performance at Malvern on 19th August, inaugurating the new Festival. A month later it was transferred to the Queen's Theatre, London, with only one minor change of cast. Cedric Hardwicke was the Magnus, Edith Evans the Orinthia. Despite much critical carping both at Malvern and in London, the play had a successful run of 238 performances, and has grown in reputation with each successive production down to the present day.]

Dear Bishop

I forgot to say, in the course of our conversation yesterday, that the main oversight in the criticisms of The Apple Cart is the failure to grasp the significance of the fact that the king wins, not *qua* king, but *qua* potential commoner. The tearing up of the ultimatum is almost a defeat for him. It is certainly a defeat for Lysistrata, whose depression the king shares when the shouting is over.

The critics have also missed the point of Boanerges's refusal to listen to a word against the Democracy which he has himself ridiculed as an instrument of popular government. The Strong Man is a democrat because Democracy places power within his reach. As Magnus expressly says, Democracy has destroyed responsible government and gives the power to (as Bunyan put it) "him that can get it." "Yourself, sir, for instance?" says Lysistrata. "I think I am in the running" replies the king. But he thinks he is in the running as Able Man, not as monarch. Only once in the whole play does Magnus assume royal authority; and that is when he cries "Orinthia: I command you." And both Orinthia and the audience laugh him to scorn.

No serious student of how monarchy and democracy actually work will demur to my handling of them. . . .

In haste
G.B.S.

To EDWARD GORDON CRAIG

Malvern Hotel. Malvern
7th September 1929

[H/3]

[Elbridge Adams had paid Edith Craig £3000 a few months earlier for the Shaw letters in her possession; there were still, however, some letters written in Ellen Terry's late years that were owned by her fourth and last husband James Carew. Edy's lesbian lover Christopher St John would eventually edit the correspondence. *Nance Oldfield* was a one-act comedy by Charles Reade revived at the Lyceum by Irving in 1891. *The Mask*, founded by Craig in Florence (1908), was a theatre arts journal; its April 1926 issue contained "The Colossus Speaks: Under This Heading Mr. Bernard Shaw Addresses An Open Letter to Mr. Gordon Craig." August Kotzebue's play *The Stranger*, adapted by Benjamin Thompson, was first performed at Drury Lane in 1798 with Mrs Siddons and John Philip Kemble; it was frequently revived in the nineteenth century.

Shaw had used the phrase "four boards and a passion" earlier in a review of T.E.Pemberton's *John Hare, Comedian*, in the *Saturday Review*, 21st December 1895. The square bracketed words in the letter were partially obliterated by the rusting of metal fasteners. Giambattista Piranesi (1720–78) was an Italian architect and pictorial painter. Craig had designed settings for the 1906 Berlin production of *Cæsar and Cleopatra* that were rejected by Max Reinhardt as unsatisfactory. Charles Ricketts did the designs for a few of Shaw's plays, most notably the sets and costumes for *Saint Joan* (London, 1924). Paul Shelving (1889–1968), principal designer for the Birmingham Repertory Company, is noted for his designs for *Back to Methuselah* (1923). He also did *The Apple Cart*. Craig had fathered two of Isadora Duncan's children.]

Dear Gordon Craig

Since I wrote to you the situation has changed. Edy has sold my letters for £3,000. It is therefore no longer possible to pretend that we are under any pecuniary pressure to publish the letters.

But as we have let them go out of our hands it is pretty certain that they will be published some day, and that they will be misunderstood unless I leave on record some elucidation of them. I have therefore completed the preface which I began when I was contemplating their publication in a collector's edition for the benefit of the executors.

I have shewn it to Edy and to Christopher, and to two extraordinary people: Lawrence of Arabia and Dame Laurentia, the Prioress of the convent here at Stanbury. Lawrence and Dame Laurentia said "There is a legend of lovability about Ellen: why disturb it?" But Christopher and Edy said "Damn the legend! this is the truth about her, which is finer than any mushy legend: nobody has done her justice before." I feel that all four are right, and that the solution is to send Ellen's letters, which are mine, to the British Museum (say) with a copy of the preface to be placed with them when they are put into the catalogue at some future date. The copyright in Ellen's letters is the property of the executors, though the material papers belong to me.

A private edition of the whole correspondence with the preface is feasible, as we have copies of all the letters except sixteen which Carew has. But now that the money consideration no longer presses I do not see why we should do violence to our instinctive repugnance to any sort of publicity until we have all passed into history—or out of it.

I want you, however, to read the preface very carefully. Edy tells me that you are at work on a memoir of Irving with incidental references to me. Now your difficulty at present is that your knowledge of the theatre jumps over a void between the eighteenth century, which you know by study, and the time when you played the boy in Nance Oldfield at the Lyceum. And, as I found out from something you wrote in The Mask, you do realize that I am not only a generation older than you in years, but in some points a full century older in personal theatrical experience; for Dublin in my boyhood was still in the eighteenth—almost in the seventeenth—century. You think I learnt my technique from an old actor named Irving, as you did. But to me Irving was a young upstart trying his hand at Barry Sullivan parts and making (at first) an appalling mess of them. The generation of playgoers which adored Henry's Hamlet and felt no deficiency in his Richelieu had never seen big acting, as Macready was too long dead, and Sullivan, after the fearful shock of having lost eight hundred pounds in three months at a little theatre in Holborn where he played The Stranger (because his suicide by poison in that gloomy play was a heartrending *tour de force* of acting) cast London out and was known only to the provinces. That was your position too. To get a vivid notion of mine, try to suppose that when you were twenty you had never seen Irving except once in a modern character part in an ordinary fashionable west-end play, and that your notions of great acting were founded on Chaliapine, and of technique on Coquelin.

Now, if you have got reoriented so far, read the preface. It will, I think, help you to understand how you, a pictorial artist with an inherited talent for acting by which you set no store, found yourself mysteriously baffled by a revival of dramatic [art] which was determined to smash the pictorial stage and go back to [four] boards and a passion, with decoration (not picture) kept in ruthless subordination to continuity and concentration of dramatic action. You will see by the correspondence (which you should read) that I wanted you as an actor, and not as the heir of your father [Edward Godwin], who was a very Victorian Piranesi. Long years after, Granville-Barker outraged you by wanting you, with my full concurrence, to act as Constantine in The Madras House instead of to Piranesify that sordid building. I forced you on the Berlin people to produce Caesar & Cleopatra there because it was full of pictures that would have delighted your father; but when you let me down, like the young idiot you then were, I saw that you cared nothing about the drama, and could not feel your art in dramatic terms. Your excuses were the excuses a tramp makes for not accepting a job; but that would not have elicited anything worse than a laugh from me if I had not understood what you did not understand yourself: that you were trying to make a picture frame of the proscenium, to replace actors by figures, and drive the dramatic poet out of the theatre. And as I was doing precisely the reverse, and the Zeitgeist carried me to success, you felt that I was the arch enemy.

So I was; but it is a pity. No author alive has given more opportunities to the theatre atmospheresuggester than I. Ricketts and Paul Shelving have found in my plays a canvas for their triumphs. I loved their art; and they loved mine: we instinctively helped one another out. But you have been driven to plough a lonely furrow in an art in which that can be done: the art of literature in the form of fascinating gossip illustrated with irrelevant marginal fancy sketches. Your mother threw herself away on your father, on Irving, on everybody who was selfish enough to sacrifice her; but you have thrown yourself away on yourself, with what satisfaction to yourself you best know.

I say all this to stimulate you to make a really interesting thing of that book, which must not be a life of Irving, of whom you can never know much that is worth recording because you were not acting-struck and he was nothing else, but, obviously, a life of Edward Gordon Craig, Teddy the Tramp, Ellen's spoilt child, champion Impostor,

Taugenichts [ne'er-do-well], Vaurien [rogue], Man who Vamped Isadora, and finally the Spoilt Child of Europe who took in everybody except the

enemy who does not reciprocate
your dislike
—if you really dislike him—

G.B.S.

To EDWARD GORDON CRAIG

Ayot St Lawrence. Welwyn
15th September 1929

[C.u/3]

[Craig's reply of 12th September was ultra-polite—and venomous. His book on Irving, already finished, contained virtually nothing of Irving's relations with Shaw, he wrote, since these were virtually non-existent and of little consequence, &c. It was typical of Shaw, he concluded, that in spite of his vaunted powers of observation, he failed to take cognizance of the obvious. Craig's typewritten letter (in the Humanities Research Center, University of Texas) finishes off with an elaborately devised, ostentatious signature. Whether designedly or not, Shaw's holograph postcard response is unsigned, though his initials subsequently were inserted by another hand.]

Yes, yes: very dainty fencing; and I acknowledge all the hits; but the practical question—my only excuse for intruding—is not disposed of by a jeu d'esprit with a beautiful signature. Elbridge Adams now says that he has bought all the outstanding letters from Carew for £400. Ellen's letters are mine materially, and yours—or the executors'—as to copyright. My letters are Adams's (to sell in the course of his business) materially, and mine as to copyright. Fifty years after my death the copyright will no longer exist and the actual letters will be accessible to all the literary ghouls. As ultimate publication seems therefore inevitable, it might be advisable ten years (say) after my or my wife's death to publish the whole correspondence with my preface and thereby realize a considerable sum for Ellen's possibly needy descendants. If you have any news on the subject speak now or be for ever silent. I cannot without *real* incivility ignore you in the matter, however unwelcome my interference may be.

The least you can do is to send me a copy of your book. If you don't, I'll buy it and read it all the same.

[G.B.S.]

To ELBRIDGE L. ADAMS

4 Whitehall Court SW1
[H/3]   17th September 1929

[Raymond Savage (1888–1964) was a London literary agent.]

Dear Mr Elbridge Adams

I am sorry you have been disappointed in the matter of the Terry letters. You are not the only victim; but when I thought that I should have to publish them for the sake of the executors, and wrote a preface of ten thousand words for the volume (which will, I hope[,] convince you that I was not trifling with the business) I had you in view as the publisher; for I did not then understand the inaction of Mr Gabriel Wells, who now explains that he was waiting for me to give him the signal under the impression that this was what had been arranged between us.

However, that does not matter now; for I shall not allow my letters to be published. You have yourself made it impossible for me to do so by paying the executors £3000 for them. How could I pretend after this that the executors are in any such need of money as would justify me in consenting to the publication? I never heard of the transaction until it was completed. Mr Raymond Savage has always been scrupulously careful to disclaim being my agent. He acted for Miss Craig, and could not without a breach of confidence tell me what he was doing for her. It was perhaps natural for you to assume that I was *au courant* with all that was passing; but I assure you that the news of the £3000 came to me as a complete surprise. Had I been consulted about it I should at once have warned you that it would alter the whole complexion of the affair.

As my part of the correspondence has now gone out of my hands it will possibly be published someday when the copyright expires. If you sell it as a whole to a *bona fide* collector or public library, and not to a dealer, I might—though I must not pledge myself—throw in as a makeweight a proof of the scrapped preface. I do not see that I can do any more; and even that, as you can well understand, would depend very much on whether the purchaser of the letters was the right sort of person or institution.

I quite see that you must feel that my withdrawal was hardly in the spirit of our friendly conversations; and I reproach myself for not having made it clear to you that the publication we were discussing, and to which I was reconciled only by my desire to do Miss Craig a substantial service, was not desired by me. The motive for that being removed, nothing remained but the possibility of making some money for myself out of the correspondence, a thing which nothing could induce me to contemplate. Under the circumstances I hope you will forgive me and that you will be able to dispose of the letters without loss. I never doubted your own pecuniary disinterestedness in the matter.

faithfully
G. Bernard Shaw

To KATHLEEN HILTON YOUNG

[C/1]

Ayot St Lawrence. Welwyn
24th September 1929

. . . I havn't a moment just now. I have had to bind myself to finish a job within six months (a Collected Edition) which I have kept hanging up since 1921; and the result is utter preoccupation and distraction.

GBS

To ROBERT S. YOUNG

[H/9; X/360]

4 Whitehall Court SW1
19th October 1929

[The forthcoming National Theatre Conference (which Shaw did not attend, though he sent a long message to be read) in London on 25th November had generated much press interest. Young was producer of the Northampton Repertory Co.]

Dear Mr Young

The nation does not care tuppence about a National Theatre. Politics, sport, religion, hospitals, education, and even to a very limited extent music and painting are popular enough to force themselves on Governments, but the theatre, no. For 20 years past the Shakespear Memorial Theatre has been begging for subscriptions by every known method of mendicity, and with the support of the most distinguished names; and its efforts have added practically nothing to the sum of £70,000 with which the late Sir Carl Meyer, a native of Hamburg, attempted to start a movement. But the movement does not move, and never has moved. I cannot honestly advise you to put your shoulder to it: you will be baffled by the national cold shoulder.

There is nothing to be done but wait until the £70,000 accumulates in the course of 50 years or so to a sum sufficient to build a theatre. Meanwhile the Stratford theatre must fill the place of a national theatre as best it can. When it is completed it will owe its existence to American money and heroworship of Shakespear.

faithfully
G. Bernard Shaw

To HILDA MATHESON

4 Whitehall Court SW1
[H/99]   29th October 1929

[Hilda Matheson (1888–1940), former political secretary to Nancy Astor, was the B.B.C.'s first director of talks; she later became director of the Joint Broadcasting Committee for recorded foreign broadcasts. Shaw had spoken on "Democracy," the third in a series of "Points of View" broadcasts, on 14th October. The text was incorporated into the preface to *The Apple Cart*, published in December 1930. *Captain Brassbound's Conversion* was broadcast on 16th December, repeated live on the 19th, produced by Howard Rose. The cast included Gertrude Kingston as Lady Cicely, Baliol Holloway as Brassbound, A. Scott Gatty as Hallam, and Charles Farrell (not the Hollywood actor) as Captain Kearney.]

Dear Miss Matheson

I had rather not make the broadcast a commercial transaction. I have never accepted payment for my work as a political speaker; and the value to me of being able to affirm this without qualification of any kind, and of calling the tune as well as playing it, is so great that it would need much more than a hundred guineas to induce me to forfeit it. I therefore return the cheque with my best thanks to the B.B.C.

As to the broadcast of Brassbound, its infamy was such that I hereby solemnly renounce, curse, and excommunicate everybody who had a hand in it. Apart from the artistic side of the affair the selection of 9.25 as the hour for raising the curtain, thus deferring the end until midnight, would have been a studied insult if any such thing as study had entered into the wretched business. The way the performers had to gabble through their parts was beyond description. Brassbound, in his highest Restoration Comedy soprano, set a pitch and a pace which

164

probably convinced the listeners-in (before they went to bed towards the end of the second act) that he was the heroine. Lady Cicely's basso profundo provided the necessary contrast and made it clear that she was the pirate. Everything that could be done to make the characters indistinguishable from oneanother, and the dialogue unintelligible, was done and done thoroughly. The cockney had evidently been born a thousand miles from Bow Bells, and had remained there until he came to Savoy Hill. The American captain's part was a series of surprises to him: he plunged into his sentences without the least notion of how they were going to end. If the producer has not already been shot, I will pay for the cartridges. The second time was not quite so bad: the hour was a reasonable one; and there were signs that after six more rehearsals the speakers would have begun to guess what on earth the whole thing was about; but the cast was a bundle of misfits; and I doubt whether anyone who listened will ever be induced by love or money to give me another trial.

I note that you declare you found it very interesting. How can you have the cheek——!

faithfully
G.B.S.

To G. S. VIERECK

[H/1]

4 Whitehall Court S W 1
6th December 1929

[Viereck had published another of his interviews, in the *New York American* on 20th October, reprinted on 10th November in the *Sunday Express*. Shaw published a disavowal of the interview in the latter paper on 17th November in spite of the fact that it had illustrated the article with a facsimile of Shaw's revision in a portion of the manuscript.]

My dear Viereck

There is only one authentic sentence in the interview; and that is "I wont be interviewed." How would you like to find in the papers G.S.V's views on love, literature, politics, art etc etc, by G.B.S.? Would you not protest that you made your living by expressing your views for yourself and not by imparting them to me for grotesque misrepresentation? You think you understand what I say; but you never do: you simply report some notion of your own which is suggested by the subjects I mention. You know nothing about music; and when I tell you something that Einstein said about Mozart you turn it into utter nonsense by substituting Beethoven for Mozart. In the case of Einstein you have the excuse that as he is not a professional journalist like myself you are doing for him something that he cannot do for himself. In my case, or in that of any writer, you have no excuse at all for giving anything more than simply news which it may be convenient to have published at my own express request. But the sort of thing you are doing now, in violation of my repeated injunctions to the contrary, and in spite of the trouble you made before by the remarks you attributed to me about the British Navy, is quite out of order. I am forced to disclaim it. I have done so in terms far more considerate than you deserve; but I have had to do it decisively.

So, no more interviews.

faithfully
G. Bernard Shaw

To SIEGFRIED TREBITSCH

Ayot St Lawrence. Welwyn
31st January [December] 1929

[C/5; X/341]

[The card, misdated, is postmarked 31st December. Shaw had been studying photos and reviews of the Max Reinhardt production of *The Apple Cart* (*Der Kaiser von Amerika*), which was first performed at the Deutsches Theater, Berlin, on 19th October, with Werner Krauss as Magnus and Maria Bard as Orinthia. A correspondent for *The Times* reported on 22nd October, "It delighted the audience and confuses the critics ... One distinguished critic says gloomily, 'Those who have walked with Shaw through half a century must take leave of him here.'" Puzzled by the hostile German critical reaction, Shaw made inquiries and soon ascertained that the text had been "barbarously cut," that several dozen non-Shavian speeches had been inserted, and that "a lot of scandalous business" had been introduced. The principal informant was Floryan Sobieniowski, which Shaw did not reveal to Trebitsch when he requested him on 29th November to tell their agent Samuel Fischer that "Reinhardt must be struck off his list of managers eligible for contracts with me. We need not quarrel with Reinhardt about it: no doubt he sincerely believes that his changes are improvements, and that the King's speech about the orbits of the stars, which is the top note of the serious side of the scene, is made interesting by the two nibbling the same stick of chocolate. But that is not how I want my plays handled; and he will not get a chance of doing it again if I can help it." He enclosed a letter for the press that "makes it clear that R's Apple Cart is not my Apple Cart" (A/5; X/341)]

The moment I saw that sublime "Bist du allein?" "Ja-a-a-a-a-!" rideau très lent, spotlight on King, orchestra plays Einsamkeit music, I knew what that double-distilled quintessence of a Schafskopf was doing with my play. That motif is completely exhausted in the first act; and the recurrence to it at the end is the blunder of an idiot who thinks he knows the author's business better than the author. But to miss the echo of the scene with Orinthia, the king going like a lamb with his unpretentious wife after fighting like a lion with the goddess—the most popular stroke in the whole play with the wives who drag their husbands to the theatre (men always want to stay at home) was a miracle of ignorant maladresse, of utter incapacity for handling serious work or even of understanding the public taste. It has been all a stupid blunder: there was the same bad press here, the same reasons and the same fools to be trampled on. Do you think *I* don't know? Tell Tina that unless she forgives me at once I will write you such letters as will drive you to murder Max and then commit suicide.

G.B.S.

To HUNTLY CARTER

4 Whitehall Court S W 1

[X/361]   1st January 1930

[Huntly Carter (d. 1942), writer and journalist, was the editor of a series of symposia surveys of sociological and cultural movements. For the survey *The New Spirit in the Cinema* (1930), Carter had solicited Shaw for an opinion on the cinema as an "Art Form," posing three questions: (1) "In your opinion should the Cinema fulfil a social function for the community?" (2) "Do you know of any particular form that would raise the level of interpretative power and with it the level of achievement?" (3) "If an 'Art Form,' do you mean a form determined by the aesthetic of technique, or by a natural aesthetic?"]

[Dear Mr Carter]

The question has no meaning for me, as art is to me only a method of intelligible or sensible expression, and art forms are processes to be carried out by instruments under the control of the artist. Art for art's sake is rather like fox hunting or skating, which have no sense except as ways of procuring food or moving from place to place, but are continued for fun by people who don't eat foxes and who, after hours of skating, take off their skates at the spot where they put them on, without having travelled in the meantime further than the opposite side of the pond.

Drama is a method of re-arranging the higgledy-piggledy happenings of actual life in such a way as to make them intelligible and thinkable. Its forms, processes and instruments include the stage, the screen, the camera, the microphone, the actor and all the other things by which the final effect desired is wrought on the senses of the audience. There is nothing new in the art of drama; but a cinema is a new art form like a new instrument added to the orchestra or a new verse form, like that in [Robert] Bridges' "Testament of Beauty." It is available, of course, for scientific demonstration also, as when it makes the month's growth of a pea visible within a few seconds.

Also it is practiced for fun like hunting. In the palmy days of acting, people found the declamation of an actor so curious and agreeable that they would crowd to hear him ranting through plays in which there was less sense than there is meat in fox.

In short, I don't quite see why you should boggle at the description of the cinema as an art form. All I can do is to make my own view clear.

[faithfully
G. Bernard Shaw]

To H. A. SILVERMAN

[H/1; X/404.e]

[Ayot St Lawrence. Welwyn]
6th January 1930

[H. A. Silverman was director of extra-mural studies at University College, Leicester, where Dr Robert Fleming Rattray (1886–1967), Unitarian minister and principal of the college 1921–31, delivered a series of university extension lectures on Shaw. Having examined a published syllabus of the course of lectures, Shaw drafted a communication to Silverman headed "Notes on Dr Rattray's Syllabus"; the two principal statements to which Shaw addressed himself were that "G.B.S. cultivated apparent indifference and swagger" and "There is an Irish streak of cruelty in him." To be napped is a slang expression meaning to receive punishment.]

I never "cultivated" anything. I was a horribly shy and diffident young man, producing an impression of brazen impudence because, I suppose, the ability of which I was unconscious asserted itself through the disadvantages and the ignorances of which I was too conscious. . . .

I dont think [the latter statement] is true. Cashel Byron, when he said that he nearly killed his first opponent because he did not know his own strength, explained the savagery of some of my early criticisms. It is true that I was, and to some extent still am, very sensitive, but on the other hand I can stand up to, and even enjoy, hammerings that drive other men to fury or reduce them to tears; and I often fail to conceive how they can be hurt by blows that make me laugh when I nap them myself.

When, as a critic or debater, I *have* to inflict pain, I do it like a dentist, with great reluctance, and with all the anaesthesia I can produce. But note that as nothing is so maladroit as any show of sparing the victim's feelings I always hit as exultantly as I can, with an air of hitting as hard as I can. I have a horror of humiliating or discouraging people. I like my man to feel that he has had a good fight and been worthy of my steel, and not that I have been showing off my good taste at his expense. That is the line that leaves the least malice.

G.B.S.

PS—Only a keen and fairly erudite musician can deal with the artistic side of my career. I was quite well educated musically and graphically.

To C. H. NORMAN

4 Whitehall Court S W 1

[C/3; X/289.e] 9th January 1930

[Akbar (1542–1605) was Mogul emperor of India from 1556, an enlightened ruler, who tolerated the varying religions of his nation, instituted reforms, and developed trade.]

Private

Charles II had manners, tact, and a precise knowledge of the cards he had in his hand and how and when to play them. So had Henri Quatre. That is all that is claimed for the fictitious Magnus. But if you want examples of sovereigns holding by sheer superiority (for the purpose) you have Elizabeth most conspicuously, and several Antonine Cæsars and feudal kings, to say nothing of geniuses like Akbar, who, being abnormal, dont count.

In The A.C. the prime minister is as able as the king: his tantrums are just as effective as the king's urbanity; and he loses the odd trick, not because he is inferior in political adroitness, but simply because the king holds the ace of trumps.

As you say, democratic rule has never been established. The reason is that it is impossible, and Demos knows it too well to let the bourgeois idealists try it.

I am disgusted at the ease with which nice clothes and a pleasant address, with rank, imposes on everybody. My infernal old scoundrel of an inquisitor in St Joan got away with it like a cathedral canon; and now here are you swallowing my gentlemanly Magnus as a god! I'm surprised at you.

G.B.S.

To C. B. PURDOM

Ayot St Lawrence. Welwyn
[H/9]   12th January 1930

[Charles Benjamin Purdom (1883–1965), journalist, author and play producer, was editor of *Everyman* 1928–32, in which, in an article "Is Shaw Played Out?" on 9th January, he stated that "Shaw shows no sign of being outworn . . . His plays are as bright to-day as ever they were." Benozzo Gozzoli (1420–97) was a Florentine painter noted for his frescoes.

Purdom, in an appendix to his study of Granville Barker (1956), listed twenty-one productions at the Court Theatre 1904–7 that were "produced" by Barker, plus five in 1907 at the Savoy Theatre. His production of *You Never Can Tell* was the revival at the Savoy on 16th September 1907. His Galsworthy productions were *The Silver Box* (Court, 1906), *Joy* (Savoy, 1907), *Strife* (Duke of York's, 1909), and *Justice* (Duke of York's, 1910). There were five Barker productions of Euripides, in Gilbert Murray translations: *Hippolytus* (Lyric, 1904), *The Trojan Women* (Court, 1905), *Electra* (Court, 1906), *Medea* (Savoy, 1907), and *Iphigenia in Tauris* (Kingsway, 1912). The Shakespeare productions were *The Winter's Tale* and *Twelfth Night* (Savoy, 1912) and *A Midsummer Night's Dream* (Savoy, 1914).]

Dear Sir

I have to thank you for an understanding article in Everyman. As you are interested in the matter of production, which all the critics now write about, let me set you right as to what happened at the Court Theatre in the days of the Vedrenne-Barker enterprise.

At the outset, whilst we were exploiting my accumulation of unacted plays, I was the producer, Granville-Barker the leading actor, and Vedrenne the business manager. I had been for years looking for an actor to play the poet in Candida; and I found him when I saw G-B in Hauptmann's Friedensfest. Though he had been nine years on the stage, he was only twentythree, and youthful looking at that, his strain of Italian blood suggesting that he had stepped out of a picture by Gozzoli. He played the poet for me at a Stage Society performance, and afterwards the American captain in Brassbound. His impersonation of the poet has never been surpassed or indeed approached within my experience. I discovered that he had written plays himself in a Meredithian style of such delicacy that theatre people, and even William Archer, could make neither head nor tail of them. As an author he was rather less like me than Debussy is like Verdi or Tchekov like Tolstoy; and it was to the actor in him that I appealed. Such parts as Eugene Marchbanks, Tanner in Man & Superman, Keegan in John Bull's Other Island, were not to be had from any other author. We were indispensable to one another; and our literary and artistic sympathies led to our becoming intimate friends, the more so as he was a lone young man in lodgings; and I was married and just old enough to be his father.

The point which I wish you to seize is that when we got to work at the Court Theatre in earnest Barker shone brilliantly as an actor, but was not thought of as a producer, and in fact did no producing work until we began to venture on other plays than mine, I doing all the producing meanwhile. His genius as a producer was waiting for its opportunity; but he certainly did not want to produce my plays, as my ring-and-sawdust comedy and Crummlesian rhetoric were destructive of the atmosphere he aimed at. Once, after some years, I left a revival of You Never Can Tell entirely in his hands for some reason; and he made a desperate attempt to make a typical G-B production of it; but its restrained elegance and fine taste only made it seem dull and underdone. Later on, as he gained breadth and strength and greater catholicity of taste he could handle my work by amusing himself with it; but he never did so when I was at hand, as he knew that nobody could do my own work as well as myself.

He found himself completely as a producer when Galsworthy came along. His Galsworthy productions were as nearly perfect as anything in our theatre can be. With Housman and Hewlett he was happy, as he was also with Gilbert Murray's Euripides; and he presently was able to get to work on his own plays. Then there was Shakespear ahead. He and I could converse in quotations from Dickens and Shakespear; and his Shakespear productions consummated his career as a producer, and restored Shakespear to the stage, as far as producing could do it with actors who were amateurs at declamation.

A Shaw production was always distinguishable from a G–B production. You make a rather acute remark about fancying that I like to see my parts overdone or guyed. I dont; but when the alternative is between crudity and nullity I encourage crudity. I must have vigor, vivacity, brilliancy of attack, naturalness, surprise, perfect audibility and intelligibility at all costs; and as actors at present are soft-trained at best, and sometimes not trained at all, the cost is often—well, what you complain of. Variety, contrast, unexpected transitions are far more important in my plays than the bourgeois refinement of the XIX century, of which I take a rather Muscovite view: at all events it is a phase of taste which, for good or evil, is passing. G–B does not feel that way: he would kill a play rather than allow it to be coarsely played. And his characteristic mood is elegiac. As mine is very much the reverse we were admirably complementary: the circumstances which divorced us were unfortunate for the London theatre. His fine artistic sense was not so specialized for the theatre as mine, or perhaps I should say for the old heroic art of acting, which had passed away before he was old enough to "take notice" as the nurses say. I was pre-Irving: he, post-Irving. As a producer I have to try to re-establish a lost technique because as an author I write for it. Until that technique is recaptured my plays will have to put up with an art which is occasionally unconcealed and seldom slickly skilful. Galsworthy's and G–B's plays are practically independent of it: they both keep within the limitations of the post-Irving theatre, whilst I demand feats that would extend Salvini, Ristori, or Coquelin. In short, I am an old-fashioned classic (or "legitimate") in my technique; and the penalty of that refusal to cut my coat according to my cloth is that neither you nor I will ever see a performance of a Shaw play as perfect as G–B has been able to shew you for Galsworthy's plays and his own.

I hope you will not find all this tedious. Your article is so interesting that I felt that I ought not to let you be derailed by ignorance of the facts. It is delightful to find you caring enough to exclaim "what an opportunity of enjoying the perfection of drama we are missing because we have no producer at work in the theatre equal to Mr Shaw in genius!" Alas! you have such a producer in Mr Shaw himself; but though he knows every trick by which a producer can impose on you, no sleight of hand can simulate executive skill, charm, and style, beyond a certain point: if the supply of them runs short all he can do is to keep your attention fixed on other things sufficiently to make you forget the possibilities that are being missed. And after all, the Macdona Players, with whom I never meddle (I have seen four performances in the course of twenty years) and who never get produced at all in my sense of the word, probably do as well as is necessary by dint of acquiring complete familiarity with the plays. . . .

All this is of course quite between ourselves. When I tell tales out of school they must not be published.

faithfully
G. Bernard Shaw

To GEORGES PITOËFF

[H/1]

4 Whitehall Court SW1
23rd January 1930

My dear Georges

Do you want to ruin me? I cannot afford another failure like that of Cæsar: it would be the end of me as a dramatic author in France. Your proposal is, as I understand from Hamon, to save two salaries by playing the King yourself and casting Ludmilla for two parts: Orinthia and the Queen. Failure would be absolutely certain as anyone in Paris knows except yourself. The case is very simple. The part of the King needs a first rate actor, with a gift of variety and vivacity enabling him to hold the audience for nearly three hours without wearying them. It is also necessary that he should be a French actor, not a foreigner. Now you, dear Georges, though you do not know it, are an execrable actor, monotonous to a maddening degree, and a foreigner into the bargain. That is why Cæsar failed. That is why Heartbreak House only half succeeded. You must put up in letters of fire over the entrance to your theatre *"At every performance, Ludmilla Pitoeff. At no performance, Georges Pitoeff. Enter without fear."*

You may ask how I, who have never seen you, can possibly know this. My friend: I am an old hand in the theatre; and I know what happens to an actor when he becomes a producer-manager. It is all over with him as an actor. Because I was told that you had made a success—God knows how!—as Hamlet, I, with great misgiving, let myself be persuaded to allow you to play Cæsar. It was the most unfriendly folly I could have committed. No tales about intrigues in the theatre could account for such a crashing, smashing, ridiculous failure, ruinous to you, ruinous to Hamon, ruinous to my reputation in France. It established you for ever as a perfectly damnable actor, absolutely the worst in the world. Nothing you can say will ever alter my conviction on that point; for Cæsar at its feeblest has always had at least a *succès d'estime*. You achieved a *four d'infamie*. That was a warning from Heaven, to you and me.

But there is something else. You do not know how to produce my plays. You murder them always by some barbarous extravagance which destroys their credibility. In Heartbreak House my instructions as to how far [to carry out] the old captain's fancy of making his workroom like a ship are precise: they do not go a step beyond what a sensible, practical man might do. By sticking up a senseless ship's mast in the middle of the room you proclaimed that the captain was in his dotage, and upset all my stage business, besides distracting the attention of the audience from the play: the very thing no producer should ever do. In Cæsar, instead of the massive solidity of Egypt you perpetrated extravagances which made the buildings look like houses of cards with figures from a nightmare. I know exactly how far to go: you do not know where to stop. It did not matter much in St Joan: nothing could prevent its success with Ludmilla (who really ought to divorce you); but your décor was XI century instead of XV: the structure looked flimsy, the atmosphere was one of weak pathetic piety instead of overbearing strength. If you had played Joan the theatre would have been burnt down and the whole company guillotined.

I must not say any more; for I never hurt an artist's feelings. But I cannot let you have the *Pot de Fleurs* [*The Apple Cart*]; nor will I consent to a revival of Heartbreak House or a production of Methuselah or Getting Married or any other play of mine until you retire from the stage as an actor and promise to play no tricks with my work as a producer.

What happens in Italy does not matter, as the audience does not understand a word of what you are saying.

cordially but resolutely
G. Bernard Shaw

To EDWARD ELGAR

4 Whitehall Court S W 1
[C/85]   25th January 1930

[Sir Hamilton Harty (1879–1941), Irish composer, was conductor of the Hallé Orchestra, Manchester, 1920–33. The performance in the Queen's Hall on 24th January included Elgar's Symphony No. 2 in E-flat, Op. 63 (1911), and Strauss's *Don Juan, Tod und Verklärung*, and *Till Eulenspiegel*.]

Harty and his Manchester men pulled off a stupendous performance of the E flat symphony last night: they seemed really to know it bit by bit instead of merely reading it: it was not a matter of the notes producing the effect (which they often dont if the players dont mean anything except to earn their salaries) but an *intended* and exhaustive real performance. H. H. was a dripping rag at the end; but he had mastered and was feeling every phrase: he was kinder to some of it than you would have been yourself.

As to that fortissimo in the rondo, which is like nothing else on earth (Beethoven nowhere!) you should have heard it. *I* never heard it before.

I write this as, if there were a question of a new record of the symphony, and you were not yourself disposed to conduct, it might be useful to know that you could trust H. H. and the Hallé band. Also it is pleasant to blow off steam after an exciting evening.

G. B. S.

To FRANK HARRIS

4 Whitehall Court S W 1

[H/3; X/279]   27th January 1930

[Frank Harris, spurred on by an itinerant American journalist Frank Scully (1892–1964), who would later take unwarranted credit for most of the work, was contemplating a Shaw biography. Archibald Henderson was busy on a revised and enlarged edition of his 1911 biography. The updated work was published in 1932 as *Bernard Shaw: Playboy and Prophet*.]

Francis

Your explanation is unintelligent. If success had gone to my head (by the way, to what part of my person did you expect it to go?) I should have jumped at the chance of making you my trumpeter. I should have flattered you and financed the great biography. I am throwing away a[n] opportunity which few men could resist.

The truth is I have a horror of biographers. The Shaw legend had become so troublesome at one time that in self-defence I had to supply information enough to Archibald Henderson to enable him to produce his huge volume, which is only a colossally expanded extract from Who's Who? But I could not force myself to read the proofs for him; and to this day it remains mostly a sealed book to me. However, it was useful to me, not only as a book of reference, but because since it appeared those who write about me have the external hang of my career much more comprehensively than in the old days when I seemed to be six different little men keeping six separate little oil shops instead of a gigantic multiple trader.

A book by you would be a very different affair, though, like Henderson, you would find it enormously more troublesome than you think. And it is not your job. Every man has a blind side; and I should catch you just on it. I am really a detestable fellow; and you have not the necessary désinvolture to do justice to my extraordinary talents and virtues and to the odiousness produced by the fact that my heart is never in the right—meaning the expected—place.

Besides, it is premature. Only two of the ladies [Jane Patterson and Florence Farr] are dead.

Think no more of it. And forgive me.

GBS

To NANCY ASTOR

4 Whitehall Court S W 1
[C/101]   7th February 1930

[Following an extended weekend visit to Cliveden, Shaw had proceeded to London to sit for the American sculptor Jo Davidson (1883–1952) at the Savoy Hotel on 6th to 8th February.]

Charlotte demanded the entire reconstruction of the bust the moment she saw it. Her criticisms were shattering; but Jo rose to the occasion and did what she wanted with a turn of the hand, leaving her contemptuously dissatisfied because my neck was too thick and the bust looked like flesh and not like flame.

It is a remarkable bit of work all the same; but tomorrow is its last day in London as it has to go off to the moulders & casters.

Post just going.

GBS

To W. R. TITTERTON

[4 Whitehall Court S W 1]
[A/4; X/362]   19th February 1930

[William R. Titterton (1876–1963), left-wing poet and playwright, had a long and varied career as a critic, journalist, and press agent. As publicist for the Old Vic, where a double bill of *The Dark Lady of the Sonnets* and *Androcles and the Lion* was to open on the 24th, he had requested a comment from Shaw on the occasion of his "first appearance at the nursing-home of Shakespeare" under the management of Lilian Baylis. "I rather agree with the world," said Titterton, "in thinking that Miss Lilian is a person of importance. If you think so too, now is the time to say it. You may help her to get Sadlers Wells going a little sooner" (H/3).]

The revival of The Dark Lady and Androcles will be my first performance under the very distinguished management of Miss Baylis; but it will not be my first appearance at the Old Vic. Towards the end of the eighteenseventies, before Miss Baylis was born, I made my debût and also took my farewell as what the Italians call a *maestro* in the orchestra of the Old Vic, under the baton of a certain Signor Samuelli, by filling up the gaps in an anything-but-full band on a grand piano at a performance of detached acts of Faust and Il Trovatore for the improvement of the masses. I flatter myself that the Anvil Chorus has seldom if ever gone with more spirit than on that occasion: anyhow, if the masses were not improved it was not my fault. I also acted as stage manager on one or two similar occasions. As the bell in the Miserere in Il Trovatore I was such a failure that the prima donna struck at rehearsal and silenced me; but what could I do with a length of gas-pipe on a string and an old poker to hit it with? The red fire with which I suggested the execution of the hero elicited thunders of applause: I cannot guess why.

Miss Baylis may therefore announce my reappearance at the Old Vic after fifty years interval. I am probably the only survivor from the previous occasion.

GBS

To FRANK HARRIS

4 Whitehall Court S W 1
[H/3; X/126]   3rd March 1930

[Shaw's prophecy was right on target. When the American publishers of the work examined galleys sent from London by the British publisher in 1931, and spotted what they feared might be deemed criminal libels, they cabled the British publisher to submit the proofs to Shaw.]

Dear Frank Harris

What a chap you are! You can of course compile a life of me as half a dozen people have done—the sort of life that can be published whilst all the parties are still alive. Something, at best, like Morley's life of Gladstone.

Also you can write an autobiography, as St Augustine did, as Rousseau did, as Casanova did, as you yourself have done, which is something more than a heavily padded Times obituary notice. A man cannot take a libel action against himself; and if he is prepared to face obloquy, and compromises no one except himself and the dead, he may even get a sort of Riviera circulation in highly priced top shelf volumes with George Moore and James Joyce. But you cannot write that way about other people. You have a right to make your own confessions, but not to make mine. If, disregarding this obvious limitation, you pick up what you can from gossip and from guesses at the extent to which my plays are founded on fact (in your Shakespearean manner), what will happen? Your publisher, believing me to be fabulously rich and an ill man to cross, will send me the MS and ask me whether I have any objection to it. Unless it is a Morley-Gladstone Who's Who job I will say that I have every possible objection and will assuredly not hold him guiltless that taketh my name in vain; and I will point out that even if I consented I could not prevent the other persons concerned from seeking their legal remedy. And then where would you be?

You must not conclude that my private life has been a very scandalous one. But I once gave some autobiographical material to an Irish American professor [T.D.O'Bolger]. He was the son of an Irish inspector of police; and he proceeded to investigate the case precisely as his father would have done. At last he produced a book about me which began by describing my mother as an adulteress and my father as a despicable fortune hunter. Of course Harpers could not dare to publish this without my consent; and equally of course I could not consent; so the unfortunate author died of disappointment, aided by pernicious anæmia, cursing me for ruining him. Now the worst of it was that I could not deny that the information I had given him bore his construction; for as a matter of fact I was brought up in a *maison à trois* (we kept joint household with a musician who was a bit of a genius as a teacher of singing and conductor, with my mother as his prima donna and lieutenant); and my father had married, at the age of 40, with nothing but a civil service pension of about £60 a year, the daughter of a country gentleman with expectations from a rich aunt who disinherited her for not marrying an earl at least. The view taken by the police inspector's son of this domestic picture was wildly off the mark; but it opened my eyes to the impossibility of conveying a truthful impression except by such a sketch of that household and those persons as I alone could attempt. In my play called Misalliance the leading young man is "the man with three fathers." I should not have thought of that if I had not had three fathers myself: my official father, the musician [Vandeleur Lee], and my maternal uncle [Walter John Gurly]. So you see, long before my own adventures began, my story took a complexion that cannot be painted at second hand. Nearly all the guessing is bound to be wrong. That is why I am afraid of your making either a ghastly mess of a biography, or a conventional affair that will add nothing to your reputation.

The prefaces to my early novels contain as much autobiography as is worth writing.

I must stop or this letter will go on for ever.

G.B.S.

To LADY RHONDDA

[A/3; X/363.e]

Ayot St Lawrence. Welwyn
16th March 1930

[An article by Lady Rhondda, "Shaw's Women," was serialized in her *Time and Tide* from 7th March to 11th April.]

My dear Lady Rhondda

I like the articles: they are very well written. I must say this at the risk of your asking whether I expected them to be badly written.

In dealing with fictitious characters you must always bear in mind that the author is not the Creator, but only a poor devil faking up simulacra to give an illusion of life to the stage. You can always safely tell him that he does not understand women, because he does not understand even his own little self, and cannot write his own history without being immediately convicted by some prosaic investigator of being all wrong about it.

Remember also that the essence of drama is conflict, either with circumstances or with others. Orestes and Pylades, Hamlet and Horatio, as men who stand by one another, are hopelessly uninteresting; and if I have not dramatized the comradeships of women, it is for the same reason as I have not dramatized those of men. In The Philanderer Grace bullies the wretched "womanly" Julia: but she stands by her against the men with a sensitive *esprit de sexe* that is lacking in the friendship of Tanner and Octavius.

179

Ann is of course a cad; but it was not *qua* cad that I called her Everywoman, but as man huntress and slave of Nature. You see, if I had allowed her a single noble moral quality—if the vanquished Tanner could have justified his surrender by any of the amenities which invite a judicious choice, the play would have been spoiled. By all means insist that Ann is a cad, or Iago a villain, or Autolycus a thief; but do not forget that they are so by dramatic necessity.

A woman who finds herself at adolescence very beautiful, or, what is not at all the same thing, irresistibly fascinating, is like a man brought up in commonplace circumstances who unexpectedly inherits a million when he is 21. Unless he is exceptionally strongminded and a good valuer he goes to the devil like the beggar on horseback. Most specially pretty women or sexually attractive women are beggars on horseback. Ann found out early enough to be prepared.

A prostitute is like a picture dealer. If he once allows himself to love and covet pictures he is ruined: he can't bear to sell them. The tragedy of the prostitute is that she dare not let herself love: she must be a woman of business in all the integrity of that calling, like Mrs Warren —or Vivie.

No more room—G. B. S.

To IRENE VANBRUGH

Ayot St Lawrence. Welwyn

[A/60; X/364]   26th March 1930

[(Dame) Irene Vanbrugh (1872–1949), wife of the younger Dion Boucicault and sister of Kenneth Barnes and Violet Vanbrugh, was appearing as Lina in Charles Macdona's revival of *Misalliance* at the Court, this being its first London production since its brief original run in Charles Frohman's repertory scheme in 1910. Others in the cast were Wilfrid Lawson as Tarleton, Hedley Briggs as Bentley, and Esmé Percy (who directed the production) as Gunner. Vesta Tilley (1864–1952) was a famed music hall performer, who specialised in swaggering male impersonations.]

My dear Irene

I looked in at the Court on Friday last. You were of course all right: frightfully competent; so you can now play with the part as you please.

Let me tell you a secret about it. Lina is the St Joan of Misalliance. She comes into that stuffy house as a religious force. She has a vocation and a training as an acrobat: the only thing of the kind—except the

Russian ballet—which now gives such training outside the convents and religious orders. She is devoted to difficult and dangerous exercises; and has a nun's grave disapproval of stunts that are not really either difficult or dangerous, and of acting and clowning. In fact she is very like a modern nun except that her sexual morality is not that of the Church: marriage is to her a sale of herself: she must be free. Her stage foundation is a grave and almost mystical beauty; and Tarleton has the surprise of his life when, touched by it, he finds that he can't buy it, even for love.

I am writing to Tarleton to say that if he would work less conscientiously for a Vesta Tilley success, with you as the representative of "the girls—the Gy—erls," he would find the scene easier for himself as well as for you.

One of the difficulties of an assumed foreign accent is that it is apt to hang itself up on one high pitched note and one characteristic cadence. Just experiment with some contralto passages.

The great final speech is effective but not yet quite impetuous enough. There should be an agony of indignant shame carrying it along like a torrent. I think that with practice you will have no difficulty in hurling it out as Coquelin could hurl out a tirade. Of course you must not really be carried away: that would knock you to pieces and make the words unintelligible; but you must seem to be so. Staccato always sounds swift, as patter singers know, though it is really deliberately done. The feeling will do the rest.

When she takes Bentley she is devoting him to death, as she devotes herself every day. Something of that should be felt by the audience; for it is to that that Bentley responds. It is a hieratic act on her part.

I say all this to keep you interested in the part. It is very jolly to be working with you.

And now for Vesta Tilley!

ever, dear Irene, your very appreciative colleague
GBS

To WILFRID LAWSON

4 Whitehall Court SW1
[S/1]   26th March 1930

[Wilfrid Lawson (1900–66), superlative character actor, also played Major Petkoff, Doolittle, Roebuck Ramsden, Sir Patrick Cullen, and Col. Craven during the Macdona 1929–30 season at the Court. He played Tarleton again in the Malvern Festival season. His most memorable Shaw performance is his Alfred Doolittle in the 1938 film version of *Pygmalion*. *Poppleton's Predicament* (1870) is a one-act farce by C. M. Rae.]

My dear Tarleton

I looked in on Friday night and found you giving a most industrious and disastrously successful impersonation of Vesta Tilley which kept the curtain so late (about half past two in the morning, I think it was) that I had not time to go round and murder you. . . .* Don't throw away a leading part for the sake of laughs that any stage funny man can get as easily as drawing corks. Every time you come on the stage you have to pick up the play and drive it, drive it, drive it for all you are worth. Tarleton picks up everything like a shot. You should not be able to get in a knife edge between his cue and his answer. Play straight and play strong. *Command* the play. All that doddering Old Poppleton farce stuff, those waits and muggings and chucklings and laughter-catchers are no good in my stuff. You have to play me as you play Shakespear: *on* the lines, not between them. I look to you to save 20 minutes on the time of performance by never leaving a moment's silence and making the audience forget to laugh in their interest in you. Otherwise we shall have a ghastly failure and it will be your doing. . . .* You must attack your job like a master. I am convinced you can do it and even do it easily, for you are a walking volcano,—and not even go all out—to get a really powerful performance which will establish you as a big man for big parts. So make up your mind that Tarleton means every word he says and never chuckles or giggles. And let yourself rip. For next time I go I shall have a revolver and I am a more resolute man than Gunner.

In great haste
G. B. S.

To LADY RHONDDA

On the road. Easter Sunday
[A/3]   [20th April] 1930
[The Shaws had driven to Edstaston over Easter, where on that Sunday they attended the unveiling of the memorial window to Charlotte's sister, Mary Cholmondeley, in the Edstaston church. They then proceeded to Buxton on the 22nd for a week's holiday.]

* The ellipsis apparently is Shaw's.

My dear Lady Rhondda

There's just one thing in the articles that I think you might elaborate; and that is the Conduit Pipe view. In my religion of Creative Evolution we are all only means to an end: in other words, Conduit Pipes. Einstein's mother was a C.P. for Einstein; Einstein is a C.P. for the theory of Relativity: and Einstein's son (if he has one) may be merely the C.P. through which the mother of the next Great Woman will be fertilized. Now to be regarded as a C.P. rather than as an end-in-oneself is not a grievance: quite the contrary: it is the foundation of respect, which is far more necessary to us than love. Complete your phrase; and make it The Conduit Pipe of the Holy Ghost (instead of the old fashioned and less accurate Temple), and you will see at once that it is a view which you should insist on rather than repudiate. When women regard their children as darling luxuries they make very bad mothers. When they regard their husbands as oaks for their ivy, or breadwinners, or bedfellows, they make bad wives. When a lovesick man says "I want a woman" as a seasick man says "I want a basin," or a woman says "I want a man" as she might say "I want a tot of whiskey," they are not rising above the C.P. view: they are falling short of it, and are being used as c.ps by Nature, who, when she has finished with them, will abandon them ruthlessly to satiety, reaction, and disgust, powerfully described by Shakespear in his sonnet on Lust. The antidote to this horror is clearly the C.P. view, which secures to both man and woman an irreducible minimum of respect.

Tanner rescues himself from entire sexual futility by this means, marrying a woman whom he has just described (to her mother) as a liar, a bully, and a whore, because he realizes that their union, being so patently willed in spite of his moralizing, must be a job of the Holy Ghost. This leaves him with a much rosier chance of a bearable life than Benedick & Beatrice.

Would you not rather be considered a C.P. for Time & Tide than an attractive female with a morbid taste for business?

There is one respect in which men know more about women and women more about men than either know of their own sex, and that is by hearsay at first hand. No woman presents herself in conversation to a man as she does to another woman; nor does a man present himself to a woman as to another man. However well I think I know a woman I always find out what my wife knows of her as well; and though there is of course a considerable overlap in our information there are ends that lie outside; so that we never think one another *quite* just in our judgments. It seems to me that there is always a point or two on which a woman will let a man deeper into her intimacy than a woman. Even if she has a woman friend to whom she finally tells everything (including things she doesn't tell to the man), yet she will tell the parts in question to a man on much slighter acquaintance. And vice versa.

As you see, I have to snatch a holiday to write a letter that is not a business letter. My real personal correspondence is always years in arrear, as probably yours is too.

ever
G.B.S.

To MOLLY TOMPKINS

4 Whitehall Court SW1
29th April 1930

[C/1; X/319]

[Molly Tompkins had attained a sufficient degree of competence as an artist to be invited to mount a show at the Galleria Brera in Milan, where it was well reviewed and, more important, several of the paintings were sold. A second show late that year, in the Leicester Galleries, London, was also well received. Shaw attended the private showing on 5th December. The *New York Times* on the following day proclaimed in a cabled report, "New American Painter a Sensation in London; Protegee of Shaw in Debut Wins High Praise." Shaw is reported as having informed a reporter that, when Molly showed him one of her works at Lago Maggiore, he had told her that it was good, but hardly a masterpiece, and that she should go to art classes and study for at least ten years. "Instead, she went right to work and this is the result. Very fine, indeed. I also told her to paint me a picture of her villa in Italy and I would give her five guineas for it. There it is." The work was described as mostly colourful flower studies and "striking nudes," which Shaw pointed out as being under the influence of Gauguin, Van Gogh and Cézanne, though, added the correspondent, "it has an independence of its own."]

But where? and have you received the letter I sent you the other day to Rome?

You hurl a letter from a Milan hotel, without place, name, or circumstance, and expect me to turn up in my best clothes, catalogue in hand, to adore your infamous masterpieces!

You have lost the light of reason. Be more explicit, tesoro!

GBS

To THE LITTLE THEATRE, AKRON, OHIO

[Y(draft)/4]

[Palace Hotel. Buxton]
1st May 1930

[The Akron Little Theatre had wired to Shaw: "Akron Ohio police refuse to consider knocking out two teeth sufficient justification for jailing. How can we attract attention to Fannys First Play."]

ASCERTAIN HOW MANY TEETH WILL SUFFICE AND ALTER TEXT ACCORDINGLY

SHAW

To NANCY ASTOR

[A/101]

Palace Hotel. Buxton
5th May 1930

[Charlotte was confined to her bed with scarlatina on 26th April, necessitating an extension of the Buxton stay for another full month, to 26th May.]

My dear Nancy

Charlotte has been washed.

I should have liked to talk to you on the telephone; but it is so situated that I cannot be sure that Charlotte will not hear what I say; and I am deceiving her (as we all are here) about her illness: she thinks she has tonsilitis, which is not alarming, whereas she really has scarlatina.

One of the tricks of scarlatina is to start on your glands when it has finished with your throat, in which event your restored normal temperature suddenly shoots up again. That is what happened to Charlotte yesterday. When I sent you my telegram she was normal and almost well. Before you read it her temperature had risen to 102° and she was in despair. She said to me very earnestly "Have I got mumps?". "No," I replied with conviction: "you havn't got mumps." This morning I did what I wanted to do on Thursday when I returned from London. I engaged a nurse. When I first suggested it Charlotte wouldn't hear of it. "I couldn't bear it," she said. "She would be trained to be cheerful and to keep up my spirits. She would WARBLE at me all the time." And so she was left to me and to the unskilled and overdriven chambermaids. But after six days without washing she welcomed the nurse, who is an excellent young woman. She does not warble; but when I took the doctor for a drive and the patient became

185

anxious for my safe return, she cheered her up with a faithful account of all the most frightful recent motor smashes in Buxton.

So Charlotte is still in bed in a fairly high fever; and the doctor says she will have two days of it, or rather the remainder of two days, one and a half having already elapsed. She is improving visibly; and the mump is yielding instead of gaining. But our departure cannot take place before the end of this week or the beginning of next. Meanwhile she is now being properly nursed and is comparatively comfortable.

The doctor declares that the case is not infectious, though a child of five might perhaps catch it. But scarlatina is scarlatina; and you must not let it into Cliveden until the last scrap of rash has peeled and been forgotten for, say, three weeks. When Charlotte *knows*, she will not let you take the slightest risk. She loves you. I am myself far from indifferent. I will send you bulletins the moment there is any news.

Goodnight & blessings
G.B.S.

To NANCY ASTOR

[A/101; X/317.e]

Palace Hotel. Buxton
12th May 1930

[Shaw made a hurried journey to London on the afternoon of 14th May, lunching with Mabel Shaw and Nancy Astor the next day, and attending meetings of the R.A.D.A. and Stage Society councils. On the 16th he travelled to Birmingham to view a performance of *Heartbreak House* at the Birmingham Rep, in preference to *Parsifal* at Covent Garden. By the 17th he was back in Buxton.]

Dearest Nancy

Charlotte is reposing and peeling and eating voraciously and getting along beautifully; but though she would dearly like to see you for a moment I dare not let you loose on her. You have not the least notion of her genius for worrying, and her conviction that nothing will be done unless she gives exact instructions just as she did in her youth to her Irish servants, and as you did to your negroes. She would feel obliged to order rooms for you, to order meals for you, to explain carefully to you how to eat them, to buy your railway ticket and see that you were washed and disinfected; and she would never believe that I was doing all this properly or that you were quite comfortable and happy without her immediate supervision. In short, you would give her an hour's happiness at the cost of a mountain of imaginary anxieties which might throw her back seriously. Her sense of responsibility is appalling. At Cliveden she is happy because running the house is not her job and she must not interfere; but here——!

The novelty of being able to read and write a little, and sleep and eat a great deal, and the blessed relief of being out of pain, is enough for her for the present. I am going up to town for a day or two mainly because she is beginning to worry about keeping me here. If I leave her she will feel that she may take her time about returning home. We must get back to Ayot: our unexpected absence has created a state of arrears in her work and mine which puts Cliveden, I fear, quite out of the question. It certainly does for me; and she wont go without me.

Now as to Thursday. Before all this happened I had invited to lunch a certain Miss Mabel Shaw (no relation), a woman with a craze for self torture, who broke off her engagement with a clergyman (he died of it) to bury herself in the wilds of Africa and lead negro children to Christ. She has a very graphic pen; and some of her letters were shewn to me. She has come home on missionary-furlough, and is to lunch with me at 4 Whitehall Court on Thursday next at 1.30. I am afraid it will be a tête à tête unless you come to protect me, with Phil or anyone else you like, or no one. It is of course mostly an excuse for seeing you. I come up by the afternoon train on Wednesday.

Charlotte is actually out of bed and installed in a chair; but after 5 minutes of my energetic conversation she had to send me away. Dont bother about bedjackets: I have been sending for them to Ayot & Whitehall and think she must have enough. She is in a state about all your work and says you mustnt be let add to it by doing things for her.

My notion of enjoying Parsifal is to have a box and sit across the back of it with my calves up on a second chair out of sight of the stage.

ever and ever
GBS

To FRANK HARRIS

[H/4; X/126.e, 279]

4 Whitehall Court SW1
20th June 1930

[Shaw's first novel *Immaturity* (1879), hitherto unpublished, was to be the initial volume in the Collected Edition, published on 26th July (Shaw's 74th birthday). Either Harris or his publisher, Victor Gollancz, had sent Shaw a completed section of the biography (apparently drafted by Frank Scully, as he claimed in his autobiography, *Cross My Heart*, 1955), consisting of 28,000 words. In return Shaw supplied Harris with a set of galley proofs of the autobiographical preface to *Immaturity*. He subsequently revised this letter of 20th June when authorising its publication in the biography, as he did several other letters.]

My dear F.H.

Don't be sentimental: it's dangerous at our ages; and it is not what the publishers want from you. Not bread and milk, but brandy, with a dash of vitriol, is what they drink at your bar.

What I sent you is only an advance proof of the preface to my first novel, 50 years old, which will be published for the first time in a collected edition of my works, 1000 sets of about 30 volumes at 30 guineas for the set. Later on it will be published in ordinary form at an ordinary price; and it is for this popular issue that I must hold the preface back from every other sort of publicity. Meanwhile, however, your private glimpse of it will put you wise as to some aspects of my boyhood. I made the additions about Lee in manuscript because it will give the proof a considerable saleable value as an autograph which may come in handy later on.

All that melodrama-bunk about my good heart and open hand must come out, because (a) it is not true (if you had ever read my books you would know that I loathe mendicity, almsgiving, and poverty, and hate the people I have to help almost as heartily as they very naturally hate me); (b) that, true or not, it will only set every beggar and charitable institution in Europe and America pestering me with appeals (I am already brutalized by shouting No every day of my life); and (c) because such stuff makes nauseous reading, utterly unworthy of you as an artist, and betrays the fact that Buccaneer Frank is only the camouflage of a sentimental donkey.

As to your question whether Lee's move to London and my mother's were simultaneous, they could not have been. Lee had to make his position in London before he could provide the musical setting for my mother and sister. But the break-up of the family was an economic necessity anyhow, because without Lee we could not afford to keep up the house. I was born in a small house in an unfashionable street (then half fields) at the edge of Dublin. No professional man of any standing could have received fashionable pupils or patients at such an address. The house had, in the basement, a kitchen, a servant's bedroom, and a pantry. On the *rez de chaussée* a parlor (a *salle à manger*), a nursery, and a "return room" which served as a dressing room for my father, and subsequently as also a bedroom for me when I grew out of sleeping in the nursery with my two sisters. Upstairs was the drawingroom and the best bedroom; and that was all. It was 3 Upper Synge Street at my birth; and one of my early recollections—co-eval with the death of the Prince Consort, when the newspaper came out with a black border— was its change to 33 Synge St when the three Synge Streets, upper, middle and lower, were amalgamated.

The house we shared with Lee, No 1 Hatch St, was fashionably placed. Being a corner house it had no garden; but it had two areas and a leads. It had eight rooms besides the spacious basement and pantry accommodation as against five in Synge St; and the rent, of course, was much higher. Without Lee's contribution it was beyond my father's dwindling means. Lee got his foot into England at a country house in Shropshire, where the lady fancied herself as an amateur *prima donna*; and he made smart acquaintances there. He had always said that he would take a house in Park Lane; and he did. No 13, it was: a narrow house, but with one fine music room.

When it was clear that he was going to stay there, and that Dublin had seen the last of him, the Hatch St house had to be given up. So my mother took a London house in Victoria Grove, way down the Fulham Road, and settled there with her two daughters, whilst I and my father went into Dublin lodgings at 61 Harcourt St. This must have been somewhere round about 1871. In 1876 I threw over my job in the office of a very superior land agent, and joined my mother in London.

I had no love affairs. Sometimes women got interested in me; and I was gallant in the oldfashioned Irish way, implying as a matter of course that I adored them; but there was nothing in it on my side; and you, as biographer, will have to face the very unHarrisian fact that I escaped seduction until I was 29, when an enterprising widow, one of my mother's pupils, appealed successfully to my curiosity. If you want to know what it was like, read The Philanderer, and cast her for the part of Julia, and me for that of Charteris. I was, in fact, a born philanderer, a type you don't understand. I am of the true Shake-spearean type: I understand everything and everyone, and am nobody and nothing.

I really must stop now.   ever
                                                                G.B.S.

P.S. Of course you will understand that the above, typed by my lady-secretary from my shorthand draft, does not answer the modern biographer's first question nor satisfy the modern reader's Freudian curiosity, which is "How did you respond to your sexual urges?" I must find a moment presently to write to you with my own hand (or typewriter) on that subject. It is a very wide and complex subject, on which a mere record of ejaculations, like that in My (Your) Life & Loves, throws no light. A more completely reticent book was never written.

To FRANK HARRIS

[A/4; X/126]

[Ayot St Lawrence. Welwyn]
24th June 1930

[The text reproduced here is that of the original holograph letter. Shaw subsequently revised the text twice, for publication in Harris's biography (1931), and later for inclusion in his *Sixteen Self Sketches* (1949). The most significant alterations for the Harris book were substitution of "gallantries" for "copulations" and "mistress" for "whore." Samuel Pepys, like Shaw, recorded his sexual adventures in his diary.]

Dear Frank Harris

First, O Biographer, get it clear in your mind that you can learn nothing about your sitter (or Biograph*ee*—) from a mere record of his copulations. You have no such record in the case of Shakespear, and a pretty full one for a few years in the case of Pepys: but you know much more about Shakespear than about Pepys. The explanation is that the relation between the parties in copulation is not a personal relation. It can be irresistibly desired and rapturously executed between persons who could not endure one another for a day in any other relation. If I were to tell you every such adventure that I have enjoyed you would be none the wiser as to my personal, nor even as to my sexual history. You would know only what you already know: that I am a human being. If you have any doubts as to my normal virility, dismiss them from your mind. I was not impotent; I was not sterile; I was not homosexual; and I was extremely, though not promiscuously susceptible.

Also I was entirely free from the neurosis (as it seems to me) of Original Sin. I never associated sexual intercourse with delinquency. I associated it always with delight, and had no scruples nor remorses nor misgivings of conscience. Of course I had scruples, and effectively inhibitive ones too, about getting women into trouble (or rather letting them get themselves into it with me) or cuckolding my friends; and I understood that chastity can be a passion just as intellect is a passion; but St Paul was to me always a pathological case. Sexual experience seemed a necessary completion of human growth; and I was not attracted by virgins as such. I preferred women who knew what they were doing.

As I have told you, my adventures began when I was 29. But it would be a prodigious mistake to take that as the date of the beginning of my sexual life. Do not misunderstand this: I was perfectly continent except for the involuntary incontinences of dreamland, which were very unfrequent. But as between Oscar Wilde, who gave 16 as the age at which sex begins, and Rousseau, who declared that his blood boiled with sensuality from his birth (but wept when Madame de Warens initiated him) my experience confirms Rousseau and is amazed at Wilde. Just as I cannot remember any time when I could not read and write, so I cannot remember any time when I did not exercise my overwhelming imagination in telling myself stories about women.

I was, as all young people should be, a votary of the Uranian Venus. I was steeped in romantic music from my childhood. I knew all the pictures and statues in the National Gallery of Ireland (a very good one) by heart. I read everything I could lay my hands on. Dumas père made French history like an opera by Meyerbeer for me. From our cottage on Dalkey Hill I contemplated an eternal Shelleyan vision of sea, sky, and mountain. Real life was only a squalid interruption to an imaginary paradise. I was overfed on honey dew. The Uranian Venus was bountiful.

The difficulty about the Uranian Venus is that though she saves you from squalid debaucheries and enables you to prolong your physical virginity long after your adolescence, she may sterilise you by giving you imaginary amours on the plains of heaven with goddesses and angels and even devils so enchanting that they spoil you for real women or—if you are a woman—for real men. You become inhuman through a surfeit of beauty and an excess of voluptuousness. You end as an ascetic, a saint, an old bachelor, an old maid (in short, a celibate) because, like Heine, you cannot ravish the Venus de Milo or be ravished by the Hermes of Praxiteles. Your love poems are like Shelley's Epipsychidion, irritating to terre à terre sensual women, who know at once that you are making them palatable by pretending they are something that they are not, and cannot stand comparison with.

Now you know how I lived, a continent virgin, until I was 29, and ran away even when the handkerchief was thrown me.

191

From that time until my marriage there was always some lady at my disposal; and I tried all the experiments and learned what there was to be learnt from them. They were "all for love"; for I had no spare money: I earned enough to keep me on a second floor, and took the rest out, not in money, but in freedom to preach Socialism.

When at last I could afford to dress presentably I soon became accustomed to women falling in love with me. I did not pursue women: I was pursued by them.

Here again do not jump at conclusions. All the pursuers did not want sexual intercourse. They wanted company and friendship. Some were happily married, and were affectionately appreciative of my understanding that sex was barred. Some were prepared to buy friendship with pleasure, having made up their minds that men were made that way. Some were sexual geniuses, quite unbearable in any other capacity. No two cases were alike: William Morris's dictum "that all taste alike" was not, as Longfellow puts it, "spoken of the soul" ["A Psalm of Life," 1839].

I found sex hopeless as a basis for permanent relations, and never dreamt of marriage in connection with it. I put everything else before it, and never refused or broke an engagement to speak on Socialism to pass a gallant evening. I liked sexual intercourse because of its amazing power of producing a celestial flood of emotion and exaltation of existence which, however momentary, gave me a sample of what may one day be the normal state of being for mankind in intellectual ecstasy. I always gave the wildest expression to this in a torrent of words, partly because I felt it due to the woman to know what I felt in her arms, and partly because I wanted her to share it. But except perhaps on one occasion I never felt quite convinced that I had carried the lady more than half as far as she had carried me: the capacity for it varies like any other capacity. I remember one woman who had a sort of affectionate worship for me saying that she had to leave her husband because sexual intercourse felt, as she put it, "like someone sticking a finger into my eye." Between her and the heroine of my first adventure, who was sexually insatiable, there was an enormous range of sensation; and the range of celestial exaltation must be still greater.

When I married I was too experienced to make the frightful mistake of simply setting up a permanent whore; nor was my wife making the complementary mistake. There was nothing whatever to prevent us from satisfying our sexual needs without paying that price for it; and it was for other considerations that we became man and wife. In permanence and seriousness my consummated love affairs count for nothing besides the ones that were either unconsummated or ended by discarding that relation.

Do not forget that all marriages are different, and that a marriage between two young people followed by parentage cannot be lumped in with a childless partnership between two middle aged people who have passed the age at which it is safe to bear a first child.

And now, no romance and above all no pornography.

G.B.S.

To OTTO KYLLMANN

Ayot St Lawrence. Welwyn
9th July 1930

[A/52]

[Kyllmann had asked if the type for the limited Collected Edition should be distributed and the texts reset for the "library edition" of Shaw's works, which would eventually be known as the Standard Edition. The War Book was *What I Really Wrote about the War* (1930), Vol. 21 of the Collected Edition. Seven of Shaw's plays were presented at the 1930 Malvern Festival including *Candida, Getting Married, Widowers' Houses, Heartbreak House,* and *The Admirable Bashville,* though the headliner that season was Rudolf Besier's new play *The Barretts of Wimpole Street.* Although the nominal director of the Shaw plays was H. K. Ayliff, Shaw attended and participated in virtually all of the rehearsals, held at the Old Vic, from 7th July until his departure for Malvern on 10th August.]

My dear Kyllman

Yes; we are bound to destroy the type [of the Collected Edition]. I shall view the operation with malignant pleasure, as I have conceived an extraordinary hatred to this particular edition, blast it!

I have just written the last stroke of the War Book. I hope to have the typed transcript in Clark's hands on Saturday morning at latest. Sheets B to N are passed for press. O to U are in type and corrected: I have only to check the corrections on the revise.

If only he will send me the 3 batches of 7 volumes each right on top of one another, and cover our expenditure with a few pence in hand.

My rehearsals for Malvern are beginning; and this obliges me to knock off working at my recent rate. I was at it from 7 [a.m.] to 10 [p.m.] on Sunday.

ever
GBS

4 Whitehall Court SW1
[H/3]   12th July 1930

Dear Elbridge Adams

I have done all I can for you. When you had recklessly given £3000 for the letters without securing the copyright, I went so far as to suggest that I might find somebody to take that bad bargain off your hands. You immediately attached the impossible condition that the letters should not be published by anyone else. You then, with your eyes wide open, deliberately spent another £3000 on the Terry copyrights, still without acquiring mine and again without letting me know what you were doing. You then began threatening to publish my letters without my license and defying me to stop you. Any less patient man than I would have thrown you out of the window into the Thames.

Instead, I tried to obtain the consent of Ellen Terry's representatives to the publication by you of a limited edition so that you might not lose your money, richly as you deserved to lose it for your unbusinesslike disposal of it. I drafted an explanation to be signed by myself jointly with Ellen Terry's children. I redrafted it to satisfy Miss Craig's solicitor. I left all the profits to be divided between you and them. I was kind to you as to a lost baby, which is what you are in business, and took care of your interests as I took care of the Terry interests. And my reward is that the Terry infants, having had your money, will neither accept my explanation nor furnish any explanation of their own, and that both you and Miss Craig now imply that the initiative in the whole affair came from me—that it was I who wanted to publish the letters; that I broached the matter to Miss Craig and forced an agent on her; that I, in short, am the villain of the piece. And you, monster of ingratitude that you are, instead of appealing to the Terry representatives to complete what you allege to be their bargain with you, repeat your threat to publish my letters without my authorization.

May I venture to ask, Elbridge, how much more of this sort of treatment you expect me to bear?

I am sending your letter to my solicitor in New York so that he may be prepared to stop you in case you should really attempt to carry out your threat. You seem to be capable of anything except taking proper care of yourself.

faithfully
G. Bernard Shaw

To JOHN MAXWELL

[F/4]

[4 Whitehall Court SW1]
[Undated: *c.* 1st August 1930]

[John Maxwell (1875–1940), formerly a Glasgow solicitor, was managing director of British International Pictures and producer of ten of the early films of director Alfred Hitchcock (1899–1980), including *Blackmail* and *Murder*. He contracted with Shaw for film rights to *How He Lied to Her Husband* on a five year licence, as an experiment, to be followed by *Captain Brassbound's Conversion* (eventually supplanted by *Arms and the Man*). One of Shaw's stipulations was that the film be directed by Cecil Lewis, formerly of the B.B.C. At Malvern Shaw was given a private Sunday screening of *Murder*.]

Dear Mr Maxwell

I have now drafted a form of agreement for my use generally, and have had our names printed in, as we may as well use the first impressions for our contract for "How He Lied." I enclose the first rough bill. Pick any holes you can in it.

I enclose also your own draft. Your clause three, though it is very cunningly put into agreements by publishers and managers[,] is quite useless as a precaution. You cannot contract yourself out of the law of the land. You and I may sign an agreement that if you commit a murder I shall be hanged for it; but the courts will hang you all the same, and send me to prison for conspiracy. All I can do is to guarantee that there is no hidden libel or plagiarism; and though this will not save you from being sued by any libeled or plagiarized person, it will enable you to sue me for damages for misleading you. But if you "published" a film which is on the face of it a seditious, blasphemous, or obscene libel, you cannot transfer your liability to the author or anyone else by any sort of private contract.

I have called B.I.P. "the manufacturers" because of the ambiguity of the word "producer," which has come to mean—say Mr Hitchcock.

I have disregarded your clause nine, as we can deal direct without any intermediary.

I shall be in London until next Thursday, after which I shall be away until October.

faithfully
G. Bernard Shaw

To THE VERY REV. H. R. L. SHEPPARD

4 Whitehall Court SW1
[H/1]   5th August 1930

[Hugh Richard Lawrie Sheppard (1880–1937) was Vicar of St Martin's-in-the-Fields (1914–27) when Shaw first met him, having been invited to lecture at St Martin's in February 1919 on Shakespeare. The requested article for the *St Martin's Review*, which Sheppard founded in 1920, was finally contributed nearly two decades later, appearing in April 1940 as "St. Martin's, Bernard Shaw and the Prayer Book." Sheppard was elevated to Dean of Canterbury in 1929, succeeding the Very Rev. Randall Davidson (1848–1930), later Baron Davidson of Lambeth; but was obliged to relinquish the post in 1931 because of a debilitating asthmatic condition. In 1934 he was appointed Canon of St Paul's. At his death Shaw eulogized (in a memorial brochure): "WHAT an actor!! ... That was what made him so tremendously effective both in the pulpit and in society and also so genuinely democratic; for the divine gift of acting knows no distinction between the stalls and the gallery: its audience is everybody within hearsay. ... [He] knew the value of his histrionic gift and cultivated it for the sake of its infinite charm and usefulness. There is no greater happiness within mortal reach than to have all the gifts for your job, and to love your job. He had that happiness."

The Shaws attended the wedding of Robert Loraine, on 15th July 1921, in St George's, Hanover Square, the fashionable church in which Alfred Doolittle, of *Pygmalion*, was married.]

My dear Dick (my secretary has done this: what I wrote was "My dear Dean")

At this moment I am so distracted by rehearsals of five of my plays for the Malvern Festival and almost as much sordid business to transact as a bishop that the mere suggestion of making an additional engagement threatens my reason. However, that will pass when I have had a bit of a holiday.

Your invitation is tempting enough as far as seeing you and Mrs Sheppard (not forgetting the big dog, who is, I trust, equal to his dignity as a decanal dog with a cathedral to guard); but what could I do with your Saturday 8.15 congregation except get you into trouble, which you are only too well able to do for yourself? From the point of view of pietistic Canterbury I am a heathen, from its political point of view I am a Bolshevik. How much of the Apostles' Creed do you suppose I believe? Do you realise that I am much more pro-Russian than Trotsky? And the worst (or best) of it is that these questions cannot be amiably side-tracked any longer. And even if this were not so

I am too old to temporize or to behave considerately: I am passing through my second youth on my way to second childhood, and find myself, to my alarm, talking very much as I did when I was twenty-five.

Some years ago (I do not know exactly how long: for age has the effect of destroying one's historical perspective, so that everything that ever happened to me seems to have happened within the last fortnight) you asked me to write in the St Martin's Review about the revision of the prayer book which I used to hear you over the wireless revising very freely every Sunday. Now a professional author knows very well that it is waste of time to talk through one's hat about revision: he knows nothing about it until he has sat himself down to the job as he would to one of his own proofs. Well, I did this; and the result was that you did not get the article. It would have blown St Martin's into Trafalgar Square.

I found that the whole book was saturated with Transubstantiation to such an extent that an attempt to eliminate it would be like an attempt to restore the spires of Chartres: the first stone taken out for numbering would have brought down the whole edifice. I had already found when my mother was cremated, and I had the Church of England service read because it seemed so mean to do the Chaplain out of his half-guinea, that the skulls and crossbones of the fifteenth century were grinning and rattling all through it in so heathenish a manner that when my sister followed my mother, I had to improvise a service and officiate myself. At a wedding in St. George's Hanover Square, my wife and I agreed that we could not have stood it, and that but for the alternative of the registrar we should have lived in sin rather than endure it. This, by the way, was not prudery: I heartily approve of the straight statement as to the purpose of matrimony in the service. But the attempt to get round the old Pauline doctrine of original sin by pretending that the affair was typical of the Union of Christ and his Church, and the vows to remain until death in a state of feeling and judgment which might and indeed must vary not only from decade to decade but even to some extent from hour to hour, were so unreal that I was not surprised to find that the parson made no more pretence of taking them seriously than any of the smart people and theatrical celebrities assembled there. The baptism service is the best; but I find people (both Roman and Anglican) asking me to act as god-father to their infants and being amazed when I reply that I cannot pledge myself to see that their children are taught doctrines some of which (the atonement, for instance) I not only disbelieve but abhor as ungentlemanly and destructive of the human conscience by putting it on the dole.

Last Easter I attended a service dedicating a window to the memory of my sister-in-law. Her husband read the lessons. One of them was that perfectly infernal chapter from Exodus [12:35-36] which describes the spoiling of the Egyptians (by borrowing their jewels and running away with them at the express suggestion of God) and the slaughter of the firstborn. It made a horrible impression on me; but the congregation took it without turning a hair because it had ceased to have any reality for them.

My general conclusion was that there was nothing to be done with the prayer-book but bury it in the British Museum Library, make a new one, and ordain that no service should remain in use without drastic revision or complete renewal for more than six years.

I am one of the Friends of Canterbury Cathedral, because your predecessor, who was almost as nice a fellow as yourself, instead of leaving me to the verger to be shewn round for half-a-crown, shewed me round himself. You cannot tip a Dean half-a-crown; but you must in decency, especially if he asked you to tea and you like him and his wife, affirm your friendship by a guinea a year representing a capital of £20. Moral: always shew plutocrats round yourself, and play Mrs Sheppard and the dog on them for all they're worth. But how can I tell your people that I am a Friend of the Cathedral because I attach an enormous value to its atmosphere when there is no service going on, and Christian and Jew, Deist and Atheist, can make their souls there without disturbance by any priest or any reminders of a rascally old tribal god with the morals of Fagin in Oliver Twist?

You see how it is. If I spoke to your people I should seem to be trying to tear off your gaiters; and I should perhaps discourage you, although my desire is to keep you in the Church so that the people may still get some genuine religion in the place where they habitually look for it. Therefore, though I shall certainly look you up when I am next in Canterbury I think it had better not be on a Saturday.

You wont, I know, mind the length of this letter; but it must stop.

Our love to Mrs Sheppard and such blessings as our very limited credit can command on yourself.

faithfully (really)
G. Bernard Shaw

To SIMON & SCHUSTER

[S/3]

[4 Whitehall Court SW1]
25th September 1930

[Simon and Schuster, an American firm of book publishers (founded 1924), had contracted for American rights to the Harris biography of Shaw.]

Dear Sirs

I am sorry if I have to upset any of your arrangements; but the Harris biography must not contain any unpublished matter by me; and the announcement that the book will contain 15000 words by me must be withdrawn. What I have done for Mr Harris is to let him see certain autobiographical matter by me which will form part of the collected edition of my works now in course of publication by Messrs Wm. H. Wise and Co. I am under contract with them to support them in any proceedings they may have to take against infringements of my copyright; and such proceedings would certainly be taken by them if you published the matter which I allowed Mr Harris to see solely for his information. I have written to him to make this clear. Mr Harris is eminently capable of writing his book himself without any further assistance from me than information as to the facts. As a business firm you are aware that a Life of me written by myself would be worth a very large sum in the book market; and such a publication as you have announced would damage my commercial interests very heavily. It is never safe to announce a publication without having the author's license at first hand. What you are good enough to call "my glorious contributions" will immediately become the subject of a lawsuit if they appear in the Harris volume; and I have no power to prevent this even if I desired to do so.

As to Mr Scully's suggestion, it does not concern me. Mr Harris can call his book what he pleases provided he does not implicate me. He is entitled to claim an old friendship with me, and to say that much of what he had written as to my early life is based on first hand information from myself; but he must tell the story in his own way and in his own words, and not in mine.

faithfully
G. Bernard Shaw

To EDWARD ELGAR

Ayot St Lawrence. Welwyn

[H/132]   28th September 1930

[Elgar's Severn Suite for Brass Band, Op. 87, derived almost entirely from the composer's old sketchbooks, was written for performance as a test piece for the 25th annual National Brass Band Championship. The orchestration, from Elgar's piano score, was made by Henry Geehl. In May 1930 Elgar asked for permission to dedicate the work to Shaw. "Naturally I shall be enormously honored," Shaw replied on 25th May; "it will secure my immortality when all my plays are dead and damned and forgotten" (A/85). On 27th September Shaw attended the band festival at the Crystal Palace, in which 189 bands from thirty-three English, Welsh, and Scottish counties participated. The championship trophy was won by Foden's Wagon Works Band, Cheshire, conducted by Fred Mortimer, whose performance was not given until after Shaw's departure. There were, in all, eighteen contestants for the trophy. Elgar, indisposed, did not attend.]

My dear Elgar

I heard the Severn Suite yesterday only eight times, as extreme hunger and the need for catching the 5–10 train at Kings Cross forced me to surrender before I had ceased finding new things in it.

If there is a new edition of the score I think it would be well to drop the old Italian indications and use the language of the bandsmen. For instance *Remember that a minuet is a dance and not a bloody hymn*; or *Steady up for artillery attack*; or *NOW—like Hell.** I think that would help some of the modest beginners who dont yet aspire to the Crystal Palace.

It is a pity you did not hear them. They had all worked like Trojans at the suite; and there was not a single slovenly or vulgar bar, nor a note muffed or missed. All keen: no professional staleness. The first three bands gave most conscientious and thorough performances; but they evidently regarded the Minuet as a variation on "Nearer, my God, to Thee." The fourth, Irwell Springs (I have seen the Irwell only far from its springs in Manchester), got it absolutely right and gave a real reading of the work, bringing down the house in earnest. I was provoked to applause; shook hands with the conductor, a most unassuming elderly gentleman named Halliwell; and promised to tell you. The seventh band gave a magnificent performance. It had a real conductor, a lanky blackavised youth in a long skirted staff officer coat

---

* The suggested instructions, set here in italics, were typewritten in red in Shaw's original letter.

200

with a red sash, who got a wonderful new phrasing for the first movement, and nearly died of the convulsions into which the work threw
him. His band had by far the greatest range of tone. He will be heard
of, this youth. Name, W. Lowes: band the Carlisle St Stephens. He
was the winner last year. This time he was not mentioned, probably
because he was too good. Irwell Springs was placed third. I did not
hear the winners: they were almost the last on the list; and they pro-
fited, I expect, by the rise of enthusiasm which continued steadily as
the work became more and more familiar, and the audience listened
harder and harder for their fancy bits.

The scoring is, as usual, infallible. You should have heard the
curiously pleasant oboe quality of the muted flugels picking up after the
cornets. The held note of the soprano cornet *in excelsis* was enormous.
These chaps have iron lips; and none of the solo cornets seemed to
have the least difficulty with the scherzo. The florid passages were all
done correctly and in a businesslike way by all the bands; and in one
band the trombones got real style into them. The solid drive of the
body of tone would have rejoiced your heart; and there was no mere
noisiness nor brassiness. (I fancy the judges, who were hermetically
sealed so that they couldnt tell which band was playing, are very
particular about this.[)]

Nobody could have guessed from looking at the score and thinking
of the thing as a toccata for brass band how beautiful and serious the
work is as abstract music.

The Columbia people wanted me to do three minutes chin music as
an introduction to the record; but I knew better than to comply: I
excused myself by demanding three hours.

I sat next one connoisseur who had, he said, sat through every contest since the thing started. A run of quavers from the basses moved
him to remark "Bit of Beethoven, eh?" I took this to be a flattering
comparison until he added "Mount of Olives, aint it?" It might have
been anything, as far as that went; but I hand on the indictment
(plagiarism) for what it is worth, that you may see how criticism is
always itself even in Brass Band circles.

I hope to hear it again from the winning band on the wireless, or on
the gramophone. The BBC should do it expressly for you. . . .

That, I think, is all for today, except Charlotte's love.

G.B.S.

To EDWARD GORDON CRAIG

4 Whitehall Court SW1
3rd October 1930

[H/3]

[Although he would have preferred that the Shaw-Terry correspondence remain unpublished, Craig informed Elbridge Adams on 29th September, he was bowing to the wishes of the other parties involved, taking consolation from the fact that publication would benefit the Terry Memorial (draft, Craig papers, Humanities Research Center, University of Texas). With this communication he sent a brief letter dated 1st October to be passed on to Shaw: "Mr Adams, our mutual friend, is as you know a little bothered by the situation. He wants to do something that you and Edith both wish to have done, so I will not stand in the way and you may rest assured that having said this I shall stick to it; and when the book containing my Mother's and your letters is published you can rely on me not to write about it in the papers or to give interviews." When, after publication of the correspondence a year hence, Craig publicly attacked the book and criticised Shaw, GBS gave Craig's letter to the journalist G.W.Bishop to publish in a self-drafted interview in *The Observer*, 8th November 1931.

Walter D'Arcy Hart (b. 1897), a solicitor partner in the firm of Gilbert Samuel and Co. and a trustee of the Ellen Terry Estate, was in charge of negotiations with Elbridge Adams and Shaw for publication of the correspondence. Edy Craig's £3000 was less than half the sum obtained by the trustees from Adams.]

Dear Mr Gordon Craig

I have to thank you for your letter handed to me by Mr Elbridge Adams.

I am afraid you have been bothered much more than was necessary about a very simple matter. It has been quite clear to me all through that the letters should not be published without your consent; but as Mr Hart and Mr Adams did not appreciate this scruple of mine I had to give them a business reason for it, which was, that if you were ignored in the matter you would be fully justified in making a public protest, against which I, at least, should have no reply. All that Mr Adams could make of this was that I wanted you to give an undertaking not to attack me in the Press and to express a *willing* consent to the publication. That is, of course, all nonsense. I took it, and take it, that your consent to the publication is like mine, a very reluctant submission to circumstances over which we have no control. The trustees, without consulting me or (as I suppose) consulting you, sold my letters and the copyright in all E. T's letters to Mr Adams for £3000; and he promptly made a contract for the publication of E. T's letters with some publisher in America. I found this a *fait accompli* on my return from the Adriatic, with Mr Adams claiming that he had been led to believe that he could have the whole correspondence for publication not only in a private edition but for a trade edition preceded by serial publication in the papers, with photographs, choice passages in thick type, and all the horrors of commercial exploitation *à l'outrance*.

I at first said that as Edy had got £3000 there was no further need for publication. Mr Adams then threatened to publish without my license and defy me to do my worst; and I had to instruct my American solicitor to convince him that it was no use trying to bluff me. But with the power to publish E.T's letters, he still has a perceptible leverage. Besides, as you have no doubt discovered, Adams has a natural gift for getting round people and persuading them that they must rescue him from the consequences of his own folly. Then there is Edy and Christopher, who, as strong Feminists, want justice done to the great woman E.T. sacrificed to the egotistical man H.I., which is the moral of the whole correspondence. And there is the promise of more money for Edy, or for the Memorial (for which, however, I do not care two straws). Under all this pressure I have said that if you feel with me that we must stifle our natural repugnance and let the thing go through I will license a limited edition of 5000 copies to be sold at five guineas a copy, all the profits, if any, to go to the trustees, who can satisfy Adams. I take nothing; but I retain my copyright, and consequently my veto on any arrangement that may seem to me undesirable. The only point on which I am a little touchy is your own point: that is, I must not be put in the position of liking and desiring a publication which I should never have contemplated for an instant if E.T. had left £100,000 instead of £20,000, or of having acted without your knowledge and consent, it being equally understood that both our consents are imposed on us by circumstances.

Beyond this I did not expect you to go; and as to your complete liberty to write about the letters, about the Lyceum, about E.T., H.I., and G.B.S., you must continue to exercise that in all respects as before. I only ask you to believe that we are alike victims of circumstances.

Do not feel obliged to reply to this: Heaven only knows what exact arrangement will be come to with Adams, and it would be waste of time to discuss the endless vicissitudes of the negotiations; but if there is any essential change in the situation I will take care that you are informed of it.

faithfully
G. Bernard Shaw

PS   You will see by my resort to initials (E. T.) that I have been reading the chapter of your Irving book which appears in that magazine, my order for the whole book not yet having been fulfilled. To me it is in some passages a very touching document, thoroughly justifying my uninvited suggestion to you to write *auto*biography, not biography.

To GEOFFREY WHITWORTH

[4 Whitehall Court SW1]

[A/1]   12th October 1930

[Geoffrey Whitworth (1883–1951) was founder and secretary (later director) of the British Drama League and editor of its journal *Drama*, for which publication he had asked Shaw to review Gordon Craig's *Henry Irving*.]

Dear Geoff
   Impossible. He has made such a lot of blunders about myself and been so nasty about them that anything by me would have to contain a lot of explanations that are of no use to the public, and some of which ought not to be published anyhow. I have had to write to him privately about them.
   But the book is so extraordinarily and beautifully right when he is giving his impressions of what he actually saw himself and really knows about that it should be reviewed by someone who is not bound to defend me, and who wont dwell on the bad half of the book, which is childishly brainless.

G.B.S.

To EDWARD GORDON CRAIG

Ayot St Lawrence. Welwyn

[H/3]   14th October 1930

[Bram Stoker was Sir Henry Irving's business manager, Louis F. Austin his secretary. The drama critic E. A. Bendall, later the Lord Chamberlain's joint-examiner of plays, served as a publicist for Irving and was believed to be in his employ. Tom Mead (1819–89) was another oldtime actor. Sam Johnson, known to Shaw from boyhood visits to Dublin's Theatre Royal, later became a member of the Lyceum company. (Sir) Charles B. Cochran (1872–1951), theatre impresario, had sponsored the Pitoëffs' production of *Saint Joan* in London the previous June.

Shaw informed Hesketh Pearson (see the chapter "Henry and Ellen," in *Bernard Shaw: His Life and Personality*, 1942) that, as Irving had "left his money in three equal parts to his two sons and a lady [Eliza Aria] for whose friendly help and care in his declining years he was grateful, [Florence] Lady Irving [his long-estranged wife], who was ignored in the great actor's will, asked Shaw to assist her in preventing the Abbey burial. Shaw wrote her several pages of diplomatic sympathy, but added that if he were her solicitor as well as her friend he should feel bound to warn her that as the widow of a famous actor buried in Westminster Abbey she could obtain a civil pension by lifting her little finger, but that as the widow of an exposed adulterer no Prime Minister would dare to put her on the Civil List. Lady Irving pocketed her wrongs and her pension."]

Dear Mr Gordon Craig

I promised to let you know of any change in the arrangements for publishing the E.T.—G.B.S. correspondence. A change has taken place.

I have elicited from Mr Adams that the Trustees entered into an agreement with him whereby they are to receive a royalty of 15% on all copies of the correspondence sold, and that he has paid them £1000 on account of these royalties and bound himself to pay another thousand within two years. This, like the sale of the letters, was effected entirely without my knowledge. On learning this I concluded that the Trustees did not intend to consult me in any way, and desired that we should all go into the matter on a purely business footing, and play our hands independently. Accordingly I proposed to Mr Adams that we should print a collected edition of 3000 copies at five guineas, sharing the cost and the profit equally. He agreed; and within 24 hours I sold the whole edition to my publishers at a discount of 40%. When the books are manufactured and distributed the money will come in; and the royalty coming to the Trustees will be over £2000, of which £1000 has already been received by them.

The question of a trade edition will then become practicable, and will probably bring further sums to the Trustees. We shall all deal as we please with our respective shares of the plunder.

We are now across the Rubicon; and it is not likely, if all goes well, that I need trouble you further about the business.

If I may intrude on you for a moment with reference to your book, I should like you, if you have to edit a second edition, to make a couple of changes. You have quite unintentionally accused me of taking a step contrary to my code of honor as a professional critic. Whilst I was earning my living in that capacity it was quite impossible for me to offer a play to any manager. The standard method of corrupting a critic at that time was either to give him £50 for an option on some play or adaptation which he had written or was about to write (this was how Wyndham and Alexander did it) or else to accept it for production at some unspecified future date, and respond to demands from the critic for advances on account of author's fees. This last was Irving's way. If I had offered him a play I should have simply been asking for a cheque; and when E. T. induced him to propose a production of The Man of Destiny to me I was embarrassed, because, as his position entitled him to command the play, I could not refuse to let him have it without gross discourtesy, and yet I knew perfectly well that he was simply buying me as he would have bought a pound of cheese, knowing that critics were seldom scrupulous about exploiting their position, and that even those who would never have dreamt of taking money from him for plays which he was obviously not going to produce would greedily accept Stoker's civilities and drink his champagne on first nights.

I was always very nice to Stoker, gratefully accepting his invitation as a personal compliment, but never appearing at the suppers.

I was as civil to Irving as to Stoker, and of course placed the play at his disposal with the most distinguished consideration; but I stipulated that it must be produced next season. Irving then asked me to come and see him; and I did. It was our only interview. He gave me all the usual and obvious reasons for putting the play on the shelf and keeping it there; and added the usual gracious hint that the inevitable delay would not apply to an advance on account of fees. A queer conversation followed, something like this. H. I. "But what does it matter to you whether the play comes on this year or next?" G.B.S. "Well, let me put it in this way. I daresay you played Hamlet when you were 25, and no doubt gave a very interesting performance. But how would you like to offer that performance today to the public as a specimen of your latest and best work? The Man of Destiny is my best up to date. But I should not like to have it represented as such ten years hence." H. I. (bothered at first, but suddenly pulling himself together and concentrating on me to impress me with his craft and resourcefulness) "These things can be explained. There are ways—ways of getting paragraphs into the Press. I know a man named Bendall"—G.B.S. "Oh yes, yes: I know all about the Press and the paragraphs: it is my profession. I know Bendall. But we must not do things that need explanation when there is no need for it. Besides, Napoleon is 27 and the lady 30. The parts will not be more suitable ten years hence."

206

And so on and so forth. In special pleading Henry had no chance against a young Fabian debater and street corner orator in full practice; and when it came to offstage acting the artificer who made Irving out of Brodribb, as you so perfectly put it, had no advantage against a rival who had made G. B. S. out of nothing. Also I knew that Shakespear was interviewing Burbage, whereas he, poor fellow, had not the faintest suspicion that Burbage was interviewing Shakespear. We both behaved irreproachably; but he afterwards told Emery Walker that I was remarkably lacking in deference, at which point Walker tactfully intimated that I was a friend of his, and the subject dropped.

No conclusion was come to, and nothing happened about it until I wrote that stupid criticism of the revival of Richard III. I call it stupid because I naïvely described Irving's performance without perceiving what was the matter with him. My play was immediately returned to me, with a curt intimation that he had no use for it. This did not surprise me, as I knew that my notice was a breach of the bargain he supposed he had made with me. But I did not know the full extent of the offence until I met Frederick Harrison, who spoke of the terrible thing I had done, and the indignation at the Lyceum about it. When I showed no sign of appreciating the enormity of my conduct, he explained "You said he was drunk." "Who told you so?" I asked. "Harry Irving. He said it would teach the old man to keep sober next time." This very Irvingesque piece of filial piety opened my eyes completely. Up to that moment I had never heard of Irving's drinking nor thought of him in that way, though theatrical gossip had informed me with great particularity how many quarts of whiskey Tom Mead consumed in the week. And I saw at once that to anyone who knew my article, with its description of Irving as not being quite himself, not answering his helm with his usual precision and concentration, and shouting at Maud Milton "Get up the stage" at the full pitch of his voice, bore that construction to anyone who knew.

I am sorry you revived this incident, even by way of denying that there was any truth in it. When an actor is accused of drinking it means that he drank as Edmund Kean and Robson drank. In that sense Irving did not drink. He went on the stage in his later days in the condition in which many London clubmen who are not teetotallers are after dinner; but that does not call for any comment.

I wrote to Irving to say that I had no objection whatever to his returning the play (which, by the way, I had never sent him: he got it from E. T.) but that as it had been announced as an item in his future program, it would not look well to withdraw it after an unpleasing notice without some dignified explanation. He immediately set Austin or Stoker to write elaborately sarcastic letters to me. I replied fiercely asking him whether he supposed I did not know who had written these letters, and what he thought would happen to his henchmen if I started that game on them. Then he completely disarmed me. He wrote me with his own hand and out of his own head and in his own not very literary style (like Queen Victoria's) a sincere little letter, the gist of which was "For God's sake, let me alone." So I let him alone and never meddled in his affairs again until he died, when his worst enemy, thinking like you that I was his Iago (I could make people laugh by calling you Roderigo; but it wouldn't be true) came to me to prevent his burial in the Abbey. It could have been done very easily; for this is a moral country, and Henry was not a moral man in his domestic affairs. I averted the danger by a stroke of diplomacy; and Henry kept his halo undimmed.

And now, to revert to the difficulty I was in as both playwright and dramatic critic. How was I to give managers access to my plays without making overtures to them. Simply by publishing them. But the reading public did not read plays. How could they, when there was nothing but French's acting edition with its technical jargon of first second and third entrances, right, left, centre and so forth? I proposed to Heinemann to publish plays in a form as readable as novels. I undertook to make an acting edition available as a prompt book and yet not containing a single reference to the stage. He assured me that it was impossible; that people would never read plays. He showed me Pinero's ledger account, in which all the sales were in batches for amateur performances. However, I persisted; and Grant Richards ventured: hence Plays, Pleasant and Unpleasant, of which E. T. had the first copy. That is the explanation of the stage directions. She did not feel insulted by them. Your notion that she would have preferred four words of cue, followed by Enter R. U. E. to R. C. without a word as to whether she was a charwoman or a queen, an old crone or an ingenue, will not wash. Later on, when E. T. read Brassbound to Henry to see whether the title part would appeal to him, his comment on the stage directions about the entry of the smuggler captain in the last act dressed in the height of fashion was a shrewd one. "Shaw put that in to make the audience laugh at me." And he was right: when Laurence created the part at the Stage Society the audience roared for a full minute.

You mention a string of parts played by Irving from which you think I borrowed my stage business. I never saw him play any of them except

The Bells, and that I saw long afterwards unintentionally when I bought one of the last stalls ever sold at the Lyceum to see Coriolanus and found the bill changed. Also I never [read] Archer's books about Irving, and never joined in the derision of his gait, as to the artistic character of which you are quite right, or his speech, as to which you are ludicrously wrong. Alexander Bell, the author of the Standard Elocutionist, spoke to me about it and was unbounded in his admiration of Irving's elocution. If you were a phonetic expert—which you ought to be, by the way—you would understand that what Irving did was to pronounce vowels as vowels and not as diphthongs. He said "gold," not go-oold nor gah-oold; and he said "Take the rope" and not "Tay-eek the rah-oop (or roh-oop)." All you could make of it was "Tek the rup"; but that is "unnly yrrr ignorance, me beu-ity." Of course it was not vernacular English; but it was not blundering; and, as you perceived, it had artistic charm.

Thank you for the correction about Napoleon's age. That howler has glared from my pages for 34 [error for 32] years; and you were the first to discover it. Also you have spotted my omission to get rid of those writing materials when I found that I could do without them. I have made both corrections.

Dont ever again couple Barry Sullivan and Salvini as a pair of barnstormers. If you had seen them you might have contrasted them; but you would never have dreamt of comparing them.

And now, finally, let me congratulate you on having produced an essay that is so exquisitely right whenever you record a direct personal impression that all your bad guesses and booberies are as dust in the balance. How you have contrived to go through the world after getting free from that utterly damned little backwater where Irving played with a theatre and made "table legs" of good actors (I saw a great deal of poor Sam Johnson in his prime) exactly as little German kinglets used to play with soldiers—how you have seen all Europe, and mixed with real live men and women, without ever bringing your experience to bear on that childish slavery, or seeing what was raging round you all the time, or shedding a single one of the ignorances and limitations of your master, is so amazing that I think you ought to leave your head to the College of Surgeons to ascertain what wonderful impressionable substance it contains instead of brains. My admiration for the good bits of the book is unbounded; but your wanderings through the real world crying always for a theatre to play with force me to remind you that that is not what a theatre is for. If you get a theatre, from Cochran or another, and play with it, it will be taken from you by a joint stock

209

company, and you will find yourself in the wilderness again. Perhaps, after all, the wilderness is your real element.

faithfully
G. Bernard Shaw

[A postscript was drafted in shorthand on the carbon copy retained in Shaw's files (it is now at Texas); the text was not included in the copy posted to Craig.]

PS. The correspondence will fill up the significant lacuna in your book as to the beautiful flower Irving put on the table of which he made you a leg. It must have been hard to be brought up under a tyranny of Terry Women—a delightful but overwhelming species, not good for a sensitive boy—but you are the son of your father, not of your mother. He, too, was an architect who built castles in the air and tried to put them on the stage. With such a father, and such a stepfather as H.I., and such a mother! what a subject for an autobiography!

Reit wunn, me beu–ity: reit wunn.

To HERBERT SAMUEL

4 Whitehall Court SW1
[A/53]   18th October 1930

[Herbert Samuel, who would in 1937 become first Viscount Samuel of Mount Carmel and of Toxteth, Liverpool, was a Liberal M.P. In 1931 he was elected Leader of the Liberal Parliamentary Party. Samuel Wallrock was treasurer for a testimonial dinner to Albert Einstein, sponsored by the Joint British Committee of Ort and Oze, organisations dedicated to the promotion of the well-being of East European Jewry, to be held in the Savoy Hotel on 28th October. Sir Arthur Eddington (1882–1944), knighted that year, was professor of astronomy at Cambridge University, a noted mathematician and astrophysicist. The Astronomer Royal was Sir Frank Dyson (1868–1939). It was Donna Julia in Byron's *Don Juan* (Canto I, stanza CXVII) who, "whispering [she would] ne'er consent, consented."]

My dear Samuel
    I have placed myself quite unreservedly at the disposal of Wallrock to do any job that a Gentile can fitly discharge; and he tells me that I am to propose Einstein's health: a tremendous honor which I should perhaps have funked if it were not that E. has once or twice written to me and spoken of me in terms which entitle me to consider myself *persona grata* with him. I will do my best.

I hesitated at first because I thought you were going to do it, and failing you, possibly Eddington or the Astronomer Royal or some big gun of science; but Wallrock told me that you had to make the appeal for the charity, and that it was not thought desirable that the bouquet should be handed to E. by another man from the same shop—that what is wanted is a non-scientific person who is a bit of a draw and a bit of a speaker; so I, swearing I should ne'er consent, consented.

But if for any reason a change in the arrangements should prove desirable, you need stand on no ceremony with me: I will fall in with the situation, whatever it may be.

faithfully
G. Bernard Shaw

To JOHN REITH

[H/99]

Ayot St Lawrence. Welwyn
20th October 1930

[Shaw's speech proposing Einstein's health was broadcast shortwave by the B.B.C. to America, being Shaw's first broadcast overseas. The domestic broadcast, scheduled for 9.40 to 10.10 p.m. on the National Programme, not unexpectedly ran over its time. The just-knighted Sir Henry Lytton (1865–1936) was for most of his career a mainstay of the D'Oyly Carte Opera Co., noted for his Ko-ko, Jack Point, and Bunthorne.]

Dear Director-General

On Tuesday the 28th I have to propose the health of Einstein (who will be present) at a public dinner given ostensibly for the benefit of a fund for the assistance of poor Jews throughout Europe. Our speeches are to be broadcast; but your people have not quite grasped the importance of the occasion. They write as if I were going to talk of Balkan politics or some such rubbish for 15 minutes. Now I have nothing to do with the Jewish charity: the appeal for that will be made quite separately by Mr Herbert Samuel. I must make a full dress oration about Ptolemy & Aristotle, Kepler & Copernicus, Galileo & Newton, gravitation and relativity and modern astro-physics and Heaven knows what, hailing Einstein as the successor of Newton, and speaking on the largest scale in the name of British culture and science welcoming the foremost natural philosopher of the last 300 years. The job should really be done by the Prime Minister; but he has left it to me; and it should be heralded with the utmost possible réclame, or we shall be branded as Philistines and have derisive comparisons drawn between the array of ministers at the banquet to the Savoyard Sir Henry Lytton and the neglect of Einstein.

I cannot do it in 15 minutes, and shall be lucky if I get out of it in 25. As to limiting Einstein, it is out of the question: we must be prepared for 2 minutes or 30 at his pleasure.

I suggest a special inset in The Radio Times, and an elastic musical program which can be adapted to whatever may happen in the hour following my rising.

faithfully
G. Bernard Shaw

To HERBERT SAMUEL

4 Whitehall Court SW 1
[A/53]   23rd October 1930
[Shaw's luncheon invitation was not accepted.]

My dear Samuel
Wallrock tells me that you are entertaining Einstein during his visit. I do not know what arrangements this involves; but it may prove convenient for you to make use of us in the matter. Here in this flat, the view over the river from which is much admired by foreigners, we can entertain six guests to lunch at a few hours notice. You and Mrs Samuel and the illustrious guest will be most welcome at any time, with any friends it may be advisable to bring.

Just make a note of this as an available resource in no way binding on you in case it should amuse Einstein or relieve Mrs Samuel for a moment of her duties as hostess.

I presume, as the visit (Wallrock says) is to be very short, Mrs Einstein is not accompanying him; but if she is, so much the better.

I hope he has learnt some English since he was here last; for my linguistic attainments are deplorable, and I cannot, like Eddington, converse with him in equations. . . .

faithfully
G. Bernard Shaw

212

To HENRY MURRAY

[4 Whitehall Court S W 1]
[C/9]   2nd November 1930

[The Irving rôles were in *Louis XI* by Casimir Delavigne, rewritten by Dion
Boucicault; *Robert Macaire* by Charles Selby; *The Bells* by Leopold Lewis;
King Charles I by W. G. Wills. Murray is unidentified.]

I dont think any actor could beat Irving's Louis XI, Macaire,
Mathias, Charles I, *et hoc genus omne*. His Shylock was remarkable,
though he made him a martyred saint. And one or two moments in his
Richard II stick in my memory. But in big straight parts, which require
what is classed as great acting, he was nothing but himself as he
fancied himself. Those who thought him great in them had never seen
great acting. Craig was in that category. Besides, he never saw Irving
from the front. And he can hardly have read Shakespear or he would
not quote with admiration Irving's absurd suggestion that he should
play Oswald like Malvolio because both were stewards.

GBS

To J. M. KENWORTHY

4 Whitehall Court S W 1
[H/1]   13th November 1930

[Joseph M. Kenworthy (1886–1953), later tenth Baron Strabolgi, a retired
Lieutenant Commander of the Royal Navy and former Liberal M.P., was
at this time Labour M.P. for Central Hull. He was the author of several
books, the current one being *New Wars, New Weapons*. Aldershot is a
principal military training centre, in Hampshire.]

My dear Kenworthy
    Thanks for the book and the friendly inscription. It is a good square
18″ hit between wind and water.
    I find when I talk to airmen that they are greatly oppressed by the
way in which they are tied to the ground by their dependence on
petrol: they always say that people do not realize what an enormous
ground force is needed to keep them going. I think they are so influenced by the contrast between the mobility of the plane and the
comparative immobility of the petrol supply that they forget that this
immobility is due to the fact that the men on the ground are organized
as soldiers in the Aldershot manner and that their supplies can be
made as mobile as themselves by air transport. Your book will be very

useful for instances of the success of airmen in doing the very things that they themselves declare they can never do. At all events it seems to me to be pretty convincing.

The extent to which people's minds run in the old groove is beyond belief except by those who have not broken their shins over it. When the first air raids arrived during the War I wrote an urgent letter to The Times suggesting that sandbagged elephant shelters should be put into all the playgrounds of the elementary schools so that the children might have a familiar place of safety to run to. To my utter amazement the editor refused indignantly to insert a letter suggesting such an unheard-of outrage on decency as an attack by civilized troops on the civilian population. I gasped, and sent the letter to A.G. Gardiner for insertion in The Daily News. He said that he had never expected to find himself in agreement with The Times on any subject; but that on this he fully and warmly agreed, and would not on any account publish my disgraceful and perverse suggestion. Of course the raids presently knocked this nonsense out of both of them, but that they should ever have entertained it shews that civilians never grasp the reality of war until it is on top of them, as it literally will be next time. If they did, war would be impossible.

The only safe Pacifists are those who, like yourself, have been trained as members of the fighting forces and are therefore by profession realists as to war. Your books are the only ones on the Labor side that are in contact with this problem, and are therefore the only ones I can read. You also know some geography: an accomplishment almost unique in political life.

So peg away: the brass hats and tarry trousers cannot finally withstand you.

faithfully
G.Bernard Shaw

To BEATRICE WEBB

[H.t/14]

Ayot St Lawrence. Welwyn
30th November 1930

[The Fabian Society's autumn lecture series was "The Unending Quest: An Inquiry into Developments in Democratic Government." Arthur Ponsonby, the newly created first Baron Ponsonby of Shulbrede, gave the fourth lecture, "The Old Bridge and the New Traffic," on 13th November. Beatrice Webb gave the fifth, "Can We Make British Parliamentary Government

Equal to Its Task?" on the 20th. Shaw finished off the series in the Kingsway Hall on the 27th with a lecture "A Cure for Democracy." The new series of Fabian Essays contemplated by Shaw did not eventuate. There was, however, a *New Fabian Essays* in 1952, edited by R. H. S. Crossman, with a preface by Clement Attlee.]

My dear Beatrice

I am not satisfied with the upshot of our conversation on Friday. I was played out nervously: I am too old for these ninety minute orations out of training, and must give them up. But Sidney was placidly aggravating to a most trying extent. What are you to do with a man who, being by profession and vocation an extraordinary and exceptional man, conceives himself a commonplace sensible Englishman living in a world of just such commonplace sensible Englishmen, and refuses to attach any importance to anything because every problem must yield to common sense in such a world. And all the time the real world is a world of cinema-poisoned ignorant romantic duffers who read the Daily Mail when they read anything at all except the serial in The Daily Herald. I, who am at least a theatrical person, and therefore far more representative than Sidney, stop short of the infatuation of believing that I am living in a world of Bernard Shaws.

What I now propose as far as the Fabian Society is concerned, is a new set of Fabian Essays on the Political Machinery of Socialism. They can appear in the Political Quarterly if the authors want to get paid; but as that would involve a dangerous delay I should prefer advancing them the money if they need it and getting the book out as soon as possible.

There should be a very good historical essay on the Party System, a very good practical one on the municipal system, an essay on the existing local government boundaries and their obsolescence and the fact that modern facilities of communication have made even regional divisions vieux jeu, an able survey of the crashing of British and pseudo-British constitutionalism all over Europe and on the essential impermanence of the dictatorial makeshifts which are bridging the landslide, a Ponsonbystic essay on the need for division of ministerial labor, with illustrations from the hopeless traffic block which has paralyzed the Labor Government, and finally an essay (? by you) with specifications and plans of the new machinery.

There you have matter for six thrilling essays which would bring the Fabian to life again.

If we are really dead, and cannot seize this opportunity, it may be that Samuel and Lothian and Lloyd George will half seize it and share the fate of those who make half revolutions. But the Labor Party, which is rapidly developing into a Bourbon Party, may incur the doom of those who make no revolutions.

And, I repeat violently, unless the Labor Party acquires an overwhelming prestige by some such quite possible and generally intelligi[ble] feat as this, it will never be able to get away with the later feat of killing Queen Anne and the coffee houses as well as Henry the Sixth and his College of the Blessed Mary at Eton opposite Windsor. The real fight will be for the souls of the children and the kicking aside of the educational stone of Sisyphus.

I shall miss the village post if I go on.

G.B.S.

To THE REV. E. W. LUMMIS

4 Whitehall Court SW1
[H/6]   10th December 1930

[The Rev. Edward William Lummis (1867–1937) was the author or translator of several books on religion. "Matamore" is a French name signifying a braggart or hector. Sir John Oldcastle (1377?–1417), a Lollard leader, friend of Henry Prince of Wales, gained the title of Baron Cobham in 1409. He later was hanged as a heretic and traitor. The Lollards ("mutterers" over prayers) were religious reformers, followers of John Wyclif. Shaw's misquotation from Ruskin is an oversimplification of what Ruskin actually said in "Natural Inspiration" (*Modern Painters*, 1856, Vol. IV, Chapter 20). Anthony Munday (1560?–1633), poet and dramatist, author of many London city pageants, and Michael Drayton (1563–1631), poet, are believed to have collaborated on *Sir John Oldcastle*, Part I, an historical drama, with Richard Hathway and Robert Wilson, published in 1600. Lummis insisted that Shakespeare had written two separate plays, a Sir John Oldcastle (Falstaff) satyr play and a Henry IV/Prince Hal history play, and then, supposedly to placate the censor, interrelated the two. Lummis was striving to re-create the two original plays prior to their fusion, and had asked Shaw to aid him in obtaining publication by providing a preface. "I do not think," Shaw wrote to him on 12th September, "that you will induce any responsible author to accept your redesigning of the Shakespearean structure as an authentic restoration. Certainly I cannot" (A/6).]

Dear Mr Lummis

A circus clown is not a real character. He is a fantasy. He is a drunkard, a glutton, a thief, a coward, a braggart, a liar, red nosed, ridiculous, kicked, beaten, exposed, tripped up and knocked down when he is not

216

tripping himself up and knocking himself over from a sheer impossibility of doing anything right. He has no social status, no family (except, anecdotically, his uncle the pawnbroker and his mother-in-law), no conscience, no property, and no proper name. Punch, Mascarille, Sganarelle, Matamore, Pistol, Bobadil, Bessus, Joey are not names: they are only epithets; and even these are too definite for the circus clown, who has no name at all.

Now this description applies exactly to Falstaff (except that he has a name and title) in the first part of Henry IV. But in Shakespear's hands he grew irresistibly into a human character. He became Sir John Falstaff, dissolute, impecunious, jolly, indulging low appetites in low company as many of his class have been and done, but quite real, and not in the least a circus clown. To the Chief Justice he says "My Lord, I will not undergo this sneap without reply . . . I say to you I do desire deliverance from these officers, being upon hasty employment in the King's affairs" [Part two: II.i.133–140]. The buffoon of Part I could not take this tone. Pistol is still Captain Matamore, a pure fantasy; but Sir John says "I would be quiet, Pistol" [Part two: II.iv.199] and throws him downstairs instead of being himself thrown down. In Shallow's house the party is quite real: the knight and the justice are not clowns but genuine human characters. Even in the end of Part I Falstaff did not dream of shirking his military duties: he did not run from Douglas as the clown ran away at Gadshill; and his beetle's ruse when he found Douglas too much for him, though it is still a circus funniment, is the trick of a fighter, not of a poltroon. Finally the whole play is spoiled by his acceptance of the king's sanctimonious rebuke, which he has no moral right to administer, and which clamors for an effective retort and a comic triumph for Falstaff.

You will now see what I mean when I say that to begin with the scenes from Part II and go on to scenes from Part I is to make the character evolve backwards. It is like transposing the early chapters of Don Quixote or Pickwick (the leading examples of the same evolution) to the end of the books. That is the real difficulty of accepting your otherwise quite plausible arrangement instead of concluding that on the accession of Cobham Oldcastle was renamed, the dancer's epilogue added, and the death of Falstaff in Henry V provided to order.

I have had to write this in scraps and in great haste. You must make the best you can of it.

faithfully
G. Bernard Shaw

217

PS   Ruskin's observation that Shakespear had no conscience s borne out by his doing for Oldcastle what he did for Joan of Arc. But have you ever gone into the evidence that the Shakespears were a Catholic family. S. made no pretence of having any religion; but he was all the more likely to accept a family bias against Lollardry if there was one. Is the Munday-Drayton play in the British Museum or the Bodleian?

GBS

PART II

1931-1936

II

(1931–1936)

The Shaws travelled extensively throughout their married life, but rarely so much or so far as in 1931 to 1936. Considering the routine dullness of Charlotte's home life, as she shouldered the domestic burden of running two households, it is not surprising that she should have craved change of scene more than GBS did, or succumbed so readily to the blandishments of travel prospectuses. The basic problem during the early years of their marriage was that the two had conflicting notions of what comprised a satisfying holiday. Shaw was fond of walking tours; Charlotte, he informed Lady Gregory, "never walks a yard when there is a vehicle—even a wheelbarrow—to be had for love or money." Thus, when he tramped the roads it was perforce with Beatrice and Sidney Webb or with Granville Barker, never with his wife. Shaw from the first was motor crazy, never more content than when zooming along country lanes on his motor-bike or traversing the roads of Britain and the Continent in one of several successive motor-cars. Charlotte, who preferred the comparative comfort of train travel, and who was happiest at sea, stoically compromised and motored with him, bringing her sister along for companionship while Shaw hobnobbed in the front with the chauffeur and did much of the driving. Frequently, however, she would encourage him to go off on his own, accompanied by the Barkers, the Webbs, J. M. Barrie, or Judy Gillmore, while she crossed to Ireland with her sister, to America with Lena Ashwell, or to Rome. People, they agreed, needed a holiday from each other as much as they needed a change of scene.

For a man who professed to dislike travel and who invariably blamed his wife for his holiday jaunts ("My wife," he told Otto Kyllmann in 1933, "has taken it into her head that she must go round the world before she dies; and I shall have to go with her"), Shaw was a complaisant traveller, putting off his packing to the very last moment yet bounding off agreeably with Charlotte to almost every conceivable part of the world. He crossed the seas to Jamaica, North Africa, Madeira, and Sweden, motored frequently through France and across Germany, Switzerland, Italy, Austria, and Scotland, and made thirteen visits to Ireland. Enthusiastically, he adjusted to all scenes and situations. At Biskra he read the Koran and rode a camel. He learned to tango in

Madeira. Aboard ship he tried his hand at shuffleboard. He made extensive notes on motoring, subsequently converting these into anonymous reports and recommendations for fellow members of the Royal Automobile Club. He took hundreds of photographs. Struggling to communicate, he tried his hand at Pelman lessons in Spanish and Italian, submitting the worksheets in his secretary's name.

His first cruise, in 1899, had been frustratingly debilitating. "Life on board a pleasure steamer," he complained from the Mediterranean to Sydney Cockerell, "violates every moral & physical condition of healthy life except fresh air ... It is a guzzling, lounging, gambling, dog's life. The only alternative to excitement is irritability." In later years, however, he seemed to thrive on sea voyages: the freedom from professional pressures, combined with open sea and sky, invariably had a beneficial effect on his creative imagination. Plays flowed freely from his pen at sea, from *Blanco Posnet* en route to Africa and *Fanny's First Play* while crossing to Jamaica to *On the Rocks* and *Geneva* in the Pacific. En route to New Zealand in 1934 he confided to Leonora Ervine that he had begun "to shoot into the air more and more extravagantly without any premeditation whatever—*advienne que pourra*," in his playwriting. *The Simpleton of the Unexpected Isles*, written in tropical climes, was, he said, "openly oriental, hieratic and insane." *The Millionairess* he admitted was conventional in form and "the theme quite stuffily matrimonial," but the dialogue, he announced, was "raving lunacy from beginning to end."

The voyages of the 1930s were enjoyed more as an end in themselves than as means of conveyance to foreign scenes. Though the Shaws travelled simply, without maid or valet, Charlotte insisted on comfort. Their agent had orders to provide them with a suite of two staterooms, large enough to contain two steamer trunks each plus valises and a quantity of small cases. The beds, where possible, were to be set against the centre wall away from portholes and doors. Isolated deck chairs were commandeered and, spurning invitations to join the captain's table, the Shaws opted for a table to themselves in a remote corner of the dining saloon. There they would, as at home, read in silence through the entire meal. Early each morning, weather permitting, Shaw would swim laps in the otherwise unoccupied outdoor pool, then take a brisk walk round the promenade deck. After breakfast on his own, for Charlotte slept late, he would settle into a deck chair for a morning session of correspondence (often in shorthand, turned over later to the ship's typist for transliteration), the reading of accumulated batches of press cuttings (which then were discarded), or play composition. Playwriting had become, he said, a Platonic exercise with him: on a long voyage "you have to work or go mad." During long months at sea neither GBS nor Charlotte ever altered their regimen: except at breakfast they never missed a meal together.

Their reading on voyages was prodigious. Each brought a capacious bookbag on the journey, crammed to the brim with recent publications acquired from Bumpus the bookseller. Once read, the books were presented to the ship's library. A list of the books presented to the *Rangitane* in 1934 indicates their eclectic taste: Lloyd George's *War Memoirs* in two volumes; Hitler's *My Struggle* (which Shaw later reported he had only sampled), J. M. Kenworthy's *Sailors, Statesmen and Others*, Lord Berners's *First Childhood*, André Maurois' *Edward VII*, biographies of De Valera, Napoleon, Sydney Smith (by Hesketh Pearson), and Cecil Rhodes, R. H. Bruce Lockhart's *Memoirs of a British Agent*, J. M. Henry's *A New Fundamentalism*, R. F. Rattray's *Bernard Shaw*, a play by James Bridie, a few novels, and several works on New Zealand, to which they were en route.

When they ventured ashore at ports on their world cruises, gaping crowds of tourists and omnipresent journalists would surround GBS, determined to hear the clever repartee expected to pour from his mouth. Accommodatingly GBS would pose for flashlight photos and Kodak snapshots, smiling bemusedly as he made an effort to respond to the unimaginative, largely predictable questions of the reporters. Charlotte, shrinking from the limelight, would usually lag unobtrusively several yards behind her husband, fleeing to ship's cabin or hotel room or waiting limousine as rapidly as possible. Only once or twice did she participate actively in an interview as when, aboard the *Arandora Star* at Honolulu in 1936, in response to the question "Do you believe that the wives of famous men should submerge their individualities in those of their husbands?" she replied with a bright smile, "Oh, but I have always done what I wanted. . . . You see, I only appear conventional on the surface. But underneath I am the most unconventional of persons."

Increasingly, as their energies flagged in tropical heat, the Shaws would decline to disembark, eschewing explorations of Bangkok or San Salvador. Occasionally they would elect to explore a port city in depth, as in Bombay, in preference to joining a dusty excursion by train to interior cities. "On examining the map," Shaw told reporters, "I find that I should hardly see anything except the inside of a railway carriage, the country is so vast."

They were not too old or weary, however, to savour new experiences.

223

In New Zealand GBS joined in a Maori singsong. A year later in Africa, at Mapumulo, he participated in a Zulu war dance, chanting and clapping along with the warriors and attempting a step or two, which Charlotte insisted was really only a jig. Aboard ship he tried square dancing. In South Africa they accepted an invitation to fly over the Cape Town peninsula for nearly an hour in a mail service Junkers monoplane of the Union Airways fleet. It was Charlotte's first flight, and the first experience of modern flying for GBS, his only previous ascents having been in a pre-war Farman biplane and by balloon. He was fascinated to learn that the Junkers had flown seven thousand feet above the Cape, at a speed of 110 miles an hour. "Incredible," he said; "how is it done?" As he questioned the pilot it became evident that he possessed an astonishing working knowledge of aviation technicalities, a knowledge that also impressed Pan American executives in Miami several years later. Charlotte too showed lively interest in the plane's operation, and volunteered that she would not object to flying all the way to the north of Africa on the return journey.

When their second world cruise ended in 1936, the Shaws disembarked for what GBS may by then have realised would be the last time. Asked by a journalist, "After visiting twenty-nine countries, what do you think would be the best country to live in?" Shaw's succinct reply was, "I should say Heaven."

To EDWARD ELGAR

[A/132]

Ayot St Lawrence. Welwyn
2nd January 1931

[Charlotte Shaw took a bad tumble while shopping in Hanover Street on 29th October 1930, cracking a bone in her shoulder and another in her pelvis, though happily not the hip joint. Until the end of the year she was obliged, as Shaw told several correspondents, "to lie up and mend herself." The Very Rev. William Moore Ede (1850–1935) was Dean of Worcester 1908–34. Shaw's authorship of a suggested revision of the National Anthem was revealed in the *New York Times*, 22nd December 1943. "V.S." is *Volti Subito*, a term used by conductors, meaning "turn quickly" at foot of a leaf of the music score. Elgar had been Master of the King's Musick since 1924.]

My dear Elgar

Charlotte got over her smash wonderfully; BUT she was no sooner on her legs again than the *other* leg—the one that had to play two parts —went on strike; and she can now do little more than hobble with a stick. But the condition is passing; and I hope another week will effect a second recovery.

Somebody who couldnt stand the grotesque contrast of your gorgeous new orchestral garment for the National Anthem with its disgraceful old literary rags has written to the Dean—your dean—Moore Ede—proposing the following amendment to the second verse.

O Lord our God arise
All our salvation lies
    In! Thy! Great! Hand! (à la Elgar)
Centre his thoughts on Thee {his / her
Let him God's captain be (Let her God's handmaid be)
Thine to Eternity
God save the {King / Queen   V.S.

Now Moore Ede thinks that his anonymous correspondent is G.B.S. But the least suspicion of such an origin would spoil everything when the Deans (the 3) put the proposal through to the King, with the Master of Music as counsellor-assessor. Ede, instead of being made a bishop, would be thrown down the stairs of Buckingham Palace. Whereas if they can all honestly swear that they don't know (if asked) or will let it be assumed that the amendment is their own (if not asked) then I should imagine the change would be well received. Moore Ede is not enthusiastic because he feels very strongly on the Indian question and finds his views exactly expressed by "Con Found Their Poll itticks," and also perhaps because Deans acquire the habit of ordering God about, and care no more for the cathedral after the first fortnight than if it were a fried fish shop; but on reflection he will see that the war killed Muscular Christianity, and that the glaringly needed change is a great chance for him.

Have you ever discussed this matter with the Family or its Head or Headess? The existing lines are hard for any Christian to stand; and how any decent contralto can bring herself to sing them after your exordium beats me.

The lumbago is deplorable: Charlotte weeps over it. Are you quite *quite* sure that your haunch bone (*alias* the Innominate) is not out of place? Did you try Pheils? he is a virtuoso on the bones; and his personal resemblance to an ophicleide would please you.

ever
G.B.S.

To EDWARD ELGAR

4 Whitehall Court SW1
[C/85]   15th January 1931
[A "cancrizans symphony" is a musical composition in which the theme or subject is repeated backwards note for note.]

Moore Ede informs me that Dean No 2 thinks that it would be simpler to omit the second verse, and Dean No 3 thinks that your version has three stanzas and that any change would involve rescoring and totally upsetting all the musical arrangements.

Sancta simplicitas!

Both of these bothered clerics think that the change had better be made next year, at Worcester.

So much the better for M.E. if it is.

They *must* consult you.

I am inclined to agree with your favorable opinion of the anonymous

226

correspondent's lines in view of the appalling limitations imposed. Imagine having to compose a sort of cancrizans symphony which would do just as well played backwards in four-bar sections as forwards!

GBS

To UNIDENTIFIED CORRESPONDENT

[S/5]

[4 Whitehall Court SW1]
6th February 1931

[Blanche Patch kept a commonplace book, in which she copied significant portions of text from Shaw's correspondence, without identification of recipient. This is one of the transcribed passages. The book is now in the Berg Collection, New York Public Library. For Gilbert Murray's League of Nations committee, see letter of 4th May 1932. Greece's demand for return of the "Elgin marbles" from the British Museum continues to the present day.]

The only excuse ever offered for Lord Elgin's plunder was that the Greeks cared so little about the Acropolis that its fragments were far safer in foreign museums than at home. When I was in Athens a proposal to demolish the little Byzantine church in the Athenian Piccadilly Circus almost provoked a revolution, though it was a serious obstruction to the city traffic, & though the citizens would have sold the Erectheum to any American cheerfully for $100. But if it can now be established that the Acropolis is being carefully protected, & that its fragments have been pieced together as you say, the government or the municipality of Athens should appeal to the League of Nations through Professor Gilbert Murray's Committee, for the return of the so-called Elgin Marbles. That is the first step to be taken; & it is one in which I have no *locus standi*.

To MOLLY TOMPKINS

[A/1; W/319]

Ayot St Lawrence. Welwyn
17th February 1931

My dear Molly

... When you meet the Granville-Barkers don't mention me in *her* presence, as you will embarras[s] him and infuriate her. She hates me with a lethal malignity which seriously damages my health if I come near her; and if by disregarding her feelings you draw any of that hatred on yourself you may not only suffer in the same way but will certainly lose the interesting acquaintance of G.B. She has detached him entirely from me. Lawrence's devotion to you is feeble compared to his to her; and he has thought the world well lost for her—and lost it, because though she has quite serious literary talent she has not an idea in her head later than 1865, and quite honestly believed that in getting him away from his old associates she was redeeming him socially and artistically. He was a playwright in the running with myself: now he is almost forgotten. The Labor Party would probably have made him a peer (they were desperately hard up for presentable men who could afford to enter the House of Lords) if he had stuck to his Fabian politics. In 20 years he has produced only two plays. One is no use: the other I have tried to persuade Barry Jackson to produce at the Malvern Festival; so far in vain; but I have hopes. I tried to get him knighted (to please *her*) at the last distribution of honors; but as he dropped the Labor Party it naturally dropped him.

So be careful how you tread. Do not broach the sore subject of G.B.S. But if you can let me have any news of him it will interest me. He has an Italian strain in him and was meant to be a man of genius.

Whatever you do, don't call her Mrs Barker. She insists on the hyphenation.

In haste for the village post.
GBS

To SYDNEY C. COCKERELL

Hotel Fast. Jerusalem
13th March 1931

[A/3]

[Shaw and Charlotte travelled from London to Marseilles, via Folkestone and Boulogne, on 3rd March, to join the Hellenic Travellers' Club tour of the Mediterranean and the Holy Land, sailing in the *Théophile Gautier* the following day. The four weeks' tour included Malta, Alexandria, Cairo, Jerusalem, Damascus, Beirut, Cyprus, Rhodes, Eleusis and Athens (with Shaw lecturing on the 29th, to a group that included the Very Rev. William Ralph Inge, Dean of St Paul's, on Greek theatre). During Shaw's three days in Jerusalem he visited the Mount of Olives, Tomb of Kings, Garden tomb, Wailing Wall, the principal temples, mosques, and churches, Via Dolorosa, Gethsemane, Virgin's tomb, Bethlehem, Nazareth, Dead Sea, Jordan, Jericho, Elisha's tomb, and Bethany.]

My dear Cockerell

Do you know any promising young craftsman or woman who could make a reliquary? A nice little lady's private reliquary, not a monster shrine.

Dame Laurentia asked me to bring her something from Calvary; but there is no credible Calvary; and what there is is not removable except by a squad of engineers backed by a victorious army. Innumerable Jew peddlers pressed me to buy rosaries, testaments bound in wood (by implication I suppose the wood of the Cross), and every conceivable trash; but I could not put her off with such stuff. So I shook the dust of fraudulent Jerusalem from my feet and went to Bethlehem, where, just outside the church of the Nativity, I picked up a little stone, a chip of the limestone rock, which may just as likely as not have felt the feet of Mary or her son, who certainly ran all over the place barefooted when he was a small boy [Cockerell has written in the margin, "Nazareth, not Bethlehem"]. What I want is some modestly precious setting or mounting for that stone, which is about the size of a young Brazil nut, but more becomingly cut; for I cannot chuck a pebble at the Abbey with nothing to distinguish it from a pebble picked up in Birmingham or Brighton.

Do not tell her anything about this. Just let me know by return to the Grand Hotel, Venice, where I expect to arrive on April the first, whether you know of anyone who would value the job.

It occurred to me to ask Kennington, who seems to be able to work in anything.

They call the new fashionable residential Zionist quarters here The New Jerusalem, quite seriously. The city is surprisingly unimpressive, considering its history and associations. Except the country I have seen nothing first rate. After Cairo, which has stupendous treasures, it is very cheap.

G.B.S.

To LAURENTIA McLACHLAN

[A/98; X/256]   St Patrick's Day in Damascus 1931

[Edward Keith-Roach (1885–1954) was district commissioner of the Jerusalem division of Palestine 1926–31.]

Dear Sister Laurentia

This Holy Land is in a queer situation from the Crusader's point of view, which is officially your point of view. The British representative in Jerusalem is also the representative, precisely, of Pontius Pilate; and when Communist Messiahs turn up, as they actually do from time to time under Russian influences, he is bound to handle the case on Pilatical lines. What would any medieval Christian saint—or say Richard Cœur de Lion—say if miraculously resuscitated in Jerusalem today? Saladin and the followers of the accurst Mahound vanquished at last by the Christian British Empire. The circumcised crucifiers of Christ scattered through the ghettos of Europe. The Cross triumphant over all the Promised Land, over Christ's birthplace, over his sepulchre, over the Mount of the Beatitudes and over the bloodstained plain (which Christ overlooked from that Mount) on which Saladin smashed the last effort of the Crusaders to resist him, over Galilee and Samaria, Bethlehem, Nazareth, Capernaum, over the waters on which he walked and the hillsides from which he preached, over Nain and Cana and Bethany, over Jordan in which he was baptized, and the unknown Golgotha on which he was duly executed according to the official routine by the predecessor of Mr Keith Roach.

So far, praised be God, Richard would say, probably adding a stentorian Hep, hep, hep!

But when Richard was further informed that the use England had made of its victory was to hand over all that sacred territory to the descendants and co-religionists of Saladin and to those of Annas and Caiphas, having promised it to both for their help in the war, and that Pontius now had his hands full with the job of keeping the peace between them, he would surely either start a new crusade or return to his tomb in disgust with a world gone entirely mad.

I ask myself whether I shall persuade Sister Laurentia to get a hundred days indulgence, a tailormade short skirt, gaiter boots, a Fair Isle pullover, a smart waterproof, a field glass and camera, a brown sun umbrella lined with red, and a Revelation suit case, and hasten hither to see for herself what she has imagined at Stanbrook. I leave the question unanswered; but I will tell you what might happen to you because it has happened to me.

You would enter the Holy Land at night under a strong impression made on you in Egypt, not by the Tutankhamen trash which the tourists are now mobbing, but by something seen under the pyramids. A pyramid is just as big as its royal builder is old; and it is always finished. If he dies a baby, there is his monument ready for him, like this: Δ . If he grows up, his tomb grows with him Δ

and so on, if he lives as long as Cheops, to △ . There was a red-haired queen who made a tomb for herself and her daughters, deep under tons of pyramid and rock, and set two great artists, Rahay a painter and Yenkaf a sculptor, to work in it. Whether the redhaired one and her brood were very fine ladies, or whether the two fine artists made fine ladies of them I do not know; but when you see that row of sculptured women come alive in a hundred candle power electric sunlight without a shadow of death or fear on their shining faces and pleasantly courteous eyes or a line or contour in their whole bodies that is not exquisite, and when you turn to their magnificently designed portraits on the wall, the impression you receive is beyond description in our lower language, as of an order of beings completely redeemed from sin and vulgarity and all the plagues of our degradation, and yet not in the least geniuses, as Michael Angelo would have made them, but girls whom you might enlist for Stanbrook without expecting them to excel in doing as well as in being. You might question their vocation on the ground that they seem to have no religion nor to need any, having achieved excellence and being content to leave it at that; but the impression would be all the more astonishing. And that to those who served them fifty tons of solid stone seemed as easy to move and handle as a little water in a spoon, gets far beyond our miracles which are wondered at as miracles and taken as divine testimonies, and lifts us into a region in which the miraculous is no longer miraculous but gigantically normal, and immortality a thing to be achieved in a turn of the hand.

Under such impressions you find yourself in the Holy Land by night, with strange new constellations all over the sky and the old ones all topsy turvy, but with the stars soft and large and down quite close overhead in a sky which you feel to be of a deep and lovely blue. When the light comes you have left the land of Egypt with its endlessly flat Delta utterly behind, and are in a hilly country, with patches of cultivation wrested from the omnipresent stones, which you instantly recognize with a strange emotion which intensifies when you see a small boy coming down one of the patches, and presently, when he has passed away, a bigger boy of about thirteen, beginning to think, and at last, when he too has vanished, a young man, very grave and somewhat troubled, all three being dressed just as Christ dressed. (Here I break off, to resume on the night of the 20th, between Cyprus and Rhodes, at sea). The appearance of a woman with an infant in her arms takes on the quality of a vision. On this first hour you do not improve. It gives you the feeling that here Christ lived and grew up, and that here Mary bore him and reared him, and that there is no land on earth quite like it.

Later on the guides try to be more exact. This, they tell you, is the stable in the inn. This is the carpenter's shop. This is the upper chamber where the Last Supper was served. You know that they are romancing—that there is not a scrap of evidence for the possible identifications and that no inn or stable ever existed in a natural cavern in the limestone rock without light or fresh air. In Nazareth you know that Mary used the well in the street because there was (and is) no other well in the town to use; but the water she drew is gone, and the new water, with taps affixed by the British mandatory Government, is anybody's and everybody's water. Everything else in Nazareth except its natural beauty as a hill town is a fraud, meanly commemmorated by an unattractive and unimpressive church. But for these frauds every stone in Nazareth would be sacred with possibilities. Because one muddy bend of the Jordan is labelled as the spot on which the dove descended, the whole river is desecrated to make trade for the stall that sells the mud in bottles. I swam in the lake of Tiberias with a pleasant sense that this, at least, was Christ's lake on which nobody could stake out the track on which he walked or the site from which the miraculous draught of fishes was hauled. It is better to have Christ everywhere than somewhere, especially somewhere where he probably wasnt.

The hills rise almost into mountains over the train to Jerusalem, which winds between them so sinuously that you can see its tail from the window. When you arrive you are surprised: the place has a flourishing modern suburban air, and the new fashionable villa-land is mentioned as The New Jerusalem. When your very modern hotel has completed your disenchantment you make for the old Jerusalem and the church of the Holy Sepulchre. And the only possible comment on it is that of Dean Inge (he is with us on this trip) "Why seek ye the living among the dead? He is not here." (When Dean Inge says the right thing it is so very right that he is privileged to say a hundred wrong things that dont matter). A sort of case can be made for the sepulchre: it is at least possible that what remains of the chamber in the rock after its smashing up by the Moslem persecutions may be the family vault of Joseph of Arimathea; but when on the same floor a few yards off they shew you Calvary (not a hill) with the sockets of the three crosses, it is irresistibly revealed to you that Saint Helena was a humbug who, when the court was ordered to turn Christian, was quite determined to outshine the Queen of Heaven by a galaxy of visions and miracles that would shew the world that Roman queens would enter the new temples as goddesses and not as Syrian peasants cradling their infants in mangers. I know that sort of woman almost as well as you must. I have seen her court in the mosaics of Ravenna, where the attempt of the imperial court ladies to look pious is ludicrously unsuccessful.

The church of the Holy Sepulchre, to eyes accustomed to western architecture of the same period, is a second rate affair; and the squabbles of the sects over their "rights" in it are not edifying. I duly squeezed myself into the sepulchre, and tipped the queerly robed priest who touched my hands with oil to the extent of five piastres, looking as credulous as I could so as not to hurt his feelings; but my thought was that you would be disappointed. For the rest of the day I damned Jerusalem up hill and down dale; and when they took me to the Mount of Olives (practically oliveless) and shewed me the famous view of the city my only comment was "Just like Buxton." But one's appreciation is more complex than that. When you stand on the stone from which the Ascension took place you feel at the same moment everything that the legend means you to feel and a purely comic amusement at the notion of Jesus going up to the highest attainable point as a taking-off place for his celestial flight. Your faith and your tourist's observation jostle one another in the queerest fashion.

Next day I discovered Jerusalem. I went to the great plain of stone on which the Temple stood, and on which the Mosque of Omar (who didnt build it) stands. And there I found the charm and sanctity of Jerusalem. Christ has been worshipped in both the mosques; Omar was a man after God's own heart; and Mahomet's horse sprang to heaven with him from the great rock which the mosque of Omar enshrines, and which is a nobly beautiful building in spite of the utterly anachronistic Corinthian capitals of the red pillars of granite which bother one all over the Holy Land, and which are so Roman and common. The Kaiser gilt the Corinthian heavily so that they might hit you harder in the eye. Mahomet respected Christ and taught his followers to do the same; and it is perhaps the failure of the Christians to respect Mahomet equally that makes Islam and Israel more impressive in the east than Christendom. Still, the history of the place is such a record of iconoclasms, massacres, persecutions, spoliations, demolitions, and

233

delendings (in Cato's sense) by Turks, Romans, and any conqueror who happened to come along, that the only general verdict possible is that of the King of Brobdingnag [in Swift's *Gulliver's Travels*]. God must feel sick when he looks at Jerusalem. I fancy he consoles himself by turning to Stanbrook.

You asked me for a relic from Calvary. But St Helena's Calvary is only a spot on a church pavement, jealously guarded, and with nothing removable about it. Where the real Calvary is nobody knows; for the hills outside the city are innumerable. The alleged Via Dolorosa I traversed in a motor car hooting furiously at the children to get out of the way. The praetorium can be reasonably identified as in the palace of Herod, which Titus kept as a fortress for his garrison when he as nearly as possible left not one stone on another of the rest of the city; but as you cannot tell where Calvary was you cannot tell the way from the praetorium to it.

So off I went to Bethlehem, a beautifully situated hill town; and from the threshold of the Church of the Nativity I picked up a little stone, a scrap of the limestone rock which certainly existed when the feet of Jesus pattered about on it and the feet of Mary pursued him to keep him in order; for he was a most inconsiderate boy when his family was concerned, as you would realize if you travelled over the distance (at least a day's journey without a Rolls Royce) his mother had to go back to look for him when he gave her the slip to stay and argue with the doctors of divinity. In fact I picked up two little stones: one to be thrown blindfold among the others in Stanbrook garden so that there may always be a stone from Bethlehem there, though nobody will know which it is and be tempted to steal it, and the other for your own self. You shall have them when I return, unless I perish on the way, in which case I shall present myself at the heavenly gate with a stone in each hand, and St Peter will stand at attention and salute the stones (incidentally saluting ME) when he has unlocked the gate and flung it open before me. At least he would if it were ever locked, which I dont believe.

I have been writing all this in scraps; but there must be an end to everything, even to a letter to you; besides, I finished with the Holy Land at Patmos, three days ago, the intervening two days having been spent among heathen idols in and around Athens. For climbing up that frightfully stony road to the top of the mountain where the Greek monastery stands I shall claim indulgence for every sin I ever committed and a few hundred which I still hope to commit. The man who wrote the Book of Revelations, who was *not* the John of the fourth

gospel (the Dean assures me that his Greek was disgracefully ungrammatical) ought to have married St Helena. I *know* he was a drug addict,
as all the wickednesses of which he accuses God, all the imaginary
horrors, all the passings of a thousand years in a second and the visions
of universes breaking into three pieces, are the regular symptoms of
drug action and delirium tremens. The book is a disgrace to the Bible
and should never have been admitted to the canon.

I began this on the 17th March and it is now the 26th! You can spend
a week of your scanty leisure in reading it, and then sell the manuscript
to Cockerell for the Fitzwilliam and endow a chapel to St Bernard at
Stanbrook with the proceeds. The writing of it has been very restful to
the soul of your brother.

affectionately
G. Bernard Shaw

To FRANK HARRIS

[A/3; X/279]

Venice—on the eve of departure for Paris
21st April 1931

[The Hellenic Travellers' Club tour ended for the Shaws at Venice on 1st
April. They stopped for three weeks at the Grand Hotel, making brief excursions to Torcello, San Lazzaro and Malamocco. From 22nd April to 6th May
they were in Paris, their return home delayed when Charlotte suddenly
developed a severe congestion in the right lung. Harris (whose letters were
being drafted for him by Frank Scully) had objected to Shaw's self-
bowdlerization of the sexual confession of 24th June 1930. Eugene O'Neill
(1888–1953), the American playwright, had been performed frequently by
West End and fringe theatres, but Shaw was as yet unfamiliar with his work.]

Man, will nothing teach you? is Nellie to mourir sur la paille after
spending her last sou on your funeral?

I tell you, if there is one expression in this book of yours that cannot be read aloud at a confirmation class, you are lost for ever. Your
life and loves are just being forgotten, and your old reputation as a
considerable and respectable man of letters reviving. This book is your
chance of recovering your tall hat; and you want to throw it away for
the sake of being in the fashion of O'Neill, Joyce, and George Moore.
And even George does not imagine that force in literature is attained
by calling a spade a f———g* shovel. Even if it were, that sort of thing

does not belong to your generation or mine, which could say all that it wanted to say without lessons from the forecastle and the barrack guard room.

So brush up your frock coat; buy a new tie; and remember that your life now depends on your being Francis Harris Esquire, editor of the Fortnightly and Saturday Reviews, from the great days of Victoria the Ladylike. Frank the Buccaneer is not a person with whom F.H. Esquire can have any connexion whatever. Bury him. If you dont, the parish will.

GBS

To SIEGFRIED TREBITSCH

Hôtel Lotti. Paris

[A/5; X/341]   28th April 1931

[*La charrette de pommes* (*The Apple Cart*) was produced by Georges Pitoëff at the Théâtre des Arts on 14th April 1931. Despite Shaw's earlier insistence that Pitoëff must not appear in the play, he cast himself as Magnus. Ludmilla, however, confined herself to Orinthia, with Jemima the queen played by Alice Reichen. Shaw attended a performance on the 24th. There is no evidence that Oscar Straus produced *The Chocolate Soldier* with a new title, let alone a new libretto.]

My dear Trebitsch

These accursed films are complicating life beyond endurance. I will not license The Chocolate Soldier under any circumstances. It would absolutely kill Arms & The Man for the screen; and it has done me quite harm enough already without that climax of injury. I have tolerated two productions of it, and had another revival made without my knowledge. I have had to defend an action taken against me by an American purchaser of the rights which, though I won it triumphantly, cost me about £1000. Attempt after attempt has been made to induce me to sell the film rights of Arms & The Man with the object of shelving it and producing The C.S. with impunity. I have defeated them all, and have steadily told them that they must provide Strauss's score with a new libretto bearing a new name—exactly what you tell me they are at last threatening to do. It is no threat to me: I am delighted (having urged it myself); for when it is done we shall be rid of The

<hr>

* The elision is Shaw's.

236

Chocolate Soldier forever; and Arms & The Man will have a chance. So cable O.S. to go ahead with the new libretto *and the new title*, as there is nothing I desire more, and there is no chance of my consenting to the abominable C.S.

I have been on the continent since the 3ʳᵈ March. When I was in Venice I seriously considered flying to Vienna; and if I had been alone I should certainly have done it; but Charlotte refuses to fly. In February I was too overworked and exhausted to attend to anything but my Collected Edition, which will be the death of me; and now I am too heartily sick of vagabondizing to think of anything but getting back. Charlotte is in bed with a bad cold; my own inside is upset; I am tired beyond words; The Apple Cart at the Theatre des Arts (Pitoeff) is ugly, silly, and incompetent; and I am in the worst of humors[.]

G.B.S.

To MURIEL F. MacSWINEY

[C/48]

Ayot St Lawrence. Welwyn
8th June 1931

[A law prohibiting abortion had generally been ignored by the courts of Germany's Weimar Republic. In 1931, however, Dr Friedrich Wolf (1888–1953), medical graduate of Bonn and Heidelberg and prolific author of proletarian stage dramas, who had issued certificates to patients attesting they were physically unfit to bear children, and Dr Else Kienle, who had performed the abortion surgery, were tried, found guilty and imprisoned. Enormous protest rose throughout Germany, particularly as they had given their services without fee to aid underprivileged women. Muriel F.Mac-Swiney, a Dubliner committed to the cause, wrote to Shaw to enlist his support. Dr Wolf, an avowed communist, emigrated to the USSR in 1933, where he published his most famous work, *Professor Mamlock*, the following year.]

It is a very difficult question. Herod's method of relieving family poverty is not easy to advocate when the method of Karl Marx is available as an alternative. In London, people of good social standing seem to have no difficulty whatever in getting rid of undesirable additions surgically on the flimsiest pretexts. I am of course quite aware of the arguments in favor of legalizing the operation; but like most operations it is not a fundamental cure: the trouble recurs. And as my business is the fundamental cure I must leave the makeshift to those who see no other way out. In short, it is not my subject; and it is not a man's subject anyhow: the women must handle it, as it is they who claim the right—or repudiate it.

G. Bernard Shaw

To UNIDENTIFIED CORRESPONDENT

[4 Whitehall Court SW 1]

[S/5]
12th June 1931

[This is another of the transcriptions in Blanche Patch's commonplace book. For Shaw's discussion of Christianity vs "Crosstianity," see the preface to *Major Barbara*.]

Your sermon interests me only as an example of the lengths to which "Crosstian" apologists will go in their quite hopeless attempts to whitewash the Roman gibbet. What do you expect me to say to such a mad remark as that "In the Cross we see God's love in action"? If by God you mean the fabulous Ogre who sought to be propitiated by human sacrifices by Abraham and Jephtha what has love to do with the affair? If you mean the God whom Jesus addressed when He cried "Why has thou forsaken me?" you suggest very strongly that the only possible answer was "Alas, my poor friend, because I have no other instrument than yourself and those who think like you; and it seems that my enemies are too many for you." But you must not muddle up the two and write nonsense to me. It is that sort of nonsense that drives people out of the churches.

Also I wish you would read the Gospels in a sane manner and not indulge in such inventions as that Jesus might have saved himself by recanting or might have rescued himself by force. He had no loophole for escape by way of recantation; and as to force, if you really believe, as a silly passage in St John's Gospel suggests, that he had only to lift his finger to make the whole Roman army of occupation, with Pilate, Caiaphas and the Sanhedrin fall flat on the ground, you are not only giving up the whole business as a fairy tale, but provoking the question why, in that case, he did not do it and thereby give the world an over-whelming demonstration of his powers instead of exposing himself to the mockery of the Jews "He saved others: Himself He cannot save. Let Him deliver him if He delight in him."

It is quite clear from the Gospel narrative that Jesus connived at his own death in the belief that he would rise again and come to glory to establish his reign on earth. Subsequent history has not confirmed his belief. If Christianity means ignoring history and perpetuating his delusion it has no future. If it means a serious attempt to popularize what is still valuable in Christ's ideas then he may really yet come to his own after centuries of failure. It may be that Crosstianity has made him such a bore, and so associated his name with manifest falsehood and superstition that his ideas can be preserved only by suppressing his connection with them. But, anyhow, dont insult him by saying that the whole value of his life would have been destroyed if he had not been hideously tortured and slaughtered.

To WALDORF ASTOR .

[A/101]

Ayot St Lawrence. Welwyn
27th June 1931

[Nancy Astor and her husband Waldorf (1879–1952), second Viscount Astor, had invited Shaw to accompany them on a journey to the USSR in July. The party was also to include Philip Henry Kerr (1882–1940), eleventh Marquess of Lothian, newspaper editor and statesman, who was Parliamentary Under-Secretary of the India Office 1931–32; Francis David Astor (b. 1912), third son of Nancy and Waldorf Astor, at this time a student at Balliol College, Oxford; and Charles Tennant. Grigory Y. Sokolnikoff (1888–194?), Soviet leader and diplomat, was ambassador in London 1929–32, where he was quite friendly with the Shaws. Harry Gordon Selfridge (1858–1947) was the American founder in 1909 of Selfridge & Co., a London department store.]

My dear Waldorf
... I have written to Sokolnikoff, asking him to order his consul to rush our papers through instantaneously. We shall need entry visas for Latvia, Lithuania, and Poland (unless we pass across the Corridor in a sealed waggon). I dont think Holland & Germany now bother about them. I have told S that we shall expect a salute of at least 101 guns on our arrival in Moscow, and that as we wish to see the torture chamber of the Tcheka he should warn them to have a victim or two ready, so that we may witness the process.

The worst snag in the scheme is the season. Does Nancy stand heat well? A railway journey through central Europe in July & early August is a test for the heat resistance of Beelzebub. September is the proper time. Even the nights are not cool now.

We must not burden ourselves with evening dress. It is not actually contraband; but it is in bad taste, and extremely suspicious. Gordon Selfridge went to the opera attired as for Covent Garden, and being not only the sole person in the theatre in that condition but in all Russia, distracted the attention of singers, orchestral players, conductor and audience to such an extent that the performance was wrecked. He did not enjoy his success as I should have done.

Have you considered the alternative of flying?

The Intourist people want to take us to central Asia.

ever
G. B. S.

To THOMAS F. GALT

Ayot St Lawrence. Welwyn

[T/1]   28th June 1931

[Thomas Franklin Galt (b. 1908), later an author, biographer, and political philosopher, had created a phonetic system of spelling for English and sent Shaw an essay on the subject.]

Dear Mr Galt

Thank you for letting me see your phonetic alphabet.

It is incomplete. You have omitted what is perhaps the most important vowel in the English language: the obscure vowel. This has driven you to transcribe Lincoln's Gettysburg speech with the word reemember in it. There is no such word. Then you have reemaening and deevoeshun. There are no such words. From Dr Johnson you give over, faeferz, and enkeraejment: three ers which do not sound in the least alike.

How would you write "My aunt was bitten by an ant in Ontario when she was singing Schubert's Ave Maria. She exclaimed 'Our Father which art in heaven!' and was overheard by Mr Fothergill the orthographer who ordered a hot compress."?

The following places are now spelt as one word. Cars Halton (Hawlton), Lewis Ham, Peters Ham, Elt Ham. Result: they are mispronounced Car-shalton, Lewi-sham, Peter-sham, Ell-tham. How are you to avoid this if you refuse to have a separate letter for sh?

The greatest difficulty in the way of spelling phonetically with our 26 letters for 36 or so sounds is that it looks like illiterate spelling.

Illiteracy is associated with poverty and ignorance; and English people cannot bear to be suspected of either. The social advantage of new letters is that they never suggest lack of education: in fact they at first suggest super education. Also they do not suggest mispronunciation, as reemember does.

What is your native dialect? You say fauskaur: I say foerskoer.

You put the case for a reform of spelling very well; but as far as I can guess from your transcripts your aural training is not yet complete enough to satisfy expert phoneticians. The vowels are the weak spots.

You will, I hope, forgive my criticism. It is the only service I can render you.

I am aware, by the way, that an exhaustively phonetic spelling is impossible by any means short of Bell's Visible Speech, which is far too slow and difficult for ordinary purposes. But a sufficient approach to it is quite practicable; and I should like to see my own works printed in reasonably phonetic spelling before I die.

faithfully
G. Bernard Shaw

To AUGUSTIN HAMON

4 Whitehall Court S W 1
[C/1]   4th July 1931

[*Too True to be Good* was commenced on 5th March, the first morning at sea on the Mediterranean tour; it was completed on 30th June. *La charrette de pommes* ran from 14th April to 29th May in its initial engagement, but remained in the repertory for over seventy performances.]

. . . Charlotte will not come with me to Russia.

I have completed the first draft of Too True to be Good, and have begun revising it and working out the stage business. It is in three acts. Lehmann & Co will be pleased to hear that it contains burglars, brigands, a stolen necklace, a military expedition and a battle actually fought on the stage. But you will have to damp their enthusiasm by adding that these stirring incidents are only pretexts for speeches of unprecedented length and solemnity. *All* the characters orate at prodigious length.

What happened to the Apple Cart at the T. des A.? Was it a failure as it deserved to be?

What are les P. doing now?

G. B. S.

To FRANK WYATT

Ayot St Lawrence. Welwyn
[A/105; X/353.e]   15th July 1931

[Frank Wyatt (1876–1943), secretary of the London Vegetarian Society, had informed Shaw, "We are trying to stop this outbreak of ox-roasting as a form of celebration on festive occasions," and requested an expression of opinion to communicate to the press.]

The ox roasting seems to me a very tame attempt to revive ancient festivities. Why not bait a bear, burn the village atheist, flog a quakeress, pillory a dissenter, duck a scold, fight a main of cocks, have a match between two oyster eaters, and do the thing in style? These feeble modern gluttons have no imagination. . . .

faithfully
G. Bernard Shaw

To HORACE PLUNKETT

4 Whitehall Court S W 1
[H/67]   16th July 1931

My dear Plunkett
I start for Moscow on Saturday, and expect to arrive there on Tuesday unless I am stopped by a revolution in Berlin. It will not be a long visit; I shall reach these shores again on the 2nd August: that is, if I am not despatched by the Soviet in the opposite direction to Siberia. My going is a bit of an accident: the Astors suddenly took it into their heads to see for themselves whether Russia is really the earthly paradise I had declared it to be; and they challenged me to go with them. I felt, at my age, that if I did not seize the opportunity, I should never see Russia at all; so I agreed. And now they have had to change their plans and nothing is left of the proposed party but myself, the Marquess of Lothian (Phil Kerr) and Tennant, the head centre of Christian Science here. (But see PPS below.) Charlotte, who has been unlucky lately in catching infections when travelling (scarlet fever at Buxton and congestion of the lung in Paris) prudently stays at home.
I was greatly tempted to go flying with you at the end of last summer; but I was under such an overwhelming necessity to get out a substantial instalment of my Collected Edition to satisfy subscribers and to write another play that I knew that I must not start a new hare

242

just then. I presume you have taken out your pilots' certificate; but do you still fly?

As far as I can make out from people who go to Russia its discomforts are quite bearable for people to whom money is no object. However, I shall be able to tell you all about that when I come back. This is of course a silly time to travel: the heat will be at its worst; but if you should take a fancy to go in September I see no reason why you should anticipate greater hardships than you have survived a dozen times in the course of your travels.

ever
G.B.S.

PS Charlotte reminds me to give you her best love.

PPS It now seems possible that the Astors will be able to come on Saturday after all.

To CHARLOTTE F. SHAW

Hotel Bristol. Berlin
19th July 1931 Sunday morning

[A/2]

[The touring party left for Russia from Victoria Station the morning of 18th July. Shaw's travel agent obtained a separate sleeping compartment for him en route, but informed him there were no "separate sleepers" on the Russian railways. Assured there were plenty of vegetarian restaurants in Moscow, he was advised, however, to carry supplementary supplies of cereal and biscuits. Each traveller was permitted to take into Russia only £30 in cash, to be declared and exchanged "at poor rates" for roubles at the border. Shaw obtained letters of credit from his bank. The tourists reached Berlin early on the 19th, departing that evening aboard the Moscow–Warsaw night express.

The British Ambassadress at Berlin from 1928 to 1933 was Etheldred (Fane) Rumbold, wife of the Rt. Hon. Sir Horace Rumbold (1869–1941). The troublesome Gertrude H. Ely, an American friend of Nancy Astor, eventually was left behind in Berlin, having neglected to obtain a visa for passage through Poland. Bobby was Robert Gould Shaw (1898–1970), Nancy Astor's firstborn and favourite son, who had been obliged to withdraw from the trip. Shaw's remark about everyone envying the absent Bobby suggests he was not privy to the secret that young Shaw had been convicted and imprisoned for a homosexual offence, a fact suppressed by all of the newspapers in deference to his stepfather, proprietor of *The Observer*.]

So far all smooth except the channel, which made me thank Providence that you had not come with me. She rolled and rolled convulsively; and I, flat on my back, rolled with her and was none the worse save for a slight and fleeting headache.

Nancy's dramatic genius enables her to enjoy her mishaps so uproariously that one can hardly grudge them to her; but she says she had a crisis last night and shrieked and then instantly went fast asleep. I, having been in the adjoining compartment, can testify that the shriek was not loud enough to penetrate the partition. There was a communicating door through which she (earlier in the evening) burst tempestuously under the impression that it led to the lavatory.

We had two hours in Brussels, which we filled up by taxying to the cathedral and then tramping the streets. They are all ardent walkers, which suits me literally down to the ground.

Except for a two hours read from 12.30 to 2.30 I got through the night bearably. I am now at the Hotel Bristol in Berlin; and a hot bath and cold shower in which I unaccustomedly indulged has almost—as you see—deprived me of the power of forming letters with my pen. We have not yet breakfasted.

Cold grey skies and rain have dispelled my fears of a roasting journey.

Berlin on Sunday morning makes a favorable impression. But all German towns do after the other ones.

* * * * * * * * * *

It is now 12 minutes to 11, and nothing done except scenes, telephonings to the Embassy, discussions as to how to spend the day, threats by David to stay in Moscow, discoveries by Nancy that she cannot go anywhere, as her maid has packed all wrong and she must repack, and at the back of it a fixed Christian Science service somewhere at 11.30, a lunch with somebody, and an afternoon with the British ambassadress, who came back from England to entertain Macdonald and now finds that she must entertain *me*.

Phil has vanished with Miss Ely, who it now appears has upset all the sleeping arrangements by joining up at the last moment instead of going separately by herself on another date.

The general distraction is indescribable. There are moments when we all envy Bobby.

I will now go out on my own and see what I can of the museums, which close early on Sunday. Later on there will be no chance of adding to this letter before we start at 18 for Warsaw and Moscow.

Bless you, dearest.

GBS

To CHARLOTTE F. SHAW

Hotel Metropole. Moscow
[A/2]   21st July 1931

[The night express crossed the Russian border at 4 p.m. on the 20th, near Negoreloje, where the visitors were transferred to a wide-gauge Russian train. Maksim Litvinov (1876–1951), Commissar of Foreign Affairs 1930–39, was a fellow passenger. Anna Louise Strong (1885–1970), who met the train at the border, was an American poet who came to Russia in 1921 as a correspondent for the American Friends Relief Mission and remained as a sympathiser to the Russian cause, publishing many books and pamphlets on the USSR (and on China). She was associate editor of the English-language *Moscow News*, in which her report appeared on 23rd July.

Shaw, in a rare instance of modesty, neglected to inform Charlotte that he was met at the Alexandrovsky railway station in Moscow by a brass band, a military guard of honour to escort him through the crowds, and a horde of welcoming Russians estimated in the thousands (most of them employees of the publishing house Gosizdat) shouting "Hail Shaw." There were dignitaries from the Society of Soviet Writers and, as representative of the Communist government, the former Commissar for Education (1917–29) and for the fine arts, Anatoly Lunacharsky (1875–1933), to greet him beneath a mass of waving banners bearing his name and portrait. It all came as a great surprise to Shaw, for, as Lunacharsky had informed the public in *Izvestia* on 21st July, Shaw had sent an advance wire to Béla Illés (1895–1974, Hungarian novelist and political writer), General Secretary of the International Union of Revolutionary Writers, indicating that "under no circumstances should he be burdened with parades, receptions, or banquets," concluding his message with the statement "I am coming for serious business" (Lunacharsky's article was published in translation in the *Labour Monthly*, London, September 1931).]

On Sunday I went off by myself and saw a bit of Berlin and a considerable selection of the best things in the Kaiser Frederick's Museum. We then lunched with a pleasant Swiss couple (at least *he* was Swiss) and were addressed by him quite interestingly on the situation in Germany for more than half an hour, during which under the eyes of the hostess I scandalously fell asleep about five times, but was awake at the end and so dramatically apt in my comments that I think I convinced her that my closed eyes indicated profound reflection.

Then the Rumbolds—ambassador, amb[dress] & their son Duncan— drove us to Potsdam at a furious speed. We were conducted through Sans Souci and rushed back to the Hotel Bristol, where the whole ground floor was crowded out with journalists and photographers clamoring and flashlighting in a manner that left Athens nowhere—a monstrous mobbery.

At 7 in the morning I looked out of my [railway car] window at Warsaw and found myself facing a battery of cameras. They apologized for the absence of Sobieniowsky and the rest of the population, having had only an hours notice of my approach.

Poland was less unlike the British Isles than any country I have ever seen. At 5 we passed under an iron arch inscribed "Communism will do away with frontiers." Meanwhile we had discovered Litvinoff on the train and become Hail-fellow-well-met with him. The clock jumped from 17 to 19 as we crossed the border. The first person who greeted me was the very goodlooking American girl of whom I have so often told the story, Miss Strong. She and half a dozen "comrades" representing Russian literature had been waiting there since morning for us. I had absolutely nothing official to do: they didnt even collect my tickets. We explored the village before the train started. Then a tempest of talk and dinner until 10, when, in the broad guage train I could at last stretch myself at full length in my bunk. I slept until 8.30. My arrival having been kept carefully secret there were only a few hundred people crowded round the carriage door to receive me with cheers and a salvo of fifty cameras. The ambassador's secretary was there to requisition me for Thursday 17 to 19. Endless introductions. Nancy, desperately mothering me and assuring everyone that I must immediately be left alone to sleep in the hotel, found me utterly out of control: I insisted on sightseeing at express speed until half an hour late for lunch. First, the hotel. Then off to Lenin's mausoleum (Nancy jibbed at going in, but ended greatly impressed), the Kremlin with inconceivable royal and priestly finery and jewelled diadems, the palace, the congress hall, and finally and amazingly the three churches where the Tsars were christened, married, & buried. Ivan the Terrible's bit of the palace was the best of it. At the end of every item Nancy clamored for sending me home to bed, but finally gave way to her loudly expressed disgust at my playing to the gallery. I smiled and waved and posed and posed—on the great gun (seated on three monster cannon balls), on the great bell, on every staircase and in every door-way. It is our first hot day: the heat is bearable but undeniably hot. I think they must have cursed me for the way I rushed them round.

At last we got back to the hotel and lunched very talkily (you can't stop talking here: Miss Strong is a perfect devil at it) until at last, at last, at last we got to our bedrooms at 14.45 to sleep until 16, when they are all to come for us to start again. And it is now 11 minutes to

16 (4) and instead of sleeping I have written all this to you. I have five minutes, perhaps, before they come.

GBS

PS Food splendid for me. Hotel sitting, bath, and bedroom en suite, couldnt be bettered. Registered trunk missing, so far, but will be retrieved. Health uproarious. Envy me.

To CHARLOTTE F. SHAW

Hotel Metropole. Moscow
[A/2]   22nd July 1931

[The Kamerny (meaning Chamber, or Intimate) Theater was created in 1914 by a theatrical radical, Alexander Taïrov (1885–1950), to break away from a naturalistic theater, creating in its place his Synthetic Theater, which placed emphasis on the individual actor, requiring of him skills in mime, acrobatics, and expressionistic techniques of performing. Taïrov's circusy *Saint Joan* (1926) was essentially a burlesque of the play, stunningly effective on its own terms. The production Shaw witnessed was a free adaptation of *The Three-penny Opera* (*Die Dreigroschenoper*), with music by the German composer Kurt Weill (1900–50) and lyrics and libretto by Bertolt Brecht (1898–1956), transposed from eighteenth century England to twentieth century American gangdom, MacHeath being metamorphosed into Al Capone. The sole scenery consisted of two reversible screens, with six swing doors in each.

Karl Radek (1885–1939), cosmopolitan Jewish revolutionary, had been expelled from the Communist Party in 1927 for leadership in the Trotskyite opposition. Reinstated in 1930 he became the chief commentator of foreign affairs in Moscow newspapers. Expelled anew in 1936, he was sentenced to ten years' imprisonment in the second Show Trial of the Great Purge, 1937. Others lunching with Shaw at the Literary Club included authors Béla Illés and Vselvolod Ivanov, Hungarian writer Lydia Seifallina, and Artashes Khalatov (1894–1938), chairman of the administrative board of Gosizdat (State Publishing House) 1927–32.]

Yesterday afternoon, drove to centres of Repose and Culture, represented by All the Fun of the Fair on a huge scale, sun bathing on the river—a colossal proletarian Lido, and infant welfare, which was simply Margaret Macmillan without Margaret Macmillan. I shook hands with people; and the crowds were incited to cheer me.

We got back late-for-dinner-hopelessly, and equally late for the Kamerny Theatre (the St Joan theatre) where they were performing an amazing and at points disgusting perversion of the Beggar's Opera, with

247

modern German music. Here I was exploited to the last inch, photographed with the manager and leading lady in the bureau (set with a collation which nobody collated), led to the middle of the front row of stalls, presented with a bouquet and a St Joan album, confronted with a gigantic banner of welcome on the stage with the whole company assembled, tears[,] cheers and laughter, gracious bows in all directions from the wretched G.B.S, and chuckles from Nancy and Phil. Horrid!

Night of terrific heat and such noise from the street—as of a London fire with a two hours continuous stream of belling engines—that I had to close the double windows and throw away the sole bed covering, consisting of an eider down which would have been warm for the South Pole. Then I slept until 9.10 and had to bath & breakfast in a scramble.

This morning the endless Revolutionary Museum, then the State Bank with an incredible treasure of crown jewels (the biggest crown has nearly 5 lbs weight of diamonds in it) and a resplendent collar and regalia of which I told them that Nancy had half a dozen like it. "Only two" said Phil, correcting me. Nancy jollies them all until they do not know whether they are head up or heels: her stock accusation being that they are all aristocrats, which does not wholly displease them.

Then the Literary Club where Nancy & I sat at a table with Lunacharsky, Radek and a crowd of authors & publishers and everybody gave Shawian performances simultaneously until Nancy dragged me away exhausted.

The heat is hellish. We shall soon be moving to Leningrad; but I have not yet copied the program from Waldorf's list.

Now I must snatch 20 minutes after-lunch nap before they come for me again.

GBS

To CHARLOTTE F. SHAW

Hotel Metropole. Moscow
[A/2]   23rd July 1931

[One of the early problems of the USSR was the menace of wandering hordes of homeless youths, necessitating the establishment of penal settlements to control them. One of the earliest such prisons was at Bolshevo, which Shaw visited. "The snag in the place," Shaw wrote to Frederick Whelen on a later occasion, "is that the criminals [*besprizorni*] will not leave at the expiration of their sentences which is just as it should be" (n.d., 1936, in Whelen's letter "G.B.S. in Moscow," *New Statesman*, 17 March 1951).

Konstantin Stanislavsky (1863–1938), actor, director, and producer, who founded the Moscow Art Theater in 1897, was one of the greatest innovators and influences in 20th-century theater, though his "method" system of acting has frequently been misunderstood and distorted. Ivan Pavlov (1849–1936), Nobel prizewinner (1904) for physiology, is remembered today almost solely for his notorious conditioned-reflex experiments on dogs. The British ambassador at Moscow was Sir Esmond Ovey (1879–1963). Lamer was the home of explorer Apsley Cherry-Garrard, just below Shaw's Corner at Ayot (the gardens abutted). Bertha M. Hammond (Ltd.) was a hair stylist in Old Bond Street.]

Litvinoff was with us all yesterday. Lunacharsky was with us today and is coming with us to Leningrad. It is dawning on us that they are seizing the opportunity to look at Communist Russia which they have never had time to see before.

Yesterday afternoon we drove out for miles and miles along the road to Siberia, but stopped at an institution for young criminals, where we dined on cabbage soup (stchi) and black bread (at least I did: the others had pounds of flesh) which I find an ideal diet. The first smile came on the faces of the criminals when I told them that I had begun by committing juvenile crimes for which I should have been sent to prison if the police had caught me.

We drove straight back to a big theatre where they were doing a film on the same subject. We were late; but the film was stopped and begun over again when the audience had been instructed to receive me with tumultuous applause, which I acknowledged in Chaliapin's best manner.

This morning we inspected a huge electric factory, where the boss wore a beautiful silk shirt and a jacket of Conduit St—Savile Row cut, and had splendidly manicured hands (he swore that the shirt wasn't silk and that his wife made it). When the work ceased for lunch we were enthusiastically mobbed in the yard, and Nancy got on a dray and schoolmarmed them in a manner utterly inconceivable by the Communist mind, to the diabolical amusement of Lunacharsky. The interpreter groaned at the utter unexpectedness of my answers to questions. At last we were dispersed by heavy rain, through which we started on a drive to a Troubetskoy house in the country, where writers, painters, scientists, schoolfolk & the like rest. I met Stanislavsky of the Moscow Art Theatre, who asked about Granville-Barker. Pavloff was not there.

After lunch Waldorf, Lunacharsky and I hurried back to the hotel to pack, as we have to travel to Leningrad tonight after a visit to the British Embassy. But we shall be back here on Sunday the 26th (a horse race is being organized in my honor for that auspicious date!) until Tuesday, when we start for the communal farms. We shall also revisit Moscow for a moment (long enough to pick up letters) on Thursday the 30th, when we start for home, coming not by Calais–Dover but by the Hook of Holland to Harwich, whence I shall drive to Ayot in time for lunch (at Lamer if desired: I get less and less tired everyday) and THEE.

GBS

PS Nancy wants to wash my hair with Lux. She says she can do it better than Bertha Hammond.

David is the beauty success of the party. He really looks like an Italian picture of the late XV century. All the Communists notice it.

To CHARLOTTE F. SHAW

[C (three cards)/2]

[Hotel de l'Europe] Leningrad
24th July 1931

[Yemelyan Pugachov (1726–75), a Cossack, proclaimed himself Peter III and led a peasant rebellion against Catherine II. Initially victorious, he subsequently was captured and executed. Aleksei Ignat'ev (1877–1954), Russian diplomat and Lt. General of the Soviet Army, was until 1937 a member of the Soviet trade delegation in Paris. Alexander Wicksteed was an English writer and Russophile, author of *Life under the Soviets* (1928). Stepan (Stenko) Razin (d. 1671), leader of a Cossack and peasant revolt, who was defeated by the czarist army and executed, is immortalised in legend and folk song, as well as in Glazunov's tone poem, Op. 13.

The cablegrams received by Lady Astor and Shaw were appeals from an emigré Dmitri Krynine (1877–?), research professor of highway engineering at Yale University, on behalf of himself and his son Paul (1901–64), to intercede with the Russians for an exit visa previously denied to his wife, so that they might be reunited. Nancy Astor made a dramatic but unsuccessful representation to Litvinov, who informed her, "Such a matter is not in my province." Efforts to reach the political police failed, and after Waldorf Astor had visited Mme Krynine and Nancy Astor had presented the cables "informally" to Soviet authorities at the Kremlin, the matter was reluctantly dropped. The sole result of the Astors' intervention was the sudden "disappearance" of Mrs Krynine when reporters sought her out a few days later.

There was, then and later, public criticism of Shaw's decision not to attempt to use *his* influence with the government, one critic recently writing: "Accounts of this episode suggest strongly that Shaw showed far less concern [than the Astors] for the fate of this unfortunate individual even while he was making speeches about the superiority of the Russian interpretation of 'freedom' to that of the West" (T.F.Evans, "Shaw in Russia," *Shaw: The Annual of Bernard Shaw Studies*, 1985).

In mitigation of Shaw's seeming disinterest it should be recognised that he had perforce become hardened to pitiful appeals, being recipient of considerable numbers of them every year; that he held a strong conviction that a guest should not abuse hospitality by embarrassing his host; and that he firmly believed that intervention by foreigners could be more damaging than useful to the unfortunates involved, as he had frequently declared in the past and would do again in press interviews in 1933 when appealed to during his American visit by the imprisoned radical Tom Mooney.

The "Ogpu" or G.P.U. was the secret "State Political Control" police force, which suppressed political crime and sought out proletarian disaffection.]

In a hotel in Leningrad where we all have Grand Ducal suites and of the name of which we are ignorant.

The man in the picture ["Emilien Pugatcheff, chef de l'insurrection des paysans en seconde moitié du XVIII siècle"] is the rebel who burnt Moscow in Catherine's time. The flames of that city are in the background; and he is recoiling from the fire of hell.

Yesterday afternoon we gabbled and consumed light refreshments at the British Embassy. Every ambassador to Russia on earth was there and was introduced to me. Several communists dropped in and made themselves at home, notably General Ignatieff, renegade Tsarist, and communist acharné. A piteous volley of telegrams from an emigré to me and Nancy, asking us to make the G.P.U. (Gay Pay Oo) send his wife to him, quite upset her, as her head is full of Bolshevik horrors in spite of what we see here, and she threatens to go to the G.P.U. when we return to Moscow and insist on their delivering up the grass widow. Alexander Wicksteed dined with us. We spent the night in the train, pleasantly enough, as the weather is ideal, warm but not torrid. On our arrival we had to mount to the roof (lift disabled) for an interminable lunch. The crowds at the station and the cinema operators, uncontrolled by police, gave no trouble: we just shoved through amicably without the least trouble. After lunch we drove about the city and went through miles and miles of pictures at the Hermitage and the interminable palaces en suite. I was and still am quite tired out by this gallery tramping. We go to the theatre tonight to see a revolutionary film; and they want me to take one of the scenes in a Lenin talkie which they are making. I must hasten to wash and dine. Nancy did wash my head in Lux at Moscow. We spend tonight and tomorrow here and return by night to Moscow, arriving Sunday morning.

GBS

[On reverse of second postcard]
This is another portrait of the same gentleman—Pugatcheff. These postcards, with at least 50 more[,] were heaped on me by the Moscow Revolutionary museum.

[On reverse of third postcard]
This ancient wooden statue of Stenko Rasin is evidently an attempt at Rodin's Balzac, made 5 or 6 hundred years before either of them was born.

To CHARLOTTE F. SHAW

	Hotel de l'Europe. Leningrad
[C (three cards)/2]	25th July 1931

["Battersea Park" was Tsarskoie Selo, known at this time as the children's village. In its pre-revolutionary mansions workers were housed on full pay for a fortnight's holiday. The text of Shaw's filmed talk on Lenin was published on 28th July in the *New York American* and in translation the next day in *Pravda*. The National Museum was, of course, the Hermitage Galleries. Lunch was sponsored there by the Writers' and Printers' Union. One of the churches visited was St Isaac's Cathedral, converted to a museum.]

Yesterday afternoon was not eventful. We were tired after the galleries, and contented ourselves with a drive round Battersea Park, or some place exactly like it except that the road was only slightly better than the old road to Sneem, and there [were] patrician villas now used as rest houses. In the evening they treated us to a selection of scraps from the most famous of their films. I slept well in the absence of Moscow's frightful slamming and tramming.

This morning an unforeseen adventure ate up half the morning. They are making a great Lenin talkie, and Lunacharski carried me off to the studio. I stage-managed and improvised (really on the spur of the moment[)] quite a good little interlude—so good, in fact, that Lunacharski was quite inspired when he made a speech introducing me. But of course my English will be lost on a Russian audience. It was a fearful lapse from holidaying; but I could not resist shewing off before the awestruck Russian talkie experts.

After the talkie I had a strenuous dose of the pictures at the National Museum. Then a lunch with the Leningrad authors who kept making speeches and asking questions, in reply to which I had to make half a dozen speeches between precarious mouthfuls. But for a jorum of tomato soup at the last moment I should have had nothing but black bread and a hard boiled egg. I saw both the big churches: one of them now an Anti-Religious museum. The British consul then gave me Russian tea with lemon and received a sermon in defence of Communism at least an hour long.

GBS

PS   Nothing remains now as far as this city is concerned, but dinner and the start for the return journey to Moscow at half past 23 (11). So goodnight.

To CHARLOTTE F. SHAW

[En route to Tambov]

[A/2]   27th July 1931. 17 (5)

[A racetrack visit, his first, including a "Bernard Shaw Handicap," occupied Shaw's afternoon of the 26th, his seventy-fifth birthday. Exhausted from the week's hectic activities he dozed in the sun much of the time, after informing his hosts "I suppose there will be only one horse in the race since there's no competition in a Socialist state." That evening, in honour of his birthday, a great celebration was held in the Trade Union Central Hall (formerly the Hall of Nobles of the Noblemen's Club), in which treason trials were held. The organising sponsors were the Society for Cultural Relations, the Federation of Soviet Writers, and the Union of State Publishing Houses. An interminably long introductory address was delivered by Lunacharsky, in which he linked Shaw to Swift and then likened him to the Russian satirist N. Shchedrin (pseudonym of Mikhail Saltykov, 1826–89). "In his youth," Lunacharsky concluded, Shaw "started to build a great bridge from the old world to the new, across which he and other people, the best endowed in mind and character, could pass today. He is now in his old age completing the last arches of this bridge and entering the new world. In this lies the worldwide historical significance of this occasion which we are celebrating with him, the occasion of the 75th birthday of this great English writer in

Moscow. (*Loud and prolonged applause*)" There was also a laudatory greeting from Maxim Gorki, kept away by illness ("the shattering blows your keen mind has dealt to conservatism and people's banality are beyond count"); Shaw returned the compliment by making a special visit to Gorki's bedside on the 29th. (Lunacharsky translation supplied to Shaw by his hosts: BL; Gorki translation by Stephen E. Wilhite, from *Pravda*.)

Kangchenjunga, the world's third highest peak, is in the Himalayas, on the border between Nepal and India.]

It is a softly hot day; and I am in a wagon-lit jogging south—whither I hardly know. Our objective is the Lenin Colony, which is a colhoz or collective farm. I think the place is called Karsinov [Kirsanov]. We left Moscow after lunch. In the forenoon I visited a flaming collection of Gauguins and Van Goghs and a little red William & Mary church, where I satisfied myself that services are going on as freely for the dwindling few that desire them as the services at St Pauls.

Yesterday, my birthday ended strenuously. We did not arrive in Moscow (from Petrograd) until 11.30, having breakfasted slenderly on a rusk, there being no restaurant car. It was very hot; and we were all faint with hunger when we got to the Stadium (out of town) for an official dejeuner, which was a champion specimen of the faked meals with which they carry off their shortages. However, there is plenty to eat in spite of there being nothing to eat. Between hunger and heat I was in anything but brilliant form, and unresistingly let the afternoon be wasted at a horse race, including one in my honor. I had to present the prize to the winning jockey. It was something in an envelope: possibly a rouble.

The evening was tremendous. In the Hall of Nobles, crammed with at least 2000 people, Lunacharsky fired off an oration in my honor which brought down the house. Other speeches followed, and before my turn came the heat and tedium had washed the virtue out of me. However, I spread myself as imposingly as I could. After my first word "Tovarische" I waited for a laugh—and got it. There were enough interpreters and students of English present to give me an occasional response; but I floundered in the middle (my mind went blank suddenly) and I had to frivol rather vulgarly before I got going again. I sat down disgusted with myself for muffing a big oratorical chance; but this morning, when I corrected the attempt at a verbatim report and cut the few lines of rubbish out, it was presentable. We then had a banquet in the green room which hardly any one sat down to. I sweltered and talked until we returned to the Hall of Nobles, where one of the Tovarishti read a translation of my speech, and, to my horror, the concert opened by a man reading several chapters from The Revolutionists Handbook (Man & Superman). Fortunately the concert was a very good one, including terrific dancing, a Liszt Rhapsody on the balalaika (!!!) and a perfect genius of a girl from the Ukraine, as great as Yvette Guilbert, who sang Ukrainian ballads with volcanic effect. Three of the men—the pianist, the accompanist, and the balalaikaist, were in evening dress, and looked unspeakably ridiculous. The concert ended, not with the Internationale, but with a tovarisch who came out and said curtly "Its over."

Nancy went on to the Embassy after swearing me to go straight to bed. To get the whole tearing business out of my head I began Scott's Ivanhoe and read it until two. When I awoke my watch had stopped. It seemed infinitely early with long shadows cast by the 2 or 3 people in the streets. But I got up; had a long wash; and finished the revision of the verbatim report before breakfast arrived. It is amazing how one keeps going here: I am at least 20 years younger. We are all well, and have been so all the time except for one brief bellyache achieved by David. And in view of my return it may reassure you to know that though we have rubbed shoulders (literally) with many proletarian crowds, including young criminals, we have not seen a single person scratching, nor had occasion to open our silly tins of Keating [a commercial brand of flea powder].

This morning Waldorf & Nancy went to the divorce court but found nothing doing.

All the western statesmen should be compelled to spend a fortnight here. Sticking pins into Soviet Russia is like cocking a snook at Kanchinjunga.

Two of your letters have reached me. When this will reach you Heaven knows: we are already 5 hours out from Moscow and have 8 hours more to roll before we reach our destination. Then it will be 3 o'clock; so we shall sleep in the train until 8, when we shall be hauled by horses for an hour to the colhoz, to spend the day there and come back to Moscow by night. I am becoming quite reconciled to railway carriage life.

I made sure of Stalin by declaring in my speech that I must see him. He has promised to receive me on the 29th.

I may be able to send you one more letter from Moscow; but after that it would be useless, as I shall deliver myself at Ayot on Sunday and a letter would not be delivered until Monday. Day will have to go to Harwich on Saturday and find out there the hour at which the Hook of Holland boat arrives in the morning. Sometime after six I think;

but some of the tables say 6.15 and others 6.55. As all the luggage will fit in the dickey the small car will do unless it is frightfully hot. A rivederci.

GBS

[Shaw's Moscow speech was delivered on 26th July, in the Central Hall of Trade Unions. An English stenogram of the speech was submitted to Shaw by *Pravda*; his corrected and amended text was published in translation in the Moscow daily on 29th July. It is here retranslated by Stephen E. Wilhite, incorporating Shaw's original phrases as reported by British and American press associations. The speech was prefaced in *Pravda* by an editorial statement: "Bernard Shaw's appearance on the platform is met by a prolonged and noisy ovation. At the outset of his speech, Shaw pronounces with difficulty the word 'tovarishchi' ['comrades'] in Russian. It comes out something like 'tovreshi' [a meaningless, typical Western mutilation of Slavic sounds], which inspires laughter and applause from the auditorium."]

Unfortunately that is the only Russian word I know. But that word has acquired a particularly friendly sound for me in the—alas—all too short time I have spent in this wonderful country. I want to use this occasion to tell you something of my personal feelings and of the friends with whom I am travelling: Lord and Lady Astor and the Marquis of Lothian. These are enormously rich people: big capitalists and landowners on the most magnificent scale. But don't blame them for that: it is not their fault. Only the English proletariat, and indeed the proletariat of the whole world, can rescue them from that situation.

You cannot imagine the courage we had to muster to risk visiting Communist Russia. Our weeping families clung to us, imploring us not to risk our lives on so dangerous a venture. And when our dear ones saw that we were still determined to set out on our journey they loaded us down with enormous baskets and parcels of food, so we wouldn't die here of hunger. They brought us bedding and all the transportable comforts of civilization. And some of them even brought us tents for fear that we would be without a roof over our heads. The railway from the frontier to Moscow is strewn with the things we threw out our carriage windows as we saw with what comfort, attention and kindness the new regime in Russia surrounded us. We don't know how to adequately express our gratitude for all that your country's Communist government has done for us. We can only say that if the

Soviet government succeeds in providing to all the peoples of the Union those same conditions which it has provided us—and we believe this is one of the Soviet government's goals—then Russia will become the most fortunate country on earth.

I would like to correct one small misunderstanding which I have noticed in the comments of several of those who've already spoken. They expressed here their hope that upon my return to England I would tell the English the full truth about Russia. For ten straight years, comrades, I have been telling the English the full truth about Russia. I didn't even wait for the Five Year Plan to be implemented. Once, when the most abominable things were being said about Russia in the capitalist West back in 1918, I sent one of my books to Lenin with an enthusiastic dedication, hoping that dedication would be published throughout Europe. I don't know what became of that book, but in any case the lines I wrote in dedication to Lenin never appeared anywhere. I know much of what you were suffering then. But from the very beginning I believed you would win through. And I knew further that, whether you were victorious or suffered defeat, it was my duty to back you to the limit.

The idea of this whole journey to Soviet Russia is not to be able to tell the English something which I didn't know before; it is so that I can answer them on those occasions when they say to me: "So, you consider Soviet Russia a remarkable country, but you've not actually been there yourself, you haven't seen all its terrors." Now upon my return I can say: Yes, I have seen all the "terrors," and I was terribly pleased by them.

We shall carry profound impressions with us as we return to England. Despite all I have just said about my familiarity with what is going on in Russia, I am not going to say that even the best hearsay acquaintance can compare with first-hand impressions, face to face with the facts. It has been an immense pleasure for me to meet several movers face to face who until now were just names to me. A week ago Lunacharsky was a well-known name to me, but now he is to me a living man. And in him I have found not only the Party member and the Communist, but beyond this something which Russians and Russians alone can give me: I speak of their ability to understand and appreciate my dramatic works with a depth and a subtlety the like of which—I must confess—I have never found in Western Europe. The illustrious name of Litvinov has also been transformed for me into a living man, and a very amicable one at that. And before I leave Moscow I intend, by hook or by crook, that Stalin shall also become a living man to me and not merely a name. Couldn't those of you who are personally acquainted with Stalin ask him to help me out in this matter?

My personal feeling in the face of your great Communist experiment, like the feeling of many others in that part of the world from which I come, is above all else a feeling of shame that England was not the first to lead the way, instead of Russia. Karl Marx said that the Communist revolution was least likely to take place in Russia. Marx believed the Communist revolution would most likely occur where capitalism is most highly developed. But you see what happened. It turned out that Russia was first. The English ought to be ashamed of themselves for not having beaten you to it. And all the nations of the West ought to share that feeling of shame with England and envy you your glory. When you carry your experiment to its triumphant conclusion—which I feel confident you will—then we in the West, we who are still just playing at Socialism, must follow in your footsteps —whether we will or no.

I find it difficult to conclude my speech. I have said all that I wanted to say to you. But as I look round me now and see all these faces with a brand new look on them, an expression you cannot see yet in the capitalist West, I feel I would like to keep on talking to you for ten hours without stop. But don't be frightened: I won't carry out that awful threat. I shall simply say to you on my own behalf and on behalf of my travelling companions: heartfelt thanks to you for the welcome you have shewn us and for the pains you have taken, which have made our journey as pleasant for us in the present as it will be memorable in the future.

(A storm of applause.)

[On 29th July Shaw was the guest of Litvinov at a luncheon in his honour, and at 8 p.m. that evening Joseph Stalin (1879–1953), general secretary of the Central Committee of the Communist Party, granted him an interview, to which he was permitted to bring the Astors and Lord Lothian, in Stalin's Kremlin office. They sat round a large table informally, with Stalin in grey tunic and black Russian top boots and Litvinov tieless in shirt sleeves. A Foreign Office official served as interpreter for what was, at two hours and twenty-five minutes, one of the longest interviews ever granted to a foreigner. The visitors having been received under an injunction against divulgence of the conversation, there were no press reports of the meeting; and as Shaw, unfortunately, did not record for Charlotte his impressions of Stalin or the gist of the interview as he freshly recalled it, such knowledge as we have of the interview regrettably is sketchy and inconsequential.

On the 30th, after a brief examination of the Red Army barracks, Shaw performed a final act of homage by visiting Nadezhda Krupskaya (1869–1939), widow of Lenin. His train left Moscow at 9.30 that evening; he passed through Stolpce on the 31st, Berlin on 1st August (where Einstein waited fruitlessly to take him for a sail on the Havel), and Liverpool Street station, London, early on the 2nd. "The traveller returned this morning," Charlotte wrote to William Maxwell, "looking well and bronzed. He says it all seems like a 'splendid, sunny dream.' He has really had the time of his life!" (A/3).]

To WILLIAM MAXWELL

[E/3]

[Malvern Hotel] Malvern
14th August 1931

[Still seeking aesthetic improvement in the typography for the new Standard Edition, Shaw was contemplating a Baskerville type for setting off emphasised words in the text to avoid the use of italics or wide-letter spacing.]

I have carefully studied the two alternatives to this Baskerville; and it seems to me by far the best. Plantin is horrible: it changes the color of the letterpress. Fournier italic is all right where italic is needed; but I still feel that if italic is to be used for the stage directions it must not be used for anything else. Baskerville struck me at first sight, as it struck you, as not being sufficiently distinctive. But I then made the curious discovery that it *is* distinctive when it is in the right place. The words *cynical* and *keystone* on the sample page do not stand out. Well, they shouldnt. But the word *before* (3rd line from foot) does stand out as it ought to. And it does not blotch the prevailing color of the letterpress or spoil the page in any way.

I therefore plump for Baskerville.

GBS

To HELEN (NELLIE) HARRIS

[A/3; X/365]

Malvern Hotel. Malvern
25th [26th] August 1931

[Frank Harris died early in the morning of 26th August, suddenly, following an attack of bronchitis. E. Merrill Root, in his *Frank Harris* (1947), claims the enclosure was a cheque for £50.]

259

Dear Mrs Harris

They have just telephoned me that you have finished the strange adventure of being married to Frank.

Death does not always select the convenient moment when there is plenty of ready money in the house to meet its expenses. Hence the enclosure. You can repay it out of the profits of the biography.

Now you can begin another life with the wisdom garnered from your first experiment; so run up the half-masted flag to the top of the staff, and away with melancholy.

ever
G.B.S.

PS   I am working on the proofs and getting the facts straight. Will you leave it to me to see it through the press?

To NANCY ASTOR

Malvern Hotel. Gt Malvern

[A/101]   2nd September 1931

[Thomas Carlyle, in his *Latter-Day Pamphlets* No. 6 (1850?), refers to "A Parliament speaking through reporters to Buncombe and the twenty-seven millions, mostly fools."]

My dear Nancy

. . . Dont worry about the sorrows and terrors of the poor things in Russia who are still foolishly trying to be ladies and gentlemen: it does not hurt them half as much to be governed by Communists as it hurts you to be governed by distillers and brewers and publicans and doctors and "forty millions, mostly fools." So buck up, and preach The Revolution. That trip to Russia would have doubly endeared you and Waldorf to me had that been possible. . . .

Bless you, dearest Nancy, and goodnight.
G.B.S.

To ADRIAN BOULT

Ayot St Lawrence. Welwyn
[A/1; X/366]   13th October 1931

[(Sir) Adrian Boult (1889–1983), former musical director of the Birmingham City Orchestra, was appointed Director of Music for the B.B.C. in 1930 and first conductor of the B.B.C. Symphony Orchestra in 1931. Shaw had heard a performance of Act III of Wagner's *Die Walküre* relayed on 12th December from the Royal Opera House, Covent Garden. The Wotan was Horace Stevens (1876–1950), Australian bass-baritone, who became celebrated for this rôle. Boult was the conductor.]

Dear Adrian Boult

Blessings on you! I have at last heard "Nicht weis'ich dir mehr Helden zur Wahl" properly conducted, and consequently properly sung, after hearing one wretched Wotan after another whacked through it as if he were the Count di Luna [in Verdi's *Il Trovatore*] trumpeting "Per me ora fatale." And at Covent Garden too! What is the world coming to?

Also "Der Augen leuchtendes Paar" taken at the right time.

And the band not a mob but a concert.

Dont trouble to acknowledge this. I thought I'd send it because people who know the difference ought occasionally to say so as a sort of tuning note.

faithfully
G. Bernard Shaw

To HELEN (NELLIE) HARRIS

4 Whitehall Court S W 1
[H/3]   17th October 1931

[Victor Gollancz (1893–1967) was the intellectual and idealistic founder (1928) of an enormously successful publishing house that specialised in leftist literature. Harris's *Bernard Shaw: An Unauthorised Biography* was published simultaneously in London and New York on 27th November. The American price was $4, nearly double what Shaw had suggested. Frank Scully, who proclaimed himself to be Harris's "Literary Secretary," had, as Shaw surmised, drafted much of Harris's supposed manuscript. Harris's *Oscar Wilde*, edited by Shaw in consultation with Lord Alfred Douglas, was finally published in England in 1938.]

Dear Mrs Harris

I have been hard at work on those proof sheets ever since I wrote to you, and have at last returned them to Victor Gollancz ready for press. They cannot be published until after the election and until S. & S. have had them for simultaneous publication in America; but they will be out sometime in November, I hope; and unless they are killed by an excessive price, as so many books have been lately, you may feel fairly sanguine as to a satisfactory sale. Gollancz agrees with me on this point, and having promised the booksellers the book at the price I suggested, eight and sixpence, finds them very keen about it. I am writing to S. & S. by this post to urge the same point.

You may think I have been a long time over this job; but I assure you it is only by putting everything else aside and working double shifts on it that I have been able to get it ready so soon. You see, Frank knew hardly more about my life history than I knew about yours; and the mixture of his guesses with the few things I told him produced the wildest results. I have had to fill in the prosaic facts in Frank's best style, and fit them to his comments as best I could; for I have most scrupulously preserved all his sallies at my expense.

Another difficulty was that though Frank was a member of the Kansas bar, nothing could ever knock into his head the subtle difference between legitimate criticism, including what is technically called "vulgar abuse," and actionable statements. The book contained two outrageous personal libels and three commercial ones; and these I have taken out, as they might have involved lawsuits which would put an end to all hope of any profit on the publication. The commercial libels were contained in a chapter full of gossip picked up at the film studio, which I think must have been written by Scully. Anyhow it had to go, as it was quite unworthy of Frank in style, and was almost miraculously wrong in every particular, besides overstepping the legal lines and making statements reflecting on the commercial management and finance of British International Films.

You may, however, depend on it that the book is not any the worse for my doctoring, and that Frank's opinions of me (which, between ourselves, you must often take with a grain of salt) are not softened or suppressed or evaded in any way.

If the book is a success, it may stimulate public interest in his other writings, especially, perhaps, in the life of Oscar Wilde, which has never been openly in the London market. Brentano, who handled it for some years in America, tells me that when Lord Alfred Douglas threatened proceedings a compromise was arrived at by which it was left on the market with the addition of a chapter by Lord Alfred correcting the statements made in it about himself. Would it not be possible to issue it here on the same condition? With the proofs of Frank's astonishing carelessness as to facts and evidence before me in my own case I can readily believe that he was even less particular about Lord Alfred; and if that is so it is a pity that the book should be driven underground if it can be saved by allowing Lord Alfred to justify himself in his own fashion. I have made as many references to it as possible with this in view, and also to My Life and Loves.

As to this, do you think it would be possible to make it conventionally presentable? You see, Frank, far from being the abandoned voluptuary he supposed himself to be, was really a mid-nineteenth-century Irish prude; and I think that the first volume, which was the only one I read (for he was much too disgusted with me for not leaving it on the drawingroom table to send me the others), could be sufficiently bowdlerized for general publication without losing any of its force or interest, or violating his intentions in any way. Fifty years ago his determination to break down the taboos and win freedom of speech about sex would have been sacred. But nowadays, when every flapper at the dinner table and every lady novelist says things that would have made Frank and myself blush like a couple of ingenues, that particular battle is won, and indeed overwon.

Besides correcting proofs I have written a postscript which must have your approval before it goes to press. I have asked Gollancz to send you a proof. In it I have not only handled Frank almost as freely as the book handles me, but made a momentary allusion to you, which you must strike out if it jars on you in any way. Frank has still some enemies surviving from old times; and I have thought it better to anticipate the worst they can say of him than to provoke them to a renewal of hostilities by leaving their grievances wholly unrecognized.

Scully has just rung me up to accuse Gollancz of wanting to appropriate my MS corrections. This is nonsense: Gollancz has behaved quite correctly and amiably; but I learnt incidentally from Scully that this letter should be addressed to the American Express Co in Paris; and though he is constitutionally incapable of making any precisely accurate statement whatever, I take a chance and address as directed....

As to the corrected proofs, I think I had better destroy them so that nobody shall ever know where the patches came in. If you like I will give you the MS of the postscript; but it is in shorthand.

Will you continue to live at Nice; and are you, all things considered, quite well and happy?

faithfully
G. Bernard Shaw

To LAURENTIA McLACHLAN

Ayot St Lawrence. Welwyn
[A/98; X/256]   25th October 1931

[While at Malvern for the third annual Festival the Shaws drove to Stanbrook Abbey, on 19th September, to deliver the Bethlehem "relic" in the silver reliquary that Shaw had commissioned from the designer J. Paul Cooper (1869–1933), noted for his gold and silversmith work in Canterbury Cathedral and numerous other cathedrals and churches in Britain, and for the small casket containing the ashes of Ellen Terry, in St Paul's Church, Covent Garden. Close to a foot in height, modelled after a mediæval reliquary, Shaw's gift consisted of "a chalice-like base decorated with conventional designs of alternate vine-leaves and bunches of grapes in repoussé work, surmounted by a conical imbricated canopy supported on four slender columns, in the midst of which rests a piece of rock of irregular shape measuring about an inch across. On the summit stands a haloed figure of the holy Child, left hand supporting the globe, right hand raised in blessing" (Dame Felicitas Corrigan, *The Nun, the Infidel and the Superman*, 1985). When Sydney Cockerell viewed it a fortnight later he noted that it lacked identification of donor or other provenance, and suggested an inscription. The prioress passed the suggestion on to Shaw.]

Dear Sister Laurentia

Cockerell is a heathen atheist: a reliquary is no more to him than a football cup.

Why can it not be a secret between us and Our Lady and her little boy?

What the devil—saving your cloth—could we put on it?

Cockerell writes a good hand. Get him a nice piece of parchment and let him inscribe it with a record of the circumstances for the Abbey Archives, if he must provide gossip for antiquarian posterity.

We couldn't put our names on it—could we? It seems to me something perfectly awful.

"An inscription explaining its purpose"! If we could explain its purpose we could explain the universe. I couldnt. Could you? If Cockerell thinks he can—and he's quite capable of it—let him try, and submit the result to the Pope.

Dear Sister: our finger prints are on it, and Heaven knows whose footprints may be on the stone. Isn't that enough?

Or am I am wrong about it?

faithfully and fraternally
Brother Bernard

PS I don't mind being prayed for. When I play with my wireless set I realize that all the sounds in the world are in my room; for I catch them as I alter the wave length receiver—German, French, Italian and unknown tongues. The ether is full of prayers too; and I suppose if I were God I could tune in to them all. Nobody can tell what influence these prayers have. If the ether is full of impulses of good will to me so much the better for me: it would be shockingly unscientific to doubt it. So let the sisters give me all the prayers they can spare; and don't forget me in yours.

To EDITH CRAIG

[A/60]

Ayot St Lawrence. Welwyn
31st October 1931

[Shaw's self-drafted interview, "Ellen Terry and Her Letters," as given to G. W. Bishop, appeared in *The Observer* on 8th November, a rebuke to Gordon Craig's just published *Ellen Terry and Her Secret Self,* in the opening page of which he accused Shaw of blind vanity and jealousy and of insulting the dead. "Craig flew away from the nest," Shaw wrote, "the moment his wings were fully fledged; and he saw very little of his mother afterwards. And he was perfectly right. He had to save his soul alive. . . . What makes this book of his so tragically moving—for if you disregard the rubbish about me, which is neither here nor there, it is a poignant human document—is his desperate denial of the big woman he ran away from and his assertion of the 'little mother' he loved. He still resents the great Ellen Terry, the woman who would have swallowed him up if he had stayed within her magnetic field, so intensely that he is furious with me because I did not tear her letters up and stamp them and her into the earth so that the world would never have known her. . . . You see, in letting that correspondence of mine with Ellen Terry be published, I made a revelation of the side of her that he suffered from; and for that he will never forgive me."

The "famous folder" was an "Annex," a separate pamphlet titled "A Plea for G.B.S.," inserted in a pocket at the back of Craig's book, in which he described Shaw as "a very large, malicious poke-nosed old woman with an idle and vindictive tongue spreading falsehoods up and down the street."

265

Writing to Shaw on 28th October Edith Craig asked forgiveness for bringing upon Shaw the "spluttered spleen" pouring out of her brother, whom she saw as a sick, tortured soul (A/4). Enid Rose (1886–?) was a disciple and defender of Craig, author of *Gordon Craig and the Theatre* (1931), to whom Shaw had written in September to disabuse her of fictions provided by Craig for her book.]

My dear Edy

Don't worry about Ted: he doesn't worry me in the least; and I shall do an interview about the whole business in The Observer which will really rather rehabilitate him, though it will also probably provoke him, as he cannot beat me, to beat Miss Enid Rose, whose yells will be music to me.

I havnt read the book, but Mr Hart sent me the famous folder, which is too babyish to do any harm.

He has not only an anti-Edy complex but an anti-Ellen one, both of which I think I understand. He does not disguise the first from himself; but he deludes himself by setting up Nell, his "darling little mother," as an excuse for attacking the powerful personality from whom he had to run away to be able to call his soul his own. Against this personality you, much disgusted with the Nell tradition, fought your way to victory and the upper hand, and can therefore do it ungrudging justice. Ted will carry his resentment to his grave unless some psycho-analyst, by revealing its true nature to him, should cure him of it.

As to the Secret Life, you said the right thing exactly; and there is nothing more to be said.

There is one feature of the affair that easily escapes notice. You were the first to read the correspondence as a whole, and to see its value. I had never done this. I had only a recollection of the letters as they were written and received thirtyfive years before. My recollection embraced the lost or destroyed letters (mine) as well as the others; and I thought them less presentable than they are, and overdid my apology in the preface. Also, being a greater egotist in my way than even Ted, I never suspected how enormously better your mother came out than I. But when I read the whole as you did, and discovered this unflattering fact, it gave me positive delight (I dont know why) and I was completely converted to your view. That explains a good deal that has puzzled E.G.C.

No room for more.

ever
G.B.S.

266

To NANCY ASTOR

[A/101]

[4 Whitehall Court SW 1]
28th November 1931

["Uncle Tom Cobleigh and all" is part of the refrain of an old ballad "Widdicombe Fair." Gandhi was in London as a delegate of the Indian National Congress, which he headed from 1924 to 1934, to the Second Round Table Conference on India. Shaw visited him on 6th November.]

Dearest Nancy

Charlotte and I have just, in a moment of insanity, taken our passages for the Cape on Christmas Eve, as the most comfortable of the Union Castle liners, the Carnarvon, sails on that day. Charlotte wants sunshine; and I, who have been working like fifty plantations of niggers since our return from Russia, will be the better for a break in my routine. The Madeira Cape route is much the shortest journey—three days—from Southampton to assured calm and summer.

You ought to see the Empire which you govern. The parliamentary Whip will be quite independent of you for five years to come. Why not come to the Cape with the whole Astor-Shaw tribe, Charles Tennant, Phil, old Uncle Tom Cobley and all. Phil could leave the Lords to an understudy: he is wasting his time as completely as Gandhi; for while they are playacting at the Round Table the real conflict of competitive murder is going on in India. If the Indians can create a situation in which, as in Ireland under Collins, the situation of the garrison becomes unbearable, then India will win. Nothing else will produce anything but Coercion Acts and martial law.

I must post this before eleven or it will not reach you until Monday. Probably it wont anyhow.

with undying affection
GBS

267

Ayot St Lawrence. Welwyn
[A/98; X/369]   29th November 1931

[Dame Anne Dowson of Stanbrook Abbey had written to inform Shaw that, following the death of the Lady Abbess on 7th November, Laurentia had been elected on 24th November to be her successor. Shaw's response was a letter in the form of an electioneering poster, comically depicting in his familiar red ink the canvassing messages of five imaginary candidates for the office of Abbess.]

Dear Sister Anne

Hooray !!!!!!! I didn't dare to write until I knew the result. I thank you most heartily for letting me know. I shall write to the Lady Abbess when I have a serious moment free.

What is an enclosed election like? This is my notion of it.

BEWARE
OF
SHAVIANS
DISGUISED
AS
BENEDICTINES
VOTE FOR
Sᴿ DIEHARD
AND
BREAD &
WATER.
MORTIFY
MORTIFY
MORTIFY

VOTE FOR
THAT OLD AND TRIED
FRIEND
OF
THE ENCLOSED
DAME LAURENTIA
AND
BREAKFAST
IN
BED
THREE
TIMES
A WEEK

VOTE FOR
Sᴿ SULPICIA
AND
SHORT
PRAYERS

SISTER
ANN
STANDS
FOR
CUTLETS
ON
FRIDAY
VERB. SAP.

ROLL UP IN YOUR THOUSANDS TO VOTE
FOR
SISTER MAGDALEN
FORMERLY OF HOLLYWOOD
THE REFORMED VAMP
SNATCH THE BRAND FROM THE BURNING

Is it really like
it?
fraternally
G. Bernard Shaw

268

To AUGUSTIN HAMON

R.M.M.V. "Carnarvon Castle"
Within 2 days of the Cape
8th January 1932

[A/1]

[The Shaws sailed as scheduled from Southampton on 24th December on a seventeen day voyage that brought them to Table Bay on 10th January, disembarking at Cape Town the following day. During the journey Shaw had drafted little more than a single chapter of *The Rationalization of Russia*; he subsequently abandoned the book. The fragment was published posthumously in 1964. The 1931 Fabian lecture series was "Capitalism in Dissolution: What Next?" Shaw's lecture, "What Indeed?" was delivered in the Kingsway Hall on 26th November. As Sidney Webb was not scheduled to give one of the series lectures or to chair a session, he presumably spoke from the floor during a discussion following a lecture.]

My dear Hamon

To get leisure to answer my letters I have had to put out to sea for a 17 days voyage.

When I left, the printer had not delivered the advance copies of Trop Vrai for rehearsal and translation; but I left instructions with my secretary to send you one when they arrived; so doubtless the play is already in your hands.

Did I send you a copy of "What I Really Wrote About The War?" If not, write to Miss Blanche Patch (the secretary aforesaid) to send you one. It might be worth Aubier's while to publish it in French, though there is very little about France in it.

I occupy my mornings on board with a book about Russia, which I call, provisionally, The Rationalization of Russia: a history of the revolution, not as to its incidents and persons, but as to its evolution in principle and practice to its present comparatively settled plan of Fabian gradualness and opportunism (Lenin–Stalinism) and nationalism (Stalinism pure). The secret of Stalin is that he is entirely opportunist as to *means*, discarding all doctrinaire limitations, and confident that Russia is big enough to achieve Socialism by itself independently of the capitalist world, which can follow his example or go its own way to perdition. This is obviously sound; for the rest of the world is waiting to see whether his experiment can succeed or not, and will not move in his direction until his success is beyond question. At the recent series of Fabian meetings Sidney Webb said that the real business of the next dozen years or so will be simply waiting for Russia to prove her case. At a later meeting I said that Socialism, Fabianism, Collectivism, Social-Democracy must now be thrown on the dust heap as

269

useless outmoded terms: we are henceforth either scientific Communists or—whatever Macdonald and Snowden (I might have added Kerensky) now are.

The crisis is curiously unreal in the face of the glut of commodities, the burning of coffee in Brazil and of wheat in America to raise prices. The plundering of Germany created a huge drift into France (reparations &c) and America (payment of money borrowed for the war) of gold, with the result that America & France made a "corner" in gold automatically, and America hoarded it helplessly. The Bank of England, unable to get gold, *broke* (this was politely called going off the gold standard) and the whole machinery of exchange deadlocked. Going off the gold standard means either reverting to barter or setting up a standard based on other commodities grouped under an index number. When this is done, and the moratorium extended to the year 5032 or thereabouts, commerce will get on its legs again. I see no reason to believe that the crisis is the Marxian crash that is to end Capitalism in world revolution. Consequently, Vive Stalin! . . .

> Best regards to you all
> G.B.S.

To THE REV. ENSOR WALTERS

R.M.M.V. "Carnarvon Castle"
Nearing the Cape
9th January 1932

[A/3]

[The mummified bodies Shaw had viewed were in the crypt beneath St Michan's Church, Dublin, and in the Bleikeller in Bremen Cathedral. The Rev. Arnold Whitaker Oxford (1854–1948), whose initials Shaw reversed, was a prolific writer of books on religion, medicine and history. He and Charles Charrington had been unsuccessful running mates in the 1898 London County Council election.]

My dear Ensor Walters

I havnt had time to answer any but business letters since my return from Russia in August; so I brought all the intimate ones in a bundle to answer on board ship. I undertook this long voyage solely to get away from my work, having no more business in S. Africa than at the South Pole, with the result that I have done an extra long days writing every day since we sailed.

The Russian situation is very interesting and fascinating from the

270

religious point of view. To be in a country where the Government is fanatically religious and insists on every child being brought up religiously, one of its religious aims being the total abolition of God, is a startling novelty, and one of those things that only a really religious Protestant can understand. They have turned the biggest church (or cathedral rather) in Leningrad (only foreigners call it so: the Commissars and Stalin invariably say Petersburgh) into an anti-God museum; and it is quite a good historical one which you would take as a matter of course in Geneva. The Belfast Corporation would make it a handsome grant; and Martin Luther would have given three cheers for it. It is in fact anti-priestcraft, anti-relic, anti-bogus miracle. The only novelties are a couple of natural mummies, like those in St Michan's church in Dublin or the church in Bremen, and these, presumed to be the bodies of two ordinary peasants, are exhibited to shew the people that the occasional preservation of the bodies of saints, like St Clare at Assisi, is not a miracle but a natural phenomenon. I said "How do you know that these are not two saints?", and scored a complete knock-out, as of course they knew nothing about them.

There is a complete consensus of testimony, Communist and the reverse, that the Russian clergy, like the English clergy in the century before their spoliation by Henry VIII, had lost their hold on the people by doing nothing but extort money and officiate in services of extravagant splendor, the most gorgeous of which are still kept up in Kieff. To convince myself that they were tolerated I dropped in at one which was being held in a church in Moscow. The priest's robes would have kept you in frock coats for fifty years; and the congregation, moaning their responses and smiting their foreheads on the ground, were fervently pious; but they were not more than fifteen all told, including myself; and *I* did not wait for the collection. What happens to them is not that they are persecuted, but that they are sold up for non-payment of rent, having lost their worshippers, like the City churches which the Church of England wants to sell, or the churches in Regent St and Great Portland St which are now shops and garages. And the priests have become laymen just as the Reverend W. A. Oxford became a doctor. Of course if a priest takes to reactionary politics he gets into trouble like any other reactionary, but as such, not as priest.

The Gay Pay Oo is an Inquisition pure and simple; and the contrast between the leniency with which ordinary police offenders are treated and the ruthlessness with which the G.P.U. "liquidates" you, using a pistol (unawares) as a humane killer, if it concludes that you are one of the Better Dead, is curious. There is no capital punishment: you can commit a murder for four years imprisonment or so. In the police courts there are—as I saw for myself—no docks, no warders, no police, no bodily restraint of any kind, women magistrates with a man and woman at the table with them to see fair. You are told to go to prison and you go, leaving the room like any member of the public; and the imprisonment, as far as I could make out, means that you are locked up at night and not let go to the Opera, doing your ordinary work all day.

It is not a cheap trip for tourists; but it would keep you in sermons for a year at least. There is no end to the odd things to be described, and the morals to be drawn. The blessed absence of ladies and gentlemen (you simply can't bear them at first when you are returning) and of the competitive commercial friction which is so omnipresent in the west that we are not conscious of it until it stops at the Russian frontier, is quite indescribable[.]

We reach Capetown tomorrow: I must go and pack.

Though we so seldom meet you are still present to me as a valued and everyday intimate friend; so give my love to your wife.

I shall be back (D.V.) in April.

ever
G.B.S.

To THE VERY REV. W. R. INGE

R.M.M.V. "Carnarvon Castle"
Nearing the Cape
9th January 1932

[A/59]

[Inge's letter of 18th December 1931 to Shaw reflected views he had expressed in a B.B.C. talk on 3rd December as part of H. G. Wells's symposium on "What would I do if I were dictator?" He was not, he said, a believer in revolutions, and could not recall one in all history that proved permanent. "Empires," he concluded, "die of indigestion, democracies of sheer folly, utopias of utter boredom" (BL). The "39 articles" are the articles of faith of the Church of England, given parliamentary authority in 1571.]

My dear Dean

Being myself that fearfully old Victorian thing a convert of Karl Marx I believe in revolutions for what they are worth. In spite of the attempts of James II and George III, the English Whig revolution was never undone. Neither Napoleon nor his little tail of effete Bourbons could bring back the marquises or get the great estates from the peasants. No Conservative Cabinet has ever dreamt of re-establishing the pocket boroughs or disfranchising Birmingham. Revolutions really can dislodge top dogs and destroy their institutions; and the Russian revolution has actually "expropriated the expropriators" so effectually that I doubt whether all the king's horses and all the king's men could set them up again even if they got the chance.

The Russians have "got religion"; and that makes them none the less formidable because one of their 39 articles is that there is no God, and that it is *not* a family secret. They have got hold of the children; and it is very easy to mould human nature if you catch it before it is set. The Russian experiment is enormously interesting and may prove historically momentous.

I write this because I find your letter among those which my intelligent secretary packed for me to answer; and I cannot let it pass without at least a wave of the pen.

Our best regards, as affectionate as she can stand, to Mrs Inge.

faithfully
G. Bernard Shaw

To EMERY WALKER

Queen's Hotel. Sea Point
Cape Town. South Africa
[A/3]   25th January 1932

[The Shaws spent nearly four weeks in Cape Town. In addition to much sightseeing, guided by Commander C. P. Newton of the Cape Town publicity bureau, Shaw spoke at several luncheons, lectured to the Cape Fabian Society for over two hours in the Town Hall on 1st February, on "The Rationalization of Russia" (the notes for which are now at Cornell), and gave a radio talk, "A Warning to South Africa," on the 6th that was, according to Shaw, the first broadcast to be relayed to all of South Africa, over some fifteen hundred miles of telephone wire. He and Charlotte took a plane ride (her first) at Maitland Aerodrome, visited the famed escapologist Harry Houdini, attended a garden party to meet General J. C. Smuts, bathed at Glencairn, and lunched with one of the principal Transvaal mine owners, Sir Abe Bailey. Dorothy ("Dolly") Walker (1878–1963) was Emery Walker's only offspring.]

My dear Walker

... This place is full of sunshine, long days, and darkies to do all the work. The gardens and old Dutch Peter de Hooghe interiors are enchanting; but the social problems—poor whites competing for un- skilled labor jobs with a black proletariat which can live on next to nothing, with no pensions nor unemployment insurance, and race war between Dutch and English—are insoluble; and I suspect that the scientific people are right (for once) in declaring that the land cannot support human life unless it extracts nitrates from the air on a colossal scale.

Russia was enormously interesting: they seem to be really pulling it off. At first they could do nothing with their American machinery but smash it (like the tricycle [Henry Hyde] Champion lent to the com- rades) but they called in the American "efficiency engineers" and the advantage of the absence of the enormous and omnipresent friction caused by the conflict of interests in the capitalist system left them such a margin for failures and breakages that—with the help of imported American hands—they have at last got into reasonable working order.

I must see you and talk to you about it when I return from this trip. There is so much to be said that I was afraid to inflict it on you when you were ill, and concluded that a visit from Charlotte alone would be more soothing.

Morris was right after all. The Fabian parliamentary program was a very plausible one; but, as Macdonald has found, parliament and the party system is no more capable of establishing Communism than two donkeys pulling different ways, one at each end, is capable of moving a modern goods train of 70 ten ton trucks.

Our love to Dolly. We shall be back about the first of April via the east coast and the Suez canal, and hope to find you in rude health when we arrive.

ever
G. Bernard Shaw

To A. NELSON

Queen's Hotel. Cape Town

[A/91]   30th January 1932

[During the Cape Town visit Shaw received a vast quantity of local correspondence, which he tried to the best of his ability to answer personally. It
became necessary, however, to resort to the familiar technique of drafting a
hasty response on the sender's letter and turning it over to a secretary to
type, transposing the message to the third person (when Shaw did not actually draft it in this manner). The secretary presumably was Commander Newton's, as the typed carbons bear the initials CPN/MP. Nelson was one of the
fortunate ones who received an autograph communication.]

Dear Sir

I know all about the Lunacy Laws. There is the same difficulty
wherever people are allowed to keep lunatics for private profit. Charles
Reade was trying to expose the abuses of the private asylums sixty
years ago; and matters seem to be much the same as they were then.

But I cannot take up the subject. My failing hands are overfull; and
there are only 24 hours in the day. You must not count on "the
supreme importance of the subject to every man and woman in S.A."
The mischief is that it is of no personal interest to any unquestionably
sane normal healthy citizen; and it is consequently almost impossible
to get the evidence of such people, all the victims being peculiar
enough to be bad witnesses.

In England, in the public asylums, the genuine desire of the authorities to get rid of the patients leads to their being occasionally discharged too soon. Dangerously mad people are often very plausible.

In cases of murder, proof of insanity should, instead of shielding the
murderer, ensure his or her execution. I have often thought that the
advocacy of this change would at least clear Lunacy Law Reformers of
all suspicion of being mere sentimentalists.

The levity with which Mental Defectives—a classification which
may be stretched to include the whole human race—are legislated for
(or against) at present is appalling.

faithfully
G. Bernard Shaw

To LADY RHONDDA

Royal Hotel. Knysna. Cape Province
[A/8]   15th February 1932

[Shaw and Charlotte left Cape Town on 7th February by automobile, their destination being Cape Elizabeth. GBS, having undergone a local driving test to obtain a South African licence, was at the wheel, proceeding uneventfully to Swellendam, Oudtshoorn, and George. At Knysna, however, on 10th February, an accident occurred. Shaw's reference to Charlotte's resultant condition conflates Mercutio's dying speech in *Romeo and Juliet* (III.i.99–100) and Hamlet's first soliloquy (I.ii.146).

The Rev. Edward Lyttelton (1855–1942), former headmaster of Eton, had written to *Time and Tide* to rebuke the editor for a review (by Lady Rhondda) of the Frank Harris biography, in which there appeared Shaw's statement that he had always associated sexual intercourse with delight, "and had no scruples nor remorses nor misgivings of conscience." Shaw and Lyttelton had then indulged in an epistolary debate, headed "Moral Detachment," in the pages of *Time and Tide* throughout December. St John Ervine, whose biography *Parnell* was published in 1925, was at work on a biography of Salvation Army General William Booth, *God's Soldier* (1934).]

My dear Lady Rhondda

I got your letter in Cape Town. All our plans for the East Coast have been upset by a sensational exploit of mine which has miraculously escaped the papers, and which you must hide in your bosom to save us from a deluge of enquiries. I hired a car to drive from Cape Town to Port Elizabeth. I negotiated several mountain ranges and gorges in a masterly manner; but on what I thought a perfectly safe bit of straight road I indulged in a turn of speed and presently got violently deflected into an overcorrected spin. I got out of it by jumping a fence, crashing through a bunker with 5 strands of barbed wire snapping one after another in a vain attempt to restrain me, and plunging madly down a steep place until I had the happy thought of shifting my straining foot from the accelerator to the brake. I got off with a crack on the chin from the steering wheel and a clip on the knee.

But Charlotte!! I can't describe it. Broken head, two black eyes, sprained left arm, bruised back, and a hole in her shin not so deep as a well nor so wide as a church door but—let me not think on't.

And she was so happy and well in the sunshine! "Nothing serious" they say. No bones broken. Nothing but days and nights of pain and shock and misery. However, the worst is over now, as the accident happened on the tenth. But the shin hole is still discharging and painful when moved; and unless it heals miraculously in the next few days I

276

Shaw in South Africa, 11 January 1932,
with Charlotte Shaw and Commander C. P. Newton

*(Photograph by Cay's Photo Service Agency; Shaw collection of
Dan H. Laurence, University of Guelph Library)*

Shaw in Tokyo, 6–8 March 1933

*(Photograph by Associated Screen News Ltd.; Shaw collection of
Dan H. Laurence, University of Guelph Library)*

Shaw in Honolulu, 16–18 March 1933

*(Photograph by Associated Screen News, Ltd.; Shaw collection of
Dan H. Laurence, University of Guelph Library)*

COMING HOME WITH THE "BUTTER."

MR. BERNARD SHAW DOES A LITTLE DUMPING.

Cartoon by Bernard Partridge, *Punch*, 12 August 1931

(Shaw collection of Dan H. Laurence, University of Guelph Library)

shall keep her here in the sun for another month and delay her return until April is well advanced. This is a heavenly climate for her.

There was a very obvious retort to Lyttelton. If it is a sin to use for pleasure the faculties that are given us for use—muscular strength for instance—then hell must be full of cricketing Lytteltons.

I did not understand about Ervine. I wrote to him and gave him a piece of my mind, as he has an Irish habit of thinking you hate him unless you tell him every week that you particularly like him. Fortunately you generally do.

Which Booth is he biographizing? Edwin the actor, or the Salvation [Army] General? He has a sort of affectionateness that makes him too kind to his subjects—for instance, Parnell—unless he despises them in the Belfast manner.

And that, dear Margaret (for I also have attacks of affectionateness) is all for the present from

your very humble and obedient servant
G. Bernard Shaw

PS   Would you mind calling me G. B. S? Mister Shaw be blowed!

To BLANCHE PATCH

[A/9]

The Royal Hotel. Knysna
17th February 1932

[Charlotte's injuries necessitated a month's recuperation. The Shaws remained at Knysna until 17th March, when they proceeded to George, where they charted a Union Airway Junker to fly them to Cape Town. At 4 p.m. on the 18th they sailed for home.]

Dear Blanche

Any travelling just now is out of the question for Mrs Shaw. I have cancelled our passages and made up my mind to stay here until the wound in her shin heals and then remain at a very pleasant place in the neighborhood called Wilderness until she is quite herself again. At best we shall be ready for the Warwick Castle, which leaves on the 18th March; but I am not very sure even of that: the case still threatens to be slow and troublesome. It has not yet taken a decisive turn.

I enclose £250 lest your funds should run dry before I return.

GBS

To H. G. WELLS

R.M.S. Warwick Castle
One day out of Capetown
[A/9]   19th March 1932

[Wells's new "Encyclopedia" was *The Work, Wealth and Happiness of Mankind* (1932). His *Science of Life* (1929), a collaboration with Julian Huxley and his son G.P.Wells, was a follow-up to *The Outline of History* (1920). Chesterton's organisation was the Distributist League. Fascination Fledgeby is a money-lender in Dickens's *Our Mutual Friend*. The "loud pedal" is the accelerator.]

My dear H.G.

The Cape Fabian Society has just presented me with a copy of your new Encyclopedia in gratitude for a great platform display of mine by which they netted £160: unheard-of wealth for them.

Having had it only for a few hours I have only sampled it to the extent of looking up half a dozen of the index references and browsing round about them. I therefore dont know whether you have dealt with a phenomenon of which I have been very conscious for some years past.

Compare Dickens and Thackeray with Wells and Shaw, and Fielding with Chesterton. All of them are troubled by social abuses and regard comedy, *alias* the chastening of morals by ridicule, as part of their business. But the moderns have tried to do what Dickens, Thack., and Fielding never dreamt of. They have deliberately tried to produce something like the Bible, the Koran, the works of Aristotle, or the Institutes of Calvin: that is, to lay down the law in religion, economics, history and philosophy for the following generations. This is the intention of my "metabiological" Creative Evolution, and my Communistic politics, with my essays on education, medicine & criminology. It is the intention of your series of Outlines. Chesterton's Romanism and his Distributive League are evidently the ruins of a scheme which was hopelessly muddled by Belloc, but which would probably not have matured anyhow because intellectual activity has always been practised by Chesterton as a sport, with the odd result that he is now dreadfully in earnest about beliefs that are intellectually impossible. So we must, alas! cut him out of the new phenomenon.

Now as between us it seems to me that though I am fully conscious of what you are doing, you are hardly at all conscious that I am doing it too. I watch your high tidemarks carefully, and begin where you leave off. When the obsolete purblind stuff which you call your education blocks your path I carefully remove it. But it never occurs to you

278

that you ought to take my proceedings seriously as part of a Shavian natural philosophy on exactly the same footing as the Wellsian natural philosophy. I am careful not to present the Shavian philosophy as alternative to and competing with the Wellsian philosophy. We are the world's family solicitors; and we should be partners. We should pool our results and adopt each other's work on this point or that. When you convict me of a superstition I abandon it. When I convict you of one, you gravely explain to the public that there is a screw loose in me.

H. G.: there isnt. When I venture to say that a thing is so, it is so. But you have to get what I say exactly, and not substitute the nearest thing in your own stock, and reject that. For instance you have in your dustbin a superstition called equal pay. You have another even more villainous superstition, or rather habit of thought, which is, that the ability to acquire capital is identical with the ability to administer it competently. And you accuse me, in a work which will have an enormous circulation, of advocating equal pay for all work, and an equal share in the administration and control of capital for everybody. You put this down and print it without ever pausing to reflect that as this is the vulgarest Jack Cade folly, Shaw, not being Jack Cade, couldnt really have said it. You cheerfully and confidently embrace the solution that I *am* Jack Cade.

Let me set this right for you. You see that the point on which the Capitalist paper Utopia has broken down grotesquely and hopelessly is Distribution.

Now, first, clear your mind of that Bromley inheritance: the notion that distribution is simply an arrangement of pay for work. The point at which distribution is supremely important is distribution among babies. Get a baby to work and be paid for it if you can.

I will not pretend that you really believe that Midas is an ideal Treasury official or Chancellor of the Exchequer. Such a belief would be an impossible extension of Jack Cadeism to a theory that all mayors who made their money in the nail and saucepan business are, before God, equally capable of the Higher Clissoldism. There is no natural association whatever between the possession of an income and the ability to spend or invest it wisely: rather is it probable that the selfish singleness of aim that makes Fascination Fledgby rich will impoverish the community if it leaves the control of his riches in his hands instead of surtaxing him and transferring the spoils to a Clissoldian Treasury.

My thesis is that a really fundamental consideration of the problem of Distribution will entirely dissociate it from payments for work or rewards of virtue, and will lead to equality of distribution by the reduction to absurdity or impossibility of every alternative. I have, in the I.W's G.S. worked the thesis out carefully and exhaustively and, so far, unanswerably. And you reject my demonstration with the commonplaces of a retired colonel in Cheltenham or Knysna C.P.S.A., and add, as a Wellsian coruscation, that I have the ideas of Jack Cade because my mother was addicted to singing. *Really*, H.G.—!!!

It is not quite so bad as the Science of Life, in which Huxley went back on his own brainiest essays in psychology, and you atavised to neo-Darwinism by denying that there is any difference between a dead body and a live one, and that only a drivelling humanitarian like Shaw could allege that there not only is a difference, but that it is the whole problem of biology.

I won't inflict another page on you; but we must pull together; for we are both in the same boat. What would you think of me if every successive work of mine contained an attack on your intellectual credit? And this not out of malice, but sheer inattention and carelessness, with complete goodwill all the time. I wish that idiot Pavlov (not unrepentant, they told me, in Russia) would devise some nice laboratory experiment to establish a Be Careful reflex in response to the word Shaw.

The bugle sounds for lunch.

ever

G.B.S.

PS I smashed Charlotte up so frightfully by shooting miraculously off the road when I was driving, and charging with the loud pedal hard down over hedge and ditch and bunker and hillside for a hectic seventy-five yards that she was in bed for a month, and then got up apparently better than ever.

To LAURENTIA McLACHLAN

[H/98; X/256.e]

4 Whitehall Court SW 1
12th [14th] April 1932

[On 16th February, as Charlotte recuperated at Knysna, Shaw informed Commander Newton that he would while away the time by writing a play—if he could think of anything. Within three days he had commenced work, but not on a play. For a third of a century Shaw had contemplated writing "a big book of devotion for modern people," as he described it for Frederick Evans on 27th August 1895, "bringing all the truths latent in the old religious dogmas into contact with real life—a gospel of Shawianity, in fact." What finally emerged, thanks in large part to Shaw's recent correspondence and meeting with the missionary Mabel Shaw, was a compact cosmic fable that effectively blended Lewis Carroll and Voltaire with the Bible. When it was completed, eighteen days later, Shaw titled it *The Adventures of the Black Girl in Her Search for God.*

The letter from Dame Laurentia to which Shaw here replied has not survived.]

Your letter has given me a terrible fright. The story is absolutely blasphemous, as it goes beyond all the churches and all the gods. I forgot all about you, or I should never have dared. It is about a negro girl converted by a missionary, who takes her conversion very seriously and demands where she is to find God. "Seek and ye shall find Him" is the only direction she gets; so off she goes through the forest on her search, with her knobkerrie in her hand. Her search is only too successful. She finds the god of Abraham, and the god of Job; and I regret to say she disposes of both with her knobkerrie. She meets Ecclesiastes (Koheleth) the Preacher, who thinks that death reduces life to futility and warns her not to be righteous overmuch. She meets Micah, roaring like a dragon and denouncing the god of Abraham as a bloodthirsty impostor with his horrible sacrifices. She meets Pavlov, who assures her that there is no god, and that life is only a series of reflexes. She meets St Peter carrying a cathedral on his shoulders. On her rushing to beg him to take care, as the weight will break his back, he assures her that it is only a paper cathedral and goes off gaily with it; but presently several others come along with paper churches, mostly much smaller and uglier, who warn her against St Peter until they begin throwing stones at oneanother and she has to run away to escape the fusillade.

Then she meets St John, who is clamoring in despair for the promised Second Coming, as he cannot die until it happens ("if I will that he tarry till I come") and he is dreadfully tired of waiting in so wicked a world. She comes to the Cross, guarded by a Roman soldier who orders her to kneel down and worship the symbol of Roman justice. She settles him with her knobkerrie and turns from the gibbet disgusted. Then she comes to the old well of the woman of Samaria, and finds your friend there, whom people call The Conjuror, as they wont listen to his preaching but like his miracles. He gives her his commandment, love oneanother; but this is not enough for her, as there are people whom she hates and knows she ought to hate; and as to loving people, even if it were always possible, she considers it a great liberty to take with them, and doesnt want everybody to take that liberty with her. When she presses this on him he begs her not to make him unhappy by reminding him of them; so they part for the moment. Her next encounter is with a scientific expedition, including some rather unpleasant women. She lays one of them out with her knob-kerrie after hearing various modern scientific explanations of the universe squabbled about.

She goes back to the Conjuror, and finds him stretched on a cross acting as model to an image carver who pays him sixpence an hour, this being the only way in which he can earn his scanty bread. He is talking to an Arab (Mahomet) who, when he complains that when he preaches to the people they stone him, though they will buy any number of wooden images of him on the cross, explains that he does not suffer in that way because though he also is a preacher, and the servant of Allah the just and merciful, he is careful to kill all those who do not believe. But this is no use to the Conjuror, who can only say that he admires such courage and practical sagacity, but is not built that way and does not feel competent to judge whether people are fit to live or not. The image maker joins in the discussion, and has a good deal to say. Finally the Arab proposes to add the black girl to his already large collection of wives, but only involves himself in a vigorous feminist argument of which he gets the worst. The girl then goes off, declaring that when men begin talking about women they are unbearable. She presently comes to a villa with a garden, which a frightfully intelligent looking but wizened old gentleman (Voltaire) is cultivating in a rather ama-teurish way. On hearing of her quest, he remonstrates with her for her audacity, and confesses that if someone told him that God was coming to pay him a visit he should hide in the nearest mousehole. Then he tells her the story of Jupiter and Semele. "Besides," he says, "you need not trouble to hunt for God: he is always at your elbow." This impresses her so much that she goes into the garden and helps the old gentleman to cultivate it until he dies and bequeaths it to her.

I am not sure that I shall not add another adventure with a person whom I shall call the Irishman; but this will be enough to give you a notion of the thing as it stands.

The truth is, dear Sister Laurentia, I have finished with all these deities, who seem to me more or less grotesque signboards announcing that the Holy Ghost is lodged within, though It is there only as It is everywhere. There are at least five different gods in the Bible; and the one I like best is the god of Micah, who is remarkably like Allah the just and merciful. As to the Churches, they live not on their own merits but on the innocent faith of millions of pious souls who clothe them with all their own highest aspirations, and think of the Pope or the archbishop always as the vicar of God on earth, or, if they know a little history, perhaps as a Hildebrand or a Gregory, but never as, say, an Alexander Borgia or one of the many Nincompopes who have been too small to hold the full papal measure of inspiration. As to the prophets, I am a prophet myself, and can sympathize with them; but if you could convince me that Jesus was a supernatural personage, as in his last distracted days he thought himself to be, I should instantly lose all interest in him. The Word does not become flesh by halves: it does not keep a trick up its sleeve and produce a Freak. I do not cry "He saved others: himself he cannot save," which is a fair taunt to a magician; I should say rather to the jeering crowd "He tried to save you, and you slew him; so now you can follow your pet Barabbas to the devil: only, as I am determined that you shall have no excuse in the hour of your ruin, I also shall point out the way to you, though you shall not catch me in your legal and ecclesiastical nets if I can help it."

And so on, and so forth.

Perhaps I should not disturb the peace of Stanbrook with my turbulent spirit; but as I want you to go on praying for me I must in common honesty let you know what you are praying for. I have a vision of a novice innocently praying for that good man Bernard Shaw, and a scandalized Deity exclaiming "What! that old reprobate who lives at Whitehall Court, for whom purgatory is too good. Dont dare mention him in my presence."

The fact is, I have such an unruly imagination that I had better change the subject. I did not feel that your election could be more than a nominal change; for you would boss the establishment if you were only the scullery maid; and now that you are the Abbess I feel comforted because you wont have to wash dishes as well as boss; and I wish you a wilful dominating interfering managing sort of Prioress so that you may henceforth have as little to do as possible except keep people's souls clean, as you help to keep that of your erring and worldly

Brother Bernard

PS Shall I send you the story or not? It is very irreverent and iconoclastic; but I dont think *you* will think it fundamentally irreligious.

To NANCY ASTOR

[A/101]

4 Whitehall Court SW1
15th April 1932

[The friend to whom Shaw cautiously referred was, of course, Nancy's son Bobby Shaw, who had emerged from prison after a four months' sentence. The term *urning*, growing out of an allusion in Plato's *Symposium* to the god Uranus, was first used by Karl Heinrich Ulrichs (1825–95), German polemicist, to refer to homosexual persons. The Carpenter "memoir" was *Edward Carpenter: in appreciation*, edited by G. Beith, 1931, with contributions by Havelock Ellis, Laurence Housman, and Goldsworthy Lowes Dickinson, among others. The play in rehearsal was *Heartbreak House*, revived by the Birmingham Repertory Company at the Queen's Theatre, London, on 25th April, with Cedric Hardwicke as Shotover and Edith Evans once again as Lady Utterword. H. K. Ayliff was the nominal director, with Shaw participating in several of the rehearsals. He lunched with the Astors finally on 5th May.]

My dear Nancy

I find myself troubled from time to time when I think of the case of our friend who got into difficulties just before our trip to Russia. I wonder has he ever studied his own case scientifically and objectively. A man may suffer acutely and lose his self-respect very dangerously if he mistakes for a frightful delinquency on his part a condition for which he is no more morally responsible than for color blindness. Also, his relatives may suffer just as cruelly from the same mistake.

During the last fifty years there has been a very large output of elaborate studies of the subject in Germany and to a less extent in England. It has been quite conclusively established that the curious reversal of the normal course of attraction is an entirely natural and genuine phenomenon which is so far from being associated with general depravity of character that some of the greatest men have experienced it (Michael Angelo, for example) and some silly-clever intellectuals actually affect it as a symptom of mental superiority though they are really quite normal.

When I was young and ignorant I had the usual thoughtless horror of it; for though I had absolutely no scruples or reticences where women were concerned, any sort of sexual relation within my own gender was repugnant and impossible: in fact I never thought of such a thing and did not want to hear about it. The subject was at last forced upon me by a special friendship which I formed with a married couple [Henry and Kate Salt] who had also a special friendship with

284

Edward Carpenter, with whom our Socialism had brought me into contact.

When I read Carpenter's Towards Democracy, which made a very fair shot at being a great poem in the manner of Walt Whitman, I at once perceived that it was womanless, and that all Carpenter's ideals of noble companionship were unisexual.

Now in our friends the married couple the man was normal; but the woman, who was affectionately fond of all three of us, and a quite good, sincere, innocent person, would not allow her husband his conjugal rights, and was always taking wild sentimental fancies to women whom she took for persecuted angels, and whom I had to unmask as liars and humbugs. At last she was troubled and on the verge of a nervous breakdown, and couldnt tell why. I told her to go and get a job in a factory, as factory girls cannot afford nerves and havn't time for them; and to my astonishment and dismay she took me at my word and went and did it. The result was excellent, though of course, being a lady, she very soon got pushed up into literate and managing work.

But she also found salvation by learning what was really the matter with her. I presume that it was Carpenter who enlightened her: anyhow she told me with great exultation one day that she had discovered the existence of the Urnings; that she was herself an Urning; and that she was very proud of it and understood everything that had puzzled and worried her before. And so she dropped the factory and sublimated her desires into harmless raptures about music and poetry and platonic adorations of Carpenter and of me and of all the nice people she came across.

This gave me a serious and humane view of the subject. It was clear that Carpenter, understanding his condition scientifically and poetically, was not degraded by it. It was equally clear that the lady, when he enlightened her, at once passed from a state of mind that threatened her reason and destroyed her happiness to ease of mind and a new and respectful interest in herself. Neither of them were in the least danger of falling into the debauchery which is a possibility of their condition exactly as it is a possibility of the normal condition.

Carpenter, being dead, yet speaketh, as you may see from the enclosed memoir and catalogue. Do you think he could be of any use in the case of our friend? However helpful his mother may be to him in some ways it is practically impossible for a man to discuss his sexual life with his parents, just as it is impossible for them to discuss their sexual lives with him. The attempt may be nerve shattering on both sides. Yet the first need is for free healthy discussion. When my late woman friend (she is dead) got enlightened she at once began to talk eagerly and interestedly and happily to me about the Urnings and herself with a quite wholesomely shameless objectivity. Now what you tell me about our friend makes me suspect that he has not reached that point and is still struggling with mischievous and tormenting shames and reticences. At all events I will chance this letter to you and leave the matter to your judgment; for in this matter Mrs Eddy, bless her, is no use; and the Bible, with its rubbish about Lot's wife, is positively dangerous.

I have written a most frightfully blasphemous religious story called The Adventures of the Black Girl in her Search for God which you will perhaps like better than the play. Both of them can be read only to a very select and intimate audience: no American ambassadors and frivolous ladies and so forth.

I shall be rehearsing like mad all next week, making lunches at fixed hours impossible; so I may not see you quite so soon as I could desire.

ever your
G.B.S.

To CECIL LEWIS

Ayot St Lawrence. Welwyn
[A/5]   18th April 1932

[Although the film version of *How He Lied to Her Husband* had received an almost uniformly devastating press when it opened in 1931, Shaw had licensed *Arms and the Man* to British International Pictures, stipulating again that Cecil Lewis was to direct the picture. Lewis was also writing the screenplay, sending portions of it to Shaw for approval. "I find this game rather fascinating," Shaw wrote to him on 17th April. "If I had time I would half rewrite the play and invent at least fifty more changes of scene" (A/5). It was evident, however, that Shaw was thinking of the film more in conventional theatrical terms than in cinematic ones. *Arms and the Man* had its world première less than four months later, at Malvern on 4th August.]

Dear Cecil Lewis

Please send the pages I have skipped to Whitehall Court.

The changes—the garden as a relief to the library and the absence of Louka from the stage during the scene of Petkoff & the photograph—are excellent. The garden should have two talking places and an urn

286

or something for Louka to dump the letters on and perhaps for occasional posing. A glade with a statue would be beyond the Petkoffs; but a well is a useful property. Anyhow, do not have the Louka–Sergius duet on the same bench as the Raïna–Bluntschli one: the former needs more privacy and romance—less obviously under the house windows.

I am not at all against your overlays on principle: I am quite eager to try them and confident of their effectiveness in the right place. But they have to be very carefully contrived; and as I have noted at Petkoff's entry in his shirtsleeves, I feel sure that an overlay spoken by a person whose presence has not been visually impressed immediately before is hopeless unless the overlaid one is a ghost.

Also the balance between full sets and close-ups should be carefully watched. I think How He Lied suffered from the audience not seeing the whole room often enough. A screen play all close-ups and groups and corners is rather like a melodrama all asides. Keep the audience well in mind of the whole room, the whole garden, even the whole landscape in which the close-ups take place.

In the stage set of the second act a valuable bit of local color was produced by a minaret, the top of which stuck up into view from a ground row, giving the effect of a valley between the garden and the mountains on the back cloth with a town in it and a mosque or two. Bung in a minaret if you can.

You may go ahead without any misgivings. I have none. I can leave the business in your hands with complete confidence—but mind! in *your* hands and not in those of the business staff or the callboy or the expert from Hollywood.

Remember that in a movie the faces alone matter; but in a talkie the voices are urgent. Raïna must be a soprano and Louka a contralto. Bluntschli must have a dry voice and Sergius a ringing one. If Nature has not made the difference Art must supply it.

GBS

To ESMÉ PERCY

4 Whitehall Court SW1
[A/3]   20th April 1932

[Percy, in desperate need, had asked Shaw for a loan, offering to give him a post-dated cheque for repayment. He had recently had a great success in a small but effective rôle in British International's film *Murder*, directed by Alfred Hitchcock.]

Dear Esme Percy

NEVER give a postdated cheque. Break fifty promises to pay if you are weakminded enough to make them and you may be forgiven; but a dishonored cheque is unpardonable and irretrievable. Never do it.

You *may* have £60 in the bank on the 16th July. You *may* win the Calcutta Sweep or the next Irish lottery. You *may* get an engagement from B.I.P. for 5 years at £500 a week.

I shall not gamble on these possibilities. I shall not lend you a farthing.

But as you demonstrated the practicability of "the entirety" of Man and Superman on the stage, and I never had the decency to say Thank You for that service I'll make you a present of £100 and leave you to await the 16th July with an easy conscience.

faithfully
G. Bernard Shaw

PS On your life, don't tell anybody.

To LAURENTIA McLACHLAN

[Ayot St Lawrence. Welwyn]
[Z/98; X/256]   [Undated: assigned to 2nd May 1932]

["In S. Africa," Shaw informed Otto Kyllmann of Constable's on 9th April, "I wrote a story, or rather a Voltairean pamphlet, very blasphemous, describing a negro girl's search for God. I think I shall add it unobtrusively to the standard edition of the short stories after turning an honest penny by serializing it if I can get anyone to venture on it" (H/64). On the 14th he sent a typescript of the tale to R. & R. Clark, confessing "I don't know what I shall do with this Black Girl story; but as it will come out in the Standard Edition Short Story volume sooner or later, it may as well be set up for it forthwith, especially as it will be a great convenience to me to have some printed copies at once; so let me have half a dozen proofs" (A/3). One of the copies was sent off to Dean Inge, with an inscription in which Shaw stated that, whether

288

inspired to write it "from above or below," he didn't know what to do with "the thing" (A/59). Another copy was sent, a day or two earlier, to Dame Laurentia, who had "demanded" to see the work. It was inscribed on the fly-leaf of the proof copy (date-stamped 20th April by the printer): "An Inspiration which came in response to the prayers of the nuns of Stanbrook Abbey and in particular to the prayers of his dear Sister Laurentia for Bernard Shaw[.]" (Stanbrook Abbey).

About a fortnight after this, Shaw sent to Dame Laurentia a little play, which she interpreted to mean that he was scrapping the work (as in fact he may momentarily have considered doing in light of his indecision as to its publication). "You have made me happy again by your nice little play," she wrote to him on 3rd May, "and I thank you from my heart for listening to me. I have read most of the book and I agree with many of your ideas, but if you had published it I could never have forgiven you. However you are going to be good and I feel light & springy again & proud of my dear Brother Bernard. You shall have more prayers by way of reward! ... I simply cannot find words to thank you for your answer to my letter, but you *know* how grateful I am" (A/2; X/369.e).]

> *Scene. God's office in heaven. Morning. The Recording Angel is writing up his books. Gabriel moodling about rather worried. Portrait of Our Lady over the mantelpiece[.] God comes in[.]*

God—Morning, Gabriel. Morning, Reck. Anything urgent this morning? Any prayers to be attended to?

Gabriel—The Abbess of Stan—

God—Again!! What a bother that woman is! What does she want *now*?

Gabriel—It's about that fellow Shaw.

God—But I've answered her prayers about him. She and her nuns pestered me about him for months. What she can see in him I can't imagine. But to please her I gave him a first class job in his own line and smashed up his wife for a month to give him time to do it.

The R. Angel (*looking up from his book*) What job was that?

God—To get Jesus off the cross. They have kept my poor boy nailed up there for nineteen hundred years, and wont listen to a word he says: they just keep on gloating over his execution. Shaw hates executions and thinks there's a lot in what Jesus says. So when Laurentia—

The R. Angel—You mustn't call her Laurentia now. She's an Abbess.

God—I shall call her what I like. She and her nuns worried me to save Shaw's soul until I was tired of hearing the fellow's name. For their sakes I did him the great honor of selecting him for the Deposition. What more does the woman want?

Gabriel—She doesnt approve of your way of saving him.

God—Not approve! She wants to dictate my ways to me, does she? I'll teach her. Put her down for five minutes in purgatory.

The R. Angel—You can t do that. Stanbury's—I mean Stanbrook's—an important place. It wouldn't do.

Gabriel—You'd better let her have her way. She's a shocking nuisance with her Shaw, I know; but she has been a faithful servant—

God—Gabriel: how often have I told you that faithful servants are the worst of tyrants? By the way, has Shaw done the job?

Gabriel—She won't let him.

God—D———

> *The scene hastily closes in; and the rest of the Divine Utterance is lost.*

To JOHN REITH

[H/99; X/367]

4 Whitehall Court SW 1
2nd May 1932

[Reith had invited Shaw to participate in a series of broadcasts to be called "Rungs of the Ladder." Despite his reluctance, Shaw eventually acquiesced, delivering the ninth talk in the series, on 11th July. His subject was parents and children.]

Dear Sir John

I am afraid that my early experiences and my later conclusions based on them would be scandalously unedifying. If ever there was a man who succeeded in spite of his incompetence for helping himself that man is myself. I never put my best foot forward, because I never put my foot forward at all. I never overcame obstacles. I never went after success; it had to come to me, such as it is. I never advertised: advertisement, like success, has been shoved on me. I have not made a tenth of the money that was within my reach at the cost of a little energy and enterprise. If I tell the truth all the ambitious parents in the country will rise up and demand your instant dispossession for unmuzzling me.

And yet I think the country should be run by imbeciles like myself, and all the energetic, shoving, selfhelping chaps shot. That would be the gist of my advice in the present emergency.

Think of your wife and child before you again let me loose on the mike.

I am shocked to see by the date of your letter that I have kept you waiting nearly three weeks for an answer. My African trip left such an accumulation of correspondence on me that I simply collapsed before it and have been moodling about over odd literary jobs ever since without an attempt to cope with the situation. Which is again very characteristic of Anti-Samuelsmiles Shaw.

faithfully
G. Bernard Shaw

P.S Wells blew in yesterday afternoon and blasphemed against the series as a fearful falling from the ideals of Hilda Matheson.

To HENRI BARBUSSE

4 Whitehall Court S W 1

[S/1]   4th May 1932

[Henri Barbusse (1873–1935), French author and editor, had asked Shaw to be a member of the organising committee of a Congress against War, along with Albert Einstein, Theodore Dreiser, Maxim Gorki, Mme Sun Yat-sen, Romain Rolland, and Barbusse, among others. The Committee of Intellectual Co-operation (C.I.C.) was created in 1921 by the League of Nations Assembly to foster appropriate international activity within the broad realm of art, science, literature, and learning. Committee members were selected by the Council of the League with a view to achieving representation of various intellectual fields as well as of different nations. One of the fifteen or twenty eminent members was Gilbert Murray, appointed at its inception; he served as its chairman from 1928 onward. After World War II its purposes and area of concern were encompassed by the programme projected at the United Nations for UNESCO. (I am indebted to Edward Connery Lathem for this information.)]

My dear Henri Barbusse

You may use my name for what it is worth in convening your Congress provided the Committee for Intellectual Co-operation of the League of Nations be invited to organise the Congress, and that we take independent action only in the event of its refusal.

The first ascertained fact that the Congress will have to deal with is that though at every military crisis, whether it be Japan—Manchuria or Poland—Danzig (the latest) a solemn protest is made by Barbusse—

291

Rolland—Wells—Shaw—Einstein—Mann—Upton Sinclair etc etc, and that nobody takes the slightest notice of it. All that happens is that our names lose all their value by futile repetition. It is with great reluctance that I give my name on this occasion; and I shall certainly not make myself ridiculous by giving it again.

I do not know whether you have noticed that we treat the League of Nations just as the bellicose Powers do. Whenever a serious international difficulty arises the Powers act precisely as if the League of Nations did not exist. We do the same. The League of Nations has a Committee for Intellectual Co-operation. It is impotent and almost useless because nobody takes any notice of it. Just as the Foreign Offices and Cabinets of Europe intrigue against one another, compete in armaments, and make alliances as if Geneva were not on the map, so Barbusse-Rolland et Cie convene their Congresses as if the League's Committee for Intellectual Co-operation did not exist. And we are repeating this slight at the moment when Gilbert Murray, on behalf of the Committee, is appealing to us to make use of it to conventulate our views by writing open letters to oneanother which it can publish as complete correspondences on definite subjects.

What is the use of firing our guns in the air? All our opponents have to do if our opposition threatens their popularity is slander us in their newspapers and kill us, or incite patriotic mobs to kill us. What we need is an effective means of defending ourselves. Reading moral lectures at Geneva will leave us just as helpless as we are at present. How are we to kill the killers: that is the real problem for our Congress to discuss.

faithfully
G. Bernard Shaw

To N. F. BARFORD

4 Whitehall Court S W 1

[H/1]   5th May 1932

[N.F. Barford, who resided at Sun Lodge, Upper Norwood, in S.E. London, was an activist in the nudist movement in Britain. The *Punch* poem, by "Evoe" on 30th March 1932, was "Little Talks for the Little Ones. II—Nacktkultur."]

Dear Sir

It is not possible for me to add sun bathing to the subjects on which I am an agitator. I cannot be everywhere and do everything. Besides, I am not a sun bather. I used to warn open air enthusiasts not to forget that direct sunlight is a powerful poison, and that in the countries where it is strongest the inhabitants avoid it and shield themselves from it sedulously. I am glad to see that you are now teaching Nudists to keep out of the sun and rejoice in cloudy days.

All the photographs which have been used to stamp me as a sun bather were taken, mostly without my knowledge or consent, on the shores of the Mediterranean or the Lago Maggiore, when I was water bathing.

I am not a complete Nudist. I am strongly in favor of getting rid of every scrap of clothing that we can dispense with. I am quite sure that the commonplaces about people dying of excessive eating and drinking need to be reinforced by resolutely iterating that they die mostly of too much comfort, which means too much clothing: in fact we need a campaign against comfort. I object also to the excessive use of clothing to produce idolatry and stimulate sexuality beyond their natural bounds. And of course I know the mischief done by making us ashamed of our bodies.

But though on all these points you have my best wishes for your success as a propagandist it seems obvious to me that as long as women menstruate and men have susceptible erector muscles they will insist on the figleaf. And, as they are not likely to desire to grow natural furs to protect them against cold, they will resort to artificial protection. Thus neither the South Sea islanders nor the Esquimaux will adopt complete nudism as a national everyday custom, though they may experiment with it, as so many people are doing now, out of a quite legitimate psychological curiosity in reaction against the morbid horror at present inculcated.

faithfully
G. Bernard Shaw

PS The Punch verses will do you no harm. You have much more to fear from the conspiracy of silence than from goodnatured ridicule.

To AUGUSTIN HAMON

[H/1]

4 Whitehall Court SW1
6th May 1932

My dear Hamon

This is a response, un peu arrierée, to your letter of the 11th February.

I shall take your advice and not call my book on Russia, if I ever finish it, The Rationalization of Russia. Also, I shall make it as short as possible. I think of calling it "This Russian Business."

If I wanted a heavy title I should call it The Evolution of Revolution. Perhaps I shall make that an alternative title, thus: This Russian Business, or The E. of R. How does that strike you?

I want to shew how a revolution made by doctrinaires, who alone have the requisite fanaticism and selflessness, evolves under the pressure of actual experience into a practical government: how points of doctrine have to be thrown to the winds in all directions and all the revolutionists who will not accept this pressure have to be shot or exiled.

Also how completely Marx was mistaken in his opinion that Communism would come first in the countries in which industrial Capitalism is most highly developed. It is precisely because in Russia there was little industry, no powerful middle class, and an enormous peasantry cultivating the soil without machinery by the most primitive methods that Communism survived the destruction of the old order. The reason was that Syndicalism, which is utterly disastrous in industry, is quite practicable in agriculture. When Lenin told the peasants to take the land (and if necessary hang the landlords) they were immediately able to cultivate the land and produce the harvest. But when the Syndicalist factory workers on their own initiative seized the factories without knowing how to work them Lenin had to shoot them and recall the old managers under the N.E.P. to keep them going as private concerns until the Communist organization had grown big enough to take them over.

I also want to deal with the Soviet government structure at its bottom and top: the bottom being the point of contact with the workers at the direct elections (the only shred of our pseudo-democracy left) and the top being the two Cabinets: the Cabinet of administrators and the Cabinet of thinkers or spiritual directors which is so ridiculously missing in the western capitalist constitutions.

Inevitably, it seems to me, this Cabinet of thinkers must come into conflict with the Third International exactly as the State came into conflict with the Church in France; indeed the strain has begun already, as I found by the assent to the remarks I made on this subject in Moscow. Trotsky, though in exile as an unteachable doctrinaire, denounces the Third International furiously.

Our own path to Communism is not so easy as Lenin—Stalin—Trotsky found it. The war had very obligingly blown up the old regime for them. "The reason we are all Mensheviks in England" I said to Stalin, "is simply that the police and soldiers are punctually paid." Unless Capitalism crashes violently enough to throw the police and soldiers starving on the streets, a revolutionary situation like that of 1917 in Russia cannot occur. The danger is that Capitalism, instead of crashing, may peter out without ever producing a revolutionary situation. We may get no further than a succession of Kerenskys or Macdonalds trying to make omelettes without breaking eggs.

Here, by the way, the police are breaking the heads of the unemployed every day, though the papers say as little as possible about it.

Decidedly, kid glove Socialism is under the weather now; and Hamon's stocks are up. . . .

As to waiting for the result of the Russian experiment, there is no respite for Capitalism in that, because the results are already quite good enough to satisfy the western proletariats; and the attempts of the press to conceal them are breaking down before the deluge of books about Russia by the tourists who are now visiting Russia in droves under the Intourist plan.

faithfully
G. Bernard Shaw

PS . . . I enclose a copy of my reply to Barbusse. People now take no more notice of a Barbusse—Romain Rolland manifesto than of the clock of Notre Dame striking twelve.

To JOHN FARLEIGH

Ayot St Lawrence. Welwyn
[A/9; X/368]   8th May 1932

[William Maxwell, having read the *Black Girl*, suggested to Shaw that the tale could make an attractive and saleable little book with the addition of some striking illustrations. For this purpose he strongly recommended a young wood engraver, John Farleigh (1900–65), whose work had attracted

Maxwell's attention. Shaw at once wrote to Farleigh, enclosing a cheque for five guineas. "It was not necessary to read the proofs carefully," Farleigh wrote in his *Graven Image* (1940), "to realize that there was a great chance for illustration: the suggestions in Shaw's letter were evidence enough. With unerring skill he had painted word pictures that would stimulate the excitement of any illustrator, and the same skill had, in this one introductory letter, made the whole job so clear that I was able to begin work without any further discussion." Raphael's painting was the Vision of Ezekiel (1518), which Shaw had viewed in Florence's Pitti Palace. Blake's little boy may have been the child reaching for a bird rather than a butterfly in the plate "Its favours here are trials" in Edward Young's *The Complaint and the Consolation: or Night Thoughts* (1797). Jean-Antoine Houdon (1741–1828), French sculptor, created more than one hundred busts of Voltaire, in various materials. Shaw had viewed on a few occasions the best known of these, in marble, done for the Comédie Française.]

Dear Sir

As I am old and out of date I have not the privilege of knowing you or your work. But Mr William Maxwell of Clark's of Edinburgh tells me that you can design, draw, and engrave pictures as parts of a printed book, which, you will understand, is something more than making a picture and sticking it into a book as an "illustration." The idea is that you and I and Maxwell should co-operate in turning out a goodlooking little volume consisting of the story contained in the enclosed proof sheets (please hold them as very private and confidential) and, say, a dozen pictures.

Are you sufficiently young and unknown to read the story and make one trial drawing for me for five guineas? That is, if the job interests you.

faithfully
G. Bernard Shaw

—Suggested Subjects—

1) The black Diana (*not* a Hottentot) going for Jehovah (as in Raphael's Ezekiel picture) with her knobkerry.
2) The same going for the god in Blake's Job.
3) The same accosting Koheleth, a very beautiful juvenile Plato.
4) The lion—"maneless" like Landseer's lions in Trafalgar Square. There used to be a delightful one named Dick in the zoo who would let you handle him as in the story.
5) St Peter carrying a full sized Gothic cathedral on his shoulders, with the black girl rushing to help him (rather like Blake's little boy rushing after a butterfly).

6) Sundry faces from the Caravan of the Curious, like the Vanity Fair jury in the Pilgrim's Progress—if you have a weakness for the ugly-grotesque.

7) The black girl and Christ at the well: proffering the cup. Christ poor and humble, but unaffected and kindly.

8) Christ posing on the cross for sixpence an hour with the image maker (say yourself) at work, and Mahomet, very handsome, looking on.

9) The black girl and Mahomet scrutinizing a miniature Venus of Milo (no bigger than a big hour glass).

10) Voltaire (after Houdon) digging with the girl looking at him over the garden gate.

11) The Irishman's dash for liberty: V. and the girl pursuing.

12) Family piece. The girl with all her children at home, with the Irishman digging, visible through the open door.

To IGNACE LILIEN

[H.c/4]

[4 Whitehall Court S W 1]
19th May 1932

[Ignace Lilien (1897–1964), Dutch pianist and composer, born in Berlin, performed mostly his own compositions in tours of the Continent and South America. To obtain Shaw's permission to compose an operatic version of *Great Catherine* he travelled to London to perform samples of his work for the playwright. The two-act comic opera, set to Siegfried Trebitsch's German translation of the play, was first performed at the Staatstheater, Wiesbaden, on 8th May 1932; Shaw declined an invitation to attend. He did, however, try his hand at the score, telling Lilien (undated draft of telegram, Bucknell) "it is teaching me to play in all twelve keys at once." Zerlina is a character in Mozart's *Don Giovanni*; the other characters appear in Mozart's *Die Zauber-flöte*, Astrifiammante being the name given to the Queen of Night in the Italian version.]

My dear Lilien

. . . I have had no news of the production at Wiesbaden. I am curious as to the effect of the music. I have the pianoforte score; but as I find it almost impossible to play in twelve different keys simultaneously, and even if I could the effect would not be like the orchestral effect, I have not yet succeeded in learning the opera. The vocal parts are not, I think, really difficult melodically; but in a work in which acting is very important, you should not demand exceptional range from your

297

singers. If you study Figaro's Hochzeit or Don Giovanni you will see that as these works require skilled comedy acting as well as singing, none of them contain a note that is too high or too low for normal voices. Don Juan, a baritone, has not even an F natural to sing; but you seem to think F sharp quite an ordinary easy note for a basso. Zerlina and Papageno are comedy parts: Astriffiamenta and Sarastro can both be played by singers who cannot act; consequently Mozart takes care that any mezzosoprano can sing Zerlina and any baritone Papageno; but the Queen of Night has to sing altissimo and the High Priest profundo.

What is your orchestra? Is it very expensive? I know what Mozart's orchestra was, and Beethoven's, and Wagner's, and even Strauss's; but when it comes to this Schönberg–Stravinsky stuff one is not sure even of the string quartette: it is just as likely to be a contrafagetto, a harp, two z[y]lophones and a celesta. What I really want to know is whether the score is one that can be played by the local theatre band in a second rate provincial town or needs a first rate metropolitan opera house or symphony orchestra.

cordially
G. Bernard Shaw

To N. F. BARFORD

4 Whitehall Court SW 1
[H/1]   2nd June 1932

Dear Sir

How can I possibly associate myself further with the movement, short of walking down Piccadilly stark naked?

A debate on the points I reserved would be quite impossible. I know better than most English people the dislike of the fig-leaf, because I was brought up in Ireland to bathe in my buff; and I felt horribly indecent when I had to wear a bathing slip in England, though I overcame that because it was evident that in no other way could mixed bathing be introduced.

But in my last letter I was not [commenting] on the general question. I gave two specific instances, one female and the other male, of occasions when nudity would be inconvenient. Has anybody ever tried to pose you with them before?

faithfully
G. Bernard Shaw

To ALMROTH WRIGHT

4 Whitehall Court SW1
[A/3]   24th June 1932

[Receiving intimations that *Too True to be Good* contained a serious medical gaffe in its first act, Shaw appealed to his friend Sir Almroth Wright, famed bacteriologist, sending a rough proof of the play with a letter inscribed across its front cover. When Wright confirmed his suspicions Shaw informed his printer William Maxwell chaffingly, "It turns out now that there is no microbe for measles; and I have to correct all those prompt copies accordingly. What good is your proof reader if he cannot spot these little things?" (A/18: 18th July 1932).]

My dear Almroth Wright

I have made a horrible mess of the first act of this by introducing a microbe in a case of measles, which is, so far, amicrobic.

Will you study the case for me, and tell me what the young lady ought to be suffering from? An American lady suggests chickenpox; but that hasn't a microbe either.

Is there any imaginary fever produced by idleness, unhealthy habits, and too much money? Park Lane fever or something like that.

your perplexed
G. Bernard Shaw

To JOHN FARLEIGH

Ayot St Lawrence. Welwyn
[A/9; X/368]   6th July 1932

[Farleigh submitted as his trial engraving the design of the artist modelling at his booth. "Good," replied Shaw on 24th May, "I think you can make a real job of it" (A/9). Vetoing several modern artists suggested to him by his German publisher and translator, he informed Trebitsch on 15th May "I want something as simple and serious as Holbein's Bible pictures but with modern beauty. I am trying a young and unknown Englishman ... who will design the picture as part of the book and not as an 'illustration' stuck into it. If he succeeds his work can be reproduced everywhere" (X/341). The work now commenced in earnest and by early July Farleigh had completed two alternative cover designs. One, a portrait of the black girl, served as the final cover; the other, a decorated paper, became (as Shaw suggested) the endpaper design.]

Dear Mr Farleigh

Yes: the portrait cover of course. What about the other for end papers?

Just consider whether she is not—for so critical a godseeker—a little too brutish. It is a quality that justifies itself completely on the purely artistic side; and I hesitate to suggest anything in the nature of a literary and intellectual irrelevance; but still, recollecting that Michaelangelo placed himself at the head of all artists by making all his subjects geniuses, I am not sure that the slightest gathering up of the corners of her mouth and squaring of the outside ridges of her brows would really damage her. I am a critic myself, and have that outside lift of my brows emphasized by what are almost secondary moustaches; and without them I should look as brainless as the Sistine Madonna. I enclose a couple of picture postcards to shew what I mean.

As to headlines have it your own way; only do nothing for the sake of consistency alone: consistency is the enemy of enterprise just as symmetry is the enemy of art. I should have a different rule for every page if it were worth bothering to that extent. Maxwell could not run his establishment without rules; but we can do as we like, short of disgracing him with his guild.

faithfully

G. Bernard Shaw

To STANLEY CLENCH

Ayot St Lawrence. Welwyn

[C/1]   6th July 1932

[Alarmed by the effects of the international economic crisis (he had seen his English sterling lose one-third of its value when exchanged for South African currency in January and his book sales in America plummet almost to zero in recent months) and troubled by the enormous expense he had incurred for the new Standard Edition settings at an inopportune moment, Shaw sought some protection for the future. Stanley Clench (1893–1961), to whom he turned for information, was Shaw's accountant and financial adviser. Many of the insurance companies offering annuities were Canadian.]

The Conversion has converted me. Make me a £10,000 proposal for an annuity payable to my wife during her lifetime and afterwards to me if I survive her. As it will be payable by your London office I presume no question of double income tax—Canadian & English—can arise.

G. Bernard Shaw

Malvern Hotel. Malvern
[H.t/46]   8th August 1932

[*Too True to be Good* was first performed at the Malvern Festival on 6th
August, following its world première production by the Theatre Guild in
Boston the preceding February. Ayliff appeared as The Elder, father of the
burglar Aubrey, played by (Sir) Cedric Hardwicke (1893–1964), a frequent
performer at the Birmingham Rep. A versatile performer, Hardwicke had
appeared in recent years in *Back to Methuselah*, *Heartbreak House*, and
Cæsar and Cleopatra, as well as in *Show Boat* and *The Barretts of Wimpole
Street*. "You will be glad to hear the play was a great success last night,"
Charlotte Shaw informed Dolly Walker on the 7th; "it was all rather curious,
& new & strange. People said 'a kind of sequel to Heartbreak House!' But it
is much more important (to my mind) than H.H. Deeper & more searching—
& incidentally, much more amusing!" (A/3).]

My dear Ayliff
    Your two interpellations, "What!" and "Your mother!!!" came so
exactly right that I have put them into the book, with a consequent
improvement on page 66. Instead of "A saint! A scoundrel, I say."
say "A saint! Say rather the ruined son of an incorrigibly superstitious
mother."
    It was stupid of me, and abominably inconsiderate to the actor, to
leave the final speech incomplete at the risk of a delay with the curtain
or a hitch in its working spoiling everything. I have now sent Cedric a
peroration which will see him through even if the curtain refuses to
descend at all. I enclose a typed copy which will fit into the last page of
the book and can be pasted in.
    I have asked Cedric, when the curtain comes down slowly on
"preach and preach" to continue declaiming at full pitch right to the
end of the peroration, but after the first few words with the curtain
down to turn his back to it and walk up stage and away through the
centre path so that the booming voice will die away quite naturally.
It is essential that it should be heard for some time after the curtain is
down, and that the words, though indistinct, should sound as if they
meant something. They dont, by the way; but they will serve.

ever
G.B.S.

To LADY RHONDDA

[A/3]

Malvern Hotel. Malvern
12th August 1932

[After an almost universal onslaught of critical vituperation, even from the usually friendly St John Ervine, Lady Rhondda's praise of *Too True to be Good* in the current issue of *Time and Tide* was especially pleasing to Shaw.]

Dearest Rhondda (Rhondda is such a lovely name, and there are such a lot of Margarets, that, if you dont mind, I shall make it your pet name)

What a magnificent article! You CAN write. Even the best of the men's articles are intolerable and unreadable piffle after it.

I wonder can I make that passage about the poor any clearer? Are you sure you havn't a family habit of classing "poor devils with only ten thousand a year" as the poor? The submerged nine tenths dont all consider themselves poor. Most of them hate the poor. The real poor hate the poor. *I* hate the poor. That I prefer them, on the whole, to the rich, doesn't affect the case in the least.

I am quite sure that the women who are going to change things are those who, like yourself, will see Capitalism damned before they will spend their lives plastering its sores and trying to clean up its messes in the name of "womanly charity." The Samaritans are no use; the Levites are no use; the only useful ones are the women who refuse to marry the fellow who let himself be robbed and won't let themselves be robbed if they can help it. And who also see the final uselessness of being bought off by becoming robbers (or whores) themselves, and who jib against the Samaritan illustration because it implies testing them by how they behave towards a man. Why did Jesus not tell the story of a certain *woman* that fell among thieves? How frightfully it dates him now!

However, you see now why Mops would have no truck with the poor, and why her great discovery was the misery of the rich. One thing at a time, you see.

GBS

To CEDRIC HARDWICKE

Malvern Hotel. Malvern
[H/1]   14th August 1932

[Mops is the patient in *Too True to be Good*, "kidnapped" by Aubrey. She was played by a superb comedienne, Leonora Corbett.]

My dear Cedric

You have created a frightful ecclesiastical scandal by mixing up the Creed with the Lord's Prayer. I had to assure the Dean [William Moore Ede] this morning when he preached on Too True at Worcester Cathedral, and quoted the peroration, that I was innocent of the outrage.

You can have the Communion of Saints, the Forgiveness of Sins, and the Life Everlasting; or you can have the Kingdom and the Power and the Glory; but you really mustnt confuse the two.

You started a military scandal also by calling the Air Force the Flying Force. There is such a thing as a Flying Fox but not a Flying Force.

In Act II you must help Mops out when she begins "This silly bitch—" by cutting in promptly with "Oh no no no no no no no no no no: damn it, Mops, be a lady." If you dont, I shall have the trouble of writing her a long speech to keep her going until you come to the rescue.

When Mops says (foot of page 68, Act III) "And then I was devoured by parasites" shiver with disgust at the word parasites.

This is all I spotted last night—at least all that you can remedy.

ever
G. Bernard Shaw

To JOHN FARLEIGH

Malvern Hotel. Malvern
[H/9; X/368]   25th August 1932

[The figure of Ecclesiastes, as Shaw here surmised, was derived by Farleigh from a frieze: the artist had failed to turn the head so that it would face the black girl. Shaw, Farleigh admitted in *Graven Image*, scored not only on this point, but "on a good many other occasions; in fact I discovered I was learning the business of illustration from the best master possible—a producer of plays, as well as author of them." The Hogarth work to which Shaw alludes is "Satire on False Perspective," a frontispiece to Joshua Kirby's book *Dr. Brook Taylor's Method of Perspective Made Easy* (1754), engraved by Luke

Sullivan. The final illustration to which Shaw refers in the letter is that of the God of Job (after Blake), carrying a book under his arm.]

Dear John Farleigh

Many apologies for my delay. I have been cobbling up my play, and could not get my mind on to the drawings in a properly leisurely way.

The lion and the Job are perfect. The other three need slight modifications. Ecclesiastes looks dead, like a figure in a frieze, because he is not looking at the girl. He also looks flat, like a profile cut in cardboard. All you have to do is to turn his head away from the spectator and towards the girl and all this will come right.

In the picture of the cathedrals you have produced an effect like Hogarth's Marvels of Perspective by not leaving a clear space between the girl's right hand and the tiny church in the distance. The result is that the girl seems to be carrying the church. Just shift the church up so that both it and the man's leg are clear of the girl's hand and arm and all will be well. You see, you cannot get aerial perspective in black and white, and are therefore dependent on scale and complete detachment.

Most important is the Christ. You have curiously reversed the relation between him and the girl. In the story he presents the cup to her; and he would obviously—since it is both a funny conjuring trick and an act of kindness—smile as he did it. But in the picture it is the girl who is the humorous conjurer with the kindly smile, and he who is accepting the cup; so you must contrive to turn the situation inside out.

The smiling Christ is a great chance for you. Most artists are so utterly floored by the problem of what Christ's face ought to express that they just make it express nothing at all and cover up the failure with a sort of abstract holiness that makes him acutely dislikeable. The first painter who is sensible and human enough to paint a Suffer Little Children with Christ smiling at a child standing on his knee will completely snuff out Holman Hunt's Light of The World. If you can paint in oils, here is your chance.

If you are not satisfied with the cover, try the effect of making the breasts a little more virginal as they are so prettily in the subject pictures. That is all I can suggest.

As to the book, clearly it should have the title JOB on it.

I shall be here for at least another fortnight.

ever
G. Bernard Shaw

To JOHN FARLEIGH

[H.t/9; X/368]

Malvern Hotel. Malvern
29th August 1932

[Shaw had enclosed for Farleigh a drawing of his concept of the flight of the Irishman from the black girl, with Voltaire looking on. "Shaw's drawings," wrote Farleigh in *Graven Image*, were "mature and highly skilful in thought and intention; their value to me lay in their intellectual clarity." Farleigh's method was to make "highly-finished drawings that closely resembled the final engraving ... I always photograph a drawing on to the block if it is elaborate in detail or is highly finished. I am thus left free to interpret as I go and, as trial proofs are taken, the ink can be removed easily from the surface of the block without impairing the photographic image beneath."

The Gregynog Press (founded in 1922) was at Newtown, Montgomeryshire. It specialised in works relating to Wales. Shaw became friendly with its chairman Thomas Jones (1870–1955), scholar and celebrated figure in government and civil service circles, who was a close friend of the Astors. Agnes Miller Parker (b. 1895), Scottish woodcut artist, who would eventually do notable work as illustrator of Hardy, Housman, and Shakespeare, was wood-engraver to the Gregynog Press 1930–33. Shaw's principal "county visit" was to Charlotte's niece Cecily Colthurst.]

Dear John Farleigh

You will see by the enclosed masterpiece what is wrong with the drawing of the flight of the laborer. My face is like the photographs they stick on to a readymade body to amuse bank holiday trippers. Also it is drawn from one of the old photographs taken on ordinary plates without a color filter, which represented me as a dark man instead of a very blond blond. The expression has not a trace of frantic terror; and the hat is an absurdity. The man is a very sophisticated metropolitan critic, and not a raw youthful laborer. Compare your own splendid portrait, full of dramatic energy and purpose, in the modeller's picture. However, you will see it all in my version; for though I am an execrable draughtsman I am a skilled and observant stage manager, always on the look-out for the right expression and movement. Keep me young, callow, fair, and scared out of my wits. Any photograph of a hurdle race will supply a study: I think he must have one leg over the gate: nothing else will give the necessary impression of headlong flight.

In the modelling picture, which is a triumphant improvement, keep Mahomet as handsome as you can: he was a princely genius. He is all right in the picture which shews him as discussing the Venus with the

305

black girl. By the way, he abhorred images, and took the second commandment *au pied de la lettre*.

In the garden gate picture, if Voltaire had a small implement—a trowel or snipper or something—in his left hand, slightly raised, it would give him a perfect air of being taken by surprise in the act of gardening by the black girl's call. As it is, he looks as if they were old friends and had been talking there for years. Stage management again!

In the caravan picture the expression of the girl is lovely; and the Vanity Fair jurymen are all that could be desired; but the man with the moustache is very like some public man—I cant remember whom —but we may chance his taking proceedings.

I shall consider the wording of the colophon, and its form. I am inclined to describe the story as *invented* by me. Why shouldnt the pictures be drawn and cut in boxwood by you? On Friday I visited the Gregynog Press, and saw some lovely wood cutting by Agnes Miller Parker. She blackens the block to begin with, and traces the design on the black with a red carbon paper. As the cuts leave the color of the wood she has the whole thing in black and white without having to make trial impressions. Is this your way?

I am off to pay some county visits and shall not be back here in Malvern until Wednesday.

ever

G.B.S.

To CLARA LEISER

Malvern Hotel. Malvern

5th September 1932

[X/370]

[Miss Leiser was writing a book, published in 1933, on the celebrated Polish baritone turned tenor, Jean de Reszke (1850–1925), considered to be the finest tenor since Mario. (See letter of 27th July 1897 to Ellen Terry.) His brother Édouard (1853–1917), a basso, was long a favourite at Covent Garden. Ernest Van Dyck (1861–1923) was a noted Heldentenor, much admired by Shaw, who predicted his success. Max Alvary (1856–98), Wagnerian tenor, was forced by illness into premature retirement in 1897. The great Italian tenor Giovanni Matteo Mario died in 1883. Shaw's statement about Jean de Reszke's high notes, claimed Miss Leiser in her book, "is refuted by other observers."]

Dear Miss Leiser

. . . You will find in my three volumes of Music in London, covering three years of the heyday of the de Reszkes, that I never ceased to urge them to give up their eternal repetitions of Lohengrin and Gounod's Faust, and bring themselves up to date by tackling the mature Wagner. At last, when some officious hanger-on tried to get up a testimonial to Jean, I contemptuously refused to sign it or to take Jean seriously until he had qualified himself as a modern first rank tenor by playing Siegfried and Tristan.

My taunts had their effect; for he presently appeared as Siegfried and sang the part as it had never been sung before, in beautifully uttered German, with Edouard as Wotan. It was such an astonishing new departure for a man who was then finishing his career that I then believed what I had been told about his having been long familiar with the Ring and Tristan in private.

When I was a youth in Dublin I heard Jean play Don Giovanni and Valentine in Faust. He was a godlike juvenile, and was easily the best I had heard in both parts. And I have not since heard him surpassed. Some years later, in London, I went to a performance of Le Nozze di Figaro expressly to hear this wonderful baritone as Almaviva. To my astonishment he had grown fat and genially stupid, and his fine high baritone had become a basso cantante, rather weak in the bass.

Of course this was Edouard, of whom I had never heard; and Jean had become a tenore robusto.

When Poles are not cretins they are sometimes very beautiful creatures; and Jean was decidedly one of the beautiful ones. And he never had a rival who was anything but a foil to him except Vandyk, who soon shouted a fine voice away, and Alvary, a remarkable Siegfried, who, though a fine actor and diseur, had no voice at all in the De Reszke sense, and seemed to be making the best of a cracked clarinet. The rest were Carusos without Caruso's voice, and seemed to have developed their larynxes by calling newspapers and announcing the names of railway stations. Jean's difficulty was his range. He could sing a ringing B natural when he was in good form; but he could only touch C, and was afraid of it. He could barely get through the duel scene in Les Huguenots, transposed half a tone down. Both Lohengrin and Die Meistersinger suited him exactly; but he was not a high note stunter, and, as far as I know, never touched the Verdi operas of the Trovatore phase.

His nearest predecessor must have been Mario; but when, as a smallish boy, I heard Mario at a concert, he was a toneless baritone with a falsetto C. He had smoked all the quality out of his voice.

I wrote quite a good deal about the De Reszkes, not, I hope, inappreciatively; and I shall read your book with lively interest when it appears.

faithfully

G. Bernard Shaw

To W. B. YEATS

Ayot St Lawrence. Welwyn

[A/1; X/371]   20th September 1932

[Yeats had approached Shaw earlier in the year with a proposal that they join forces to found an Irish Academy of Letters, both to reward literary achievement and to organise writers for the purpose of battling against literary censorship in Ireland by the Catholic Church. Principally for the latter purpose Shaw agreed to the proposal, with the understanding that he would not be expected to take an active part in the academy's management. The men they selected to join them as founding members were George W. Russell (AE), Lennox Robinson, Seumas O'Sullivan, Oliver St John Gogarty, Frank O'Connor, F. R. Higgins, and Michael O'Donovan. At the first meeting of the academy, on 14th September, the members present (which included everyone but GBS) unanimously elected Shaw president, Yeats vice-president, and Russell secretary/treasurer. Despite his protestations Shaw was induced to accept the office, serving until succeeded by Yeats in 1935. On the death of Yeats in 1939 he was re-elected to the office for a further year.

Seventeen additional founding "Academicians" were nominated at the meeting, including Sean O'Faolain, Liam O'Flaherty, Edith Œ Somerville, Austin Clarke, St John Ervine (at Shaw's insistence), James Stephens, James Joyce, and Sean O'Casey. The latter two were among the six nominees who declined the invitation (drafted by Shaw). Eleven "Associates" were also nominated, acceptances being received from, among others, Eugene O'Neill, T. E. Lawrence, Helen Waddell, and J. M. Hone. Sir John Pentland Mahaffy (1839–1919), first professor of ancient history and, later, provost of Trinity College, Dublin, was, according to the *DNB*, "a remarkably versatile writer of great shrewdness and sagacity," his extensive output of scholarly works dealing mostly with the history and literature of the classic Greeks. He was one of Dublin's most colourful and popular personages.]

My dear Yeats

I am against myself as President. The President should be also Resident, and should be a man with a presence who loves gassing at public banquets, state unveilings, and foundation stone layings. The

308

chairman of the Council, who should be a man of business, and who under the rules is often changed, cannot always fill the bill. I am really a London man; and I loathe public functions: there is everything against me. Assuming that you also are no Mahaffy, what about Russell? He is on the spot and has the requisite Jehovesque beard and aspect.

ever
G.B.S.

PS Anyhow if I am to be President there *must* be a resident Vice President, which is d——d nonsense.

To JOHN REITH

4 Whitehall Court S W 1
[H/99; X/367]   30th September 1932

[For years Elgar had been contemplating a third symphony, fragments of which he and his violinist friend and colleague William H. Reed (see Shaw's letter of 17th August 1934) performed for the Shaws when they came to tea at Marl Bank, Elgar's home in Worcester.]

Dear Sir John

May I make a suggestion?

In 1823 the London Philharmonic Society passed a resolution to offer Beethoven £50 for the MS of a symphony. In 1827 the Society sent him £100. He was dying; and he said "God bless the Philharmonic Society and the whole English nation."

This is by far the most creditable incident in English history.

Now the only composer today who is comparable to Beethoven is Elgar. Everybody seems to assume either that Elgar can live on air, or that he is so rich and successful that he can afford to write symphonies and conduct festivals for nothing. As a matter of fact his financial position is a very difficult one, making it impossible for him to give time enough to such heavy jobs as the completion of a symphony; and consequently here we have the case of a British composer who has written two great symphonies which place England at the head of the world in this top department of instrumental music, unable to complete and score a third. I know that he has the material for the first movement ready, because he has played it to me on his piano.

Well, why should not the B.B.C. with its millions do for Elgar what the old Philharmonic did for Beethoven? You could bring the third symphony into existence, and obtain the performing rights for the B.B.C. for, say, ten years, for a few thousand pounds. The Kudos would be stupendous and the value for the money ample: in fact if Elgar were a good man of business instead of a great artist who throws his commercial opportunities about *en grand seigneur*, he would open his mouth much wider.

He does not know that I am meddling in his affairs and yours in this manner; and I have not the faintest notion of what sum he would jump at; but I do know that he has still a lot of stuff in him that could be released if he could sit down to it without risking his livelihood.

Think it over when you have a spare moment.

faithfully
G. Bernard Shaw

[Acting on Shaw's suggestion the B.B.C. offered a commission to Elgar, which he accepted in December, consisting of a payment of £1000 at the start plus £250 quarterly for a year or until completion, whichever came sooner. Elgar died on 23rd February 1934, the symphony uncompleted.]

To RUTLAND BOUGHTON

[C/2]

Ayot St Lawrence. Welwyn
5th October 1932

I'm afraid I can't be in London on the 11th. I *must* stay down here and work. Besides, what's the use of talking? You can compose real music: why waste your time making chin music?

Of course Wagner, after Die Walküre and the first two acts of Siegfried, went back to roaring blazing grand opera. Götterdämmerung should have an alternative title

or

The Relapse of the Teetotaller

GBS

310

To RUTLAND BOUGHTON

[C/2]

Ayot St Lawrence. Welwyn
11th October 1932

[Boughton was founder of the Glastonbury Music Festival in 1914.]

What you have to rub in is that opera is impossible in any complete artistic sense under commercial conditions. Your Glastonbury performances were enormously better than anything ever seen at Covent Garden. There is more promise of a really enjoyable Lohengrin in our provincial pageants than in all the schemes of [Sir Thomas] Beecham. When we have Communism at plenty of leisure, with money enough to provide our own houses and costumes with a little over for the treasury we shall just begin to make opera live.

Dont contradict what you agree with because it is not stated in your own words. Anybody who cannot see and hear that the first act of Die Walküre and the second of Tristan is music drama and the second act of Götterdämmerung overloaded Rienzibub doesnt know chalk from cheese! *I DO.*

GBS

To R. & R. CLARK

[C/3]

Ayot St Lawrence. Welwyn
25th October 1932

[The letter to Shaw presumably had been written by William Maxwell.]

I cannot leave so long and elaborate a letter unanswered; but I assure you that Liza *did* marry Freddy, and that Higgins never married anybody.

It does not follow in the least that Liza and Higgins were sexually insensible to one another, or that their sensibility took the form of repugnance, or that her combination of hatred and rebellion with doglike fidelity was exactly what it would have been had her instructor been a woman; but the fact stands that their marriage would have been a revolting tragedy; and that the marriage with Freddy is the natural and happy ending to the story.

G. Bernard Shaw

To ST JOHN ERVINE

4 Whitehall Court SW1
29th October 1932
[H/5]

[Ervine had reviewed *Too True to be Good* in *The Observer* on 9th October, posing the question: "What right has an old man to throw up his hands and surrender every belief he holds? That game soldier, Shaw, who has hitherto valiantly put up his fists and been the foremost in every fight, is now whimpering in corners and assuring his followers . . . that they had better all lie down and die. . . . Better indeed that [he] should have died a dozen years ago than live to write this whining play . . . [in which he] recants all his beliefs." Charlotte, on the same day, wrote passionately to Ervine, insisting the play was one of revolt: "Everything . . . points to the fact that there *is* a 'way of life,' & that all these people, some consciously, some unconsciously, are struggling to find it." With much prescience she anticipated that "in the future . . . it will be understood that this is among G.B.S.'s *big* plays. The voice of one crying in the wilderness!" (Janet Dunbar, *Mrs. G.B.S.*, 1963).

Too True to be Good had a run of 47 performances in the West End before it was withdrawn on 22nd October. It had earlier played for a fortnight at the Birmingham Rep following its eight performances at Malvern, and it toured the provinces after London, with Greer Garson replacing Leonora Corbett as the patient, until 10th December. Nora was Ervine's wife Leonora. T.E. Lawrence served as Shaw's model for the character of Private Meek.

Shaw's quotation of Lassalle was an aphoristic improvement. In a courtroom speech in his own defence Lassalle castigated a foe, the writer Max Wirth, by telling the court that if Wirth "wished to call me an unoriginal compiler, as I have called him, he would merely arouse enormous laughter from every scholar who knows me. But when I use the term to him, every expert knows how enormously true it is, and therefore my words come upon his head with crushing force" (Georg Brandes, *Ferdinand Lassalle* (London, 1911; first published in Danish, 1877).]

My dear St John

Please note that the modern psychologists, when classifying mental defectives and criminals, put in the lowest sections those who cannot distinguish between similars and dissimilars. When you place me in this class, the laugh is on you, not on me. Never forget Lassalle's retort to the professor who criticized him, "If I call you a fool all Europe will believe me. If you call me a fool all Europe will laugh at you." If your characteristic rashness did not betray you into rushing into every debate without thinking, you would start with the assumption that I can distinguish between similars and dissimilars and have therefore observed that Einstein's mind is more developed than that of the village idiot, and that he is better at mathematics than I, who spent years of

312

my childhood vainly trying to solve the problem "a herring and a half for three ha'pence: how many is that for elevenpence?"

That has nothing to do with the question whether there exists anything in nature corresponding to the popular conception of a Great Man. In Ayot St Lawrence, they believe that the London police stop the traffic for me individually when I want to cross the street. This convinces them that I am a Great Man, and leads them to invest me with all sorts of fabulous attributes. All my correspondents who have grievances believe that I have complete and absolute control of the leader page in The Times, and that I am their potential Saviour and Redeemer. When Jesus turned the water into wine at the wedding feast they immediately concluded that he was a Great Man and could raise the dead. In my neighborhood they voted for the National Government at the last election because they believed Macdonald and Snowden to be Great Men: that is, persons who could do no wrong, like the King.

Conversely, you have the Monsters: Lenin, Mussolini, Karl Marx, the Kaiser, and all the anti-Christs of history.

Now, is this a valid currency of human values? I say that it is a spurious and enormously mischievous one. I say that there is nothing in the human species that corresponds to it. So do you. But the moment I say it bluntly you throw a fit and shriek out that I am denying the difference between the captain of a canal barge and the horse. Are you not ashamed? This comes of wasting years of your life on Parnell and General Booth, about whom all that need now be said can be fitted into ten pages.

And now, to prevent your filling the next Observer with a scream that I have slandered Booth as a murderer, an atheist, a libertine and a liar, let me hasten to assure you that I like the little I heard from him (the story of Major Barbara will be the only interesting chapter in your book) and that I really believe what his Commissars said when I put it to them, that he would have fought just as hard for the poor and their salvation if there had been no other world for him than this.

I suggested to Nora that you could get two or three useful Observer articles out of Too True instead of yapping about pessimism and despair, for which you owe me so many million apologies.

As you are not a bacteriologist you had better let the microbe alone; but as so many duffers have raised the cry of The Doctor's Dilemma over again, you might expatiate on the fact that the dilemma in Too True is that of the unfortunate doctor forced by his patients' folly and ignorance and his own dependence on them, to humbug them. There is not a hint of this in the old play, nor of the possibility which has been all along overlooked by the germ theory pathologists: namely, that the bacillus has been infected and transformed by the disease which has attacked the patient, instead of being itself the disease.

Then what about worrying mothers? About one per cent of my correspondents say that they no longer exist. The rest complain that they are all over the place, and bless me for exposing them.

Again, you have been a soldier, and know what colonels are, and have no doubt been puzzled by the fact that colonels are often able men, like my colonel in Too True, also admirals, and that it is this ability that has brought them to the top; and yet the colonels are all impossibles and the admirals all more or less mad. In Too True I take advantage of the amazing case of Lawrence to suggest the reason. Nobody has ever touched this before: the critics have seen nothing in it but my being " down on the army " or " down on the doctors " as usual.

Thus I make you a present of enough to keep you going in The Observer for a month; and all you do is to complain that I have disturbed you and that you dont like being disturbed. You are getting a Devon brain: perhaps that is why you look so healthy. But you must trot out your London brain for me. Nora resists the climate better. I—but I have no time for more.

In haste
GBS

PS By the way, you might put in a plea for a National Theatre & for municipal theatres à propos of Too True. It was drawing over £1000 a week (a pre-war gold mine) when it came off. In America it came off after 12 weeks roaring business because the receipts dropped to $6500. In 1894 the takings for Arms & The Man averaged £135 *a week*. At the Court (Vedrenne & Barker) £600 a week was prosperity. Now, anything under £1600 a week comes off as a failure. Rub in the utter ridiculousness of such a situation.

To BLANCHE PATCH

[E.u/2] [4 Whitehall Court SW 1]
[Undated: *c.* 4th November 1932]

[A man named Wallace H. Salter had written to Shaw on 2nd November, enclosing for his opinion a synopsis of a book in opposition to Einstein's doctrines, which had been rejected by several publishers. The reply, drafted for Blanche Patch to deal with, was written on Salter's letter. The Australian-born Col. Arthur Lynch (1861–1934), physician, author, Nationalist M.P. from West Clare 1909–18, and commander of British troops in Ireland in 1918, was also in the anti-Einstein camp (see letter of 6th December to Lynch). American physicists Albert A. Michelson (1852–1931) and Edward Morley (1838–1923) demonstrated in 1887 that there is no absolute motion of the earth relative to an ether. From this ether-drift experiment the theory of relativity was developed.

Dr Thomas Young (1773–1829) was an English physician and physicist, whose researches contributed to development of a wave theory of light. George Francis FitzGerald (1851–1901), Irish physicist, was responsible for a theory of the effect on the shape of a body by its motion through the ether. Henrik Lorentz (1853–1928), Dutch mathematical physicist, worked on phenomena of moving bodies, which helped to substantiate the relativity theory.]

Say I am not an adherent to the general theory of Relativity. I am not a mathematician and do not understand it. I rank Einstein as a man of genius from personal observation and from certain propositions of his which are within my comprehension; but you and Colonel Lynch and the other anti-Einsteinians must fight it out with him yourselves: I must not make myself ridiculous by interfering in a discussion that is outside my province.

As the whole progress of mathematics from its ancient simplicities to what we call its "higher" modern developments has been effected by assuming impossibilities and inconceivabilities, your line of argument does not seem to me conclusive. Since the Michelson-Morley experiment in its original form demonstrates that the velocity of light, the motion of the earth round the sun, and the ether, are all fictions (an incredible conclusion) there has arisen a demand for some new stroke of mathematical nonsense to save the situation. And it is not possible to dissociate mathematical nonsense from physical nonsense when the problem is one of astro-physics. Newton, Leibniz, Young, Fitzgerald, Lorentz and Einstein are all Nonsensists; but you cannot dispose of Einstein by this statement any more than you can dispose of Michael Angelo by calling him an Illusionist.

To ARTHUR LYNCH

Ayot St Lawrence. Welwyn
[H/9]   6th December 1932

[Lynch's book was *The Case Against Einstein* (1932). John Tyndall (1820–93), Irish physicist, was professor and, later, superintendent of the Royal Institution; one of his principal works was *Six Lectures on Light* (1873).]

Dear Colonel Lynch

As I am not a mathematician, propositions expressed in algebraic notation are lost on me; and I should make myself ridiculous if I interfered in a controversy which I cannot follow to the ultimate conclusions.

I have read your confounded book straight through as far as page 123, and stolen glimpses at the final chapters. I shall persevere: for the quarrelsomeness of the book makes it readable (though it's a fault); and the brain work in it makes it worth reading. But before I go further, tell me this.

Suppose me standing on the Barnet by-pass road at ten in the morning. A huntsman, trotting at twelve miles an hour, is approaching me. A car passes him at sixty miles an hour: and, at the moment of passing, the huntsman sounds his horn and the chauffeur honks his klaxon.

Twelve hours later I am in the same spot. A bicyclist comes towards me round a bend pedalling at twelve miles an hour. Just as his light comes into view he is overtaken by a car travelling at sixty miles an hour.

My common sense, sophisticated by my boyish studies of Young and Tyndall, tells me that the sounds of the horn and the klaxon, and the rays from the lights of the car and the bicycle, will, respectively, reach my ears and eyes simultaneously. Einstein agrees. But I gather that you contend, as a matter of common sense, that the car's rays and roars will reach me in one fifth of the time taken by those of the huntsman and the cyclist.

That is to say, the velocity of light is a function of the velocity of the material body from which the light is projected. Do you really mean this? If not, why do you quarrel with Einstein for side-tracking the Michelson-Morley experiment (which proved that either light has no velocity or the earth is motionless in space) by cheerfully proposing to call the velocity of light Zero?

Again, you accept the infinitesimal calculus equally with Einstein. But surely this takes you off the ground of common sense. The procedure you describe of halving the halves to infinity is not a common sense procedure: it proves that Achilles can never overtake the tortoise if he allows him even a millimetre start, which is blazing nonsense. As used by astronomers it assumes that there is a measurable distance between two points which are in the same place. The differential calculus assumes that a curve is a series of straight lines. Is your house any less a glass house than Einstein's; and if it is not is it safe to throw stones at him? I, the layman, may laugh at you both as long as I keep off the mathematical grass; but you put one foot on the gravel and one on the grass: a dangerous position if the grass begins to move, as mathematical grass does on the smallest provocation.

There is another point which puzzles me; but I forget it for the moment; and this letter is already too long, especially as I am probably as muddled about it all as Einstein.

But I would like to know incidentally whether you accept Newton's law of rectilinear motion. My experience as a boy throwing stones at cockshies on Dalkey Hill conclusively proved that there is no such law, and that nothing on earth will make a body in motion go straight. I proved it in my own person in a fog in Hyde Park before the paths were railed in. Having set myself in motion at the Marble Arch towards Knightsbridge I found myself quarter of an hour later at the fountain close to the Arch. The hypothesis of gravitation therefore seems to me to be entirely superfluous; and I was naturally impressed to find Einstein arriving at the same conclusion by mathematical paths. Does the curved universe mean anything more than that the law of motion is curvilinear?

A final criticism. The many kind people who have undertaken to explain my views to the world have invariably explained them all wrong. Therefore I cannot admit that you are controverting Einstein when you are controverting somebody who is idiot enough not to allow Einstein to speak for himself.

Now set me right when you next have an hour to spare; for I am utterly without authority, and perhaps without faculty in this matter.

In haste
G. Bernard Shaw

P.S. You will probably be underrated and academically ignored all your lifetime, like Samuel Butler. But if you *will* treat those who cannot see your points as moral delinquents, and cannot pass a respectable university figure head without instinctively fastening your teeth in his calf, how can you expect them to make as much of you as of the affable Einstein? It takes a long time to walk from Hyde Park Corner to Putney Bridge if you stop to fight every man you meet on the way.

To G. K. CHESTERTON

[E/1]

4 Whitehall Court SW 1
3rd December 1932

[Shaw had commenced to distribute advance copies of *The Adventures of the Black Girl in Her Search for God.*]

Dear G.K.C.

This wont be published until the 5th.

Tell the Vatican that something must be done about the Bible. It is like the burden on Christian's back [in Bunyan's *Pilgrim's Progress*] at present; only it won't come off.

GBS

To W. BRIDGES-ADAMS

[A/87]

[4 Whitehall Court SW 1]
8th December 1932

[When Fordham Flower (1904–66), chairman of the executive council of the Royal Shakespeare Theatre at Stratford-upon-Avon, appealed to Shaw to stage a Shakespearean production at the theatre, he replied "I'm too old; and I dont like appearing before the public in any line (professionally) except that of author. Even when I produce my own plays I never let the fact be announced. Besides . . . it would take far too much time. The utmost I could do would be to take a few rehearsals and suggest a few of my stage tricks, if the real producer wouldn't mind . . . That is all I do now for Barry Jackson: Ayliff roughs it all out for me. If B.A. would do that I could perhaps put in a useful touch or two" (C/1: 13th July 1932). Working on Shaw's "perhaps," the theatre's director Bridges-Adams managed eventually to extract a reluctant commitment from Shaw to stage (with Bridges-Adams at his side) a production of *Macbeth* the following spring. When, however, Bridges-Adams discovered from a press report that the Shaws were about to embark on a world cruise he worriedly communicated with GBS to inquire whether this meant a withdrawal from the spring commitment.

The Shaws' world tour aboard the Canadian Pacific liner *Empress of Britain* commenced at Monaco on 16th December, with stops at Naples (including visits to Pompeii and Mount Vesuvius), Athens, Haifa, Port Said, and an inland excursion in Egypt, the last week in December, touring Cairo, Luxor, and Aswan.]

Good Lord! I quite forgot that I shall be too late for Stratford. I am irrevocably committed to the trip round the world; and it ends at

318

Southampton on April the 18th!!! You must either put off Mac to the summer season or else produce him yourself. You'd have had to do nine tenths of it for me anyhow.

What a sell!

G. Bernard Shaw

To LOWELL BRENTANO

At Sea. World Cruise
[H/106]   6th January 1933

[Having reboarded the ship at Suez on 1st January the Shaws were now two days out of Bombay, where they would spend a week in sightseeing, followed by briefer visits to Ceylon and several of the East Indies islands. (It would be interesting to know whether Shaw visited Florence Farr's grave at Colombo.)

Lowell Brentano (1895–1950), editorial director and officer of the publishing house of Brentano's 1918–33, subsequently became a successful author of novels, plays, and film scenarios. His father Simon died in 1915, when he was succeeded as president by Lowell's brother Arthur (1858–1944). Despite the firm's economic crisis it was not forced into bankruptcy until March 1933, when it was bought out by the firm of Coward, McCann. In the same year its retail outlets were gobbled up by a Chicago bookseller Adolph Kroch. Shaw was the only author–creditor who, because of the ironclad terms of his contract, received 100% of the moneys due to him, the others having to be content with about 35¢. in the dollar.

The firm of Dodd, Mead & Co. had in that year contracted to become Shaw's American publisher, its first Shaw publication being *The Adventures of the Black Girl in Her Search for God* in February 1933. Dodd, Mead remained Shaw's publisher until his death and for more than thirty years thereafter.]

Dear Lowell Brentano

Now that I have at last a moment's leisure on board ship I must send you a line to express the wrench to my personal feelings which my change of Publishers cost me. I held on as long as I could with any sort of prudence—in fact longer; but you will probably not appreciate this until you are forty years older. An older hand than you would have known that the report you sent me about the action of your Bankers was decisive. I made every possible enquiry in quarters which, if not actively friendly, were at least quite disinterested; but I could get no scrap of reason for hoping that the Bankers would not foreclose in February, and involve me without benefitting you.

319

If you can transfer your stock of my books to Dodd Mead before your creditors remainder them at waste paper prices, so much the better.

I do not know what is happening or what is going to happen; but I assume that there is some chance of the bookshop's going on under the old name. If you sell the goodwill you will, I suppose, be pushed out on the grounds that the family management has not been successful since the death of your father. You evidently over-capitalised in anticipation of an extension of business that did not take place. Now, they'll blame you and your relatives for the crash; and it might be well for you in making a settlement to do your best to avoid being both squeezed out and prevented from using your name in any future adventures.

Whether Dodd Mead will do any better for me in the way of distribution remains to be seen. They gave up book selling long ago, and therefore do not enjoy the discount which enlarges the fund out of which royalties come; so I am changing my plan and accepting lower royalties on a guaranteed minimum circulation. Our 1931 results were so bad that I foresaw that I must either make some change, or accept the position of an extinct volcano in America.

All this is only to help you to think your affairs over. We, my wife and I—are distressed at the possibility of you—you two—finding yourself in a difficult financial situation which my action will not tend to improve.

But it really couldn't be helped; so feel as charitable as you can about it; and do not forget that there is nothing like three or four bankruptcies for building up a big fortune nowadays.

faithfully
G. Bernard Shaw

To RABINDRANATH TAGORE

R.M.S. Empress of Britain
[A/107; X/372]   [Bombay] 10th January 1933

[While most of the passengers entrained for Delhi and Agra the Shaws remained in Bombay the entire week the ship was in port, concentrating on visits to several temples (notably two Jain temples), gardens, and the zoo, with an excursion to Elephanta Island to view the famous cave temples. The Bengali poet and Shaw had last met at a luncheon held for Tagore during a visit to London in January 1931.]

My dear Rabindranath Tagore

Unfortunately I am not really visiting India; but the ship in which I am going round the world to get a little rest and do a little work has to put in at Bombay and Colombo to replenish her tanks; and on such occasions I step ashore for a few hours and wander about the streets and such temples as are open to European untouchables.

The organizers of the tour urge me to see India by spending 5 days and nights in a crowded railway carriage and being let out for a few minutes occasionally to lunch at a hotel and see the Taj Mahal; but I am too old a traveller to be taken by such baits, and too old a man ($76\frac{1}{2}$) to endure such hardships without expiring.

My only regret is that I shall be unable to visit you. My consolation is that the present situation in India will not bear being talked about. I understand it only too well.

faithfully
G. Bernard Shaw

To NANCY ASTOR

Empress of India [Britain]. Bombay

[C/101; X/373]   13th January 1933

[On the reverse of Shaw's postcard is a portrait of his hostess, identified in his engagement diary on 12th January as "Atizabegum."]

This is my latest conquest.

We are alive; but that is all. We started tired to death, hoping for rest; but this ship keeps stopping in ports where the water is too filthy to bathe in and shooting us ashore for impossible excursions to see the insides of railway carriages, and be let out, like little dogs, for a few minutes exercise and a glimpse of a temple or a hotel meal or a cobra–mongoose fight. We absolutely refused, and were roasted for a week at Luxor and are now roasting at Bombay for another week.

The Begum on the other side, a lion huntress acharnée, concentrated all the native nobility on me at a grand reception full of Nizamesses and Indian highnesses; and oh my! can't they dress, these native plutocrats. The place blazed with beauty. The British are right to boycott them (there was only one white real lady, spouse of a Chief Justice); for the dusky damsels would not leave their daughters an earthly.

I have been hung with flowers in the temples and drenched with rosewater and dabbed with vermilion in the houses; and the ship is infested with pilgrims to my shrine. Charlotte and I curse the day of our birth and the hour of our sailing incessantly. Our sole comfort is to think of THEE and wish we were within reach of you.

G.B.S.

To THE REV. ENSOR WALTERS

[H/3; X/374]

R.M.S. Empress of Britain
At Sea. 4th February 1933

[The *Empress of Britain* was en route from Singapore to Bangkok (where the Shaws declined to go ashore). "Que diable fait il dans cette galère?" ("What the devil was he doing in that galley?") is a frequently iterated phrase in Shaw's writings, from Molière's *Les fourberies de Scapin* (1671). Iphigenia, daughter of Agamemnon, and Jephtha's daughter (Judges, 11) were sacrificed by their fathers to propitiate their gods. Robert G. Ingersoll (1833–99), American attorney, was a famed agnostic. John James (Jack) Lawson (1881–1965), later first Baron Lawson of Beamish, was a miner who became a Labour M.P. for Chester-le-Street, Co. Durham, 1919–49. His autobiography *A Man's Life* was published in 1932. The book Shaw promised to send Walters was *Doctors' Delusions* . . . (Standard Edition, 1932).]

Dear Ensor Walters

I am writing this in the Gulf of Siam after inspecting a remarkable collection of religions in Egypt and India. The apparent multiplicity of Gods is bewildering at the first glance; but you presently discover that they are all the same one God in different aspects and functions and even sexes. There is always one uttermost God who defies personification. This makes Hinduism the most tolerant religion in the world, because its one transcendant God includes all possible Gods, from elephant Gods, bird Gods, and snake Gods, right up to the great trinity of Brahma, Vishnu and Shiva, which makes room for the Virgin Mary and modern Feminism by making Shiva a woman as well as a man. Christ is there as Krishna, who might also be Dionysos. In fact Hinduism is so elastic and so subtle that the profoundest Methodist and the crudest idolator are equally at home in it.

Islam is very different, being ferociously intolerant. What I may call Manifold Monotheism becomes in the minds of very simple folk an absurdly polytheistic idolatry, just as European peasants not only worship Saints and the Virgin as Gods but will fight fanatically for their faith in the ugly little black doll who is the Virgin of their own Church against the black doll of the next village. When the Arabs had run this sort of idolatry to such extremes [that] they did without black dolls and worshipped any stone that looked funny, Mahomet rose up at the risk of his life and insulted the stones shockingly, declaring that there is only one God, Allah, the glorious, the great, and pinning himself to the second Commandment that no man should dare make a graven image of Allah or any of his creatures. And there was to be no nonsense about toleration. You accepted Allah or you had your throat cut by somebody who did accept him, and who went to Paradise for having sent you to Hell. Mahomet was a great Protestant religious force like George Fox or Wesley. The main difference between the opposition of Islam to Hinduism and the opposition between Protestant and Catholic is that the Catholic persecutes as fiercely as the Protestant when he has the power; but Hinduism cannot persecute, because all the Gods—and what goes deeper, the no Gods—are to be found in its Temples. There is actually a great Hindu sect, the Jains, with Temples of amazing magnificence, which abolish God, not on materialist atheist considerations, but as unspeakable and unknowable, transcending all human comprehension.

So far, it is all simple enough for anyone with religious sense. But when you are face to face with the Temples and the worshippers, you find that before Mahomet and the founder of the Jains were cold in their graves, the institutions and rituals they founded began to revert to the more popular types, and all the Gods and no Gods became hopelessly mixed up, exactly as the Apostles backslid when Jesus was killed. In the Jain Temple you find shrines and images, and baths where you must wash all over before you may enter the shrine and adore the image. If you can find an intelligent Priest who is a real Jain theologian, you say "How's this? A God in the Jain Temple!" He explains to you that the image is not a God, but a portrait of one of their great Saints; and that the man just out of the bath prostrating himself is not worshipping but expressing his respect for the memory of the late eminent Ensoramji Waltershagpat. But it is like Dean Inge trying to explain away St. Pauls. It is perfectly plain that the image is a super refined Buddha, and that Jainism and Buddhism have got hopelessly mixed. Jain Buddha is attended by sculptured elephants. You ask what they mean, and are told that they are purely ornamental works of art. Then your eye lights on an image of Ganesh, the Hindu God with the head and trunk of an elephant. On the point of exclaiming "Que diable fait il dans cette galère?", you remember that you must not put your

323

courteous host in a corner, and politely hold your tongue, but think furiously.

It is always the same: outside the few who have religious sense, and who are equally at home and equally estranged in all the Temples of all the faiths, there is the multitudinous average man. What he demands from the founder of his faith is, first, miracles. If, like Mahomet, you rebuke him and tell him that you are not a conjuror, or, like Jesus, turn on him furiously with "An evil and adulterous generation seeketh after a sign," it will not matter: when you have become famous through your preaching, and cured the sick by healing their minds and thereby curing their bodies, your average man will invent miracles enough for you to eclipse St. Anthony of Padua. Then he will make you his God, which means that he will beg from you, and, when he is properly frightened of you, make sacrifices to propitiate you, even to the extent of killing your daughter (Iphigenia or Miss Jephtha) to please you; but he will soon begin to cheat by substituting a ram for his son, and finally making the sacrifice purely symbolic and imaginary. And it is through this, and not through the principles of the founder of his faith, that you must get at him if you are to make a decent human being of him. In Jamaica and Rhodesia all the good negroes and their great ministers and leaders are Fundamentalists. If you rubbed Bradlaugh and Ingersoll into them, you would probably not only shock but demoralize them. You find the same thing in our mining villages. Read "A Man's Life" by Jack Lawson, Labour M.P. The Dean of Worcester made me read it. You must start, however, with a knowledge of what the underground world was before Methodism came and saved it. In those days the men were demons and the women savages. Jack Lawson was a demon and his mother was a savage (it was by the grace of God that she did not maim or kill the ten children whom she had to bring up, mostly in one room); but they were honest, upright demons and savages, with solid characters; and it was Methodism that did that for them. I very much doubt whether Shavianism would have been equally successful.

Methodism has done this without magnificent temples: it houses God very shabbily. Prelacy houses him magnificently: so much so, that the poor man cannot feel really at home there. But the value of big building for getting hold of the popular imagination was powerfully impressed on me at Baalbek, Delphi, Eleusis, and Karnak, where Jupiter, Apollo, and the Egyptian Gods had colossal Temples. People stare at these ruins and wonder at the prodigious feats their builders achieved, handling blocks of stone weighing several tons as if they were

324

bricks, and raising them hundreds of feet to the tops of giant pillars as if they had got far beyond our baby steam cranes. But the really impressive thing about them is not the enormous labour and expense lavished on building them, but the still more amazing labour, care, and cost spent on smashing them. You have in that a convincing testimony to the influence they exercised over the imagination of the people. The Arabs, the Protestants of the East, could have built a hundred splendid mosques with the labour that made good their resolution that of the tremendous temple of Jupiter at Baalbek not one stone should be left standing on another, and to leave Apollo homeless at Delphi and Eleusis. What our Puritans did to our Cathedrals was mere schoolboy mischief in comparison. The rage that accumulates in religious hearts when these wonders of architecture become dens of thieves and substitute sensuous ritual for the search for God must have risen to earthquake force when it scattered Delphi.

To take you back home for the moment, I ought to be sympathetic about Mrs. Walters' operations; but these things infuriate me; I can do nothing but swear uselessly. When I get back to London I must send you a book of mine—a reprint of old articles—which will explain my views as to authorised medicine and surgery. It can cure nothing; but it can produce a condition of anxiety and terror in the household— to say nothing of money strain—that can be guaranteed to include everyone who cares for the patient in the list of casualties. However, life is enormously and abidingly strong: it beats the Doctors nine times out of ten. And then they claim the credit of their own defeat. I wish you both most earnestly a safe delivery.

I haven't a "Black Girl" here to autograph for you; but that can be remedied on my return in April.

as ever
G. Bernard Shaw

To THERESA HELBURN

Empress of Britain. At sea
Meridian Day between 13th–14th March 1933
[A/7]   on the Pacific

[At Manila on 9th February the Shaws lunched with the governor, Theodore Roosevelt (son of the ex-president). They then sailed to Hong Kong and Shanghai (where they visited Mme Sun Yat-sen (1890–1981), widow of the Chinese revolutionary leader), travelling by train to Beijing (Peiping) for

325

three days. The ship next proceeded to Kobe and Yokohama, where Shaw had tea with the minister of war General Sadao Araki (1877–1966), attended a performance of *Noh* in his honour, visited labour leaders and members of the Socialist People's Party, and called on the prime minister, Makoto Saito (1858–1936). Leaving Japan on 9th March, the *Empress of Britain* headed south for Honolulu.

The sponsor of Shaw's New York lecture in the Metropolitan Opera House on 11th April was the Academy of Political Science, a non-profit organisation that sold seats to its members only, at minimum prices to cover expenses. There was, however, considerable speculation in tickets. Thomas W. Lamont (1870–1948), senior partner of J. P. Morgan & Co. and a trustee of the Academy, was Shaw's host and escort the night of the lecture. *Village Wooing*, provisionally titled "The Red Sea," was a short play, in "three conversations," commenced by Shaw on 2nd January, while crossing that sea, and completed on the Indian Ocean three weeks later. *On the Rocks* was begun in the Gulf of Siam on 6th February; Shaw made little progress on it during the voyage, and it was not completed until July, at Ayot. The Theatre Guild did, in fact, "drop" Shaw after producing one more of his new plays, *The Simpleton of the Unexpected Isles*, in 1935, though it briefly revived *You Never Can Tell* in 1948.]

My dear Terry (which I still maintain should be Tessie)

It is odd that in spite of the blazing publicity of this tour round the world I cannot knock into people's heads the fact that I am *not* going to spend a month in New York and address large audiences every night after days spent in being lionized to death. The ship is timed to land me in New York at noon on the 11th April. After letting the press do its worst I have to convince the authorities that I am eligible for admission to New England. When I carry that point I have to address as many Americans as the Metropolitan Opera House will hold for about an hour for the pecuniary benefit of the Academy of Political Science. If not lynched, I shall take refuge with the Lamonts for a while before escaping back to the ship to sleep. At noon next day I sail for Cherbourg and Southampton. In the meantime about a thousand people will try to see me on particular business—perhaps you among them to relieve the horror of it. And that's all. Absolutely all.

Now it is obvious that any attempt to exploit this sensation must be made *after* my departure, when people are talking about me. A performance in competition with me on the 11th would be the last word in managerial ineptitude. A previous production would involve not only this, but the possibility of a failure, or at least a deluge of hostile criticism, which would discount me heavily. Therefore on your life nothing until I am gone.

326

What could you do anyhow? Give a single performance of Methu-selah or Man & Superman in "the entirety" and lose a lot of money! Far better leave the performance to me and let the Academy of Political Science fill its pockets and leave mine emptied; for I shall not take a cent out of America on this visit, though the agents are ruining themselves with wireless offers of "the first five thousand dollars."

... I can do nothing in the fashionable theatre at present prices. I shall leave it quite out of account henceforth. The play I am now engaged on is only for *publication* with Too Good [*Too True to be Good*]. The one I finished in the first weeks of the tour, when I was too dog tired for anything but child's play, is only a comedietta for two people in three scenes, which will fill out the volume between the other two. It is time for the Guild to drop me, and for me to cease costing the Guild more than I am now worth to it.

I shall send this by air mail from San Francisco so that it can fly straight to you whilst I loaf round through the Canal. I doubt whether there is a service from Honolulu.

ever
G.B.S.

To LOWELL BRENTANO

R.M.S. Empress of Britain
approaching Honolulu from Japan

[A/106]   14th March 1933

[Brentano's had published its last Shaw title, a trade edition of *What I Really Wrote about the War*, in March 1932.]

Dear Lowell Brentano

It is no use making schemes to make fortunes out of my publicity: I am not going to wear myself out in that particular way, as Charles Dickens did. People are hurling offers over the wireless of "the first $5000" at me daily; and if the Academy of Political Science handles the affair properly my appearance in New York at the Metropolitan Opera House will keep it in funds for a year to come; and the Inland Revenue collectors will try to hold me up for surtax. But I shall leave New York poorer than I came; for I shall not touch a cent, directly or indirectly, of the booty. And I shall stay on the east coast, not, as they all suppose, for a month, but for 24 hours exactly, arriving at noon on the 11th April and sailing for Europe at noon on the 12th. I shall come from San Francisco and Los Angeles via the Canal; so that by airmailing this letter from Frisco I can get it to you a few days before my arrival.

I am very sensible of the friendly way in which you have helped the transfer to Dodd Meads; and if I were forty years younger there is no saying what we might do together; but my sands are nearly run out; and I have no time for moneymaking, nor any desire for the limelight except to get out of it. My brief appearance in New York will be to say some unpopular but necessary things to your people before I die.

I shall have to keep as quiet as possible on the 11th and sleep on the ship; for to tackle and hold a big audience for an hour at 77 is—though with care I can do it—something that will use up all my forces.

I am rather horrified at the threatened spectacle of a publisher turning playwright. Now if it were the other way—!

Who is to support your wife—and *you*?

ever
G. Bernard Shaw

To ETHEL WARNER

R.M.S. Empress of Britain

[S/1]   14th March 1933

[Ethel Warner was director of the Academy of Political Science. Shaw's lecture "The Future of Political Science in America" was broadcast in its entirety (as stipulated by Shaw), its running time of an hour and forty minutes thoroughly exhausting him. "I thought I had got through the lecture and the appalling press and camera riot on the ship next day without turning a hair," he wrote to Warner from London on 15th May; "but two days later nearly all my remaining teeth came loose and untouchably sore. Fortunately they quieted down and fastened up again quickly; but I shan't do it again: I am too old for these feats of endurance" (S/1). True to his word Shaw accepted no future lecture invitations, though he occasionally until his very last years made an impromptu little speech for some occasion or other and continued until 1941 to accept invitations from the B.B.C. to broadcast.

The brief reception at the Lamonts' New York townhouse, following Shaw's lecture, lasted less than three-quarters of an hour; Shaw was back aboard ship a few minutes past midnight.]

Private
Dear Miss Warner

As my wireless messages have been brief I had better enlarge on them a little.

328

The lecture at the Opera House will be the only public appearance I shall make on this tour. I make this exception to my rule of privacy because the Academy of Political Science is the most important institution in the United States. My contention will be that nothing but political science can save civilization in America now; and that political science involves an almost complete scrapping of the present constitution and a reconstruction on diametrically opposite principles. I have consented to speak to the largest possible audience because I wish to make as much money as possible for the Academy; and it must be fully understood that I speak at my own expense and leave America without having touched a single cent, directly or indirectly, of the gate money, the broadcasting fee (if any), or whatever else may be paid by the American public to hear or see me.

I am not going to read a paper. My address will be extemporized; and I cannot undertake to correct reports nor to supply the press with notes in advance. I shall hardly speak for less than an hour; and in so big a place this will be quite enough for me at my age (77). I must have rest and silence for some hours before the speech; and after it I must go back to the ship to bed except for a few words in private at the Lamonts'. So do not turn on a hundred people to shake hands with me.

If the Radio will take on my whole address and arrange their microphone so as not to hamper me, and will pay the Academy adequately therefor, I have no objection. But it must be that or nothing. They will try to substitute "a few words" from the President and a few echoes from me. They won't get them; and you must warn them beforehand that it is useless to ask me for them. A broadcast from me to America is no novelty. What would be a novelty would be a speech from me that said nothing; and I shall take care that such a thing does not happen. I have been bored with it too often to take my turn as a bore.

Keep the tone of the affair as serious as you can; and if, as I presume, the Academy has no State endowment, make the most of the occasion to get one, or at least to make a hullabaloo about not getting one.

I think that is all I need trouble you with until we meet. . . .

Many thanks for your activities in this rather thankless business.

faithfully
G. Bernard Shaw

To THOMAS MOONEY

Casa del Mar. San Simeon

[S/41]   27th March 1933

[Thomas J. Mooney (1882–1942), American militant labour leader, was convicted for alleged responsibility for a bomb explosion during a San Francisco Preparedness Parade in 1916, which killed nine persons and injured many others. He protested his innocence then and later, and eventually was pardoned, but not before he had served more than twenty years behind bars. When word of Shaw's imminent visit to California was received, Mooney wrote to him in Japan to urge that he visit San Quentin prison and make a public statement about Mooney's case to the press in San Francisco. A defence committee further urged Shaw to address a giant rally under its sponsorship to urge a pardon from the governor. "Sorry," came Shaw's cabled reply to the committee, "Interference Communist foreign celebrity would not help Mooney" (S(Y)/41: 8th March 1933).

This response was consistent with Shaw's public position that foreign interference was harmful rather than beneficial to the petitioners, and helps to explain why he did not add his voice to Nancy Astor's in 1931 to aid the appeal of the Krynines. In 1932, when Fenner Brockway asked Shaw to protest to the Hungarian minister of justice against the imminent hanging of the revolutionary poet Fritz Karik, he replied, "Shall I ever persuade you, Fenner, that the surest way to hang a political prisoner is to call in the foreigner to help him?" (A. Fenner Brockway, *Inside the Left*, 1942: 25th August 1932). To officials of the World Committee for the Relief of Victims of German Fascism he warned: "People here get into a state of political agitation and take up the case of some prisoner or other accused by a foreign government, and without the slightest consideration of the fact that they are damaging the unfortunate prisoner—never considering the effect of their proceedings on the prisoner in question. Take the case of Sacco and Vanzetti. Any chance they had of not being electrocuted was cut off by foreign agitation got up denouncing American justice and that kind of thing. ... Continually using these unfortunate prisoners abroad as a stick with which to beat a government seems to be cruel and inconsiderate" ("Mr. G. B. Shaw and the [Leipzig] Prisoners," *The Observer*, 24th September 1933).

When questioned by reporters about the Mooney case in San Francisco Shaw declined as "a visitor" to express an opinion on the merits of the case, but his indignation was apparent as he added, "I cannot pretend that I am not shocked at having any person put into a vault for 16 or 17 years." Unfortunately, he continued, "Mr. Mooney has been made a political martyr. I would like to see the case treated as simply from a humanitarian angle. I would be afraid to go to see him because it might do him more harm than good. ... My sole concern would be to get Mr. Mooney out of that vault" ("Shaw Bests Army of Interviewers," *New York Times*, 25th March 1933).

When he arrived at the Hearst ranch at San Simeon he indited "the sort of reply" to Mooney that "I thought best calculated to help him if he sent it to the press. I shewed it to W. R. H[earst]. at the Ranch. He agreed" (C/3: 27th September 1933, to S. K. Ratcliffe).]

Dear Mr Mooney

You have combined two of the worst pieces of luck that can happen to a man in a civilized country.

All civilized countries now have an elaborate theory of criminal law. If when a crime is committed something cruel is done to somebody and the public can be persuaded that this unfortunate somebody is the person who committed it, then the rest of the community will be "deterred" from committing similar crimes by the fear of suffering similar cruelty. All our judges and juries (except those who are naively vindictive) cling to this theory to justify the atrocities in which they take part every day.

The advantage of the theory is that it does not matter in the least whether the person who is hanged or flogged or imprisoned is the real culprit or not. The deterrent effect is precisely the same in either case.

The disadvantage is that if the guilty party cannot be found, the police have a very strong incentive to substitute an innocent one and to persuade themselves that the substitution is a genuine detection. And the judge and jury have the same incentive to support the operation. Even those who are not quite self-deluded or imposed on say "It is expedient that one person die for the people."

Consequently the fact that though ten people were killed by a bomb and a victim was sacrificed "pour encourager les autres" it by no means follows that the selected victim—yourself—ever saw that bomb. But you would have the satisfaction of believing that your fate had put a stop to bombing were it not that many more bombs have been thrown since your conviction than in the same number of years before it. That is your first stroke of bad luck.

The second is that your friends have boosted you as the champion and martyr of the Proletarian Revolution. Consequently your release would be the greatest misfortune that could happen to them. What use is a martyr when he no longer suffers? Also your release would be a political defeat for the dominant capitalist classes, for the police, and for the courts. The door that was locked on you is thus double-locked by your friends and triple-locked by your opponents.

Now I have no interest in the theory of deterrence. And I do not consider it humane to use you as a stick to beat Capitalism. My sole concern with you is to get you out of prison. If somebody would bomb the Mooney Defence Committee out of existence—if it were made a crime to mention your name in the papers—if only you could be allowed to take your true present position as an amiable elderly gentleman whose career as a Labor pioneer was cut short many years ago by a verdict vaguely remembered as having been much questioned at the time, and whose imprisonment has gone to a length which is now out-of-date and shocking, then perhaps the remonstrances I have made in response to Press inquiries might have some effect. I still have some hope that they may be listened to in spite of everything.

I very greatly regret that my short stay on the west coast, and my fear of associating you with my own political views, which are much more extreme than yours, have prevented me from paying you a visit which would have been personally most interesting to me and would have varied prison routine to you for a moment.

Wishing you a speedy release, I remain, dear Mr Mooney,

faithfully yours
G. Bernard Shaw

To WILLIAM RANDOLPH HEARST

San Simeon
[A/81]   28th March 1933

[The Shaws were guests of Hearst and his mistress Marion Davies from the 24th to the 27th. Shaw's letter was an inscription in Hearst's copy of *What I Really Wrote about the War* (New York, 1932), written immediately prior to his departure. During their visit they were surrounded by a bevy of Hollywood starlets and intimate friends of Davies, Shaw luxuriating in the indoor and outdoor swimming pools and enjoying his proximity to the exotic animals and birds with which the ranch was stocked. Asked by a fellow guest his opinion of the castle-like central structure, "This," said Shaw, "is the way God would have built it, if He'd had the money" (Walter Wanger, *You Must Remember This*, 1975).]

My dear W.R.

Nobody will ever know what we two really wrote about the war.

Think of the articles we wrote which before the ink was dry were too late to print as the military and diplomatic situation changed from hour to hour like a kaleidoscope jolted by every cannon shot!

And oh! think of the truths we might have told but had to keep to ourselves lest our countries should be involved in the scandal and ruin that would have followed!

Well, we both got into honorable trouble early in the war and kept in it to the end; so we have nothing to be ashamed of except our connexion with the human race, which was not just then doing itself much credit.

G. Bernard Shaw

To KENNETH MacGOWAN

R.M.S. Empress of Britain
At Sea in the Caribbean
[A/109]   [nearing Havana] 7th April 1933

[Kenneth MacGowan (1888–1963) was a story editor and associate producer at RKO Studios. In 1947 he became head of the Department of Theatre Arts at UCLA. RKO was negotiating with Shaw for rights to several of his plays, including *Captain Brassbound's Conversion* for Ann Harding (1901–81), *The Devil's Disciple* for John Barrymore, and *Saint Joan* for its electrifying new young star Katharine Hepburn (b. 1907). With the advent of sound George Arliss had become one of the screen's giants, winning the 1929–30 Academy Award for his performance in *Disraeli*.]

Dear Kenneth Macgowan

I got your wireless on the high seas, and intended to see you at Hollywood about it. But as luck would have it I missed San Francisco and Los Angeles and Hollywood. Except for an hour or so at Culver City with Metro-Goldwyn-Mayer I was either at W.R. Hearst's ranch or in the air all the time.

You will find that R.K.O. doesn't mean business when it comes to the point. They held me up for a year over Arms and the Man when they were operating in London through Basil Dean; and I shall not take up the question of Brassbound or Candida with them until I have some evidence that they know what they are doing. Somebody has told them that I am a man with a publicity name and a story to sell them to play with. They think all they have to do is to say "How much?" and toss me a cheque, and then hand over my play to the bell boy to arrange as a movie with spoken sub-titles and a due salting of kisses and socks on the jaw.

In spite of the promising work done by Arliss in the serious screening

333

of plays *as such* I don't believe that Hollywood is within ten years of tackling my stuff. And the British experiments with it are hopeless: they have no money and want to put in minutes (mostly wasted) where months are needed.

faithfully
G. Bernard Shaw

To THE NEW YORK PRESS

[R.M.S. Empress of Britain]
[New York harbour]

[U(E)/9; X/455]   [Undated: assigned to 11th April 1933]

[When a battalion of reporters scrambled aboard the ship upon its arrival in New York they were confronted with a message Shaw had hastily written and given to his biographer Archibald Henderson to post for him; and found, when they persistently sought out his stateroom, that the captain had placed the ship's master at arms as a guard before the door. Shaw eventually relented and allowed himself to be photographed, but he declined to be interviewed until he had had a long drive through Manhattan, across the George Washington Bridge, and down the Jersey Palisades, returning to New York via the Holland Tunnel; and until he had delivered his address that night in the Metropolitan Opera House. The press had to be content to wait for their interview until the morning of the 12th, just before the ship set out on its Atlantic crossing. The tour ended for the Shaws at Southampton on 19th April.]

The New York press may return to its firesides and nurse the baby until tomorrow morning, except the enterprising section which came on board at Havana, and discussed everything with me for an hour and forty minutes. Today I am in training for the Metropolitan Opera House tonight, and may be regarded as deaf and dumb for the moment.

With regrets and apologies.

GBS

To THE EDITOR OF *WORLD'S PRESS NEWS*

[4 Whitehall Court SW 1]
[X/375]   [Undated: *c.* 29th April 1933]

[Hannen Swaffer (1879–1962), ardent socialist and one of Britain's most flamboyant journalists, was during his long career a pioneer gossip columnist, editor of several London dailies, theatre critic for the *Daily* and *Sunday Express*, and until his death contributor of a weekly column to the *World's Press News.*]

Dear Sir

My friend Mr. Swaffer is wrong on one point only. I did not talk twaddle to the reporters. I overwhelmed them with my most serious wisdom and my most sparkling wit.

They reported, not what I said, but the nearest thing in their own mental repertory. In some cases the two matched rather poorly.

But let me tell you an old theatre story about Macready. When he was rehearsing *Macbeth*, the actor who had to announce that Birnam Wood was coming to Dunsinane showed a painful lack of interest in that miracle.

Macready gave him a thrilling demonstration of how his lines ought to be delivered. The actor simply said, "I suppose you expect ten pounds a night for acting. I get twenty-five bob a week. Give me your ten pounds and I will show you."

In the capital cities I visited I saw too many free-lances who were evidently in the position of that actor. I should like to impress on our newspaper proprietors and editors that if they want adequate reports (which I am afraid they don't) they can get them by paying adequately for them, and that any other sort of reporting should be rigidly excluded from the columns of reputable newspapers.

G. Bernard Shaw

To SIEGFRIED TREBITSCH

4 Whitehall Court SW 1
[H/5; X/341]   12th–15th May 1933

[Adolf Hitler (1889–1945), leader of the National Socialist German Workers' (Nazi) Party from 1921, had just been appointed Chancellor. By the year's end he had become dictator of Germany. Hermann Goering (1893–1946), Hitler's principal aide and, at this time, Prussia's premier, did not carry out

335

his threat to parcel out the Junker estates to the peasantry. The first perform-
ance of *Too True to be Good* in Mannheim was marred by Nazi taunts of
"Jew Shaw" until quelled by the police. Alfred Rosenberg (1893–1946),
German Nazi leader and ideologist of the party, in 1933 headed the Nazis'
just established Foreign Policy Office. During a recent visit to England he
had been castigated in the press and subjected to angry demonstrations by
London Jews. Dr Alfred Kerr (1867–1948), influential theatre critic, and
Julius Bab subsequently emigrated, the former to England, the latter to
France and then to the United States.]

My dear Trebitsch

I have not had a moment free for private correspondence since I
landed until today (the 12th).

My first impulse was to write you a long and fierce letter for publication in the German press, bringing all my guns to bear on Hitler's
stupid mistake in trying to make political capital out of the Judenhetze,* and on his attempt to cover up the essentially Communist
character of his proclamation of compulsory labor and his nationalization of the Trade Unions (the first being pure Bernard Shawism and
the second borrowed from Russia) by a senseless denunciation of
Marxism. For in such a crisis as the present you have either to hit back
and hit hard, or else accept the situation in an attitude of complete
submission.

But on reflection I saw that I could not involve you in such a controversy, not only because you would run all the risks of it and I none,
but because your sympathies, except to the extent to which they are
Bohemian artistic sympathies, are Junker sympathies. You believe all
the rubbish the newspapers print about Russia.** Although the 1914
war began by the mobilisation of Imperialist Russia against Germany,
and the Bolsheviks stopped that war by the peace of Brest Litovsk and

---

* All through my tour the first question put by the press at every port was about Hitler.
I said that a statesman who began by a persecution of the Jews was compromised as hopelessly as an officer who began by cheating at cards. But I approved of the subsequent
edicts. I admitted that the Germans had as much right to exclude non-Germans from
governmental posts as the Americans to reserve the presidency for Americans, but insisted
that displaced Jews should be compensated and not driven out penniless by hounding the
mob to attack them.

** The Russians, in their desperate struggle to civilize their hundred million peasants,
have been forced to spend recklessly on education, and they have probably overcapitalized
in machinery, with the result that they may have run short of food for the moment. But
the stories told by the runaways when they find that there is a good market for anti-
Communist lies are quite worthless as evidence of the collapse of Communism, though
some of the tales of individual and accidental hardships may be true enough. But even
these are trifles compared to what is happening in England and America. In New York
well dressed gentlemen are begging in the streets desperately and shamelessly.

336

were denounced for it by their Allies, who accused them of being in the pay of Germany, you would, if you could, restore the Imperial government in Russia and go back to the anti-Russian situation of 1914. If the Junkers were wise and farsighted instead of being blinded by class prejudice and dread of losing their properties they would say that as they have nothing to fear diplomatically from a Communist Russia and everything to fear from an Imperialist Russia, it is their interest that Russia should remain Communist even if Germany remains Capitalist. But they are not wise; and the consequence is that they have made a combination with Nazi Hitlerism, which derives all its electoral strength from the sentimentalized and Chauvinized Socialism of the city proletariats. They have made Hitler dictator for four years only to find themselves left out of his councils and his distribution of public posts, and the situation dominated by Colonel Goering, a Socialist who is determined to break up the big Junker estates in the east and give them to the peasants (just as Lenin did) to secure their support for Fascism.

You have not analyzed the position because you hate politics, and are quite unaccustomed to and inexpert at the sort of political controversy in which I am as practised as I am in playwriting. You had better keep out of the melée as much as possible. If you are pressed as to why you translate me, who am a notorious Communist, and a strenuous upholder of the present regime in Russia, you must say that you are not concerned with all that—that you have introduced me to Germany as a great artist, and that all you know about my present attitude is that though I may have expressed the greatest contempt for the Judenhetze I have been the first to applaud Hitler's two great steps as to compulsory labor and the trade unions when the whole British press are denouncing them savagely, exactly as I supported Mussolini when he too was being denounced as the most infamous of usurpers and tyrants. But you are not committed to my opinions: all you know is that I have a right to be heard, and that to pretend that my artistic works should not be read in Germany because of my opinions is as ridiculous as to make the same objection to translations of the works of Tolstoy or of the Koran. But whatever you say or do, you must be careful not to shew the least sign of being intimidated, or of caring one snap of your fingers what anybody thinks or threatens.

As to silencing me, that is not possible. I can neither refuse to receive the press when I visit a foreign country nor educate them to report what I say correctly. If the consequences prove ruinous to both of us I cannot help it; but let us wait until we really are ruined. My ruin has been announced so often that I am no longer afraid of scarecrows. If

337

they worry you about it say "All I know is that Shaw is the greatest man who ever lived and everything he says must be right." They wont shoot you: they will treat you as a privileged lunatic.

On the voyage I wrote a comedietta for two persons, which would occupy about one hour in performance, and a very long political play of the Apple Cart kind, which I still have to finish and cut down into reasonable length. I shall not take any trouble to have them performed, but publish them in the same volume as Too True.

By the way, what has happened to that play? Is it true that the Nazis interrupted performances with shouts of "Down with the Jew Shaw!"?

Tell dear Tina that Vichy water, though no use in bottles, is radio-active when you drink it straight out of the ground. It does wonders for livers, but may be good for other organs as well.

In haste, as usual
G. Bernard Shaw

P.S. 15th May 1933. Rosenberg has just returned to Berlin overwhelmed by the avalanche of execration brought down on Hitler by the persecution of the Jews. Meanwhile I receive piteous letters from Jews, notably Alfred Kerr and Julius Bab, asking me to help them. But how can any private purse help in a wholesale catastrophe like this one? . . . All this is written without reserve as you are on French soil. Is there any risk in Austria of your letters being opened, or of your being boycotted? I dare not write a line frankly to anyone in Germany.

How much are you a Jew? I know that you are a practising heathen; but do any of your kinsfolk go to the synagogue?

Excuse all the marginal scrawlings; but the situation changes almost from hour to hour.

To ELSIE BELLE CHAMPION

Ayot St Lawrence. Welwyn
15th May 1933

[C/4; X/377]

[Elsie Belle Champion (1873–1953), widow of the socialist leader Henry Hyde Champion, ran a literary agency and bookshop in Melbourne, which licensed Shaw's works in the Antipodes. Gregan McMahon (1874–1941) founded the Melbourne Repertory Theatre in 1910–11, its productions being performed mostly by well-drilled amateurs. It was a casualty, however, of the

First World War. In 1929 McMahon formed a new semi-professional company in Melbourne, staging several of Shaw's plays including the first performance in English of *The Millionairess* in 1936. The McMahon Players gave five performances of *Too True to be Good* in the Garrick Theatre between 1st and 8th April 1933, the reviewer for the Melbourne *Argus* on 3rd April reporting that Shaw's "collected edition of lectures" was "admirably played"; the notice was captioned "Long Sermons and Short Witticisms."]

The alleged failure of Too True in London has to be qualified by the fact that it was drawing over £1000 a week when it was taken off. This would have paid with economical management; but unfortunately the management was extravagant, and, with several other enterprises on hand, was getting out of its depth and had to curtail and reconstruct. The first step of its retreat was the dropping of Too True, which, however, though dead, yet speaketh.

I must add that though the play has everywhere produced exactly the sensation described in your letter, it has also been bitterly disparaged by the press and avoided by the fashionable public. It is all right in large theatres charging moderate prices; but it is not a London West End play, nor a Boulevard or Broadway one.

Congratulations to Gregan on doing it justice. I hope it won't ruin him.

G.B.S.

To W. B. YEATS

4 Whitehall Court S W 1
[C/5]   18th May 1933

[The Irish government in May 1933 suppressed sale and circulation of the *Black Girl* in Ireland, describing it as "in its general tendency indecent and obscene." At the Irish Academy of Letters special meeting on 29th May it was reported that the Minister for Justice, Patrick J. Ruttledge (1892–1952), had told a deputation from the Academy he had read the work and could himself see no reason for its being censored. He would, he said, take the matter up with the Board of Censors. On 3rd August a letter was read in which the minister stated that after full consideration he had decided not to revoke the prohibition order. When the Academy demanded to know the reason for the ban, it was informed by Ruttledge, according to minutes of the 29th August meeting, that it was not usual for the ministry to offer reasons for the banning of any book other than those given in the official gazette. When Shaw expressed doubts as to the advisability of legal action, the issue was allowed to die.]

Tell the Committee not to forget John Farleigh's illustrations. The reverend censors are not nudists, and probably regard a nude negress as the last extremity of obscenity.

The best line to take is that the book completely justifies the Church in its objection to throwing the Bible into the hands of ignorant persons to be interpreted by their private judgment.

GBS

To EDWARD ELGAR

4 Whitehall Court SW 1

[H/85]   30th May 1933

[Elgar flew to Paris (it was his first plane trip) to conduct his violin concerto, Op. 61, in the Salle Pleyel on 31st May. The soloist was sixteen-year-old Yehudi Menuhin. The Malvern Festival's fifth season saluted "Four Hundred Years of English Drama," ranging from *Gammer Gurton's Needle* and Dryden's *All for Love* to Henry Arthur Jones's *The Dancing Girl* and a new play by James Bridie, *A Sleeping Clergyman*. As in 1931, there was no play by Shaw. The Shaws attended the Hereford music festival from 5th to 8th September, which included performances of Elgar's *The Kingdom* and *The Dream of Gerontius*.]

My dear Elgar

Why Paris? I recommend Peiping (çi-devant Peking) where you must go to the Lama temple and discover how the Chinese produce harmony. Instead of your laborious expedient of composing a lot of different parts to be sung simultaneously, they sing in unison all the time, mostly without changing the note; but they produce their voices in some magical way that brings out all the harmonics with extraordinary richness, like big bells. I have never had my ears so super-satisfied. The basses are stupendous. The conductor keeps them to the pitch by tinkling a tiny bell occasionally. They sit in rows round a golden Buddha fifty feet high, whose beneficent majesty and intimate interest in them is beyond description. In art we do everything the wrong way and the Chinese do it the right way.

At Tientsin they had a Chinese band for me. It consisted of a most lovely toned gong, a few flageolets (I don't know what else to call them) which specialised in pitch without tone, and a magnificent row of straight brass instruments reaching to the ground, with mouthpieces like the ones I saw in the Arsenal in Venice many years ago: brass

Shaw at Metropolitan Opera House, New York, 11 April 1933

*(Photograph by New York American; Shaw collection of
Dan H. Laurence, University of Guelph Library)*

Too True to be Good, Guild Theatre, New York, February–March 1932:
Ernest Cossart, Beatrice Lillie, Hope Williams, Leo G. Carroll

(Photograph by Vandamm Studios; Shaw collection of Dan H. Laurence, University of Guelph Library)

Ellen Pollock as Sweetie in *Too True to be Good*,
Malvern Festival, August 1932

*(Photograph by Sasha, Pall Mall; Shaw collection of Dan H. Laurence,
University of Guelph Library)*

Shaw on the beach at Mount Maunganui, New Zealand, 28 March 1934

(Photograph by Jack Duncan; Shaw collection of Dan H. Laurence, University of Guelph Library)

saucers quite flat, with a small hole in the middle. They all played the same note, and played it all the time, like the E flat in the Rheingold prelude; but it was rich in harmonics, like the note of the basses in the temple. At the first pause I demanded that they should play some other notes to display all the possibilities of the instrument. This atheistic proposal stunned them. They pleaded that they had never played any other note; that their fathers, grandfathers, and forbears right back to the Chinese Tubal Cain had played that note and no other note, and that to assert that there was more than one note was to imply that there is more than one god. But the man with the gong rose to the occasion and proved that in China as in Europe the drummer is always the most intelligent person in the band. He snatched one of the trumpets, waved it in the air like a mail coach guard with a posthorn, and filled the air with flourishes and fanfares and Nothung motifs. We must make the B.B.C. import a dozen of these trumpets to reinforce our piffling basses.

Then there is the Japanese theatre orchestra. I daresay you fancy yourself as a master of orchestration; but you should just hear what can be done in the way of producing atmosphere with one banjo string pizzicato and a bicycle bell. But the Chinese will reveal to you the whole secret of opera, which is, not to set a libretto to music, but to stimulate actors to act and declaim. When there is a speech to be delivered, the first (and only) fiddler fiddles at the speaker as if he were lifting a horse over the Grand National jumps; an ear splitting gong clangs at him; a maddening castanet clacks at him; and finally the audience joins in and incites the fiddler to redouble his efforts. You at once perceive that this is the true function of the orchestra in the theatre and that the Wagnerian score is only gas and gaiters.

At this point of writing I learn from the papers that you are flying to Paris to conduct for that amazing young violinist. He is worth it.

I have nothing on at Malvern this time; but we will go down to hear the old plays and cheer up Barry, who has just had to go to bed again, having racketed about too soon. We have also taken out our stewardships for the Hereford Festival; so we shall meet on or near your native heath.

How does the symphony get on? Dont you think you could get two into the time? Remember, you have to catch up on Beethoven.

always
G. Bernard Shaw

To W. NUGENT MONCK

[A/1]

Ayot St Lawrence. Welwyn
4th June 1933

[Nugent Monck (1877–1958) was founder of an amateur company, the Norwich Players, in 1911. Just after the war he converted the interior of the Maddermarket Theatre, Norwich, into an Elizabethan playhouse, where he produced the work of most of the Elizabethan dramatists, including the full Shakespeare canon, staging and appearing in most of the plays himself. There were nine performances of each new production, the actors being unidentified. Many of Shaw's plays were staged there by Monck.]

Dear Nugent Monck

I feel strongly tempted to come and hear Henry VI. It was the great success of this play that set Shakespear up in his profession when it was first produced; and I have always held that it is capable of repeating that success today.

It is now a long time since I have seen you, or the cathedral, or the Maddermarket. . . .

Keep this dark; or I shall be overwhelmed with demands for lectures and lunches and all sorts of publicities that would spoil my visit.

I shall have a car and chauffeur; and my wife will accompany me; so I shall not be travelling en garçon. Bath room suite, with sitting-room and two bedrooms, is the sort of thing, if Norwich runs to it.

faithfully
G. Bernard Shaw

To KATHARINE HECHT

[C/1]

4 Whitehall Court S W 1
9th June 1933

[Katharine Hecht, daughter-in-law of Shaw's friend Max Hecht (1844–1908), financier and theatre investor, had presumably written in reference to Shaw's "Halt, Hitler!" questionnaire-interview published on 4th June in the *Sunday Dispatch*.]

As the Nazis are shouting "Down with the Jew Shaw" in the German theatres, and as a protest against the persecution would have much less value from a Jew, it is necessary for me to emphasize the fact that I am a Gentile, and an Irish Gentile at that, to clear myself of any suspicion of a pro-Jewish bias. I even claim a pro-Nazi, or at least a pro-Fascist bias, to give greater weight to my protest. Otherwise I should seem to be only using the Jew as a stick to beat Hitler, as some of our papers are obviously doing.

G. Bernard Shaw

To ELLEN POLLOCK

[C/1]

Ayot St Lawrence. Welwyn
14th June 1933

[Ellen Pollock (b. 1903), who had played Sweetie in *Too True to be Good*, soon became one of Shaw's favourite actresses, appearing in more Shavian rôles than any of her contemporaries. Shaw here was subtly wooing her, ultimately successfully, for a small but effective rôle, as Aloysia Brollikins in *On the Rocks*, produced by Charles Macdona in London the following November.]

There isn't a woman's part worth tuppence in the wretched thing. You would be wasted on the best of them; so unless you are destitute and out of a job when the time comes—if it ever does—for production I shall not dare to offer you the one little part which I confess I should like you to play.

GBS

To JULIUS BAB

[H/110]

4 Whitehall Court S W 1
29th June 1933

Dear Julius Bab

This is a horrible business; but what can I possibly do? I was greatly distressed when your letter reached me simultaneously with others to the same effect from victims of the persecution. I set aside my work to write an article strongly denouncing the persecution and pointing out that it was not a part of Fascism or any other ism, but a pure phobia, and that it had done the greatest damage to the Nazi cause abroad. I gave this article in the form of an interview to a journalist on whom I could rely to get it published in England and America, and disposed of to Reuters for exploitation on the Continent as far as the Nazi censorship allowed.

343

And now that the article has appeared here and in America, what good has it done? None, as far as I can see, except to the journalist.

I gave your name and address as one of the sufferers to two of the people who are organising relief funds here; but I was informed that it was very difficult to send relief directly, as it would probably be confiscated. And unfortunately one of these gentlemen, a Jew, was so enraged by the persecution that he was furiously attacking the Germans, as such, in terms that recalled the madness of 1914.

The persecution cannot last; and I hope it has already abated. But the magnitude of the catastrophe is beyond individual help: one can only shrug one's shoulders helplessly and try to think of other things. It seems mere mockery to write this to you and to the others who share your misfortune; but perhaps it is better than complete silence. Can you suggest anything?

> faithfully
> G. Bernard Shaw

To LAURENTIA McLACHLAN

[H/98; X/256]

4 Whitehall Court SW 1
29th June 1933

[A strong response from Dame Laurentia to the first-edition copy of the *Black Girl* inscribed to her on 14th December 1932: "Dear Sister Laurentia This black girl has broken out in spite of everything. I was afraid to present myself at Stanbrook in September. Forgive me," was delivered to Shaw at Bangkok in early February. "The Jackdaw of Rheims" is the most famous of all the *Ingoldsby Legends* (1840–47) by the poet Richard Harris Barham (1788–1845), who published under the pseudonym Thomas Ingoldsby.]

Dear Sister Laurentia

I have a wretched tale to tell, and can only hope that you will laugh at it.

I was ridiculously surprised at your reception of The Black Girl story, which I innocently took to be a valuable contribution to the purification of religion from horrible old Jewish superstitions; and even my callousness was pierced by finding that it had shocked and distressed you. On the ship going round the world I wrote you a long letter about it, but could not feel sure that it might not wound you again, and so tore it up.

Then I wrote you another, with the same result after a few days reflection. But at the third attempt I succeeded, or thought I did. It was a long letter; and as I had no typewriter to make it legible for you I wrote it in shorthand for the ship's stenographer to transcribe. Alas, you never received it; for the next thing that happened was a ludicrous catastrophe.

On that ship were hundreds of foolish Canadian and American worshippers of my publicity. Publicity worship sets great store by relics. The notebook in which I had drafted your letter (and others) vanished from my deck chair; and the offer of a guinea to any steward who could find it for me had no result. Your letter is in the collection of some devoutly Shavian thief. Your only remedy is anathema and major excommunication like that which brought the Jackdaw of Rheims to its senses; and for this you are too kind-hearted. Our consolation must be that the thief probably cannot read shorthand; and if he (or she) calls in an expert it cannot be published without infringing my copyright, of which offence certain former legal proceedings of mine have established a wholesome dread in America.

I will not try to reproduce the letter: the moment has passed for that. Besides, I am afraid of upsetting your faith, which is still entangled in those old stories which unluckily got scribbled up on the Rock of Ages before you landed there. So I must go delicately with you, though you need have no such tenderness with me; for you can knock all the story books in the world into a cocked hat without shaking an iota of *my* faith.

Now that I think of it, it was a venial sin to write me such a cruel letter; and I think you ought to impose on yourself the penance of reading The Black Girl once a month for a year. I have a sneaking hope that it might not seem so very wicked the tenth or eleventh time as you thought it at first. You must forgive its superficial levity. Why should the devil have all the fun as well as all the good tunes?

ever your
Brother Bernard

To EMMELINE PETHICK-LAWRENCE

4 Whitehall Court S W 1
[H/52; X/376.e]   4th July 1933

[Emmeline Pethick-Lawrence (1867–1954), wife of the former Labour M.P. and financial secretary to the Treasury under Snowden, F. W. Pethick-Lawrence (1871–1961), invited Shaw to speak at a meeting the following

November in Central Hall, Westminster, which would deal with the question, "Should Married Women Earn?" When Lady Rhondda, in a letter to Mrs Pethick-Lawrence, expressed amazement at Shaw's refusal, he replied: "I quite understand Lady Rhondda's attitude, and sympathise with it. But I am a man, and know how careful women have to be in dealing with men. I support the right of married women to earn. But when it is fully established the women must be careful not to let the men live on their earnings. They will do so if they get half a chance" (*Daily Telegraph*, 3rd November 1933).]

My dear Mrs Pethick Lawrence

Sybil Thorndike has sent on your letter of the 23rd June. Nothing will induce me to speak at a meeting to demand rights for women. I have lost no opportunity of giving The Cause a lift in my writings, and have only just sent off a proof in which I have put in a strong word on the strange survival of celibacy in the Education Office. But, as I have repeatedly explained, my personal vanity will not allow me to be led in triumph by eloquent militant women, and exhibited peeping out between their skirts to squeak out a little patronising piece to the effect that in my masculine opinion they should be indulged with this or that concession, and then patted on the head by them as a good little knight errant and sent home to bed. In the old militant days I saw Zangwill and Laurence Housman and the rest making themselves ridiculous in this manner, and resisted all attempts to lure me into sharing their fate. A pretty figure I should cut at 77 in the Queen's Hall demanding rights for married women. The couvade would be more dignified.

But this will not impress you so much as the fact that the meeting would be entirely spoiled and its significance discounted by the crowd that follows me about caring not two straws whether I am advocating Purdah or Promiscuity. Of speakers you have no shortage: you can easily lay your hand on half a dozen who can wipe the floor with me.

I should be inclined to carry the war into the enemies' country by demanding the exclusion of celibates (except pupil teachers under 20 in elementary schools) from the teaching profession.

A more important matter in these days when the general disgust with Parliament threatens to make the vote quite valueless is the point I used to insist on during the suffrage campaign, but could not gain any notice for—bar some violent abuse from women who had no room in their heads for anything but votes. I maintained that as the vote might not secure the return of a single woman to Parliament, and did in fact secure the return of one only at first, women should agitate for a pro-portion of women on every governing body, whether elected, co-opted, nominated, or picked up in the street like a coroner's jury, provided only their sex was unquestionable. Do not Mussolini, Hitler & Co make you think occasionally that perhaps I was right? What we now have is the spectacle of women's votes keeping women out of Parliament, and Liberia, the negro republic, reviving the slave trade.

What a world!

faithfully
G. Bernard Shaw

To FLORYAN SOBIENIOWSKI

Malvern Hotel. Malvern

[A/2]   24th July 1933

[At a meeting of the Wexford Bee-Keepers Association, Dr G.E.J.Greene on 29th December 1932 proposed that Shaw's name be dropped from the list of members as a consequence of blasphemies about Christ and His Apostles in the *Black Girl*. "A man who made observations that struck with sarcastic ridicule at the very foundations of Christianity," said Dr Greene, "should not be associated even remotely" with their society (*The Times*, 30th December 1932). The matter was adjourned to the following month's AGM, at which time, by a show of hands, the members decided not to hear Dr Greene, and fellow apiarist Shaw remained a Life Member in good standing. It was the Irish Academy of Letters, not the Irish Society of Authors, that sent a deputation to the Minister for Justice.]

Dear Sobieniowski

In England the sale of the Black Girl, roughly 100,000 copies, has not been interfered with in any way. My publisher, Constable & Co, are first rate. My printers (Clarks of Edinburgh) are first rate. There has been, as far as I know, no suggestion of prohibition, prosecution, or censorship of any kind.

The same is true of the United States, where my publishers, an old firm of unchallenged piety and respectability, Dodd Mead & Co, have never dreamt of any difficulty arising.

The County Wexford Bee Keepers' Association is, as its name implies, a harmless little Irish society of village honey sellers of which I happen to be a life-member, which means that on some occasion I gave them a donation of a few guineas. One of their number who had read the Black Girl proposed my expulsion. The rest ridiculed the notion, and he left the room without finding a single supporter. I enclose a letter received (by chance) this morning to shew that I am still a highly esteemed member of the W.B.A.

347

In Ireland (the Irish Free State only) the ultra-clerical Censorship banned the book too late to injure the sales. The Irish Society of Authors sent a deputation to the responsible member of the Cabinet, who said that the objection was not to the book but to the illustrations, which exhibited a nude negress. W.B.Yeats, the poet, then displayed to the Minister a photograph of the ceiling of the Sistine Chapel, full of nude figures. The Minister expressed his surprise (at the profligacy of the Popes, apparently) and the question remains under discussion; but as the Irish Censorship bans many books and authors unchallenged in Poland I do not expect it to give way to a Freethinker of Irish Protestant birth.

In Germany the book is held up because the publisher, Fischer, is a Jew. Trebitsch, brought up as a Protestant, is the son of a Jew. Nazis call me "the Jew Shaw," though I am a Gentile of the Gentiles. Attacks on my books in Poland would be pure Hitlerism.

In France the story has been published (by Éditions Montaigne) without a word of protest.

That is the whole story as far as my information goes.

The Bee Keeper tale of my expulsion, though untrue, was circulated all over the world because it was so extraordinarily ridiculous.

The weather here is as hot as elsewhere, which is unusual in Malvern.

GBS

To LAURENTIA McLACHLAN

Malvern Hotel. Malvern
[H/98; X/256]   24th July 1933

["The fact is," Dame Laurentia wrote on 13th July, "our points of view are so different, that talking, or writing, round the subject can be of little use. The only way to comfort me would be for you to withdraw the Black Girl from circulation, and make a public act of reparation for the dishonour it does to Almighty God. . . . I ask you this first and foremost in the interests of your own soul. I have made myself in some sense responsible for that soul of yours, and I hate to see you dishonour it. . . .

"You know how I value your friendship and how truly I have believed in you. Is this precious thing to be sacrificed to a book that is unworthy of you?" (X/369).]

Sister Laurentia

You are the most unreasonable woman I ever knew. You want me
to go out and collect 100,000 sold copies of The Black Girl, which
have all been read and the mischief, if any, done; and then you want
me to announce publicly that my idea of God Almighty is the anti-
vegetarian deity who, after trying to exterminate the human race by
drowning it, was coaxed out of finishing the job by a gorgeous smell of
roast meat. Laurentia: has it never occurred to you that I might possibly have a more exalted notion of divinity, and that I dont as a matter
of fact believe that Noah's deity ever existed or ever could exist? How
could it possibly comfort you if I declared that I believed in him. It
would simply horrify you. I know much better than you what you
really believe. You think you believe the eighth chapter of Genesis; and
I know you dont: if you did I would never speak to you again. You
think you believe that Micah, when he wrote the eighth verse of his
sixth chapter, was a liar and a blasphemer; but I know that you agree
heartily with Micah, and that if you caught one of your nuns offering
rams and calves and her first-born (if she had one) as a sacrifice to
Jehovah you would have her out of the convent and into the nearest
lunatic asylum before she could say Hail, Mary. You think you are a
better Catholic than I; but my view of the Bible is the view of the
Fathers of the Church; and yours is that of a Belfast Protestant to
whom the Bible is a fetish and religion entirely irrational. You think
you believe that God did not know what he was about when he made
me and inspired me to write The Black Girl. For what happened was
that when my wife was ill in Africa God came to me and said "These
women in Worcester plague me night and day with their prayers for
you. What are you good for, anyhow?" So I said I could write a bit but
was good for nothing else. God said then "Take your pen and write
what I shall put into your silly head." When I had done so, I told you
about it, thinking that you would be pleased, as it was the answer to
your prayers. But you were not pleased at all, and peremptorily forbad
me to publish it. So I went to God and said "The Abbess is displeased."
And God said, "I am God; and I will not be trampled on by any
Abbess that ever walked. Go and do as I have ordered you." I said
"How is she to know that this is not the work of the devil?" "Well"
said God, "if she has not sense enough to know the difference between
my work and the devil's I must have a talk with her." Then Jesus cut
in and said "Do, Lord; for this man, though he is a great fool and
should never be let come near a convent, has taken me off that abominable Roman cross and out of the Chamber of Horrors into the principal

349

show room; so that people will now perhaps begin to listen to my teachings instead of gloating over my agonies." "Well," I said "I suppose I must publish the book if you are determined that I shall; but it will get me into trouble with the Abbess; for she is an obstinate unreasonable woman who will never let me take her out in my car; and there is no use your going to have a talk with her; for you might as well talk to the wall unless you let her have everything all her own way just as they taught it to her when she was a child." So I leave you to settle it with God and his Son as best you can; but you must go on praying for me, however surprising the results may be.

your incorrigible
G. Bernard Shaw

PS Cockerell's friend Sir Emery Walker made a good end on Saturday— was apparently mending comfortably when he just gave a couple of gulps and died. This will be a relief to C., who had to visit him a good deal, as they were old friends and had been business partners. Walker was a most amiable man; but he had lived his life; and it was time for him to die.

And for me also; so do not be unkind to me.

We are here in Malvern as usual for the Festival, though I have no play in the bill this year. There is a miracle play, The Conversion of St Paul, to which you should come with all your nuns.

To OTTO KYLLMANN

[Malvern Hotel. Malvern]

[E.u/64]   [Undated: assigned to 26th July 1933]

[Shaw's note was written on a page proof of the New York lecture, with a title-page reading: "THE POLITICAL MADHOUSE IN AMERICA AND NEARER HOME *A Lecture With an Explanation by* BERNARD SHAW 1933". Kyllmann instructed Clark's the next day to make the suggested alteration. John Farleigh designed lettering for the book's cover (printed paper boards, with a glassine wrapper), but was otherwise uninvolved in its production. When published, it contained no illustrations.]

This won't do, because it suggests an anonymous lecture with an explanation by me. As the whole book is by me there is no need to mention the explanation, as there would be if it applied to a book by somebody else. And there is no publisher's imprint, a pernicious and illegal innovation. The design is all right; but the designer was not supplied with the proper copy. If he is Farleigh, better send him the accompanying corrected page, and ask him to fill in with a picture of me kicking the statue of Liberty off its pedestal.

Drawn by Shaw on a proof leaf.

To OTTO KYLLMANN

Malvern Hotel. Malvern

[A/52; X/391.e]   2nd August 1933

[*The Political Madhouse in America* bore the legend "Price One Florin" on
its cover when published on 29th August.]

When selling a cheap line the first rule is to mark the article with its
price in plain figures. A book by me *might* cost anything up to 7^s/6^d;
and people will be afraid to ask for it unless they know that two bob is
the limit.

Nothing on earth will make a flat tint of white on green look well.
A flat white bit of paper on a tea-rose bush would look like litter.
Orange on green would be all right. If the lettering is to be white the
ground must be Worcester blue. Black would recall the Black Girl and
is therefore ruled out. The green on white, especially that particular
shade of green, gives the book an Irish Roman Catholic air, repellant
to all good Protestants.

If the figure 2/- looks too haberdashery Farleigh might add another
line PRICE ONE FLORIN. "Two shillings" looks and sounds cheap
and nasty, but Florin is Apostolically Imperial and attractively novel.

One should study bookbuyer's psychology.

GBS

To W. B. YEATS

4 Whitehall Court SW1

[H/1]   4th September 1933

My dear Yeats

You can't prosecute a Government: the King can do no wrong. It
is conceivable that a publisher whose stock had been made unsaleable
by a censorial ban might apply to the courts for an order to the censors
to withdraw the ban on the ground that it was an infringement of
public liberty; but the procedure would be expensive and the decision
almost certainly in favor of the censor. If the application went the
whole hog in asking for a declaration that the censorship is unconstitu-
tional the action would be magnified; but so also would be the expense
and the certainty of a triumph for the enemy.

You say that the Academy cannot leave the matter where it is; but
what can it do? When the *force majeure* is on the other side it is the
greatest of mistakes to attempt any sort of compulsion. Articles and

Miltonic essays may be hurled at the Government if the editors and publishers can be induced to print them: that is all. And even that will be a waste of time. I shall not protest: if the Churchmen think my book subversive they are quite right from their point of view. Only, as the word obscene can hardly apply to my text, I wish some member of the Dail would ask Mr Ruttledge whether, if I issue a special edition for Ireland with the negress depicted in long skirts, the ban will be withdrawn.

always
G. Bernard Shaw

To KENNETH MacGOWAN

[4 Whitehall Court SW1]

[Y/109]   27th October 1933

[Negotiations were proceeding smoothly for *The Devil's Disciple*, with Shaw's terms (ten per cent of gross receipts and five year licence) accepted by Mac-Gowan on behalf of RKO on 6th December. Shaw had balked, however, at a proposal of an eighty minute running time for a film version of *Saint Joan*, which he insisted was "suitable only for grand single feature program" (Y/109: 20th October, to MacGowan). Consequently, Katharine Hepburn ended up with Barrie instead of Shaw, in *The Little Minister* (1934).]

FLAT TEN QUITE REASONABLE WITHOUT ADVANCE FIVE YEARS QUITE USUAL IN MY AGREEMENTS JOAN WITH BATTLES AND SIEGES WILL LAST 240 MINUTES TELL THEM WITH MY LOVE TO STOP HAGGLING AND GET TO WORK . . .

SHAW

To SIEGFRIED TREBITSCH

4 Whitehall Court SW1

[H/5; X/341]   21st October 1933

[Hitler had just withdrawn from the Disarmament Conference (first convened at Geneva in February 1932) and from the League of Nations. Engelbert Dollfuss (1892–1934), Austrian chancellor, opposed unification with a Germany under the Nazis. Austrian Nazis assassinated him in 1934.]

353

My dear Trebitsch

You must keep your head clear about this Nazi business. Hitler's withdrawal from the League of Nations and the Disarmament Committee is a masterstroke; and no German, whether he be Austrian or Prussian, can refuse his hearty approval without placing himself in a hopelessly false position. You, as an Austrian, must be in favor of the repudiation of the Treaty of Versailles, and the refusal of any German or Austrian government to remain in any league or international committee in an inferior position. It is by taking this stand that Hitler has rallied the whole German nation to him, and made such an impression in Austria. And on these points you should support Hitler without reserve. It is only by making this clear that you can repudiate Hitler's Judophobia, and his persecution of Social-Democrats and Communists as such, and declare that an Ausgleich is impossible until the German Nazis discard this irrelevant and discreditable side of their program.

Whatever you say, dont treat the question as if Hitler and Dollfus were two gamecocks, and you were backing Dollfus.

The enclosed [statement for *Europäische Revue*, Berlin, on Hitler's withdrawal from the League of Nations] may amuse you. I have to make it clear that in Hitler's last big move I am entirely on his side and against English anti-German Jingoism.

I hope you have arrived safely in Vienna and that Tina finds you looking the better for your journey.

always
G. Bernard Shaw

To KENNETH MacGOWAN

[4 Whitehall Court SW 1]
[Y(draft)/73]   10th November 1933

CONTRACT WILL CONTAIN EXPRESS STIPULATION THAT DICK SHALL NOT BE REPRESENTED AS IN LOVE WITH JUDITH AND SHALL MAKE HIS DECLARATION TO THE CONTRARY WITH ALL POSSIBLE EMPHASIS STOP JUDITH IS PITIABLE AND RATHER CONTEMPTIBLE NOT FLAMBOYANT IF THIS IS AGREED GO AHEAD WITH SCRIPT AND PUBLICITY SEND LONDON ADDRESS

SHAW

To MARGARET MACKAIL

4 Whitehall Court SW1
[C/83; X/378]   11th November 1933

[Margaret Mackail, eldest daughter of Sir Edward Burne-Jones and wife of the classical scholar John W. Mackail (1859–1945), had presumably solicited Shaw to lend his name to an appeal for a children's hospital.]

Yes: by all means. But as the world is not at present fit for children to live in why not give the little invalids a gorgeous party, and when they have eaten and danced themselves to sleep, turn on the gas and let them all wake up in heaven?

G. Bernard Shaw

To JOHN BARRYMORE

4 Whitehall Court SW1
[S/111; X/379]   14th November 1933

[John Barrymore, writing to Shaw on 30th October, hinted that he would vastly prefer to come to England with his family and work in a film there directly under Shaw's supervision and guidance than to make the film in Hollywood. By implication he may have been seeking to get *The Devil's Disciple* or any other Shaw play for himself, cutting RKO out.]

Dear John Barrymore

I am out of the film world here, being Victorian and very old, and yet too advanced for the poor things. Until lately the film work done here was not as good as at Hollywood. It is better now, and will be better still later on, as it is the English way to do nothing until others have made all the experiments and found out the way, and then go ahead with it strongly. And it may be that the development of the movie into the international talkie may operate in favor of the studios which are within easy reach of Paris, Rome, Berlin etc. as against remote Hollywood.

On the whole, I think it is not so much the question of which is the best professional centre as to where you would like to live and have your children educated. And that takes a good deal of consideration. I dare not advise you. The world is in such a mess at present; and our profession is such a desperately precarious one at all times that one can only laugh when one is advised to act prudently.

R.K.O., through Macgowan, has been sounding me on the subject

355

of films for a year past. I suggested The Devil's Disciple as the best selection, provided you could be induced to play Dick Dudgeon. This has just come to a head; and my terms are accepted; but there is one stipulation which I have sprung on them too lately to receive a reply. That is, that Dick must not be represented as being in love with Judith. If you have read the play you will understand that Judith is a snivelling little goody-goody, as pathetically pretty as she pleases, and spoilt and conceited enough to imagine that Dick has faced the gallows for her sake instead of "by the law of his own nature." But the least suggestion that he was prowling after her instead of standing up to her husband would belittle him unbearably and reduce the whole affair to third rate Hollywood sobstuff. Unless I can knock this into R.K.O. the bargain may fall through; but by the time you receive this you will either have been offered the engagement, which will shew that my stipulation has been accepted, or else the deal is off.

faithfully
G. Bernard Shaw

To BASIL LIDDELL HART

[H/129]
4 Whitehall Court SW1
15th December 1933

[(Sir) Basil Liddell Hart (1895–1970), author and military correspondent for the *Daily Telegraph* 1925–35 and later for *The Times*, had sent Shaw the manuscript of his book *T. E. Lawrence: In Arabia and After* (1934). For Feisul I, see headnote to letter of 31st May 1923 to Stanley Baldwin.]

Dear L. H.

I have read the chapters that are in question . . .

If I were the author I should rewrite these chapters . . . because they violate my rules as a playwright: that is, abstracting stage technique, a story teller. One of the most important of these rules is that you must not introduce, or even mention if you can avoid it, any character who is not a live wire in the story. You have discarded this rule recklessly. Those chapters are like mess tables at dinner: they are crowded with officers who might as well be sentries or lorry drivers for all they have to do with the story. Why do you insist on introducing them all to me? I dont want to know them; I forget their names before I have turned the page; they do not carry the tale a step farther. Some of them you introduce as nonentities, which is a reason for not introducing them.

Others you introduce as nuisances, which only makes you one more enemy, and is an abuse of the literary pillory, as nothing comes of it. All this is mere military shop of the worst kind. Your speciality is serious military shop, which I take to be military art and science.

Now the point which is obscured by the intrusion of all these military boobs or even capable officers who only cross the stage and disappear, is that the professional soldiers all faced the Arabian problem as one of forces detached from the west for a military occupation to conduct regular operations against the Turkish regulars, and to hold down the natives meanwhile. [Field Marshal Sir William] Robertson saw it this way, and decided against it. He was perfectly right. . . . The professional soldiers were all right from their point of view. This needs to be made quite clear (it is not fair to imply that poor Robertson was a fool merely because T.E's subsequent triumph made him look like one); and, when it is clear, then the interesting question arises, at what point did T.E. get his illumination as to keeping the regulars out of it and starting a gangster campaign with Arab gunmen on British money, with Feisal as figure head . . . I dont know when this occurred: no doubt it smouldered for some time before it burst into flame. My guess is that it was the meeting with Feisal that produced complete conviction. (I have just met T.E. and asked him. He says it was even later than the meeting with Feisal, and that he made this plain in the Seven Pillars.) The chapters in my opinion should concentrate on this situation and be cleared of all the military supers. No matter how interesting some of them are, they have no business in the book unless they played a decisive part in the history of the revolt.

I have read the addenda you have just sent. I think you had better make it clear that the charming voice is not the voice of an orator, and that T.E., in spite of his interest in history, has apparently none whatever in politics and is almost aggressively indifferent to the arts of the platform. The enthusiasts who think he may yet redeem Israel as a Messiah or a Mahomet have nothing to go on . . . [T]hough there is no saying what T.E. might or might not do if he gave his mind to it, he has shewn no sign of having ever given his mind to revolutionary politics and seems much more interested in Ezra Pound than in Karl Marx.

I write this in great haste; and you must not mind if it is all criticism. . . .

faithfully
G. Bernard Shaw

357

To NAOMI MITCHISON

4 Whitehall Court S W 1
20th December 1933

[A/112]

[Naomi Mitchison (b. 1897), daughter of J. S. Haldane, was a prolific writer of fiction. When an enthusiast of her work decided her name should be proposed for the Nobel Prize for Literature, she petitioned Shaw to supply her with a testimonial for submission to the Swedish Academy. Shaw had earlier written such a letter (unsolicited) recommending Upton Sinclair for the prize, "and thereby probably extinguished any chance he ever had of getting it" (A/112: 15th December 1933, to Naomi Mitchison).]

My dear Naomi

Damn it, no: I can't do this. You don't "go in for" the Nobel Prize as if it were a Cross Word competition. It is supposed to come as a spontaneous recognition of effulgent excellence, visible at Stockholm like the sun in the heavens. It cannot be asked for nor canvassed for. Of course it *is* asked for: a number of persons expressed their opinions that Thomas Hardy and Upton Sinclair were eligible; but this was general news that was assumed to be within the field of the Academy's attention. I never heard of any individual writing to the Academy "Take my tip: Naomi for the Nobel." As to saying simply that you are an author, that would imply that the fact is a secret instead of a European phenomenon. It would do more harm than good, and would be a horrible solecism: at least that is what I feel about it.

Your wangler must think of something else. Can't she write a private letter and quote me?

You should never rewrite a book. It's much shorter to write another.

In haste: this is a yell
rather than a letter
GBS

To SIEGFRIED TREBITSCH

4 Whitehall Court S W 1
22nd December 1933

[H/5; X/341]

[Werner Krauss (1884–1959), noted Austrian actor who had played King Magnus, was apparently seeking official approval for Max Reinhardt to direct *On the Rocks* at the Deutsches Theater despite the fact that Reinhardt, a Jew, had cautiously left Germany in March 1933 and been removed as head of the

Deutsches Theater a month later. Mrs Baker-Eddy was Mary Baker Eddy (1821–1910), founder of the Christian Science movement.]

My dear Trebitsch

I am very uneasy about this business of On The Rocks and Reinhardt. If he is let go within ten miles of the play, he will turn it into an intrigue between the Prime Minister and his secretary, and use the table as a cover for indecent liberties between the Duke and Aloysia. My reputation suffered greatly in Germany from his version of The Apple Cart. You must just tell W.K. that I will not have On The Rocks produced by Reinhardt. Tell him I have too much respect for his great talent and dignity as an artist to allow him to be placed under the direction of our friend Max, who revels in pornographic farce and has no respect for actors and actresses. . . .

Now as to politics. I tried to dissuade you from going to Berlin; but I guessed that you would go; so I fired my shot in the Europaisches Revue just in time. I am informed that Colonel Goebbels, on being asked why my plays were out of favor, declared that I am *persona gratissima* in Berlin, and that my plays are welcome "when they are not opposed to Nazi principles."

You must bear in mind that Hitler began his career as a strong pro-German and anti-Slav, all for the Ausgleich and against Jugo Slavia and Czechoslovakia and the rest of the non-German elements. This was hopeless under Franz Josef and the Archduke; but when the war cut off the Jugoslavs and Czechoslavs, and left Vienna like a starving shepherd whose sheep had all run away, the case for the Ausgleich—Hitler's case—was enormously strengthened. Mussolini objects because his Brenner frontier is an ethnological outrage, easier to maintain against poor crippled Vienna than against a united and belligerent German Reich. Hitler, who needs Mussolini's friendship just at present, does not want to stir up this question; but it will arise inevitably sooner or later. I think if I were in your place I should advocate a union with Germany, which would please Berlin, though I should denounce anti-Semitism and all the nonsense about Nordics and Latins as bogus ethnology and bad biology.

Fascism, or the organisation of the State as a hierarchy of industrial and professional corporations, is right as far as it goes; but what real power will the corporations have unless they own the land and control the industries—unless, that is, the State is Socialist as well as Fascist? Therefore the persecution of Socialists as Socialists is even sillier than the persecution of Jews *qua* Jews; for if Fascism is to come to anything it must come to Communism finally. The alternative is a bourgeois republic in which the Corporations would be the tools of the financiers and their industrial allies just as the parliamentary Cabinets are. If you meddle in politics at all, keep these leading considerations in your head. You may be challenged to explain my views, if not your own.

As to the title of On the Rocks you must, I think, use the words uttered by the Admiral and Blee [about being "off the rocks" or "on the rocks"] . . . The title must give the situation, and not any particular person. Why not Auf dem Trocknen?

I have been trying to write this letter for weeks past; but the production of the play and the arrears of business and correspondence that accumulated during the rehearsals made it impossible for me to write anything longer than a postcard. Even now I have to write hurriedly, in great distraction; so you must make allowances. My new volume, containing three plays [*Too True to be Good, Village Wooing,* and *On the Rocks*] and two important prefaces has just gone to press, and will be published here [on 15th February 1934] as soon as the American edition is ready. What about Fischer?

always
G. Bernard Shaw

PS. On the back of this sheet you will find the answers to your questions about the text of On the Rocks. . . . You suggest Mrs Baker-Eddy as a future heroine. But she is in On the Rocks as the lady doctor!

To W. B. YEATS

Ayot St Lawrence. Welwyn
[C/5]   14th January 1934

[The Irish Academy, through Yeats, had invited Shaw to adjudicate the 1933 Harmsworth Award. When he declined, John Masefield was invited in his stead, and accepted.]

This prizegiving business has no sense in it. It is a schoolmaster's job. He can give 10 marks for grammar, 10 for punctuation, 10 for history (if any), 10 for geography, 10 for accuracy of imagination, 10 for good taste, 10 for orthodoxy, 10 for quantity (or brevity), 10 for probability, 10 for shocklessness, & 20 for soporificity.

Failing a schoolmaster, get a boxing referee, accustomed to declare winners "on points."

Anyhow you wont get *me*.

The prize should be for the worst English novel. That would at least amuse the public. Donkey races are always popular.

G. Bernard Shaw

To ROBERT YOUNG

[Ayot St Lawrence. Welwyn]
[X/380]   14th January 1934

[Young was fishing, successfully, for a publicity release for his Northampton Repertory Company production of *A Doll's House*.]

The adjective "epoch making" is so hackneyed that it has almost lost its literal meaning; but Ibsen's Doll's House was really "epoch making." Young people today cannot imagine the impression it made in England in 1889. It was the same all over Europe. The stage has never been quite the same since. It killed Queen Victoria, though she never saw it and probably never read it.

G. Bernard Shaw

To CHARLES A. SIEPMANN

4 Whitehall Court SW1
[A/99]   18th January 1934

[Charles A. Siepmann (1899–1985) was director of talks for the B.B.C. from 1932 to 1935. He later became professor of education at New York University. Shaw's talk was the fifth in a series titled "Whither Britain?" broadcast on 6th February. In April the Labour Party issued it as a pamphlet titled *Are We Heading for War?*]

Dear Mr Siepman

I was disappointed when they told me that I had taken 34 minutes to make the record. I had read it to my wife the night before in 31. If the result is not satisfactory I can have another shot at it.

May I suggest that now is the time to turn on Sir Oswald Mosley, if you have not already included him. He is said to be a very good speaker; and he puts real work into his speeches.

You will have to warn the politicians that their platform bunk is no use on the wireless. They are so accustomed to stoking up audiences of excited partisans that they have no notion of how to handle millions of innocent non-politicians sitting quietly by their firesides. Besides, the mike gives away the least insincerity mercilessly.

I did not feel at all neglected; and I beg you never to think it necessary to attend to me. Treat me just as you would the man who comes to read the gas meter or wind the clocks; and do not let me waste your time, which must be pretty heavily taxed.

I have been approached by a firm of publishers about the broadcast. But why on earth doesn't the BBC publish these series itself just as it does the Listener and the year books and the other things? It could appoint some publisher as its official agent: for instance, Stanley Unwin, who has absorbed Williams & Norgate, who published for Herbert Spencer and other highbrows.

faithfully
G. Bernard Shaw

To KENNETH MacGOWAN

Ayot St Lawrence. Welwyn
[C/109; X/379]   22nd January 1934

[Gene Fowler, in *Good Night, Sweet Prince* (1954), misidentified the recipient of this postcard as John Barrymore. Shaw had stipulated in the agreement that he have script approval. A copy of the screenplay of *The Devil's Disciple* had now been sent to him.]

— Private —

I am sorry for the delay of the D's D.; but it is inevitable. As you know, the differences between first rate work and shop routine are often microscopic and seem to the routineer to be quite unimportant; but they are just what the first rate man earns his eminence by. I have only glanced through the opening pages of the scenario; but it has been enough to convince me that I must put in about a months work (or leisure) on it before any attempt is made to rehearse or shoot it. I can only hope that when I return to London in May I shall have something to send you on which you can set to work.

I see I shall have to educate Hollywood. It means well; but it doesn't know how to make an effect and leave it alone. It wallows in it fifteen seconds too long, and then starts to explain it. It can't find the spiritual *track* of a story and keep to it. And it can't tell a story. I've never yet seen an American film that was intelligible to me all through. And it doesn't know the difference between a call boy and a playwright.

G.B.S.

To SIDNEY WEBB

Ayot St Lawrence. Welwyn
[A/14; X/391.e]   30th January 1934

[Beatrice Webb's illness and catastrophic market conditions had put a severe drain on the Webbs' finances. Shaw, sensing their need, instructed his banker to pay £1000 into Sidney Webb's account. "I am overwhelmed," Webb wrote to Shaw on 29th January, when informed of the credit by his bank. "If there is no mistake in the amount, and if it is really a gift—well, words fail me to express our gratitude. It comes most timely to remove our anxieties. . . . It is a long time since we first met at the Zetetical Society [in 1879] . . . It led to nearly half a century of a friendship & companionship, which has been most fruitful to me. I look back on it with wonder at the advantage, and indeed, the beauty of that prolonged friendship. Apart from marriage, it has certainly been the biggest thing in my life; which without it would have been poor indeed" (A/2).

Shaw had recorded his "Whither Britain?" talk on 13th January. Simultaneously with the recorded broadcast to England on 6th February, he delivered the talk live for relay to the NBC network in America.]

My dear Sidney

The figure is correct; and of course the money will come in handy; but the function of the cheque is purely therapeutic. Nobody can resist the bucking effect of a thousand pounds in a lump; and my clinical instinct told me that this was the moment to administer it. The minutest push towards recovery is so priceless that thousands are as twopences in comparison. Beatrice will laugh at this; but it is biologically quite sound. . . .

The balancing instinct in Nature is remarkable. Alarmed at her work in 1856 she produced you three years later as my complement. It was one of her few successes.

We shall be away only three months—back in May.

I am dead beat, as I have been working pretty continuously for the

363

last nine months; and so is Charlotte; but the last voyage was a success as to our health; and I daresay this one will be no worse.

Note that my broadcast this day week, being from a record, is illegal in America. So I shall have to speak it all over again for the benefit of the Americans whilst the wax record is quacking it out to the British Isles. Beatrice should bear this in mind next time she broadcasts, if there is any question of America.

GBS

To SIEGFRIED TREBITSCH

[4 Whitehall Court SW1]

[E/5; X/341]   5th February 1934

[*England erwache* is a translation of the title of the song "England, Arise," with lyrics by Edward Carpenter, sung at the end of *On the Rocks*. The final German title for the play was *Festgefahren*. The Shaws began another long sea voyage on the 8th, sailing from Tilbury in the RMS *Rangitane*, their destination New Zealand.]

Yes: I think "England, erwache" a *much better* title than On the Rocks, though it seems odd that it should be preferred in Germany. So by all means adopt it.

We start for N.Z. this week: on Thursday the 8th. The voyage will take 4 weeks; we shall be a month on shore; and then 4 weeks return voyage will land us back again in England about the middle of May.

Miss Patch will remain on duty meanwhile.

I am in a fearful hurry packing.

Our love to Tina.

Auf wiedersehen!

GBS

To NANCY ASTOR

Passing Southampton or thereabouts

[A/101]   9th February 1934

[The Shaws had lunched with the Astors in London on the 6th, preparatory to their departure; other guests were Lloyd George and Elisabeth Bergner. Sean O'Casey (1880–1964) and his wife Eileen had become good friends with the Shaws. GBS had read all of O'Casey's plays and seen London performances of a few of them, notably *The Silver Tassie* ("What a hell of a play!"

he wrote to O'Casey), produced by Charles Cochran in 1929. O'Casey's newest play *Within the Gates* opened two nights earlier at the Royalty Theatre.]

Dearest Nancy

I find that we call at Plymouth for mails; so I am able to send this note to you . . .

Sean is all right now that his shift from the Dublin slums to Hyde Park has shewn that his genius is not limited by frontiers. His plays are wonderfully impressive and *reproachful* without being irritating like mine. People fall crying into one another's arms saying God forgive us all! instead of refusing to speak and going to their solicitors for a divorce.

The sea has been flatter than the round pond; but Charlotte is not yet up (11 a.m.) and woke up only for a moment to tell me to send her fondest love to you.

She isn't lonely. Any woman married to me would be only too glad to be in that enviable state.

Pity you are not in Plymouth. I could wave to you.

sempre
GBS

To KENNETH MacGOWAN

Mid Atlantic—outward bound
[A/109]   15th February 1934

[The *Rangitane* was six days away from Kingston, and eight from the Panama Canal. It stopped at Pitcairn Island on 5th March, crossed the international dateline on the 14th ("Dies non" Shaw entered for this date in his pocket diary), and arrived in Auckland on 15th March.

Lester Cohen (1901–63) was an author whose novel *Sweepings* was filmed by RKO in 1933 in his own adaptation, the latter being described by Richard B. Jewell in *The RKO Story* (1982) as "stuffy and lugubrious." His screenplay for *The Devil's Disciple* was abysmal. The next year, deprived of Shaw, he did his damndest to wreak havoc on Somerset Maugham's *Of Human Bondage*.]

Dear Kenneth Macgowan

I have now read through Mr Lester Cohen's play; and I must tell you at once that the deal is off. I part with R.K.O., I hope, on the friendliest terms; but we are hopeless incompatibles artistically. You will hardly be surprised at this. I am an old and highly skilled and experienced hand in the making of stage effects. They are blundering novices, with the technique of the lecturer and the magic lantern. They are entirely illiterate, and think that eighteenth century English must be changed into Hollywood slipshod to be intelligible. They have no suspicion that even Hollywood slipshod must be speakable and rhythmical before it is any use to an actor. They cannot distinguish between dramatic poetry by a first class author and a paraphrase by the nearest chatterbox. They deal with a famous author for his publicity without the faintest sense of the quality of his work. They put the artistic work —except the photography—into the hands of unskilled fans, and have consequently no technique; only a tradition of blunders which make the simplest story unintelligible, and waste miles of film on senseless details which only check the impetus of the drama and distract the spectator. And to make time for these they omit the crucially interesting passages.

Someday they will have to face the difficulty that if they undertake to film a first class play, they must either take it as it is, as they would take the work of any other expert, or else get a first rate author to produce it: a practical impossibility, as first rate authors have their own work to do. It is sometimes possible, however, to find young men —future first classes like Shakespeare cobbling up Henry VI—with taste and talent enough to be trusted with the production of fine work. Failing such, there is nothing for it but to assume that the author knows his job, and stand or fall by it. That is, of course, unless the author can stand by and produce his work himself, which is the ideal plan.

I cannot do this: I am too old; and the very few effective years which remain to me must not be squandered in studios. As to revising RKO versions written apparently to show me how RKO would have done it, I cannot be expected to lend a hand to my own murder. If RKO were to order a picture from, say, Augustus John, I have no doubt that they would have it at once repainted to their taste by a local sign painter; but if they asked Augustus to touch up the sign painter's work and put his name to it he would probably find a better and more congenial use for his time in painting new masterpieces.

When I went into this matter I was dealing with you on the strength of your published work. I do not know why you handed me over to Mr Lester Cohen, who seems to me a very different sort of writer. That RKO thinks him superior to you I can well believe, as they evidently think him very far superior to me. They might be right; but his ways are not my ways; and there is no accounting for tastes. I suggest they commission him to write a play of his own to fill the gap left by my withdrawal of The Devil's Disciple, which will either remain unfilmed or go into the hands of a corporation which likes it better than RKO.

I presume you have copies of the scenario and that I need not return the one you sent me. The truth is, I have scrawled it with comments which do more justice to my own feelings than to the work of my fellow-playwright Mr Cohen. . . .

And now I shall begin a new play and forget and forgive. RKO can do the forgetting and I the forgiving.

sincerely
G. Bernard Shaw

To G. M. HENDERSON

RMS Rangitane
Wellington to London
[A/113]   18th April 1934

[There are fewer surviving letters in this period than for any other of Shaw's voyages of the 1930s, and most of them consist merely of acknowledgments of books (several of which were donated to the ship's library) and photographs; some inconsequential publishing business; and a condolence message. George Macdonald Henderson (1876–?) was a New Zealander who later (1948) published a book *The Antecedents and Early Life of Valentine Savage, Known as Taina.* "Pakeha" is the Maori term for a member of the white race, meaning "foreigner." Shaw, having expressed the belief that most Maori music was adapted from European sources, was persuaded to attend a private concert at the home of a Maori, Guide Rangi, in Whakarewarewa (Rotorua), on 28th March. Although a condition of his attendance was that he could depart after performance of the first piece, which was entirely of Maori origin, he and Charlotte remained for the entire evening.]

Dear Mr Henderson
The truth is I had to fight the tendency to assume that I had come to N.Z. to study the Maoris. The Pakeha was my game.

At the School of Arts and Crafts near Auckland (or was it Rotorua?) I found a Maori workman who could sing Maori music—*not* Maori words to the tune of Just a Song at Twilight. It was practically a Gregorian chant with a touch of the pibroch, not primitive music, but almost effetely civilized music.

367

At the tourist concert at Rotorua, which I was induced to attend only by a promise of at least one turn of genuine Maori music, they gave us some rhythms without melody. Some of them were Spanish. These they gave with great precision and enjoyment, as they did all the German waltz tunes (early XIX century) and *ländler* and barcarolles in which they delight. In Auckland a half blooded lady treated me to several of these without, as far as I could gather, the least suspicion that she was not singing the primitive music of her remotest half-ancestors.

I was interested in the Maori vowels; but so much of the poetry has been printed with translations that I did not worry about it.

Many thanks for your letter.

faithfully
G. Bernard Shaw

To NANCY ASTOR

RMS Rangitane
Wellington to London
[A/101; X/373.e]   28th April 1934

[The civic reception at Christchurch was headed by Mayor D. G. Sullivan, a Labour MP. Shaw's broadcast on 2YA, Wellington (New Zealand Broadcasting Service), on 12th April, was titled "Shaw Speaks to the Universe." Sir Frederic Truby King (1858–1938) was founder of the Royal New Zealand Society for the Health of Women and Children and of the Karitane Hospital. He was director of child welfare 1921–27. The En-zeds (i.e., N.Z.) were the ruling European (white) inhabitants of the islands.]

My dear Nancy
    If the engines dont break down again (the ship is too full) we should be in the Thames on the 17th. But I am not sure. We lost a day in starting to take a lot of what are called naval ratings. They turned out to be human beings. Perhaps we shall dump them at Plymouth, though we do not stop there officially.
    When we are near enough to know with some sort of exactness the day of our arrival I will send Miss Patch a wireless.
    Although New Zealand actually has a law prohibiting the landing of any person who has recently visited Russia I had the same Royal Progress as we had in the U.S.S.R. After a week in Auckland I positively refused to visit any other city except Wellington, from which I

had to sail. Nevertheless at the last moment I made a dash south for Christchurch. The Mayor waylaid us 30 miles out; and after a civic reception (broadcast) I returned to Wellington a pitiable old wreck, and only escaped a second one by inviting the Mayor to lunch and pleading extreme exhaustion.

I wish you and Waldorf had been with us. There is a municipal milk supply in Wellington, and an amazing maternity welfare institution centering on a strange old genius, Sir Truby King, with the result that the infant mortality rate in N.Z. is *less than half* the English rate. I wished extremely you had been with me there. And the agricultural problems would have filled all Waldorf's time. You both ought to have a look at this queer Empire at close quarters. Tramping the deck for exercise and playing childish deck games is not worse than the division lobbies. The En-zeds are intensely imperial-patriotic, and call England HOME. Their devotion takes the form of expecting us to exclude all butter and wool except theirs; to wage tariff wars against all Powers refusing to do likewise; to fight all Asiatic States who demand access to the island[,] which is piously Victorian but [which] resolutely birth-controlling British inhabitants resolutely refuse to populate; and to allow all their exports freely into England whilst they pile up protective duties against us and buy freely from Czechoslovakia, China, and anywhere else where we are undersold.

If England makes an alliance with Japan, which lots of our Diehards are quite capable of doing, the United States will have to make a counter-alliance with Russia, and then Australasia will have to chuck the silly Empire and join the U.S.A. Likewise Canada. But you have to get into the Pacific to realize how possible this is. If Russia were to relapse into predatory Capitalism and Communism to be rooted out of China, a dangerous situation would develop with terrific rapidity. Consequently it is our business to back up Communist Russia and China for all we are worth. But people think I say this because I am a Communist, whereas it is the most obvious Conservative Balance-of-Power diplomacy. I must therefore leave it to you and Waldorf to wave the red flag.

I am flying this letter from Panama to New York; but it wont reach you more than a few days ahead of ourselves. Charlotte is longing to see you. I am moderately eager myself.

sempre a te
G. Bernard Shaw

To APSLEY CHERRY-GARRARD

RMS Rangitane
Wellington NZ to London
[A/3]   1st May 1934

[The play and a half that Shaw had written were *The Simpleton of the Un-expected Isles*, commenced on 16th February, eight days out from London, and completed " In the open Pacific Lat. 16° 28′ Long 106° 19′ " on 26th April; and *The Millionairess*, begun the next day. Shaw completed the draft of the latter on 10th May. The *Rangitane* docked at Plymouth on 17th May. The Wilson book was George Seaver's *Edward Wilson of the Antarctic* (1933), with an introduction by Cherry-Garrard. (Sir) Joseph Kinsey (1852–1936) was shipping agent in New Zealand for Scott's expedition in 1910. The Governor-General of New Zealand was Charles Bathurst (1867–1958), first Baron (later first Viscount) Bledisloe of Lydney.]

My dear Cherry

We have just crossed the line in the cloudy English looking weather usual in this no-latitude; and by flying this letter to New York from Panama, which we expect to reach tomorrow, we can get it to Lamer a few days ahead of our landing. We are late, as we had to wait for a crew of naval ratings before leaving Wellington, and in mid-Pacific one of our engines went out of action and slowed us down for a day or so; but if nothing else untoward happens we shall be at Ayot on Whit Sunday.

The weather has been remarkably quiet. The channel was as smooth as a billiard table; and we have not missed a single meal. The ship is the steadiest I ever was on. I have written a play and a half up to date and read a good deal, including the Wilson book, which, with your assistance, seems to me pretty well done. It also gives you a show which was impossible in your own book, which must have left many readers wondering who C-G. was, and how the devil he came to be with the expedition. The picture is without shadow, except one counts hard-ships: a little malice would have been a relief occasionally; but on the whole the job is as good a one as is possible while there are survivors; and evidently there is nothing but good to be said of Wilson.

After an exhausting reception in Auckland I insisted on all cities being struck out of our tour; but at the last moment we made a dash for Christchurch, where we looked up Kinsey and were received by him with shouting geniality. He has abandoned the house you remember and now lives in a street of villas, where he collects everything with appalling indiscriminateness. He was greatly pleased at our seeking him out, and at your remembering him.

As "persons who have recently visited Communist countries" can be refused landing by the Government, there was lively press discussion as to what would happen to me; but my reception was overwhelming. The dockers cheered us as we came down the gangway; the Governor General entertained us; the cities invited us to civic receptions; the universities invited me to give one of their annual orations; the Maoris serenaded us with their native music, which turned out to be "Just a song at twilight"; my broadcasts were carte blanche without a hint of censorship: in short, I escaped by the skin of my teeth from dying of my vogue. Charlotte blooms like the rose, and was idealized by N.Z. to its heart's content and her occasional exasperation.

More when we meet. The weather reports from England have been hideous; but we hope to find you completely re-established.

GBS

To DINO GRANDI

[U(A)/1]

Ayot St Lawrence. Welwyn
28th May 1934

[(Count) Dino Grandi (b. 1895), former minister of foreign affairs, was Italian ambassador to Britain. Shaw's Italian agent, as well as translator since the death of Antonio Agresti, was Cesare Castelli. The Rt. Hon. Sir Henry Norman (1858–1939), coal magnate, former journalist, and would-be playwright, was married to the Hon. Florence McLaren, sister-in-law of Christabel, friend of Charlotte.

Grandi's effort to obtain censorship concessions for Shaw in Italy had repercussions when, in November 1935, the press reported the Minister of Propaganda at Rome as saying that Shaw was the only playwright besides Shakespeare to be exempted from "intellectual counter-sanctions" because "he is the most brilliant and anti-British of all living British dramatists." Shaw immediately issued a rejoinder through a reporter for the *Manchester Guardian*, which was published on 29th November 1935: "It is very flattering to be associated with Shakespeare, but I could not accept authorisation to perform my plays on the ground that I am 'the most anti-British' of writers. I consider myself one of Britain's best friends, and would refuse to have my plays performed on that ground. I have instructed my agents not to apply for any exceptions in my favour to the Italian intellectual counter-sanctions. I am quite friendly to Italy, but I cannot accept the position of an anti-British author."]

371

Excellency

I have to thank you infinitely for what you have done for me in the matter of the Censorship. I have communicated the substance of your very kind letter to my Italian agent, who will henceforth revere me as privilegiatissimo. I have only just returned from New Zealand or I should have made this acknowledgment sooner.

My wife is in bed with bronchial trouble. It is not serious; but for the moment we are not accepting any invitations for evenings. The truth is, we are too old to dine out. Once a year perhaps we may dine with very ancient friends like the Normans; but you know what happened to me even at their house. Your lady graciously came and spoke to me. I lost my head completely and tried to speak in Italian (which I cannot speak). The result was a stammering in very bad French (I am the worst of linguists—not like you, who speak English better than any Englishman). It was evident to the Signora Grande that I was very drunk; and the conversation ended abruptly before I recovered my presence of mind. That is what happens to old old men when they dine out instead of going to bed. My wife and I have decided that the age limit for dining out is 75. Beyond that they are bores and dotards. And alas! Charlotte and I are nearer 80 than 75.

But we can still keep up a sort of ghastly affectation of youthfulness until about 4 in the afternoon; and if at any time you are giving a quiet luncheon party, and two of your guests disappoint you at the last moment, we should not shrink from the two vacant chairs.

Our days in London are Thursdays, Fridays & Saturdays. The rest of the time I work in the country.

You must visit the Pacific to get the true orientation of Japan. If England makes an alliance with Japan (as some of her anti-Stalins would like) the British Empire will crack up like a dropped basin. Australasia will join Canada in an alliance with the United States against the Jap; and the U.S. will be forced into an alliance with Russia. The way has been paved by Litvinoff. Have you considered what Italy will do in such an event? If you have, dont tell me, as I am incapable of keeping diplomatic (or any other) secrets.

faithfully and gratefully
G. Bernard Shaw

To CHRISTINA WALSHE

4 Whitehall Court SW1
30th May 1934

[Christina Walshe, like Rutland Boughton, had espoused communism. Shaw's reply to Philip Snowden was a letter headed "Our 'Communists,'" in the *Daily News*, 12th June 1925. Elgar had died on 23rd February.]

My dear Christina

What more can I do for Communism than I am doing? I went to Russia to be able to speak with the authority (such as it is) of the man who has been on the spot. Since then I have gone round the world and paid a special visit to New Zealand, shouting that I am a Communist and urging in season and out of season that even on the most old-fashioned Balance of Power diplomatic lines it is our interest to back up Communism in Russia and China. I have given every scrap of my support for what it is worth to Russia. I did so in the black days of 1921, when I sent Lenin a book of mine with an inscription, lithographs of which can still be obtained in Moscow. There is no public man in England more completely committed to Communism, and in particular to the support of the Russian system, than I.

But the whole value of my support depends on my behaving sensibly and understanding what I am talking about. When Philip Snowden denounced "the Communists" as angrily as Hitler denounces "the Marxists" I protested publicly against this confusion of tongues, pointing out that if the Labor Party was not Communist it was nothing. I knew perfectly well that "the Communists" were making intolerable nuisances of themselves and doing no good whatever, because they did not know the A.B.C. of their political business, and were mostly not really Communists at all, but only incorrigible frondeurs. When a bunch of them were arrested and imprisoned for six months I went bail for Gallagher; but I knew that he had no business to be in the dock, and had put his head in the lion's mouth unnecessarily and uselessly. He and the rest were also in the hopelessly false position of being in the pay of Moscow and recognizing it as their Vatican, thereby not only placing themselves at the mercy of the police as agents of a foreign Power, but making any sort of headway in a strongly Nationalist country like England impossible. Communism in Britain must be as British as the Fabian Society before it can have the slightest weight internationally. In short, your "Communist Party" as it calls itself, behaves in such a way that I could not touch it without losing the little

373

influence I have in fighting the battles of Communism and of Russia *contra mundum.*

Now, as I gather from your letter and from other sources, the C.P. thinks of nothing but fighting the Fascists. But they should not have attacked the Fascists. Before any serious changes can be made in England, the Parliamentary party system, with its mask of democracy, liberty, and all the rest of it, must be smashed, and replaced by a constitution which will have a good deal in common not only with the Russian constitution but also with our own municipal government and with the Corporate State of Mussolini and the National Socialist State of Hitler. As against our Parliamentary pretences Communists, Fascists and Nazis have a common cause. The blind attack on Fascism in the name of Liberty is not Communism: it is oldfashioned Radicalism and Anarchism.

Consequently I will not give you money to fight the Fascists: I had much rather give it to Rutland, who, after some years of obscurity as a pig farmer, is trying to resurrect himself and Glastonbury in Gloucestershire, and making raids into London as a teacher of singing. Now that Elgar is gone, all the other composers emerge from his mighty shadow and go up one. Besides, public memory is very short in politics; and Rutland the Communist never made as much impression as Rutland of The Immortal Hour; so perhaps there may yet be more Festivals with dresses and scenes designed by you.

I see that your letter is dated the 8th April. I presume you know that I have only just returned from New Zealand and that your letter has had to wait all this time not only unanswered but unread. I was glad to receive a sign of life from you.

faithfully
G. Bernard Shaw

PS Besides, dear Christina, if you pick up the jargon of pseudo-Communism, a horrible inheritance from the bad translations of 1848–62, you will become a BORE, and be avoided by all your friends like the plague, besides getting committed to Class War and General Strike and the thick end of Internationalism and all the other exploded blunders of XIX century pre-Fabian revolutionism.

To R. & R. CLARK

[C/3; X/289]
4 Whitehall Court S W 1
9th June 1934

A schoolboy writes to me pointing out a hideous mistake in the Too True volume on p. 155 in the cross head.

Seventh commandment (adultery) should be sixth commandment (kill).

What is Edinburgh coming to when they dont know even the numbers of the commandments?

Mend the plate instantly, and blush.

GBS

To JOHN REITH

[H/99]
4 Whitehall Court S W 1
22nd June 1934

[Since 1930 Shaw had been chairman of the B.B.C.'s Advisory Committee on Spoken English, which was undergoing structural changes and a revision of its duties and responsibilities. Arthur Lloyd James (1884–1943), professor of phonetics, was linguistic adviser to the B.B.C. and secretary of the committee. Dr C. T. Onions (1873–1965), noted philologist and fellow of Magdalen College, Oxford, was a member of the committee.]

Dear Sir John

It would suit me very well indeed to arrange the meeting as you suggest. It is essential that the newcomers should be received and the new phase inaugurated by you.

My main difficulty as chairman—the one which will eventually make me impossible in that capacity—is that I am beginning to forget people's names quite ridiculously. At Emerson's funeral, Longfellow, who was overwhelmed with grief, said to the man next him "Sir: will you be so good as to remind me of the name of that dear friend of ours whose loss we are now lamenting." It will come to that with me presently.

When the Irish Academy of Letters was founded I managed to get a rule registered that the average age of the Committee of Management should not be allowed to exceed—I think it was 65; but at any rate it was a means of shoving off the octogenarians who persist in "lagging

375

superfluous." Lloyd James might keep this admirable precedent at the back of his mind when he drafts the standing orders.

I think that in the case of members domiciled at universities outside London, we ought to pay railway fares. A first class return ticket and afternoon tea, in addition to our most distinguished consideration, might prevent them from following the example of Onions and asking why the B.B.C., wallowing in millions (as they all believe) should not pay them a thousand a year apiece for teaching us how to speak with an Oxford accent.

always yours
G. Bernard Shaw

To PAUL KORETZ

[S/4]

[4 Whitehall Court SW 1]
[Undated: *c*. 13th July 1934]

[Paul Koretz (1885?–1980), international copyright lawyer, was negotiating for Eberhard K. Klagemann (b. 1904), of the Berlin firm Klagemann-Film der Tobis-Rota, for German-language rights to film *Pygmalion*. French actress Gaby Morlay (1890–1964), a reigning star of the Parisian stage, was under consideration for the rôle of "Elisa" in a French film version, the scenario for which had been written by Albert Rièra (b. 1895), principal assistant director to Jean Vigo on the films *Zéro de Conduite* (1933) and *L'Atalante* (1934). Shaw's terms for a film were ten per cent of the gross; for foreign films half of this sum was ceded to the translator of the original play.]

Dear Dr Koretz

Many thanks for your letter of the 9th [July].

It has been clear to me ever since the movies were extinguished and repressed by the tax that the old movie system of dealing in world rights must be modified greatly. But the movie world is hard to move; and its brains are still working in movie crowds and are likely to remain there for the next twenty years.

Your list of places in which you would exploit the film would not alarm me if I could feel sure that it would be intelligible to German or German speaking audiences only. On this condition I should not object to the exhibition of the film in the United States and anywhere else in North and South America where there are colonies of Germans. Unfortunately the practice of tacking on translations to films enables a national film to spoil the market for the other nationalities. You say that it is "solely in Italy" that this occurs. But I have seen it occur with a German film in London.

Take the case of Italy. I have on my desk a proposal for a Franco-Italian film of Pygmalion featuring Gaby Morlay–Elisa. The scenario, by a Monsieur Riera, is complete and in my hands. It is possible that I may accept this proposal. But in that case your film must not circulate throughout Italy, though it would be in its natural home inside the pre-war frontier save the Pusterthal. But I must not endanger my present friendly relations with the Italian government by sanctioning any poaching.

In spite of these difficulties I hope we may be able to come to an agreement. My work requires cultured handling; and though the Germans are already badly demoralized by Hollywood, still a demoralized German with some remains of culture is better than a British or American barbarian with no culture at all. So if we cannot agree it will not be over any ill will on my part.

As to our friend Trebitsch, you have corrupted him by an offer of twenty million shillings, for which Ted would sell his soul and mine and yours as well. Therefore you had better leave Trebitsch out of the question and deal with me for all the licenses necessary. I propose that you pay me ten percent interest [instead] of five and guarantee me a minimum of £1000 sterling out of the first years takings. If you agree to this I can buy Trebitsch's interest. Thus I and not you will have to pay an advance for all others fees. My ten percent will not be payable until you have received the money from the exhibitors. The agreement to be limited to five years.

The draft agreement you have sent me has amused me quite as much as you guessed it would. It asks for the guarantee that the play is not in the public domain anywhere in the world. Is there any civilized country except America in which the lawyers do not know that Russia, covering one-sixth of the globe, is all public domain, and that there are plenty of other States which are not parties to the copyright convention? But I can easily draft an agreement that will not qualify us for the lunatic asylum.

Please reply at your convenience. I will pacify Trebitsch. Besides Ted has gone to Karlsbad.

faithfully
[G. Bernard Shaw]

To WILLIAM H. REED

[X/381]

[Malvern Hotel. Malvern]
17th August 1934

[W. H. (Billy) Reed (1877–1942), violinist, was for many years concertmaster of the London Symphony Orchestra. "The material for a third symphony had been in Elgar's mind for years," Reed wrote in *Elgar as I Knew Him* (1936), which Shaw edited for publication. "Some of the themes and ideas are written down in his scrap-books, in various guises ... In the latter part of 1933 he began to get all these fragments—in some instances as many as twenty or thirty consecutive bars—on paper, though they were rarely harmonically complete. A clear vision of the whole symphony was forming in his mind." Elgar wrote the full exposition of the first movement, as well as the main themes of the slow movement and fragments of the last two movements, on single staves for Reed to play on the violin while he filled in the harmonies on the piano.]

[My dear Reed]

What is a symphony? A hundred years ago it was a composition in a clear symmetrical pattern established by Haydn and called Sonata Form. Now if half a symmetrical design is completed, any draughts-man can supply the missing half. If Haydn had died during the composition of one of his symphonies, and had left notes of its themes, and a hint or two of its bridge passages, Beethoven could easily have contributed a perfect Haydn symphony from them as an act of piety or a musical *jeu d'esprit*.

On the same terms any educated musician could construct an unfinished Rossini overture.

But no composer of symphonies nowadays adheres to the decorative patterns. The musical romances and extravaganzas of Berlioz, the symphonic poems of Liszt and Strauss, and the tone-dramas of Wagner could not have conformed to symmetrical decorative patterns: they had to find expressionist forms; and to reconstruct a lost expressionist composition from a fragment would be as impossible as to reconstruct a Shakespeare sonnet from the first two lines of it.

All the great symphonies after Beethoven are as expressionist as Wagner's music-dramas, even when, as in the Symphonies of Brahms and Elgar, the skeleton of the old pattern is still discernible. All possibility of reconstruction from fragments or completion from beginnings is gone.

Consequently, though Elgar left some sketches of a third symphony

378

and was actually at work on it when he died, no completion or reconstruction is possible: the symphony, like Beethoven's tenth, died with the composer.

> faithfully
> G. Bernard Shaw

To GEORGINA MUSTERS

Malvern
[E/1] 21st August 1934

[During the annual Malvern visit, as Shaw was driving his saloon on a Worcester road, a motorcyclist travelling with his wife in a side-car swung out to avoid ploughing into a stationary vehicle and smashed into the bumper and wing of Shaw's car. Though GBS was unhurt, the cyclists, a Mr and Mrs Hubert Paxton, sustained minor injuries. Much concerned about their condition, Shaw could not be persuaded to depart until he had been reassured they were not seriously hurt and would be able to get home unassisted.]

The smash had no effect on us at all: my big car did not feel it, though its bumpers and one mudguard crumpled a bit. But the unfortunate cyclist and his wife and his motorbike shot up into the air, the bike in six separate fragments, and came down all over the road, fortunately not under the car. I was driving at the time. It was over before I could do more than catch sight of them and give them up for dead. I half think they must be, though they dont know it yet.

> GBS

To THE NUNS OF STANBROOK ABBEY

4 Whitehall Court SW1
[H/98; X/256] 3rd October 1934

[Misconceiving a souvenir card celebrating Dame Laurentia's golden jubilee as a nun for a memorial card (it read: IN MEMORY OF SEPT. 6 1884–1934 DAME LAURENTIA McLACHLAN ABBESS OF STANBROOK), Shaw penned a touching letter of condolence to the nuns of her order.]

To the Ladies of
  Stanbrook Abbey

Dear Sisters

Through some mislaying of my letters I have only just received the news of the death of Dame Laurentia McLachlan. I was in Malvern from the end of July until the 16th September, and I never passed through Stanbrook without a really heartfelt pang because I might not call and see her as of old. But I had no knowledge of the state of her health and no suspicion that I should never see her again in this world.

There was a time when I was in such grace with her that she asked you all to pray for me; and I valued your prayers quite sincerely. But we never know exactly how our prayers will be answered; and their effect on me was that when my wife was lying dangerously ill in Africa through an accident I wrote a little book which, to my grief, shocked Dame Laurentia so deeply that I did not dare to show my face at the Abbey until I was forgiven. She has, I am sure, forgiven me now; but I wish she could tell me so. In the outside world from which you have escaped it is necessary to shock people violently to make them think seriously about religion; and my ways were too rough. But that was how I was inspired.

I have no right to your prayers; but if I should happen to be remembered occasionally by those of you who remember my old visits I should be none the worse for them, and very grateful.

faithfully
G. Bernard Shaw

To LAURENTIA McLACHLAN

Ayot St Lawrence. Welwyn
[A/98; X/256]   7th October 1934

["I have made a superhowler about Stanbrook," Shaw told Sydney Cockerell on 17th October, his letter of condolence having been answered by "Laurentia herself! Happily she said I was to resume my visits. But I felt as if a soul had been dragged back from felicity. Which is queer, as of course I dont believe anything of the sort" (A/3).]

Laurentia! Alive!!

Well!!!!!

Is this a way to trifle with a man's most sacred feelings?

I cannot express myself. I renounce all the beliefs I have left. I thought you were in heaven, happy and blessed. And you were only laughing at me. It is your revenge for that Black Girl.

Oh, Laurentia, Laurentia, Laurentia, how *could* you.

I weep tears of blood.

Poor Brother Bernard

To MARION PETERS

[4 Whitehall Court SW 1]

[U(E)/2]   16th October 1934

[Marion Peters, of the West Texas Gas Co., Plainview, Texas, who collected branding irons as a hobby, had inquired how, since Shaw indicated his personal contempt for branding cattle with hot irons, he would place a cabalistic mark on the cow so that it would remain a permanent mark of identification for the lifetime of the animal. Although Peters signed his name with a "Mr", Shaw addressed the letter to "Miss Peters."]

Paint it on them, you idiot.

You can put your name on your handkerchief without using a red hot poker, can't you?

G. Bernard Shaw

To BASIL BLACKWELL

[4 Whitehall Court SW1]

[X/382]   25th October 1934

[When Constable's published Shaw's *Complete Plays* in one volume in 1931 they assured booksellers that the book would never be reprinted. In 1934, however, Shaw contracted with Odhams Press to publish an edition to be offered at bargain prices, as a sales promotion, to its readers by the *Daily Herald*. It would, wrote Basil Blackwell (1889–1984), leading Oxford bookseller, "help those booksellers (already sufficiently penalised) who are charged by their customers with a breach of faith, if you could arm them with a statement exonerating them from complicity" (*Publishers' Circular*, 3rd November 1934). On receipt of a letter of complaint a month earlier from the Retail

Booksellers, Stationers and Allied Trades Employees' Association, Shaw replied that "in New York I have sold editions of two books [*Intelligent Woman's Guide* (1928) and the *Black Girl* (1933), both to the Book-of-the-Month Club], of 50,000 each, to Book Clubs to distribute *as a bonus* to their subscribers free, gratis, and for nothing. Of these 100,000 books not one went to the public through the hands of a bookseller; yet no bookseller had a word to say about it" (I/1: 5th October 1934). The Book-of-the-Month Club had additionally obtained 50,000 copies of the Terry-Shaw correspondence from Putnam's in 1932, by arrangement with Elbridge Adams.]

Dear Basil Blackwell

In future, when a customer asks you for a book of mine, say "Thanks very much," wrap the book up nicely in paper for him (or her), take the money, give the change, say "Thanks very much" over again, and bow the customer out.

If, out of pure gratuitous incontinence you prefer to enter into conversation and give unsolicited assurances, of an obviously idiotic character, about my business intentions, you do it at your own risk; and if it turns out subsequently that I never had any such intentions, you will have to exonerate yourself as best you can.

I have given Constables a letter to the effect that they took no part in the *Daily Herald* transaction, except to oppose it with all their might. I can do nothing for the booksellers but tell them not to be childish.

In America I have lately had two orders of 50,000 copies each from book clubs, to be given away to their members *for nothing*, as a bonus. Of course, I accepted both.

I am looking forward to an order from Woolworths for a sixpenny edition.

Would you, Basil, refuse such business, if it came your way?

And have you no bowels of compassion for the millions of your fellow countrymen who can no more afford a twelve-and-sixpenny book than a trip round the world? You should see some of their letters.

I am really surprised at you. When we met at Bumpus's, you seemed quite an intelligent youth.

faithfully
G. Bernard Shaw

[Blackwell, after quoting the Lord Chief Justice's remarks to Falstaff in *Henry IV Part 2*, rejoined on 29th October: "My 'level consideration' is that Constable's edition . . . was sold to the bookseller, and by the booksellers to the public on the assurance that there would not be a reprint; that this assurance ('idiotic' perhaps, but neither invented nor suggested by the booksellers) was given with your knowledge and consent; that later, according to your letter, business opportunity jumping with your generous impulses, you authorised a reprint; that this practice leaves you with the halfpence, your publishers and the booksellers with the kicks" (*Publishers' Circular*, 3rd November 1934).]

To HESKETH PEARSON

4 Whitehall Court SW 1
[H/3; X/383.e]   26th October 1934

[Pearson was researching for a joint biography of Gilbert and Sullivan, published in 1935. Shaw had become familiar with the works of Serge Prokofiev (1891–1953) principally through performances broadcast by the B.B.C. The "darned Mounseer" is a phrase in Richard Dauntless's ballad solo "I shipped, d'ye see, in a Revenue sloop," in *Ruddigore* (1887).]

Dear Hesketh Pearson

Your letter reminds me that I said nothing about Gilbert and Sullivan. I never met Sullivan. I did meet Gilbert once or perhaps twice shortly before his death. He was quite friendly; but all I remember of our conversation is that he complained of the way people invented illnatured witticisms and attributed them to him. He instanced the famous description of Tree's Hamlet as "funny without being vulgar," which Tree invented himself and then fathered on Gilbert.

I do not know to what extent you are a musician; but this is a musician's job. Sullivan has been gaining ground and Gilbert losing it since they died. The reason is that when they started Gilbert was new and unique: he had absolutely no rivals. But Sullivan was hard up against Offenbach, whose music was like champagne, and also against Auber, whose Fra Diavolo was a masterpiece. Sullivan was a church organist; and when I in my teens heard Trial By Jury, which stands out as Pickwick stands out in Dickens, its harmonies struck me as most unexpectedly churchy after Offenbach.

Offenbach and Auber are now forgotten; and Sullivan's music is as light as air beside Elgar's or Prokovieff's.

Besides, Sullivan's vein was never worked out: he was as good at the end as the beginning. But Gilbert, fundamentally a sentimentalist who never learnt the value of his own satire, got worked out very desperately. People used to say that the two quarrelled about a carpet, which was very silly nonsense. But when Gilbert could give Sullivan nothing

383

better to set to music than The Darned Mounseer, Sullivan, who was always a serious musician, must have felt deeply offended in his art.

D'Oyly Carte asked me to write a libretto for Sullivan. He even said I might choose my own composer if I would do it. I trifled with the idea for awhile; but I always found something better to do. George Edwardes had a try also; but that, too, came to nothing; and I escaped all the attempts to make me a comic opera librettist.

But are you really going on with this job?

faithfully
G. Bernard Shaw

To H. G. WELLS

[H/26]

[Ayot St Lawrence. Welwyn]
[Undated: *c*. 4th November 1934]

[Shaw's review of Vol. 1 of Wells's *Experiment in Autobiography* and Dean Inge's *Vale* appeared under the heading "H. G. Wells and the Dean" in the *Daily Herald* on 8th October. The *Confessions* (1781–88) of Jean-Jacques Rousseau (1712–77) and Goethe's *Aus meinem Leben, Dichtung und Wahrheit* (1811–22) are celebrated autobiographies. In his reference to Webbian "devices" Shaw may have been using the term in its Sam Weller—Pickwickian sense ("dewises"). Rosminian philosophers are disciples of Antonio Rosmini Serbati (1797–1855), an Italian priest and philosopher, who sought to reconcile Roman Catholic dogma with modern political and scientific thought. Thomas Davidson (1840–1900) was an American philosopher who in 1883 founded the Fellowship of the New Life, from which the Fabian Society sprang.

A verbatim report of H. G. Wells's interview with Stalin appeared as a supplement in the *New Statesman* on 27th October. O.K. was Odette Keun, a Dutch-Italian ex-nun whom Wells described as his "prostitute-housekeeper," and whom he set up in a south of France villa. "H. G., infuriated by my comment on the Stalin interview in The New Statesman," Shaw informed Lady Rhondda on 3rd November, "tells me I have a sister soul in O.K. and that she and I ought to get together before it is too late" (H/8).]

Dearest H. G.

What have I done to God that he should plague me with you in this fashion? I seem to spend my life rescuing the victims of your outrageous onslaughts and seeming to remonstrate with you and make fun of you whilst I have to boost you subtly all the time.

When I wrote the Inge-Wells review I had read nothing but the scraps in the Daily Herald; so of course it was not a review at all but a flagrant blurb to stimulate sales. I refused to review the second volume because I had fired my shot and did not want to spoil it by making the stage mistake of trying to repeat a successful effect.

Besides, the second volume of an autobiography is not good game for a friendly reviewer. A child knows what happens to it; and people tell it the truth about itself, or at least about its effect on them, quite brutally. It knows every corner of its little back yard of a world. And by the time it is old enough to write an autobiography its people are dead. Consequently the worst autobiography is interesting and moving in the pre-adult stages; and the best loses terribly in intensity and reality afterwards.

This is not merely or even chiefly because the truth affects too many living persons (some of them vindictively litigious) to be printable. It is mainly because the adult does not know the world into which he enters, and nobody ever tells him the truth or shews his hand to him dispassionately. Once, when a breakdown of my car held me up in Nancy for fifteen days I read Rousseau's Confessions in the original from end to end. There were heaven knows how many volumes. I might have saved myself the trouble for all I can remember of his routine after he became a notorious philosopher and Madame de Warens [Rousseau's mistress and protector] a superfatted wreck in the distance both of time and space. Goethe as a child and youth is interesting; but he bores himself so frightfully later on that he tails off into long accounts of people he came across who are now forgotten.

You keep up the interest for me because your sketches in the Goethe manner are of people whom I have known, and incidents in which I have played a part. But they confirm what I have just said. When you burst into the Fabian Society and played Old Harry there, you did not know where you were or where we were. WE (the old gang) were hard at work bringing a magnificent revolutionary conception down to tin tacks and gas and water municipalism, to black and white Bills, to Webbian "devices." We were exploiting our piffling congregation, which we well knew could never exceed (as it never did) two thousand harmless middle class people who did not go to church and practised birth control, to "permeate" the Opposition-local-Associations and foist Newcastle programs and the like on the parties and newspapers. And you, trying to drag us back—forward, as you saw it—to the magnificent dream which had had its day long before you dreamed it, were disgusted with such trifling and with Pease's shabby little office. Nothing but a senseless discord could come of such a misunderstanding.

385

You are still wrong about our origins. The little group of Rosminian philosophers formed by Davidson was led out of dreams of Perfectionist colonies in Brazil by the hard common sense of Bland, whose section became the F.S. and was spied out in the London chaos by me. I had already spied out in the same chaos an unassuming figure named Sidney Webb. I have a genius for casting plays; and I picked him as my leading man and forced my acquaintance on him. I had discovered Olivier through Henry George and the Land Reform Union. I made them join the Fabian, where they immediately took the practical lead out of the hands of Bland and his Blackheath group, whom they would have driven out of the Society but for my determination to keep Bland in it, as he had a valuable point of view which we were apt to forget, and was *au fond* on the right side in spite of his being very trying as a censorious libertine. He had a long struggle with poverty, living at times on the half guinea a week that the Weekly Despatch paid her [Edith Nesbit, wife of Bland] for poems, some of which were inspired by ME. But at last I was offered a weekly feuilleton job at £5 a week (I think); and I managed to persuade the editor that Bland was the heavenborn man he wanted. It turned out that I was right; for Bland never looked back from that moment, and held his own as "Hubert," champion feuilletonist [of the *Daily Chronicle*] and breadwinner, until he died.

You think that when you came along you antagonized me; but you are wildly wrong. As leaders neither you nor Webb looked the part as well as, for example, Hyndman (why didnt you describe Hyndman?); but I did my best to keep you in the Society. My nearest to a real quarrel with the Webbs was when I forced them to recognize that Ann Veronica [Amber Reeves] and you had the upper hand of them because they could not expose you without discrediting the London School of Economics by a sexual scandal. Bland was savagely furious with you because you tried to shake the resistance of Rosamund [his daughter, another of Wells's amours] by citing the example of her parents. A debate between you and Bland would have been a butchery: one with Webb would have been very painful. I was the obvious alternative; but they mistrusted me deeply (and quite rightly) because they knew that I was a Wellsite as far as it was possible for anyone to be a Wellsite in the face of your wild behavior. There was no fear of not defeating you: you were sure to defeat yourself hopelessly every time you opened your mouth or put pen to paper. But you could be let off too easily; and I forced myself on the Executive Committee as its champion only by explicit pledges that I would be unsparing in my exaction of a complete and uncompromising surrender. What I did not say was that I should also exact from you a pledge that you would not leave the Society if the vote went against you.

So you see the story cannot be told; but there has never been any antagonism to you on my part, because, mere natural liking apart, I am free from your besetting fault of ridiculously underrating your contemporaries. From Marx and Webb to Stalin, your gibes are amazing in their triviality: in fact you are very like Marx in this respect. However, I would not have you other than you are. All the idols are the better for having an occasional brick shied at them.

O.K. has missed her chance: she should have written a funny description of H.G. in bed. She has an amazing command of English and is clever, but not clever enough to avoid exhibiting herself as a child crying for the moon and a deeply resentful abandonnée. I am defeating the well meant but mistaken efforts of Lady R. to bring us together.

I must stop this babble: the village post goes at six thirty; but of course I have not said half enough about the book.

GBS

To GERTRUDE PARRY

[H/56]

4 Whitehall Court SW1
19th November 1934

[Dr William J. Maloney (1881–1952) had written a book, just then being circulated in manuscript among publishers in America and not published until 1936, entitled *The Forged Casement Diaries*, which argued that the British Government had forged diaries allegedly kept by Sir Roger Casement at Putamaya, to despoil his memory with "evidence" that he was homosexual and thus discredit him as a martyred hero. His cousin Gertrude Bannister, now Mrs Sidney Parry, wrote to Shaw to ask him what if anything he knew about the book. Admiral Sir Reginald Hall (1870–1943) was director of the intelligence division of the Admiralty War Staff 1914–18. Lloyd George's *War Memoirs* were published 1933–36.]

Dear Mrs Parry

I have read Dr Maloney's book. It is a monument of zealous industry; but it does not clear the ground: it rather overcrowds it. It takes more trouble to put the British Government in the wrong than to put Roger in the right. It begins with five chapters to prove in the abstract what nobody doubts in the concrete: that is, that governments use

Press propaganda to further their policy and whitewash their operations. This I found unreadable; and nothing disables a book more completely than an unreadable opening.

What the case needs is a special pleader who will stick to his brief with his eye on the jury all the time, and not an abstract political essayist nor a nationalist partisan; and unfortunately Dr Maloney begins as the one and ends as the other, using Casement as a stick to beat a regime which has been extinguished by the establishment of the Irish Free State, and which is consequently regarded by the reading public as a back number. The book that is needed to rehabilitate Roger must be written on a carefully cleaned slate. Dr Maloney has written his on one crowded with old sums.

There is nothing either peculiar or in any sort of dispute about the trial and execution. No vindication is needed as to anything that was pleaded in court. There is no excuse for going all over that now except as an illustration in a treatise demonstrating the need for an international or neutral court for such trials. What *is* peculiar to the case and what is at issue is the fact that Roger was grossly defamed, and the intervention of many of his most influential political sympathisers to obtain a reprieve prevented, by the circulation of a report that a nasty diary, proving him to be a disgustingly unpleasant person, had been found in his possession. Admiral Sir Reginald Hall, Director of the Intelligence Division of the Admiralty War Staff, exhibited photostats of pages from the diary at his office, thereby making the Government responsible for the report and taking it out of the category of idle gossip.

It is now contended that the documents exhibited as portions of a diary of Casement's own life were transcripts made by him of certain evidence in one of the Putumayan scandals which he was knighted for exposing, and that the diary of which they were assumed to form part has never been produced nor proved to exist.

This is the case, the whole case, and nothing but the case. The introduction of any other controversial matter only confuses it and gives the defence excuses for riding off on exciting but quite irrelevant questions. Dr Maloney has done his utmost to obscure it by dragging in every side issue he could lay his pen to. For example, he has devoted a chapter to shewing that according to the theory of the British constitution, every department and every minister must have been fully cognisant of and a party to the proceedings of Admiral Sir Reginald Hall. But to dwell on this purely academic assumption at the moment when Mr Lloyd George's memoirs have shewn its utter unreality is to deprive the book of all authority, and start a fusillade of refutations which the public will accept as refutations of Roger's claim to rehabilitation. No book will serve his memory unless it is completely impartial and as far as possible silent on every other issue except that of the authenticity of the diary. The Government must be cornered by a committee of Roger's relatives and friends and asked to produce the diary for examination in its completeness if it exists. A refusal would leave the Government in an indefensible position, as there can now be no diplomatic reason for secrecy. The formation of such a committee is the first step; and it must not approach the Government as a hostile Irish political demonstration. It must assume that now we are at peace the Government will be anxious to remedy any injustice that may have sprung from the necessities of war and the old unhappy relations between England and Ireland.

Everything will then depend on the action of the Government. If it refuses, then a book calling for judgment against it through default would be in order. If on the other hand the documents are produced and examined, the Committee should publish a report of their conclusions. But no indictment should be published until the Government has had a full opportunity of answering it. They *must* answer it if it be made in proper form. If it is not made in proper form the impropriety will be the Government's excuse for refusing to answer without admitting that it is in default.

When the matter has been disposed of in a correctly judicial way then Dr Maloney can let loose all his invective against the Government for its part in it. But until then his book can do nothing but harm, and may make a really satisfactory rehabilitation impossible for years to come.

This is my considered opinion, the best I can arrive at.

always yours
G. Bernard Shaw

To JOHN MAYNARD KEYNES

4 Whitehall Court SW1
[H/17; X/384]   30th November 1934

[Wells's interview, together with correspondence by Shaw, Keynes, Ernst Toller, and others, which appeared in succeeding issues of the *New Statesman* was published on 5th December as *Stalin-Wells Talk*, too rapidly for Keynes

389

to make the suggested revisions, even if he had desired to do so. He did write to the editor Kingsley Martin, however, to report Shaw's reticence. "Presumably," Keynes wrote, "you got his permission some time ago. I fancy the old gentleman is weak and ill," and he repeated Shaw's statement about being "still in bed." What he did not know was that Shaw had collapsed in a dead faint on 24th November, the doctor diagnosing his ailment as a "not serious" heart attack. Confined to bed for several days, he initially slept straight through for sixty hours. Kingsley Martin (1897–1969), formerly on the editorial staff of the *Manchester Guardian*, was editor of the *New Statesman* 1930–60.]

Dear Maynard Keynes

I am not at all easy about Kingsley Martin's proposal to reprint all that stuff in The New Statesman. I should put my foot down on it at once but for H.G.[,] who has an infatuated belief that he has put Stalin in his place and given me an exemplary drubbing, whereas it is equally clear to me that he has made a blazing idiot of himself.

It is represented to me that you, too, are anxious for the reprint, which makes it still more difficult for me to object. However, if you insist, I suggest that you should recast what you said about Marx being a back number, as this will certainly be misunderstood, though of course Marx is an old story to you, as he is to me. But look at the facts. When I read Marx 50 years ago, I could not find an English translation of Capital in the British Museum, and had to read him in Deville's French translation. Today the book is the best seller among the serious books in the Everyman Library, and the world is gasping at the Russian revolution, which was put through by men who were inspired by Marx more directly and exclusively than the Reformation by Luther and Calvin or the French Revolution by Rousseau and Voltaire. In such a situation it is impossible for a sociologist of any standing to write about Marx as forgotten and negligible. I have picked Marx's mistakes to pieces as meticulously as anybody; but I am always very careful to reserve the fact that he was an Epoch Maker.

Besides, the Class War is perfectly sound as a proposition in political physics. It is not disposed of by saying that the lines of disruptive strain do not follow the lines between classes; but that the strain is there and can be got rid of only by the abolition of "real" property is beyond all sane question. At present Marx's demonstration of the blind ruthlessness of capital in the pursuit of "surplus value" (practically of cheap labor) is producing a dangerous conflict between our obvious balance-of-power interest in an alliance of England and France with Russia and the U.S.A. and the class war pressure to join with Japan in the exploitation of Manchuoko.

Your article reads as if you had never heard of all this; and therefore, if it is to be reprinted, I think you ought to revise it sufficiently to avoid this impression.

I have offered H.G. to write his part in the affair for him and give him a good show; but he says I must "take my medicine," bless his innocence.

I write with difficulty, very incompetently, as I am still in bed, tired out and run down to nothing, but convalescing all right so far.

faithfully
G. Bernard Shaw

PS I think the core of the affair—the report of the interview—a complete disappointment considering the eminence of the parties. Why give it a pretence of importance by making a book of it?

To HENRY S. SALT

Ayot St Lawrence. Welwyn
7th December 1934

[A/4]

[Shaw was getting on "splendidly," Charlotte reported to Otto Kyllmann on 7th December, from Ayot. "We came down here on Wednesday last & he has made great strides since—went for a good walk this morning (a lovely day) & is beginning to lose his cough, which was very bad! My only trouble is that he is as troublesome as a patient as he is to his publisher! *Nothing* will make him prudent—nothing!" (D/52). The William Morris centenary was celebrated on 20th October with the inauguration of a memorial village hall at Kelmscott, attended by the Prime Minister Ramsay MacDonald, Shaw, Cockerell, Lady Mary Murray, Lord Olivier, Sir Frederick and Lady Keeble (Lillah McCarthy), and William Rothenstein, among others. Shaw in a brief address dubbed Morris, who he said was hard to classify, St William of Kelmscott. G.Bell and Sons published three of Salt's books early in the century. It is doubtful if Shaw had more than a second-hand acquaintance with the works of Sigmund Freud (1856–1939), though he made frequent reference to him in the later correspondence.]

My dear Salt

Cold be blowed! I just dropped down dead in the middle of a telephone conversation; and it is the greatest pity on earth that I revived like Lazarus. I was literally tired to death: hadnt had even a Sunday off for months and months; and I slept for three days on end.

The Morris celebration was most edifying. You should have heard us singing Onward, Christian Soldiers, which I led with stentorian vigor. Morris was turning in his grave round the corner. Olivier was alarmingly sardonic; but he held his peace, and the villagers thought it was all werry capital. May provided a stupendous tea, which spread all over the garden and offices, as the house was hopelessly overcrowded.

Has Bell left any successor in the publishing world who would speculate in the Great Understanding? The kinship idea irresistibly suggests a chapter on your relations with your father. Were you ever reconciled? I do not believe a bit in Freud's facile jealousy theory of feuds between father and son; but long before Freud was heard of I held that Nature had introduced an element of antipathy into kinship as a defence against incest. So please be careful to explain that kinship unites only when it is distant (a dog being a dearer friend than a man) and sunders when it is close.

But really the human race is beyond redemption. . . .

as ever
G.B.S.

To FRANCIS YOUNGHUSBAND

[4 Whitehall Court SW 1]
[H.c.u/9]   28th December 1934
[Sir Francis Younghusband (1863–1942), soldier, diplomat, explorer, and religious mystic, was founder of the World Congress of Faiths in 1936, and was author of numerous inspirational books and pamphlets. The pamphlet he sent to Shaw probably was *Philosophy, Science and Religion*, a tract published in 1929. Agapemone is alluded to in Act III of *Too True to be Good*, Shaw's stage direction calling for a grotto above which "some scholarly soldier has carved . . . in Greek characters the word Αγαπεμονε, beneath which is written in red chalk THE ABODE OF LOVE . . ."

Sir Arthur Pinero died on 23rd November. The royal wedding was that of Prince George (1902–42), newly-created Duke of Kent, fourth son of George V, who married Princess Marina of Greece at Westminster Abbey on 29th November. H.G. Wells's *The Open Conspiracy* (1928), sub-titled *Blueprints for a World Revolution*, was described by its author as "a scheme for all human conduct." The Oxford Group was a religious sect led by the American evangelist Frank Buchman (1878–1961) at Oxford University; it led in 1938 to creation of the Moral Re-Armament movement.]

Dear Sir Francis

I start for a trip round South America on the 16th, and am not due back until the 1st April.

I have had a good deal of experience in trying to induce men of different faiths, and what is much more difficult, of the same faith to work together in response to the constant clamor for unity and fellow-ship. But nothing ever got done until the "fellows" divided themselves into small sections according to their speed of brain, their general knowledge, their facility in social intercourse as well as to their possession of a common object or program. Spiritual men (and women) are extraordinarily quarrelsome. In your pamphlet you speak of "men of burning faith in the redeeming power of love"; but when you ask them to work with people whom they do not and cannot love or who do not and cannot love them you find that the world is not an Agapemone but a place in which dislikes and antipathies are so common and so strong that the real problem is not superfluously to unite people who love oneanother, but to hammer it into them that their dislikes do not give them the smallest right to be unjust or uncivil to oneanother.

My fellow playwright Arthur Pinero, whose death the other day passed almost unnoticed amid the rejoicings over the royal wedding, once signed a letter to me "with admiration and detestation." That was the truth; but it did not prevent him from treating me with the most scrupulous consideration, nor, though I knew his feeling quite well, prevent me from persuading the Asquiths that he should have a knighthood.

Compare this with the conduct of H. G. Wells. We are old friends; and we like oneanother as well as any two mortal men can. What is more we have so many public objects in common that there is no excuse for our quarrelling. Yet he behaves in public as if I were his bitterest enemy.

Our spiritual men have hardly a good word to say of oneanother. Karl Marx changed the mind of the world more extensively than Jesus or Mahomet; but he abused everyone who was not his abject disciple so fiercely and implacably that he kept only one friend [Friedrich Engels] without whom he would have starved. It is nearly always so. Many ordinary men cannot bear contradiction, especially if, like H. G. Wells, they have had no sisters; but the geniuses whom you would

393

combine cannot bear agreement, perhaps because it is an assertion of equality. Yet they are all for unity: "proletarians of all lands, unite," and for combination in The Open Conspiracy. If you get them on your platform (no easy job) they would utter the noblest sentiments. Get them round a table to agree on a basic manifesto or spend half a crown of public money and most of them will make frantic scenes and dash out of the room after hurling their resignation at you.

If I joined you there are two questions which I should put as tests for admission to the fellowship. 1. On what public grounds would you shoot your next door neighbor, excluding those already recognised by our criminal court? 2. If you do not believe in hell or in the direct administration of the world's business by a just and omnipotent God, what are the minimum conditions on which you would grant the privilege of living in civilized society?

People who have not faced these questions will never change society on public grounds: at best they will only rave like the old Bolshevik prophets in the Bible. The changes are made by daring rogues with axes to grind. Note how instantly the Russians had to face the two questions when they had to build from the ground up.

Nobody ever mentions the real problems. Here we are, as Disraeli put it, two nations, rich and poor. The rich, as Tolstoy said, will do everything for the poor except get off their backs. The poor do not want the rich to do anything for them except get off their backs and leave them to take care of themselves. When this big difficulty comes in at the door love flies out at the window.

Just now there is quite a crop of attempts to form world fellowships. H. G. Wells's Open Conspiracy is open for a subscription of five shillings. They all invite me to join. A few years ago, when the Oxford Group was booming, I was invited to join that because I was civil enough to it to admit that its magic spell of sacrificing all ones hatreds to Jesus was a great improvement on the older plan of adulterating and cheating all the week in the glorious certainty that all the guilt could be washed off one's soul (though not off the gingerbread) by a bath in the blood of the lamb next Sunday. But when it comes to something more practical than being "nice" to Fundamentalists and Salvationists, and patting them on the back for improvements in morals produced by their spells—when, for example, the question arises whether their compulsorily educated children in the State schools are to be taught to worship a savage old Bedouin idol, the gloves come off, and you find these nice people ready to cut oneanothers throats sooner than tolerate such education on one side or relinquish it on the other. It is no use pretending that such conflicts can be avoided by keeping the proceedings on a spiritual plane: they are the outward and visible signs of inward and spiritual grace.

But I must not bother you any more with what you must know as well as I do. It will perhaps amuse you more to read an unpublished play of mine [*The Simpleton of the Unexpected Isles*] which will show you that I, too, have found in the east a quality of religion which is lacking in these islands.

faithfully
[G. Bernard Shaw]

To A. LLOYD JAMES

[C/99]

Ayot St Lawrence. Welwyn
30th December 1934

Pronunciations heard from broadcasters & noted in my pocket diary during 1934.

Formidd'able (for'midable)
Combattíng (rhyming to matting)
Drāymer (American for drahma)
Ak'kumen (? akēw'men)
Harast' (harassed, rhyming to past)
Kal'liber (calibre ? caleebr)
Serriments (Cerements – Hamlet ? seerments)
Gal'lant (licentious ? gall<u>ant</u>')
Quan'dery (? quandāīŕy)
Trapēz'ing (for the Irish trapesing which rhymes to shape-sing).

I fancy we have settled some of these.

In spite of the virtuosity with which the musical items are announced, we still get Figure-oh for Feegahro, Corśe-a-cough for Korsah'kof (I think) and worst of all Die Walküre with the stress on the ü instead of on <u>Val</u>.

G.B.S.

To SIEGFRIED TREBITSCH

[C/5; X/341]

4 Whitehall Court S W 1
10th January 1935

[Charlotte had booked an eight-week South American tour for January in order to get the ailing GBS away from mid-winter England. Just after the turn of the year she too was stricken, her temperature rising unaccountably and refusing to budge. "These last few days she has been decidedly mending," Shaw informed T. E. Lawrence on 28th January, "but it was a near thing. She hurt her shin packing. It woke up the old South African wound and produced blood poisoning. Three doctors, 1, local g.p., 2, Harley St homeopath (Sir John Weir), 3 [William] Cooper the osteopath. Yet she lives!" (C/1). She was not fully convalescent until the end of February. A substituted second cruise to Africa was delayed until mid-March.]

The Irish Free State has repudiated the British citizenship of the Irish people. The question then arose, what is the status of Irishmen living in England? The press asked me whether I intended to take out papers of naturalization to make me legally an Englishman. I said that I had the whole world to choose from and could just as easily become a Russian as an Englishman. I said if I changed at all (which of course I have no intention of doing) I should choose the country where I was most highly appreciated. I warned England that Russia might win in that competition. I made no allusion to Maxim Gorky. The joke seems to be taken seriously by some of the German journalists. It does not matter: Russophobia is a folly that will soon pass.

My journey has been put off until the 26th by a sudden illness which has prostrated Charlotte. I had to cancel the South American trip, and engage for another tour round Africa to the Dutch East Indies. I hope she will recover in time for it. What a world of mishaps!

GBS

To A. TROYTE GRIFFITH

[C/114]

4 Whitehall Court S W 1
20th January 1935

[A. Troyte Griffith (1864–1942), an architect who resided in Malvern, was a longtime friend of Elgar and one of the subjects of the "Enigma" variations. A Ralph Vaughan Williams (1872–1958) article on Elgar in *Music and Letters*, January 1935, had made reference to "vapourings by . . . G. B. Shaw," in a refutation of Shaw's charge that Hubert Parry had led a clique with the principal aim of keeping Elgar down.]

I was surprised at V. W. suddenly sticking his knife into me; I must take some opportunity of conciliating him; for he has no reason to class me with litterateurs who write on music without knowing anything about it. I was still more surprised at his backing up the university clique to the extent of pretending that they received E.E. with open arms. But on looking him up in Grove [*Grove's Dictionary of Music and Musicians*] I find that he is a survivor of the clique himself. Heaven help him!

Still, his article and Reed's are the only ones with anything real in them in the symposium.

GBS

To FREDERICK C. OWLETT

4 Whitehall Court SW 1
[H/1]   22nd January 1935
[Frederick C. Owlett, a member of the Globe-Mermaid Association interested in restoration of ancient playhouses, was author of monographs on Thomas Chatterton and Francis Thompson.]

Dear Mr Owlett

I cannot imagine anything more idiotic. Take my own case. My career, in so far as it is connected with any theatre, is connected with the Court Theatre in Sloane Square. It had every drawback that a nineteenth century small theatre could have; and that is saying a good deal. Even after it was reconstructed in bits it was, from the author's point of view, a damnable place. Conceive, if you can, a body of Shavian enthusiasts in the year 2235 proposing to reproduce the Court Theatre on its present site! It would make me turn in my grave.

What warrant have you for supposing that the old Globe was any more Shakesperean than the Court is Shavian? He may have loathed it and cursed it at every rehearsal for its inconveniences.

But suppose he liked it and was satisfied with it. What would the London County Council say to its sanitation? Or its exit doors? What would a producer say to its lighting, or a modern audience say to its seats or the pit with a clay floor and nothing to sit on? By the time you had made the compromise between a bear pit and an inn yard fit for modern use it would be no more like Shakespear's Globe than the baths of Caracalla are like a private suite at the Ritz.

397

A model to present to the Victoria and Albert Museum would be interesting enough; but haven't they got one? Poel had something of the sort constructed. Perhaps that is in the London Museum.

Anyhow, this Resurrection Pie project of yours is utter folly in its present form.

candidly
G. Bernard Shaw

To AUGUSTIN HAMON

4 Whitehall Court SW1
13th February 1935

[H/1]

[Benjamin Franklin's maxim, prefixed to *Poor Richard's Almanack* (1757), is "Experience keeps a dear school, but fools will learn in no other." Henry Deutschmeister (1903–69), who later became head of Franco London Films, appears to have been the would-be producer of the French film version of *Pygmalion*. The Dutch version, produced by Rudolf Meyer for Filmex Cinetone of Amsterdam and directed by the German-born Ludwig Berger (1892–1969), was first screened in Amsterdam in March 1937.]

My dear Hamon

The business is a complicated one.

The invention of the movie (film muet) was enormously profitable because the audience was the whole world.

The invention of the talkie (film parlant) involves the nationalization of the film and the end of the world audience.

The film corporations are still trying desperately to maintain the old movie system of world rights. Nothing but experience will teach them to face the new situation; for, as Benjamin Franklin said "Experience is the costliest way of learning; but it is the only one of which fools are capable."

France is trying to keep the movies alive for her millions of negroes; but this will not last because (a) movies are no longer produced by the manufacturers, and (b) there are negroes enough to make talkies acted and spoken by negroes* in their own language (negroes are wonderful actors) reasonably profitable. Pending this development the French talkie has the run of French Africa.

Now for the political side of the question.

---

* Shaw's secretary had typed the word "niggers," which Shaw altered in holograph.

All the new States into which the war has broken up Europe are fiercely protectionist. They not only put every difficulty in the way of importing anything that they can produce themselves, but also in the way of exporting rentes of any kind. At present many of them have to admit foreign films because they have none of their own manufacture. But this will not last, because nothing is easier than to start a film studio. The old pre-war movie industry reckoned without frontiers. The post-war talkie industry has filled Europe with frontiers which are all the more jealously guarded and strengthened because most of them are in the wrong place.

Worst of all, there is no sign of any relaxation of anti-semitism. Logically it has nothing to do with Fascism. But the human race is imitative rather than logical; and as Fascism spreads anti-semitism spreads. A British subject selling the rights in a French film of his play to an exiled German Jew is behaving very imprudently unless the bargain is one of an outright sale for a big lump sum.

Spain, which includes all South America that is not Portuguese, will soon be in the field with Spanish or Argentine or Chilean films. Until then, English and American films will hold the field. There is not a single French speaking State in South America.

Then there is the general consideration that France is not for me the centre of the universe, as it naturally seems to you. On the whole I should be a richer man today if France had never existed; and you would certainly be in a stronger position if I had never existed. The French bourgeois doesnt like either of us. To make France the centre of operations for any work of mine would be the act of a lunatic on my part.

As to the German film I have at last obtained an assurance that my fees will be sent to me if I employ German firms to manufacture and distribute. I have accordingly got rid of Fox Films and arranged for a new contract.

As Holland has started making films I have a contract in hand with a Dutch firm; and here again I am faced with all the claims outside Holland and the Dutch East Indies that Deutschmeister makes, and have to say No just as I have said it to him. The nationalisation of the talkie gives a lot of trouble; but it has the advantage in the case of a failure that the eggs are not all in one basket.

I hope Pitoeff is still sending you royalties. The Simpleton is in rehearsal in New York and also in Warsaw. It will not be produced here until the Malvern Festival in August.

All my arrangements have been upset and my work interrupted by the very serious illness of my wife, who nearly died of blood poisoning when we were about to start for South America. She is now convalescing though still in bed; but I cannot deny that it has been hard to attend to her and to Herr Deutschmeister at the same time, to say nothing of you and Henriette. Under the circumstances the intervention of Pitoeff must be regarded as providential.

always
G. Bernard Shaw

To THERESA HELBURN

4 Whitehall Court S W 1
[H/7]   15th February 1935

[Elisabeth Bergner (1897–1986), who emigrated to England in 1932, was a Viennese actress, star of many of Max Reinhardt's productions. She created Joan on the Berlin stage in 1924; it was one of her greatest successes. Her husband Paul Czinner (1890–1972), whom she had wed in 1933, was a Hungarian stage and film producer-director, who had entered into negotiations with Shaw for screen rights of *Saint Joan*, to star his wife. Alla Nazimova (1879–1945), sultry Russian actress noted for "heavy" rôles, was startlingly miscast as Prola in the Theatre Guild's New York production of *The Simpleton of the Unexpected Isles*.]

—Private—

My dear Tessie

I am glad that I have at last a correspondent at Hollywood who has some sense. There is no question of my attitude changing: all my plays are in the market for filming, and have been ever since Hollywood began to realize, however feebly, that a talkie is something more than a movie with spoken sub-titles.

But there is a good deal more for it to realize besides. For instance, that the talkie has killed the old system of buying the world rights from the author. I have just concluded an agreement for a German film of Pygmalion. But under the existing law the film must be made and distributed by Aryan German firms. Else the necessary German permission for the export of my royalties would be refused by the Government. Fox Films might have had this job, including the English language rights, if they had consented to guarantee my German royal-

400

ties; but they threw the whole affair back on my hands with the remark that they are not interested [solely] in the English language rights of Pygmalion.

Another example. R.K.O. makes proposals for the filming of The Devil's Disciple with John Barrymore as the star. But when they submitted a scenario I had to cry off: it was quite impossible; and I then saw that I must make my own scenarios, as Hollywood is not within half a century of knowing how to handle my stuff. I accordingly made a scenario of Pygmalion. The German studio (Klagemann) jumped at it, and, when Fox backed out, agreed with me for the German language.

Then came the great question of the St Joan film with Elizabeth Bergner. I had to make the scenario for that; for nobody could cut the dialogue and write the new scenes except myself. A Hollywood studio would have given the job to the bellboy and been firmly persuaded that his hokum was real good screen stuff which would carry my literary tosh to victory.

R.K.O. did not get as far as the bellboy. Their notion of a scenario was a man lecturing on a series of pictures, like the old dioramas of my youth.

I contemplate the popular Hollywood productions in despair. The photography is good, the acting is good, the expenditure is extravagant; but the attempt to tell a story is pitiable: the people expend tons of energy jumping in and out of automobiles, knocking at doors, running up and downstairs, opening and shutting bedroom doors, drawing automatics, being arrested and tried for inexplicable crimes, with intervals of passionate kissing; and all this is amusing in a way; but of what it is all about neither I nor anyone else in the audience has the faintest idea. Scenically, histrionically, photographically, and wastefully, Hollywood is the wonder of the world; but it has no dramatic technique and no literary taste: it will stick a patch of slovenly speakeasy Californian dialect upon a fine passage of English prose without seeing any difference, like a color blind man sticking a patch of Highland tartan on his dress trousers. When it gets a good bit of stuff it takes infinite pains to drag it down to its own level, firmly believing, of course, that it is improving it all the time. So you see it is not very easy for me to deal with Hollywood; and it will probably end (or begin) with European productions of my plays, adapted to the screen by myself.

I have no notion of what they are doing with The Simpleton in New York, except that they muffed their attempt to get Mrs Patrick Campbell and got Nazimova instead. I have a horrible fear that they will use

Honolulu costumes (or no costumes) instead of Indian ones, and present the four phantoms as brown savages with nothing on but garlands of flowers.

Will you tell them that if they want to abbreviate the title for an electric sign, they must call it The Simpleton, and not The Unexpected Isles?

Many thanks for your letter. I presume you are doing business for Columbia and not wasting your young life in the studio. You must be quite priceless; for I have yet to find anyone connected with films who has the faintest notion of what the word business means.

faithfully
G. Bernard Shaw

To SYDNEY W. CARROLL

Ayot St Lawrence. Welwyn
[H/9]   16th February 1935

[Sydney W. Carroll (1877–1958) journalist and stage producer, had presented Shaw's *The Six of Calais* at his open-air theatre in Regent's Park, in a bill with *Androcles and the Lion*, in July 1934. His newest production was *Henry IV Part 1* at His Majesty's Theatre on 28th February, with pantomime and revue comic George Robey (1869–1954) in his first Shakespearean rôle as Falstaff, directed by Robert Atkins (1886–1972), a former actor who had served his apprenticeship under Beerbohm Tree and performed with Forbes-Robertson and Sir Frank Benson. Charles Surface is a character in *The School for Scandal*.]

Dear Sydney Carroll

Many thanks; but dont waste two first night stalls on an extinct pressman: I'll look in later when the thing has fallen into shape. I loathe first nights, though I appreciate being asked to them.

Now about those damned men in buckram. The tradition of them has been lost—unless Robey has picked it up somewhere. The way to get the climax and bring down the house is this.

It is no use merely mentioning the men in buckram: all you get by that is two or three duty laughs from members of the Shakespeare Reading Society. Falstaff must act the fight all through with the crowd round him. There must be a crowd; for as he illustrates his feints and thrusts they have to get out of his way pretty quickly. The climax comes with

    "I followed me close, came in foot and hand [illustrating], and—

with a THOUGHT!!!!! [Here he stops and does a magnificent whirl round, cutting down an imaginary adversary at each step. The crowd scrambles and tumbles out of the way. He does this as perfectly correct sabre play with his left hand on his hip. He ends up facing the prince on guard, and adds] SEVEN—of the eleven—I paid. [He waits for an instant in this attitude, and then, as an afterthought, suddenly throws up his left arm like a foil fencer. It is this last movement that gets the laugh and completes the culminating situation. Robey will know how to do it].["]

The other point to be careful about is the character of the prince. To play him like Charles Surface is a common and fatal mistake. He is a hateful character, terribly able and sure of himself, selfish, cruel, and without the slightest kindly feeling for the people he amuses himself with. Falstaff's mistake on this last point, and his humiliation when he presumes to act on it when his Hal becomes king, is latent in the First Part, like the ruthless whipping of poor old Quickly and the hanging of Bardolph; but Shakespear takes care to affirm it in the shock of that menacing outburst at the end of the second scene, when, after rattling away as Prince Hal, he suddenly, the moment Poins's back is turned, throws off the *faux bonhomme* and shews his true character in "I know you all, and will a while uphold &c. &c." When that comes, the stage ought to darken and a sinister red lime glow on the demon of the piece.

This is very important, because if the prince tries to snatch the sympathetic comic lead from Falstaff he is bound to fail and damage the whole play in doing so.

The high politics of the play can be saved from tediousness only by playing them very energetically and seriously, with a thorough understanding that all the nobles are scoundrels out for killing the two cleverer scoundrels, Hal and his worn-out father. Falstaff is by contrast a decent soul.

Francis the drawer cuts no ice nowadays: he is an intolerable bore. I should cut him out ruthlessly, thus. "Score a pint of bastard in the Half Moon or so. I am now of all humors that have shewed themselves humors since the old days of Goodman Adam to the pupil age of this present 12 o'clock at midnight; but I am not yet of Percy's mind &c. &c. &c.["]

Ask Robert what he thinks of these suggestions; and excuse my prolixity: it is always dangerous to start me on Shake.

always yours
G. Bernard Shaw

To THE REV. J. BARLOW BROOKS

4 Whitehall Court SW1
[C/1; X/384]   2nd February [March] 1935

[J. Barlow Brooks (1874–1952), a Methodist minister and specialist on Lancashire dialect, was the brother of Shaw's early Fabian colleague and friend
Sam Brooks (1871–1930), an agitator for improved factory and living conditions for workers. Shaw's letter of condolence on the death of Sam activated
a correspondence with the Rev. Mr Brooks, who on 27th February 1935
informed Shaw of his retort to a preacher who said, "A man who does not
desire a future life loves nobody."]

The preacher you quote was probably thinking of a fact that every
table rapping spiritualist can confirm: namely, that the desire to communicate with a lost and beloved friend or relative is the strongest
incentive to believe in personal immortality among people who are free
from the mere vulgar fear of death which leads to the common pretence
that it does not exist.

This pretence will not stand examination. Those who maintain it
make it a condition that the person who survives for ever and ever shall
not be like themselves, but an ecstatically happy and sinless soul with
nothing to do but enjoy being happy in a celestial city where nobody
works and everybody wears beautiful clothes and the sun shines always.
In this fairy tale there is no real continuity nor identity with Tom and
Dick, Fanny and Sally. The so-called immortality is accepted only on
impossible conditions of transfiguration and depersonalization.

As to real immortality—persistence of the individual with all his
limitations and imperfections and memories to all eternity, I do not
desire it, not only because no sensible man desires what he knows he
cannot get, but because nothing more horrible can be imagined than
the doom of the Wandering Jew and the Flying Dutchman.

G. Bernard Shaw

To THE REV. J. BARLOW BROOKS

[Savoy Hotel. Bournemouth]
[C/1; X/384]   [Undated: assigned to 8th March 1935]

["Why shouldn't life after death be evolutionary," Brooks had replied, "and
therefore relieved from monotony?" The Nunc Dimittis "Lord, now lettest
thou thy servant depart in peace" is the song of Simeon (Luke 2:29–32)

performed as a canticle in the liturgies of various churches. Shaw and Charlotte holidayed for a week in Bournemouth.]

There is not a scrap of evidence for post mortem evolution. How many feet high would an oak tree be in the year 193,500,000,000,000,000 if it went on growing for ever and ever?

To an intelligent and reasonably modest person the grapes are really sour. If you are too young to look at yourself and say Enough, look at ME, and your Nunc Dimittis will deafen the congregation.

GBS

To MRS PATRICK CAMPBELL

[H/4; X/160]

[Ayot St Lawrence. Welwyn]
17th March 1935

[*The Simpleton of the Unexpected Isles* opened in New York on 18th February; it survived for only forty performances. It was the drama critic Percy Hammond (1873–1936) who had written in the *New York Herald-Tribune* on 19th February, "Like a dignified monkey, he climbs a tree and pelts us with edifying cocoanuts ..." The Polish press, Shaw informed William Maxwell in September, labelled the play "The Unexpected Failure of The Aged Simpleton." *Escape Me Never* by Margaret Kennedy (1896–1967), with Elisabeth Bergner making her first London appearance, opened in December 1933 and ran for eight months. Shaw carried to Africa with him a typescript of the draft of *The Millionairess*, which he had written on the 1934 voyage under the provisional title *His Tragic Clients*, to trim, revise, and provide with stage directions. It was finally sent to the printer in July.]

Stella, Stella

How often must I tell you to take on as many enemies in front as you please, but never to leave one behind!

As it turns out you are lucky to have missed the part of Prola—not, O most Just God, Pralo—for the critics have fallen on it with such fury that it has flopped completely and is now playing to the Guild subscribers only, which means $8000 a week for a few weeks and then, extinction. The politest notice describes me as a dignified monkey shying cocoanuts at the public. However, that does not account for the failure; for the critics went just as savagely for Margaret Kennedy's play with Elisabeth Bergner, and it has had an overwhelming success. I have just had the flashlights of the production, which was lavish and earnest, but all wrong. Nazimova, in *your* part, appears as a slinking sinuous odalisque. She should have been straight as a ramrod: an Egyptian goddess. My four wonderful young Indian deities, clothed to the wrists and ankles in silks and bangles, and full of mystery and enchantment, came out simply as a naked cabaret troup in the latest Parisian undress. And so on and so forth. When I am not on the spot the harder they try and the wronger they go.

However, that is not what I have to scold you for. You should not have snubbed The Guild even if they were in the wrong. You are not their governess; and it is very important for you that they should be very sorry they missed you, and very eager to get you another time. You should have touched your hat and trusted for a renewal of their esteemed orders. But they were not in the wrong. If you want New York engagements it is your business to live within half an hour of Broadway exactly as it is the business of a London stockbroker to live within half an hour of Capel Court. And it is because you want engagements as a film actress that you live within half an hour of Hollywood. This almost forces you to choose between the two branches of the profession unless you are prepared to pay travelling expenses; for you cannot expect New York to pay travelling expenses from California just as you could not expect London to pay travelling expenses from the Hebrides. You must either live on the spot or get to it at your own expense. That is hard lines; but it is business; and you must not insult The Guild for being businesslike.

To offer you a part without sending you the book would, I grant you, have been a little disrespectful if the play had been by some nobody; but damn it, Stella, a play by *me*—by ME—by ME!!!!! What were you dreaming of?

All this is to guide you in your ways in future; for it always makes me uneasy when I think how very likely you are to *mourir sur la paille* if you persist in governessing people and quarrelling with them. Quarrelling DATES: it drags one back to Whistler. Governessing is pure Croydon.

In short you shouldnt have left that poor young lady at The Guild offices with a sore derrière by dealing a quite useless parting kick instead of sending her a bouquet and saying how flattered you were by being honored by an invitation to act for the leading highbrow theatre in the U.S. if not in the world.

How do you like being tutored? Well, that's how other people feel when you lecture them.

As you apparently do not keep a press agent one never knows what you are doing or where you are. As for me I am repulsively old, as I fancy you realized suddenly when last we met. . . . We start next Thursday (21st March) for a voyage round Africa, and shall not be back in England until the middle of June.

And that's all my news, except that I shall spend the voyage finishing a play I began a year ago called *The Millionairess*.

The machine having suddenly gone out of order I must stop just when I am beginning.

GBS

To WILLIAM MAXWELL

Rolling down the Spanish coast for Gib.
MV Llangibby Castle

[S(A)/3]   23rd March 1935

[The Shaws sailed from Tilbury on the 21st, proceeding to Gibraltar and thence to Palma, Marseilles, Genoa, Port Said and Suez. The Webbs' new book was *Soviet Communism: A New Civilisation?*]

We had a smooth Channel; and the Bay looked smooth, but was crossed by an Atlantic swell which caused the ship to make all-but successful efforts to capsize every half minute or so; and though we are getting used to it, and the cold has abated, we are still squeamish. I have, however, put in two good days work on the Millionairess and on Webb's Russian proofs.

This calls for no reply; but in case anything unexpected should turn up I am overtakable via Miss Patch and Air Mail at Marseilles, Genoa, and Port Said. All being well, we shall land at Durban, Natal, on the 29th April, spend a while there, and sail in a bigger ship, The Winchester Castle, on the 15th May, round the Cape to Cape Town, Madeira & Southampton. I shall be accessible all the time by wireless.

Ugh! this ship does roll damnably.

always yrs
G. Bernard Shaw

To THE THEATRE GUILD

[A/6]
In the Red Sea outward bound to Durban
7th April 1935

[The ship was now somewhere between Port Sudan and Aden, crossing the equator on the 10th. The Shaws spent a few days at Mombasa, then sailed down the coast to Zanzibar, Beira and Lourenço Marques. They disembarked at Durban on the 28th, where they remained for a three-week visit. Then, on 24th May, they boarded the *Winchester Castle* at Cape Town for a seventeen-day return cruise to Southampton. The settings for the Theatre Guild production of *The Simpleton* were designed by Lee Simonson.]

Dear Theatre Guild

I am sorry The Simpleton has flopped so completely. The returns I saw before leaving seemed to indicate that no soul in New York outside your subscription list crossed the threshold of the theatre.

The flashlights shewed me that you had done your very best for the play; but you did it all wrong. I should have made you send Simonson to Bombay for a month, not only to see the Elephanta caves, but to feel the sex appeal of the women, especially the Parsee ladies, and the enchantment of the temple gods, especially the Jain no-gods.

In India nudity, which we ridiculous westerns still think the climax of S.A. (in spite of our everyday experience of sunbathing) means simply poverty. The Indian enchantress is dressed in wonderful silks right up to the wrists and ankles, finishing off with circlets of gold. The Simpleton depends on the reproduction of this Indian magic on the stage. Simonson, being an American savage, saw nothing in it but a chance for a Hollywood cabaret quartet, utterly prosaic, utterly Broadway in its scanty dress, and as nearly as possible utterly nude. No magic, and no sex appeal except that flaunted in every restaurant.

Nazimova saw herself as a Javanese dancer, sinuous, slinking, the perfect odalisque. Prola should be as rigid as an Egyptian queen: all steel and straight lines. Now Prola is the leading part in the play: no Prola, no play. Nazimova tried to substitute something else; and it was something she could not supply; for she is *not* a Javanese dancer; and no actress can act one.

It is a pity your attempt to capture Mrs P.C. for the part failed. I have told her that you were not to blame: if people want New York engagements they must live within half an hour of Broadway, and she shouldnt have snubbed your very polite lady correspondent; but she would have given the part the peculiar distinction it needs: a quasi intellectual distinction, not an exotic one.

The play I am at present at work on, The Millionairess, is a star play for a very vigorous actress, very much as On the Rocks was a star play for the leading actor (or The Apple Cart); but the play in itself is no more likely to please the popular taste than The Simpleton; and I shall not press it on your attention until you are prepared to announce a season of my failures to give New York an opportunity of apologizing.

I expect to arrive in England on the 15th June. Until then I shall be a wanderer on the face of the earth.

faithfully
G. Bernard Shaw

To LAURENTIA McLACHLAN

On the Equator. 82° in the shade
On the east coast of Africa

[H/98; X/256]   12th April 1935

["Since you ask about my latest play," Shaw wrote to Dame Laurentia on 25th January, "I risk the last remnant of your regard for me by sending you a copy. If only you can get over the first shock of its profanity you may find some tiny spark of divinity in it. You may ask why I write such things. I dont know: I have to. The devil has me by one hand and the Blessed Virgin by the other" (H/98; X/256). "You are quite right," the abbess replied on the 7th, "in believing that I should discover divinity under the profanity, and with very much I am in full sympathy, and heartily amused. Is it necessary though to be so offensively profane when satirizing vice and the British Empire? Need you use words of Scripture? It seems to me you could be quite as convincing without wounding the reasonable susceptibilities of those who believe in God with their whole hearts as I suspect you yourself do. I see the play is unpublished and I hope it will remain so ... Whatever happens you absolutely must omit the allusion to the Immaculate Mother ... You know, as well as I do, that we do not worship her as God" (A/2; X/369).

"I have again," Shaw confessed to Sydney Cockerell on the 12th, "shocked Laurentia, who says that the finest religious passage in my new play made her blood boil and that it must come out" (C/9). "I wish," he added to Cockerell on the 28th, "we could take Laurentia to the east, and make her pray in all the Divine Mother's temples" (A/9).]

Cara Sorella Laurentia

You are a puzzle to me with your unexpected rages. I ask myself, since I know that one becomes eminent in the Church through capacity for business more easily than by capacity for religion, "Can

Laurentia be a completely irreligious (or areligious) managing woman who becomes boss in a convent exactly as she would become boss in a castle or in a laundry?"

McLachlan? That suggests a clan of Covenanters to whom the worship of the B.V.M. is a damnable idolatry to be wiped out with claymore and faggot. Has Laurentia got that in her blood? If not, why in the name of all the saints does she fly out at me when I devoutly insist that the Godhead must contain the Mother as well as the Father?

Or is it merely personal? So many women hate their mothers (serve them right, mostly!) and see red when the cult of maternity arises.

You want me, as if it were a sort of penance, to say a lot of Hail Maries. But I am always saying Hail, Mary! on my travels. Of course I dont say it in that artificial form which means nothing. I say it in my own natural and sincere way when She turns up in the temples and tombs of Egypt and among the gods of Hindustan—Hallo, Mary! For you really cannot get away from Her. She has many names in the guide books, and many disguises. But She never takes me in. She favours Brother Bernardo with special revelations and smiles at his delighted "Hallo, Mary!" When I write a play like The Simpleton and have to deal with divinity in it She jogs my elbow at the right moment and whispers "Now Brother *B*. dont forget *me*." And I dont.

But then you come along in a fury and cry "How dare you? Cut all this stuff out, and say fifty Hail Maries."

Which am I to obey? Our Lady of Stanbrook or Our Lady of Everywhere?

When you are old, as I am, these things will clear up and become real to you. I wonder whether, if Raphael had lived to be old like Michael Angelo, he would have given us something less absurd than the highly respectable Italian farmers' daughters he imposed so smugly on the world as visions of the B.V.M. Never have I stood before one of his Madonnas and exclaimed Hallo, Mary! Raphael made the adoration of the Mother impossible; but his view was so frankly and nicely human and fleshly and kindly that in the Dresden Madonna he produced for all time the ideal wet nurse, healthy, comely, and completely brainless.

On the other hand there is the giantess–goddess of Cimabue with her magnetic stare, a much deeper conception, but with just a little too much of the image and too little reality to be as approachable as the Egyptian goddesses of the great period.

In short, the Christian Maries are all failures. This suggests that the Jains were right in excluding God from their ritual as beyond human

410

power to conceive or portray. At least that is their theory; but in practice they have in their shrines images of extraordinary beauty and purity of design who throw you into an ecstasy of prayer and a trance of peace when they look at you, as no Christian iconography can.

I said to the pundit who shewed me round "Those images are surely gods, are they not?" "Not at all" he said, "they are statues of certain very wise men of the Jains." This was obvious nonsense; so I pointed out that a man kneeling in the shrine (having first washed himself from head to foot) was clearly praying to a god. "Pooh!" said the pundit with enormous contempt, "he is only a heathen idolator."

It is in these temples that you escape from the frightful parochiality of our little sects of Protestants and Catholics, and recognize the idea of God everywhere, and understand how the people who struggled hardest to establish the unity of God made the greatest number of fantastically different images of it, producing on us the effect of a crude polytheism.

Then comes the effort to humanize these images. The archaic Minerva becomes the very handsome and natural Venus of Milo. The Cimabue colossus becomes the wet nurse. Bellini's favorite model becomes as well known to us in her blue hood as any popular actress. Leonardo, Michael Angelo, Correggio (once, in the dome in Parma) lift these leading ladies, these stars of the studio, for a moment out of the hopelessly common; but on the whole, wisdom is with the Jains.

I have been getting into trouble by backing up a proposal to give Christ's Cathedral in Dublin to the Catholics, leaving St Patrick's to the Protestants. The two cathedrals are in a poor neighborhood within a stone's throw of one another. St Patrick's was restored by Guinness the brewer, Christ's by Roe the distiller. The drunkenness of the poor Catholics paid for both: why should they not have at least one?

But my individual opinion is that cathedrals should be for all men, and not for this or that sect.

By this time we have passed the equator, and it is time for me to stop blaspheming.

Bless you, dear Laurentia.

G. Bernard Shaw

To SYDNEY C. COCKERELL

Ayot St Lawrence. Welwyn
[A/3; X/289.e]   25th June 1935

[Following a spill from his motor bike "Boanerges" (a gift from the Shaws) on 14th May, T.E. Lawrence lingered unconscious for 142 hours, then died on the morning of the 19th. The Shaws received the news in Durban, where Shaw was queried by a pressman as to what he thought the nation owed to Lawrence. "What about Westminster Abbey?" said Shaw. "His country, which refused him a small pension, owes him at least a stone" (*Natal Mercury*, 20th May 1935). Charlotte's personal grief is evident in a letter she wrote to Dolly Walker on 24th June: "The South African papers made a giant deal of it but there was not the vulgar excitement there has been here [in England]. How he suffered from that all his life! I am not sure this is not better for *him*. He always dreaded pain & the idea of death (as a sort of sign of defeat!), and now, you see, he has got off without knowing anything about it. I somehow cannot feel he is really gone—he seems to be here in this little house [in Ayot] he came to so often" (A/3). And in 1939 she admitted to Dolly it was "the strangest contact of my life" (A/3).]

My dear Cockerell

I could have sworn that your visit with Lawrence about Doughty and the visit on which you took away the picture [the Augustus John portrait of Shaw donated to the Fitzwilliam Museum] were separate and unconnected events. On looking up my documents I find that you were right.

My memory is excessively theatrical. It arranges everything for the stage. This is artistically a great improvement; but as police evidence it is worthless.

ever
G.B.S.

To SIEGFRIED TREBITSCH

4 Whitehall Court SW1
[H/5; X/341]   27th June 1935

[Oswald Pirow (1890–1959), a member of longtime Prime Minister James Hertzog's "inner cabinet," who piloted the States Act of 1934 through the South African parliament, was minister of defence and transport 1933–39.]

My dear Trebitsch

When I was in S. Africa, the Minister for Transport, Mr Pirow (note the Teutonic name) made a public appeal for white immigrants to keep up the white population. If the Germans are offended by the charge of sterility implied in this appeal, it is to Mr Pirow they must look and not to me.

It is alleged in certain quarters in Africa, Australia, and New Zealand, that white families become degenerate and extinct in the third generation. This is certainly not true of all white families under all circumstances; but Mr Pirow's appeal proves that, as in New Zealand, the white people do not multiply as the colored people do. I at first attributed this to Birth Control, but was assured that the white natives *want* more children.

One day, in conversation with an able public man, a doctor by profession, I remarked on the fact that although the day was one of unbroken sunshine, the sun went down at 5.15, almost without twilight, and left us in darkness until 7.30 in the morning! "We are glad of it" he said. "We get too much sunshine."

It immediately occurred to me that the effect of excessive sunshine on white skins might have something to do with white sterility. If so, the remedy is clearly pigmentation, which can be brought about most easily by interbreeding with the colored races. Germans in Africa do not object: there are plenty of half breeds in what used to be German Africa.

Talk about "the negro" is mere ignorance. The colored races are as different as Prussians from Bavarians, or as Baltic Celts from Viennese. German "poor whites" (for instance, the only half human charcoal burners) are shockingly inferior to Zulus.

In Hawai, in New Zealand, and in Jamaica, there are hardly any pure bred natives left. The white man, however "Nordic," cannot resist the very attractive native women. Even in the United States the fanatical boycott of "the tar brush" is being relaxed to an extent which astonishes old Americans. We may live to see a Reichskanzler with a Zulu, Bantu, or Hawaian wife.

Tell Colonel Goering with my compliments that I have backed his regime in England to the point of making myself unpopular, and shall continue to do so on all matters in which he and Hitler stand for permanent truths and genuine Realpolitik. But this racial stuff is damned English nonsense, foisted on Germany by Houston Chamberlain. The future is to the mongrel, not to the Junker. I, Bernard Shaw, have said it. And if Germany boycotts me, so much the worse for German culture.

ever
G. Bernard Shaw

413

PS Give this to the press, but not until you are safely back in Vienna. It will be a magnificent advertisement if they dare print it. If not, send copies privately to Goering and Hitler.

To HERBERT M. PRENTICE

Malvern Hotel. Malvern
[H/3]   28th July 1935

[Herbert M. Prentice (1890–1963) was until 1940 a principal stage director of the Birmingham Repertory Theatre. He staged most of the Malvern productions from 1934 to 1937, including the 1935 *Misalliance* and the first English production of *The Simpleton*. Shaw was attending dress rehearsals prior to the season's opening on the 29th. Despite his statement after viewing the *Misalliance* rehearsal that Tarleton was "hopeless," Shaw wrote to Wilfrid Lawson on 21st August to say "I enjoyed both your Gilbey [in *Fanny's First Play*] & your Tarleton enormously, all the more because you are not a bit like either & yet got away with both magnificently" (S(A)/1).]

Dear Herbert

Here is a note or two about Misalliance.

Lina's costume is frightfully wrong: those riding breeches are not only ugly but they suggest the equestrienne, which is just what she is not. She should have a complete acrobat's performing suit, skin tight from head to foot, as brilliant as possible, but not loud, as she has to be very dignified and refined. There is no other costume in the least like an acrobat's; and unless her costume proclaims her profession and incidentally overwhelms Mrs Tarleton all her distinction is gone.

Gunner is wrong also. He must look extremely respectable in the shop assistant's style: black coat, carefully brushed, white collar, black tie, white shirt, grey trousers, and bowler hat, if not a tall one. His speech must be that of a shopman, not of a rough. If the wardrobe does not run to this, he might wear a neat blue serge suit and bowler hat with the white collar and black tie and white shirt; but the other would be better.

Tarleton is hopeless. He should be a handsome, imposing figure with white hair, nearer seventy than sixty, a king of men in his line. But Lawson has become so completely the slave of his box of tricks that he has lost his instinct for make-up (if he ever had any) and produces no impression except that he has been too lazy to dress himself for the

414

part. I am afraid to say anything to him lest I should upset him alto-gether. He will get through on the one funny mannerism which seems to be his whole stock-in-trade; but it is a pity; for he really has, or used to have, some histrionic guts in him.

The rest of my notes I can impart myself at the final words rehearsal.

Take care of yourself. I was really horrified when I learnt that you had to drudge at the wretched Simpleton again for Birmingham.

faithfully
G. Bernard Shaw

To JAMES BRIDIE

Malvern Hotel. Malvern
[H/1] 8th August 1935

[James Bridie (1888–1951) was the pseudonym of a Scottish doctor Osborne Henry Mavor, who became a successful dramatist. Invited by Paul Czinner to revise Shaw's scenario for *Saint Joan*, the cautious Bridie wrote to GBS to determine whether it would meet with his approval. Despite his threats, Shaw continued to negotiate with Czinner into the following year. Elisabeth Bergner had recently appeared in the film *Catherine the Great*, directed by Czinner, with Douglas Fairbanks Jr. as her leading man.]

My dear Bridie

You have blown the gaff with a vengeance. Your letter came just in the nick of time as I was about to discuss the contract with the com-pany. I have now cried off the film, and excommunicated Czinner with bell, book, and candle.

I made a complete scenario for Joan myself, with new scenes, new speeches, all the necessary cuts, and everything ready for the screen except such minutiae of the shooting as can be done only in the studio. Czinner professed himself delighted with it. Not a word has ever been said as to any departure from it.

And now, your letter!

There is only one thing to be said on Czinner's side; and that is that he had the sense to select you as his collaborator. For that be all his sins forgiven; but it is clear that he does not see the play as I see it, and that puts him out of the question as a director.

I have just seen the film in which Elizabeth plays Catherine II. It was curious to see how completely and unconsciously she made Catherine a scheming Jewess instead of a German princess rising by sheer gravitation.

Any chance of seeing you here in Malvern this year?

always yours
G. Bernard Shaw

To JAMES BRIDIE

[C/1]
Malvern Hotel. Malvern
12th August 1935

Shinner is perhaps more shinned against than shinning; but he told two whoppers. No contract has yet been executed. And no carte blanche as to the scenario was either given or implied. And why, if he wanted more scenes to gratify his anti-rigidity craze, did he not ask me for them? Why did he, without consulting me, invite another famous author into a collaboration which would double the commercial burden of the authors fees on the enterprise?

Send him a bill for £500 at once, just to larn him.

GBS

To LAURENTIA McLACHLAN

[H/98; X/256]
Malvern
30th August 1935

[The edition of Lawrence's *Seven Pillars of Wisdom* that Shaw sent was the first commercially published one. *The Millionairess* was a first proof, inscribed: "This is one of my entirely profane works; so you must read it in an unprofessional spirit." Dom Basil Messinesis was a Benedictine monk to whom Dame Laurentia had introduced GBS and Charlotte.]

Dearest Sister Laurentia

You cannot imagine how delighted I was to find you shining in all your old radiance before the cloud of illness came upon you. If ever I write an opera libretto, it will be rather like Die Zauberflöte; but I shall call it The Merry Abbess.

As I drove back here it was a magically lovely evening, or seemed so to me. I felt ever so much the better for your blessing. There are some people who, like Judas Iscariot, have to be damned as a matter of heavenly business; and it is clear that I may be one of them; but if I try to sneak into paradise behind you they will be too glad to see you to notice me.

I sent the Seven Pillars yesterday, and now enclose The Millionairess, which will make you rejoice in your retreat.

I promised to send that handsome young Dom Basil a book, and have actually bought it for him; but for the moment I have mislaid the address he gave me. It will turn up presently.

always your
Brother Bernard

To WILLIAM SAROYAN

Ayot St Lawrence. Welwyn
23rd September 1935

[U(E)/123]

[William Saroyan (1908–81), a young American playwright and short story writer of Armenian extraction, had sent to Shaw from his home in Fresno, California, some of his one-act plays, which may have included the early version of *My Heart's in the Highlands,* an expanded text of which was produced by the Theatre Guild in April 1939. In a further note on 15th November (U(E)/123) Shaw proclaimed Saroyan to be "a new and remarkable talent." Five years later, Saroyan won and rejected a Pulitzer Prize for drama.]

[T]hey are very good: good everyway: character—action—musical talk (style)—modern screenable technique—full range of interest—sound economic and political foundation—all alive-O—make me feel like an ancient classic on the shelf.

Go ahead, hard, William: you are I T.

G. Bernard Shaw

To G. W. BISHOP

[H/83; X/385]

4 Whitehall Court SW1
10th October 1935

[G. W. Bishop had written to Shaw in his capacity as president of the Critics' Circle. Shaw lectured to the Circle in October 1929 and attended its dinner in honour of J. T. Grein in December 1932, at which he responded to St John Ervine's toast to "Our Visitors."]

Dear George Bishop

I accept with my best bow the honor magnanimously conferred on me by the Critics' Circle; and I promise not to abuse it by blighting the reunions of the circle by my abhorrent presence.

When the circle was formed about a hundred years ago I joined it, to the great consternation of its members. But as I never, as far as I can remember, paid any subscription, and certainly never received any notice of its meetings, I think I may take it that though I was never formally expelled, I may now take my place as a new recruit.

faithfully
G. Bernard Shaw

To A. A. ROBACK

[X/386]

4 Whitehall Court SW1
16th October 1935

[Dr Abraham Aaron Roback (1890–1965), a Freudian psychopathologist, of Cambridge, Mass., was the author of numerous books, including *The Psychology of Character* (1927).]

Dear Sir

In reply to your letter of the 1st instant, I am not qualified to contribute to the Freud volume. When I was young I rejected all the standard books on psychology as worthless. I said that a science of psychology was impossible because it could be established only by the personal confession of the workings of the human imagination which nobody would make, and which would be unprintable in any case. Dr Freud proved that I was right as to the science, but quite wrong as to the difficulty of obtaining the confessions and the permanence of the

Victorian prudery which inhibited their publication. But that does not qualify me to contribute to a serious work on psycho-analysis. I must therefore excuse myself.

Many thanks for the invitation.

faithfully

G. Bernard Shaw

To SIEGFRIED TREBITSCH

Ayot St Lawrence. Welwyn

15th December 1935

[H/5; X/341]

[Shaw was preparing to embark on a west-to-east round-the-world cruise, the last foreign journey he and Charlotte were destined to make. Gabriel Pascal (1894–1954), a flashy, self-confident, impecunious Hungarian, with a paucity of film credits as a producer-director, had turned a mesmerising eye on Shaw and in a trice convinced him to entrust to the exotic foreigner the English-language screen rights to *Pygmalion*. There was, however, nothing really surprising about this: it was merely an extension of Shaw's lifetime fascination with and predilection for all the vagabonds and tinkers and drunkards, the scoundrels and sharpsters whom, with eyes fully open, he had permitted to reach into his pocket. The antecedents of the ingratiating Pascal were, among others, Pakenham Beatty and Charles Charrington, Hubert Bland and Edward Aveling, Frank Harris, Charles McEvoy and Floryan Sobieniowski; and Shaw's tolerance of them is reflected both in Morell's injunction to his wily father-in-law in *Candida*: "So long as you come here honestly as a self-respecting, thorough, convinced scoundrel, justifying your scoundrelism, and proud of it, you are welcome," and in Lord Henry's assertion, in Wilde's *The Picture of Dorian Gray*, that Dorian would always be fond of him because "I represent to you all the sins you have never had the courage to commit."

Alexander Korda (1893–1956), founder and head of London Film Productions, first brought artistic distinction and commercial success to the British film industry in the mid-1930s.]

My dear Trebitsch

Klagemann must wait. I sail for the Pacific on the 22nd January; and it is utterly beyond my possibilities to complete a scenario of Caesar and Cleopatra before then. Even if I had nothing else to do it would be difficult: as it is, I have about two months work to jam in by hook or crook. Besides, I have not made up my mind about C. and C.: I may decide on another play. Anyhow there can be no question of a scenario

419

or an agreement until my return in April. And whether the agreement will be with Klagemann I cannot say until I have seen the Pygmalion film.

I have disposed of the English film of Pygmalion to Gabriel Pascal, whom I think you have met. He has been trying to get the Klagemann film over for me; and one was actually sent; but it was so badly worn— so "rainy"—that Pascal sent it back. He expects to have a new one to shew me on Thursday next. Until I see this I cannot judge whether I can depend on Klagemann to understand my artistic planning for the screen.

Korda is out of the song: I shall see no more of him now that I have closed with Pascal. He is too busy on other jobs to be of use to me in the way I want. He would certainly not entertain Jitta at present.

The film business has not so far proved very lucrative. Klagemann sends me elaborate accounts and says that the money is enclosed with them; but this part of the affair is wholly imaginary: not a rap has reached me. I daresay this can be explained; but meanwhile I am heavily out of pocket by the transaction.

For the moment you and Tina must starve. Shall I lend you £500 on account pending some transaction between us for your translation rights? If so, send me a wire with the single word Yes; and I will remit.

as ever
G. Bernard Shaw

To SIEGFRIED TREBITSCH

[H/5; X/341]

Ayot St Lawrence. Welwyn
30th December 1935

[A Viennese correspondent reported in *The Observer* on 22nd December that the world première of *The Millionairess* would take place in Vienna's intimate Akademie Theater, and offered a garbled synopsis of the play. The first Viennese performance was on 4th January 1936. The correspondent could, unknown to Shaw, have had easy access to a copy of the play, for it had been published in German on 19th December.]

My dear Trebitsch

I am appalled at your unhappy bargain with Klagemann. You will get nothing, because in the film business [it] is not the manufacturer who makes the profit but the distributor. The manufacturer is ruined

420

unless he has shares in the distributing company, which of course he takes care to secure before he does the work. As Klagemann is no novice he must have known perfectly well that he was taking advantage of your innocence when he offered you a profit sharing agreement—unless indeed you asked him for one, in which case he is entitled to plead Caveat Emptor.

A notice of The Millionairess has appeared here in The Observer and made me rather nervous, because, though its quotations from the text prove that the writer had access either to the prompt book or to the rehearsals, his account of the plot is extraordinarily confused and incomplete. Are you sure they are not tampering with it? If you allow them the smallest latitude they will spoil it and the play will be a ghastly failure. If they have found the right woman for Epifania, and she sticks faithfully to her part as I have written it, it will be a success; and you will make some money. But if you let them talk you into accepting the smallest variations, the danger of failure will be very great. The play is not like the Apple Cart. Infamous as Reinhardt's travesty of that play was, it at least made money, though it dragged my reputation through the mud. But this cannot happen with The Millionairess. Unless it is pure Shaw, it is doomed.

I have not yet seen the Pygmalion film: the exhibition has been put off until next Friday the third January. Pascal has told me some things about it that make me uneasy. I have your solemn assurance that it follows my scenario exactly; but Pascal denies this. If Klagemann has betrayed me, and humbugged you into believing that his changes dont matter, I shall not trust him again.

All film adventurers denounce one another as crooks, mostly quite justly. To my great surprise Pascal made an exception in the case of Klagemann, who is, he says, a gentleman. He claims to have met you, but no more. He is a Hungarian, apparently a man of birth and education, and an extraordinarily clever and dramatic talker. He reminds me of Frank Harris, though he has certainly been better brought up. I am taking a big chance with him; but I should have to do that with anybody. Artistically he is vehemently Antisemite, which just suits me; for it is always the Jew who thinks he knows better than I do how to put a play on the stage or screen. He is equally vehemently pro-Jew in business. He says "In the studio, no Jews. In distribution and exhibition, all Jews." So I have given him a Pygmalion contract for the English language; and now, advienne que pourra, as Baudricourt said [in *Saint Joan*].

I hope to write a new play on my voyage (22 Jan. to 6th April). It would pay me better to turn my old plays into scenarios; but that takes as long or longer. I wish you could write scenarios: then we could retrieve your shattered fortunes.

How, exactly, was your income cut off? On what ground can the German government pillage an Austrian subject? I want to know this politically as well as personally.

Be sure you tell the Academie management that if they alter a single word or incident in The Millionairess they shall never have another play of mine to murder.

ever
G. Bernard Shaw

To FLORYAN SOBIENIOWSKI

Ayot St Lawrence. Welwyn
[H/4]   7th January 1936

[Shaw and Pascal finally viewed the German *Pygmalion*, which had been allowed to enter the country "in bond," on 4th January, in a hired projection room in Endell Street. Jenny Jugo (b. 1905), a Viennese actress, made films until 1950.]

Dear Sobieniowski

. . . Klagemann of Berlin has made a film of Pygmalion which has had a great success. In spite of a most explicit contract binding him to follow my scenario exactly, he has made dozens of changes; and every change is a blunder. He has introduced a horse race at which Eliza fights a rough. Also a ping pong table (table tennis) tournament. The thing is beyond description; but Jenny Jugo, as a female circus clown not in the least like Eliza, carries it through by her high spirits. Fortunately Klagemann has it for the German language only; so you may threaten the direst vengeance if any attempt is made to introduce it into Poland.

Are there any Polish films home-made? I have given the English film license for Pygmalion to Gabriel Pascal, who has some artistic flair. Have you ever heard of him?

faithfully
G. Bernard Shaw

To SIEGFRIED TREBITSCH

4 Whitehall Court S W 1

[H/5; X/341]   16th January 1936

[*The Millionairess* was not banned in Germany. It was eventually produced in Munich on 15th August 1936, and in Berlin the following December, with Joseph Goebbels (1897–1945), minister for propaganda and "national enlightenment," in the audience.]

My dear Siegfried

You will certainly drive me crazy with your changes of front. You assured me repeatedly that I need have no fear; that Klagemann was a perfect gentleman and that my scenario was being faithfully followed in every particular. And all the time, as you now tell me, you were in Berlin in a nest of scoundrels fighting to prevent them from making changes even more monstrous than those they have actually made! If you had given me the smallest hint of this I could have tackled K. before it was too late. But you kept patting me on the back and telling me not to worry—that it was all right—and that the film would be just what I wanted it to be. And this, you say, was to save me from being disturbed by your conflicts with K!

Klagemann very wisely says nothing. He has sent more money: that is his best argument.

Why should not the hundred stages of Germany produce The Millionairess? If the Pygmalion [film] is not banned, why should The Millionairess be banned? In any case persecutions do not last for ever. What I feared was that you had property which had been confiscated.

Since writing the above I have received your letter of the 14th, in which you promise me that when you come to London in October you will tell me how you have been deceiving me for the last 30 years.* But the present trouble is about your deceiving me for the last 30 weeks. Why dwell on your past crimes?

I must make my own scenarios to avoid intolerable complications. You forget that I have to deal with all the countries on earth, with authorised translators in several of them. If I had to arrange for a rake-off for you in all these countries in addition to what my translators could claim the transaction would be impossible. But it does not matter, as Klagemann is the only bidder for C & C [*Cæsar and Cleopatra*]; and I do not propose to trust him with another film.

---

* Here Trebitsch inserted a marginal note, dated Zürich 15. Oktober 1953, which (translated from the German) reads: "This alludes to cuts I allowed in order to assure success and to attain productions."

If Koretz will give me the name and address of any film producer who is not a crook (according to all the others) I shall be obliged to him. This particular one has deeply engraved on his frontal sinus the vertical wrinkles which are made by the human conscience. What a contrast with you, who have no conscience whatever!

your long suffering
G. Bernard Shaw

To AUGUSTIN HAMON

[H/1]
4 Whitehall Court SW 1
20th January 1936

[Italy had invaded Abyssinia (now Ethiopia) in 1935. The territory remained under Italian control until liberated by British troops in 1941. Danakil is the Arabic name for the Afars, a proud, independent, and fierce people of northeastern Ethiopia and Djibouti, nominally Muslim.]

My dear Hamon
Many thanks for the articles, which I return. But they do not touch the question of the present war. In European politics you may be anti-Mussolini and pro-Stalin in the conflict between Fascism and Communism. So may I. But in the conflict between Danakil savage and civilized Italian you must, as a civilized man, be on the Italian side. Otherwise you find yourself in a position which is fundamentally indefensible, and in which you will for the first time in your life be heartily supported by the Liberals, the Imperialists, the right wing of the Labor Party (that is, the Trade Unionists), the Militarists, the Pacifists: in short, with the massed reaction that has always been anti-Hamon.

You must not fall back on the old notion that I stand for Italy merely to épater le bourgeois. I have been compelled to think the matter out very carefully by the fact that my wife is furiously pro-Abyssinian. Nothing but the strongest conviction could induce me to write letters to The Times which distress her. But in the face of the scalp hunting North American Indian, the head hunting Dyak, the cannibal Maori, and the testicle hunting Danakil, European civilization must stand solid. Capitalism versus Socialism, clericalism versus anti-clericalism, Fascism versus Sovietism do not come into the question at all. To take

424

the side of the Danakil out of hostility to Mussolini would be an act of opportunist scoundrelism which would make the European situation very much worse than it already is, and do no good in the long run to the Danakils.

always yours
G. Bernard Shaw

To BLANCHE PATCH

S.S. Arandora Star
Approaching Miami Beach
[A/4]   3rd February 1936

[The Shaws sailed on 22nd January from Southampton. During the Atlantic crossing Shaw worked to clear away two obligations: prefaces for the Limited Editions Club's *Great Expectations* (1937) and for May Morris's *William Morris: Artist, Writer, Socialist*, II (1936), the preface separately published in the United States as *William Morris as I Knew Him* (1936).]

Dear B.P.

The enclosed Dickens preface is finished. I have a Morris preface in hand; but it has not gone far enough to send. No play yet.

The day after I wrote the Madeira card we had a most infernal storm. To my great disgust I was violently sick for the first time since my Jamaica trip in—was it 1911?

Nothing else to record.

G. Bernard Shaw

To CLARA HIGGS

[S.S. Arandora Star]
[X/387]   10th February 1936

[Clara Higgs (1874–1948) had been the Shaws' housekeeper at Ayot and her husband Harry (1874–1961) the gardener and occasional chauffeur since 1904. The photo was taken aboard ship on 4th February. During the two days they were in Miami, Shaw toured the Pan American Airways base and he and Charlotte visited the physical culturist Bernarr Macfadden (1868–1955) and dined with the physician John Kellogg (1852–1943) at his Miami Springs sanatorium, before moving on to Havana.]

Dear Mrs Higgs

Here are all the American journalists and photographers interviewing me on our arrival at Miami last Tuesday.

We are quite well, though the heat here in the Caribbean Sea is terrible. Tomorrow we pass through the Panama Canal into the Pacific Ocean, which will be cooler.

We hope you are all well at Ayot.

G.B.S.

To BLANCHE PATCH

S.S. Arandora Star
Gulf of Panama
[A/3]   20th March 1936

["We have been having quite a good time," Charlotte wrote to Apsley Cherry-Garrard as they neared Mexico on 10th March. "Charlie Chaplin at Honolulu, a fine trip from San Francisco to the Grand Canyon, & now confronting a trip to Mexico City—high up—5 days" (C/3). She and GBS had been unable to see Marion Davies during their few hours in Los Angeles, though they had chatted on the telephone. The "enclosed" presumably was a communication from her, received in Mexico, appealing to Shaw to let her play Eliza in a film of *Pygmalion*. A new play, *Geneva*, finally was begun on 11th February as the ship passed through the Panama Canal; it was completed two days before the *Arandora Star* docked at Southampton on 6th April.]

Dear B.P.

I think it would be well to let Gabriel Pascal see the enclosed. Marion is by far the most attractive of the stars who are not really eighteen.

We came through the Mexican excursion pretty hardily; but the heat here is infernal (86 in our cabins). I try to write plays falling asleep between every sentence.

The ship goes back through the canal tomorrow. We shall land and go across by rail with some friends who live in Panama.

I see that you are at last having scraps of sunshine in London; but the winter record was appalling.

This is the last post which (by air) can get to England before us.

GBS

To MAY MORRIS

Ayot St Lawrence. Welwyn
[A/2]   13th April 1936

[Shaw had been reading proofs of May Morris's *William Morris*, Vol. II: *The Socialist*, in which his preface would appear. It was published in June.]

I have gone through all these proofs, and suggested corrections in pencil as they occurred to me. But I do not presume to dictate. I have a certain system of punctuation which has no authority except in so far as it is founded on the Authorized version of the Bible, which is not consistent. I have not attempted to impose it on your text all through; but in one or two points I have interfered, apparently unwarrantably, because of one or two fads of mine.

In the Bible there is not from beginning to end a single dash or inverted comma. If you met with either in it you would be shocked.

If you read one of Sheridan's comedies in the original edition, you will find no stops except full stops and dashes—predominantly dashes.

If you could read Sidney Webb's proofs you would discover that he has a mania for inverted commas which would make them unreadable if I did not cut out 99% of them. It is a sort of tic that afflicts writers.

I argue that if the Bible could do without dashes and inverted commas, both being disfigurements of the printer's work, any book can.

You are a reckless dasher; and though you have to quote titles continually you have not decided on a usage and stuck to it. Sometimes you use italics: sometimes you use single inverted commas—distracting things and hardly ever necessary. It does not matter having some variety; but when you discard the italics & use roman you will find that capitals are quite sufficient without inverted commas, and much handsomer.

My own contribution, which runs to about 12000 words, follows in another enclosure with a letter which will require your special attention.

GBS

To ST JOHN ERVINE

4 Whitehall Court SW1
28th April 1936
also the 11th May 1936

[H/3]   delayed by having to hunt up dates for you

[The book Ervine sent was *People of Our Class: A Comedy in Three Acts*, in
the manuscript of which Shaw had made some revisions. Two of his letters
were incorporated into the preface.

Paul Czinner had, unwisely, submitted Shaw's scenario to a newly created
office for Catholic Action (an organisation embracing lay activities of the
Roman Catholic church) at the Vatican, and eventually received a report
from Monsignor M. Barbera, S.J., dated 27th August 1935. "If the final film
appears to be according to the truth of the story," Barbera wrote, "and does
not contain anything against the prestige of the Roman Catholic Church, the
Catholic Action (Azione Cattolica) will declare that the showing of such a
picture has not met with any objections from the Catholic Authorities" (BL
50633). The hitch was that Father Barbera found serious violations of
"historical fact" by the "mocking Irishman" and declared it was impossible
to approve of the screenplay without substantial changes. Shaw, in his remarks to Ervine, was inaccurate in saying the film had been "stopped by the
Papal censor," for Catholic Action was not an official body of the Church;
and whether or not Hollywood's self-censorship organisation, the Hays
office, was "directed from the Vatican," it was in no way implicated in
Barbera's decision.

Shaw's recollection that his father lived into his eighties is an astonishing memory distortion, as George Carr Shaw, born in 1814, was only in his
seventy-first year when he died suddenly in 1885.]

My dear St John

Dont. When you have had as many biographies written about you as
I have, you will learn that there is only one way to flatten out their
distorting mirrors, and that is to write an autobiography or else get at
the proof sheets of the biographers and rewrite them.

I have done both. I went through Henderson's proofs and corrected
a good many of his worst American misunderstandings. In Frank
Harris's book, all the facts, of which he knew nothing, are by me. Its
account of my mother's family and of my marriage are not to be found
elsewhere.

But I have written enough direct autobiography to cover all my
childhood and my life until I became a public character. First, there is
a preface to my first novel, Immaturity, published in 1931 [1930], fifty
years after it was written. But from this I omitted the musical history

428

of my mother, which was my real education, a point that only a biographer completely equipped musically could understand. I have supplied this omission in a preface to a reprint of my early musical criticisms (signed Corno di Bassetto) which is now in the press. Besides this I have written a sketch called Morris as I Knew Him as a foreword to the two new volumes of Morris's collected works, which contains an episode not otherwise discoverable. Anyone who reads these documents, and perhaps the correspondence with Ellen Terry, will know as much as need be known of my personal circumstances and adventures.

What there is still room for is a compendium and a criticism of my doctrine; and you would make a horrid mess of this because you would never have the patience, even if you could afford the time, to equip yourself for the task. My economic doctrine is Communist; and now that Communism has got on its legs at last in Russia, you splutter against it like the General [Major-General Gregory March] in your play. My religious creed is Creative Evolution, the biological side of which involves the controversy which began with Butler's attack on Darwin, and has since reached gigantic proportions. In this you have never shewn any interest. On the religious side, you splutter again, amusingly but nonsensically, demanding a proper Belfast God, and not a creative purpose in the universe that proceeds by trial and error and produces appalling evils by the errors.

Now spluttering, as you do it, makes very good reading, and sometimes gets a splash or two in on the right spot; but it is neither exposition nor criticism. And a criticism of my doctrine should be as cautious and laborious as a criticism of Calvin's institutes. What I have tried to do is to bring my readers up to date and a little further in their economic, scientific, and religious grounding. Even if your violent prejudices and reckless rashness were treated by Nora making you take a spoonful of laudanum every hour, all you would achieve would be a compendium of my own statements unless you had some fundamental criticism of my position and were nerved by it to tackle the job savagely. But that is not the situation. You contemplate nothing but a good-natured potboiler.

I am not really a good subject, because all the fun that is to be got out of me I have already extracted myself. You can't write a funny book about Mark Twain or about Chesterton: they have both been there before you and reaped the field too thoroughly to leave any gleanings worth gathering.

I got the book safely on my return, with its preface. That intensely incompetent body, the Dramatists' League of America, has out of sheer slavish imbecility, made a usage of giving managers a rake-off on film rights; but nobody as yet has had the audacity to try that game on me. What is worse than the League is the Hays censorship, which is directed from the Vatican, with the result that the St Joan film has been stopped by the Papal censor, whose ignorance of secular history is surpassed by his ignorance of Catholic doctrine. The poor devil's salary is probably $750 a year, for which he is expected to exercise the wisdom and omniscience of God Almighty.

I hope you are both well, as this leaves me at present, thank God for it.

always yours
G. Bernard Shaw

PS As to the dates you asked for, I think Agnes died in 1876. Lucy held out until a few years after the war. My mother died in 1913 or thereabouts. She was over 80. My father died at the same sort of age; but as he was 20 years older than she, he must have died somewhere in the eighties or nineties. The registers of St Bride's, which was demolished, and where I was baptized, were stored in the Four Courts, and perished in the troubles. But see the enclosed chits.

I will send you a copy of Immaturity and—as soon as I can get it—a proof of the Bassetto preface.

[*Additional notes attached to letter*]

Oliver Cromwell's daughter Bridget married General Fleetwood. Their daughter Frances married Captain Fennell of Cappoquin. Their daughter Elizabeth married Daniel Markham. Their granddaughter married Robert Shaw, whose eldest son William Shaw was Shaw of Sandpits, Co. Kilkenny, my greatgrandfather or thereabouts.

These Shaws were descended from Macduff the Unborn, through his third son Shaigh.

I am also descended from everybody who was alive and fertile in these islands in the XVII century and earlier; but old Noll [Cromwell] and Macduff are my selections.

All my mother's people were county family folk, except her mysterious grandfather, who was a pawnbroker—luckily for me, as I just escaped starvation on the last scrap of his money.

As my mother and Lucy were cremated at Golder's Green, and my father's grave is kept in repair in Mount Jerome, and I have somewhere a mislaid photograph of Agnes's grave in the Isle of Wight after Lucy got it repaired, the dates of their deaths are all ascertainable with pedantic exactitude; but at Golder's Green the books must be consulted, as the ashes were scattered on the flower beds.

Granville-Barker was the sole witness at my mother's incineration. At my sister's there was an unexpected crowd; and I had to improvise a service and officiate myself.

My mother was baptized in December 1830, married in June 1852, and died before the war in 1913 or thereabouts, possibly 1912, at her villa in Park Village, next door to Albany St Barracks. My father died in his lodging in the suburbs of Dublin, south side, out Donnybrook way. After I left him in 1876 I never saw him again except for a few days when he paid us a visit in London—the only holiday he ever took in his life as far as my knowledge goes. I have no dates except his marriage and a notion that he was 39 when he married. That would give 1813 for his birth. As he lived to be over 80, his death must have been in the nineties. Buried in Mount Jerome, where his tombstone no doubt gives the date.

My sister Agnes died in the Isle of Wight in 1876. She was one year older than I. She was unmarried.

My sister Lucy died in 1820 [1920] at Champion Cottage, Champion Hill, S.E.5. She was three years my senior. She married one Charles Butterfield, member of a family of Irvingites (the apostle Irving, not the actor). They soon separated. Many years later she discovered that at the time of their marriage he was entertaining a supplementary bride. In a fury she divorced him (or rather I did). After this they got on very well together until his death [in 1916]. No children.

To EDITH EVANS

[H/3; X/316]

4 Whitehall Court SW1
22nd May 1936

[The Elephant and Castle Theatre was a playhouse in the south of London, devoted originally to popular melodrama. In 1932 it was converted into a cinema. Edith Evans joined the Old Vic repertory, October–December 1936, appearing as Rosalind, the Witch of Edmonton, and Lady Fidgett in *The Country Wife*. Shaw had written *The Millionairess* with Evans in mind for Epifania, but all efforts to obtain a commitment from her failed until 1940, when H.M. Tennent Ltd. sent it on a pre-London tour. When the Globe Theatre was blitzed, the London engagement was cancelled.]

Edith, Edith

You ARE a daisy. You treated poor Charles [Macdona] and all the managers who have ever done anything for me as outcasts, and insisted on an ultra fashionable west end production. I have cleared the ground for that and got rid of them all for you. And now you offer me as a climax of magnificence, what? repertory at the Old Vic! Not even a run at the Elephant and Castle.

Dearest, I cant afford it. I have not written a potboiler since The Apple Cart; and I must make some money out of The Millionairess or drop the theatre. The Old Vic can have the play in repertory as much as it likes when it has been squeezed dry at the west end, but not before. The successes in Vienna, Prague, and now in Milan and Rome are hopeful; and I ought to strike while the iron is lukewarm. The spring season is lost: and if I let the autumn season go after it I shall get badly behindhand with my business.

And now you tell me that you have signed on with Lilian [Baylis] for the autumn season!

I have a young and beautiful Epifania raging to play the part: it is with the greatest difficulty that I escape, when we meet, without giving her a contract. I keep staving her off with allegations that it is your play. Her name is Leonora Corbett. Can I frighten you with her?

Between you I am a most distracted man. Do make up my mind for me.

GBS

To W. NUGENT MONCK

4 Whitehall Court SW1
[H/1]   29th May 1936

[Monck had scheduled Dekker's *The Shoemaker's Holiday* at Norwich as its Silver Jubilee production in late June. The Shaws attended performances of *The Magic Flute, Così fan tutte, Don Giovanni, The Marriage of Figaro*, and *The Abduction from the Seraglio* at Glyndebourne on 24th to 28th June.]

Dear Nugent Monck

Most unluckily you have fixed up The Shoemaker for the last of the Glyndebourne Mozart performances, the only week in which all the operas can be heard and for which I have been able to secure tickets. As I learnt my trade from Mozart, and may never have another opportunity of hearing his works presented in this way, I cannot give him up for Dekker, for whom I do not give a damn (comparatively), nor even for the Maddermarket, whose 25th anniversary is a great triumph for you, as no insurance company would have given a policy covering it for more than 25 days when it started.

We promise to turn up on the 50th anniversary if we live long enough.

My wife desires me to send you her specially kind regards.

faithfully
G. Bernard Shaw

To FRANCES CHESTERTON

4 Whitehall Court SW1
[A/1; X/136]   15th June 1936
[Gilbert Chesterton died the previous day. Mrs Chesterton (1875–1938), sufficiently provided for, did not avail herself of the proffered help, but was (Chesterton's secretary later reported to Dan H. Laurence) "very moved at the generous offer." Shaw, concerned lest her refusal be a matter of pride, called on Blanche Patch to unearth all of Chesterton's letters from the files to be returned to Mrs Chesterton, thus enhancing the value of Shaw's correspondence already in her hands if she had to resort to a sale.]

Dear Mrs Chesterton

It seems the most ridiculous thing in the world that I, 18 years older than Gilbert, should be heartlessly surviving him.

However, this is only to say that if you have any temporal bothers that I can remove, a line on a postcard (or three figures) will be sufficient.

The trumpets are sounding for him; and the slightest interruption must be intolerable.

faithfully
G. Bernard Shaw

To H. A. GWYNNE

4 Whitehall Court SW 1
[H/59]   22nd June 1936

[Howell Arthur Gwynne (1865–1950), editor of the *Morning Post* 1911–37, had invited Shaw to contribute to a series, "What Next?"]

Dear Mr Gwynne

The difficulty about What Next is that nobody knows, and anyone who thinks he does is sure to write a silly article.

I do not practise now as a journalist unless there is something I want badly to say. Even if it paid me instead of costing me money on balance as it does, I am now in my eightieth year; and my experience of octogenarians who imagine themselves as good as ever when they are actually outmoded bores is rather intimidating.

I do not know exactly what has happened to the class catered for by the old Morning Post; but there is a change in its literary appetite. The country house, the rectory, the Guards Club, the half-enobled plutocracy are all there, apparently as solid as ever; but they are not so stuck in their old grooves when they go a reading as they used to be: they are demoralised by a press which is politically and morally all over the shop. The Times doesnt know where it is, and hasnt for a long time past. Though you are ten years younger than I, you must sometimes sit back and ask yourself What Next for the Morning Post. I can only say again that I dont know.

However, I am very obliged to you for your invitation to contribute; and if I want to fire a shot that can with any propriety be discharged from your deck I shall avail myself of your hospitality very gratefully.

faithfully
G. Bernard Shaw

To EBERHARD K. KLAGEMANN

[4 Whitehall Court SW 1]
[F.u/4]   [Undated: *c.* 1st July 1936]

[Shaw evidently had contracted for release of the German *Pygmalion* only in German-speaking countries, ruling out geographical areas where there were significant colonies of Germans, as in South America. The credited scenarists of the film are Heinrich Oberländer and Walther Wasserman.]

Dear Mr Klagemann

Very well: please continue to hold my fees until it is again possible to export them.

My information about South America came from an agent [Lawrence Smith] who, though he did not possess the Spanish rights, nevertheless invited proposals for a Spanish version of the film. The reply was that your film had spoilt the market.

I have to apologize for having left a letter of yours unanswered. The explanation is that it arrived when I was absent from London and has only just come into my hands. I gather from it that you are under the impression that you discarded my scenario in favor of one which followed the original stage version more closely. Now it is true that your scenario writer took the trouble to put in the things I had carefully left out, as well as leaving out several things I carefully put in. But as the great art of storytelling, whether on the stage or on the screen, is to know exactly what to leave out and what to leave in, every one of these breaches of contract was an artistic blunder. If you study the effect of your film at the actual performances you will find that all attempts to drag in matters and people that are mentioned but not shewn in both my scenario and the original play—Doolittle's wife, the lesson in phonetics, the dance at the party, &c. &c.—are failures, and that the successful parts are precisely those with which I had nothing to do, representing Eliza as a violent tomboy, always a popular figure in knockabout farce. I congratulate your librettist on the fun he has got out of this; but there was really no need to put my name to it. When he has learnt that a dramatic surprise, such as the entry of Doolittle, should not be spoilt by telling the audience beforehand that it is going to happen, he may become quite an effective playwright.

faithfully
[G. Bernard Shaw]

To ERNEST THESIGER

Malvern Hotel. Malvern
[H/40]   24th July 1936

[The Malvern Festival company proposed making a presentation gift to Shaw to celebrate his eightieth birthday. "Shaw was furious," Thesiger later informed Dan H. Laurence. "I told him he lacked the art of accepting gracefully." This was Shaw's response.]

My dear Ernest

Let me explain about birthday presents. I am not at all insensible to the good feeling that prompts them; but I like them to be useful and friendly. Also they should be personal. A presentation into which the subscribers have been blackmailed is abhorrent to me. It results in some silver atrocity that I dont want—that no human being could ever possibly want (except to pawn)—and that I shall never see again. For instance, the Nobel Prize. Eight ounces of solid gold, with a stamp of less merit than a postmark. I havnt the faintest notion of where it is; and its possession has never given me a moment's gratification.

Also, as Charlotte and I have as much money as is good for us there is no use giving us anything expensive, as we have naturally bought all things of that sort for ourselves.

Subject to these sensible limitations I should be much gratified to receive a personal present from every member of the company who would like to give me one. Only, it must be a Woolworth present, a threepenny one. I should have a whole basketful of useful or amusing presents, which would give Charlotte and myself the greatest pleasure. And the donors would have the fun of buying and selecting them at Woolworth's regardless of expense.

As for me, I am under much greater obligations to my actor-collaborators than they to me; so I shall give £100 to the Actors Benevolent just to shew that I know my place.

By the way, what's the address of the A.B.? I hope you dont know, but some less fortunate star may.

Do you approve? I think it an ideal settlement.

always yours
G. Bernard Shaw

To WENDY HILLER

[H.t/1; X/388.e]

Malvern Hotel. Malvern
17th August 1936

[*Saint Joan* was performed at Malvern for five performances, with Wendy Hiller (b. 1912), who had recently made a noteworthy stage début in *Love on the Dole* (London and New York), as Joan, concurrently with her Eliza in *Pygmalion*. Shaw's dissatisfaction with her interpretation may be deduced from his inquiry to the B.B.C. producer Hamilton Marr a day earlier as to whether Sybil Thorndike might be available for a forthcoming radio production of the play. Wendy Hiller, recalling that season, recently impressed upon an interviewer that there had been only a month's rehearsal at Malvern for all the plays combined. "Young people," she said, "look at me and obviously don't believe me when I tell them it was six rehearsals and, if you were lucky, you got through half a dress. One day when I said 'G.B.S., we've only had six rehearsals,' he said, 'Well, it's a very good play, dear. If you can't have six weeks, six [days] will do.' In other words, 'Get on with my play and shut up.' " Shaw's personal supervision had been confined to a word rehearsal in a vacant swimming bath. He "told me to hurry up and get on with it, there was no time to try and act with it. Then we managed half a dress rehearsal, but it went on too long so G.B.S., who had brought out his great big gold watch and timed the Inquisitor's speech as he always did, snapped it shut and went home" (Holly Hill, "Saint Joan's Voices: Actresses on Shaw's Maid," *Shaw: The Annual of Bernard Shaw Studies*, VI (1986).]

My dear Wendy

I had another look at St Joan and saw you trying your pet stunts for all they were worth. They failed completely, as I told you they would; but I saw what you were driving at, and can now explain to you why they failed.

What you have conceived is a cataleptic Joan who, in her highest moments, goes up out of the world into a trance. Such an effect is n impossible on the stage if the author has prepared it properly. I he play began with Joan in the fields with her sheep, hearing the b , and going into a trance of ecstasy ending in a sleep from which e would be awakened by village folk who would discuss this str e power of hers, so that the audience would learn about the tran and be able to recognize their symptoms, then you might produce electric effect by making such a trance the climax of the cathedr ene and of the trial scene too, to say nothing of the epilogue.

Without such careful preparation the e ct is quite impossible. To the unprepared audience the trance ap rs a collapse, unaccountable and disappointing. When you coll ed at the last moment of the cathedral scene, with victory just thin your grasp, the man next me threw up his hands in despa and exclaimed "Good God!!!" To those who remembered S l Thorndike's exit it was worse than disappointing: it was inf ating.

In the last speech of the trial, where you have in a few sweeping words to paint a landscape of a frosty morning in the country in the lambing season, and you suddenly try a cataleptic convulsion in which not one word is audible or intelligible, you are simply puzzling.

437

In both cases the result is a complete and astonishing knock-out.

However, it is a bit of experience for you. One gets experience by making mistakes. In future, when you want to put something into your part that is not in the play, you must ask the author—or some other author—to lead up to the interpolation for you. Never forget that the effect of a line may depend, not on its delivery, but on something said earlier in the play either by somebody else or by yourself, and that if you change it it may be necessary to change the whole first act as well.

Now I can't rewrite Joan for you, though it would be great fun. I must be faithful to her as well as nice to you; and Joan wasnt a cata-leptic. She was forcible and sure from beginning to end, and never played pianissimo—you[r] pet pianissimo, which, dearest, you have not yet got the art of making perfectly audible. So deny it to yourself if you can in this play.

When you come on in the trial scene, kick the chain from step to step instead of dragging it. Let the kicks be heard before you come on; and when they take it off do not rub your ankle pathetically; but bend your legs at the knee and stretch them as if you were going to take on the whole court at all-in wrestling. And call the man a noodle heartily, not peevishly. Get a big laugh with it.

And now go your way in the strength of the Lord; but do not wholly despise the instruction of the old bird

G.B.S.

To NICOLAS SLONIMSKY

[X/389]

[Malvern Hotel. Malvern]
2nd September 1936

[Nicolas Slonimsky (b. 1894) is a Russian-born composer, conductor, and respected musicologist.]

Dear Sir

Within my lifetime there has been a complete liberation of modula-tion from its own rules. All the composers, great and small, have now availed themselves fully of this. New modes have been tried, like the whole tone (or organ tuner's) scale of Debussy; and the obsolete modes have been played with a little. But all this music was in terms of some tonality or other, however sudden and frequent its modulations and transitions might be. And the harmonic practice was so free that the scale became a 12 note scale with nothing of the old tonality left but a keynote. Still, as long as there was a keynote there was no fundamental difference between Bach and Richard Strauss.

Schönberg tried to get loose from the keynote by writing pieces in listening to which you could not guess which was to be the final chord, because there was no tonal cadence. The revolutionary young composers rushed in at this new game and dropped key signatures; so that their scores were a mass of accidentals; but Schönberg exhausted the fun of this and relapsed more and more into tonality. This drift is apparent in all the big composers now. It is hard to say that the symphonies of Sibelius are in this key or that; but when we come to know his symphonies by heart as we know those of Mozart and Beethoven they will appear as tonal to us as Elgar's.

In short the post-Wagnerian anarchy is falling into order as all anarchies do pretty soon; and I expect soon to hear the Wagnerian flood of endless melody getting embanked in the melodic *design* of Bach and Handel.

faithfully
G. Bernard Shaw

To C. H. NORMAN

4 Whitehall Court SW 1
4th September 1936

[H/83]

[Stinie Morrison (1882?–1921), a foreigner who may have been, in 1911, a victim of British xenophobia, was convicted of the murder of a Frenchman on Clapham Common despite his ability to produce some evidence of an alibi. After he failed in an appeal his sentence was commuted to life imprisonment. Henry Daniel Seymour (1892–1931), a commercial traveller, was executed on 10th December 1931 for the murder-by-stabbing of Alice Kempson, a widow, in Oxford on 1st August of the same year. On 6th November 1930 Alfred A. Rouse (1894–1931) to create an impression of his own death, strangled an unidentified stranger and set fire to him and the car with petrol; the "Blazing Car" murderer was hanged at Bedford on 10th March 1931. The Irish-born Charlotte (Mrs Frederick John) Bryant was hanged at Exeter Prison on 15th July 1936 for the murder of her husband. Shaw was in error in his statement that Mrs Bryant's guilt had been assumed "by herself as well as by everyone else." From the moment of charge until her execution she insisted that she was innocent. The peculiarity of her case, Norman argued, was that no crime actually had been committed.]

439

Dear Clarence Norman

As long as the Deterrence or Terrorist theory of punishment prevails, judges and police authorities will hold, more or less consciously, that every murder must be followed by an execution to deter others from doing likewise. Whether the person executed has had anything to do with the murder does not matter in the least, as the hanging of an innocent person is just as terrifying as the hanging of a guilty one. Therefore the police have every inducement, if they cannot find the guilty party, to pick out some bad character and frame up a case against him or her. Stinie Morrison died in prison after serving 15 years of a commuted death sentence, the commutation having taken place because there was absolutely no evidence that he had committed the Clapham murder, though there was evidence enough to prove that Stinie was a dangerous person who would be better dead. Another undesirable person was hanged for the Oxford murder, the evidence being that (a) he was in Oxford when the murder was committed, (b) that he had purchased a chisel as an appropriate instrument for cutting the lady's throat, and (c) that his character was bad and his behavior that of a guilty person. As the police were after him for a theft he had committed, this last point was capable of another explanation; but it helped to hang him all the same.

A British jury will always hang a prisoner whose conduct is improper. They must; for otherwise they would be condoning improper conduct. In the case of the burnt out murder car, the survivor was convicted of murder because he kept two connubial establishments. Had he been a respectable monogamist nobody would have blamed him for the conflagration.

It is useless to insist that these people were innocent. You cannot get any sympathy for them: the feeling is that they deserved hanging whether they were guilty in the particular instance or not. Nobody regrets the death of Mrs Bryant: her guilt was assumed from the first quite spontaneously, apparently by herself as well as by everyone else. God knows why; but it was so. So do not waste your time trying to rouse any compunction for her execution: the point to hammer at is that the dice are loaded against the prisoner by the Deterrence theory, which also explains the desperate reluctance of the Home Office to admit a miscarriage of justice . . .

faithfully
G. Bernard Shaw

440

To BEATRICE WEBB

Malvern Hotel. Malvern
[H/14]   4th September 1936

[Late in 1934 Stalin began a campaign of political terror that led to the show
trials and purges that commenced in August 1936 and extended into 1938.
Leon Trotsky (1879–1940), revolutionary leader, who had clashed with
Stalin, been expelled from the party (1927) and banished from the USSR
(1929), was at this time in exile in Norway; he later went to Mexico, where
he was assassinated in 1940. Grigory Y. Sokolnikoff was suddenly expelled
from the party and arrested in 1936, charged with Trotskyite treason and
conspiracy. At the second show trial in 1937 he was sentenced to ten years'
imprisonment and vanished.

John Felton (*c.* 1595–1628) assassinated the Duke of Buckingham at Portsmouth. François Ravaillac (1578–1610) assassinated Henry IV of France in
1610. Leon F. Czolgosz (1873–1901) was the anarchist slayer of the American
president William McKinley in 1901. (On another occasion Shaw corrosively
referred to this as his favourite incident in history!) The Spanish Civil War,
five years after the founding of the Republic, broke out with a military revolt
by General Francisco Franco (1892–1975) in July 1936, against liberal and
socialist elements in government.]

My dear Beatrice

This Russian business is very puzzling. It looks like a Popish Plot
without any Titus Oates, or another witch burning epidemic. An
assassination of Stalin could do nothing but make him a national saint
like Lincoln, and make Trotsky for ever impossible. If he came back
it would be as "the priest who slew the slayer and shall himself be
slain." Why should Sokolnikoff lend himself to such insanity even if
Trotsky were mad enough for it? And what grip has Stalin on his
fabulous dictatorial power except his efficiency and popularity? One
can understand his being killed by a Felton, a Ravaillac, or a Cholgosh
(I forget the spelling); but a conspiracy to kill him by level headed
men like Sokolnikoff suggests the one real danger to Communism: that
its leaders have not minds of the necessary size to take it in and are
relapsing into pre-Marxian conceptions of politics. Was the new
constitution a symptom of this, or was it only a stupid attempt to
conciliate western prejudices instead of deliberately shocking them at
every topical point until they collapse under the moral bombardment?

I suppose we must wait until we get some authentic news.

The Spanish explosion is much more important than the Abyssinian
affair, which was merely an incident in the inevitable erosion of tribal
savagery by police and engineering. It is part of a movement begun in

441

Ireland by [Sir Edward] Carson and the military caste: the deliberate refusal to accept the democratic substitution of the ballot for the bullet. The class war will be fought out with ball cartridge, not with Labor programs. At present the Spanish Government is only a Kerenskyan muddle fighting a solidly prejudiced rebellion with all the reactionists in Europe at its back; but after the Russian success against overwhelming odds anything may happen.

Well, après nous, le deluge.

We shall meet in London on the 26th, nicht war?

GBS

To EDITH EVANS

Portmeirion Hotel
Penrhyndeudraeth. North Wales
[E/3; X/316]   14th September 1936

[*The Seagull* ran at the New Theatre from 20th May to 22nd August. Shaw had seen it early in the run, before John Gielgud (b. 1904), referred to here as "Gg," was succeeded by Ion Swinley. The director was Theodore Komisarjevsky (1882–1954), a Russian who emigrated to England in 1919. He had staged productions in London of *Uncle Vanya*, *Ivanoff*, *The Three Sisters*, and *The Cherry Orchard*, several of which Shaw had seen. Gilbert Miller (1884–1969) was a London and New York theatrical manager, son of Henry Miller. Leon M. Lion (1879–1947) was an inexhaustible actor-manager who, from the time he entered management in 1918, had presented over sixty plays in London. The play in which Granville Barker made love to Mabel Terry Lewis was Somerset Maugham's *A Man of Honour*, produced by the Stage Society in February 1903.]

Here I wander distractedly to shake off maddening Malvern before returning home next week. It is raining cats and dogs—real Welsh rain. I have lost all interest in the wretched potboiling Millionairess: only a lingering interest in you after all these Leonoras and Wendies still binds me to it. It is rather late in the day for any enthusiasm on the part of Gilbert M. What about C. B. Cochran? he has always declared himself ready at a moment's notice. So has Leon M. Lion, whose resources appear inexhaustible.

I went to The Seagull, and disliked it extremely. You kicked it round the stage; and Gg killed it dead every time he walked on. Tchekov is not in the Terry blood. Komisar has lost his old Russian touch: he filled the last act with pauses of the sort that are bearable

442

only in a first act when there is no hurry and the audience is willing to speculate a little on dumb shows. And anyhow the dumb shows are unintelligible and uninteresting. The passionate bits were ghastly: they reminded me of Granville Barker trying to play a love scene with Mabel Terry Lewis years ago, or Loraine refusing to conceal his hatred of Lillah in Man & Superman [at the Court Theatre, May 1907]. You may ask me how I account for the run. I can only explain it by your prodigious draw. And at any rate you *acted*. Gg's nullity was stupendous, considering that the man *can* act when the stuff suits him.

> faithful still
>
> GBS

We return home early next week if not sooner.

To THE EDITOR OF *THE TIMES*

[H/2]

[4 Whitehall Court SW1]

[Undated: October 1936]

[This corrected typescript, though signed by Shaw, appears to be a draft copy. At the top Shaw has added and circled the date "Oct 1936" and inserted a note "Refused by The Times as it might be mischievous in India."]

Sir

May I call attention to the very unfortunate coincidence of riots in Bombay with riots in the east end of London, and the contrast between the treatment of the Indian and British rioters. The Indians are to be flogged: the Britons are to be dealt with in the ordinary civilized manner. Why is this distinction made at a time when our hold upon India in the face of a strong nationalist movement depends so much on our pretension to be a highly civilized power conferring its humane institutions on a relatively primitive region? Surely we should be particularly careful to give the Indian nationalists no excuse for complaining that they are treated as slaves and not as citizens of the Empire.

I notice these things because I was brought up in the nineteenth century, when the abolition of corporal punishment was a recognized mark of advancing civilization. But sixty years in England have convinced me that this view is obsolete and that the Englishman loves flogging. Its revival was advocated at first as a substitute for imprisonment; but in practice it soon became a vindictive addition to it. Not

443

long ago a criminal [James Spiers] was sentenced to ten years imprisonment *and* a flogging. He committed suicide [in Wandsworth Prison, on 3rd February 1930]. Nobody protested or seemed at all concerned about the incident.

Therefore, though I cannot conquer my ancient prejudice against flogging as a depraved taste and a demoralizing practice, I am not now raising the question whether rioters should be flogged or not. I am only pointing out that it is invidious to flog them in Bombay if we do not flog them equally in Bermondsey or Barking.

yours truly
G. Bernard Shaw

To MATTHEW FORSYTH

4 Whitehall Court SW1
[H/115; X/390]   3rd November 1936

[Matthew Forsyth (1896–1954), actor and director, was staging the first performance in England of *The Millionairess*, with his repertory company in the De La Warr Pavilion, Bexhill-on-Sea. It opened on 17th November, with Jane Bacon as Epifania, for a single week. Harry Nicholls (1852–1926), former Drury Lane pantomime comedian, was for several years a member of William Terriss's Adelphi Theatre company. He appeared in Gertrude Kingston's 1912 revival of *Captain Brassbound's Conversion*.]

Dear Matthew Forsyth

The sweater and his wife speak Whitechapel cockney. I have given up trying to write these dialects phonetically: it cannot be done with our alphabet. When Harry Nicholls, a great cockney comedian, played Drinkwater in Captain Brassbound's Conversion for me, the attempt at phonetic spelling puzzled him so much that he had to write out the part in ordinary spelling before he could learn it. The pair would ordinarily be Jews; but you must carefully avoid any suggestion of this at present, as it would drag in current politics.

Deary will do as well as darling; but anything that sounds comic must be avoided. The woman's quiet crying must give a hopeless pathos to the end of the scene. Clare Greet could do this perfectly. The danger is that if you tell a younger actress to play cockney she will conclude that she has to be funny, which would ruin the scene. There is not a gleam of fun in these two poor devils.

444

If you want to waste a salary, or if you have a young utility actor on your hands eating his head off, he could introduce the characters. But there is a difficulty. The appearance of a clerk and his attempt to pronounce Epifania's tongue twisting name, would utterly wreck her tragic entrance. Here, therefore, you must be content with a telephone and a selfclosing door. But all the other entrances can be announced as much as you please. I now always use a telephone to save a servant's salary and avoid having a player hanging about at rehearsal with nothing to do. Nobody ever complains.

I shall come down to one of the matinees if I possibly can. Perhaps Sir Barry will come with me.

faithfully

G. Bernard Shaw

To J. KINGSTON BARTON

[H/1]

4 Whitehall Court SW1
10th November 1936

[Shaw and Dr Barton of St Bartholomew's Hospital, close friends in their early London years, had not crossed paths for decades.]

My dear J.K.B.

This is a very neat arrangement of yours; but I assure you I have already done everything that I can in the way of converting income into annuity for the security of myself and my wife. We have no children to provide for; but we have a crowd of old servants and destitute relatives. Even if I made Barts my residuary legatee it would have to wait a long time before the last of these (an immortal race) went underground.

But why should I leave my money to be spent on guinea pigs, stolen dogs, torture chambers call[ed] laboratories, and all the other expenses of mechanistic surgery, pseudo-medical voodoo, and all the other fruits of the idiotic claim that the pursuit of knowledge is exempt from all moral law. The result is the modern doctor cant cure anything: cant even correct a dislocation, and tells you—as a bright young practitioner in South Africa assured me lately—that in a few years all child births will be effected by section.

Yet the other day, when I asked a brilliant young surgeon (an M.C.) what manual training he had had, he replied "None whatever."

For years I agitated for the laicization of the G.M.C. and have at last succeeded in getting *one* layman put on; but what can he do single-handed against a trade union of the worst type. No, dear J.K.B.: I know too much about it—probably more than you do, bar clinical experience.

Almroth Wright claims my support for St Mary's, because I got a lucrative play (The Doctor's Dilemma) straight out of his laboratory there, and put him into it as the principal character. Can Barts trump that?

Besides, there is my own profession and its schools, ready to swallow a thousand such fortunes as mine.

At a performance of a comparatively recent play of mine called Too True [to be Good] a doctor was sitting behind me. The first act takes place in a sick room. It shews how foolish and ignorant parents force doctors to prescribe things that they know to be quite useless. The doctor whispered to me "Every medical student ought to see this play before he starts in private practice." In short, I have spent a good deal of my life in trying to reform the medical profession. It says in effect "We dont want your amateur advice: we want your money." It wont get it.

Happily doctors never take their own prescriptions nor practise the rules of hygienic conduct they lay down for their patients. That explains why you have survived to be 82, and, I gather, are still hale and hearty. I look fairly well for my age; but it is only a stage effect: my faculties have all gone to pot.

What is your son? A doctor?

always yours
G. Bernard Shaw

To AUGUSTIN HAMON

4 Whitehall Court SW1
[H/1]   21st November 1936

[Shaw had provided Gabriel Pascal on 14th November with a formal introduction to Hamon: "This is to introduce to you Mr Gabriel Pascal, who is authorized to produce an english film of Pygmalion and who is prepared to undertake the french film as well. His proposal is by far the most eligible that has been made to me; and if he can settle with you for the use of your translation I shall accept it. Meanwhile he wishes to make your acquaintance and

446

to discuss the affair with you. I recommend him to your distinguished consideration" (H/1).]

My dear Hamon

Prenez garde. Monsieur G.P. m'amuse énormement. Il est parleur et son imagination est prodigieuse. Bref, fabuliste incomparable.

However, I like the fellow; and I have placed him "on the map" by giving him a contract to produce the English film of Pygmalion. He has planned half a dozen magnificent schemes for the fulfilment of this contract (which expires presently) but not one of them has come to anything. He now swears that he has arranged everything with an American company for making a film in March next. He has no studio and is a pure adventurer; but he may be able to carry the effort through for me. In the film world they are all adventurers more or less.

He has no contract for France; but I promised him that if he could arrange for the manufacture of the French version simultaneously with the English one, I should not object; but that he must buy your consent to use your translation.

Unfortunately for him your letter has let the cat out of the bag as to his intentions of playing me false about the scenario. He is strictly bound by his agreement to use my scenario and not to depart from it by a hair's breadth. He knows that I loathe the German film, a grotesque and stupid travesty, introducing among other things a vue des courses. He knows that I am determined not to allow Higgins to be represented as the lover of Eliza. His scene of jealousy between Higgins and Freddy, which makes Higgins a lover at once, shews that he intends to cheat me on this point also. I am not surprised; for though his own artistic sense is unusually fine, he is as weak as water, and will let himself be led into any sort of folly by the film people unless I hold him in a grip of iron.

When he calls on you on Monday you must apologize to him most sympathetically for having unintentionally upset the apple cart by asking me about the jealousy scene and the racecourse scene. Say that immediately on my hearing of this I have written to you by air mail announcing a rupture definitive between G.P. and G.B.S.; so that anything that passes between you at the interview must be conditional on his appeasing me and pledging himself to adhere to my scenario to the uttermost comma.

Then let him talk. He will amuse you as he amuses me.

In haste
G. Bernard Shaw

447

To CHARLOTTE ROGERS

[H/3]
4 Whitehall Court S W 1
27th November 1936

[Aunt Charlotte Rogers, in Carlow, Ireland, was once again proving her expertise as a sponger.]

Dear Mrs Rogers

I will see you through as to the dentures; so you need not be economical in ordering them.

I send you £5; but you must bear in mind that I am rather a mean sort of man about money, and that if you can always get out of a difficulty by writing to me for £5, you will very soon be in a difficulty every month, then every week, and finally every day. So do your best to live within your income, no matter what coals cost.

faithfully
G. Bernard Shaw

To ELIZABETH ROBINS

[H/3]
4 Whitehall Court S W 1
28th November 1936

["I hadnt the least idea that you and Mrs B. [Annie Besant] had ever met," Shaw wrote to Elizabeth Robins on 17th November. "She was what Ibsen calls an episode in my life, and I in hers. It came to nothing. Nothing *from the inside* ever did come to anything with her: she was a public person first and last" (C/3).]

My dear Elizabeth Robins

I dont consider the [Herbert] Burrows incident in the least a Key incident in A.B's career. He was only one of many lame dogs whom she helped over stiles; and like all the other men with whom she was associated, including myself, he left no trace on her mind.

Besides, it really cost her nothing to give him a bedroom in her house and take his insane excitability in her strong hand. She liked doing things of that sort. And quite a lot of people do kind personal things of that sort. It is not to be compared with her action in the [Bryant & May] match strike. She was sitting in her office behind a Fleet Street shop when in walked a group of London's poorest of poor girls. They told her of their five shillings a week and their "fossy jaw" and all the rest of it, and said they had heard that she was a noble minded lady who could help them to make their sorrows known. And she went bang into it without a moment's hesitation. That was a job beside which her humanity to Burrows was the merest trifle. I described to you what it meant. I went with her by way of escort when she took the bags of silver down to Charrington's great hall in the Mile End Road to distribute it in strike pay. All the way there in the cab she was in hysterics from sheer exhaustion. I did all I could to soothe and pet her; but when we arrived I had made up my mind that her condition was hopeless and that I should have to take the meeting in hand myself.

But a big meeting was the elixir of life to her. She sailed into the hall as if she were fresh from six weeks holiday, and took command of that multitude of palpitating girls like an extremely self possessed queen, with her voice in its best order, low and quiet and irresistibly authoritative.

If you want to shew the quality that made her great, dwell on her pugnacity. She was not only helping the girls: she was fighting, not Bryant & May, who were only names to her, but oppression, starvation, compulsory prostitution and all the villainies of capitalism.

After "Bloody Sunday" she wanted to go to Trafalgar Square the next Sunday and overwhelm the police. At the Council meeting G. W. Foote and I had to oppose her, as there was not the faintest possibility of the attempt ending in anything but more broken heads and sentences of imprisonment. She moved her fighting resolution in a magnificent speech which swept us all away in thunders of applause. Foote's speech and mine in moving the amendment were received in dead silence with shame and loathing. But our descriptions of the barricade warfare they would have to be prepared for if they decided to march to the square were unanswerable; and though she got all the applause we got all the votes. She must have thought us a filthy lot of cowards. But the police courts gave her plenty to do for many weeks.

She was great in impulse and in action; but she contributed nothing to the doctrines she preached here. I know too little of her Indian career to say whether she achieved anything original theosophically. She was not an original thinker, just as Napoleon was not an original soldier.

I should have written before; but I am distracted with odds and ends of business, and urgent work waiting to be finished.

By the way, dont spend too much time over A.B. That is one of the dangers of biography.

always
G. Bernard Shaw

To F. E. LOEWENSTEIN

[C/3; X/391]

4 Whitehall Court SW1
10th December 1936

[Dr Fritz Erwin Loewenstein (1901–69), who had come to London in 1933 as a refugee from Germany, with a Ph.D. from the University of Würzburg, had written to Shaw to indicate a desire to compile a bibliography of his published works.]

I am really the last person to consult; for I dont keep an opus list; and my recollection of the literary work I did for the Fabian Society is hopelessly imperfect and confused.

I cannot even remember the names of former bibliographers.

All I can do is to look through the draft of your bibliography when you have completed it, and see whether I can add anything to it.

G. Bernard Shaw

To HUGH BEAUMONT

[H/116]

4 Whitehall Court SW1
17th December 1936

[Hugh "Binkie" Beaumont (1908–73), one of the most powerful theatre managers in England, was managing director of H.M. Tennent Ltd. He had contracted for a new production of *Candida* to star Ann Harding, and to be directed by Irene Hentschel (1891–1979), former actress and the wife of the drama critic Ivor Brown. Shaw had agreed to participate in the rehearsals, which meant that as usual he was taking over. "I must stick to the rehearsals for a week," he wrote to Beaumont on the 11th, "so as to save waste of time and get the stage business firmly settled, book in hand. Then they can knock off for Christmas and to swallow the words. I have had a talk with Irene H, who will be in the program as producer. I hope to make the job as easy as possible for her" (A/116).

The first rehearsal, on 14th December, was chaotic. To obtain all the promotional value he could squeeze from the presence of a celebrated author and a glamorous Hollywood star, Beaumont had invited a large contingent of the press. As Shaw strode in, Hentschel remembered, with "the vigour of a hurricane," lights flashed and cameras clicked from all parts of the auditorium and stage. Shyly and nervously, Hentschel gathered her players round her and started to map out preliminary moves, Shaw "standing amid the shadows ... look[ing] like an emaciated giant. ... Within seconds he seemed to have grown another couple of feet in height. 'This is all wrong,'" he shouted, unaware that Beaumont's designer had altered the shape of the set since he had seen the original plans. Hentschel attempted, amid the hubbub, to explain the changes, but Shaw would not listen. In exasperation he started to depart. "I suggested that he should take over and show us what he wanted. This he did and began to place the actors, making them enter through our fire-place and gaze through a shut door instead of a window. After half-an-hour he suddenly grew tired ... and swept out, leaving an exhausted company and a panic-stricken producer" (Irene Hentschel, "Producing for Shaw and Priestley," *Drama*, Winter 1964).

Beaumont sought vainly to placate the trembling woman, urging her to proceed with the rehearsal. Instead, she went home, rang up Shaw, and announced she was going to resign. He laughed, told her to do what she liked, even to have a trap-door if it appealed to her. "You can't hurt a play of mine," he assured her. Moments later he penned a letter to her: "On reflection, the temptation of escaping this terrible corvée is too much for me ... I shall retire and leave you to work your will. ... So you have seen the last of me at the Globe; and I hope they will all be happier with you than with your superannuated G. Bernard Shaw" (T/1).]

Dear Hugh Beaumont

... As to the production I should like to be assured that you and your partners have fully considered the situation, as otherwise you may consider later on that I have let you down by abandoning the work to Miss I. H.

The business of a producer is to carry out the author's design. Miss I. H. says "Oh no: I am going to carry out a new design of my own." In the normal course you would say "That is not what you are engaged for; so we must replace you by some producer who will give us Shaw and not I. H." And I, in the normal course, should insist on this.

But, instead, we both agree to take a sporting chance and let her try her plan, knowing that my plan is sure fire and hers untried and unknown to us. It may produce misfits between the business and the dialogue that may be very awkward, especially as the producer cannot,

451

as I could, alter the dialogue to fit the new business; and heaven knows what would happen then.

Now I am taking this chance with my eyes open. But it will be more serious for you than for me if the play flops. Nothing can shake my reputation or that of the play; a flop will not ruin me; and I can afford to indulge myself by letting Miss I. H. have her chance now that I am too old for the drudgery of rehearsals. But you stand to lose a lot of money if things go wrong; and I am not sure that your eyes are as wide open as mine; for I doubt if you have given much thought to the matter; and you might with some justice reproach me for not making the case clear to you if the results should prove disappointing.

However, as I have already said, the play, if it gets its grip, will stand a much greater degree of inadequacy than we have any reason to fear from Irene. So let her rip by all means if you feel like it.

So now my conscience is no longer uneasy; and I must apologise for having eased it at such length.

As to pressmen, a little experience will convince you that you may as well shut up your theatre as throw the stage open to them. Treat them as I do. You need not be afraid of offending them: they must have legitimate news or perish; but you must control it.

faithfully
G. Bernard Shaw

PART III

1937-1943

III

(1937–1943)

Shaw, said Chesterton, was "a splendid republican . . . The interest of the State is with him a sincere thirst of the soul." He reacted to Democracy, which he called Mobocracy, much as did D. H. Lawrence, who had argued, "The secret is to commit into the hands of the sacred few the responsibility which now lies like torture on the mass. . . . Leaders—this is what mankind is craving for"; and he spent much of his life seeking to prove Democracy a fraud. Parliament was, in Shaw's view, merely a defence against any government at all, a political mad-house. "You send a Government to govern the country," he argued, "and send an Opposition to prevent them from doing it, and all that you call discussion in Parliament means simply obstruction." A State dominated by a majority party of politically naïve talkers who dont know their business is not a State at all, said Shaw. "It is a mob."

Influenced by the ideals of Carlyle and Nietzsche, what Shaw envisaged was a great modern State with a competent ruler, a neo-Platonic philosopher-king. In his preface to *Three Plays for Puritans* (1901) he had predicted the degeneration of the democratic attitude into a pathetic romantic illusion, at which instant "the brute force of the strong-minded Bismarckian man of action, impatient of humbug, will combine with the subtlety and spiritual energy of the man of thought whom shams cannot illude or interest." It is not surprising, therefore, that he proclaimed Julius Cæsar to be the greatest man who ever lived. His own stage rulers, from Cæsar to Magnus and Good King Charles, were not rulers "with the capacity of village headmen" attempting vainly to govern empires, but powerful, intelligent, charismatic men, not subject to the caprices of the masses but non-despotically dedicated to the public weal, personifying a high aristocratic tradition of political leadership. "Irishmen," St John Ervine commented, "are natural lovers of dictators. The Irish are believers in aristocracy—they are the most devout lovers of royalty in the world." And Shaw belonged to the Irish ascendancy, albeit the "downstart" segment of it.

Not infrequently Shaw's statements concerning the Fascists may be discerned as inverted critical gibes at the seesawing Labour politics of Ramsay MacDonald's government. "One of the best things Hitler has said," Shaw informed an interviewer in 1934, "is, 'Decisions which

455

are made by majorities are decisions for which no man is responsible.'
Therefore you cannot have responsible government so long as you have
decisions by majorities. . . . I think Hitler was perfectly right when he
said that."

Mussolini and Hitler were to Shaw merely new dictators supplanting
old ones. Irresponsible, predatory financial dictators had, in the Great
War and again in the 1929 stockmarket crash, morally and economically
bankrupted the world and sacrificed millions of innocent men. Britain,
Shaw argued, was even then under the dominance of thousands of
dictators, who called themselves employers and landlords, and whose
powers were greater and touched the populace more fundamentally than
those of any political dictator. Further, said Shaw, they were nationally
irresponsible, not professing to seek anything more than their own
individual profit. It was the necessity to bring these corrupting despots
to heel that had resulted in the election in modern Europe of political
dictators by overwhelming majorities.

Having defended Mussolini a decade earlier, Shaw in the early 1930s
showed similar respect for Hitler. Nor was he alone in his regard for the
messianic man of action. Lloyd George, impressed by the constructive
achievements of the Nazis that he had been shown during a visit to
Hitler in 1936, called him "unquestionably a great leader," not, as had
been charged, "a mechanical moron." The Prince of Wales publicly
advocated friendship with Germany, provoking scandal by openly
socialising with the Nazi leader. Even Winston Churchill was moved to
admit that he "admired" Hitler for being a champion of his nation's
pride. To Shaw Hitler (in his *Mein Kampf*) was "the greatest living
Tory, and a wonderful preacher of everything that is right and best in
Toryism," but as a Messiah he was a failure, succumbing to the "rabble
of . . . ruffians." In the end he was, said GBS, "a doomed Impossibilist,"
making it necessary to "disable the aspirant to the government of the
earth" by crushing his Third Reich.

Behind Shaw's interest in Hitler was a concern for Germany itself,
"the centre of gravity of the Protestant North in Europe," which in so
many ways had been his spiritual home and his teacher, and which
(though he never publicly alluded to it) was the ancestral home of his
maternal antecedents, the Gurlys. With rare prescience he had, in 1914
in *Common Sense about the War*, urged a spirit of "sans rancune" when
the victory came, only to see Germany left prostrate and humiliated by
the Treaty of Versailles, cowering under the awful threat of a resump-
tion of the war. Shaw, who had preached a collectivist creed for half a
century, was one of the first to articulate prominently that Fascism was

456

a legatee of the nineteenth century's rebellion against Capitalism, and that it was "the only visible practical alternative to Communism." Add to this his doctrine of the Life Force and of the Superman, and it is not difficult to see why he would look favourably upon the social and political experiments practised by the dictators, and upon such moves as Hitler's early nationalisation of the trade unions.

Accused by Churchill of having become "airily detached," of having blinded himself to reality; and confronted with examples of brutality and ruthlessness in Italy, Germany, and the U.S.S.R., Shaw countered that this was often the price for social change by violence, and pointed to the excesses of the French Revolution's reign of terror, which anticipated modern totalitarian purges. A revolutionary movement, he argued, is a revolt against cruelty; but when the insurgence comes to pass and its adherents discover that the expected millennium has not been realised, they turn reactionary in their frustration, suspending liberties. That was why Shaw advocated a gradual, constitutional transition to Socialism, recognising that violence would retard the development of the economy and deter the transition.

Moreover, he noted, mob violence, beatings, torture, castration and other mutilation, culminating in victims being hanged or burned alive, were popular sports in "democracies" like the United States, many of whose community and national leaders tacitly sanctioned lynchings and the reign of terror imposed on Negroes, Catholics, and Jews by the cross-burning, white-hooded Ku Klux Klan, and whose president had in 1932 ordered federal troops to fire on unarmed veteran "bonus army" marchers in the nation's capital. Man's survival in the twentieth century, GBS insisted, would require wholesale revision of morality and ethics, of thought and behaviour.

His sympathy with the Fascists eventually waned when they manifested a denial of individual responsibility. As one who had long preached equality and social justice, Shaw was unsympathetic to the concept of Aryan supremacy, and it was, finally, on the attendant issue of anti-Semitism that he was moved to draw the line, calling the Nazis' Judophobia "a very malignant disease," which "destroyed any credit the Nazis might have had." A party, he averred, "which condescends to the phobias [of its most rabid citizens] must be desperately hard up for a program. 'No program: try a pogrom' must be," he told the *Jewish Chronicle*, "the very last resource of a mentally bankrupt party." His final judgment on the Fascist Right was, "Whom the gods would destroy they first make dotty."

His unwavering allegiance to the Revolutionary Left probably had its roots in his Irish heritage, which, as Harry Slochower commented in *No Voice is Wholly Lost* (1946), "contained the tradition of Catholic communality and that of political dissidence." The Soviet experiment, in any event, won Shaw's complete admiration. It astonished him that its detractors should speak of the Revolution as if it were "a transient riot headed by a couple of rascals," for it was futile to deny the "monumental triumph of the Bolshevik Revolution. You might as well argue with an earthquake." For half a century he had preached that only by economic salvation does one free the mind and the spirit, and it was his firm conviction that Communism alone could eventually accomplish this, the Russians being free from the illusion of Democracy.

Yet he did not blindly give blanket endorsement to its tenets and its methods: he was never a doctrinaire communist, and he was never moved to join the Communist Party. He shared the Soviet principle of social justice and economic equality, of a classless society, but heretically he rejected Marxist determinism and the principle of historical necessity. The errors of the Soviet government he criticised as bluntly as he did those of the British government, as when in 1925 he condemned the Third International, insisting it had done more harm to Russia than Rasputin did; or when after his 1931 visit he reported that there was no free press in Russia and no cameras "except official ones." He turned a blind eye, however, to Stalin's abuses of authority, and insisted that Russian Communism was the greatest political experiment in all history. As he proclaimed in his famous address to his Russian hosts in Moscow on his 75th birthday in 1931, he staunchly believed that "when you carry your experiment to its triumphant conclusion—which I feel confident you will—then we in the West, we who are still just playing at Socialism, must follow in your footsteps—whether we will or no."

To R. & R. CLARK, LTD.

4 Whitehall Court SW1
[A/18]   11th January 1937

[The "little amusement" was a revised fifth act for Shakespeare's *Cymbeline*, published as *Cymbeline Refinished*. Eventually it was produced, not at the Shakespeare Festival Theatre, but by Ronald Adam at the Embassy Theatre, Swiss Cottage, on 16th November 1937, the play being billed as by William Shakespeare and Bernard Shaw.]

This little amusement may surprise you.

It arose out of a proposal made at the last meeting of the Stratford-on-Avon committee to revive Cymbeline.

I said they had better let me rewrite the last act; and to my surprise they jumped at it. Curiosity, no doubt; but it stuck in my mind like a mosquito until I actually perpetrated the outrage.

There will be a tiny preface.

GBS

To MARIE ROLLAND

4 Whitehall Court SW1
[A/3]   19th January 1937

[Marie Koudachev (d. 1986) became, in 1934, the second wife of the writer Romain Rolland (1866–1944), who had a passion for music and taught musicology and art before concentrating on a writing career. Rolland's principal literary creation, Jean-Christophe Krafft, a musical genius of German parentage, is modelled in part on Beethoven. Shaw's letter is inscribed on the flyleaf of *William Morris as I Knew Him*, New York, 1936.]

Dear Madame Roland

I think this booklet—only a chapter in the two English volumes lately published here by May Morris—may interest you.

William Morris was one of the greatest men of our genre that the world has produced; but as he came just a generation before Romain, and absolutely refused to have anything to do with modern music, I do not suppose that they had any personal contacts.

I told him in vain that Die Meistersinger was the very thing he wanted in music. He had a very pleasant singing voice and an infallible ear; and medieval music touched him to tears; but the sound of a steel framed grand piano infuriated him, very justly.

Anyhow, this will not take very long to read.

> faithfully
> G. Bernard Shaw

To HERBERT BREWER

[S/117]   [Undated: January 1937]

[Herbert Brewer (1897–1968) was an eugenist introduced to Shaw by J.B.S. Haldane as one whose "ideas on eugenics were by far the most striking contribution to that subject which had been made in recent years" (quoted by Brewer in a letter to C.P. Blacker, 20th January 1937: Wellcome Institute for the History of Medicine). Hermann J. Muller (1890–1967), American geneticist and 1946 Nobel winner for physiology, was the author of *Out of the Night: A Biologist's View of the Future* (1935). To aid Brewer, a socialist, who earned his living as a postal clerk in Maldon, Shaw enclosed a cheque for £100.]

Dear Mr Brewer

All right: go ahead.

Dont be apologetic. Dont even mention popular prejudices: walk through them as if they wern't there.

When I, who have no children, & couldnt have been bothered with them, think of all the ones I might have inseminated!!!

And of all the women who could not have tolerated me in the house for a day, but would have liked some of my qualities for their children!!!

I should, however, have made it a condition that neither the origin nor the destination of the spermatazoon should be known to the parties.

I have ordered Muller's book.

> faithfully
> G. Bernard Shaw

To HENRY S. SALT

[C/3]
4 Whitehall Court S W 1
11th February 1937

Have you seen the recent news that boys flogged in the police courts now provide themselves with pocket money by exhibiting their weals at a penny a look?

The flagellomaniacs overlooked this incitement to juvenile delinquency.

What a world!

GBS

To M. J. MacMANUS

[H/48]
4 Whitehall Court S W 1
13th February 1937

[M. J. MacManus (1891–1951), author, bibliographer, and journalist associated with the *Irish Press*, was proprietor of the Dublin Book Agency. He later provided a biographical chapter for *G.B.S. 90*, edited by Stephen Winsten (1946). Shaw's article, "The Casement Documents," dealing with William J. Maloney's *The Forged Casement Diaries*, appeared in the *Irish Press* on 15th March 1937.]

—Private—

Dear Mr MacManus

I am not Minos judging which particular circle of hell the Asquith Cabinet of 1916 should spend eternity in. I simply want to remove a stain from Casement's reputation. When that is done Maloney Minos can push his face as far as he can and as hard as he likes.

Meanwhile, however, it ought not to be hard to obtain from the present Cabinet a statement to the effect asked for in my letter. Casement being safely hanged and the Irish question settled, there is no further need to blacken his name. The English are not vindictive as we are: they commit every atrocity on Monday when they are alarmed, and forget it with perfect goodnature on Saturday when the danger is passed.

What I advise accordingly is that we get some friendly M.P. to sound the Government as to whether, in view of the Putamayo explanation, they have anything against Casement's private character, pointing out how very unkind it is to his relatives to leave the matter in doubt when the documents are locked up in the Foreign Office. I see no

461

reason why John Bull should not give that assurance in his best genial and gentlemanly manner.

But what I understand you and the Irish Press demand from John is a full public confession that he is a forger, a liar, a slanderer, a plotter, a sneak, and a murderer. I think it is unreasonable to expect that from John; and I am quite sure that not only will you not get it, but you will revive the diary scandal without being able to disprove it.

The matter should be handled by Mr de Valera. What does he think about it?

faithfully
G. Bernard Shaw

Many thanks for your letter.

To SIDNEY WEBB

[D/14]

Ayot St Lawrence. Welwyn
21st March 1937

[The Russian writer Count Aleksey Tolstoy (1882–1945), a distant relation of Leo Tolstoy, was an honoured artist of the Soviet Union. Ivan M. Maisky (1884–1975), a Soviet diplomat, who would later participate in the Yalta and Potsdam conferences, was ambassador of the USSR to Great Britain from 1932 to 1943. On 13th March he had addressed the second National Congress of Peace and Friendship with the USSR on the position of Russia in international affairs. The lyric Shaw cites is from an 1878 music hall song by G. W. Hunt, at a time when Britain contemplated aligning itself with the Turks in their war against the Russians.]

... We had Alexis Tolstoy to lunch yesterday (at his own suggestion), also his wife and a member of the Communist Party as interpreter. It was quite a success: very nice people, converted emigrés, she goodlooking and perfectly dressed, his literary career remarkably like mine.

I fired off what you called my paradoxes (why?) at them with great effect. We parted with the most cordial au revoirs.

Maisky's speech was a paraphrase of "We dont want to fight; but by Jingo if we do, We've got the guns; we've got the men; and we've got the money too." I suggested a translation into Russian.

GBS

To CYRIL CLEMENS

[H/52; X/405.e]

4 Whitehall Court S W 1
1st April 1937

[G. K. Chesterton wrote for the *Daily News* from 1901 to 1913. The "review of Scott's Ivanhoe" is probably a misrecollection of Chesterton's "The Position of Sir Walter Scott," a critical overview, in the *Daily News*, 10th August 1901, in which he wrote: "Probably the most thoroughly brilliant and typical man of this decade is Mr. Bernard Shaw. In his admirable play of 'Candida' it is clearly a part of the character of the Socialist clergyman that he should be eloquent, but he is not eloquent, because the whole 'G.B.S.' condition of mind renders impossible that simplicity which eloquence requires."]

Dear Cyril Clemens

I am very highly gratified by the award you announce in your letter of the 28th February. A Mark Twain medal is something worth having.

I cannot remember when I first met Chesterton. I was so much struck by a review of Scott's Ivanhoe which he wrote for The Daily News in the course of his earliest notable job as feuilletonist to that paper that I wrote to him asking who he was and where he came from, as he was evidently a new star in literature. He was either too shy or too lazy to answer. The next thing I remember is his lunching with us on quite intimate terms, accompanied by Belloc.

Our actual physical contacts, however, were few, as he never belonged to the Fabian Society nor came to its meetings (this being my set), whilst his Fleet Street Bohemianism lay outside my vegetarian, teetotal, non-smoking tastes. Besides, he apparently liked literary society; and it had the grace to like him. I avoided it and it loathed me. But of course we were very conscious of oneanother. I enjoyed him and admired him keenly; and nothing could have been more generous than his treatment of me. Our controversies were exhibition spars, in which nothing could have induced either of us to hurt the other.

By the way, since you connect the medal with my sketch of William Morris, it may interest you to know that Morris was a confirmed Mark Twainer: he rated Huckleberry Finn as one of the world's great books, and read it over and over again.

faithfully
G. Bernard Shaw

To THE FEDERAL THEATRE

4 Whitehall Court SW1
[W(H)/393]   22nd May 1937

[The Federal Theatre project of the United States Government had, since 1935, been headed by Hallie Flanagan (1891–1969), of the Vassar College Experimental Theatre, who had been invited by the director of the Works Progress Administration, Harry Hopkins, to found a federal theatre. An immense success, the project produced everything from Eliot's *Murder in the Cathedral* to Marlowe's *Doctor Faustus* and the young Orson Welles's voodoo version of *Macbeth*. Milton Shubert (1900–67) had held a licence from Shaw since August 1936 to produce *On the Rocks* in New York, after out-of-town tryouts, for "an uninterrupted series of at least fifty consecutive performances." When the Shubert Organisation cancelled the agreement, the Federal Theatre produced the play at Daly's Theatre, New York, on 15th June 1938, for a run of 66 performances. Several thousand performances of Shaw's plays were presented throughout the United States over a period of two years with no more formal contract than this single letter of blanket approval.]

I cannot let you have On The Rocks until Mr Milton Shubert has given it a send off by his New York production, or until his failure to produce next autumn makes an end of his contract with me.

Now as to the rest of the repertory, will you kindly, to start with, put clean out of your head all the silly legends that the American newspapers keep repeating about me, and regard me, if you possibly can, as a fellow creature?

I know quite well what you are up against in this undertaking. It is useless to hope that you can find "groups with a high degree of skill in acting and direction" everywhere. You may not be able to find them anywhere. The plays will be murdered more or less barbarically all the time. That happens on Broadway too; and you must take what you can get in the way of casting and direction just as if you were a fashionable manager. So far from avoiding Negro casts you will be very lucky if you can get them; for Negroes act with a delicacy and sweetness that make white actors look like a gang of roughnecks in comparison.

You must leave the Theatre Guild out of account, and deal directly with me. The Guild people are my very good friends; but their object in life is to prevent anyone except themselves doing my plays; and their interference is quite unnecessary. I want them to perform my plays and not to complicate my business affairs.

They tell me that your theatre, being a federal institution, is unable to move without miles of red tape being consumed, and that money can be extracted from it only after signing nine receipts. They also seem to think that every production will be a separate transaction involving a special licence and weekly payments and acknowledgments. That will never do for me. As long as you stick to your fifty cent maximum for admission, and send me the accounts and payments quarterly, or half yearly if you prefer it, so that I shall have to sign only four or two receipts a year, and forget all about you in the meantime, you can play anything of mine you like unless you hear from me to the contrary as in the case of On The Rocks, which will soon be at your disposal like the rest.

Can you arrange things in this fashion for me?

Any author of serious plays who does not follow my example does not know what is good for him. I am not making a public spirited sacrifice: I am jumping at an unprecedentedly good offer.

faithfully
G. Bernard Shaw

To O. A. FORSYTH-MAJOR

Sidmouth
[H/102]   27th May 1937

Dear Sir

Lawrence called on us at Whitehall Court one frightfully cold day, dressed as usual in his aircraftman's uniform with nothing over it. When he was leaving I took down a very warm overcoat which I had never worn and put it on him. He was about to protest; but it was so comfortable, and, being much too long for him, so oriental, that he went off quite happily in it instead of half frozen as he was when he came in. I have no recollection of his returning it; but as it now hangs on its old peg, still unused by me, he must have done so when the summer came.

His assumption of the name Shaw had nothing to do with me. When he was enlisting he gave a name which happened to be that of the officer who was on duty at the time. He remonstrated, knowing quite well, of course, that the name was an assumed one. Lawrence then decided to open the telephone directory at random and take the first name of four letters his eye lighted on. This was Shaw; and so he became T. E. Shaw.

faithfully
G. Bernard Shaw

To CECIL LEWIS

Passfield Corner
chez les Webb
[H.c.u/4]   5th June 1937

[Jeff Lazarus was a Hollywood film producer, at Paramount Studios. The film the Shaws had seen was *The General Died at Dawn*, produced by William Le Baron and directed by Lewis Milestone for Paramount, from a screenplay by Clifford Odets. The cameraman was Victor Milner. Gary Cooper (1901–61) and British actress Madeleine Carroll (1906–87) were two of Paramount's top stars.]

My dear Cecil

Your description of the attitude and function of Lazarus has replaced the coffin lid on him and on Paramount as far as I am concerned. I know all about his notion of the art of filming; and I can only echo his matter-of-fact sister and warn you that it stinketh.

Now listen to me. I sat out a film at Sidmouth (where we have just spent a month) in which Gary Cooper and Madeline Carroll kept having their photographs taken for an hour or so, just as I have seen a hundred similar exhibitions before. The photographs were very good, and the lighting and scenery first rate. Madeline was very handsome; and the success with which her natural hair was made to look like a dazzlingly shiny wig and flashed at me until I could hardly help screaming to her for God's sake to take it off, was unforgettable. Fortunately it was relieved by a fascinating series of Chinks and negro train attendants, also beautifully photographed and lighted, and each looking like a whole detective story in himself, with a parallel series of sinister Americans, whom Gary Cooper socked on the jaw from time to time without ascertainable provocation. It was really beautifully done; and it held the audience as a picture book holds a child. The camera men and the producers had put their hearts and souls into their jobs.

But the interest was entirely pictorial and utterly undramatic. My liking for pictures was gratified to the full: my dramatic side was only exasperated by the splendor of the opportunity for telling a story and the pitiful amateurish bungling of the attempt to do it. I left the theatre without the faintest notion of what it was all about. I could not make out why Gary Cooper socked those innocent and picturesque people on the jaw. As to Madeline, her transitions from being a virtuous heroine to being a crook's decoy were so bewildering that Cooper at last socked *her* on the jaw without affecting in the least her infatuation for him. From time to time they made inarticulate noises with American accents, with all the consonants left out. Not one word could I understand, nor could Charlotte. The affair was in effect a movie, not a talkie: a movie without the qualities which the old movies derived from the speechlessness.

Now set your analytical faculty, if you have any, to tabulate all the techniques involved in these extraordinary exhibitions. You have the camera technique, the electric light technique, the face making technique, the costumier's technique, the picture composer's technique, the picture maker's technique (employing builders, architects and their draughtsmen), and the technique of the stage management. Contemplating this list you will realize the abysmal ignorance of the impostors who talk of the technique of the screen as if it were one thing. Contemplate it further, you will understand how easy it is in the excitement of all these techniques and their triumphs of execution, to overlook the one technique that is not in the list and is nevertheless the technique for which all the others exist, and without which their exercise has no meaning. Omit 1; and the audience become children turning over the pages of a splendid picture book. Up to a certain point it pays. Most of the studios seem to live by it. But in such studios the dramatist can find no place. They know that they can do without him; and as he upsets them very painfully by insisting on their several magics being made subordinate to his, they despise him, hate him, baffle him, and finally kick him out as a creature who knows nothing about their job.

Nevertheless, they presently want a continuity to set them to work, and a name to flash on the screen beneath the growling lion and the crowing cock. They sent a boy round to Whitehall Court for "the rights" of The Devil's Disciple. If they got them they would make a picture book of the play. The picture book might be a very gorgeous one. Dick would be very handsome; and the close-up of Uncle Titus and Uncle William would suggest all the characters in America's darkest fiction. Judith's eyebrows would be shaved off and replaced by a proper Hollywood pair. Burgoyne surrendering to Gates on the field of Saratoga and marching out proudly with the honors of war, would provide a glorious spectacular finish. All the scenery of New England would be used up in the transformation of my five little scenes into five hundred. Anderson will die at Saratoga and stain an anachronistic Old Glory with his blood, leaving Judith to fall into Dick's arms and make him unhappy for ever after. And nobody at the end would have the faintest notion of what it was all about.

They dont even know, poor devils, that there is such a thing as a dramatic technique.

Now do you begin to understand the matter, and to understand me, and to understand yourself. Get drama and picture making separate in your mind, or you may make ruinous mistakes.

If Lazarus would like the D's D to do his utter damndest with for three years or so, I am open to an offer, not less than five figures, nor too small ones at that.

I have plenty of friendly things to tell you; but this essay has quite exhausted me for today.

Have you found out Hollywood yet? I was talking to Mary Pickford about it the other day. . . . And I see that Mrs Patrick Campbell has taken my advice and moved to New York to be within reach of her proper work.

I am the better for the month at Sidmouth: so is Charlotte.

always yours
[G. Bernard Shaw]

Definitely, if you are going to be there, and can put over a front office scenario on Paramount and see it through without interference from ambitious office boys and other amateurs, I will let you rip and be content with a modest ten per cent and a time limit of three years from the date of release. But it must be for the English language only and for the English speaking countries.

To ADA TYRRELL

4 Whitehall Court SW1
[A/9]   8th June 1937

[The "infant" was Ada Tyrrell's daughter Geraldine (Deena) Hanson (1890–1980), in her later years a patroness of the arts in Dublin, who held a literary salon. Shaw's broadcast was "Schools," addressed to Sixth Form students, on 11th June.]

My dear Addie

You certainly have had a narrow escape from a literary career; for you write better than any of the family. I tried the bit of autobiography on my wife and found that it fascinated her and held her to the end.

I was amazed to learn that I made a superior impression in my boyhood. I remember your deriding me for using long words and on one occasion objecting very properly to my nails being black. Up to that time I had supposed that black was the natural color of nails. It gave a sort of finish to their outline.

We went and had tea with the Budleigh Salterton infant, very agreeably. Now that we are back in town we must manage to have a glimpse of her mother; but for the moment we are distracted with arrears of all sorts.

I am to broadcast at 3.35 on Friday—to the young!

GBS

To JOHN G. MOORE

[U(C)/89]

Ayot St Lawrence. Welwyn
23rd June 1937

[Edward VIII (1894-1972) had renounced his throne in December 1936 to be free to marry Wallis Warfield Simpson (1896-1986), an American divorcee. Shaw's correspondent in Hollywood sent a photocopy of the postcard to Upton Sinclair, marked "*Not* for publication."]

The British people and the London parliament were not consulted, and are wholly blameless in the matter.

The king refused to sacrifice his domestic and religious freedom, and abdicated. The royal family settled the affair among themselves.

There is no evidence that the Prime Minister [Stanley Baldwin] was allowed any say in the business. He had to keep crying Tomorrow to the clamorous House of Commons until it was arranged over his head, when he announced the arrangement in a speech of such sentimental eloquence that the nation was persuaded that it was all his doing.

G.B.S.

To HERBERT M. PRENTICE

[C/3]

4 Whitehall Court SW1
8th July 1937

[Prentice was rehearsing *The Millionairess* for the 1937 Malvern Festival, with Elspeth March as Epifania. Pond's was a popular brand of cosmetics, whose manufacturer advertised endorsements by society beauties.]

Eppy's speech should be peculiar to herself; but she must not be a stage foreigner, as that lingo is always grossly incorrect. She is exotic and essentially tragic all through. She should speak perfect English—too perfect, as a foreigner who has been thoroughly taught speaks it, but with the tragic rhythm of Mrs Siddons. At least that is how I should tackle it. But she must do it in her own way as best she can.

Her first dress should be a costume of black with touches of white, with a very white make-up and plenty of dark under the eyes. She can be a blaze of fashion and Pond as proprietress of the hotel.

GBS

To MRS PATRICK CAMPBELL

4 Whitehall Court SW 1
[H/4; X/160]   11th August 1937

[James Agate (1877–1947), the most celebrated dramatic critic in London, wrote for the *Sunday Times* 1923–47.]

My dear Stella

My antiquity, now extreme at eighty-one, has obliged me to make a clearance among my papers and take measures generally for my probably imminent decease. I find that I have done a very wicked thing: I have kept all your letters in spite of my rule never to keep anything but necessary business memoranda. I kept Ellen Terry's because her handwriting made pictures of them which I could not burn: it would have been like burning a mediaeval psalter or a XV Century French Book of Hours, I have no such excuse in your case. They *would* not be burnt, I suppose.

Now, if I keep them, the next thing that may happen after I die is their sale by my trustee to Gabriel Wells for the benefit of my estate, with incalculable subsequent adventures. Your only control over them will be your copyright in them, which will make it impossible for anyone to publish them for fifty years after your death without your authorization.

There is only one thing to be done—to send the letters back to you so that you may have the complete correspondence in your hands. This will add to its value if you have to sell it. Gabriel who has a mania for buying letters of mine (he has bought thousands) tells me that he would buy without hesitation but that you make impracticable conditions. But what conditions can you make except those that the law secures for you? Legally I have not the right to make copies of your letters; and I have not done so and shall not do so, as I should certainly die of angina pectoris during the operation. But you ought to make and keep copies of them before you part with them (if you do) as otherwise you will have a valuable copyright which you will not be able to use because you will not be able to supply the text; and the owners of the letters as material objects will be able to blackmail you for access to them.

As the last address that I had is a Hollywood one, and the interview that was lately published by James Agate placed you in New York, I asked Stella where you were. She gave me the last address she had; but as it was three months old I cabled you for confirmation. Your reply has arrived.

I learn incidentally that the quondam chancellor has made you a great-grandmother. Fancy that! as Tesman says [in Ibsen's *Hedda Gabler*].

I shall wait long enough to give you time to reply by post. If you dont, I shall send the letters on.

I rejoice to learn from the things you said to Agate that you ought not to have said that you are still Stella. I wish I were still Joey; but I have to be content now to play Pantaloon.

> always yours
> G. Bernard Shaw

PS I intended to buy from one of the fashionable locksmiths and safe manufacturers a beautiful jewel box big enough to hold the correspondence. But this would involve difficulties at the custom house and affidavits and deuce knows what. The only safe and easy plan is just to stuff the letters into a vulgar set of registered envelopes and post them to you. So you must just buy the box yourself and send me the bill. And if you decide to have the whole correspondence typed as a simple precaution against fire you must let me pay for that too, as it will cost as much as a new hat.

To MRS PATRICK CAMPBELL

Ayot St Lawrence. Welwyn
[A/4; X/160.e]   14th August 1937
[George Cornwallis-West published several books, including three novels and a book of reminiscences, *Edwardian Hey-Days* (1930), cordially received by the reviewers. None, however, could by any stretch of the imagination be termed a "best seller."]

471

My dear Stella

I have now, with infinite labor and a little heartbreak, packed all the letters, from the polite one to dear Mr Shaw in 1901 when you wouldnt be Cleopatra, to your last cablegram, into six compact envelopes: five of them the official registration ones and the sixth an ordinary one such as typed playscripts fit into without folding. When you have received the six you have received the whole collection and *nothing else*. I underline the nothing else because you need not open the envelopes until you want to deal with the letters, which will be meanwhile conveniently packed for you. The official envelopes are fairly stout.

I cannot remember anything in these letters that could hurt anyone except, perhaps, those concerning George's bankruptcies and infidelities. But all letters need editing. I have given Ellen Terry's letters to the British Museum; but they were not all printed nor unedited. For instance, her description of Mrs Kendal as "my idea of hell" could hardly be published during Dame Madge's lifetime. And Gordon Craig had to be considered.

There can be no question of publication in our case until Charlotte's ashes and mine are scattered in the gardens of one of the crematoria in which I hold shares. After that, the correspondence will be a valuable literary property which may be helpful to Stella junior if not to yourself. By the way, have you made your will? If you die intestate George will enjoy full marital rights over your property. Unless you divorce him you must expressly disinherit him unless you intend him to enjoy the widower's portion. I have not seen him of late; nor have I seen any new books reviewed as from his pen, though he once perpetrated a best seller. I infer that he is provided for....

You understand that if Charlotte survives me she will become the absolute owner of all the papers in my possession. Your letters would be a rather embarrassing legacy for her. She knows I am giving them to you, and approves.

And so, blessed be your days, dear Stella.

GBS

To MURIEL MURRAY

4 Whitehall Court SW1
[H/118]   19th August 1937

[Muriel Murray (1906–59), despite the severe handicap of cerebral palsy, held a post as acquisitions librarian at Northwestern University, Evanston, Illinois.]

Dear Madam

In somewhat belated reply to your letter dated the 2nd April of last year, what I object to is the doctrine that any atrocity is justifiable if we learn something by it. As there is no conceivable horror from which something may not be learnt, there is no extremity of cruelty and villainy to which this doctrine, which is the current doctrine of professional science today, may not lead. I contend that the pursuit of knowledge in the physiological laboratory as well as out of it, is subject to the common moral law, and that if the research worker can see no other means of proceeding except by way of cruel experiments, he must just wait until he has found a humane path, failing which he must just do without the desired knowledge. This takes a bit of thinking, which is troublesome, whereas any fool can vivisect and cook his experiment to suit his theory. All laboratory experiments are put-up jobs.

Far from "repeatedly and dogmatically branding vivisection as utterly useless," however, I have done my utmost to stop silly anti-vivisectionists from taking this line. Even if every vivisection that has ever been made could be proved to be misleading and useless, as many of them have been, yet there is nothing to prevent the next one leading to a great discovery. The same thing can be said of a volcanic eruption, an earthquake, a war or any other calamity. But people who made a profession of inducing or imitating such disasters would get short shrift.

You speak of living in a community which has swallowed science whole. Nothing could be more unscientific. It would be silly to swallow the philosophy of the great artists wholesale; but that philosophy is just as much a part of science as the mutilation of guinea pigs; and anyone who is unacquainted with it and its divinations is an ignorant person, however eminent he may be as a physiologist or mathematician.

faithfully
G. Bernard Shaw

To OTTO KYLLMANN

Victoria Hotel. Sidmouth

[H/64]   23rd September 1937

[Having enjoyed their May sojourn in Sidmouth, with excursions to Lyme Regis, Dorchester, Exeter, Axminster, and Exmouth, the Shaws returned on 22nd August for a holiday that extended into early October. Odham's Press not only took over whatever stock was left of the *Prefaces* in the Leighton-Straker warehouse, but contracted for an enlarged second edition of 20,000 copies in 1938.]

My dear O.K.

Let me now explain my sudden attack of business rapacity, and why you must now as fast as you can get out of my debt and keep out of it.

Charlotte and I have been heavily preoccupied with our positively last wills and testaments, which are at last executed and safe in the strong rooms of our respective solicitors.

It is mine which concerns Constable & Co. I am now in my 80second year, which means that my death may occur at any moment: indeed, actuarially, I am dead already.

Suppose I die tomorrow, or this afternoon (motoring on these Devonshire lanes is hazardous), what happens to you? You will find yourself not in the hands of Charlotte or any friendly and squeezable private executor, but in the grip of the Public Trustee, whose mill grinds quickly and grinds exceeding large. It would be a case of your money or your life: cash down or Portugal St. [Bankruptcy Office].

It was this new situation which I felt bound to present to you in as violent a manner as possible. Strictly speaking you should insure my life for the debt; but the premium would be colossal.

Meanwhile I cannot pretend that I am suffering any serious personal privation for lack of the money; so you may take a week or two to consider it. I did not mean it to arrive as a welcome home: I had no idea that you were returning from Ireland. Why did you go to that fantastic country? There are worse places, provided you can always get away from it.

We shall probably stay here until the end of the month or thereabouts.

A letter from Odhams just arrived informs me that they never took on the prefaces, but that if I have a large remainder on hand they will get rid of it for me on terms to be arranged. Have we any such remainder?

always yours
GBS

To ALFRED DOUGLAS

[H/64; X/394]
4 Whitehall Court SW 1
8th October 1937

[Robert Harborough Sherard (1861–1943), a devoted friend of Oscar Wilde since they first met in 1883, despite his aversion to homosexuality, had recently published *Bernard Shaw, Frank Harris and Oscar Wilde* (1937), an angry attack on Harris's biography of Wilde, which Sherard proved "by fact" was full of "malicious" lies and fictions. Douglas had provided a preface for it. Shaw's preface for a new edition of the Harris biography was already drafted. The biography, he informed Hesketh Pearson on 28th February 1934, "is still, as far as I know, by far the best literary portrait of Oscar in existence, simply because Frank was the best writer who tackled the job, and because he knew Wilde well personally. Sherard's picture of Wilde [as presented in two earlier studies] is obviously false; you can say of it what William Morris said of the Droeshout portrait of Shakespear: 'we know it's not like Shakespear because it's not like a man' " (A/3). Sir Rupert Hart-Davis characterises Sherard's portrait of Wilde as "loyally naïve."]

Dear Lord Alfred

Nellie Harris is on the rocks, as you may imagine, having sold everything saleable that Frank left. I cannot adopt her, but that funny book of Sherard's has given me a cue for a preface to a new edition of the Life and Confessions of O. W.

This book, as you know, has never been published in England because the publishers were afraid of litigation from you. I can quite easily edit the book so as to make it quite inoffensive to you; or, alternatively, delete all references to you, if you would prefer that. But on examining the last American edition (1930, Covici Friede) I find that you actually contributed a long letter—practically a very readable chapter—to this edition. Do you wish this to be included in the english edition; and, if so, will you give Nellie the necessary authorization?

Both the style and the matter of this letter make it a valuable attraction; but much as I appreciate its extraordinary candour I am not sure that some of it will not suggest more than it really means. And Frank's reply, to say the least, is not gracious.

Anyhow, let me know how you feel about the matter.

By the way, I have owed you a letter about the poems for a long time; but it is quite a job, and I have not yet had time to sit down to it. You certainly have a first rate talent for the most difficult forms of verse: sonnet sequences come from you as easily as limericks; but where's your epic? If I could sing like that in words I should by this time have left more verses than Shelley did. It is not as if, like poor

475

Henley, who had a bit of a gift too, only coarser, you had nothing to say. Are you lazy?

faithfully
G. Bernard Shaw

To ALFRED DOUGLAS

4 Whitehall Court SW 1
2nd November 1937

[H/64; X/394]

[Douglas urged Shaw on 12th October to wait until his new book *Without Apology* appeared in November before coming to a decision about a reissue of Harris's biography, and declined to approve of the Covici edition, which he had never seen, until he received a copy. This American edition was a reprint of the original, unrevised but with the addition of "the hitherto unpublished and full confession by Lord Alfred Douglas" (publisher's brochure: Dan H. Laurence Shaw Collection, University of Guelph). Douglas apparently informed Shaw in the same letter that his letters to his father (the "confession") were published without authorisation; a leaf of the letter, unfortunately, is missing.

Arthur Ransome (1884–1967) published *Oscar Wilde: A Critical Study* in 1912. "The idle singer of an empty day" was a self-description by William Morris in the opening stanza of *The Earthly Paradise*.]

Dear Lord Alfred

It is clearly not possible to prevent publication of Harris's book now. Nellie must live, even if you and I have to support her; and an advance of £350 on a 15% royalty has already been offered; so that the teashop in Nice promises to materialize.

I was greatly relieved to learn that your letters in the Covici edition were not intended for publication. But they contain a description of your father which is not only irresistible as literature but is a vital part of the history of the Wilde affair. I should very much like to work it in somewhere.

It is as I said possible to cut you out of the book altogether if you feel that way about it; but it would make a frightful hole in it; and it would miss a chance of setting you right at last. I still stick to my old opinion that Harris's portrait of Oscar is by far the most vivid we have. Ransome's is far more respectable and judicial; and Sherard's little account of the spaniel like attachment that made him at last unbearable is pitiful and sincere; but neither of them can push the trenchant Frank off the stage; his power of assertion and readability will carry the day

476

with posterity if posterity ever troubles itself about any of us. It is important to get Harris right: he is unsuppressible.

I must go over his stuff and see what can be done to make it harmless to the innocent. As you know, I have already had the job of editing his biography of myself so as to get the facts right without taking out the pepper and salt. As the man was dying the book fell to pieces at the end; and at the beginning it was full of stupendous inventions, as he knew nothing about my early life. Consequently a good deal of it is autobiography on my part, with the advantage of making Harris say one or two things that I could not decently say myself.

But before I tackle this job (I have already written a preface in which I have great fun with R. H. H. [error for R. H. S.]) I should like to know whether you wish me to depict you as well as I can and let Frank have the credit of it, or else leave you out of the saga altogether, which would be a great pity and would not remedy the wrong done you by the previous edition. . . .

I agree that to ask a poet to write an epic is rather like asking an explorer to live all his life on the summit of Mount Everest. There are scraps of downright doggerel even in Shelley's Prometheus; and Scott's worst is laughable. Still, there is plenty of good music in the middle of the voice, and much to be said for the idle singer of the empty day.

I knew *him*, by the way, pretty well.

> faithfully
> G. Bernard Shaw

To CHARLES MacMAHON SHAW

[U(H)/4]

Ayot St Lawrence. Welwyn
17th November 1937

[Charles MacMahon Shaw (d. 1943), an Australian cousin, one of the six sons and two daughters of Shaw's paternal uncle Walter Stephen Shaw (1822–?), who had emigrated to the Antipodes, had written a book entitled *Bernard's Brethren*. It was published by Constable in 1938, with Shaw's notes and disclaimers set as rubricated comments on facing pages. A revised text of Shaw's letter was published in 1949 in *Sixteen Self Sketches*.

Charlotte Greene was a well-known Dublin hostess, whose stepson Arthur was married to George Carr Shaw's sister Frances (Aunt Fanny), a drunkard. Uncle William (1811–74?), the reformed drunk, was the oldest son, preceded by five daughters. Uncle Henry (1819–84) was the eleventh of the fourteen siblings. Shaw's Aunt Emily (1821–95?) was married to the Rev. William G. Carroll (d. 1885), her first cousin; their unmarried daughter Emily ("Tah") (1854–1945) was the last survivor of the five Carroll children.

Frederick Gorringe, Ltd., was a drapery emporium in the Buckingham Palace Road, in which generations of schoolchildren were reluctantly fitted with public-school uniforms; it expired in the late 1960s. Rhoda Broughton (1840–1920) was a popular writer of rather audacious novels. For reference to Lucy Carr Shaw's books (there were two), see letter of 13th August 1913 to M. E. McNulty.]

Dear Cousin Charles

I have now been through your typescript; and though it must be corrected scrupulously as to the facts, it must be left as it is in style and form. Any attempt to polish you by giving it a conventional professional air would quite spoil it, as it would wipe your personality and character out of it, and make it dull and unreadable.

All the fiction in it must be cut out ruthlessly. In this business if you are not naively veracious you are nothing. Besides, you do not know the ground well enough to invent credibly. In Australia society is much more promiscuous than it was in Ireland in the nineteenth century. The Shaws were snobs necessarily, like all their class; but you have to bear in mind the different sorts of snobbery. When my father told me I must not play with a schoolfellow whose father kept a shop he was telling me what all fathers in his position had to tell their sons to prevent them making undesirable acquaintances. When I was told that all Roman Catholics went to hell it was impossible for me not to infer that Papists were an inferior species with whom a Protestant Shaw could not fitly associate. Here were two lines strictly drawn, the first between wholesaler and retailer, and the other between the Church of Rome and the Episcopal Church of Ireland, which was then the established Church of Ireland. No Shaw could form a social acquaintance with a shopkeeper or a Roman Catholic; and naturally the Shaw parents impressed that fact on their children and thereby made snobs of them.

But there is another department of snobbery which is less compulsory; and your book is amusingly full of it. This is the snobbery of the clan, the conviction that "the Shaws" were a superior race with dominant noses, either belonging to or connected with the landed gentry. To an Irish Shaw this was not a snobbish illusion: it was a fact of natural history and of social order. We jib at the word middle class or bourgeoisie just as the Hobart police chief did: we belong to the aristocracy. That is the sort of snobbery you can take to Australia, as my uncles did. All you can do with it is to make goodnatured fun of it. In a post-Marxian age it will not wash.

Your attempt to prove that my father did not wreck his marriage by drinking is the most desperate enterprise in the book; and it has led you to libel him atrociously by comparing him to the father of Samuel Butler. Butler feared and hated his father intensely, with good reason, as his father's notion of bringing him up in a godly way was simply to beat the humanity out of him and the Latin grammar into him. Now nobody—not even my mother—could hate my father, or fear him. When I remember occasions on which I was inconsiderate to him I understand perfectly how Dr Johnson stood in the rain in Lichfield to soothe the same remorse. He was unlucky and untrained and unsuccessful; and he could not conquer his miserable drink neurosis (for it did make him miserable) until he fell down on our doorstep in a fit which gave him a thorough fright and made him understand that he was destroying himself. From that time onward he drank no more.

When nevertheless we all deserted him, he must have found himself much happier; and I am much indebted to you for giving me the evidence of this: to wit, that he was able to renew his relations with his brothers and sisters. Two things had completely detached him from them. First, the drink neurosis. At one of the family parties at Bushy Park he got so drunk that it became a question whether he was not socially impossible. Then there was a party given by the Greens. The same thing occurred; and he was finally blacklisted. We were no longer visited by or invited by his brothers and sisters; and I no longer saw anything of my cousins.

This was hard enough on him; but what was harder was that he could not find society in his own house. In my Bassetto book I have described how we made a joint household with Lee, my mother's musical colleague. His energy and enterprise reduced my father to almost complete nullity. When his children had grown too big for him to play with, and the suspense as to whether he would come home drunk or sober never ceased, he got practically no comfortable society from them. His relatives did not want to see him; and my mother did not want to see his relatives: she was interested only in people who could sing, and they were mostly Catholics, not proper company for the Protestant caste of Shaw. I leave you to imagine the effect you produce on me when you take your stand firmly on the ground that no Shaw could possibly be anything so vulgar as a drunkard and that therefore I must be a freakish liar. If you had been through that time with me you would not see anything in it to joke about. But dont rush to the other extreme and conclude that all the Shaws were inebriates. Only three out of the eleven drank; and two of them, my father and William, suddenly gave it up long after their cases seemed hopeless. Whether the lady did I dont know: I never met her and heard nothing about her except malicious gossip.

Now consider the sequel when I, at 20 years of age, the last member of the family to live with my father, deserted him like the others and fled to London. It really was the consummation of a blessed relief for him. Aunt Bessie, with her Catholic rabble of singers, and her devotion to Lee, was gone. His diabolical son, who, in the middle of the religious revival produced by the visit of Moody and Sankey to Dublin, had written a letter to Public Opinion practically declaring himself an atheist, had gone too. It was now certain that George had really given up drinking. What was there to prevent the return of the reprobate to the clan? You tell me they took him back and made him as happy as we had made him wretched. Those lunches with Henry on Sundays were unheard of and impossible whilst we were with him. He was received by the Carrolls as a wit of the first order: when I found Emily Carroll, the only survivor of Aunt Emily's brood, at Eastbourne the other day, she told me all sorts of things that he used to say. I cannot believe that he ever wanted to see us again; but it happened that Lucy was in Dublin when he died, which he did in the happiest manner. He had a slight attack of pneumonia, and was recovering from it quite successfully when one morning he sat up in bed too suddenly and fell back dead with a clot stopping his heart. It never occurred to me to go to his funeral—not that I could have afforded it if it had.

Our indifference to oneanother's deaths marked us as a remarkably unsentimental family. And your determination to find us full of Victorian sentiment, including romantic beauty for all the women and dauntless courage for all the men, has culminated in the fancy sketch of my sister Lucy's life and character which is not only untrue, but the very opposite to the truth. Lucy, away from home, was everybody's darling: she broke many hearts, but never her own. Why, when she was middleaged, she married Butterfield I cannot tell you: my best guess is that she liked his family, who were pillars of the Irvingite Church and highly respectable commercially solid people. Butterfield's mother had discovered that the pleasantest place to live in is in bed, where she remained for 15 years or so until she died. Lucy had always fought shy of the opportunities her good looks and her singing gave her of getting into upper ten society: she knew that she had neither the money nor the social standing to be comfortable there, and very wisely kept among people who looked up to her and petted her rather than those who looked down their noses at her. She had no use for the Shaw pretensions, nor for the Gurly country-gentlemanism, and was therefore suspected at home of low tastes socially. Yet she hated Bohemianism and was ashamed of it. Now it happened that bedridden Mrs Butterfield saw what was the matter and set herself to give Lucy the social training she had felt the want of; for my mother, herself tyranically overtrained, left us all to train ourselves; and Lucy, who had always resented this neglect, was greatly relieved when Mrs Butterfield made her fully conscious of it and won her eternal gratitude by teaching her how to behave herself.

Butterfield was a little dumpling of an ex-insurance clerk (the Butterfields were up to their necks in insurance) whose pretty little face seemed to be sculptured on a bladder of lard. His one ambition was to be a leading tenor in light opera. His clerkship in the colonies enabled him to save £50; and with this sum he bribed the manager of a touring light opera company to allow him to sing the principal tenor part for one night. After this, I suppose, they could not very well turn him into the street. He sang with difficulty; but still he could sing a bit; and his tastes made him quite at home in that theatrical stratum. He was addicted to gambling and to women. And so in the course of time he met Lucy and married her. She soon got tired of him and banished him, resuming her way of living as a free spinster. This had gone on for some years when she learnt accidentally that at the time of her marriage he had been living with another woman. In a burst of fury she came to me and said she must have a divorce. As she had already practically divorced him I suggested that the operation was superfluous; but she was determined to be legally rid of him; and he was quite willing to leave the petition undefended if all claims for alimony or damages were waived. Accordingly, the divorce went through, and Lucy resumed her spinster name.

Then came the Shavian touch. Later on Butterfield turned up again, older and presumably lonely and at a loss for somewhere to spend his evenings. Lucy was goodnatured enough to tolerate him as a waif and stray, though as a husband she had found him unbearable. So he became a frequent visitor until he died, when his place was taken by his very capable brother Douglas Butterfield, who was manager of one of London's monster multiple shops, called Gorringes. Lucy survived them all without shedding a tear. Our parents had been dead a long time. I was the only immediate relative left; and I visited her only at very long intervals when there was some business to discuss. One afternoon when her health was giving some special anxiety I called at her house and found her in bed. When I had sat with her a little while she said "I am dying." I took her hand to encourage her and said, rather conventionally, "Oh no: it will be all right presently." We were silent then; and there was no sound except from somebody playing the piano in the nearest house (it was a fine evening and all the windows were open) until there was a very faint flutter in her throat. She was still holding my hand. Then her thumb straightened, and she was dead.

The doctor came in presently; and, as I had to go and register the death, I asked him what cause of death he would put in the certificate, adding that I supposed it was tuberculosis, from which she had suffered for many years following an attack of pneumonia which had ended her stage career. He said no; that her tuberculosis had been completely cured. I said "What then?". He replied "Starvation." I remonstrated, assuring him that I had provided for her better than that. He then told me that since the war they had never been able to make her eat enough. During the air raids an anti-aircraft gun, planted just outside her garden, had broken all the windows and crockery in her house, and shell-shocked her badly. They took her away to Devon, out of range of the German bombers; but she never recovered her appetite. Not knowing her circle of friends I did not invite anyone to her cremation at Golders Green; but when I got there I found the chapel crowded with her adorers. In her will she had expressly forbidden any religious service; but with all those people there I could not have her thrown on the fire like a scuttle of coals; so I delivered a funeral oration and finished by reciting the dirge from Cymbeline because

"Fear no more the lightning flash
Nor the all dreaded thunder stone["]

so nearly fitted what the doctor told me.

Lucy had literary faculty enough to have one or two stories, written in the style of Rhoda Broughton, accepted by The Family Herald. In middle life she perpetrated a book of which one of her admirers, who happened to be a publisher, brought out an edition. I believe I still possess a few copies, the remainder of that edition. You can have one if you wish to have your illusion about Lucy finally blighted; for it is so utterly cynical that it revolted my mother and almost shocked even me. It is supposed to be a series of letters addressed by an old woman to a young one advising her as to her conduct in life.

The rest you must discover from my notes on your typescript, as I must get back to my own work now. They will give you some eye openers as to the family which you have been able to idolize to your heart's content in Australia.

faithfully
G. Bernard Shaw

To WALTER RUMMEL

4 Whitehall Court S W 1
[C/1]   24th November 1937

[Walter Rummel (1882–1953), noted Berlin-born pianist, student of Leopold Godowsky and friend of Debussy, had written from Brussels to invite Shaw to attend his forthcoming recital in the Wigmore Hall.]

You forget how old I am.

How well I, ancient journalist-critic, know those recitals, infested with bearded octogenarians, all deadheads, who haunt the places where they once played or came to hear their pupils play! Outside one imagines a waiting string, not of Rolls Royces, but of coffins.

You want me to become one of these spectres. I wont. I would not cross the street to hear Liszt play a duet with Schnabel.

My presence or absence will not make a shilling of difference. Try all you can to get a broadcast. Make records, records, records. Put money in thy purse. The Wigmore cemetery will only empty it.

GBS

To A. LLOYD JAMES

4 Whitehall Court S W 1
[H/99]   2nd December 1937

[At a meeting of the B.B.C.'s Advisory Committee on Spoken English on 20th July, it had been suggested that the equerry of the royal stables at Buckingham Palace be consulted as to the pronunciation of "landau."]

Dear Ll. J.

It will be a blessed relief to the Committee to have a meeting without me.

Were I present I should protest violently against lárgess. Nobody ever uses it now within my hearing; but the older generation who had literary tastes and read the Waverley novels sometimes substituted it for tips or backsheesh. They always pronounced it with the stress strongly on the second syllable, as any gentleman or lady would. Largesse pronounced in this way cannot be mistaken for any other word. Pronounced as the consultant members recommend, it would be mistaken for largest.

POLKA has always been pronounced poalka. Why pollka? Gaseous I pronounce gáysius, Tussore tussóar (but the vulgar form is as recommended); Wenscut is new to me: I should say wainscot if I ever said it at all; Lándaw should not be referred to Buck, as there may be a German tradition there, and there can be no question about the received English pronunciation; I say baróak, errewdight, and errewdition; and I never say celeriac at all, not knowing that there is any such word, but now that it is revealed I shall call it turnip celery.

The other recommendations seem to me innocuous.

faithfully
G. Bernard Shaw

To AUGUSTIN HAMON

[H/1]
4 Whitehall Court SW1
8th December 1937

[Shaw had seen Ludmilla Pitoëff as Joan in the French production when it was performed in London at the Globe Theatre, in June 1930. Katharine Cornell (1893–1974) co-produced and starred in a new production of *Saint Joan* in New York in March 1936. Madame Pitoëff's Joan, recalled the reviewer of *The Times* on 26th November 1934, "not the herald of Protestantism and individualism, but a saint of the Catholic calendar breaking through the order of natural law, clearly belonged to another play—an essentially religious work of dramatic art suggested to M. Pitoëff, its producer, in the course of a brilliantly ingenious reading between the lines of Mr. Shaw's *St. Joan*."]

My dear Hamon

I hope you had a pleasant voyage and are now being comfortably ensoleilled in the south.

I can do nothing about St Joan for the present. A custom has sprung up in Paris of exhibiting foreign films there; and not until the foreign film has been a success will the French firms venture on a French one. At least that is what I am told by Czinner (Czinner is Elizabeth Bergner's husband), who cannot get the money to make an English film of St Joan unless they may exhibit it in Paris without any translation of the text into French.

I am not swallowing this without a grain of salt; but in the case of a European vedette like Elisabeth Bergner I have consented to try the experiment of allowing the film to be shewn in Paris without any "dubbed" translation or explanation on the chance that the French firms will then wake up and give us a French St Joan instead of a Judeo-German one, or a Russian one speaking French with a foreign accent.

I have made scenarios both for Pygmalion and Joan. They are not "shooting scenarios," which are purely technical specifications for the camera men; but they are complete in all other respects. The Pygmalion one will keep you busy for the present.

As to Pitoeff, you have no notion of how she falsified the play. Of course, being a very exceptional actress, she was able to make a Porte St Martin success of the Inquisition scene. So could any actress worth £10 a week. But it was to destroy that sort of St Joan that I wrote the play. I told her quite frankly that she had given a wonderful representation of a scullery maid being sentenced to a fortnight's imprisonment for stealing a pint of milk for her illegitimate child; and I have no reason to suppose that she could do anything better now.

Bernstein was exactly right when he said that her success was due to the fact that her every word and gesture was a flat contradiction of the Shavian text.

I shall wait until the Bergner film has had a turn in Paris, and until perhaps Katharine Cornell has included Paris in her world tour; and then we shall see what the French firms say about a genuine French Joan. . . .

faithfully
G. Bernard Shaw

To MARGARET EPSTEIN

[4 Whitehall Court S W 1]
[H.c.u/2]   29th December 1937

[Margaret Epstein (d. 1947) was the wife of the sculptor (Sir) Jacob Epstein (1880–1959), to whom Shaw had sat for a bust, commissioned in 1934 at the behest of A.R.Orage by an American woman, Mrs Blanche Grant. Mrs Epstein, in a letter to Shaw on 14th December, claimed Orage had later reported that Shaw did not like the completed bronze, that it was considered "offensive" to his household, and that he was unlikely to purchase a cast of it. Epstein, in his autobiography *Let There Be Sculpture* (1940), recalled that "Shaw was puzzled by the bust ... He believed that I had made a kind of primitive barbarian of him. Something altogether uncivilised and really a projection of myself, rather than of him. I never tried to explain the bust to him, and I think that there are in it elements so subtle that they would be difficult to explain. Nevertheless, I believe this to be an authentic and faithful rendering of George Bernard Shaw physically and psychologically." Shaw eventually did pay for a casting, but immediately presented it to the Theatre Guild.

Zsigmund Kisfaludi-Strobl (1884–1975), better known as Sigmund de Strobl, had sculpted Shaw at Malvern in 1932. Epstein's "Consummatum Est" was exhibited at the Leicester Galleries in 1937. Chaim Weizmann (1874–1952), world Zionist leader, became first president of Israel 1949–52. The Yugoslavian sculptor presumably was Ivan Meštrović (1883–1962), known for vigorous, dynamic images, and lionised on the occasion of his first exhibition, in the Victoria and Albert Museum, in 1915. He had two additional exhibitions in London in 1918.]

Dear Mrs Epstein

Only Orage the Irresponsible could have said that or supposed that I would throw an Epstein bust back in the sculptor's face as a thing of no value. Of course I never thought of doing anything of the kind. I could at least have sold it and given Jacob the price.

What happened was this. Jacob, as you know, is a savage, always seeking to discover and expose the savage in his sitters and often betrayed by the fact that his sitters are not savages. When he said to me "I will shew you what you really are" I knew quite well that he would do his utmost to represent me as an Australian Bushman. The result was a very remarkable bust; but as I am neither an Australian nor a Bushman, my wife, when she saw a photograph of it in the papers, absolutely refused to see it or to have it in her house on any terms. And she expressed her feelings very emphatically to Orage, and indeed to everyone who mentioned the bust to her.

Something else happened as well. A Hungarian sculptor, Sigismund Strobl (or de Strobl) came over with a commission like that of the American lady; and I gave him sittings down at Malvern. He turned out to be one of the finest sculptors in Europe. But he was a civilized man who was not in the least interested in the Shavian Bushman who may or may not have lived in Australia fifty thousand years ago, and very much interested in the dramatic poet and philosopher Bernard Shaw. He produced accordingly a beautiful bust of a man of genius (Michael Angelo made all his sitters geniuses) with comedy in one side

486

of his mouth and philosophy in the other, the whole bearing a flattering resemblance to Bernard Shaw at his best.

My wife was naturally delighted. She made him carve it in hard Austrian marble and gave it the place of honor in her drawingroom. With it before her Jacob's Bushman was like a blow in the face. I did not re-act quite so simply. I knew Jacob understood quite well what had happened. Jacob had done what he wanted to do as successfully as Strobl had done what *he* wanted to do; but as Jacob was at his old game of illustrating a biological theory and debunking civilized mankind, whereas Strobl was honestly working on the facts and making the highest of them, he won the heart of my wife, who did not want to see me debunked. She will never forgive Jacob; and the Bushman will never darken our doors. But that does not console me for the loss of it. There are plenty of things to be done with it besides setting it up in Whitehall Court as a foil to Strobl's masterpiece. What is the name and address of the American lady. I have quite forgotten both. I should not like her to think that I did not appreciate what she did for us.

What interests me at an exhibition of Jacob's work is always the work in which the truth breaks through the biological theory, which began as a phallic obsession and held him back for years. It does, sometimes. The head of a young revolutionist in the Consummation show. It did in the Weizmann bust. He is always picking out the women models on whom he can lavish exquisite modelling in detail but on the whole make them lizards, not women. Why do you let him do it?

Please dont think that I want to see him overwhelmed by commissions from royalties and aristocrats who ask only to be made to look like ladies and gentlemen, that being in fact all they are. It would keep his pockets full but waste his time as Strobl's is largely wasted. But the princesses and peers are authentic and the bushmen and lizards are not. It is sometimes an allowable ironic joke to take a lady with a thrice lifted baby face and expose her as the reptile she really is, as that Jugo-Slavian sculptor whose name I forget (I forget everything now) used to do when he was fashionable for a while in London years ago; but it should be only a joke, not the whole of the sculptor's practice. One Chaim Weizmann as such is worth a dozen bushmen labelled Bernard Shaw.

If all this makes you angry just think how you would feel if you ordered a statue of Jacob to remember him by, and you received instead a statue of Ishmael!

faithfully
[G. Bernard Shaw]

487

To JOHN A. HUGHES

[H/73]

4 Whitehall Court SW1
5th January 1938

[John A. Hughes (*c.* 1883–1942), formerly an Anglican clergyman, was a member of the Society of Friends, well known in the Yorkshire area as a producer of amateur drama. Henry B. Sharman was an educator, author of *Records of the Life of Jesus* and other theological works. John Masefield wrote several religious dramas, including *Good Friday* (1917), *The Trial of Jesus* (1925), and *The Coming of Christ* (1928).]

Dear Mr Hughes

Tell Dr Sharman not to attempt a modern Passion play. It has been repeatedly suggested to me and carefully considered by me. And the soundness of my conclusion has been proved by John Masefield's drama. On the stage Jesus comes out as an arrogant lunatic, dull, speechless, and too intolerable to be pitiable until they torture him. Pilate and Annas carry off all the honors. No doubt that is the truth of the matter; but a real madman with a ridiculous delusion cannot be a hero of tragedy (Lear and Ajax [in *Troilus and Cressida*] have no delusion of their own greatness) and a passion play without Jesus as the hero is impossible.

faithfully
G. Bernard Shaw

To MARY CATHARINE INGE

Ayot St Lawrence. Welwyn
[C/59]
18th January 1938

[Mary Catharine Inge (1880–1949), née Spooner, was the wife of the Dean of St Paul's.]

Dare you tell Himself that one of the surprises of Moscow is that Lenin was a delicate blonde who might have been your twin? Only you are a little bigger and not so fragile.

You might have knocked me down with a feather when I saw him.

Stalin, with his Georgian eyes and frank smile, is the lady killer as far as looks go; but he is said to be a model of domesticity, virtue, and innocence.

Instead of making himself President he remains a nondescript nobody. He knows what Lawrence of Arabia found out, that he that is least among you is master of all the rest.

This is only an excuse for sending you our loves.

GBS

To ALFRED DOUGLAS

Ayot St Lawrence. Welwyn
[A/64; X/394]   25th January 1938

[Aided by Douglas, Shaw had extensively revised and amended both the preface and (silently) the text of Harris's biography of Wilde.]

Dear Lord Alfred

At last I have finished this job for Mrs Harris. By this post I send to the publishers (Constables) the edited copy for Frank's Oscar Wilde, with a preface by me running to 18000 words or so in the form of a reply to Sherard's Shaw–Harris–Wilde explosion.

Your marginal notes and letters have been of great assistance. I agreed with all of them practically. What I cannot understand is why Harris would not accept them and get rid of the libellous character of the book.

I think Wilde took you both in by the game he began to amuse himself [with] in prison: the romance of the ill treated hero and the cruel false friend. Once you see the character of this make-believe, all his lies and your imaginary crimes become merely comic.

I take it that the book of which you wrote to me—or shall I say threatened me with?—is not yet published. So much the better: you had better hold it back until mine is out; for not only will you have the last word, but as I have made out a much better case for you than you can decently make out for yourself you will be able to avoid spoiling it. . . .

In great haste
G. Bernard Shaw

To G. S. VIERECK

4 Whitehall Court S W I
[H/108; X/395]   27th January 1938

[Viereck had sent Shaw the American edition of his book *The Kaiser on Trial*
(1937). Shaw's letter was published as preface to the English edition (1938).
Helmuth von Moltke the Younger (1848–1916) was Chief of the German
General Staff in 1914. His muddling of attack plans at the outbreak of war
slowed the offensive and frustrated the Kaiser's hopes for an early decisive
victory.]

Dear Sylvester Viereck

I congratulate you on The Kaiser on Trial. It is a new method in the
writing of history, and by far the most effective and readable one, as
instead of the usual academic efforts to be impartial it presents all the
partisans doing their worst and very best, and leaves the reader to find
the verdict. It says a great deal for the Kaiser that he sanctioned this
procedure, knowing that it involved a statement of everything that
could be said against himself by his lowest assailants. Most monarchs
expect to have it all one way; and many of them never find out that
there is any other way.

On the whole Wilhelm comes out of it pretty well for a man thrust
by the accident of birth into a part which was not only extremely
difficult, but to a great extent imaginary and flatly impossible.

To my mind his highest, but, as it proved, his most tragic point was
reached when, in 1914, he saw that the enemies of Germany had
ambushed her, and that his only chance was to secure the neutrality of
the western Powers and swing all his forces to the east for a square
fight with Russia. England and America would have had no excuse for
attacking him in the rear; and though there was the fatal inheritance
from 1871 of Alsace-Lorraine and the savage hatred of Poincaré, who
could not speak of 1871 without screaming with rage, yet it might not
have been easy to induce the French to go to war without the backing
of England on behalf of the detested Tsardom.

But what made any such move impossible was that the Kaiser's
command of the army was not a real one. Napoleon was able to swing
his army from Boulogne, on the eve of invading England, to Austerlitz.
Wilhelm had no such command. He came up against Moltke (the
lesser Moltke) who, when he was asked to change his old pigeon holed
plans for an attack on France through Belgium and a rush to Paris,
plans which broke down completely in practice, simply began to cry,
having no room in his head for new ideas. But Wilhelm had the idea;

and that, I think, gives him some claim to be ranked as the best brain in the government of Germany then.

What he could not know was the mind of Grey, because Grey did not know his own mind, which was bent on war with Germany at all hazards after Wilhelm dared to build a German fleet. In any sane country Grey would never have been trusted with any public office after his connivance in and defence of the Denshawai atrocity, and after his repeated proofs that he was incapable of telling the truth on any political subject because he never knew what the truth was: his brains being those of a naturalist, not of a diplomatist. The Press never criticized him, and repeated at least once a month that he was a perfect gentleman. The war was the price that England paid for encouraging Grey's folly and callousness in dealing with Egypt; and now her rule there has gone where it deserved to go.

I used to say when I was asked how long the war would last that it would last 30 years, and be ended by the soldiers going home in disgust, as the Russians did. I argued that the central powers could not be blockaded, as they were fully self-sufficient. A military decision was impossible: all the great offensives and their incidental victories came to nothing. What I did not foresee was that the Germans could starve themselves by withdrawing too many producers from industry and sending them to the trenches. There could be only one end to that; and the Emperor, having been the idol, was inevitably made the scapegoat. You have knocked some of that nonsense on the head. As to the withdrawal to Holland, it needs no apology any more than Louis Napoleon's withdrawal to Chislehurst. What possible good would it have done to anyone to return to Berlin without any power and with the assurance of the army that they could not protect him against being mobbed and probably murdered? It was an admirable piece of common sense and a happy ending for a monarch who had done nothing to deserve an unhappy one.

You have done a big job splendidly: I shudder when I think of the labor it must have cost you. It is a mine of information, and is both dramatic and judicious: an unusual combination. Again, my congratulations.

faithfully
G. Bernard Shaw

To UNIDENTIFIED CORRESPONDENT

[E/83]

[4 Whitehall Court SW1]
5th February 1938

[Shaw had been requested to affix his name to an appeal, the full text of which read:

"The renewed outbreak of air bombing of densely populated cities in Spain and the resultant slaughter and maiming of hundreds of non-combatant men, women, and children have filled the civilised world with horror. The under-signed, representing diverse sections of the British nation, implore the leaders of Republican and Nationalist Spain, for the sake of the Spanish people and in the interest of humanity, to abandon by express agreement the deliberate bombing of civilian populations."]

I am afraid I cannot sign this. The notion that the killing of civilians, women & children is worse than the killing of soldiers can be held only by horrified people who have not thought out the subject. The object of war is to vanquish the enemy; and its method is to kill as many of them as possible. The civilian is the enemy just as much as the soldier; and it is very undesirable that he (or she) should be immune from the horrors faced by the soldier. Such an immunity perpetuates war as an institution and prolongs its campaigns. Its abandonment is a great step towards the abolition of war as a glorious institution[.]

G. Bernard Shaw

To BEATRICE WEBB

[H/14]

Ayot St Lawrence. Welwyn
6th February 1938

[Sidney Webb was felled by a stroke, in January 1938, from which he never fully recovered, remaining partially paralysed with his speech impaired. Confined to Passfield Corner, he could read but had difficulty writing. In celebration of Beatrice Webb's eightieth birthday Shaw had accepted an invitation from Henry Wilson Harris (1883–1955), editor of *The Spectator*, to write a tribute, published as "Beatrice Webb, Octogenarian" on 21st January. Kingsley Martin, on finding that Shaw was already committed, invited H. G. Wells to pen an article for the *New Statesman*; this appeared as "Mrs. Webb's Birthday" on 22nd January. Éamon De Valera's news-paper was the *Irish Press*, founded in 1931. His speech on vocational organisa-tion may have been that of 11th May 1937, in Dáil Éireann, on the constitu-tion of Ireland. Shaw's letter in *The Times* on 5th February was captioned "Italians in Abyssinia."]

492

. . . Sidney has given us rather a fright. We are the only members of the old gang left; and we shouldnt do such things. Our numbers are up now: and we should arrange to die quietly in our beds of heart failure. I am already in good practice, as it takes me 25 minutes to walk a mile, and the least hill or a flight of steps slows me to a crawl. I suppose it is best for you to be alone at Passfield with nobody to bother you, except your invalid; but somehow it does not feel that way to us: the impulse to stand by is so strong that it needs an exercise of conscious reasoning to stifle it.

However, the alarm is over: if Sidney can talk he is all right. I sleep a lot now in the daytime: make him do the same.

The Ervines were much disappointed at not meeting you as promised at lunch. My conversation with you over the telephone was not really a conversation; for the line was out of condition and I could not catch what you were saying. I caught Wells's name; but I did not then know that Kingsley Martin had gone to him for an article when Wilson Harris forestalled him with me; so I had no clue to your mention of him.

I took up De Valera's Irish paper the other day (Charlotte subscribes to it) and found that the new Irish senate is an experiment in vocational organization which is interesting and praiseworthy. I gathered nothing of this from the English Press. De V. made a long and important speech about it.

Did you see my little letter in The Times yesterday?

I think we ought to tackle the Jewish question by admitting the right of States to make eugenic experiments by weeding out any strains that they think undesirable, but insisting that they should do it as humanely as they can afford to, and not shock civilization by such misdemeanors as the expulsion and robbery of Einstein.

The prevailing thoughtlessness is damnable. . . .

G.B.S.

To GABRIEL PASCAL

4 Whitehall Court S W 1
[H/1; X/396, 400.e]   24th February 1938

[Pascal filmed three endings for *Pygmalion*, including one that conformed to Shaw's screenplay. The final, romanticized ending dissatisfied Shaw, but he stoically acceded to it. Laurence Irving (b. 1897), grandson of Sir Henry Irving, was a scenic designer for stage and screen. "Nepomuck" was Shaw's original name for the Hungarian phonetic expert, Higgins's former pupil, at the Embassy ball. In the film he became Count Aristid Karpathy. The rôle was superbly performed by Esmé Percy. Despite the "insult to Hollywood," Shaw was awarded an Oscar for his screenplay at the Motion Picture Academy ceremony a year later.]

My dear Gabriel

I have given my mind to the Pygmalion film seriously, and have no doubt at all as to how to handle the end of it. Anthony is a talented and inventive youth; but he doesnt know the difference between the end of a play and the beginning. Just when the audience has had enough of everything except the ending between Higgins and Eliza, to go back to the dirty mob in Covent Garden and drag back Doolittle after he has been finished and done with would produce a boredom and distraction that would spoil the whole affair. As to taking Higgins and Eliza out of that pretty drawingroom to be shaken up in a car it shows an appalling want of theatre sense and a childish itch for playing with motor cars and forgetting all about the play and the public. So away all that silly stuff goes.

Will you impress on Laurence Irving that the end of the play will depend on him? Not only must the drawingroom be pretty and the landscape, and the river if possible, visible through the windows with the suggestion of a perfect day outside, but the final scene on the embankment at Cheyne Walk must be a really beautiful picture. Its spaciousness must come out when the car is driven off. Irving must eclipse Whistler in this.

I am sorry I have had to stick in the flower shop; but it need not cost more than it is worth and you will save by getting rid of the wedding rubbish. It is not a Bond Street shop but a South Kensington one: half florist's, half greengrocer's and fruiterer's with a fine bunch of property grapes for Freddy to weight for a lady customer. The counters can be made for a few pounds: scales can be hired; and the building can be faked out of any old junk. Everything unsightly can be covered in flowers.

I timed the dialogue in the Nepomuck scenes last night. Actual speaking occupies 68½ seconds, practically nothing.

Our advertising line must be an insult to Hollywood all through. An all British film made by British methods without interference by American script writers, no spurious dialogue but every word by the author, a revolution in the presentation of drama on the film. In short, English *über Alles*.

I am looking forward to seeing you tomorrow.

faithfully
GBS

494

To HANNEN SWAFFER

[4 Whitehall Court SW 1]
[H/1]   26th February 1938

Dear Hannen Swaffer

I cannot tell you the exact date of my death. It has not yet been settled. When it is, I shall be settled too. You must be content to know that as I am in my 82nd year, my number is up, and the cremation furnace may make an end of me at any moment, to the great relief of many worthy persons.

Your second question, how do I intend to leave my money, is complicated by the fact that, as you rightly surmise, I do not know how much money I have to leave. Most of my time is spent in earning and collecting money for the government, national and municipal. They do not pay me a commission.

As to the disposition of my property after my death, you had better write an article on the curious custom of making wills. I don't know whether you have ever tried to make one. I am old enough to have made several; for wills become obsolete with surprising rapidity, considering that each is intended to be final. I have known men of great possessions who had to make new wills every year. I cannot be bothered like that; but the result is that my will is never up to date. My last one is quite recent.

As to how it disposes of my property I need only tell you that my experience has convinced me that the surest way to ruin young people is to offer them the faintest hope of an inheritance. But this does not apply to old people whose bolt is shot nor, of course, to widows and children whose livelihood is dependent on the life of some owner of property. My property will therefore be charged with annuities which will postpone its final disposal until other people than myself are extinct. But when that happens I should like to do something for the English language, for English speech and manners, for the science of phonetics, for the methods of personal training which may be described as yogas. And how that can best be done is a problem which you are welcome to solve for me if you can.

faithfully
G. Bernard Shaw

To SIEGFRIED TREBITSCH

[H/5; X/341]

4 Whitehall Court SW1
18th March 1938

[Shaw's article "And So—Heil Hitler," in the *Evening Standard* on 17th March, took the position that the Anschluss (Hitler's march into Austria on 12th March, culminating in its annexation by Germany on the following day) was born of the infamous Versailles Pact. The Trebitsches had fled to Prague a few days later. Shaw subsequently insisted that the article and congratulatory messages sent by him to colleagues in Austria and Germany were intended to be helpful to them in living among or escaping from the Nazis.]

My dear Trebitsch

We are glad to hear that you are safe in Prague. I have just instructed my bankers to send you a draft on Prague for the Czechoslovakian equivalent of 1200 German marks. Yesterday all London was placarded with "Bernard Shaw" "Heil, Hitler!" in the biggest capitals. At the same time I sent you a postcard congratulating you on the glorious achievement of the Anschluss by your fellowcountryman the Führer.

And now you reproach me because I did not write letters pointing out that you are a Jew marked out for Nazi persecution.

You say that I am the only one of your friends who has not done this. In that case I am the only one of your friends who is not a mischievous fool. As for you, you have many merits and talents; but in politics you are the most thoughtless idiot in Europe. You are furious with me because I did not betray you to the police, who are pretty sure to read all your correspondence.

I hope my unfeeling conduct helped you to get a passport. Let us hear about your adventures when you have time to write.

ever
GBS

To MRS PATRICK CAMPBELL

[H/4; X/160]

4 Whitehall Court SW1
18th March 1938

My dear Stella

Now that you put me to it, I find this business of the letters much more complicated than I thought. I can do no more than confirm to you the gift of the pieces of paper on which your letters to me are written. The pieces of paper on which my letters to you are written are your property without question.

I can also declare, and do hereby declare, that my executors will be acting according to my wishes if, after my wife's death and mine, they consent to the publication of the letters for your benefit, or, if you also are no more, for the benefit of your daughter Stella. Failing her, the interest in the letters becomes an unencumbered part of my estate.

This is all I can do at present. If I become a widower I may be able to make the situation clearer by a codicil to my will; but if she becomes a widow this will not be possible. She will inherit the copyright in my letters with all my other copyrights; and you may regard it as certain that she will not consent to publication, and had better not be reminded of the existence of the correspondence. On her death the copyrights will go to the Public Trustee; and then publication will be possible.

The position will then be that nobody can publish without your consent, because only you will possess the letters; and in any case you have the copyright in the letters written by yourself. This makes you mistress of the situation to the utmost extent now possible. But you must hold on to the letters.

I strongly advise you to have two copies of the correspondence typed in sections of three or four letters at different offices so as to prevent the possibility of surreptitious copies. Send one copy to Stella and tell her to take special care of it. This will act as a fire insurance. You keep the originals yourself. The third copy will do for the printer; and if it also is kept in a separate place it will be an additional insurance against loss by theft, fire, accident, carelessness or the like. I have no copies myself, nor have I ever shewn your letters to anyone.

I think this is all I have to say, except that as you are nine years younger than we are your chances of surviving both of us are fairly good.

always
GBS

PS If the copying is inconveniently expensive send the bill to me.

To ALFRED DOUGLAS

Ayot St Lawrence. Welwyn
[H/64; X/394]   18th April 1938

[Douglas's *Without Apology* was published on 6th April; one of the author's copies was posted to Shaw as a gift. Reginald Turner (1869–1938) was a member of Wilde's circle who befriended him in France on his release from prison; he achieved a modest success as a novelist. For "the Daventry plot" see the letter of 4th November 1900 to Frank Harris. Seth Pecksniff is a hypocrite and Montague Tigg a swindler in Dickens's *Martin Chuzzlewit*. Harris's four papers were *The Candid Friend, The Motorist and Traveller, Vanity Fair*, and *Modern Society*; his two articles on Shaw in *Vanity Fair* ("Ruskin and Wells: Shaw and Carlyle" on 17th July 1907 and " 'First Aid to Critics' By George Bernard Shaw" on 11th September 1907) are both signed "Frank Harris." Lady Jessica Sykes (1856–1912), journalist and author, daughter of George Cavendish-Bentinck, was the wife of Sir Tatton Sykes. Wilde was not incarcerated at Wormwood Scrubs (Shaw retained the old spelling) but at Reading. Shaw's gift to Douglas in reciprocation was a just-published book by Albert Einstein and Leopold Infeld, *The Evolution of Physics*.]

Dear Lord Alfred

The book is extremely readable: I enjoyed it very much. And it is quite convincing as to your entire sincerity as a writer of Confessions and your innocence in the Wilde affair and generosity in your relations with him.

But you have not got the hang of Harris. There are in the story two George Washingtons: one who could not, and the other who would not tell a lie. One was Harris; the other was yourself. In your case this dangerous virtue was a trifle compared to the tragedy produced by your father. But Harris was ruined by it. Sherard describes him as trumpeting lies all over the place. That is exactly what he should have done to establish his place in London society. What he did do was to trumpet the truth all over the place and make himself quite impossible.

All the recriminations about lying are traceable to the lying of Wilde (his bread depended on it) when he gave up writing. He was living on you, on Harris, on Ross, on Turner (who was Turner?), on all his old theatrical friends to whom he sold the Daventry plot exactly as Sheridan sold shares in Drury Lane Theatre. It was a necessary part of the game that you should each be persuaded that all the others had left him to starve. He convinced Harris that you had never given him a penny. He convinced you that Harris had cheated him basely over Daventry. And so on with all the rest. Harris believed him when he

498

wrote his life of Wilde. You still believe his tales about Harris. And Harris died convinced of your mendacity. In truth there was only one masterliar in the case; and he was Oscar.

Let me again remind you that I am an Irishman. I know that there is no beggar on earth as shameless as an Irish beggar. I have seen them beg when they are perfectly well off—beg from poor people. And I know that flexibility which enables an Irishman to charm you to your face, and tear you to pieces the moment your back is turned. When I said that Oscar was incapable of friendship (as you understand it) I knew what I was talking about.

Harris disliked you, and said so frankly. Another man would have disparaged you to gratify his dislike. Harris alone placed you at the top of the tree, and never retreated a step from that estimate. It was this knowledge of the difference between chalk and cheese, and this courage in trumpeting his opinion that made Harris's editorship of The Saturday Review the success it was. Whatever he was he was neither a liar nor a hypocrite; and you and Sherard owe his ghost an apology for dismissing him as a combination of Pecksniff and Montagu Tigg.

But there is one thing that you perhaps do not know. You accuse him of a specific attempt to blackmail you. His notions of business morality were so American that it is possible that he regarded blackmail as one of the legitimate ways of making money out of journalism. But he behaved exactly as if he knew nothing of the attempt. He took no notice of your attacks in your paper; and was genuinely astonished and hurt by your treatment of him at the Café Royal.

Perhaps you do not know that Harris collapsed as a writer very much as Wilde did. He was the nominal editor of at least four papers after The Saturday, and no doubt drew a salary for the goodwill, such as it was, of his name in the bill. But that was all they got out of him. The first of them, The Candid Friend, engaged him for a day or two in a vain attempt to rally his old Saturday staff round him; but it was run by Lady Jessica Sykes, a clever woman and a heavy drinker, until it perished. As to Vanity Fair, it contained an article abusing me up hill and down dale over the signature F.H. It did not contain a sentence that he could have written or would have written. Finally he found himself in prison for stuff that he knew nothing about.

Are you quite sure that he knew anything about the attempt to blackmail you? When he was banished by the war and had really to edit a rag called Pearson's Magazine he reprinted any mortal screed of his sooner than write fresh stuff. The Saturday finished him as a writer just as Wormwood Scrubbs finished Oscar. His attempt to write a book about me was pitiable. Drink and pneumonia disabled him. He was never drunk to my knowledge; but then he was never sober in my fashion.

As to your final denunciation of me as a dangerous man, you are quite right: I am as fatal to retired majors and pensioned governesses [as] I could possibly desire to be, though they wont die, damn them! How is it that the fragment of mind that you exercise is so first rate whilst all the rest prefers The Patriot to The New Statesman? But I bear no malice: I am used to it; and the Harris preface will be my revenge. By the way, it ought to be issued as edited by Lord Alfred Douglas; for I agreed with all your notes and made no attempt to improve on them. The book is now perfectly presentable; and I hope its publication will do you a service as shewing for the first time that the Queensberry affair was your tragedy and, comparatively, Wilde's comedy.

I enclose a little present. Einstein is a poet.

G.B.S.

To ALFRED DOUGLAS

[C/64; X/394]

Ayot St Lawrence. Welwyn
25th April 1938

[Philip Melancthon (1497–1560), German religious reformer, was a fellow worker of Martin Luther at Wittenberg.]

I forgot to say that the Einstein book is not a joke. Just put it by until you feel the necessary curiosity about the revolution in physics which has taken place in our time. You see, the whole Catholic philosophy is founded, on its scientific side, on Aquinas, who was founded on Aristotle, a pagan whose works were made virtually canonical in the XIII century. Nowadays a Catholic who is ignorant of Einstein is as incomplete as a thirteenth century Dominican ignorant of Aristotle.

The protest against scientific physics was led by Luther, Melancthon, and the Protestants generally. Religion without science is mere smallmindedness.

GBS

Sculpture by Sir Jacob Epstein, June–July 1934

(Photograph: Shaw collection of Dan H. Laurence, University of Guelph Library)

Robert Donat and Rosamund John in
The Devil's Disciple, Piccadilly Theatre, London, July 1940

(Photograph by Angus McBean; Shaw collection of Dan H. Laurence,
University of Guelph Library)

Pygmalion: film production, 1938 (detail)
(O. B. Clarence, Everley Gregg, Leslie Howard, Wendy Hiller, Marie Löhr)

(Shaw collection of Dan H. Laurence, University of Guelph Library)

Dame Laurentia McLachlan

*(Shaw collection of Dan H. Laurence,
University of Guelph Library)*

Nancy Astor

(Reading University Library)

Gabriel Pascal

*(Shaw collection of Dan H. Laurence,
University of Guelph)*

F. E. Loewenstein

*(British Library of Political
and Economic Science)*

To H. K. AYLIFF

Ayot St Lawrence. Welwyn
[C/9]   10th May 1938

[George Villiers (1877–1955), sixth Earl of Clarendon, former Governor General of the Union of South Africa, was announced to succeed Lord Cromer as Lord Chamberlain on 1st July. He held the appointment until 1952. Despite Shaw's concern, *Geneva* was licensed as submitted, with no textual changes required. The only undertaking sought was that the actor playing the dictator Battler should not be made up to impersonate Hitler.]

Geneva is finished as far as the dialogue is concerned; but to cut it to the bone and get it through the press for rehearsal copies will be a job long enough to run up to and into June.

Then there is the question of the censorship with a new Lord Chamberlain. The play is a lampoon with Hitler and Mussolini unmistakably on the stage, and a thinly disguised Austen Chamberlain as the British Foreign Secretary.

Until Limbert has a license we cannot be sure of anything except, at worst, the publicity for the Festival of a refusal. At best it will be a rush for you. All the parts demand considerable powers of oratory. The heroine, a vigorous young Camberwell typist, must be a capable and pushing comedian . . .* How are you?

                                                        GBS

To FRANK WYATT

                                    4 Whitehall Court S W 1
[U(A)/105; X/397]   28th June 1938

["Collapsed in London," Shaw noted in his engagement diary on 4th June. "I suddenly found," he recalled in a letter to Lady Kennet on 17th February 1947 (H/1), "that bits of road I had always thought level were unclim[b]able mountains and six stairs impossible." Pernicious anæmia was the diagnosis of the pathologist Dr Geoffrey Evans (1883–1951), treatment for which consisted of a prescribed series of fifteen muscular injections of hæmopoietin (liver hormone) in what Shaw described as "the lumbar regions." For six weeks, until 15th July, he was invalided at Whitehall Court, stretched out indolently on a sofa. Frank Wyatt of the London Vegetarian Society, having read a distorted report of the illness in the *Daily Express*, shot off a telegram of inquiry to Shaw, who instantly drafted a disclaimer, published in the *Express* on the 29th.]

* Shaw's ellipsis.

Dear Sir

The headline "G.B.S. takes meat after 50 years" is a mistake. My diet remains unchanged.

But I am experimenting (or letting the doctors experiment) with the injections that have made "pernicious anæmia" harmless. At first it involved eating impossible quantities of liver. Now the manufacturing chemists sell what they declare is a quintessence of which one cubic centimetre equals 30 ounces or pounds or tons of liver. When squirted into a thick muscle it acts as a hormone which sets up a rejuvenated supply of red corpuscles. So far it has had that effect on me. I like trying all these games, though I never take the usual recommendation to back them up with beefsteaks and whiskey.

Has anything been done in the way of vegetable hormones? We must keep step with this endocrine-hormonic development. My strong guess is that much more effective hormones could be extracted from acorns than from cods' livers.

faithfully
G. Bernard Shaw

To HESKETH PEARSON

4 Whitehall Court SW1
[H/3; X/373.e]   4th July 1938

[J.M.Barrie died on 19th June 1937. He and his wife Mary (Ansell) (1862–1950) were divorced in 1909 after she admitted to an affair and ran off with the writer/critic Gilbert Cannan, who subsequently abandoned her. Despite her behaviour Barrie came to her financial aid when in 1919 he learned she was in straitened circumstances, and left her a tax-free annuity of £600 a year in his will. Of the five orphaned Davies brothers whom Barrie adopted, only one died in the war. This was George (d. 1915).]

Dear Hesketh Pearson

I have been a complete invalid, forbidden to touch a pen, for a month past, passing the time in reading [Pearson's autobiographical] Thinking It Over and other masterpieces.

I was always on affectionate terms with Barrie, like everyone else who knew him; but though I lived for many years opposite him in the Adelphi and should, one would suppose, have met him nearly every day, we met not oftener than three times in five years in the street. It was impossible to make him happy on a visit unless he could smoke like a chimney (mere cigarettes left him quite unsatisfied); and as this made our flat uninhabitable for weeks all the visiting was on our side, and was very infrequent.

I fancy Barrie was rather conscious of the fact that writers have no history and consequently no biography, not being men of action.

His wife's elopement, and the deaths of some of his adopted children in the war, were the only events in his life I knew of. Though he seemed the most taciturn of men he could talk like Niagara when he let himself go, as he did once with Granville-Barker and myself on a day which we spent walking in Wiltshire when he told us about his boyhood. He said that he had bacon twice a year, and beyond this treat had to content himself with porridge. He left me under the impression that his father was a minister; but this was probably a flight of my own imagination.

In The Author [Autumn 1937] I wrote a little obituary sketch when he died. It contained all I had to say about him for public consumption.

He had a frightfully gloomy mind, which he fortunately could not afford to express in his plays. Only in child's play could he make other people happy.

You will have a bit of a job to make a full sized biography for him; but I daresay you will manage it if anybody can. I really knew very little about him; and yet I suspect that I knew all that there was to be known about him from the official point of view.

Do you know his quondam wife? If you dont you will hardly be able to do justice to him in his domestic capacity.

How little we may know of the people we think we know is illustrated by the fact that I never knew you had ever appeared on the stage until I read your book the other day. The funny part of your story is that though you were an out-and-out Bardolator you took no interest whatever in acting as an art, and left me persuaded that you must have owed your stage vogue to your good looks solely.

Constable & Co are issuing a British edition of Harris's Oscar Wilde. To save his widow from destitution I have edited it and written a preface in which I have made hay of Sherard's recent book as good-naturedly as possible. He called Harris a liar on every page without convicting him of a single falsehood, contradicting himself outrageously all the time. Still, a very honest book, recklessly written.

faithfully
G. Bernard Shaw

[Pearson replied a day later that after spending a few weeks "ploughing through" Barrie's "morbid" writings he had lost interest in him as a subject and was abandoning the project (S/3).]

To ALMROTH WRIGHT

4 Whitehall Court SW1
[H/1; X/394.e]   5th July 1938

[Lord Alfred Douglas had entered St Mary's Hospital, Paddington, for possible surgery. Sir Almroth Wright, upon receiving Shaw's letter recommending Douglas to his personal care, informed him that Douglas had been
given a private accommodation and been examined by the hospital's most
skilled surgeon, who deemed the operation inadvisable. Douglas was
promptly discharged.]

My dear Sir Almroth

Yesterday a patient went into the Almroth Wright Ward for an
operation. Being, as he says, "slightly frightened" he begs me to pray
for him. I am [in] some doubt as to whether my prayers to heaven
would be much of a recommendation; but a prayer to you to be kind
to him seems practical. He is Lord Alfred Douglas, whose father, old
Queensberry, ruined him (purposely, he believes) by announcing that
he was being corrupted by Oscar Wilde. He was a very beautiful youth
and a quite considerable poet; and he stuck to Wilde through thick and
thin, with the result that he never shook off his father's imputation,
though he was victorious in all the lawsuits that followed. He is now a
pious Catholic and a teetotaller, but he still has an infantile complex
that is amusing, especially as he is quite conscious of it himself. Tell
the students that he is not a homosexualist, and that his brother the
Marquess is a great figure in the hospital world.

I am at present floored by pernicious anaemia. They are injecting
liver hormone; and my blood count is running up (probably because I
am resting) but for the moment I am *hors de combat*.

GBS

To GILBERT MURRAY

4 Whitehall Court SW1
[A/1]   8th July 1938

[Shaw's letter was inscribed on the half-title of a proof copy of *Geneva*.]

Dear Gilbert Murray

You may remember our correspondence about the Intellectual Co-
operation Committee. It ended in my being invited to write letters to
the Committee about nothing in particular, for burial, apparently, in

the Committee's pigeon holes. I made one or two efforts to induce Barbusse, Romain Rolland & Co, to make use of the Committee instead of firing off manifestoes of which nobody took any notice. They repudiated the suggestion as "bourgeois."

Finally I produced THIS.

I was driven to the conclusion that the Hague court, *not* the Geneva Assembly, is the possibly operative organ, and its weapon (or "sanction") so far, Excommunication.

What do you think?

G. Bernard Shaw

To WILLIAM GERHARDI

4 Whitehall Court S W 1
[H/5]   11th August 1938

[William Gerhardi (1895–1977), British novelist, who later spelled his name Gerhardie, had appealed to Shaw for assistance in obtaining an exit permit from the USSR for his sister's husband, a Russian citizen. Lady Muriel Paget (1876–1938) was a philanthropist involved in relief for British subjects in Russia 1924–38. Sir Robert Vansittart, first Baron Vansittart (1881–1957), British diplomat, was Undersecretary of State for Foreign Affairs 1930–38.]

Dear Mr Gerhardi

I am afraid nothing can be done beyond what you have done already. The notion that I am persona grata with the dictators is one of the Shaw myths. I have a long experience of foreign agitations to procure the release of political prisoners in Italy, Germany, America and Russia: I am always asked to take a hand and assured that the word from me will do the trick. The result is always to make it worse for the unfortunate victim, as foreign interference is not only resented as such, but taken as additional evidence of disaffection.

No doubt if I could guarantee from personal knowledge the entire devotion of Mr and Mrs Misernuke to the Communist regime and their abhorrence of Lady Muriel Paget and the British peerage generally, I could put the case to Maisky (not to Stalin) with a view to having Mrs Misernuke sent home; and if Vansittart and the rest had not tried and failed it might weigh the tenth part of a scruple towards getting a passport for her; but as that is out of the question I can do nothing.

I may add that in one or two cases where I have procured passports to or from Russia for Britishers in trivial difficulties they have let me down so completely by subsequently abusing the Russians tooth and nail that I am not sure that there is not a heavy black mark against me in Kensington Gardens.

You see, as to Misernuke, we have absolutely no right to interfere at all. He is a Russian; and the Russian government will regard any foreign interference as an impertinence. And I presume your sister, by marrying a Russian, has acquired his nationality. Unfortunately so many English ladies who have done this have sympathised, not with Bolshevism, but in effect with the reaction against it, that they are classed and treated as suspects, and their husbands are imprisoned for not marrying native communists.

I am loth to pass by on the other side; but I do not see how I can act with any beneficial effect.

Callously, alas!
G. Bernard Shaw

To HENRY S. SALT

4 Whitehall Court SW1
[H/3]   29th August 1938
[Walter Savage Landor (1775–1864), poet and essayist, ended his "Dying Speech of an Old Philosopher, Jan. 31, 1849":

> "I strove with none, for none was worth my strife.
> Nature I loved, and, next to Nature, Art;
> I warmed both hands before the fire of Life;
> It sinks, and I am ready to depart."]

My dear Salt

How are you? I get letters from disciples who have visited you from time to time which reassure me as to your existence; but your old activities are much missed at present, the world being given over to orgies of flogging and vivisection, by which latter I am supposed to be benefiting because in June last I collapsed with "pernicious anæmia" or whiteness of blood. My own view is that I am by nature a white-blooded man; and after lying on a sofa and doing absolutely nothing for six weeks I got rid of my angina pectoris and locomotor ataxy and other disablements and shewed signs of a new lease of life (of sorts). Meanwhile the doctors, called in by my distracted wife, had begun by "ordering" me beef and whisky, a prescription which I received with the thumb to the nose. However, they guaranteed a cure if I allowed them to squirt into the muscles of my seat a hormone extracted from the livers of countless unspecified fish or animals by a process which gets rid of the liver tissue and leaves the mysterious hormone which reds the blood. To this treatment I responded so promptly that I challenged the doctors to become vegetarians and, when they had a vegetarian patient, thank God for him instead of "ordering" beefsteaks and brandy.

I then studied the subject and discovered that the Chinese had for 2000 years past treated anæmia with ravens' livers, and that the modern hormones have been arrived at by thousands of experiments on dogs, and that many of them are extracted from unappetising materials which I shall not nauseate you by particularising.

But I am bound to admit that the letters I have received from all sorts of cranks urging me to try all sorts of cures are some of them more revolting than the hormones. The latest is the most agreeable. It is a dose of claret every day for a month.

I have also learnt that the stuff they stab and squirt into my unfortunate posterior, called Pernemon forte, is dangerous. It has done me no harm so far and has taken all the credit of my recuperation. A milder mixture is called Campolon. I keep demanding extracts of acorns or oranges or something vegetarian.

H. G. Wells, who is diabetic, wont take insulin, and seems to get on quite well without it on a diet.

My most distressing complaint is Anorexia, or dislike of food. I regard this as a hint that I have lived quite long enough. I am as ready to depart as Landor, and, if I were not a married man and could do as I pleased, would not lift a finger to survive.

And now, what about yourself? Have you another book in you? I daresay I have another play, but not a necessary one. I must send you a copy of Geneva when I get a fresh supply printed: the theatre has absorbed all the first crude batch.

as ever
GBS

To GABRIEL PASCAL

The Impney Hotel. Droitwich
[H/1; X/396.e]   1st September 1938

[The Shaws were en route to the Worcester Music Festival for performances of the Bach *St Matthew Passion*, Mendelssohn's *Elijah*, Elgar's *The Music Makers*, *The Dream of Gerontius*, and violin concerto, and Vaughan Williams's

Dona Nobis. Greta Garbo (b. 1905) had recently been named best actress by the New York film critics for her *Camille* (1937). Mae West (1892–1980) was known to Shaw as a name only: there is no evidence he had seen any of her films. Robert Donat (1905–58), highly respected young British stage and screen actor, would shortly star in West End productions of *The Devil's Disciple* and *Heartbreak House*. Cecil Trouncer (1898–1953), one of Shaw's favourite actors, had appeared with Bergner in *Saint Joan* at Malvern. Shaw saw this production on 20th August and *Geneva* two nights later.

Carlo Confalonieri (1893–1986), Roman Catholic prelate, was personal secretary to Pius XII for nineteen years. He later was elevated to cardinal. John Hay (Jock) Whitney (1904–82), financier and publisher/editor of the *New York Herald Tribune*, later was U.S. Ambassador to the Court of St James's (1957–61). David O. Selznick (1902–65), head of Selznick International Pictures, had expressed interest in Pascal's next film following the warm critical reception of *Pygmalion*. No film was made of *The Devil's Disciple* until after the deaths both of Shaw and Pascal. Scott Sunderland appeared as Colonel Pickering in the Pascal *Pygmalion*.]

My dear Gabriel

Now is the time to be careful—extraordinarily careful. The success of the Pygmalion film will set all Hollywood rushing to get a rake-off on the next Shaw film. Where the carcass is, there will the eagles be gathered. No American feels safe until he has at least five other Americans raking off him, most of them contributing nothing except their entirely undesirable company. They get so settled in that way of doing business that they do not understand how a European with a cast iron monopoly under his own hat can play his game singlehanded. So again I say be careful, or the film will make a million and yet leave you with a deficit.

Elizabeth Bergner, though she drew full houses at Malvern, was such a hopeless failure as Joan that I told her she must drop the film project. The play is therefore free; but the Californian suggestion of Miss Garbo for Joan is—well, Californian. If the heroine of the play were the Blessed Virgin they would probably have suggested Miss Mae West. We must have Wendy. There is no gratitude in business; and it would be the height of folly to quarrel with her after we have made her a star of the first magnitude. Somebody else would get her and exploit the work you have done with her. She cannot refuse the part, which is unique; and even if she did, or if she dropped dead, I could produce two young English provincial Joans who would be better than any Hollywood siren.

As to Caesar, the difficulty is to find an actor capable of filling the part. Robert Donat is far too young. The best heavy lead on the

English stage is Trouncer, who played the policeman in Pygmalion, and ought to have played Higgins. He has just had a tremendous success as Bombardone in Geneva. The sole objection to him is that he has not Caesar's beak and shape of head. But he is our only big gun. His Inquisitor in Joan is first rate. Caesar must not be a *primo amoroso*.

As to conciliating the Vatican, that is utter nonsense. What Czinner calls the Vatican (that is how he lost the film) is some petty official who has a list of words which must not be used by film actors. He objected to "halo" because it is religious, and to "babies" because it is sexual. I make it an absolute condition that the Catholic Action shall be entirely ignored, and the film made in complete disregard of these understrappers of the Church. Really responsible Catholics will not object to the film; but it is not fair to consult them about it, as it is one thing to welcome a film and quite another to guarantee it as orthodox. When the play is filmed it will be irresistible. The Hollywood simpletons say that none of the twenty million American Catholics will go to see it. When the Catholic Action can keep these Americans out of the saloons and gambling casinos and Ziegfeld Follies I shall believe in its power to keep them away from St Joan. Until then, we go ahead.

Do not approach Monsignor Gonfalonieri; but if you happen to meet him you can explain to him the utterly silly and impossible objections, grossly insulting to me, which were made in America, and say that the play led to great hopes in England among Catholics of my conversion to The Faith. The play practically wiped out the scurrilities of Mark Twain and Andrew Lang which were formerly the stock-in-trade of Protestant writers on the subject. But whatever you do, do not ask him for any official expression of approval. Say that nobody, not even the Pope, could be made answerable for Shaw.

Is it really necessary to trouble Messrs Whitney and Selznick? Why not ask your British bankers to back you on the strength of Pygmalion's succès éclatant? Failing them there are lunatics in London who, excited by the press notices, will back anything filmable to any amount if it has our names attached. We must shew the Hollywood distributors that we are independent of them as far as capital is concerned. They threaten not to distribute, as they did in the case of Pygmalion; but when it comes to the point they MUST distribute, not only for the immediate profit but because we are insuppressible and they would be unwise to quarrel with us. They will always hope to land us next time, and feel foolish if they are left out this time.

I shall be at this address until after the 24th September: possibly a week or two longer. Meanwhile I am in no hurry to see the film: it will be quite time enough when it is released and on show at the picture palaces.

Scott Sunderland could play Burgoyne in the Devil's Disciple [T]he rest of the cast can be as American (eighteenth century) as you like. Scott has played Britannus in Caesar very satisfactorily.

That is all for the present—and quite enough too.

Congratulations on the conquest of Venice!

G. Bernard Shaw

To SIEGFRIED TREBITSCH

Ayot St Lawrence. Welwyn

[C/5; X/341] 13th September 1938

[The Trebitsches were now in France, attempting to obtain French citizenship.]

Pascal's address is 10 Bolton St, Piccadilly, London W.1. Do not run after him: tell him you will be in London in October and that if that is too late he must come to Paris. He has *diable au corps* and is always rushing all over the globe. With my agreement in his pocket he cannot be short of money. He is a demonic genius in his way. It is useless and frightfully expensive, to keep up with his meteoric movements. As he *must* deal with you, you need not worry.

GBS

To LAWRENCE LANGNER

4 Whitehall Court SW1

[H/7; X/312] 20th September 1938

[Deeply distressed by Shaw's *Geneva*, Langner responded to it in a letter of several pages on 26th August in which he took Shaw to task for making the character of The Jew "a pitifully inferior mouthpiece to express his case, thus playing into the hands of the breeders of racial hatred by ranging yourself unconsciously on their side." St John Ervine, he said, had once told him that Shaw had more profoundly influenced his generation than any other man: "The effect of your influence has been exactly the opposite of that of the dictators. You have preached tolerance, justice, love of the common man, freedom, economic fairness, elevation of women; and, in England and America, at any rate, your disciples are numbered by the millions. Yet you

510

seem to justify Fascism with its intolerance, racial hatred, economic slavery, degradation of women, fanning of the war spirit, etc., mainly on the ground that its dictators are 'Supermen' and the Supermen 'get things done.'" He concluded by hoping Shaw would forgive the prolixity of his letter "and will understand its spirit, which I am sure only echoes the thoughts of millions of others who love you as I do, and have had their lives and thoughts influenced so strongly by you" (Langner, *The Magic Curtain*, 1951).

"Sheeny," origin unknown but nineteenth century, is an opprobrious term for a Jew, which gained racist implications in the 1930s.]

Dear Lawrence Langner

Can you wonder at Hitler (and now Mussolini) driving out the Jews? Here am I who have written a play in which I make ruthless fun of British Cabinet Ministers, of German and Italian Dictators, and Cockney young women, of the Buchmanite Oxford movement, of Church of England bishops, and of the League of Nations. Everyone laughs. Not a voice is raised in their defence.

But I have dared to introduce a Jew without holding him up to the admiring worship of the audience as the inheritor of all the virtues and none of the vices of Abraham and Moses, David and Isaiah. And instantly you, Lawrence, raise a wail of lamentation and complaint and accuse me of being a modern Torquemada.

You ask me how I would feel if the British Government burnt my books because I am an Irishman, and then put Irish characters on the stage and made fun of them. Lawrence: the Irish *have* banned my books; and in John Bull's Other Island I myself have been far less kind to the Irish characters than I have been to the Jew in Geneva, who is introduced solely to convict the Nazis of persecution. But you will not allow him to do exactly what an able Jew of his type would do when Gentiles were swallowing a terrifying Press canard: that is, go into the money market as a bear speculator and make his fortune.

You really are the most thoughtless of Sheenies. However, to please you, I have written up the part a bit. Musso let me down completely by going anti-Semite on me; and I have had to revise the third act to such an extent that you may now put the copy I sent you in the fire as useless, or, better still, sell it as a curiosity. Only 40 copies of it ever existed; and most of them were worn to tatters at rehearsal in Malvern. So go in as a bull speculator.

Meanwhile wait until I send you a revised copy. You may shew it to the Guild; but they had better leave it to the Federal Theatre and the 50 cent public, who are a much steadier source of income to me. Why doesnt the Guild come to terms for a revival of The Apple Cart with Cedric Hardwicke, who made a tremendous success with it in London whilst it went for nothing in New York?

Have you ever considered what would have happened to the United States if the Ku-Klux-Klan had found as competent a leader as Hitler? There is a play for you in that.

yours as always
G. Bernard Shaw

["If I am really one of the most thoughtless of 'Sheenies,'" Langner retorted on 7th October, "then you are one of the most inconsistent of 'Micks.'

"Since you are rewriting the part of Mussolini, I hope that you will make it quite clear that his anti-semitism does not spring from any nobler source than the fact that he believes it is a good way to stir up the Arabs against the British. This shows the tremendous value to the world of having supermen dictators, who at the stroke of a pen, can sacrifice the future of thousands of individuals on the altar of racial superiority."

Concluding that Shaw was descended from the "black Irish" mixture of Celt and Spaniard "from which most of the men of genius of Ireland have been produced," particularly from the Spanish Maranos, or converted Jews, Langner proclaimed "the truth will out. You too are a Sheenie . . ." (Langner, *The Magic Curtain*, 1951).]

To HESKETH PEARSON

[C/3]

4 Whitehall Court S W 1
8th October 1938

[Pearson had suddenly substituted Shaw for Barrie as his next biographical subject.]

Don't.

I have got everything out of myself that there is to be got. My autobiography by Frank Harris has left nothing to be gleaned. The huge biography by Archibald Henderson laid his life waste, as I warned him it would.

I need inbunking, not debunking, having debunked myself like a born clown.

I shall dissuade you personally any time you like to see me. You have only to ring up Whitehall 3160.

G.B.S.

To LADY KENNET

4 Whitehall Court SW 1

[H/1]   8th October 1938

[Lady Kennet's bust of Shaw is now in the Russell-Cotes Art Gallery and Museum, Bournemouth.]

My dear Kathleen

I hope you have not smashed your masterpiece in a fury at my delay in answering. When I was at Droitwich in August and September I got several press cuttings with photographs of the bust; and I saw at once that my collapse as your model was a Godsend, and that just because you had got away from me you had achieved something quite different from Rodin, Troubetskoy, Davidson, Strobl, and Epstein, who had me staring them in the face up to the last minute. Result, pure portraiture.

In Droitwich I was conscious of Shakespear's ridiculous monument in Stratford Church, within an hour's drive of me. The bust on it helps the Baconians by making people say "Did this thing write Lear?" Then I thought of Swift's monument in St Patricks cathedral in Dublin (my native town) with its famous inscription about his lacerated heart. And all this was because I was haunted by our statue in some cloister wall or nave, *not* about my lacerated heart; for the organ hardly exists. As we motored round Worcestershire endless jingles kept running in my head. All that survives of them is this.

WEEP NOT FOR OLD GEORGE BERNARD: HE IS DEAD
AND ALL HIS FRIENDS EXCLAIM "A DAMNED GOOD
  JOB!"
THOUGH RANKING GEORGE'S CELEBRATED HEAD
HIGH IN THE MORE UNCOMMON SORTS OF NOB.
LONG AT ITS IMAGE KATHLEEN'S HAND HAD PLIED
UNTIL ONE DAY THE LORD SAID "NO, MY LASS:
COPY NO MORE: YOUR SPIRIT BE YOUR GUIDE:
CARVE HIM SUB SPECIE AETERNITAS:
THUS, WHEN HIS WORKS SHALL ALL FORGOTTEN BE,
YET SHALL HE SHARE YOUR IMMORTALITY."

The only thing to be done now is to design the whole tomb. It is the only one in which I could lie quietly.

Anyhow, you see why I did not write at once.

G. Bernard Shaw

Your husband, to whom commend me, could improve considerably on the above.

513

To C. H. NORMAN

[C/3]
4 Whitehall Court S W 1
8th October 1938

... Hitler has so far proved himself a good judge of how far he could go without having to fight. When he went an inch too far in his Memorandum and realised that we were digging trenches, mobilising the fleet, and drifting helplessly into taking him on, he promptly sent for Chamberlain and climbed down the necessary inch [at Munich, in September]. Musso must have pulled him up pretty decisively. Italy could not have gone to war on such an issue. I did not share the general terror. ...

G.B.S.

To H. C. DUFFIN

[H/52]
4 Whitehall Court S W 1
2nd November 1938

[Henry Charles Duffin (1884–1974) was preparing a revised second edition of his study *The Quintessence of Bernard Shaw*, first published in 1920. Shaw read, emended, and trimmed the manuscript.]

Dear Mr Duffin

Obviously when a passage is unsatisfactory the shortest way to deal with it is not to enter into long explanations but to correct or rewrite it. This not only explains the error but does the job. If the job is sufficiently done there is no reason why you should not accept it just as you would accept a proof reader's correction and be thankful that you have not to do it over again. That is, unless you can do it better, in which case do it better and be damned.

The notion that every sentence in the book must be your own and not the proof reader's corrections is to me the scruple of a selfconscious amateur or an idiot. What you agree with you can appropriate when it is not stolen but offered to you to be appropriated. If you dont agree you can reject it. If you partly agree you can rewrite in your own way. Anyhow when you are offered friendly help you can either take it or leave it. I have sent books of mine to half a dozen people for criticism and correction (people who would have had to read it in any case), and let their corrections stand as if I had made them myself when I could not improve on them.

If I write you a critical letter pointing out this or that misunderstanding[,] a publisher may as a matter of business tell you that a letter from me would sell better than your book; and that if he can get such a letter he does not care two straws how disparaging the letter may be to you or the book. He may even go so far as to say that he will publish the book with the letter but not without. In that case the royalty on the book clearly belongs to me; and you are entitled to no more than a few shillings per thousand words for the labor of writing the rest of the stuff and for the loss of your selfrespect. But the question does not arise, as I forbid the publication of the letter absolutely and shouldnt have written it if I had foreseen that you would be so stupid as to let any publisher see it.

My omission of the Candida chapter from my enclosures was unintentional; and now I dont know where it is. If it turns up presently I will send it to you; but its proper place is the dustbin, as it was the fruit of a performance which is now happily forgotten.

Waste no more of your time and mine over this book. Either adapt my amendments or reject them as you think fit; but make up your mind that the publishers must take it or leave it as your book, and not mine. Otherwise you will drive yourself mad and starve; and I will simply swear at you.

faithfully
G. Bernard Shaw

To MARY LAWTON

4 Whitehall Court SW1
[H/23; X/398]   11th November 1938

[Mary Lawton (d. 1945), an American actress who had appeared in Shaw's play *The Philanderer* in New York 1913–14, was co-author and editor of *The Paderewski Memoirs* (New York, 1938). Shaw's letter was published as foreword to the English edition in 1939. The drawing of Paderewski by Edward Burne-Jones is reproduced in Malcolm Bell's *Sir Edward Burne Jones* (1909). Egon Petri (1881–1962), Busoni's pupil, who performed duets with him in recitals, later became a distinguished concert artist. Anton Rubinstein (1829–94) was the celebrated Russian pianist and composer. Friedrich Wieck (1785–1873) was a German teacher, whose most successful student was his daughter Clara, wife of Robert Schumann. Theodor Kullak (1818–82), Polish pianist, was one of the nineteenth century's most outstanding teachers.

515

Sigismond Thalberg (1812–71), Austrian pianist, was the rival of Liszt. Charles Hallé (1819–95), German-English pianist, is better known as an executive artist, founder (1857) and longtime conductor of Manchester's celebrated Hallé Orchestra. Artur Schnabel (1882–1951), noted concert pianist and composer, was a student of Leschetizky.]

Dear Mary Lawton

Though you have deserted the stage for literature your impersonation of Paderewski in this book of his and yours must rank with your greatest achievements as an actress. It has every quality of a great autobiography. It actually sent me to the index of the four volumes of my musical criticisms of 50 years ago to see what I had said when Paderewski swooped on London and was immediately drawn as an archangel by Burne Jones. I am glad to find that I made no mistake about him: he appears in my notices as the greatest pianist of that time. He has forgotten them all except one which annoyed him; and therefore he appears in the book, as far as I am concerned, as a monster of ingratitude; but I can explain that misunderstanding.

I think it was during Busoni's last visit to London that he invited me to a concert to hear an arrangement of his compositions played on two pianos by himself and Egon Petri. I said to him "There is only one thing on earth more damnable than one grand piano, and that is two grand pianos." Busoni understood this at once. "That is true" he said; "but we cannot do without it."

This had not occurred to anybody when Paderewski arrived in London. The louder the music the better people liked it—or pretended to like it; for there was a frightful lot of pretence about the vogue of classical music in Victorian days. Rubinstein, his most famous predecessor, waved his arms furiously in the air and pretended to bang the piano like a savage. You see, there had been a change in the instrument. The old wooden pianos which made the fame of Broadwoods, and for which Beethoven and Chopin composed, had been supplanted by a monster called the iron grand, now a steel one. Leschetizky, the greatest teacher of that day, realized that a steel piano needed steel fingers to play it. He taught Paderewski a touch undreamt of by Wieck or Kullak, and made him the Stalin of the iron grand. Paderewski did not know that this was a novelty in London. In the book he describes Clara Schumann to you as a poor old lady who could not play a fortissimo. And indeed she was old then and had gouty fingers; but she could still make a simple scale beautiful in a way of which Paderewski had apparently no conception. He says he played Schumann's fortissimo passages fortissimo; but he does not know that the fortissimo of the iron monster under his steel fingers, whilst it would have drowned ten Clara Schumanns, would have sent Schumann into the street with his fingers in his ears. My mother's favorite pianist was Thalberg (I never heard him) and next to him Hallé. Liszt and Rubinstein bridged the change. I never heard Liszt; but I heard many players of his school. Rubinstein I did hear. He was an extraordinary player, but not to be compared to Paderewski in comprehension of the great composers: he played Beethoven like a bear. Paderewski was a civilized player who brought fine culture and mental grasp to his work: he would have thrown aside the steel monster and become a great conductor if a conductor could then have earned the revenue of a prince as a great pianist did.

You have told the tragic story of how he came to hate the piano; but the odd part of it is that he seems to think that this hatred was pathological: it does not seem to have occurred to him that the steel concert grand is a hateful instrument: the cardinal fact of which Busoni was aware. Possibly Schnabel knows it too; for neither of them cultivated the Leschetizsky touch, nor does Walter Rummel. Perhaps Paderewski has left it behind: I have not heard him play this many years. The Siegfried who dealt a mortal wound to the steel dragon was Arnold Dolmetsch. When he resuscitated the clavichord and the viols he made the steel concert grand and the Leschetizsky touch unbearable. I taught myself how *not* to play on a Bord pianette; and though for 40 years past Steinway grands, Erard grands, and Börsendorfers have been easily within my means I am still content with a cottage Bechstein, though I have a new inside put into it every time I quite murder it. I also have a clavichord which I cannot play, as its touch is too far ahead of Leschetizsky to be handled by me, my own touch having been formed (like that of the infant Paderewski, by the way) by playing the bass in duets thunderously with my sister. I know too well what he means when he says that you become a pianist not by playing but by working. I have always played at the piano, never worked at it.

I await the second volume with an interest and curiosity that is extraordinary considering my age (I am older than your hero). I was in my forties when I studied Paderewski the pianist. Now in my eighties I want to hear about Paderewski the President. When he played the Emperor Concerto the difference between him and all his rivals was that he played it presidentially. So much so that it was quite natural for Poland to make him President in 1918 after his great American campaign. We want to know all about that; for how so great an artist could endure even for a single year as he did in 1919 our parliamentary

517

politics, which can have suggested nothing to him but cats fighting on the keyboard is a bit of history that has not yet been made known to us.

> Enough, dear Mary.
> G. Bernard Shaw

To H. K. AYLIFF

[C/9]
4 Whitehall Court SW1
19th November 1938

[*Geneva*, produced by Roy Limbert and staged by Ayliff, opened at the Saville Theatre on 22nd November, transferring to the St James's Theatre on 27th January 1939. It achieved a London run of 237 performances, thereafter touring the provinces, with Shaw frequently making textual revisions to keep abreast of international developments.]

If you are satisfied, I shant intrude, so that it may be wholly and indisputably your production. I should only upset the company.

I will not even come up for the first night. I have had enough of first nights, and had rather see it when it has settled down to its best—that is, if it survives the fortnight.

Take the author's call, and say "The author is not in the house, thank God!"

> GBS

To HOWARD C. LEWIS

[A/1]
4 Whitehall Court SW1
25th November 1938

[Howard C. Lewis (1890–1952) was vice-president of the American publishers Dodd, Mead & Co., a position he had held since 1928. It was Lewis who took the Shaws on a whirlwind motor tour of New York City and the Jersey Palisades on their one-day visit in 1933. He had written for permission to grant approval to a request by the American Foundation for the Blind to record *Candida* as a talking record.]

I dont approve at all. I never object to Braille, because the blind can't read the play in the ordinary editions. But they *can* go to ordinary performances. And I strongly object to the existence of records made without any guarantee of the quality of the performance. It is one

518

thing to record a performance by Miss Katharine Cornell and her company. That would be available for the whole English speaking world, blind or seeing. But a record made by a firm of nobodies with a cast of nobodies!—no, damn it, no no no no NO !

... Excuse this scrawl.

GBS

To AUGUSTIN HAMON

4 Whitehall Court SW 1
[C/1; W/406.e]   26th November 1938

As to les Pitoeff—convenu.

We have always been too civil to the boulevard and the Français. In London I bombarded the West End theatres with criticisms which now fill three volumes [*Our Theatres in the Nineties*, 1931], and are still read, before I got on the map as a writer of plays. Feuilletons of 2000 words a week for years were needed to establish a convention, not so much that Ibsen was the greatest of the moderns as that Sardou was obsolete and ridiculous.

I make nearly £300 a year in tantièmes from what they call the petits théâtres here: mostly desperate adventures by ouvriers and petty bourgeois amateurs: très pauvres.

In America I allow *all* my published plays to be performed by the Federal theatres (state endowed to relieve unemployment among actors) on condition that the highest price charged for a seat is 50 sous. So by all means encourage the acteurs syndiques.

G.B.S.

To HESKETH PEARSON

4 Whitehall Court SW 1
[A/3; X/399]   2nd December 1938

Dear Hesketh Pearson

Unfortunately I cannot prevent anyone from writing about me, from the briefest scurrilous paragraph to the most pretentious biography.

But no sane publisher will touch a biography or essay unless (a) he has some assurance that I am not going to be unpleasant about it, and (b) the author's name is a guarantee of readability.

So you may go ahead with my blessing. There is no one else in the field.

G. Bernard Shaw

To LADY LONDONDERRY

[H/120; X/407.e]

4 Whitehall Court SW1
17th December 1938

[A terse entry in Shaw's engagement diary on 16th December reads "FLOP!" It signifies that, arriving to lunch that day in the Park Lane home of Lady Londonderry, Shaw startled the distinguished gathering by suddenly keeling over in a dead faint, apparently the result of a hormone injection he had received that morning. Refusing further inoculations, he substituted daily dosages of a naturist concoction called Hepamult. Whether or not the remedy was efficacious, the anæmia and its symptoms vanished.

Edith Lady Londonderry (1879–1959) was the wife of Charles Vane-Tempest-Stewart (1878–1949), seventh marquess of Londonderry, former Conservative M.P. and Secretary of State for Air. *Sidonia von Bork, die Klosterhexe* (1847–8) was a novel (ostensibly a factual account of a trial for witchcraft at Stettin in 1620) by Pastor Wilhelm Meinhold (1797–1851), which Shaw had read in the Kelmscott Press edition (1893) in a translation by Oscar Wilde's mother, Speranza, titled *Sidonia the Sorceress.* "Aimeekee-gee" appears to be a Shavian treatment of the name of Sister Chigi, a trained nurse called in to assist him. Lady Mairi Stewart was the youngest daughter of the Londonderrys. "That book" was Lady Londonderry's *Retrospect* (1938).]

My dear Sidonia

Circe was A sorceress, and, I think, a small woman, like Aimeekee-gee, though very unlike her in character. Besides, she was very far from being respectable. THE sorceress was Sidonia—Sidonia the Sorceress; and if I may have a name for you all to myself I will have Sidonia, as you look her, every inch.

I was extraordinarily lucky in flopping where I did yesterday. Inconvenient for you, but ideal for me. I had just given up my coat and hat and umbrella when I found that I could not stand, and put my hand against the wall to steady myself. Next thing I knew I was flat on my back with Charles, unaccountably looking 20 years younger than when I saw him last, kneeling by me and trying to rub some warmth into my cold hand, which was very comforting. I was perfectly happy in spirit, though physically convinced that if I moved I should be sick. I felt quite willing to lie there for a month, but could not forget that this would hardly be a suitable arrangement for the household. I had presence of mind enough to say How dye do to Charles, who presently transported me to the library, where I became completely conscious of you, looking so resplendent that I concluded I was delirious and never thought of saying Howdyedo. You are an amazing pair. You said that Mairi Mairi (quite contrairy) was to have sat beside me at lunch; and I was on the point of saying "Why doesnt she come and sit beside me now" when it occurred to me just in time that the still possible spectacle of her idealized celebrity being violently sick might make her a cynic for life.

Your footman was evidently a non-Aryan refugee doctor in disguise: he was immensely capable and did not leave me until he had planted me safely in bed; and Sister Chigi was a jewel. Today I am quite well —exceptionally well, in fact. It did me a lot of good seeing you both.

That book will get you into trouble by one immortal sentence. "Now" sez you "you very rarely see anyone who looks like a lady." You should be careful how you tell the truth so recklessly: the poor things can't help themselves; and they are really better than that upholstered fraud the Victorian lady, whom, by the way, you dont in the least resemble and happily dont remember. I, being 82½, do.

All that you say about Ramsay [MacDonald] is timely and true. I knew him in his old Socialist days before you were born. He was not really a Socialist in the academic sense: he was a seventeenth century Highlander who was quite at home in feudal society and quite out of it among English trade unionists. As a leader of English labor he was, as Beatrice Webb put it, a façade: amid chieftains and ladies bright he was himself.

There is one very serious omission in the book, which could be remedied in the next one. There would be a tremendous sale for *The Greatest Man I Ever Met*, by Sidonia the Sorceress.

A wonderful box of flowers has just arrived and thrown Charlotte into transports. She said quite spontaneously "They are so well grown and healthy and beautiful, like herself." That just hit it off.

I shall miss the post if I go on.

G. Bernard Shaw

To ROY LIMBERT

[C/3; X/289.e]

Ayot St Lawrence. Welwyn
24th December 1938

[In late November Shaw commenced a draft of what was to become *In Good King Charles's Golden Days*. He did not complete it until the following April.]

I never know what a play is going to be until it is finished. What I am aiming at so far is an educational history film. The people will wear XVII century costumes regardless of expense, numbers, and salaries. It may be beyond the resources of Malvern even if Pascal does not get in first. So do not commit yourself too exactly.

We are snowed up here. Frost and snow agree with me: I hope they do with you.

GBS

To ASHLEY DUKES

[A/4]

Ayot St Lawrence. Welwyn
3rd January 1939

[Stanley (now first Earl) Baldwin had launched a fund for Jewish refugees in a broadcast appeal on 8th December, which raised half a million pounds within eight months. The arts were asked to participate in various fund-raising activities on a designated Entertainments' Day. The League of Dramatists called upon its members to contribute a percentage of their royalties for all performances on this day: the donations came to a paltry £61.1.10. Ashley Dukes was a member of the League's executive committee.]

Ashley

What the devil does the League of Dramatists mean by throwing over the sternest traditions of the Society of Authors and interfering in the private charities of its members?

I refuse violently to take part in this attempt to tax us for the benefit of Lord Baldwin's Fund, and that too in a manner so silly that the richest of us may escape the contribution, having nothing running, whilst the poorest who may for once in his or her life be enjoying a scarce or solitary catch-on will be mulcted in £30 or so. Have we no desperate hangers-on to the Royal Literary Fund or the Pension Fund who need a benefit of this kind as badly as the Jews?

Have you not yourself had to come to the rescue of individual refugees? If not you are luckier than I.

522

I am not in the camp of the Anti-Sheenies; but what of our members who are?

Tell the Committee with my compliments that they are sentimental idiots, and have grossly overstepped their function in this business.

almost indignantly
G. Bernard Shaw

To ROY LIMBERT

[H/3]

4 Whitehall Court SW 1
5th January 1939

[*The Apple Cart* had its world première in Warsaw on 14th June 1929, at the Teatr Polski. *In Good King Charles's Golden Days* was first performed at the Malvern Festival on 12th August 1939 for six performances. A new production opened at the New Theatre, London, on 9th May 1940, following a pre-West End trial run that commenced on 15th April at the Streatham Hill Theatre. The contemplated film was never made.]

Dear Roy

In the Tube the other day I was horrified to see Geneva described on the bills as mercilessly "guying" all the dictators. Now this is just what Geneva doesnt do: it flatters them enormously. And a guying play is not attractive. You should have a strip pasted over that mistake, inscribed *London's deepest play and funniest harlequinade.*

The returns, though slightly rocky, are good enough to go on with for a while provided they dont rock any more.

I found the [Saville] theatre, which I had never been in before, comfortable but ugly. There is too much heavy brown in the color scheme. Next time they paint it they should call in an artist to make a new color scheme.

As to World's Premières, I am dismayed to find that you have got Barry's complaint. He has never forgiven me, and probably never will, because The Apple Cart was produced first in Warsaw. That event brought us a most useful set of preliminary paragraphs for Malvern and London; and it never occurred to me that he could take any other view of it. But he nearly died of it.

And now you are in the same frenzy about Charles!

I do not see how Pascal can get ahead of you with a film release; but I will not stop any production, whether in the studios or on the Continent, merely to get the words "world première" into the bill at

523

Malvern, where it will not draw an extra penny. I cannot work my business that way. And their value for your prestige is quite imaginary. Their absence will not be noticed; but if you get in first, which is quite likely, so much the better. Only, dont promise.

Also, with a film in contemplation, I am planning the thing regardless of expense—there are seven big salaries in it already—the cost may be a bit too stiff for Malvern.

At the Saville see that they keep Geneva on the high horse. No more guying stuff.

GBS

To BEATRICE WEBB

[C/14]
Ayot St Lawrence. Welwyn
17th January 1939

[Shaw's sources for *Good King Charles* included Sir Arthur Bryant's *King Charles II* (1931). Bryant also published a three-volume biography of Samuel Pepys (1933–35). Sir Isaac Newton (1642–1727), mathematician and natural philosopher, and George Fox (1624–91), a religious leader who founded the Society of Friends, were principal characters in *Good King Charles*, which was subtitled "A True History That Never Happened." Act III of *Geneva* was broadcast by the B.B.C. on 23rd April 1939, from the stage of the St James's Theatre, following the reading of a synopsis of Acts I and II provided by Shaw.]

I have Bryant on Charles.

I will look him up on Pepys; but I want to keep Pepys out of it, as he is in it anyhow by strong association, and I have no new light to throw on him.

Charles I have to invent all over again. Newton and Fox I have only to put on the stage, as they are strangers there, and are far too little known.

I am getting on with it.

They are going to broadcast 20 minutes of Geneva!

GBS

524

To SIEGFRIED TREBITSCH

Ayot St Lawrence. Welwyn

[H/5; X/341]   31st January 1939

[The Trebitsches in Nice had been summoned to the apartment of relatives, Leopold Lipschütz (1870–1939), prominent Austrian journalist, and his wife, who had failed to respond to their bell. When a concierge forced an entry, they were discovered dead in a double suicide compact. Hitler had made a speech on 30th January. Emil Ludwig (1881–1948), German writer in exile, lunched with Shaw on 20th January. Ludwig, Shaw had written to Trebitsch on 26th January, "believes as you do that H. is an illiterate semi-idiot; that Mein Kampf was written for him by other people; and that he knows no language except an Austrian dialect, and very little of that. . . . In spite of Hitler's crazy anti-Semitism and anti-Bolshevism, der Führer is a man to be taken very seriously" (H/5; X/341).]

What a frightful experience! Next time you have to break a door open do not take Tina with you. Nowadays we are accustomed to read about such things and hear about them; but to *see* them upsets one for days. The effect will pass away, as such effects always mercifully do; but in the meantime dont talk to her about it: there is nothing to be done but rock her in your arms and kiss her. That is what I should do if Charlotte had such a shock.

Suicide, the last extremity of egotism, is sometimes justifiable and even obligatory. But under all ordinary vicissitudes of fortune it must be ruled out. One should not do it in a hotel, but in some place where the police will find the body and dispose of it. I am not sure that one should not commit half a dozen murders first, since it can be done with impunity; but the difficulty is to secure for the victims the fair trial to which they are entitled. Still, suicide is so unnatural that you will feel that Leopold's way out is not really open to sane men. It is mystically barred.

You see, I was right about Hitler. His speech was a wonderful performance: nobody else in Europe could have made it. Of course the part about the Jews was stark raving nonsense: he is mad on that subject; but the rest was masterly. Naturally you have no reason to love him; but nothing is more dangerous than to underrate your adversary; and, believe me, it is childish to think of Hitler as E.L. does: Adolf leaves the next ablest statesman in Germany nowhere.

Even if it were not so, what possible good can come of my reviling him as all the anti-Nazi papers and talkers are doing? If I joined in the vituperation I should do no good to you or anyone else; and I might do you a great deal of harm. . . .

525

Charlotte is very much moved at Tina's distress; but, I repeat, it will not bear talking about. . . .

GBS

To THEA HOLME

[C/1]

4 Whitehall Court SW1
2nd February 1939

[Thea Holme (1907–80), an actress with a well-established West End and provincial reputation, was rehearsing in the Oxford Repertory Players production of *Saint Joan*, opening on 20th February. In later years she became custodian of Carlyle House, in Chelsea, for the National Trust. Shaw's diplomatic omissions of the names of the two offending actresses were standard procedure with him when resorting to open-to-view postcards.]

Private

As Joan spoke a provincial French to which we have no clue except that she pronounced goddams as godons no British dialect is more appropriate than another.

The safe course is to speak straight English impetuously, with just a touch of rough country dialect (any that you happen to know, but not Irish) here and there in the Court scene to distinguish her as a country girl from the Dauphin and the court people. But just the touch or two I have indicated is enough. Any attempt to make a character part of Joan and keep up an artificial pronunciation all through would be disastrous.

Don't let Joan snivel. She is always the adventurous impetuous masterful girl soldier: even her despair is an angry despair. She has also the ecstasy of a saint; but the blubberings of—— and ——— are all wrong. Sybil was right.

G.B.S.

To MATTHEW EDWARD McNULTY

[A/4]

4 Whitehall Court SW1
3rd March 1939

[Accompanying Shaw's letter was a formal receipt: "Received from Edward McNulty Esquire the sum of One Hundred Pounds alleged by him to be due to me from him."]

526

My dear Mac

You must be crazy. I have not the faintest recollection of any such transaction, and dont believe it ever took place.

But I am delighted to know that you can afford to sling hundred pound cheques about like this.

My acceptance of the cheque gives me the right to do as I please with it. So if you dont mind I'll put it in the fire.

GBS

To HESKETH PEARSON

4 Whitehall Court SW1
[H/3; X/373]   15th March 1939

[For the "horrible scene" between Jenny Patterson and Florence Farr, see the letter of 1st May 1891 to Florence Farr.]

Dear Hesketh Pearson

At the age of 12 or thereabouts I was with two other boys on the seaside slope of Torca Hill, Dalkey, when the question arose whether it would not be a lark to set the gorse on fire. Boy number 3 remonstrated strongly, but, being unable to prevail, bolted down the hill to the road, where he was arrested by the police, who saw a terrific conflagration raging and a boy running away. It is the innocent who suffer. I and boy number 2, appalled by the burst of flame which sprang from our match, bolted up the hill (we both lived higher up), where I learnt presently that number 3 was in custody.

It was outside my code of honor to let another bear the burden of my guilt; so I put on my best jacket and called on the landlord of the hill, Mr Hercules Macdonnell, who received me on the terrace of his villa with a gravity equal to my own. I orated as described with an eloquence beyond my years, and finally received a letter to the police inspector to say that the matter could be let drop. I duly delivered this, and found that number 3 had been released. The fire had meanwhile been extinguished by the neighbor's gardeners.

I have not the faintest recollection of what I said on this occasion, but have no doubt that my fondness for long words and my budding literary gift stood me in good stead with Hercules's sense of humor.

Mrs Patterson was my model for Julia; and the first act of The Philanderer is founded on a very horrible scene between her and Florence Farr. I did not lose my temper on that occasion: I kept it for several hours; but the strain was unforgettable, and I never saw Mrs

527

Patterson again nor answered one of the storm of letters and telegrams that lasted for months afterwards. And she never forgave me. This was not vindictiveness on my part: I left her £100 in my will, which she never inherited as she died long ago, in memory of her kindness to me during our intimacy; but it was clear that I could not go through life pursued by an ungovernably jealous woman making violent scenes whenever I spoke to any other woman. She was amazingly jealous, not merely in love but in every other relation in life, regardless of sex.

I can keep my temper under ordinary injuries, though woe betide those who, like Jenny, push the strain too far; but it makes me quite savage to hear a work of art—a play, opera, or symphony—murdered.

G. Bernard Shaw

To THERESA HELBURN

4 Whitehall Court SW 1
[C/7]   21st April 1939

[Erik Charell (1895–1974) was a Berlin producer of musical extravaganzas at the Grosses Schauspielhaus. In London in the early 1930s he successfully produced two operettas, *White Horse Inn* and *Casanova*. The Theatre Guild had for years sought to win Shaw's approval for a musical treatment of *The Devil's Disciple*, their original candidates being the team of Richard Rodgers and Lorenz Hart. Kurt Weill was now in America, where he had had his first popular success, *Knickerbocker Holiday* (libretto and lyrics by Maxwell Anderson), following a failure with Paul Green's *Johnny Johnson* (one of his finest scores).]

My dear Tessie
    After my experience with The Chocolate Soldier nothing will ever induce me to allow any other play of mine to be degraded into an operetta or set to any music except its own.
    Mr Eric Charall's name was unknown to me until I saw it in your letter.
    I saw a musical version of The Beggar's Opera in Moscow by a German composer: probably Mr Kurt Weill.
    He shall NOT touch The Devil's Disciple.
    Make the same reply to all composers.
    Hands off!
    Is the Guild still alive? What about Geneva, now painfully approaching its sixth month in London?

G.B.S.

To CATHERINE SALT

Ayot St Lawrence. Welwyn
[A/4]   8th May 1939
[Henry Salt's second wife, Catherine Mandeville, was now his widow.]

Dear Mrs Salt

Thank you for the report. I received several press cuttings of it.

You may smile when I say that Henry was one of my most intimate and valued friends, seeing that at least 30 years have passed since I last called on him, though I have never been long out of reach of him. Yet it is so.

In the last century, when he was married to a queer wife who fell in love with every woman who was kind to her (or who told her lies enough) and who tolerated as friends Henry, Edward Carpenter and myself, I was quite at home with them at Tilford, Oxted, and once in Yorkshire; but when she died and he got really married and happy, and I also married and had to keep my wife out of Kate's way, we both began a new and separate life and never got together again, though we corresponded on the old intimate terms.

He was, and I am, too old to desire reasonably to live any longer; but you will miss him for a while before you benefit by the release.

I know he was not too well off; but I hope he has left you enough to carry on with.

faithfully
G. Bernard Shaw

To HERBERT WHITELEY

4 Whitehall Court S W 1
[H/9]   7th June 1939
[Whiteley was a music scholar, who had published a pamphlet or two; he is otherwise unidentified. The Besses o' the Barn was a well established brass band.]

Dear Sir

In my father's time brass instruments were socially fashionable. My uncle [William Shaw] played Annie Laurie on the ophicleide (a monster keyed bugle) in the drawingroom at Bushy Park at parties there. A band of gentlemen amateurs played weekly at Lord Ely's gate on the Dodder (All this took place in Dublin before I emigrated in the

529

year 1876. I was born in 1856.), my father assisting with his trombone. The cornet was called the cornopean, and the tuba the bombardon, with the accent on the doan. The soprano cornet, now revived as such by the Salvation Army, was the cornetto: it needed an exceptional lip. All the old instrument firms fifty years ago regretted those gentlemanly days.

I did not return to the Crystal Palace after dinner on the Severn Suite day [27th September 1930]. You ask how many bands I heard play it. About fifteen thousand I should say.

The Besses etc. etc. will not perish; but they must improve their programs and their scoring and playing.

faithfully
G. Bernard Shaw

PS One of my uncles [Walter Gurly] having presented me with a cornet which he no longer cared to play (he was settling down in a country practice as a doctor) I learnt the instrument from an Englishman named Kennedy, and had just mastered it when someone told me that it would make it impossible for me ever to be a singer; so I presented it to my instructor and abandoned all ambition to excel in that department.

To JOHN FARLEIGH

Ayot St Lawrence. Welwyn
[A/9]   26th June 1939
[Farleigh was commissioned by the Gregynog Press to engrave a frontispiece portrait of Shaw for its edition of *Shaw Gives Himself Away* (1939), a collection of autobiographical miscellanea.]

Dear John Farleigh
Your masterly drawing is a faultless drawing; but it is not a frontispiece; and it has deprived me of brains and of humor. My moustache turns up; and my eyes, which must fix the spectator frontispecially, are thoughtful eyes.

I am forced to suggest what I mean by the execrable drawing on the obverse of this board, which has the advantage of getting rid of that damned photograph. You can impart the requisite technical propriety to what it may suggest to you.

I want it to wipe out the Droeshout portrait of Shakespear, of which

530

Morris said "We know it's not like Shakespear because it's not like a man," but which nevertheless made an indelible impression as a frontispiece.

G. Bernard Shaw

To GABRIEL PASCAL

Ayot St Lawrence. Welwyn
[A/1; X/396]   24th July 1939

[The letter was written as a testimonial to assist Pascal in his application for British citizenship.]

Dear Gabriel Pascal

Now that you have shifted the artistic centre of gravity of the film industry from Hollywood to Middlesex I hope you will shift your nationality in the same direction.

You have your choice of all the world except the place where you were born. The operations of Herr Hitler have closed that to you. The next best place for you is the British Empire with residence in London. It would be a calamity for British films and for me and for yourself if you chose California. England is the place for you: your work and all the employment it gives are there; and the new departure you have

531

made so successfully in film drama would have been impossible in America.

Besides, you will be far more at home with us. California is not suited to a Magyar de la vieille roche.

always yours
G. Bernard Shaw

To JOHN FARLEIGH

Ayot St Lawrence. Welwyn
[A/4; X/289.e] 8th August 1939

[A week earlier Farleigh had repaid a loan of £100.]

My dear Farleigh
Paying a forgotten debt is honest but thriftless.

The division of the spoils between us has been glaringly unjust; and £100 conscience money would ease my mind about it. Accept your own cheque as a readjustment of the bargain. . . .

My eminence as an author had better be alleviated by my infamy as a draughtsman; so you may expose me to your heart's content [in *Graven Image*, 1940].

GBS

To R. & R. CLARK

4 Whitehall Court SW1
[A/18] 19th August 1939

[Shaw frequently called for corrections and revisions in the plates of the Standard Edition. One of his most significant revisions was the alteration of the final lines in *Pygmalion*, which occurred in the 1939 reprints of the *Androcles-Overruled-Pygmalion* volume and of *Pygmalion* as a separate volume.]

—Some corrections—

Page 279–80 of Pygmalion: standard edition.
Delete the last 5 lines of 279 and the first two on 280
Substitute the following.
MRS HIGGINS. I'm afraid youve spoilt that girl, Henry. I should be uneasy about you and her if she were less fond of Colonel Pickering.

HIGGINS. Pickering! Nonsense: she's going to marry Freddy. Ha ha! Freddy! Freddy! Ha ha ha ha ha!!!!! [*He roars with laughter as the play ends*].

(I should like to have a dozen pulls of the corrected page to send to the acting companies.) . . .

GBS

To GABRIEL PASCAL

4 Whitehall Court SW1

[H/1; X/396.e]21st August 1939

[Pascal was preparing a screen treatment of *Major Barbara*. Samuel Goldwyn (1882–1974), American film producer, had a predilection for eminent authors as scenarists for his films.]

My dear Gabriel

I enclose the breakfast scene to follow the river scene. I expect I shall have a lot of new scenes to join the 3rd and 4th acts.

I have read the Undershaft–Sardanapalus scenes you and Lawrence [Irving] mapped out. You and he must have got frightfully drunk in Hollywood to conceive such a thing. Stephen and Cusins playing baccarat and Undershaft living like a second lieutenant just come into a legacy, with nautch girls all complete, is beyond the wildest dreams of Sam Goldwyn. I cannot put on paper the imprecations with which I hurled it into the waste paper basket; so unless you kept a copy it is dead. However, never mind: I shall give you plenty to do in the Perivale scenes.

I hope I did not seem too impossible on Saturday; but I had given that agreement long and careful consideration and made up my mind like granite. If I give way an inch you give way a foot, and everyone else gives way or grabs all over the place until the whole business goes to pieces. There must be a rock somewhere in the shifting sands; and I have decided to be that rock.

It is of the first importance that the money for Barbara shall be advanced on Barbara and for Barbara alone. I know the artistic value of your indifference to money; but if I gave you more than one agreement at a time you would raise the last penny on the whole lot and spend it on the first, leaving yourself penniless for the rest, whilst I

533

should be tied up for years. I want you to have these great successes without utterly ruining you. Hence my obstinacy on the point of one agreement at a time.

your adamant
G. Bernard Shaw

To HESKETH PEARSON

[A/3; X/373]
Hotel Esplanade. Frinton-on-Sea
4th September 1939

[The Shaws went on holiday to Frinton-on-Sea on 29th August, remaining there until 29th September. Shaw's review of William Ralph Inge's *Outspoken Essays*, headed "Our Great Dean," was published in *Everyman*, 22nd November 1919; he later included it in *Pen Portraits and Reviews* (1931) in the Collected Edition. Curiously, Shaw makes no mention to Pearson of Britain's declaration of war with Germany a day earlier.]

Dear H. P.

Have I hurt your feelings? It was unintentional; but I meant to convey that you must produce a biography, not a birthday book.

When an old colonel (British) called on Beethoven in his latter days and offered him a commission to compose something like his Septet (an infantile work) Beethoven dismissed him with imprecations. But if the colonel had asked him to name his favorite symphony the result would have been the same. Favorite is the wrong word. The births of Fanny and of Methuselah were things that happened. Fanny was a potboiler; and Methuselah was an important work, for the moment impracticable commercially. I know that as well as you do. But I have no birthday book feeling about it.

Dickens had a birthday book preference for David Copperfield because he had put certain experiences of his own into it; but he knew quite well that Great Expectations was a better book and Little Dorrit a bigger one.

Plays which I wrote completely in the air (Heartbreak House was one of them) interest me more than the potboilers written for immediate production like You Never Can Tell; but I really have no sentimental preferences.

As to Inge, read his Outspoken Essays and my review of it headed Our Great Dean. And never mind his pre-Marxian political economy.

534

Labor politics are not his job. When he is on his job he is easily one of the first minds in England. Remember: you have to account for my admiration of him.

G. Bernard Shaw

To BLANCHE PATCH

Hotel Esplanade. Frinton-on-Sea

[H/4; X/104.e]   5th September 1939

[Shaw's letter in *The Times* that morning was "Theatres in Time of War."]

My dear Blanche

We have been a good deal concerned about you since we came down here; and the possibilities we discussed included your coming to Frinton. Ayot was excluded as a refuge because the servants are away holidaying and will not be back until the end of the month. For the moment, however, your Sussex experiment has solved the problem; so there is nothing more to say until we see how it will turn out.

There are no shelters in Frinton. When that wicked false alarm was sounded on Sunday night I was wakened and urged to get up and crowd with the other people downstairs, where one lady was proclaiming that "passages" are safe. I absolutely refused to budge. As there are no safe places in Frinton and the beds are very comfortable, besides being respectable places to die in, I advised everyone to follow my example. Presently the All Clear sounded and settled the question except for the people who took it for a fresh alarm. I slept in peace for the rest of the night.

I should have done the same at Whitehall, as I have no reason to believe that the club basement is bombproof; and your account of it confirms my guess at its horrors.

I have a furious letter in today's Times which will clear up your mind as to your duty to your country. Theatres and films will be needed most desperately for the soldiers on leave and for the evacuated children. You cannot possibly be more usefully employed than in helping Gabriel and myself with the Barbara film and keeping the theatres going. And you will be giving people pleasure instead of helping to kill them. So you may give your conscience a complete rest as to all that.

I am actually trying to persuade Cecil Lewis, now in control at

535

Number ten group R.A.F. Gillingham, Kent, to declare himself a conscientious objector and insist on employment at the B.B.C. or in the films or some other branch of the entertainment industry. He is in a very dangerous place, close to the Chatham dockyards.

Mrs Shaw has been in bed all day with a bad relapse, possibly the result of Sunday night. She has given me many messages for you which I must leave to your imagination, as I shall lose the post if I go on.

G. Bernard Shaw

To BLANCHE PATCH

Hotel Esplanade. Frinton-on-Sea
[A/4; X/104.e]   6th September 1939

[Margaret (Mrs Fred) Day was the wife of the Shaws' chauffeur. Mrs Colthurst was Charlotte's niece Cecily.]

Another alarm at 7 this morning. Nothing happened except a flight of British planes along the coast. I slept through it.

Mrs Shaw is much better.

Heaps of children here carrying gasmasks. They are having the time of their lives. They do not understand bathing, but take to paddling like ducks. Mrs Day has had one planted on her. Mrs Colthurst has twentyeight on her hands at her son-in-law's place in Somerset. Her comment is "They smell awful."

Make the best arrangement you can at Granby Court. I will pay all war expenses.

GBS

To KENNETH BARNES

Hotel Esplanade. Frinton-on-Sea
[A/3; X/401]   9th September 1939

Dear Kenneth

Why not carry on? I see no reason on earth why the R.A.D.A. should close for a single day. We kept going last time with only eight male students and a crowd of girls.

The difference of your case was that you were of military age and had not yet "given your proofs." Now there can be no question that no work that you can do is of greater national importance than yours and no one can do it nearly so well.

The ridiculous funk which has closed the theatres and ordered the abolition of light will soon pass: all the sooner the more institutions carry on without turning a hair.

Why not have a shot in the correspondence in The Times? Point out that the shortage of shells in 1914 does not exist today, but the action of the authorities is creating a worse shortage: the shortage of theatres. It is our business to make a resounding ballyhoo about it.

I expect to be here until the 30th, when the hotel closes.

G. Bernard Shaw

To CONSTABLE & CO.

Hotel Esplanade. Frinton-on-Sea

[C/64]   17th September 1939

[Feliks Topolski (b. 1907), Polish artist, came to London in 1935. He received a commission in 1939 to provide illustrations for the Constable edition of *Geneva* (1939), followed by *In Good King Charles's Golden Days* (1939), and the Penguin edition of *Pygmalion* (1941). "I have seen Topolski," Shaw informed Floryan Sobieniowski; "an astonishing draughtsman: perhaps the greatest of all the Impressionists in black and white" (n.d., 1938, in a proof of *Geneva* now in Warsaw: text courtesy of Prof. Julian Krzyzanowski).]

I have added a new scene to Geneva which is a great improvement, as the play lacked a solid climax. It contains the declaration of war and the betrayal of Battler by Bombardone and Flanco, a fact of which the press and the Cabinet seem idiotically unconscious.

If you have to reprint the Topolski edition this new scene must be added.

Maxwell will add it in his standard text. . . .

GBS

To BEATRICE WEBB

Hotel Esplanade. Frinton-on-Sea

[A/14]   17th September 1939

[Eduard Beneš (1884–1948) resigned as president of Czechoslovakia in October 1938 when Germany occupied the Sudetenland. From 1939 to 1945 he was president of the Czechoslovakian Government in England. The defiant cry of Georges-Jacques Danton (1759–94), the French revolutionary, cited by Shaw, is from a speech of 2nd September 1792, when France was threatened with invasion by allied Austrian and German forces under the command of the Duke of Brunswick, in an aborted effort to crush the Revolution.]

My dear Beatrice

... This is a pleasant place; but we have had a terrible time with Charlotte's lumbago, which is the form taken by a nervous breakdown, induced, I fear, by seeing me drop dead three times in the last year or so. The outbreak of war produced a very painful relapse; but the local doctor has taken her in hand; and today and yesterday she is out of bed and apparently recovering.

I am robustly well (for my age) and have written not only a new scene for Geneva (declaration of war by Hitler and his betrayal by Mussolini and Franco, so far idiotically unnoticed by press and Cabinet) but some stupendously expensive pictures for the film of Major Barbara.

Why have we lived so long? One war was enough.

There is a point at which continuous successes will make a man believe that he can achieve anything. As I read it, this point was reached when we let Hitler get away with Czechoslovakia. Until then he had calculated accurately how far he could go without fighting. But when France let him into Prague he lost his head, and, like Danton, cried "l'audace, l'audace, et toujours l'audace." Now, if we go through with it, he will go to St Helena and Benes to Prague. The worst of it is that we had a good case for Prague, and now have to fight for the corridor, where he has the good case.

But what concerns us is the unintended consequences of the war, like the Russian consequence in 1917. Stalin, having to take one or other of the belligerents by the scruff of the neck, was right to take Hitler; but I do not know what the Soviet is driving at. Obviously it cannot desire either a British or German hegemony.

Have you seen Maisky lately? If so, what does *he* say?

And are you both bearing it well, in spite of the firing at Borden? At all events you have been spared the billeting of the young hooligans. Mrs St John Ervine sends us an appalling account of their arrival in Devon; and our doctor says "Same here." The wireless suppressed this side of it shamelessly.

G.B.S.

Charlotte is not yet well enough to write.

538

To NANCY ASTOR

[H/101; X/373]
4 Whitehall Court SW1
28th September 1939

[Shaw's statement that "the war is over" reflects a view he would enlarge upon in an article "Uncommon Sense about the War," published in the New York *Journal-American* (headed "'War is Over,' Shaw Says") on 6th October and in the *New Statesman* a day later. It was reproduced in full in the U.S. *Congressional Record* after extracts were read from the floor of the U.S. Senate on two separate occasions.

The statement that it was the British who invented concentration camps refers to the removal "for safety" of Boer women and children to large camps in 1901 as the British, in pursuit of the war in the Transvaal, cordoned off districts and cleared them up by mobile columns while burning the Boer farms. A scandal arose back home when the reformer Emily Hobhouse, after a visit to the camps, revealed the heavy death rates and the great distress visited upon the inhabitants.

Geoffrey Dawson (1874–1944), editor of *The Times* 1912–19 and 1922–41, following the appearance of "Theatres in Time of War," published Shaw's letter captioned "Poland and Russia," in which he described Hitler as "Stalin's catspaw," on 20th September.]

My dearest Nancy

I think it is time for you, as a sensible woman trying to keep your political household of dunderheads and lunatics out of mischief, to get up in the House and point out the cruelty of keeping up the pretence of a three years war when everyone who can see three moves in front of his or her nose knows that the war is over. The pretence is ruining people in all directions at home and slaughtering them abroad.

The thoughtlessness of our guarantee to Poland has left us without a leg to stand on. Most unfortunately we pledged ourselves to go to her aid WITH ALL OUR RESOURCES; and when it came to the point we dared not use the only resource that could help her (our air bombers); for we had not a soldier within hundreds of miles of her frontiers nor a sailor in the Baltic; and a single bomb from us on the Rhine cities or Berlin would have started a retaliation match which would have left all the cities of the west in the same condition as Madrid and Warsaw. We should have warned the Poles that we could do nothing to stop the German steamroller, and that they must take it lying down as Chekoslovakia had to, until we had brought Hitler to his senses.

Fortunately our old pal Stalin stepped in at the right moment and

539

took Hitler by the scruff of the neck: a masterstroke of foreign policy with six million red soldiers at its back.

What we have to do now is at once to give the order Cease firing, and light up the streets: in short, call off the war and urge on Hitler that Poland will be a greater trouble to him than half a dozen Irelands if he oppresses it unbearably. But we must remember that as far as Poland's business is anybody's business but Poland's, it is more Russia's business and Germany's than ours. Also that we cannot fight Germany *à l'outrance* without ruining both ourselves and Germany, and that we cannot fight Russia at all (neither can Hitler). The diehards who are still dreaming of a restoration of the Romanoffs and Bourbons and even the Stuarts, to say nothing of the Habsburgs, must be booted out of politics.

We should, I think, at once announce our intention of lodging a complaint with the International court against Hitler as being unfitted for State control, as he is obsessed by a Jewish complex: that of the Chosen Race, which has led him into wholesale persecution and robbery. Nothing should be said about concentration camps, because it was we who invented them.

I write this at Frinton in Essex; but we return to Ayot to-morrow and shall perhaps see you soon. Charlotte has had a terrible time here, but is much better this last week.

Waldorf might wave the red flag a bit in the House of Lords. Chamberlainism is no use on earth to him; and he might incidentally give America a lead. Geoffrey has heroically inserted two letters of mine in The Times, and has a third in his locker. I am deeply obliged to him.

Proletarians of all lands, unite!

The Labor Party is making the damndest fool of itself.

Our best love to you both.

In haste—packing
G. B. S.

To JOHN MAYNARD KEYNES

Ayot St Lawrence. Welwyn
[H/17]   5th October 1939

[Keynes, concerned about some suspected misstatements of fact in "Uncommon Sense about the War," had suggested to Kingsley Martin that the article be submitted to the censor, Hugh Pattison Macmillan (1873–1952), later Baron Macmillan of Aberfeldt, who was Minister of Information 1939–40. This proved unnecessary when Shaw acquiesced in some deletions before publication. Keynes's wife was the ballerina Lydia Lopokova, who was firmly anti-Stalinist though she and her husband were longtime close friends of the Russian ambassador Ivan Maisky.]

Dear Maynard Keynes

A thousand apologies for having misled you yesterday over the telephone. I am too old and too deaf for normal treatment on that instrument: only a set oratorical performance reaches me effectively.

Kingsley Martin had told me the day before that you wanted to take my article to the Censor, and that the risk of his suppressing it, and even the paper itself, was so great that I was sure to object. I hastened therefore to assure you that I had no objection in the world to its being shewn to the Censor (presumably Macmillan) and to the whole Cabinet, as I was sure that they would rise up and call me blessed for saying what they all wanted to say, but dared not. It never occurred to me that you might not connect this with my conversation with Martin, and so might suppose that what I meant was that the article should go no further than the Censor and the Cabinet. I am sorry. I could not have restricted my circulation to that extent even if I had not been convinced that it would be of notable public service, and that you would be jolly glad to have had it for the N.S. before the end of next week. It had already left my hands beyond recall.

When Martin told me later that you could not bear my description of the betrayal of Italy I told him to cut it out. It was necessary to a complete statement of the case; but I had already said it in The Times, which left me no excuse for rubbing it into you if you were sensitive on the point.

But the explanation of our not having come to an understanding is that of all you said to me over the phone I caught only one sentence; and that was when I asked you were you warcrazy, and you replied very slowly and doubtfully that you didnt *think* you were.

You must always remember in dealing with me that I am an Irishman and you an Englishman: that is, that you have a miraculous power of doing stupendous things without letting yourself know what you are doing, wheras I, destitute of that power, know what you are at all the time. So you must always bear with me. I am sometimes useful.

Our best regards to Lydia. Does she rejoice in the triumph of the Red Flag? Or do you never mention it to one another[?]

G. Bernard Shaw

To GABRIEL PASCAL

[A/1; X/402.e, 396.e]

Ayot St Lawrence. Welwyn
21st November 1939

[Walter Hudd (1898–1963) was a first-rate character actor, who created Sergeant Meek in *Too True to be Good* (1932) and was appearing as Battler (Hitler) in *Geneva*. He proved despite his age to be an excellent Stephen in the filmed *Major Barbara*. Peter Shirley was played by Donald Calthrop (1888–1940), who died during the filming, necessitating some tricky doubling and dubbing. A Rossini quartet and chorus from *Moses in Egypt*, with new lyrics supplied by Shaw, was to have been televised on a huge screen in a scene at Perivale St Andrews, but was not filmed, presumably to reduce accelerating wartime costs. Katharine Cornell did not play Barbara in America; in 1941 she produced and starred in *The Doctor's Dilemma*, with Raymond Massey as Ridgeon and Bramwell Fletcher as Dubedat.]

Dear Gabriel

I am much relieved to have you safe in Salcombe instead of worrying yourself to death here. You needed the change; and the news that it has been a success rejoices me.

Your notion of a scene representing the conversion of Shirley by Barbara is the very worst I ever heard. Shirley is not converted: the bitterness of his lot is that being an atheist sacked as "too old over forty" he is driven by starvation to beg a crust from the Salvation Army. Get Shirley out of your mind: there is just enough of him in the play. Beware of the temptation to overdo every good effect. Enough is enough: another word and enough becomes too much: the fault of Hollywood.

Besides, such a scene would collide with the Mog Habbijam—Bill Walker scene, and wreck both, besides spoiling Barbara's conversion scene with Bill. Big effects must not be repeated.

Why does Hudd want such a disagreeable part as Stephen, on which he will be thrown away? Why not give him Lomax? Scott Sunderl^d, by the way, would be an ideal Cholly if only he could *act* him instead of *being* him.

I dont believe that links and bridges are needed to connect the acts for filming. The audience will make the jump exactly as they do in the theatre.

I left undone an important bit of Barbara: the words for the Rossini quartet. I have now done them and will send you a fair copy when Blanche types it. It has been a horrid job. Nothing would have been easier than to write a few pretty verses; but to fit them to Rossini's notes and accents, and to provide open vowels for the big recurring portamento was the very devil; and the result is queer, but singable. I almost drove my wife mad bellowing it over and over on Sunday night.

Stephen must be a complete prig—the dictionary gives saputello; but I dont know whether that is the real equivalent. It is always bad economy to waste an agreeable actor on a charmless part: that is why I think a better use might be made of Hudd.

Who is your Shirley now?

I must stop. Stay as long as you can in Salcombe.

Katherine Cornell now wants to play Barbara with Maurice Evans in the spring in New York; and this, I think, will be good business for us; so I have told her I am enchanted.

Whoosh!
GBS

To C. H. NORMAN

4 Whitehall Court SW 1

[H/83]   20th December 1939

Dear Norman

I have not exactly "joined the fight-it-out Party." I said everything I could get published, and some things that I couldnt, to bring about a truce and a conference; but I might just as well have been singing Tipperary. So, the facts being the facts, I said: "Very well: you are going to fight; so that is settled. Now we shall see what we shall see." If that is what you call joining the fight-it-out Party, have it so.

Perhaps our best excuse for fighting is that as the government has no case, and a perfect genius for furthering itself in the wrong, it had better trust to its fist. The objection is that in a simple dogfight neither Germany nor the Allies can win though both can and will get badly bitten. Besides, the war is not popular; nobody knows what it is all about. The taxation, the evacuations, the conscription and rationing, are producing every degree of unpleasantness, from acute inconvenience to downright ruin.

I seem to be the only person who understands the Finland complication because I am Irish, and Ireland is the British Finland. If England is threatened from the west, she will have to swallow all her virtuous indignation and re-occupy Ireland exactly as the Russians have occupied Finland. The expulsion of Russia from the League not only gives

Russia a free hand, but raises the question why England did not refer the Polish case to the League before aggressively starting a new and quite distinct war.

Anyhow if we fight to the bitter end and are beaten we have no mercy to expect. We dont deserve it; and if we did we shouldnt get it.

Really what we are fighting for is prestige. If we had allowed the Polish war to end with a victory for Hitler, it would have deposed us from our position as first fiddle in Europe.

What else had we to expect from a government of grown-up public schoolboys and a trade union Labour opposition?

G. Bernard Shaw

To IVO GEIKIE-COBB

[H/1]

4 Whitehall Court SW1
6th January 1940

[Ivo Geikie-Cobb (1887–1953) was a physician and surgeon who wrote and broadcast under the pseudonym Anthony Weymouth. He joined the B.B.C.'s Overseas Service Department at the start of 1940, writing and editing scripts and participating in some of the broadcasts. Sir William DeCourcy Wheeler (1879–1943), Dublin-born surgeon with an international reputation, was Shaw's cousin once removed, being a grandson of George Carr Shaw's brother Henry.]

Dear Mr Cobb

Sir William Wheeler tells me that you want to get a message from me to the Colonies. I never send messages: my speciality is keeping my mouth shut when I have nothing to say or at least think I had better not say it. Just at present the difficulty with the Colonies is that we have had nothing from them but the usual bunk from the political careerists. This is probably representative enough for Canada and New Zealand, but not for Australia and South Africa, where there is a good deal of anti-British and pro-American or anti-British pro-Dutch feeling to be reckoned with. I know of the existence of this, but not how strong it is. Even in New Zealand there is sufficient anti-Japanese feeling to produce a break with the Empire if we went too far in the Far East.

In short I do not know the ground well enough to justify my pontificating on the subject; and I am no use for recruiting speeches.

Before giving you the trouble of calling on me I think it better to give you these reasons for writing me off as a wash-out.

faithfully
G. Bernard Shaw

To G. M. TREVELYAN

4 Whitehall Court SW1
20th January 1940
[C/3]

[Sir James Jeans (1877–1946), astronomer, physicist, and author of *The Universe around Us* (1929) and other popularised scientific works, did the logarithms for *Good King Charles*. The astronomer Sir Arthur Eddington "gasped at the perihelion of Mercury," Shaw noted on 7th December 1939 in his inscription to H. G. Wells in a copy of the published text; "but as it is a sure stage laugh (like Weston super Mare) I could not sacrifice it" (A/119). Despite the assistance of experts, the play was full of blunders. In making mathematical calculations Shaw added Leap Years instead of subtracting them. Catherine of Braganza refers to Portsmouth when it should be Cleveland; and John Calvin's death was placed in the seventeenth century instead of the sixteenth (he died in 1564), so that James refers erroneously to Calvin as "[going] to hell sixteen years ago."]

The play was read by two astronomers (Jeans & Eddington), by the omniscient Webbs, and the entire person[n]el of the Malvern Festival. They all swallowed the Calvin blunder without a grimace. I was quite right about it myself; but most unfortunately instead of trusting to my historical instinct (the true method) I foolishly looked up the date in the Enc. Br. and of course was set wrong, misreading the century because my head was full of the seventeenth. I dont know why I made Charles say he couldnt remember his father. I didnt believe it; but at 83 1/2 (my present age) I find myself doing all sorts of silly things. Jeans corrected my ridiculous logarithms.

Thanks for the corrections.

GBS

To HAMILTON MARR

4 Whitehall Court SW1
[H/99]   15th February 1940

[Hamilton Marr (1900–40) was head of programme copyright at the B.B.C. Act I of *Arms and the Man* was eventually performed, unedited, on Home Service radio on 14th March. The reference to "overseas people" relates to the performance of the play in three parts, on 14th, 18th, and 21st April 1939, on the Empire service.]

Dear Mr Hamilton Marr

I will not consent to the omission of a single word or comma from the first act of Arms and the Man. You can find 40 minutes for a Church service. You can find 45 minutes for a Brahms symphony. You can find 60 minutes for the most damnable variety of muck or for one of your intolerable rechauffés of obsolete drivel from the XIX century. Well, if you want me you must find 40, 50, 60, and if necessary 180 minutes for me, or else do without me. Tell these overseas people that their thirty minute arrangements are not applicable to works of art, but only to tripe, which can be cut up and supplied by the pound.

If that is clear I may remark that the first act of Arms and the Man should take 27 minutes, which allows 3 for fluffing.

G. Bernard Shaw

To G. S. VIERECK

4 Whitehall Court SW1
[H/1]   8th March 1940

[Arthur Neville Chamberlain (1869–1940) succeeded Stanley Baldwin as Prime Minister in 1937. Sir Austen Chamberlain was his half-brother. It was Neville Chamberlain, a preacher of avoidance of war by appeasement, who agreed to the Munich pact in September 1938 that resulted in the partition of Czechoslovakia. He resigned in May 1940 after a vote of confidence (which he won by 281–200) clearly revealed the extent to which he had lost support. He was succeeded by Winston Churchill. St Helena was Napoleon's last address. Camden Place in Chislehurst, Kent, was the residence in exile of Napoleon III (1808–73) and his consort Eugénie; while Doorn, in the Netherlands, was that of Kaiser Wilhelm II.]

Dear G. S. V.

Blood is thicker than all the water in the Atlantic; and I know too well how hopeless it would be to try to convince you or any other echt

Deutscher that the Chamberlains are the most absurdly and naively sincere statesmen on the face of the globe. Hypocrisy is the last feat they could possibly perform even if they thought it necessary for God's Englishmen to resort to such an expedient. What hypocrite would talk as I have made Austen talk in Geneva? But Austen could talk like that by the hour. When he came back from the League of Nations he actually did say in Parliament "Of course the British Empire comes first with me." What hypocrite would have given himself away so confidently? Hypocrisy is always carefully logical.

I think I made Hitler give a better account of himself than he has ever done in real life. He is a very difficult character to dramatize because of his incongruous assortment of qualities. His Nordic anti-Semite rubbish is Houston-Chamberlain at secondhand in theory, and in fact the reaction of his resentment complex to the circumstance that he has never been able to impose himself on the Jews. Also he has failed to hypnotize the Marxists, and has therefore abused them and attempted to head the capitalist movement against Communism whilst establishing himself by National Socialism: a contradiction which has finally landed him in a very unstable alliance with Russia. The people he has impressed are the ultra-Prussian Conservatives and the simple everyday idolators. But he has lifted Germany from the gutter into which the Allies kicked her into the most dreaded power in Europe; and a man who, himself started in the gutter, has been able enough to do that without a single Napoleonic victory must be ranked among the great men (a fabulous species by the way).

But he is in a tight corner. When England, bogged by her own blundering, is at last provoked to say "For one or both of us the hour has come," her ablest and toughest adversary will have all his work cut out for him to keep out of St Helena or Chiselhurst or Doorn.

You are safe in America. Do not take sides. You can do nothing to help Hitler or hinder Chamberlain, though you can damage yourself if you try; so sit tight as a 100% American.

GBS

To SIEGFRIED TREBITSCH

Ayot St Lawrence. Welwyn
[H/4; X/341]   11th March 1940

[Trebitsch, temporarily in Monaco, he and Tina having settled into the Hotel Winter Palace at Nice a month earlier, was contemplating an April visit to England. Michael Kantorowitz (1877–1961), Russian-born theatrical agent, represented Shaw from a base in Switzerland. Kurt Reiss (1901–74), a Swiss publisher and literary agent, proposed filming *Pygmalion* in Swiss-German dialect. Wilhelm Viktor Krausz (1878–1959) was a celebrated portraitist in Vienna; he later became an American citizen.]

My dear Trebitsch

This is the first sensible letter you have sent me since the Dispersal. I have been making inquiries, and find that "apartments" have disappeared from London economy, and that people who formerly lived in them now live in hotels or in "service flats" like mine in Whitehall. It is interesting to learn that this is true of the Riviera also, and that you can patronize hotels and save Tina the burden of housekeeping and finding servants with a good conscience.

In London, however, you could have three weeks at a *good* hotel with all meals included for what it costs for bed and breakfast at the Dorchester. You would not have jazz bands and crowds of actresses and smart women every night at supper: the company would be bourgeois and not all in evening dress at dinner; but there would be solid comfort, entire respectability, and good public rooms to write in. The Victorian hotels which were within my recollection famous as the best in London—the Langham and Charing Cross, for instance—are not "smart" (smartness was not considered respectable by the old Queen); but they are as good as ever; and you can stand up without knocking a hole in the ceiling with your head. Fifty years ago you would have thought them the last word in luxury. That is one of the advantages of being old: what was good enough for Franz Joseph and Victoria is good enough for us.

We are now in summer time; and the black-out does not begin until half past seven. You can go to a cinema or a theatre matinée without being blinded or run over; and if you come when there is a moon the risks are negligible. In April there will be still more daylight. As to the war, the Powers are still very wisely afraid to bombard each other's capitals; and London is the safest place in the west of Europe except perhaps Monte Carlo. But this security may not last: there is uncertainty enough about it to make it impossible to say whether you ought to come here next month unless you have more pressing business than to see two people whose united ages amount to 167. We cannot believe that we are interesting enough to make the journey worth while for our sakes alone. Still, it would be a change for you which would probably do you good. My only doubt is whether I may not have to take Charlotte away for a few weeks after Easter, as she also has had a hard time through a hard winter and talks of going to the Isle of Wight to recuperate. However, she is so much better now that she can hold out at home until the holidays are over. If you can afford the journey we must arrange it somehow. Pascal still assures me that you are a millionaire.

Is Monaco a neutral state like Switzerland from which you can communicate with Vienna?

It is impossible for me to name a lump sum as the price of the Swiss–German dialect rights of Pygmalion. I do not know whether they are worth twopence or two thousand pounds or twenty thousand. Kantorovich should be able to advise us. But I prefer my ten per cent arrangement. Meanwhile Kurt Reiss must let me know whether he accepts our scenario as it stands, and will undertake to follow it exactly. I have heard nothing from him since you sent him the script.

As to the word fluxions in Charles there may not be any German version of it. What happened was that Newton invented the differential calculus (and infinitesimal calculus) for his own convenience when he was a young man, and said nothing about it. He called this mathematical method Fluxions because it enabled him to determine the rate at which a continually changing quantity—a *flowing* quantity—changes. Later on Leibniz invented the same method independently; but his figuration (notation) was so much easier to work with that it was adopted by all the mathematicians and called the calculus, or the infinitesimal calculus, or the integral calculus, or the differential calculus, whilst Newton's word Fluxions was dropped. The Muret-Sanders dictionary gives for Fluxions the same word, for Equinox das Aequinoktium, and for Notation das Bezeichnungssystem. The ducking stool is a long plank on wheels with a chair at the end. Women who were scolds and shrews were tied in the chair and dipped into the pond or river until they were half drowned.

I received Krauss's visit but refused to sit to him. There are too many portraits of me in the world. Foreign painters imagine that if they can paint Shaw their fortunes will be made. If I let them do it they find that they have wasted their time painting a picture that nobody will buy; and they come back to me begging me to buy it. Therefore I always refuse to sit unless the painter can produce a commission from some rich client for a portrait of me. Frau Krauss, who must have been brilliantly pretty when she was young, tried all her blandishments on me; but I was adamant.

You must not mind my hardheartedness. Charlotte and I are old and in our second childhood. We can no longer feel things [except little things]* as you do, which is very fortunate for us, because human misery is so appalling nowadays that if we allowed ourselves to dwell on it we should only add imaginary miseries of our own to the real miseries of others without doing them any good. When the inflation of the German currency ruined the middle classes after the treaty of Versailles I received hundreds of heartbreaking letters from Germans telling me all about their wrecked lives and begging for sums from five shillings to five hundred pounds or even for an abusive postcard which they could sell as an autograph. I had to harden my heart until it was like that of a professional torturer and executioner; and I have not yet recovered from that anaesthetic, nor shall I dare to until this war is over. But I am none the less conscious of your misfortunes, and of how much more they afflict you than they would me, who have been really poor as you have never been.

I could live on £2 a week; but Tina could not, nor Charlotte, nor you.

I think I have now answered all your letters; and Heaven knows when I shall have time to write again. But we are always glad to hear from you.

G. Bernard Shaw

To LAWRENCE LANGNER

[H/7; X/312.e]

4 Whitehall Court SW 1
3rd April 1940

[*Geneva*, presented by Maurice Colbourne and Barry Jones in association with Gilbert Miller, at the Henry Miller's Theatre, New York, on 30th January 1940, after brief engagements in Canada, was blasted by the reviewers and expired after a fortnight. *Saint Joan* was not filmed until years after Shaw's death, and then with a screenplay by Graham Greene supplanting Shaw's own, which the producer-director Otto Preminger later said he didn't know existed. Katharine Hepburn had an enormous success in the Theatre Guild's production of Philip Barry's *The Philadelphia Story* (1939), which she repeated a year later in the film version. She finally played Epifania in *The Millionairess* in London and New York in 1952.]

Dear Lawrence Langner

I rejoice to hear that the Guild is up on its feet again. I had given it up as finished. It has, as you know, dropped me as an author. I did

---

* The square brackets are Shaw's.

not blame it, as my plays did not seem to be bringing it any luck. The Press attack on Geneva and its flop has not improved matters. However, the sensational success of the Pygmalion film has suddenly brought me into vogue as a screen expert (I was supposed to know nothing about the cinema); and this bears on the Hepburn question.

St Joan has been pretty thoroughly exploited lately by your new niece, Kit [Katharine Cornell]. That irresistible lady called on me when she was last in London, and put me in her pocket in five seconds, not to mention that she had made a pot of money for me while the Guild was turning down my plays one after another and throwing me into the arms of the late lamented Federal Theatre. Is it not a bit soon to start a fresh tour of St Joan on the heels of such a charmer?

Besides, I have a St Joan film coming on with Wendy Hiller as the star—she who did so well in Pygmalion. Until this is released I cannot put up a rival Joan against Wendy. If Hepburn can act—and as she has been playing successfully for the Guild I take it that you are satisfied that she can—she would be a formidable rival. I never feel that I have any moral right to lock up a part against anyone who feels called on to play it, and has fairly won an artist's right to try it; but business has its rights too; and when I have given Pascal an agreement on which he must raise $500,000 to film the play I cannot reasonably do anything that could spoil his claim. So, until the film is released, I am afraid I must hold up the play unless Miss Hepburn can persuade Pascal that her performance would be a help. Kit easily persuaded him that his film of Major Barbara, now in hand, would be helped by her appearance as Barbara with Maurice Evans; but then Kit could persuade anybody to let her do anything. She only gave it up because she could not find an actor good enough for Undershaft.

Meanwhile my play The Millionairess, with Edith Evans in the title part, is next on the list at the Globe Theatre in London. In the original version I made the woman a boxer; but, on the stage, that was unconvincing and unladylike. So I have made her a Judo expert. Judo is what we vulgarly call jiujitsu, which is magnificently spectacular. The part requires just such a personality as Miss Hepburn. Has she ever read the play? . . .

Give my regards to the faithless Terry if she still remembers me. Have you any new plays ready, and does your own particular theatre still exist?

G. Bernard Shaw

To LEONARD ELMHIRST

[H/130]

4 Whitehall Court S W 1
5th April 1940

[Leonard Elmhirst (1893–1974) and his wife purchased the rundown Dartington Hall Estate, in Totnes, South Devon, in 1925, to found an experiment in rural industrial research and education. He was a founder trustee and, from 1931, chairman of the Dartington Hall Trust. Portions of *Major Barbara* were eventually filmed in Dartington Hall.]

Dear Mr Elmhirst

Don Pasquale (Gabriel Pascal) is his unique self. Having seen him and heard him you know as much about him as I do. His birthplace was in Hungary and is now in Roumania. He has been a child in Florence, dividing his time between swimming in the Arno and haunting the picture galleries. He has been a cavalry officer. He has been an actor at the Burgtheater in Vienna. Finally he became a maker of films. He thinks in millions. He is naturalized as an Englishman. He speaks all languages, preferably Italian.

He called on me without introduction or references of any kind, and, as I have learnt since, without a farthing of capital in hand. I made what enquiries I could, with unsatisfactory results: nothing definite but everybody afraid of him.

At a second interview I took a big chance and handed him an agreement authorizing him to film my play Pygmalion, thus enabling him to raise a credit of £60,000. Being quite reckless about money when artistic considerations are at stake he spent more than that on the film; but its success was overwhelming. It has put him at the tip top of the film world; and I who was supposed to be hopeless on the screen, am now the desired of Hollywood.

People say "He needs watching." The truth is, he needs nursing; for though he is more acute than the business men and financiers with whom he has to deal, he cares too little for money, and too much for art, to spend his time and wits in fighting them; and I have to use my own powers to put the screw on for him occasionally. He has never humbugged or cheated me in any way: I have to choke him off when his imagination suggests some gorgeous folly; but I recognize in him the Magyar gentleman; and he has not let me down.

I do not know what took him to Dartington: I am quite guiltless of letting him loose on you; but now that he has found you out he is enchanted with the great hall and the other attractions of the place, and believes he can use them in the film of my play Major Barbara on which he is at present working. I am much indebted to you for allowing [him] to make use of you in this way. As there is no limit to his imagination and to his powers of transmogrification you must keep your eyes on him lest he should make Dartington disappear from the earth like a transformation scene in a pantomime. You may be quite frank with him: in fact it is impossible to deal with him on any other terms.

It was a great disappointment to us that you were away when we last visited Dartington. Better luck next time.

always yours
G. Bernard Shaw

To ADA TYRRELL

4 Whitehall Court SW 1
[H/1; X/136]   17th April 1940

[Mrs Patrick Campbell died at Pau on 9th April, at the age of 75. Mrs Tyrrell was living with a daughter at Budleigh Salterton in Devon.]

My dear Addy

Yes: she is dead; and everybody is greatly relieved: herself, I should say, most of all; for the last pictures of her are not those of a happy woman. She was not a great actress; but she was a great enchantress, how or why I dont know; but if she wanted to capture you you might as well go quietly; for she was irresistible. Unfortunately she was professionally such a devilish nuisance that nobody who had been through a production with her ever repeated that experience if it were possible to avoid it. She made a great success for Pinero and another for me; but though we both wrote plays afterwards containing parts that would have suited her to perfection, we did not cast her for them. She did not know how to live with real people in the real world. She was a hybrid, half Italian, half suburban Croydon; and the transition from one to the other was bewildering. Though her grandfather ran a circus and her mother rode in it and was never anglicised, there must have been a strain of nobility on the Italian side; for she could behave finely on occasion. She enchanted me among the rest; but I could not have lived with her for a week; and I knew it; so nothing came of it. She was kind to Lucy, who in some ways could walk round her. Orinthia in The Apple Cart is a dramatic portrait of her. R.I.P. . . .

553

I am glad to gather from your letter that you are still unimpaired. When you come to London let us know. We shall arrange a meeting.

always yours affectionately

G.Bernard Shaw

To C. H. NORMAN

Ayot St Lawrence. Welwyn

[C/4; X/289.e]   22nd April 1940

Yes; but what about America? It was the U.S.A. that won the last rubber. Neither they nor the U.S.S.R. may be able to keep out of it this time either. History always repeats itself and yet never repeats itself. . . .

GBS

To H. K. AYLIFF

Ayot St Lawrence. Welwyn

[H/46]   5th May 1940

[The Roy Limbert—Emile Littler production of *In Good King Charles's Golden Days*, bound for the West End, was being polished up during a week's engagement at the Golders Green Hippodrome following its initial engagement at Streatham Hill on 15th April. The cast included Ernest Thesiger as Charles, Cecil Trouncer as Newton, Herbert Lomas as Fox, Irene Vanbrugh as Queen Catherine, Eileen Beldon as Nell Gwyn, Amy Veness as Mrs Basham, William Hutchison as James, Daphne Heard as Barbara, Bruno Barnabe as Kneller, Ina de la Haye as Louise, and Betty Marsden as Sally. Isabel Thornton played Mrs Basham at Malvern in August 1939. Margaret Yarde (1878–1944) was a character actress with dozens of West End and provincial theatre credits; she appeared the previous January as Mrs Hardcastle in *She Stoops to Conquer*, at the Old Vic. Isabel Thornton and Alec Clunes replaced Amy Veness and Bruno Barnabe by the end of the week. H.R.Hignett was playing the Bishop in *Geneva*, now in the twenty-fourth week of its London engagement.]

Dear Ayliff

I saw the show yesterday at Golders Green. My general impression is that it was not quite up to West End concert pitch; but then I am old and deaf; and the box was high up and out of the line of fire from

554

the stage; and I was hiding at the back of it; so I will not back my opinion that most of it was a bit underplayed.

An unexpected exception was Kneller, with whom you seem to have worked a miracle; for he came out brilliantly. I should not have thought of changing him.

The housekeeper was dangerously weak: the part needs Thornton or Margaret Yarde. I found no fault with Miss V.: she was quite good up to her weight, but was not heavy enough, not enough of a terror.

James is too young and pretty: he would [be] all right as Monmouth, but not as the uncle who beheaded Monmouth. His claim to be more popular than Charles was quite credible. He should be an elderly admiral with awkward manners.

Charles's first entrance missed fire through a lack of the large condescending courtesy and charm that should captivate Fox and Newton. He seemed an unattractive young man instead of a very attractive elderly one. Throughout he lacked gaiety of heart and regal ease: the picture was that of an unhappy man rather than of a carelessly happy and resourceful one. Ernest could get this in a turn of the hand, I should think.

Eileen was too conscious of being Nell Gwyn; and it was partly her fault that the Dryden scene was a failure. Instead of trusting to her own charm and playing straight, with a staggering change to extravagant artificiality when she recites, she did exactly the opposite, and was artificial when she was not supposed to be acting and startlingly natural when she spouted Dryden's wildly unnatural lines. James made matters worse by gabbling his quotation in his most colloquial manner. Explain to him that all royal personages are carefully taught to speak carefully and correctly.

I should give Charles the centre of the stage for the great pessimistic speech, which should act as a grand exordium for the formality of the rest. The change from Eileen's spouting to her "Then somebody says something," a sure laugh, went for nothing.

Newton and Fox got the last inch out of their parts; and, surprisingly, Sally caught the pitch of the house and the style of the text so well that she played Mrs Basham off the stage.

Cleveland was not tall enough, nor superb enough in ruined beauty, to make her bygone reign over Charles credible. Make her prouder in her bursts of rage if you can: she is intelligent enough. Haughty is the word.

Louise all right.

I think this is all. Of course what is against us is that the memorizing work is very hard, and the emotions of a quite unaccustomed kind: consequently it has been impossible to get the best out of most of them; so I am not too hopeful of playing to capacity.

Still, it was only a matinée on a hot afternoon; and it will be more forcible on the night. All the same I dont envy you your job, and thank my stars that I have had you to throw it on to.

In great haste—I have had to supply Limbert with some dialogue to get Begonia [Alison Leggatt] off the stage in Geneva when her part stops. He thinks it is killing her to sit for so long silent; but she is the first actress I have met who wouldnt rather be on the stage silent than off at the fall of the curtain.

G. Bernard Shaw

PS. I think—and Mrs Shaw agrees vehemently—that James is a hopeless and dangerous miscast: you cannot make either an old salt or a James II of him. As you are unhappily changing Kneller why not coach James in Kneller, and get a new James? I wish I could think of the right man.

[*On the back flap of envelope*] Hignet would be the man; but I suppose he is playing in Geneva. James was essentially an *old* man, as Charles was a young one.

To VIRGINIA WOOLF

4 Whitehall Court SW1
[H/5; X/408.e, 409]   10th May 1940
[Virginia Woolf (1882–1941) the novelist and her husband Leonard Woolf (1880–1969), author, journalist, Fabian Socialist, and founder of the Hogarth Press, were leading members of the set known as the Bloomsbury Group. Another of its members was the artist Roger Fry (1866–1934), whose biography Mrs Woolf was writing.]

My dear Virginia

I do not remember the occasion described by Roger; and I could hardly have dismissed art so very summarily from consideration as a social factor as if I had just looked into it as a foreign subject for five minutes or so. As a matter of fact I am an artist to my finger tips, and always contend that I am a highly educated person because I had continual contacts with literature and art, including music, in my childhood, and found school and its Latin and Greek grind nothing but a brutalizing imprisonment which interfered disastrously with my real education. Now that I am nearly eighty I am more convinced than ever that an æsthetic education is the best now available, and that the neglect of the æsthetic factor in science has deprived it of its claim to be scientific.

Probably what Roger heard me say was that nothing fundamental can be done by art until the economical problem is solved. I am fond of saying that 12 hours hunger will reduce any saint, artist, or philosopher to the level of a highwayman.

I think my first private meeting with Roger was also my first meeting with Elgar. We three lunched with Madame Vandervelde, then wedded to the late Belgian Socialist Minister. Elgar, who had enjoyed my musical criticisms when he was a student and remembered all my silly jokes, talked music so voluminously that Roger had nothing to do but eat his lunch in silence. At last we stopped to breathe and to eat something ourselves; and Roger, feeling that our hostess expected him to contribute something, began in his beautiful voice (his and Forbes Robertson's were the only voices one could listen to for their own sakes) "After all, there is only one art: all the arts are the same." I heard no more; for my attention was taken by a growl from the other side of the table. It was Elgar, with his fangs bared and all his hackles bristling, in an appalling rage. "Music," he spluttered, "is written on the skies for you to note down. And you compare that to a DAMNED imitation."

There was nothing for Roger to do but either seize the decanter and split Elgar's head with it, or else take it like an angel with perfect dignity. Which latter he did.

I have a picture by Roger which I will give you if you care to have it: a landscape.

I wish we could see more of you and Leonard; but we two are now so frightfully old that we no longer dare to offer our company as a treat to friends who are still in the prime of life.

There is a play of mine called Heartbreak House which I always connect with you because I conceived it in that house somewhere in Sussex where I first met you [in 1913] and, of course, fell in love with you. I suppose every man did.

always yours, consequently
G. Bernard Shaw

["Your letter," Mrs Woolf replied on 15th May, "reduced me to two days silence from sheer pleasure. You wont be surprised to hear that I promptly lifted some paragraphs and inserted them in my proofs. You may take what action you like.

557

"As for the falling in love, it was not, let me confess, one-sided. When I first met you at the Webbs I was set against all great men, having been liberally fed on them in my father's [Leslie Stephen's] house. I wanted only to meet business men and (say) racing experts. But in a jiffy you made me re-consider all that and had me at your feet. Indeed you have acted a lover's part in my life for the past thirty years; and though I daresay it's not much to boast of, I should have been a worser woman without Bernard Shaw. That is the reason—I mean the multiplicity of your lovers and what you must suffer from them—why Leonard and Virginia have never liked to impose themselves upon you. But we have an intermittent perch . . . in London; and if ever Mr Shaw dropped his handkerchief—to recur to the love theme —we should ask nothing better than to come and see you. . . . Heartbreak House, by the way, is my favourite of all your works" (H/2).

There was no visit; Virginia Woolf committed suicide the following year.]

To ROY LIMBERT

[C/3]
Ayot St Lawrence. Welwyn
19th May 1940

[*In Good King Charles's Golden Days* opened at the New Theatre, London, on 9th May. Audiences, however, were sparse, and the play was withdrawn after 29 performances. Limbert toured the play again in 1948–49, and presented it at a resurrected Malvern Festival in 1949.]

There is nothing for it but to wait until a) the war settles into the old routine of leave providing huge audiences every night, or b) blue blazes for everybody makes an end of all the questions.

I forgot all about the first night, and did not realize the situation at the New until your letter arrived.

It is all right now we are thoroughly frightened. England never does anything until that happens; but, when it does, then Lord help her enemies!

GBS

To FELIKS TOPOLSKI

[C/3; W/289]
Ayot St Lawrence. Welwyn
[Undated: assigned to 20th May 1940]

[Topolski was illustrating *Pygmalion* for Penguin Books.]

The costumes do not matter chronologically, because by the time the book is finished and in circulation the fashions of today will be as obsolete as those of 1913. But 1913 will give you Eliza's shawl and hat with three ostrich figures [feathers], now quite vanished; and the Rosettian Mrs Higgins in her Burne Jones costume and Morrisian drawingroom. I think I have photographs of Mrs Morris and of the original production that would help.

The men's dress has not changed much, except that Higgins should have a frock coat and tall hat instead of a lounge suit and Derby.

GBS

To BEATRICE WEBB

Ayot St Lawrence. Welwyn
[C/14]   17th June 1940

[Henri-Philippe Pétain (1856–1951), French soldier who became Marshal of France in 1918, was the new premier of Unoccupied France (1940–44). He had ordered the French Army to stop fighting and called on Hitler to conclude an honourable peace settlement. Churchill broadcast a message that evening, in the course of which he said: "What has happened in France makes no difference to our actions and purpose. We have become the sole champions now in arms to defend the world cause. We shall do our best to be worthy of this high honour. . . . We shall fight on unconquerable until the curse of Hitler is lifted from the brows of mankind."]

We must not let Adolf give Socialism a bad name. We are National Socialists, and for Socialism in a single country as against Trotsky; and we cannot too strongly insist that we are not objecting to German

Socialism but to persecution and bogus Racialism, which are completely foreign to Socialism and incompatible with it, and have been attached to it illogically and insanely by the Führer. I was horrified when The New Statesman made the slip of denouncing Natl. Soc^lm as the enemy instead of Hitlerism.

I have just heard Churchill on the wireless, evidently badly floored. He should have said more or said nothing; but it is impossible to blame him; for what can any of us say until we know the terms obtainable by Petain? If, as is possible, Adolf has had enough, and is uneasy about his home front and about Russia, there is no reason why we should not be a party to the bargaining if not to the bargain.

Come for a week-end any time you like.

G.B.S.

To WINSTON S. CHURCHILL

[T/122]

[Ayot St Lawrence. Welwyn]
[Undated: June 1940]

Dear Prime Minister

Why not declare war on France and capture her fleet (which would gladly strike its colors to us) before A.H. recovers his breath?

Surely that is the logic to the situation?

tactically
G. Bernard Shaw

To DODD, MEAD & CO.

[H.c.u/1]

4 Whitehall Court SW1
19th June 1940

[Almost from the inception of its association with Shaw, the publishing house of Dodd, Mead & Co. had acted more as an agent than a publisher, pocketing half the royalties and fees for previously published Shaw works licensed to other houses, and issuing a variety of reprint editions of the plays from the cheaply acquired plates of William H. Wise's collected Ayot St Lawrence Edition (1930–32), while resisting investment in new Shavian publications. Despite his threats Shaw retained Dodd, Mead as his American publisher until his death. The Shaw Estate did not cancel the self-renewing contract with the firm until 1983.]

Dear Dodd, Mead & Co.

The war has knocked the postal service into a cocked hat. Your letter in reply to my ultimatum, though dated the 26th April, did not reach me until June, though some later letters had arrived in good time; and at last I had concluded that I had struck you dead, and must act at once to make sure that my notice to quit on the 31st December would reach you soon enough. So I instructed my Counselor at Law, Mr Benjamin H. Stern of 1 East 45th Street, to put the notice through formally.

Now comes your letter. I understand it completely; but it only confirms my decision not to continue on the old terms. What it comes to is that you would like to cease publishing my old books and simply to levy a tax of 50% on my royalties from the operations of other publishers. That, dear Dodd, is not business: you would not dream of allowing me to stop writing books and to levy a tax of 50% on all the other books you publish. Let me put my situation to you.

Most books, bar Bibles and Shakespears, have a lifetime of 18 months. The publisher has to risk the cost of manufacture, and must fix the price at a figure which will bring back his money plus the necessary profit on a sale of between one and two thousand copies. The transaction ends with the sale. There is not much in it for the publisher; but it keeps the shop open even when the profit is negligible. Poor business: why does the publisher do it? Because he is gambling on the chance of, say, one in six or ten of the books proving a best seller. This does actually occur: hence the publisher's automobile and other luxuries, which are permanent whilst the author only acquires expensive habits which ruin him when the book is over and the publisher goes on to the next boom.

Meanwhile the publisher has found out that the author is an imbecile in business and so poor and so desperately anxious to see himself in print that he dare not say No to any condition imposed by the publisher and will sell all his rights, film rights, performing rights, translation rights, and his soul and body into the bargain for $50 cash. It is greatly to the credit of the publishers that they do not kill the goose that lays the golden eggs every time, since there are always more geese to kill. But they get together in their autos and agree to demand 50% of the author's income over and above the winnings of the gamble.

Now all this does not apply to my case. I have a reputation which makes the sale of a few thousand copies of anything I write a certainty. The publisher runs no risk of loss of his capital, nor need he advance any; for the printers and binders, hampered by plants which are eating their heads off when they are not busy, will give credit until the sale bring[s] in the money. There is no need to spend anything worth mentioning on advertisement: my publicity advertises itself. The publisher contributes nothing but a fractional part of his overhead and sales machinery. The author has to write the book, which costs him many months of work, and has only that book to fall back on whereas the publisher has hundreds of books. To the 50–50 business the publisher contributes absolutely nothing at all.

Naturally in England I having always more money lying at my bank on deposit at next to nothing per cent than enough to manufacture my books at a profit of 300 per cent, and being neither a born imbecile nor ignorant and incapable in business, I publish on commission. Constable has no printers or binders bills to pay; he has the use of the money from the sales for many months and he finally keeps 15% of it for the fractional part of his overhead that I cost him. He is on velvet; yet he tries his hardest to get me on to a royalty basis. I have allowed him to have some books on a "half profit" arrangement by which he pays for everything and gives me half of the surplus of sale over cost of manufacture (no overhead). My last two plays were published by him on this system because he found a wonderful illustrator at his own cost and for the first time chose the type and designed the book subject to my approval.

These two books with their illustrations you refused to publish in the U.S.; and I should have forfeited the U.S. Copyright had I not registered them as "dramatic compositions" in Washington in typescript. But if I had found another publisher for them you would have demanded 50% without a blush!

Dodd, Dodd, Dodd: what sort of fool do you take me for?

Any capital you invested in me you invested with your eyes open and our agreement before you. You had to make it good within five years; and the operations of [William] Wise were reserved. I have asked for no advances; and you have had every advantage that you could expect from books that live for two years or less. But my books are not for an age but for all time, provided, that is, that the $2.50 editions are followed by cheaper ones and travelled and canvassed and advertised in all sorts of ways that are beyond your resources. You have refused to take any such risks, very wisely; but for your refusal you demand 50% of my royalties. The proposition bereaves me of breath. I will see you in heaven first.

We must either make reasonable arrangements or else part good friends. There is no reason why you should not continue to do my *de luxe* business and skim the cream off my new books before they go into the cheap market with the rest of my old junk, though if you run your prices up to $5 I shall expect more than 15%. But in the cheap market there is room for one author and one publisher; and in that I must be completely free. If I have to give up either the *de luxe* market or the cheap market I shall give up the *de luxe* market and bid farewell for ever to old established responsible publishers. Think it over.

Forgive the brevity of this letter: I havent time to write at greater length.

[yours faithfully
G. Bernard Shaw]

To IVO GEIKIE-COBB

Ayot St Lawrence. Welwyn
[A/1]   24th June 1940

[(Sir) Stephen Tallents (1884–1958), Overseas Services Controller of the B.B.C. 1940–41, had suggested that Shaw be invited to broadcast a talk amplifying a statement in a recent newspaper interview that the British must fight to the last ditch. Geikie-Cobb relayed the invitation, and within a few days Shaw personally delivered a text to his office. When the talk was submitted to the Minister of Information, Alfred Duff Cooper (1890–1954), later first Viscount Norwich of Aldwick, he returned the manuscript to Tallents with the words "I won't have that man on the air." Geikie-Cobb (as Anthony Weymouth) published the banned broadcast, called "The Unavoidable Subject," in his *Journal of the War Years and One Year Later* (1948). After visiting Shaw on 21st June to explain the situation, Geikie-Cobb noted in the journal, "No one who knows him and appreciates the humanity which prompts his actions can do otherwise than admire him. 'A prophet, etc.' Yes. We don't like people who have been right long before we ourselves have even seen the point. Shaw, the prophet, will yet—and very shortly—come into his own. Shaw, the man, is completely and irresistibly lovable."]

Dear Mr Weymouth

No use my trying to broadcast my notion of what we are fighting for when the P.M. is committing himself to Back to 1919, and the Information Ministry wont let me broadcast at all. I shall have to confine myself to articles in The Daily Worker.

Besides, the situation has gone beyond ultimate discussions. If I were P.M. I should declare war on France and instantly capture the French fleet, which would presumably surrender without a shot if it were assured that the declaration was pro forma.

I do not believe in the blockade, as it sets all Europe against us and starves every European country *except* Germany. We shall have enough to do to avoid being blockaded ourselves.

I am afraid you must keep me out of Portland Place if you wish to keep yourself in it, which I consider highly desirable.

G. Bernard Shaw

To ADA TYRRELL

[C/1]

4 Whitehall Court S W 1
27th June 1940

No holidays this year nor perhaps next. No petrol, no money, and a strong moral obligation to stay where we are and pretend that we don't care a dump for Adolf the Conqueror. So I shall carry on as usual, Saturday afternoon to Wednesday morning at Ayot St Lawrence, and Wednesday noon to Saturday afternoon at Whitehall, wondering how I shall pay my taxes next January, and writing words of wisdom to which nobody pays the slightest attention. . . .

Excuse the postcard. I cannot afford the extra penny for an envelope.

G.B.S.

To GABRIEL PASCAL

[U(A)/121]

4 Whitehall Court S W 1
28th February [June] 1940

[Military service had decimated the ranks of young actors available for Cusins. Stephen Murray (1912–83) had impressed Shaw by his performances in *Misalliance, The Simpleton of the Unexpected Isles*, and *On the Rocks* at the Malvern Festival 1935–36. Alec Guinness (b. 1914) made a dazzling success as Hamlet in a modern-dress production at the Old Vic in 1938; he did not make his screen début until 1946. Although Pascal strongly desired Leslie Howard for Cusins, Shaw was firm in his opposition to this casting, not only because Howard was too old, but because Shaw had disliked his interpretation of Higgins. The rôle eventually went to Rex Harrison (b. 1908), young, handsome, and debonair, who had rapidly earned a reputation for his stage appearances in *French without Tears* (1936) and *Design for Living* (1939) and film appearances in *The Citadel, St Martin's Lane*, and the just-completed *Night Train to Munich*.]

564

My dear Gabriel

Don't give way to fancies about my moods. I am a proper tracksman and not a gentleman-amateur with moods. When there is a job to be done I do it, as you know, without waiting for moods. But this thing that you want is

W R O N G

and mustn't be done. The play must begin with two people, rousing interest in two *new* couples, all six piling up the interest in Undershaft, the protagonist. Then they must go away one after the other until even Lady Britomart goes and leaves Stephen to finish the sequence *alone*. It would be utterly spoilt if you introduced the two couples before Brit & Stephen have prepared their appearance. The unity of place must be kept unbroken throughout: a change to the nursery would break it, and cost a new scene which would do nothing but mischief. So put it out of your too active mind.

The stills are splendid. Barbara must keep sunny—no Maiden's Prayer business—until the blow of Bodger's Whiskey falls.

I expected the trouble about Cusins. Stephen Murray is, I suppose, unobtainable; but there is a young actor named Guinness whom you ought to see. L.H. is quite out of the question: be adamant on that. If you cannot get the right man, take the bull by the horns and change Hudd to Cusins. He is wasted on Stephen, who is much easier to cast.

> In great haste to catch the post: therefore
> brusque,
> G.B.S.

To GABRIEL PASCAL

4 Whitehall Court SW 1
[H/1; X/396.e]   6th July 1940

["I agree dramatically with what you say about the unity of place," Pascal replied on 3rd July, "but leave it to me, without going into polemics, to keep my faithfulness to you as artist, and at the same time to cut away when that is demanded by the iron law of movement, which is the basic element of the cinema (and the reason why it is also called 'movies'). So please have faith in my judgment where to intercut short movements, always respecting your dialogue. I only do it in extreme necessity" (S(H)/121).

Pascal's backers were unsuccessful in their effort to supplant him with Anthony Asquith as director of the uncompleted film. Leslie Howard was

565

co-director, with Asquith, of *Pygmalion*. Charles Moss Woolf (1879–1943), Managing Director of General Theatre Corporation, and Nicholas Davenport (1895–1979), financial journalist and economic adviser, shared a financial interest with film titan J. Arthur Rank in *Major Barbara*.]

My dear Gabriel

As I feared, you have made a worse financial mess of Barbara than you did of Pygmalion. Things have now come to a crisis at which the film has already cost twice what it should. Yet it is still unfinished. The financiers wont go on; the cast is exhausted and sulky; and you have lost your head. And the financiers' notion of saving the situation is to call in Anthony Asquith, L. H. having opened his mouth too wide!

Now here are my instructions, which you must obey like a lamb. You will finish screening my script *without a single retake*, until you have it complete. When it is finished, and not until then, you will go through the rushes and be satisfied with what is good enough, no matter how much better you could make it if you had another hundred thousand pounds and another six months. Any sequences that are really unpresentable you can then retake. Nobody with any artistic or technical pretensions is to be allowed to interfere with you; but Woolf and Davenport must stand over you with revolvers and stop you ruthlessly if you waste a penny or a foot of film by attempting to take anything twice over. The cast must absolutely refuse to do anything twice over. You must finish, finish, finish at all sacrifices until *a* Barbara film is ready for release, no matter how far it may fall short of *the* film of which you dream.

If you do this Woolf and the bank will recover their lost confidence in you; the cast will recover their spirits; and Davenport may be able to induce them to go on when they see that they are no longer throwing good money after bad.

This is clear and exact: will you do it or wont you?

If you would like to come to Ayot St Lawrence on Sunday at 12.30, so that we can have an hour before lunch for a glorious row, do so (let me know tomorrow); for I can stand up to you and none of the rest can. The situation is desperate; and you alone can retrieve it by doing seriously what I tell you.

Ring up Whitehall tomorrow.

Your thoroughly alarmed and now iron jawed
GBS

To RONALD GOW

4 Whitehall Court S W 1
[H&A/1]   [Undated: *c.* July 1940]

[Playwright Ronald Gow (b. 1897) is the husband of Wendy Hiller. "Gabriel
Pascal was full of new ideas for altering *Major Barbara*," Gow informed
Dan H. Laurence on 13th January 1986, "and I had been forced to listen
to them. At one time there was to be a night-club scene with 'lovvly vimmen'
and I sent Pascal some of my own ideas. Unknown to me Pascal showed
these to Shaw. Hence the letter from Shaw in which I have been blamed
for things I didn't do and which were quite a surprise to me. But it does
represent Shaw's declaration of freedom to write his own script—which
must have surprised Pascal as well." Mary Pickford (1893–1979) and Douglas
Fairbanks (1883–1939), whose "perfect marriage" was dissolved five years
earlier, were teamed on the screen only once, in *The Taming of the Shrew*
(1929).]

Dear Ronald Gow

Pascal sent me the enclosed. I had, however, anticipated you by
making my own scenario.

When you come to do this sort of job for yourself, as you very likely
will, you must be very careful how you introduce your characters. The
star plan is to talk about them before they appear so as to make the
audience curious to see them, and sufficiently informed about them to
save them the trouble of explaining their circumstances. But as some
of the characters must begin the play and cannot be prepared in this
way, you must either fall back on the Parisian wellmade play formula
and begin with a conversation between the butler and housemaid or
else start the characters with a strongly assertive scene, like Richard III.

In Barbara Lady Britomart introduces herself like Richard; but
Todger Fairmile (who, by the way, does not appear at all in the play)
is introduced very effectively by Shirley and Walker. In your version
you have thrown away all the introductions and presented Todger as a
nobody.

You have also quite disregarded building up the interest to the
climaxes of the play, cutting it up into little pieces like a jig saw puzzle,
but assuming that it did not matter in what order you put them together again. The havoc you wrought by this is not to be described.
It is not the story that matters but the way it is told. You think that
it is the story that matters and not the way it is told. That delusion
will be your ruin if you really entertain it, which you probably dont on
reflection.

The moral is, never work to a ready made plot unless you are merely manufacturing a detective play. Let the play grow naturally and it will come right. Cut it in bits and force it into a pattern, and you will get nothing but a mechanized abortion.

The legalization in England of marriage with a deceased wife's sister or husband's brother is quite recent and did not exist at Cusins's birth. It knocked Barbara out of date; but as it also knocked out Hamlet I left it as it was in good company.

It is no use trying to shift the interest of a play to adapt it to a lower class of audience. The result is neither the one thing nor the other: it is spoiled for both audiences. And of all such attempts the most hopeless is to deshavianize and Hollywoodize a Shavian play. Barbara & Cusins will not do as Mary & Doug.

Tell Wendy to make them dress the sister as brilliantly as possible, as Barbara has to get her effect by dressing *against* her. The secret of effective dressing, as Ellen Terry knew, was never to be in the fashion: that is, like everybody else, but always like nobody on earth.

Excuse this scrawl
G.Bernard Shaw

To EDITH CRAIG

4 Whitehall Court SW1
17th July 1940

[I.hc.u/9]

[Edith Craig and Christopher St John, in a joint letter on 3rd July, requested a message for a commemorative ceremony on 21st July, the twelfth anniversary of Ellen Terry's death. Shaw's letter was read at the "little reunion of people" and symposium, in which Edith Evans was a participant. The Barn Theatre commemorative performances at Smallhythe each year had been curtailed by the war, hence the revised format of the ceremony.]

My dear Edy

The ancient Pagans, who had a much keener sense of public decency than we have, used to close all their civilized temples when they went to war, and keep only the Barbarian ones open. I am not at all sure that you ought not to close the Barn Theatre, Ellen's temple, for the duration. Possibly the military authorities will close it under the Emergency Act. They would if they had any sense; for no matter how often and how loudly we recite the warlike slogans from Richard the Second and Henry the Fifth, those of us who are old enough to have heard Ellen telling us that "the quality of mercy is not strained" have only to recall her voice to become incapable of killing the Germans or anyone else. The worst we can wish even for Mr Hitler himself is to hear him told off by Ellen, not in a railway carriage, but in the court of the Doge in Venice.

My own excessive age, though it tends to make me an intolerable bore, personally repulsive to the young, gives me one advantage over them. I can remember Ellen and all her contemporary rivals as young creatures in the first bloom of their youth. They are all dead now; so we are free to speak all the evil of them that we could not utter during their lives without hurting their feelings very illnaturedly. I can still feel the shock that Johnstone Forbes-Robertson gave me when I heard him allude to the fascinating Madge Robertson as Old Mar Kendal.

There is not such a thing as an actress type: any sort of woman may be an actress; but Ellen was not a sort of woman: she was absolutely unique, and so extraordinarily unlike Madge that I was not surprised when she said, not at all illnaturedly, "Mrs Kendal is my idea of hell." I once tried to talk to Mrs Kendal in her own house, but could not get in a word edgeways, though I was by no means an exceptionally silent man. She talked so well and so continually that she never listened, and consequently never learnt anything except her stage parts, with the result that to the day of her quite recent death she spoke of Irving as a ridiculous young pretender, and of the cinema as a vulgar penny gaff with which no selfrespecting player could possibly be connected.

The greatest English-speaking contemporary of Ellen and Madge was the Irish-American actress Ada Rehan, whose extraordinarily beautiful voice and noble style made her irresistible in Shakespear. And this brings me to the interesting question of how far the tiptop actresses of the last half of the nineteenth century differed from Sybil Thorndike and Edith Evans today. I can best answer this by a scrap of history. When I wrote Captain Brassbound's Conversion for Ellen, my American agent Elisabeth Marbury took it on herself, without my knowledge, to recommend it to Ada Rehan. Ada snubbed her ruthlessly, demanding what she meant by sending her a thing that was not a play at all, and had only one woman in it, and she an old one. By an old woman Ada meant any woman over eighteen. Years later, when her career, as it proved, was closed, I read Brassbound to her. It excited her to an extent that amazed me. At the end she rose and strode up and down the room, protesting incoherently. "You do not know" she said. "This is something new. We were expected to be young, to be willowy, to be beautiful. It is wonderful stuff; but it is different." Then she added, with a professional touch, "And oh! the man's part is so good."

The truth is, the stage in the nineteenth century had become so completely differentiated from the living world outside that there were no real women in the plays except heavily caricatured low comedy ones; and what the leading actresses had to do was to provide an embodiment of romantic charm and keep it up with an air of being human and soulful without having a single touch of nature in the lines and gestures dictated by the author's script. This was not an easy job. Ellen Terry, Madge Robertson, and Ada Rehan had to acquire a technique of which our young actresses have no conception, because they had to make bricks without straw. What the author asked for was charm without brains; and unless they could smuggle in something of their own between the lines the play could not succeed. When in my first play I made the heroine lose her temper and half strangle the parlormaid I produced an uproar that raged in the London press for a whole fortnight. I could never have induced Ellen or Madge or Ada to do such a thing on the stage: it had to be done by a young and very imperfectly professionalized actress who was in full revolt against the romantic conventions, and who heartily agreed with an aphorism of mine which ran "Home, sweet home, is the girl's prison and the woman's workhouse ['Maxims for Revolutionists']." She belonged to a sect called the Revolted Daughters, a classification now forgotten. I believe the first revolted daughters must have been the daughters of great actresses of the old school; for to live in the same little house with a mother of overwhelming vitality, and a vocal technique capable of dominating a thousand people in a theatre, must have made it difficult for their children to call their souls their own, even when their mothers were as lovable off stage as on, which was not always the case.

In between the nineteenth-century actresses and the twentieth-century ones came the *fin de siècle*: notably Lena Ashwell and Mrs Patrick Campbell, whose death only the other day brought her back into the headlines and awoke poignant memories of her. When both these actresses began, the theatre had been so knocked to pieces by Ibsen and by my half strangled parlormaid that they had to teach themselves and develop their own technique. By Mrs Kendal's standards Lena Ashwell had no technique at all; but her salary was Mrs Kendal's salary multiplied by ten. Mrs Patrick Campbell cared too little for plays and playacting as such to be always a great actress; but she was beyond all question a great enchantress, how or why I do not know, as her attraction was a quite unaccountable magic operating infallibly on men and women alike. Unfortunately, she was possessed of a devil who obliged her to torment everybody whom she did not care to fascinate, with the result that the production of a play in which she played was an experience so terrible for the manager, the author, and her fellow players that however much money she made for them, or however long their engagements lasted, nothing but the direct necessity could ever induce them to go through it again. She had made a small fortune for George Alexander and for Arthur Pinero; but when I wrote Pygmalion for her, Alexander, foreseeing its success, offered to engage for me any actress I could name in the whole world, at whatever price, except only Mrs Patrick Campbell, as he was prepared to die in the workhouse rather than go through another London run with her. And Pinero's Iris, which she would have played to perfection, went to an American actress [Fay Davis] who was full of solid character: just what Iris should never have suggested. Pygmalion proved my greatest London success so far; but though Mrs Campbell was exactly what I wanted for the part of Hesione Hushabye in Heartbreak House, and a later part: that of Orinthia in The Apple Cart, was such a vivid sketch of herself that I read it to her and altered what she disliked in it before letting anyone else see it, I did not cast her either for it or for Hesione because I was afraid that she would wreck the production, and set everyone in the theatre by the ears; and my plays are too risky to take chances like that. I have said picturesquely that she was possessed by a devil; but what was really the matter with her was a lack of *savoir vivre* so complete that she never learnt how to live in the real world. Forbes Robertson's criticism of her as "very limited" technically was so true that once at rehearsal, when I asked her to take a step forward to get out of the way of another character—a trivial thing that any skilled actress would have done mechanically—she harangued me to the effect that a great actress never repeated a movement until I was provoked into calling her "a Belsize Park amateur." I am ashamed of having forgotten myself as a producer to this extent; but it gained me the eternal devotion of Marion Terry, who was on the stage at the time and whose opinion of Mrs Campbell's technique it exactly expressed. I nearly died of keeping my temper with Mrs Campbell professionally, though off the stage there was not a cloud in the sky. Like Barrie and everyone else whom she wanted to ensnare I was in love with her; but as I never imagined that I could possibly live in the house with her for two days, I resisted all her attempts to make me elope with her; and our relations remained quite innocent to the end. She was not in love with me nor with anyone else; but it amused her to give proofs of her power to upset everyone, whether it was an actor trying to play his part instead of being her courtier, or a husband who presumed to give first place to his wife. Yet with all this she had her noble moments, and without being at all extravagant could not keep the money she earned, because she gave too much of it away. She died unknown to our younger generation, and would have died penniless but for an income left her by the late Mrs Bridget Guinness, another enchantress and even a more beautiful one. The two enchantresses enchanted one another; and Mrs Guinness's last request to her husband was, in King Charles's phrase[,] "Let not Stella starve."

This intermediate generation of leading London actresses of the *fin de siècle* had the advantage of complete emancipation from male management. Ellen Terry and Ada Rehan had to attach their careers to those of Henry Irving and Augustin Daly; and Mrs Kendal was inseparable from her husband, who was a popular actor-manager. Most unfortunately for them these three managers remained untouched by the new movement in drama, which enormously increased the importance of women and consequently the opportunities for actresses. All the good pioneering actresses like Janet Achurch and Elizabeth Robins, who, without theatres or backers, had either to ruin themselves financially every time they created one of the great Ibsen parts or, like Alma Murray and Florence Farr, find a woman pioneer in management, of which species there was only one, Miss Horniman; and she, after a single experiment in London which let me loose on the British stage, shook the dust of London from her feet, and started the system of professional repertory theatres which has since played so important a part in British theatrical development. Only you yourself, dear Edy, and the much less enterprising Stage Societies, were left to enlighten the poor old metropolis.

Lena Ashwell and Mrs Campbell did not suffer from this slavery to unprogressive male management. Lena's career was not identified with any management; and no management could stand much of Mrs Campbell.

As to our stars of today, the male actors who would have been their managers and the dictators of their destinies fifty years ago are now their mere appendages. Try to imagine Ellen Terry bringing the script of [St John Ervine's] Robert's Wife or [Emlyn Williams's] The Corn is Green to Irving, who found The Man of Destiny and Captain Brassbound's Conversion, the most appallingly old fashioned star plays I have ever perpetrated, too advanced for him. The effort paralyzes me: the pen drops from my hand. So no more today from

yours always, dear Edy
[G. Bernard Shaw]

572

4 Whitehall Court SW1
[H/1]   15th August 1940

[Donat, who toured as Dick Dudgeon in *The Devil's Disciple* with the Old
Vic the preceding autumn, was appearing in a revival at the Piccadilly
Theatre, which opened on 24th July. The staging was by Milton Rosmer,
who appeared as Burgoyne. Roger Livesey (1906–76), a fixture in the West
End in the 1930s, was Anthony Anderson. Rosamund John (b. 1913), whose
stage and screen career had barely commenced, played Judith. James
Sheridan Knowles (1784–1862), author of *The Love Chase* (1837), was an
Irish-born dramatist, cousin of Sheridan.]

Dear Robert Donat

I saw the show yesterday. It was a queer experience; for the play
was simplified and changed in unexpected ways. You had an immense
success as a good-natured blackguard, always a popular character on
the stage. As the years go on you will add other sides of the Devil's
Disciple to that simple one, and end up as a tragic figure, sardonic,
sensitive, a fanatic and a gentleman, until you have built up the complete Richard, by which time you will be over sixty; and the play will
be drawing £200 a week.

However, you are doing very well for both of us meanwhile. Sufficient for the day is the success thereof.

The new feature in the play was the discovery that the minister,
announced as having married a pretty wife, had in fact married an
escaped lunatic. The effect is queer and rather funny; but it is hard on
poor Livesey to have his big scene stolen from him by a madwoman
screaming him off the stage. Milton's speciality as a producer is Pace,
Pace, and nothing but Pace; no play, but Pace; and the same pace and
tone for everybody with all the cues picked up and fielded like cricket
balls by a county eleven at play. The slow-witted dazed Christie
[Jonathan Field] was so swift and mercurial that he only needed a few
more lines to eclipse you as the genius of the family. The first act is
totally unintelligible until your entry. Hard on you, as you have to
burst into a picture without a background. Not my fault, I assure you.

Why on earth is [Henry] Caine cast for Swindon (anybody can play
Swindon) instead of for the sergeant, who is very important and just
the part for him? And why is his exit speech, which gingers up the
British retreat, cut? And why is the capable old lawyer Hawkins
represented by his junior clerk [William Murray]?

The staging of the last scene is very poor. Milton has evidently

573

never been hanged by the military. I hope he will be, just to larn him.

After your exit in the second act there should be no black-out. The curtain should come down for a moment during which a continuous drum-roll (not too loud) holds the audience, and then rise on the half-darkened stage with the candle guttering out. The faint is horribly mismanaged; she should drop like a stone. The directions are plain; but nothing will persuade Milton that I know my business.

This is a nice cheerful letter; but it must come to an end. The returns are all right. Hurrah!

yours faithfully
G. Bernard Shaw

PS Your Squire Wildrake dress is wrong. Richard cares too much for his father not to be dressed in enough black to be accepted by the sergeant as a possible parson. And he should be of a superior class to the rest in his own right.

Tell Uncle William [Edgar K. Bruce] that he is much the best of the lot.

To GABRIEL PASCAL

4 Whitehall Court SW1
[H/1]   16th August 1940

Dear Gabriel

I think it would be unwise to give the Americans a Hepburn impression of Joan immediately before Wendy. It might make Wendy quite inacceptable. The present impression is one left by Cornell, which will be on the whole helpful. I shall therefore not license any American Joan until the film is safely established.

I saw The Devil's Disciple on Wednesday. The production is so outrageously bad that if I could have done so without breaking my neck I should have jumped from my box on to the stage and rehearsed it before the audience. On the screen it would be quite impossible. The minister's wife, instead of being a pretty nonentity, is a raving madwoman. The whole affair is provincial, and second-rate at that. The final scene with the gallows is ridiculous. I wish I had seen it earlier: I would not for worlds have let you get an impression of the play from it.

The secret of its success is plain enough. Richard, instead of being a tragic figure and a complicated character, is played by Donat as a goodnatured blackguard: always a popular part on the stage. The rest is mere "support" for him. This simplifies the play and secures an Elephant and Castle success thanks to Donat's popularity (he does it very well); but it would not make a Pascal success; and there is no proof in it that Donat can give us the real Devil's Disciple.

I left the theatre without saying a word in praise of the performance; and I have written to Donat about it in terms which make my opinion of it quite clear. I have no objection to his being present at the screening: in fact I should like to meet him. Probably he is right about an American actor being desirable for Richard; but the part is on the plane on which there is no nationality. The sergeant and the two British officers would have to be English. With Trouncer as Anderson and either Thesiger or Arliss as Burgoyne I could make a production that would astonish the simpletons who think the show at the Piccadilly a good one.

I dont think Madame Charlotte will venture to make a day of it at Denham; but if we could drive there for an hour or so at half-past four or five I daresay I could persuade her to come. But when I am in London I can always run down by train.

G. Bernard Shaw

To ALFRED DOUGLAS

4 Whitehall Court S W 1

[H/64; X/394]   28th August 1940

[John Bright, Liberal statesman, fought for political, financial, and religious reform. Benjamin Disraeli (1804–81), first Earl of Beaconsfield, was one of Britain's greatest nineteenth-century prime ministers. The final paragraph is added in holograph.]

Importunate Childe
    ... We also sleep through the raids. My wife does not give a damn for bombs, but dreads shelters and prefers death to getting up and dressing. After all bed is the proper place to die in.

Why do you recommend me to go to Russia? I've been there. It is a paradise: no ladies and gentlemen there.

The Catholic Church is like democracy, an eternal ideal, noble and beneficent as such; but all attempts to manufacture it in the concrete reduce it to absurdity. Read my old play John Bull's Other Island. Father Keegan is an ideal Catholic; and he is "silenced" for his pains.

Father Dempsey is the very parochial reality. Democracy was great in the XIXth century, when Gladstone and Bright and Dizzy [Disraeli] and your father believed in it. What is it now when every fool and every flapper has a vote? Government by the unqualified, chosen by the if possible less qualified. Russia shoots such impostors. Can you blame her?

I made surprise visits to churches in Russia, and found priests in gorgeous vestments blazing away, with congregations genuflecting, prostrating, smiting the ground with their foreheads as if the Vatican had annexed the Kremlin; but there were only about 15 worshippers, including myself; and I left before the collection.

Miss Patch has made a frightful mess of this letter. She must be out of sorts. Forgive her.

G. Bernard Shaw

To STEPHEN GWYNN

[H/73]

4 Whitehall Court SW1
28th August 1940

[Stephen Gwynn (1864–1950), Irish poet, novelist, and journalist, was an M.P. from 1906 to 1918 and a member of the Irish Convention 1917–18. The book he had edited was *Scattering Branches: Tributes to the Memory of W.B. Yeats* (published in July). Shaw and Yeats were at Coole Park together in August 1910. Maud Gonne McBride (1866–1953), celebrated beauty who acted in Yeats's *Cathleen ni Houlihan* (1891), later became a revolutionary. The Shaws had seen the Abbey Players' production of *Kathleen ni Houlihan* on a triple bill with Lady Gregory's *The Workhouse Ward* and Shaw's *The Shewing-up of Blanco Posnet*, presented in London under the auspices of the Stage Society on 5th December 1909.]

Dear Stephen Gwynn

I have just found a letter from you dated the 21st September which I should have answered at once and didnt. As at my age (84) I forget everything in ten minutes, the occurrence is not unusual; but as yours is a special case I feel specially apologetic about it.

Somehow I cannot write about Yeats in the way proper to the volume you have in hand. I was always on very good terms with him personally; but I was not on literary terms with him; did not read enough of him to pontificate about his work; and did not get into his movement at all. At first he amused me because of Gilbert's entirely

576

unsuccessful attempt to put Wilde on the stage as Bunthorne in Patience. Bunthorne was not a bit like Wilde; but he presently came to life in the person of W. B. Y., who outBunthorned him enough to make him seem commonplace. Not until I spent some time in the house with him at Lady Gregory's, years later, did I learn what a penetrating critic and good talker he was; for he played none of his Bunthorne games, and saw no green elephants, at Coole.

One of my most vivid memory pictures is of a pitch black night in Chancery Lane (of all places) when into a circle of light under an arc lamp there suddenly stepped, walking towards me, Yeats with his wing of raven black hair swinging across his forehead and Maud Gonne, dazzlingly beautiful in white silk, both of them in evening dress. The pair were quite beyond description. I was invisible in the dark as they passed on; and of course I did not intrude. That was the only time I ever saw her.

The Abbey Players were enormously interesting, both technically and poetically, and brought me into closer relations with him. At Kathleen ni Houlihan my wife filled the box with her tears; and though I was by that time a hardened professional in the theatre I was quite touched by it. But Ireland meant something then that cut no ice outside the island of saints; and to this day I cannot place Yeats objectively enough to attempt an appreciation of him.

He was given to elaboration to such an extent that instead of letting well alone he sometimes spoilt his rhythms trying to make them supersubtle. I allow myself only a proof, a revise, and a final revise to check the corrections, not to make fresh ones. I am too tidy to adopt Shakespear's plan of never blotting a line, but going on to the next play without wasting time on revising Hamlet instead of writing Macbeth.

If I were a professor and not a practitioner I should write you an analysis of the difference between Moore and Yeats. As it is I can find nothing suitable to say.

always yours
G. Bernard Shaw

To C. H. NORMAN

Ayot St Lawrence. Welwyn
[C/4]   18th September 1940

[The Shaws had returned to Ayot from London a day before the start of Germany's air bombardment (see next letter) early in September. They remained at Shaw's Corner until August 1941, when they visited the Astors at Cliveden. Blanche Patch, frightened away from London by the violent air attacks, joined them in the country on 11th September. The *Major Barbara* "newsreel" was actually a trailer or "visual prologue," filmed at Denham on 12th September, to be screened in American film theatres by way of advertisement for forthcoming showings of the film.

Romain Rolland, an internationalist who took a neutral position during the first world war, wrote articles in Switzerland urging the French and the Germans to recall their cultural past, and calling upon their intellectuals to cease screaming at each other and act in a civilised manner. These articles were collected in 1915 as *Au dessus de la mêlée* (*Above the Conflict*).]

All well in the little village, with no shelters and only a squeaky siren which sometimes echoes Harpenden [a nearby town] (audible here in a west wind) and sometimes doesnt. So far, no damage.

I got the muzzle off unexpectedly in a newsreel for America to advertize the film of Major Barbara. I had some fun with it; but in my 85th year I can only *planer au dessus de la melée* like Romain Rolland when the siren does not remind me that I am crawling *au dessous des bombiers*.

Perhaps it is as well that none of them know what they are fighting for except a victory. There will be a deuce of a mess when they find out; so let us hope they wont, and that the war will reduce itself to absurdity presently.

All the French generals of 1914–18 detest us. An alliance in the field is a perpetual squabble.

GBS

To [OTTO KYLLMANN] CONSTABLE & CO.

[C/64]

Ayot St Lawrence. Welwyn
24th September 1940

[The German blitz of London commenced on the evening of 7th September when enemy raiding planes penetrated to the heart of the city and set fire to the Surrey docks. High-flying aircraft, eluding searchlights and anti-aircraft weaponry, hovered over the city all night, killing over four hundred people, seriously injuring some fifteen hundred, and causing much property damage. All-night raids became commonplace now, as the Battle of London continued unabated for a considerable period. On 18th September an incendiary bomb struck the quire stock warehouse of the Leighton-Straker bindery, destroying nearly ninety thousand unbound sets of sheets of Shaw's works, plus their dustwrappers.]

The Germans have done what Constables have never succeeded in doing. They have disposed of 86,701 sheets of my works in less than 24 hours.

Have we enough bound stock to go on with? Leightons have not told me how much bound stock they hold—if any.

On the afternoon before the Blitzkrieg started, Mrs Shaw had a fall and hurt her knees so severely that I had to help her about. She is mending slowly.

Meanwhile, a good excuse for me to skulk down here and look on at the firework display over London 30 miles off. However, we have a pipsqueak siren that echoes all the alarms and an occasional bomb near enough to make us jump. We have no shelter and no fire brigade; but our beds are fairly comfortable.

How about you?

GBS

To ROBERT DONAT

[H/1; X/411]

Ayot St Lawrence. Welwyn
9th October 1940

["Bow Wow acting," or "Yapping," is a term denoting a declamatory style of performing. Forbes-Robertson was indispensable for *Cæsar and Cleopatra*, Shaw informed J.E.Vedrenne in 1905, as "Caesar is a big bow-wow part of the leading legitimate first magnitude" (Sotheby sale, 13th November 1929). "As a producer," Shaw stated in his preface to Lillah McCarthy's *Myself and My Friends* (1933), "I went back to the forgotten heroic stage business and the exciting or impressive declamation I had learnt from old-timers like Ristori, Salvini, and Barry Sullivan. . . . I was continually struggling with the conscientious efforts of our players to underdo their parts lest they should be considered stagey." *The Devil's Disciple* toured the provinces for eight weeks following its London engagement. Shaw's reference to "the Adored" indicates he was aware of Donat's offstage infatuation with his leading lady.]

Dear Robert Donat

As you are starting again on tour, and may have to do some rehearsal with new people and local supers, let me give you a few hints about Bow Wow acting which became extinct before your time, but which I remember quite well, and for which I have written many of my plays, including The Devil's Disciple.

In a play in which you are the star, and in which your entrance is prepared by the beginners instead of, as in Richard III, being started by the star himself, coach the beginners very carefully so that they make the audience understand the situation and be interested in you before you come on. Remember that for the first five minutes or so the audience is quite in the dark and has not got its ears in; so that the speeches and business must be slow and very distinct. If they are gabbled through and slurred as if they didnt matter, and must be got over as fast as possible, which is what happened at the Piccadilly, they might as well be cut right out, leaving the star to face an audience which knows nothing about him instead of all about him.

Never make your entry into a crowd, and form merely one of it. The star must always be a figure apart. When you enter in the first act, everyone must be sitting down except Uncle William at the extreme side. There should be a long, awkward, solemn pause of silent prayer for the dead, broken only by Christy's lumpish (not smart) "Here's Dick." The door opens (no kick) and there stands the D's D in black, silent and saturnine, surveying the family. Except for the sudden chucking of his hat at Christy, which makes everybody start, he is slow, sardonic, bitter, picking out each relative for an insult. Not until Anderson says "You are in the presence of my wife" (or whatever the line is) is he surprised into being a gentleman, and dropping his acting for an instant.

You will see that this entry is entirely spoiled if Richard bursts into a mob of relatives and becomes one the mob. They must all sit, Uncle William out of the line of sight. The funeral atmosphere must be kept up carefully. Otherwise, Richard has nothing to play against.

Never have a scene or an object on the stage that the audience cannot help looking at instead of the players. No matter whether it is a gallows or a stray cat or an obtrusively painted backcloth, the effect is disastrous. That monstrous gallows reduces the actors to insignificance. It should be, as I directed, upstage on the O.P. side and presented so that Richard and not it shall be conspicuous when he mounts the cart. I say the cart, which should be drawn in by two of the soldiers, who stand by to pull it away when the signal is given. Actually, soldiers do it with a kitchen table instead of a cart, but that would get an undesirable laugh on the stage. The method of hanging exhibited at the Piccadilly was absurdly impossible.

As to the Adored, I do not know whether you dare say anything to her except to assure her that her name will rank with that of Sarah Siddons in the annals of the theatre; but if I were producing I should ask her whether she has ever heard of a clergyman's wife going to a house of mourning in a white skirt. I should then instruct her to put on, over her more intimate undies, a pair of stays, a heavy flannel petticoat reaching to her ankles, a white petticoat of stiff linen with "Russian embroidery" round the hem, reaching to her instep, and a black skirt reaching to the ground. I should then say "Now dart about the stage like Puck starting to put a girdle round the earth in 40 minutes if you can." I should then get a first-rate make-up artist from the film studio to make her look not a day over twenty. The parson must be convicted of marrying a much too young and pretty girl, and not of having married his grandmother.

Then, as to the acting, I should try to make her begin by remembering her superior station as the minister's wife, and *condescending* very nicely to Mrs Dudgeon, who isnt having any. I should teach her, when she has a tragedy part, not to plaster the tragedy all over the part before it begins, and produce the impression that she is an escaped lunatic.

And I should tell her uncompromisingly that if she tried to steal the end of the second act from Anderson by bawling all over the stage and ruining his vital scene, I should have to sack her. It is hard enough for Anderson to produce the necessary volcanic effect with the utmost help she can give him. With her playing against him, it is impossible. She must be in weak, hopeless, pitiable despair all the way through, not raising her voice for a moment, and obeying his orders in dazed astonishment. When he goes out, the stage should still be all amazement at the transformation; and her last words will give her the curtain she now shouts for in vain.

You say that the Sergeant [Grenville Darling] did not omit his big exit with the drum marking time for British Grenadiers and the soldiers sticking their chins up. If so, he did it *sotto voce*; for I didnt hear it.

That is enough for the present. It is as much as I can tell you by letter; but it is enough to effect a considerable change if you take it all in. Anyhow, I can no more today.

G. Bernard Shaw

PS   Tell Mrs Dudgeon [Janet Barrow] not to be really crying when she enters to the guests. She holds her handkerchief to her eyes as a matter of form, but is boiling with fury inside.

Make as much as you can of the impression that Anderson's magnanimity makes on Richard before the supper scene. That is why he finds it impossible to betray him.

I am staying in the country at present; but do not bother to write.

To WILLIAM J. PICKERILL

[H/119]

Ayot St Lawrence. Welwyn
10th October 1940

[Although many of Shaw's letters from this period were written on stationery printed Whitehall Court, all were written from Ayot. (Sir) William J. Pickerill (1892–1955), English-born conductor and bassoonist, was conductor of the Cape Town Municipal Orchestra, South Africa, 1926–46. Sir Henry Wood (1869–1944) was the venerable founder and conductor of the Queen's Hall Promenade Concerts from 1895 until the bombing of the hall in 1941; he carried on at the Royal Albert Hall until 1944. Wood helped to form the B.B.C. Symphony Orchestra in 1930.]

My dear Pickerill

Presumably the municipality has by this time learnt the lesson that we learnt in London in August 1914: that patriotism in music does not pay. War broke out then when our London Promenade concerts had just started for the season. At once all German music was struck out of the program. Mozart, Beethoven, Mendelssohn and Wagner, were classed with the Kaiser and banned. Everyone applauded this patriotic gesture; and for three nights Sir Henry Wood's orchestra played to an empty house. On the Thursday Sir Henry announced a Wagner program.

The hall was crowded.

Since then our concerts have been totally unpatriotic but highly popular. I suggest that you at once announce Mozart's E flat Symphony with a note in the program "Can it be believed that the country which produced this great composer, the friend of all the world, can now produce nothing better than the degenerate Adolf Hitler?" Or Mendelssohn's Italian symphony with "If Mendelssohn were alive today he would be sharing the exile of Einstein." Or the Good Friday music with "Herr Hitler delights in this music and believes himself to be a blend of Parsifal and Lohengrin. The Gestapo kept Wagner out of Germany for twelve years; and the king who welcomed him back was certified as mad."

But perhaps you had better play all the German classics and say nothing about it. If those members of the municipality who have no music in their souls object, shew them the balance sheet, as Sir Henry Wood did.

faithfully
G. Bernard Shaw

582

Ayot St Lawrence. Welwyn

[H/36]   23rd October 1940

[William Joyce (1908–46), Anglo-American propagandist who broadcast from Germany during the second World War to undermine Allied morale, was known as Lord Haw Haw because of his exaggerated drawl. He was tried after the war as a British traitor and hanged. Begonia Brown is a character in *Geneva*; the epitome of commonplace suburban womanhood, she is secretary to the International Committee for Intellectual Co-operation. The "Penguin sixpenny" became the Constable ten-shilling *Everybody's Political What's What?* in 1944. Murray's translation of Sophocles' *Antigone* in rhyming verse was published in 1941.]

My dear Murray

We are here in a village where there are no shelters, no fire brigade, no guns, nothing warlike except a searchlight and a little siren which explodes every ten minutes or so. As the raiders are highly scientific, and fly blindly by their instruments, they begin every night by bombarding us in the firm conviction that they are making direct hits on Churchill's hat when as a matter of fact they are missing mine by a mile or two and shaking the house to remind us that there is a war on and that we are all in the front line.

I began by being pigheaded and refusing to let them disturb my routine of $3\frac{1}{2}$ days in the country and $3\frac{1}{2}$ in town every week. This alarmed Providence for my safety. The day before the Blitz, as we were starting for town as usual, Charlotte fell and hurt her knees so badly that she had to be helped upstairs, and the journey to London was out of the question. She is well now; but the pigheadedness has been bombed out of us; and we havnt been up to Whitehall Court for seven weeks. We can see fireworks here from our windows, which is quite enough for us. Two of our windows and a door panel have been smashed by one of the 12 hits in the Whitehall district; but here we only get shaken. We console ourselves with the mathematical chances against our being hit; but the facts, as usual, ignore mathematics and strongly support the theory of a mystical human polarization by which some people attract bombs and torpedoes, and others repel them.

The village people all call the war senseless; but as they are as helpless as you and I there is nothing for it but fatalism, which the wireless calls our heroism, and a strong objection to allow Ittler to control our destinies. The childishness of the politicians is appalling. Churchill occasionally tells as much of the truth as he safely can over the wireless. Then he takes an audible gulp of his favorite stimulant and, with a

583

preliminary yell, gives the gallery a peroration and denounces Nazi scoundrels who actually bomb civilians, women and children. He is immediately followed by the news announcer, who begins by describing how the R.A.F. has rained bombs on the railway stations of Berlin etc. etc. In a sardonic mood one can turn on the Rome Radio, or Haw Haw, and listen to the news over again, with the names reversed, but the moral indignation an exact echo. But this poor amusement does not bear its daily repetition.

The clamor for a statement of war aims (as if anybody had any aims except with guns) does not interest me. What it comes to is a statement of the conditions on which we will stop fighting; and what we can demand with any hope of success depends on the odds for or against our winning the fight. When the odds are ten to one in our favor we can clearly demand much more than when they are merely even. When they are against us we cannot demand anything: we can only beg for mercy. At present the odds seem even or thereabouts; consequently I think Churchill is right when he decides that the position is not yet good enough to demand as much as will be on the cards if we get the odds on our side.

But why does not the League of Nations take the initiative? It is true that the Assembly does not exist, and cannot be resuscitated until the Powers consent to assemble. It would be no use if they did, as from the first it has been reduced to absurdity by the rule that its decisions must be unanimous. The fact is that when Chamberlain declared war it never even occurred to him that he should have referred the case to the League. So much for the Assembly.

But Begonia Brown still exists, and is indestructible as long as the Committee exists. What is to prevent her pointing out that it is not for the belligerents to declare their aims, which are necessarily selfish. It is for the intellectual élite to demand in the name of civilization why they are disturbing the peace of the world, and what they hope to gain by the senseless and horrible bombing match which they are at present carrying on. In England Hitler is exterminating the natives at the rate of 233 a day. There are 40 millions to be exterminated. Begonia can do arithmetic enough to demonstrate that at this rate it will take 470 years to finish the job, or, since the extermination of the women would be sufficient, say 235 years. Similar figures confront the R.A.F. The Committee can ask whether ministers entering on such programs can be regarded as sane. Then the Committee can state the minimum requirements of civilization as impartially as it can.

During the Four Years War Barbusse, Romain Rolland and Co, kept

584

asking me to sign some such manifesto. I told them that as they were nobodies the thing should be done through the Committee, of which they had never heard. Rolland wanted us to *planer au dessus de la melée*; and though I made fun of this it is what the Committee should try to do.

In "Geneva" I made fun of the Committee; but in such a way as to make this the first step to its publicity and popularity.

Roughly, do you think anything can be done in this direction. Are its members young enough? You are 74. I am 84. And we both know too much.

I am trying to write a Penguin sixpenny stating the facts that persons ought to know before they are allowed to vote or present themselves for election. They may have any opinions they like as to how to deal with the facts; but they must know the facts. Any person using abstract terms should be disqualified at once: measures not mouthings should be the rule. At present we are governed by people who do not know the world they are living in: the Old School Ties have the mentality of Edward III, and the Merchant Taylors that of Henry VII, whilst adult suffrage enables them to get elected by irresistible majorities with no political mentality, but with a strong snobbery which loves the Old School Tie and its associations.

This letter is too long: I must stop.

My love to Lady Mary.

Oh, I forgot. The filming of Major Barbara, now just completed, convinced me that the old beginning would not work, as nobody with the punch of Lady Britomart was available. So I had to begin with the first meeting of Cusins and Barbara, including his courting and proposal, all in ten minutes or thereabouts!!! It seemed impossible; but it came off quite well. I had to add dozens of new scenes. I wonder what you will think of them. It is so new to have a production-cost-limit of £200,000 instead of £200.

I await the Antigone. It is something to think about—and I often do think about it that though I have lived in the thick of a revolutionary burst of playwriting activity in London, the only plays that seem to me likely to survive it are the old Greek ones in your translations.

Do you ever see Granville-Barker now? He is not allowed to have any communication with me, as his Helen sticks pins into wax images of me; but we are—on my side certainly, as I suspect on his also—as good friends as ever.

enough

G. Bernard Shaw

... There goes the wretched siren.

To ALFRED DOUGLAS

Ayot St Lawrence. Welwyn
[H/64; X/394]   9th November 1940

[Douglas, violently anti-Irish as a result of Eire's position of neutrality in this war as in the last one, had underwritten the cost of a pamphlet *Ireland and the War against Hitler*, which consisted of an introduction by himself and a reprint of most of a chapter, "The Sinn Fein Rebellion," from Hervey de Montmorency's *Sword and Stirrup* (1936). Shaw had just given a self-drafted interview on the problem of the Irish ports to the journalist W. R. Titterton; it was published in the *Sunday Graphic* on 17th November as "G.B.S. to De Valera: 'Call in Britain,'" one of several interviews or articles on the subject that Shaw provided for British and American journals during this period.]

Impossible Childe

It is a relief to learn that the pamphlet is not an out-of-date attempt at Orange propaganda paid for with more or less secret service money, but an act of pure folly on your own private part. You certainly are a jumping sillybilly.

Now listen to me. At present it does not matter the millionth fraction of a tupenny damn what the Shinners and the Black and Tans did before the treaty. They are done with and mostly dead. Collins burnt the chateaux (including the one in which my wife was born) and the police stations. The Tans burnt the creameries and shops: I saw a champion sample of their work in Mallow. Collins, with the people on his side, had the better of the burning: the gentry dared not prosecute, and could only write privately to say that they were done. Collins won, and was immediately shot by his countrymen for it. I made his acquaintance a few days before his end. His nerves were in rags: his hand kept slapping his revolver all the time he was talking pleasantly enough. But all that is now ancient history: nobody with the least grip of the present situation has any time for it.

De Valera is in a frightfully difficult situation. The last thing he desires is a conquest of Ireland by Nazi Protestant-Atheists. But if he calls on England to fulfil her treaty obligations and re-occupy the Irish ports with British troops and British ships, he annuls Ireland's neutrality and not only infuriates the I.R.A., which he might in extremity dare to defy, but provokes Hitler to make Ireland the cockpit of the war, which would suit England down to the ground but which no Irishman could justify himself in doing. He must do just what he *is* doing: that is, stick to Ireland's neutrality and take his chance of an invasion. Fortunately invasion seems off just now; and Dev may win through;

586

but if it happens, then Churchill must reoccupy Ireland. It will be willy nilly for him, for Dev, and for the I.R.A. If Dev fought he would have to fight on four fronts, against Hitler on the west, Churchill on the east, Belfast on the north, and the British navy on the south, and to forfeit all the American support and sympathy which is still as important to Eire as when it helped with the treaty. What can he do but sit tight and let events take their course.

The situation is dangerous, but has the advantage that it offers an opportunity for the first time to unite Ireland, not in support of England, but against Hitler, which comes to the same thing.

And this is the moment you choose to dig up the rotten apple of discord and throw it in again to revive the strife of Shinner and Black and Tan! Can you imagine anything more thoughtlessly stupid and wicked?

And to put it all on poor innocent St Jude——!

If you go on I shall be tempted to use strong language. Burn that mischievous trash, and never mention Ireland to me again.

GBS

To ALFRED DOUGLAS

[H/64; X/394]

Ayot St Lawrence. Welwyn
14th November 1940

Childe, Childe

Politically you have the brains of a grasshopper; and you have far too much courage. If the Douglases had had less courage and more commonsense they would now be the royal house of Scotland. Providence, knowing how valuable my life was going to be, took care that I should be born a devout coward. As a boy I was horribly ashamed of my poltroonery; now I am thankful for it. Samuel Butler wrote a book called Luck or Cunning. Some day I shall write one called Pluck or Cunning.

The Irish question is going to be a very vital one. If the submarine campaign on the west coast of Ireland continues to be successful, and we come as we did before within five weeks of being starved out, we *must* seize the Irish ports or surrender. Obviously we will not surrender for the sake of the I.R.A.'s beautiful eyes. We will exterminate the whole four millions of Irish in Ireland first.

Your notion of dealing with this situation is to rake up old dirt to

587

set the Irish by the ears again, and to call De Valera a skunk and declare that you do not care two damns about his difficulties. How much farther will that get you or anyone else, do you think?

De V. is not, as a matter of passionate fact, a skunk. He is an ex-schoolmaster of unblemished character who, when, like you, he had more courage than commonsense, risked his life in the Easter rising, and escaped hanging by the skin of his teeth. He is where he is because Ireland needed a schoolmaster very badly and had enough of hanged heroes. His difficulties, about which you do not care two damns, happen to be England's difficulties as well. If I were in his place I should probably write a very private letter to the P.M. as follows[:] "Dear Churchill: I cannot give you the ports because I should provoke an I.R.A. rising and lose such power for good as I have. I cannot prevent you from taking the ports, as I have only four millions to your forty, and you have America at your back this time. So for God's sake *take* the ports as nicely as you can as a temporary forced loan, promising to give them back when our common enemy the atheist Hun is disposed of. Faithfully, Eamon de Valera.["]

What have you to say to that, courageous but idiotic Douglas? Which cat, by the way, are you going to bell?

GBS

To WENDY HILLER

[H/1]

Ayot St Lawrence. Welwyn
4th December 1940

[Dame Wendy, according to her husband Ronald Gow, has always been puzzled by Shaw's first statement in this letter, and suspects that Pascal invented her dislike to camouflage reasons of his own. (Sir) William Walton (1902–83), celebrated composer of orchestral music and opera, wrote film scores for *Major Barbara, Henry V, Hamlet*, and *Richard III*. Deborah Kerr (b. 1921), who portrayed Jenny Hill in the film, had just appeared in the screen version of *Love on the Dole*, which Gow and Walter Greenwood had dramatised for the stage from the latter's novel. Wendy Hiller had made a notable West End début in the play in 1935, which she repeated in New York before coming to Malvern in 1936 for her appearances as Joan and Eliza.]

My dear Wendy

Pascal tells me that you dislike the river scene in Barbara, and that he is not pressing you to do it.

Now this will make no difference to the film, as it can do without it without drawing a penny the less; but it will make a difference to you professionally which I want you to consider carefully.

In the stage version of Barbara the incidents of the night following the second act are not shewn. They are described in a few words next day; and Barbara is thus left in full possession of the audience's imagination. But in the screen version this is entirely altered. There are several new scenes for Cusins and Undershaft, and a grand show with band and chorus for Mrs Baines. Without a strong contrabalancing scene for Barbara she is wiped out, and Mrs Baines steals the play from her.

You dont really want this to happen, do you? It is true that the river scene is a bit of claptrap which any melodramatic leading lady could play with Walton's music and a Thames-by-Moonlight scene to back her; but the people in front know nothing about that: for them it will be the climax of the shelter scene and of Barbara's catastrophe, giving her a sensational share in the story of that night, and keeping her in her place as the star turn. That is what I wrote it for. Think it over before you throw it away. I strongly advise you to make Pascal take it and shew it to you on the screen. You can then decide the question of cutting it out for yourself.

You see, you are in the dreadful position of having made such an enormous success as Eliza that the public will expect you to do it every time; and you must leave no stone unturned to fulfil that very un-reasonable expectation. In Pygmalion Eliza is the whole play: all the other characters revolve round her and help her; and none of the women are her rivals in any way. In Barbara this is not so: all the other characters are her rivals professionally; and Sybil Thorndike [as Mrs Baines] can do a tremendous lot with half a dozen lines, especially in a religious part which suits her own saintly temperament. So think it over once, twice, fifty times; and then do exactly what you please. You must have good critical faculty; for your eyebrows are exactly like mine.

faithfully
G. Bernard Shaw

PS Somebody told me the other day that Love on the Dole has been filmed with Jenny Hill as the heroine. Is this true? If so, what were you and Ronald thinking of to let it happen. Of course the part is actress-proof up to a point: nobody could fail in it. But what you did beyond that point made all the difference. Has Pascal driven you mad?

To HESKETH PEARSON

[A/3; X/454.e]

Ayot St Lawrence. Welwyn
12th January 1941

[Shaw added to the final chapter of Pearson's biography the verse he had inscribed in the copy of the Kelmscott Chaucer he presented to Rodin:
  "I have seen two masters at work, Morris who made this book,
    The other Rodin the Great, who fashioned my head in clay:
    I give the book to Rodin, scrawling my name in a nook
    Of the shrine their works shall hallow when mine are dust by the way."]

Not on your life, Hesketh.

What I have written I have written in your character, not in my own. As an autobiographer I should have written quite differently. There are things that you may quite properly say which would come less gracefully from me. I have carefully avoided altering your opinions except where you had not known the facts and some deduction of yours had to be suppressed as a non-sequitur. For the rest I have either retained or paraphrased, leaving you to reparaphrase if I had misinterpreted.

You can of course in a foreword say that as you know me personally your authority for much hitherto unpublished information is G.B.S. himself at first hand, and that you have consulted me on doubtful points sufficiently to feel confident that your readers will not be misled in matters of fact. A good deal that could not have been made public before has been released by the parties passing from life into history.

But if a word is said to connect me with the authorship of the book or its first proposal or its commercial profits I shall be driven to the most desperate steps to disclaim it. It must appear as Harris's book did, to which I contributed a good deal to save his widow from destitution. If you are not prepared to father my stuff, you can rewrite it; but you must not publish it as mine. You have more than enough ipse dixits in inverted commas to carry you through without that outrage.

Besides, what you propose would concentrate all the reviewing and all the credit with publishers on me, and shove you into the background. . . .

I am adding an important document about Rodin which will hold up the last chapter for a day or two longer.

GBS

To FELIKS TOPOLSKI

[H/3] Ayot St Lawrence. Welwyn
27th January 1941

[Topolski had suggested one of his spider-monkey-squiggle drawings of Shaw for the wrapper of the Penguin edition of *Pygmalion*, which he was illustrating. It was published on 19th September 1941 in an edition of 94,500 copies, in the standard Penguin format. *The London Spectacle: Seen by F. Topolski* (1935) is a volume of caricatures and cartoons, with marginal notes and introduction by D.B. Wyndham Lewis.]

Dear Feliks

People see the cover of a book on the shop counter or bookstall for nothing. It makes no money for the publisher or the author unless it tempts people to buy the book. A drawing of a ridiculous old man may amuse them; but it will not suggest that the book is worth reading: on the contrary, it will put them off it. 99% of the people who buy Penguins know nothing and care nothing about authors; but many of them have heard that Pygmalion is a good story. The young ones like to imagine the writer of such a story as young and beautiful. To exhibit him as old and repulsive is like throwing a bucket of water in their faces. No doubt Maxwell and the Penguin people think your drawing great fun. But Maxwell will not buy the book. Neither will the Penguin people. Unless we can make 100,000 complete strangers buy it, it will flop. The author will make no money; the publisher will lose a lot; and the artist will be blacklisted as very clever but no good commercially. So draw us something attractive, and keep me out of it. Your job, I repeat a thousand times, is to sell the book, not to caricature me, however cleverly.

Have you ever seen the old frontispiece to The Pilgrim's Progress, with Bunyan's head and shoulders big and black in the extreme foreground, fast asleep and dreaming, with his vision of the progress in the air above him. What about Eliza asleep over her basket of flowers in the foreground, and Eliza at the ambassadors reception in the air above her? Eliza poor and dirty must be pathetic, not ugly: Duchess Eliza must be beautiful enough for a magazine cover. That gives the whole story. When the papers review the book you can easily sell your caricature to them.

As to the illustrations generally they are first rate as leftovers from your wonderful volume on London. As illustrations to a story they must surely be the very worst on record from an artist of your calibre. The play concentrates on three intensely individualized characters, and a few fairly distinct ones. In the drawings these characters hardly exist.

591

At their first appearance they might be anybody sketched in the street. At their second they are quite different persons. Nobody would suppose that you have ever read the play. I have made some detailed notes on the proof sheets, which I return herewith.

However, I am not disappointed. I daresay the critics will complain that I have not written up to your illustrations, which will quite justify themselves as an independent feature. Pygmalion will serve as an excuse for them. I shall have my revenge when you write a book and I illustrate it.

Our best regards to your lady.

faithfully

G. Bernard Shaw

To NANCY ASTOR

Ayot St Lawrence. Welwyn

30th January 1941

[H/101]

[Press reports of Mrs Patrick Campbell's will had alluded to the Shaw correspondence and to their relationship. Shaw screened the cuttings he received to keep Charlotte from seeing any of the references. Blanche Patch resided at Ayot until July 1943, when the Shaws resumed residence at Whitehall Court to enable the Ayot servants to have a holiday. She returned in June 1944 when a V-bomb blew in the study window at Whitehall Court. Nancy Astor's residence in Plymouth was No. 3, Eliott Terrace.]

My dear Nancy

I put you off on Tuesday partly for your own sake. Calling here on your way to Plymouth is much the same as calling at the North Pole on your way to Monte Carlo. I enclose an itinerary to keep by you for future excursions.

Charlotte had better be left alone just now. She has had a bad return of her lumbago and has been bedridden for weeks, well enough except for the dread of bringing on the pain by moving about, and raging because of the confinement and helplessness. Her nerves are all in rags; but she is just beginning to venture on a little movement; and until she has lost her dread of a return of the pains I dare not let her face the excitement, however joyful, of a sudden visit from you. She will tell you herself when she feels well enough to entertain you. At present the mere suggestion of your coming sets her worrying. As Miss Patch is staying with us we have no spare room now. The village pub would not be good enough for you. You would be caught in the black-out and certainly killed. We cannot get the things you ought to have to eat. All nonsense, of course; but terrible to her in her present condition. A few days ago a friend of ours drove into an unlighted refuge at 35 miles an hour and smashed his car to pieces in the dark. Charlotte is convinced that if you could not get back by daylight the same would happen to you.

As to those letters, my press cuttings are carefully handpicked before they go upstairs, so nobody here except Miss Patch and myself is worried by them. The huge success of my correspondence with Ellen Terry was a tremendous temptation to Stella, who would have had to beg her bread but for the £500 a year left her by Bridget Guinness; but I was adamant as to their publication, though I reminded her that she could always sell the originals to private collectors. But she would neither do that nor divorce George, who offered her an alimony of £800 a year. When we are all dead the letters will help to pay for the education of her great grandchildren. She must have left plenty of others, the copyright of which will expire 50 years after the death of the writers. They will be available for publication on certain terms 25 years after.

A letter written by her to me just before her death began "Dear dear Joey" and on the last day on which she was intelligible she said something about me; so there was no malice between us. Her doctor said he could cure her of her pneumonia—had cured her, in fact, but, said he, "I cannot keep alive a woman who has no intention of living."

Is it worth while to have been an enchantress when the charm no longer works? She had many gifts but no *savoir vivre*.

We have had no bombs here since the middle of November, when we had eight within a stone's throw. We are without any shelter or fire brigade or protection of any sort; but so far we are more frightened than hurt. We have not been in town for months. Miss Patch had to go up on Tuesday and walked into four alerts. At Whitehall Court we have had a window or two broken. We heard that No 4 had been hit, and we are now a bit anxious about Elliott Terrace, but hope that God will take care of his own.

GBS

593

To BEATRICE WEBB

Ayot St Lawrence. Welwyn
[H/14]   17th February 1941

[Throughout the war years, from 1939 to 1945, Shaw found an outlet for his articles and letters to the editor in the pages of *Forward*, a Glasgow socialist weekly edited by Emrys Hughes. The "last three" articles dealt with De Valera and the problem of the Irish ports in wartime. In the early months of 1941 Shaw prepared a *R.A.D.A. Graduates' Keepsake & Counsellor* for students of the Royal Academy of Dramatic Art, for which he provided an unsigned introduction and edited the "messages of advice" he had obtained from actors, managers, and friends of the theatre. Copies were printed by R. & R. Clark at Shaw's expense.

H. G. Wells had organised the Sankey Committee for a new Declaration of Human Rights of Man. A "trial statement" was published in *The Times* on 23rd October 1940; in the same year Penguin issued as a "Special" volume (No. 50) Wells's *The Rights of Man, or What Are We Fighting For?* Shaw's list "of things rulers must understand" developed into *Everybody's Political What's What?* Richard Albert Wilson's *The Birth of Language: Its Place in World Evolution and Its Structure in Relation to Space and Time* was first published in 1937. Shaw was so enthusiastic about it that he provided a cogent preface for a paperback edition in 1941, issued as *The Miraculous Birth of Language.*

Anderson war shelters were built of corrugated steel, half above and half below ground. Shaw's shelter was his glass-enclosed hut, built on a pivot to allow for maximum sunlight, in which he worked at the bottom of his garden. It was originally constructed as a retreat for Charlotte.]

My dear Beatrice

Charlotte has had another very bad bout of lumbago and has been in bed for many weeks. She cannot write, as her back will not stand the writing posture; but she can now come downstairs for meals and will soon, I hope, be able to get about out of doors. Neither of us has been in London since the blitzing began. Blanche lives with us, and is a great comfort.

Up to the middle of November we had a searchlight here, and were consequently under fire. After a grand bombardment in which we had 8 H.E. [High Explosive] bombs in the village (one in the next garden) and incendiaries *ad lib*, the searchlight was taken away; we ceased to be a military objective; and we now see and hear the raids on London 30 miles off; but nothing has since come near enough to keep us awake. I have bought a stirrup pump, two longhandled spades, and a load of sand; and I am ordering a ladder (all quite useless with no one to handle them except a rheumatic gardener of 75 and an ancient author

594

of 85) so as to get incendiaries out of the gutters when they roll off the roof into them. I therefore cannot be reproached for not taking precautions. I am thinking of buying one of the new portable indoor shelters for our dauntless Irish parlormaid [Margaret Cashin] who sleeps just under the tiles regardless of bombs.

I am very occasionally moved to write something about the war. I do not send it to The New Statesman because I do not want to embarass Kingsley Martin: one editor is enough for one paper. I send the stuff to Forward, which is very glad to have it, and to Hearst, who pays me £100 for an article, though he can have them for nothing. I enclose the last three. Send them back to me at your convenience. I have written nothing for the stage since Charles, and will perhaps not write for it again. I have been kept busy all the winter with three jobs. 1. Revising a biography of me by Hesketh Pearson, which will contain some hitherto unpublished matter that has been set free by the deaths of Mrs Besant and Mrs Patrick Campbell. This took me rather longer than writing the book myself. 2. Writing for the Royal Academy of Dramatic Art a booklet full of advice for beginners on the stage to be presented to our students when they finish their course and get their diploma. When I proposed this to the Council they naturally said "Write it yourself." It was a funny job; but I felt it had to be done. 3. Something in our line. The Wells Bill of Rights left me out of all patience with abstractions on which Stalin and Lord Halifax are perfectly agreed. Also I am convinced that what is the matter with everybody is ignorance, and every day read something about our own time which occurred without my ever hearing a word of it. But there is no remedy for it. No statesman can ever know the facts of the moment at which he must act: he will not learn them for at least 20 years, and then only some of them. He must guess by instinct and knowledge of human nature and history. The wisdom of the people is a myth. Democracy should secure them a means of ventilating their grievances and give them a choice of *qualified* rulers every four or five years. Anything more means the sort of government we have, or worse.

The problem to be solved is the qualification. I cannot solve it, nor can anyone else; but somebody must begin with a minimum list of things rulers must understand, no matter what their conclusions may be. I am drafting such a list, leaving those who can to amend it. If I ever finish this beginning I will send it to you and Sidney before I publish it.

This has just been interrupted by another job. Professor Wilson at the University of Sascatchewan in the city of Saskatoon (of which I had never heard) sent me a book called The Birth of Language, which was so up to date and emancipated from the damnable post-Darwinian Materialism cum Determinism, that I immediately urged Dent to publish a cheap edition, and offered to write a preface. This preface has taken me a goodish while; but I have just finished the first draft of it, and will have a copy made for the Passfield criticism.

I work at this job until lunch in my shelter in the garden (not an Anderson one), sleep for an hour or so after lunch and then go out carrying a chopper and a saw and do amateur woodman's jobs or cut up firewood until the black-out, when I come indoors again and write letters until dinner. I am very old and ought to be dead. My failing memory plays me the most terrifying tricks. I am losing weight so fast that I shall presently have totally disappeared. I look when stripped like a native in a famine picture, an imperfectly concealed skeleton. I am still 6 feet high; but I weigh only 9 stone, my old weight having been between 10 stone 8 lbs and 11 stone.

I could tell you lots of other senilities, and what is much more interesting some new young growths; but this is enough for one letter.

I cannot write as I used to or invent stories; but I can still gossip quite smartly, and am less discursive and excessive than I was in my prime.

Your account of Sidney is very encouraging.

Obituary: William Maxwell's wife and Stephen Sanders: no doubt you know of these already.

Both our loves to both of you.

GBS

To OTTO KYLLMANN

Ayot St Lawrence. Welwyn
[H/64]   24th February 1941

[J. G. Wilson was manager of John and Edward Bumpus Ltd., booksellers in Oxford Street, from whom Shaw made most of his book purchases. The tax system imposed graduated rates on gross income, with only the highest portion of a large income taxed at the maximum rate of eighteen shillings (later nineteen and six).]

Dear O.K.

I am stoney broke, and have paid my January taxes only with the help of the insurance money I got when my books were burnt at

Leighton's. On the 25th March you must send me my accounts and pay me up to the 31st December. Wilson tells me that my books are being bought for the soldiers; so you must have a few pounds in hand for me.

I would not press you but for the appalling misfortune of my having received within one financial year £25,000 from the Pygmalion film. This put me into the millionaire class, in which I am taxed 18/- in the pound not only on the £25,000, but on my wife's income and everything else as well. The U.S.A. also takes 15%. Result, ruin. If I were younger I should abandon authorship and become a publisher.

Are you co-operating with Dent in his plan of pricing books at sixpence and a shilling in paper covers? He tempts me assiduously to let him include me in his Everyman library. I have had to let Pygmalion be penguined. My days of respectable publishing are over, I fear.

For many months past I have been hard at work on jobs that will not bring me in a penny. I have earned nothing but a couple of casual hundred pounds from the Hearst Press for articles.

Unless you go into the sixpenny business, for which you are quite unfitted, we shall end together in the workhouse.

Charlotte has been very ill in bed for many many weeks, and is recovering very slowly.

This is a nice cheerful letter. I have put off writing it as long as possible; but as you do the same with your payments (very properly) it serves you right.

always yours
G. Bernard Shaw

To HANNEN SWAFFER

Ayot St Lawrence. Welwyn

[H/3]   24th February 1941

[Swaffer, for reasons of political conviction, damned *The Apple Cart* up hill and down dale in his review of it following its first performance at Malvern in 1929, and at every opportunity thereafter. Britain leased to the United States in September 1940 a number of naval and air bases in Newfoundland and the Caribbean islands in return for fifty U.S. destroyers of First World War vintage.]

PRIVATE.

Dear Hannen Swaffer

... I congratulate you on escaping from your fifties—the worst decade of life—into the sixties, which you will find much healthier and happier. Certainly I did.

Dont forget, by the way, that I am nearly 85. It dates you to speak of the Shavian perversity: young people now regard me as a quite obsolete back number. To them what you call my perversities and paradoxes are platitudes. They always were; but as I took some care to know what I was talking about while all the others were splutterbunking I astonished them by not saying exactly what they were shouting. The perverse Shaw is as dead as a doornail: he is replaced by a more or less venerable dotard.

If I may risk infuriating you (God knows why!) by reminding you of The Apple Cart, I may claim that what occurred in that play as an extravagance—I mean the return of the United States to the British Commonwealth, which the clever king saw was really an annexation—this business of the naval bases and the drawing together of the republican plutocracies is an instalment of my prophecy coming true. You were too good a republican to endure my giving the best part to the king; but you are also a Socialist; and where will your Socialism be if republican plutocracy becomes the totalitarian ruler of Europe. Then the fun will begin in earnest. I shall be dead; but you may have another quarter century to take you into the thick of it. So look ahead and forget the cliché of the *fin de siècle*.

always yours
G. Bernard Shaw

To GEORGE CORNWALLIS-WEST

Ayot St Lawrence. Welwyn
[H/2]   26th February 1941
[Cornwallis-West had remarried once Stella Campbell's death released him from his bonds. The solicitors were F. M. Guedalla & Co. Mrs Campbell's daughter had borrowed £100 from Shaw to send to her mother's companion, Agnes Claudius, at Pau to pay for the funeral. The enclosed pamphlet is unidentified.]

My dear George

Delighted to hear from you: now that we are being bombed all over the place one always wants to know whether you are alive and where you are. Branksome is rather a good choice, as Bournemouth is near enough to be convenient and far enough to draw Jerry's fire without having the windows broken. Here in this village we had a searchlight, and were consequently bombed until the middle of November, when the searchlight was taken away and we have since been able to enjoy in perfect peace the spectacle of London on fire thirty miles off.

The sale of Stella's furniture begins tomorrow at Harrods. She seems to have kept the whole houseful and never paid for the warehousing. So Harrods are selling it up. D.D. and Guedalla (the solicitor, not the author) seem to think that I might possibly buy it all in and present it to Mrs Beech (Stella II); but I can imagine nothing wickeder, as she has been bombed out and left with nothing but the clothes she had on her back. The sale may perhaps leave something for her after Harrods' claim is satisfied; and the disposal is the very best thing that could happen to her: it will finish the process of getting rid of her famous mother and have a turn at being herself.

As to the will, Stella was so amazingly lacking in *savoir vivre* that it was always hard to guess whether simple ignorance or devilment actuated her. She had a good press for the will; but as my wife, who has suffered much from lumbago lately, was ill in bed, I took care that the press cuttings that reached her were carefully handpicked first; so no harm was done. The worst of it is that as Mrs Beech could make a pot of money by publishing the correspondence I seem to be robbing her by refusing to sanction it. Stella, who wanted to eclipse the Ellen Terry letters, did her best to persuade me, but in vain: I told her she could always sell the letters as material objects but must not publish them.

She bore no malice; for her last letter to me, written shortly before her death[,] began "Dear dear Joey"; and she talked about me to the last. Considering that when she asked me to pay her way back from Paris to London I said I would as soon pay the devil's passage, and my language as to her treatment of you had been equally emphatic, her conduct to me may almost be described as magnanimous. She was in such straits finally that I had to go to the rescue with the expenses of her illness and funeral; but Mrs Beech scrupulously sent me two cheques for £20 each, and never noticed that they were not presented!

The doctor said that the pneumonia was quite curable, but that he could not save the life of a woman who had no intention of living. Her good looks were gone; and yet only a few months before her death she fascinated Pascal the film genius.

The war is unspeakable: read the enclosed pamphlet.

I hesitate to ask to be remembered to your partner. One of a woman's worst trials must be putting up with her husband's old friends; and they really should not be so damnably old as we are. I shall be 85 in July. I am no longer a desirable acquaintance, but can still write a bit. We havent seen London since September.

always yours
G. Bernard Shaw

To RONALD KIDD

Ayot St Lawrence. Welwyn
6th March 1941

[C/102; X/410]

[Ronald Kidd (d. 1942) of the National Council for Civil Liberties was the editor of the journal *Civil Liberty*. He was writing a book *The Fight for a Free Press*, published the following year. *The Times* that morning announced a B.B.C. ban on actors and musicians who had participated in a pacifist People's Convention. The ensuing uproar led to questions in Parliament and an eventual lifting of the ban by Churchill on 20th March. The Government had suppressed publication of the *Daily Worker* the previous January.]

The whole managing staff of the B.B.C. should be sacked instantly. Here we are in thick of a war which we claim to be fighting as the champions of western democracy. Daily we throw in the teeth of Germany and Italy the reproach that they have abolished the rights of public meeting and free speech. And this is the moment selected by the B.B.C. to give the world an exhibition of British Nazi-ism gone mad. Just on top of the suppression of a newspaper too! Europe will hear all about it from Herr Goebbels and Mr [William] Joyce. We liquidate our looters, whose mischief is comparatively negligible. When shall we learn to liquidate our fools?

G. Bernard Shaw

To H. G. WELLS

Ayot St Lawrence. Welwyn
15th April 1941

[H/26]

[Wells's *Babes in the Darkling Wood* (1940) was described in its preface as a "dialogue novel of contemporary ideas." Churchill had said in an address on 27th March to the Central Council Meeting of Conservative and Unionist Associations (*not* broadcast, but published in *The Times* on the 28th), "It is because of the interests of national unity that I have forborne to produce a catalogue of war aims or peace aims; every one knows quite well what we are fighting about, but if you try to set forth in a catalogue what will be the exact settlement of affairs in a period which, as I say, is unforeseeable; if you attempt to do that you will find that the moment you leave the sphere of pious platitude you will descend into the arena of heated controversy. That would militate against the efforts which we are making, and we could not in justice to our country take such a step" (Churchill, *Complete Speeches*, VI, 1974).

The verse Shaw recited to Stalin is from Valentine Blacker's "Oliver Cromwell's Advice" (1834). On 1st March 1941 the Red Army captured the Finnish city of Vyborg on the Isthmus of Karelia; the Finns signed a peace treaty twelve days later that ceded to the USSR the territories earlier demanded. When the Irish Free State was set up by treaty in 1921, Britain retained control of three ports: Cork Harbour, Lough Swilly, and Berehaven. These were transferred to Ireland in 1938 after a negotiated settlement. The new Irish Constitution of 1937, which proclaimed Eire to be "a sovereign independent, theocratic State, belonging not to the Commonwealth but 'to the most Holy Trinity,'" as Shaw commented in *Forward*, 11th January 1941, emphasised Roman Catholicism as the religion of the majority of the Irish people.

Benedetto Croce (1866–1952) was a famed Italian philosopher, statesman, and historian. Responding the next day to Shaw's reaction to Pavlov, Wells informed him that the scientist "was invincibly like you. You will probably be compared by posterity. He talked about as well but wrote damnable prose" (*GBS 90*, ed. S. Winsten, 1946). Imperial Chemical Industries Ltd. in the early days of the war leased the spacious Ayot House as a country refuge for its employees. Frank Richard Wells (1903–83), H.G.'s son, was a film maker, who produced over a hundred educational and documentary films.]

My dear H.G.

I have just finished The Babes, which was impossible until everyone else had finished it first. You are not dead yet (I am, unfortunately): there are luminosities and subtleties that are newly born as well as the old Wellsian faculty.

I was specially tickled by your onslaught on brass tacks, because I am trying to write a book with the express object of bringing your Declaration of Rights down to these useful articles. Churchill was absolutely right the other day in his broadcast when he said that if he declared his war aims the united nation behind him would split into fifty irreconcilable factions.

My book is a little list of the things a person ought to understand (no matter what his or her conclusions may be) before being trusted with a vote or put on the panel as eligible for public work of this or that grade.

You are less splenetic than you were. The British spleen that broke out occasionally and upset your valuations is mellowing a bit. This is very noticeable in your description of Stalin. I rate him higher than you do. He was equal to two very big opportunities of going wrong. The first was Socialism in a single country versus Trotsky's world revolution. The second was collective farming versus the moujik. His choice and the success with which he carried it out rank him as the greatest living statesman. Collective farming is the only chance for our agriculture; but we stick helplessly to the moujik and the Kulak. Stalin would not have a dog's chance in a British constituency. He made a favorable impression on me when I met him in 1931. The attentive silence in which he listened to us until we had said everything we had to say and the goodhumor with which he laughed at us when his turn came (for he did laugh at us) could not have been improved on in point of pleasant manners and grasping of the situation. Lothian's proposal that he should invite Lloyd George to Moscow with a view to his leading the progressive Liberals to the Left of the Labor Party as a Party of scientific Socialism simply amused him, though he cordially invited Ll. G. to come and see for himself. When Lady Astor told him that the Soviet knew nothing about handling children of five years he was outraged. "In England" he said "you beat children[.]" But Nancy went for him like a steamroller and ordered him to send a sensible woman to London to learn the business. The moment he saw that she knew what she was talking about he made a note of her address, and presently dumped not one but half a dozen sensible women on her doorstep. This trifle impressed me; for I thought his noting the address was mere politeness. I, who had heard nothing of Lothian's proposal until he paid it out to Uncle Joe, had nothing to say; but when Astor, who is by temperament a born Communist, gave him assurances that Russia had many friends in England, I asked him whether he had ever heard of Cromwell, and quoted the refrain of the old song

> "So put your trust in God, my boys;
> And keep your powder dry."

He knew all about Cromwell, and intimated that at any rate he would keep his powder dry. He was very friendly; and as I was treated all through as if I were Karl Marx risen from the grave, I did not see the rough side of anybody or anything. But there was no attempt to humbug me. They were too full of their achievements to dream of any need for that, especially as they were convinced that Capitalist England was in comparison a Chamber of Horrors.

I was prepared for Finland, as Ireland is the British Finland, and I have said ever since the Treaty that in the event of a world war England would have to re-occupy Ireland militarily, or at least take over the ports, for the duration. Churchill and Roosevelt may still have to do it if the battle of the Atlantic continues to go against us. The only novelty about Finland was the unprecedented fact that Russia took only what she needed instead of taking back the whole place as any other Power would have done.

Talking of Ireland, were you aware that in 1937, when the ports were given back, the ownership of Eire was formally and explicitly transferred to The Most Holy Trinity? I discovered that a month ago. Had you ever heard of it?

I think you and Benedetto Croce are not civil enough to Karl Marx. I have myself pointed out his purely academic mistakes; but as he was unquestionably an epoch making philosopher who changed the mind of the intellectually conscious world, attempts to belittle him fail and belittle their authors.

To balance it I dismiss Pavlof as a supremely damned fool. But he seems to have been as civil to you as Uncle Joe was to me, for which I give him one good mark. His personal resemblance to me I take as an unpardonable liberty. Your difficulty about him is fundamentally due to the fact that you were educated by your schooling, which you carried to its end by becoming a teacher and crammer. My education was entirely aesthetic: I learnt nothing at school, and loathed it. It kept me from becoming a young gangster; but it did this by imprisoning me; and I have never forgiven it. I have at last come definitely to believe that all effective education is aesthetic, and that the Materialistic Mechanistic science which you had to get up for school purposes was all wrong. As an aesthetic worker I claim to be scientifically a biologist and an economist, my laboratory, or rather my observatory[,] being the whole world in which the events are not put-up jobs (see Love and Mr Lewisham) and, barring mere accidents, their cause is always in the future and never in the past. In short I understand why we differ; so there is no harm done, as I am careful to say nothing about it; for the idea must not get about that the Wellsians and Shavians have any differences. They are in fact the same body.

We are quiet here. Up to last November we had a searchlight here, with the result that every raid began on us: we have several craters to shew. But I.C.I. took a house here. The searchlight was taken away.

Whether the two events were connected I dont know; but since then we have had no bombs. Frank [Wells] is nearer the viaduct, which is a target; but it is of less importance now that there is an alternative line. We presume you are well, as anything happening to you would be in the papers. I havent been in London for months. My imagination is nearly dead; I forget everything in ten minutes; and my weight has fallen to 9 stone; but I keep up a stage effect of being an upstanding old man. I am not unhappy in spite of this senseless war, though I ought to be dead, and am not in the least troubled by that fact.

always yours
GBS

PS I havn't written a play for nearly two years. I am by no means sure that I shall ever write another.

As the Babes was really an exhaustive letter to me, this is an acknowledgment, and need not be acknowledged, as you must have something better to do.

Read my letter in today's Times ["A King's Spelling: Letters and Sounds"]. It is not about the war.

To ROY LIMBERT

Ayot St Lawrence. Welwyn

[C/3]   [Undated: assigned to 1st May 1941]

[Limbert, despite the wartime cancellation of the Malvern Festival, kept the local theatre open. The reply to his invitation to Shaw to speak was written on one of the stereotyped-message postcards: "Mr Bernard Shaw is obliged by advancing years to discontinue his personal activities on the platform."]

How old do these people suppose I am? I shall be 85 in July. Do they want an old dotard with his artificial teeth dropping out at every second sentence to stoke up Malvern patriotism? If so, surely there must be a local Oldest Inhabitant available. Anyhow, NO.

G.B.S.

To JOHN ROWLAND

[C/3]

Ayot St Lawrence. Welwyn
3rd July 1941

[John Rowland (b. 1907), journalist and author, published "The Truth about Bernard Shaw" in the *Rationalist Annual* (1942).]

This is not a war for Xtian civilization. It is a war to disable an aspirant to the government of the earth, by name Adolph Hitler. This, and nothing else, is its object.

Do not add octogenarians to your visiting list. Make young friends: they keep longer.

G.B.S.

To PAUL KORETZ

[F.u/2]

[Ayot St Lawrence. Welwyn]
[Undated: *c.* mid-July 1941]

[Koretz, who had set up practice in New York, was about to transfer his headquarters to Hollywood. Apparently he had been appealed to for assistance by Siegfried Trebitsch, desperately seeking avenues for additional income. For the libretto of the film version of *The Chocolate Soldier* Metro-Goldwyn-Mayer substituted the play *The Guardsman* (1910) by the Hungarian dramatist Ferenc Molnár (1878–1952), the rights to which it already owned. It opened at the Astor Theatre, New York, on 31st October 1941. *Arms and the Man* became one more of Pascal's many abandoned projects. The Trebitsches obtained French citizenship in the summer of 1939.]

Dear Dr Koretz

I cannot understand on what ground Trebitsch can claim an interest in the English version of the Chocolate Soldier. He can claim an exclusive right to translate Arms and the Man into German; but the English version was translated from the libretto of Jacobsohn without any apparent reference to Trebitsch's Helden. That version infringes my copyright; and I now, after allowing two or three fortunes to be made out of the opera without interference, make its producers pay me a nominal fee of one shilling per performance in acknowledgment of my licence to perform it. I exercise my right to forbid absolutely any filming of the C.S. until Arms and the Man has been filmed and has exhausted its vogue.

To Oscar Strauss's music I have no claim whatever; and I have repeatedly declared that if a different libretto were fitted to it, and the

605

title changed, I should have no ground for interference. You now tell me that this hint has been acted on by calling in Molnar, a very competent original playwright, to refit the music with a new libretto; and you suggest that their right to do this may be disputable. It would be if Molnar's libretto infringed my copyright at any point; but if it did not I should not risk an action at law.

Meanwhile the intention to produce the C.S. in its old form has been abandoned, as Gabriel Pascal objected on my behalf, and as a lawsuit on the point had been decided in my favor in London when a similar proposal was made by an American who had bought the musical rights. My right to prohibit was not disputed.

Trebitsch wants me to withdraw my prohibition and allow him to profit by the result; but I cannot see that he would have any claim; and in any case I am pledged not to allow the C.S. to be filmed until Pascal has filmed Arms and the Man and fully exploited it.

I am very sorry for poor Siegfried: his position is desperate. Even if the war taxation left me any money to send him I should not be allowed to send it without a permit which is only granted when the payment is absolutely necessary for business purposes. As a refugee in Switzerland he is not allowed to work as a journalist and do anything that could be done by a Swiss. He asks me to do the most contradictory and impossible things, as if I were the British Government and could get him visas and passports in all directions. In the same letter he asks me to get him passports for the USA, and then gives me reasons why he cannot go there. His acquisition of French nationality seems to have done him more harm than good. He has always been so well off that he does not know how to live without plenty of money[.] I cannot imagine how he could live in the U.S.A. even if his wife could be persuaded to venture on the voyage. He tells me his clothes are worn out, and in the same breath complains that the jewellers are not offering enough for an old fashioned tiara of diamonds which I thought he must have sold long ago. I do not know what advice to give him. Do you?

I am glad to hear from you, and to infer that your own position is still solid. I count you as a special friend as Trebitsch does also.

faithfully
[G. Bernard Shaw]

To KENNETH BARNES

[H/3; X/401.e]
Ayot St Lawrence. Welwyn
23rd July 1941

[On 26th July, his eighty-fifth birthday, Shaw formally resigned from the R.A.D.A. Council, informing Sir Kenneth Barnes: "Though I am ten years beyond the usual age for retirement I have been able to persuade myself that my lagging was not wholly superfluous; but 85 is the limit set by public decency as well as by my infirmity, and I must now make room for a younger councillor" (H/3). On the same date he submitted his resignation from the Executive Committee of the Shakespeare Memorial National Theatre. "I am acting after the most careful consideration," he wrote to the Hon. Secretary, Geoffrey Whitworth, "and beg the Council to accept my resignation as inevitable and my decision as unchangeable. My name can remain in the bill as a member of the General Committee. I shall thus be available for consultation if any occasion should arise" (Whitworth, *The Making of a National Theatre*, 1951).]

My dear Kenneth

. . . I understand your dismay at my threatened resignation; but you must endure my going hence even as my coming hither. The years are inexorable: you cannot imagine how dotty I am, though I can still write a bit. I resigned my chairmanship 5 years ago, and should have done it ten years ago. To hold on until ninety would be ridiculous. . . . You must accustom yourself to a Shawless council. Better too soon (which it isnt) than too late.

I am afraid we shall get nothing substantial from America [in financial assistance] without a touring company and a lecturer for the universities, which we cannot afford. Our only chance of escaping reckless mortgaging is a sudden collapse of the war. That may happen. Our notion that Hitler was going to have a walk-over in Russia was only an aftermath of the silly lies we have been telling ourselves about the U.S.S.R. for twenty years. Germany is getting frightfully hammered before and behind, with worse to come; and she cannot stand it for long. The air war, in which the vanquished cannot surrender and the victor has to run away, is reducing war to absurdity: nobody wants it to go on. Anyhow war never does what it is expected to do. Nothing that I can see except utter desperation could have induced Hitler to take on Russia when he was fighting Britain and America. He must have felt certain that Stalin would do what he (Hitler) would have done in Stalin's place: that is, go for him when he was exhausted by the fight in the west. . . .

G. Bernard Shaw

607

To J. UNSWORTH

[X/413]

Ayot St Lawrence. Welwyn
29th July 1941

[J. Unsworth, assistant secretary of the Warrington Committee of the People's Convention, had sent a copy of K. E. Voroshilov's *Stalin and the Red Army* (Moscow, 1941); Shaw's reply was inscribed on the fly-leaf of the book, which was sold for £2 at a meeting in Warrington on 10th August.]

Dear Mr Unsworth

Thank you for lending me this book.

I was, however, aware of the extraordinary military ability and general force of character displayed by Stalin when he saved the revolution in 1918–20. Without him Lenin could never have held Russia against a Capitalist world in arms.

When I met him in 1931 I knew that I was face to face with the ablest statesman in Europe; and the personal impression he made on me did not change my opinion. I still rank Stalin first, Roosevelt second, and the rest nowhere.

I cannot address a meeting for you. As my 86th birthday occurred last Saturday I no longer try to move assemblies.

faithfully
G. Bernard Shaw

To KATHARINE CORNELL

[H/123]

Ayot St Lawrence. Welwyn
30th July 1941

[Katharine Cornell, one of the most celebrated American actresses of her generation, first appeared in *Candida* in 1924. It was later included in her repertory in a national tour in 1933–34, and staged again in New York in 1937. Her New York production of *The Doctor's Dilemma*, directed by her husband Guthrie McClintic (1893–1961), had just concluded a run of 121 performances, the longest American engagement of the play and the most profitable anywhere. In September 1941 it commenced a national tour of several months' duration. Bramwell Fletcher, who played Dubedat, was in his late thirties. The original Minnie Tinwell in 1906 was Mary Hamilton.]

Delectable Katharine

I took the success of The Doctor's Dilemma as a matter of course, with you in it. I got the photographs: they look all right except that Dubedat is fifty years too old. He should be a beautiful stripling who looks 18, though he is in fact a few years older, and not in the same street with the other men, morally or physically.

Jennifer is a sort of woman I hate: one who never looks facts in the face, and lives in a lying dream. My favorite female in the play is Minnie Tinwell, daughter of joy and shyboots, who can steal the play in two minutes if she is put to it. In the original production she was played to perfection by the daughter of an American bishop. When you go on tour, double the two parts: there will be time for you to change after your exit in the second act, and you save a salary. I could find a dozen Jennifers more easily than one Minnie.

As to filming Candida, I strongly advise not to do it until the war is over and taxation back to reasonable levels. I have made nothing out of The Doctor's Dilemma: all the dollars you send me are sold to the British Treasury, which will take every cent of the price, and more, back from me in Income Tax and Surtax. Something of the same kind must be happening to you, or very soon will. Candida can wait: you will be irresistible in it at 70 as you are now; and I will be able to live on your earnings as I have done so often before. If only I had written another part good enough for you!

So you remembered my 86th birthday. I was born 50 years too soon.

I notice that you ask a percentage on profits. Have you noticed that I ask a percentage on receipts? There may be no profits; and there are always receipts; and the profits can never exceed the receipts. And the receipts can always be ascertained, whereas it may take ten lawsuits to settle what the profits are. Ask Guthrie whether he has considered this?

your oldest author
G. Bernard Shaw

To C. WALTER SMEE

Ayot St Lawrence. Welwyn
[S(H)/1]   9th August 1941

[C. Walter Smee (b. 1890) was a chartered accountant, of the London firm of F. Rowland & Co.; he later formed his own company. The New York solicitor was Benjamin Stern. None of the four plays mentioned by Shaw was filmed by Pascal, or by anyone else during the remaining nine years of Shaw's life.]

Dear Mr Smee

Pascal starts for America next Monday, the 10th inst. I can explain the situation less volcanically.

I do not know what are the legal implications of the word Evasion; but I presume that any man in business may legitimately shut up his shop if he cannot keep it open without sacrifices which he cannot afford, and wait to re-open it until the market considerations are more favorable. My business as a playwright is the licensing of performances and film exhibitions in consideration of royalties on the receipts. If I suspend the issue of licences until the market recovers I take it that I am within my rights, and that you may abet me without being disqualified as an accountant or shot as a traitor, notwithstanding that we wilfully prevent a flow of dollars to this country which the Treasury wishes to secure.

The Pygmalion film brought me in the first year £25,000, being 10% on the money paid by the exhibitors to the distributors. Therefore the proceeds must have considerably exceeded £250,000, of which, after deducting the American distributors commission of say, 25% (they are glad to take 17½% now that Shaw is ranked as a gold mine), enough came to this country from America to make the Treasury very keen on our going ahead. The Canadian Government and the Royal Bank of Canada are equally keen.

But the receipt of £25,000 in one year has ruined me by putting me into the class which is allowed to retain only sixpence of every pound it receives. My 25,000 sixpences did not pay the rent of my flat in Whitehall. Pascal is similarly ruined. The Treasury and Canadian Government now ask us to produce four new films in the next two years: Arms and the Man, St Joan, Captain Brassbound's Conversion, and The Devil's Disciple. I reply that I cannot afford to. They may argue that it is my duty to the country to consent, as I am no worse off than other rich citizens; but this does not apply, as I do not possess an income of £25,000 a year which will persist after the war, but am gambling on a windfall that may not materialize; for any film may flop and thereby be made worthless for the rest of my life. Authors should be allowed to average their income for 20 years for taxation purposes. The other day an author took the Inland Revenue into court on the question whether his copyright, which he had sold, was not capital and therefore exempt from taxation as such. But the court decided against him. I must therefore either go out of business for the duration or else devise some arrangement whereby I may legitimately defer coming into taxable possession of any royalties on the said four plays until the national expenditure falls below its present level of 12 millions a day. Meanwhile I can live on my capital and on my normal earnings.

Instead of the usual 5 years contract by which the producers are bound to pay me 10% of the money paid by the exhibitors to the distributors month by month I want the following conditions. The first charge on these receipts to be the formation of a reserve fund of 20% deposited in the Royal Bank of Canada to secure the fees of the author and director. This charge to have priority of all other private liabilities, and the director's half share (10%) to be prior to the author's. This reserve fund must be in the nature of a trust for the benefit of G.B.S. and G.P.; but it must not stand in their names or confer taxable possession on them until they demand it or some part of it from Pascal Films Ltd. and are duly paid by that firm.

An alternative plan would be a formation of a limited Liability Company by G.B.S., G.P., and the British or Canadian Government or the bank, its capital assets being 4 licences, G.P's services as director, and money advanced by the Government or the bank or by private speculators, the dividends of G.B.S. and G.P. to be limited to 10% each, and their shares classed as preference shares.

Again alternatively, if I sold my interest in the four copyrights for five years for promissory notes for £25,000 each, payable five years from the dates of release of the films, would the notes be taxable as securities in my possession? Can an unliquidated security be taxed?

These are all the expedients I can think of at present. Whatever the solution arrived at it will be stipulated that [of] all the dollars earned by the films in America 50% shall be offered for sale to the Treasury here.

If when you have recovered from the perusal of this letter you have any advice to give me, I shall appreciate it. But Pascal has his New York solicitor, who is also my solicitor, at work on the problem; and I am sending a copy to him accordingly.

faithfully
G.Bernard Shaw

To SIEGFRIED TREBITSCH

Cliveden (until the 30th)
Taplow. Bucks.
17th August 1941

[A/5; X/341]

[The Shaws had left Ayot for Cliveden on 12th August to allow the servants to have a much-needed holiday.]

My dear Trebitsch

Your letter[,] dated my birthday and full of reproaches, reached me today, having taken 22 days in transit.

You think now that in the old days I wrote to you every week. The truth is that you were always complaining that I did not answer your letters, exactly as you are complaining now. But then I did often leave you unanswered for months, whereas I now answer every letter promptly. Only, you expect the answer in two days. It arrives—when it arrives at all—in three weeks, during which you curse me every morning for my neglect.

The worst of it is that though I have many things to say to you I may not write them, as the Censors would probably object. All I can say is that the end of the war seems much nearer than it did, and that it will be an end favorable to you personally.

The "cruel change" which you accuse me of is real enough: it is the change from the vigor of my prime to the callousness and impotence of old age. Has it not yet occurred to you that I am now a very old man? It is amazing how people who have read in the newspapers that I am 85 write to me asking me to do things impossible to anyone over 40. You are just as thoughtless as they are.

I know your difficulties and have thought a good deal about them; but as to compassion! what can you expect from an octogenarian with the world falling into ruins round him?

However, keep on reproaching me. It relieves your feelings and amuses me. *All* your letters have been and shall be answered. Our best regards to Tina.

G. Bernard Shaw

To GILBERT MURRAY

Ayot St Lawrence. Welwyn
[H/36]   5th September 1941

[Murray reported on 26th July that he and Lady Mary were "completely bowled over" by most of the filmed *Major Barbara*, though they found the ending unsatisfactory. The tragic moment in the film when Barbara casts her bonnet into the water "moved and thrilled" him (X/289). Pascal's originally edited print of the film ran for 137 minutes, but distributors both in the United States and Britain made unauthorised cuts, to the detriment of the movie, which in varying markets and at varying times ran: 121 minutes (British première, 1941); 115 minutes (United States première); 100 minutes (New York revival, 1964); 95 minutes (Toronto Film Society screening, 1973), as reported by Bernard Dukore in the Shaw *Collected Screenplays* (1980).

Tito Pagliardini (1817–95) was a phoneticist and vocal teacher with whom Shaw was acquainted in his last years. George Skelton Terry's book was *Duodecimal Arithmetic* (1938).]

My dear Murray

Your letter of the 26th July moved me to go to St Albans at the sacrifice of some scarce petrol to see the Barbara film. These provincial picture houses believe that they must have at every performance two films and the news reel. To make room for this they cut the last third of the film all to pieces, and left Barbara's and Undershaft's position so hopelessly confused that I am inundated with letters accusing me of making Barbara sell out, and glorifying a scoundrelly war profiteer. You may have seen the film uncut. If so, there was nothing else in the program except the news reel. If there was another film then Barbara was cut.

As I write plays as they come to me, by inspiration and not by conscious logic, I am as likely as anyone else to be mistaken about their morals. It seems to me that what Barbara finds out is that the ancient Greek (whoever he was) who said "First make sure of an income and then practise virtue" was rightly preaching natural morality. Clearly the conversions of Snobby Price and Rummy Mitchens by "the bribe of bread" were not worth the few pence they cost. It was Barbara's business to get rich with Cusins while he fed the poor with honestly earned wages, and then, when their bellies were full, see what she could do with their souls, if she still thought herself qualified for that impertinence.

Thatt (as Bridges spells it), and the rule that until you have abolished

613

poverty you have done and can do nothing but tinker with the wreck-age, is what comes out of the play for me.

The enclosed book, originally called The Birth of Language, seemed to me worth boosting with a preface and a revised title to secure a cheap edition here. I grow more and more intolerant of official religion as I grow older, and also more convinced that a negative attitude to-wards it is no use. People rightly object to having their minds just emptied, no matter how poisonous the contents are. Better die of drink-ing brandy than of thirst. The only thing we have to fill up with is Creative Evolution; and Professor Wilson is strong and positive on that point.

The preface is nothing but an expansion of my Spelling Reform letter to The Times. I calculate that I have lost four years of my pro-ductive life writing superfluous letters. I could have written at least three good plays in four years.

Old Tito Pagliardini converted me many years ago to duodecimals. That also has an overwhelming economic side that has never been urged. The defeat of the French is probably due to their counting their money in three ha'penny francs and writing the results in decimals. An American named Terry has published a table of duodecimal logarithms. He ought to get a Nobel Prize for it.

G. Bernard Shaw

Almroth Wright said the other day that translations are contemptible, as nobody could possibly quote them. I cited the English Bible and your version of Euripides to confute him. He said you were the original poet masquerading as Euripides. He declared that he could quote you by pages, but that he had compared some of the finest of those pages with the alleged originals without discovering the faintest resemblance. Not being a Greek scholar I could not contradict him. I did not want to, in fact.

To I. J. PITMAN

Ayot St Lawrence. Welwyn
[H/1]   16th September 1941

[Isaac James (later Sir James) Pitman (1901–85), grandson of the founder of the Pitman system of phonography, was chairman of Sir Isaac Pitman & Sons, Ltd., 1934–66. In 1940–43 he was acting Squadron Leader in the R.A.F. After Shaw's death he served as an adviser to the Public Trustee for the carrying out of Shaw's wishes for the design and publication of a proposed British alphabet. David Kirkwood (1872–1955), Labour M.P., and William Gallacher, Communist M.P., both represented Scottish constituencies, the former Clydebank Dumbarton Burghs, the latter the Western Division of Fife.

Among the designers of systems of shorthand were William B. Gurney (1777–1855), official reporter to Parliament from 1813; Samuel Sams, author in 1812 of *A Complete and Universal System of Stenography*; Samuel Taylor (fl. 1786–1816), deviser of a universal system of stenography, of which Pitman's system is an adaptation; John Matthew Sloan and Émile Duployé (1833–1913), creators and publishers of a system of shorthand that rivalled Pitman's; and John Robert Gregg (1867–1948), creator of the Gregg shorthand system in common usage in the United States.]

Dear Mr Pitman

If you take up this spelling business it may get a move on after lying fallow for a generation, as you are evidently the grandson of your grandfather, and a chip of the old block.

My contribution ["A King's Spelling" *The Times*, 15th April] has been the turning right-side-up of the enormous economic case for the reform, which is the only one strong enough to move mountains.

But the English (like other peoples) are no sooner convinced of the need of a reform than they assume that it must be violently catastrophic and instantaneous. Much of my life as a propagandist has been spent on curing converts to Socialism of the notion that the program will be capitalism in full blast on Saturday, revolution on Sunday, and Socialism complete on Monday. My collaborator Sidney Webb at last succeeded in establishing "the inevitability of gradualness" as a slogan. The next step in Spelling Reform must be the extension to it of that slogan. Our converts will begin with a vision of the old spelling everywhere on Tuesday, the conversion of all typewriters, monotype machines, and printing plants generally on Wednesday, and on Thursday the appearance of The Times and of Government publications in the new phonetic alphabet of 42 letters. Which will of course make the scheme utterly incredible and impossible.

What I visualize is the designing of an alphabet of 42 letters plus a few double consonants as you suggest, and the casting of a fount of type to enable it to be printed. Then the compilation and publication of a manual like your New Era Pitman instruction book. Then the issue of a propagandist journal, or the planting of a section about the New British Writing (N.B.W.) in an existing journal or even a newspaper, like the Gaelic sections in the Irish papers. Then the publication of some modern books in the N.B.W.: not the Bible and Shakespear, but

615

Wells, Shaw, and Gilbert Murray's version of the Greek classic drama. The authors could permit this just as they permit Braille editions. If the results were encouraging enough, inventors would set to work on typewriters with three letters on each type bar instead of two and similarly modified monotype and linotype machines. The old spelling and the new would run side by side until the old faded out and the new became official. *The old spelling must not be altered.*

The money would be provided by a Society of private subscribers with such legacies and endowments as it could get from enthusiasts; or the scheme could be taken up by the Pitman firm or the Orthological Institute. It would finally pay its own way if it proved irresistible.

There could be no bickering about detail *once the alphabet was launched*, because people could spell as they speak and be encouraged to do so. (See, however, my first postscript hereto.) A Pitman writer can write the word future ⌎ or ⌎ as he pleases. Standard forms would establish themselves naturally; but at no time will there be any reason why a private Bill in Parliament drafted by Mr Kirkwood or Mr Gallacher should be spelt like one drafted by Mr Churchill, provided both are equally intelligible.

In short, the thing must grow just as Pitman has grown.

But if I were a Pitman director, I would try to extricate it from its obsession with the art of verbatim reporting, which finally drove both Sir Isaac and Henry Sweet into the blind alley of reporting shorthand. They ceased to be phoneticians and became mere speed merchants. English cannot be written at the speed at which it is spoken; but with years of practice "conditioned reflexes," as Pavlov called them, can be established between spoken words or phrases and marks on paper called grammalogues, and contractions which leave the reader to guess whether vl means novel or navel or nevertheless or envelope or voluntary or involuntary or what not. Henry Sweet got so clever at this sort of guessing that after seven years of it he dismissed me as mentally defective because I could not decipher postcards written in his Current Shorthand. Pitman is now devoted entirely to imposing these reflexes on its students. 200 of them may enable a girl typist to take down from dictation the clichés of an ordinary office. 2000 may be needed for a gallery reporter who has to keep going for 15 minutes. Heaven knows how many are needed by a law reporter who has to stick it all day, and sometimes report several barristers at a time. The girl typist may qualify in a few months, the gallery man a year or two, the law reporter

616

five or seven years. The old Gurney men used to be apprenticed for seven years.

Now for this purpose it was quite unnecessary to invent either Pitman or Sweet. Any system—Pitman, Sweet, Gurney, Sams, Taylor, Sloan-Duployan, Gregg or which not—will serve equally well: Charles Dickens could report verbatim as well as any Pitmanite. Pitman triumphed in England because Sir Isaac was the best business organizer; but Gregg has captured the U.S.A. similarly. Had Henry Sweet had your business ability or, like your grandfather, enjoyed that superhuman power of working 16 hours a day for 30 years which enables anyone possessing it to do anything, he would have snatched quite a lot of lucrative business from Pitman's. Being, as he was, the most cantankerous of Oxford University satirists, his shorthand got no further than a lithograph in his own handwriting of the very ill-arranged manual he produced. But it may yet be discovered and boosted by some speculator envious of the success of Pitman and Gregg.

Now for one person who writes enough to care whether the word "though" is to be spelt with six letters or two, there must be at least a thousand who, like myself, neither need nor desire to write as fast as a speaker can speak, but who can add years to their working time by using the Pitman alphabet. I have done so ever since I could afford to pay a secretary. I save years of time and tons of paper by it. All my plays and books for the last 40 years have been written with it. But Pitman put the most disheartening difficulties in the way of my learning it. He engaged me in a desperate and impossible effort to write from 120 to 160 words a minute. Now the top speed at which I write averages ten words a minute. I can take as much time as I please over a sentence; and the arguing of it into its final form may take ten minutes or more. If I have written 1200 words in two hours I have done a good day's work. Pitman insisted that I must do 15,000! To achieve this unnatural feat, which an author (as distinguished from a reporter) never has to perform, he loaded my memory up with 60% of grammalogues and phraseograms and contractions which only held me back, as I could write 20 words in full while I was thinking how to contract 3 or four, and made my shorthand illegible not only by other people but by myself. Yet, staring Sir Isaac in the face, was the case of Dickens, who, though he had made his living as a verbatim reporter, had to write all his books at full length in longhand (you can see them at the Victoria and Albert Museum) because he could not hand his verbatim stenography to anyone else to transcribe for him.

Now I can write a book in Pitman's alphabet, and not only have it

617

transcribed by my secretary, but when I am abroad and she is not with me, can hand it to the nearest shorthand typist, who transcribes it without the smallest difficulty. I did this in South Africa with my book entitled The Adventures of a Black Girl in Search of God. The young lady found my 1870 shorthand old-fashioned in some particulars, as some changes had had to be made to renew the copyright; but she produced a typed copy ready for the printer. For thirty years I have written t-h-o-u-g-h with a single stroke of the pen, and all the articles, prepositions, conjunctions, and auxiliary verbs with ticks and dots and half circles, at my average rate of ten words a minute for two hours a day, writing all the longer and less frequent words legibly in full. I began by using all the grammalogues I could remember; and two or three of them still cling like bad habits; but the rest of the 60% shed themselves gradually and unconsciously until I now write nearly every word (except the ticks and dots) in full and separately even when their grammalogues still come back as reflexes.

The saving in manual labor has been enormous: you can calculate it if you practise such feats. My shorthand writing is not impaired by my age. I can write it legibly in the train, which I cannot do in long-hand; and I am independent of typewriters, dictaphones, and all such heavy and expensive apparatus.

Therefore were I a Pitman partner I should set up a department for Authors' Shorthand, not on speaking terms with the reporters' depart-ment, and having separate pages in the [Pitman's] Journal. I should advertise in The Author and urge the importance of the system to all authors, laying stress on the fact that unlike reporting shorthand (which is virtually all contractions and grammalogues) it is easy to learn, and can be taught to the laziest author in a few weeks. Almost all the typing office[s] have someone who can read it more easily than longhand, which is often very illegible—sometimes, as in the cases of Mrs Sidney Webb (Lady Passfield), Lady Astor, and the late Cunninghame Graham, positively cryptographic.

Its only disadvantage for you is that it has enabled me to write you an inordinately long letter. You can, however, keep it until you retire from business and have time for it.

faithfully
G. Bernard Shaw

PS There is one exception to my statement that there would be no squabble about details. There would be if the alphabet were thrown open to discussion. A few master spirits must decide it and get it de-signed by an artist both for print and handwriting, in which the nt endings should figure. It must be presented to the mob of spelling cranks as a *fait accompli*, as the Pitman alphabet was. There was a long-handwriting in the Pitman Manual of 1840.

PPS The economic argument applies so strongly to duodecimal arithmetic that Sir Isaac's agitation for it might be revived. . . .

The word AGE which you cite was "simplified" by Henry Sweet into EIDZH!! Five letters instead of two.

To CHIEF SOLICITOR, H. M. TREASURY

Ayot St Lawrence. Welwyn
[G/1]   16th October 1941

[Shaw's correspondence with the Treasury may have been prompted by prosecutions of George Arliss and Noël Coward for alleged currency violation.]

Dear Sir

I have to thank you for your letter. Since then I have been looking into my foreign securities, and find that I possess 185 5% Preference Stock Shares in the Buenos Ayres Western Railway, and £600 (nominal) in the San Paulo R.C. Railway, and Japanese 4% Loan returning a gross interest of £87–4–0. Are these of any interest to H.M. Treasury? The South American ones seem to be worthless at present.

Also I find that my New York solicitor holds some money of mine which he invests and transfers as seems best to him from time to time. His last remittance of interest, amounting to only £23–18–6 for the year, is described by him as "the Walton Estate Mortgage." It must be held in his name, as I have taken no part in its acquirement and know nothing more about it. But it is a dollar security; and I can instruct him to sell it for what it is worth and send me his cheque on his New York bank payable in dollars for the result, if that would be of any service.

The rest of my capital is in home securities.

faithfully
G. Bernard Shaw

To NOËL COWARD

Ayot St Lawrence. Welwyn

[H/1; X/414]   26th October 1941

[Coward had been charged with having violated currency regulations by maintaining and using an American bank account after the outbreak of war, "when new laws had made it compulsory to declare any money held overseas to the Treasury, and illegal to spend any of it without prior permission." Though insistent that he was unaware of the law and that neither his British nor American accountants had brought it to his attention, Coward was about to heed the advice of an eminent attorney Dingwall Bateson to plead guilty in hopes of receiving a lighter fine, when Shaw's letter reached him (Sheridan Morley, *A Talent to Amuse*, 1969). Shaw had given similar advice, after the fact, to George Arliss on 27th September. "Guilty or Not Guilty," he wrote, "is not a question of fact, though of course the facts must be ascertained before the court can arrive at any decision at all. But when the facts are established the question of guilt remains entirely open. If you were firing at a target for practice as a Home Guard, and your bullet missed the target and killed me, and you said 'I cannot deny it: I killed him: I plead guilty' the judge would have to sentence you to death. You would of course plead Not Guilty, and be acquitted on the ground that the killing was an unintended accident. If the jury disliked me enough, they might even bring in a verdict of justifiable homicide" (H/58). He recommended that Arliss consult his solicitors about a retrial or revision of sentence on the ground that he had entered a Guilty plea under a misapprehension.]

Dear Noel Coward

The other day George Arliss, being in trouble about his American securities, pleaded Guilty under the impression that he was only admitting the facts and saving the Lord Mayor useless trouble. There was nothing for it then but to fine him £3000.

He should have admitted the facts and pleaded Not Guilty, being as innocent as an unborn lamb. Guilty or Not Guilty is not a question of material facts. Of course the facts have to be established before that question arises; but when they are admitted or proved they leave the question of innocence or guilt unsettled. There can be no guilt without intention. Arliss knew nothing about the Finance Clauses, and did not even know that he owned American securities. He was Not Guilty, and should have said so and thereby put his defence in order.

Therefore let nothing induce you to plead Guilty. If your lawyers advise you to do so tell them that *I* advise you not to. You may know all this as well as I do; but after the Arliss case I think it safer to warn you.

G.B.S.

["I can't tell you how touched & grateful I am for your wise & most kindly advice which I will most certainly follow," Coward replied two days later. "I need hardly tell you I am completely innocent . . . & have done the best I could since the war began to work for the country. I intend to fight this tooth & claw & feel most enormously encouraged by your great kindness in writing to me" (A/3; X/414). Eventually he was found guilty of two related charges, for one of which he was fined £200 and for the other £1600.]

To F. E. LOEWENSTEIN

Ayot St Lawrence. Welwyn
[E/4; W/289]   14th November 1941
[Loewenstein had asked for permission to found a Shaw Society. It survives to the present day, with Ellen Pollock as its president since 1957.]

The Browning Society was a terror to Browning.
Shelley was dead.
Shakespear was dead.
I shall soon be dead.
We all provided a rallying point for the co-operation and education of kindred spirits and a forum for their irreconcilable controversies.
So go ahead; but dont bother me about it. I am old, deaf, and dotty. In short, a Has Been.

G. Bernard Shaw

To LAWRENCE LANGNER

Ayot St Lawrence. Welwyn
[C/7; X/312]   28th November 1941
[There was no further Theatre Guild production of Shaw until 1948, when it revived *You Never Can Tell*, with Leo G. Carroll as the Waiter.]

William Brady also wants to revive You Never Can Tell with a magnificent cast; but I am sufficiently ruined already by Katharine Cornell's revival of The Doctor's Dilemma and the Pygmalion film, with royalties taxed 27% in the States and 95% here. I shall have to let Gabriel film Arms & the Man to keep him alive; but that is all for the duration: I may die at any moment now; and what is to become of all the people provided for in my will if my property is swallowed

621

up by this infernal war? Dont mention another production to me unless you can guarantee a flop worse than The Apple Cart or the Unexpected Isles. However, I rejoice in the recovery of the Guild from its phase of apparent slow extinction. It sounds more like its old self now.

G.B.S.

To ALFRED DOUGLAS

Ayot St Lawrence. Welwyn
[H/64; X/394]   27th December 1941

[Joseph Montague Kenworthy became tenth Baron Strabolgi of England on the death of his father in 1934.]

Dear Childe Alfred

Swift was not born in Surrey. He came of British stock (York and Leicester) and was related through his two grandfathers to Dryden and Herrick; but he was born in Dublin, schooled in Kilkenny, graduated at Trinity College[,] Dublin, did not set foot in England until he was 22, and of the 78 years of his life spent ten in London, ten back and forward between London and his benefice in Trim, and 58 in Ireland.

Of my 85 years twenty have been spent in Ireland and 65 in England; and yet what mortal power could make an Englishman of me? The climate of Ireland and its society will stamp an Englishman for life; but nothing will erase the native stamp on an Irishman.

I learn from a letter in The Irish Times that Eire is a Gaelic translation of Ireland, which is still the correct name of the island in the English language.

Russia is rather in a fix about Japan. When she offered us the same non-aggression trading pact that she made with Hitler, we contemptuously refused, and made no secret of our hope that some day we should be able to rally Germany and Japan to the sacred task of smashing the Bolsheviks and making a new Partition of Russia among the western Capitalist powers. Japan had more sense, and made the offered pact. And as she has not attacked Russia Stalin has no excuse for a breach of neutrality. And we can hardly ask him to take on another front when we have taken no notice of his suggestion that we should do this ourselves. Nobody but Strabolgie has said we ought to. So for the moment Stalin can do nothing but help China all he can without declaring war, as we did in Spain when we made the horrible mistake of securing victory for Franco, with the result that Franco will probably sell Spain to Hitler for Portugal, and give us a fearful job in the Atlantic.

When you say that I will become a Catholic you miss the point that I am already an ultra-Catholic, being a Communist of sixty years standing. Rome is behind me, not before me. Am I an Aztec that I should eat the god, or a child that I should believe the Apostles' creed, or a tribal savage that I should worship an idol like Jehovah and offer blood sacrifices to appease him? As to becoming a Christian and letting Jesus suffer for my sins, damn it, Childe, I have still some instincts of a gentleman left. I have never said these things to you before because you had better have the Roman faith than none, and Jesus was right when he refused to attack the established religion of the Jews on the ground that if you tried to rid a field of wheat of its tares you would pull up too much of the wheat with them. Still I am shewing you my background just for a moment so that you may understand that you are up against a modern Catholicism compared to which the Vatican is only a little meeting house in a village, preaching an impossible Protestantism.

My book, which I thought would be finished this year, is a mess of senile ramblings and repetitions. I shall never get it into any very orderly sequence. But perhaps my second childhood may go down with the mob better than my maturity did.

Time for me to die, Childe, time for me to die. But I can still saw logs. I am really proud of the pile of them in the garden, though nobody will ever call them immortal works.

Lady Keeble (Lillah McCarthy) is a nailer at reciting sonnets: the BBC should have found that out. Instead of boring me with small talk she declaims them at me by the dozen—knows them all by heart.

Enough.

GBS

To R. & R. CLARK

Ayot St Lawrence. Welwyn
[C/3]   8th January 1942
[The first chapter of *Everybody's Political What's What?* was posted to William Maxwell on 4th January, with a request for specimen pages and a warning, "*Not* Fournier." "I expect," Shaw concluded, "we shall fall back on solid Caslon, like the Intelligent Woman's Guide" (A/3). Maxwell

obliged with specimens of several type styles. The artist Eric Gill (1882–1940) designed a dozen printing types, with names ranging from Perpetua and Solus to Joanna and Jubilee.]

I am not convinced by Baskerville, Plantin or Bembo or Imprint that they are as good as Caslon. You said there was a type designed by Eric Gill with a name which I forget—a pretty name.

I still cling to Morris's rule of no leads and the largest face. 11 point is not big enough to satisfy me. What about 12 or 13. I presume the machines are limited to one size.

I should like to see a page—or a dozen lines would do—in Caslon or any of the other new types that are available on the machines. I have seen a lot here and there.

GBS

To R. & R. CLARK

[Ayot St Lawrence. Welwyn]
[C/3]   [Undated: assigned to 16th January 1942]

[The *What's What?* was not adopted by any book club, English or American.]

My wife is much taken by the swank of Plantin and so was I at first; but it is not economical and I think it is tiresome to read because it is crowded and shouts at you all the time.

My final choice is Bembo, which is very readable and quiet. Have you anything against it? It is economical.

For the sake of my domestic peace I should like to see a whole page of my first chapter, standard edition size, set up in (a Plantin and (b Bembo.

It is possible that the Left Book Club, or one of its rivals, might select the book for sale to their members at half a crown, and order ?ooo copies. You might bear this in mind.

Have you any preference yourself?

GBS

To A. W. TUKE

[A/1; W/387]

Ayot St Lawrence. Welwyn
17th January 1942

[Anthony W. Tuke (1897–1975), general manager of Barclay's Bank 1931–46, was a trustee of the Historic Churches Preservation Trust and a church-warden of Ayot church. William Archer (1866–1941) was carpenter for the Brocket Arms Estate. The gravedigger Richards is not remembered by the present villagers.]

My dear Churchwarden

I used to pay £2–2–0 pew rent whenever your predecessors dunned me for it. They stopped doing this for some reason: perhaps because I had to pay £20 to keep the tower of the old abbey church from falling, and later on £100 to preserve the Lyde tombs and colonnade of the newer church.

Now that I have succeeded our late neighbor Archer as the Village Atheist and the late gravedigger Richards as the Oldest Inhabitant the occasion seems a fit one for resuming the two guinea arrangement.

My wife desires to contribute a fiver to the liquidation of the debt. Also her best regards to Mrs Tuke.

I renew my offer to defray the cost of removing the three trees which now hide and disfigure the classic front of the church as soon as labor can be found to do it.

The parishioners will not consider this generous on my part, as they believe me to be a millionaire. You, being a banker, know better. A windfall of £29,000 (estimated in the newspapers as £55,000) has cost me £50,000 in taxes. I shall live this year on overdraft, and may yet die not only in this parish but on it.

Wishing you a more solvent New Year than I can hope for myself—

faithfully
G. Bernard Shaw

To IVO GEIKIE-COBB

[C/1; X/415]

Ayot St Lawrence. Welwyn
21st January 1942

[The B.B.C. was considering a performance of Handel's *Messiah* in which the original instrumentation would be restored; Geikie-Cobb sought to interest Shaw in introducing the performance. Victor-Charles Mahillon

(1841–1924) was a Belgian music scholar whose family manufactured musical instruments. A collector of ancient instruments, he made copies of many of them, anticipating the modern trend toward re-creation of "original performances." Mozart's arrangement and adaptation of *Messiah* for new instrumentation was first performed in March 1789. For Shaw's views on the Atonement see his preface (1916) to *Androcles and the Lion.*]

1. No: it wouldnt do. Messiah cannot be performed with its original instrumentation. For this you need to have at least half a dozen oboes specially made with special reeds to double the violins. Henry Wood has one that Mahillon made for him.

2. Handel is dead and cannot put in the original harmonies he supplied on the organ.

3. Without these the original score is dull and inferior to Mozart's version of it.

4. The subject of the work is the Atonement; yet it can still make people cry who, like myself, abhor the Scapegoat doctrine as perniciously demoralizing and ungentlemanly.

5. I should have to say all this; and A. W. would get the sack.

The Soviet War News is sent to me daily. Thanks all the same.

G.B.S.

To DOUGLAS R. ALLAN

[H/99]

Ayot St Lawrence. Welwyn
6th February 1942

[Douglas R. Allan (1904–62), a B.B.C. performer turned producer, was preparing for the Home Service a schools broadcast of *Saint Joan* consisting of a dramatic reading of scenes with special insertions written by Shaw as connective tissue, to be read by Allan as narrator, on 10th February. (Sir) Felix Aylmer (1889–1979), highly regarded character actor, appeared as Warwick in the Old Vic revival of *Saint Joan* in 1934.]

Dear Mr Douglas Allan

I return the script for the St Joan School Broadcast with some amendments, and an alternative version of the Narrator's part. Your version seems to me to be too critical and to assume that the listeners know all about it already, which is a fatal mistake. Also it treats the narrator as an announcer. He should be treated as an actor taking part in the performances: you should give it to one of your best speakers. I suggest Aylmer. Dunois should be your best leading juvenile with a pleasant tenor voice, contrasting as strongly as possible with Baudricourt's, which should be a robust baritone or bass. The steward's voice should be that of a weak old sniveller. And for heaven's sake, dont give the part of the page to a woman and make him the principal boy in a pantomime. He must be a real boy.

I have given the Narrator about 200 words more than in your script; so you must allow him a couple of minutes more. Any attempt to hurry them up will end in their all speaking at the same excessive pace and spoiling the broadcast. Contrast of pace and pitch and tone color are even more important in a broadcast than on the stage, where they are all-important.

faithfully
G. Bernard Shaw

When my version is fair-typed, will you be so good as to have an extra carbon made and sent to me.

To SIEGFRIED TREBITSCH

England
19th February 1942

[H/5; X/341]

[Trebitsch had deliberately misled Shaw into believing he was practising frugality by living "modestly" in Lausanne, when in actuality he and Tina were domiciled in Zürich at the costly Dolder Hotel.]

My dear Trebitsch

Your letter dated the 25th January arrived on the 14th February. And a postcard which I sent to you on the 2nd April last, addressed to a hotel at Montreux, has just been returned to me, though it was passed by the censor. In the face of such dates you must not blame me when you get no reply to your letters. The replies are on the way, and will arrive perhaps when the war is over.

Do not torment yourself with the delusion that you should have remained in England. You would have been interned in a concentration camp in the Isle of Man; and though you would have been released after some months your situation would have been much more difficult than it is in Switzerland even if you had escaped the Blitz. On the whole you are better off in Lausanne than you would be in London.

I have done all I could to obtain a permit to send you £100 through United Artists or through my bankers. I pleaded that you had been the means of transferring a good deal of money from Germany to England; that you were not a Nazi but a Jewish refugee; that an exception should be made in your favor etc etc; but it was all in vain: the Treasury was obdurate and maintained that any action which would have the effect of transferring money to you would be against the defence regulations.

In any case I could do very little; for my own financial situation is difficult enough, as you may judge from the fact that when the enormous success of [the] Pygmalion film put £29,000 into my pocket, the Chancellor of the Exchequer took £50,000 out of it. Another such "success" and I shall be poorer than you are.

As to The Chocolate Soldier my lawyer maintained that though there is no copyright in titles yet the three words were a plagiarism of the text of Arms and the Man. But it was impossible to claim that your title "Helden" or the words "praliné Soldat" had been used in the English version. I could not in any case have started an expensive and very doubtful lawsuit on such a point. Finally they did what I myself advised them to do. They took an entirely different and very good comedy by Molnar as their libretto, and made the hero and heroine sing Oscar Strauss's musical numbers, in which I have no copyright whatever. This new version has been performed in London; and not one of the press notices said a word about Arms and the Man. So the affair is closed as far as I am concerned. It is still possible that the old German version may be revived; and in that case, when the war is over, you could claim a royalty; but there is no present help nor much future promise in this. I never believed that you could get anything out of the business. The only way I could have helped you in it was by consenting to the filming of the old version on condition that the bribe they offered you to persuade me was paid to you; but I was pledged to Pascal not to allow such a filming, and anyhow it would not have been a decent transaction.

I could say much more; but the uncertainty of this ever reaching you and the pressure on my writing time on my new book and other matters obliges me to stop. Your miseries, which I dare not think about, may end sooner than we expect. If they dont, we shall be companions in misfortune.

always yours
G. Bernard Shaw

To KINGSLEY MARTIN

Ayot St Lawrence. Welwyn
[H/92]   10th March 1942

[The United States had entered the war in December 1941 following the Japanese attack on Pearl Harbor. Hong Kong, also attacked on 7th December, surrendered to the Japanese on Christmas Day. Enemy troops crossed the Johore Strait into Singapore on 8th February 1942; the British command surrendered the city and the island on 15th February. "Steady, boys, steady" is a lyric by David Garrick (in *Heart of Oak, c.* 1770).]

Dear Kingsley Martin

Steady, steady, steady. You need a holiday. Take a week now or you will have to take months later on.

An editor must never let the news upset him. If he does so he will be lost exactly as a school teacher is lost if she allows herself to become fond of her pupils, or a Bond Street picture dealer if he lets himself care so much for pictures that he cannot bear to part from them. To him the collapse of the British Commonwealth in the far east must be as much in the day's work as the collapse of the Spanish empire in South America or Gibbon's Decline and Fall. The last regrouping of the world must be to him like the last murder or the last opening of Parliament: news and nothing but news. He must be as good a judge of news as a licensed victualler must be of liquor; but he must remember that a public house will kill its keeper if he drinks, and that a newspaper will kill its editor if he cannot announce the Day of Judgement without turning a hair.

I know no more than you what is going to happen or what path the human race will follow, as the world is not inhabited by Bernard Shaws exclusively or even largely, any more than by Kingsley Martins. We shall not be consulted, and can only look on at the antics of Homo Insapiens, and keep up a running commentary on them. When they say that the "loss" of Singapore is the end of the world, we can point out that Singapore stands just where it did, and is no more lost than the United States were when Cornwallis surrendered to Washington. We can, however, add that if Hong Kong and Singapore are retaken by the Chinese we shall have to buy them back; and it is by no means certain—it is certainly not reasonable—that the Chinese will consent to sell to a western Power at any price. If Australia is saved by the United States and not by us, Australia may decide to become a United State herself and change the Union Jack for the Stars and Stripes. We may have to let India go just as we had to let Eire go in 1921, and even go farther and become a sovereign independent federation. If so it will all be news for you; and to the born editor news is great fun, even as the capsizing of a boat in Sydney Harbor is great fun for the sharks. It will be your livelihood. Do not let yourself be rattled by a word in a familiar private letter.

I have advised the nations to adopt Communism, and have carefully explained how they can do it without cutting one another's throats. But if they prefer to do it by cutting one another's throats I am no less a Communist. Communism will be good even for Yahoos.

But what you need is a day off, not another letter from me. Clifford Sharp let himself be rattled by the sinking of the Lusitania and then drank himself to death. Yet the Lusitania did not matter a damn beyond bringing in America on our side. Hong Kong and the rest are more serious; but they are not the end of the world. So again steady, boys, steady, to fight and be conquered again and again.

GBS

["Dear Capt. Shotover," Martin replied on 12th March, "I hope they have kept up the quality of the rum for you when you slip away at the sound of a question you don't want to be bothered to answer. The Captain did not wait till old age to evolve this trick, but always scored with a shot or rather a volley of shots over his shoulder when anyone tried to disturb his own line of thought. Anyone would think from your last letter that it was I who was rattled over Singapore or what not, and not you who had added a note to your first letter which showed that you were all groggy at the knees. In my original letter I merely remarked that Russia might win the war, that the British Empire and Germany might lose it, and the dreams of G.B.S. and others be fulfilled. I had known that the loss of Singapore was coming ever since the 'Prince of Wales' and the 'Repulse' were sunk and the American Navy put out of action at Pearl Harbour. Nothing that has happened in the Far East has surprised me . . . and now bold as brass or Bernard Shaw you write me a solemn epistle about the proper detachment of an Editor. My letter was an exclamation mark occasioned by the surprising picture of your "if, if, if," combined with a rebuke that I was in fact the kind of detached unfeeling creature that you now tell me an Editor ought to be. Time for another glass of rum. A noggin all round, me included" (H.c.u/92).]

630

To ADA TYRRELL

[C/9; X/351.e]

Ayot St Lawrence. Welwyn
20th March 1942

I am still alive and very apologetic for staying so late. Charlotte still suffering from lumbago. We have slept in our beds every night war or no war, and our rations are sufficient for us. But we cannot move about much, and are for all social purposes deaf dotty and half dead. Glad to hear from you all the same[.]

Lucy, having no children, appropriated yours, and did the spoiling, leaving you to do the smacking. Like a grandmother. You saw more of her and knew her better than I did. Things musical came so easily to her that she never learnt how to work hard professionally.

And the way we were brought up, or rather not brought up!!! It doesnt bear thinking of. . . .

GBS

To KENNETH BARNES

[E/3]

Ayot St Lawrence. Welwyn
7th July 1942

I quite agree with the auditors that we have come off jolly well after 2 years.

As for me, I am ruined—living on overdraft for the first time in my life.

GBS

To E. STRAUSS

[H/1]

Address until the 14th
Cliveden. Taplow
Maidenhead
4th August 1942

[The Shaws made what was to be their final visit to Cliveden from 21st July to 14th August. The Viennese-born Erich Strauss (b. 1911) came to England in 1938. A chartered accountant and economist by profession, he was the author of numerous books, including *Bernard Shaw: Art and Socialism* (1942), a Marxist account of Shaw's social and economic writings.]

Dear Mr Strauss

Our friend Gollancz has sent me your book about me; and I have enjoyed reading it, as is natural considering how high you rank my work for its thought and its art. You are evidently a connoisseur in both departments; so much so indeed that I should like to know your age and record, and will certainly look them up in Who's Who, when my visit here is over, and I get back to my books and references at home.

Having written this far I went to look for a Who's Who here, and found one. You are not in it, which is what I expected, as I guessed you as a very clever beginner, young enough to be much more up to date than my earlier critics and commentators.

You must be a young man; for an older one could never have undertaken the appalling task of reading nearly all my books, including the five novels which nobody would publish and which nothing could now induce me to read, though they are branded on my memory far more deeply and agonizingly than much that I have written since.

Now let me tell you where you have [made] a mess of the job. You have taken for your framework what you call my development, and got frightfully mixed up between [s]imple matter of fact and stages in that development. You demand happy endings, which you call "solutions" to all my plays and treatises; and when you dont get them, you infer failure, disappointment, embitterment, disillusion, and even despair on my part, and cannot understand why in the face of these catastrophes I still stick to my Socialism. Assuming (without noticing it) that all capitalists, plutocrats, bosses, and top dogs generally must be exactly alike; and finding that they are not exactly alike in all my plays, and are in fact all different types, you infer that here also my whole outlook on society has again changed catastrophically, and cannot make out why I have not changed from a Fabian into a diehard. All this has led you to write several passages of poppycock. You should read Benedetto Croce and get cured of mistaking classifications for men. It is necessary sometimes: for instance, Karl Marx had to lump men into two classes, bourgeois and proletarian, to such an extent that you wonder whether he ever in his life had met and spoken to a real workman or a real employer; but a playwright cannot work in that way: his types must never repeat oneanother. Leontes must not be a repetition of Othello.

Also you cannot make out why I, being a Republican and a Communist, do not write plays in which all the kings are villains and all the Socialists angels. That is the very crudest dramatic practice, and is never convincing. Molière made the mistake, when he wrote an anti-clerical play [*Tartuffe*], of making the priest in it a common scoundrel. This proves nothing: there are scoundrels in every profession. When I want to chasten a profession I always take it at its best, not at its worst. Morell is a first rate clergyman: Magnus is a first rate king:

Mrs Warren is a first rate procuress and a good mother. You conclude that I must have begun as a pandar, been converted to Christian Socialism, and later to royalism.

On the same lines you think that because I applauded Mussolini and Hitler until they went off the rails, and contrasted their effectiveness and that of the two Napoleons with the impotence of the British Parliament, I became a worshipper of dictators and despaired when they went wrong. But I do not shoot a dictator until he sells out. And I do not become an Imperialist when I point out that Louis Napoleon could and did rebuild Paris whilst the British Parliament could not even build a bridge over the Severn.

You find that several of my characters are myself. Novices often say so. And of course it is true in the sense that Hamlet and Macbeth are both Shakespear. They both speak his language, and cannot think nor feel anything outside his consciousness, just as Pip and David Copperfield are both Dickens; and so are Jo Gargery and Mr Pumblechook. But the playwright meets other people and observes them. The portrait painter puts something of himself into every portrait. When you look at the famous portrait of Charles V you say at once "That is a Titian." But you had better not say "Charles V was Titian" if you value your standing as a critic. In Man and Superman I used the Socialist leader Henry Mayers Hyndman as a model and drew a pen portrait of him. And you declare that it is a portrait of myself. You say the same of my sketch of Napoleon in The Man of Destiny. They are both Shaws in the sense that Reynolds's Mrs Siddons and his Dr Johnson are both Reynoldses, but in any other sense such an identification reduces criticism to absurdity.

As a Socialist it is my business to state social problems and to solve them. I have done this in tracts, treatises, essays and prefaces. You keep asking why I do not keep repeating these propositions and principles Euclidically in my plays. You might as well ask me why I dont wear my gloves on my feet or eat jam with a spade. And when you make all these thoughtlessnesses the basis of a tragedy of ambition (a blind lust which I never felt in my life), disappointment, failure and despair, your book gets out of all relation to the facts, much more to the poetry of my life and work.

All the same you are a clever lad from the point of view of 86; and if I come across your next book I shall probably read it.

faithfully
G. Bernard Shaw

To SYDNEY C. COCKERELL

Ayot St Lawrence. Welwyn
21st August 1942

[C/78; X/277]

I must drop you a line as Charlotte cannot write easily. We have just spent three weeks with the Astors at Cliveden; and the Canadian medical service at the military hospital there took her on for a thorough overhaul in a businesslike way: Xray, blood sample, life history all complete. Verdict: suffering from the effect of an accident in her teens, and incurable because the only treatment—steel corsets, plastic jacket, immobilization for months—is bearable by men under forty only. No danger to her life beyond that of all octogenarians; but she will be an invalid as far as medical science goes: a sentence of lumbago for life.

We are very difficult of access here except for people with cars and supplementary petrol. It is such a business that visits tend to be longer than Charlotte can bear; but she is getting used to her condition and will, I hope, soon be normally sociable. Then we can settle something: it is time for us to meet. I am damnably old; but as well as can be expected at 86. I can still write a bit.

G.B.S.

To HERBERT MORRISON

[Ayot St Lawrence. Welwyn]
[Undated: c. 25th August 1942]

[F.u/4]

[Herbert Morrison (1888–1965), later Baron Morrison of Lambeth, Labour M.P. for East Lewisham, was Home Secretary 1940–45 and Minister of Home Security, as well as a member of the War Cabinet. On 5th April 1942, Easter Sunday, a constabulary patrol car in Belfast was fired upon by a group of I.R.A. men as a diversion to draw police away from an area where a banned ceremony commemorating the 1916 Rising was to be held. In the ensuing gun-battle a police constable was killed and the leader of the I.R.A. unit, Tom Williams, was wounded before the group surrendered. All six of the men involved in the shooting were convicted and sentenced to death. As no Republican in Northern Ireland had ever been executed, the threat of a mass hanging and of its possible repercussions set off protests, demonstrations, and appeals all over Ireland and Britain. On 22nd August an appeal to the courts was dismissed, and on the 28th the appeal to the House of Lords was refused. Three days later, however, just four days before the date set for execution, five of the men received reprieves. Williams, the leader, though he had not fired the shots that killed the constable, went to the gallows on 2nd September in the Crumlin Road jail.

634

"God Save Ireland," by Timothy D. Sullivan, is sung to the tune of "Tramp, Tramp, the Boys are Marching." The "Indian arrests" refers to the arrest of Gandhi earlier in August.]

Dear Mr Herbert Morrison

I am being urged to address you on the subject of the Belfast sentences with a view to having the case reviewed in the House of Lords. The practical effect of such a step would be to take the case out of your hands and leave it in those of the Judicial Committee.

Now the only chance of a reprieve for the condemned men lies in H.M. the King's prerogative of clemency as to the exercise of which you are privileged to advise him.

The Judicial Committee has nothing to do with the prerogative or with the considerations of policy and sentiment on which it depends. Its business is to declare the law in the case; and as the sentence in question is beyond all dispute lawful and the verdict and sentence in perfect order, reference to the Committee must result in the hanging of the condemned men: that is, in the very event which its advocates want to avert.

I also want to avert it, because I am old enough to remember the parallel case of the Manchester Martyrs, who were hanged in a batch because one of them, in breaking the lock of the prison van with a pistol shot, accidentally killed a police officer at the other side of the door. The sentence was good in law; but the executions gave so much trouble afterwards that less harm would have ensued if the victims had been pardoned, pensioned and decorated. I do not want to see the ghosts of the Manchester Martyrs reviving as the Belfast Martyrs to the strains of "God Save Ireland, said the Heroes" and a stirring up of all the old bad blood and Anglo-Irish mischief. If I had any influence with you—I do not pretend to have any—I should use it to persuade you, if any persuasion was necessary, to intervene with an act of signal clemency from which the actual slayer might or might not be excluded.

The Manchester case had no effect beyond these islands and Irish America. But in the present crisis, with Dr Goebbels at the radio, a similar tragedy, coming on top of the Indian arrests and the Flogging Act, would be inopportune.

Forgive me for troubling you with this letter. I could not refuse to let you know my opinion for what it is worth; and I had rather write to you personally than to The Times.

faithfully
[G. Bernard Shaw]

To JOHN WARDROP

[H/1]

Ayot St Lawrence. Welwyn
3rd September 1942

[John Wardrop (b. 1919), a young Scottish journalist, whose ardour for Shaw verged on idolatry, injected himself into the dramatist's life in 1939, commencing a bizarre relationship between an impetuous, immature, hypertensive but deeply sincere youth and an irrepressibly mischievous, frequently curmudgeonly old man that continued until, in the last year of Shaw's life, Wardrop emigrated to America. The story of his entrance on the scene is best told in Wardrop's own words, as recollected for Shaw in a letter probably written in 1942, reproduced here from an undated transcription supplied by Blanche Patch:

"On the 17th December 1939 I arrived, like the hero of fiction, in London with something around a shilling in my pocket and a picture in my heart. I had no plans, no friends, no job, and no knowledge whatsoever of the way from Victoria (which I have a vague notion is the place where the bus on which I travelled . . . dropped me off) to Whitehall Court, the only destination of the slightest interest to me.

"I arrived at Whitehall Court without incident and sent up my card (my National Union of Journalists' card with its record of arrears of contributions all complete) which Miss Patch returned per the hall porter with the information that you were away in the country (I did not know your habits so well then).

Taking myself off—I must have looked a sight, with my crumpled collar and fast-growing beard, the products of an uneasy night in a bus which took about 17 hours to make the trip from Edinburgh, I bought a bar of chocolate —and hied me to a pawnbroker's over the river where I received the magnificent sum of 2s 6d for a perfectly good coat for which I paid 50/– on the instalment plan.

I found digs (on credit). I wrote to you and you replied and then I rang you up and practically insisted that you see me after my astounding—to me— journey.

Anyway that started it. After that you could not get me out of your hair. Yet it took about two years of incessant letters and occasional visits to sufficiently impress you with my superb quality that you, entirely out of the blue, planked down on me a bunch of 'Whats What' proofs and told me, in effect, to get cracking."

By mid-1942 Wardrop was grooming himself to be Shaw's literary executor, by undertaking the editing of some of Shaw's fugitive writings and correspondence, thus becoming the sworn enemy of his rival Dr Loewenstein. Shaw, who found Wardrop amusing and entertaining, continued to be indulgent.

The woman Wardrop visited was Erica Cotterill, now calling herself Erica May Saye and residing on a North Devon farm, where she raised two adopted sons. His companion on the visit was a woman some fifteen years his senior with whom he was emotionally involved. Though Shaw knew the two were not married he tactfully referred to the woman as Mrs Wardrop, both in conversation and correspondence, as a protection to her reputation; and chose for reasons of his own to address her by her confirmation name Veronica rather than by the Christian name by which she was usually known. Quite fond of her, Shaw would, when in London, drop in unannounced at her residence in Park Village West (adjacent to the house in which his mother had lived), and stay and chat for an hour or two. It was to her home that Shaw retreated on the day of Charlotte's death in September 1943.]

Dear John Wardrop

I am very glad you have both seen E. C. and appreciated her. Nobody who had not seen her and known her could possibly believe in her existence, or understand how I felt about her.

But you can only guess at what she was like when she was young; for she must in thirty years have acquired some sort of *savoir vivre* in this world of tribal conventions or she would have been locked up as a madwoman. She was not mad; but she was overbred and refined to such an extraordinary degree, so sensitive and yet so utterly fearless in acting on her own superiority without being conscious of it, that she seemed mad to people who could not take her measure. If a man interested her she would walk into his house at any hour: mostly in the middle of the night; take possession of him as if his astonished and outraged wife did not exist; and be quite unconscious of any reason why she should not sleep with him and live in the house as long as she wanted to. When she was put out (there was nothing else for it) she would sometimes sleep in the woods, sometimes unexpectedly produce a motor bicycle from the hedge and ride off God knows where after with great difficulty persuading it to start. She would go into any cottage and sit down there uninvited, deeply offending the cottagers by this liberty and yet holding them spellbound by her exquisite un-usualness. Once, when I was walking home at night with Forbes-Robertson, she suddenly appeared and joined us as a matter of course. To keep step with us she made every fifth step a half step, startling us every time she did it and making her walk a sort of mazurka. F.R. stood it for a while, and then said Good Night decisively and bolted across the street into the darkness. She took no notice: he was not her mark. She simply intended to walk with me to the end of the world, for ever and ever. How I got away from her I do not remember: I must have broken loose just as F.R. did; for I was caught in the toils of this world and this age; and she was already in the Celestial City centuries ahead.

It was dreadful to have to shake her off in this way, knowing that she was not mad but born before her time.

Her literary talent was as extraordinary as herself. I had not read three sentences when I saw that here was a style and touch never put on paper before; and I told her that she could become a great writer before I discovered that fatal aphasia I described in my last letter. I turned her head by this rash judgment. She wrote book after book and had them printed at her own expense. I have three or four of them somewhere. Who they were about nobody could tell: I knew only that it was sometimes Rupert Brook, sometimes me, sometimes God knows who, all mixed up in the same chapter as unnameables. Yet not without a senseless charm.

I was anxious about her money; but concluded that she was mad only NNW, and could take care of herself. Be kind to her: she is a nonpareil.

GBS

Presumably her parents are dead. She had a terrible hate-fixation against her father. Freud would have made a good deal of its effect on her sexual conduct.

To JOHN WARDROP

[C/1]

Ayot St Lawrence. Welwyn
4th September 1942

[Wardrop was by now serving as Shaw's editorial assistant and proof reader for the *What's What?* for which Shaw paid him a fee of £30. For months he diligently worked his way through the galleys and pages, spotting contradictions, eliminating duplications, and correcting factual blunders.]

Please send me your synopses of my chapters. I cannot remember what I have already written and am hopelessly bogged.

I must get the book finished by hook or crook. Your *précis* (as much of it as you have done) will save me days of trouble.

GBS

To F. E. LOEWENSTEIN

Ayot St Lawrence. Welwyn
[H/83]   11th September 1942

[Shaw's statement that the Dickens Fellowship was "much dreaded" by Dickens's daughter Kate Perugini is one he also made in a letter to the *Times Literary Supplement*, published on 27th July 1935 as " 'This Ever-Diverse Pair.' " It is difficult to believe that Mrs Perugini would have carried politeness in public to the extent of being a very active president of the Fellowship for a quarter of a century! Moreover, the Fellowship was not a nineteenth-century society; it was founded in 1902. Loewenstein's bibliographical essay "A Collection of Shaviana" appeared in the *TLS* on 22nd August. He earned his doctorate at the University of Würzburg with a dissertation on Japanese prints. The Shaw Society's membership, Shaw was informed on 19th September, consisted of "about forty members" (H.c.u/83). Loewenstein did not "give up" his projected Shaw Society exhibition intended for Shaw's 86th birthday; he merely bided his time until he could set into motion a more ambitious scheme that led to the Ninetieth Birthday Exhibition at the National Book League in 1946. The "Fabian letters" were Shaw's correspondence with the Fabian Society, in the archive of that society (many subsequently were sold to help pay off debts), over which Loewenstein and Wardrop were contending, though more at issue was their rivalry over a never-published collective volume of papers, essays, and pamphlets to be called *Shavian Socialism*.]

Dear Mr Loewenstein

You are too young to understand what I felt when you announced the formation of a Shaw Society. I was already an active young lion of letters in the eighties, which is to you a remote and largely incomprehensible historical period, when I saw the foundation of the Browning Society and the Shelley Society. The Browning Society was the most talked about; for it succeeded quite unintentionally in making its hero ridiculous. It was always described in the newspapers as a gang of long haired young poetasters. It was really a conventicle of elderly Evangelical ladies, though the founder, F. T. Furnival, was an aggressive Victorian Agnostic. Furnival induced these ladies to join the Shelley Society when he founded it later on; and when at the first big public meeting of that Society I rose and introduced myself as "like Shelley, a Socialist, atheist and vegetarian," they were unspeakably horrified. Two of them resigned on the spot.

Furnival put me down as a member of all his Societies without consulting me, as I could always enliven a meeting. Shelley was dead; but

639

Browning, very much alive, contemplated the proceedings of the Society which bore his name with feelings that can only be guessed, because he kept rigidly aloof.

The Societies did not survive into this century, except one, the Dickens Fellowship, much dreaded by Dickens's daughter (Kate Perugini) whom I knew. She had to be polite to the Fellowship in public; but she never told it the things about her father that she told me. But the Fellowship never achieved the notoriety of the Browning Society, which was unique as a society devoted to a living author. Furnival's death made an end of all his societies; and they are now forgotten except by octogenarians.

Suddenly you broke the peace by announcing a Shaw Society. I was to share the fate of Browning. Well, you were too young to know what you were doing. I bore you no malice and bear none. But, like Browning I lie low and take no responsibility for the proceedings of the Society. My only hope is that nobody will join it, and therefore there will be no proceedings. I have heard of three members; but they have all left. What is your present membership?

I see by The Times Literary Supplement that you are a very competent bibliographer: you know much more about my writings than I can remember. Is bibliography your profession? If so can one make a living out of it? Or are you a man of property? How old are you? Are you married? I have heard you spoken of as *Dr* Loewenstein: is that correct? If so what was your university, and are you a doctor of divinity, of letters, or law? Forgive these questions: you are under no obligation to answer them.

I have to thank you for so promptly giving up the projected Shaw exhibition at my request.

This letter has been too long delayed; but I am very old (in my 87th year) and have a book in hand which will never be finished if I indulge in private correspondence. Some letters have to be written to keep my business going; and even these I have to neglect. But I read letters, though I can answer only a few of them. The more interesting a letter is the longer it take[s] to answer; so my best correspondents are the worst treated.

As to the Fabian letters I can only say again that until somebody goes through them and makes a *catalogue raisonné* we can discuss them only without knowing what we are talking about. Most of them must be obsolete ephemerals. I never keep copies of my letters; and I regard the keeping of letters as, on the whole, a mischievous habit. Dickens did so for some time, and then burnt the lot at Gadshill. I tear them up

on the spot or when they are answered unless there is some special
reason for keeping them.

faithfully
G. Bernard Shaw

To D. KILHAM ROBERTS

Ayot St Lawrence. Welwyn
[H/2]   17th September 1942

[Denis Kilham Roberts (1903–76), a young barrister with literary pretensions, became secretary of the Society of Authors, following the retirement
of G. Herbert Thring, in 1930; he retained the post until his own retirement
in 1963. Emlyn Williams (1905–87), actor and playwright, was the author of
Night Must Fall, filmed by Metro-Goldwyn-Mayer in 1937. Roberts's response to Shaw's third paragraph was that the situation applied only if the
author in question were resident abroad.]

Dear Mr Kilham Roberts

A point of enormous importance to authors has been raised by the
war taxation. My royalty on the Pygmalion film brought me in over
£20,000 in the first year, and thereby subjected me to income and
surtax at the rate of 19/6d in the pound not only on those royalties but
on my entire income, plus my wife's. Within the two years affected by
this apparent windfall I had to pay £50,000 to the Exchequer because
of my supposed good fortune. Another such stroke of luck would ruin
me. The royalties due to me from the Barbara film must also exceed
£20,000; but I have refused to touch them until all production
expenses, amounting to £235,000, are paid off. I am doing all I can to
prevent anyone paying me anything lest I should be utterly ruined.

In short, the author who has a windfall of £20,000 plus one farthing
once in 86 years is taxed at the same rate as the plutocrat who enjoys a
settled income of over £20,000 a year from the cradle to the grave.

Now comes the purpose of this letter. An accountant assures me
that an author's rights are his capital. Consequently if he sells his rights
outright or for a fixed period, the price he receives is not taxable as
income any more than the price obtained by a sale of stocks. If I had
sold my Pygmalion film rights for £30,000, I should not have been
taxed on that sum.

What is the legal position of this? What is the practice (Emlyn
Williams and others are reported to have sold film rights for lump

sums)? The Society, if it has not ascertained this[,] should obviously do so, taking counsel's opinion if necessary. Members are entitled to an answer.

To bring the matter to a head, I, as a member, demand an answer.

Perhaps you have gone into it and can answer straight off. I have an offer on hand which depends on it.

> faithfully
> G. Bernard Shaw

To NANCY ASTOR

[H/101]

Ayot St Lawrence. Welwyn
22nd October 1942

[One of the Ayot housemaids, Violet Pond, had received a call-up notice for national service. Ernest Bevin (1881–1951), Labour M.P., was Minister of Labour and National Service 1940–45. Alfred Rosenberg was now Reich Minister for the Eastern Occupied Territories; he was executed at Nuremberg in October 1946. "The Brains Trust," first broadcast by the B.B.C. in January 1941 as "Any Questions?" was a programme, with Donald McCullough as Question Master, in which noted public figures responded to questions submitted by listeners. It rapidly became one of the outstanding popular programmes of all time. J. C. Smuts's address to the assembled members of both houses of Parliament on war aims and the peace, in which he stated "The stage is set for the last, the offensive phase," and called for the fullest help for Russia, was recorded for broadcast by the B.B.C. on 21st October.]

My dear Nancy

Double double toil and trouble: they are taking away our housemaid on the 28th of November; and our one remaining maid will probably give us notice rather than stay singlehanded: she certainly would if she were a sensible Englishwoman. Charlotte is distracted; but I have not fired all my guns yet, and may intimidate the local people by a battery of figures. My income tax for the duration so far amounts to over £90,000. My copyrights, which cost the country nothing, have brought in over $100,000 paid to myself direct; and this is only ten per cent of all the dollars imported on the job. From the Barbara film I have had nothing; but it has brought in at least half as much. I can satisfy an accountant that I have brought over a million and a half dollars to London for nothing but my signature to an agreement. But I have lost money by the transaction, and have had to work seven days a week all the time with only Blanche Patch to help me, managing the business and making fresh copyrights to make more dollars to pay our debt to America.

I hope this will make the local people sit up. If it doesnt I must appeal to Bevin personally and ask him to tell them that my work is of national importance, and that I am not to be interrupted or molested.

I tell you all this stuff so that you may tell him that if he breaks up my home I shall dump myself and Charlotte and Blanche on your doorstep at Cliveden and spend the rest of my life there.

I have not enough skill in Christian Science to cure Charlotte's worrying. I hardly like to ask her what on earth it matters what happens to us in the few months that are left to us of 86 years. Even if we freeze or starve to death we have had our day, and should scorn to lag super-fluous. I find this a cheerful way of looking at it: she doesnt: I only seem to be making light of her sufferings—which, by the way, are pretty bad. I dont believe that corset fits scientifically.

I have been reading Hitler's Mein Kampf really attentively instead of dipping into it. He is the greatest living Tory, and a wonderful preacher of everything that is right and best in Toryism. Your Party should capture him and keep him as a teacher and leader whilst check-mating his phobias. On the need for religion, on the sham democracy of votes for everybody, on unemployment and casual labor, he is superb. The book is really one of the world's bibles, like Calvin's Institutes (written when Calvin was 23), Adam Smith's Wealth of Nations, Marx's Capital: it has changed the mind of the reading world. We must lick his rabble of Rosenberg's and ruffians; but we really mustnt hang him. But there is not much danger of that: when his army cracks, he will turn up in Ireland, renting the Vice Regal Lodge like Louis Napoleon at Chislehurst or the Kaiser at Doorn; and who can touch him?

Where he has failed is in not making the occupied countries the better for his coming, as Julius Caesar managed to do in Spain. To put it another way, he has failed as Messiah. His army service suited him and made him a Terrorist and a tough. His smattering of cheap science (which is not a Tory subject) filled his head with a crude notion of "the survival of the fittest" which would justify the ruling of the U.S.A. by a Congress of grizzly bears. And so he will be a failure. But then most of the Messiahs have been failures, though they had their points all the same.

I see we shall hear your voice from the Brains Trust next week. They have just been discussing why America has got along with fewer wars than Europe. None of them pointed out that the Americans were so busy killing one another with revolvers and bowie knives, to say nothing of lynchings, that they had no time for killing anyone else except redskins. Murder is sporadic in Europe and endemic in America. How far is this still true?

I must stop. You must be pretty busy just now; but we cannot resist giving you a hullo occasionally.

always your
G. Bernard Shaw

We listened in to Smuts. A very proper well spoken piece; but he probably delivered it in 1899 with "British" changed to "Boer" and "Hitler" to Rhodes.

Do tell Churchill and Ll. G. that the House of Commons way of speechifying is pitiably ridiculous through the mike. Stopping for ten seconds between every word to wonder what the devil you can say next ("thinking on one's legs") is not made good by uttering the word when it comes as if it were an oracle, especially when it is only a preposition or conjunction.

To ST JOHN ERVINE

[H/3; X/136.e]

Ayot St Lawrence. Welwyn
31st October 1942

["My intention in writing this book," Ervine informed the reader in the foreword to *Bernard Shaw: His Life, Work and Friends* (1956), "is to tell the story of Bernard Shaw's life from my personal knowledge of him, with such additions of fact as are essential to proper understanding of his career. I began to write it long before his death, but put it aside because I had work of my own to do; but he knew that I had begun it, had, indeed, read what I had written, and he hoped that I would one day finish what I had begun because, so he said, 'You will understand the Irish side of me better than anybody who is not Irish.' "

Charlotte's illness was at last identified as osteitis deformans, commonly known as Paget's disease. Ervine's *Spectator* review that week was of Pearson's biography, "the most readable" of all Shaw's biographies, "because its author has wisely let Mr. Shaw do most of the talking." For Moody and Sankey see the letter of 24th January 1896 to Henry Pease. For Francis Place see letter of January 1902 to T. H. S. Escott. The new book (*Everybody's Political What's What?*) was, Shaw told Lillah McCarthy on 24th October

644

1942, "a sort of Child's Guide to Politics, as the world is being ruined not by its well meant wickednesses, but by its want of elementary education" A(/4).]

Dear St John

I return the aborted biography, which I read through last night. It is hopeless; and I will tell you exactly why. Like Beatrice Webb you seem interested not in individuals but only in their classes. Yet she, though disliking people who were not typical of their classes and dismissing them as unmanageable accidents, admitted their existence, and, after some natural repugnance, put up with me and found a class for me as "a sprite."

But you have given a masterly description of my class and treated me as typical of it. Now unluckily the Irish snob-Protestants are not interesting to British readers. A book about them would be simply a dull book about dull people, even when written by you. It would be like a book about Molière on the assumption that he was typical of the rich shopkeeper class under Louis XIV, or about Voltaire on the assumption that he was a typical product of Jesuit education.

Class bringing-up not only stamps its types but on rare occasions provokes violent reactions against itself. I was always in intense reaction against the Shaw snobbery: I exceeded in the opposite direction, derided my relations, and before I reached my teens quite deliberately stopped saying my prayers and proclaimed myself an atheist. Besides, the atmosphere in which I grew up was a Roman Catholic atmosphere. Lee had no creed: I have heard him mention religion: he conducted Mendelssohn's Protestant music and the Catholic masses with impartial perfection. The Amateur Musical Society was made up, singers, orchestra and all, from his pupils and anyone whom he heard playing an instrument. . . . Now God, less impartial, had ordained that most of his pupils should be Catholics, and some of them shopkeepers. Acquaintance with these people and glimpses of their homes soon cured me of the inculcated belief that Catholics all went to hell and had no refinement nor manners nor culture. My mother actually made the acquaintance of priests, and several times sang in "chapel." Many of these people were more cultivated than my relatives, being picked for their musical tastes. The Shaws could play all sorts of instruments "by ear," and could harmonize any popular tune with three chords, tonic, dominant, and subdominant; but their musical tastes were primitive: only one uncle [William] joined Lee's orchestra. He played the ophicleide. My father, who "vamped" on the trombone, was ineligible, as he could not read music.

645

Art is a great solvent of bigotries and snobberies. The result is always a more or less Bohemian society; and I became what I can describe only as an unconvivial Bohemian. Being unconvivial I was not even a typical Bohemian. Representation of me as a typical Protestant snob is widely off the mark anyhow. Sociology is not biography. Genius abolishes it. If I am not a genius I am not worth a biography. If I am a genius you must keep your spotlight on me and your ambers only on Protestant Dublin.

I am amazed to find that you have actually read my novels. I could never believe that they were enjoyable. Unfortunately they are not unreadable: people rash enough to begin them go on to the end, and resent the experience all their lives.

We keep up affectionate interest in you and Leonora; but we are too old to presume on our ancient attractions. Charlotte's *osteitis deformans* is incurable: she is often in pain, and moves about very slowly and not far. I was vetted lately and reported sound; but that means only that when I go I shall go all at once. We are both deaf; and the number of familiar names that we cannot remember increases; in short, we are considerably dotty. I have resigned everything, committees, chairmanships, etc., and work at my book as hard as I can lest I should not live to finish it. I seldom go outside the curtilage, and for exercise just saw firewood for an hour or less in the garden. I can still write a bit; but that is all. Unlike Ibsen I can still remember the alphabet.

The enormous success of the Pygmalion film, and the war taxation, has all but ruined me: since 1938 I have paid the Government more than £90,000 in income tax alone. I am living on my capital, and desperately trying to get out of the millionaire category (19/6 in the £) by staving off the royalties due to me on the Barbara film, which, though a flop compared to Pygmalion, owes me at least £15,000.

Altogether we have reason to feel very grateful to you for not dropping our acquaintance. Forgive senile garrulousness.

ever yours
G. Bernard Shaw

PS I have just read your Spectator review. You have muddled up Moody & Sankey frightfully. They were Protestants, which completely excluded Catholics from their meetings and therefore put the class issue quite out of the question in Ireland. My jejune contempt for the Revivalists was purely intellectual, and had nothing whatever to do with Protestant snobbery. In England the Welsh "dissenter" takes the place of the R.C. in Ireland; but in Ireland a country gentleman may frequent Methodist meetings just as I went to a Methodist school without derogation. It suffices that he is a Protestant.

You are always readable; but you have no intellectual conscience. Francis Place tells us that his father never passed by one of his children without hitting it. You do the same with your aversions. You really shouldnt have any.

To R. D. BLUMENTHAL

Ayot St Lawrence. Welwyn
10th November 1942

[C/3; X/341]

["I am afraid I can do no more," Shaw wrote to Siegfried Trebitsch on 28th September, after exploring every avenue for release of controlled and frozen funds in London, Paris, and Switzerland. Responding to Trebitsch's desperate but melodramatic threat to resort to a suicide poisoning, Shaw concluded: "I strongly deprecate veronal: it is much wiser to die of starvation, because somehow one *doesnt*. We shall both survive this bloody business" (H/5; X/341).]

Trebitsch and his wife are still in Lausanne at the Hotel Beau Site.

They are in desperate circumstances, all the worse because T. has not the faintest notion of how people with small incomes live. And he has no income at all. The last of his wife's jewels are now sold. He has £600 to his credit at the Westminster Bank; but as it was lodged in the Paris branch (now closed) he cannot touch it. I have exhausted every dodge to help him—tried the Foreign Office, the Board of Trade—but without success; and I cannot make him understand the difficulty.

His first step, which was to become naturalized in France, was only an additional complication. His project of going to America came to nothing. He has laid in a store of veronal to poison himself and Frau Trebitsch; but even that does not come off.

I give him up: I can do no more.

GBS

To ELLEN POLLOCK

[H/1]

Ayot St Lawrence. Welwyn
10th November 1942

[Ellen Pollock was touring with Baxter Somerville's company in *Major Barbara*; the Undershaft was Michael Golden. Beatrice Connell was Ellen's error for Lena Connell, well-known feminist and photographer of the suffragist movement, who had sent her a portrait of Shaw. *Village Wooing*, with Ellen as "Z" and Leslie Banks as "A," was broadcast by the B.B.C. on 28th August. "The boy" was Ellen's son Michael Hancock (b. 1929), with whom Shaw had played at Malvern in 1932.]

Dear Ellen Pollock

As to how to play the long silence of Barbara in the last act it is clear as a matter of technique that you must do just nothing and leave the whole scene to Undershaft. If you as much as twinkle an eye-lash to draw the attention of the audience from him to you you shake his hold on it and raise hopes that you are going to cut in: hopes that only disappoint. He has to carry the scene through by fixing the entire attention of the house on himself.

As to what she feels about it, that is quite another matter. One night at the Court Theatre Lady B. [Rosina Filippi] went asleep while Louis Calvert was declaiming; and everybody thought it was a clever stroke of acting until her cue came and it was discovered that she really was fast asleep. Now this would never do for Barbara. She is not horrified: her Salvation Army experience has accustomed her to shocks; but she is now suffering the supreme tragedy of being forsaken by God and seeing her father put the army in his pocket.

But her father has rescued her from her despair by suggesting to her that though Bill Walker has shewn her that the conversion[s] of penniless Rummy Mitchens and Snobby Price are worthless, he has been converted himself even more deeply than Todger and Mog, who were not penniless.

From that moment she has a new light, and begins first to suspect and then to realize that Undershaft is right, and that it [is] the full fed people who need conversion. In the third act she listens with the most intense attention to Undershaft, and at last grasps the situation and makes her final confession of faith.

I dont remember Mrs Beatrice Connell; but I do remember Lena Connell, who, having taken some excellent photographs of me before 1913, took another set after I had rehearsed Pygmalion at His Majesty's with Tree and Mrs Campbell. They had to be destroyed because they

648

resembled an old dog after a fight, which was how I felt and no doubt looked.

The story about the lecture is no doubt true. It was one of my platform tricks. I had quite a bag of them.

The broadcast of Village Wooing came across very well.

Modern dress or period does not matter, except to the men who have to buy their own modern clothes, whereas period is costume. As period is always wildly wrong you can design your costume to suit yourself: nobody will know the difference. I have great hopes of you as a Shaw specialist.

We are both frightfully old (86) and my wife is permanently invalided.

The boy must be growing up. Does he promise well? Or are you tired of him? Boys have to be morally weaned after six.

faithfully
G. Bernard Shaw

To BEATRICE WEBB

Ayot St Lawrence. Welwyn
[H/14]   26th November 1942

[Hesketh Pearson's biography was published by Collins on 26th October. The open letter to Hitler did not materialise. Beatrice's nephew (The Rt Hon. Sir) Stafford Cripps (1889–1952), Labour M.P., was Leader of the House of Commons in 1942 and Minister of Aircraft Production 1942–45. Anthony Eden (1897–1977), later first Earl of Avon, was Secretary of State for Foreign Affairs 1940–45 and Leader of the House of Commons 1942–45. He became Prime Minister in 1955. Sir John Maynard's book was *The Russian Peasant; and Other Studies* (1942). Shaw and biologist Julian Huxley (1887–1975) indulged in a running debate on "Bernard Shaw as Biologist" in the correspondence columns of *The Listener* from November 1942 to March 1943.]

My dear Beatrice

At last the publishers of Pearson's book have sent me a spare copy which I couldnt afford to buy, or I should have written sooner. Here it is.

I can't think of any news that you have not already had from Blanche [Patch] or from the newspapers. I have not come to the end of my book which in its nature can, like the Annual Register, never be finished; but I must stop somewhere or I shall die or outrun Maxwell's stock of paper; so I shall stop now.

I am seriously thinking of writing an open letter to Hitler, and sending it to The Observer, which has asked me for an article. This is the result of reading Mein Kampf right through attentively and seriously. It is a curious combination of an extraordinarily penetrating observation and comprehension of the political and psychological situation with epileptic phobias and conviction of the eugenic value of racial inbreeding. The war, in fact, is a war between inbreeding and cross breeding, between mongrels and pedigrees; and Hitler has the courage of his convictions to a sublime height which has nerved him to stake a world war on it. Altogether a very remarkable fellow this Hitler, though a doomed Impossibilist. . . .

Cripps seems to have missed the flood tide of his fortunes. I dont know him well enough to size him up: in fact I dont know him at all; but it seems to me that he could have stopped the arrest of the Indian Congressmen and the flogging business if he had threatened to resign, and should have resigned anyhow. As it was he lost his head. Parliament kills everyone except careerists: Hitler saw that as clearly as Dickens did a century ago.

Eden seems to have been converted more or less: he is a very different man from the Eden of ten years ago.

Have you read Sir John Maynard's book? It is the only one that touches yours [*The Truth about Soviet Russia*, 1942] in importance. Its cataloguing of the mistakes of the Bolsheviks, which will all be repeated here if we do not take warning by them, is invaluable. I shall tell serious inquirers to read the Webbs and read Maynard. Do you agree?

I was sorry to hear that you had not been so well lately. I hope that trouble is over or at least eased.

Do you take in The Listener? I am having a bit of a scrap with Julian Huxley in which Wells is implicated. They insist that I am a brainless emotionalist incapable of reasoning and ignorant of science. I tell them that their materialist neo-Darwinism is only an anti-clerical backwater which has no connection with real science. My book rubs this in very hard. I read Pavlov very thoroughly (nobody else could or did, I believe) and found it a tissue of ridiculous nonsense founded on a set of disgustingly cruel experiments—25 years of them, all failures.

I think that is all for today.

G. Bernard Shaw

To GRACE GOODLIFFE

Ayot St Lawrence. Welwyn

[S/1]   3rd December 1942

[Grace Goodliffe, of Burnfoot, Co. Donegal, was both a distant cousin of
Shaw and a relation of Neville Chamberlain. Sir Robert Shaw, whose funeral
Shaw attended, died on 19th February 1869; Shaw was in his thirteenth
year. Henry W. Pickersgill (1782–1875) was a highly-reputed English portrait
painter; his portrait of Sir Robert Shaw, the second Baronet, is reproduced
in F. E. Loewenstein's *Bernard Shaw through the Camera* (1948). (Sir) Bernard Vidal Shaw (1891–1984), was from 1925 to 1936 resident magistrate in
Mombasa; the Shaws were his guests in April 1935 while cruising round
Africa.]

Dear Cousin Grace (alas! four or five times removed)

Come now: have I been so very unkind to the family? I say nothing
of having made their name famous throughout five continents: poachers
and tinkers have done as much. They never did anything for me (why
should they?); but I have never been ashamed of them, never disowned
them, made no illnatured fun of them, and saved the destitute among
them from the Poor Law even to the second generation of cousins. My
sole offence was that some sixty years ago I wrote somewhere that my
family had "revolved round an obscure baronetcy." Not a "nebulous"
baronet as you have it. I was not thinking of the Recorder but of his
brother then reigning at Bushy Park, the second Sir Robert, my
father's second cousin. And I made amends later on by confessing that
the obscure ones had bowled me out by serving with great distinction.

I was at Bushy Park only once; but I was so sensible of its charm (I
loved the eagle on the parapet and cherish a photograph of the house);
and that was when I was taken to Sir Robert's funeral. I got no farther
than the hall where the oak coffin was. I never had the slightest prejudice against the brothers; for Sir Robert was specially kind and attentive to my mother; and my father always spoke highly of the Recorder,
and appealed to my sympathies for him because, my father said, he
suffered from a perpetual headache.

The story about the drums and whistles is obviously impossible (a
Shaw story never lost anything in the telling); but I suggest a foundation for it. My father was not the only inebriate in the family. My uncle
William (Barney Shaw) outdid him both as a drinker and smoker,
though, like my father, he at last reformed completely in this respect.
Now in those days it was the fashion for gentlemen to play wind
instruments. Professional musicians were not engaged to entertain

651

evening parties: the guests provided their own music. Barney played the ophicleide, a monster keyed bugle now obsolete. My mother described him to me standing on the ottoman in the middle of the drawing room at Bushy Park and playing Annie Laurie with great expression. My father played the trombone. At the Ely Gate on the Dodder a whole band of gentlemen of which they were members used to give open air concerts. My father was a member; so was Barney. But the two enlisted two others in a brass quartet which on Sundays strolled about the country playing all the popular tunes "by ear." They sent the hat round and collected a store of pennies which, on their return in the evening, they dropped into the charity box at the Mercers Hospital.

I imagine that what happened was this. When my father was blacklisted at Bushy Park, Barney may have shared his fate for the same reason. It would be a first rate stroke of Shavian humor to take the quartet into the park and treat Sir Robert to a serenade. This would have been entirely possible, easy, natural, and inoffensive. And it did not involve the sober Shaws who still enjoyed Sir Robert's hospitality and of course took his side in the affair. The story no doubt grew into the fable about the whole family parading with drums and whistles, which is utter nonsense.

At all events my father's weakness cut me off completely from the family while I was still a child; and after that one funeral visit I never again saw the eagle on the parapet. I bore no malice; but I formed no family attachments. But I was greatly interested in our descent from the Thane of Fife (Macduff) and in the drop of Cromwell's blood that leavened the original Kilkenny Shaws of Sandpits, who split into Cork Shaws and Dublin Shaws. An old weekly paper called The Whitehall Review published a portrait of Eyre Massey Shaw, Captain of the London Fire Brigade, which was strikingly like me, though my grandmother, a Carr from Wexford, had brought into the family a broader nose than Eyre Massey's, which was thinner. He was a Cork Shaw. The Carr nose is now all over Australia, whence Charles Shaw, the author of Bernard and His Brethren, descended on me. I was amused at his collection of fables, and could not believe they would interest anyone outside our circle of family jokers; but my publishers enjoyed them so much that they accepted his book and actually advanced him £200 on it. In Australia, he tells me, it sold like hot cakes. I contributed flat contradictions of the fables with corrected versions of some of them. So you see we are a more amusing family on paper than in real life. Charles would have it that the second Sir Robert's bachelordom was caused by his love for my Carr grandmother; but this was quite new to me. A Mr. [J.] Bellingham-Warner has just sent me a photograph of a picture of Sir Robert (presumably the first) by Pickersgill. He says it was in the B-W family until 1930, when they sold it to one George Taylor of New York. I suppose he bought it on its merits as a work of art, which is considerable.

You must bear in mind in dealing with your distant cousins that there is a world of difference between being born in Bushy Park in the direct line of the landed gentry and being born in Synge Street as the son of a younger son of a younger son, with the Bushy Park traditions and social pretensions and no money to support them on. The feudal system with its primogeniture made no provisions for younger sons. In my twentieth year I changed from being a Shaw in Dublin to being a "middle class" nobody in a London suburb and, when my Irish clothes wore out, a very shabby one at that. And though you have not read my many writings and still live in the landed gentry atmosphere of the seventeenth century you must not leave quite out of account what people call my genius, which is critical as well as creative. I read Karl Marx 14 years before Lenin did, and preached Red Communism every Sunday through the length and breadth of England while Bushy Park was quietly going to church at Rathfarnham without dreaming that Queen Anne was dead. But I did not hate my relatives nor cut them (no Marxist could think in that way) and dont see why they should hate or cut me. As a matter of fact none of them did. When I was in Africa in 1935 I found another Bernard Shaw in Mombasa in whose house I spent some pleasant days; and if I had gone as far up country as Nairobi I should perhaps have met your brother there though it was preaching like mine that drove him from hearth and home.

But I am glad to learn that Shaws are still happy in the old house that will perhaps be less lovely for awhile when it becomes the rest house of a Trade Union or Co-operative Society or possibly a hotel. It will be happier than ever when both rich and poor have passed away, and a Shaw will be a fossil in a historical museum.

Meanwhile you did not guess rightly my feeling on receiving your letter. It was very welcome; and though I am no longer a Shaw but only a maker of Shavians you may count on me as

always yours faithfully and cordially
G. Bernard Shaw

P.S. The reviews of Hesketh Pearson's book treat my family pretensions with great respect, and say they account for "MY ARROGANCE"!!!

To O. B. CLARENCE

[Ayot St Lawrence. Welwyn]
[X/416]   [Undated: *c*. late 1942]

[Veteran actor O.B.Clarence (1870–1955), who created the rôle of the Inquisitor in the 1924 first London production of *Saint Joan*, had apparently been seen by Shaw in the Stage Society production of Hauptmann's *The Coming of Peace*, on 10th June 1900, in a translation by Janet Achurch and Dr Charles E.Wheeler; and later in St John Hankin's translation of the Brieux play *The Three Daughters of M. Dupont* (1905). Elsie Fogerty (1865–1945), C.B.E., known to all as Fogey, was founder of the Central School of Speech Training and Dramatic Art. She was a familiar figure at most of the Malvern Festivals. Barker's Spanish translation was of the Serafin and Joaquin Alvarez Quintero play *Fortunato* (1928), in which "Clarty" had the title rôle (with John Gielgud in a very minor one). Shaw's letter was a response to Clarence's request that he "write a few lines by way of a blessing" for his autobiography *No Complaints* (1943), in which it was published.]

Dear O.B.

You can have no notion of what the London theatre was like when I came from Ireland and began business in it. Though there were no schools like the Royal Academy of Dramatic Art and Elsie Fogarty's Central Training School, actors who had been "through the mill" were highly skilled technically; but they knew no world outside the theatre, and were bewildered and scandalized if they were engaged to play a character with any politics or religion or even any intellect. And because they did not want such parts they of course insisted that the public did not want them. As the people who did want them gave up going to the theatre, the London playgoer had ceased to represent the public, and bore out the opinion of the actors. Besides, stage technique was a product of the stuff they had to perform, which consisted of adaptations of Parisian "constructed" plays, with the same old plot about the same old triangle, and about as much real life in them as in a clockwork mouse. Such plays, having no life of their own, had to be animated by the players. The heroines being only dolls with nothing real to say, the leading lady had to make the most of her personal charm, and to conceal the emptiness of her dialogue by throwing away her lines and looking unutterable things between them. The comedians had to acquire the same trick, getting their laughs not by their lines but by making funny faces between the lines.

This technique was not merely useless for real drama but destructive of its stage effect. I found myself between mature players who would not accept my parts in plays, or, if they did, were as much ashamed as

654

if they had been driven to accept Poor Law Relief, and who on the stage spoiled their parts and prolonged the performances drearily by using their old technique, and beginners who were carried away by Ibsen but did not know their business until they had picked it up in forlorn hopes like the Stage Society. In time, Ibsen's plays and mine produced their own technique, which was also the Shakespearian and Shavian technique. You had to get your lines across in their full meaning and leave them to get their effect without interrupting the performance to look unutterable things or to mug, just as in Shakespeare. The first acting successes made in my plays in London were by Louis Calvert, an old Shakespearian who was with difficulty persuaded to appear in modern dress, and Granville-Barker, a young genius who simply could not act a constructed Parisian play.

An odd effect of these foreign mechanistic plays, which gave the actors no characters to act, and forced them to exploit their personal attractions, was that the playgoers would not let their favourites act even when they wanted to, as most of them did. Handsome men like George Alexander and Lewis Waller could attract audiences, not as Hamlet or Peer Gynt, but as George and Lewis and nobody else. Ellen Terry and Mrs. Patrick Campbell were not allowed to disguise themselves and pretend to be other people: playgoers paid their money to see Ellen and Stella and only secondarily to see a play. And this reacted on the playwrights, who could get their plays performed only by dropping all pretence of creating characters and, instead, simply wrote parts for the personalities of the stars. It ended in the actors being unable to act and the authors unable to write.

But human nature would not be denied for long. There arose a generation of born actors who could not help acting, and born dramatic poets who could not trade in clockwork mice even if they starved for it. The flood tide began with Ibsen; and at last a night came in which *John Bull's Other Island* was played by royal command with the stalls full of Cabinet ministers and duchesses, and the Kendals, playing with a French clockwork mouse at the old Avenue Theatre, took sixteen shillings at the pay boxes, and had to go into the provinces to live on their reputation. Henry Irving was so completely out of date on his literary side that he had not even reached the clockwork mouse stage and was still in the eighteenth century. The last time I visited the old Lyceum Theatre he was playing to a house so thoroughly "papered" that when I asked for a stall at the box office, the ticket was handed to me with an air of dreary resignation which changed to stupefaction when I actually put down a golden half sovereign and a sixpence for it.

Irving returned to the provinces penniless, and died there, because he would not play Ibsen or Shaw, and had played-out all the Shakespeare parts for which he was not too old.

It was at a Stage Society performance that I saw a young actor in a small "silly ass" part, in which he twiddled what is now known as a Charlie Chaplin cane. Probably you forget it; but that young actor was O.B. Clarence; and I at once noted him as the real article. Yet as so often happens, it was twenty years before I could secure him for a part in one of my own plays. He was always engaged elsewhere, notably in Barrie's plays, and once, very delightfully, in a Spanish play translated by Granville-Barker, in which he represented a quite unathletic white collar clerk driven by unemployment and the hunger of his children to take a job with a variety star, who stood him up against a target and outlined his figure on it with bullets. Nobody else on the stage could have played that part as you did.

When you played the Inquisitor in *St. Joan*, you accepted the part without comment and played it "on your head." Thirty-two years before, when my first play was first performed, I could not have persuaded any experienced actor to undertake a speech seven minutes long. His limit would have been seven seconds. After the first rehearsal of a play of mine [*You Never Can Tell*] by a fashionable London company one of the ladies threw up her part because there were "no laughs and no exits" in it; and one of the gentlemen did the same because he was not in the first act and had to deliver a very serious talk in the third. Years after, when that play had become almost as infallible a potboiler as *East Lynne*, he [Allan Aynesworth] was driven to play that very part, and made his best success in it; but when he wrote his memoirs he concealed this disgraceful experience, and expatiated on his triumphs in plays and parts that nobody remembered.

What tickled me when I began producing my own plays was that the critics at first pooh-poohed me as a pamphleteer who had no theatre sense, and, when that would no longer wash, gave me credit for the most audacious and startling innovations, the truth being that I was only reviving the old operatic declamatory technique of which the public favourites of the cup and saucer school knew nothing. The Inquisitor's speech is an operatic solo as much as "Il balen" in Verdi's *Trovatore*. There is nothing I like better than composing arias, cavatinas, and grand finales for good actors. My technique I had learnt, not in the cup and saucer school, with its "reserved force" which was so welcome to actors who had no force to reserve, but from Salvini and Ristori, and from Barry Sullivan, last of stage supermen, whose three thousandth appearance as Hamlet was all in the night's work for him, and who was outraged if he finished the week with less than three hundred guineas in his pocket. He died leaving £100,000. Had he not kept away from London he would have lost that sum to the ground landlords as Irving did.

Beside my knowledge of the stage methods of those great guns I had my practice as a public speaker. When they told me that the public would not endure long speeches I told them that I made speeches from sixty to ninety minutes long every week or oftener to full houses without hearing a single cough; that the public liked nothing better; and that its favourite subjects were politics and religion. When they wanted to do their big scenes upstage I said I always spoke right down on the float, with the chairman, whom I was supposed to be addressing, behind me like the operatic prima donnas who poured out their passion over the opera house as close to the audience as they could get whilst the tenor who was making love to them had to chanter *à l'épaule* quite out of their sight. The cup and saucer experts thought this unnatural. So it was; but it brought down the house and gave the players command of the audience and not of one another. I used all the old techniques quite easily and effectively. I used the ancient Greek technique in which the actor declaimed from a tribune before an immovable front scene of architectural magnificence. I used the circus technique of ringmaster and clown as Molière did. I used the Christy Minstrel technique of President in the middle and Bones and Johnson at the corners. I used the Elizabethan technique with an inner stage formed by "traverses." (I picked this up at Ober Ammergau.) I used Granville-Barker's revival of the apron stage with doors in the proscenium. I used Reinhardt's trick of using the floor of the house as well as the stage for entrances and exits, mixing up actors and audience. The only technique I did not condescend to was the french window in the centre with two or three doors at each side which served for the old entrances between the wings. *Candida* in one room, with one door through which all the entrances and exits were made, was considered untheatrical, ignorant, and almost indecent. That was almost my only innovation in stage management.

The greatest novelty of the day in the theatre began in Ibsen's *Doll's House*, which, though a constructed play in the French manner, ended astonishingly not with a dénouement but with a discussion of the play. In *Candida*, which is *The Doll's House* with the tables turned and the wife not the husband's doll but the husband the wife's baby, the heroine, when the play is over, instead of bringing down the curtain

657

says simply, "Let us sit down and discuss all this." Ellen Terry said it couldn't be done: the audience would just get up and leave the house. But the audience didn't: it only gasped; and the discussion became the big scene of the play. But this was no daring novelty; the most popular play on the English stage is *Hamlet*; and Hamlet does nothing all the evening but discuss. Certainly he sees a ghost and commits four murders; but they are momentary and are not even discussed. All serious drama is discussion: the critics called it "all talk" and "no action" in vain. As H. G. Wells said when he chose novel writing instead of play writing, "On the stage nothing can happen."

But I am forgetting the scarcity of paper and writing you a letter longer than the Inquisitor's speech. The rest is silence.

always yours
G. Bernard Shaw

To HESKETH PEARSON

Ayot St Lawrence. Welwyn
[H/3]   18th January 1943

[Dodd, Mead & Co. had proposed to Hesketh Pearson that he edit a volume of Shaw's selected correspondence. Ashley Dukes (1885–1959), Fabian, playwright and critic, founded London's Mercury Theatre (1933) for production of off-beat theatre and ballet; the ballet teacher Marie Rambert was his wife. James Rennell Rodd (1858–1941), first Baron Rennell, poet and scholar, was a member of the diplomatic service and, later, a Conservative M.P. James L. Lindsay (1847–1913), 26th Earl of Crawford and 9th of Balcarres, astronomer and bibliophile, had been M.P. for Wigan.]

Dear Hesketh

The success of your book has driven the whole trade mad. They all want a book about me, a film about me, anything about me. This will soon evaporate; but my correspondence is a serious problem. I have written an enormous number of letter[s] in my long lifetime, none of them unnecessary (there has never been time for that) and therefore never absolutely vapid and unreadable. That, I suppose, is why so many of them were preserved even before they had any value as autographs. But as I have never kept copies they are scattered over the earth like wrapping paper over the Malvern Beacon after a bank holiday. However, one serious attempt was made to collect them. A

Hungarian Jew named Gabriel Wells, a famous dealer in rare books to whom thousands of pounds were as sixpences, began offering fancy prices for Shaw letters, and accumulated bushels of them before he got tired of trying to persuade me to edit collectors' editions of them. He employed Ashley Dukes to make a selection; but Ashley selected theatrical ones with Janet Achurch as the leading lady; and I did not want to repeat the Ellen Terry success and figure as a theatrical celebrity instead of as an artist philosopher. Gabriel Wells still presumably has his mountain of letters which will be scattered again at his death, which cannot be very much more distant than my own. The copyright in them remains a part of my estate which will some day be valuable.

But I strongly advise you to fight shy of the job, though it will be done someday by somebody. It would take as long as half a dozen biographies; and overloaded as it would be with Wells's profits and my royalties there would not be enough money in it. I could not possibly co-operate even if I were alive: it would take all my time; and I shall never again have any to spare for picking up my old droppings.

I suggest that you write to Dodd Mead to say that you quite agree with them, and have gone into the matter with me; but that the upshot has been as stated in a letter from me, copy of the above relevant part of which you enclose. You see no prospect of being able to undertake the work on any terms that any publisher could afford to offer you, and must leave it to some enthusiast with private means enough to take as labor of love.

As to giving the names of correspondents that would take me at least a year if I could remember them, which I can't.

I enclose the Dodd Mead letter. They are a respectable high priced firm, too well established to need the prestige which a big academic publication would cost them. But they are all right.

faithfully
G. Bernard Shaw

Rennel Rodd is dead. He shared with me the regards of Jenny Patterson, who was on affectionate terms also with the then Crawford of Balcarres. *Honi soit* &c &c.

To D. KILHAM ROBERTS

Ayot St Lawrence. Welwyn
[H/2]   22nd January 1943

[There was no American film treatment of Harris's biography of Oscar Wilde, though Leslie and Sewell Stokes's play *Oscar Wilde*, first performed at the Gate Theatre, Dublin, in 1936, had been produced in New York, with Robert Morley in the title rôle, in October 1938. The "play by Barrie" may have been a skit performed at the Cinema Supper on 3rd July 1914 (see letter of 30th December 1916 to William Archer).]

Dear Mr Kilham Roberts

The success of Hesketh Pearson's book about me has produced a crop of applications for the film rights. A film founded on the book would involve the impersonation of me by an actor. What is the law on the subject—if any? Have I a copyright in my own person at common law? Can I prosecute an actor for impersonating me? Presumably I can sue for damages if I suffer pecuniarily by the performances; but it may not be possible to prove this, as it might on the contrary stimulate the sale of my books and the vogue of my plays.

Have I any remedy or power to prevent by applying to the courts for an order or otherwise. These questions do not concern me alone. The American success of a film founded on Harris's Life of Oscar Wilde, in which Lord Alfred Douglas and other living persons must have been impersonated, will create a demand for such performing rights, and make it necessary for us to ascertain our legal position. I have refused my consent to be filmed either in my own person or anyone else's; but I do not know what I could do if they went ahead in defiance of my wishes. I have been staged in a play by Barrie; and my make-up copied in performances of my own plays; but this was nothing to fuss about. The films raise the question in a very serious form.

faithfully
G. Bernard Shaw

PS I claim no rights in Pearson's book, though I had some hand in it. I want to know my position on the assumption that I have no such rights.

[The answer Shaw received from the Society of Authors, written on 26th January, in the absence of the ailing Roberts, by the assistant secretary M. Elizabeth Barber (1911–79), was that there is no right of privacy under English law and that, as a result, Shaw could take legal action against an impersonator and/or a film company only if the impersonation of him were

660

of such a nature as to constitute a libel upon his reputation. In the United States, however, an Act had been passed that in certain cases granted the right of privacy denied to him in England.]

To R. KINGSLEY READ

Ayot St Lawrence. Welwyn
[H/101]   28th January 1943

[R. Kingsley Read (1887–1975), a language specialist, later produced *Quick-script: Its Alphabet and Manual with a General Introduction to Reformed Alphabetic Writings* (1966). It was Read who judged the competition for the design of a new alphabet established by the Public Trustee in fulfilment of Shaw's testamentary request, and who assisted in its final creation and publication in 1962. Charles Kay Ogden (1889–1957) founded the Orthological Institute (1927) and, twenty years later, the Basic English Foundation. He had recently sent to Shaw a copy of Kenneth Searight's *Sona: An Auxiliary Neutral Language* (1935), of which, he admitted, only seventeen copies had been sold in seven years. "Whittaker" appears to be Shaw's error for Kenneth W. Littlewood, who had sent him a pamphlet of a system of "Pidgin" that had received favourable reaction from the Ministry of Information (it does not turn up in the British Library catalogue). Sir Richard Paget (1869–1955), second Baronet, was a barrister and scholar, who had published a letter, "English Usage," in *The Times* on 31st December 1942. A typescript of Read's "Manual" was ready for Shaw's inspection in July; it was published subsequently as an *Introduction to Sound-writing*, being "a self-instructor on the subject" for teachers.]

Dear Mr Kingsley Read

If you let yourself be drawn into the general question of phonetics you are lost. Stick to your special contribution: every step you take outside it will be a false step. Your department is English Writing Reform: the Greatest Labor Saving Reform in the world. You have nothing to do with universal languages, with reporting shorthand systems, nor to interfere with the old writing and spelling in any way: you simply make it possible to write English economically with a single unequivocal letter for every spoken sound. Your alphabet is a 42 letter alphabet; but it is not new nor untried: it is the alphabet of Pitman and Henry Sweet, and has been found sufficient for all practical purposes for a hundred years past. The only novelty is in the shape of the letters, which are for use by everybody and not for reporters; but they owe something to Pitman and to Sweet's criticisms of Pitman.

661

They do not represent English speech exactly, because no two Englishmen have the same vowels any more than the same thumb prints, and an alphabet capable of exactly representing the speech of a million Englishmen would have to contain sixteen million letters. But this does not prevent every Englishman understanding what every other Englishman says; and experience has proved that an alphabet of 42 letters is phonetic enough to enable every Englishman to understand what every other Englishman writes.

Your business is to provide such an alphabet, and save your country the appalling waste of time involved in spelling the two sounds in the word *though* with six letters instead of two, to take one instance out of thousands. All you claim is to have done this, and made your script attractive in appearance without dots or crosses or diacritical marks of any kind. You have proved that the thing can be done by designing the needed new lettering; and the ulterior views and interests which have hitherto led all the public discussions of phonetics up the garden path do not interest you.

This is your line; and you must set your teeth and stick to it. If the above statement of it suits you, you can copy as much of it, verbatim or paraphrased, into your correspondence as you please, provided you give no hint that I have had anything to do with it.

And dont alter your script to please or conciliate anybody. Dont mention any living person. Dont argue: just repeat your assertions and demonstrations. Above all, dont dream of anything so mad as waiting until you have compiled a dictionary. If you do, you will die unpublished and unheard of.

faithfully
G. Bernard Shaw

PS

Ogden gets two or three new alfabets every week. He put into Basic English and financed and published a system called Sona. Less than a dozen copies were ever sold; but it cured Ogden of his taste for such adventures. Besides, his Orthological Institute is on the rocks financially through the war. You must not be surprised if you do not hear from him.

Whittaker is simply a competitor against you for any interest or help that may be available. Dont attempt to co-operate with him. You must go ahead on your own; and so must he. Your script will be available for his Pidgin; but the two are independent.

Sir Richard Paget is your friendliest mark for correspondence; but you will be best singlehanded.

662

In writing the Manual, dont explain it or expatiate on radicals or on anything else that interests only specialists. Sona was a terrible example of a book killed dead by this mistake. Just state the object of your script, and display it with samples of well known texts written in it.

To MANNING D. ROBERTSON

Ayot St Lawrence. Welwyn
[S(H)/48]   [Undated: *c*. 3rd February 1943]

[Manning D. Robertson (1887–1945) was an Irish architect and town planner. The Cat's Ladder was a steep, narrow muddy path (later supplanted by a ladder-like wooden stairway) leading to a house on the upper reaches of Torca Hill. Ard Sunnas was a house adjacent to Torca Cottage.]

Dear Mr Robertson

... I grew from ten to fourteen on Torca Hill; and the scenery— Killiney Bay to Bray Head and the Wicklow Mountains from the front of the house, and Dublin Bay from Dalkey Island to Howth Head from the back garden, made a deep impression on me. I am very susceptible that way; and I count it as a factor of the first importance in my real education, which was essentially aesthetic.

Your sketch shows the place as very little changed. The cottage, of which I have a late photograph, has had a left wing built on to it. The houses marked Lohengrin and San Elmo did not exist in my time, but Mount Henry at the top of the Cat's Ladder and St Germans at the foot of it were there, also the group of three houses of which the cottage was one.

On the heath in front of these three there was a stone tower with a pump locked up in it, called The Provost's Pump, not marked on your plan. None of this was fenced in; and no question of rights of way ever occurred to us. In my photograph of the cottage there appears a wire fence opposite our gate as if some enclosure had been made; but I am glad to gather from your letter that it has now been acquired as common land, which in effect it always was, though on the Torca road, a couple of hundred yards north of Ard Sunnas, there was a gate across the road and a gate lodge occupied by a family named Fox. But this was never closed.

Dalkey Hill to the south of Torca was walled off as the private park of the Warren family, who, however, gave written orders of admission to the local gentry in virtue of which I had the run of the hill. I was shocked when in later years, as the guest of Sir Horace Plunket at Foxrock, I found that this was not included in Kilkenny Park; and I rejoice to learn that it is now to be added to it. It was sometimes called Telegraph Hill, from the castellated building at the top, formerly, I suppose, provided to signal a Napoleonic invasion.

Do not, for Heaven's sake, plant the hill east of Torca Road with trees; they will shut out the view to sea and spoil the unrivalled amenity of the three houses. Except for commercial purposes one tree to the acre is quite enough. In my time Dalkey Hill was burnt right down to the white granite; and it would lose half its charm if it were covered up with black pines. There is nothing better than granite and heather for roaming.

Many thanks for your letter and the tracing. I shall never see the place again; but it is extremely vivid in my memory.

faithfully
G. Bernard Shaw

PS All the stone walls built during the Famine to provide employment should be demolished. Such corridors as the road from Donnybrook to Stillorgan should be made illegal.

To HUGH BEAUMONT

[H/116]

Ayot St Lawrence. Welwyn
7th February 1943

[*Heartbreak House* was to be revived by H. M. Tennent at the Cambridge Theatre on 18th March 1943, with Robert Donat as Shotover and Vernon Kelso as Hector. (Sir) Beverley Baxter (1891–1964), a Canadian author and journalist, was on the staff of the *Daily Express* in 1921; he later became its editor-in-chief. Contemporary reports of the first London performance of *Heartbreak House* lay the blame for the delay between Acts II and III on faulty stage machinery. Henry Marriott Watson (1863–1921), an Australian, was a prolific popular novelist.]

Dear Hugh Beaumont

Tell Donat, on the cue "I hope so," to bring down the curtain with a commanding "Well said, child. They will awaken your country's sleeping soul." Try this at the next rehearsal; and let me know whether it does the trick.

There must be no interval between Acts II and III. This is frightfully important. At the first performance I had made the change from the interior to the exterior so instantaneous that except for the briefest possible blackout Hector's exit from the house and his entry into the garden were practically continuous. But on the night the arc light went wrong; and it took 35 minutes to get it going. This catastrophe wrecked the performance hopelessly except for a roar of laughter when Hector said "How is all this going to end?" The unfortunate critics all declared the play intolerably long, as in effect it was. Beverley Baxter made a heroic attempt to boost it; but it drew only £500 a week, and as soon as possible Fagan withdrew it and replaced it by She Stoops to Conquer, which drew absolutely nothing at all and shut up the shop. So make sure Acts II and III are continuous.

Also see that the cues for the bombs are thoroughly understood. At Birmingham, where the play had a great success, it finished on the first night without a single explosion. Barry Jackson then took his managerial call and was getting on with his speech when suddenly Bang Bang went a tremendous cannonade and blew Barry off the stage. Beware of these contretemps: the play seems to have some attraction for them.

Who is playing Hector? His make-up has always been a difficulty. If we could get a photograph of the late novelist Marriott Watson (his daughter was on the stage and may have one), it would solve the problem: for he looked like Athos, Aramis and D'Artagnan rolled into one: Ellie would certainly have fallen in love with him and believed all his stories. And yet he was obviously a modern gentleman.

Let me have a note of the cast: I know only the three ladies and the captain.

In the program I think it would be appropriate to call the play a fantasy in the Russian manner as it was at first. And for Heaven's sake dont let them George me. Professionally I am Bernard Shaw.

> faithfully
> G. Bernard Shaw

When you have a couple of stalls or a box to spare, invite Beverley Baxter in recognition of his championship of the first production.

The aeroplane noise is made with a vacuum cleaner.

The BBC does shell bursts rather well. How?

To NANCY ASTOR

[C/101]

Ayot St Lawrence. Welwyn
13th February 1943

[Through the connivance of Lady Astor, abetted by Blanche Patch, the local authorities had received instructions from Ernest Bevin's office to exempt Violet Pond from national service. In the following June, however, she declined further exemption and departed from Ayot.]

Violet is respected until the 27th May.

The sweets arrived happily just when my ration gave out. I gobble them with much gusto.

Tell Winston to stop talking alarming nonsense about unconditional surrender. Make him explain that the surrender cannot be unconditional, but that we shall dictate the conditions. As to whether "we" includes Uncle Jo[e], the less said just now the better.

GBS

To MARJORIE DEANS

[H/1]

Ayot St Lawrence. Welwyn
22nd March 1943

[Marjorie Deans (1901–82), assistant to Gabriel Pascal and script writer, handled much of his business and correspondence during this period. Pascal claimed to have signed Greta Garbo to play Saint Joan in his projected film. Ann Casson (b. 1915) toured in 1943 as Vivie Warren and Raïna Petkoff, and in 1944 as Ann Whitefield and Joan.]

Dear Marjorie Deans

It was finally decided between Gabriel and myself that G. G. was out of the question for various reasons; and not a word more passed about her until your last letter arrived just after a cable from Gabriel to say he had signed an agreement with her, not mentioning her name. Now I had made up my mind that the new Joan must not be an old Hollywood star no longer in her first youth, but a new Englishwoman on the threshold of a career; and the one I have in view is Ann Casson, Sybil Thorndike's daughter, who looks the part and is of the right age.

However, as the G. G. arrangement, like all Gabriel's arrangements[,] will probably come to nothing anyhow, we need not bother about it yet.

I think it is evident that if Cornell is to be filmed as Candida—and

I know of nobody better—she must be left to her husband's direction, and Gabriel must drop the play. But I have done nothing about this so far, as I want to stave off any more films until the war is over.

The situation is a ticklish one. Gabriel has achieved the surprising feat of going to America at the height of his reputation, fortified by a monopoly of my plays for filming, and coming back with nothing done and nothing doing. What are we to do with him? Anyhow it is clear that he must give up the notion of confining himself to my stuff. How is he to live? . . .

faithfully
G. Bernard Shaw

To RONALD GOW

[Ayot St Lawrence. Welwyn]
[E/1]   1st April 1943

[Gow was doing a screen treatment of Howard Spring's novel *Fame is the Spur*, which had as its background the rise of the Labour Party, its central character mirroring Ramsay MacDonald. The project was subsequently abandoned; another version, written by Nigel Balchin, was produced in 1947. Gow had written to ask if it was true that Shaw had instructed Keir Hardie and other early Labour members entering Parliament, "Whatever you do don't behave like gentlemen. The House of Commons is a gentleman's club, and if you play their game they've got you."]

I have no recollection of saying this; but it was good advice on a reasonable interpretation. Keir Hardie was so much one of nature's gentlemen himself that he never could understand that a Cabinet Minister (Sir Edward Grey for instance) was not only deliberately lying but leading the House to believe that Hardie was lying.

But the Labor members never asked me for advice. Why should they? If they had, I should have warned them to be very careful to eat like gentlemen when they were confronted with dinners of five courses, and not wreck their health (as some of them did) by making a full meal of each course.

G.B.S.

To SIDNEY WEBB

[H/14]   29th April 1943

[Beatrice Webb died the following day. Barbara Drake (1876–1963), her favourite niece, was an ardent Fabian and social research worker, who co-edited Beatrice's unfinished book *Our Partnership* (1948) with Margaret I. Cole. Shaw's article on 10th March 1943 was a review of the first two volumes of Marx's *Selected Works* edited by V. Adoratsky, "What Would Marx Say about Beveridge?" Sydney Olivier, first Baron Olivier of Ramsden, died on 15th February 1943. The "Essayists" were the seven contributors to *Fabian Essays in Socialism* (1889).]

My dear Sidney

Not having heard from Beatrice for some time I feared she was ill, and would probably have written to Barbara at the County Council for news of her but for your letter. In particular there was an article on Marx which was extracted from me by The Daily Herald, and which I wrote mainly for your amusement, as it made out that the Soviet government was a disastrous failure until it was Fabianized on your lines by Lenin and Stalin, whom I hailed as the arch-Fabian. I thought this would have drawn a letter from Beatrice; and when I heard nothing I began to be anxious.

At our ages we can only wait the event that cannot in any case be far off. There seems nothing that I can do; but if there is tell Barbara to let me know.

Charlotte is so crippled and invalided with this wretched *osteitis deformans* that there is not much joy in life for her. The doctors can do nothing. I am vetted by them as sound in wind and limb; and I hope to be able to finish my book. Though I hardly ever go outside the curtilage I saw firewood for an hour or so every day; but my blunders and forgettings and repetitions and omissions are pitiable: my corrections are estimated by Maxwell at 75% of the cost of setting-up. I really ought to be dead. Olivier, some time before the end, wrote to me that he never left the house, and agreed with the priest in John Bull's Other Island that this world is hell, and that we are here to expiate sins committed in a former existence. You and I are now the sole surviving Essayists.

The war is interesting all the same, diabolical, senseless, useless as it now seems. A mere trifle in history; but I am rather curious to see how it will end; and so no doubt are you.

So let us hold on as long as we can.   as ever

                                                                       GBS

Blanche Patch is having her Easter holiday; so I have to do my own typing as you may guess by the look of it.

To JOHN MAYNARD KEYNES

Ayot St Lawrence. Welwyn

[H/17]   7th May 1943

[Keynes wanted an obituary article on Beatrice Webb for the *Economic Journal*. Shaw's *Picture Post* article of 13th September 1941, "Two Friends of the Soviet Union," was reprinted on the dust-wrappers of the two-volume second edition of the Webbs' *Soviet Communism* (1941) and as a preface to their *The Truth about Soviet Russia* (1942). In 1947 Beatrice's ashes, mixed with Sidney's, were interred in Westminster Abbey, the first time in its history that husband and wife had been buried together at the same ceremony.]

Dear Maynard Keynes

You are the fourth editor who has pressed me for a Beatrice obituary. I cannot do it, for two reasons. First, only the other day an article I wrote on the Webbs got a large circulation in The Picture Post; and Beatrice reproduced it in a pamphlet and an edition of a book which covered all the ground that the P.P. is too popular to reach. That shot my bolt as far as the public life of Beatrice is concerned.

Second, I knew her too well and saw her too closely at home to get her into her distant perspective as a great woman. If I wrote about her intimately I should write gaily; and that would not have the funeral solemnity proper to the present occasion.

Her ashes should go to Westminster Abbey, which is now much too masculine.

She was not noticeably strong in economics. She was, to her great credit, a selfmade ethical Socialist, and not a convert by Marx or Mill or any other economist. I never could persuade her that it was fundamental in the Manchester School that *Laisser-faire* must make unemployment impossible because demand is insatiable, and that as neither of these propositions were borne out by the facts, the Manchester School was a convicted failure. That is the sort of economic argument she never used.

I think you must write her obituary yourself or find some very competent understudy. . . .

as ever

G. Bernard Shaw

669

To VERA GARGAN

[A/4]
Ayot St Lawrence. Welwyn
15th May 1943

[Vera Gargan had reported the death of her father Matthew Edward McNulty, who had resided with her in Dublin following retirement from his banking position in Newry.]

My dear Vera

It was very kind of you to wire me the news. It came to me by telephone; and I, being old and deaf, could make nothing of your name. I have to address this to your father, knowing it will come into your hands.

He was in his 87th year, like myself; and at that age it is time to rest; so there is no occasion for sadness. He had a good long time to enjoy his life in his own way after escaping from his drudgery in the Bank of Ireland.

Is there such a thing as a photograph of him in his later years? I should like to see it. I will return it.

If there is anything I can do for you, let me know.

faithfully
G. Bernard Shaw

To GABRIEL PASCAL

[H/1]
Ayot St Lawrence. Welwyn
24th June 1943

[J. Arthur Rank (1888–1972), later first Baron Rank of Sutton Scotney, was chairman of the Rank Organisation 1941–62 and, subsequently, its president; he became the most powerful film maker in Britain. Pascal, on the strength of his contract with Garbo, was able to interest Rank in financing *Saint Joan*, as well as *Cæsar and Cleopatra* and *The Doctor's Dilemma*. Shaw encouraged Pascal to hold out for a salary plus ten per cent of the gross receipts. When Rank demurred, Pascal withdrew the percentage demand. Eventually plans for *Saint Joan* were cancelled, the British Government having indicated it would be injudicious to produce, during wartime, a film that showed the British burning a French patriot.

Cæsar and Cleopatra was produced at Dublin's Abbey Theatre on 24th October 1927. The designer of its scenery and costumes was D. Travers Smith.]

670

My dear Gabriel

Wash out everything I said to you last Saturday. A.R. is not an innocent novice: he has been in the game for 15 years, and is chairman of ten companies engaged in it. He is a director of nearly 60 companies. I am more anxious than ever to have a look at him; but what I have learnt since we met entirely changes my view of the situation. Do not let yourself be entangled in his companies by becoming a shareholder. Have a separate agreement for each production, your remuneration to be a royalty on the gross and not a share of profits, with advances, non-returnable, for you to live on, and a deposit of capital by the shareholders sufficient to cover the utmost cost of the whole production. Do not bind your future activities in any way.

You will notice that Korda, in becoming a film speculator, has ceased to be an artist, just as so many good engineers, in becoming mining speculators, have ceased to be engineers: a miserable deterioration ending sometimes in their ruin.

On reflection I am against putting C and C, or any other production, in front of St Joan. I cannot afford to have two films running at the same time; and I think the distraction of public expectation by starting a new and less popular hare would be an error of artistic judgement. There is plenty to do on St Joan beside the Loire scene, which you will not be ready to do before the spring.

I have a set of flashlights of the Dublin production of C and C for your inspection, as the Egyptian scenery is so good that you might find the designer useful. I can easily find out who he is. . . .

We are expecting you on Saturday the 3rd July, with or without A.R.

always yours
G. Bernard Shaw

To WILLIAM A. ROBSON

Ayot St Lawrence. Welwyn
[H/13]   3rd July 1943

[Robson had written a lengthy appreciation of Beatrice Webb for publication in the journal *Public Administration,* in which (citing a passage in *My Apprenticeship*) he alluded to her "artistic strain . . . which suggests that she could have been an imaginative writer if she had been so minded." Rosalind (Rosie) Dobbs (1865–1949) was the youngest of Beatrice's sisters.]

671

Dear Robson

There is only one thing in your excellent article which you must change.... The notion that Beatrice supplied the facts and Sidney put them into literary form is wildly wrong. Webb combines extraordinary ability with an equally extraordinary simplicity of character that makes him so indifferent to purely artistic considerations that nothing could ever induce him to study writing or public speaking as a fine art. This grew on him so much that when he was in Parliament he made the best informed and wisest speeches there without taking the trouble to make them audible or intelligible three yards off. He could make himself perfectly clear in writing; but beyond that he would not go. He had no patience with people who wanted airs and graces as well.

Beatrice was much more complex. You have rightly said (page 4) that she was something of an artist. There was not only an artistic strain in her, but a gipsy strain which came out in the amazing career of her younger sister Rosie Dobbs, painter and wanderer. When Beatrice was not satisfied that she had made her case clear she handed the chapter to me (if I was within reach) to redraft. You can see from her autobiography that she had an artistic style, and needed no help on that side....

We two are dreadfully old, nearer 90 than 80, and one of us (the lady) an invalid badly disabled physically; but always glad to hear from you.

faithfully
G. Bernard Shaw

To EMRYS HUGHES

[C/1; W/417]

4 Whitehall Court SW1
13th August 1943

[Emrys Hughes (1894–1969), son-in-law of Keir Hardie, was editor of *Forward* 1931–46. He had requested an article on the downfall of Mussolini, whose resignation had been requested on 24th July by the Fascist Grand Council, followed by his arrest and imprisonment in the Abruzzi Mountains, which supposedly ended the Fascist regime. Shaw's scepticism was justified: rescued in a spectacular parachute raid by German commandos in mid-September, Mussolini set up a Fascist regime in the north of Italy.

The Shaws had returned to Whitehall Court, for the first time in nearly three years, on 26th July, Shaw's 87th birthday, to allow the servants to spring-clean Shaw's Corner and take their holiday. The return to Ayot was postponed due to the illness of the cook, Clara Higgs.]

Before writing an obituary always make sure that your man is dead.

Napoleon came back from Elba; and his subsequent extinction was, as his extinguisher Wellington testified, "a very near thing."

It is not yet clear that by sacking him the Italians have done more than jump out of the frying pan into the fire.

I had rather not prophesy until I know.

So for the moment, MUM ! ! !

GBS

To HUGH BEAUMONT

4 Whitehall Court S W 1
[A/116]   29th August 1943

[Having attended a matinée of *Heartbreak House* on 18th August, Shaw wrote two days later to Edith Evans to commiserate with her for having (as Hesione) to "pull the play through against four hopeless miscasts, including a faded maiden aunt as your youthful rival and a Shotover who is obviously a leading juvenile in a stuck-on beard." The play, he concluded, "should be billed as Half Heart House" (X/316). To Robert Donat he wrote on the same day: "You're too young. The matinee idol shines through the obviously false beard and draws the money. But he daren't be stormy because that would give the audience away completely; and Shotover is nothing when he is not stormy. So he has to play the Vicar of Wakefield. ... You should play Hector and let the callboy play Shotover. ... Play young parts while you are young: you won't be convincing in them when you are old. You were not born old, as some actors are" (X/411).

The other "miscasts" included Deborah Kerr (Ellie), Vernon Kelso (Hector), Amy Veness (Guinness), and Francis Lister (Randall). Acceptable to Shaw were the performances of Isabel Jeans (Ariadne), J. H. Roberts (Mazzini Dunn), and George Merritt (Mangan). John Burrell was the director, Cecil Beaton the costume designer. The play closed on 9th October. Freda Jackson (b. 1909) had made an early success at Stratford and the Old Vic.]

Dear Hugh Beaumont

I see by the returns that H. H. is dropping slowly to death. I saw it at the Wednesday matinée the week before last. It was a dull performance, considering what the play can do at concert pitch. The miscasts,

673

which are really very bad, killed it. Donat, though he is popular, is, as I knew he would be, too young for Shotover, and not right for the character anyhow. Ellie and Hector, though they are intelligent and do their best, are hopelessly out of it; and nothing can get the play right if they are wrong. Randall works honestly for his salary; but not having the Foreign Office touch he is quite undistinguished. Guinness is all wrong. Edith, Isabel, and Roberts are all right; but except when they have the stage to themselves they have nobody to play up to them except Mangan, who is good. There are certain details of dress and business that can be remedied: I have written to Burrell about them.

I know that the war time difficulties are very troublesome. There is only one way of checking the rot in the receipts; and that is to have another first night and set of notices, with Donat as Hector, Freda Jackson as Ellie, and Ayliff as Shotover (he is playing it in Birmingham and is the only possible Shotover I know except Trouncer, who is engaged at the Hayma[rket]).

But if you let the run die a natural death we shall not have done so badly. I am not complaining, only criticising, which is my special job.

G.B.S.

To DANIEL MACMILLAN

[X/105]

[4 Whitehall Court SW 1]
11th September 1943

[Daniel Macmillan (1886–1965), chairman and managing director of the publishing house of Macmillan & Co., was a descendant of Alexander Macmillan (1818–96), who with his brother Daniel (1813–57) co-founded the firm in 1845, and of George A. Macmillan (1855–1936), second son of Alexander. The history of the house was being written by Charles Morgan. For Shaw's correspondence with Macmillan 1880–85 and with the other publishers mentioned, see *Collected Letters 1874–1897*. The "hereditary" publisher in Bedford Street was G.P. Putnam's Sons.]

Dear Mr Macmillan

I have read the galley slips you sent me concerning myself in Mr Morgan's history of Macmillans with interest and a very agreeable measure of astonishment.

I had no idea that the reports on novels I submitted were so appreciative. I consider them highly creditable to the firm's readers; for they make it clear that what was wrong was not, as I thought, any failure to spot me as a literary discovery, but the strangeness at that time of my valuations. In fact they thought more of my jejune prentice work than I did myself; for I really hated those five novels, having drudged through them like any other industrious apprentice because there was nothing else I could or would do. That in spite of their disagreeableness they somehow induced readers rash enough to begin them to go on to the end and resent that experience seems to me now a proof that I was a born master of the pen. But the novel was not my proper medium. I wrote novels because everybody did so then; and the theatre, my rightful kingdom, was outside literature. The coterie theatres in which I first reached the public as a playwright did not then exist.

But of course I did not understand all this at the time. My recollection, until your letter arrived, was far less encouraging. I began, not very wisely, by calling on all the publishers in person to see what they were like; and they did not like me. I did not like myself enough to blame them. I was young (23), raw, Irish from Dublin, and Bohemian without being in the least convivial or self-indulgent, deeply diffident inside and consequently brazen outside, and so utterly devoid of reverence that a phrenologist whom I asked what my bump of veneration was like replied "Why, it's a hole!" Altogether a discordant personality in the eyes of the elderly great publishers of those days, a now extinct species. As I had a considerable aesthetic culture, and the English governing classes, of whom I knew only what I had picked up from Thackeray and Trollope, had none, they were barbarians to me; and I was to them a complete outsider. I was in fact outside the political world until I had written the first three of my novels; and when I came in I came in as a Marxist, a phenomenon then inconceivable even to Mill, [John] Morley, [Sir Charles] Dilke, Auberon Herbert, the Fortnightly Reviewers, the Positivists, the Darwinians, and the rest of the Agnostic Republicans who represented the extreme left of the most advanced pioneers in the eighties of the last century. The Transvaluation of Values in which I was an obscure pioneer can hardly be imagined nowadays by people under 70. I was a Nietzschean and an Ibsenist before I had ever heard of Nietzsche or Ibsen.

In view of all this you will see that Macmillans were very much ahead of the older publishers (I tried them all) in recognising my talent. They corresponded with me a little; and George Macmillan tried to soften my rejection by Alexander, who didn't like me personally, by sending me a long report by Morley, who turned me down as a victim of undigested Ruskin, of whom I had read little or nothing. [George]

675

Meredith turned me down for Chatto [error for Chapman & Hall] without extenuating circumstances. Blackwood accepted my first novel; but afterwards reneged, to the distress of his oldest reader. Smith Elder were polite and asked to see future efforts. None of the rest would have anything to say to me; and even those who gave some attention to my first attempt found its successors more and more impossible. When William Archer made Stevenson read *Cashel Byron's Profession*, and he and Henley applauded it, Bentley, who had refused it, sent for it urgently, and was furious because it was no longer at his disposal; but that was after I had given up novel writing, having designed a mighty work which I found myself too ignorant to finish; so I let its opening section go as *An Unsocial Socialist*. The novels, printed as padding in Socialist magazines, got pirated in America; and when I, being ashamed of them, tried to suppress them, they broke out in spite of me as persistently as they had suppressed themselves before.

Macmillan's attention and George's kindly civility certainly made a difference to me. There are so many amateurs sending in crude MSS to publishers and managers that no beginner can be sure that he is not one of the hopeless failures until his work is accepted, or he has had at least some response indicating that he is not quite out of the question. If Macmillan had simply declined with thanks like nearly all the rest, I should have had to set my teeth still closer.

I am now one of the few who personally remember the Grand Old Men of the publishing world of that day: Alexander Macmillan, Longman, and Bentley. They were so powerful that they held the booksellers in abject subjection, and were denounced by Walter Besant and his newly organised Society of Authors as remorseless sharks. When they died and were succeeded by their sons, the hereditary system did not always work as well as it did in Bedford Street; and the booksellers got the upper hand. John Murray's Byronic prestige was so select that I did not dream of trying him until years later, when I was an author of some note and had already helped to bankrupt three publishers. I offered him *Man & Superman*. He refused in a letter which really touched me. He said he was old-fashioned and perhaps a bit behind the times; but he could not see any intention in my book but to wound, irritate, and upset all established constitutional opinion, and therefore could not take the responsibility of publishing it. By that time I could command sufficient capital to finance my books and enter into direct friendly relations with the printers (this began my very pleasant relations with Clarks of Edinburgh). I took matters into my own hands and, like Herbert Spencer and Ruskin, manufactured my books myself, and induced Constables to take me "on commission."

Walter Besant never understood that publishing, like Insurance and turf bookmaking, is a gamble, with the important difference that whereas an insurer can employ an actuary who will tell him the odds at which chance becomes mathematical certainty, and a bookmaker who bets against every horse can lose on one only and is being supplanted by the tote, the publisher has to take chances which are incalculable, and must therefore play with all the advantages he can get, leaving the author to take care of himself. Besant assumed that a successful book ought to pay for itself only, not knowing that it has to pay for several others which, though they keep the shop open, barely repay the overhead and the cost of their manufacture and sometimes lose even that. A loss of 100% on the swings makes a large hole in a profit of 300% on the roundabouts. If both authors and publishers understood this there would be much less friction in their dealings. But the publisher often knows everything about publishing practice and nothing about its economic theory, whilst the author as a rule knows nothing about either, and is constitutionally unfit to conduct his own business. I served for ten years on the Society's Committee, and know the ropes pretty well.

faithfully
G. Bernard Shaw

To H. G. WELLS

4 Whitehall Court SW 1
12th September 1943

[C/26]

Charlotte died this morning at 2.30. You saw what she had become when you last visited us: an old woman bowed and crippled, furrowed and wrinkled, and greatly distressed by hallucinations of crowds in the room, evil persons, and animals. Also by breathlessness, as the osteitis closed on her lungs. She got steadily worse: the prognosis was terrible, ending with double pneumonia.

But on Friday evening a miracle began. Her troubles vanished. Her visions ceased. Her furrows and wrinkles smoothed out. Forty years fell off her like a garment. She had thirty hours of happiness and heaven. Even after her last breath she shed another twenty years, and now lies young and incredibly beautiful. I have to go in and look at her and talk affectionately to her. I did not know I could be so moved.

Do not tell a soul until Thursday when all will be over. I could not stand flowers and letters and a crowd at Golders Green.

G.B.S.

To ALFRED DOUGLAS

4 Whitehall Court SW1
[C/64; X/394] 15th September 1943

[The music of Handel performed at Charlotte's funeral ceremony was Part II, No. 32 ("But Thou didst not leave His soul in hell") of *Messiah* and "Ombra ma fù" from *Serse*.]

A mass does nobody any harm; and I may for all I know have been living on prayers for years past. But my wife's orders in her will were "No flowers; no black clothes; no service." So this morning at Golders Green not a word was spoken; but Handel gave the music he set to "nor didst Thou suffer thy Holy One to see corruption" for the comittal, and "Ombra mai fu" (vulgarly known as Handel's Largo) for the voluntary. Who could ask for more?

Handel was her favorite composer.

Miracles of rejuvenation occurred and made the end touchingly happy, making grief and sorrow impossible. Envy me; but dont condole. I am exaltedly serene and vigorous.

G.B.S.

To LILLAH AND FREDERICK KEEBLE

4 Whitehall Court SW1
[C/4] 18th September 1943

It was quite happy: at 86 and 87 the end is all in the day's work, discussed, prepared, and painless, though none the less deeply felt.

We'll talk about it some day.

G.B.S.

678

To LADY MARY MURRAY

[H/36]

4 Whitehall Court SW 1
21st September 1943

[In the Personal column of *The Times* on 20th September a notice appeared: "MR. BERNARD SHAW has received such a prodigious mass of letters on the occasion of his wife's death that, though he has read and values them all, any attempt to acknowledge them individually is beyond his powers. He therefore begs his friends and hers to be content with this omnibus reply, and to assure them that a very happy ending to a very long life has left him awaiting his own turn in perfect serenity."]

My dear Lady Murray [Blanche Patch's typing error?]

It was not a bit sad: the vigorous serenity with which I made all the arrangements was almost indecent. The end was most blessedly better than we had expected and I had feared. This evil disease—*osteitis deformans* they call it—began in 1939, disguised as lumbago. It is slow degeneration and collapse of the bony structure that finally crushes the lungs until they can no longer do their work, and the patient dies of pneumonia. The doctors cannot cure it (nor anything else, for that matter). It bows the neck, cripples the limbs, shortens the breath, furrows the brow, makes walking and breathing impossible, and transfigures the best looking woman into a witch out of the Ingoldsby Legends until you would not be surprised to see her ride off on a broomstick.

Charlotte was enduring the slow but inexorable advance of all this when, about a month ago, her distress was increased by hallucinations which filled her room with intruders. She was perfectly reasonable about them, insisting that I should call up the Whitehall Court manager and housekeeper and ask them why they let these people up; but she could not believe that they were not real until I told her that she had become clairvoyant, and that though she saw them in the room, they were really in Australia or elsewhere.

Still, her life had not become quite unbearable when on the evening of the 10th, when I was taking her from the dinner table, I was astonished to see that her deeply furrowed forehead had smoothed: there was not a wrinkle in it. And when she spoke her voice was what it had been in her happiest, most lighthearted, moments before she was ill I knew in my soul at once what this meant; but the relief was so blessed, and the change so magical that I could think of nothing but that her distresses were over and we were still together. I got her to bed and settled her for the night earlier than usual, quite happy.

Next day she looked as she did when I first met her 45 years ago. I stayed with her every moment I could; and she talked to me incessantly, like a pleased child, babbling unintelligibly, but understanding what I said to her. I told her that she was getting well; that all our troubles were over; that she had recovered all her good looks. I heaped on her every endearment I could find words for; and she was delighted, and only once was puzzled for an instant and said "Why do you say that?" I was more deeply moved than I had known myself to be capable of being, but not in the least painfully.

This lasted all Saturday; and again I bade her goodnight early and left her happy.

On Sunday morning at a quarter past eight, the night nurse woke me with a cheery shout of "Your wife died at half past two; but I thought I wouldnt wake you." There is always some comic relief on these occasions. It did not hurt, and was quite a success.

But the miracle went on. Six hours after she drew her last tiny breath, she had thrown off twenty more years, and was younger than I had ever known her. She was classically beautiful. I remembered what York Powell wrote to a friend in 1898 "Shaw has married a woman with a face like a muffin," and thought "What would he say if he saw her now?" It was a busy day; but I could not resist the impulse to go into her room and look at her and talk to her, though I knew that she had thrown me off with her married life and all the rest of her sense life, her troubles and distresses.

On Monday there was nothing but a beautiful wax figure: I could not talk to it: she was gone. On Tuesday it was ready for the Golders Green furnace.

In her will she wrote "No flowers, no black clothes, no service." Yet I wore my one black suit because she liked it; and though not a word was spoken, the organist made the right atmosphere for me by playing Handel, her pet composer. Nobody was there beside myself but my secretary, Blanche Patch, and Lady Astor, who could not stay away. I was quite happy. All's well that ends well.

Some months ago I said to her one day "Why do we see so little of Gilbert Murray? Have you turned against him?" If he had heard how vehemently she repudiated this suspicion he would have been amply assured of her high regard for him. What made me ask was that she had lost her interest in another famous man; and when I asked her why, she said "I have not turned against him; but he is *such* an infernal liar!"

I am afraid I have written you an immoderately long letter (I have let everyone else off with a postcard); but somehow I had to, lest you should think that I am in sorrow instead of very much the reverse.

always yours and Gilbert's
G. Bernard Shaw

To SIDNEY WEBB

4 Whitehall Court SW 1
[C/14]   27th September 1943

[At her death Charlotte left to Shaw a life interest in the income from her estate, and bequests to her niece Cecily Colthurst and several of her long-time friends. The bulk of the estate after Shaw's demise was to be placed in Irish trusts administered by the National City Bank of Dublin, the money to be used "in its uncontrolled discretion": (a) To make grants to founda-tions or institutions having as their object the bringing of masterpieces of fine art within the reach of the Irish people; (b) To teach self-control, elocution, oratory and deportment, the arts of personal contact and social intercourse, and the other arts of public, private, professional and business life to Irish men and women; and (c) To establish a chair or readership at an Irish university to give instruction in those subjects.]

Charlotte's will contains a legacy to you of £1000. The lawyers will deal with this when they have obtained probate, unless by any chance you want it sooner, when it will be forthcoming at any moment. . . .

I am executor and trustee jointly with the National Provincial Bank. The residual after my death goes to Ireland for public purposes, less £20,000 to her niece, which I shall let her have at once.

I am pretty full of business; but the book is getting finished at last.

G.B.S.

To DONALD McLEOD MATHESON

4 Whitehall Court SW 1
[A/126; W/418]   5th October 1943

[Donald McLeod Matheson (1896–1979) was secretary of the National Trust.]

To the Secretary of the N.T.
Dear Sir

I own the freehold of a ten roomed house in the village of Ayot St Lawrence in Herts, where I have lived for the last 35 years—longer than in any other of my residences. I am now in my 87th year, and about to make my last will.

The house stands in a plot of some two acres. There is a detached garage and greenhouse, and scraps of kitchen garden, orchard, and lawn, with a belt of trees.

Has such a trifle any use or interest for the National Trust?

> faithfully
> G. Bernard Shaw

To WILLIAM MAXWELL

[A/3]

Ayot St Lawrence. Welwyn
24th October 1943

[Shaw returned to Ayot on 21st October. Maxwell, who had received a warning letter from the anxious Blanche Patch, wrote to Shaw to caution him against making a precipitate decision to appoint John Wardrop as his literary executor.]

My dear Maxwell

Dont apologize: your counsel is always welcome, and highly valued. I fished for it: didnt I?

I refer back one or two points for further consideration. 1. A triumvirate of three sages would cost more than the income from my works, which are not for all time, but for the remnant of my days plus fifty years. 2. As they would never agree, except negatively, they would operate as a Shaw Suppression Society, realizing nothing but their subconscious intention. 3. The greatness of any literary work does not create a directly proportionate need for nursing it. On the contrary, the greater it is, the more it takes care of itself no matter who handles it. Shakespear and Blake had no literary executors. 4. Only a Shavomaniac who prefers my interests to his own and will be to me what Watts Dunton was to Swinburne, Hall Caine to Dante Rossetti, [John] Severn to Ruskin, or (I forget the name [James Gillman]) to Coleridge. 5. He must be young enough to reach the twentyfirst century before he is 80. 6. He must not only be a fancier of letters, but a bit of a lawyer and a man of business, preferably a Scot. 7. He must be married to a woman who does not regard me as his worst enemy and that of her children.

When you have duly weighed these seven points, you will see how my choice has been narrowed down until Wardrop leads the field by a head.

At your next visit I will try to contrive that he shall by a happy accident drop in at the same moment.

G. Bernard Shaw

To WILLIAM MAXWELL

4 Whitehall Court SW 1
[H/4]   3rd November 1943

My dear Maxwell

I have no intention of making J.W. my literary executor. How do I know what his condition will be when he is forty? He may have enough business of his own to leave him no time for mine. Or he may have taken to drink. No: I shall make the Public Trustee my literary executor, with a recommendation to employ J.W. to do the work and have the custody of the papers. If he goes wrong, the P.T. can sack him.

I cannot hit on any better arrangement. The job is quite within the capacity of a young man, subject to certain rules which I can establish definitely. I repeat, there is no nursing or building up to be done: my vogue will go its own way without any handling.

G. Bernard Shaw

To STELLA BEECH

4 Whitehall Court SW 1
[H/1]   8th November 1943

[Pat was Stella Beech's son Patrick. The friend was Lord Alfred Douglas, who sold twenty-five of his Wilde letters to Quaritch for £200. These subsequently were sold to the dealer A.S.W. Rosenbach, who then re-sold them to the collector John B. Stetson, Jr. Whether the Rosenbach purchase came to as much as Douglas claimed is conjectural.]

My dear Stella II

I am shy of presuming on my friendships with people's mothers, as they do not always approve of the relation. But of course I never thought of you as Missis Beech and I dont believe you ever think of me as Mister Shaw, at arms' length. My particular friends always call me G.B.S.

As to the letters, I attach no importance to the actual sheets of paper and the handwriting: it is what is written that matters, not how it was or where it was written. Some letters have no literary or historical value, and are treasured as relics, curiosities or keepsakes; but that is quite negligible when they are historical documents. I therefore see no objection to the sale of such letters as curiosities, and advise you and Pat to think twice before you make a sale impossible by presenting the originals to the British Museum, which is the readiest and best way of doing it. But if you two were to be hit by the same bomb, the market price of these scraps of paper might make all the difference to the widow and the children, who could sell them without the smallest indelicacy.

A friend of mine who had corresponded with Oscar Wilde and had 30 of his letters was so hard pressed for money that he sold them to Quaritch for £350. Quaritch's executors sold them for £2000! Think of it for a moment from the point of view of throwing away your grandchildren's education perhaps.

As to the photostats, they are the surest sort of fire insurance. Keep one set in your house and another in Pat's. Dame Lyttelton might keep another to make assurance doubly sure. As to destroying the rest (if any) you must not do that without the consent of your co-trustees; but it is not desirable to have copies unlocated.

Keep every scrap of my writing you have. As to what should be included when the letters are published that must be settled when the time comes. No use bothering about it at present. . . .

always yours
G. Bernard Shaw

To DONALD McLEOD MATHESON

[H/126; X/418]

4 Whitehall Court SW 1
10th November 1943

[James Lees-Milne (b. 1908) was a member of the National Trust staff 1936–66 and a much-published author. The "ardent Shavians" were John Wardrop and Veronica.]

. . . Pressure of affairs makes it uncertain when I shall return to Ayot; but when I do I shall inform Mr Lees-Milne and appoint a visit.

I have in mind a gentleman who will probably be my acting literary executor. He and his wife are very anxious to reside in the house and to shew if off to visitors. They are ardent Shavians and can afford the tenancy; so I should like to discuss this with Mr L-M.

G. Bernard Shaw

To ADA TYRRELL

[C/1]

4 Whitehall Court SW1
21st November 1943

[Judy Musters insisted it was untrue that Shaw's mother never crossed his threshold: she visited Adelphi Terrace on a few occasions (when Judy, then Georgina Gillmore, was Shaw's secretary), and she and Judy spent a weekend with the Shaws at Harmer Green. Barker was visiting at the same time, for a single night. Gladys (Mrs Harold) Fitz-James was Mrs Tyrrell's niece; she converted to Roman Catholicism and became an Irish nationalist. Shaw gave money to Mrs Tyrrell, secretly, in 1944 to pay for Gladys's hospital expenses. Maud Clarke (1863–1950) was Mrs Tyrrell's sister.]

My dear Addie

I forgot to send you back Gladys's letter. Here it is.

Lucy used to call my wife Carlotta; and Gladys picked it up from her. But there was no love lost between them. Charlotte dreaded and disliked my very unconventional family; and I took care not to force them on her. When a woman marries at 40, she is confronted with a crowd of friends and relatives who know her husband ten times as well as she does. They make her a stranger in her own house. So I kept them off until we had been married long enough for her to know me better than any of them, and invited only my political acquaintances who were also hers.

As my family took no particular interest in her and had plenty of friends of their own, they let her go her own way without worrying themselves or me about it, with the result that after the first few civilities to put us on speaking terms neither Lucy nor my mother ever crossed the threshold of our dwelling. There was no bad blood; but it happened so quite naturally.

Charlotte remembered you and Maud, and would have been always glad to see you had you come along.

always yours
GBS

685

To BLANCHE PATCH

Ayot St Lawrence. Welwyn
[C(F)/4]   21st December 1943

I have been discussing the question of C. F. S's clothes with Mrs Higgs. I have given her the underclothes, as they fit her. There are two fur cloaks. I have sent the newest to Mrs Colthurst. The other seems to me just as good. The gems of the collection are two evening dresses which she took to Cliveden and are too dressy for use by anyone except Pascal's guests at Claridge's.

Mrs Higgs admitted that they are far above the pretensions of common people but said she could not bear the idea of their going to strangers. I had exactly the same feeling. I told her that I wanted to give them to you; and she agreed warmly; so they are being sent to you. I do not know whether they are hopelessly oldfashioned or not; but they look good enough to dazzle Onslow Court or the Ritz. Mrs Higgs thinks that combinations are so oldfashioned that only C. F. S. and herself wore them or even knew what they were. There are still a lot of wraps and summer coats to be disposed of, and a box of jewelry which you might perhaps look through here when the days are longer.

G. B. S.

To GEORGINA MUSTERS

Ayot St Lawrence. Welwyn
[C/1]   [Undated: assigned to 22nd December 1943]

There has been a great plundering of Charlotte's wardrobe, in which you have come off badly because you and she were not of a size. Almost everything at Whitehall Court went to the Theatrical Ladies Guild, where it was sorely wanted. Here the underclothing goes to Mrs Higgs as her traditional right. A fur coat goes to Mrs Colthurst: Charlotte promised it to her. She would have inherited all the chattels had I had the decency to die first. Two evening dresses of the smartest splendour, worn only at Cliveden, have gone to Blanche Patch, who sups sometimes in the film world and other dressy places; and for you Mrs Higgs has rescued a handsome shawl (it would make an imposing bedspread) and a showy jacket or cape which first belonged to Charlotte's sister, whose elegant figure was nearer yours. They will arrive as soon as the G.P.O. has recovered from the Xmas traffic.

There is still some less distinguished booty left.

G. B. S.

To JOHN WARDROP

[C(F)/73]

Ayot St Lawrence. Welwyn
22nd December 1943

Maxwell has sent me page proof of signatures A to K [of the *What's What?*] without my corrections but with yours. He should not have had the sheets marked by you at all. If I have to read the nine sheets through critically all over again it will mean weeks of drudgery. I have told him that there must be some mistake and that I will do nothing until he pulls a fresh proof from the type as it actually stands, as I cannot believe that my corrections were not made.

I have not the slightest intention of doing anything so foolish as to name an official biographer. My intention is to leave all documentary evidence finally to the British Museum, where all the would-be biographers can find it and do their worst or their best. . . .

I await your next lucid interval.

G.B.S.

To THE SHEFFIELD SHAW SOCIETY

[E/83]

[Ayot St Lawrence. Welwyn]
31st December 1943

[The Sheffield Shaw Society was the first regional group of the Shaw Society, meeting in the Sheffield Educational Settlement.]

Please remember that the works that are so delightful and interesting to you all, are to me nothing but a lifetime of toil; and that the subject of Bernard Shaw bores me to distraction. Loewenstein is to me an unholy terror: a man to be avoided beyond any other fellow creature. As I cannot dissolve nor extinguish the Shaw Society, and have brought it on myself by my writings, I must put up with it; but I implore it to enjoy or discuss my output without bothering me about them. I am very old and still have much work to finish. My sole need and desire is to be let alone.

G. Bernard Shaw

PART IV

1944-1950

IV

(1944–1950)

"I never grieve," Shaw iterated in letters of condolence, "and I never forget." The death of Charlotte affected him deeply (a book-shop assistant recalled him as being "extraordinarily 'caved in'" a month or so after his wife's death, looking "very sad"); yet notwithstanding St John Ervine's recollection that "he was so desolate after her death that the poor old man was lost," there was no Dickensian "prostration of a spent giant" discernible in him. Resiliently adjusting to solitary life in an isolated country village, Shaw not only cleaved to the work-and-exercise regimen that had sustained him for nearly three-quarters of a century, but enlarged it. With the valuable editorial assistance of John Wardrop, who patiently and diligently expunged repetitions, divagations and errors from the galleys, he saw *Everybody's Political What's What?* through the press. He resurrected a play manuscript he had abandoned in 1937 and completed it as *Buoyant Billions. Major Barbara* was revised for a Penguin "Screen Version" edition and *Geneva* expanded to four acts for the Standard Edition. Between 1944 and 1950 he contributed over four hundred articles, messages, letters, and self-drafted interviews to newspapers and journals, and kept up a correspondence of several thousand letters and postcards a year. Aided by Dr Loewenstein he compiled, edited, and provided fresh matter for *Shaw on Vivisection* and *Sixteen Self Sketches*, and he serenely prepared for death by making the revisions to his will necessitated by Charlotte's passing, appointing the Public Trustee as his executor and disposing of Shaw's Corner to the National Trust.

His ninetieth birthday was the occasion for an unprecedented degree of festivity, with hundreds of gifts and messages from wellwishers who included among their number Winston Churchill and Éamon De Valera, Ireland's Taoiseach, whose greeting was composed in Gaelic.* From the world press there flowed a profusion of obituary-like encomiums. A Festschrift (*GBS 90*) was issued by his publishers, and a large-scale exhibition on his life and work mounted at the National Book League. Performances of his plays were staged throughout the

---

* "An céad go mairir i bhfus agus an tsíoraíocht sna flaithis" ("The first hundred years of life growing and eternity in heaven"). [Frank Gallagher papers, National Library of Ireland, MS 18,375.]

birthday week in virtually every state of the U.S.S.R. A dinner in his honour, held in New York and broadcast to the nation, was sponsored by the *Saturday Review of Literature*, with tributes by Lawrence Langner of the Theatre Guild, Maxwell Anderson, Deems Taylor, and Henry Seidel Canby, and a special segment of the popular radio show *Information Please*, questions for which had been submitted by Shaw's admirers. Radio Eireann, apologising that it was handicapped by a lack of professional talent in Ireland and of readily available amateur talent for a performance of a Shaw play, instead scheduled a birthday talk by the journalist M. J. MacManus. The B.B.C. broadcast *The Man of Destiny* and selected readings from other plays; but its coup was an unexpected television appearance by the celebrated nonagenarian, which Denis Johnston had cajoled him into filming. "I must do some talking," Shaw informed Johnston, "so do not rush your camera men and take me by surprise."* The result was a spellbinding final glimpse of the He-Ancient as for the record he again rattled off ("I call it my pianola roll," he told a friend) his views on success, age, and happiness, and gave advice to the young, telling them "the way to have a happy life is to be too busy doing what you like all the time, having no time left to you to consider whether you are happy or not."

Denis Johnston on a later occasion deplored the fact that Charlotte had not survived GBS. "It would," he said in a B.B.C. interview in 1954, "have saved his latter years from some situations which can hardly be spoken about, but which I hope are being described privately for posterity, because it makes a fantastic ending to the life of a very great man that is almost as sardonic as the last days of Swift." What Johnston was alluding to was the swarm of predators, spongers, and adulators that descended upon Ayot St Lawrence when Charlotte was no longer there to shield him, resulting, as Johnston privately described it in 1954, in "a plain bloody sordid scramble for the rights to be regarded as the only friend of an old celebrity who had no friends."

What Johnston failed to realise was that, even in Charlotte's lifetime and despite her best efforts to protect him from imposition, Shaw perversely had encouraged the kind of attentions, petitions and depredations to which he now was subjected in his last years; and that he was perfectly capable of purging offenders when it suited him to do so. Young John Wardrop, who had come on the scene in 1939, appears to have recalled to Shaw his own early self, remembered as "diffident on the inside and consequently brazen outside." Barely out of his teens

---

* 3rd July 1946: by permission of the Board of Trinity College, Dublin.

and exuding a passion for Shaw's ideas and style, he amused Shaw by his puppylike eagerness and adoration. It was GBS who, ignoring Charlotte's expressed annoyance at Wardrop's presence at Whitehall Court, actuated the relationship and initiated the suggestion that the young man become his literary executor (though he may only have been indulging his propensity for wilfully misleading admirers). Wardrop was given a latchkey to the flat so that he might have access, in Blanche Patch's absence at Ayot, to draw up lists of the books there. He was authorised also to remove to his home two outdated account books to study and the contents of ten files of business documents to be re-organised at his leisure. Wardrop might, in fact, have remained the favoured one and have attained his goal if Dr Loewenstein had not unexpectedly gained the ascendancy, eventually eclipsing him.

At the start of the war Loewenstein was interned on the Isle of Man as an enemy alien, but subsequently was allowed to take employment in a factory as a motor-mechanic trainee. A twice-married man with three children to support, he was desperate for money. Parading his circumstances before Shaw, he assured GBS that he did not intend to beg or borrow money, though he was not above "borrowing books" (an ironic phrase in view of later circumstances) for the preparation of his bibliography. Shaw, unaware that Loewenstein had unguardedly informed Blanche Patch at their initial meeting that he had "as many tricks as a monkey" when he wanted to get his way, succumbed to the refugee's blandishments, inviting him to Ayot and giving him *carte blanche* to examine the contents of all the file boxes and storage cupboards. Immediately, Loewenstein gained a foothold at Ayot, was appointed Shaw's "authorised bibliographer and remembrancer" (with delusions of becoming a latter-day Boswell), and was given an upstairs sitting room for working space. With a servility and unction that Uriah Heep might have envied, dubbing Shaw "The Master," Loewenstein quietly and efficiently went about the business of raiding for his own collection (sold in 1953 and now housed principally in American university libraries) the filed and shelved Shaviana he was being paid to catalogue for his bibliography and for Shaw's testamentary gift to British libraries.

Inevitably the exuberant, ingenuous young Wardrop and the soft-spoken, artful Loewenstein clashed, both within the Shaw Society and in their dealings with GBS. Loewenstein, anxious for Wardrop's return of borrowed materials, prodded Shaw to recall them. Peremptorily, as if Wardrop had in some way been an offender, Shaw demanded their return. Most of the promptly restored items, including the 1898–1928 account books, surfaced after Shaw's death in Loewenstein's possession.

Perhaps from a sense of guilt that he had misled Wardrop into un-realistic expectations, Shaw offered to pay the tuition fees to enable him to qualify as a barrister, though the young Scot had never so much as matriculated. The scheme, unfortunately, was complicated by the inter-vention of military obligations. At the same time Shaw was enticed into paying university fees for Molly Tompkins's son Peter, as well as for the son of his newly acquired bohemian neighbours at Ayot, Stephen and Clare Winsten, who had showered attentions upon him, encouraging him to sit for Mrs Winsten, an artist, and to commission from her a statue of Saint Joan for his garden. From Shaw's friendly intercourse Winsten eventually fashioned three books, each tainted by distortion, inaccuracy and deception, including extended passages from Shaw's published works passed off as responses in conversation; misquotation; and correspondence cited out of context, with deliberate juggling of chronology and recipient. The Winstens did not remain long at Ayot, however, and departed with only a few of Shaw's unpublished manu-scripts, one of which was published posthumously as *My Dear Dorothea*, edited by Stephen and illustrated by Clare.

Loewenstein's arch-enemy and most formidable adversary was Blanche Patch. For nearly a quarter of a century she had served Shaw without on any occasion succumbing to his spell, bragging to anyone willing to listen that she cared nothing for Shaw's writings and opinions and had never been influenced by him in the slightest. Their relations, as St John Ervine once noted, "were as impersonal as those of an adding machine to a dictaphone." Moreover, life at Ayot during the war years had been painfully frustrating, for she loathed the isolation and quiet, considered Charlotte "a very bad tempered old lady," and thought her employer an unutterable bore, informing Nancy Astor in 1944 that she longed "to forget GBS and all his works." Yet, inspired by the 1943 marriage of the aged Lloyd George to his erstwhile secretary, she schemed almost from the day of Charlotte's death to get Shaw to wed her, appealing to his close associates for assistance. She was, however, no more successful in this intrigue than in her efforts, mostly via poisonous letters, to banish "the non-stop smoking German Jew."

Though Shaw took note of her pique he maddeningly encouraged the daily presence of the interloper, who took up lodgings in nearby Wheathampstead for five days a week, walking nearly three miles each morning to Shaw's Corner, where he pried and poked, accepted tele-phone messages, and took over much of the correspondence. Miss Patch became so allergic to him and so disgruntled by his usurpation of her prerogatives that she was moved finally to pack up and abandon Ayot, leaving Loewenstein with a clear field. Only Alice Laden, the new housekeeper, known locally as St George's dragon, stood up to Loewenstein, to the extent of ordering him emphatically to stay out of the kitchen. He brought his lunch with him thereafter in a paper bag and a thermos jug, eating on the back porch.

With the passing years Loewenstein grew increasingly bloated with a sense of his own importance, conjuring up publishing projects and self-aggrandising publicity stories, boasting that he eventually would take possession of the "Shaw Shrine" at Ayot as its curator. To his dismay, the post went to Alice Laden after the Public Trustee, on the day of Shaw's death, quietly ordered that he remove himself immediately from the house and not return. For the second time in his life Dr Loewenstein became a displaced person.

To D. KILHAM ROBERTS

[Ayot St Lawrence. Welwyn]
[H/2]   5th January 1944

[The playwright Edward Percy (who was also Edward P. Smith, M.P.) undertook to lead a small deputation from the Society of Authors to the Chancellor of the Exchequer to discuss the subject of the present burden imposed on British authors resulting from double taxation on income derived from the U.S.A. Shaw was asked to join the delegation. His views on income tax subsequently were incorporated in letters to the editor of *The Times*: "The Coming Budget" on 1st February 1944 and "The Author's Gamble" on 18th January 1949. The "toil, envy, want" quotation is from Samuel Johnson's *Vanity of Human Wishes* (1749). Sir John Anderson (1882–1958), later Viscount Waverley, was Chancellor of the Exchequer 1943–45.]

Dear Kilham Roberts

I could not take this on ... even if I were not so damnably old, because you have no case. There is no double tax on my American income: I pay only on the net left me when the American Revenue has done its worst. What America keeps is free of British income tax. Our real grievance is a very substantial one. We authors provide for our old age, when we can afford to do it at all, by windfalls, which occur sometimes once in a lifetime, and at best at intervals of, say, fifteen years. All the rest of the time we live from hand to mouth, suffering "Toil, envy, want: the patron and the gaol." Yet when once in a way we get £25,000 by a best seller or a hit on the films, we are taxed on it exactly as a millionaire with a settled unearned income of £25,000 is taxed. At present the rate is 19/6 in the £, which means that we collect the money for the government for a commission of sixpence in the £, which does not pay for our work and our overhead; and we die in the workhouse leaving our widows to follow us there, and our children uneducated.

This is a monstrous injustice, and acts as a tax on our capital from which capitalists as such are exempt. Formerly it was mitigated a little by taxing us on a three years average; but this is now abolished.

I myself, once a rich and exceptionally lucky author, am now overdrawn at the bank for the first time in my life by some £20,000; and instead of doing all I can to get my plays performed I am doing all I

697

can to keep off the stage and reduce my income to a figure at which the rate of tax would be bearable.

I have known cases—for instance, William Archer with his one success, The Green Goddess, and the author [Richard Whiteing] of No 5 John Street [1899]—for whom an average of 40 years would have been fairer than of three; but John Galsworthy got it into his head—heaven knows how!—that the three years average was robbery (his income had fallen, I suppose) and the authorities were only too glad to abolish it.

Why not work up this very real grievance, which the new film industry has made acute, and drop the notion that we have to pay two income taxes, which Anderson could deny and make us look foolish without the least difficulty?

> faithfully
> G. Bernard Shaw

To GEORGINA MUSTERS

Ayot St Lawrence. Welwyn

[C(F)/1]   30th January 1944

[Shaw informed Judy Musters on 23rd January that the net result of Charlotte's leaving him her separate property was that "without being a penny the richer, I have to pay £40,000 to the govt, and Heaven knows what to the lawyers and valuers ..." (A/1). Mrs Musters, in response, condoled with him in his poverty and offered him the hundred pounds in her bank account to save him from starvation.]

Your calculation is not quite exact. I am giving Mrs C. [Cecily Colthurst] her £20,000 at once. This, with the Estate Duties will dispose of about £75,000. You say I am left with £100,000 worth; but not only is that figure too high by £25,000, but the income from it, which is all that I inherit, will all go in taxation—more, in fact, because the sixpence in the pound left to me will not pay my expenses. So you may have to lend me the £100 you offer after all. . . .

> GBS

To E. MARGARET WHEELER

Ayot St Lawrence. Welwyn
[T/9]   9th February 1944

[E. Margaret (Mrs Charles) Wheeler (b. 1908), of Workington, Cumberland, wrote to Shaw on 22nd January 1944 in response to his preface to R.A. Wilson's *The Miraculous Birth of Language*, informing him that she was a housewife, with four small children and a husband in India, who had attempted to devise a compromise "half and half" alphabet. On 2nd February, in another letter, she launched unexpectedly into a discussion of a very personal problem: her belief that her small daughter had been accidentally exchanged at birth with another infant born at the same time, in a Nottingham nursery home, to working-class parents (Blanche and Fred R——), who could not be convinced to submit their child to blood and other tests. Thus commenced an odd correspondence that continued for six years, until March 1950. Some thirty-five years after its commencement the story was filmed as a sixty-minute documentary, *Mix-Up*, directed by Françoise Romand, featuring interviews with all the family members, including Valerie (raised by Margaret and Charles) and Peggy (raised by Blanche and Fred).]

Dear Mrs Wheeler

You are an exceptionally intelligent woman; so be careful. . . .

Now as to the changeling child. If I were the other couple I should say "By all means let us have the tests and find out which child is whose; but on the strict understanding that the two couples shall retain the children they have adopted and grown fond of and that these infants shall never be psychologically wrecked by being told about the tests until they are at least 40, if at all." William Morris (the poet) used to say "It is very hard to say who are the best people to bring up children; but it is quite certain that the parents are the worst." I have known cases of mothers loving "strange" children and positively disliking their own.

Now in this case the two children are loved by parents they have acquired, whether by accident or in the course of nature does not matter. If they were disliked I should say change by all means, though not until the children had been given opportunities of forming a new attachment and welcoming the change. But as it is, there is no excuse for the change; and it would be a crime to upset the children by giving them the smallest hint of its possibility.

The future intercourse of the two couples, by the way, will be very interesting. Almost a group marriage in fact.

I must apologize for having exceeded the limits of a postcard.

faithfully
G. Bernard Shaw

699

P.S. I am tempted to write a play on the Judgment of Solomon, in which he will discover that the woman who gave up the child to save its life was not its mother, and that the other *was*, and disliked it.

With an eye to the future remember that children should not be *only* children: they should have brothers and sisters as well as parents.

Also note that the maternal passion does not always wake up at the first birth. I know a woman who hated her confinements, and did not love their results, until her fourth child, whom she adored.

To AUGUSTUS JOHN

Ayot St Lawrence. Welwyn
[H/1; X/419]   26th February 1944

[Bernard Law Montgomery (1887–1976), Field Marshal (later first Viscount Montgomery of Alamein), commanded the Eighth Army 1942–43 during campaigns in North Africa, Sicily and Italy. In 1944 he was appointed Commander-in-Chief of British and Allied armies in Northern France. Through his *aide-de-camp* he extended an invitation to Shaw to visit him while sitting to Augustus John for his portrait. Chauffeured in an official car from Ayot, Shaw came to John's studio on 26th February: the interview lasted for a full hour.]

Dear Augustus John

This afternoon I had to talk all over the shop to amuse your sitter and keep his mind off the worries of the present actual fighting. And as I could see him with one eye and you with the other—two great men at a glance—I noted the extreme unlikeness between you. You, large, tall, blonde, were almost massive in contrast, with that intensely compacted hank of steel wire, who looked as if you might have taken him out of your pocket.

A great portrait painter always puts himself as well as his sitter into his work; and since he cannot see himself as he paints (as I saw you) there is some danger that he may substitute himself for his subject in the finished work. Sure enough, your portrait of B.L.M. immediately reminded me of your portrait of yourself in the Leicester Gallery. It fills the canvas, suggesting a large tall man. It does not look at you, and Monty always does this with intense effect. *He* concentrates all space into a small spot like a burning glass: *it* has practically no space at all: you havnt left room for any.

Now for it. Take that old petrol rag that wiped out so many portraits of me (all masterpieces), and rub out this one until the canvas is blank.

Then paint a small figure looking at you straight from above, as he looked at me from the dais. Paint him at full length (some foreground in front of him) leaning forward with his knees bent back gripping the edge of his camp stool, and his expression one of piercing scrutiny, the eyes unforgettable. The background: the vast totality of desert Africa. Result: a picture worth £100,000. The present sketch isnt honestly worth more than the price of your keep while you were painting it. You really weren't interested in the man.

Dont bother to reply. Just take it or leave it as it strikes you.

What a nose! And what eyes!

Call the picture INFINITE HORIZONS AND ONE MAN.

Fancy a soldier being intelligent enough to want to be painted by you and to talk to me!

always yours
G.B.S.

To AUGUSTUS JOHN

Ayot St Lawrence. Welwyn
[H/1]   27th February 1944

[Montgomery, who found Shaw "most amusing, and with a penetrating brain," was of a mind with him about the portrait: "I did not like the portrait when completed," he recalled, "since I reckoned it was not like me" (X/419). Eventually John sold it to the University of Glasgow for "a good price."]

My dear John

Having slept on it I perceive that part of my letter of yesterday must be dismissed as an ebulition of senile excitement; for as a matter of business the portrait as it stands will serve as the regulation one which its buyers bargained for and are entitled to have (plenty of paint and the sitter all over the canvas). And between ourselves it has a subtle and lovely Johannine color plan which must not be thrown away.

The moral would seem to be to finish the portrait for your customers and then paint the picture for yourself. Only, as he certainly wont have time to give you a second set of sittings you must steal a drawing or two made from the chair in which I sat.

The worst of being 87–88 is that I never can be quite sure whether I am talking sense or old man's drivel. I must leave the judgement to you.

as ever, but doddering,
G. Bernard Shaw

701

To W. L. MULRY

[E/1]

[Ayot St Lawrence. Welwyn]
22nd March 1944

[William Leo Mulry (1889–1954), an attorney with the New York law firm of Sullivan & Cromwell, wrote to Shaw on 17th February 1944, jocularly addressing him as "George" and appending the signature "Bill," to request a "true copy of the Last Will and Testament of THE LATE AND LAMBASTED MISSUS." Shaw's reply was a handwritten note on Mulry's letter. Charlotte's well-intentioned bequest to Ireland, referred to as the "Eliza Doolittle bequest" and the "Erin Go High-Braugh Scheme," became the subject of much criticism and spleen.]

The relevant clause of the will has been quoted verbatim in the American papers. It has been misunderstood only by simpletons who thought they were being accused of eating peas with a knife. Probably they do.

Mrs Shaw left her residual estate to Ireland solely because she was born there, and wanted to suggest and endow a grossly neglected branch of education. The subject is a serious one; and the people who are making fun of it are proving their need for the training it contemplates.

G.B.S.

To E. MARGARET WHEELER

[T/9]

Ayot St Lawrence. Welwyn
25th March 1944

[Mrs Wheeler had enumerated, on 21st March, seven reasons for her suspicions concerning the nursing home and its staff, and indicated she had written to "Fred" only after submitting a draft of the letter to her solicitor.]

Dear Mrs Wheeler

Your letter alters the case a little. Hitherto you have dwelt on so-called "scientific" blood tests which would cut no ice in court. You would not accept them yourself if they went against you. Your insistence on them is a proof of your belief in your case; and the refusal of the other party to submit to them suggests that they are less convinced on their side, though they may be acting on advice on the ground that they also would not accept the test if it went against them. Anyhow I do not believe that the court would act on it. So let us dismiss the blood test from consideration.

The new evidence which you now mention is on a very different footing. It is of the kind that weighs in court; and if you can get the necessary testimony to establish it you have a case strong enough to justify you in public opinion for bringing an action.

But of what sort of action I have not the least notion. It may be that you can apply for a writ of Habeas Corpus to deliver the body of Peggy from the custody of Fred into yours, and enable you to turn Valerie out of doors. As the two cannot be rechristened, Peggy can become Valerie only by paying £10 for a deed poll. I am curious as to what the actual procedure will be. Solicitors can usually be depended on in matters of practice; but they are often bad lawyers. Now this case is so extraordinary that there is virtually no practice to refer to: it is therefore a matter for counsel's opinion.

Of course it had better be settled out of court if possible. But it seems to me that only two settlements are possible. One is for you to drop the affair altogether and accept the situation as it is (and this apparently you wont do). The other is to just change the children back again by reciprocal consent (and this, apparently, Fred and Blanche wont do).

This deadlock may bring the case into court either by Fred suing you for jactitation of parentage, or you suing him for a writ of *habeas corpus* or whatever the appropriate procedure may be called. In either event the affair will become known to the children; and the two concerned will become suspected intruders in the homes, which will be bad for them and for the other children too. This means that a change would be the best upshot. Unless, indeed, the two children could be made wards in chancery and taken out of their alleged parents' hands altogether on Morrisian principles.

Altogether a very difficult case, for which there is no harmless solution possible.

By the way, I am excluding from consideration the possibility which has occurred to me once or twice that the whole story may be a romance invented to interest me and make you interesting. Bright women are sometimes fearful liars.

You are evidently an attractively intelligent woman with a ready tongue and pen. You are able to get round bank managers, solicitors, literary celebrities, and susceptible males generally with great ease; and you know it. You are what experienced men call a dangerous woman. This does not matter with me: I have been a dangerous man myself; and I know the game, and at 88 am proof against it. Be careful. Your solicitor is certainly wrong if he maintains that jactitation of parentage is not annoyance. I should not in his place have passed the words in your letter to Fred which suggested that my letters were favorable to your case, and that his letters were such as he would not like to have made public. But he has probably given you up as uncontrollable. . . .

This is all I have to say, except that I pity Peggy if she has to live with an overwhelming and exacting mother. I have known too many daughters and sons who have been crushed in that manner.

I am neglecting my proper work to write all this. Clever of you to induce me to do it.

G. Bernard Shaw

To STELLA BEECH

Ayot St Lawrence. Welwyn

[A/1; X/420]   28th March 1944

[Surviving receipts from Shaw to Stella Beech between 1940 and 1943 indicate she repaid in full the sum she had borrowed for her mother's funeral costs. The last payment was made by cheque in the amount of £31.4.9, on 8th December 1943. Shaw, however, never cashed any of the cheques.]

Dear Mrs S. Mervyn Beech (as you prefer we should begin)
If this blitzing goes on, the front will be by far the safest place.

You must not feel distressed about what you call your debt: you have paid it honorably to the uttermost farthing. But I had my rights and duties in the matter too. I was her best friend: you were only her daughter, a whole generation removed. It was for me, not for you, to render first aid. So everything is just as it should be.

Dont bother about Pat's whereabouts: I will communicate through you if necessary.

your obedient servant
Mister G. Bernard Shaw
(G. B. S. is shorter.)

To SIDNEY WEBB

Ayot St Lawrence. Welwyn

[H/14; X/151.e]   2nd April 1944

[Charlotte's solicitor for many years was E. W. Wykes (1883–1964), of Lawrence, Graham & Company. Charles Trevelyan's home was at Cambo, Morpeth, Northumberland. For details of the Carlow property and negotiations for its transfer, see letter of 15th May 1944. (Dame) Margaret Cole

(1893–1980), Fabian writer and lecturer, and her husband G.D.H.Cole were close friends of the Webbs. She later edited portions of Beatrice's diaries, as well as a book *The Webbs and Their Work* (1949). A memorial appeal for Beatrice had been started.]

My dear Sidney

I have just signed a second batch of forms for Charlotte's solicitor. As they are all connected with her stocks and the sales thereof I have some hope of the legacies being paid before we are all dead. Meanwhile, if you are at all pressed, I can lend you a thousand pounds as a private transaction between us without bothering about all that nonsense of an assignment which would be necessary if we did it in the form of my advancing the legacy.

Charlotte's death has been a financial disaster for me. During our marriage her property doubled in value, as she quite unintentionally made a profit out of our arrangement by which she paid the house-keeping bills and I paid the rents, the travelling expenses and cars, and gave her £1200 a year cash. She saved and invested, with the result that whereas she had £4000 a year when we married she had £8000 when she died, on which I paid the supertax.

Now as we lived on our joint incomes my inheritance of her property did not enrich me by a single farthing. But I had to pay £40,000 death duties. Altogether I have had to pay considerably more than £100,000 to the Exchequer since 1939. I have just sold out £30,000 War Loan to clear my personal overdraft; but I still [am] overdrawn heaven knows how much at the National Provincial on Charlotte's account which is a Trust.

So much for the popular belief that I am rolling in money as a consequence of having been left £150,000. However, I am on velvet compared to many others broken by the war. I am not yet really insolvent. So enough of this.

I am greatly bothered by having to make a new will. I am giving Ayot to the National Trust as a show place straight away, reserving a life interest as Trevelyan has done with Wallington. I am trying to hand over my Carlow property to the municipality, but find it almost impossible to effect this in such a way as to prevent its being sold again into private hands or used to relieve the rates. What I want is to start a public fund for experimenting in Innovations of Public utility.

You can imagine the feelings of my solicitors and agents confronted with such lunacy.

I am living alone here in Ayot; but I like being alone. After being taken care of devotedly for 46 years I rather enjoy being free to take care of myself. I work longer and later than Charlotte would ever have allowed me to; and a marked improvement in my health and vigor since her death shews what a strain her four years illness was, though I was not conscious of it at the time. I have finished the book at last. Though I had to cut it short abruptly to prevent its going on for ever I found on casting it up that it contains 180,000 words. You will find it unreadable, as it contains nothing that you dont know already. I cannot read books on Socialism. The thing began with Wells's Declaration of Rights, which had to be brought down to tin tacks if it was to be of the smallest use.

I see, by the way, that H.G. is ill.

I wish we—you and I—did not live so far apart. I am forbidden to take the car farther than ten miles, and am allowed petrol enough for that distance only. And as I am older (88) physically than mentally anything like a long drive fatigues me overmuch. I am pretty dotty in the way of making all sorts of mistakes and omissions and forgetfulneses but I can still write presentably provided I revise the proofs. The only news I have from your neighborhood is an occasional line from Bertha Newcombe.

I am still trying to convince Margaret Cole that Beatrice must have a visible monument, and that it should be a monument to the Webbs and not to one of them alone. My latest suggestion is that if the fifty thousand asked for is forthcoming, a couple of thousand of it should be spent in a statue of Sidney and Beatrice on the same pedestal, to be sculpted by Lady Kennet of the Dene (Scott's widow) and placed on the Embankment by the L.C.C. [London County Council]

The rest of the money (if any) could found scholarships earmarked for proletarian schools, with Eton and its like absolutely barred. Eton and the new secondary schools should meet only in street fights.

This is all for the present. Dont bother to answer at any length: I shall look for no more than three lines at your entire convenience.

G.B.S.

To PATRICIA DEVINE

Ayot St Lawrence. Welwyn
3rd May 1944

[H/1]

[Patricia Devine, twenty-two year old daughter of Mary Devine, the tenant of Shaw's birthplace at 33 Synge Street, Dublin, wrote to ask for information about his family's occupancy of the house. Shaw, in replying, misread her name as Patrick. The photo he sent was a recent one from a sitting to Yosuf Karsh of Ottawa. The birthplace (originally No. 3 Upper Synge Street) was one of eleven residences built and leased in the 1840s by William Moyers adjacent to his timber yard and works.]

Dear Mr Devine

Are you the tenant of 33 or a paying guest?

I ask because I have a portrait of myself which I could send over (if I could get the necessary permit) to be placed in the house to amuse American and other visitors if there are any, and if the lady of the house does not find them an unbearable nuisance.

The house may have been altered or added to since my time there. It then contained in the basement the kitchen and servant's bedroom, on the street level the parlor (front) and nursery, and upstairs the drawing-room and best bedroom. At the back there was a return of two rooms, the lower our pantry, and the upper my bedroom, which served also as my father's dressingroom. In the high walled garden, with Moyers's building yard behind the back wall, and continuing the return, the primitive sanitary arrangements of those days consisted of an ashpit (dustbin) and a privy, used by males only, the ladies being provided for by commodes in their bedrooms. No bathroom, of course.

On the other side of the street there were no houses to the left of that directly opposite us. The rest was a big field, blotted out by hoardings plastered with advertisements.

I revisit the place sometimes in a dream, but always as an old stranger, not as a boy.

When I was round about nine or ten years old we left Synge Street to live at number one Hatch Street.

For some inscrutable reason we considered Upper Synge St the fashionable end, and spoke to people who lived in Harrington St, but not to dwellers in Middle or Lower Synge St, nor even in Lennox St.

faithfully
G. Bernard Shaw

To THE SECRETARY, FOOD RELIEF CAMPAIGN

[Ayot St Lawrence. Welwyn]
[H/105; X/421]   6th May 1944

[Shaw had been invited to participate in a meeting in the Caxton Hall, London, on 8th May, in which Sir Richard Acland, Vera Brittain, and R.R. Stokes, M.P., were to speak on behalf of the Food Relief Campaign.]

We must realize that the Anglo-American alliance will come out of this war with a terrifying reputation not only in enemy countries but in allied ones. Our air warfare strikes friends and foes alike; and instead of gaining rich cities and subjugating industrious populations we reduce the cities to heaps of rubble, and leave those of their inhabitants whom we do not kill without the means of practising their industries. The fact that this horror has been forced on us by circumstances may excuse us; but it does not lessen the terror of it; and terror breeds hatred and brings us into mortal danger of a world combination to deprive us of our destructive power. From this nothing can save us but a conspicuous humanity in all our dealings with the victims and the vanquished. In 1918 we maintained the blockade after the Armistice and starved millions of children. If we do that again we shall deserve the worst that may happen to us later on. This time we must feed the children at all costs and hazards. Every meal they eat at our table will be a premium of the very safest form of insurance against another war.

G. Bernard Shaw

To ARTHUR BLISS

Ayot St Lawrence. Welwyn
[H.t/1; X/422]   7th May 1944

[(Sir) Arthur Bliss (1891–1975), director of music for the B.B.C., whose most notable film music was for *Things to Come* (1935), had been asked to compose the score for *Cæsar and Cleopatra*. Gustav Holst (1874–1934), English composer of *The Planets* (1914–16), had written much "quite serious Sanscrit music," including choral hymns from the Rig Veda and an opera *Sāvitri* (1908). Emanuel Schikaneder (1751–1812) was the librettist of Mozart's *Die Zauberflöte*. The bucina was a Roman wind instrument, presumably a straight trumpet (or tuba), of which the modern trombone is a descendant. "One look at [the director, Pascal] made it self-evident that he would never be a sympathetic collaborator," Bliss later wrote, "and I withdrew from the assignment" (X/422).]

Dear Maestro

In Heaven's name, no Egyptian music. It would not even be sham Egyptian: it would be sham Aida. It must all be Blissful and British. If you feel tempted, think of what Messiah would have been if Handel had felt bound to compose Jewish and Syrian music to it, what Figaro and Don Giovanni would have been if Mozart had gone Spanish, or

708

The Magic Flute if he had gone Egyptian. Or even what my play would have been if I had Latinized Caesar's dialogue.

Of course, if Pascal wants a ballet for the banquet scene, you can amuse yourself by giving it a fanciful turn in the direction of the Nile as you conceive the Nile, just as Mozart and Beethoven composed "Turkish" marches with *grosse caisse*, cymbals, triangle and piccolo; or Gounod did a very lively farandole, Bizet a real Spanish song and dance, and Meyerbeer some Russian short rhythms in L'Etoile du Nord. These larks are jolly and harmless. But Holst's quite serious Sanscrit music! No: damn it, no.

Write your Blissfullest, and your imagination will give the music the necessary cast without your knowing it. After all, there is a complete difference of atmosphere between Figaro and Zauberflöte which I am sure was automatic.

This letter is quite unnecessary: it wont alter a single demisemiquaver; but as you mentioned the matter and may possibly be led to think that I want my play Aida-ized, I must disclaim any such folly. Let yourself rip in your own way and it will all come right. Pascal will be Schickaneder, of course; and there will be sub-Schicks all over the place, each believing that he knows better than you what is needful; but you are master of the situation.

Pascal runs after every new notion; but he always comes back to the right thing in the end.

I suggested to him an ophicleide for the Roman bucina partly because my uncle played it, but also because it has the peculiar tone that made Berlioz call it a chromatic bullock, quite different from the tuba. The tuba is only a bass saxhorn. The ophicleide is a monster keyed bugle.

Bach trumpets, which are keyed posthorns, have also a different and rather pleasant difference from the ordinary orchestral trumpet and can reach higher notes. But military bugles have their points too. And cavalry trumpets.

All of which you know better than I do.

Dont bother to answer. In fact I should have begun with Dont trouble to read.

G.B.S.

[V(H)/48; X/423]

[Ayot St Lawrence. Welwyn]
15th May 1944

[A.J.V.Fitzmaurice had succeeded his father William, who died in 1928,
as Shaw's estate agent in Ireland.]

Dear Sir

Will you be so good as to bring the following matter before your
Council?

I am the landlord of a property in Carlow which I inherited as the
greatgrandson of the Thomas Gurly whose monument is in one of your
chief churches. It was formerly a considerable property, but it now
yields a net revenue of only £150 a year. When it came into my hands
I received nothing but the legal ownership, a bundle of mortgages, and
several dependent relatives. As I have cleared off the mortgages, and
provided otherwise for the surviving relatives, there are now no
encumbrances except the head rents.

I am an absentee landlord, having spent out of the 88 years of my
life only one day in Carlow. The estate is managed by Major A.J.V.
Fitzmaurice of 1 Leinster Crescent.

These are the bare facts. The economic situation is that Carlow has
to send my share of its rent to England, where it is confiscated by the
British Government to defray the expenses of military operations which
include the recent bombing of the Vatican. Carlow clearly loses by this
arrangement.

I therefore propose to hand over the property to the Carlow municipality for the common welfare.

I find, however, that this step, being unusual, is not easy. Nobody
seems to know how it is to be done. If I proposed to leave the property
to some relative who might, like my grandfather, mortgage it to the
last farthing and leave it in a ruinous condition, I could do it without
the least trouble. But to leave it to a public body for the public benefit
seems to be impossible when the public body in question is a municipality.

I have served for six years as municipal councillor on a London
Borough Council governing a quarter of a million people. I therefore
know the difficulties from the inside.

What I would beg the U.D.C. to consider is this. Suppose I make a
gift of the property to the Council on Trust for purposes which exclude
its sale to private owners, the use of its revenue to relieve the rates

directly, or for almsgiving in any form, confining it to improvements, house modernization and experimental innovations, embankment of the river Barrow, and, generally, for progressive work which would not otherwise be undertaken, would the Council accept the Trust, and establish a standing committee or subcommittee to administer it?

You may say that the property is too small to be worth considering for such purposes. I should reply that it represents solid land, the importance of which to a city is not fairly measurable by the income of its private landlord, and that I can stipulate that it shall not be a closed Trust, but be the nucleus of a civic improvement Fund well advertized and open to all citizens who desire to follow my example, but, like myself, do not know exactly how to do it. It should not bear my name nor that of any other individual nor of any creed or political party. Its income could be left to accumulate within the limit allowed by the law against perpetuities to any extent thought necessary. Would the Council take it on these conditions?

I should perhaps mention that if it refuses, the property will pass after my death to the National Gallery of Ireland, to which in my boyhood in Dublin I owed much of my Art education, which enabled me to earn a living as critic before I made my mark as a playwright. It will therefore not be lost to Ireland in any case.

But Carlow is clearly entitled to the first offer.

faithfully
G. Bernard Shaw

[Shaw's letter was placed before the Carlow Urban Council for consideration at a special meeting on 23rd May, at which time it was unanimously resolved: "That the Council accepts the offer contained in Mr. Shaw's letter . . . That the Council expresses its warm appreciation of Mr. Shaw's very generous gift, and that consideration of the manner in which the conveyance of the properties shall be taken over by the Council, or by Trustees on its behalf, be deferred until such time as full detailed particulars of the properties be made available to the Council's Solicitor . . ." When it was discovered that there was no law in Ireland enabling the gift to be accepted by the Council, Shaw asked in 1945 for such a law to be enacted.]

To F. E. LOEWENSTEIN

[A/83]

Ayot St Lawrence. Welwyn
16th June 1944

[Shaw had commissioned Loewenstein to complete his bibliography. In due course the commitment was expanded to include the organising of Shaw's archive for eventual presentation to the British Museum and the London School of Economics, and the free-lance employment of Loewenstein for various other duties, making him, in effect, a useful general factotum at Shaw's Corner. In this letter Shaw was indulging in a favourite sport, inventing names for people's initials; this time, however, he had confused the initials.]

Dear Loewenstein

You must not rush this matter. You must make a definite offer to do such and such a job in or within a certain period for a professional fee of £100 as bibliographer. Any incidental secretarial work had better be quite voluntary and gratuitous, and therefore unmentioned.

What do E & L stand for—? Emmanuel Lazarus?

And are you a Doctor of Law or Philosophy or Letters or Divinity or what?

I may have occasion to describe you in some formal document.

GBS

To SYDNEY C. COCKERELL

[C/97]

Ayot St Lawrence. Welwyn
27th June 1944

[As indicated here, Shaw bequeathed to the Public Trustee the means of financing a reformed English alphabet along lines he had suggested in his lifetime, to be carried out by any qualified and responsible body, corporate or individual, that would take certain defined steps in its direction. When in 1957 the Trustee informed the High Court of Justice, Chancery Division, that he was unequipped to deal with the matter practically, the Lord Justice the Rt. Hon. Sir Charles Harman (1894–1970) issued a declaration that this provision in the will was legally invalid; the moneys were consequently diverted to the three residuary legatees.]

I dare not delay the execution of my widower's will until the new alphabet is organized. All I can do is to leave my residuary estate to accumulate for 20 years (the perpetuity limit) with power to the Public Trustee to finance any body or individual who will take on the job to his satisfaction: I am defining and limiting it exactly. Failing any response the estate goes to the British Museum, the National Gallery of Ireland (to pay for my education) and the Royal Academy of Dramatic Art. At worst this will advertise the alphabet.

Drafting the will has been more trouble than ten plays; and it comes to just what I might have done the day after Charlotte's death.

I am making a present of my Irish estate to the Urban District Council of Carlow.

Unloading, in fact.

GBS

To GABRIEL PASCAL

Ayot St Lawrence. Welwyn
[H/1; X/424]   1st July 1944

[The filming of *Cæsar and Cleopatra* had begun on 12th June after several weeks of rehearsals and pre-production activity. Shaw visited the Denham set on 25th April and again on 29th June. Britannus was played by Cecil Parker (1897–1971), a striking performer who had just completed a three-year West End appearance in Noël Coward's *Blithe Spirit*. Vivien Leigh (1913–67), rapidly becoming a star of the first magnitude, had come to the film direct from a run of 474 performances at the Theatre Royal, Haymarket, in *The Doctor's Dilemma*.]

My dear Gabriel

You have surpassed yourself in this production already in one scene. When it is all finished it will lick creation.

There is one thing wrong with the desert sky. The stars and planets are all the same size and brightness, like pinholes. You should have engaged an astronomer to correct this. It is the only thing that gives away the artificiality of the scene.

Britannus is so hopelessly wrong that he will hold up all the scenes in which he appears until he is redressed. I enclose a suggestion of what he should look like. At present he is a handsome young military man instead of an elderly academic literary secretary, very unlike all the others. He must have an academic gown.

But I pity poor Rank. The film will cost a million. On Thursday there were hundreds of men in the studio; and only twelve at most had anything to do but take snapshots and pick up scraps of my conversation for sale to the papers. Most of them did not do even that much. Were they all on the payroll?

And the retakes! with Vivien gabbling tonelessly such sounds as cummineechoo and oaljentlmin! Does she always go on like that; or should I have had her here to drill her in the diction of the part?

However, I am beginning to complain, which is monstrously ungrateful; for the film promises to be a wonder.

sempre a te
GBS

To GILBERT MURRAY

Ayot St Lawrence. Welwyn

[H/36]   4th July 1944

[Jean-Baptiste Racine (1639–99) wrote his comedy *Les Plaideurs* in 1668. Surviving fragments of Menander's *The Arbitration* (*Epitrepontes*) had been translated by Murray with "conjecturally filled" gaps; the work was published in 1945. In 1942 Murray had published a similar reconstruction of fragments of Menander's *The Rape of the Lock* (*Perikeiromenê*). *Badinguet-Cartouche* (*c.* 1870) was a book of satires on Napoleon III. Pisistratus (d. BC 527) was Tyrant of Athens, 554–527. No publication of the World War I marching song has been located. General Dwight D. Eisenhower (1890–1969), Supreme Commander of the Allied Expeditionary Force in Western Europe, 1944, became President of the United States in 1953. A "Safe Conduct" leaflet, bearing General Eisenhower's signature, was dropped in large quantities over enemy territory, giving instructions to German soldiers on how to surrender. Strobl's bust of Lady Astor was later repaired and presented by Shaw to the House of Commons.]

My dear Murray

It is a great relief to learn that nothing is the matter with you except the troubles of the incipient Struldbrug. I, ten and a half years farther on the declivity, exceed you in blunders and forgetfulness by the square of that distance. Ibsen at last forgot how to write, and spent hours making pothooks and hangers in vain efforts to learn over again. I shall come to that presently; but I am a little consoled by discovering that though my childish acquirements are perishing, my very latest developments are still young.

Now as to Les Plaideurs (Racine's title, wasnt it?). It is enormously better than The Rape, just as Twelfth Night is better than The Comedy of Errors, Menander being more accomplished in his maturity than he was as a beginner. It is almost a XIX century Parisian "well made" play. The only difference is that in Scribe and Sardou the five acts have been compressed into three, the unity of place has been discarded, and the long lost babes have been sidetracked by adulteries and duels. But the interest is not technical except for playwrights: it is important as evidence that bourgeois society is just what it was in 320 BC: it makes me feel as I did 45 years ago, when Grant Allen read to me a page of history and challenged me to guess who the hero was. I said "Obviously Napoleon III." It was not Badinguet: it was Pisistratus. So much for Progress!

After reading a few pages of your translation I automatically began scrawling alternative scansions all over it as if it were my own, but in pencil so that you can rub them out. I am very sensitive to any flaw in blank verse: I really have Shakespear's ear. For some reason or other people who have much Latin and more Greek always take contemptuous liberties with blank verse as if they did not matter in so easy a metre. But they do matter, because the metre is so easy and elastic that on the very slightest trifling with it it ceases to be verse at all. Take these lines from Hamlet

GHOST.   The serpent that did sting thy father's life
                    Now wears his crown.
HAMLET,   Oh, my prophetic soul!
                    My uncle!
Can you imagine Shakespear writing
GHOST.   The serpent that did sting thy father's life
                    Now wears his crown and weds his wife
HAMLET,   Oh my!
                    Prophetic soul: my uncle!
Yet you do this and similar things unblushingly. To end a line with a possessive pronoun and begin the next with its object is a literary crime. It is not verse; and its intrusion into verse is unbearably unpleasant. Shakespear, who exhausted the possibilities of blank verse, never did it.

Take another trick. In the Four Years War the American soldiers improvised a marching song which began

Mister
McKinlay
he aint done
no wrong
He went down
to Buffalo
way Michigan
along

in the last verse this became
    Cholgosh
    They took him
    and puthimintheelec
    tric chair
    They shocked him
    so hard that
    they shocked off all
    his hair
Now a very sparing use of this verbal ellipsis is tolerable in blank verse. Beethoven in a bar of 16 semiquavers sometimes got in an extra one or two by grouping 3 as 2 or 7 as 5; but the effect is always musical and is never frequent. But you do it again and again in successive lines, though to do it twice in succession makes stumbling prose of the passage. You not only torture the line: you torture me.

You will now understand my scrawls. They are mostly attempts to get a caesura in the right place. Forgive them if you can.

What Greek grammar would you recommend to a beginner in that language? Is there such a thing as a good one? Schoolbooks are the worst books in the world: they make education a hated torment.

I am greatly pleased with Eisenhower's military disregard of Churchill's unconditional surrender slogan in his offer of a detailed list of conditions to the German soldiers.

My Whitehall flat has been blasted again, this time by a Robot. A window in my study was shivered into smithereens, my front door blown in, the grandfather clock prostrated, one of Charlotte's Tang horses shattered, and—*comble de malheur*—Strobl's bust of Lady Astor done in.

Our devastation of Europe is almost beyond endurance. And they call it a Savings Campaign!

My book is printed, and will be published presently if the binders can get the necessary labor.

                                                    G. Bernard Shaw

PS   I could not in any passage draw the line between Menander and Murray. The translation is perfectly homogeneous. It would act quite well.

To E. MARGARET WHEELER

Ayot St Lawrence. Welwyn
[T/9]   10th July 1944

[It had been suggested to Mrs Wheeler, apparently by her new solicitor, that she sell Shaw's letters to cover court costs of an action against the R——s; she refused, however, to consider this, and the letters remained a prized possession then and later. The Dublin family of Shaw's childhood recollection was that of George Ferdinand and Ellen Shaw, parents of Ada Tyrrell.]

Dear Mrs Wheeler

The serial keeps up its interest. Pray continue it when you feel disposed and have time. I never object to people turning an honest penny by selling my letters, as the sale does not convey any power to publish them. Silly people buy old postcards of mine of no interest whatever at London West End bookshops for a guinea. But prices vary. At Sothebys, such wares have slumped as low as six shillings per letter for a bundle. But you need not bother about this, as our correspondence does not concern me at all, and concerns you very intimately. For this reason I destroy your letters (a great pity) lest they should be found after my death and make mischief for you.

Let me now repeat and explain my warning to you not to prove your case legally and publicly.

If you do, Fred will be obliged to say "Here then: take your brat and be damned; and give me my own child." The children, violently uprooted and transplanted, must know all about it. Nothing short of this can possibly happen if the case is proved in court. Do you wish it to happen or not? If not, you must be content with the establishment of a private understanding between the two families, leaving them as they are. If you intend to become a political woman this will be better for Peggy as you may become a notable and even very useful politician, and a very bad mother.

I note that Fred instinctively took the first step towards a group marriage.

Children and mothers from different houses can see a great deal of one another without much or any intercourse between the fathers. In my childhood I and my sisters were very intimate with a family in the next street, playing together as if we were the same family; and our mothers were on intimate terms; but as far as I know our fathers never met one another.

Another case known to me is of a family in which the parents had each been twice married and had children by both marriages. The

717

result was a household of children of three distinct families, sisters and brothers, half sisters and half brothers, all mixed up. One of them assured me that it did not make the smallest difference: they felt and behaved towards one another exactly as if they were equally akin.

Complete separation and group marriage are only the possible extremes: many degrees (for instance, reciprocal adoption) are possible on the scale between them. There is much to be said for leaving things as they are. You cannot have them both ways.

This is enough of my wisdom for one letter. Quite a good six shilling's worth.

G. Bernard Shaw

To F. E. LOEWENSTEIN

Ayot St Lawrence. Welwyn
[E.u/3]   20th July 1944

Dont send me things I have to return.

Dont remind me of my birthdays.

Dont hunt up my relatives.

Dont mention the Shaw Society to me.

Dont forget that I am fully occupied with my present and future and have no time to attend to my past over again.

To CLARA M. KENNEDY

Ayot St Lawrence. Welwyn
[H/1]   24th July 1944

[Clara M. Kennedy was secretary of the Women's Missionary Association. Shaw here, as elsewhere on several occasions (see letter of 28th August 1896 to Ellen Terry), misquotes Carlyle's *Sartor Resartus* (1831). The passage in the chapter "The Everlasting Yea" reads: "America is here or nowhere." Shaw may have been thinking of one of W. Somerset Maugham's South Seas tales, such as "The Vessel of Wrath," filmed in 1938.]

Dear Miss Kennedy

What a letter! Where have I ever suggested that the missionary vocation is a neurosis? I am a missionary myself on the home front. I was a boy when Carlyle wrote "Here and now is thine Australia"; so I did not cross the seas to preach my gospel. My friend Henry Salt, a humanitarian home missionary, when he wrote his autobiography, called it "Seventy year[s] among savages." You should read my plays again.

718

The greatest women in them are missionaries: the love scenes are re-placed by conversion scenes: the only male professional missionary in them is a blameless and entire[ly] amiable character. Before I took the theatre by storm I discussed African missionary work with H.M. Stanley, the explorer who found Livingstone and converted Mtesa, the native king of Uganda, to Christianity. Many years later I corresponded with and met one of the missionary women on your list, who had an extraordinary gift of description. She told me about her work in Rhodesia. I will not tell you which she was, because her passion for what worldly women call selfsacrifice (it was to her a luxury) led to an incident which I have made use of in my tale of The Black Girl, and which I suspect you of mistaking for a disgraceful neurosis.

So you see I am not so ignorant of African missionary work as you imagine. It demands rare qualities: courage, enterprise, tact, devotion, independence, managerial ability in handling children and adults, and, in women, the build of a *maitresse femme*, the very opposite of the neurotic woman. But it is very dangerous and responsible work. Jesus was a missionary who sent his disciples as missionaries "to the ends of the world"; yet he warned them that if instead of adding Christianity to the established religions they tore them up by the roots and tried to substitute their own (the besetting sin of missions) they would root up the wheat as well as the tares, and leave their converts without any real religion at all. Mtesa, Stanley's convert, lived to curse the day on which he had admitted the rival Christian missions to his country. My friend from Rhodesia told me wonderful stories of how she had trained her black girls to live in a perpetual dream of the actual presence and leadership of Christ; but she could not tell me anything of what hap-pened when the girls grew up and found that the dream was a fairy tale mostly of my friend's own invention. The Bible perished in the hand of my Black Girl when she tried all the gods in it and found more rest for her soul with Voltaire than with any of them.

You have a lot of thinking to do before you find rest for your soul. Read all my books again to start with.

faithfully
G. Bernard Shaw

PS I have not thanked you for your letter, which interested me. Your instances of educated Presbyterian missionary women all end in their being engaged, not in turning Voodoo negroes into good Presbyterians, which is what the money was subscribed for, but in turning primitive tribesmen into civilized wage slaves, and forcing unhealthy clothes and tinned food on them.

The Rhodesian lady made their children happy in a fool's paradise—which is the kindest way to govern ignorance and superstition—but people like Maugham and myself cannot accept this as a final solution in view of the fact that the civilization we are imposing is at present busy committing suicide.

To GABRIEL PASCAL

[H/1; X/424.e]

Ayot St Lawrence. Welwyn
28th July 1944

[Claude Rains (1889–1967) early in his career had toured Australia in *You Never Can Tell* and in 1914–15 was Barker's general manager for an American tour. In 1933 he virtually abandoned the stage for films, returning only occasionally in his late years. The Gaumont-British newsreel of 26th July, forty-six seconds in length, was presented the next year to the B.B.C. archive.]

My dear Gabriel

In the sketch of Britannus I rushed off to you I painted his eyebrows black. They should of course be yellow. The wig, moustache, and whiskers can all be made on a frame which he can put on like a helmet: it cannot be stuck on with spirit gum. The color should be auburn or downright yellow.

As to the music I can make nothing of the orchestral score you have sent me. I advised Bliss to compose a complete C.&C. suite for use at orchestral concerts, and to let you use such parts of it as you may require to accompany the film. You are quite right in ruling that when my music begins his must stop. Thus we need a nocturne for the opening of the Sphinx scene; but it must die away into silence when Caesar arrives at the Sphinx and contemplates it before he speaks. And there must be no more until the scene is over. Any "melodrame" during the dialogue you must cut out ruthlessly: it is detestably inartistic: neither drama nor opera. The BBC has reduced it to absurdity. I urged Bliss not to be oriental but just Blissful to his heart's content. As a taste for his music, like all new music, has to be acquired, we must not lightly turn it down. Have you recorded any of it? It is impossible for me to say anything until I have heard more of it than I can finger out from the very unreadable score.

Try to impress on C.R. that unless the other characters are made the very most of—they are all minor figures who are there only to build him up—he will lose heavily. A star who is jealous of his support throws away half his lustre.

720

I am not sorry that there is a time limit for both C. and Cleo: time limits are badly needed in the studio, as the temptation to retake is so strong when the director is a real artist: in short, when he is Gabriel Pascal.

Hitler celebrated my birthday by smashing my bedroom window with a bomb; and in the afternoon I had to do a newsreel about it.

I think there must be a definite break in the continuity after the lighthouse scene; but I will study it and see what can be done with the help of your suggestions.

come sempre
GBS

To I. J. PITMAN

Ayot St Lawrence. Welwyn
[H/1]   7th August 1944

Dear Mr Pitman

The other day a will in which the testator had left his property to endow Community Centres was taken into court by his next of kin. The judge, who had never heard of Community Centres—or if he had probably thought them seditious—ruled that the bequest was senseless and that the case must be dealt with as an intestacy. I must run the risk of the same ignorant and prejudiced judge having the same opinion of my will. But my next of kin will not move in the matter; for I have been careful to provide alternative destinations for my residual estate in the event of the alphabet scheme being annulled.

I cannot guard against litigation over my definition of a British alphabet; but as I attach much more importance to advertisement of the need for the alphabet than to the success of my attempt to provide it my ghost will be perfectly satisfied if the lawyers and litigants keep the subject in the headlines for the twenty years perpetuity limit.

As to the 42 letters no definition of them is possible; for there are as many different vowels in use as finger prints; and there are always fastidious phoneticians who want different spellings for too, two, and to. I myself am often tempted to write Robert Bridges's thatt to distinguish it from that. I propose to get out of the difficulty by prescribing the alphabet of Henry Sweet, who, though he was an impossible fellow who called your phonography "the Pitfall System," and reduced his own Current Shorthand to illegible absurdity by trying to make it available for verbatim reporting, was the foremost English phonetician of his day, and actually had a "Readership" created for him at Oxford. He never forgave the University for not giving him the Chair of English literature.

I cannot see that sh, ch, etc are diphthongs. Having no letters to spell them we try sticking in an h to indicate them, just as the Poles stuck in a z to spell their very frequent ones. This enabled us to spell Engli*sh Ch*urch; but it set us miscalling Lewis Ham and Peter's Ham Looey Sham and Peter Sham.

My father was fond of pronouncing Stephens as Step Hens because he disliked a man of that name. My name has only two sounds: there is no s at the beginning nor ooh at the end. The sounds are simple: there is no double gesture of the tongue.

faithfully
G. Bernard Shaw

To JAMES LEES-MILNE

[C/126; W/418.e]

Ayot St Lawrence. Welwyn
12th August 1944

["I am in mortal dread of dying" before the transfer of the deeds to Shaw's Corner to the National Trust, Shaw wrote on 22nd March (E/126) to James Lees-Milne, then acting secretary of the Trust. The vesting deed in the house was finally signed on 26th June; but by August Shaw was still involved in organising and rearranging its contents, as he would continue to be until he disposed of the contents of the London flat in 1949.]

... I am trying to arrange matters so that I can leave the entire contents of this house to the Trust except what I specifically dispose of otherwise by will. I shall transfer from London all the pictures and statuettes and busts that are there to titivate Shaw's Corner as a show place. The Trust can sell what is superfluous to pay for repairs.

But everything is in a mess at present. I will let you know when they get into better shape.

G.B.S.

To LAURENTIA McLACHLAN

Ayot St Lawrence. Welwyn
[A/98; X/256]   4th September 1944

[Shaw's letter was written on the fly-leaf of a copy of *Everybody's Political What's What?*]

I hope this will not arrive late for your Diamond Jubilee tomorrow. It is too late for mine by twenty years: I was eightyeight last month but one. The saint who called me to the religious life when I was eighteen was Shelley.

But you have lived the religious life: I have only talked and written about it.

You ask me how I am. I must reply, the better for your prayers; for, deaf, and doddering and dotty as I inevitably am at my age, I am astonishingly well, much weller than I was a year ago.

Look at my portrait: it was taken this year. You would still know me if you met me. I wish you could. I count my days at Stanbrook among my happiest.

G. Bernard Shaw

To ANN CASSON

Ayot St Lawrence. Welwyn
[C/1]   8th September 1944

[Ann Casson succeeded her mother Sybil Thorndike in a 1944 touring production of *Saint Joan*, directed by her father Lewis Casson, which went from the provinces to the King's Theatre, Hammersmith, and on to the Continent, in 1945–46. Shaw had earlier encouraged the casting, writing to Sybil Thorndike on 9th February 1942: "She has the authentic St Joan tradition; and I look to her to rescue the part from the snivelling Bergners and Pitoeffs who do nothing but cry and leave out all the strong lines" (C/1).]

You are in exactly the right humor for it; for J. is a volcano of energy from beginning to end, and never the snivelling Cinderella, born to be burnt, that all the others—except the first—made her.

So go ahead with my blessing; and be sure not to wear yourself out before you begin.

Not that you could, even if you tried; but still, keep a bit always in reserve.

GBS

723

To SYDNEY C. COCKERELL

Ayot St Lawrence. Welwyn
[X/277]   29th September 1944

[There is no London monument to Shaw, nor even a commemorative plaque in the British Museum, to which he made one of the largest single gifts of any donor in its history.]

My dear Cockerell

As to Westminster Abbey I have no fancy for it: it is an extremely miscellaneous Pantheon, but I should probably be more welcome there than in St Patrick's Cathedral in Dublin, where Swift flourishes his epitaph. But the matter will not be in my hands. The instructions in my will are that (a) I am to be cremated, (b) that my ashes are to be inseparably mixed with those of my wife, now in custody at Golders Green with that in view, and (c) that the mixture is to be scattered in the garden here unless in the opinion of the Public Trustee (my executor) a more eligible disposal of them be available.

I have requested that no inscription on any monument to me shall imply that I belonged to any established religious denomination, my own belief being in Creative Evolution, and that the monument itself shall not take the form of a cross, or any other instrument of torture.

Charlotte, in her will, directed that her ashes should be taken to Ireland and scattered on the Three Rock Mountain; but when the war made the journey too arduous for my old age, and our friend Father Joseph Leonard, whom I should have asked to deputize for me, could hardly be expected to consecrate the whole mountain for the whim of a Protestant lady of no recognized religious faith at all, I proposed the arrangement in my own will as above. It pleased her, and she agreed.

What I should like as a London monument is a replica on the Embankment of the full length statue of me in my platform pose as an orator by Troubetskoy, which is now in the National Gallery in Dublin. When I am forgotten it will still commemorate Troubetskoy, who was a great sculptor. For a tomb in a cathedral or cloister wall I should recommend the half length by Lady Kennet of the Dene (Captain Scott's widow).

My bust by Strobl I have bequeathed to the Shakespear Memorial National Theatre to place in the foyer as the bust of Voltaire by Houdon is placed in the foyer of the Théâtre Français. The Troubetskoy busts in the Tate and the Theatre Guild of New York I leave to them respectively with a reversion of the latter to the Metropolitan Museum should the Guild be dissolved.

724

I have more to say on other subjects, but will say it in a later letter.

G. Bernard Shaw

P.S. My nationality is confused by the fact that out of my 88 years, only 20 have been lived where I was born. Correctly, I am an Irish Londoner; but I retain my Irish citizenship and nature, and am still a foreigner with an objective view (invaluable) of England, that "distressful country" in whose public service I am a missionary.

To THE REV. G. REYNOLD WALTERS

[S/9]

[Ayot St Lawrence. Welwyn]
[Undated: c. October 1944]

[The Rev. Gordon Reynold Walters (1878–1963), Curate of St Andrews, Uxbridge, 1944–48, married Shaw's second cousin Mary Ethel (Shaw) Davis (1880–1962), a widow since 1938, late in 1944. Shaw had both ages wrong, as Walters was then 66 and Mrs Davis 64.]

Dear Mr Walters

The proposed marriage of a gentleman of 70 with a lady of 58, who have known one another for 40 years, is not a matter to be decided on the advice of a perfect stranger to you (aged 88) who happens to be a second cousin of the lady. If you are lonely you must take your chance of presently wishing you had remained solitary.

Naturally I should like somebody to take Ethel off my hands. Can you really do so? When she was married to the late Sebastian Davis, I always had to make both ends meet for her in her housekeeping accounts; and though she always contended that he was too sensitively independent to be told of this he must have known it. At the end she was worked so hard nursing him and keeping the house without servants that he would certainly have killed her had he not been considerate enough to die himself first. As a widow she blossomed like a rose. I cannot advise her to risk repeating this experience. Can you afford a settlement?

No doubt you will do your best to make her happy; but what guarantee have you that she will make you happy? She is amiable enough with me; but I have never lived with her, nor seen her oftener than two or three times a year for half an hour at a time. And how could she afford to quarrel with me?

I am supposed to be a very rich man, and was in fact very comfortably off until the war taxation and the death of my wife, which cost me more than £60,000, changed all that. My last will, which I am not likely to change, leaves my entire property, subject to certain annuities and pensions to the Public Trustee for public purposes: my kindred have no expectations from me. If you marry Ethel you must marry her entirely for her own sake. It may be for her own sake you should not marry her.

I can say no more: I have no *locus standi* in the matter.

G.B.S.

To JOHN ARABEN

Ayot St Lawrence. Welwyn
[H/3; X/289.e]   1st November 1944

[John Araben of Belfast was writing a biography, which does not appear to have been published, of Dr Henry R.Parker, of Trinity College, Dublin, who was headmaster 1867–71 of the Wesleyan Connexional School (now Wesley College) in Dublin, at which Shaw was a student. Shaw attended his first class on 13th April 1867, a few months prior to Parker's arrival. In 1947, when G.V.Crook, grandson of Dr Robert Crook, predecessor to Parker, made a similar inquiry, Shaw sent him a slightly abridged and truncated text of the same letter in reply, neglecting to alter the reference to "77 years later" in the penultimate paragraph.

Harry Furniss became a cartoonist for *Punch* and illustrator of complete editions of Dickens and Thackeray. Though Shaw contributed *Passion, Poison, and Petrifaction* to his *Annual* in 1905, they never had more than a slight acquaintance in their adult years. The cruel Edward Murdstone marries David's widowed mother in Dickens's *David Copperfield*.]

Dear Sir

As I was only 11 when Parker came to the Wesleyan Connexional School in succession to Dr Robert Crook, and as I left that school soon after, I am afraid I can say nothing about him that could be fairly quoted in a serious biography. I was never in the classes which he took; and my only contacts with him were when I was "kept in," and had to get as best I could through a dozen lines or so of Virgil before I was released, the hearing being conducted by the headmaster, cane in hand.

And it was an appalling cane of a kind that had never been seen in the school before. "Tips" with a common yellow cane were in daily use under Dr Crook; and the maximum number was six; but they did not hurt more than a boy of ordinary fortitude could endure without wincing, and had no deterrent effect whatever.

When Parker appeared armed with a long lithe chestnut colored oriental cane, which had evidently cost much more than a penny, and slashed our hands with it mercilessly, he established an unprecedented terrorism. He was young (really too young), darkly handsome: a perfect Murdstone. I think, however, he soon found that he was carrying his youthful terroristic logic too far. He never used his cane on me, though he had every excuse for doing so; but he had what no schoolmaster should allow himself to indulge: a dislike of stupid boys as such. However, the terrible cane was kept enough in reserve to make his reign bearable during the short time I was under it.

His reign did not last long. The school was so utterly incompetent as a teaching institution that a man of his stamp could have lost no opportunity of getting out of it. I was taken away from it because my clerical uncle [William Carroll], who had grounded me in Latin grammar quite successfully in my childhood, examined me and discovered that I had learnt nothing and forgotten a good deal at the Wesleyan. The school was not then the co-educational Wesley College of today. It was in an old private house, next door to the mansion of Sir Benjamin Lee Guinness, with a big schoolroom at the back of the playground, where the stables used to be. It was the cheapest of the Dublin Protestant schools of any social pretensions, and could not afford to give adequate attention to the number of dayboys and boarders it took on. The classes were too large: the teachers, untrained in pedagogy (they had never heard of such a word) were mostly young men waiting for a ministry. There was really no teaching. Latin and Greek were the only subjects that were taken seriously: history, geography, arithmetic and Euclid, were in the curriculum; but education meant Caesar, Virgil, and Homer. The method of teaching was never to teach, but to set lessons and sums without a word of explanation. In the large classes the utmost examination possible in the lessons meant one question for each boy in alphabetical order, or at most two. If you could answer the questions or do the sums, or construe the few lines that fell to your lot, you passed unscathed: if not, or if you talked in class or misbehaved, you were marked in your judgement book for caning by the headmaster. Manners and dress were not taught: the boarders (we dayboys called them the skinnies) could appear with their shoes unlaced and their collars unpresentable without rebuke. Such discipline and study as there was, were learnt and enforced at home; for we were all snobbishly respectable, and would not speak to one unfortunate outcast whose father was a pawnbroker.

Clearly the school was no place for a man of Parker's calibre; and I am not surprised to learn that after a few equally brief experiences in other public schools he finally settled in a private school of his own.

Since my departure from the Wesleyan in 1867 [1868] I never heard of him again until your letter arrived 77 years later. I am glad to learn that he made good when he matured.

Harry Furniss was at the school with me. I do not think he was in Parker's classes, being too young; but he produced a "Schoolboys' Punch," in which I remember a cartoon in which Parker figured. Parker was pleased with it, and encouraged Furniss. He also, by the way, took in, and actually brought into the schoolroom, a savagely satirical illustrated journal of that day called The Tomahawk. I cannot conceive Dr Crook tolerating such literature.

This is all I can tell you that has any bearing on your memoir. You know, I presume, that in Ireland in 1867 there were only two sects: Protestant and Roman Catholic. No other dissent counted. If you were a Protestant it did not matter whether you were Methodist, Baptist, Congregationalist, Plymouth Brother or what not. The fact that a boy went to the Wesleyan did not mean that his parents were Methodists. My people were all members by baptism of the then established Episcopal Church of Ireland.

faithfully
G. Bernard Shaw

To MARJORIE DEANS

[A/1]
Ayot St Lawrence. Welwyn
10th November 1944

[The woman Pascal had brought to visit Shaw, and of whom he was briefly enamoured, was a young American actress. Marjorie Deans was very much in love with Pascal, and he was certainly fond of her, but whether or not they ever were lovers is uncertain. Shaw's almost fatherly concern for Pascal is evident in this letter.]

Dear Marjorie Deans

The situation is one that will work itself out: nothing that any of us can do can alter it now.

I shot my own bolt pretty hard and straight when the pair visited me on Sunday, and I found that the lady was not, as the gentleman had given me to understand, a potential housekeeper and home comfort, but a clever ambitious girl with a religious vocation which led her to want above all things to star as Saint Joan. Incidentally she is in love with G., but not so deeply as not to be able to tell me so without any embarrassment.

I decided at once that she was right for Joan and wrong for Mrs G., and said emphatically that I could not go on with a director married to an actress whom he would have to shove into all my leading lady parts. And when I had a word alone with him while she was tidying up I found that he had misgivings as to his success as a husband. I suspect that he had already found out at Mumfords [Pascal's country estate] that neither of them fitted into the vision of home life. As for her, she was so delighted at my seeing her as St Joan that if I had been 40 years younger she would have fallen for me and forgotten all about G.

And so, I repeat, the situation must work itself out. The best you can do—the wisest—is to get out of their way as completely as possible, *and let it*. There is nothing a man dreads so much as a woman who cannot do without him. Relieve him of that fear and see how the twain will come out of their present acid test of living together.

That is all I can say so far, except that the more brilliant the lady's career, the more undesirable that her bracelets should be manacles. Let her therefore have every possible praise and encouragement.

GBS

PS Your letter is in the fire.

To GABRIEL PASCAL

Ayot St Lawrence. Welwyn
[H/1]   16th December 1944

[Pascal, having failed to obtain Prokofiev, Walton, Bliss, or Benjamin Britten for the scoring of his film, finally enlisted the services of Georges Auric (1899–1983), a member of the group known as Les Six, who had produced notable film music for René Clair's *A Nous la Liberté* (1931) and Jean Cocteau's *L'Eternel Retour* (1943). Britten (1913–76), then at work on *Peter Grimes*, had provided music for the B.B.C.'s *Pericles*, broadcast on 21st February 1943 as the first of a series "The Four Freedoms" by Louis MacNeice, who had asked Britten to create "an impression of early Greek music."]

The music for the Caesar film should not be difficult if we can get the right composer. The only snag in it is that the right composer would be too good for a job of incidental theatre music of no use in the concert room. Therefore what we should do is to let the composer see the film, and ask him whether he finds in it the program for an orchestral

729

suite: Overture, Desert Nocturne, Barcarolle, March, Egyptian Music Lesson, Banquet, Triumph ending in Calm Sea and Prosperous Voyage, with perhaps Til Eulenspiegelish character numbers labelled Ftatateeta and Britannus, making a complete independent work to be broadcast or performed at the Three Choirs and other Festivals. This would belong exclusively to the composer: all we should need would be his licence to have suitable parts of it fitted to the film, and his help in arranging it, and adding a few fanfares and scraps of "*melodrama.*" For this of course he would be paid; and he would be left in possession of a musical property as lucrative as Grieg's Peer Gynt suite. This would be well worth the best composer's while if he felt inspired by the subject.

The question remains, who is the best man? I was very much struck by a broadcast of a classical play (Greek) with music by Benjamin Britten. It had style and great refinement. He handled his trumpets beautifully; and his manner was not the lawless post-Wagnerism that now sounds so tiresomely oldfashioned, but in the tradition of Gluck, Berlioz, and Chopin. It had the forgotten quality of elegance. And it was all original: he will not plant any ersatz Aida on us.

Do, pray, sound him on the subject. In the form which I suggest the proposition would be good business for him; and a view of the film may rouse his artistic interest. He need not complete the suite for publication in full score and concert performance until he has experimented with its themes in the studio and seen us through. This part of the work must be put through at once, or the release will be held up very seriously.

> faithfully
> G. Bernard Shaw

To E. MARGARET WHEELER

Ayot St Lawrence. Welwyn
[T/9]   27th December 1944

[Mrs Wheeler's solicitor went into gales of laughter, she reported, when she showed him one of Shaw's letters, and informed her that while Shaw's interpretation of law was fine as far as it went, he was in error on the vital issue of annulment of registration of the birth. The children, she added, had not been enlightened as to the situation.]

Dear Mrs Wheeler

Let us take it that you are right on the parentage question. You have given me enough evidence: I am convinced.

730

I am not sensitive to your lawyer's amusement in the way of being hurt or offended by it. But on more than two or three occasions I have had my instructions misunderstood by solicitors obsessed with the notion that I am a clown whose favorite joke is to call black white, and that nothing I say is to be taken seriously. I have to come down pretty sharply on solicitors who laugh in the wrong place.

My point was that the possibility of your taking legal action was not the only one to be considered. The registered father may take action against you for molestation or jactitation. He will not do this unless you make the situation unbearable for him; but you may do this if you let it upset you too much; and it is your solicitor's business to realize this and keep you within bounds. It is no laughing matter.

Your separation from your man being inevitable let us see whether there is not something to be said for it instead of making the worst of it. Many couples need a long holiday from one another very badly. Six years seems a long time to you; but to me who have been a grown-up man for sixty, it can be spared quite profitably at your age. Neither of you can ever know the value of your marriage until you have been deprived of it for a while. You are both developing all the time and becoming new people; but you cannot notice this, and may get tired of one another, if you see one another so often and know one another so continuously that you don't notice this slow process. After six years absence he will have a new wife and you a new husband. You will actually be rejuvenated by your relief from child bearing, which develops the child at the expense of the mother. And either he will have conserved his energies by being faithful, or he will have run through a whole seraglio of substitutes and found how much better life was with you than with any of them.

There's something to be said for it after all.

But don't throw it all away by worrying too much about this change-ling business. Peggy is being well loved and looked after; and most of her life will be just the same school life as she would have with you. Of course this will not console you completely; but don't think of the case as worse than it really is.

In twelve short years there will be no Peggy, but, instead, a budding woman fighting for her independence against a tyrant mother, and needing a sympathetic unauthoritative aunt above all things.

Decidedly there are more points of view than one of every situation; so do not let yourself get stuck in one of them.

And that is all I have time for tonight.

G.B.S.

731

To OTTO KYLLMANN

[H/64]

Ayot St Lawrence. Welwyn
30th December 1944

[Constable's payment of £10,000 was largely from sales of 85,000 copies of the *What's What?*, which it had published on commission. The Penguin screen version of *Major Barbara* was not published until July 1946. The Oxford World's Classics edition of *Back to Methuselah*, with preface and text extensively revised and an added postscript "After Twentyfive Years," was also delayed until 1946. Shaw had just that month given approval to the War Department for publication of an edition of 6600 copies of *Selected Plays* (*Androcles*, *Pygmalion*, and *Saint Joan*, with their prefaces) in an "Edition for the Forces," published in 1945. It was followed in the same year by an edition of 4000 copies of the *What's What?*]

Dear O.K.

Ten thousand pounds! What a magnificent swank!

And you nearly persuaded me that, like Walter Scott and Mark Twain, I should be ruined by the bankruptcy of my publisher.

If you can chuck money about like that I can well believe that your excess profits are so enormous that the few pounds the Exchequer leaves you out of the Whats-[What] are less than nothing to you.

But, damn it, you are on velvet compared to me. Out of your ten thousand £8619–16–11 has already gone to the Treasury; and more than the rest will follow it next June. Meanwhile I have paid the cost of manufacture, and the best part of four years work. Who would be an author on such terms? Who would not be a publisher?

The Penguin Major Barbara (screen version) is now in print: I am correcting it. Ditto the Oxford U. Press World Classic Methuselah. The *carte blanche* I have given to the Government to reprint anything of mine for the soldiers may mean a distribution of samples that will act as the big advertisement that I have never yet ventured on[.] I wish you were in the cheap classic line; but I cannot honestly advise you to go beyond your present highpriced groove, which is a very necessary one.

I shall not wish you another hellish new year; but I am afraid we are in for it. As Europeans we are ruined: how we shall get on as islanders remains to be seen. Bootyless battles do not pay.

I have settled into a routine here in which the months fly like minutes. And as the days are at last lengthening I shall soon perhaps see you again.

GBS

To JOHN WARDROP

[Ayot St Lawrence. Welwyn]

[F.u/3]   [Undated: 1944–5]

[Dating of this letter is conjectural; but it seems, by internal evidence, to come shortly before Shaw's letter of 17th February 1945 to Veronica as well as a letter of 12th February 1945 to Blanche Patch, in which he exaggeratedly informed her, "At a word of encouragement he loses his head and believes that he is my literary executor and owns me and my house and you and my books and is my oldest and dearest friend, my brother, my heir: in short, myself. Sit on him" (A/9).]

Your letter is an alarming one: I perceive that I am ruining you, & should at once drop you decisively for ever.

As you know, I own a property in Ireland which I am supposed to have inherited through my uncle from my maternal grandfather. As a matter of fact I bought it from the mortgagees & left the pawnbrokers to sell the chattels. But long before this I had seen this property spoil the lives of every young person who could imagine that they might possibly inherit it, even if half a dozen lives of nearer relatives stood in the way. They all assumed that their destiny was to be idle welldressed ladies & gentlemen & that earning a living was something quite beneath them. I have had to support several of them.

I made up my mind that this curse must be lifted from the property if it ever came my way, & that it should not descend on any other property I might come to possess. And I have not changed it.

And now the curse has attacked you; your letter betrays the familiar symptoms at their worst. You are to have my house & everything in it, including my Rolls Royce car, which you are already driving in your dreams. You need take no further care for your future or [Veronica's]: you are my heir, handsomely provided for & need never again give a thought to John Wardrop.

Well, happy as the dream is, I must wake you up. I havent the smallest intention of leaving you anything except an introduction to my Trustees as a possible tenant for the Ayot house, & a possible assistant & agent. I hope it will not be worth your while to take on such drudgery for long, if at all. I shall most certainly not leave you a £2000 motor car that cost £37–10– for Taxation alone, & eats up petrol at the rate of a gallon every 17 miles. You will hardly be able to afford a baby Austin for years to come.

I fully intended to make use of your infatuation & give you every convenient chance of becoming a Shaw expert; but now your castle in the air is growing at such a rate that I must knock it down with an almighty kick or it will be your ruin. It will do you no harm to have a hobby; but having a hobby is one thing & earning a living another. Literature is one of the hobbies by which a living can be earned by the lucky ones; but if the literature is not your own literature you can kill the 2 birds with one stone only by (a) taking a university degree & becoming a publisher or (b) going into business as a publisher or bookseller.

So there!

To LADY RHONDDA

[H.t/8]

Ayot St Lawrence. Welwyn
1st January 1945

[Lady Rhondda had been divorced from her husband Sir Humphrey Mackworth, seventh Baronet, since 1923.]

Dear dear Rhondda

I also think of you occasionally quite apart from the weekly reminder by T & T. [*Time and Tide*]

By all means write about me; but take care to exclude the notion that you disagree with me. You dont disagree with me at all about anything. As to democracy we both agree with Herodotus, who arrived at our conclusions about democracy three or four thousand years ago. You will find lots of people quarrelling violently with people who hold exactly the same opinions because their approach to them is different and they dont give the same reasons for them. Also because they dont know what they are quarrelling about.

Just at present there is an intolerable noise and confusion made by shouting words that nobody thinks of defining. Fascism is nothing but State financed private enterprise. The capitalists have stolen the clothes of the Socialists; but, not understanding the transaction, they are shrieking for the destruction of Fascism, in which we are up to the neck as far as big business is concerned. We are clamoring for Democracy, by which we mean the British parliamentary system, under which real democracy is impossible. Democracy means nothing but running the country for the benefit of everybody, which can be done only through a natural division of labor, getting government done by the percentage of people who are capable of it, and who, for lack of specific talent (say for playwriting), have nothing better [to] do. But nobody understands the job. Think of those duffers in parliament

734

wasting their time and their tempers trying to reduce the price to be paid to the landlords for State purchased land because they were too ignorant of the ABC of economics to know that taxation falls ultimately on rent, and that the tax collector would take back from the landlords every penny they were paid.

Oh, Rhondda, I am devilishly old; and though the booksellers have bought 135,000 of my book I am not sure that you should not editorially write me off as obsolete as far as the readers of T&T are concerned. As to the mob, it has not caught up with me yet. Sixty years ago I said that what agriculture needed was a minimum wage of £2 (it was then thirteen shillings) and that employers' liability should be a State liability. Ministers are passing as great statesmen for saying that now; but all that is remembered about me is that I was a jocular lunatic, and presumably am so still.

I am again a bachelor, and can go to bed when I please. Why dont you write about this? You also have been married and are now free. The subject has never been treated.

G.B.S.

To LEONORA ERVINE

[C/3]

Ayot St Lawrence. Welwyn
5th January 1945

[Shaw's fortunate acquisition at Shaw's Corner, in September 1944, was a Scots housekeeper, Alice Laden (1901–79), a woman who had nursed Charlotte at Whitehall Court in her last illness. Her salary was fixed at £2.15.0 a week.]

I discar[d]ed anthracite years ago. Have you tried coalite? It is light to carry, clean to handle, smokeless, slateless, and when kindled by firewood burns with a steady hot glow that is much more satisfactory than the vicissitudes of a raw coal fire. I use it now exclusively for my sittingroom open fires. The others are electric.

The only exercise I am able for now in the 89th year is sawing wood into blocks to burn with the coalite, and occasionally walking a mile or two.

Our old servants could not stand another winter here, and retired in September. I had the good luck to find efficient modern substitutes (if only I can keep them); but the neighboring gentlefolk are all being overworked as their own general servants. I wish I could share my luck with you.

G.B.S.

To BRIAN DESMOND HURST

Ayot St Lawrence. Welwyn
[H/4]   9th January 1945

[Brian Desmond Hurst (1900–86) was an Irish-born director of British films. Although he apparently directed some scenes of *Cæsar and Cleopatra*, and contributed to its screen treatment, his work was uncredited.]

Dear Mr Hurst

I am sorry; but I am afraid it cannot be done. The agreement which controls the Caesar film contains a clause making it of the essence of the contract that the film is to be presented as a Pascal–Shaw film solely and indivisibly. The scenario is by me: the artistic direction is by Pascal; and no suggestion is to be made that our functions have been shared by transcript writers or co-directors of any sort. Without such clauses I should have all sorts of duffers and deadheads foisted on me as collaborators. You should have informed yourself on this point before you took the job.

You must find some other title in the bill than co-director or any other sort of director. When I produced my plays in the theatre, I made no mention of that fact in the program, but let the stage manager be named as such. If you are named as screen manager, or deputy super-intendent or anything else you can invent without infringing the clause, I shall not grudge you that publicity. But please note that the scenario of Caesar is my work. Anything you have contributed to it, though it may suggest a title for you, must not be described as scenario. I am not unfriendly; but experience has convinced me, as it will soon convince you, of the need for undivided publicity and responsibility in direction.

faithfully
G. Bernard Shaw

To NANCY ASTOR

Ayot St Lawrence. Welwyn
[C/101]   20th January 1945

[Nancy's close friend Philip Kerr (Lord Lothian) died in December 1940. Blanche Patch, who found Ayot St Lawrence too cold and isolated in winter (and Loewenstein maddeningly in favour), returned to London before Christmas.]

These excursions are wildly impossible for me at my age, even if I were not loaded with business that I cannot deal with apart from my

736

papers. Miss P., losing her sanity by living in a shopless village with one very old man of whom she must be very tired, has braved the bombs and returned to London, which makes my presence here still more compulsory. The postal arrangements are worse than ever, my letters arriving half an hour *after* the one daily collection; so that I cannot answer by return.

You must get a younger understudy for Phil. My next journey will probably be to Golders Green [crematorium]; and you should in common prudence replace me betimes, however inferior the substitute.

G.B.S.

To DOROTHY EAGLE

Ayot St Lawrence. Welwyn
[H/1]   23rd January 1945
[Dorothy Eagle was a grand-niece of Emily Carroll (Cousin Ta[h]), oldest daughter of the Rev. William Carroll and Shaw's Aunt Emily.]

Dear Mrs Eagle

You need have no scruples: the money was my cousin Ta's from the last quarter day, and was meant for the cost of her dying as well as of her living. If the doctor and the undertaker have left you out of pocket let me know.

Ta had £50 a year of her own when I discovered her in Eastbourne, and was eking it out by giving lessons in the dead languages and in Hebrew. A year after I came to her aid I asked her how the lessons were going. She said "Lessons! I dont give lessons: I live like a lady." In her day (and mine) ladies were not supposed to work for their living. I am glad I made things that much easier for her.

I do not know in what securities the capital of the £50 was invested; but as it may be intact still you must look after it.

Your father writes that her landlady was good to her. Was she left anything? If not, is there any acknowledgment we ought to make?

faithfully
G. Bernard Shaw

737

To BLANCHE PATCH

[H.t/9]
Ayot St Lawrence. Welwyn
17th February 1945

My dear Blanche

Wardrop has just burst in on me, with a suit case, frantic about Loewenstein, and announcing that he had come to sleep here and live with me to protect his property (ME) against the Jew. He assured me that you entirely agreed with him. Of course I have packed him back to London after bullying him into comparative deflatedness if not into sanity.

With these lunatics to deal with we two must have a look at the whole situation.

I am a finished man, and will die tomorrow or next day; but I have done such an enormous mass of work in the last sixty years that there is a mountain of litter to tidy-up. That job is quite beyond us. Since the tidying-up of Charlotte's affairs forced me to face it I have been looking about for somebody who would drudge through my papers for hardly less than two years for six or seven hours a day and be docile enough to like doing it.

For us to do it ourselves is quite out of the question. Our day-to-day current work is quite enough for us. You are still far from being describable as an old woman; but I am a very old man, and can only manage three hours a day at literature or business. We must find somebody who can make it a whole time job for at least a year or eighteen months.

I have been feeling about for that somebody of late years. I tried J.W., and went so far with him as to give him the run of the house [at Whitehall Court] and a latchkey.

Now read the enclosed green sheet, which I have carboned because I mean to send a copy to Mrs W.

I should perhaps have discussed the situation with you more fully; but it did not develop itself fully until the weeks L. has lately spent here brought me to a final decision about him.

In haste to catch the Sunday post—

G.B.S.

To BLANCHE PATCH

[H.c.u/9]
[Ayot St Lawrence. Welwyn]
[Undated: assigned to 17th February 1945]

He proved impossible. He was too young, too excitable. The slightest encouragement turned his head. The slightest inattention or suggestion that I have anyone else to consider than himself amazed and infuriated him. A rebuff prostrated him to the verge of suicide. He assumed not only the position of my literary agent but of my son and heir. He lacked neither brains nor devotion, but age, experience, training, and polish. He was declassed, too good for one level and not schooled enough for the other. I concluded that what he needed was a profession. The obvious profession for him is the law; and I am considering whether I shall make him the necessary grants-in-aid to see him through the years of study and polishing before he can be called to the bar.

Meanwhile another candidate has arisen in the person of F.E.L. I began with a violent prejudice against him because he arrived as the founder of The Shaw Society which threatened to become a nuisance to me. I remembered my old experiences in the Shelley and Browning Societies, and fought him off for a long time. But he made good in spite of me. He is fully matured, twice married with a grown-up daughter and an infant one, university trained with his head split open in duels and the degree of doctor of philosophy, and a mania for bibliography which has taken the special form of Shaw bibliography. And at that abominable drudgery he is now working seven hours a day for five days a week in my house in Ayot. He has captured the tidying-up job by sheer fitness for it; and we must both go on with him until it is finished.

That is the exact situation at present as to J.W. and F.E.L.; and we must accept it whether we like it or not because the tidying-up is, like the war, imperative and must have priority at all hazards.

To BLANCHE PATCH

[E.u/4]
Ayot St Lawrence. Welwyn
21st February 1945

My braces are in the last stage of ruin. Mrs Laden tried to buy me a pair, but was told that I must get a permit or else be satisfied with utility braces, which she considers unworthy of my dignity.

Last time I bought any I bought three pairs. So will you look through my wardrobe and see if there are any left. They may be in one of the small drawers on the left side of my big looking glass.

If there are none I am afraid you must buy me a utility pair; for the utility of braces is extreme. Without them my dignity would disappear altogether.

To E. MARGARET WHEELER

Ayot St Lawrence. Welwyn
[T/9]   1st March 1945

[Mrs Wheeler had expressed disagreement with Shaw's views on methods of raising children as cited in the *New Statesman* on 10th February, from a letter originally published as "The Care of Children: Hospital and other Training" in *The Times* on 2nd August 1944.]

Dear Mrs Wheeler

Send me no more evidence: I am convinced; and I hate having to send back documents. But the photographs are against you; for the sheet of four dozen prints marked Valerie are like you, though very unlike the two separate ones—the scowling baby ones—also marked Valerie. The rest are like all children.

One of the puzzles in the case is why you waited for eight years to get into a state about Peggy. I take it that at six a child ceases to be its mammy's doll and darling, and begins to draw away from her as an independent individual. Also it enters on school life, which is a rival to home life. I have known cases in which women have had no maternal passion for their first three children and have adored their fourth; but to do without *the same child* for eight years and then suddenly feel that its possession is an absolute necessity is something new to me. I am not arguing the point: I am only warning you that the R———s will argue it if you take them into court and they are as determined as you are to have and hold the child.

I enclose a copy of The Times correspondence, a stupid snippet from which kept you up until four in the morning. My point was that hospital nurses and hospital discipline simply kill children, and that maternal massage (cub licking) is a necessity for them. All that you say is quite true (I have discussed it most interestingly with a mother of three successfully grown-ups); but the difficulty about our family system remains: adults need quiet, order, and cleanliness; and children need noise, dirt, and destructiveness; yet they both need one another's company to some extent. People who can afford it send their children to school to get rid of them, and are glad when holidays are over. And, as I have dwelt on so emphatically in my last book, child life must be organized and educated by the State in sections within which the children never grow up, whereas in families the children are always growing up; so that by the time the parent has learnt how to handle a child of five it has become a child of eight requiring different handling.

The percentage of intelligent women (say ten) to which you belong may get away with their job fairly well if they have aptitude enough to make its drudgery endurable; but parentage is a skilled craft anyhow, different from school teaching and sick nursing; and as the child needs all three, the first two continuously, the organization of child life is a complicated business which so far is only very crudely attempted by compulsory education in day schools.

A lady of my acquaintance maintains that young children are affected by the moods of their mothers, and that when the mother is depressed or in trouble the child wakes up crying in the middle of the night. Have you ever had any such experience?

She says also that children are "kept in their place" much more severely in the north of England than in the south. I should say that of Scotland but not of Cumberland, which seems to me as soft a place as Devon. But then I have been there only once, very briefly, to lecture.

What were your parents? I want to get your class antecedents, though you, like me, are a freak and have transcended them.

I am called away. Do not sit up until four to answer unless you also lie in bed until twelve, which is improbable.

G. Bernard Shaw

To NANCY ASTOR

Ayot St Lawrence. Welwyn
13th April 1945

[C/101]

[Lady Astor, distressed by whining complaints from Blanche Patch of the supposed "battening" on Shaw by Loewenstein and, more recently, Stephen and Clare Winsten, who moved in next door to Shaw's Corner, had sought to convince Shaw that he needed a live-in companion. Like Patch, Nancy Astor was virulently anti-Semitic, and where the former vented her spleen mostly on Loewenstein, Nancy focused upon the Winstens, aspersing the "distinguished artist" who made scenes and her "Polish Jew" husband, who, Nancy charged, "extract[ed]" money from Shaw for dubious art works (A/2: 3rd September [1946]).]

I see. Having neither wisdom nor character I am to be placed in the care of someone gifted with both, selected by you, and willing to act as my keeper and office boy. Splendid.

However, there is no hurry: I am getting along fairly well as I am. I have in me the makings of a first rate hermit. Even a bit of an oracle.

Only, as you wont consult me I can hardly be of any use to you, except to amuse you occasionally.

Mrs P.C. with her last breath called me Joey, and in her last letter Dear *dear* Joey. I am glad she got that much out of me. And now you also——!!

G.B.S.

To THE EDITOR, *STRAND MAGAZINE*

[C/5]

Ayot St Lawrence. Welwyn
2nd May 1945

[John Burdon Sanderson Haldane (1892–1964), author of *New Paths in Genetics* (1941), was professor of biometry at London University. A Marxist philosopher, he later emigrated to India and took citizenship there. Dr Maurice Ernest (1872–1955), a homœopath, was the author of *The Longer Life: A Critical Survey of Many Claims to Abnormal Longevity* . . . (1938).]

Thanks for the invitation; but I cannot write an article on How to Live Long, because I dont know.

I have just done it: that is all; but how or why I can tell you no more than a cabbage can tell you how or why it grew.

Get some popular biologist who has studied a thousand cases to do it. J.B.S.Haldane would suit. But why not Dr Maurice Ernest, author of The Longer Life . . . on *Why has Shaw Lived 30 Years Longer than Shakespear?*

That would drag me in all right.

G.Bernard Shaw

To ÉAMON DE VALERA

[T(H)/127; F/2]

Ayot St Lawrence. Welwyn
5th May 1945

[Éamon De Valera had been Prime Minister and Foreign Minister of the Irish Republic since 1932. "Taoiseach" is Irish Gaelic for leader or chief, and in Irish politics stands for Prime Minister. It was Shaw's country solicitor at Luton, Ivo L. Currall, who, when Shaw was told there was no legal machinery in Ireland for dealing with such a disposition as he had proposed to the Carlow Urban Council, suggested he should ask De Valera to get a special Enabling Act passed through the Dáil.]

Dear Taoiseach

Is it possible to pass an Act enabling every Irish municipality to establish and administer a voluntary Civic Improvement Fund open to all citizens who have property which they desire to give or bequeath to their country instead of to their next of kin, who, like the relatives from whom I inherited my own Irish property, may exploit, mortgage, and ruin it, and demoralize themselves in the process.

The circumstances under which I venture to intrude on you with this question are as follows.

I own a small house property in Carlow and a shop in Wexford. Years ago I gave the principal building in Carlow, the old Assembly Rooms, to the town; and it is now a flourishing municipal School of Art. Last year I offered the entire estate to the District Council on condition that they establish a permanent Voluntary Civic Improvement Fund open to all contributors and administered by the Council. The offer was accepted enthusiastically; but it has broken down on the condition. I believe that the establishment of such a fund is within the Council's powers and is the right way to effect it, having consulted Lord Passfield (Sidney Webb) who is probably the best available authority on local government. But as it is a novelty invented by myself, the Council is not only afraid to adopt it without an empowering Act, but wants that Act to be peculiar to my case, and to sanction, not my proposed fund, but an ordinary charitable Trust, which of all things I am determined to avoid, as it would set no example and end in nothing being done with the revenue of the estate but apply it to the reduction of the rates: in effect making it a present to the Carlow landlords, on whom the rates finally fall, without benefiting the country or improving the town. I am an old municipal councillor and an economist; and I know. I must therefore withdraw my offer unless that Act is passed to assure the Council, (a) that its compliance with my conditions will not be *ultra vires*, and (b) that it shall not be limited to my estate nor to Carlow nor set up an ordinary trust (a Shaw Charity), but a step in general legislation for all Eire and a suggestion and recommendation to all Ireland and for that matter to all the civilized world.

This clearly makes it your business and not mine. If it were an affair of a private Bill promoted to effect a single transaction in the old-fashioned way I should have no excuse for troubling you with it. Unless you come to the rescue I shall die (I am on the verge of my ninetieth year) and my Irish property will fall into my residuary estate (less death duties) and be shared with certain English institutions figuring in my will as it stands at present.

My late wife, who was devoted to you, holding you to be the greatest living Irishman except one, made a will leaving all her property, subject to a life interest for me, in trust to an Irish Bank, for the development of Irish culture, specifying branches in the manner of charitable trusts, including some (the provision of orchestral music for instance) which have since been completely covered by the wireless. Her solicitors, like the Carlow solicitors, assured her that this was the only legal way of carrying out her intention. I am afraid it will prove a legal way of very largely defeating it. I shall certainly not adopt it myself. Only by making it an affair of State, quite impersonal to myself, can I justify my calling your attention to it.

> faithfully
> G. Bernard Shaw

To ÉAMON DE VALERA

[T(H)/127]

Ayot St Lawrence. Welwyn
5th June 1945

[De Valera notified Shaw on 2nd June that the Minister for Local Government agreed with Shaw's view as to the desirability of providing for establishment of local Civic Improvement Funds, and was preparing legislation shortly to be submitted to the Government. If these proposals were approved by the Government, which they undoubtedly would be, a Bill could be introduced in the Dáil soon thereafter.]

Dear Taoiseach

Splendid!

It would have taken thirty years to get as far in this unhappy country. Many, many thanks.

> faithfully
> G. Bernard Shaw

To EIRENE LLOYD JONES

[X/425]

[Ayot St Lawrence. Welwyn]
[Undated: *c.* 25th June 1945]

[Eirene Lloyd Jones, daughter of Thomas Jones (chairman of the Gregynog Press) was a parliamentary Labour candidate for the Welsh borough of Flint in the General Election on 5th July. She lost, 27,800 to 26,761, to the Conservative candidate Lt.-Col. N.Birch. Shaw's views on the Coupled Vote were incorporated in the just-written preface to *Good King Charles* in the Standard Edition, not published until 1947.]

My dear Eirene

I rejoice to hear that you are up for election on July 5. The chances are at least ten to one against Flint finding a better candidate. Your record, like your father's, is very far beyond that of the average Parliamentary candidate.

As you know, I attach vital importance to the presence and participation of women on all public authorities. No Government can be representative or democratic in the absence and disfranchisement of women. I have had the experience of sitting on public committees with women; then, by a change in legislation, with women excluded; and again, by another change, back again, besides much experience in private societies with women colleagues; and I know what I am talking about when I say that men cannot be trusted to behave themselves properly in the absence of women when the interests of their better halves are concerned. I gave great offence to the wilder suffragettes of forty years ago by saying that their war cry of Votes for Women, if attained, would keep women out of Parliament—as it did at first completely, and still does to the extent that the present proportion of men to women there is 600 to 14, instead of as it should be to make it representative of the country. My own remedy for that monstrosity is to make the electoral unit not One Man One Vote plus One Woman One Vote, but a man AND a woman—a Coupled Vote: all votes for a single candidate being invalid. This, and this alone, will secure the representation of men and women in equal numbers.

I must not try to commit you to this as a plank in your election platform: too many women—even Welshwomen—would be foolish and ignorant enough to vote against it. I mention it only to show how strong is my experienced conviction of the urgent necessity for more women at Westminster.

Women with your qualifications and antecedents do not grow on the gooseberry bushes; and I hope Flint will rally to you and be proud of

745

you. Your first-rate election address will enable the electors to know exactly where they stand with you, which is more than most constituencies will be able to say on polling day. You will not let them down; and I wish you an overwhelming majority.

affectionately
G. Bernard Shaw

To E. MARGARET WHEELER

[T/9]
Ayot St Lawrence. Welwyn
28th June 1945

[The Duke of Wellington criticised lack of military discipline in several of his dispatches and letters, particularly railing at "impunity" in the dispatch of 28th November 1812 to officers commanding divisions and brigades.]

Dear Margaret Wheeler

Your mind is giving way under your grievance. Why do you plague me with these unnecessary copies of dull letters when I have told you that I have had quite enough evidence of the change. Enough is enough: dont, I beg you, bother me with any more, or with the old stuff over again. Think rather of the coming reunion with Major Charles, who is perhaps already on the seas or in the air on his way home.

I still do not consider the evidence good enough for a court of law; nor do I see on what issue it can be raised there. It is no use telling Mr R—— that you desire a friendly settlement if you finish with a threat of proceedings. What proceedings? How is the writ or the charge to run?

I see nothing for it but reciprocal adoption. And for that you must depend on the awakening of a feeling in the R——s that they have the wrong child, and want the right one.

The one very important point on which you are silent is how Peggy and Valerie feel about it. They are not packets of sweets to be labelled with certain addresses and delivered there by the errand boy. At eight years old they are human beings with likings and dislikings.

To get away from this overworked subject let me ask you why, when you and I are obviously perfectly agreed on some matter, you always open it by announcing that our opinions are contrary and irreconcilable. Are you a quarrelsome devil?

That incident of the scissors, for example. You should have clouted yourself for not taking the scissors with you when you left the room. You might as well have left a loaded cannon. What child would not have pulled the lanyard!

When children or adults have to be managed, the time factor dominates the situation. When something has to be done and done at once (or not done) it is no use preaching at great length (as you do) that if the said children and adults had been properly and kindly brought up they would have done the right thing spontaneously. If they will respond to nothing but kicking and swearing they must be kicked and cursed. Ask any fighting mate in the merchant service. If as often happens, the occasion is one which the child is too young to understand it must be made to obey without understanding; and if it wont obey for love it must be made to obey for fear; and perfect fear casteth out love. Army discipline, like all terrorism, is sometimes unnatural, unjust and cruel; but the great Duke of Wellington said "Anything is better than impunity." He knew.

Bear all that in mind before you start lecturing me about managing human beings, young or old.

I send back the letters to you to inflict on some other victim. This letter of my own is not an enjoyable one; and I am half disposed to tear it up, as I certainly should if I kept it until tomorrow. But let it go: I believe you like quarrelling.

G.B.S.

To MAURICE MOYNIHAN

Ayot St Lawrence. Welwyn
[V(H)/127] 12th July 1945

[Maurice Moynihan (b. 1902) was private secretary to De Valera, and later Secretary to the Government. He signed his name in the Gaelic, as Muiris Ó Moimhneacháin. On 5th July he sent to Shaw a copy of the Local Authorities (Acceptance of Gifts) Bill, 1945, which had been introduced into the Dáil. "The Bill," he wrote, "has for its aim to enable local authorities to accept, hold and administer, gifts of property, provided they adopt a Civic Improvement Scheme. An attempt has been made to define 'civic improvement' to include anything which tends to improve the amenities of the area of a local authority or is conducive to the welfare of the inhabitants or any class of them. Care has been taken over this definition so that a gift will be used to initiate improvements and will not be absorbed into the general assets of a local authority for the direct relief of rates" (T/127). The Bill was passed, and Shaw's gift was accepted by the Carlow Urban Council. Conveyed on 13th August 1945, it consisted of seventeen parcels of land in and around Carlow, including a burial ground known as "The Graves."

Although Shaw had been prepared to relinquish his life income in Charlotte's estate, he changed his mind when E. W. Wykes, Charlotte's solicitor, advised him that if he did so the matter would first have to be brought before the courts to determine whether or not the bequests were valid charitable bequests, and that Shaw would have to be a party to the action. It was not until a year after his death that the action was at last taken and the bequests upheld in the courts.]

Dear Sir

I have to thank you for the copy of the Acceptance of Gifts Bill, which meets my case exactly. I am strongly in favor of the managerial system. It is the best available cure for the jobberies of the gombeen men and for the way in which local councillors who have never handled large sums of money sit dumb and helpless before items of £20,000 and hold all-night sittings wrangling over eighteenpence for refreshments.

My wife, who died in 1943, left her property, producing a gross income of £8000, to me for life and then to Ireland in the form of a trust for the culture of music, literature, and the fine arts generally. The trustees at present are myself and the National Provincial Bank of England. When I die the National Bank of Ireland takes up the trust and administers it.

I am prepared to renounce and release my life interest straightaway and allow the whole property to go to Ireland at once. This is quite simple; but the effect will be that the estate will go, not to the Irish Nation, but to the National Bank's executors' department, which can do nothing with it but found scholarships at the Academy of Music and Hibernian Academy, and make grants to individuals of its own choice. This was the best my wife could do in the absence of an Irish National Trust, a Ministry of Fine Arts, or any other national organ doing for the nation what the new Bill will do for the municipalities. I would much rather give over the estate to Mr de Valera's government than to the National Bank; but I have no choice in the matter. The situation should be considered in view of the possibility of forming an Irish National Trust; so I trouble you with these details on the chance of your being able and willing to mention my case as illustrating the need for further development.

faithfully
G. Bernard Shaw

Note how legible my signature is at 89. Yours is utterly inscrutable. I dont know who I am writing to.

Up the Republic!

To HAROLD LASKI

4 Whitehall Court S W 1
[S/92]   27th July 1945

[Shaw paid a rare visit to London in mid July for a meeting with the Public Trustee and consultation with his accountant Stanley Clench, as well as lunches and social meetings with Roy Limbert, Gabriel Pascal, Feliks Topolski, Doris Thorne (daughter of Henry Arthur Jones), Cecily Colthurst, Sydney Cockerell, and the Winstens. He returned to Ayot just after his 89th birthday.

Harold Laski (1893–1950), political scientist and author, was a professor at the University of London from 1926. Joseph Lane and Frank Kitz (1849–1923), joint-founders (1882) of the Labour Emancipation League, were members of the Social Democratic Federation who broke away with William Morris in 1884 to found the Socialist League. Kitz became co-editor of the Socialist journal *Commonwealth*.]

Dear Laski

... Morris was in one respect in the same position as myself in the movement. We were both Aestheticists having to work with hopeless Philistines. I was the worse off because Morris had a circle of artist friends acquired in his early days or attracted by his reputation as a poet. But the Fabians were Philistines unalloyed. When Bertha Newcombe designed a title page depicting a nymph holding up a lamp, they rejected it because the nymph had no petticoats, and were deeply shocked. When I proposed that we should publish Wagner's Art and Revolution and Oscar Wilde's essay on Socialism as tracts, they simply did not know what I was talking about. Morris and I were thrown together in spite of the difference between Fabian tactics and those of the Socialist Leaguers; and when I smashed up Max Nordau in a review now entitled The Sanity of Art, a job which Morris could not do himself but was very glad to have done for him, he admitted me at once to a real intimacy.

He held on paying the way of the [Socialist] League because the Fabian middle-class Philistinism was unendurable to him, and because there was something Chaucerian about the primitive simplicity of Joseph Lane and Frank Kitz and the rest of the League: pilgrims and

Autolycuses that attracted him in spite of their absurd futility as modern politicians. But when their antics forced him to give up financing them, and the League at once collapsed, he said that he had no doubt the change would come about in Mister Webb's way and not in Kitz's or Lane's. The Chaucerian fancy is important, because only a very bad judge of character and capacity could have mistaken the Leaguers for statesmen. Morris was a very good judge of men—so good that he saw clearly that the sophisticated politicians were even more hopeless than the romantic tinkers and costers, and that the House of Commons was impossible as an organ for Socialism.

None of us foresaw then that the revolution would be achieved in Russia (of all places!) by a minority of excessively sophisticated Marxists; and that they would make every possible catastrophic mistake until they were driven by sheer force of facts to establish the present Russo-Fabian state. Nor did the Fabians foresee that the State Socialism they were offering to the workers would be foozled by them and grabbed by the Capitalists, producing the new phenomenon called Fascism which is bridging the real "interval between two barbarisms."

We shall see now whether the Labor majority in the House of Commons, which the newspapers call power, will be overwhelmed by it. . . .

Morris would not bother about theories of value and philosophies of history: he went straight through to the fundamental issue and took his economic stand on the basic fact that the capitalists are damned thieves who live by robbing the poor. He declared that his book conversion was, like Webb's, effected by John Stuart Mill, whose first verdict against Communism was, he maintained, against the evidence. When I apostatized by rejecting Marx's Ricardian value theory for that of Jevons (which is much more socialistic) Morris was induced to sign a disavowal of me by Hyndman & Co; but he did this as a Communist defending a Communist and did not pretend to know anything about the theorizing of Ricardo, Marx, Jevons and Wicksteed. No theories could get over the simple fact that the rich lived by robbing the poor and got nothing by it but ugly unhappy lives.

All this you probably know as well or better than I do; but a first hand witness is always worth hearing. It is well to get it from the horse's mouth, even when, as mostly happens, the horse does not know what he is neighing about.

G.B.S.

To OTTO KYLLMANN

Ayot St Lawrence. Welwyn
[C/64]   14th August 1945

[The Standard Edition volume *Geneva, Cymbeline Refinished,* & *Good King Charles* was delayed by Shaw's revisions, labour shortage, and, finally, corrections necessitated in the prelims to eliminate faulty publishers' addresses. The new play was one Shaw had commenced at sea on 17th February 1936 as *The World Betterer*, but quickly abandoned. He re-commenced it at Ayot on 2nd August 1945 as *Old Bill Buoyant's Billions.* Its title being altered briefly to *A World Betterer's Courtship*, it finally became *Buoyant Billions* when completed on 20th November 1946.]

Sorry I missed you when I was in town; but what could I have said anyhow? Even if the Whatswhat is finished, there is the Geneva volume to be printed, and the preface to it has been knocked to pieces by the atomic bomb and must be rewritten. Also I have begun a new play. And though Maxwell says there is paper enough available, there is not labor enough: he could not get the jubilee Methuselah out on my birthday.

The Penguin Major Barbara (screen version) is passed for press and is sticking there apparently. I must Penguinize and Odhamize and perhaps Everyman-Dentize (he is always at me for a volume) because our prices are too high for people with less than £1000 a year; but I always hold back until our lemon is squeezed dry and the book not worth your shelf room, whilst the demand for a decent edition is actually revived by the vogue of the cheap one. The gallery success helps the stalls.

G.B.S.

To BLANCHE PATCH

Ayot St Lawrence. Welwyn
[A/4]   19th September 1945

[Giulio Aristide Sartorio (1860–1932), Italian painter, engraver, and sculptor, was commissioned by Charlotte Payne-Townshend in 1894 to do a pastel portrait of her, originally intended to be a gift for Dr Axel Munthe. Gustave De Smet (1877–1943) was a Belgian expressionist painter.]

... When the car next comes up it can transport hither the big Sartorio portrait of C.F.S. and the Augustus John portrait of me. Also the head of Balzac by Rodin in bronze and the two owls from the drawingroom mantelpiece.

751

The odd little picture by De Smet in the study over the dictionaries might also come with the statuette of the Jap sawing a log.

This is part of my policy of leaving all my works of art of any interest either in Ayot for the National Trust or to some public gallery.

Of course they need not come all at once. Begin with the Sartorio and John portraits and the Balzac-Rodin bronze.

G.B.S.

To C. H. NORMAN

[C/4]

Ayot St Lawrence. Welwyn
24th September 1945

[Bergen-Belsen was a notorious Nazi concentration camp in Germany, established in July 1943 both as a prisoner-of-war camp and as a Jewish transit camp. Nearly forty thousand prisoners (including the young diarist Anne Frank) died here before it was liberated by the British in April 1945.]

I agree, of course: these lynchings are disgusting. I think W.J. [William Joyce] would have done better to throw over his lawyers and claim that a man has a human right to choose his side in a war, and that as he changed his domicile and was perfectly frank about it he was in order.

If our Imperialists rush us into a war with Russia, where will our Socialists be?

Belsen was obviously produced by the incompetence and breakdown of the military command. The concentration camps are always left to the refuse of officers' messes, for whom the job of feeding and sanitating the deluge of prisoners is too much. The result is always the same more or less.

G.B.S.

To STANLEY CLENCH

[C/1]

Ayot St Lawrence. Welwyn
2nd October 1945

All that we said about a bank as Trustee, or the Royal Exchange[,] is a wash-out.

It must be the Public Trustee, whom I have already discussed my will with.

752

The whole affair will take a bit of arranging, as the P.T. has to accumulate £20,000 for my fad of a British alphabet; but I think I can do it.

GBS

To CLARE WINSTEN

Ayot St Lawrence. Welwyn

[A/9]   5th October 1945

[Shaw's neighbours Clare Winsten (b. 1898?) and Stephen Winsten (b. 1897) had become almost daily visitors to Shaw's Corner, the one sketching him while the other engaged him in conversation. Stephen Winsten edited *G.B.S. 90*, published on Shaw's ninetieth birthday in 1946, and wrote three books on Shaw, the first of which, *Days with Bernard Shaw*, was publicly criticised by its subject in 1949. Clare Winsten had proposed a sculpture of Saint Joan for the garden at Shaw's Corner. Commissioned for £400 and moulded in bronze, it was erected in 1947. Christopher was the Winstens' son.]

My dear Clare

What an incorrigible megalomaniac you are! Do you suppose I want a white stone ghost of Joan, ten feet high, to haunt the twilight in my little garden? You can get the stone, you say: can you get and keep three hefty labourers to handle it, and a military lorry to carry it? Can I do the same?

You say you must know the material you are modelling for. Well, ask Christopher what particular brand of bakelite it will be. It wont be Portland stone nor bronze. Zinc or pewter or lead perhaps if plastics are impossible. It must be portable anyhow.

But this is not a contract. All I can say is that if you can in your spare time turn out a figure that appeals to me and will fit into my garden I shall be tempted to bargain with you for it. It mustnt be an alteration of anything you have done. It mustnt weigh more than a pound or two. It must amuse you to produce it; this is *not* a commission. You suggested it yourself.

However, plasticine, of which you may consume some tons in your experiments (if you make any), costs money; and even in your spare time you must eat. I will take a chance and put £50 in your hands for current expenses. Let us see what will come of it.

G.B.S.

To BLANCHE PATCH

[A/4]

Ayot St Lawrence. Welwyn
13th October 1945

When Hubert Bland was dying he said to his daughter Rosamund "If there is not money enough for John's education, ask Shaw." So I financed John through Cambridge into the medical profession; got into the way of spending some of my spare money in that way; and paid the schoolbills of Frederick Evans's son and Peter Tompkins. They were all more or less Pygmalion experiments.

When the case of J.W. came up, I was a bit staggered. As the unqualified son of a licensed victualler he had no status; and he lost his head when I let him try his hand as assistant secretary and was completely ousted by Loewenstein, doctor of philosophy. There was nothing to be done with him but either drop him or make a qualified professional man of him. He was willing to matriculate and qualify for the bar, and fairly confident that he could get through the examinations. He estimated the cost as £5000. I could not swallow that; but the experiment tempted me. I plunged and gave him £2000.

The result remains to be seen. Meanwhile he is offstage.

GBS

To HARRIET COHEN

[H/2]

Ayot St Lawrence. Welwyn
22nd October 1945

My dear Harriet

The Music Cure is no use: put it out of your head. Even if it were not quite obsolete, it would have to be done by a popular actress, with the music played on a record intensified by the microphone to a thunder which no pianist could produce from the bass octaves in the A flat polonaise. So you are out of it anyhow.

Years ago I told Walter Rummel that a pianist ought to be a lecturer at home and abroad as far as his or her knowledge of languages would go. For instance:—

Ladies and Gentlemen: I am going to play you a sonata. Several of you will want to know what a sonata is. Well, before Beethoven changed it it used to be a pattern; and a pattern in sound is like a pattern on paper: it is an ornamental design in which the parts repeat and balance another like the lyre under this piano where the pedals are. They are what you

754

call tunes. They are like lines of verse, where the rhythm—the ringle-jingle—appeals to your taste for beauty, for symmetry, for danceability.

Let me quote you a verse from Sullivan's opera H.M.S. Pinafore. The sailors have to sing

> We are sober steady men
> And quite devoid of fee-are
> In all the Royal N
> None are so smart as we are

Let me play you the first two lines. Now how does Sullivan go on? He just simply repeats the first two lines note for note, though the words are different.

You may think that this simplest of patterns is used because the words are comic. But here is the most pathetic of the songs of Ireland: The last Rose of Summer. The pattern is the same. It has nothing to do with the meaning or mood of the words.

A sonata is only a more elaborate pattern. It has no philosophy, no drama, no meaning: it is a straight and simple appeal to your admiration of a beautiful design in sound pattern. Roughly it consists of two tunes called the first and second subjects, a centre section called the free fantasia in which the composer plays all sorts of pretty or amusing tricks with scraps of the two tunes, and finally a repetition of the tunes. I will play you a simple sonata by Mozart and point out to [you] as I play where the two subjects and the fantasia begin and end.

Mozart was such a mighty genius that he could compose sonatas in his childhood without being taught. He grew up into being a dramatist, a poet, and a thinker; and he put his drama, his poetry, and his thought into sonata form as far as that was possible; and with him all things were possible in music.

Then came Beethoven. All the musicians thought him mad because he used the sonata form not to present agreeable sound patterns, but to express in music his moods, which were gigantic, sometimes stormy to hurricane force, sometimes uproariously jolly to the pitch of buffoonery, sometimes pastoral, often lovely. You listen to Beethoven to share his mighty or magic moods, not to enjoy sound patterns and royalty ballads.

I will play you one of his great sonatas. Now that you know what to look for in it you will hear how completely it differs from the earlier sound patterns. And you will be on the way to understand why Wagner threw over sonata opera altogether and composed immense music dramas.

Talking of Wagner, do you remember the bells in Parsifal. Listen to their four notes: how they haunt you after your first hearing of them. Listen. Tum tum tum tum, Tum tum tum tum: how solemn they are and beautiful! Let me play them faster. Faster. Faster.

["]Falsacappa, voici ma prise" &c &c

That is from Offenbach's opera bouffe The Brigands. The same notes, the same harmony; but how different. Let us go back to the Wagner version and finish on that.

Let me play you one of Bach's choral preludes, transcribed for the piano by myself. I have not changed the speed, nor altered it at all; but have you recognized in it the policeman's song from the Pirates of Penzance?

And so on: I have no room and no time for more. But you see the idea: a piano lecture, not merely a recital. A specialty that would take you out of the mob of finger acrobats.

GBS

Excuse my blundering typing. I am very old, and can do no better.

To SIDNEY WEBB

Ayot St Lawrence. Welwyn

[H/14]   26th October 1945

[Shaw's review of Margaret Cole's *Beatrice Webb*, under the caption "The History of a Happy Marriage," appeared in the *Times Literary Supplement* on 20th October. H. G. Wells died on 13th August 1946; Shaw's generous notice, "The Man I Knew," appeared in the *New Statesman* on 17th August. Wells, belying Shaw's description of him as a man without malice, pre-wrote an acidulous obituary of Shaw, which appeared in the British and American press in November 1950.]

My dear Sidney

When they asked me to do the Cole book I rather shrank, feeling that I knew too much to do justice in a couple of thousand words. But as I also felt that I could not trust Beatrice to anyone else I took it on to secure the human touch[.]

I had hardly finished it when Kingsley Martin wrote to say that H. G. Wells is dying, and would I write an obituary for the Statesman, to be kept in cold storage until he passed out. It also is a delicate job; but I have done it. . . .

I am very groggy on my legs, and without a stick, or even with one, stagger like a drunk and incapable, and cannot go far. Otherwise I can still keep up appearances and write a bit, though I make all sorts of mistakes and blunders, as you may see by my typing; and I forget names so desperately—even Napoleon and Shakespear have become uncertain—that when I write history I have to do it with an encyclopedia at my elbow.

Curiously though, I have developed a talent for business, and am arranging my affairs with a bossy competence that surprises me. They all treat me as a Great Man now: even De Valera passed an Act to legalize my method of municipalizing my Irish estate. I have sold out some of my gilt edged stocks and bought ten-year annuities in separate Canadian offices. I am throwing superfluous money about to some extent; so if you want any let me know.

The war and the atomic bomb have produced a situation which is far beyond the political capacity not only of our new rulers but of mankind. I seriously think that unless the term of the human prime of life can be extended to 300 years, and political careers begin instead of ending at our age, which is biologically possible, we shall be superse[ded] by some superFabian species capable of behaving decently.

I hope you are properly looked after at home. I have been lucky enough to secure a first class housekeeper (Mrs Laden, Scotch) to succeed the Higgses retired.

My last remaining tooth is to be extracted tomorrow.

GBS

This bachelor life with nobody to consult but myself—eat when I like, go to bed when I like, work when I like, order the house and garden as I fancy, and be solitary (or social) all to myself—suits me very well; it actually develops me at 90!

Set against this all the things I should never have done if I had not had to consider Charlotte. Quite a new experience for both of us.

To OTTO KYLLMANN

[C/64]

Ayot St Lawrence. Welwyn
21st November 1945

[Paper shortages, combined with the destruction of the Leighton-Straker storage warehouse, resulted in most of Shaw's Standard Edition volumes being out of print at the end of the war (which Shaw celebrated without ceremony at home). And the need for R. & R. Clark to concentrate on the Oxford University Press *Methuselah* and the Penguin "Shaw Million" (ten titles to be issued in an edition of 100,000 copies each, in celebration of Shaw's ninetieth birthday) resulted in further delay in the reissue of the Standard Edition.]

All our plans are knocked to pieces.

Penguins will issue a million copies of your list in 10 volumes on my 90th birthday (26/7/46); and to this I must give priority, leaving us nothing except the new Standard Geneva-Charles volume; and even that can wait a bit if it must.

This is an atomic bomb; but it will advertize and pay the Standard in the long run.

GBS

To BLANCHE PATCH

Ayot St Lawrence. Welwyn
[H/9]   23rd November 1945

[Incensed by Loewenstein's gradual usurpation of what she saw as her responsibilities and prerogatives, and noting from the cash book how much money Shaw was paying out to him, Blanche Patch had finally been moved to complain that she was underpaid and that Shaw was unappreciative of her services and loyalty. Slapping back at him in Eliza Doolittle fashion she accused him of insincerity and maliciousness. Though she was scornful of all "GBS's triplets—War, Win and Loew," it was Loewenstein who remained her principal bugbear: "I admit," she wrote to Shaw, "that while lacking all the things required from a secretary he possesses the racial knack of knowing how to extract money. In the past 18 months he has had £745 from you in addition to his percentages, payments from newspapers for news of you, and subscriptions from members of the Shaw Society. Not so bad for one who was earning £4 a week when he came to you while I have remained static since 1932 though everything costs almost double what it did then . . ." (S/1).]

My dear Blanche

You have given me a jolt at last. We have been together all these years, during which you have transcribed almost every word I have written; and you have seen nothing in them but a love of teasing: a form of cruelty which I specially abhor and have never practised. To save you from being written off as the stupidest woman on earth I must give you a testimonial.

You are Shawproof; but you are not in the least stupid. That you are sober[,] honest and industrious and have been for countless years in your present post goes without saying. You are intelligent, sensible, self-reliant, kindly, useful, competent, and almost unbelievably even-tempered and self-controlled. You are the least vain and touchy woman

758

in the world. The trouble you have NOT given me, and the help you HAVE given me are immeasurable. And no man knows your value better than I do.

It has been a great advantage to us both that you have been completely unaffected by my doctrine and my philosophy, and held your own against it, unswamped by my personality as the Wardrops and Loewensteins and Shavians have been. But it has had one drawback. You have mistaken my philosophy for mere fun and malice. I am horrified, and beg you to reconsider the malice.

Now let us come down with a crash to your salary, which has nothing to do with your merits. Smee, who has a likeable soft spot in him, started the notion that you are underpaid. He even discussed it with Stanley Clench, hoping that he would remonstrate with me. He did. I went into the question with him. He finally agreed that you are on velvet.

I thought a good deal about it. I could not go on raising your salary for ever. I stopped when you had enough for comfortably ladylike life, with a pension that would leave you rather more after my death. For emergencies and luxuries you always could depend on me for a grant-in-aid. When Charlotte's death and the near prospect of my own created a mass of extra work I took on Loewenstein to do it. He works seven hours a day for less than your modest stipend. Your figures will not stand auditing.

I now intend to relieve you and myself of all the licensing business by handing it over to the Collection Bureau of the Society of Authors: all you will have to do is to enter its settlements twice a year in the cash book. Smee will do the rest of the accountancy. If you are pressed for money you have only to suggest a grant.

Will that satisfy you? If not, what will?

G. Bernard Shaw

As L. opens my letters you may like marking some of them Personal.

To BLANCHE PATCH

Ayot St Lawrence. Welwyn
[A/3]   30th November 1945

[Arrangements were made for the Society of Authors to assume the tasks on commission of licensing and collecting royalties for Shaw's theatrical and publishing business at the start of the new year. Startled by the promptitude

759

with which more of her erstwhile responsibilities and prerogatives had been stripped from her, Patch desperately attempted to delay the unexpected transition. Shaw had assumed the cost of education of Christopher Winsten.]

My dear Blanche

I dare not wait six months: my days are too narrowly numbered. The Society of Authors must take over on the 1st January; and you will be kept busy enough during the ensuing six months knocking the change into the heads of the theatre people and sending on their letters. I have redrafted the sheet of terms and ordered a new printed postcard accordingly.

As F.E.L. buys things for me; and I pay him for them by cheque (I have made him open an a/c at New Oxford St) you must not conclude that he gets a lot of money from me for nothing. What is for himself he earns quite hard. The sums I have invested in John Wardrop and Christopher Winsten are far beyond any that F.E.L. with his daughter to educate and his two rents to pay, has got out of me. So far, I should be poorer without him.

G.B.S.

To J. J. McCALL

[C/91; X/426]

Ayot St Lawrence. Welwyn
4th December 1945

[J.J. McCall was a journalist on the staff of the Glasgow *Sunday Mail*. Shaw's principal visits to Scotland occurred in 1924 (13th July to mid-September) and 1925 (17th July to early October). Flora MacDonald (1722–90) was a Hebrides farm girl adopted by gentry who aided Prince Charles Stuart, the Young Pretender, to escape after the Battle of Culloden (1746).]

Except for a few weeks at Pitlochrie and Lough Erne (where a whale rose to blow within a yard of me when I was swimming in it) I have traversed Scotland only as a motoring tourist from the border to utter Shetland. Of Glasgow I had a Saturday night: the entire male population was drunk to the last man.

I first heard the Glesca dialect from a lady in a railway carriage, richly dressed in clothes that might have been Flora MacDonald's. It fascinated me.

William Morris was fond of saying "The Irish have all the virtues; and I dont like them. The Scots have all the vices; and I like them." (He said Scotch, not Scots; but I must not forget my manners.) And that is exactly how I feel. I am very susceptible to bonnie Scotland, and set great store by my Scots-Stratford upon Avon descent from Shaig, young son of Macduff, who was of no woman born, and delighted my boyhood by his tremendous stage fights with Barry Sullivan, last of the great English speaking tragedians.

G.B.S.

To R. J. HAYES

Ayot St Lawrence. Welwyn
[H/48; X/339]   6th December 1945

[Richard J.Hayes (1902–76), librarian and bibliographer, was Director of the National Library of Ireland 1940–67. "Dear Bernard Shaw," he wrote, "I can think of no better place than the National Library of Ireland for your manuscripts and first editions. Can you?" (Henry Boylan, *A Dictionary of Irish Biography*, 1978).]

Dear Sir

Your invitation as national librarian is in the nature of a command.

I have only a few early MSS, dating from my beginning as a novelist, too poor to afford a typewriter. I am having them tidied up and bound; and when this is finished you shall have them.

Then came my period as a journalist–critic with a typewriter, writing weekly feuilletons which the printer did not return with the proofs.

Finally I became a man of means, a playwright with a secretary who could decipher Pitman's phonography if written as I wrote it, without too many reporter's contractions. Since then my works have been drafted in that script and the drafts systematically destroyed though I kept the draft of Saint Joan because it bore some notes of the various dates and places of its composition. It is now in the library of the British Museum, of which I made daily use for many years before I married at the age of forty.

Have you any agency in London to which I can consign the novels or shall I send them to you direct by parcel post separately, as they are too heavy to go together by that service.

faithfully
G.Bernard Shaw

PS   I do not collect first editions: I destroy them to suppress their blunders. Other people collect my letters. Keeping them is a mischievous habit. Dickens burnt all his at Gadshill very wisely.

To FLORYAN SOBIENIOWSKI

Ayot St Lawrence. Welwyn
[S/1]   25th December 1945

[To enable him to renew his literary contacts Sobieniowski had been given temporary employment in the London embassy of the Polish People's Republic, which had supplanted the Polish Government-in-Exile. Moss Bros., then as now, was a popular men's clothing emporium.]

Dear Sobieniowski

I was not joking about the Embassy. You MUST dress well or you will lose the job. Go at once to Moss Bros., 20 King St., Covent Garden, and tell them frankly that you are hard up, and can they make you look respectable for five or six pounds. They are accustomed to do that sort of thing for actors, being in the theatre district. They may have a readymade suit, or even a secondhand one in good condition, that would fit you. Anyhow, get rigged out like a diplomatist at once; and do not spend a penny of the enclosed cheque on anything else until you look like an attache or even like an ambassador. . . .

On the first of January I hand over my business to the Society of Authors here. It will collect my royalties from Szyfman, and keep you out of temptation.

You must take my age seriously. There is practically no difference between 35 and 60; but between 65 and 90 the difference is enormous; and you must reckon accordingly and not try to tomfool me with compliments.

G. Bernard Shaw

To WILLIAM ROWBOTTOM

Ayot St Lawrence. Welwyn
[H.u/9; X/152]   5th January 1946

[William Rowbottom wrote from Leeds on 2nd January that he was "a soul not only in torment but so angry and desperate that it is using every ounce of energy in me to fight off the urge to kill my children and myself. I did not decide that that was the best way to deal with the situation in a moment of unbridled anger . . . I have given the whole matter all the calm thought possible long enough ago and all the time struggling desperately to go the other way—to find a satisfactory way out. But the whole thing is beating me. I never did care for sloppy sentiment and useless pity—it is sense I want— wisdom—that is why I write to you. I do not think there is a saner man in the country than you—nay—there cannot be anywhere.

"So I do not appeal to you as a kind, soft-hearted and soft-headed man—but as a fellow human who is eminently sane knowledgeable and clever. . . . [W]ill you consider the case and advise me? Will you be the one man out of about forty seven million to help me to avoid committing a terrible crime—as the vast majority would call it?" (A/9).

Thomas John Barnardo (1845–1905), Irish-born surgeon and philanthropist, established a number of orphanages for waifs from the streets, whom he educated to prepare them for good citizenship. More than 55,000 children were aided by his efforts in his lifetime. Dr Barnardo's Day Care Centres now flourish.]

Dear Sir

Killing yourself is a matter for your own judgment. Nobody can prevent you; and if you are convinced that you are not worth your salt, and an intolerable nuisance to yourself and everyone else, it is a solution to be considered. But you can always put it off to tomorrow on the chance of something interesting turning up that evening.

As to killing the children, it would be the act of a madman or a murderer. They may have the happiest dispositions. They may be born to greatness: the children of good-for-nothings (Beethoven and Isaac Newton for instance) have grown up to be geniuses. My father was a failure: only his latest years (he was longlived) could be called happy. I am conceited enough to believe that it is just as well that he did not kill me in a fit of low spirits. Instead, he relieved himself by drinking occasionally, though it only made him worse.

Have you consulted a psychologist? Soul torment is not a philosophy: it is a disease, and usually cures itself after a time. A quick medicine for it may be discovered tomorrow. Read the autobiography of John Stuart Mill, who gives a graphic description of a long fit of depression which passed away completely and was the prelude to an illustrious future.

Life, happy or unhappy, successful or unsuccessful, is extraordinarily interesting; and children left destitute by their parents do not die of starvation but are taken care of in Barnardo homes or public institutions or adopted. These are sometimes more wisely and kindly treated than they would have been at home, especially if their parents are morbid patients who think it would be kind to kill them.

In short, dear sir, dont be a damned fool. Get interested in something.

faithfully
[G. Bernard Shaw]

To ROBERT HO TUNG

[H/1]

Ayot St Lawrence. Welwyn
15th January 1946

[Sir Robert Ho Tung (1862–1956) was a wealthy Hong Kong industrialist and philanthropist, whose residence "Idlewild" the Shaws had visited on 13th February 1933 during their world tour in the *Empress of Britain*. Prompted by Sir Robert's letter, Shaw described the visit in an essay "Aesthetic Science," published later in the year in *Design '46*:

"He took me upstairs into what in England would have been a drawing room. It was a radiant miniature temple with an altar of Chinese vermilion and gold, and cushioned divan seats round the walls for the worshippers. Everything was in such perfect Chinese taste that to sit there and look was a quiet delight. A robed priest and his acolyte stole in and went through a service. When it was over I told Sir Robert that I had found it extraordinarily soothing and happy though I had not understood a word of it. 'Neither have I,' he said, 'but it soothes me too.' It was part of the art of life for Chinaman and Irishman alike, and was purely esthetic." The temple was incorporated into Act III of *Buoyant Billions*.]

My dear Sir Robert

I am overjoyed to learn from your letter that you are alive and well in the house where you so hospitably entertained me when I passed through Hong Kong in my voyage round the world. My late wife ... never forgot the caress of welcome she received from lady Ho-Tung, and declared that only a Chinese hostess was capable of such affectionate courtesy in all the world. We both regarded you as quite special friends and were anxious about you during the troubles.

I have a copy of the photograph and will have a copy made and sent to you.

I am now very old (90) and still too busy to think of the past, but when I do, nothing soothes me more than the recollection of that service in your celestial private temple and the afternoon we spent together.

G. Bernard Shaw

To P. J. HERNON

[H/131; W/427]

Ayot St Lawrence. Welwyn
10th February 1946

[P. J. Hernon (1889–1973), City Manager and Town Clerk for the Corporation of Dublin, wrote to Shaw on 7th February, by direction of the City Council, to inform him a resolution had been adopted at the monthly meeting on the 4th "That the Lord Mayor, Aldermen and Councillors of the City of Dublin request Mr. George Bernard Shaw to honour the citizens by accepting an invitation to become a Freeman of his native City" (X/427).]

Dear Dr Hernon

Your welcome letter dated the 7th has just reached me.

I shall be gratefully proud to become an honorary freeman of my native city.

I have hitherto evaded credentials from foreign sources: Dublin alone has the right to affirm that in spite of my incessantly controversial past and present I have not disgraced her.

I am too old to be present; but there is so little of me left that it will hardly be missed. Better leave my ancient vigor to the imagination of young Ireland and the photographers of fifty years ago.

faithfully
G. Bernard Shaw

To JOHN W. DULANTY

[Ayot St Lawrence. Welwyn]
[Undated: April 1946]

[F.u/4]

[John Whelan Dulanty (1883–1955), High Commissioner for Eire 1930–50, became first ambassador of the Republic of Ireland in Britain in July 1946. Shaw's gift to the National Library of Ireland included bound copies of the surviving manuscripts of four of his five novels written between 1879 and 1883 (*Immaturity, The Irrational Knot, Cashel Byron's Profession,* and *An Unsocial Socialist*), plus the fragment of a sixth novel commenced in 1887 but rapidly abandoned.]

Dear Mr Dulanty

The National Library of Eire has put in a claim for my manuscripts. All I had kept were over 60 years old and in unpresentable condition. Every page had to be detached, cleaned, mounted on expensive paper and bound by an eminent specialist at a cost of £120, the result being a pile of volumes each weighing about 8 lbs, leaving me faced with the problem of how to transport them to that most inaccessible of countries, Eire.

The National Library instructed me to dump them on you; and I now await your consent and instructions. I cannot pack the books (they would be unmanageable by me in the parcel) but I can put them into my car and deliver them at any address you may indicate within reach.

Besides the books I have a portrait by a second-rate contemporary and teacher of Reynolds of an entirely undistinguished ancestor of mine, which I have promised to send to the head quarter of the Shaw clan at the seat of Sir Robert Shaw, Bushy Park, Co. Dublin, to add to the family picture gallery there. The transport authorities seem to transport nothing but merchandise and ask a hundred unanswerable questions about it. Is there any short cut available?

I blush to bother you with all this. It cannot claim any priority if you are very busy.

I have just given all my Irish property to the towns in which it is situate. To make this operation practicable I had to have a new Act, devised by myself, passed through the Dail. I hope another will not be necessary to transfer the books.

> faithfully
> [G. Bernard Shaw]

To R. J. HAYES

[A/48; X/339]
Ayot St Lawrence. Welwyn
23rd April 1946

[Douglas Cockerell (1870–1945), brother of Sydney Cockerell, was a noted book binder, designer, teacher, and manufacturer of binding materials. Shaw's insistence, here and elsewhere, that his post-1885 manuscripts had not survived was either an extraordinary case of forgetfulness or a colossal, self-protective lie. Shorthand or holograph drafts and/or revised and corrected typescripts survive for all but seven of the fifty-one plays in Shaw's canon, plus those of many of his non-dramatic works.]

Dear Sir

I have this day handed eleven huge volumes of my early manuscripts to the High Commissioner Mr J. W. Dulanty, who has most kindly undertaken to place them in your hands.

I must apologize for their condition. They were so dirty that it was necessary to clean every page separately and mount it on durable drawing paper. This was very thoroughly done by the late Douglas Cockerell, the prince of English bookbinders; but when the renovated and fortified pages were bound up, the result was four trumpery novels in volumes as pretentious looking as the most priceless codices, and requiring ten times as much shelf space.

All I can say is that it will be quite easy to detach the leaves from their mounting and pack them in a box befitting their merits, leaving the Cockerell volumes blank for worthier uses.

The reason there is nothing later than 1885 is that after that I wrote in Pitman's phonography and destroyed the original Pitman drafts and typescripts and proofs when they had served their turn.

yours very apologetically
G. Bernard Shaw

To JAMES M. BARNES

Ayot St Lawrence. Welwyn
3rd May 1946

[C/1]

[James M. Barnes (b. 1907), a young grocer in the local co-op at Blackburn (he later became the owner of four licensed betting shops), was a theatre enthusiast so enamoured of the Theatre Workshop (headed by an obscure producer named Joan Littlewood) struggling for survival in a converted church in his town that he appealed to Shaw to aid the starving but determined performers.]

Bless your innocence, these catastrophes occur every week in the theatre. Actors alternate opulence with insolvent destitution as plays succeed or fail all their lives.

My business is to take and make money out of theatres: never to put money into them. If I broke that rule I should be a pauper.

Your business (or pleasure) is to pay for your seat. Go beyond that and you will die in the workhouse.

You have done more than you can afford. Well, do no more. Theatre business is a gamble at enormous odds. If you meddle, your two daughters will have to support you as charwomen. The Workshop people will pull through somehow: they are used to it.

G. Bernard Shaw

To SYDNEY C. COCKERELL

[Ayot St Lawrence. Welwyn]
[Undated: assigned to 3rd May 1946]

[C/4; X/277]

[Sydney Cockerell, a persistent and methodical man, was again sounding Shaw out on funerary possibilities.]

My ghost would be bored by big buildings like the Abbey or St Patrick's Cathedral (next Swift) in Dublin. I need seasons: trees and birds. What I should really like would be a beautifully designed urn on a little pedestal in the garden here in Ayot with Charlotte and myself inside listening for the first cuckoo and the nightingale and scenting the big cherry tree.

Can you suggest a sculptor? Clare Winsten, a very gifted one, lives here. Do you know her?

G.B.S.

To DON BATEMAN

[W(C)/428]

[Ayot St Lawrence. Welwyn]
[Undated: *c.* 1st May 1946]

[Don Bateman, author and journalist, had asked for a statement on the first anniversary of V-E Day, the day on which in 1945 the surrender of Germany was officially announced, ending the war in Europe. Shaw's pronouncements on the atom bomb first appeared in the *Sunday Express*, 12th August 1945 (and a week later in the *New York Journal-American* as "Atom Bomb Too Deadly for War, Asserts Shaw"), and in a letter in *The Times* on 20th August.]

I shall take no part in the celebrations. Victory is very far from being won yet; I am deadly tired of the war. The atomic bomb scare, which produced the second armistice, is nothing to be proud of! However, any excuse is good enough for a spree; so let those rejoice who feel like it. Sprees are not in my line.

G. Bernard Shaw

To E. NORMAN MEREDITH

[H/73]

[Ayot St Lawrence. Welwyn]
16th May 1946

[E. Norman Meredith was the husband of Shaw's half-cousin Georgina (Rogers), who had written to Shaw from Dublin to ask him to underwrite the purchase of a house for herself and her husband by diverting the income from the family properties in Ireland, unaware that he had already disposed of them. "I note," Shaw responded to her on 16th May, "that you consider that to ask anyone for money whenever you are in want of it is a base action. As this is exactly what you did, Gurly like, when you had to find a new house, I am amused. I cannot afford to buy you a house . . . Don't be offended at my ways: you will soon get used to them; and we will both remain reasonably affectionate half cousins" [H/73]. Under his will Shaw left a small annuity each to Mrs Meredith and her brother Eames Rogers.]

Dear N-M

... As to the immediate money question, your wife's notion that it can be solved by drawing on the Carlow property (she is a thorough-bred Gurly in this respect) is a delusion. That property, which has wasted and blighted and blasted so many lives, is no longer mine: it belongs now to the towns of Carlow and Wexford; and not a penny will ever come again into my pocket or the Gurly pocket or that of any private person who does not earn it.

Now I cannot give away whole properties and keep on their families as well. I had to support Georgina's mother and all her aunts except well-to-do Mrs Hamilton all their lives. Now that they are gone and the property gone too I must close the account and retire absolutely from my appointment as Earthly Providence of the Gurly clan.

However, this need not interrupt our friendly relations. If you need a reasonable lift over a difficult moment I daresay I can manage it for you. How much will see you through?

G. Bernard Shaw

To WILLIAM MAXWELL

4 Whitehall Court. SW1

[H(signed by Patch)/3]   31st May 1946

[The Ninetieth Birthday exhibition, organised by Douglas Leighton, ran from 26th July to 24th August, at the National Book League in Albemarle Street, London. The honours Shaw spurned were the Companion of Honour and the Order of Merit. Ella was Maxwell's spinster daughter and only sur-viving child (after the death of his son in the first world war). Blanche Patch transcribed the letter in London from shorthand sent from Ayot, added her own postscript, and signed it for Shaw.]

My dear William

Do not succumb to the Shaw influence. The 26th July has not the smallest importance beyond that of any other day in the year. I shall spend the day as usual in solitary work and meditation. Nothing will induce me to take part in any of the celebrations with which I am threatened. I do not think the Book League should associate the open-ing of the Albemarle Street house with the name of any individual author, especially such a very controversial one as I.

I have asked the Government, not for a title or a C.H. or O.M., but for an Act which the Parliament of Eire has already passed for me. Blanche can tell you about it.

I have refused to receive a delegation from Dublin to present me ceremonially with the honorary freedom of the city with its crowd of photographers and journalists and speechmakers. If I yield an inch I shall simply be killed with kindness, well meant but lethal. Even you and Ella I would rather see on another day. Why spoil the uniqueness of your visit on my 80th?

pp G. Bernard Shaw
Blanche Patch.
Secretary

PS by B. P. This letter arrived this morning with the following foot-note. "You had better locate him and hand him this letter, signed per pro. Tell everybody to the same effect. I can stand no more of this foolish fuss."

I must explain to him that the Book League rooms have already been open to other exhibitions, and that the Prime Minister was simply to open the Shaw exhibits. In all probability G. B. S. will be in town on the 26th, not because of the birthday, but because of Ayot servants' holidays.

To ANNETTE CURNEN BURGESS

Ayot St Lawrence. Welwyn
6th June 1946

[C/38]

[Several members of the board of directors of the Academy of Political Science, seated on stage behind Shaw during his April 1933 lecture at the Metropolitan Opera House, New York, were financial tycoons. Shaw, however, was not introduced to any of them until the reception later that night at the home of his host Thomas Lamont. Annette Curnen Burgess was an American political worker.]

You must never think of me as speaking or writing with my tongue in my cheek. I did not get my reputation by playing the fool, though I may clown a bit occasionally for fun, as laughter is good for me and for everybody. But I abhor insincerity, and believe what I preach. When I spoke at the Opera House I had no suspicion that the men I was criticising were all sitting on the stage behind me. I found it out at supper with them afterwards. What they got from me was the straight-forward truth as far as I could ascertain it. The truth is sometimes the funniest joke in the world until it is thoroughly found out.

G. Bernard Shaw

To BERMAN-FISCHER VERLAG

[Ayot St Lawrence. Welwyn]
[S.u/5]   14th June 1946 (by registered letter)

[Gottfried Berman-Fischer (b. 1897), publisher (based in Stockholm) and author, was the son-in-law of Shaw's German publisher Samuel Fischer. A copy of Shaw's letter was sent to Siegfried Trebitsch.]

Dear Sirs

In the course of certain changes in my publishing arrangements which the war has imposed on me I have been informed that your firm claims to represent that of S. Fischer late of Berlin, which for many years acted as my German publishers and agents. I cannot admit this claim. The S. Fischer firm was liquidated as non-Aryan under the Nazi regime and has not been revived. Its licence to publish my works, if there exists any documentary evidence of it, was not negotiable nor transferable: it was peculiar to Mr S. Fischer, who was personally known to me. The fact that Dr Berman married his daughter and conducts a publishing business in Stockholm gives him no legal claim to succeed to the business of his father-in-law. No sane author would place his German business in the hands of a Stockholm publisher.

If I have been and remain a party to any transactions with the new and independent Berman firm I must now give you notice that any publishing licence granted to it is hereby withdrawn by me as from the earliest moment at which such withdrawal is legally possible.

You must not regard this as an unfriendly act on my part nor as reflecting in any way on your competence and standing as publishers. It is imposed on me by political conditions which have obliged my translator Siegfried Trebitsch, in Switzerland, to conclude agreements with Swiss publishers and agents who require assurances that you are no longer in the field.

I have no recollection of ever signing an agreement with S. Fischer. I certainly never assigned my copyrights. I have never assigned a copyright nor granted a licence without power to withdraw it at the end of five years or at any time thereafter at six months notice. Herr Trebitsch never had power to commit me further than this. But, I repeat, I do not believe there was any written agreement.

faithfully
[G. Bernard Shaw]

To PATRICK O'REILLY

Ayot St Lawrence. Welwyn

[W(C)/429]   [Undated: July 1946]

[Patrick O'Reilly, a Dublin dustman, sent Shaw a ninetieth-birthday gift on behalf of the fifty-six members of the Bernard Shaw Branch (Dublin) of the Irish Labour Party, of which O'Reilly was chairman.]

A golden shamrock!

What a charming gift!

It is on my watch chain, and shall remain there until I myself drop off it.

G. Bernard Shaw

To G. E. EVANS

Ayot St Lawrence. Welwyn

[B/1; W/430]   21st July 1946

[George Eyre Evans, a bookseller (The Celtic Book Co.) in Cardiff's Queen Street Arcade, was author and editor of several works on local history and genealogy.]

Try all the creeds, and believe as much of them as suits you. If you find the rituals agreeable, you can attend them and pay your way by putting sixpence (or what you can afford) into the collection. Do not expect any of them to explain the universe to you. None of them can. But all of them may be good for your soul, more or less.

I do not myself belong to any denomination but I find a cathedral a good place for contemplation. I can even endure the service if the music is good and the preacher has something to say and says it well.

G. B. S.

To JOHN MASEFIELD

Ayot St Lawrence. Welwyn

[C/3]   24th July 1946

I shall not come to the opening of the N.B.L. exhibition. My official excuse is that I have to reserve that afternoon for my signature to the roll of honorary freemen of the City of Dublin.

But anyhow my presence would embarrass Inge and [your]self, to say nothing of the other speakers—if any.

I may drop in when it is all over; but I am doubtful as to how much I shall be able to get about in London. I'm very groggy on my legs.

G.B.S.

Holograph poem just arrived: a treasure.

[The Poet Laureate John Masefield, president of the Society of Authors, who presided at the formal opening of the National Book League exhibition on 26th July, read a verse tribute written for the occasion (it was published the next day in *The Times*), and told the distinguished assemblage, "We are met to-day to do honour to one of the greatest living brains, one of the clearest minds, now living in this planet." The exhibition was opened, in the absence of the Labour prime minister Clement Attlee (1883–1967), by the Very Rev. Dr. W. R. Inge. Despite Shaw's "official excuse," he made a surprise appearance at the exhibition in the late afternoon, mingling sociably with Sydney Cockerell, Gabriel Pascal, William Maxwell, Otto Kyllmann, and other friends, amid cameras and flashlights, for three-quarters of an hour. During its month's run the exhibition attracted over six thousand visitors.]

To P. J. HERNON

[S/131; X/431]

Ayot St Lawrence. Welwyn
25th July 1946

[The Scroll of Freedom, presented to Shaw at Whitehall Court the next afternoon, was illuminated by Alice O'Rourke. The Roll of Freedom was conveyed for Shaw's signature by Hernon and the clerk of the Dublin Council, T. J. O'Neill. According to a report in *The Times* on 27th July, Shaw "was shown an old parchment roll which bore the signatures of his father and grandfather, both of whom were freemen of Dublin."]

Dear Dr Hernon

Thanks for your letter of the 23rd. As nothing is to happen tomorrow, and the birthday will be stale or forgotten in August, I cannot believe that it will be a sufficient excuse for an event so important as a visit of the Lord Mayor to London.

Besides, there seems to be some confusion about the legal position. I take it that there is no further question of conferring the Freedom on me. That has already been done by resolution of the whole Corporation with my grateful consent. I am, therefore, already an Honorary Freeman; and the signing of the Roll is only an official form. Suppose I die today or tomorrow (I am actuarily dead already), I cannot sign the Roll; but that will not cancel the decision of the Corporation.

The obtaining of the signature is clearly your function. It is not an act of the Corporation, but simply a registration. There has been some confusion about this. It gives the Corporation the clear choice between quietly sending you to get the roll signed, and making a State affair of it with all possible publicity. In my opinion this is more than the delayed occasion will bear. It has already been made the most of.

I am not raising difficulties; I am pointing out those that might arise, and clarifying the situation as an old hand in municipal affairs.

And at my age (90), unable to travel, and quite unprovided with the means of entertaining distinguished guests and important delegations, I can undertake nothing beyond appearing for an hour or so, probably in a bath chair, if at all.

G. Bernard Shaw

To EDWARD J. DENT

[A/1]

Ayot St Lawrence. Welwyn
26th July 1946

[The musicologist Edward J. Dent (1876–1957) had contributed the chapter "Corno di Bassetto" to the just-published *G.B.S. 90*, in which he said of the soprano Therese Tietjens (1831–77), "She was typically German in her personal ungainliness, but still more so in her tragic sincerity." Shaw had heard her sing ("in bad voice") in *Messiah* at the Albert Hall on 18th December 1876, as reported in his unsigned notice in *The Hornet* nine days later. Tietjens until her death was reigning soprano of all of London's principal opera houses.]

Dear Edward Dent

You have got back to my date surprisingly well.

Page 125 reminds me of Tietjens. She was adored by those who, like my mother, heard her when she was young and slim.

But by the time I heard her, she was enormously fat: 19 stone at least I should say; and her voice, though it still had some magnificent middle notes left, was stale. She damaged it badly by attempting Donizetti's Favorita, and forcing her chest voice up to

Yet she warned my mother earlier to beware of this before all things.

Her size was the effect of colossal meals. I was the first critic to take

774

exception to this, and insist that a singer should train like a jockey or a pugilist, and Isoldas of 80 be banished from opera. It was then considered the proper age for a prima donna.

G. Bernard Shaw

To F. E. LOEWENSTEIN

[E.u/3; W/289]

[Ayot St Lawrence. Welwyn]
[Undated: *c.* 29th July 1946]

[There were more than two hundred pieces of mail awaiting Shaw's arrival at Whitehall Court on his birthday, and hundreds more at Ayot on his return, including eighty pieces that arrived on the 29th. Most of these were never seen by Shaw, having been examined and destroyed, under his order, by Loewenstein and Stephen Winsten.]

F.E.L.
Throw away all the birthday ones.
They make me sick.

To LAURENTIA McLACHLAN

[A/98; X/256.e]

[Ayot St Lawrence. Welwyn]
30th July 1946

[Lady Cockerell was the former Kate Kingsford.]

Dear Sister Laurentia

For the past week I have had over 100 congratulations a day. But for two strong men who have worked hard tearing them up for me I should never have been 90. Saving your reverence I do not give a damn for congratulations. But prayers touch me and help me. It is good for me to be touched. Stanbrook prayers must have some special charm; for I never forget them.

On the birthday I had a word with Cockerell. He is beginning to look a bit oldish; but he can walk without a stick, which I dare not attempt, as the police would charge me with being drunk and incapable. However, I am quite happy in my garden, where the weeks race past like minutes: their speed is incredible. I can still write a bit, and have plenty to do.

Lady Cockerell keeps her good looks magically. Many many years ago she went to bed; found it comfortable; and has lain there in a sort of glory ever since. I have never pretended to believe that there is or ever was anything the matter with her.

I wonder ought we two to have done the same!

G. Bernard Shaw

To WINSTON S. CHURCHILL

[F.u/4; X/289.e]

[Ayot St Lawrence. Welwyn]
[Undated: August 1946]

[Churchill, defeated by the Labour Party in July 1945, was now leader of the Opposition. Cobdenism was a philosophy of free trade first promulgated by Richard Cobden (1804–65), economist and politician, who believed in minimum government domestically and minimum foreign intervention. Henry Broadhurst (1840–1911), pioneer labour leader and Liberal M.P., grew disenchanted with trade union development in his late years. Walter M. Citrine (1887–1983), later first Baron Citrine of Wembley, was general secretary of the Trades Union Congress 1926–46. John Burns (1858–1943), a Progressive who was M.P. for Battersea, 1892–1918, refused to join the Independent Labour Party. He was the first workman to achieve cabinet rank; Shaw immortalised him as the cabinet minister Boanerges in *The Apple Cart*.

The National Health Service Bill was enacted in November 1946. It had its third reading in the House of Commons on 26th July and its first in the Lords on 29th July. The Rt. Hon. (Col.) Walter Elliot (1888–1958), Conservative M.P., represented the Kelvingrove Division of Glasgow from 1924 until his defeat by Labour in the 1945 general election. William Francis Hare (b. 1906), fifth Earl of Listowel, was Labour Party whip in the House of Lords; he served as Postmaster-General 1945–47.

The shorthand draft may be incomplete.]

My dear Churchill

I was very glad to receive your friendly birthday message. This in your case is a cordially personal feeling, but it had also pleased me as the only other message I had from anyone of your political eminence was from Eamon de Valera!

No man of action has any chance of being a British prime minister until a war frightens the electorate out of its chronic dread of government interference and preference for guaranteed fanéants like Ramsay and Baldwin and their like. But the worst of military glory is that the electorate, understanding only the glory and the fear of defeat, forces their leader either to keep feeding them with it and go from Austerlitz to Moscow, Leipsic, Waterloo and St Helena, or, like the first Churchill and Wellington, chuck soldiering and become political nobodies like Lloyd George.

The alternative is to keep the electorate excited by programs so popular that the Blimps and reactionaries in general cannot withstand them.

In short, Disraeli's invention and your father's creed: Tory Democracy; for since Socialism killed Laissez-faire Liberalism (Cobdenism) stone dead, the Socialists have failed to carry out the Fabian program worked out for them by Webb and Shaw, partly through incompetence (Ramsay's Cabinet could not meet because none of the members were on speaking terms, and [Philip] Snowden [Chancellor of the Exchequer] hated Ramsay above all men) and partly because the Socialists, having a program but no money[,] had put themselves under the thumb of the Trade Unions, which had money but no program except to exploit the Cobdenist system exactly as the financiers and employers were doing, believing that Trade Unionism could beat them at that game. The effective Trade Union leaders, from Broadhurst to Citrine, have been and still are, thoroughgoing Tories (Broadhurst hated and dreaded John Burns); and no collaboration was possible between Citrine and Maxton. Observe that these toughest of Tories are not democrats: the trade union secretary is the most absolute dictator left on earth; and the card vote reduces the T.U.C. [Trades Union Congress] to utter absurdity democratically.

What, then, is the situation you are confronted with. Socialism has become Fabianism [since] Lenin announced his N.E.P. [New Economic Policy] quarter of a century ago. The N.E.P.[,] forced [on] the Bolsheviks by bitter experience[,] proved that I was right when I warned the world of young Socialists [against] their notion of Capitalism in full swing on Monday, revolution on Tuesday, and Communism in full swing on Wednesday, and established Webb's Inevitability of Gradualness as the only alternative to civil war. There is no longer any issue between Cobdenism and Socialism: Cobden as a world architect is

777

dead as a door nail; but he will come to life again when Socialism has gone far enough to raise the question of individual freedom for leisure. Meanwhile the Communist basis of all possible civilization must be accepted by all parties and leaders who know what they are talking about. From the police station in the next street to the Cabinet, the Treasury, the War Office, the Admiralty, the Air Force, the Bench and the Crown, the rock foundation of all possible systems is pure Communism; and the man who questions this knowingly is no gentleman. You have been a soldier and a Commissar all your life: your books will belong to the Commonwealth 50 years after your death, like mine. The controversies of the future will be between the people who want to work 12 hours a day and be free for private enterprise or private leisure at 40 and those who want to work 4 hours a day in a five-day week, and retire at 70. (All the would-be artists and philosophers will grow out of this party).

I do not suggest that you should revive the cry of Tory Democracy. But what about Democratic Aristocracy, fiercely critical, not of Communism, but of Labor Legislation. The National Health Act imposes crude trade unionism on the doctors, who will impose the forty inoculations now imposed on soldiers and travellers on everybody, at half a crown a dose. Your fellows had a first-rate chance of taking a lead from Colonel Elliott, and shewing up the Labor Party as a trade-union dictatorship, and enlisting the dread of doctors that is now rife in all classes. On rationing they had better have proposed the communization of bread and milk than come out second to the Labor backbenchers in criticism. Listowel and Dalton on the Budget should have been attacked fiercely for not giving us back the penny letter and ha'penny postcard instead of overcharging us scandalously for postage and giving the plunder to lighten the surtax. There is no end to the games that Domestic [error for Democratic] Aristocracy might play to get in front as the popular party and keep there.

You have never been a real Tory: a foundation of democracy and a very considerable dash of the author and artist and the training of the soldier has made you a phenomenon that the Blimps and Philistines and Stick-in-the-Muds have never understood and always dreaded.

[G. Bernard Shaw]

To LUCY PHILLIMORE

[C/3]

Ayot St Lawrence. Welwyn
30th September 1946

My dear Lion

On Monday the 7th I come up to Whitehall Court for at least a week. On Wednesday the 9th, at 2.30, the St Pancras Borough Council holds a grand meeting to make me its first honorary Freeman. They ought to invite you, and even to make you their first honorary Freewoman.

Anyhow note that I shall be in reach for that week. We must meet.

G.B.S.

To PETER WATTS

[H/99]

Ayot St Lawrence. Welwyn
3rd October 1946

[Peter Michael Watts (1900–72), former Old Vic stage manager, was from 1941 a B.B.C. producer. *Man and Superman* was broadcast on the Third Programme on 1st October and repeated the following night. Act III ("Don Juan in Hell") was re-broadcast on 7th October; the play *sans* Act III was repeated on 1st November. Denis Johnston (1901–84), Irish dramatist and former managing director of the Dublin Gate Theatre, joined the B.B.C. in 1936.]

Dear Mr Watts

What has become of the music in the hell scene of Man & Superman? It is needed as a blessed relief to the cackle as well as for its proper effect. There was nothing on Monday but a faint moaning, probably an interference from another wave length.

If you cannot add it to the record you must get the theatre orchestra to stand by. At the entrance of the statue the two first chords of the overture to Don Giovanni must crash out fortissimo in the broadest measure. When the devil appears the opening staves of Le Veau d'Or, the song of Mephistopheles from Gounod's Faust, rattles out. At the end, when Ana cries "A father for the Superman" the band bursts out with "unto us a child is born" from Handel's Messiah, and makes a resounding and triumphant finish.

These passages are readymade without any alteration; but the music to the change from the Sierra requires arrangement.

The reading of my stage directions at full length is damnably stupid.

779

They are mostly directions to the scenepainter, to the producer, to the actor making-up and dressing: promptbook stuff that has nothing to do with the audience and is an intolerable interruption, intrusion, and distraction in a performance. Only at the beginnings of the acts are their descriptive passages needed; and even then they should be drastically cut. I have not time to do the cutting myself; but you can get Denis Johnston to go through them and reduce them to the barest and quickest indication of entrances and exits, and, above all, not to speak them as if they were part of the play, but to interpolate them sharply and authoritatively so as to make it clear that he is an announcer, not a character in the drama.

Your credit as a producer is bound up with these changes, damn you.

The play is too long unless played as a matinée in the afternoon and finished after the second interval after dinner. Otherwise it is best as it was planned, on separate days with the hell scene all by itself.

Do not treat my printed text with blindly superstitious reverence. It must always be adapted intelligently to the studio, the screen, the stage, or whatever the physical conditions of performance may be.

G. Bernard Shaw

To CLARE WINSTEN

[C/9]

Ayot St Lawrence. Welwyn
6th October 1946

Dear Mrs Winsten

It having been agreed between us to decorate the dell in my garden with a statue of Joan of Arc designed and modelled by you and now in process of manufacture, the cost of material and casting in bronze being meanwhile at my expense, I enclose my cheque for £350, being my second contribution to such cost, and at your disposal until the work is completed to your satisfaction.

G. Bernard Shaw

To CHARLES LATHAM

[E/125]
[4 Whitehall Court SW 1]
[Undated: *c*. 9th October 1946]

[Charles Latham (1888–1970), first Baron Latham of Hendon, a chartered accountant and Labourite, was leader of the London County Council 1940–47. Shaw's note is written at the foot of a copy of the agenda paper that admitted the bearer to a special meeting of the Council of the Metropolitan Borough of St Pancras, on 9th October, to bestow upon Shaw the Honorary Freedom of the Borough "in recognition and appreciation of his eminent services to local government whilst serving as a member of the St. Pancras Vestry and the St. Pancras Borough Council from February, 1897, until November, 1903, and in manifestation of the very high regard and esteem in which he is held by the citizens of the Borough for his valued and learned contributions to intellectual thought, and philosophy, literature, and the cultural arts, in the advancement of which he has attained eminence, distinction and world-wide fame of the highest order."

An unfortunate tumble and injury to his leg, just before the ceremony, however, resulted in a cancellation of his appearance. Instead, he made an acceptance speech from his bed, which was relayed to the meeting from Whitehall Court by the B.B.C.]

Dear Lord Latham

I wasnt there; but the mike spoke for me.

G. Bernard Shaw

To THE INFORMATION MINISTER

[F.u/4]
[Ayot St Lawrence. Welwyn]
25th October 1946

[There was no Ministry of Information in October 1946, it having been succeeded on 1st April by a newly created Central Office of Information, a non-ministerial department. Director-General of the COI was Australian-born (Sir) Robert Brown Fraser (1904–85), a former journalist associated with the Information Ministry since 1939. Herbert Samuel (the Privy Councillor referred to in Shaw's letter), first Viscount Samuel of Mount Carmel and Toxteth since 1937, had sounded Shaw out on the possible award to him of the Order of Merit: no actual offer, however, was made. Shaw's "formal reply," repeated at the end of his letter of 12th November to Samuel, was quoted *in extenso* by Blanche Patch in a letter to *The Times* on 3rd September 1952.]

781

I have been sounded by a Privy Councillor (not a member of the Government) as to whether I would accept the Order of Merit if it were conferred on me. I must not treat this as public or official; but as it has been made a matter of reproach to the authorities that at ninety years of age I still remain undistinguished by any place in the Honors List the present Government may desire to make it known that there has been no omission or prejudice on its part, and that I was offered a knighthood by the Labor Prime Minister on my 70th birthday 20 years ago, and that the superior distinction of the Order of Merit is now at my disposal.

My formal reply runs as follows.

"Deeply grateful as I am for the award of the highest distinction within the gift of the Commonwealth, yet the nature of my calling is such that the Order of Merit in it cannot be determined within the span of a single human life.

Either I shall be remembered as long as Aristophanes and rank with Shakespear and Molière, or I shall be a forgotten clown before the end of the century.

I dare not anticipate the verdict of history. I must remain simply Bernard Shaw."

I leave the publication of this information at your discretion and in your hands. I have no right to take any action in the matter nor any desire or objection either way. But the Government may or may not care to clear itself of any suspicion of neglect or prejudice.

faithfully
[G. Bernard Shaw]

To EMMELINE PETHICK-LAWRENCE

[Ayot St Lawrence. Welwyn]
29th October 1946

[H/48]

[Parliamentary representation by women has always been weak; forty years after Shaw commented on the disproportion of 40 women to 600 men and called for a coupled vote, the number following the 1987 General Election is 41 out of 650 members.]

Dear Lady Pethick Lawrence

How jolly to have a hail from you!

I have been thinking of you for some time past as a possible supporter of a project which I am suggesting for adoption by the old Suffragettes and young recruits.

782

I got into trouble with the movement over Votes for Women by saying that the effect of it would be to keep women out of Parliament; and sure enough not a single woman got in at the first election under Adult Suffrage. First rate candidates like Mary MacArthur and Margaret Bondfield were defeated by male nobodies. The enfranchised women voted against them.

And now, after a quarter of a century, in Parliament, instead of an equal proportion of women and men, there are 40 women and 600 men. Votes for Women has been much worse than a failure: it has guaranteed an enormous masculine majority, as I foresaw.

I maintained that what is needed is a constitutional amendment making the electoral unit, not a man OR woman, but a man AND a woman. No vote for a man to be valid until coupled with a vote for a woman. I call this The Coupled Vote. What do you think of it? It will at least give the defeated women a sensational program and bring it back into life and topicality.

My warmest regards to your good man, who stands as ever high in my esteem.

G. Bernard Shaw

Excuse the erasures. I am too old to do anything correctly.

[Lady Pethick-Lawrence replied on 6th November: "I am astonished at the boldness of your suggestion and consider it as a great sign of your amazing youth and optimism. . . . [Your vision] stretches our faith to the utmost limit. Your dissatisfaction with the effect of the women's vote is also a challenge to my own easy going complacency. I feel thankful to have had any part in a Movement which within forty years has accomplished something like a world revolution without afflicting any physical injury on the life or limb of an opponent, but I must furbish up my dreams afresh, stimulated by your letter" (H.c/48).]

To HERBERT SAMUEL

[Ayot St Lawrence. Welwyn]
[H/53] 12th November 1946

[After a visit to Shaw at Whitehall Court on 15th October, Samuel immediately wrote down his recollections of the conversation, which ranged from T.E. Lawrence to the Liberal Party and women, from Russia to Jewish agents. Asked about the O.M., Shaw responded: "There are thousands of people doing excellent public service . . . in complete obscurity, and who never get recognised and could not be. So why should others be singled out? ... Besides, if I were to accept, I might at any time do something monstrous that would bring discredit on the Order. I might even be hanged" (T/53).]

My dear Lord Samuel

I do not object to titles: I agree with all you say about them. I have begged them for others, for Pinero, for Barry Jackson, and am still begging them. As a Socialist looking forward to a great multiplication of public servants doing invaluable work for which there is neither recognition nor profit, I am all for red ribbons, uniforms, titles, and even garters to distinguish citizens of eminent service from routineers and slackers, provided they are not hereditary.

I regard honorary university degrees as very proper for unofficial eminent men, national and international, in art and scholarship. When a Scottish University sounded me as to whether I would accept a degree I refused, not because I object to degrees but because they wanted to make me a doctor of law instead of literature, which was absurd. I was offered a chair of drama in a northern English University. I refused on the ground that I am not a professor but a practitioner, and could not undertake the necessary lectures. In short I really have no prejudices masquerading as principles in the matter.

But each case is none the less an individual case in which the recipient must have a say. I need no publicity: I have already much more than my fair share of it. I shall have my period of staleness and out-of-dateness for years after my death (it is beginning already); but an O.M. will not save me from this. And I cannot admit that the Order of Merit in dramatic poetry can be determined by any mortal king or Government. I am jealous of my name to that extent, and cannot bear to be merged in any official rank, however high. ...

                                                            Bernard Shaw

To ROY LIMBERT

                                                    Ayot St Lawrence. Welwyn
[A/3]   18th November 1946
Dear Roy

I finished the new play [*Buoyant Billions*] for the 1947 Festival (if it ever comes off) yesterday. It is so bad that I ought to burn it; but it will serve your turn for a few performances.

It is shortish, and will perhaps leave room for another short one in

784

the same performance. Could you persuade Sybil Thorndike to play Great Catharine?

There are 12 characters and 3 scenes, costing more than they are worth.

Keep this deadly dark until your full announcements are ready.

I shall not be able to get printed copies for some time, as labor is so short.

G.B.S.

To LAURENCE IRVING

[Ayot St Lawrence. Welwyn]
[H/1]   28th November 1946

[Laurence Irving (namesake of the uncle who died in 1914), was writing a biography of his grandfather, *Henry Irving: The Actor and His World* (1951). The playwright F. A. Marshall until his death in 1889 was Henry Irving's play editor. Louis F. Austin (1852–1905) was his secretary, Bram Stoker his business manager. The actor-managers to whom Irving was successor were Richard Burbage (*c.* 1567–1619), Thomas Betterton (*c.* 1635–1710), David Garrick, Charles Kemble (1775–1854), and Edmund and Charles Kean. Shaw's reminiscences of Barry Sullivan inspired his article "Barry Sullivan, Shakespear and Shaw," in the *Strand Magazine*, October 1947. William Macready first produced and starred in Edward Bulwer Lytton's *Richelieu* (1839). Shaw in his Dublin youth had seen Irving as Digby Grant in James Albery's *Two Roses*, which was performed at the Theatre Royal 15th to 27th May 1871, and Sullivan in *Hamlet* on 6th October 1873.

Irving's statue (1910), sculpted by Sir Thomas Brock (1847–1922), was erected behind the National Gallery of Art (diagonally opposite the Garrick Theatre in Charing Cross Road), paid for by donations from fellow-members of the theatre. Among Irving's productions were W. G. Wills's *Charles I* (1872), *Eugene Aram* (1873), *Faust* (1885), and *Olivia* (1891); H. D. Traill and Robert Hichens's *The Medicine Man* (1898), and Alfred Lord Tennyson's *Beckett* (1893). Kate Terry (1844–1924), a fine classical actress, was Ellen's older sister.

As Shaw was certainly cognizant of Henry Irving's adulterous relationship with Eliza Aria, his statement to Laurence Irving that he did not know the reason for Lady Irving's ire must be recognised as a further example of his old-fashioned sense of propriety and tact regarding women's reputations.]

Dear Lawrence Irving II

You will have no difficulty with the letters written *to* H.I., as they are all genuine. It is the replies, which are mostly frauds, that will belie his character. When actors can write, or have any business capacity,

785

they are pushed off the stage into literature or into business management as, for instance, Cochran and Barry Jackson have been. H.I. could neither write nor manage; and, as an actor, he was accustomed to have his words written for him by Shakespear or by some living nonentity whose just remuneration he estimated at 15 shillings an act (or was it five?), the fifth act being sometimes written while the first was being played. Yet he had to pay as much as a fixed fee of £34 a night to Sardou because the alternative was a royalty which gave him away when business was bad and he was playing to papered houses. He considered my ten percent royalty grossly extortionate.

It was a great merit in him that instead of employing common press agents to write for him, he hired literary men of distinction, notably Frank Marshall, L. F. Austin, and Bram Stoker, who were at home in good society, where they turned the conversation on to him and talked him up. Austin was specially active in this way. They wrote his speeches and lectures, and crushed his opponents with brilliantly sarcastic letters when this was needed. They made for him an entirely fabulous reputation as a man of profound learning. Like all the old actors, he slipped in the most puzzling way from complete illiteracy to the scraps of shrewdness and wisdom he had picked up from Shakespear and the plays he had acted.

As to management, Bram Stoker and others did that for him. Management does not matter in the theatre, where the profits are either 100% per performance or 100% loss. When H.I. was being robbed, and knew it, he enjoyed the complete mastery of the situation and abject reverence for "the Governor" which this knowledge gave him. And so he reigned in great dignity and splendor until the final crash came and he had to take perforce to the road, penniless, played out in London, old, and obsolete, but with a tremendous reputation to exploit in the provinces. He had held out in London for thirty years, a quite unprecedented feat, to appreciate which you must compare Macready (8 years) and Barry Sullivan, much greater actors, the last of the super-human school dating from Burbage and Betterton, and including Garrick, Kemble, and the two Keans, especially Charles, who may be said to have invented H.I's game. Barry Sullivan matured his powers in America and Australia, and, having attempted London management in his middle age, abandoned it after a few months for the provinces, where he soon never finished a week in the provincial cities without £300 in his pocket. He left £100,000 when he died. Though by far the greatest actor of his day he remained a stroller to the end, and even for stage equipment and modern literature did nothing. Press agents and the splendors of Lyceum scenery and costume, to say nothing of theatres in which the old pit was supplanted by half guinea stalls, were as unknown to him as the shape of the earth was to Moses.

When writing for readers who know nothing of the theatre behind the scenes the difficulty is to avoid making H.I. appear an impostor with a reputation manufactured by Austin and Co. But it is an actor's profession to be an impostor. Nobody expects him to write his own parts. Nobody should expect him to write his own letters or lectures. Barry Sullivan, who wrote no letters and delivered no lectures, simply had no national publicity, only about a dozen intense local reputations which never became metropolitan. London publicity is a perfectly legitimate part of an actor-manager's business; and H.I's talent for it is all to his credit.

What was wrong with him was that he was as much out-of-date as Burbage would have been in his plays. When I first saw him (I was a boy then) in The Two Roses, I felt "This is the man for me": he seemed born to play ultra-modern parts. A combination of Irving and Ellen Terry and Ibsen seemed to have been sent by Providence to revive the rotting theatre of that day. When at the Lyceum, instead of following up his success in The Bells with modern plays he went back to the Barry Sullivan repertory in which, lacking Sullivan's extraordinary physical and technical qualifications, he could not act the big parts, and had to depend on his queer personality, which fascinated the public, I was disappointed. I remember saying to Alexander Bell, the author of the Standard Elocutionist, who was pleased with H.I's studied articulation, that he reminded me of nothing but a boiled silk hat. So I began with a prejudice against him through the disappointment of a strong fancy for him. To anyone who had seen Sullivan's magnificent Richelieu, Henry's antics in the part were unbearable; but to his young fans, who had never seen Macready nor heard of Sullivan, the antics were fascinating. They did not know what great acting was; but here was an intense personality that enchanted them. I, a Dubliner, had seen Sullivan in his prime, though not in his youth. I did not see Macready; but my father had seen him as Coriolanus. I asked him what it was like. He said "Like a mad bull."

There was no mad bull about H.I.; but there was a man who was like no other man. His statue at the back of the National Gallery is entirely unlike him because the sculptor has aimed with success at making him like an ordinary gentleman instead of caricaturing his unique peculiarity. Of the grace and power of Sullivan's thousand times repeated Hamlet or the terrible truculence of his Richard he had nothing; but he had H.I.: a grotesque figure like the portraits of Paganini, with a shambling dance for a walk, and a voice made resonant in his nose which became a whinny when he tried to rant. Those who would not admit that he was a great actor could not deny that he was an irresistible curiosity. It took him some years before he realized his limitations sufficiently to become more of an actor and less of a curiosity. This compensated to some extent for the wearing off of his attractive novelty.

Now the older an actor grows the more dependent he becomes on moving with the times and producing plays in the latest fashion. And this is just what an actor cannot do; for as he is on the stage every night, and can never "go to the play," he ends by knowing nothing of the contemporary theatre. When H.I. should have been playing Ibsen and Shaw he could not get beyond Wills and Traill and the Laureate Tennyson, whose genius was not dramatic. Shakespear was always ready to his hand; but he mutilated the plays so horribly to make them one-part-plays instead of galaxies of characters, that all the connoisseur critics were disgusted; and the reporter critics who had never read Shakespear could not make head or tail of the stories of the plays and were bored.

Now it would be a mistake to attribute this to vulgar professional jealousy of his fellow actors; for he always engaged the best actors he could get. He cut their parts and stage-managed them into relative insignificance not through jealousy but through his naïve belief that to do so was his right and duty as "the governor" and his sincere conviction that their parts did not matter and that his did. Kate Terry denounced him to me as a supreme egotist; but what she took to be egotism was pure ignorance and not illnature. He was not, as far as I can make him out, a bad sort. This point is a bit subtle, and will need careful handling in any biography of him.

I must stop here, assuming that you know from my public correspondence with Ellen Terry, all about The Man of Destiny affair. Also you probably know of the implacable Irish hatred your grandmother had for him and how she would have prevented his burial in Westminster Abbey if I had not taken her in hand and headed her off. How he had offended her I do not know.

I should like you to know that my fight to have women on the Council of the Royal Academy of Dramatic Art began by my nominating your mother year after year for election. She would have been an ideal member; but when at last I succeeded she was gone.

I am having a search made for my correspondence with H.I. If it is successful I will send it to you with typed copies for you to keep, as you may desire to present the originals to the British Museum, which is the proper place for them.

G. Bernard Shaw

To F. E. LOEWENSTEIN

[Ayot St Lawrence. Welwyn]
[E.u/73]   [Undated: *c.* 1st December 1946]

[Shaw's note was written across the lower half of a letter to Loewenstein from David Marcus (b. 1924), co-editor of *Irish Writing* (Cork), suggesting 1500 to 2000 words from Shaw for a forthcoming number. Marcus's letter implies that Shaw had earlier encouraged him to believe he would be receptive to the invitation, or that Loewenstein had done so on behalf of Shaw.]

I know nothing of contemporary Irish writers. I left Ireland 70 years ago; and Sean O'Casey, in whose works I am not up to date, is the only living specimen known to me.

I am not qualified to write the desired article and flatly WONT

To M. A. ST CLAIR STOBART

[H/9]   8th January 1947

[Mabel Annie (Boulton) St Clair Stobart (1862–1954), founder of the Women's Convoy Corps in the first world war, was a writer on women in war and a spiritualist.

Shaw did not return to London from the end of 1946 until his death in 1950, remaining in residence at Ayot St Lawrence except for hospitalisation at Luton after the accident that ultimately proved fatal. His address has therefore been deleted as redundant for this and subsequent letters.]

Dear Mrs Stobart

The late Rev. Dick Sheppard suggested that I should revise the Prayer Book, as there were certain passages in the lessons which he would not have read in his church.

I tackled the job, but found the book so saturated with the superstition of the Atonement that even after the most drastic excision of the savageries you quote it remained intolerably obsolete and mischievous. I gave it up as hopeless before the question of revision was raised in the House of Commons, and was swept away by such a majority, led by Joynson Hicks, that no political Party or individual has ever dared to mention it since. I am not sure that it is not the savage part that will live as a social necessity. When Mahomet achieved his great feat of converting the Arabs from a crude idolatry of "sticks and stones" to a fanatical belief in one living God, he found that this elimination by no means produced better conduct on their part: rather did it set them running wild in the matter of ordinary social morality. He was forced to re-invent hell and dictate a new Bible for which he claimed divine inspiration. It was a very frightful hell, of disgusting diseases and no houris; but it was the sort of place that the Arabs could understand and believe in; and it put the fear of God into them.

A lady friend of mine advised one of the new rulers of Ireland, now out of office, to adopt a certain policy, which he, as a devout Catholic, considered Machiavellian. He would have none of it. The lady asked why. He replied "Because I happen to believe that there is such a place as hell." The rulers of Europe no longer believe in hell; but the history of the last thirty years suggests strongly that the sooner they believe in it again, the better for the world. People must be governed according to their credulity and pugnacity. Vengeance is mine, saith the Lord; but vengeance there must be or there will be no morality. Ireland believes in hell; Ireland kept out of the war.

So you see this is hardly the moment for your attack on the Prayer Book, unanswerable as it is. It is dying a natural death with us (we are not now a church going people); but we have reason to regret that Hitler had no fear of hell. As for myself, I have written my creed and bible for those whom it suits, and will spend no time cooking the old one.

To hear from you was a pleasant surprise.

G. Bernard Shaw

To J. W. ROBERTSON SCOTT

[H/8]   8th January 1947

[J. W. Robertson Scott (1866–1962), veteran journalist of the *Pall Mall Gazette* 1887–93 and the *Westminster Gazette* 1893–99, was a writer on and activist in rural affairs, editor of *The Countryman*. Kemal Atatürk (1881–1938) was the founder of modern Turkey.]

Dear Robertson Scott

The temperance tract is excellent. But the question is a puzzling one and needs deeper scientific study. I have found by experiment on myself that a single glass of wine reduces, not my selfcontrol, but, as you also have noted, my selfcriticism to such an extent that when writing drunk I let ten sentences pass as final where when sober I should have let only two. I find this out when the proofs come to be corrected. I conclude that in all artistic work, only a teetotaller can produce the best work of which he is capable.

But very few workers ever do their best. Their second or third best is good enough; and they are happier when they are selfsatisfied with it. The Germans describe a drunken man as *selig*: happy. Their beer does them no harm and does society no harm. Good enough is good enough: only the leaders and geniuses need do their utmost; and the necessary proportion of these is only five per cent or thereabouts. An army of Napoleons or a fleet of Nelsons would be as disastrous as an army with no general or a fleet without admirals. And without his beer or his rum an infantry soldier or a marine might become a mutineer.

On the other hand it is unquestionable that we can overdraw on our vital capital and achieve extraordinary feats by dosing ourselves with brandy. Edmund Kean, Frederick Robson, and Charles Dickens (on his last American tour which killed him) did this. It brought them supreme fame, called immortality, as actors; but they died before they were 60.

Then there are the soakers, who are never drunk, though they live on whisky, of which they consume every day enough to keep us two comfortably drunk for a week. The most successful adopter of this diet was Ataturk; but we need go no further than the House of Commons to see it led by veteran soakers.

Then there are kindly husbands and wives who are jolly and amiable "under the influence" but so miserable, quarrelsome, and unbearable without stimulants that when they are persuaded to take the pledge their spouses have to set them drinking again to endure life with them.

I wrote many years ago that drink is the chloroform that enables the proletariat to bear the painful operation of living. I am still convinced that, as the failure of Prohibition in America proved, simple abstinence is not the remedy, we must get at the troubles that drive men to drink, and produce a state of life in which the taste of alcohol is disagreeable and the influence uncomfortable.

Meanwhile I think that we do not advertise enough. The law of libel makes it dangerous to plaster the walls with "Guinness is bad for you"; but we could at least try to persuade people that the need for Guinness or Haig is a symptom of low vitality of which they should be ashamed instead of glorying in it.

That is all I have to say about it. I have been an observer of alcoholism since I was a small child, as my father, though in theory a teetotaller, had drink fits occasionally. His case was one of a solitary neurosis. He was not convivial.

I know a lady teetotaller who drinks five cups of tea every morning and has no other breakfast. I have known Australian tea dipsomaniacs who would have been better and lived longer on a normal allowance of beer.

G. Bernard Shaw

To ARTHUR C. CLARKE

[C/1; X/432]   25th January 1947

[Arthur C. Clarke (b. 1917), scientist, explorer, and popular science-fiction writer, had sent a copy of the *Journal* of the British Interplanetary Society (founded 1933), of which he was chairman, containing the text of a lecture he had given. Shaw instantly joined the Society as a Life Member! Geoffrey Raoul de Havilland (1910–46), aeroplane designer, while testing the experimental DH 108 jet plane over the Thames on 27th September 1946, had put the plane into a dive, reaching the highest speed man had yet attained; but supersonic flutter as the plane passed through the sound barrier caused it to break apart.]

Many thanks for the very interesting lecture to the B.I.S. How does one become a member, or at least subscribe to the Journal?

When de Haviland perished here the other day it seemed clear to me that he must have reached the speed at which the air resistance balanced the engine power and brought him to a standstill. Then he accelerated, and found out what happens when an irresistible force encounters an immovable obstacle.

Nobody has as yet dealt with this obvious limit to aeronautic speed as far as I have read.

G.B.S.

To ARTHUR C. CLARKE

[A/1; X/432]   31st January 1947

[Clarke replied on 27th January: "Although the precise cause ... is still unknown, it seems likely that the accident was due to some structural failure. As you say, the limit of speed is set when air resistance equals engine thrust.

But the latter can always be increased with more powerful motors, so there is no absolute limit—only a limit for any particular type of machine. . . . In the vacuum of space, of course, where the rocket works at maximum efficiency, there is no resistance and no speed limit at all. A motor of any power could build up any speed as long as its fuel supply could be maintained" (X/432).

This was, Clarke later admitted, oversimplification, as there is "a natural limit of speed—that of the velocity of light. However, as light travels almost a million times as fast as sound, I felt justified in ignoring this complication in the (vain) hope that Shaw would do likewise." Shaw's reply, said Clarke, "remains one of the most baffling communications I have ever received . . . hopeless confusion" (X/432).]

I am not convinced about de Haviland. It is necessary mathematically to have a zero to count from to infinity, positive or negative, Fahrenheit or Centigrade; but the zero is not a physical fact: it is only a convention; and infinity means only the limit to human counting. I approach the subject, being a dramatist, first from my knowledge of the man, and my conviction that he would accelerate to the utmost of his engine if air resistance stopped him. And this would smash his machine as it actually did smash, in spite of all assumptions that speed cannot exceed the velocity of light and that above the stratosphere is sheer vacuum, both of them mathematical convictions [conventions?] and not scientific facts.

Besides, what proof is there that he was above the stratosphere when his machine broke up?

However, this may be my ignorant crudity; so do not bother to reply.

GBS

To JOHN G. FITZGERALD

[U(H)/48; X/433]   12th April 1947

[John G. Fitzgerald, secretary of the Dalkey Development Association, had proposed that a new public park adjoining Killiney Hill be called Bernard Shaw Park, and that a plaque be erected on the nearby house in which Shaw had spent a number of his boyhood years. The then owner of Torca Cottage, Dr J. K. Craig, consented to the erection of a plaque, designed by the Dublin architect Vincent Kelly, paid for by public subscription. It was unveiled on 6th December 1947.]

Dear Mr Fitzgerald

It is monstrous that Dalkey Hill, called in my time Telegraph Hill from the little castle on top, should be a private domain, as Killiney Hill was for so many centuries. But it must not be called Bernard Shaw Hill. Not only would that be a clumsy ugly title, but out of the question because the men of Ireland are mortal and temporal and her hills eternal.

But a plaquette at Torca Cottage, if the present proprietor does not object, would gratify me, and be all I deserve. I owe more than I can express to the natural beauty of that enchanting situation commanding the two great bays between Howth and Bray Head and its canopied skies such as I have never seen elsewhere in the world. They are as present to me now as they were 80 years ago.

I think the hill, which is not a park, should be called Torca Hill. Killiney Hill, Torca Hill, and Dalkey Island, sound well as a group, like the British Malverns.

G. Bernard Shaw

To AUGUSTUS JOHN

[A/104]   10th May 1947

[Shaw's letter was written on the reverse of a photograph. Hugh Dalton was Chancellor of the Exchequer 1945–47.]

Dear Augustus John

I'm too old for sittings: half an hour would finish me. And I can't put you up here for a month: domestic labor wont run to it.

As you may see by this photograph, taken this month, I have no longer any outline and am just like any other old man with a white beard.

At 90 one must be counted as dead: there is no getting away from it, even to be immortalized by a great painter.

Lapps are not in my line. The little spare cash that Dalton leaves me is all bespoke.

G.B.S.

To ELLEN POLLOCK

[C/1]   23rd May 1947

[Ellen Pollock, anxious to have the rôle of Eliza in a new staging at the Lyric
Theatre, appealed to Shaw. By this time Diana Churchill had been cast, but
was subsequently forced by illness to withdraw. Shaw had recognised the
stage potential of Charles Laughton (1899–1962) when in 1923 he rehearsed
him as Higgins in scenes for a student production of *Pygmalion* at RADA.]

I do not dictate casts nowadays. I did not choose the lady. I am too
out-of-date.

The tradition of middle aged Elizas and *primo amoroso* Higginses is
detestable. Eliza should be really 18, and Higgins a Charles Laughton
type.

G. B. S.

To JAYANTA PADMANABHA

[X/434]   4th June 1947

[Jayanta Padmanabha sent Shaw cuttings of articles he had published in the
Ceylon Daily News on Florence Farr's last years in Ceylon, where she was
first principal of a college founded by (and named after) his grand uncle Sir
Pannamballam Ramanathan (1851–1930). It was the latter who had persuaded her to come to the Orient in 1912.]

[Dear Sir]

I am much indebted to you for sending me the articles on Florence
Farr. They have astonished me. I thought that Yeats and I knew her
through and through, as far as there was anything to know. I now see
that we did not know her at all. Your great-uncle, of whom we had
never heard, opened her mind and developed the real woman. I should
have said she was the last woman on earth to become the authoritative
head of a college, or to break her way out of the little cliques in which
she figured in London, and find a spiritual home in philosophic India.
I was wrong. I was the wrong man for her, and I am deeply glad that
she found the right one after I had passed out of her life. Again, thank
you a thousand times for enlightening me.

[G. Bernard Shaw]

To J. C. TREWIN

[H.u/3]   [Undated: assigned to 9th June 1947]

[Shaw was here responding to a request from the drama critic and theatre historian J. C. Trewin (b. 1908) for illustrations of Frank Harris's earthy manner of speech. On the envelope bearing the message Shaw wrote in red pencil "*Highly Personal.*" Lady C.C. was Lady Colin Campbell (1858–1911), a journalist who succeeded Shaw as art critic of *The World*.]

SAMPLES AS DESIRED
X and F.H. meet at the stage door of Wyndham's Theatre.
X. What on earth are you doing here, of all places?
F.H. I am going to read a play to Wyndham.
X. Ah, well, he is half a century out of date; but he is a really great comedian; and you may pick up a hint or two from him.
F.H. The pump will give water if you PEE in it.

ANOTHER OCCASION
X. By the way, do you know Lady C.C.
F.H. DO I know that fat arsed bitch! ! !
[the lady was in fact a tall woman who laced so tightly that she was dorsally on the Hottentot side. She was a famous beauty, and had no doubt snubbed F.H.]*

No typing or printing can convey the effect of F.H's resonant voice, audible to everyone within a range of hundreds of yards indoor or out, and of his perfect elocution. No man could express scorn as he could in the language of a buccaneer but with the bearing of a prophet.

He could not understand why publishers would not commission him to write a Life of Christ, whom he regarded as the nearest thing to himself that humanity had ever produced.

To JOHN TAYLOR

[A/1; W/435]   6th July 1947

[John Taylor (b. 1924), a young journalist, was at this time editor of the trade journal *Tailor and Cutter*.]

The greatest artists are not careless of their dress.
Rodin, who worked at his modelling like an old plasterer, went out of doors looking like his contemporary King Oscar of Sweden.

* Shaw's brackets.

796

Paul Troubetskoy, his great rival as a sculptor, looked every inch a Russian prince.

William Morris, described by Andrew Lang as "like a ship's purser[,]" wore a blue lounge suit and a blue shirt and collar dyed by himself, and would not tolerate a mirror in his house. But he was not careless or slovenly. Very much the opposite.

Augustus John, regardless of convention, but not careless, and presentably like his namesake the Apostle.

Thomas Hardy. Nobody would have guessed his profession from his clothes. He dressed like the architect he first was.

Sir John Lavery. Louis Philippe whiskers, but Victorian polite dress.

John Collier. Always correct sartorially.

All these are from personal observation.

Ibsen (whom I never saw) was very particular, and might have passed for an ambassador.

I wore colored collars years before anyone except Morris dared; but I could not bear a tie of the wrong color; and I now look fairly in fashion, though I do not allow my jackets to be lined and padded.

G. B. S.

To WILLIAM J. PICKERILL

[H/119]   13th August 1947

[The letter was drafted in shorthand at Ayot on 11th August, transliterated and typed by Blanche Patch on Whitehall Court stationery on the 13th, then returned to the country for signature.]

Dear Pickerill

It is impossible to foresee how any story will do as an opera. One would not suppose that The Flying Dutchman and Parsifal would suit the same composer equally well. There is no promise in Figaro of Don Giovanni; but Mozart must have discovered Handel's organ concerto in G minor in between; and lo! the statue music. Any good story will make a good opera if the composer is competent.

You will notice that I use the word opera, not music drama. I do so because you say in your letter that there will be no arias nor cadenzas. Let me implore you on the contrary to compose nothing else. Tristan is famous; but we are all sick of the wamblings it started. My late wife,

797

whenever I treated her to Tristan, said "Do stop that caterwauling." Composers for the last fifty years have been writing Beethovenian mood music on the assumption that their moods are as interesting as those of Beethoven or Sibelius; and Wagner's unprepared 13ths are old hat. The word is now Back to Handel and Mozart, to dramatic recitative, good tunes, and lovely arias, but without the old sonata-form repetitions. Even Back to Rossini and Meyerbeer! anything rather than shapeless moody wambling and dreary ugliness by way of profundity.

I am an old militant Wagnerite; but now I switch off the overture to Tannhäuser and switch on the overture to William Tell. I can get some pleasure out of Maritana, but not out of the latest wambledy-dambledy.

By all means come to England and try to get in at Glyndebourne; but let it be as an African composer who has had enough of Brahmsism. You must break new ground with what was best in the old.

G. Bernard Shaw

To LORD KENNET OF THE DENE

[A/1]   16th August 1947

[Hilton Young, Lord Kennet, had written to tell Shaw of the death of his longtime friend Kathleen Lady Kennet on 25th July.]

My dear Kennett

The news reached me by wireless on my birthday, and instantly reduced the monstrous pile of letters and cards to dust and ashes.

But it did not hurt. I rejoice in Kathleen, dead or alive. I never grieve; and I never forget. Some 85 years ago I heard that my mother's aunt had died. I fled into the garden and cried for half an hour, believing that I should cry in agonized grief all the rest of my life.

Then I recovered so completely that even at six years old I made a mental note of the fact that those who cry forget, and those who never grieve remember.

And I have heard some rare howling in my time.

So I do not condole. I have always ranked you as a poet. I rank myself that way. I was deeply touched by your writing to me.

GBS

To I. J. PITMAN

[C/1]   18th August 1947

[Pitman had visited Shaw in Ayot on 5th August.]

No: I never contemplated designing the alfabet myself. There must be no amateur work in the job: the designing must be done by a professional artist-calligrapher. The difficulty is to find one able to invent as well as write.

Your own inventions are excellent; but calligraphy as a handicraft is not your profession.

I am dead against any mixture of Johnsonese and Phonetic. We must get the Bible (latest American Revision) into Phonetic: it would look blasphemously horrible in misspelt etymological Johnsonese. The two alfabets must be quite distinct from the start. The period of bi-scripture will pass.

G.B.S.

To ARTHUR COX

[E/1]   8th September 1947

[Arthur Cox (1891–1965) was head of a firm of Dublin solicitors, in St Stephen's Green, who drew up a contract between Shaw and Irish Productions Ltd. (also known as Irish Screen Art Ltd.) to produce film versions of Shaw's plays and erect film studios in Ireland, the first film under the agreement to be *Androcles and the Lion*. Cox was one of the directors of the limited company, along with Dan Breen (1894–1969), Irish Republican, who represented Tipperary in the Dáil 1932–65; the accountant E.J.Shott; and the architect John J.Robinson. Shaw signed and returned the contract on 8th September, accompanied by a press release he had drafted. The latter, apparently unpublished at the time, was reproduced in Bernard Dukore (ed.), *Collected Screenplays of Bernard Shaw* (1980).]

I propose that this should be sent to the Press agencies in Ireland (if any) and in England and America.

It is important that no names should be mentioned except mine. Pascal is a foreigner. Dan is still too much a firebrand Republican.

GBS

Mr Bernard Shaw, interviewed by a Press representative, supplies the following information.

799

"I have had in mind for a long time the fitness of Ireland as a field for film industry. The climate, the scenery, the dramatic aptitudes of the people, all point that way. The present domination of Hollywood over the enormous influence of screen pictures on the mind of the world is to me deplorable: it is creating a barbarous sock-in-the-jaw morality on the whole world from which Ireland must be rescued. Having already municipalized my Irish landed property I am ready to give Ireland the first call on my valuable film rights. I have in fact actually executed an agreement which will have that effect if the project meets with the necessary public approval and financial private support. Already I have been met more than half way in both respects. An experimental company, to be known presently as Irish Screen Arts Limited, is now in existence with sufficient Irish capital to exploit certain film rights of mine until it is in a position to build the necessary studios to operate exclusively in Ireland: a work which might well be undertaken by the Irish State. That is as far as the matter has gone at present.

My friend Arthur Rank has no part in the affair, all the capital being Irish; but I hope his many picture houses, in which his strength lies, will be filled with Irish films to make up for the threatened restrictions on the import of Hollywood ones. Hollywood itself may prove a good customer."

To GABRIEL PASCAL

[A/1]   8th September 1947

[Maurice Evans (b. 1901), English actor who became a reigning star of the American stage, had visited Shaw in June to obtain his approval for a new production of *Man and Superman* in America. It opened in New York on 8th October, where it achieved a critical acclamation and a run of 295 performances, followed by a cross-continent tour.]

My dear Gabriel

I have executed the agreement and sent it back to Cox, who should have sent it directly to me.

You have now to make your own agreement with the company. My agreement makes you indispensable: that is all I can do for you. So take care of yourself. A share of the profits (strictly defined) would give you an interest in keeping down the expenses; but it should not take the place of royalty and production fee (or salary) and expenses.

I do not want to see you. I do not want to see
                    ANYBODY.
I find that when I have a visitor my work falls into arrear for half the day. I have a book to see through the press—two books in fact—no, three!!! I have a production to arrange for Evans in America, and a revival of You Never Can Tell for London at Wyndham's. There is the Irish business to draft and redraft. Pressing private correspondence for which I have to keep my afternoons turns up by every post. I want to go on with my literary work, even to write another one now that my new one has not finished quite so badly as I feared. Mrs Laden is going away to Aberdeen for a holiday.

Keep away, Gabriel. Keep away EVERYBODY. Come only when there is the most pressing necessity unless you want to kill me.

                                        G.B.S.

To HAROLD LASKI

[S(H)/97]   12th September 1947

[Shaw's "Sixty Years of Fabianism" was published in the Jubilee Edition of *Fabian Essays in Socialism* (1948); it was not, however, a "new" essay, having earlier appeared in the *Fabian Quarterly* (April 1944) as "Fabian Failures and Successes," in celebration of the Fabian Society's sixtieth anniversary. When the editor of the new edition of the *Fabian Essays* sought to place Shaw's "postscript" at the front of the book to increase its saleability, Shaw crushed the idea in a letter to the Society's assistant research secretary, Margaret Locke, on 23rd May 1947: "This is not going to be a Shaw book for Shaw fans. They have all read the Essays, and are mostly dead. The Essays are for people who are curious about Socialism, and do not care a dump for the old driveller who edited the volume, and whose senility is very expensively proved by the appalling proof corrections. . . . Let me have the revise before I die" (A/35).]

Dear Harold Laski

You share the popular delusion that I am a millionaire. I have not a rap to spare over and above my expenses: the Exchequer sees to that. Anyhow what use is research to Fabians? We have solution enough for the next 20 years. Our business is to preach, push, and permeate, not to hunt up history, of which we know more than enough. The old Essays, to which I have just contributed a new one, are still in advance of the situation. You will find it hard to say much more. The Labor

Cabinet is hardly yet ready for sixth form schoolbooks. Anyhow you may write me off as a dried up well, especially as to my imaginary millions.

G. Bernard Shaw

To P. J. A. SCOTT-MAUNSELL

[E.u/4; X/289]   19th September 1947

[P. J. A. Scott-Maunsell was secretary of the London branch of the Anti-Partition of Ireland League. Shaw's note was written on the reverse of Scott-Maunsell's letter. Dr Loewenstein apparently communicated the text in his own hand and preserved Shaw's original, adding a memo: "This text used as model for printed card to come. 19.9.47." The stereotyped postcard was never ordered.]

I take no sides in Irish party politics, and have repeatedly declared my conviction that Ulster Protestant Capitalism, which will never yield to Catholic Republican agitation, will undo Partition when it is out-voted by organized Labor, and can fortify itself against Socialism only by an alliance with the agricultural proprietors of Eire.

To GABRIEL PASCAL

[C/1; X/396.e]   24th September 1947

[A resolution by the Association of Cine-Technicians in 1946, censuring Pascal "for the inordinate length of time taken to produce *Cæsar and Cleopatra*," called for him to be "only allowed to make pictures in this country subject to special control." This, plus the withdrawal of J. Arthur Rank from further financial investment in Pascal productions due to the disastrous over-run of costs on the film, making it the biggest financial failure in British film history, forced Pascal to seek new financing abroad. His negotiations eventually involved the United States, Ireland, Malta, Mexico, and Italy, where he negotiated for a film of the life of St Francis, for which he then besought Shaw to provide an original screenplay. Not until two years after Shaw's death did he produce another film, *Androcles and the Lion*, in Hollywood; it was the least successful of his Shaw films.]

I think we had both [better] leave Saint Francis alone. You do not care a rap about him; and my view of him and of Savonarola and of

802

Jesus is that their propaganda of Holy Poverty and amateur Communism was mischievous and ignorant. This would not suit the Italians.

As to Saturday or Sunday or any other day come if you must: I cannot shut my door to you.

GBS

To CLARA M. KENNEDY

[C/1]   27th September 1947

[Shaw's postcard was cited by Miss Kennedy in a debate on missionaries organised at Marylebone by the Women's Missionary Society in early October; see "Missionaries in Fiction," *British Weekly*, 16th October 1947.]

You have wasted your ink. The Black Girl is in no sense an attack on missionaries as such; and if you publish a statement to the contrary you will discredit your own cause, as 9 out of 10 readers will conclude that if I am against missionaries as such there must be something gravely wrong with them.

I am myself a missionary.

Fifty years ago half the Free Churches had already become Voltairean and renounced what they called "the commercial theory of the atonement." The black girl's search led her to this goal; and her search is the subject of the book, not an attack on anybody.

G.B.S.

To GABRIEL PASCAL

[H/1; X/396.e]   2nd October 1947

[During a visit to Shaw on 28th September, Pascal revealed that he had been quietly married at Amersham the preceding week. On 18th October he brought his Hungarian actress bride Valerie Hidveghy to Ayot.]

My dear Gabriel

I do not see how I can collaborate with the Italian authors of the St Francis scenario. I have strong views as to the character of St Francis, who was an apostle of Holy Poverty, whereas my doctrine is that poverty is a social crime and the root of all evil for individuals. In any version made by me the saint would appear, not altogether as a hero but as a wellintentioned but dangerously mistaken enemy of the

Vatican, who, had he lived longer[,] would have shared the fate of Savonarola, Hus, and Jesus. My heroine would be St Clare.

The result would be a film which the Church might find it hard to sponsor; so I think I had better let it alone. The necessary revision of the existing scenario had better be made by some practised Italian playwright who accepts the popular view of St Francis as an example to all the world of holy living.

I should like to have a look at the comedy you mention as a substitute.

G. Bernard Shaw

To NANCY ASTOR

[C/101]   21st October 1947

B.P. spent the weekend here. She was at the top of her form. I could detect no trace of the half starved, raggedly dressed, cruelly exploited, moribund victim I had been led to expect from recent conversations.

So be easy.

GBS

To SIDNEY R. CAMPION

[W(C)/436]   23rd October 1947

[Sidney R. Campion (1891–1978), barrister, journalist, and author, was from 1940 head of the Press and Broadcast Division of the General Post Office.]

No man can direct any disposal of his ashes that is not available equally for Tom, Dick, or Harriet. His will cannot contain a clause that he is to be buried in a fane reserved for nationally eminent persons.

I have directed that my ashes shall be mixed inseparably with those of my late wife, and inurned in our garden.

G. Bernard Shaw

To S. K. RATCLIFFE

[C/3]   7th November 1947

[Sidney Webb died on 13th October. Shaw pre-recorded on 5th November a self-written dialogue between the theatre manager C.B. Cochran and himself, to be broadcast on St John Ervine's B.B.C. programme "A Pageant of Plays and Players" on 12th November. It was Shaw's last broadcast.]

You need not hesitate about the public speaking. I recorded a broadcast the day before yesterday. A pitiable effort, but good enough. I'm 91. I retired from the platform at 85.

I saw Webb only two or three times after his stroke. It altered his handwriting for the worse, and put an end to his work though not to his omnivorous reading. He walked as usual but not without a nurse, as he was not sure that if he fell he could get up again. His speech was so very slightly affected that only very intimate old friends noticed it. In short, quite presentable.

As a public speaker he had long become impossible. Practising it as an art was not in his extraordinarily simple character. Part of his immense efficiency was due to his never doing anything better than was necessary: a limit fatal to fine art on the platform. Beatrice told me that it was useless to remonstrate about his growing inaudibility: she had tried in vain.

I never expected to survive them.

G.B.S.

To ROBERT HO TUNG

[H/I]   13th November 1947

[Sir Robert had sent Shaw a pair of jade cufflinks, delivered through the offices of Sir Leslie Boyce of the U.K. Trade Mission. In October he wrote to thank Shaw for sending him the "Aesthetic Science" article. The "scene painter" (actually, the designer) for *Buoyant Billions* was the Winstens' daughter Theodora (b. 1917).]

Dear Sir Robert

Your letter reaches me just after I have finished a play in which I have introduced a private temple like the one in which I spent with you an hour which I have never forgotten and never shall forget.

Old English houses contained what are called Meditation Parlors which fulfilled the purpose of your beautiful temple until modern barbarism profaned them as smoking rooms. Now the barbarians smoke all over the house.

The scene painter wants to know what your temple is like. Have you by any chance a photograph of it? Or of the priest in his vestments?

My wife died in 1943. She, too, never forgot the caress with which Lady Hotung received her that day.

I am very old (91). If I forgot to acknowledge the lovely jade ornaments it must have been because I believed I had done so. My memory cannot be depended on for more than ten minutes. I make blunder after blunder, and can only hobble instead of walk.

I wish you a prosperous voyage to America and a safe return. You will rank always as one of my special friends.

G. Bernard Shaw

To BETTY PRITCHARD

[F.u/4]   [13th November 1947]

[A revised text of this letter was multigraphed by Dr Loewenstein for circulation in the manner of the stereotyped postcards. Miss Pritchard lived in Lewisham.]

Dear Miss Pritchard

You may punctuate as you please, and you must let me punctuate as I please.

The most profusely punctuated book in the English language is the Bible; but it is not consistent grammatically and mixes semicolons and colons, and ors or nors in the same verses. The worst punctuator in the world was Sheridan, who had only one stop: a dash. There is no established practice. Few authors get as far as a colon.

In my own practice of conjunctions a semicolon comes when the nominative changes or is repeated, and a comma when it does not. He was drunk, but not disorderly. He was drunk; but his brother was sober.

The Bible translators sometimes followed this purely grammatical rule, but were apt to substitute a colon, which I use artistically and not grammatically. I use the semicolon when the nominative is changed or when it is repeated. "Thou shalt not take the name of the Lord thy God in vain; for the Lord will not hold him guiltless that taketh His name in vain."

Punctuation is mostly idiosyncratic: there are childish simple rules such as "but is always preceded by a semicolon." It may be preceded by any stop or no stop. So may any other conjunction. But it is admissible that a writer's practice should be consistent, so that anyone reading it aloud at first sight should know how the sentence is going to turn. Playwrights especially must see to this, as their lines are meant to be spoken.

Whatever system you adopt or invent, please dont bother me about it. I am too old a dog to learn new tricks.

[G. Bernard Shaw]

[H.c.u./2]   2nd December 1947

[De Valera, who had seen *Cæsar and Cleopatra* (specially screened for him by Pascal in August 1946) and written to say he'd enjoyed it, was most enthusiastic about the Irish film project. When there were signs, even before the signing of the contract, that the deal was foundering, he wrote to beg Shaw to have faith in the Irish principals involved. The linchpin, however, was Joseph McGrath (1887–1966), millionaire financier who founded the Irish Hospital sweepstakes in 1930; when he, upon advice that the venture had no financial chance of success, limited his support to a small fraction of what had been expected from him, the scheme collapsed.

The Dáil dissolved on 12th January 1948, polling occurring on 4th February. For the first time since 1931 there was a serious challenge to De Valera's position. His party, Fíanna Fáil, won only 68 seats, 11 fewer than a majority. With the support of opposition groups, the leader of the Fine Gael Party, John A. Costello (1891–1976), was elected to succeed Dev as Taoiseach after sixteen years of rule.]

Dear Taioseach

This is to let you know that the film project has fizzled. After doing its utmost to raise the necessary capital in Ireland it has got £41,000, including £10,000 from MacGrath, who will give no more. The odd £1000 has been borrowed by Dan Breen, who ought to have known better.

This utter failure was concealed from me, not to say painted up for me considerably, until last week, when I saw the minutes of the Board meeting. For filming purposes they might as well have collected 41,000 farthings. To start with less than a million and a half in certain prospect and a quarter of a million in the bank would be financial folly. The company should be wound up at once. Its contract with me must be torn up in any case.

Leaving me out of the question, however, there is an alternative possible. Screen Art Limited could hold on to its £41,000, giving up all high art pretensions and film producing plans, and getting capital from Hollywood, or from the Rank organization, or wherever else it can, and concentrating on building studios in Ireland to be let to any film manufacturing company on purely commercial terms in the ordinary course of business. As the supply of studios is short, and S.A. Limited has bought through Pascal some equipment, it might succeed on these lines and put Ireland on the map commercially if not aesthetically.

I think this would appeal specially to Mr Robinson and attract the many capitalists who regard my name as a highbrow drawback, and the

Catholics, lay and clerical, to whom I am a notorious and dangerous Freethinker.

This needs no answer. You have so much to think about, especially with a General Election threatening, that I jot down my own thoughts to save you as much trouble as possible.

[G. Bernard Shaw]

To BARBARA DRAKE

[H/8]   8th December 1947

[Barbara Drake was editing, with the help of Margaret Cole, Beatrice Webb's unfinished book *Our Partnership* (1948). The ashes of the two Webbs were re-interred in Westminster Abbey on 12th December.]

My dear Barbara

My postcard was not naughty. You will be misunderstood if you say that Beatrice disagreed with Jesus but did not dislike him. The contrary is the truth. She did not disagree with him on any point on which it is now possible for anyone as capable as she was to agree with him; but she had a constitutional dislike for that sort of man, just as she had of the Irish and of the Chinese. She had a double dislike of me both as an Irishman and an individual whom she could not classify. . . . Sidney had his dislikes too; but he was so reticent about them that it was years before I found them out.

Anyhow, dont say that Beatrice was unchristian. She was; but the word by itself is too much associated with selfishness.

G. Bernard Shaw

To WERNER KRAUSS

[W(C)/452]   9th December 1947

[Werner Krauss, distinguished actor who had appeared in expressionist silent films, was made an Actor of the State for his participation in a few propaganda films under the Nazis, notably the anti-Semitic *Jud Süss* (1940), adapted from the novel by Lion Feuchtwanger (1884–1958). Tried by the Stuttgart de-Nazification Court in 1948, he presented to the court, through counsel, a response received from Shaw to his request for an opinion on the justification for his trial. Krauss, previously acquitted by two de-Nazification courts, was found guilty as "a minor offender" and fined the equivalent of £125 by the German Court of Appeal. A distorted text of Shaw's message, re-translated from the German translation, was published in Britain.]

All civilizations are kept in existence by the masses who collaborate with whatever governments are for the moment established in their country, native or foreign.

To treat such collaboration as a crime after every change of government is a vindictive stupidity which cannot be justified on any ground.

G. Bernard Shaw

To E. MARGARET WHEELER

[S/9]   6th January 1948

Dear Mrs Wheeler, not to say Margaret or Maggie or Meg,

What you need is a Lady Not Lift Little Finger Forty Dollar a Month Chinaman, formerly available in San Francisco, but probably now extinct.

Beatrice Webb's half an hour a day for housekeeping was of course founded on two servants and a thousand a year unearned income. She was extraordinarily incapable with her hands. Her handwriting was a mass of scrawls and scratches that could be understood only by smelling and guessing; for reading it was impossible. If she took up a pencil she soon bit it into splinters: if a flower, she tore it to strips. These things she did automatically, not intentionally. If she had tried to do housework she would have wrecked the building.

You ask how she could tell how long it takes to make a bed and dust a bedroom if she never did it herself, and whether her cook was honest or not if she never cooked herself. Well, how do you know what you should pay for your boots or your watch? You never made a pair of boots nor a watch. Everything in daily use has a market price, arrived at in a way that you will understand when you study economics or read my criticism of Marx's theory of value. Meanwhile dont ask me foolish questions.

Beatrice certainly gave tremendous value for the housework that was done for her. I have just succeeded in having her cinders buried in Westminster Abbey: do you suppose she did nothing to earn this tribute?

As to how she employed her leisure: she was a tremendous walker, and was ruthless in making me and Sidney accompany her every day. She could walk us off our legs. For years we bicycled; but one day Sidney fainted and fell off his machine; and she never let him mount a bicycle again, and took to walking. I used to mend all the punctures and all road repairs, and inspect and tighten up their brakes and saddles, which would have soon come to pieces without me, as they were both incapable of doing anything mechanical: they just sat on the grass and enjoyed looking on at my operations.

They were a great pair in a great partnership; but it was not a typical marriage, nor was mine; for both marriages were childless. You must study your own marriage: it is the real thing. But do not jump at the conclusion that we knew nothing about children and normal family life. We were not parents; but we had been children with parents. Beatrice was the youngest but one of nine sisters. I was the youngest of three children: I had two sisters. So was Webb: he had a brother and a sister. My father was 40 when I was born. It is amazing how parents forget their experiences as children. Women treat their grown-up daughters as if they were still infants. I have known two famous and rich women both of whom had one daughter. One of the daughters ran away with the chauffeur: the other married an earl before she was mature enough to be married at all. Both had only one object: to escape from the nursery. Both mothers, by the way, were Americans; but English mothers are just as bad. This does not mean lack of affection: it often means too much; for it makes escape seem heartless. You say you want to be a mother to your own child. What sort of mother? Mrs. Fred might do the job better. Children may be and perhaps should be made pets (live dolls) until they are six; but then they must be handed over to the school teacher: to get rid of them for most of the day rather than to have them educated. Your kids are growing up and becoming independent human beings. Don't try to keep them too much under your thumb. It is very difficult to know exactly how much children need guidance and how much they should be told to think for themselves. How much do you tell them what to do when they come running to you to save them that trouble? If ever a foundling baby is left on your doorstep, and you adopt it, you may find yourself loving it better than your authentic children, some of whom you may come to dislike very thoroughly.

Your category of philosophers is first rate; but you add a complaint that no living philosopher fits exactly into his category, nor is indifferent to his material and animal wellbeing. Well, nobody fits into a category. We are all hybrids; and must put our material and animal wellbeing first. If you demur to this next time you reach your highest plane fast for 12 hours and you will think of nothing but food. There are shorter ways which I forbear to mention. A world betterer may be a great glutton. Peter the Great, infernally cruel, was a great world betterer. Ibsen drank. I asked a German lady who had attended Liszt's piano class, where her sister was a pupil, what he used to say to her. She said they never talked, because she always sat as far from him as possible. I asked her why. Her reply was "Er war nie gut gewaschen."

Your notion of a play in which the audience hears what the characters say conventionally, but also hears what they really feel and think, is one for which I can devise no technique except the old asides. What makes my plays unlike others is that my characters say what they feel and would not say in real life. Hence the description of B.B. [*Buoyant Billions*] as a comedy of no manners.

When you read something you do not understand do not stop to puzzle over it. Skip it and go on to what you do understand. Later on the obscure passage will be quite clear if you are capable of it: if not it is no use bothering about it.

I must stop....

G. Bernard Shaw

To LAWRENCE LANGNER

[Y/7; X/312]

[London: sent by Blanche Patch]
10th January 1948

[The Theatre Guild was contemplating a revival of *You Never Can Tell*, with rehearsals to commence late in January. Shaw's interest in the American presidential election of 1948 was focused on the left-wing Progressive Party candidate, Henry A. Wallace (1888–1965), former Vice President (1941–45) "All Europe," Shaw told an interviewer for the *Michigan Daily* (25th February 1948), "and America slandered Russia for twenty years, then slobbered over her when Hitler attacked her and she became our ally, and the moment the war was over began slandering her again. After that can you wonder that she mistrusts us? Wallace is the only candidate whose election would allay her suspicions."]

PRODUCE NOTHING OF MINE UNTIL PRESIDENTIAL ELECTION IS OVER. SHAW.

To ALAN S. DOWNER

[H/9]   21st January 1948

[Alan S. Downer (1912–70), teacher and theatre historian, was a professor of English at Princeton University 1946–70. Sir William Davenant (1606–68) and Nicholas Rowe (1674–1718) were poets laureate and dramatists; Rowe was also the first modern editor of the works of Shakespeare.]

Dear Mr Downer

I cannot sufficiently urge you to repress your impulse to write a chronicle of the English theatre. That has been done and overdone many times and to do it over again would not only involve hours of dry-as-dust research for you, but bore your readers (if you had any) to such a degree that they would never read another book of yours.

There is plenty for you to do without rehashing Jonson, Rowe, Davenant, Pepys, Johnson, Cibber's Apology and the lifelong diary of Macready. The tradition of heroic acting in Shakesperean tragedy did not end with Macready nor include Irving: it ended with Barry Sullivan (1821–91), perhaps the greatest of them all, and certainly the most successful. What there is for you to do is to take up the subject of theatre economics, of which there are two phases to be recorded. First, why did Barry Sullivan, after his early successes in America, Australia, and in London, shake London's dust from his feet, and play only in the English provinces, Ireland, and Scotland? It was because his forerunners all finally exhausted their London vogue there in a few years and were driven back to the road. The wellknown London manager Hollingshead declared that Shakespear spelt ruin; and nobody contradicted him. Speeches longer than 20 words were considered impossible. Meanwhile Sullivan in the provinces was playing Hamlet, Richard, Macbeth, and Lytton's Richelieu over and over again to crowded houses, making £300 a week. He played Hamlet, his favorite part, more than 3000 times, and died a very rich man. Irving held out in London for thirty years and was driven back to the road penniless.

Second, the tremendous economic change made by the cinema. When I began, the running expenses of a performance at a fashionable London theatre were at least £80, and the greatest possible total receipts £300: a terrific gamble. For a big success it was necessary to sell 100,000 seats. This does not mean 100,000 playgoers. 100,000 people might go once to see the chariot race in Ben Hur. They would not go to see a play of mine at all. But if 20,000 people would go five times or 10,000 people 10 times, first class plays had a chance; and all the capital needed to produce a play and insure salaries for a fortnight was £2000 at most.

Compare cinema figures. The film of my play Caesar and Cleopatra cost £600,000. The art of the theatre never changes; but a play on which such a sum can be spent profitably is very different to one by an author limited to £2000 or less. And the players' salaries are stupendous. Here is something for you to write about. Better than stale stories about Garrick, eh?

Holding a mirror up to nature is not a correct definition of a playwright's art. A mirror reflects what is before it. Hold it up to any street at noonday and it shews a crowd of people and vehicles and tells you nothing about them. A photograph of them has no meaning. They may be in love with one another, they may intend to murder one another. They may be husbands and wives, parents and children, or doctors and patients, in the most comic or tragic relations to one another; but the mirror or photograph tells you nothing of all this, and cannot give the playwright any material whatever. Shakespear's mirror was for the actor, to teach [him] not to saw the air and look like nothing on earth. The playwright has more to do than to watch and wave: the policeman does that much; but the playwright must interpret the passing show by parables.

My stage directions are explained by yet another change for you to deal with. When I began no publisher would touch a play. The only printed copies were technical prompt books, full of " *Enter O.P. to L.C., kills her and Exit R.U.E.*" utterly unreadable, and much of it unintelligible. As I could not get my plays performed and could not offer them to managers because I was a critic, I had to get them published. I had to make my stage directions practicable without ever mentioning the stage, and as readable by novel readers as by prompters and property men. Read them in that light. Now plays are published as freely as novels. My doing.

Now you have plenty to go on with.

G. Bernard Shaw

To E. A. PRENTICE

[W(C)/437]   3rd February 1948

[E. A. Prentice, a serviceman in the Royal Air Force, had apparently requested approval for setting *Pygmalion* to music.]

I absolutely forbid any such outrage.

If Pygmalion is not good enough for your friends with its own verbal music, their talent must be altogether extraordinary.

Let them try Mozart's Cosi fan tutte, or at least Offenbach's Grand Duchess.

G. B. S.

To ROLFE BOSWELL

[C/4]   3rd February 1948

[Rolfe Boswell was on the staff of the New York *Sun*. In *The Star* on 17th May 1889 "Corno di Bassetto" had written: "I am always inclined to believe in a violinist who can play Wieniawski. Beethoven and Mendelssohn were great composers of violin music. There is all the difference in the world between the two." The Prokofiev sonata presumably was the D major (Op. 94a), first performed in 1944. The principal violin composition of the Finnish composer Jean Sibelius (1865–1957) was his violin concerto in D minor.]

I have not changed my distinction between Beethoven and Wieniawski.

Elgar was at first almost a violin virtuoso. I asked his orchestral leader Billy Reed whether Elgar wrote sympathetically and easily played parts for the violin. He replied emphatically NO. The composer may be a fiddler, but his instrument is the orchestra, not the violin.

But have you heard the violin sonata of Prokovieff? A humorous masterpiece of authentic violin music. Sibelius *impersonates* every instrument.

                                                          G.B.S.

To EMIL LUDWIG

[H/110]   13th February 1948

[Emil Ludwig, a Jew who had gone into voluntary exile from Germany in 1907, was the author of numerous "humanized" biographies, including those of Goethe, Napoleon, and Jesus. In Nazi Germany he was labelled an enemy of the state and his books were burned. He died in Switzerland (his adopted home) on 17th September 1948.]

My dear Ludwig

Before Freud was ever heard of I dismissed all the standard books on Psychology as worthless, because, as I declared, genuinely scientific work on the subject would be so indecent that nobody could possibly print it or even write it.

I did not then believe that a human being so utterly void of any sort of delicacy as Freud could exist. But apparently I created him; for I have lived to see him come not only into existence but into vogue. I am now expected to explain that I was never carnally in love with my mother, nor ever hated my father nor wanted to murder him.

Still the fellow was of some use, if only by making the scientific discussion of sex possible by making the unmentionable mentionable.

I did not know that you are an invalid, and hope you have not got into the grip of the doctors and become a chronic case. What is wrong with you? A year's illness demands a change of doctors or a change of diet, or both.

Give my very special regards to Frau Ludwig whom I hold in high esteem and affection.

G. Bernard Shaw

To SALLY LUTHER

[Y/73; X/438]   23rd February 1948

[Sally Luther, a journalist employed on the Minneapolis *Star Tribune* and a publicist for the Civic Theatre, cabled to Shaw: "Pygmalion opens here Wednesday as supreme effort of struggling Minneapolis Civic Theatre. Controversy rages over ending. Shall we use Mrs Pat Campbell's line What size and make villagers happy or shall we leave them in Shavian suspension?" Despite Shaw's interdiction the "happy" ending was used.]

I absolutely forbid the Campbell interpolation or any suggestion that the middleaged bully and the girl of eighteen are lovers.

Bernard Shaw

To JOHN REITH

[H/99]   25th February 1948

[Lord Reith had retired from his position as the B.B.C.'s Director-General. The "scraps" of Elgar's Third Symphony are reproduced in facsimile in William H. Reed's *Elgar as I Knew Him* (1936), which Shaw had a hand in editing.]

Dear Lord Reith

You cannot deplore your departure from the B.B.C. more than I did; for I knew by long political observation that though in this country one gets to the front as an able man of action, once there his only way to political power is to convince the Government that he will not use it to do anything that can possibly be left undone. Macdonald began as the most intransigent Socialist in the movement. He became P.M.

as what Beatrice Webb called him: a façade. Baldwin could be trusted to promise everything and do nothing but get photographed with a pipe in his mouth.

You have never shaken off your reputation as a man of action; and nothing but another war will ever make you a P.M. It took that to do the trick for Lloyd George and Churchill when the foe was at the gate.

The Elgar affair was magnificent on your part; but on his it was a failure. He tried to compose a symphony, and produced a few scraps which he played for me at his house in Worcester, where I was a frequent visitor: he playing the piano and Reid (Billy Reid now dead) the fiddle. I could make neither head nor tail of the stuff. There was certainly no big theme in it.

The fact is he was dying. For some years, his spine had been visibly going wrong, getting humped at the neck. My wife urged him to consult an osteopath; but no persuasion could induce him to resort to a doctor who was not on the British register: that was his sort of snobbery. It cost him his life.

He was given to complaining that his fame made people expect him to work *honoris causa* and left him unpaid and in want of money. I told him that my business as a playwright obliged me to keep a large balance at my bank for emergencies and that if he was ever at a loss up to a thousand it would make no difference to me, only to the bank. He presently wrote to me for it, alleging a domestic financial crisis. I paid up; and immediately he bought a car for £800 and made a present of it to Miss [Mary] Clifford, his very attractive secretary.

I of course wrote it off as irrecoverable; but when he died he left his daughter [Carice] a settled income, but no ready money. I had to rake out my cheque and put in a claim against his estate for the thousand as a loan. It was allowed; and I transferred it to his daughter's private account and saved the situation for her.

What he did with your donation I do not know. Probably bought a Rolls Royce with it.

You may find this peep behind the scenes instructive when you are at work on your autobiography [*Into the Wind*, 1949]. It needs no answer.

G. Bernard Shaw

816

To FANNY HOLTZMANN

[H/1; X/439.e]   5th April 1948

[Fanny Holtzmann (1903–80) was a New York attorney who specialised in
motion picture and copyright cases. Among the clients she represented were
Gertrude Lawrence, Noël Coward, Clifton Webb, and Fred Astaire. She and
Gertrude Lawrence (1898–1952) had been using their combined powers of
persuasion to convince Shaw to let them musicalise *Pygmalion*.]

My dear Fanny
    Stop cabling crazy nonsense.
    What you need is a month's holiday.
    Noel could not conceivably interfere in my business.
    My decision as to Pygmalion is final: let me hear no more about it.
This is final.

GBS

To M. BAXTER

[H/9]   17th April 1948

[Dr M. Baxter (1904–71) was secretary of the recently-formed H. G. Wells
Memorial Fellowship Scheme.]

Dear Dr Baxter
    I think the Wells Committees suggestions need further consideration.
    First, I detest the practice of making presents to ourselves in the
shape of hospital beds and lectureships on the pretext of commemorating the great. A memorial should be a public monument having no
further utility whatever, like the Scott monument in Edinburgh. A
statue on Primrose Hill, a bust in Hanover Terrace, or even a mulberry
tree in Regent's Park, would be a genuine memorial.
    But let that pass.
    A Wells Fellowship for the promotion of his ideas is recommended;
but what were his specific ideas? Those which took any practical form,
the division of our absurd local government areas into planned regions,
the tank, the radio-active bomb, need no promotion. His declaration
of Human Rights was not a step in advance of Jefferson and Tom
Paine 175 years ago, and left him in despair. He chalked up many ideas,
but ran away from them when anyone proposed to put them into
practice. He attacked his best friends at home and abroad furiously,
denouncing Fabianism and Marxism, the Webbs and Stalin, recklessly. Finally his spleen made him, though once the most readable and

hope inspiring of authors, almost unreadable and very discouraging.

In short, he was a great author and should be commemorated, but the last man on earth to be the subject of propagandist lectureships, or indeed of any permanent organization.

What we need is money, a sculptor, and a site.

G. Bernard Shaw

To ELLEN POLLOCK

[H/1]   22nd May 1948

For the moment this poor old crock, overworked to the limit, desires only to be left alone. Why do you want to see me in my decrepitude?

Think of me as I was when I was young and beautiful.

GBS

To SIEGFRIED TREBITSCH

[H.t/5; X/341]   23rd May 1948

[Shaw had discouraged Trebitsch from making another pilgrimage to Ayot.]

... [Y]ou are not coming and that ... is a relief. You dont understand the British dislike of Empfindlichkeit and Sentimentalität. I have had to forbid Pascal to kiss me, as he did at first to the scandal of the village. As to Webb, he was my oldest and best friend as well as my political partner. You think I saw him every day. As a matter of fact, though he lived within a three hours motor drive from me I did not see him for years before his death; and we exchanged very few letters. But our feelings were quite unchanged, as mine are towards you. I never shook hands with Webb in all my life; and I dont want to shake hands with you nor to contemplate your wrinkles. You want to shake my hand and contemplate my wrinkles and my infirm steps so badly that you think it worth while to visit London at a cost that you can afford no more than you can keep a steam yacht just to satisfy your Empfindlichkeit. You must understand that in England this is sentimental nonsense: I have no patience with it; and if we cannot remain good friends without it we had better not pretend to be friends at all.

Of course Tina does not notice your wrinkles: she sees you every

818

day. But you are not a bit like your old self; and neither am I. However, you are still Siegfried Trebitsch; and I can keep my regard for you without seeing you for a hundred years.

Now do you understand?

G.B.S.

To CONAL O'RIORDAN

[K.t/8]   28th May 1948

[O'Riordan died three weeks later, on 18th June. Iago, in Verdi's *Otello*, sings "La Morte è il Nulla" in the Act II aria "Credo in un Dio crudel ..."]

Dear Conal

Are you still alive? You and I are overdoing it: it is time for us to clear out. My hope when I go to sleep every night is that I may never wake; but I have such a lot of work still to do that I seem unable to shuffle off.

I shall not be surprised if you find yourself in the same difficulty; for the doctors are often wrong.

I am not a bit unhappy: old age, though [I'm] a bit tired of it all, is quite cheerful; so I wont condole.

As Verdi's Iago says "La morte e nulla."

G.B.S.

To THE VERY REV. W. R. INGE

[H.t/59]   28th May 1948

[Dean Inge was in hospital for prostate surgery from 2nd May to 11th July. Accompanying Shaw's letter was a typewritten note to Mrs Inge (addressed as Catherine by Shaw, though Kitty to everyone else): "Do as you think best about posting the enclosed or burning it. I leave it to your judgment, as my own is Ga Ga and not to be trusted."]

I have been turning to the bulletins in the papers every morning first thing, and resisting the temptation to bother Catherine for more precise information. I dont know what precisely is the matter; but I conjecture prostate. If so, you have already found that it is an abominable operation; but when the pain is over the recovery is complete: nobody ever dies of it; and it leaves one much jollier. I am not writing

819

from experience but from observation: the last example was my Printer: and he is another and better man.

I know that the contingency of death does not trouble you. For you as for me "la morte e nulla." But I am sure you share my very lively objection to pain, which drives us to the surgeons who, never having been operated on themselves, and associating operations pleasantly with guineas, are apt to promise that they are painless. So it is as well to have lay evidence.

At 92 I am very groggy on my legs; but I still have my wits about me, or imagine I have. I sleep well, always in the hope that I may not wake again; but I am not in the least unhappy.

Old age is not unhappy. I have talked to three centenarians about it: all three women. One said "What is it but buttoning and unbuttoning?" and amused herself by arranging her funeral. The second said it was like being a child again: little things amuse you. The third did not discuss it, but chatted normally. Not one of the three was otherwise than cheerful. They were all resigned to live as long as they must, and had given up hoping for death with all the other vanities.

The confusion of tongues is rampant in political oratory: one can hear nothing but the wheezing of windbags who do not know what they are wheezing about. The first need of the moment is a Catechism and a Dictionary.

This is enough of me for one morning. Dont regard it as that haunting terror, a letter that must be answered.

I have to type my letters because I write like a child making pot-hooks and hangers, very slowly.

G.B.S.

To GENE TUNNEY

[S(H)/9]   9th June 1948

[Joe Louis (1914–81), the "Brown Bomber," was American heavyweight champion 1937–49, who defended his title twenty-five times. He arrived in London on 24th February 1948 for an exhibition tour that earned him $80,000 by the time he left England on 27th March.]

Dear Gene

It may amuse you to hear that when Jo[e] L. arrived here it was announced that the only people he wished to visit were myself and Winston Churchill.

Woodcut engraving by John Farleigh, July 1949 (unpublished)
(Burgunder Shaw Collection, Cornell University Library)

Shaw at Ayot St Lawrence, 1948

(Photograph by H. E. Brooks; Shaw collection of Dan H. Laurence, University of Guelph Library)

Shaw and Jawaharlal Nehru, Ayot St Lawrence, 29 April 1950

(Photograph by F. E. Loewenstein?; Burgunder Shaw collection, Cornell University Library)

Shakes versus Shav, Malvern, July 1949
Waldo S. Lanchester marionettes

(Shaw collection of Dan H. Laurence, University of Guelph Library)

The whole British Press made a rush for me (probably also for Churchill) to learn the date and place and hour and minute of the visit.

I said I had not heard from Mr Louis; but two comparatively unknown persons like myself and Mr Churchill could not but feel flattered by a visit from a world-famous head of his profession.

This redoubled the clamor for the date. I repeated that I had not heard from the champion; but that he and Mrs Louis would be welcome in my house after his tour, when there could be no question of advertizing ourselves. It would be strictly private: no photographers, no reporters, no interviewing, only we three for the pleasure of meeting one another.

And that was the last I heard of it. I have no reason to believe that J. L. knew about the stunt at all, or had ever heard of me or of Winston.

I am told that the tour was a failure, and am not surprised; for exhibition spars in soft gloves draw no gates here: they are out-of-date and forgotten; and our sporting crowds know nothing about boxing. What they pay for is bashing. Louis got his $100,000 (reputed) for nothing.

I hope you are all well at home, as I hold you in affectionate remembrance.

I am damnably old (92) and ought to be dead.

GBS

To ERIC BENTLEY

[H/52; X/440]   11th June 1948

[Eric R. Bentley (b. 1916), theatre historian, dramatist, critic, and teacher, published *Bernard Shaw: A Reconsideration* in 1947. The Cromwell reference is to a remark made to a Monsieur Bellièvre, quoted in the *Mémoires* (1717) of Jean-François de Gondi, Cardinal de Retz: "One never rises so high as when one does not know where one is going." Despite Shaw's insistence that he did not see the Webbs' *Decay of Capitalist Civilization* until after its publication, Beatrice Webb's diaries for September and October 1922 indicate that Shaw "amended" Part I, "pointed and perfected" the first proof, and added "one or two paragraphs of his own where he thought we had not made our meaning clear" (British Library of Political and Economic Science). The typescript of the introduction was so extensively amended and corrected by Shaw as to constitute a rewriting. Bentley's statement that Shaw revised the proofs was drawn from a prefatory acknowledgment by the Webbs in the 1923 edition; he did not amend the statement in his revised edition of 1957.]

Dear Mr Bentley

There are two sorts of books I cannot read: books about Socialism and books about myself. But people have been bothering me lately for my opinion of your essay; and I have dipped into it, and found it by far the best critical description of my public activities I have yet come across.

Let me tell you a few things you have missed. Wide as was the range of the Webb interests, there was one sort of human animal they had never met, and indeed had never been able to conceive as possible until they met me. That animal was the Irishman. Webb was ready for anything or anybody: he had a very few personal dislikes which he never indulged by doing an injury to their objects; but he had no hatreds nor even prejudices, and he took me on cheerfully as all in the day's work, and actually liked me in spite of my novelty, and valued the new light I threw on all his readymade beliefs. Besides, as we had the same frame of reference, there was nothing to puzzle him in my mental methods.

Beatrice was full of hatreds and class prejudices. She could not bear people whom she could not class. She despised the poor middle class, and was for a long time kept aloof from the Fabians by social and intellectual snobbery. She hated the Irish. She hated the Chinese and always championed the Japanese against them. She hated the Chinese because they were unaccountable, incalculable, and could not be classified. To her, actors, in whom she took no interest, were insincere vagabonds and literary nobodies.

I, as an Irishman, a genius, and a born and incurable actor, was trebly abhorrent to her; and it is enormously to her credit that instead of detaching her husband from me as Mrs Granville-Barker did, she forced herself to receive and tolerate me because I was Sidney's loyal friend and had dramatized him as the ablest man in England: a thing he was utterly incapable of doing for himself.

When she found that I was no trouble in the house, and very useful in literary work, she put herself quite at her ease with me by classifying me as a Sprite, and we became thorough friends: in fact until I married I was practically a member of her household.

As such I was a grindstone for the Webbs' wits, and they for mine. Nothing is idler than discussion of how much of the Fabian work was theirs and how much mine. My Irish approach to a subject was so different to theirs, and my insistence on thinking it out to its final meaning and consequences so opposed to their British agreement with Cromwell that no man goes farther than he who does not know whither he is going, that they argued every step so fiercely that visitors who witnessed our daily battles could not believe that we could ever speak to oneanother again, and were amazed to find us on the friendliest terms at the next meal.

All this time I was writing 2000 words of art criticism every week and arguing every sentence down to its final point with the analytical faculty that was my special gift as a critic. It stood me and the Webbs in good stead whenever they asked me to write a summary of their argument into one or other of their chapters.

Now it is evident that the result of this unique collaboration was neither pure Webb nor pure Shaw juxtaposed, but Webb and Shaw amalgamated.

But note carefully that it ceased when I married, after which I no longer lived with the Webbs for months at a time, but only visited them or lunched with them for occasional days. Failure to grasp this has led you into a flat mis-statement of fact at the top of page 21, where you write that I revised The Decay of Capitalist Civilization. I never saw nor discussed a word of it until it was published, when I immediately objected that its call for two parliaments, political and industrial, should have been for dozens of industrial parliaments and an initiative politbureau with nothing to do but think. I thought the book should have gone much farther, and ranked it as their least thought out book.

I was no longer writing weekly critical feuilletons; but in casting my plays I was continually up against the differences in human ability, whilst the Webbs were continually up against the average man with whom legislation has to deal. With my springing on the Fabians of the case for equality of income, and the reduction of it to a basic income sufficient to make all the classes intermarriageable and Carnegie, Rockefeller, and Caruso fortunes negligible, the Webbs had nothing to do: they were as much surprised by it as anybody; but they saw its soundness and accepted it.

The Webbs['] anti-Marx phase and subsequent conversion is a fable. It was I who, though a confirmed Marxist, was determined that Fabianism should be presented as entirely British. Marxism and Wagnerism were being presented in a horrible jargon of dictionary-translated Hegel and Schopenhauer which was neither English nor German. Webb had come to Socialism through John Stuart Mill. So had Morris. Beatrice was a Socialist self-made. Olivier was a Comtist. Henry George had converted thousands to Collective Thinking. So had Ruskin. That is why Marx is not even mentioned in Fabian Essays. I alone postulated that an English movement must be conducted in the English language. I was myself an artist in literature. Webb, though he wrote and read enormously, never thought of himself as an artist, never aimed at artistic perfection, and never wasted a minute when he had done his job well enough. He was the simplest of souls, and the ablest: a phenomenally rare combination. He ended by making the best speeches without taking the trouble to make any but the nearest listeners hear them. That was why he made so little impression in Parliament, where acting (of which he was incapable) and skilled oratory are everything. In his Fabian days he was an effective speaker because his voice was naturally loud enough. But a platform artist he never was.

This is as much as I have time to write. It may help you when you revise.

faithfully
G. Bernard Shaw

To GEORGINA MUSTERS

[H.t/9]   4th July 1948

[Jiddu Krishnamurti (1895–1986), ascetic Indian philosopher, was adopted at thirteen and educated by Dr Annie Besant, who created the Order of the Star in the East in 1911 with Krishnamurti as its World Teacher. As teacher and author of some three dozen books, he advocated spiritual liberation through austere self-knowledge.]

My hand writing is now so slow and tiresome to me that I have fallen back on doing a good deal of my own typewriting; but I note that you will be available in July [to deputise for the holidaying Blanche Patch]. . . .

I once met Krishnamurti. He was the most beautiful human creature I had ever seen. Both his beauty and the attempts of Mrs Besant and the Star-in-the-East group to make a Messiah of him would have turned the head of any ordinary mortal; but he kept his wits about him and defeated them all. I have never read anything of his doctrine that I disagree with.

G.B.S.

To SIEGFRIED TREBITSCH

[H.t/5; X/341]   8th July 1948

[The Trebitschs had moved into a comfortable but modest apartment on
Zürich's Dufourstrasse. The Schauspielhaus, Zürich, was preparing for the
world première production of *Buoyant Billions*, which opened on 21st
October for fifteen performances. *Zu viel Geld* (*Too Much Money*) was
Shaw's choice of title for the German translation, in preference to the management's suggestion of *Zu viel Zu viel*. *Kaiser Diokletian* (1922), an unpro-
duced play by Trebitsch, dealt with the Roman militarist and reformer who
seized power and was proclaimed emperor by his army in AD 284.]

My dear Trebitsch

I have revised B.B. drastically, cutting out Thirdborn altogether as
he has no character and says nothing that cannot be said by the others.
Also I have greatly improved the mathematician, and deleted much
superfluous dialogue. I will send you the revised version as soon as it
is printed. What do you intend to call it? In English the word buoyant
means not only floating in water as a cork does, but, when applied to a
human being, energetically highspi[ri]ted, gaily superior to misfortune.
And Billionen is a familiar and quite intelligible German word which
came into use during the inflation after 1918. I am assured of this by
Loewenstein who, as an echt Berliner, maintains that you do not know
a word of German, and speak and write a barbarous Austrian dialect.
His suggestion of DER BILLIONEN SPRUDEL seems to me
acceptable.

As to your change of address I told you years ago that this was inevitable, and that you and Tina could no longer afford to live in hotels
of the Dolder class and put up in Park Lane in London instead of
Bloomsbury. But you have not yet learnt the lesson: rich habits are
hard to shake off. Tina cannot imagine I have not unlimited money.

But it is astonishing how soon one gets used to cramped flats. On a
sea voyage one has to live in a cabin no larger than a pantry on shore.
In two days one feels quite at home in it. In Hietzing you were never
unhappy because your house was not a royal Schloss; and you will not
be unhappy in your new flat because it is not a Dolder suite. Here in
England there is such a shortage of houses and servants that ladies like
Tina are scrubbing and cooking[,] sleeping and eating, in single rooms;
but they seem all the better for it. If only you were both younger I
should not pity you.

If you have made Diocletian sufficiently topical (Stalin or Tito in
disguise) this may prove the moment for it.

                                                             G.B.S.

                                                                825

To DODD, MEAD & COMPANY

[H.t/1; X/441.e]   12th July 1948

[Although the phrasing suggests that Shaw scrawled his initials for the designer in the midst of the letter, they appear only in their normal position at the foot.]

Dear Dodds

Drown your designer. There is nothing so ugly in print as a combination of type with ordinary handwriting. If I were a great artist-calligrapher like Michael Angelo, whose handwriting was more beautiful than any fount of type, then a lithograph of my holograph would make any book an art treasure. As it is, it would make any book a disgusting curiosity, like binding it in the skin of some famous murderer.

Your designer ought to know this as well as I do. If he has an incurable fancy for my initials, here they are as I scrawl. They make a sort of butterfly pattern. Let him redraw them artistically and repeat them all over the page as he would in a wallpaper; and the result would be a presentable end paper for the inside of the cover.

I have changed the title to SIXTEEN SELF SKETCHES partly because there must be no suggestion of a full dress Autobiography, and also because a title must be easy to speak, easy to spell, and unmistakeable to pronounce.

Autobiography is a hard word. Many people are uncertain about both the spelling and the pronunciation.

The illustrations will follow when Maxwell gets them done.

I shall be 92 on the 26th. Please do not congratulate me. Wish me no returns.

G.B.S.

To E. MARGARET WHEELER

[T/9]   22nd July 1948

Dear Mrs Twodimples

. . . Literature is not the only tool of the artist and poet. The reason I do not write love plays like Romeo and Juliet, Tristan and Iseult, Francesca di Rimini, and Deirdre is that they are the business of Mozart and Wagner, Gounod and Puccini, after whose music Juliet's spoken verses, except for their verbal music, are like the quips of a lawyer's clerk. The words spoil the music. Michael Angelo wrote reams of sonnets; but what are they beside the speechless prophets and sybils in the Sistine Chapel? Is there any written or writable description that makes you see the Venus of Milo or the Hermes of Praxiteles? Do the gardeners' catalogues with which Milton padded Paradise Lost do for you what Turner and Monet did with a few dabs of paint?

Well, what is your other talent if you except your literary talent? Can you compose music? Can you draw? Can you carve marble or model clay? I never wanted to be a writer. I wanted to be a painter. I wanted to be a musician. But I couldnt draw. I couldnt compose. If anyone had taught me I could have been a mediocre artist or painter or actor or singer or pianist. But nobody taught me; and I was a born writer. You must use the talent you have, not the talent you have only a taste for. You cannot really taste the talent you are born with, just as you cannot taste water because it is always in your mouth. . . .

G.B.S.

To ROY LIMBERT

[A/3]   12th August 1948

Dear Roy

Broadcasts absolutely barred.

Never let a play be broadcast until it is so hackneyed that all play-goers have seen it in the theatre. People who make its acquaintance through the mike consider that they know it and need not pay to see it on the stage.

But when they *have* so seen it, a broadcast may revive a desire to see it again. So old plays, yes: new ones never.

G.B.S.

To JAWAHARLAL NEHRU

[H/124; X/442]   18th September 1948

[Jawaharlal Nehru (1889–1964), India's first prime minister, guided his nation through its early stage of independence. He wrote from New Delhi on 4th September, recalling that he had heard Shaw lecture at Cambridge when he was an undergraduate there, and as he had been moulded by his reading of Shaw and had always felt close to him, he asked for permission to visit when he came to England in October. "If I have the privilege to meet you," he concluded, ". . . it will be to treasure a memory which will make me a little richer than I am" (X/442). By the time Shaw's response reached India and then followed the already-departed Nehru to Paris it was too late to include a visit in Nehru's itinerary. He eventually came to Ayot on 29th April 1950.

Shaw's visit to India was part of the itinerary of his 1931 world cruise with Charlotte. Mohammed Ali Jinnah (1876–1948), leader of the All-India Moslem League, which agitated for a separate Moslem state, became governor general of Pakistan after the partition of India in 1947 created an Islamic state with British dominion status. It became a republic in 1956, six years after India had achieved complete independence.

Eire was formally inaugurated as the Republic of Ireland on Easter Monday 1949.]

Dear Mr Nehru

I was greatly gratified to learn that you were acquainted with my political writings; and I need hardly add that I should be honored by a visit from you, though I cannot pretend that it will be worth your while to spend an afternoon of your precious time making the journey to this remote village, where there is nothing left of Bernard Shaw but a doddering old skeleton who should have died years ago.

I once spent a week in Bombay, another in Ceylon; and that is all I know at first hand about India. I was convinced that Ceylon is the cradle of the human race because everybody there looks an original. All other nations are obviously mass produced.

Though I know nothing about India except what is in the newspapers I can consider it objectively because I am not English but Irish, and have lived through the long struggle for liberation from English rule, and the partition of the country into Eire and Northern Ireland, the Western equivalent of Hindustan and Pakistan. I am as much a foreigner in England as you were in Cambridge.

I am wondering whether the death of Jinner will prevent you from coming to England. If he has no competent successor you will have to govern the whole Peninsula.

faithfully
G. Bernard Shaw

To ROBERT WILLIAMSON

[A/3; X/443]   3rd October 1948

[Shaw learned to ride a bicycle in 1895; for a description of his first efforts see his letter to Janet Achurch, 13th April 1895. The bone shaker, the earliest crank-and-pedal bicycle (*c.* 1865), was a heavy all-metal machine, weighing over thirty-five pounds and lacking rubber tyres. The penny farthing (*c.* 1885) was a very tall bicycle, with one large and one small wheel. Robert Williamson, journalist and publicist, was press officer for the bicycle show opening on 18th November.]

I remember the bone shaker and the penny farthing very well, but, being by profession a man of genius, could not afford a bicycle until I was 40, by which time both had been superseded by the safety bicycle with pneumatic tyres. I rode this until 1908, when I took to motoring. I had ten years of it.

Bicycling is like other exercises as far as bodily health is concerned: that is, harmless if you dont do too much of it. It is the effect on the mind of the extension of the day's travel from a few miles to a hundred that gives the bicyclist such an enormous advantage over the pedestrian, to say nothing of the saving in boot leather.

When a ride of fifty miles and upward is undertaken the cyclist must walk all the hills for the first hour, and postpone all heavy eating until the ride is over. A beefsteak is almost disabling. A thin slice of brown bread with currant jam and a cup of tea or a glass of shandygaff is quite enough.

To learn biking try to stand a penny on its edge. Impossible when the penny is stationary, easy when it is rolling. Once convinced of this, rush the machine and jump on. Jump off or fall off when it stops. Keep on at this until you *suddenly* find that you can balance. Do not expect to improve with practice. You wont. The change from hopeless failure to complete success is instan[tan]eous and miraculous.

G. Bernard Shaw

To BRUCE BYROLLY

[E/73]   9th October 1948

["Few people," a student named Bruce Byrolly had written from Waterbury, Conn., on 5th October, "realize the magnificence and beauty of the pipe organ, and of Mr. Bach's great works for that instrument. Surely, Mr. Shaw, you can not deny that during some time in your life you have been moved to passion of a celestial nature by organ music." Shaw's reply was written on Byrolly's letter.]

The modern organ with its mixture stops and equal temperament tuning (or mistuning) is a horrible instrument.

Bach's organ music should be played on flupipe organs with mean tone tuning. So should Handel's. There are still some in old village churches.

G. Bernard Shaw

The modern high pitch is of course all wrong for XVIII century key instruments.

To FANNY HOLTZMANN

[K/1]   [Undated: assigned to 15th October 1948]
[Kasha is buckwheat, a staple grain in the diet of many Russian Jews in America.]

My dear Fanny

By all means send me a packet of kasha: I cannot get it here. But dont send anything else eatable. The conviction current in America that we are all starving here is not true—YET. My fans in the U.S.A. send me hampers of the common necessaries of life, mostly things that I never eat. They are all purchasable here.

It is not worth coming to England to see the little that is left of me; but come if you will: I shall have the better of the exchange.

GBS

To THE DEPUTY EDITOR OF THE TIMES

[H/47]   28th October 1948
[The deputy editor (Shaw addressed the letter in error to the sub-editor) of The Times was Alfred Patrick ("A.P.") Ryan (1900–72), who had recently joined the staff after several years with the B.B.C. Shaw's letter, "Basso Continuo," which concerned orchestral basses, appeared in The Times on 25th October.]

PRIVATE
Dear Sir

As you are the most powerful and effective power in determining English literary usage in the world may I have a word with you?

In my Basso Continuo letter you added the definite article to the title of Handel's Oratorio. This is customary; but it is incorrect. The title of the work is Messiah, not *The* Messiah, which conveys a different shade of meaning.

I have given up ending my letters with yours truly, yours faithfully, yours sincerely, and yours etc. They are simply a nuisance and waste a line of space. I suggest that The Times should cut them out altogether. Next to their omission I should prefer the old dignified "Your obedient servant." But their total disuse would save tons of ink, acres of paper, and much embarassment as to how far the writer should go in the way of intimacy.

One more point. A most discourteous practice is beginning to call the chief Russian statesman Mister Stalin. This is inexcusable. He is Marshal Dhugashvili or Generalissimo Vissionarovich; but under no circumstances should the soubriquet which he has made famous be mentioned or written with a prefix, as if he were a small shopkeeper. Wellington did not mean to be complimentary when he called Napoleon Boney; but at least he did not call him Mister Boney, nor did French grognards call him Monsieur le Petit Caporal.

It is for you to decide these matters; for what you do, goes.

G.B.S.

To FLORA ROBSON

[H/1; X/444]   15th November 1948

[(Dame) Flora Robson (1902–84) was contemplating a British tour, as Lady Macbeth, which she had performed in New York that year, and as Lady Cicely in *Captain Brassbound's Conversion*, in which she had appeared at the Lyric Theatre, Hammersmith, in October. This letter provides insight into how Shaw might have staged *Macbeth* at Stratford in 1933 if he had not reneged on his commitment to William Bridges-Adams.]

My dear Flora

. . . Most Lady Macbeths imagine that the sleepwalking scene is the great scene. It isnt. Anybody can play it. It plays itself.

The scene that takes out of you all that you have in you is the one in the first act (I suspect Mrs Siddons primed herself for it with a pint of porter); for all star Macbeths try to steal it by swaggering instead of cowering in a chair and crying piteously "I prithee peace. I dare &c" in the desperation of a henpecked man, while she towers over him, storming and raging and dominant. But if he will not play down you must play up and let yourself go for all you are worth; for you must get on top at all costs; and that will pretty well finish you for the evening.

But the other big scene (the dagger one) is yet to come. The difficulty here is to shew that she is drunk without making the audience

831

laugh. The rest is easy: you may be exhausted after the termagant scene; but you have not to let yourself go out again: anyone can say "Give ME the daggers." She is still the dominating shrew, but only contemptuous this time.

I must stop. When I start stage managing I am apt to go on for ever.

G. Bernard Shaw

To ETHEL M. EDGEWORTH

[S(H)/108; X/445]   25th November 1948

[Ethel M. Edgeworth, apparently a composer and musicologist with an interest in folk music, had written from Tullow, Co. Carlow, Ireland. Malcolm Lawson, musician acquaintance of Shaw in the 1880s, was choral conductor of the Gluck Society.]

Dear Miss Edgeworth

I was a musical critic 60 years ago. Now I am an old ghost of 92, quite unable to do anything to help you.

Cecil Sharp's collection of Somersetshire songs had such success that if you provide an effective piano accompaniment (not the dreary rum-tum tacked on to Moore's Melodies) you might induce a Dublin music publisher to take them up, or even a London or Edinburgh one. Malcolm Lawson's Scottish melodies must have paid their way.

The difficulty in collecting these airs from peasants, who alone know them, is that they regard all music and everything pleasant as forms of debauchery, and will not confess to any knowledge or practice unless you can convince them that you are as abandoned a profligate as themselves. They are confirmed in this by the words they sing to the airs, which are sometimes unfit for publication, and quite often senseless.

They also consider certain songs as their individual property: such and such a song is Mrs. Murphy's and is sung by her only; and such another Paddy Kelly's, and so on.

Moore, who sang by ear, changed the tunes unconsciously; but as he was a real poet, often at his best in fitting words to them he immortalized them. The Red Fox became "Let Erin Remember" and beat the Marseillaise all to nothing. "Silent, O Moyle, be the roar of thy waters" is unforgettable. If only he had had a Cecil Sharp to compose the accompaniments!

That is your chance.

G. Bernard Shaw

To J. R. TILL

[A/1]   30th November 1948

[J. R. Till (b. 1911) had written to Shaw concerning a question in the most recent English Language and Literature Final Honours Examination at Oxford: "What are, or what would have been, the chief differences in values and in emphasis between Shakespeare's *Antony and Cleopatra* and the same theme had it been treated by Bernard Shaw?"]

A stupid question: the themes are not the same. The shallow romantic soldier Antony and Cæsar the genius are as different as possible. The real contrast is between the Shakespear-Plutarch Cæsar, a megalomaniac with his head turned by popularity, and the Shaw–Mommeson–Goethe great man.

If I had been foolish enough to touch the fullblown Cleopatra after Shakespear I should have been bothered as to how to reconcile her splendid end with her flight from Actium. But I daresay I should have found a way out. I always do when it comes to the point: never sooner.

G.B.S.

To BLANCHE PATCH

[A/73]   11th December 1948

[Due to complications beyond his control John Wardrop was unable to pursue his law degree. After working in London as an advertising agency copywriter, he emigrated to the United States in 1950, where, starting with the lowest editorial-grade post in the Washington-based Bureau of National Affairs, he became within a dozen years advertising manager of its publication *Report for the Business Executive*, and eventually director of marketing of the books division.]

Wardrop wrote me several pages quoting my works to shew that I owe it to my character and reputation to give him £3000 to start with in America.

I tore the letter up. He shall get no further echo out of me.

GBS

To THE REV. JAMES P. SHERWIN

[F.u/4]   [Undated: 1949?]

[The Rev. (later Archdeacon) James P. Sherwin (d. 1960, "at a great age"), was the parish priest of St Kevins, Harrington Street, Dublin.]

Dear Father Sherwin

My late sister Lucy at one time decided to be on the safe side when the judgment day came, and accordingly went to Mass on Sunday morning and to a Protestant church for the evening service. Your letter suggests that the Rev William Carroll, Emily's father, was to the same extent an undenominational Christian. Was this so?

He was the first Protestant clergyman to declare himself a Home Ruler. Emily told me that he was a Republican. Altogether an exceptional man, of whom my father used to say that he would have been a Bishop if only he had been able to keep his temper.

St Kevins did not exist in my time: the north side of Harrington St was incomplete: only a few houses at each end. Is there a photograph of St Kevins obtainable by alms in any form? If so I should like to see one. Tell the verger, or whoever looks after the bookstall.

[G. Bernard Shaw]

To THE REV. H. COTTON-SMITH

[S/1]   [Undated: 1949]

[The Rev. Harry Cotton-Smith (1865–1952), Vicar of Nettleham, had written to Shaw to chastise him for use of a split infinitive in a review published in the *Saturday Review* on 13th April 1895, subsequently collected in *Our Theatres in the Nineties* (1931). The offending passage read: "I have twice had to resign very desirable positions on the critical staff of London papers of first-rate pretension—in one case because I was called upon ... to write corrupt puffs of the editor's personal friends, with full liberty, in return, to corruptly puff my own. ..." "Excuse one only 84 years old," wrote the sender, "daring to criticise one [nearly] 94 years young, but being a member of Trinity College, Dublin (your own city) we have a kind of 'Alma Mater' in common."]

Only from T.C.D. could come the obsolete and illiterate notion that "split infinitives" are not idiomatic and classical English. They are as correct as "split indicatives." If you must pontificate, reserve your encyclicals for mis-placed 'onlies,' which are irritatingly prevalent.

G. B. S.

To THE REV. H. COTTON-SMITH

[S/1]   [Undated: 1949]

["Now," replied the Reverend, "you are defending a sort of *double* split. The preposition 'to' is used as an indicative of the infinitive. It is unjust to interpose an adverb between the 'to' and the expected verb. Would a Frenchman dare to split 'parler bien' into 'parl-bien-er'? In German, would you write 'zu-zurück-schreiben' for the correct 'zurück-zu-schreiben' ('to back answer' for 'to answer back')? As to obsolete illiterate notions from T.C.D., would you ever hear 'split infinitives' at the lectures of Salmon, Bernard, Ball, Bury, Mahaffy, or Dowden?"]

Well, why not a double split, or a treble quadruple quintuple centuple split? Nothing wrong with splits as such, is there? Justice is not in question: 'back answer' is already current as 'back-chat,' neither being just or unjust. Your job (or hobby) is to make grammar logical. By all means go ahead for all you are worth. But what is grammar? Usage. Whose usage? The usage of the best masters of language. I am one of the best ten now living: Salmon, Mahaffy, Dowden etc. are not in the same street with ME. What I write goes. Q.E.D.

G.B.S.

To RUTLAND BOUGHTON

[C/2]   4th January 1949

The point to make is that no country in the world exempts science or anything else from State control.

Even the ordering of Prokovief to compose like Balfe and Sullivan is no worse than the fact that the 1st performances of Don Giovanni and Tristan in London were held up for 30 years.

Talking all over the shop about biology and Materialism cuts no ice and confuses the issue. I analyse until I discover that issue, and stick to it.

I wish the others would.

GBS

To IVO L. CURRALL

[H/1]   5th January 1949

[Ivo L. Currall (1902–66), a Luton solicitor, carried out several legal jobs for Shaw, mostly dealing with producing rights and copyrights. An ardent Shavian collector, he willed his collection to the Royal Academy of Dramatic Art. In early January 1949 Currall received a letter from another fanatical Shavian, Allan M. Laing, a Liverpool journalist, who had just read Stephen Winsten's newly-published *Days with Bernard Shaw* (dated 1949, but published in December 1948): "In the recorded talks I continually came upon phrases, opinions and anecdotes already printed in Shaw's works or in books about Shaw, and it pains me to think that G.B.S. is so short of conversational matter that he has to repeat all this to Winsten . . . [O]n the whole the book gave me a feeling of embarrassment on Shaw's behalf" (A/1). Currall communicated the information to Loewenstein, who passed it along to Shaw. Once Shaw had been stimulated to glance into the book he found sufficient inaccuracy to warrant his sending a letter to the *Times Literary Supplement*, which published it on 15th January. "In hardly any passage in the book," he wrote, "as far as I have had time to examine it has Mr. Winsten's art not improved on bare fact and occurrence by adding the charm of his own style to the haphazard crudity of nature." To the dramatist Robert E. Sherwood, who quoted Shaw's *TLS* letter extensively in his notice in the *New York Times* on 27th March, he complained that "W. in his confounded book spoilt more good stories than any writer that ever lived. He has no sense of comedy, and is out of his element in Shawland" (*New York Times Book Review*, 1st May 1949).

The William Hazlitt quotation, with minor amendment, is from "The Conversations of James Northcote, Esq., R.A.," first published in the *New Monthly Magazine* 1826–27 and, revised and enlarged, in book form, 1830.]

Dear Ivo Currall

I have read your letter to F. E. L.

Hazlitt said "What made me dislike the conversations of learned or literary men was that I got nothing from them but what I already knew, and hardly that; for they poured the same ideas and phrases and cant of knowledge out of books into my ears, as apothecaries' apprentices made prescriptions out of the same bottles; but there were no new drugs or simples in their *materia medica* to cause me to feel that I learnt from listening to them."

This explains why there are two sorts of books that I cannot read: books about Socialism and books about myself. I read enough of Winsten's 1946 book, "G.B.S. 90," which he edited, to ascertain whether or no he is a competent writer, and was satisfied that he was. But I did not read a word of the book you write about. I was assured by him and by the publishers that it contained no copyright matter of mine and was within their statutory privileges.

I infer from your letter that this was a blazing lie; but what can I do? The book is out; and W. has had advances on his royalties. To take proceedings would cost me endless time, which is in my case money.

Besides, the Winstens are a remarkable and talented family, the only people in the village I can talk to or can talk to me. Winsten began with 3 years as a Conchy in 1914 [imprisoned in Wandsworth]. His wife Clare is a sculptress and can draw or paint anything. Their son is a precocious mathematician now in Cambridge, who took his degrees when he was still a boy. They are Bohemian Anarchists who have been in everything and know everyone in each Movement. They are vegetarians and are always striking moral attitudes, but are thoroughly goodnatured. I try to bully them into business habits. You should be their solicitor.

That is the situation. You see how impossible it is for me to do anything about the copyright.

G. Bernard Shaw

P.S. I have since looked through the book and found such blunders in it that I think I must write to The Times Literary Supplement about it. . . .

The photograph of my [supposed] first meeting with my future wife is one which I took myself of her meeting with Henry Salt when she had been married to me for a year. That is a sample.

To RUTLAND BOUGHTON

[C/2]   7th January 1949

[*Maria Marten*, an anonymous popular melodrama of the nineteenth century, was filmed four times, in 1902, 1913, 1928, and 1935. No record has been found of a film version of J.B.Buckstone's *The Wreck Ashore* (1830).]

There is no evidence that Proko has been ordered to compose like Wagner & Beethoven. HE DOES. What they want is Maritana or The Bohemian Girl. We denounce them for such Philistinism, and then order the subsidised film companies to produce screen plays like Maria Marten and The Wreck Ashore.

This is dead on the points now at issue, which are (a) that Soviet rule is a horrible slavery to which Englishmen would never never never submit, and (b) whether science is any free-r here than in Moscow. Or—for instance, music.

The post-Beethoven composers use music to express their moods, and have none worth suppressing. I prefer Rossini. You dont know the difference between a concerto and a toccata[.] But you can knock out a good tune sometimes. The B.B.C. should revive Alkestis[.]

G.B.S.

To LAURENCE IRVING

[H/1]   18th January 1949

[For Shaw's negotiations with Henry Irving for performing rights to *The Man of Destiny*, see correspondence with Ellen Terry *c*. 26th August 1896 and later.]

Dear Lawrence Irving II

Although I came to know the Charringtons pretty intimately I never heard of any communication between them and H.I. It occurred before my time with them. I am not surprised to learn that Janet borrowed money from him: she borrowed money from everybody she could get into any sort of touch with.

If the £100 loan had come from anyone else than H.I. it would have been an act of extraordinary generosity and a tribute to Ibsen; and it was very generous of H.I. anyhow. But I cannot believe that it had anything to do with Ibsen. It was part of H.I.'s mixture of policy with sardonic humor to buy everybody. He liked to see them selling themselves and bought them partly to gratify that taste. He knew he was being robbed; but would not sack the robbers because it put them in his power and at his command. He tried to buy me, and believed I had come to sell myself. But he did not always buy the right people, and, being as I think, both kindly and princely, he spent too much at the game and ended his Lyceum run penniless.

He enjoyed playing sinister parts; but if you get to the bottom of him I think you will find an amiable and honorable personality. Kate Terry thought him a thoroughpaced egotist (she told me so) but everybody is an egotist; and she probably knew him only at secondhand. I hope he will come from your hands attractively; but it will be a subtle job.

G.Bernard Shaw

To WALDO LANCHESTER

[A/64]   20th January 1949

[Waldo S. Lanchester (1897–1978) and his wife Muriel had for a number of
years operated the Lanchester Marionette Theatre in Malvern, where it was
an adjunct to the Festival Theatre productions. Shaw, at its opening in 1936,
made a short speech in thanks after Barry Jackson formally opened the
theatre. When Lanchester in 1949 suggested that Shaw write a play for
puppets, he readily assented.]

Dear Mr Lanchester

I will send you a dialogue presently; but it may not be suitable, as I
do not know how much acrobatics puppets are capable of.

Do not elaborate the scenery: it distracts the attention of the
audience from the actors. As I see it now there will be no scenery: only
a background, floorground, and ceiling (if any) of rich dark green stuff,
or even black velvet. For Shakespear must begin with a speech
addressed directly to the audience, as Richard III does, explaining who
he is.

However, we shall see.

GBS

To ARTHUR DAVIES

[E/2]   21st January 1949

[Arthur Davies of Santa Monica, California, had inquired whether the
appearance or existence of an apparition had ever been proved to Shaw's
satisfaction "beyond any doubt."]

Never. But I once walked into a room and saw myself sitting at an
escritoire. As I stared, I vanished.

GBS

To F. N. HORNSBY

[H/1]   16th February 1949

[F. Noël Hornsby (1903–75) was managing director of Whitehall Court
1931–60.]

Dear Mr Hornsby

I am now more than half way through my 93rd year; and it is unlikely that I shall ever see London again. I have not come up for some
years now.

Under such circumstances it is a monstrous extravagance for me to pay a thousand a year for a five room flat when all I need is a study for Miss Patch to work in, a lavatory, and perhaps a bedroom in case I should be burnt out here and need a place to sleep in an emergency. If at the same address so much the better.

I could warehouse or sell my furniture unless by good luck some millionaire or ambassador should need a furnished residence in a hurry.

Will you be so good as to turn this over in your mind at your convenience and oblige me with a suggestion?

The matter is not instantly pressing; but as I am actuarially dead it is bound to come up presently.

G. Bernard Shaw

PS. My notion is that as you must have applications for furnished flats in Whitehall ... it might pay us both if you were to buy my furniture and transfer me to a cheaper two-room flat. You could leave the furniture in 130, to which it is very suitable, or store it in the basement.

To WILLIAM J. PICKERILL

[H/1]   17th February 1949

Dear William Pickerill

It was my uncle who played the ophicleide. I once mastered the cornet, but gave it up when I was told that it would spoil my singing voice.

I now think that the orchestral bass (the weak spot) will be reinforced not by the ophicleide but by the bass saxophone, on which it is possible for a virtuoso to play demisemiquavers prestissimo; so that we may at last hear Beethoven's florid basses as he meant them to be heard and not as a senseless blare.

Thanks to the wireless Palestrina is much better known than he was; but adequate performances are rare as only celibate male singers after years of practise together can do his polyphony justice. Monteverdi, much easier, is becoming quite fashionable.

I note June as a happy month.

G. Bernard Shaw

To ELIZABETH CORBETT

[H/25]   25th February 1949

[Elizabeth Corbett, who lived in the neighbouring town of Hitchin, was concerned for the education of her eldest son, then seven, in the light of the Attlee Government's proposal that public schools should be reduced in number and eventually abolished.]

Dear Mrs Corbett

If you have an income of at least four figures from property or professional earnings, or both when, as often happens, a successful professional man marries a woman of property, then the routine of preparatory school, public school, and university for both children is practically inevitable.

If you have no such resources, and are living from hand to mouth in the best house you can afford, then to stint your expenditure to put your children through the university routine would be senseless snobbery, both for you and for them. The first thing to do for them is to give them the best furnished home you can afford, with books, pictures, a piano, and an atmosphere of culture, a garden if in the country with pets, so they may not grow up afraid of dogs and cats. Bicycles of course.

This comes before everything else in education. With it children without any schooling will grow up presentable human beings with both intellectual and artistic possibilities. Without it neither Eton nor Oxford can leave them any better than sporting barbarians. But the common Elementary School and the Grammar School are available, and a great relief to their mothers. For the boy clever with his hands there is the Polytechnic. For the brainy boy who reads, there are scholarships. For the athletic there are boys' clubs with gymnasia. There are corresponding opportunities for girls.

Children should be brought up to associate and converse on easy terms with all classes, but also to distinguish clearly between classes and sets, and to seek and find and associate with their natural sets. The owner of a Derby winner now meets Einstein occasionally at public dinners on neighborly terms; but neither could endure the same club or the same set. Young people should find society according to their tastes and mental capacities for its own sake, and not for social promotion.

G. Bernard Shaw

To I. J. PITMAN

[H/1; X/446]   3rd March 1949

[Dr Mont Follick (1887–1958), Labour M.P. for Loughborough 1945–55 and a Fabian, was sponsor of a Spelling Reform Bill recently introduced into the House of Commons. Pitman sent a copy to Shaw, and asked for a letter he could read in the House, in which Shaw would set down his views. "This," replied Shaw in a covering letter on 3rd March, "is the best I can do in the way of a letter that will not tire the house and may amuse it. . . . There must be free competition between the old and the new. Follick's demands for compulsion will wreck the Bill unless you support it only as to be amended. He is a schoolmaster, not a politician" (A/1). Shaw's letter was read in the House on 11th March, but had little effect; the motion for a second reading of the Bill was defeated 87–84.]

Dear Mr Pitman

The Bill as it stands with its compulsory and exclusive items is impossible; but it can be made practicable in Committee; and its defeat would be an international calamity.

Nevertheless the House will be frightened off, as it always has been, by the cost of replacing scrapped printers' plant and typewriters, re-arranging and reprinting dictionaries and encyclopedias, transmogrifying the Bible and all the masterpieces of our literature. It has never taken into account the hard fact that a British alphabet of 40 letters would make it possible by rational spelling to save 20% *per minute* in time and labor, and that 20% per minute is more than half a million per cent per year. If that figure does not make Sir Stafford Cripps as keen on Spelling Reform as Mr Follick nothing will.

But a beginning can be made with existing plant. The addition of 14 letters to the present alphabet can be obtained provisionally by handsetting with 14 of the letters turned upside down or with borrowings from the Greek alphabet which all considerable printers stock. By this device school primers can be rationally spelt and children enabled to spell as they pronounce and have their mispronunciations corrected by their teachers.

Although I did not begin writing plays until I was 40, I have written 17 more plays than Shakespear did, besides bulky political treatises bringing Socialism up to date, and a mass of critical essays in Art and Science, to say nothing of letters to The Times. Such an output would have been utterly impossible had it not been drafted in Pitman's 40 letter phonographic alphabet. Keep your eye on your father, Isaac; and he will pull you through.

But perhaps you had better not mention this in debate, as honorable members may not be quite unanimous in regarding my activities as a boon and a blessing.

G. Bernard Shaw

To RUARI McLEAN

[A/1; X/447.e]   28th March 1949

[Ruari McLean (b. 1917), typography and book designer, solicited Shaw's aid in getting "the correct facts about your early interest in typography" for a short account of English modern book design he had been commissioned to write for the British Council. Nicolas Jenson (d. *c.* 1480) was a French engraver and printer who perfected roman type. William Caslon (1692–1766) was an English type founder whose very legible type, in use until about 1800, was later revived by the Chiswick Press.]

My acquaintance with [William] Morris led me to look at the page of a book as a picture, and a book as an ornament. This led to a certain connoisseurship in types and typesetting. I chose old face Caslon as the best after Jensen. I discarded apostrophes wherever possible (dont, wont, cant, shant &c but not Ill shell hell for I'll, she'll, he'll) and banished mutton quads between sentences because they made "rivers" of white in the black rectangle of print. I was particular about margins. When I visited Chantilly I turned over every page of the famous Psalter.

All this began with Morris and his collection of MSS. The Kelmscott Press came afterwards when I already knew what he was driving at.

For my Standard Edition I changed from Caslon to Plantin because the small type I had to use in Caslon was very troublesome to keep clean. I fought linotype and monotype for some time because it would not justify as well as hand set could be made to do; but at last, as always happens, the machine outdid the hand, and got all the best types on it.

I think this is all you want to know.

GBS

To PATRICK O'REILLY

[U(H)/48; X/448]   30th March 1949

[O'Reilly had for several years collected sixpences and shillings along his
dustman's route to pay for a plaque to be erected on the façade of Shaw's
Synge Street birthplace, with an inscription that would read in part: "You
gave your services to your country unlimited, unstinted and without price."
Shaw, vetoing the "blazing lie," sent a substitute inscription to C.G. Sawier
the engraver, which read simply: "Bernard Shaw, author of many plays, was
born in this house 26 July, 1856."]

Dear Mr O'Reilly

Your inscription is a blazing lie. All my political services have been
given to the British Labor movement and to International Socialism.
And I have lived less than 20 years in Ireland and more than 78 in
England. And for all you know I may be hanged yet.

I am sending to Mr Sawier a proper design and inscription: the only
one I will consent to.

The consents of the tenant, the landlord, and the Corporation must
also, I presume, be obtained. The tablet must therefore bear no inscription of opinion as to my merits or demerits, and must state only
the unquestionable fact that I was born in the house.

All the same I fully appreciate your kind interest in the matter.

G. Bernard Shaw

To PATRICK O'REILLY

[E.u/73]   [Undated *c*. 2nd April 1949]

[O'Reilly had requested this information on behalf of an acquaintance,
William J. Jacob of Dublin.]

The mill at the end of Rutland Avenue, Dolphins Barn, which was
in ruin when I last saw it, and has probably now disappeared, was run
by my father's firm (Clibborn & Shaw). I played in it and in the big
field adjoining when I was a boy, but never lived there. There was a
warehouse on the avenue front, and a shop where corn, wheat, flour
and locust beans were retailed to the villagers.

The mill never paid its way; and nobody took it on when C & S.
abandoned it.

The waterwheel or some scraps of it may still be there.

To B.B.C. HEAD OF PLAYS DEPARTMENT [VAL GIELGUD]

[F.u/4]   [Undated: assigned to 8th April 1949]

[Val Gielgud (1900–81), who was head of both Television and Sound Drama, contributed the chapter "Bernard Shaw and the Radio" to *G.B.S. 90* (1946). *Candida* was recorded for the "Curtain Up" series on the Light Programme, broadcast on 30th March and repeated on the Home Service on 2nd April. "Please note," Shaw wrote to M. Elizabeth Barber of The Society of Authors on 8th April, "that I have instructed the B.B.C. to destroy its record of Candida; and do not authorize it to broadcast any play of mine in future without consulting me. It was a silly failure, and will probably kill the play for the next few years. What becomes of these records? They should become the property of the author: otherwise what is to prevent the holder from hiring them out all over the place?" (H/2).

As a consequence of Shaw's criticism, broadcasts of the play that had been scheduled for the Overseas Service were cancelled. The performers of the ill-fated performance included Edith Evans as Candida, Emlyn Williams as Marchbanks, Andrew Cruickshank as Morell, and Hugh Manning as Lexy. The producer was Archie Campbell, the announcer Dermot Cathie.]

Dear Director

Please destroy the Candida record: it is a hopeless failure; its broadcasting has probably killed the play for the next few years. It is underplayed all through; and the end completely sacrificed by [the] delivery by Morell as a casual remark of "D' you mean me, Candida?" instead of the thunderstruck "Do you mean M E, Candida" which is the climax of the play, and the explanation of the finish. Such a blunder shews that neither the actor nor the producer has the least notion of what the play is about.

The announcer omits all the entrances and exits; and as Lexy's voice is undistinguishable from Morell's, no listener can make out which of them is speaking or who is on the stage and who not.

E. E. is badly miscast: she was very clever in the second [act]; but the part makes nothing of her, and she can't make enough of the part: it is not in her line.

You must not broadcast my plays until you get an experienced Shavian producer. You have one at hand in Esme Percy.

Emlyn did not change from the colloquial to the hierarchic when he stood revealed as the stronger of the two: "Out, then, into the night with me!" sounded like "I think I will go out for a bit of a stroll."

845

The tapping of a typewriter does not sound like the rattle of a machine or the banging of a weaver's loom. It was half-way between.

You really are a pack of duffers.

[G. Bernard Shaw]

To JULIUS GOLD

[H/112]   22nd April 1949

[Dr Julius Gold (1883–?), a retired orchestral player and music theorist, had written from California on 3rd April to chastise Shaw: "[Y]ou irritate me intensely when you discuss the formulary side of music in terms of 'textbook jargon.' . . . [T]he charm of at least two studies [*The Sanity of Art* and *Sixteen Self Sketches*] otherwise fascinating was spoiled for me when I found you dealing with a subject in which only bona-fide scholars trained by practice and experience are genuinely skillful. . . . I read both essays with something more than mere academic interest or simian curiosity, only to find a musical terminology clipped and barbarized and bearing just the semblance of the scientific language it debases" (fragment of typed letter, Shaw's Corner).

Alfred Day (1810–49), music theorist and surgeon, wrote his *Treatise on Harmony* in 1845. Sir Frederick Ouseley (1825–89), professor of music at Oxford, published *A Treatise on Harmony* in 1868. Sir John Stainer (1840–1901), also a professor of music at Oxford, was the author of *A Theory of Harmony* (1871). Johann Bernhard Logier (1777–1846), German pianist and teacher, is noted for *Logier's Thoroughbass* (London, 1818). Mozart's *Kurzgefasste Generalbass-Schule* (Vienna, 1818), popularly known as *Mozart's Succinct Thoroughbass*, is listed as a doubtful or suppositious work in the British Library's catalogue of printed music.

The expression *mi contra fa est diabolus in musica* ("mi against fa is the devil in music") was the mediæval rebuke of the tritone. Shaw erred in his statement that Beethoven's Prometheus overture opened with a diminished seventh; it was a dominant seventh. Sir George A. Macfarren (1813–87) presumably reproached Hermann Goetz (1840–76), a now-neglected composer for whom Shaw had a high regard, in Macfarren's programme notes for the Philharmonic concerts. Arrigo Boïto (1842–1918) was an opera composer, best known for his *Mefistofele* (1868).]

Dear Dr Gold

We dont disagree on anything that matters; but your hobby is nomenclature; and you make ends of the verbal tools that to me are only means.

The text books in my time were Day, Ouseley, and Stainer. Day's pseudo-scientific nonsense was tried later by Scriabin and Bartok but produced nothing that could be called music; and they had to drop it. Ouseley was pedantic, and made no real advance on Logier's Thorough-bass, which Logier himself knocked into my mother. Stainer was simple, sensible and historically sound, and was the man for me.

What has actually happened is that the pedants began by harmonizing horribly in consecutive fifths whilst the folk insisted on thirds and sixths. The composers found that thirds sounded sweet; but when they tried three major thirds on top of the dominant, they found that *mi contra fa diabolus est*. It was Monteverde, I think, who tried making [the] top third minor; and found it bearable and dramatic when it was prepared and resolved. It caught on, and culminated in Mozart's "*Trema, trema, scelerato*" in Don Giovanni.

Then the youthful Beethoven discarded preparation and resolution and began his Prometheus overture by blasting the opening chord with the diminished seventh unprepared in the bass. You are too young to remember how strangely impressive it sounded; but I shall never forget it. With the diminished seventh it was easy to modulate into any key; and Schubert and Weber used this to sugar music with inharmonic changes until Beethoven disparaged their works as strings of diminished sevenths.

Wagner, nauseated by the sugar, stuck on another major third and set his trumpets blaring major unprepared ninths. I can remember how they also sounded. It was utterly unlike music; for the orchestras, accustomed to Rossini and Donizetti, could not play it musically, only noisily. From these unprepared major ninths Wagner went on to elevenths and thirteenths in Tristan; but there he had to stop; for the next step brought him back to the starting point; and to what Beethoven had done recklessly in the Eroica: that is, sound all the notes in the major scale simultaneously in one tremendous crash. Nowadays any fool can write any combination or progression he likes without being reproached for bad musical grammar as Macfarren reproached Goetz on the authority of Cherubini.

The result has been that many fools began composing so execrably that we are now glad to switch them off and listen to The Bohemian Girl, Maritana, and the overture to William Tell. Oscar Wilde used to say that we should never dress in the latest fashion because it will be out of date in six months. And sure enough consecutive fifths now sound unbearably out of date, even by Boito, Busoni, and Cyril Scott.

All this is not theory: it is history; and my language is quite correct in terms of it. My numbering from triads to thirteenths is a necessary part of it. You regard it as moral delinquency because your passion for nomenclature drives you to give a different name to every numerable item. Tonic and dominant and subdominant, mediant and submediant, lydian and mixolydian, supertonic and Italian sixth, *etc. etc. etc. etc.* are to me a verbal farrago of which Bach knew nothing, though he used them all. I asked Elgar what text book he could recommend. He said he knew nothing about text book composition, but that the scrap of paper called Mozart's Succinct Thoroughbass was worth looking at because it taught the 4 to 3 suspension.

The snag in your system is that a student forced to learn all the names instead of listening to music and learning only its notation and how to decipher a figured bass, hates music all the rest of his life unless his vocation is irresistible, in which case, like Bach and Elgar, he needs no teacher, knows nothing of names, and everything of sonorities.

Forgive so long a letter. You provoked it by accusing me of reprehensible error and ignorance instead of allowing me my own frame of reference, and Stainer's.

G. Bernard Shaw

To NANCY ASTOR

[H/101]   8th May 1949

My dear Nancy

You must positively not come on the 13th. If you will not let me manage my work and my household in my own way you must not come at all. I have arranged with Mrs Laden that there are to be no visits for the next three weeks; and no visits there shall be.

All this nonsense about my having to be looked after, and the job bequeathed to you by Charlotte, is a worn-out joke which you are beginning to believe in yourself. Let me hear no more of it. You need looking after far more than I do; and nobody knew this better than Charlotte, except perhaps your unfortunate secretaries. You must upset your own household, not mine.

I write in great haste, and am rather angry with you for forcing me to put my old foot down and make you understand that in this house what I say, goes.

As the keeper of a mental patient you are DISCHARGED.

Quite unchanged nevertheless.

G.B.S.

To DANIEL G. DAY

[E/4]   9th May 1949

[Daniel G. Day had written to Shaw from Chicago.]

I have no "view" of death: it is a fact like the rising of the sun every
morning and has simply to be faced, not argued about. The dread of it
does not trouble me in the least (quite the contrary) though it has
corrupted all the religions with escapist fables of immortality which
comfort even murderers on the scaffold.

                                                                               GBS

To BLANCHE PATCH

[H.t/3]   23rd May 1949

[The Whitehall Court transfer to a smaller flat had commenced. As Hornsby
declined to purchase Shaw's furniture, it was consigned to Phillips, Neale &
Co. for auction. Most of the books were auctioned by Sotheby & Co. on
25th July. The Nellie Heath portrait of Shaw, eventually located, was sold
in July at Sotheby's.]

Good Heavens, my dear Blanche, do not dream of "sorting things
out." It would take you months, and probably kill you. And the furniture MUST be got out on Wednesday.

Just empty the drawers out in a heap on the floor higgledypiggledy.
Loewenstein will sort out. He says you proposed to send the drawers
down; but that is nonsense; the bureaux cannot be sold without the
drawers. Do what I say. The study will look untidy for a while; but
it cannot be helped: everything that you cannot do without in 116 must
go, and go TOMORROW as you receive this. There can be no waiting
for the 24th June. It must be possible for you to send for Judy [Mus-
ters] and go to bed on Wednesday night and stay there for a week or
so until you are thoroughly rested.

If necessary Mrs Laden can come up and help. I have not forgotten
for a moment that the move must not be too much for you.

The big bookcase must go, measurements or no measurements. Also
the bureaux, but not the picture cabinet, and perhaps not the filing
cabinet if you will need it. The Ceres desk, the writing table, and the
typewriter stand you will want.

What I have said to H. about my expectation of life is not sentimental rubbish: it is to impress on him that I can not take a long lease

of 116 or buy furniture at my age. It is a matter of business. In his own interest he must be able to get back the flat ready for reletting as soon as possible after my transfer to Golders Green.

Keep the clock for yourself by all means.

If the Nellie Heath portrait is anywhere in the flat it is in the cupboard in the kitchenette; but I now think I must have sent it back to her as a picture she might possibly sell. So bother no more about it.

G.B.S.

To ROY LIMBERT

[H.t/3]   12th July 1949

[Rehearsals had begun for the Malvern Festival production of *Buoyant Billions*, directed by Esmé Percy, who brought several of the performers to Ayot to obtain Shaw's directorial advice at first hand. Frances Day (1908–84), a brisk blonde former showgirl from East Orange, New Jersey, had appeared since 1925 in British cabaret, variety, farce, and films. When signed for Malvern she was starring in the London revue *Latin Quarter*; "She" (Clementina) was her first serious rôle in the theatre. After six scheduled performances at Malvern the production was transferred, with original cast intact, to London, where it survived for only forty performances. "He" (Junius) was played by Denholm Elliott (b. 1922), the Native by Kenneth Mackintosh.]

Dear Roy

I have met Esme Percy, Frances Day, the Native, and the He at the Winstens, and gone over the Panama scene with them.

There are two things you have to procure, regardless of expense. One is a fancy dress of great beauty and strangeness for F.D. Theodora [Winsten] will design it.

The other is a saxophone record of some wellknown air, played by a first rate artist, not as a comic squeak as the jazz bands have it, but properly played and enchanting enough to hold the audience and the two men enjoying it until the snakes and gaters start. The Londonderry air or any other familiar tune of which there is a good record obtainable will do; but it must be a very pleasant classical record, not a jazz.

You must get the chairs from Parkes, and let Esme and Theodora select them. These three points are of vital importance. They may make all the difference between a flop and a success; and a flop will cost you the London option.

F.D. is all right if she is properly handled: a born actress. But she has no conception of her part as yet; and her notion of playing the sax herself and wearing slacks and so forth is out of the question. HE has good looks and the necessary charm; but he has been trained to gabble his words so as to get over all that dull stuff as fast as possible, and must be coached to make the most of them, and never to hurry, as the play is on the short side, and if gabbled will not only bore the audience to tears but be over too soon.

The NATIVE knows his job, and will do it well. F.D's travelling dress and her Orinthia dress had better be designed by Theodora. I cannot sufficiently impress on you the importance of this dress designing. It is a stroke of pure luck that the foolish girl has peroxided her hair white, and produced a bizarre effect that will fit into her two parts; but she will soon find it necessary to shave her head clean and let her hair grow naturally again, wearing wigs until this happens.

Percy was all wrong about the stage business; but I think I convinced him of this and got him on to the right lines. He thought he should keep the players moving and changing sides. My players should never move except to get on or off the stage. Essentially my plays are church services: the spoken word is everything and what people call action nothing.

This is enough for you [to] take in one dose.

G.B.S.

To ADA TYRRELL

[H/1]   14th July 1949

[For an earlier reference to Aunt Ellen (Whitcroft) see headnote to Shaw's letter of 23rd April 1885 to R. Frederick Shaw. Marie C. Stopes (1880–1958), scientist and writer, was president of the Society for Constructive Birth Control and Racial Progress, and a longtime acquaintance of Shaw.]

My dear Addie

. . . That portrait of me with my cheeks in my hands was not meant to suggest grief. You are quite right in believing that I am not a griever. When I was a very small child in Synge Street and news came that my mother's Aunt Ellen was dead I went out into the garden and cried, broken hearted, for a long time (it seems to me at least half an hour), and was terrified by my belief that I should go on crying all my life. But to my astonishment I cried away all my grief in that half hour; and I have never grieved since. This taught me that people who cry and grieve never remember. I never grieve and never forget. When Charlotte died, and people wrote to me sympathizing with my grief and loneliness, I tore up their screeds and cursed them up hill and down dale. I like being alone because I can always tell myself stories, and so am never lonely.

The portrait was meant to shew what I am like in my old age, and to express the thoughtfulness of a profound philosopher.

Do people write to you telling you how to live for ever, or at least to be 100? Marie Stopes assures me she will live to be 140, because she drinks a pint of sea water every day for six weeks. A Russian woman, a famous athlete, is equally sure that the secret of longevity is never to eat anything at all.

You were always notably young for your age, even in your childhood. I am groggy on my legs and pretty deaf; but I pretend to be deafer than I am so that others must answer the telephone calls. . . .

And that is enough for today.

G. Bernard Shaw

To ST JOHN ERVINE

26th July 1949

[H/3]   —93 today—

[The reference to his childhood address was a Shavian lapse: the birthplace address was 3 Upper Synge Street, renumbered 33 Synge Street years later. James Craig (1871–1940), first Viscount Craigavon, was a Unionist M.P. from Belfast 1906–21, who became first prime minister of Northern Ireland 1921–40. Ervine's *Craigavon: Ulsterman* was published later in 1949. The only letter from Horatio Nelson (1758–1805) that has been noted with a text along the lines of Shaw's apparently embellished recollection is one Lord Nelson wrote to Emma Hamilton on 19th May 1799: "I am now perfectly the *great man*—not a creature near me. From my heart, I wish myself the little man again!" (Geoffrey Rawson, ed., *Nelson's Letters*, 1960).]

My dear Sinjon

May I respectfully remind you that when Lincoln was shot (just at the right moment, like Gandhi) my age was 9 years, and my views on the subject so little in demand that I did not take the trouble to form any. . . .

My first experience of addressing a public assembly occurred when I was still so small that when my father took me for a walk he had to carry me in his arms when I tired. One evening we were caught in a heavy shower on the quay. We made a rush for a portico; and all the passers-by did the same. I was carried. The building with the portico had been plastered all over with advertisements by the bill stickers. Seated on my father's shoulder I began to read the advertisements aloud. The sensation I created was immense. The Southern proletariat mostly could neither read nor write; and to see and hear an infinites[i]-mal child read print, hard words and all, was miraculous. But I was not shewing off. It seemed to me that when I was confronted with print I was expected and bound to read it aloud like a lesson.

I remember also being puzzled by my father's habit, when we took a side car home, never to tell the jarvey to drive to 33 Upper Synge St. He always said "Drive in the direction of the Three Rock Mountain,["] (much as if, wanting to be driven to Putney, one told the taxi-man to drive in the direction of Portsmouth). But it was not so silly as it sounded; for all the jarvies knew the road to the 3 Rock. It passed the end of Synge St, which they did not all know.

I tell you these senile anecdotes because you seem to imagine that I issued from my mother's womb a fully fledged G.B.S. But I have not much else to tell you. I am again unable to walk far. I am as I was under the portico; and there is nobody now to carry me. I have survived my second childhood and got my second wind. My routine of sleeping and working never varies; and the months pass like minutes.

The news that you are writing a biography of Craigavon leaves me curious as to how a genius of your calibre could venture on such an unnatural enterprise after one look at that walking monument of obstinate mindlessness. He concentrated into a single enormity all that is most hopeless in Ulster. Not even a reactionary; for reaction means movement; and he was immovable. He had one useful quality: you could always depend on him. That is my impression of him, founded entirely on his photographs: in fact I know nothing else about him. As to Parnell, he made himself purposely disagreeable to the estate office where I was cashier; so I started with a prejudice against him which I never quite got over without reasoning myself out of it. He was a humanitarian, and, like most humanitarians, an implacable hater. I do not think of him as a great man; but that species is fabulous. One of my favorite documents is the letter in which Nelson wishes he were not a great man, as it is the fans who have all the fun and the idol who has all the trouble.

I also had my books burnt in a fire at the binders. I got £2000 insurance; so there must have been a lot of them.

I have cleared out of my flat at Whitehall Court: all my furniture and pictures and books are being auctioned. But the address remains: I have taken a smaller and cheaper flat downstairs as an office for my secretary and a bed for myself in case of emergency. But I shall probably never see London again and dont want to.

Enough. Love to Leonora.

G. Bernard Shaw

To M. ELIZABETH BARBER

[H/2]   26th July 1949

[The Society of Authors had had discussions with the B.B.C. and with British Actors Equity about recent television developments, as Shaw was informed a day or two later. The project broached by Gertrude Lawrence, however, was more ambitious than anything that had yet been attempted, and finally came to nothing.]

Dear Miss Barber

Has the Society yet discussed the new and difficult developments in television? I already have a proposal to allow an actual stage performance of Pygmalion to be televised on full sized screens all over the world. Authors' fees for such a performance must be fabulous compared to anything now being charged. Audiences of many millions paying nothing at the doors, and next to nothing for their licences and receivers, are something new that requires the most careful consideration. Has anything been done?

It is conceivable that later on such performances may be put on for a run, just as advertisements are repeated day after day; but that has not come yet as far as I know. But it will come; and then the author may charge a fixed fee per night; but for the moment a prodigious fee for a single performance is what we have to settle.

I should be glad to hear from you on this question, as Miss Gertrude Lawrence is pressing me about it. She has had the same offer.

G. Bernard Shaw

To ELLEN POLLOCK

[C/1]   29th August 1949

[Ellen Pollock had thought of acquiring as a memento one of the books in the sale of Shaw's library, and sought his opinion as to which lot she should bid on. By the time he replied the Sotheby sale was a month in the past.]

Damn it, I am not a dealer in relics. As a baptized Irish Protestant, I abhor them.

If you worship them our ways will lie for ever apart.

Collectors are among the plagues of my life.

Dont.

GBS

To FRANCES DAY

[S/1]   29th August 1949

[D.E. was Denholm Elliott; Donald Eccles was his father in the play. Frances Day also played Orinthia in *The Apple Cart* during the Malvern season; she never performed in *In Good King Charles's Golden Days*.]

My dear Frances

I am expecting a letter from D.E. (Junius) asking me to cut the love interest out of Buoyant Billions, and add to his part all the good lines that are now in yours. My reply to both of you will be borrowed from the third act of Pygmalion.

It is amazing how players of genius, like you, can be such hopeless idiots as they mostly are when they try their hands as playwrights. To do what you want would be to break your part's back and make the disappointed audience want to break yours. During the first half hour of a play the audience will put up with anything because they are occupied in finding out who the people on the stage are, and where they are, and what the situation is. Explaining all this to them is often the dullest drudgery actors can have to do. They have to prepare the entry of the star and create interest in him/her.

Junius and his father are just holding the audience long enough to make your appearance a delightful change after the boredom of the explanations.

And you want to do the boring yourself. You are a born actress, Frances; but oh, what a damned fool!

I have just settled with Roy for the immediate London production

855

... on the condition that you are to play the lead. If the result is a success, there will, I hope, be later revivals of The Apple Cart with you as Orinthia and Hardwicke as Magnus, and of course Charles with you as Nell or Braganza. There are some perfect parts for you, if you make good as a serious actress, as I judge you can. But you will probably have to shave bald and wear wigs until your hair grows again in its natural colour, whatever that may be. ...

G. Bernard Shaw

To DEREK TATHAM

[E/4]   16th September 1949

[Celebrities frequently are victimised by tasteless anecdotes foisted on them by publicists, raconteurs, or conscienceless gossip columnists, the same apocryphal tales surfacing generation after generation. Sheridan Morley, for example, in a biography of Gertrude Lawrence recounted that the Sitwell family believed a number by Noël Coward in a revue *London Calling!* (1923) was a parody of themselves; that Osbert Sitwell allegedly "remarked acidly that as he was leaving town for the weekend he would have to miss the show, since it would doubtless have closed before he got back"; and that Coward responded that the revue was "in for a long run and he would be happy to place a stage box at the Sitwells' disposal from which they could see the show with *all* their supporters."

A quarter of a century later, essentially the same anecdote was ascribed to Shaw and Churchill. "I intend to use the following story," wrote Derek Tatham (a journalist?) to Shaw; "have you any objections? It is said that when Bernard Shaw's new play ... was being rehearsed at Malvern, the author sent Winston Churchill two complimentary tickets suggesting that the latter may like to use one and give the second to a friend—if he had one. Mr. Churchill, it is rumoured, thanked the famous playwright for the tickets and said he would attend the opening performance. The other ticket he would give to a friend for the second performance—if there was one." Shaw's reply was written on Tatham's letter of 15th September.]

The above is not only a flat lie but a political libel which may possibly damage me. Publish it at your peril, whether in assertion or contradiction.

G. Bernard Shaw

856

To GRACE GOODLIFFE

[F.u/83; X/351.e]   [Undated: assigned to 25th October 1949]
[The ancestral home of the Shaws of Bushy Park later became the headquarters of a religious order of Catholic nuns. Robert Shaw, a young relation,
who served in the Navy, subsequently emigrated to Kenya.]

Dear Cousin Grace

I'm afraid the only chance for the Bushy Park house is to become a
hotel, sanatorium or college, or to be bought or leased by a Trade Union
[or] Co-operative Society as a rest house. That is what is happening to
some of the English country houses, which has made Sidney Webb say
that instead of demolishing them we should build a hundred more.

If the place were mine I should send round an attractively illustrated
prospectus of it to the leading labor, educational, and health authorities
on the chance of the house being saved in this way. Its abandonment by
the Protestant Shaws is inevitable: it is better to be an M.P., mayor or
magistrate in Kenya than a pariah dog in Eire. We should not dream
of being Empire Builders; but Commonwealth building is a different
matter, and is our proper business next to earning our bread and butter.
I have nothing against Robert for his emigration.

It is just as well that we should be transplanted; for united as we
were against all outsiders, we poor relatives inside the clan quarreled
incessantly and were incorrigible snobs. I shall not be sorry to see the
Catholic bourgeoisie elegantly housed in the park; for my mother, who
was a famous amateur singer, found that Providence gave good voices
and musical faculty quite indiscriminately to Catholics and Protestants.
The priests invited her to sing when there were special musical services in their chapels. The concerts of the Amateur Musical Society
were rehearsed in our house; and the tenors, baritones, basses, and
sopranos[,] as it happened, were all Catholics. Shaws were no use: they
were musical enough to [play] all sorts of popular tunes on all sorts of
musical instruments by ear, my father the trombone, Uncle Barney the
ophicleide, Aunt Emily the cello &c &c: they were hopelessly unclassical
in their tastes and no use for opera, oratorio or symphony. In this way I
learnt early that the Catholic bourgeoisie, instead of being, as I had
been taught, an inferior class on its way to hell, was in fact more cultivated and much kinder and better mannered than the Protestant. And
so, politically, I approve of sale of the park and even of the Eagles. But
none the less I feel the heartbreak to you of the alienation[,] and perhaps
demolition, of the lovely house in which you spent a happy childhood.

The house where I spent my not at all happy childhood has just been decorated with a tablet commemorating my birth there. I would see it blown to smithereens without the faintest regret, in fact, with exultation.

So hurray for Kenya, Tasmania, and Australia as the places for future Shaw conquests.

[G. Bernard Shaw]

To SYLVIA BEACH

[U(C)37; X/449.e]   13th November 1949

["I tried to read Finnegan," Shaw wrote of Joyce's *Finnegans Wake* to Malachy Leonard of Dalkey in April 1948, "but found it would take more time to decipher than it seemed worth" (E/73). Eighteen months later he responded to the same question, this time to the Paris publisher of Joyce's *Ulysses*.]

... I tried Finnegan's Wake, but had to give up after a page or two because I had not time to interpret it. I might have persevered when I was 20; but at 93 time is precious and the days pass like flights of arrows.

I suffered from monthly migraines until I was 70. Too much protein in the old vegetarian diet probably. I now live on chopped raw vegetables and have no headaches. Try it.

G. Bernard Shaw

To FRANCES DAY

[S/1]   13th December 1949

["Shall I be an old man's darling" was a music hall song popularised by Gracie Fields. The young virgin Abishag the Shunamite was brought to the aged, stricken King David to "cherish him" and "lie in [his] bosom, that my lord the king may get heat" (I Kings, I, 1–5). Bettina was a name assumed by Elizabeth Brentano (1785–1859), Countess von Arnim, in *Letters to a Child* (1835), which purported to be a correspondence (mostly spurious) between herself and Goethe.]

Phairest Phrances

Tut tut! Harsh? Nonsense. You do not understand the situation. I will be explicit.

You want to come down here and play with me. To flirt with me. When one is still an elderly youth of 70 romance is still possible with

858

Old Men's Darlings, Shunamite women, Bettinas and the like. But for old skeletons of 90 they are unnatural, abhorrent, unbearable. The word is "keep off. Get out."

But our sacred professional calling continues. It is my business to spot histrionic genius, and encourage it. It is your business to read all the best plays in search of parts that you feel you could play and would like to play. That is why I was glad to send you the books, though I never try to shove my works down people's throats by making presents of them. I thought you had sent them to me to be autographed (I was told so) but now that you have them you must read them religiously. Then you can sell them and buy more plays with the money.

You need not read the prefaces: they have nothing to do with the play.

You will always interest me as a spotted genius. But keep the old skeleton out of sight and touch as much as you can. His skinny presence is best left to itself. Only in his dreams is he young. Do not disturb them.

G. Bernard Shaw

To GEORGINA MUSTERS

[C(F)/1]   8th January 1950

[Judy Musters had protested against a statement by Shaw, quoted in an evening newspaper, about priests working on the superstitions of their flocks. Walter Bagnal Gurly's sister (Shaw's great aunt), a convert to Catholicism, became an abbess.]

I am not an Irish priest. You are not a nun, as your grandaunt was. What would you do if you were?

There are priests who are as primitively ignorant and superstitious as their flocks. There are others who are tyrants and scoundrels. They are not in question. What about Jesus, Mohammed, Inge? What about the millions of peasants and proletarians who without their Gods and miracles will cry "Religion is a pack of lies: we may do as we like now."

Think, child, think.

GBS

To UNIDENTIFIED CORRESPONDENT

[F.u/4]   24th January 1950

[The correspondent appears to have been an attorney or agent representing Nuovo Rinasciamento Films, Rome.]

Learned Sir

It is not possible for me to make all the changes your clients desire. I know that in film business the distributors get the lion's share at the expense of the Producers and Authors. They shall not get it at mine. My percentage is on what the Exhibitors pay the Distributors. I have the monopoly; and it is for the Producers to bargain accordingly with the Distributors.

I never sell my rights: I retain them all intact, and proceed by licensing their exploitation. My licence is never for the world but always for the language only: for example, Clause 4 leaves me free to license native productions in any country except Italy. There must be no dubbing. It is my policy to encourage native film production and prevent its being barred by foreign films, especially American ones.

If you were to wait for my royalties until the production expenses were recouped I should be making a profit sharing agreement with a speculator with no guarantee, which is quite out of the question in my case.

If your clients cannot afford these terms I shall regret it, but shall have to dispose of Androcles elsewhere; for if I altered them for one I must alter them for all.

If they are accepted I will send you a separate agreement for the Italian language.

Always yours with my best consideration

[G. Bernard Shaw]

To GABRIEL PASCAL

[C/1]   6th March 1950

[Pascal's original negotiations with Mexican film makers were for a production of *Androcles and the Lion*, to be designed by Diego Rivera and to star the comedian Cantinflas (stage name of Mario Moreno, b. 1911). Six days before Pascal's departure for Mexico Shaw changed his mind.]

On thinking it over I conclude that the Mexican experiment had better be with Blanco Posnet acted by popular Mexican actors in

Spanish, and, if you find when you arrive there that they have a good enough leading man and lady, The Man of Destiny. No English rights nor players. All my other plays would be too foreign in Mexico.

GBS

To GABRIEL PASCAL

[H/1]   10th March 1950

[Rodolfo Usigli (1905–79), renowned Mexican playwright and critic, was an acquaintance of Shaw.]

There is not time to consult with Belgrave Square. The ambassador can do nothing. I enclose the agreements. With them in your pocket you can arrange everything. The name you have given me for the Company is not sufficient: an agreement cannot be made with a studio: only with a person or body of persons. . . .

If Usigli makes the translation he must be billed as the translator and not as Editor nor Adaptor nor script writer: only as Translator.

We must take our chance as to security, and be content with the President's letter, of which I have a copy. But the President lasts only until the next election or until he is assassinated; and his successor may be against the film business.

However, we can do no better. Any breach of the contract leaves us free to make a new one as best we can.

If Ipeca complains that we did not submit a draft before asking them to sign on the dotted line, say I *did* submit one, and it was returned without comment or objection.

Bon voyage!

G.B.S.

To SYDNEY C. COCKERELL

[H/4; X/277]   10th April 1950

[The books Shaw had been reading were Peter Quennell's *John Ruskin: the Portrait of a Prophet* (1949) and Oswald Doughty's *A Victorian Romantic: Dante Gabriel Rossetti* (1949). John Guille Millais (1865–1931) had written of Ruskin in *The Life and Letters of Sir John Everett Millais* (1899). Ruskin's wife obtained an annulment of her marriage to him, not, as Shaw stated, a divorce.]

My dear Cockerell

Mrs Patrick Campbell slipped on the ice in America and broke a knee cap. It didnt disable her on the stage nor noticeably in private. I think they spliced it with silver wire. The worst of old age is the way one tumbles about. I have had several falls; but so far my technique of stage falling has saved me from any serious damage; and I do not now venture into the garden without a stick.

I have little time for reading now; but I have somehow contrived lately to read Peter Quennell's life of Ruskin and Doughty's life of Rossetti. The revelation of Ruskin as a lifelong monster milksop is astounding, and hardly bearable. Millais alone ticketed him accurately, having the advantage of being married to the quondam Mrs Ruskin, who divorced him for an entirely false impotence, the truth being that he was abnormally sexed. I gather that you did not come across him until he was a violent dotard, with sane intervals which you were lucky enough to hit on.

The Rossetti book is so spun out with repetitions that it is hardly possible to read it straight through; and on the whole D.G.R. comes out of it, in spite of his charm and talent, as a socially impossible and unpleasant untrustworthy and dishonest modern Casanova.

Morris comes into both books as the biggest man of the lot, in spite of his epileptic rages, his gout, and his final tuberculosis. At first he looked up to D.G.R. as his leader and superior almost as unquestionably as he took Chaucer for his master and himself for the idle singer of an empty day; but when I knew him he had found D.G.R. out, and though he spoke of him with a certain wonder at his ability as a money maker and a copious letterwriter (Morris hated writing letters and would not read them over to correct them) he disliked him.

There must have been a moment in which he realized that there was no such person as Topsy, and that William Morris was the rightful king of the Rossettian gang.

Doughty's notion that he was jealous of Rossetti's love for Mrs Morris I do not believe for a moment. All the jealousy Morris was capable of he reserved for Burne-Jones, the slightest disparagement of whom he could not bear. Anyhow D.G.R's portraits of Janey were indispensable.

I must stop: the subject is inexhaustible.

GBS

862

To MAUNG OHN

[F.u/4]   [Undated: *c.* 1st May 1950]

[Maung Ohn, president of Burma, requested on 19th April (through the Burmese Embassy in London) an audience with Shaw for his prime minister Thakin Nu, who wished to pay his respects during a visit to England in May. Thakin Nu (b. 1907), later known as U Nu, was an independence leader who became Burma's first prime minister in 1947 (transfer of sovereign power from Britain to the Union of Burma occurred on 4th January 1948). Shaw had been receiving out-patient treatment of radiant heat for lumbago, at the Welwyn Victoria Hospital, intermittently since 1947. He underwent eleven treatments between 1st and 13th May 1950.]

Dear President Maung Ohn

I greatly regret that I am unable to receive the visit with which your Premier proposes to honor me. I am at present being treated in hospital for an attack of lumbago which is very disabling at my great age (93.9). Also there is a shortage in my domestic staff which makes it impossible to entertain distinguished visitors with due respect to their eminence.

But as I am only a skeleton of my former self, and have nothing to say that I have not written, Mr Thakin Nu will lose nothing, and save an afternoon of his valuable time, by leaving this remote village and its oldest inhabitant unvisited.

                                        your Honour's Obedient Servant
                                        [G. Bernard Shaw]

To HENRIETTA R. HAYTHORNTHWAITE

[H/9]   3rd May 1950

[Henrietta R. Haythornthwaite (d. 1954) was a distant relation of Shaw by marriage, being a granddaughter of Eliza Townsend, a kinswoman of Charlotte's grandfather. She appears to have had an acquaintance with the latest generation of Bushy Park Shaws. The book Shaw sent to her (now in the Burgunder Shaw Collection at Cornell University) is F. E. Loewenstein's *Bernard Shaw through the Camera* (1948). Shaw's grandparents were Frances and Bernard Shaw; he was a Dublin solicitor. The Roundtown bungalow had been converted to a dispensary. Robert Shaw, after wartime naval service, joined his father in Kenya, where he was farming; his brother John elected to enter Sandhurst.]

Dear Cousin Hetty

The snaps [she had sent] are atrocious: they were taken with a Brownie camera and should have been exposed for at least two or three seconds instead of a twentieth. I have asked the Leagrave Press to send you a book of photographs relating to myself. On page 27 you will find a picture of Bushy Park. I believe I have a better one somewhere, but cannot lay my hand on it just now.

Roundtown was not a row of little houses: it was a single circular bungalow in which my grandmother dwelt in what I as a small child considered great state. My dead grandfather's yeomanry sword and helmet hung over the door by way of escutcheon.

Thanks for all your news, which, by the way, did not include the Nairobi household. When I last heard from Robert he was in training at Dartmouth. Is he now in service in the Navy?

G. Bernard Shaw

To SEAN O'CASEY

[H/1; X/450]   6th May 1950

[Eileen O'Casey and John Dulanty had visited Shaw at Ayot on 14th January. The "first flower ... first gem" allusion is from Thomas Moore's "Remember Thee!"; the "hope for a season ... freedom shrieked" couplet is from Thomas Campbell's *The Pleasures of Hope* (1799). Thaddeus Koskiusco (1746–1817), Polish general who aided the American revolutionary cause, led an unsuccessful insurrection against foreign invaders of Poland in 1794.]

My dear Sean

Eileen, still lovely as ever, gave me a photograph of the lot of you which pleased me so much that I have had it framed and look at it quite often. Your marriage has been a eugenic success: the Heir Apparent is a stalwart who must count me as a Struldbrug, which is what I actually look like. I keep my wits about me much better than my legs: that is the best I can say for myself.

Ireland, no longer under Dublin Castle and Grand Jury government, cannot now brood on her wrongs for cash from America and heroic and romantic sympathy from the rest of the world. In the old days we were the first flower of the earth and the first gem of the sea, our only rival being Poland, where hope for a season bade the world farewell, and freedom shrieked when Kosciusko fell. Now we are an

864

insignificant cabbage garden in a little islet quite out of the headlines; and our Fianna Fail Party is now The Unionist Party and doesnt know it. I have nothing to tell them except that the Ulster capitalists will themselves abolish the Partition when the Labor Party is strong enough to threaten them with an Irish 1945 at the polls, and they must have the support of the Catholic agricultural south to avert it. But all they do is to send me medals of the Blessed Virgin, guaranteeing, if I say a novena, that she will give me anything I ask from her, to which I reply that the B.V. needs helpers and not beggars.

I have no news for you except the quite uninteresting item that I am having a bout of lumbago. They are trying to bake it out of me by Radiant Heat.

G. Bernard Shaw

To BLANCHE PATCH

[E/9]   19th May 1950

[Blanche Patch resided in Queens Gate until her death in 1966; for her it represented gentility.]

By the way, I should have said in my letter about your salary an address in Queens Gate is as much beyond your means and needs as Whitehall Court is beyond mine. The day may come when we shall both have to move.

GBS

To PETER & IONA OPIE

[H/1]   8th June 1950

[Peter Opie (1918–82) and his wife Iona (b. 1923) were authors and editors principally of works on children's life and literature. They were in process of compiling the *Oxford Dictionary of Nursery Rhymes* (1951), and asked Shaw for recollections of his childhood songs and rhymes.]

BERNARD SHAW'S
NURSERY RHYMES

The usual ones: Baba black sheep, Old Mother Hubbard, Pop goes the weasel, Simple Simon, Jump Jim Crow, Little Jack Horner, Georgie Porgie pudding and pie, &&&&&&

865

God made Man and Man made money
God made bees and bees made honey
God made Satan and Satan made sin
And God made Hell to put Satan in.

There was an old man and his wife was a woman
                Ritoody I ah Ritoody I ah
There was a loaf in the press and twas gone when I ate it
                Ritoody I ah Ritoody I ah
I had a big dog and he barked when I bet him
                Ritoody &&&&

Hunkydorum titherum tie
A tailor's goose it cannot fly.

Sundry couplets by Dr Watts: for instance
It is a sin to steal a pin
&c&c&c

Dumpitydoodledum big bowwow
Dumpitydoodledum dandy
    I composed this myself to sing when petting
    our dog Rover. It was my Opus 1.

                              GBS

To ADA TYRRELL

[H/1]   8th June 1950
[Maud Clarke was Mrs Tyrrell's last surviving sister. Ada Tyrrell, a year older than Shaw, lived to be a centenarian. Shaw's final will was signed on 12th June, witnessed by Harold O. White (1909–80), master printer of the Leagrave Press, Luton, and his wife Marjorie.]

My dear Addie
  Maud was wise to die; for old age is bearable only when there is nothing else wrong with one's body.
  As you say, I am lucky in having no relatives to plague me; but I have on my hands a mass of business from which I cannot, like most men, retire; for when I leave it to an agent I have to undo it and do it right myself. If you build a house, you know where it is, and can live in

it, or let it and live on its rent. But when I write a book or a play, which is my way of building a house, that book or play is my property in every civilized country in the world except Russia. I cannot live in it, but must let it over and over again, not for years but for weeks, and not only bargain about it every time but protect it against pirates everywhere.

Just now I am recovering very slowly from an abominable attack of lumbago, and laboring at my very complicated last will and testament in daily dread of dying before I have executed it. Such are the worries of an old author.

I have to keep 20 printed postcards to deal with my correspondence: the enclosed specimens will amuse you.

You and I will soon be the oldest inhabitants of the globe. It is perhaps as well that we cannot meet; for even if I could walk farther than my garden, and that only with a stick, and long distance motoring is beyond my powers, I had rather be remembered by you as Sonny than as the ghastly old skeleton of a celebrity I now am.

Enough! This letter is only a grumble. I write it because I am always glad to hear from you, and must play up when your welcome postmark appears on the breakfast table.

G. Bernard Shaw

To PAUL ROBESON

[H/128]   13th June 1950

[Paul Robeson (1898–1976), consummate singer, actor, and humanitarian, was a vice-chairman of the Progressive Party, on whose ticket Henry A. Wallace had run for president in 1948. Shaw had "campaigned" for Wallace in a series of interviews, being the first to propose his candidature in the British press. Robeson's criticism of the United States Government's racist practices in a series of radical and inflammatory speeches abroad resulted in the decision of the State Department, under executive order from the president Harry Truman, to revoke his passport, in effect placing him under house arrest for the next eight years. A Supreme Court decision restored travelling rights to him in 1958. Robeson may have been planning to run for office as a counterthrust to the Government's effort to gag him.]

My dear Paul

If you connect my name and reputation with your campaign, and invite me to speak for you in the U.S.A. as Wallace's silly committee did at the Presidential election, you will gain perhaps two thousand votes, ten of them negro, and lose two million. The rest will ask (if they ask or care anything at all) "Who the hell is Bernard Shaw?"

In the U.S.A. an enormous majority of those who know that I exist, know me as an Irish foreigner, a Red Communist, a friend and agent of Stalin, an Atheist, and in literature a joker who thinks himself a better playwright than Shakespear and made a reputation by calling black white. Keep me out of it; and do not waste your time courting the handful of people whose votes you are sure of already. Play for Republican votes and episcopal support all the time; and when you get a big meeting of all sorts, dont talk politics but sing Old Man River [a song from Jerome Kern's *Show Boat* that Robeson had made world famous].

always your SINCERE friend
G. Bernard Shaw

To GABRIEL PASCAL

[H/1]   18th June 1950

[Pascal, despite Shaw's prognostications, outlived him by less than four years, his death occurring on 6th July 1954, at the age of sixty.]

My dear Gabriel

Another fiasco! Have you brought back the agreements? If not, the case is very serious; for if they have been executed Mexico has a hold on us under the clause which provides that if you are unable *or unwilling* to direct, a substitute shall be agreed on. I gather from your letter . . . that you have the agreements and can put them in the fire, leaving us quite free; but I should like to be sure of this; so let me know positively.

Meanwhile there is nothing on hand but Androcles. I will make no more agreements until we see how you get on with the Milan people. I dread another fiasco.

I have been uneasy about you lately. You are laying out your life as if I were sure to live another fifty years, and putting all your eggs in that quite illusory basket accordingly. It is extremely unlikely that I shall live another three years, and not certain that I shall live another three days; and when I die your connexion with me will have been a mere episode in your career. You will have half your life before you which you must fill up with new friendships and new interests and activities. Otherwise you will starve. Never forget that dealings with

868

very old people can be only transient. Make young friends and young clients. Look for a young Shaw; for though Shaws do not grow on the gooseberry bushes there are as good fish in the sea as ever came out of it. Anyhow you must live in your own generation, not in mine.

Devotion to an old crock like me is sentimental folly.

GBS

To ESMÉ PERCY

[C/3]   12th July 1950

[*Farfetched Fables*, written in July and August 1948, was produced under the sponsorship of the Shaw Society at the Watergate Theatre (a private-club theatre and therefore, in Shaw's eyes, not "publicly" performed), for thirty performances commencing 6th September. It was designed by Feliks Topolski and staged by Esmé Percy.]

Farfetched (not Fabulous) Fables is not a regular play. It is a string of short scenes in which all the characters can be played by the same little group of half a dozen amateurs changing their dress and makeup between each. They represent different people in different periods. There are corresponding changes in the scenery.

The piece is not intended for professional production, but for amateurs with unlimited time for rehearsal, making their own dresses and painting their own scenery. Also shifting it.

It is no job for you. You cannot afford it.

G.B.S.

To ESMÉ PERCY

[C/3; X/289.e]   19th July 1950

[Performances of *Farfetched Fables* had originally been scheduled to commence on Shaw's 94th birthday at the end of July.]

What is this production of F.F. going to be? I did not bargain for a regular West End first performance; and it must not be announced as such. The Gate must call it X performances to celebrate my birthday,

THE WATERGATE THEATRE
presents for THE SHAW SOCIETY
the first production on any stage of

Farfetched Fables

BY BERNARD SHAW

conducted by ESME PERCY (President of The Shaw Society)
and illustrated by FELIKS TOPOLSKI

THE PLAYERS are led by Miss Ellen Pollock

Time : To-day and Possible To-morrows

THE FIRST FABLE
A Public Park, London

Park Attendant . .	Patrick Graucob
Young Woman . .	Margaret Manners
Young Man	Eric Batson
An Excitable M.A.M.	Dominic Clauzel

THIRD FABLE
Outside the Anthropometric Laboratory, I.O.W.

Girl	Barbara Carter
Tourist	Charles Rennison
Matron	Marion Everall
A Shrewd M.A.M. . .	Eric Batson
Tramp	Martin Starkie

SECOND FABLE
At the War Office, London

Secretary	Rosemary Carvill
C. in C.	Howard Bourgein
Lord Oldhand of the Foreign Office.	Michael Sherwell

FOURTH FABLE
At the Diet Commissioners, I.O.W.

Commissioner	Esme Percy

INTERVAL OF TEN MINUTES

FIFTH FABLE
At the Genetic Institute, I.O.W.

Shamrock	Michael Sherwell
Rose	Ellen Pollock
Herm	Esme Percy
Thistle	Patrick Graucob

SIXTH FABLE
Sixth Form School, I.O.W.
Scheduled Historic Monument

Teacher	Ellen Pollock
Youth 1	Charles Rennison
Maiden 5	Marion Everall
Youth 3	Ray Jackson
Youth 2	Geoffrey Sasse
Maiden 4	Margaret Manners

Production Manager . .	Bill Honeywood
Stage Director . . .	Rosemary Carvill
Assistant Stage Managers	Lois Mallinson / June Epstein
Publicity	Paul Sheridan

Costumes made by Rosemary Carvill, assisted by Rosamund Ross and Hilary Virgo. Dressing room fittings made by Eugene Leahy. Back Projection by Newton & Co. Flourescent lighting by Thorn Electrical Industries Limited.

ADELPHI ARTISTS, 11 BUCKINGHAM STREET, W.C.2.

making it clear that what is in hand is a special limited run at a coterie theatre. Another fiasco like that of Buoyant Billions would damage me seriously.

GBS

To ST JOHN ERVINE

[H/3] 19th July 1950

[For an example of Shaw's borrowing from *The Importance of Being Earnest*, compare Jack Worthing's reaction to Miss Prism's presumed motherhood with that of Jack Tanner to Violet Robinson's condition in *Man and Superman*.]

My dear St John

Do not let yourself be trapped into the silly cliché that The Importance is Wilde's best play. It's a mechanical cat's cradle farce without a single touch of human nature in it. It is Gilbert and Sullivan minus Sullivan.

The other plays—except, of course, the boyish [Duchess of] Padua —have the conventional woman-with-a-past plot of their day; and the feeling of which they are full is a bit romantic: but the characters are all human, and their conversation the most delightfully brilliant in the annals of the English stage, knocking Congreve and Sheridan into a cocked hat.

Remember that nothing is more ridiculous than artists' opinions of one another. I have a collection of these verdicts (knowing the parties); and they are absurd beyond belief. I was present at all the Wilde first nights, and enjoyed them intensely, except The Importance, which amused me by its stage tricks (I borrowed the best of them) but left me unmoved and even a bit bored and quite a lot disappointed.

A week from now I shall be 94. Yet the day before yesterday I began a new play: a very little one. I cannot write big plays now. I could if my old big ones had left me anything to say; but they havnt: my bolt is shot.

This is all I have to say just now.

Love to Leonora.
GBS

To SYDNEY C. COCKERELL

[D/4; X/277]   27th July 1950

[The *Autobiography and Journals* of the historical painter Benjamin R. Haydon (1786–1846), edited by Tom Taylor, were first published in 1853.]

Yesterday was simple hell. The Times statement that I was "resting" elicited a yell of rage from me. The telephone and door bell never stopped. The lane was blocked with photographers all day. None of them would take NO for an answer. Fortnum & Mason made huge profits on giant cakes, gorgeous and uneatable. The Post & Telegraph services staggered under their burdens. . . .

I am reading Haydons Autobiography & journals. Morris was wrong for once when he said that Haydon cut his throat because he "found himself out." It was Morris himself who found himself out as a Rossettian painter. Haydon was the most extraordinary genius of them all.

G.B.S.

To HENRIETTA R. HAYTHORNTHWAITE

[C/9]   4th August 1951 [1950]

[The Gothic-windowed cottage of Shaw's grandmother is in a section of Terenure originally called Roundtown because of a circle of round-fronted cottages built in 1801 where the road to Templeogue begins. Shaw was in error in his belief that it was his grandmother's house and not the whole community that was known as Roundtown. (Joyceans will know that it was outside Matthew Dillon's house in Roundtown in 1887 that Leopold Bloom and Marion Tweedy first met Stephen Dedalus, "a lad of four or five in linsey woolsey.") Raheny (now incorporated into Dublin) was a suburban village north of Dublin on the road to Howth.]

Builder unknown. Probably the one who built the Raheny replica [of it]. Photos quite useless now.

House front very white. Yeomanry equipment hang up inside

GBS

872

To FREDERICK MAY

[X/451]   [Undated: assigned to 8th August 1950]

[Frederick May, a lecturer in the Department of Italian at the University of Leeds, was secretary of the Pirandello Society. Shaw first met Pirandello on 13th November 1923; the "loquacious" friend was Edward Storer (1882–?), a United Press staff correspondent in Rome, who published several articles on Pirandello in British journals. Lady Lavery's dinner occurred on 26th June 1925. The "extravagant dictum" by Shaw, not located, was cited in an article, "Pirandello Confesses ... *Why and How He Wrote 'Six Characters in Search of an Author,'*" in the *Virginia Quarterly Review*, April 1925.]

When I met Pirandello he was accompanied by a friend (or courier) so extremely loquacious that his incessant monologue cut us both completely out of the conversation. At a dinner later at Lady Lavery's I was seated next Mr Winston Churchill, far apart from Pirandello who pontificated in Italian. We had no tete a tete at all.

I have no recollection of the extravagant dictum you quote; but I rank P. as first rate among playwrights, and have never come across a play so *original* as Six Characters [in Search of an Author].

[G. Bernard Shaw]

To M. SCHILLER

[H/83]   25th August 1950

[The unidentified Dr M. Schiller had taken it upon himself to serve as a go-between in an effort to obtain the mounting of *Saint Joan* at the Comédie Française. "I shall always be able to reproach the Théâtre Français, in its national representative capacity," Shaw had written to Augustin Hamon on 16th September 1932, "with having abandoned St Joan and Cæsar and Cleopatra to a foreigner at a coterie theatre after they had been produced by all the leading national theatres in Europe" (H/1). Now, though he did not forbid Schiller from communicating with the Paris theatre, he offered little enthusiasm or optimism, even when Schiller forwarded to him a letter received from P. A. Touchard, Administrator General of the Comédie Française, dated 25th July, in which he indicated that such a project "me séduit beaucoup" (H/13). The final decision, Touchard cautioned, rested in the Comité de Lecture; and the Committee's subsequent lack of interest is reflected in the fact that no Shaw play has yet been performed by a French company at the Comédie Française, though the Old Vic's production of *Arms and the Man* had a brief celebratory engagement there just after V-E Day.

For a reference to Hamon's 1907 Brussels lecture at the New University, see Shaw's letter to him of 9th January 1907. Rémy de Gourmont (1858–1915), noted French critic, philosopher, novelist, and exponent of the symbolist movement, stated in his feuilleton in *La France* on 27th February 1913 that Shaw was "le seul génie dramatique de la présente heure européenne."]

Dear Dr Schiller

I strongly advise you not to spend much time persuading Touchard to produce Saint Joan at the Français. If you succeed it will probably be on such conditions that I shall refuse to authorize it. He has already said that he thinks it should be in the hands of Madame Pitoeff, which shews that he has the same false notion of the play as a Porte St Martin melodrama with Joan in tears all the time and half burnt already on her first entry, like all the other French Joans.

As to the translation, what you say has been said of all my translators. A suburban accent does not matter: the players can speak their parts as elegantly as they please. Hamon's style was that of an essayist rather than of a playwright. But at least he did not cut out all the Shaw and all the true Joan, and substitute Scribe and Sardou, which is, I suspect, what Mons. Touchard wants. You may have to wait until by some miracle the Français hits on a Shavian director.

The sole advantage in the Français for me is that the company is trained in declamation by the Molière tradition; and if I, as Hamon contended, am *le Molière de nos jours*, their style would serve me fairly well, as Shakesperean players do in England.

I remember the Brussels Candida very well. Hamon delivered some very solemn lectures at the university about my work, and, having no sense of comedy, had a terrible shock when he first heard his translation performed at the Théatre de la Monnaie. He had no suspicion that Burgess is the *drole* of the piece; and when the audience saw the fun, Hamon exclaimed "*Mon Dieu! On rit. Tout est perdu.*"

Remy de Gourmont and others praised the translation highly. D'Humières denounced it as the work of a *primaire*. They had, as far as I know, nothing to gain by flattering him. His ultra-revolutionary politics may have pleased them.

G. Bernard Shaw

To BLANCHE PATCH

[H.u/9]   3rd September 1950

[Blanche Patch was working on her memoirs, published in 1951 as *Thirty Years with G.B.S.*, but had not confided to Shaw that the book was being ghostwritten by his publicist acquaintance Robert Williamson, to whom she was feeding copies of letters and other memorabilia. Kate Hodgman and her sister Emma were employed for many years as the Shaws' house parlour-maids.]

My dear Blanche

Make a very sparing use of the letters; and quote nothing that has not some point of special interest. Mere itineraries like those of Charlotte's you have sent me would dull your book unbearably. Never quote for the sake of quoting. Do not write a sentence that does not carry on your story.

Remember always that the only readable part of an autobiography is the writer's childhood and adolescence. Adult lives are all the same. Repetition, repetition, repetition: Wesley's sermons, George Fox's church stormings, Tunney's prizefights, each a repetition of the other, become alike tedious. Tell your own story from your cradle to your engagement as my secretary (including your question to Kate [in 1920] "Does he throw things at you"); and then fill up not with letters but with tales of the players and authors and socialists and other noted people you have met, keeping me out of it as far as possible because all the tales about me have been published over and over again. Dont bother about style: tell your story unaffectedly in your own way. Stuck-on style is no style at all, and hatefully unreadable.

To LIONEL AMES

[W(H.t)/387]   4th September 1950

[Captain Lionel G. Ames (1889–1971) was a neighbour at Ayot, whose home "Amesbury" was adjacent to Shaw's Corner.]

Dear Lionel Ames

I thought of you very sympathetically on Saturday when the west wind was smoking you out. You will have your revenge when the wind goes south and smokes me out. I know of no remedy for the autumn bonfires, which have smoked for all my 94 years and thousands of centuries before that.

I have had to lop my two giant elms, as they were dangerous, and my ash, which died a natural death last winter. This makes the smoke a bit worse this year; but it will soon be over. Every log worth saving from the fire will be carted away.

I shall be burnt up myself presently; but the fumes will get no farther than Golders Green. . . .

G.B.S.

The End

[Most of the posthumous reports of Shaw's accident in September 1950 and of the events that followed are unreliable. Alice Laden's recollections, in at least three interviews between 1950 and 1968, swelled imaginatively with each telling, contradictory in many of the essential details. Moreover, she reported statements as having been made by Shaw in her presence at Ayot which had actually been addressed earlier to hospital staff, as recorded in the press (where Mrs Laden presumably read them). John O'Donovan, in his 1983 study of Shaw, conjured up a graphic but mythic image of GBS, knapsack strapped to his back, falling Finnegan-like from a ladder, while pruning greengage trees. Most of the compilers of books and calendars of Famous Last Words have presented as Shaw's final utterance a statement ("If I survive this, I shall be immortal") that he had made more than a month before his death (it was reported in the *Daily Express* on 5th October 1950), which would have necessitated an extraordinary and uncharacteristic taciturnity on his part in the weeks of life that followed. His doctor presented as gospel the celebrated Shaw–Churchill exchange, allegedly recounted to him by his patient, though GBS had twice refuted the canard on earlier occasions. And for years rumours circulated that Shaw received the last rites and was received into the Church of England on his deathbed.

The present account, which seeks to separate fact from fiction, is compiled from contemporary correspondence, including that of Mrs Laden, Blanche Patch, F. E. Loewenstein, and Nancy Astor; hospital records; reports published in London, Welwyn, Luton, Hatfield, Dublin, and New York newspapers; and interviews, personal, telephonic, and written, with, among others, Judy Musters, Lady Astor, Miss Patch, and Denis Johnston.]

In the late afternoon of Monday, 10th September, Shaw drew from his pocket the pair of secateurs he carried on garden walks and compulsively grabbed at a hedge to prune away a projecting branch. In doing so he overreached, lost balance, tripped over the edging along the garden path, and went tumbling. Margaret Cashin Smith, the former housemaid who had returned a couple of days earlier to look after GBS while Alice Laden went on holiday, was summoned from the house by an emergency whistle Shaw carried with him; she found him sprawled on the ground in pain. Assisted by her husband she helped him into the house and phoned the local physician, Dr Thomas C. Probyn of Kimpton, on whose instructions she despatched the chauffeur Fred Day to fetch a radiologist. With the aid of a portable X-ray machine the specialist determined that Shaw had fractured his left thigh. He was sedated for the night; arrangements were made to transport him next morning to the Luton and Dunstable Hospital; and Alice Laden, who had just reached Aberdeen, flew back to take charge of the suddenly disrupted household.

Deposited for the journey in the Letchworth ambulance on a stretcher, a bright and cheerful GBS joked with the attendant as the driver slowly traversed the fifteen miles of country road to avoid bumps. Shaw was deposited in a single-bedded, carpeted and curtained private room with deep French windows and a balcony overlooking the Chiltern Hills (at a cost of £2.14.0 a day), where he settled down with a book from the small library he had brought with him. The hospital was instantly inundated with calls, the operator Peggy Howarth reporting next day that she had had inquiries from India, Germany, the United States, Australia, and virtually every corner of the British Isles. A second operator was brought in to deal with the overtaxed switchboard. Reporters crammed the anterooms, overwhelming Mrs Laden as she bustled in with a supply of Shaw's specially woven wool blankets and sheets and the pyjamas he had forgotten to bring with him. The hospital's boardroom was placed at the disposal of the pressmen, to whom regular bulletins were delivered. When local accommodation was exhausted, a few of the reporters were found room in a jail cell at the police station.

On the evening of the 11th the resident orthopædic surgeon, L. W. Plewes, joined together the broken surfaces of the neck of the thigh bone, while the patient slumbered under a general anæsthetic. The operation, it was later stated, was one designed to reduce the immobility of the injured limb to a minimum. Rather than case the leg in a plaster cast, as was generally done, the doctor had inserted a metal pin, joining the two sides of the fractured bone, which allowed Shaw to move the leg in bed. No mention was made in the post-surgery announcement of the fact that the anæsthetist had had to plaster Shaw's beard to his face to get the mask on after he had vehemently objected to a partial shave.

The hospital's medical director, Dr S. D. Purcell, pronouncing the operation a success, reported that Shaw was not on the danger list. He was, in fact, quite perkily awake by six in the morning, on the 12th, proclaiming he was hungry, and protesting, when a wash basin was brought to his bed, that he had already been washed the night before. He demanded—and received— a receipt from Sister Elizabeth Gallagher, the night nurse, for the last two washings lest some one "come along in five minutes and give me another one. Too much washing is not good for antiques." The morning newspapers not yet having been delivered, Shaw wheedled Sister Gallagher into bringing a portable wireless from the nurses' quarters, telling her "I must have the news; I feel so out of touch." Upon hearing a B.B.C. report of the death of General Smuts, his mood changed instantly. "I feel sad, sister," he announced; "I think I will go to sleep."

Complete rest and quiet remained the order for this day and the next, with no one but Alice Laden permitted to visit, and even she was allowed entry only for two minutes, to bring fresh fruit from the garden at Shaw's Corner and some of GBS's special breakfast grains. The bulletin of the 13th assured the world that he was comfortable and his progress satisfactory. He asked for pen and stationery (though no letter dated after the accident has been located) and for dahlias from his garden. Two doctors and two nurses lifted him from the bed, encouraging him to take the weight on his sound right leg, and supporting him upright for thirty seconds. Asked to move the injured limb, he discovered he could swing it slightly with little pain. By the time Mrs Laden arrived the exhausted GBS was again asleep. On the 14th he was out of bed for a full minute, but reportedly told the doctor, "It will do you no good if I get over this. A doctor's reputation is made by the number of eminent men who die under his care." Blanche Patch, arriving from London to find him in good spirits, carried away eighty letters and wires with instructions as to their acknowledgment. Eventually there was so much correspondence that Mrs Laden undertook to write responses to anxious inquirers like Sir Robert Ho Tung in Hong Kong.

Among the telegrams was a request from Radio Eireann's "Celebrities' Choice," asking Shaw to select a recording to be played for him. "Play the tune the old cow died of," he shot back. Ignorant of this classic Irish colloquialism implying that a tune was hardly the relief he required at the moment, the station announced it couldn't locate a song called "The Old Cow Died," and substituted Connie Foley's version of "The Wild Colonial Boy."

On the 15th there were hints of a setback, with a London urologist, Dr Alec W. Badenoch of Bart's, summoned to deal with "a worsening of a longstanding difficulty with the renal outflow." Temporary measures were adopted to relieve the bladder and kidney condition. Shaw did not have his first real visitor until the 17th, when his cousin Judy Musters was admitted for a few minutes; shortly thereafter Roy Limbert was refused admission. On the 18th Shaw listened to a broadcast of *Saint Joan*, without comment. He indicated anxiety to get home; but on the 21st he was subjected to further surgery, to deal with the renal problem. Out of bed again on the 23rd and allowed to sit in a chair for ten minutes, he enjoyed a surprise visit from Frances Day. The next morning he was allowed to sit at the window for half an hour, where he gazed out at the Dunstable Downs. Lady Astor, earlier denied admission, returned on the 25th in her chauffeur-driven Rolls Royce, laden with gladioli and dahlias, which Shaw made her carry away again as the room was already crammed with flowers, including roses from the Winston Churchills and a large pot of cyclamen from Constance Cummings and her husband Benn Levy. Nancy bristled with anger at discovering that Frances Day had been admitted as a visitor before her, and the nurses hustled her out. She managed, however, to put on a good show for the journalists and photographers, who had by now become frustrated in their efforts to photograph Shaw in his room, despite offers to the administrators as high as a thousand pounds.

A final bulletin was issued on the 27th, announcing "satisfactory progress," but the kidney condition continued to cause anxiety, and Shaw fretted and chafed at the delayed departure. He was, however, able to stand on the injured leg for five minutes on 2nd October, and, after he had refused to permit additional surgery for the damaged condition of the kidneys, the doctors gave him his discharge. After twenty-four days of hospitalisation, he was suddenly and secretly removed on 4th October, with only one reporter, R. Foulkes of the *Luton News*, aware of the departure. Wrapped in a tan dressing-gown, with two hot water bottles tucked in beside him, Shaw ignored the questions directed at him, maintaining stolid silence as he was carried on a stretcher to the waiting ambulance for the return journey to Ayot St Lawrence.

As the ambulance approached the front drive of Shaw's Corner, just after 5 p.m., Mrs Laden signalled to the gardener Fred Drury and the chauffeur Fred Day to unroll a 20 × 15-foot canvas screen before the door to conceal from the curious onlookers, including the omnipresent photographers, the spectacle of Shaw being removed from the ambulance. A high, narrow bed with a wooden headboard had been placed in the ground-floor dining-room, facing out from the inner wall to enable GBS to see the garden through the windows. He was made comfortable by Sister Florence Horan of the Royal Free Hospital, who had (along with Alice Laden) nursed Charlotte in her last illness, and Sister Jean Howell of King's College Hospital.

He slept most of the next morning and afternoon, though he allowed a momentary visit from Dr Loewenstein and ate some soup and fruit-sweets at dinner. In the days that followed he seemed to rally, being allowed out of bed for about an hour and a half, sitting in a chair on the back verandah when the weather permitted. He dictated instructions to Blanche Patch, including a request that a substantial cheque be sent to the hospital to compensate the telephone operators and other staff for the extra labours his presence had brought upon them. There were visits from Veronica and Eileen O'Casey. Frances Day bustled in and out; and Shaw even consented to an interview with his journalist friend F. G. Prince-White, a Hearst correspondent, on the occasion of his first wheelchair jaunt into the garden on the 12th. Shaw was "not now the scintillating sage," said Prince-White; "a gentleness is on his face now, a softness in his once-piercing glance," as he said quietly "I don't think I shall ever write anything more." Mrs Laden too had noted the alteration. The verbal fencing he had hitherto enjoyed indulging in with her had diminished; mostly he lay brooding and silent, glancing impatiently at newspapers, occasionally taking up a book for a moment or two, listening to the six o'clock news and a bit of music on the Third Programme. Nancy Astor was the first to reveal publicly his pessimistic frame of mind, informing the press after a visit that Shaw had told her "I wish I were dead."

A glimmer of his former self could be detected, however, in his final conversation, on 25th October, with Judy Musters, who recorded his words in shorthand immediately upon leaving the sick room. "Think of the enjoyment you've given," Mrs Musters reminded him, "and the stimulus . . ." You might, said Shaw, chuckling, "say the same of any Mrs Warren." In a moment of reminiscence about his marriage, he commented "I used to think the children were what mattered in marriage but no: its the companionship that matters." It was now, he concluded, time for him to go: "I believe in life everlasting; but not for the individual." When another visitor, Valerie Pascal, responded with a small moan to his quiet statement "I am dying finally," he demanded of her "How much longer do you want me to lie here paralysed and be watched like a monkey by those outside?"

He weakened perceptibly toward the end of the month, declining to leave his bed. Shortly after signing his name shakily to a tax document brought to him by Miss Patch (who steadied his wrist as he wrote), he relapsed, running an alarmingly high temperature brought on by the kidney dysfunction. The nurses patiently moistened his mouth with a glycerine solution, but no effort was made to provide intravenous nourishment. Would-be visitors were denied admission, but on the 31st both Nancy Astor and Frances Day, ignoring the remonstrances of Mrs Laden and the nurses, made their way to Shaw's bedside, fighting like cats, as Frances Day later described it to Denis Johnston, each seeking the star rôle as chief mourner. "He is very, very tired," Lady Astor told the pressmen as she emerged an hour later; his final words to her, she reported, were "Oh, Nancy. I want to sleep, sleep." Before lapsing into a coma at 3 a.m. on 1st November, his last words, uttered with a quiet sense of relief, were "I am going to die."

He remained in a coma for twenty-six hours, his strongly beating heart refusing to give way. In the morning the Rev. R. J. Davies, rector of Ayot St Peter, visited the house and, at Mrs Laden's urging, recited the 23rd Psalm over the unconscious and slow-breathing GBS. A noon bulletin stated that he had had a peaceful night, but that his strength was ebbing. Dr Loewenstein, who maintained a vigil in the next room through the night of 1st November, was the first to learn that Shaw had breathed his last at 4.59 a.m. on All Soul's Day. Mrs Laden walked bare-headed down the mist-shrouded path to inform the reporters gathered at the wrought-iron gates, "Mr Shaw has passed on." A hand-written bulletin on Shaw's own notepaper, composed by H. G. Prince-White, was fixed to the gate shortly thereafter. It read:

Mr Bernard Shaw passed peacefully away at one minute to five o'clock this morning, November 2.

From the coffers of his genius he enriched the world.

Gabriel Pascal, hastening to the scene, was confronted with the news upon his arrival that morning at London Airport; he burst into tears, then emotionally announced he would write and produce a film of Shaw's life. Lady Astor, "making an exhibition of herself, as usual, about [Shaw], and behaving as if she was the widow," as Sir Henry Channon noted in his diary that evening, took charge at Shaw's Corner, stage-managing the final scene. "I think you ought to see him. He looks so lovely," she announced to the pressmen, and led them into the house to view and photograph the body. Half an hour later, at noon, the Rev. Mr Davies, invited by Mrs Laden, conducted a brief service at the bedside, attended by a few women of the village, come to pay their last respects. The body was then transferred to the Chapel of Rest, in Welwyn, where it was clad by the mortician in a two-piece suit of mauve silk pyjamas, chosen as his "favourites." By Lady Astor's instruction a death mask was made; this was secreted for years in the British Museum by order of Shaw's executor, but was at last exhibited in 1977.

Before the day ended, millions of words of tribute had been published in the press of all the civilised world. Messages streamed in from President Harry S. Truman, Pandit Nehru, Ireland's Taoiseach (John A. Costello), the Executive Board of UNESCO, Arnold Zweig (representing the German Democratic Republic Academy of Arts), André Maurois, Dean Inge, and the British–Soviet Friendship Society. In New York, unprecedentedly, Broadway theatre marquees and the bright lights of Times Square were blacked out for several minutes. Theatre audiences in Australia rose for two minutes' silence. The actors and directors of the Swedish National Theatre delivered a statement to the British Ambassador in Stockholm expressing gratitude "for Mr. Shaw's wit, satire, social criticism, and dramatic information during a long and stimulating creative life." To its discredit there was no formal sign of tribute from the British theatre profession, though Sybil Thorndike and Laurence Olivier paid personal homage, the latter describing Shaw as one who, "true to his text," had "made of the theatre 'a factory of thought, a prompter of conscience, an elucidator of social conduct, an armory against despair and dullness, and a temple of the Ascent of Man.'"

Equally conspicuous was the absence of any official statement from the Independent Labour Party, though the Labour (and Fabian) Prime Minister, Clement Attlee, who, unlike Churchill, had overlooked Shaw's ninetieth birthday and been silent throughout his final illness, was at last moved to declare, "We Socialists who knew him as a fellow-worker revered him for the many years of devoted service and effective support by word and pen that he gave to our movement."

In an appreciation broadcast by the B.B.C. on the night of Shaw's death, St John Ervine provided what was probably the most indelible impression of GBS, in a recollection of him as a great laugher, who "laughed with his whole body. He threw his shoulders about while the laughter ran up his long legs and threatened to shake his head off. That is how I like to remember him."

On 5th November, en route from Welwyn to Golder's Green, the hearse carrying Shaw's remains stopped at Ayot St Lawrence to allow a spray of rosemary to be placed on the coffin. Sent by Christopher St John, it bore a note, "Rosemary from Ellen Terry's garden, for remembrance of her partnership with 'Bernie.' " At 4 p.m. on 6th November, in the high-ceilinged, brick-walled, chrysanthemum-decorated West Chapel of the Golder's Green Crematorium a brief funeral service was conducted. Despite Shaw's desire that the service be private, three dozen relatives and friends were admitted by cards issued by the Public Trustee, including several cousins (Judy Musters, Ethel Walters, George Gamble, James Cockaigne Shaw and Bernard Vidal Shaw), Charlotte's niece Cecily Colthurst, Lady Astor, the Gabriel Pascals, Pakenham Beatty's daughter Cecilia Livia, Otto Kyllmann, Ebba Low, the Irish Ambassador (Frederick H. Boland), Lennox Robinson (representing both Dublin's Abbey Theatre and the Irish Academy of Letters), Blanche Patch, Dr Loewenstein, Mrs Laden, Dr Probyn, Margaret Cashin Smith, Fred Day, Shaw's nurses, and F. Wyndham Hirst, the Public Trustee.

The music, played on a mammoth pipe organ, had been chosen by Shaw himself: the hymn at the start of Humperdinck's *Hansel and Gretel* overture, the *Libere me* from Verdi's Requiem, and extracts from Elgar's *The Music Makers* and the Nimrod variation from the *Enigma Variations*. It was relayed to the cloisters and Garden of Remembrance, where some five hundred admirers were gathered, one of them a leader of the Women's Social and Political Union, Mary Leigh, who unfurled the purple, green and white flag of the suffrage movement, announcing, "G.B.S. was one of our best friends during our fight for the vote. He visited us in prison and gave us all the support he could." In a final irony, the police quietly but firmly bustled her out of the courtyard, which was strewn with wreaths from William Randolph Hearst, the Polish Writers' Association of Warsaw, and the Executive of the Communist Party of Great Britain.

On Shaw's grey-draped plain cremation coffin, as it was carried in and rested on a teakwood stand, was a bronze urn at its head containing

Charlotte's ashes. Scattered upon the coffin were a few rose petals mingled with laurel leaves, placed there by Sir Sydney Cockerell, who, in lieu of a eulogy, read to the gathering the final words of Mr Valiant-for-Truth, from Bunyan's *Pilgrim's Progress*:

" 'My Sword I give to him that shall succeed me in my Pilgrimage, and my Courage and Skill to him that can get it. My Marks and Scars I carry with me, to be a Witness for me that I have fought his Battles, who now will be my Rewarder.'

"When the Day that he must go hence was come, many accompanied him to the River side, into which as he went, he said 'Death, where is thy Sting?' And as he went down deeper, he said 'Grave, where is thy Victory?' So he passed over, and the Trumpets sounded for him on the other side."

As the mourners, led by a red-eyed Nancy Astor, her head bowed in grief, departed into the dusk to the organ strains of Walford Davies's "Solemn Melody," Shaw's coffin was consigned to the furnace, the ashes later being deposited in a small rectangular bronze casket to await disposal. Even before his death the question had arisen of burial in Westminster Abbey, though the Dean of Westminster, the Very Rev. A. C. Don, subsequently stated he had never been formally approached on the subject. The Dean of St Patrick's, Dublin, requested that Shaw's remains be returned to Ireland for burial in the cathedral beside the grave of Swift. Lady Astor informed the press that Shaw's final injunction was that "I want my ashes mingled with my wife's. After that you can do what you like." As Clause 3 of Shaw's last will and testament, however, stated "I prefer the garden to the cloister," the Public Trustee took this as a mandate, finally, to consign the ashes to the garden at Shaw's Corner.

The quiet ceremony at Ayot St Lawrence, at 1.15 p.m. on 23rd November, was attended only by the Public Trustee and his deputies W. L. Limb and B. L. Davies, Dr Probyn, Charlotte's executor (W. E. Pierce), Mrs Laden, and a news-agency reporter representing the press and the public. The Public Trustee mingled the ashes of Charlotte and GBS on the oak sideboard in the dining-room and Dr Probyn carried them out to the garden, where he strewed them over the sloping lawn and, in circles, round the statue of Saint Joan and the revolving hut in which Shaw had spent so many of his working hours.

886

Corrections and additions for
Collected Letters 1911–1925

The first numeral refers to page, the second to line. There are separate line counts for headnote and text. Recipient is indicated when more than one letter appears on a page. H indicates Headnote, T text.

xvi: 17	For "Physical" read "Psychical"
24: 3	Shaw's "without" is an error; the sense requires "with"
87: 5	(Shaw, 28 April) for "Thirlmore" read "Thirlmere"
159: 1	For "thing" read "some thing"
166: T, 33	For "than" read "that"
168: 28	For "forego" read "forgo" in line 11 of sonnet
281: 6	(Durham) For "48-years" read "48-hours"
308: H, 8	(Gregory) For "Sarah" read "Sara"
347: H, 4	For "3rd" read "2nd"
382: H, 7	(Poel) for "State Society" read "Stage Society"
409: 23–24	Williamstown (Williams College) is in Massachusetts, not in New Hampshire
411: H, 4–5	(Faversham) Charles Evans Hughes ran *opposite* Wilson and lost. He later became chief justice of the U.S. Supreme Court
471: H, 5	(Wells) For "1836" read "1536"
480: 10	For "master" read "mastered"
492: 4	For "How" read "Now"
509: H, 1–3	(Plunkett) Plunkett's assistant was (Francis) Cruise O'Brien, a member of the Irish Convention secretariat
515: 20	For "ease" read "case"
515: 39	For "17th" read "16th"
516: 4	(Blumenfeld) Inverted commas following "anticipated" should rightfully precede "Sinn Féin"
547: T, 18	(Plunkett) For "or" read "of"
548: T, 12	(Hamon) For "one his" read "one of his"
618: H, 2	Wane B. Wells was editor of the first *Irish Statesman* 1919–20. Russell edited the revived journal 1923–30
631: 14	For "there is wealth" read "there is [not] wealth"
639: T, 7	(Bassett-Lowke) For "wise to" read "wise enough to"

687: H, 13	(Trebitsch) For "1881" read "1880"
797: 35	For "Beatu" read "Beata"
803: H, 4	(Lawrence) John E. Mack in *A Prince of Our Disorder* (1976) says Lawrence claimed his father did *not* change his name by deed poll
830: 10	For "gentlemen" read "gentleman"
842: H, 1	(Salt) For "not" read "never"
890: H, 3	For "Pitöeff" read "Pitoëff"
907: H, 6–7	Alter to read "William Maxwell Aitken"
921: T, 9	For "*fou*" read "*four*"

Correction for
Collected Letters 1898–1910

871: H, 2	(Vedrenne) *Just Exactly Nothing* was the working title for *Fanny's First Play*, not *Misalliance*

Correction for
Collected Letters 1874–1897

238: H, 8	It was Ada Russell, also an actress, who became Amy Lowell's companion, not Ada Rehan

Index of Recipients

Irving, Laurence (the younger), 785, 838

James, A. Lloyd, 395, 483
John, Augustus, 700, 701, 794
Jones, Eirene Lloyd, 745
Jones, Henry Arthur, 26

Keeble, Lillah (McCarthy) and Frederick, 678
Kennedy, Clara M., 718, 803
Kennedy, W. S., 41
Kennet, Lady (Kathleen Hilton Young, formerly Scott), 22, 28, 163, 513
Kennet, Lord (Edward Hilton Young), 798
Kenworthy, J.M., 213
Keynes, John Maynard, 389, 540, 669
Kidd, Ronald, 600
Klagemann, Eberhard K., 434
Koretz, Paul, 376, 605
Krauss, Werner, 808
Kyllmann, Otto, 12, 78, 193, 350, 352, 474, 578, 596, 732, 751, 757

Lanchester, Waldo, 839
Langner, Lawrence, 510, 550, 621, 811
Laski, Harold, 749, 801
Latham, Charles, 781
Lawson, Wilfrid, 181
Lawton, Mary, 515
Leahy, Maurice, 50
Lees-Milne, James, 722
Leiser, Clara, 306
Levinson, Jesse, 61
Lewis, Cecil, 286, 466
Lewis, Howard C., 518
Liddell Hart, Basil, 356
Lilien, Ignace, 297
Limbert, Roy, 522, 523, 558, 604, 784, 827, 850
Little Theatre, Akron, Ohio, 185
Loewenstein, F.E., 450, 621, 639, 712, 718, 775, 789
Londonderry, Lady (Edith Vane-Tempest-Stewart), 520
Low, Ebba, 32
Lucas, E.V., 147
Ludwig, Emil, 814

Lummis, Rev. E.W., 216
Luther, Sally, 815
Lynch, Arthur, 316

McCall, J.J., 760
McCarthy, Lillah: see Keeble
McCulloch, C.B., 35
MacDonald, J. Ramsay, 74, 79
McEvoy, Charles, 35
MacGowan, Kenneth, 333, 353, 354, 362, 365
Mackail, Margaret, 355
McLachlan, Dame Laurentia, 229, 264, 280, 288, 344, 348, 380, 409, 416, 723, 775
McLaren, Christabel, 113
McLean, Ruari, 843
MacManus, M.J., 461
Macmillan, Daniel, 674
McNulty, Matthew Edward, 121, 526
MacSwiney, Muriel F., 237
Marr, Hamilton, 546
Martin, Kingsley, 629
Martin-Harvey, John, 30
Masefield, John, 772
Matheson, Donald McLeod, 681, 684
Matheson, Hilda, 164
Maxwell, John, 195
Maxwell, William, 7, 129, 259, 407, 682, 683, 769
May, Frederick, 873
Meredith, E. Norman, 768
Mitchison, Naomi, 358
Monck, W. Nugent, 342, 432
Mooney, Thomas, 330
Moore, John G., 469
Morris, May, 427
Morrison, Herbert, 634
Moynihan, Maurice, 747
Mulry, W.L., 702
Murray, Gilbert, 504, 583, 613, 714
Murray, Henry, 213
Murray, Lady Mary, 679
Murray, Muriel, 473
Musters, Georgina (Judy Gillmore), 379, 686, 698, 824, 859

Nehru, Jawaharlal, 827
Nelson, A., 275

GENERAL INDEX

COMPILED BY T. F. EVANS AND FRANCES GLENDENNING

Barrie, Mary (Ansell), 502-3
Barrow, Janet, 581
Barry, Philip, 550
Barrymore, John
    and proposed film of *The Devil's Disciple*, 333, 355-6, 362, 401
Barrymore, Lionel, 134
Bartok, Béla, 846
Bartolucci, Candida, 49-50
Barton, Dr J. Kingston, 445-6
Basic English Foundation, 661-2
Basile, Carlo Emanuele, 100
    Discorsi Fascisti, 71
Baskerville (type), 259, 624
Bateman, Don, 768
Bathurst, Charles, later Baron Bledisloe of Lydney, 370-1
Bax, Arnold, 92
Bax, E. Belfort, 57
Baxter, (Sir) Beverley, 664-5
Baxter, Dr M., 817
Baylis, Lilian, 177, 432
Bayreuth, 129
B.B.C.: 3, 24-5, 164-5, 195, 201, 211, 261, 272, 309-10, 341, 361-2, 375-6, 383, 436, 483, 536, 538, 546, 600, 623, 625-6, 642, 648, 665, 692, 708, 720, 729, 779, 781, 804, 815-16, 845, 854, 880, 882, 885
B.B.C. Overseas Service Department, 544, 563
B.B.C. Symphony Orchestra, 261, 582
Beach, Sylvia, 858
Beaton, Cecil, 673
Beatty, Vice-Admiral Sir David, 63
Beatty, Cecilia Livia, 885
Beatty, Pakenham, 50, 419, 885
Beaumont, Hugh (Binkie), 450-1, 664, 673
Bebel, August, 73
Bechstein (piano), 92-3, 95, 517
Becket, Thomas à, 70
Beech, Patrick, 683-4, 704
Beech, Mrs Mervyn: *see* Campbell, Stella Patrick
Beecham, Sir Thomas, 311
Beerbohm, Sir Max, 27

Beethoven, Ludwig van, 29, 144-5, 166, 175, 201, 298, 309-10, 341, 378-379, 439, 459, 516-17, 534, 582, 709, 716, 754-5, 763, 798, 814, 837-8, 840, 847
Beggar's Opera, The: *see* Brecht, Bertolt
Begum, The ("Atizabegum"), 321
Beith, G., (ed.): *Edward Carpenter: an appreciation*, 284
Beldon, Eileen, 554-5
Belfast Corporation, 271
Belgium, 490
Bell, Alexander: *The Standard Elocutionist*, 209, 787
Bell, G., and Sons, 391-2
Bell, Malcolm: *Sir Edward Burne Jones*, 515
Bell, Melville: *Visible Speech*, 241
Bell, Dr Robert, 54-5
Bellhouse (boy in Dublin), 87
Bellièvre, M., 821
Bellingham-Warner, J., 653
Bellini, Vicenzo, 411
Belloc, Hilaire, 278, 463
Belsen: *see* Bergen-Belsen
Bembo (type), 624
Benckendorff, Aleksandr Konstantinovich, 42
Benckendorff family, 42-4
Bendall, E. A., 204, 206
Benedict XV, Pope, 62
Beneš, Eduard, 537-8
Bennett, Arnold, 54, 92, 118
Benson, Sir Frank, 402
Bentley, R. (publisher), 676
Bentley, Eric: *Bernard Shaw: a reconsideration*, 821
Bergen-Belsen, 752
Berger, Ludwig, 398
Bergner, Elisabeth, 364, 401, 484-5
    in *Saint Joan* in Berlin, 400
    "hopeless failure" in *Saint Joan* at Malvern, 508, 723
    in *Escape Me Never*, 405
    in *Catherine the Great* (film), 415-16
Berlioz, Hector, 378, 709, 730
Berman-Fischer, Gottfried, 771
Berners, Lord: *First Childhood*, 223

Brewer, Herbert, 460
Bridges, Robert, 24, 613, 721
   The Testament of Beauty, 168
Bridges-Adams, William, 318–19, 831
Bridie, James (pseudonym), 223
   A Sleeping Clergyman, 340
   invited to revise film scenario for *Saint Joan*, 415–16
Brieux, Eugène, 654
Briggs, Hedley, 180
Bright, John, 575–6
British Broadcasting Corporation: *see* B.B.C.
British Commonwealth, 601, 629, 782, 857
British Empire, 230, 369, 409, 531, 544, 547
British International Films, 262
British International Pictures, 195, 286, 288
British Interplanetary Society, 792
British Museum, 135, 159, 198, 218, 390, 472, 684, 687, 712–13, 724, 761, 789, 884
British-Soviet Friendship Society, 884
British Union for the Abolition of Vivisection, *Experiments on Animals*, 58
British Weekly, 113, 803
Brittain, Vera, 707
Britten, Benjamin, later Baron Britten of Aldeburgh
   music for radio play by MacNeice, 730
   Peter Grimes, 729
Broadhurst, Henry, 776–7
Broadwood (piano), 516
Brock, Sir Thomas, 785
Brockway, A. Fenner, later Lord Brockway, 132
   Inside the Left, 330
Bronson, Betty, 134
Brooke, Rupert, 638
Brooks, Rev. J. Barlow, 404
Brooks, Sam, 404
Broughton, Rhoda, 478, 482
Brown, Ford Madox, 107, 109
Brown, Ivor, 450

Browne, Charles Farrar: *Artemus Ward: His Book*, 22–3
Browning, Robert, 621
Browning Society, 621, 639–40, 739
Bruce, Edgar K., 574
Brunswick, Duke of, 538
Bryant, (Sir) Arthur, 524
Bryant, Charlotte (Mrs Frederick John), 439–40
Bryant and May match strike, 449
Buchman, Frank, 393, 511
Buckingham, Duke of, 441
Buckstone, John: *The Wreck Ashore*, 837
Buddha, 323
Bull, Stanley W., 23
Bumpus, John and Edward Ltd., 223, 382, 596–7
Bunin, Ivan, 40
Bunyan, John, 89, 157
   tercentenary of, 113
   The Holy War, 88, 113–14
   Pilgrim's Progress, 88, 113–15, 297, 306, 318, 591, 886
Buoyant Billions: *see* Shaw—Plays
Burbage, Richard, 136, 207, 785–7
Burgess, Annette Curnen, 770
Burlington Arcade, 80
Burma, 863
Burne-Jones, Sir Edward, 107–8, 355, 515–16, 559, 862
Burnham, Viscount: *see* Lawson, Harry
Burns, John, 777
   model for Boanerges in *The Apple Cart*, 776
Burrell, John, 673–4
Burrows, Herbert, 448–9
Busoni, Ferruccio, 515–17, 847
Butler, Samuel, 317, 429, 479, 587
Butterfield, Charles, 431, 480–1
Butterfield, Douglas, 481
Byrolly, Bruce, 829
Byron, George Gordon, Lord, 676
   Don Juan, 210

Cade, Jack, 279–80
Cæsar, Julius, 43, 455, 643, 727, 833
Cæsar and Cleopatra: *see* Shaw—Plays
Caine, Sir Hall, 682
   Recollections of Rossetti, 106–7

Caine, Henry, 573
Caligula, 62
Calles, Plutarco, President of Mexico, 62
Calthrop, Donald, 542
Calvert, Louis, 648, 655
Calvin, John, 390, 545
  Institutes, 278, 429, 643
Cambridge Theatre, 664
Cambridge, University of, 13, 827
Campbell, Alan Hugh (Beo), 151-2
Campbell, Archie, 845
Campbell, Lady Colin, 796
Campbell, Patrick (grandson of Mrs Patrick Campbell), 153, 156
Campbell, Mrs Patrick (Beatrice Stella Tanner), 91, 132-3, 150-3, 155-156, 401, 405, 408, 468, 470-2, 496-7, 570-2, 593, 595, 599, 655, 742, 862
  tells Shaw to tear up *The Apple Cart*, 155
  in *The Matriarch*, 148-9
  in *Lady Patricia*, 152
  death of, 553, 598-9
  portrait in *The Apple Cart*, 133
  My Life and some Letters, 592
  in *Pygmalion*, 648, 815
  "You were right, Sandwich and all," 133
  model for other characters, 157
Campbell, Stella Patrick (Mrs Mervyn Beech *or* Stella Mervyn Campbell), 149, 471-2, 497, 598-9, 683-4, 704
Campbell, Thomas
  The Life of Mrs Siddons, 46
  The Pleasures of Hope, 864
Campion, Sidney R., 804
Canby, Henry Seidel, 692
Candid Friend, The, 498-9
Candida: *see* Shaw—Plays
Cannan, Gilbert, 502
Canterbury Cathedral, 196, 198, 264
Cantinflas (stage name of Mario Moreno), 860
Cape, Jonathan, 110
Cape Town Municipal Orchestra, 582
Čapek, Karel, 112-13

Capitalism, 44, 58, 73-6, 270, 279, 294-5, 302, 369, 424, 457, 750, 777
Capital Levy, 81
Capone, Al, 247
Captain Brassbound's Conversion: *see* Shaw—Plays
Carew, James, 158-9, 161
Carlisle St Stephen's Band, 201
Carlow Urban District Council
  transfer of property to, 704, 710-11, 713, 743-4, 747-8, 766, 769
Carlyle, Thomas, 120, 455, 498, 526
  Latter-Day Pamphlets, 260
  Sartor Resartus, 718
Carnarvon Castle (ship), 267, 270
Carnegie, Andrew, 823
Carpenter, Edward, 529
  Towards Democracy, 284
  song by, sung in *On the Rocks*, 364
Carpentier, Georges, 130-2
Carr, J. Comyns: *Tristan and Iseult*, 826
Carroll, Emily (Aunt Emily), 480, 737, 857
Carroll, Emily ("Tah"), 478, 737
Carroll, Leo G., 621
Carroll, Lewis, 281
Carroll, Madeleine, 466
Carroll, Sydney W.: presents *The Six of Calais* and *Androcles and the Lion*, 402
Carroll, Rev. William George, 478, 727, 737, 834
Carson, Sir Edward, 442
Carter, Huntly (ed.): *The New Spirit in the Cinema*, 167
Caruso, Enrico, 307, 823
Casanova, 106, 178, 862
Casement, Sir Roger, 461
  "forged" diaries of, 387-9
Cashel Byron's Profession: *see* Shaw—Novels
Cashin, Margaret: *see* Smith, Margaret Cashin
Caslon (type), 129, 623-4
Caslon, William, 843
Casson, Ann, 666, 723
Casson, (Sir) Lewis, 37, 723
Castelli, Cesare, 371

Dalton, Hugh, later Baron Dalton, 80–1, 778, 794
Daly, Arnold, 155
Daly, Augustin, 572
Daly's Theatre, New York, 464
Danakils, 424
D'Annunzio, Gabriele: *Francesca da Rimini*, 826
Danton, Georges-Jacques, 537–8
Darling, Grenville, 581
Dartington Hall, 552–3
Darwin, Charles, 280, 429, 596, 650, 675
Darzens, Rodolphe, 123–4
Davenant, Sir William, 811–12
Davenport, Nicholas, 566
Davidson, Jo, 176, 513
Davidson, Dr Randall, later Baron Davidson of Dundee, 196
Davidson, Thomas, 384, 386
Davies, Arthur, 839
Davies, B. L., 886
Davies, George, 502
Davies, Kathleen, 18–19
Davies, Marion, 109–10, 332
   wishes to play Eliza in film of *Pygmalion*, 426
Davies, Rev. Richard James, 883–4
Davies, Walford, 886
Davis, Fay, 571
Davis, Kathleen, 19
Davis, Mary Ethel (Shaw), later Walters, 725–6, 885
Dawson, Geoffrey, 539–40
Day, Alfred: *Treatise on Harmony*, 846
Day, Daniel G., 849
Day, Frances, 856, 858–9, 881–3
   in *The Apple Cart*, 851, 855
   in *Buoyant Billions*, 850–1, 855
Day, Fred, 21, 22, 536, 879, 882, 885
Day, Margaret (Mrs Fred), 536
"D.D.": *see* Lyttelton, Dame Edith
Dean, Basil, 333
Deans, Marjorie, 666, 728
Debussy, Claude, 171, 438, 483
Deck, Richard, 48, 121
De Forrest, Lee, 37
Dekker, Thomas, 433
   The Shoemaker's Holiday, 432
   The Witch of Edmonton, 431

De La Haye, Ina, 554
Delavigne, Casimir, 213
De La Warr Pavilion, Bexhill-on-Sea, 444
Democracy, 73, 81, 101, 157, 164, 455, 458, 575–6, 595, 600, 734, 777–8
Dempsey, Jack, 130–2
Denshawi, 491
Dent, Alan, 149
Dent, Edward J.: article in *G.B.S.* 90, 774
Dent, J. M., and Co., 597, 751
Design '46, 764
De Smet, Gustav, 751–2
Despard, Charlotte, 67
Determinism, 596
Deutsches Theater, Berlin, 166, 358–9
Deutschmeister, Henry, 398–400
De Valera, Éamon, 67, 223, 462, 492–3, 586–8, 594, 691, 742–4, 747–8, 757, 777, 807
   Gaelic greeting for 90th birthday, 691
Devil's Disciple, The: *see* Shaw—Plays
Deville, Gabriel, 390
Devine, Mary, 706
Devine, Patricia, 706–7
Dickens, Charles, 121, 327, 617, 639–40, 650, 691, 761, 791
   David Copperfield, 115, 534, 633, 693, 726–7
   Dombey and Son, 120
   Great Expectations, 425, 534, 633
   Little Dorrit, 534
   Martin Chuzzlewit, 498–9
   Nicholas Nickleby, 171
   Oliver Twist, 198
   Our Mutual Friend, 278–9
   Pickwick Papers, 17–18, 30–1, 217, 383–4
Dickens Fellowship, 120, 639–40
Dickinson, Goldsworthy Lowes, 284
Dictionary of National Biography, 308
Dilke, Sir Charles, 675
Directory, French, 68
Disarmament Conference, 353
Disraeli, Benjamin, later Earl of Beaconsfield, 120, 394, 575–6, 777
Distributist League, 278

Eisenhower, General Dwight D., 714, 716
Eisenstein, Sergei: *Potemkin* (film), 132
Elephant and Castle Theatre, 431–2, 575
Elgar, Carice, 816
Elgar, Sir Edward, 174–5, 200, 225–6, 373–4, 378–9, 383, 397, 439, 557, 814–16, 848
 wishes to dedicate work to Shaw, 200
 first meeting with, 557
 "Cockaigne Overture," 101–3
 The Dream of Gerontius, 340, 507
 Enigma Variations, 396, 885
 The Kingdom, 340
 The Music Makers, 507, 885
 Shaw suggests B.B.C. commission, 309–10
Elgin marbles, 227
Eliot, T. S., 118, 464
Elizabeth I, 62, 81, 169
Ellen Terry and Bernard Shaw: a correspondence: see Shaw—Other Works
Ellen Terry Memorial Institute, 134, 136, 202–3
Elliott, Rt. Hon. Col. Walter, 776, 778
Elliott, Denholm, 850, 855
Ellis, Havelock, 118, 284
Elmhirst, Leonard, 552
Ely, Gertrude H., 243–4
Ely, Lord, 529
Embassy Theatre, Swiss Cottage, 459
Emerson, Ralph Waldo, 375
Empress of Britain (ship), 318, 320, 322, 326
Encyclopædia Britannica, 12, 21, 545
Engels, Friedrich, 67, 393
Enghien, Duc d', 69
Episcopal Church of Ireland, 478
Epstein, (Sir) Jacob, 513
 bust of Shaw, 485–7
 Let There be Sculpture, 486
Epstein, Margaret, 485–7
Erard grand (piano), 517
Ernest, Dr Maurice, 742
Ervine, St John, 308, 312–14, 418, 455, 493, 510, 691, 694, 871, 885
 "Mr Moses Shaw," review of *Back to

Ervine, St John—*contd.*
 Methuselah, 95–8
 Parnell, 276–7, 313
 God's Soldier, 276–7, 313
 on *Too True to be Good*, 302, 312–13
 People of our Class, 428–9
 Robert's Wife, 572
 Bernard Shaw: his Life, Work and Friends, 644–5
 review of Pearson biography, 644
 Shaw considers the biography by Ervine "hopeless," 645
 "A Pageant of Plays and Players" (B.B.C. programme), 804
 Craigavon: Ulsterman, 852–3
Ervine, Leonora (Mrs St John), 96, 222, 312–14, 429, 493, 538, 646, 735, 871
Escott, T. H. S., 644
Etherege, Sir George, 127
Eton College, 216, 706, 841
Euclid, 633
Eugénie, Empress, 546
Euripides, 171, 614
 tr. by Gilbert Murray, 614
 Electra, 170
 Hippolytus, 170
 Iphigenia in Tauris, 170
 Medea, 170
 The Trojan Women, 170
Europäische Revue, 359
Evans, Caradoc, 9–11
Evans, (Dame) Edith, 432, 568–9
 in *The Apple Cart*, 149–50, 157
 in *As You Like It*, 431
 in *Candida* (B.B.C. sound broadcast), 845
 in *The Country Wife*, 431
 in *Heartbreak House*, 284, 673–4
 in *The Millionairess*, 431
 in *The Seagull*, 442
 in *The Witch of Edmonton*, 431
Evans, Frederick H., 280, 754
Evans, Dr Geoffrey, 501
Evans, George Eyre, 772
Evans, Maurice, 543, 551
 in *Man and Superman*, 800–1
Evans, T. F.: article, "Shaw in Russia," 251

906

Fox, William, studios, 121–2, 400–1
France, 69, 73, 538, 559–60, 563, 578, 873; *and see* Shaw—Travel
France, La, 874
Francesca da Rimini: *see* D'Annunzio
Franco, General Francisco, 441, 538, 623
Franco London Films, 398
Franco-Prussian war, 18
Frank, Anne, 752
Franklin, Benjamin, 398
Franz Ferdinand, Archduke, 359
Franz Joseph, Emperor of Austria, 359, 548
Fraser, Sir Robert Brown, 781
French Revolution, 390, 457, 538
French, Samuel, 208
Freud, Siegmund, 190, 391–2, 418, 638, 814–15
Frohman, Charles, 180
Fry, Roger, 556–7
Fundamentalists, 324, 394
Furniss, Harry, 728
 Annual, 726
Furnivall, Dr F. J., 117, 639–40

Galen, 58–9
Galileo, 211
Gallacher, William, 101–3, 373, 615–616
Gallagher, Sister Elizabeth, 880
Galleria Brera, Milan, 184
Galsworthy, John, 84–5, 170–2, 698
Galt, Thomas F., 240
Gamage's, 80–1
Gamble, George, 885
Gammer Gurton's Needle, 340
Gandhi, Mohandas K., 267, 635, 852
Garbo, Greta, 508, 666, 670
Gardiner, A. G., 214
Gargan, Bernard Talbot, 121
Gargan, Vera, 670
Garrick, David, 46, 785–6, 812
 Heart of Oak, 629
Garrick Theatre, Melbourne, 339
Garson, Greer, 312
Gatty, A. Scott, 164
Gauguin, Paul, 184, 254
Gaumont-British News, 721

Gay, John, 144, 247, 528
Gay Pay Oo: *see* OGPU
Gazzetta del Popolo, 68
G.B.S. 90: *see* Winsten, Stephen
Geehl, Henry, 200
Geikie-Cobb, Ivo, 544, 563, 625
 publishes banned broadcast by Shaw, 563
General Election (June 1929), 141, 776
General Election (October 1931), 262, 313
General Election (June 1945), 745
General Election (Irish, 1948), 807–8
General Medical Council, 446
General Post Office, 154, 804, 872
General Strike (1926), 101, 103
Geneva: *see* Shaw—Plays
George III, 272
George V, 118
George VI, 635
George, Henry, 386, 823
Gerhardi, William, 505
German Communist Party, 42
Germany, 3, 20, 25–6, 29, 63, 237, 244, 335, 343, 348, 359, 400, 413, 422–3, 450, 456, 467, 490, 496, 505, 600, 607, 814: *see also* Hitler
Gestapo, 582
Gibbon, Edward: *Decline and Fall of the Roman Empire*, 629
Gielgud, John
 in *Fortunato*, 654
 in *The Seagull*, 442–3
Gielgud, Val: article, "Bernard Shaw and the Radio," 845
Gilbert, Sir W. S., 383
 and Sullivan, Sir A., 871
  H.M.S. Pinafore, 755
  The Mikado, 211
  Patience, 211, 577
  The Pirates of Penzance, 756
  Ruddigore, 383–4
  Trial by Jury, 383
  The Yeomen of the Guard, 211
Gill, Eric, 624
Gillman, James, 682
Gillmore, Arabella, née Gurly, 65

Gillmore, Georgina (Judy), Mrs Harold
    Chaworth Musters, 65, 221, 379,
    685–6, 698, 824, 849, 859, 878,
    881–2, 885
Gladstone, William Ewart, 74, 120, 178,
    576
Glasites, 50
Glastonbury Music Festival, 311
Glazunov, Alexander, 250
Globe-Mermaid Association, 397
Globe Theatre, Shaftesbury Avenue, 33,
    431, 451, 484, 551
Globe Theatre, Southwark, 397
Gluck, Christoph W., 730
    Orfeo, 8
Gluck Society, 832
Glyndebourne, 432, 798
Godfrey, Dan, 101
Godowsky, Leopold, 483
Godwin, Edward, 160, 210
Goebbels, Joseph, 359, 423, 600, 635
Goering, Hermann, 335, 337, 413–
    414
Goethe, Johann Wolfgang, 385, 814,
    833, 858
    Aus meinem Leben, Dichtung und
        Wahrheit, 384
    Faust, 100, 785
Goetz, Hermann, 846–7
Gogarty, Oliver St John, 308
Gold, Julius, 846–8
Golden, Michael, 648
Golders Green Cemetery, 54, 430–1,
    876, 885–6
Golders Green Hippodrome, 554
Goldsmith, Oliver
    She Stoops to Conquer, 554, 665
    The Vicar of Wakefield, 115, 673,
        (adapted as Olivia), 785
Goldwyn, Samuel, 533
Gollancz, Victor, 187, 261–3, 631
Gonne, Maud: see McBride, Maud
    Gonne
Goodall, Edyth, 15–16
Goodliffe, Grace, 651–3, 857
Gorki, Maxim, 254, 291, 396
Gorringe, Frederick, Ltd., 478, 481
Gosizdat (State Publishing House), 245,
    247

Gosse, Sir Edmund
    Father and Son, 127–8
    Life of Congreve, 127
Gosse, Philip, 127
Gounod, Charles, 709, 826
    Faust, 177, 307, 779
Gourmont, Rémy de, 874
Gow, Ronald, 567
    Love on the Dole (film), 588–9
    screen version of Fame is the Spur,
        667
Gozzoli, Benozzo, 170–1
G.P.U.: see "Ogpu"
Grand National, 341
Grandi, (Count) Dino, 371–2
Grant, Blanche, 485, 487
Granville Barker, Harley, 3, 82–3, 118,
    221, 227–8, 249, 431, 503, 585,
    655, 657, 685, 720
    Shaw's opinion of, 170–3
    The Madras House, 160
    translation of Fortunato, 654, 656
    in Candida, 171
    in Captain Brassbound's Conversion,
        171
    in Friedensfest, 171
    in John Bull's Other Island, 171
    in Man and Superman, 171
    in A Man of Honour, 442–3
Granville Barker, Mrs Harley (Helen
    Huntington) 227, 585, 822
    Shaw "blasted and bewitched" by, 83
    insists on hyphenation, 228
Gray, Mary (of Martin-Harvey Com-
    pany): in The Shewing-up of
    Blanco Posnet, 30
Great War: see War of 1914–1918
Greek drama, 657
Greek Orthodox Church, 62
Greek theatre: Shaw lectures on, 228
Green, Paul, 528
Greene, Arthur, 477
Greene, Charlotte, 477, 479
Greene, Dr G. E. J., 347
Greene, Graham, 550
Greenwood, Walter: Love on the Dole,
    588–9
Greet, Clare, 444
Gregg, John Robert, 615–17

Harris, Frank—*contd.*
261–2, 475–7, 489, 503, 660;
preface by Shaw, 475, 489
Mr and Mrs Daventry, 498
editor of various publications, 498–9
articles on Shaw in *Vanity Fair*, 498
examples of "earthy speech," 796
death of, 259–60
Christ—"the nearest thing to him-
self," 796
Harris, Helen O'Hara (Nellie), 105–6,
235, 259–64, 475–6, 489
Harris, Henry Wilson, 492–3
Harrison, Frederick, 207
Harrison, Rex, 564
Harrod's, 599
Hart, Sir Basil Liddell: *see* Liddell
Hart
Hart, Lorenz, 528
Hart, Walter D'Arcy, 202, 266
Hart-Davis, Sir Rupert, 475
Harty, (Sir) Hamilton, 174–5
Harvard University, 13
Hathway, Richard, 216
Hatton, Thomas, 138
Hauptmann, Gerhardt, 3
*The Coming of Peace (Das Friedens-
fest)*, 171, 654
Havilland, Geoffrey Raoul de, 792–3
Hay, William Montagu, tenth Marquis
of Tweeddale, 49
Haydn, Franz Joseph, 378
Haydon, Benjamin R., 872
Hayek, Max, 16–17
Hayes, Richard J., 761, 766
Haymarket, Theatre Royal, 152, 674,
713
Hays Office censorship, 428, 430
Haythornthwaite, Henrietta R., 863–4,
872
Hazlitt, William, 836
Heard, Daphne, 554
Hearst, William Randolph, 104, 109–10,
331–3, 595, 597, 885
Heartbreak House: *see* Shaw—Plays
Heath, Nellie: portrait of Shaw, 849–50
Hecht, Katharine, 342
Hegel, G. W. F., 823
Heine, Heinrich, 191

Helburn, Theresa, 128, 325–6, 400, 528,
551
Hellenic Travellers' Club, 228, 235
Henderson, Archibald, 64, 176, 334
Table-Talk of G.B.S., 9
Bernard Shaw: Playboy and Prophet,
9, 175, 428, 512
article, "My Friend, Bernard Shaw,"
37
Henderson, George Macdonald, 367
Henley, W. E., 476
Henri IV, 169, 441
Henry, Prince of Wales, later Henry V,
216
Henry VI, 216
Henry VII, 585
Henry VIII, 271
Henry, J. M., 223
Henry and Co., 147
Henry Miller's Theatre, New York, 550
Hentschel, Irene
produces *Candida*, 450–2
article, "Producing for Shaw and
Priestley," 451
Hepburn, Katharine, 551, 574
proposed film of *Saint Joan*, 333, 353
in *The Little Minister* (film), 353
in *The Millionairess*, 550–1
in *The Philadelphia Story*, 550
Herbert, Auberon, 675
Hereford Music Festival, 340–1
Hermitage, Leningrad, 251–3
Hernon, P. J., 764–5, 773
Herodotus, 734
Herrick, Robert, 622
Hertzog, James, 412
Hewlett, Maurice, 171
Hichens, Robert: *see* Traill, H. D.
Hidveghy, Valerie: *see* Pascal, Valerie
Higgins, F. R., 308
Higgs, Clara and Harry, 425–6, 673,
686, 757
Hignett, H. R., 554, 556
Hildebrand, Pope, 283
Hiller, (Dame) Wendy, 442, 508, 551,
568, 574
on inadequate rehearsal time, 437
in *Love on the Dole*, 436
in *Major Barbara* (film), 568, 588

Japanese music, 340–1
Jaurès, Jean, 73
Jeans, Isabel, 673–4
Jeans, Sir James: does logarithms for *In Good King Charles's Golden Days*, 545
Jefferson, Thomas, 817
Jellicoe, Admiral Sir John, 63
Jenson, Nicolas, 843
Jesuits, 645
Jevons, Stanley, 750
Jews, 51, 198, 210–11, 238, 336–8, 342–4, 348, 354, 358–60, 413, 421, 444, 457, 493, 496, 510–12, 522–3, 525, 540, 547, 623, 752, 783; *see also* Anti-Semitism
Jewish Chronicle, 457
Jinnah, Mohammed Ali, 828
Jitta's Atonement: see Shaw—Plays
Joachim, Joseph, 93–4
Joan of Arc, 53, 56–7
John, Augustus, 366, 700–1, 794, 797
  portrait of Shaw, 412, 751–2
John, Rosamund, 573, 579–81
John Bull's Other Island: *see* Shaw—Plays
Johnson, Edward, 799
Johnson, Sam, 204, 209
Johnson, Dr Samuel, 46, 48, 115, 240, 479, 633, 697, 812
Johnson–Malone editions of Shakespeare, 129
Johnston, Denis, 692, 779–80, 878, 883
Jones, Barry, 550
Jones, Doris Arthur (later Thorne), 26, 749
Jones, Eirene Lloyd, 745–6
Jones, Henry Arthur, 26, 749
  The Dancing Girl, 340
  article, "My Religion," 27
Jones, Thomas, 305, 745
Jonson, Ben, 217, 812
Joseph of Arimathea, 232
Joyce, James, 178, 235, 308
  Finnegans Wake, 858, 878
  Ulysses, 858, 872
Joyce, William ("Lord Haw Haw"), 583–4, 600, 752

Joynson-Hicks, Sir William, later Viscount Brentford ("Jicks" or "Jix"), 74–5, 112, 789
  raid on Arcos Ltd., 67
  censors *The Well of Loneliness*, 110, 116
Joynes, J. L., 106–7
Jugo, Jenny, 422
Jutland, Battle of, 63

Kaiser: *see* Wilhelm II
Kaiser Frederick's Museum, 245
Kamerny Theatre, Moscow, 247
Kantorowitz, Michael, 548–9
Karik, Fritz, 330
Karsh, Yosuf, 707
Kautsky, Karl, 42, 67, 70
Kean, Charles, 785–6
Kean, Edmund, 207, 785–6, 791
Keeble, (Sir) Frederick, 21, 391, 678
Keeble, Lady: *see* McCarthy, Lillah
Keith-Roach, Edward, 229–30
Kellogg, John, 425
Kelly, Vincent, 793
Kelmscott Press, 520, 590, 843
Kelso, Vernon, 664, 673
Kemble, Charles, 785–6
Kemble, John Philip, 46, 158
Kempson, Alice, 439–40
Kendal, Dame Madge, 472, 569–70, 572, 655
Kennedy, Clara M., 718, 803
Kennedy, Margaret, 405
Kennedy, W. S., 41–5, 67
Kennet, Lady: *see* Young, Kathleen Hilton
Kennet of the Dene, Lord: *see* Young, Edward Hilton
Kennington, Eric, 229
Kent, Duke of (Prince George), 392–3
Kentish, Agatha, 14
Kenworthy, Joseph Montague, later Baron Strabolgi, 622
  New Wars, New Weapons, 213
  Sailors, Statesmen, and Others, 223
Kepler, Johann, 211
Kerenski, Aleksandr, 43, 270, 295, 442
Kern, Jerome, 868
Kerr, Alfred, 336, 338

915

Loewenstein, Dr Fritz Erwin—*contd.*
758–60, 775, 789, 802, 806, 825, 836, 849, 878, 882–3, 885
"A Collection of Shaviana," 639
Bernard Shaw through the Camera, 651, 863
"a man to be avoided," 687
raids Shaw's archive, 693
appointed "authorised bibliographer and remembrancer," 693
Logier, Johann Bernhard, 846–7
Lollards, 216, 218
Lomas, Herbert, 554
London, Battle of, 578
London, City of, 271
London County Council, 397, 668, 706, 781
election (1898), 270
London Film Productions, 419
London Film Society, 132
London Missionary Society, 53, 55
London Museum, 398
London Music in 1888–89: see Shaw—Other Works
London Philharmonic Society, 309–10
London School of Economics and Political Science, 151, 386, 712
London, University of, 82–3, 742, 749
London Vegetarian Society, 242, 501
Londonderry, Edith, Lady, 520–1
Londonderry, Marquess of, 520–1
Longfellow, Henry Wadsworth, 192, 375
Longman (publisher), 676
Lonsdale, Frederick, 15
Lopokova, Lydia (Lady Keynes), 541
Loraine, Robert, 196, 443
Lord Chamberlain, 14, 111, 133, 204, 501
Lorentz, Henrik, 315
Lothian, Lord: see Kerr, Philip
Louis, Joe, 820–1
Louis XIV, 645
Louis XVI, 103
Louis Napoleon: see Napoleon III
Louis Philippe, 797
Low, Ebba, 32, 885
Lowes, W., 201
Lucas, Edward Verrall, 147

Ludwig II, of Bavaria, 582
Ludwig, Emil, 3, 525, 814
Lummis, Rev. E. W., 216
Lunacharsky, Anatoly, 245, 248–50, 252–4, 257
Lunacy Laws, 275
Lusitania, sinking of, 630
Luther, Martin, 271, 390, 500
Luther, Sally, 815
Luton and Dunstable Hospital, 879
Luxembourg, Rosa, 42, 44
Lyceum Theatre, 158–9, 203–4, 207, 209, 655, 787, 838
Lynch, Col. Arthur, 315–16
Lyric Theatre, Hammersmith, 831
Lyttelton, Dame Edith ("D.D."), 132–133, 150, 599, 684
Lyttelton, Rev. Edward, 276–7
Lytton, Edward Bulwer, first Baron Lytton of Knebworth, 159, 785, 812
Lytton, Sir Henry, 211–12

Macarthur, Mary, 783
Macaulay, Rose, 118
McBride, Maud Gonne, 67, 576–7
McCall, J. J., 760
MacCarthy, (Sir) Desmond, 117–18
McCarthy, Lillah (Lady Keeble), 21, 391, 623, 644, 678
in *Man and Superman*, 443
Myself and My Friends, 579
McClintic, Guthrie, 608–9, 667
McCulloch, Christina B., 35
McCullough, Donald, 642
Macdona, Charles, 14, 180, 343, 432
Macdona Players, 51, 172, 181
MacDonald, Flora, 760
MacDonald, J. Ramsay, 3, 5–6, 18–19, 24, 58, 74–5, 79, 81, 84, 101, 104, 141, 211, 244, 270, 274, 295, 313, 391, 455, 521, 667, 777, 782, 815
Macdonnell, Hercules, 527
Macduff, Shaws descended from, 430, 652, 761
McEvoy, Charles, 35, 419
MacFadden, Bernarr, 14, 425
MacFarren, Sir George A., 846–7

Martin-Harvey, (Sir) John
  in *The Devil's Disciple*, 30
  in *The Shewing-up of Blanco Posnet*,
    30–1
Marx, Karl, 18–19, 70, 102, 237, 258,
    270, 272, 294, 313, 357, 373, 387,
    441, 602–3, 632, 653, 668–9,
    675, 742, 750, 809, 817, 823
  Capital, 390, 643
  Selected Works, 668
  "an Epoch Maker," 390
  "changed the mind of the world," 393
Marxism, 101, 104, 336, 458, 534, 547,
    817
Mary, Blessed Virgin, 9, 50, 232, 234,
    322–3, 409–10, 508, 865
Masefield, John, 360, 488, 772
  verse tribute on ninetieth birthday,
    773
Mask, The, 158–9
Massey, Raymond, 542
Materialism, 596, 835
Matheson, Donald McLeod, 681, 684
Matheson, Hilda, 164–5, 291
Matteoti, Giacomo, 43, 69–70, 72, 74–6
Maturin, Eric, 95
Maude, Cyril, 37
Maugham, W. Somerset, 365, 442, 718,
    720
Maung Ohn, 863
Maurois, André, 884
  Edward VII, 223
Mavor, Osborne Henry: *see* Bridie,
    James
Maxton, James, 101–2, 777
Maxwell, Ella, 769
Maxwell, John, 195
Maxwell, William, 7, 129, 259, 295–6,
    299–300, 311, 405, 407, 537, 591,
    596, 623, 649, 668, 682–3, 687,
    751, 769–70, 773, 826
May, Frederick, 873
Maynard, Sir John, 649–50
Mazzini, Giuseppe, 38, 69
Mead, Tom, 204, 207
Meinhold, Pastor Wilhelm: *Sidonia von
    Bock, die Klosterhexe*, 520
Melancthon, Philip, 500
Melbourne Repertory Theatre, 338–9

Menander, 716
  The Arbitration (tr. Gilbert Murray),
    714
  The Rape of the Locks (tr. Gilbert
    Murray), 714
Mendelssohn, Felix, 582, 645, 814
  Elijah, 507
Mensheviks, 295
Menuhin, Yehudi, 340
Meredith, E. Norman, 768–9
Meredith, George, 171, 676
Meredith, Georgina: *see* Rogers,
    Georgina
Merritt, George, 673
Messinesis, Dom Basil, 416–17
Meštrović, Ivan, 486–7
Methodism, 322, 324, 404, 647, 728
Metro-Goldwyn-Mayer, 333, 605, 641
Metropolitan Museum, New York, 724
Metropolitan Opera House, New York,
    326–7, 329, 334, 770
Metropolitan Police, 41
Mexico, 62, 426, 441, 802, 860, 868
Meyer, Sir Carl, 163
Meyer, Rudolf, 398
Meyerbeer, Giacomo, 191, 709, 798
  Les Huguenots, 144–5, 307
Michael Angelo, 231, 284, 300, 315,
    410–11, 486, 825–7
Michelson, Alberta, 315–16
Milestone, Lewis, 466
Mill, John Stuart, 669, 675, 750, 823
  Autobiography, 763
Millais, Sir John Everett, 861
Millais, John Guille: *The Life and
    Letters of Sir John Everett
    Millais*, 861
Miller, Gilbert, 442, 550
Miller, Henry, 442
Millionairess, The: *see* Shaw—Plays
Milner, Victor, 466
Milton, John, 353, 827
Milton, Maud, 207
Minneapolis Civic Theatre, 815
Misalliance: *see* Shaw—Plays
Misernuke, Mr and Mrs, 505–6
Mrs Warren's Profession: *see* Shaw—
    Plays
Mitchison, Naomi, 358

Murray, Lady Mary, 391, 585, 613, 679
Murray, Muriel, 473
Murray, Stephen, 564–5
Murray, William, 573
Music Cure, The: *see* Shaw—Plays
Music in London: *see* Shaw—Other
    Works
Musical forms, 92–3, 378–9, 754–5
Musical instruments, 82, 92–5, 144–5,
    200–1, 297–8, 516–18, 529–30,
    625–6, 651–2, 708–9, 814, 829–
    830, 840, 846–8, 850, 857
Mussolini, Benito, 5, 18, 38, 41–5, 64,
    68–70, 72, 74–6, 79–81, 313, 337,
    347, 359, 374, 424–5, 456, 501,
    511–12, 514, 538, 633, 672
    "My Twenty-four Hours: Life and
    Work," 41
Musters, Judy: *see* Gillmore, Georgina
Myers and Co., 120

Napoleon Bonaparte, 42–3, 68–9, 80–1,
    209, 223, 273, 449, 490, 546–7,
    633, 673, 757, 791, 814, 831
Napoleon III (Louis Napoleon), 70,
    491, 546, 633, 643, 714–15
Natal Mercury, 412
National Anthem, 225–6
National Bank of Ireland, 748
National Book League exhibition (1946),
    639, 691, 769–70, 772–3
National Brass Band Championship, 200
National Broadcasting Corporation
    (U.S.A.), 363
National City Bank of Dublin, 681
National Congress of Peace and Friend-
    ship with the U.S.S.R., 462
National Council for Civil Liberties, 600
National Gallery, 115, 785, 787
National Gallery of Ireland, 28, 191,
    711, 713, 724
National Government (1931), 313
National Health Service Bill, 776, 778
National Library of Ireland, 761, 765–6
National Provincial Bank, 681, 705, 748
National Socialist German Workers'
    party (Nazis), 335–6, 343–4, 348,
    353–4, 359, 456–7, 496, 547, 600,
    752, 771, 808

National Theatre, 163–4, 314
National Theatre Conference, 163
National Trust, 526
    offer of house to, 681–2, 684, 691, 705,
    722, 752
Nazimova, Alla, 400–1, 405, 408
Nazis: *see* National Socialist German
    Workers' party
N.B.C.: *see* National Broadcasting
    Corporation
Negri, Pola, 121–2
Negroes, 186, 398, 413, 457, 464, 719,
    868
Nehru, Jawaharlal, 827–8, 884
Nelson, A., 275
Nelson, Horatio, Admiral, 791, 852–3
Nelson, Thomas, and Son, 78
N.E.P.: *see* New Economic Policy
Nero, 62
Nesbit, Edith, 386
Neue Freie Presse, 29, 37, 63
Newcastle programme, 385
Newcombe, Bertha, 706, 749
New Economic Policy (N.E.P.), 104–5,
    294, 777
New Fabian Essays: ed. R. H. S. Cross-
    man, 215
New Gallery, 79
New Statesman, 249, 384, 389–90, 492,
    500, 539, 541, 560, 595, 740, 756
New Theatre, 442, 523, 558
Newton, Commander C. P., 273, 275,
    280
Newton, Sir Isaac, 211, 315, 317, 524,
    549, 763
New York American, 37, 63, 165, 252
New York Herald-Tribune, 405, 508
New York Journal-American, 539, 768
New York press, 334
New York Public Library, 144, 227
New York, Supreme Court of the City
    of, 21
New York Times, 184, 225, 330, 836, 873
New Zealand: *see* Shaw—Travel
New Zealand Broadcasting Service, 368
Nicholas II, Tsar, 103
Nicholls, Harry, 444
Nicholson, Ivor, 109–10
Nietzsche, Friedrich, 455, 675

921

Paget, Lady Muriel, 505
Paget, Sir Richard, 661-2
Pagliardini, Tito, 613-14
Paine, Thomas, 817
Pakistan, 828
Palestrina, Giovanni Pierluigi da, 840
Pall Mall Gazette, 790
Palmstierna, Erik Kule, Baron, 32-4, 52
Pan American Airways, 425
Paramount Pictures, 134, 466, 468
Paris Commune (1871), 72
Parker, Agnes Miller, 305-6
Parker, Cecil, 713
Parker, Dr Henry R., 726-8
Parkes, 850
Parkins and Gotto Ltd., 143
Parliamentary system, 374
Parnell, Charles Stewart, 313, 853
Parry, Sir Charles Hubert H., 396
Parry, Gertrude (*née* Bannister), Mrs Sidney, 387
Pascal, Gabriel, 426, 493, 507-10, 522-523, 531, 533, 535, 542, 549, 552, 564-5, 574-5, 588-9, 599, 609-611, 613, 666-7, 670-1, 686, 708-709, 713, 720-1, 728-30, 736, 749, 773, 799-804, 807, 818, 860-1, 868, 884-5
   screen versions of *Arms and the Man, Cæsar and Cleopatra, Major Barbara, Pygmalion,* and *Saint Joan: see* Shaw—Plays
   intends to make film of Shaw's life, 884
Pascal, Valerie (*née* Hidveghy), 803, 883, 885
Pascal Films Ltd., 611
Passfield, Lord and Lady: *see* Webb, Sidney and Beatrice
Passion, Poison, and Petrifaction: see Shaw—Plays
Patch, Blanche, 93, 109, 138-9, 154-5, 189, 269, 273, 277, 314-15, 364, 368, 407, 425-6, 433, 535-6, 542, 576-8, 592-4, 636, 643, 649, 666, 669, 680, 682, 686, 693-5, 733, 736-9, 751, 754, 758-60, 769, 781, 797, 804, 824, 833, 840, 849, 865, 878, 880, 883, 885

Patch, Blanche—*contd.*
   Thirty Years with G.B.S., 875
   kept a commonplace book, 227, 238
   relations with Shaw and her opinion of Shaw and wife, 694
   "virulently anti-Semitic," 741
Patriot, The, 500
Patterson, Jane (Jenny), 176, 189, 527-8, 659
Pavlov, Ivan, 249, 280-1, 601, 603, 616, 650
Pax, Paulette, 38
Paxton, Hubert, 379
Pearl Harbor, 629-30
Pearson, Hesketh, 475, 503, 512, 519, 527, 534
   Bernard Shaw: His Life and Personality, 205, 590, 595, 644, 649, 653, 658, 660
   Gilbert and Sullivan, 383-4
   The Smith of Smiths, 223
   Thinking it Over, 502
Pearson's Magazine, 499
Pease, Edward R., 385
Pease, Henry, 644
Pelman lessons, 222
Pemberton, T. E., 158
Pen Portraits and Reviews: see Shaw—Other Works
Penguin Books, 537, 583, 585, 591, 594, 597, 691, 732, 751
   "Shaw Million," 757-8
People's Convention, 600-8
Pepys, Samuel, 190, 524, 812
Percy, Edward: *see* Smith, Edward P.
Percy, Esmé
   stages *Mrs Warren's Profession*, 14
   in *Misalliance*, 180
   Shaw refuses post-dated cheque, 288
   in *Murder* (film), 288
   in *Pygmalion* (film), 494
   "an experienced Shavian producer," 845
   produces *Buoyant Billions*, 850-1
   produces *Farfetched Fables*, 869
Perugini, Kate, 639-40
Pester Lloyd, 112
Pétain, Henri-Philippe, 559-60
Peter the Great (Russia), 810

Retail Booksellers, Stationers and Allied Trades Employees Association, 381–2

Retz, Jean-François de Gondi, Cardinal de, 821

Reuters, 343

Revolutionary Museum, Moscow, 252

Reynolds, Sir Joshua, 633, 766

Rhodes, Cecil, 223, 644

Rhodesia, 719–20

Rhondda, Margaret Haig Thomas, Viscountess, 45–8, 182–4, 346, 384, 387, 734
  article, "Shaw's Women," 179
  praises *Too True to be Good*, 302
  reviews Harris biography of Shaw, 276
  Shaw's pet name for, 302

Ricardo, David, 750

Richard I, 79, 230

Richards, Grant, 208

Richards (gravedigger at Ayot St Lawrence), 625

Ricketts, Charles, 160
  designs for *Saint Joan*, 158

Rièra, Albert, 376–7

Rig Veda, 708

Ristori, Adelaide, 172, 579, 656

Rivera, Diego, 860

Rivera y Orbaneja, Miguel Primo de, General, 17–18

Rivers, William Halse R., 71–2

R.K.O. Studios, 333, 353, 355–6, 365–7, 401

Roback, Abraham Aaron, 418

Roberts, C. and A. (Whitwell) Ltd., 21

Roberts, Denis Kilham, 636, 641, 660, 697

Roberts, J. H., 673–4

Robertson, Madge: *see* Kendal, Madge

Robertson, Manning D., 663–4

Robertson, Field Marshall Sir William, 357

Robeson, Paul, 867–8

Robey, (Sir) George, 402–3

Robins, Elizabeth, 448, 572

Robinson, John J., 799, 807

Robinson, Lennox, 308, 885

Robson, (Dame) Flora, 831

Robson, Frederick, 207, 791

Robson, William A., 671–2

Roche, Raphael, 54–5, 60

Rockefeller, John D., 823

Rodd, James Rennell, later Baron Rennell, 658–9

Rodgers, Richard, 528

Rodin, Auguste, 28, 252, 513, 590, 751–752, 796

Roe (distillers), 411

Rogers, Charlotte, née Gurly, 65, 448

Rogers, Eames, 768

Rogers, Georgina (Mrs E. N. Meredith), 65, 768–9

Rolland, Romain, 291–2, 295, 459, 505, 584–5
  Au dessus de la Melée (*Above the Conflict*), 578

Rolland, Marie, 459

Roman Catholics and Catholicism: *see* Catholics

Roman Empire, 43, 89, 281

Romand, Françoise, 699

Romanoffs, 540

Roosevelt, Franklin Delano, 603, 608

Roosevelt, Theodore (son of ex-President), 325

Root, E. Merrill, 259

Rose, Enid, 266

Rose, Howard, 164

Rosenbach, A. S. W., 683

Rosenberg, Alfred, 336, 338, 642–3

Rosmer, Milton, 573

Rosminian: *see* Serbati

Ross, Robert, 498

Rossetti, Dante Gabriel, 82, 106–9, 559, 682, 861–2, 872

Rossini, Giacchino Antonio, 378, 542, 838
  William Tell, 798, 847

Rothenstein, (Sir) William, 391

Rothermere, Lord, 113

Round Table Conference on India, second, 267

Rouse, Alfred A., 439–40

Rousseau, Jean-Jacques, 178, 191, 390
  The Confessions, 384–5

Rowbottom, William, 762–3

Rowe, Nicholas, 811–12

Shaw, George Bernard—*contd.*

on sex and reproduction, 96–7, 119, 190–3, 263, 460

dines at Claridge's, 103

no objection to witness box, 116

"Freethinker," 117, 808

on personal appearance and clothes, 121, 530, 796–7

typefaces and book production, 7, 129, 147–8, 259, 295–7, 300, 350–2, 591–2, 623–4, 826, 843

boxing, 130–2

comments on old age, 150–6, 375, 470, 487, 495, 549, 569, 576, 578, 596, 598, 600, 604, 612, 621, 623, 646, 649, 672, 701, 706, 714, 723, 735–6, 738, 756–7, 762, 764, 774, 794, 805–6, 818–21, 828, 830, 850, 859, 862–4, 866–8

on marriage and divorce, 150, 154

form of name, 154, 277, 665, 683

National Theatre, 163–4

on style of Shaw production, 172

on biography and autobiography, 175–6, 178, 385, 428, 450, 512, 519–20, 590, 687, 826, 875

portraits and sculptures, 28–9, 176, 412, 485–7, 513, 530, 549, 700, 724, 751, 794, 849–52

first appearance at Old Vic, 177

lack of deference and veneration, 207, 675

explains stage directions, 208, 813

"hundreds of photographs," 222

first experience of modern flying, 224

on crime and punishment, 248, 271–2, 275, 331, 440, 443–4

appreciates prayers, 265, 775

drafts election poster for nuns, 268

on modern authors, 278, 789

"We are the world's family solicitors," 279

equal pay and distribution, 279

on feminism and female suffrage, 302, 322, 346–7, 745–6, 782–3

"I hate the poor," 302

elected President of Irish Academy, 308

Shaw, George Bernard—*contd.*

on party for children—"turn on the gas and let them all wake up in heaven," 355

advises B.B.C. on publishing, 362

not "anti-British," 371

"I am the worst of linguists," 372

asked to write libretto for Sullivan, 384

fascination with vagabonds and scoundrels, 419

at sister's cremation, 430–1, 482

"I am rather a mean sort of man," 448

"I dont keep an opus list," 450

never a doctrinaire communist, 458

avoided literary society, 463

last will, 474, 495, 497, 528, 682, 691, 705, 711–13, 721–2, 724, 726, 733, 752, 768, 866–7, 886

declines to sign Spanish Civil War Appeal, 492

awarded an "Oscar," 494

"I am an Irishman," 499, 541, 543, 725

"I bear no malice," 500

obituary jingle, 513

emends Duffin manuscript, 514–15

refuses to contribute to Entertainments' Day, 522

on world premières, 523

on suicide, 525, 647, 762–3

on musical versions of plays, 528, 813

on wartime billeting of children, 536, 538

on broadcasting of plays, 546, 827

will not consent to cutting, 546

on hotels in London, 548

"I could live on £2 a week," 550

"History always repeats itself," 554

"Why not declare war on France?", 560

"never work to a ready made plot," 567

returns to Ayot, 577

destruction of unbound sheets of books, 578–9

on Bow Wow acting, 579

war damage, 583, 592–4, 716, 721

may not write for the stage again, 595, 604

Shaw, George Bernard—*contd.*
discontinues personal activities on platform, 604
stereotyped postcards, 604, 867
"This is not a war for Xtian civilization," 605
on translation, 614
subscription to church, 625
on duty of editor, 629
on letter writing, 640, 831
on House of Commons speechifying, 644
"Parliament kills everyone except careerists," 650
as public speaker, 657
value of letters, 659, 707, 761
return to Whitehall Court, 672
"subject of Bernard Shaw bores me," 687
"I never grieve," 691, 798, 852
pays tuition fees for friends' children, 694
cannot read some books, 706, 822, 836
birthplace, 706–7, 844, 852
again a bachelor, 705–6, 735, 757, 852
newsreel, 720–1
suggestions for monument, 724, 767–768
on braces, 739–40
gives manuscripts to National Library of Ireland, 761, 765–6
offered freedom of Dublin, 765, 773
asks for Act of Parliament, 769
possibility of award of Order of Merit, 769, 781–4
never sells rights, 771, 860
joins British Interplanetary Society, 792
plaque on Torca Cottage, Dalkey, 793–4
"Keep away EVERYBODY," 801
"I am myself a missionary," 803
direction for disposal of ashes, 804
advises against writing history of theatre, 812
"I was a born writer," 827
"a foreigner in England," 828
on bicycling, 828–9
on split infinitive, 834–5

Shaw, George Bernard—*contd.*
leaves Whitehall Court, 839–40, 849–850, 853–4
has no "view" of death, 849
"my plays are church services," 851
on house at Bushy Park, 857–8
nursery rhymes, 865–6
bungalow at Roundtown, 863–4, 872
"Dont bother about style," 875
final accident and death, 878–86
"If I survive this I shall be immortal," 878
death mask, 884
obituary tributes, 884–5
funeral service, 885–6
disposal of ashes at Ayot, 886

PLAYS

The Admirable Bashville, 193
Androcles and the Lion, 176–7, 402, 532
preface, 626
proposed films, 799, 860, 868
Hollywood film, 802
"Edition for the Forces," 732
The Apple Cart, 125–6, 132, 156, 169–170, 338, 409, 421, 432, 455, 622, 632, 856
Margaret Bondfield as model for Powermistress General, 45
described by Shaw, 128–9
manuscript of, 138–9
world première in Warsaw, 146, 150, 523
first production at Malvern, 150, 157
transfer to West End, 157
reference to "Beo" Campbell, 151
Mrs Patrick Campbell as model for Orinthia, 133, 148–9, 156, 553, 571
Mrs Patrick Campbell tells Shaw to tear it up, 155
designs by Paul Shelving, 158
preface, 164
German production, 166, 358–9, 421

931

Sunday Express, 111, 165, 335
Sunday Times, 470
Sunderland, Scott, 542
  in Cæsar and Cleopatra, 510
  in Pygmalion (film), 508
Sun Yat-Sen, Mme, 291, 325
Surtees, Virginia, 107
Swaffer, Hannen, 335, 495, 597-8
Swedish National Theatre, 884
Sweden, 32-4, 98
Sweet, Henry, 155, 616-17, 661, 721-2
  the word "age" was "simplified"
    into "eidzh," 619
Swift, Jonathan, 253, 513, 622, 692, 724,
    767, 886
  Gulliver's Travels, 234, 714, 864
Swinburne, Algernon Charles, 106-9,
    682
Swinley, Ion, 442
Switzerland, 814
Sykes, Lady Jessica, 498-9
Sykes, Sir Tatton, 498
Syndicalism, 294
Synge, John M.: Deirdre of the Sorrows,
    826
Synthetic Theater, 247
Szalai, Emil, 112
Szyfman, Arnold, 762

Tagore, Sir Rabindranath, 320-1
Taïrov, Alexander: produces Saint Joan,
    247
Tallents, Sir Stephen, 563
Talma, François-Joseph, 123-4, 126
Tate Gallery, 107, 724
Tatham, Derek, 856
Taxation of land values, 81
Taylor, Deems, 692
Taylor, George, 653
Taylor, John, 796
Taylor, Samuel, 615, 617
Taylor, Tom, 872
Tcheka, 43, 239
Tchekhov, Anton, 7, 171, 442
Teatr Polski, Warsaw, 146, 523
Temperance, 790-2
Tennant, Charles W. J., 82-3, 239, 242,
    267
Tennent, H. M., Ltd., 431, 450, 664

Tennyson, Alfred, Lord, 785, 788
Terriss, William, 444
Terry family, 442
Terry, Dame Ellen, 134-6, 158-62, 194,
    202-10, 264-6, 306, 382, 470,
    472, 655, 658-9, 718, 785, 787-8,
    838, 885; see also Ellen Terry
    Memorial Institute
  reads Captain Brassbound's Conver-
    sion to Irving, 208
  twelfth anniversary of death, 568
Terry, George Skelton: Duodecimal
    Arithmetic, 613-14
Terry, Kate, 785, 788, 838
Terry, Marion, 571
Thackeray, William Makepeace, 120,
    152, 278, 675, 726
Thakin Nu, 863
Thalberg, Sigismond, 92-3, 516-17
Théâtre de la Monnaie, Brussels, 874
Théâtre de Monte Carlo, 38
Théâtre des Arts, 38, 123, 236-7, 241
Théâtre des Mathurins, 38, 76-7
Théâtre Français, 51
Theatre Guild, 28, 134, 301, 326-7, 400,
    406, 408, 417, 464, 486, 511-12,
    550-1, 621-2, 692, 724, 811
  Shaw suggests production of Geneva,
    528
Théâtre Hébertot, 123
Theatre Royal, Dublin, 204, 785
Theatre Workshop, 767
Théophile Gautier (ship), 228
Thesiger, Ernest, 435-6, 575
  in In Good King Charles's Golden
    Days, 554-5
Thiers, Louis-Adolphe, 18-19, 70
Third International, 18, 69, 295, 458
Thirty-nine Articles (Church of Eng-
    land), 272
Thomas, Margaret Haig: see Rhondda,
    Viscountess
Thompson, Benjamin, 158
Thompson, Francis, 397
Thorndike, (Dame) Sybil, 37, 346, 569,
    666, 785, 884
  in Major Barbara (film), 589
  in Saint Joan, 437, 526, 723
Thorne, Doris: see Jones, Doris Arthur

941

Thornton, Isabel, 554-5
Three Choirs Festival, 105, 730
Threepenny Opera, The: see Brecht, Bertolt
Thring, G. Herbert, 641
Tietjens, Therese, 774
Till, J. R., 833
Tilley, Vesta, 180-2
Time and Tide, 45, 179, 183, 276, 302, 734-5
Times, The, 6, 68, 166, 178, 214, 313, 347, 356, 424, 434, 443, 484, 492-3, 535, 537, 539-41, 594, 600, 604, 614-15, 635, 661, 697, 740, 768, 773, 781, 830-1, 842, 872
    notice of wife's death, 679
Times Literary Supplement, 111, 639-40, 756, 836-7
Titian, 49, 633
Tito (Josip Broz), 825
Titterton, W. R., 176, 586
Titus, 234
Toller, Ernst, 389
Tolstoy, Count Aleksey, 462
Tolstoy, Count Leo, 7-8, 28, 109, 171, 337, 394, 462
Tomahawk, The, 728
Tompkins, Henry, 99
Tompkins, Laurence, 8, 83, 100, 228
Tompkins, Molly, 7-8, 82-3, 99-100, 184, 227-8, 694
Tompkins, Peter, 7, 83-4, 694, 754
Too True to be Good: see Shaw—Plays
Topolski, Feliks, 749
  Shaw's opinion of, 537
  illustrates published plays, 537, 558-559, 591
  designs *Farfetched Fables*, 869
Torquemada, 511
Tory democracy, 777-8
Touchard, P. W., 873-4
Tournées Ch. Baret, 98
Townsend, Eliza, 863
Townsend, Horace, 138
Trade Union Central Hall, Moscow, 253, 256
Trade Unions, 74, 336
Trades Union Congress, 776-7

Traill, H. D., collab. with Robert Hichens, 785, 788
Treasury, H.M., 41, 279, 610, 619-20, 732
Trebitsch, Siegfried, 20, 30, 37, 146, 166-7, 236, 297, 299, 335-8, 348, 353-4, 358-60, 364, 377, 396, 412, 419-24, 496, 510, 525-6, 547-50, 605-6, 612, 627, 647, 771, 818-19
  Helden (Arms and the Man), 605
  Jitta's Atonement, 37, 420
  Kaiser Diokletian, 825
Trebitsch, Tina, 20, 37, 167, 338, 354, 364, 420, 510, 525-6, 547-50, 605-6, 612, 627, 647, 818, 825
Tree, Sir Herbert (Beerbohm), 383, 402
  in *Pygmalion*, 648
Trevelyan, Sir Charles, 704-5
Trevelyan, George Macaulay, 545
Trewin, J. C., 796
Trinity College, Dublin, 308, 622, 692, 726, 834
Triple Entente, 42
Tristan and Iseult: see Carr, J. Comyns
Trollope, Anthony, 675
Trotsky, Leon, 19, 105, 196, 247, 295, 441, 559, 602
  The Defence of Terrorism, 103
Troubetskoy, Prince Paul, 28-9, 58, 84, 100, 249, 513, 724, 797
Trouncer, Cecil, 508, 554, 575, 674
  "The best heavy lead on the English stage," 508-9
Truman, Harry S., 867, 884
Tuke, Anthony W., 625
Tunney, Gene, 130-1, 137, 820-1, 875
Tunney, Polly, 130, 137
Turati, Filippo, 42, 73-5
Turner, J. M. W., 827
Turner, Reginald, 498
Tutankhamen, 230
Twain, Mark (pseudonym of Samuel L. Clemens), 12, 64-5, 429, 509, 732
  Huckleberry Finn, 463
Tyndall, John, 316
Tyrrell, Ada, 5, 86, 468, 553, 564, 631, 685, 717, 851-2, 857, 866

Tyrrell, Robert Yelverton, 86

Ulrichs, Karl Heinrich, 284
Ulster: *see* Northern Ireland
UNESCO, 291, 884
Union Airways, 224, 277
Union of State Publishing Houses, 253
United Artists, 627
United Nations, 291
United Press, 873
United States of America, 5, 128, 381,
    457, 490, 505, 512, 519, 554, 597,
    629, 643, 660, 802, 811–12, 830,
    860, 864, 867–8, 884; *and see*
    Shaw—Travel, *and* Hollywood
University College, London, 117
University degrees, honorary, 13, 784
Unsocial Socialist, An: *see* Shaw—
    Novels
Unsworth, J., 608
Unwin, (Sir) Stanley, 362
Usigli, Rudolfo, 861
USSR: *see* Soviet Union

Vanbrugh, (Dame) Irene, 36
    in *In Good King Charles's Golden
        Days*, 554
    in *Misalliance*, 180–1
Vanbrugh, Violet, 36, 180
Vandervelde, Emile, 73, 557
Vandervelde, Jeanne E. (Lalla), 557
Van Dyck, Ernest, 306–7
Vane, Sir Francis Fletcher, fifth
    Baronet, 75
Vane-Tempest-Stewart, Charles: *see*
    Londonderry, Marquess of
Van Gogh, Vincent, 184, 254
Vanity Fair (ed. Frank Harris), 498
Vansittart, Sir Robert, later Baron
    Vansittart, 505
Vanzetti, Bartolomeo, 71–2, 76, 330
Vatican, 318, 373, 428, 430, 509, 576,
    623, 710, 804
Vatican Council (1869–1870), 67
Vedrenne, J. E., 3, 23, 170, 579
Vedrenne-Barker seasons, 170, 314
Vegetarianism, 20, 108, 242, 501–2, 507,
    858
Veness, Amy, 554–5, 673

Venus de Milo, 297, 305, 411, 827
Verdi, Giuseppe, 144, 171, 885
    Aida, 708–9, 730
    Il Trovatore, 49, 177, 261, 307, 656
    Otello, 145, 819
Veronica (confirmation name of "Mrs
    Wardrop"), 637, 684–5, 733,
    738, 882
Versailles, Treaty of, 354, 456, 496, 550
Victoria, Queen, 58, 120, 208, 236, 361,
    548
Victoria and Albert Museum, 398, 486,
    617
Viereck, G. S., 13, 63, 165, 546–7
    interview: "Shaw looks at life at
        Seventy," 52–3
    The Kaiser on Trial, 490
Vigo, Jean, 376
Village Wooing: *see* Shaw—Plays
Villiers, George, sixth Earl of Claren-
    don, 501
Virgil, 726–7
Vivisection, 58, 473, 506, 691
Volney, Comte de, 18–19
Voltaire, 89, 281–2, 288, 296–7, 305–6,
    390, 645, 719, 724, 803
Voodoo, 719
Voroshilov, K. E., 608

Waddell, Helen, 308
Wagner, Richard, 101–2, 298, 306, 341,
    378, 439, 730, 823, 837
    Art and Revolution, 749
    The Flying Dutchman, 404, 797
    Die Götterdämmerung, 310–11
        alternative title suggested, 310
    Lohengrin, 307, 311, 582
    Die Meistersinger, 144–5, 307, 460
    Parsifal, 186–7, 582, 755–6, 797
    Das Rheingold, 341
    Rienzi, 311
    Der Ring des Nibelungen, 145, 307
    Siegfried, 307, 310
    Tannhäuser, 798
    Tristan und Isolde, 145, 307, 311, 775,
        797–8, 835, 847
    Die Walküre, 261, 310–11, 395
Waite, J. M. (ed.): *Self Defence, or The
    Art of Boxing*, 131

943

Walker, Dorothy (Dolly), 273–4, 301, 412
Walker, (Sir) Emery, 207, 273–4, 350
Wallace, Henry A., 811, 867
Wallace, General Lew: *Ben Hur*, 812
Wallace, William Vincent: *Maritana*, 144, 798, 837, 847
Wallas, Graham, 42
  reads proofs of *Intelligent Woman's Guide*, 80
Waller, Lewis, 655
Wallrock, Samuel, 210–12
Walshe, Christina, 18–19, 373
Walters, Ethel: *see* Davis, Mary Ethel
Walters, Rev. Ensor, 270, 322–5
Walters, Rev. Gordon Reynold, 725–726
Walton, (Sir) William, 588–9, 729
Wanger, Walter, 332
Ward, Artemus: *see* Browne, Charles Farrar
Wardrop, John, 636–8, 682–5, 687, 691–694, 733, 738–9, 754, 758–60, 833
Warens, Mme de, 191, 385
Warner, Ethel, 328
War of 1914–1918, 63, 75, 214, 295, 339, 456, 482, 490–1, 499, 578, 584, 708, 714–16
War of 1939–1945, 291, 534, *passim*
  end of war, 757, 768
War Department: "Edition for the Forces," 732
Warren family, 663
Warwick Castle (ship), 277
Washington, George, 44, 498, 629
Wassermann, Walther, 434
Watergate Theatre, 869–70
Waterloo, Battle of, 777
Watson, Sir Henry Marriott, 664–5
Watts, Peter Michael, 779
Watts(-Dunton), Theodore, 106–7, 682
Waugh, Arthur, 10
Webb, Beatrice, 54, 104, 215, 221, 363–364, 386, 441, 466, 492–3, 521, 524, 537–8, 545, 558–9, 594–6, 618, 645, 649–50, 672, 705–6, 809–10, 816–17, 821–3
  lectures to Fabian Society, 214

Webb, Beatrice—*contd.*
  illness, 363
  death, 668
  ashes interred in Westminster Abbey, 669, 808–9
  Shaw reviews Cole biography, 756
  "a self-made ethical Socialist," 669, 823
  "artistic strain" and "gipsy strain," 671–2
  My Apprenticeship, 671
  Our Partnership, 668, 808
  "double dislike of Shaw," 808
  Diaries, 821
Webb, Sidney, later Lord Passfield, 19, 104, 215, 221, 269, 363, 384–7, 427, 462, 545, 558, 595–6, 668, 672, 681, 704, 743, 750, 756, 809–10, 817–18, 821–2
  Shaw's estimate of, 81, 822–4
  "placidly aggravating," 215
  "half a century of friendship and companionship," 363
  "mania for inverted commas," 427
  suffers stroke, 492–3
  "the inevitability of gradualness," 615, 777
  death, 804–5
  ashes interred in Westminster Abbey, 808–9
Webb, Sidney and Beatrice, 466, 558, 706, 817
  The Decay of Capitalist Civilisation, 821–3
  Soviet Communism: A New Civilisation?, 407, 669
  The Truth about Soviet Russia, 669
  Shaw suggests monument, 706
Weber, Carl Maria von, 847
Weekly Dispatch, 386
Weill, Kurt, 247, 528
  wishes to make musical of *The Devil's Disciple*, 528
Weimar Republic, 237
Weir, Sir John, 396
Weizmann, Chaim, 486–7
Welles, Orson, 464
Wellington, Arthur Wellesley, Duke of, 673, 746–7, 777, 831

944

Williams, Michael, 62
Williams, Ralph Vaughan, 397, 507
  Dona Nobis, 508
  article on Elgar, 396
Williams, Tom, 634
Williams and Norgate, 362
Williamson, Robert, 828–9, 875
Wills, W. G., 788
  King Charles I, 213, 785
  Olivia (adapted from Goldsmith), 785
Wilson, J. G., 596–7
Wilson, Richard Albert: *The Miraculous Birth of Language*, 594, 596, 614, 699
Wilson, Robert, 216
Winchester Castle (ship), 408
Winsten, Christopher, 694, 753, 760, 837
Winsten, Clare, 741, 749, 768, 837, 850
  sculpture of Joan of Arc, 694, 753, 780, 886
Winsten, Stephen, 741, 749, 758, 775, 850
  ed., *My Dear Dorothea*, 694
  ed., *G.B.S. 90*, 691
  "fashioned three books, each tainted," 694
  Days with Bernard Shaw criticised by Shaw, 753, 836–7
Winsten, Theodora, 805, 850–1
Wirth, Max, 312
Wise, William H., and Co., 199, 560, 562
Wolf, Friedrich, 237
Women's Missionary Association and Society, 718, 803
Women's Social and Political Union, 885
Wood, Sir Henry J., 92, 582, 626
Wood, Mrs Henry, 656
Woolf, Charles Moss, 566
Woolf, Leonard, 556–8
Woolf, Virginia, 118, 556
  Shaw "fell in love with," 557–8
"Woolwich Infants," 131
Woolworth's, 382, 436
Worcester Cathedral, 225–6, 303, 324

Worcester Music Festival, 507
Works Progress Administration, 464
World, The, 796
World Committee for the Relief of Victims of German Fascism, 330
World's Press News, 335
World War I: *see* War of 1914–1918
World War II: *see* War of 1939–1945
Wright, Sir Almroth, 299, 446, 504, 614
Wyatt, Frank, 242, 501
Wycherley, William: *The Country Wife*, 431
Wyclif, John, 216
Wykes, E. W., 704, 748
Wyndham, Sir Charles, 206, 796
Wyndham's Theatre, 796, 801
Wynne, Lewis (pseudonym): *see* Bostock, John S. L. W.

Yale University, 13, 250
Yalta Conference, 462
Yarde, Margaret, 554–5
Yeats, W. B., 4, 33, 308, 339, 348, 352, 360, 577, 795
  Cathleen ni Houlihan (spelled "Kathleen" by Abbey Theatre), 576–7
Yenkaf (Egyptian sculptor), 231
You Never Can Tell: *see* Shaw—Plays
Young, Edward, 296
Young, Edward Hilton, later Baron Kennet, 22–3, 513, 798
Young, Kathleen Hilton, later Lady Kennet, 22–3, 28, 163, 501
  bust of Shaw, 513, 724
  suggested statue of Webbs, 706
  Shaw hears of death of, 798
Young, Robert S., 163, 361
Young, Thomas, 315–16
Younghusband, Sir Francis, 392–5
Yugoslavia: *see* Shaw—Travel

Zangwill, Israel, 346
Zetetical Society, 363
Zinoviev, Grigory, 18–19
Zweig, Arnold, 884